Welcome to the Kitchen & Bath Source Book . . .

We are proud to present this 1991 edition of the Kitchen & Bath Source Book. It is *the* book for anyone interested in the vast array of products available for today's kitchen and bathroom.

The Kitchen & Bath Source Book is designed to save you time, money and energy in selecting the right products for the look you want to achieve. Design ideas are presented with a listing of all the products you'll need to complete the room and where to find them. Included in these pages you'll find:

Thousands of color pictures and design ideas from the leading manufacturers in the kitchen and bath industry.

An easy to use reference section for locating the products to meet your design requirements.

A complete listing of where to buy the common and not so common products that may interest you.

If you are a homeowner, designer, dealer or remodeler, the Kitchen & Bath Source Book is for you!

I am confident that this book will become one of the most valued sources you have in order to help in the planning, design and selection of products for your upcoming kitchen and bathroom projects.

Sincerely,

Gordon Macomber
Publisher

If you don't use one of these...

you better use one of these.

Maybe even all of them, if you're dreaming of a special new kitchen. Because you should ask a lot of the firm you hire to make that dream a reality:

• Will they spend the time to understand what you really want?
• Can they provide new and exciting ideas for making your kitchen look and *work* better?
• Will they do top-quality work at a fair price?
• Do they offer all the services you need?
• Do they have a showroom where you can see the latest trends and products?

Working with a member of the National Kitchen and Bath Association is the only way to be certain you'll get the right answer to each of these questions. So why test your luck?

Go with a sure thing — the total professionalism of every NKBA member. It's the best way to get exactly what you want.

Now that's our idea of a charmed life.

For information on NKBA members in your area, and how to get our new 24-page brochure full of great kitchen ideas, call toll-free: **1-800-FOR-NKBA.**

©1990, NKBA   687 Willow Grove Street, Hackettstown, New Jersey 07840 FAX: (201) 852-1695

KITCHEN & BATH SOURCE BOOK

International Standard Book Number — 1-879163-00-4

STAFF	Gordon Macomber, President/Publisher Russell G. Barone, National Sales Manager Cathy Combs, Production Manager Nancy Bullock, Production Assistant Judy Hamilton, Publisher's Assistant
OFFICE	MBC Data Distribution Publications 3901 West 86th Street, Suite 330 Indianapolis, IN 46268 Tel: 317-875-7776 FAX: 317-875-8029

SALES OFFICE

Boston, MA
Dennis McHale
508-384-8111

Cleveland, OH
Phil Ertel
216-397-0564

California, Northern
Bruce Ortiz
714-522-6604

Minneapolis, MN
Brian Stang
612-935-5785

California, Southern
Jim Dalton
714-672-2534

Philadelphia, PA
Jeff Sanderson
317-875-7776

Chicago, IL
Tom Milazo
708-299-1707

KITCHEN & BATH
SOURCE BOOK

NO COMPETITION

Oceana

Now that you've discovered the secret of Paradise-Relax!

As a dealer-distributor for Paradise Luxury Baths, you will have an exclusive area in which to offer our exclusive whirlpool products, luxury acrylic baths with a revolutionary 20-year limited warranty.

PARADISE LUXURY WHIRLPOOL BATHS OFFER:

- The Comfort of a Spa, the Convenience of a Bath
- High Velocity Spa Jets
- Mirror Finish ICI "Perspex" Acrylic
- Extraordinary 23" Depth and Comfort
- 20 Year Limited Warranty

If you think a world without competition sounds like Paradise . . . it is!

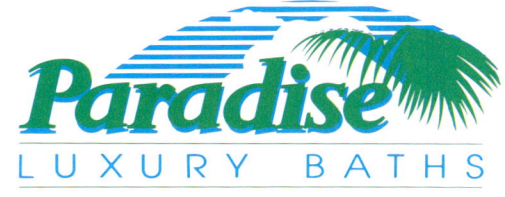

For details: P.O. Box 127, Mercer Island, WA 98040 • U.S. 1-800-232-2552 Cda. 1-800-835-7844

Kitchen & Bath Source Book

Table of Contents

See the subscription card in the back of this catalog to receive the 1992 edition of Kitchen & Bath Source Book.

FORM MEETS FUNCTION TO BRING YOU MORE THAN JUST SINKS

Blancotec 1½ bowl, white

BLANCO offers entire food preparation centers integrating the finest European design and craftsmanship with ergonomic function.

Choose from our family of complementary sinks, faucets and cooktops for the discriminating consumer.

Our sinks are available in high quality stainless steel and 5 colors in quartz composite.

Please send for our Blanco Design Guide to see our complete line of sinks in a wide array of styles and colors. Write to Blanco, 1001 Lower Landing Road, Suite 607, Blackwood, NJ 08012. Or call 1-800-451-5782.

Blancotec 1½ bowl, stainless steel

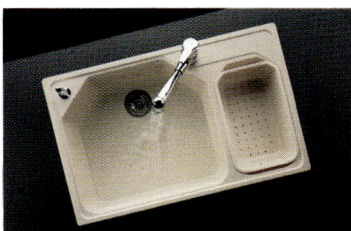

Blancotec 1½ bowl, ivory

Blancotec 1 bowl, stainless steel

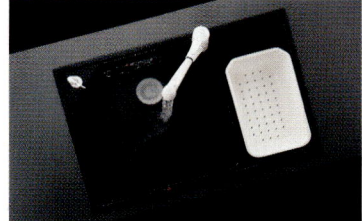

Blancotec 1½ bowl, black

INDEX OF MANUFACTURERS

INDEX OF MANUFACTURERS

INDEX OF MANUFACTURERS

This is.... REV·A·SHELF® INC.

ADD VALUE...

to your cabinets by installing convenience accessories in your display models. Contact us @ **800-626-1126** for assistance in gaining access to greater profitability. Accessories will increase the volume of your cabinet sales.

Rev-A-Shelf is the leading manufacturer with the most complete product line of kitchen cabinet and drawer utilizers.™ Our products are easily installed in new or existing frame and frameless cabinets. Enhance your cabinet sales by offering your customers the #1 cabinet organizers/utilizers™ from Rev-A-Shelf. Also available is a full color easel display brochure for your showroom.

Kidney
Our shelves come in 4 sizes – 18", 24", 28", and 32" and can be adjusted to any height required. Decorative chrome plated shaft system and hardware provide a "unique" corner base product. Single shelf Rev-A-Trays provide rotating efficiency to fixed shelf cabinets.

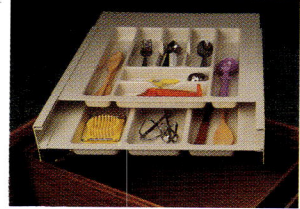

Extra Drawer Kit
Our **NEW GLOSSY EXTRA DRAWER KIT** allows you to double the available drawer space in most kitchens. This product is designed to be custom cut to fit all drawer sizes (even metal drawer boxes) and requires no fastening. Our Glossy Tray provides ample space for cutlery and cooking utensils.

Tip-Out
Every kitchen should be equipped with sink front storage. Our TIP-OUT products are available in a wide variety of polymer trays in many colors and our easily installable concealed hinges provide the ultimate in function.

Blind Corner Base Shelves
Blind base cabinets have always been a storage nightmare until you utilize our storage system. Three size shelves with various bracketry and slide-out features provide a very accessible option to any cabinet.

Rev-A-Shelf has many more unique space saving products. Remember, our products are engineered, not just manufactured.

REV·A·SHELF® INC.
Your Total Accessory Source!

2409 Plantside Drive • Jeffersontown, Ky. 40299 • 502-499-5835 • FAX 502-491-2215

PRODUCT INDEX OF MANUFACTURERS LITERATURE

PRODUCT INDEX OF MANUFACTURERS LITERATURE

Amana®
ALL THE RIGHT PIECES

Because you're always looking for an edge in design, Amana offers you innovative products that can elevate your latest work from great to spectacular. The pieces of the puzzle belonging to Amana are an easy fit into your next project.

1-800-843-0304
AMANA FAST FACTS

Call Amana's toll-free number today to receive the most current information promptly on the products you are specifying.

The pieces all fit together when you specify Amana.

Amana has the image, products, and sales and service network to support your design specifications.

Look to Amana for the solution to any of your puzzles, from the casual to the elegant, from the simple to the complex.

■ *Refrigerators:*
Freezers on the top
Freezers on the bottom
Side by side
Freestanding
Built-in

■ *Freezers:*
Chest
Upright

■ *Ranges:*
Freestanding
Slide-in
Electric or Gas

■ *Radarange® Microwave Ovens:*
Full-Size Countertop
Built-in
Microwave Convection
Compact

■ *Dishwashers*

■ *Dehumidifiers*

1-800-843-0304
AMANA FAST FACTS

Call Amana's toll-free number today to receive the most current information promptly on the products you are specifying.

Synergy

- Room Air Conditioners

- Cooktops:
  Quartz Halogen
  Solid Disk
  Electric Downdraft
  Gas Downdraft

- Wall Ovens:
  Single Electric
  Double Gas

- Washers & Dryers

- Central Heating & Cooling Products

KOHLER COLOR COORDINATES PARTNER

DESIGN BY REFINEMENT

*From traditional to
contemporary design,
Amana has the appliances
for your specific projects.*

*Our products are built with
integrity to ensure quality
and your satisfaction.*

Amana
A **Raytheon** Company

Form No. 0928
Printed in U.S.A.

© 1990 Amana Refrigeration, Inc.
Amana, Iowa 52204

1-800-843-0304
AMANA FAST FACTS

*Call Amana's toll-free number today to receive the most current
information promptly on the products you are specifying.*

SCANDINAVIAN EXCELLENCE

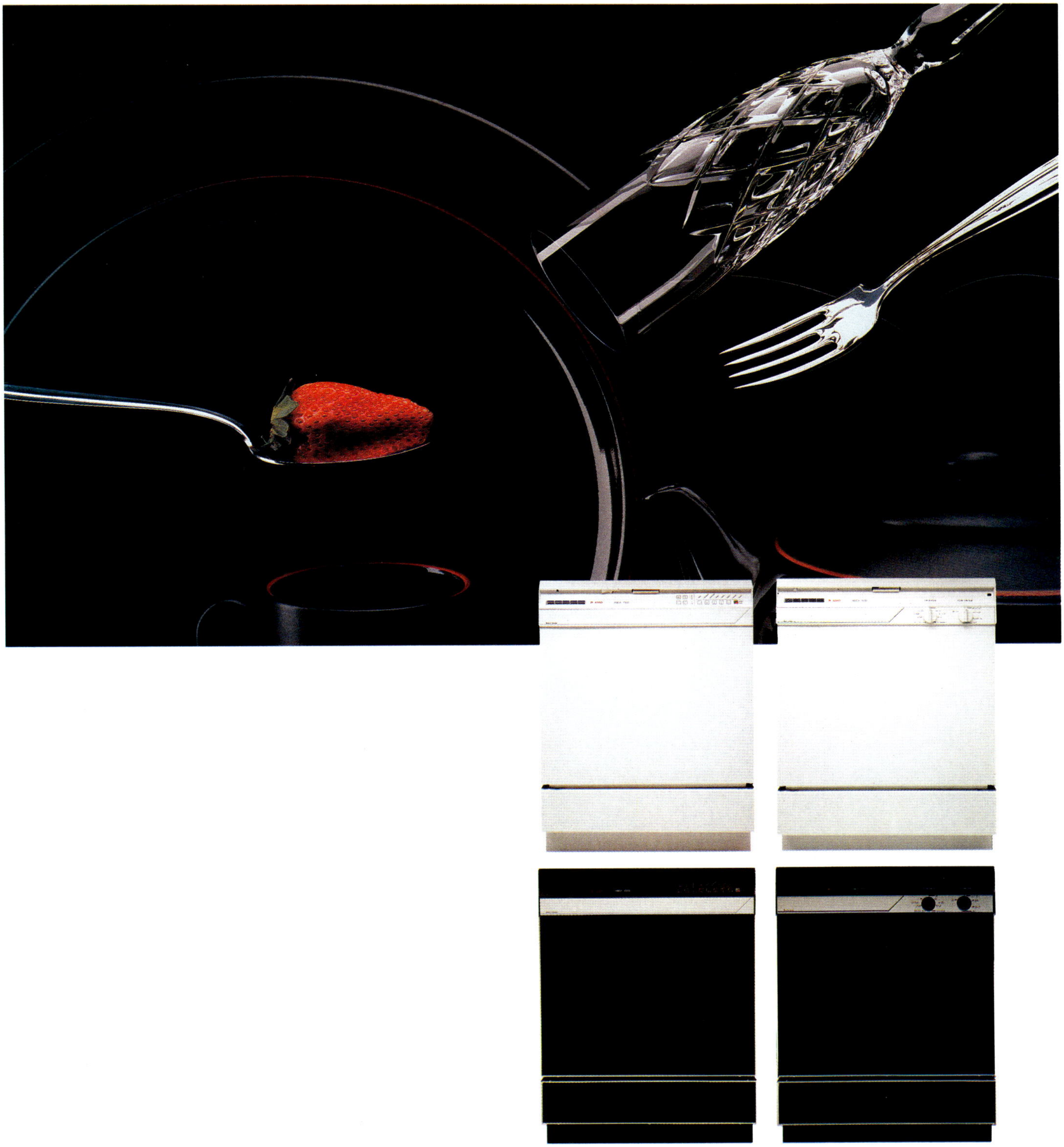

QUIET, EFFICIENT, ECONOMICAL WITH SUPERIOR CLEANABILITY

Asko Asea dishwashers are built for people who appreciate quality from start to finish. People who value a unique design which makes handling easier and improves results. People who understand that excellent overall economy comes from low operating costs and a long life.

The combination of Swedish design and Swedish engineering skills together with the experience gained in manufacturing quality appliances for nearly four decades has enabled us to produce the world's finest quality dishwashers. Sold internationally, our excellent products have an unrivaled track record for efficiency and reliability. Asko Asea dishwashers have been specifically designed and built to last economically and quietly well into the 21st century.

THE MOST IMPORTANT FEATURES ARE NOT ALWAYS VISIBLE

SPARKLING RESULTS The wide range of washing programs and water temperatures provides for "squeaky clean" sparkling glasses and dishes and super clean pots and pans. The Asko Asea washing system continually ranks the highest in test results according to the National Swedish Board for Consumer policies.

KIND TO YOUR DISHES The baskets are coated with Rilsan, a long-lasting graphite-nylon material which protects them from wear and corrosion and is kind to your dishes at the same time. Even the ends of the tynes are double coated for added protection.

WATER & ENERGY EFFICIENT 4.7 gallons of water is all that is required to wash 14 complete place settings with the normal wash program. Low water consumption and short running time saves energy too. Running a full Asko Asea dishwasher is actually cheaper than washing the same dishes by hand.

ROOMY & FLEXIBLE The basket's interior racks are adjustable and can hold up to 14 complete place settings. There are folding shelves in the top basket, specially formed holders for stemware, and a handle on the lower basket makes loading and unloading even easier.

RELIABLE The circulation pump and drain pump are each driven by a separate powerful motor. Designed to last for a long, long time.

VERSATILE INSTALLATION You are not limited to European metric cabinets or standard American cabinets as the Asko Asea can be easily installed in both types of cabinetry. Trim kits, front kits and many accessory items are available to make yours a custom installation.

CHILDPROOF A hidden childproof lock located just under the door handle can be used to keep tiny hands out of the dishwasher and away from accidents.

BASED UPON QUALITY The base pan is pressed from a single piece of hot-dipped galvanized steel sheet. No corrosion, no leakage. Pumps, motors, valves, etc. are isolated on the one piece base pan for quietness and serviceability.

EVERY MACHINE IS TESTED METICULOUSLY Most of the manufacturing process is robotized and automated. This results in high, uniform quality. That's not all. Every single machine is thoroughly tested before it is allowed to leave the factory. The entire wash program is run without short cuts. All functions are tested. Only excellent engineering, superior design, careful construction and stringent testing allows Asko Asea to document the reliability of the product with longest-strongest warranty in the industry; 2 year parts and labor, 5 years on functional parts, and 10 years on the stainless steel tank and door panel. For full details see the Asko Asea warranty.

UNIQUE DESIGN

STAINLESS No other dishwasher offers better quality materials. The inner casing, filters, pipes and spray arms are made of genuine 18:8 surgical-quality stainless steel. Not only is it hygenic, but supremely durable as well.

REMOVABLE BASKET INSERT The rear plate insert in the lower basket can easily be removed, leaving plenty of room for large bowls and pots and pans. The cutlery basket is also easy to remove and is designed to accommodate all shapes of utensils.

WORLD PATENTED VENT is open only during drying. Being closed at other times locks in odors, noise, vapor and heat. The grille is designed so the steam is directed outwards, away from cabinets and counter tops.

UNIQUE FEATURES

WORLD'S QUIETEST The units have thick insulation everywhere, even in the door. This not only results in virtually silent operation, but also keeps the heat inside and energy consumption down. Insulation plus a number of engineering design innovations make the Asko Asea the quietest of all brands tested according to standards of the National Swedish Board for Consumer Policies.

CONVENIENT PUMP Should the separate drain pump need cleaning at any time, simply remove the lower panel and kick plate. Drain the pump through the short hose and clear the pump. A convenient way to save service calls.

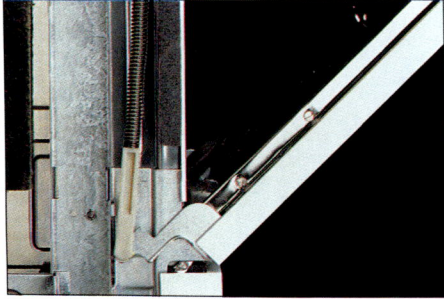

BALANCED DOOR The perfectly balanced door is one example of Asko Asea quality and attention to detail. Two durable compression springs ensure that the door stops exactly where you release it and they won't weaken through years of use.

THE STRENGTH BEHIND THE NAME

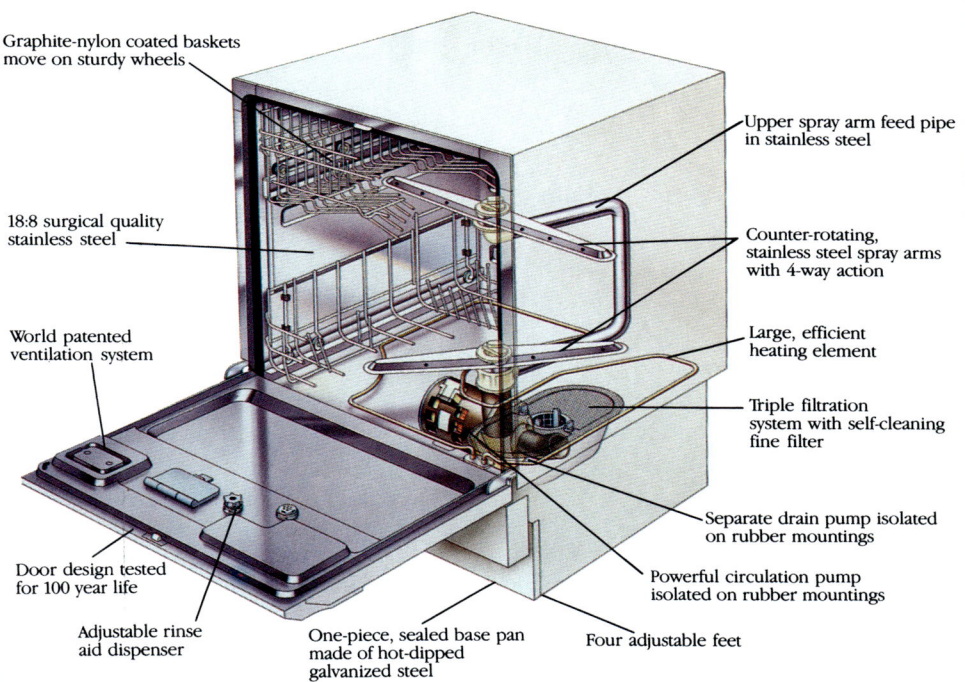

Graphite-nylon coated baskets move on sturdy wheels

Upper spray arm feed pipe in stainless steel

18:8 surgical quality stainless steel

Counter-rotating, stainless steel spray arms with 4-way action

World patented ventilation system

Large, efficient heating element

Triple filtration system with self-cleaning fine filter

Separate drain pump isolated on rubber mountings

Door design tested for 100 year life

Powerful circulation pump isolated on rubber mountings

Adjustable rinse aid dispenser

One-piece, sealed base pan made of hot-dipped galvanized steel

Four adjustable feet

Super Cleaning System™

Asko Asea's new patent-pending Super Cleaning System,™ allows for the use of less water while still achieving the best cleaning results. After the pre-wash, any food particles are removed from the filter automatically and pumped out the separate drain system. This means that the main wash always begins with clean water. The triple filtration system works throughout the wash cycle to remove even the smallest particles and can be easily removed for cleaning when needed. Dishes washed in clean water get sparkling clean.

SUPERIOR SPRAY SYSTEM One of the secrets behind the excellent washing results with low water consumption is the unique 4-way spray system. The upper spray arm sprays both upwards and downwards with a constant pressure due to solid pipe water feed. There is no water tower to reduce washing efficiency and steal usable space. The lower spray arm sprays up with a more powerful pressure to clean more heavily soiled items. It also sprays down to clean the filter and wash the soil into the drain sump. The spray arms are counter rotating, which enhances washing action.

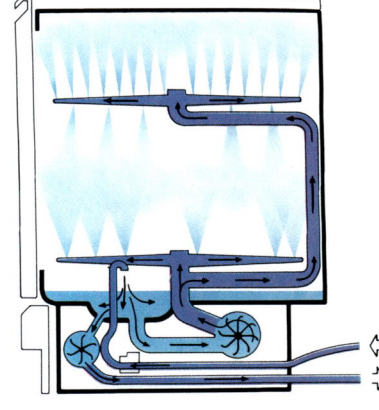

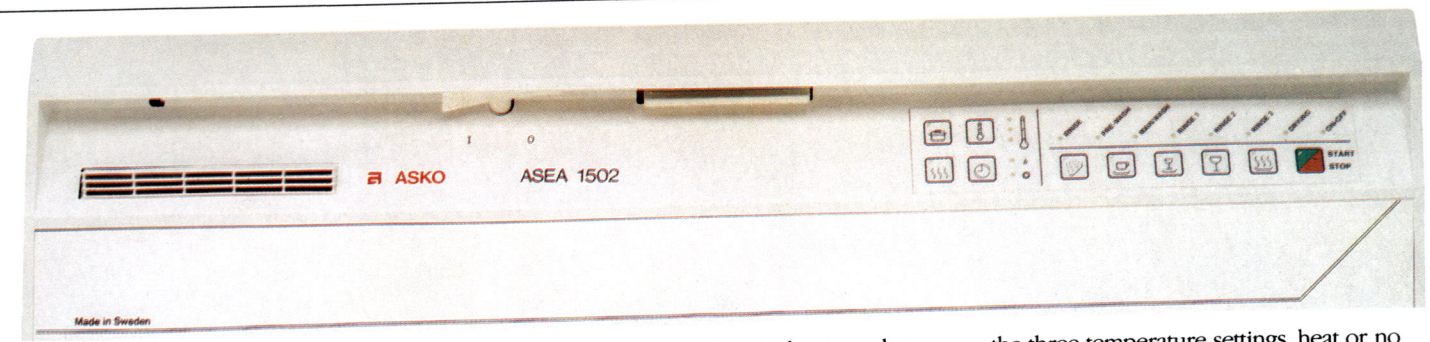

If you are not content with anything but the best, you should take a look at the Asko Asea 1502, the most technically sophisticated dishwasher. This machine washes dishes so quietly, you can hardly hear it. And water consumption is just 4.7 gallons during a normal cycle which means it is also economical.

Its computer-operated control system also improves reliability by reducing the number of moving parts.

You operate the 1502 by touching the program symbols on the panel. Indicator lights show which cycles are included in the chosen program. You can also select one of

the three temperature settings, heat or no heat dry or the special refinement of a delay start time. It also has a unique memory feature. The indicator lights show which of the over twenty programs was last used. Just touch start if you want to run the same program again.

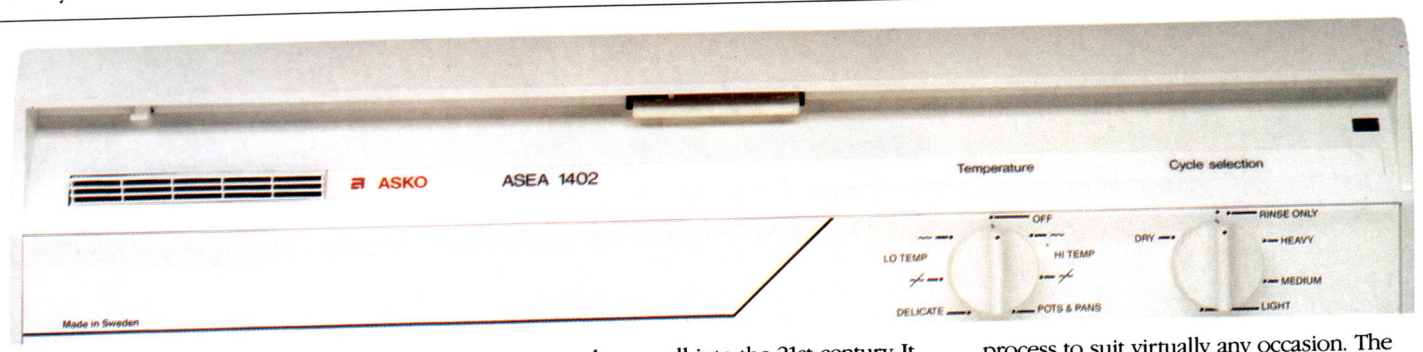

If you are looking for a dishwasher with outstanding overall economy, top class performance and many practical refinements which make it really easy to operate, then the 1402 is for you. You will have a dishwasher

you can rely on well into the 21st century. It is the same basic construction and washing system as the 1502. With twelve different washing programs and choice of two temperature levels, you can select a dishwashing

process to suit virtually any occasion. The 1402 has the capacity to cope with large families or festive occasions, but still consumes a minimum amount of energy, water and detergent.

SPECIFICATIONS AND DIMENSIONS

The Asko Asea 1402 and 1502 dishwashers are designed to fit both American and European dimensions. Trim strips packed with each

unit allow for installation in standard 24″ wide openings. The leveling legs allow height adjustment for most installations, and

the toe space is adjustable to accommodate both European and American cabinet installation.

	AMERICAN	EUROPEAN
	Inches	Millimeters
A	32¼	820
B	23½	595
C	22⁷⁄₁₆	570
D	32¼-35	820-890
E	22⁷⁄₁₆ min.	570 min.
F	23½-24	595-608
G	4-6¾	100-171
H	4	100
I	8¼	210

SUPPLY: Both electrical and water supply should enter the opening on either side within an area 4″ from the back and 8″ from the floor. Supply must run from the back along the left side. Allow enough to accommodate this with the necessary bends.

WATER: Water pressure should be 18 to 176 PSI connected to the hot water supply. The supply line should be ⅜″ O D copper tubing. A ⅜″ NPT female connection is attached to the fill valve.

ELECTRICAL: 120 volt; 60 Hz.; 15 amp properly grounded circuit is required. No other appliance or outlets should be on this circuit. Connection can be either non-metallic cable or conduit.

...KO U.S.A., Inc. retains the right to vary the ...del specifications at any time. All facts were ...rate at time of printing. These units are ...by Underwriters Laboratories Inc.

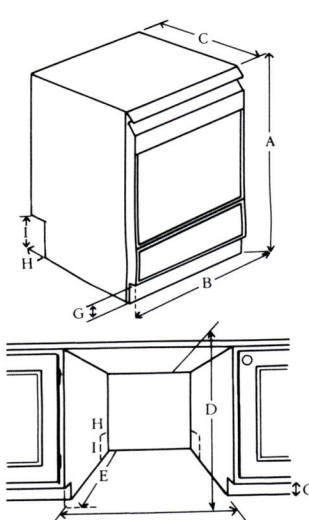

CUSTOM PANELS

For standard non-raised panels, use ¹⁄₁₆ in. up to ³⁄₁₆ in. material. Cut to fit:

	Inches	Centimeters
Upper Panel		
Width	23¼	59
Height	17¹³⁄₁₆	45.5
Lower Panel		
Width	23¼	59
Height	4¹¹⁄₁₆	12

For custom raised panels, the decor trim will accept up to a ³⁄₁₆″ flange. The raised panel can be mounted on a backing sheet cut to fit as above. The raised portion should fit inside the dimensions as indicated.

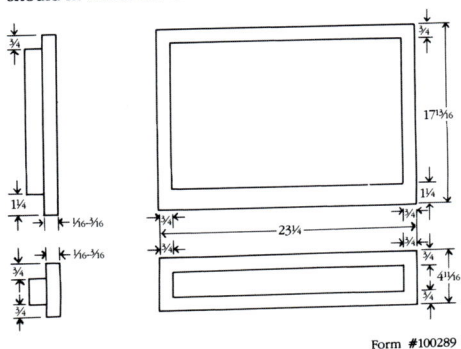

ASKO ASEA

ASKO USA, Inc., 903 N. Bowser, #170, Richardson, Texas 75081, 214-644-8595

Form #100289

The Creda Collection

Combination circulaire oven

CSO 200 SERIES

THE ULTIMATE COMBINATION OVEN, THAT
GENUINELY COMBINES TRADITIONAL FAN OVEN
COOKING WITH THE SPEED OF MICROWAVE.
A CIRCULAIRE FAN CONVECTION OVEN, AN
ADVANCED MICROWAVE AND
BROILER – ALL BRILLIANTLY COMBINED IN ONE
SPACE SAVING WALL OR UNDER
COUNTER OVEN, OFFERING 5-OPTION COOKING
VERSATILITY AND INCREDIBLE COOKING SPEED.

*Select convection oven, broiler or microwave
individually, or combine microwave/convection
oven or microwave/broiler for exceptional
cooking speed with natural browning and finish.*

*Circulaire fan convection oven with auto
control, providing even heat distribution for full
oven usage with no basting or flavor transfer.*

*Advanced 600W microwave, with high, low, roast
and defrost power options, plus auto defrost
program.*

Broiler in top of oven with half-on facility.

*Electronic temperature probe senses when roasts
are perfectly cooked and, along with
combination oven programs and auto control, will,
at the end of the cooking time, automatically
switch to keep warm.*

*Sophisticated yet simple-to-use digital display;
12 hour delay and minute timer, pre-set
power levels for 9 combination cooking programs
ensures perfect results.*

MODEL CSO 200 SERIES, AVAILABLE IN BLACK OR WHITE FINISH.

Solarspeed ceramic cooktops

EHH 200 AND EHH 250 SERIES

BEAUTIFULLY SLEEK AND PRACTICAL
SLIMLINE COOKTOPS IN ONE-PIECE CERAMIC GLASS,
EACH INCORPORATING 2 SOLARSPEED
HALOGEN ELEMENTS FOR EXCEPTIONAL RESPONSE
AND CONTROL.

*Incredibly tough ceramic glass top – the
ultimate in uncluttered style and easy cleaning.*

*2 Solarspeed halogen elements for immediate
visual cooking response and exceptionally even heat
spread, plus 2 radiant elements.*

*30" model with staggered format for optimum pan
usage and rest space, with power-on and
cooktop hot indicator lights.*

*24" model with 2 large and 2 regular elements,
offering 3 power outputs, and power-on
indicator light.*

*Slimline profile to fit over a drawer or Creda
undercounter oven. Controls can be positioned left
or right.*

The Creda Collection

THE CREDA DOMINO COOKTOP SERIES

This comprehensive range of Modular, design-integrated cooktops offers a versatility of cooking styles which enables personal creative flair to flow through.

There is a range of seven Dominos:

◆ A Gas Sealed Burner Domino - offering a large 10,000 BTU high efficiency burner alongside a regular 5000 BTU Burner.

◆ A large 12000 BTU Wok Domino for those who enjoy food with an oriental flavor.

◆ A Solid Element Domino offering two fast solid element burners - one at 2000W and one 1500W.

◆ Electric Halogen Domino. This Domino has an 1800W Halogen element and a 1200W Quickstar element, offering direct visual response and an attractive easy to clean surface.

◆ Barbeque Domino. A powerful 3000W element enables the user to barbeque whatover the weather. Lava stones ensure even heat spread and fat absorption.

◆ Deep Fryer Domino. With a powerful 2000W heating element for rapid warm up, frying becomes easy with this unit. Thermostatically controlled from 0 - 320°F with a safety temperature cut out. This unit also has a 4 litre oil bath which is easily removable for cleaning.

◆ Downdraft Domino. This unit is an ideal complement to the Deep Fryer and Barbeque keeping the kitchen free of smoke and steam. The unit comes with either an internal or external motor to suit all installations.

All Domino units come in an attractive stainless steel finish, with a choice of lids either Stainless, White or Black.

All units have an appealing easy to clean glass fascia with simple controls complete with on/off indicator lights.

◆ 7 units offering versatility of cooking methods

◆ Elegant European Styling

◆ Easy to install

◆ Stylish Stainless Steel finish with a choice of lids

Stainless   White   Black

PRODUCT SPECIFICATIONS

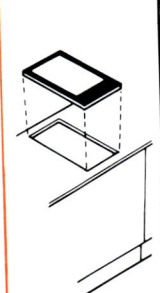

DOMINO COOKTOPS - STAINLESS STEEL		GDS103	GDW103	EDD203	EDS203	EDF203	EDB203	EDH200
OVERALL DOMINO	WIDTH	11 13/16"	11 13/16"	3 1/4"	11 13/16"	11 13/16"	11 13/16"	11 13/16"
	DEPTH	20"	20"	20"	20"	20"	20"	20"
COUNTERTOP APERATURE	WIDTH	11 1/16"	11 1/16"	2 3/8"	11 1/16"	11 1/16"	11 1/16"	11 1/16"
	DEPTH	19 5/16"	19 5/16"	19	19 5/16"	19 5/16"	19 5/16"	19 5/16"
HEATING ELEMENTS (LOAD)					3500W	2000W	3000W	3000W
HEAT INPUT	LARGE BURNER	10,000BTU	12,000BTU		2000W			1800W
	REGULAR BURNER	5,000BTU			1500W			1200W
VOLTAGE (60hz)		120V	120V	120V	240V	240V	240V	240V
APPROXIMATE SHIPPING WEIGHT (lbs)		14	12	4	16	23	23	15

WARRANTY

Creda appliances are guaranteed against faulty material or workmanship, for two full years from the date of original purchase.

If any part is found to be defective within the warranty period, we, or our Service Agent will replace or at our option, repair that part free of charge for materials and labor.

Creda INC 5700 WEST TOUHY AVE., CHICAGO IL 60648
TEL: (708) 647-8024

The Creda Collection

THE CREDA DOMINO COOKTOP SERIES

The Creda Collection

CREDA TELESCOPIC DOWNDRAFTS
ETD 303 & 363

FOR THE PERFECT COOKTOP COMBINATION

Creda now offer the perfect combination for cooktop cooking, either a Creda Gas or Electric Cooktop complemented by a Creda Telescopic Downdraft.

The new Creda Telescopic Downdraft comes in two sizes 30″ and 36″. Unlike most downdrafts however the covers are a full 30″ or 36″ wide giving a perfect flush finish when placed with your cooktop.

◆ The Creda ETD rises to a height of 7″ above the cooktop extracting all steam, smoke and smells without affecting either the food being cooked or the energy efficiency.

◆ The Creda ETD rises smoothly by just touching the cover above the hidden button. When extraction is complete, by just touching the button, the telescopic extractor lowers to the cooktop level where the cover falls flush for a perfect finish.

◆ The Creda ETD has a complete range of covers to choose from; aluminium, glass and ceramic.

◆ Infinite speed control switch located conveniently at the side.

◆ Both Creda Telescopic Downdraft units have a powerful 500 CFM blower which uses standard 6″ round ducting - making installation an easier task.

◆ Full 30″ or 36″ covers.

◆ Covers available in aluminium, glass, ceramic.

◆ Complements all Creda cooktops.

◆ Telescopic extractor with infinite speed control.

◆ Suitable for conventional, island & peninsula kitchen design.

PRODUCT SPECIFICATIONS

CREDA TELESCOPIC DOWNDRAFTS	ETD 303	ETD 363
VOLTS	120	120
AMPS	4.0	4.0
CFM	500	500
DUCT	6″round	6″round
FILTER	Aluminium (replaceable)	Aluminium (replaceable)
ELECTRICAL	Std. - 3 prong grounded cord	Std. - 3 prong grounded cord
WIDTH (with cover)	30″	36″
DEPTH BENEATH WORK SURFACE	28³/4″	28³/4″

The system will operate most efficiently when the duct work does not exceed 40ft of straight duct (Round Elbows = 6ft of straight duct, 90⁰ Elbows = 8ft of straight duct, Transitions = 2ft of straight duct.

COVER SPECIFICATIONS

	COLOUR	SIZE
ALUMINIUM	Satin or Black	30″or 36″
GLASS	White or Black	30″or 36″
CERAMIC	White or Black	30″or 36″

WARRANTY

Creda appliances are guaranteed against faulty material or workmanship, for two full years from the date of original purchase.

If any part is found to be defective within the warranty period, we, or our Service Agent will replace or at our option, repair that part free of charge for materials and labor.

Creda INC. 5700 WEST TOUHY AVE., CHICAGO IL60648
TEL: (708) 647-8024

The Creda Collection

CREDA TELESCOPIC DOWNDRAFTS
ETD 303 & 363

Specifications

ELECTRIC DOUBLE WALL OVEN EDO 200 SERIES

BLACK EDO 200/WHITE EDO 202

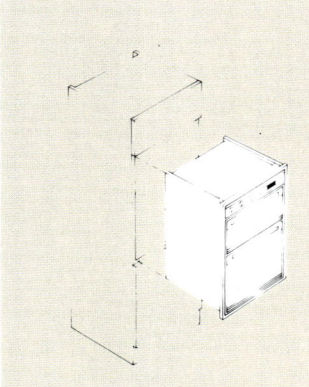

- PORCELAIN ENAMEL BROILER PAN AND RACK
- REMOVABLE DROP DOWN DOOR FOR EASY CLEANING
- FULL SIZE OVEN WINDOW AND LIGHT
- SIDE OPENING REVERSIBLE DOOR
- THREE OVEN RACKS
- PORCELAIN ENAMEL MEAT PAN AND ANTI-SPLASH TRAY
- ILLUMINATED CONTROL PANEL

	HEIGHT	WIDTH	DEPTH	LOAD W
OVERALL OVEN	34⁷/₈″	23½″	22¼″	5500
CABINET APERTURE (MIN. DIM.)	34³/₄″	22½″	22³/₈″	
BROILER		14¼″	9⁷/₈″	2900
TOP OVEN	8¼″	17″	17⅛″	1920
MAIN OVEN	15″	15⁷/₈″	15³/₈″	2500
CAPACITY BROILER	139 IN²			
TOP OVEN	1.39 CU.FT.			
MAIN OVEN	2.12 CU.FT.			
TOTAL LOAD				5500
VOLTAGE			240V, 60Hz, AC	
AMPERAGE				23A MAX
APPROX. SHIPPING WT. (LBS)				152

ELECTRIC SINGLE WALL OVEN ESO 200 SERIES

BLACK ESO 200/WHITE ESO 202

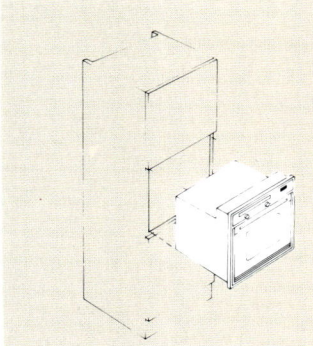

- REMOVABLE DROP DOWN DOOR
- THREE OVEN RACKS
- PORCELAIN ENAMEL BROILER/ MEAT PAN WITH TRAY
- ILLUMINATED CONTROL PANEL

	HEIGHT	WIDTH	DEPTH	LOAD W
OVERALL OVEN	23″	23½″	22¼″	3000
CABINET APERTURE	22⁷/₈″	22½″	22³/₈″	
CAPACITY BROILER	139.5 IN²			2900
OVEN	2.12 CU.FT.			2500
TOTAL LOAD				3000
VOLTAGE			240V, 60Hz, AC	
AMPERAGE				12.5A MAX
APPROX. SHIPPING WT. (LBS)				110

COMBINATION CIRCULAIRE OVEN CSO 200 SERIES

BLACK CSO 200/WHITE CSO 202

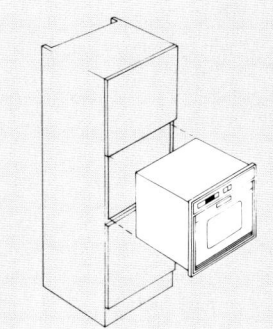

- Full size oven window and light
- Drop down door
- Ceramic broiler/meat pan with tray
- Illuminated control panel

	HEIGHT	WIDTH	DEPTH	LOAD W
OVERALL OVEN	23"	23½"	22¼"	4050
CABINET APERTURE	22⅞"	22½"	22⅜"	
CAPACITY BROILER	129.4 IN²			2330
OVEN	1.8 CU.FT.			2500
MICROWAVE OUTPUT 600W				1450
VOLTAGE				240V, 60HZ, AC
AMPERAGE				16.9A MAX
APPROX. SHIPPING WT. (LBS)				113

SOLARSPEED CERAMIC COOKTOPS

EHH 200 AND EHH 250 SERIES

30" SOLARSPEED CERAMIC COOKTOP BLACK EHH 200/GRAY EHH 202

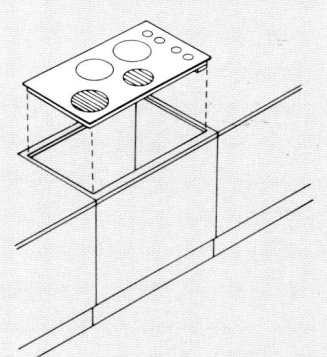

	WIDTH	DEPTH
OVERALL COOKTOP	30⅜"	18½"
COUNTERTOP APERTURE	29½"	17¾"
4 HEATING AREAS 1 x 7" DIA. Halogen Element		LOAD 1800W
1 x 5¾" DIA. Halogen Element		LOAD 1200W
2 x 7" DIA. Radiant Element		LOAD 1800W
VOLTAGE		240V, 60HZ, AC
AMPERAGE		27.5A MAX
APPROX. SHIPPING WT. (LBS)		35

24" SOLARSPEED CERAMIC COOKTOP BLACK EHH 250/GRAY EHH 252

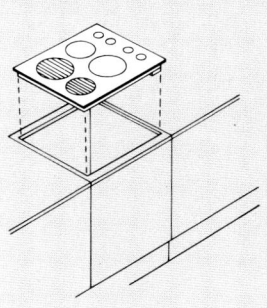

	WIDTH	DEPTH
OVERALL COOKTOP	22⅞"	20⅛"
COUNTERTOP APERTURE	22⅛"	19⅜"
4 HEATING AREAS 1 x 7" DIA. Halogen Element		LOAD 1800W
1 x 5¾" DIA. Halogen Element		LOAD 1200W
1 x 7" DIA. Radiant Element		LOAD 1600W
1 x 5¾" DIA. Radiant Element		LOAD 1200W
VOLTAGE		240V, 60HZ, AC
AMPERAGE		24.2A MAX
APPROX. SHIPPING WT. (LBS)		31

36" GAS GLASS COOKTOP BLACK GGH 100/WHITE GGH 102

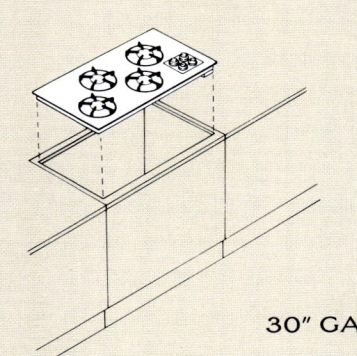

	WIDTH	DEPTH
OVERALL COOKTOP	36"	21"
COUNTERTOP APERTURE	33"	16½"
VOLTAGE	120V, 60Hz, AC	
AMPERAGE	0.005A MAX	
HEAT INPUT High Efficiency Large Burner	10,000 BTU/HR	
High Efficiency Regular Burner	6,000 BTU/HR	

30" GAS GLASS COOKTOP BLACK GGH 150/WHITE GGH 152

	WIDTH	DEPTH
OVERALL COOKTOP	30"	21"
COUNTERTOP APERTURE	26½"	16½"
VOLTAGE	120V, 60Hz, AC	
AMPERAGE	0.005A MAX	
HEAT INPUT High Efficiency Large Burner	10,000 BTU/HR	
High Efficiency Regular Burner	6,000 BTU/HR	

AGA Design Certified, and suitable for LPG conversion using a simple AGA Design Certified conversion kit. Ask your Creda dealer for details.

CREDA DOMINO COOKTOPS

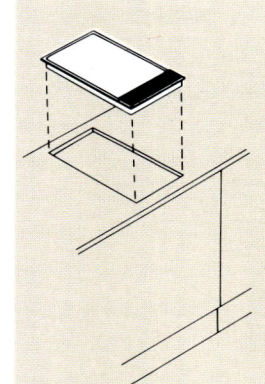

DOMINO COOKTOPS – STAINLESS STEEL		GDS103	GDW103	EDD203	EDS203	EDF203	EDB203	EDH200
OVERALL DOMINO	WIDTH	11¹³/₁₆"	11¹³/₁₆"	3¼"	11¹³/₁₆"	11¹³/₁₆"	11¹³/₁₆"	11¹³/₁₆"
	DEPTH	20"	20"	20"	20"	20"	20"	20"
COUNTERTOP APERTURE	WIDTH	11¹/₁₆"	11¹/₁₆"	2³/₈"	11¹/₁₆"	11¹/₁₆"	11¹/₁₆"	11¹/₁₆"
	DEPTH	19⁵/₁₆"	19⁵/₁₆"	19"	19⁵/₁₆"	19⁵/₁₆"	19⁵/₁₆"	19⁵/₁₆"
HEATING ELEMENTS (LOAD)					3500W	2000W	3000W	3000W
HEAT INPUT	LARGE BURNER	10,000BTU (GDS103)	12,000BTU (GDW103)					
	REGULAR BURNER	5,000BTU (GDS103)						
VOLTAGE (60Hz)		120V	120V	120V	240V	240V	240V	240V
APPROXIMATE SHIPPING WEIGHT (LBS)		14	12	4	16	23	23	15

5700 West Touhy Ave., Chicago IL60648.

Tel: (708) 647 8024

Convection Plus
Self-Cleaning Built-In Ovens
Made in America

DACOR takes great pride in presenting the "Convection Plus" electric built-in oven. Its sophisticated simplicity of styling, ease of cleaning and unique cooking features make the extraordinary Convection Plus a pleasure to have in your kitchen.

The 30″ Convection Plus, available in either black or white, offers you many special benefits. One of these is the combination of self-cleaning convenience with convection cooking. The oven cleans itself during the self-cleaning cycle, eliminating even the toughest baked-on soil.

Another significant benefit of the Convection Plus is its enormous capacity of 3.4 cu. ft. Never has a convection oven designed for home use offered so much cooking capacity. The three 24-inch wide racks adjust to six different positions. The uniform air circulation of the DACOR oven enables you to fully load the racks and prepare foods in quantity...a feature not available in a standard oven. Pizzas, cakes, cookies, biscuits, muffins and frozen convenience foods can be prepared on two or three racks at the same time.

cooking flexibility...sophisticated simplicity of design

"Pure convection" cooking in a 30" oven is another exclusive of the Dacor Convection Plus. Five different cooking modes gives you complete versatility and enable you to prepare delicious meals conveniently, efficiently and quickly. "Standard Bake" offers you the best in conventional baking, preparing your favorite recipes just the way you like them... "Standard Broil" is a quick and flavorful way to enjoy hamburgers, chicken, chops and steaks. The three modes of "Pure Convection," "Convection Bake" and "Convection Broil"

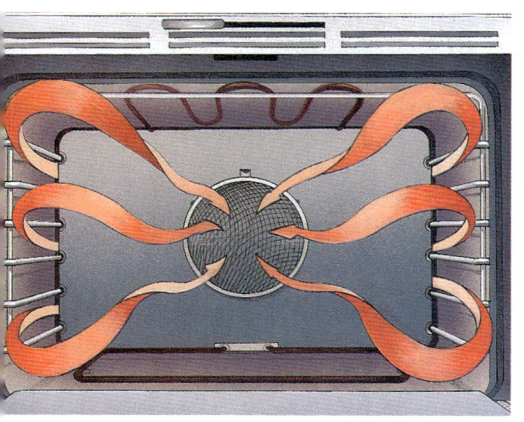

are a passport to special cuisine. Convection is the fan-circulated hot air process employed by professional chefs. "Pure Convection" uses a third element outside the oven cavity to heat the air before it is evenly circulated throughout the cooking compartment by a powerful fan. This equalizes the temperature, eliminates hot and cold spots, and results in very uniformly cooked food.

When cooked by convection, roasts have their juices sealed in, making them more moist and tender and perfectly browned without basting or turning. Breads are evenly textured with golden crusts. Pastries and desserts of all types are superior when baked in the circulating heated air. Convection is also excellent for delicate foods which do not get overly dry. Convection broiling is ideal for broiling extra-thick steaks or chops and also a quick method of broiling fish. Since the DACOR broiler is thermostatically controlled, you can

adjust the broiling temperature in both the convection and standard modes to accommodate whatever you are broiling.

Another advantage of the convection process is its saving of time and energy. The flow of heated air circulating throughout the Convection Plus cooks the food faster and at lower temperatures than in conventional ovens.

A special plus of the DACOR oven is an unique "Defrost Mode" which speeds up the process of defrosting. Using only the fan, the oven defrosts food far faster than would take place in the refrigerator or on the counter.

The ultimate in cooking versatility and capacity are two ovens either stacked or side-by-side. You can use different cooking modes in any combination of convection and/or conventional modes to cook a variety of courses at the same time. The DACOR Convection Plus also enables you to cook with gas and bake with electricity by placing it under a DACOR cooktop.

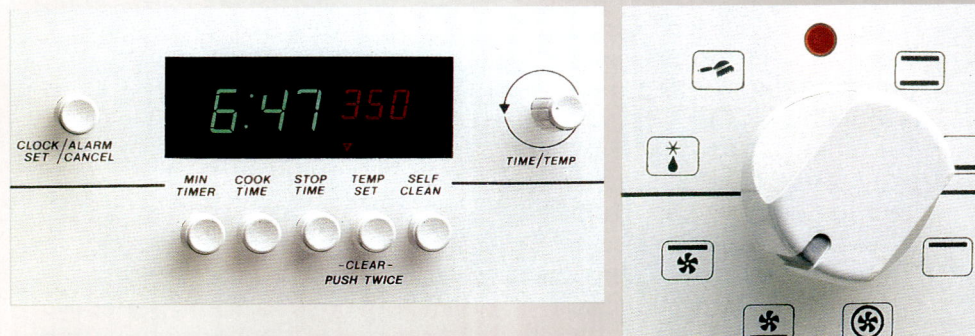

dacor

The Convection Plus control panel is extremely easy to operate. It is uncluttered with just one selector switch controlling all of the cooking functions. Each of the oven's eight functions is symbolized for ease of reading.

The digital electronic clock/timer allows you maximum flexibility and freedom. Its "Delayed Time Cooking" feature allows you to start your cooking at a pre-designated time without your presence. Come home to delicious meals cooked while you are working or enjoying other activities. Most important—the clock is easy to understand and operate. Just preset the cooking time required and the time you want your cooking completed. Then select the desired cooking mode and the appropriate temperature. The clock does the rest by counting down the cooking time and either automatically shutting off the oven with a pleasant audible sound or reducing the heat to 150° which keeps the food at serving temperature.

The control panel also has a separate control for the oven light which enables you to observe the food through the see-through window without opening the door and losing heat. An added feature of the Convection Plus is high density insulation which prevents heat loss and insures a cool exterior.

All DACOR products are covered by one-year warranty. Constant product improvements make some features and specifications subject to change without notice.

LISTED

Lit. No. L80140   © August, 1989, DACOR   Printed in U.S.A.

Cabinet Planning: Convection Plus (Model 305)

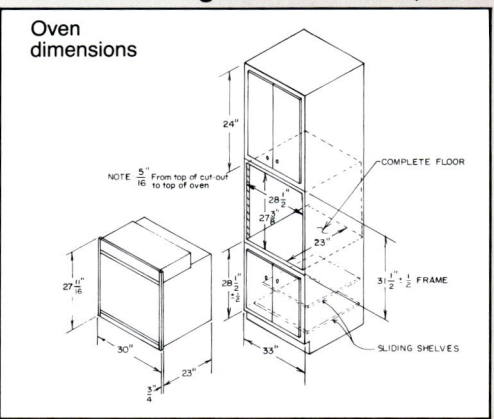

Oven dimensions

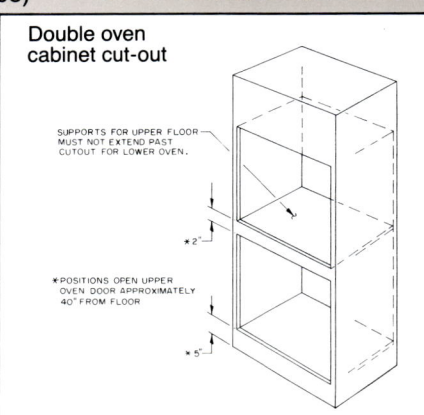

Double oven cabinet cut-out

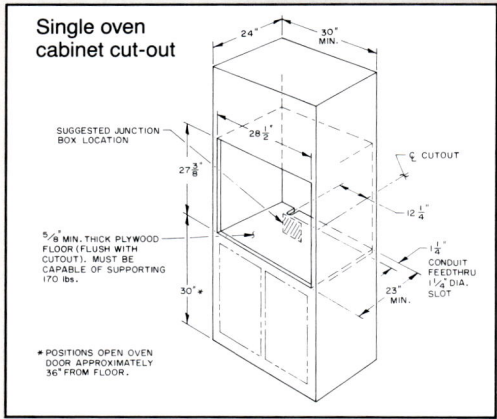

Single oven cabinet cut-out

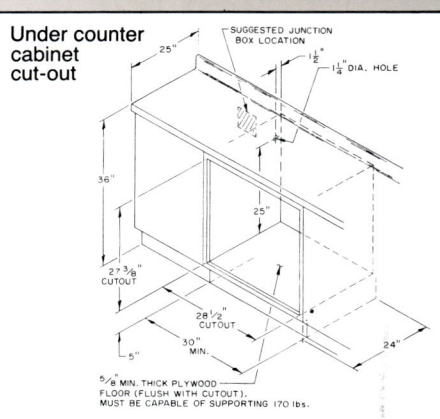

Under counter cabinet cut-out

Maximum Connection Load 5 k.w. @ 240 V 20 amps.

dacor
A reflection of your good taste.™

950 South Raymond Avenue
Pasadena, California 91109
(818) 799-1000

THE DACOR SMOOTH TOP

Cooking with Style and Performance

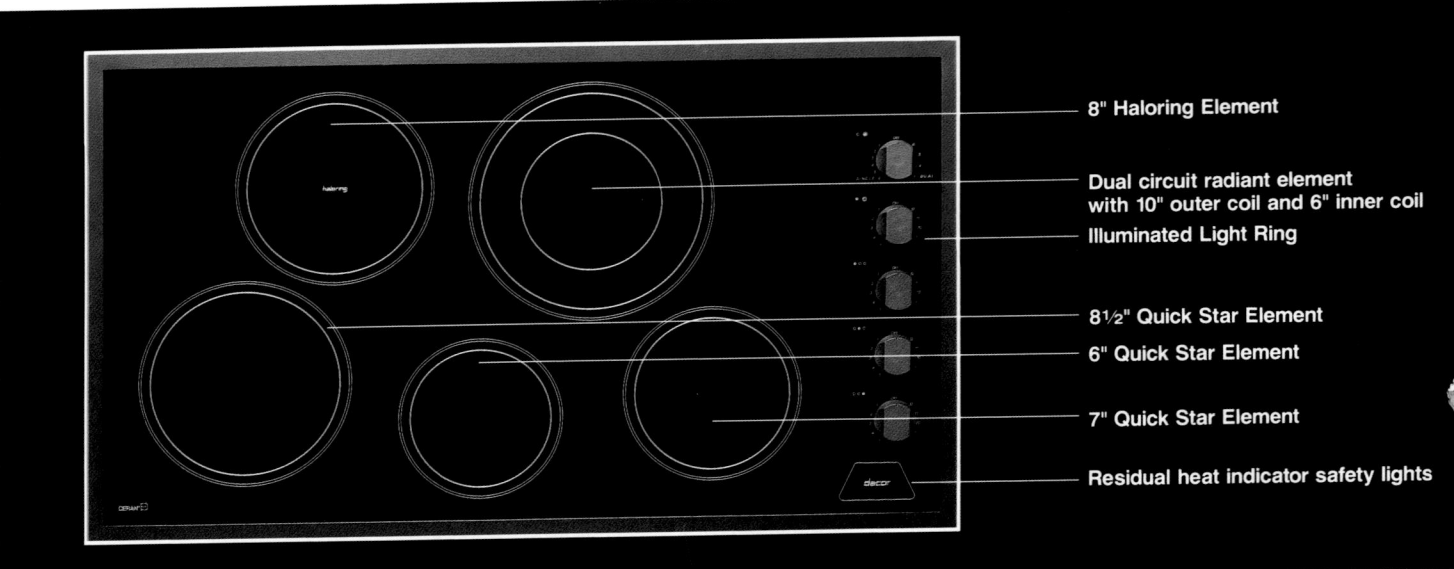

8" Haloring Element

Dual circuit radiant element
with 10" outer coil and 6" inner coil

Illuminated Light Ring

8½" Quick Star Element

6" Quick Star Element

7" Quick Star Element

Residual heat indicator safety lights

Smooth Top Five (CET 365)

Cooking with Style and Performance

The black Ceran® glass surface of this new cook-top is fashionable, functional, and easy to clean. The DACOR Smooth Top Five also offers you that something extra you have come to expect from DACOR—a fifth element for added cooking capability.

The surface of the cooktop is just one smooth piece of Ceran glass. There are no protruding elements or separate control panel. When the elements are on, they glow through the translucent glass.

Sleek and sophisticated, the DACOR Smooth Top becomes the centerpiece of the countertop. The elegant steel black frame which surrounds the Ceran panel provides an almost seamless transition between the cooktop and the surrounding surface. The Smooth Top coordinates with virtually any material used for the countertop.

The cooking surface is made to stay attractive through years of use. Normal use will not mar the surface, and the color of the Ceran tends to mini-mize any scratches that might occur.

All DACOR appliances are Made in America

Unique Combination of Elements Designed with Your Cooking Needs in Mind

The Smooth Top Five is a 36" cooktop with five elements; the Smooth Top Four is a 30" cooktop with four elements. These elements are spaced so that there is plenty of room between them to accommodate most cooking needs.

There are three different types of elements for maximum cooking flexibility. A new type of element is the 8" Haloring of 1800 watts which provides an instant visual heat response. An infrared lamp encircles a radiant coil for extremely uniform heat distribution on the cooking surface. This results in reduced boiling times and improved cooking performance.

A Dual Circuit radiant element in effect is two elements in one. You can use the single inner coil of 6" (1000 watts) alone or in combination with a larger diameter outer coil of 10" (2400 watts) on the Smooth Top Five and 9" (2000 watts) on the Smooth Top Four.

The third type of Smooth Top element is the Quick Star featuring a star shaped pattern in its center. This element provides a visual heat response within three to five seconds. There are three Quick Stars on the 36" five element model. They are 6" (1200 watts), 7" (1400 watts) and 8½" (1900 watts). The two on the 30" four-element model are 6" (1200 watts) and 8½" (1900 watts).

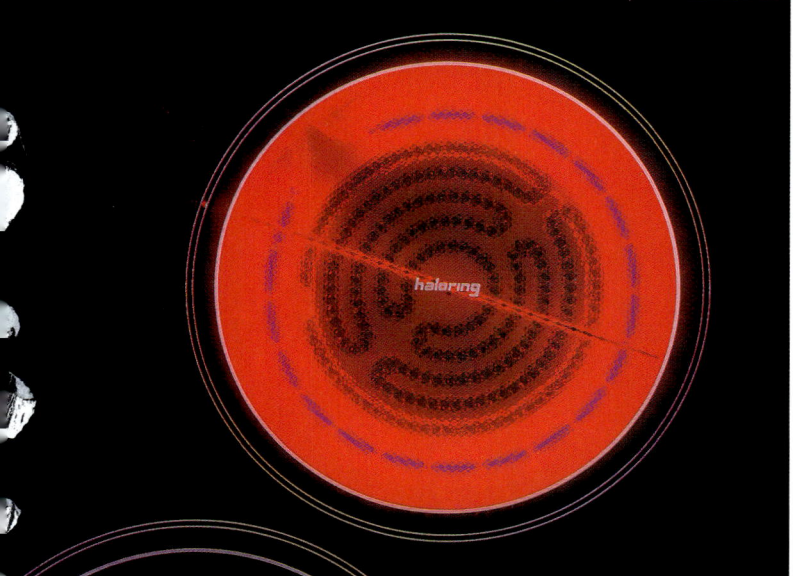

Haloring Element

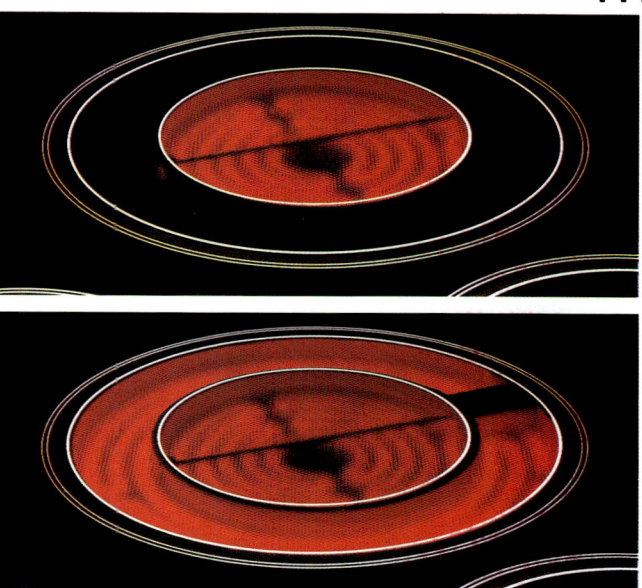

Dual Circuit Radiant Element

Why so many different size elements on the DACOR Smooth Top? Maximum versatility and greatly reduced boiling times! You can now match your different size pots and pans to the same size cooking element. This is not only quick and efficient— it saves time and money.

Unique Controls for Safety and Precision

The control for each element is encircled by a distinctive red light ring which illuminates when the element is in operation. You always see when the element is on even in other areas of the kitchen. The special residual heat indicator lights are another safety precaution. They remain illuminated to alert the user to hot cooking surfaces. All controls feature infinite power control for setting precise cooking temperatures and reversible direction for easy operation. These controls must be pushed to turn as an added safety precaution.

Quick Star Element

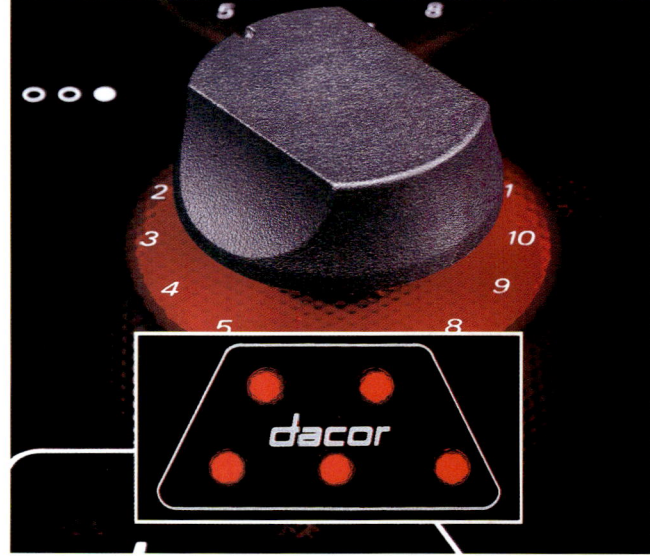

Illuminated Control and Residual Heat Indicator Lights

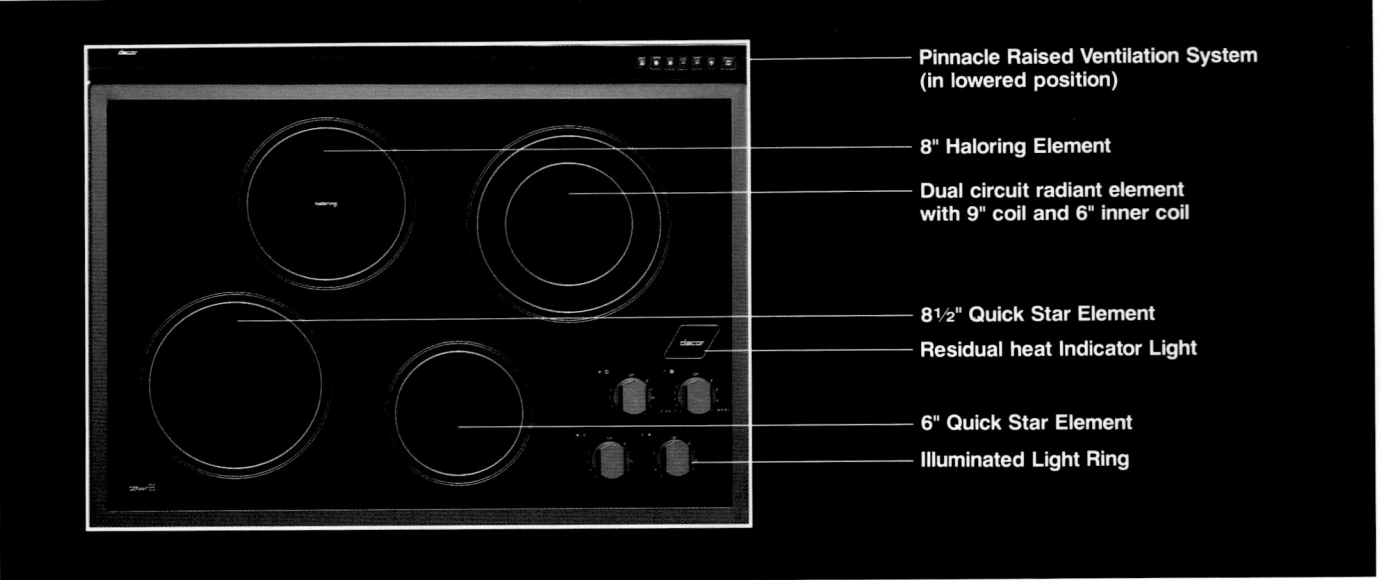

Pinnacle Raised Ventilation System
(in lowered position)

8" Haloring Element

Dual circuit radiant element
with 9" coil and 6" inner coil

8½" Quick Star Element

Residual heat Indicator Light

6" Quick Star Element

Illuminated Light Ring

Smooth Top Four (CET 304)

Unique Performance Characteristics

The special characteristics of the DACOR Smooth Top make it an ideal cooktop surface.

The composition and thickness of Ceran® transfers radiant and infrared heat readily which reduces boiling time and improves cooking performance through increased temperature uniformity. The heat is transmitted directly upward so even while one cooking zone gets hot, the rest of the cooktop surface remains cool. The Smooth Top concentrates heat where you want it and keeps it away from where you do not.

All of the elements are equipped with automatic limiters to ensure that the cooktop will not overheat or cause empty pots and pans to melt or damage the cooking surface.

The smooth surface of the DACOR Ceran cooktop makes moving cookware across the cooktop both safe and easy. Also, the seamless surface is easy to clean and maintain.

Ventilation Flexibility

The DACOR Smooth Top may be used with either DACOR's overhead or downdraft ventilation systems.

Overall Dimensions*

CET 304B 30" x 21" x 4"
CET 304B with 4400/6600 downdraft ventilation system 30" x 22¾"
CET 304B with Pinnacle ventilation system 30" x 23¼"

CET 365B 36" x 21" x 4"
CET 365B with 4400/6600 downdraft ventilation system 36" x 22¾"
CET 365B with Pinnacle ventilation system 36" x 23¼"

Cut-out Dimensions*

CET 304B 29¼" x 20¼"
CET 304B with 4400/6600 downdraft ventilation system 29¼" x 22⅜"
CET 304B with Pinnacle ventilation system 29¼" x 22⅝"

CET 365B 35¼" x 20¼"
CET 365B with 4400/6600 downdraft ventilation system 35¼" x 22⅜"
CET 365B with Pinnacle ventilation system 35¼" x 22⅝"

Maximum Connected Load

CET 304B 6.9 K.W. 30A. 240V.
CET 365B 8.7 K.W. 40A. 240V.

*Note: These dimensions are not intended for use as final installation specifications. Refer to installation instructions packed with unit for complete information. Constant product improvement makes some features and specifications subject to change without notice.

Cooking on a DACOR Smooth Top does not require special pots or pans. For best results:
● match the diameters of the cookware with approximately the same size element
● use cookware with slightly concave, smooth thick bottoms
● use clean dry cookware

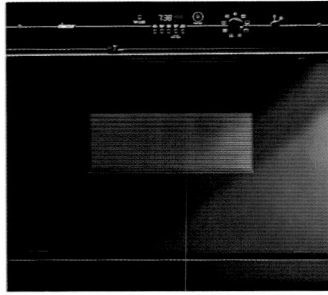

The perfect complement to your DACOR Smooth Top is the DACOR Convection Plus 30" self-cleaning oven. Offering unmatched useable capacity with extraordinary cooking capacity, it may be placed in the wall or under your Smooth Top.

A reflection of your good taste.™

Distinctive Appliance Corporation
950 South Raymond Avenue, Pasadena, California 91109
(818) 799-1000

LISTED

Lit. No. L-85221   © October 1990, DACOR   Printed in U.S.A.

Pinnacle™ Raised Ventilation System

dacor

"A reflection of your good taste."

More ventilation efficiency and more cabinet storage space

The Pinnacle is available in two series. The RVC series has a blower rated at approximately 600 CFM. It mounts to the vent plenum in the rear of the cabinet. The RVR series uses a remote power system rated at approximately 1000 CFM which provides efficiency for the longer-than-normal duct runs of external wall or roof installations.

Equally as important as efficient ventilation is adequate storage space for your kitchen needs. That's why DACOR has designed the Pinnacle to take a minimal amount of cabinet space underneath your cooktop area. While other ventilation systems may dominate the cabinet, the slim profile of the Pinnacle gives you the added value of almost a full cabinet for storage of kitchen utensils. The RVC series leaves approximately 80% of the cabinet underneath the cooktop for storage and the RVR series, approximately 95%.

RVC series for use with 5600 P3 cabinet blower

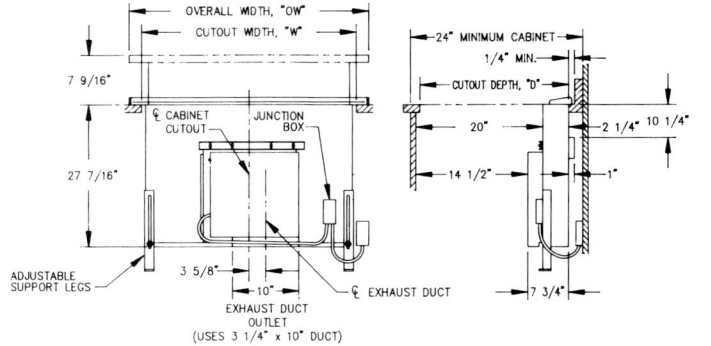

RVR series for use with 4400 P3 remote blower

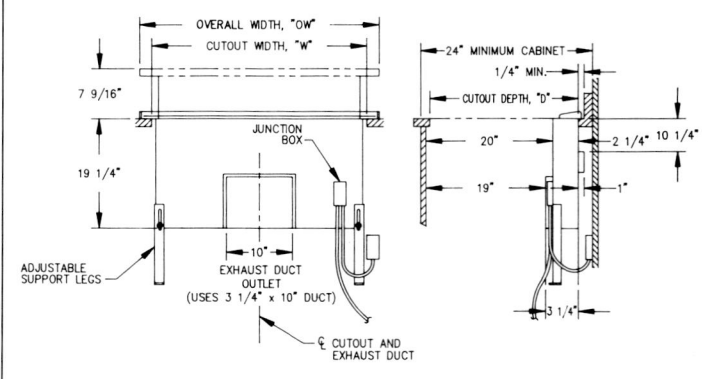

CUT-OUT/OVERALL DIMENSIONS

Model	Cut-out Dimensions		Overall Dimensions	
	W	D	OW	OD
RV 30	27½″	2⁵⁄₁₆″	30″	2½″
RV 36	33½″	2⁵⁄₁₆″	36″	2½″
RV 46	43½″	2⁵⁄₁₆″	46″	2½″
CET 304 with RV 30	29¼″	*22⅝″	30″	23⅛″
CET 365 with RV 36	35¼″	*22⅝″	36″	23⅛″
ECC 36 with RV 36	33½″	22⅜″	36″	23″
ECC 46 with RV 46	44¼″	22⅜″	46¹⁄₁₆″	23″
GC 30 with RV 30	27½″	21³⁄₁₆″	30″	23″
GC 36 with RV 36	33½″	20¹³⁄₁₆″	36″	23″
GC 46 with RV 46	43½″	22⁵⁄₁₆″	46¹⁄₁₆″	23″
GGC 304 with RV 30	27½″	21¹³⁄₁₆″	30″	23″
GGC 365 with RV 36	33¾″	21¹¹⁄₁₆″	36″	23″

★ Notched cut-out required, see installation instructions.

These dimensions are not intended for use as final installation specifications. Refer to installation instructions packed with unit for complete information.

dacor

***A reflection of your good taste.*™**
950 South Raymond Avenue
Pasadena, California 91109 (818) 799-1000

Lit. No. L85223
© November 1990, DACOR
Printed in U.S.A.

LISTED

Euroflair. The only line of European appliances that is, indeed, a complete line.

With Euroflair, we have created perfect symmetry. A series of modular units that can be used in infinite combinations. Gas and electric hobs (or cooktops to Americans) can be combined with electric grills. Maybe you'll want to suggest a third oven for entertaining. Perhaps a wine cooler in addition to the refrigerators and freezers.

However you configure Euroflair, the look will be stunning. Because each piece fits flush with surrounding cabinetry. And comes in colors like black, white, almond, gazelle, and stainless steel. Or custom panels.

The beauty of these appliances is that they perform as flawlessly as they look. We realize some people cook while others create. So each cooktop, oven, refrigerator, freezer, wine cooler and dishwasher has a specialty designed to enhance the cook's performance.

These appliances are crafted in Sweden, Denmark, Switzerland and Italy for authenticity that can't be matched.

But the fact that Euroflair is imported exclusively by Frigidaire tells you that your customers will never be left alone. Because Euroflair is backed by the entire Frigidaire service network.

To receive your free Euroflair information packet call 1-800-272-7992.

A MODULAR COLLECTION OF EUROPEAN KITCHEN APPLIANCES.

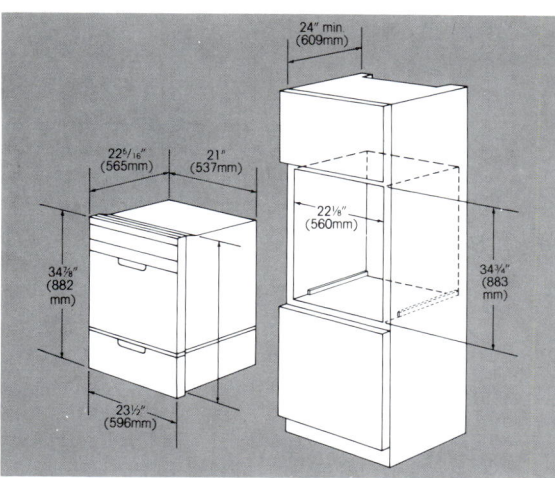

RGCF97E-Double Oven Built-in Wall Oven. 240V/60 Hz.

Upper oven, convection and conventional (Top/Bottom Heating) • Lower oven, conventional (Top/Bottom Heating) • Five selector settings for lower oven • Seven selector settings for top oven • See through black glass doors • Temperature probe on upper oven with Fahrenheit readout at timer • Atomizer to introduce moisture into upper oven • Electronic clock with timer and oven programmer • Euro-clean catalytic oven surface • Oven lights in both ovens • Two Baking/Broiling pans and four racks.

Interior space: upper–2 cu. ft., lower–1.6 cu. ft.

Available in White, Almond, Black and Gazelle.

Total Amps: 27.9.

RGCF94E-Built-in Electric Wall Oven. 240V/60 Hz.

Convection and conventional oven (Top/Bottom Heating) • Illuminated glass control panel • Seven setting selector control • Electronic clock with timer and oven programmer • Euro-clean catalytic oven surface • Oven lights • Baking/Broiling pan and three racks • See through black glass doors.

Interior space: 2 cu. ft.

Available in White, Almond, Black.

Total Amps: 14.2.

RGCF95E-Deluxe Built-in Electric Wall Oven. 240V/60 Hz.

Convection and conventional (Top/Bottom Heating) • Temperature probe with Fahrenheit readout at timer • Atomizer to introduce moisture into oven • Illuminated glass control panel • Seven setting selector control • Electronic clock with timer and oven programmer • Euro-clean catalytic oven surface • Oven lights • Baking/Broiling pan and three racks • See through black glass doors.

Interior space: 2 cu. ft.

Available in White, Almond, Black and Gazelle.

Total Amps: 14.2.

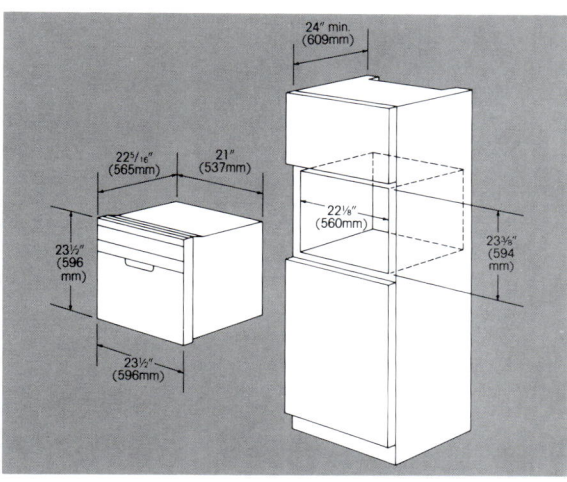

CAUTION: Consult installation instructions before making final cuts.

RBUGCF95E-Built-Under Electric Oven. 240V/60 Hz.

Convection and conventional oven (Top/Bottom Heating) • Illuminated glass control panel • Seven setting selector control • Two standard and two sensor surface unit controls • Electronic clock with timer and programmer • Atomizer to introduce moisture into oven • Temperature probe with Fahrenheit readout at timer • Euro-clean catalytic oven surface • Oven lights • Baking/Broiling pan and three racks • See through black glass doors.

Interior space: 2 cu. ft.

Available in White, Almond and Black.

Combines with RBF139CE, Electric Glass-Ceramic Hob (Cooktop), or RBSF129E, Electric Hob (Cooktop).
Total Amps: 47.9.

Accessories available on all oven models:
• White oven handles
• Professional perforated Teflon baking tray

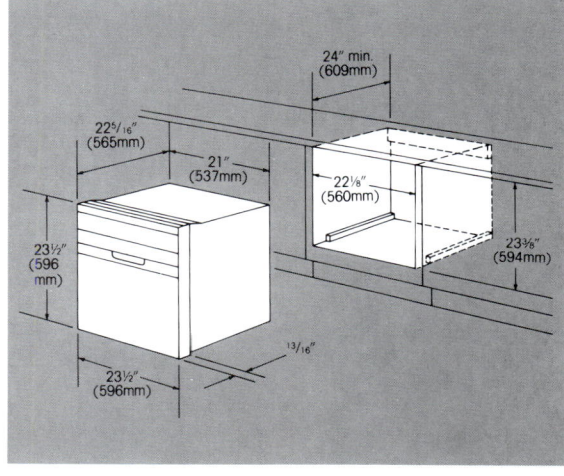

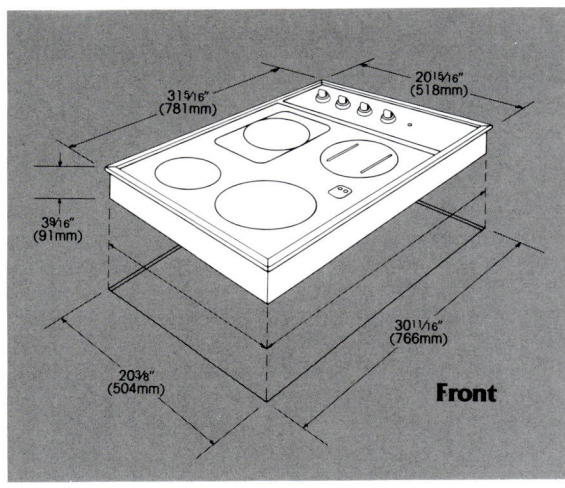

RBF136CL-Halogen Glass-Ceramic Hob.
• Four burners, I halogen element • 6½" x 11½" right rear element can be used for large pans when knob is in max position • Hot surface indicator lights • Hi-temp thermal safety switches • Integrated controls.

RBF139CE-Electric Glass-Ceramic Hob (Cooktop). 240V/60 Hz.
Glass-ceramic hob with radiant heating elements • Includes warming area • Cooking and warming zones indicated by graphic outlines • Hot surface indicator lamps • One 9", two 7¼" and one 6" cooking zones • Pan sensor on rear 7¼" and 6" cooking zones.

Combines with RBUGCF95E Built-Under Electric Oven or CBEF4E Control Panel.

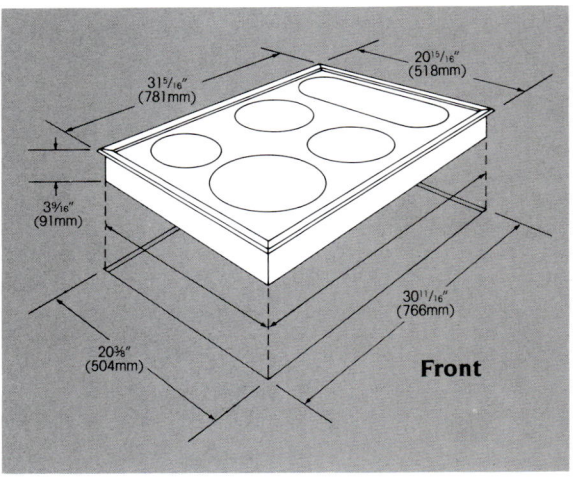

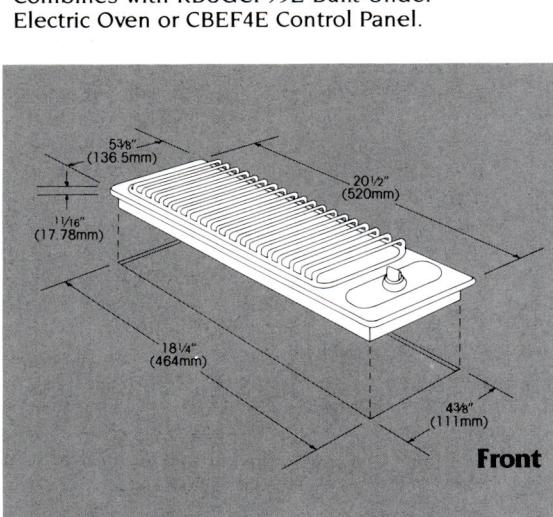

Downdraft ventilator (Top RDTPK)
• Provides extraction into outside air or ventilation flue • Grill is chromium plated and removable • Black painted frame • Infinite fan control • Interior blower (RDIP) 450CFM or exterior blower (RDEP) 900CFM • Dishwasher safe filter • On/off light.

CAUTION: Consult installation instructions before making final cuts.

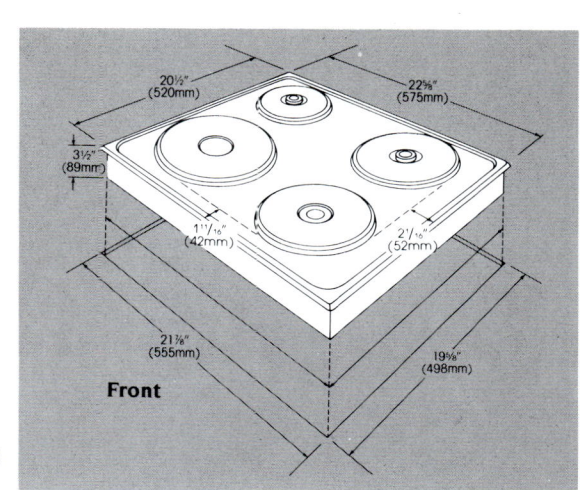

RBSF129E-Electric Hob.
240V/60 Hz.

Four sealed cast-iron heating elements; one 6″ with pan sensor, two 7¼″ including one with pan sensor, and one 9″.

Combines with RBUGCF95E Built-Under Electric Oven or CBEF4E Control Panel.

Available in White, Almond, Black, Gazelle and Stainless Steel.

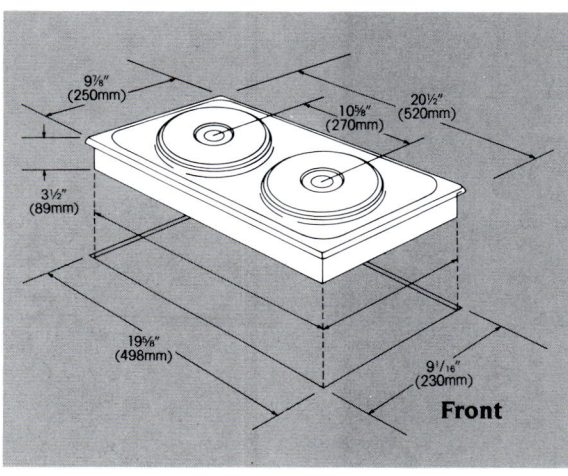

RBSF117E-Electric Hob.
240V/60 Hz.

Two sealed cast-iron heating elements, one 7¼″ and one 6″.

Combines with CBEF2E Control Panel.

Available in White, Almond, Black, Gazelle and Stainless Steel.

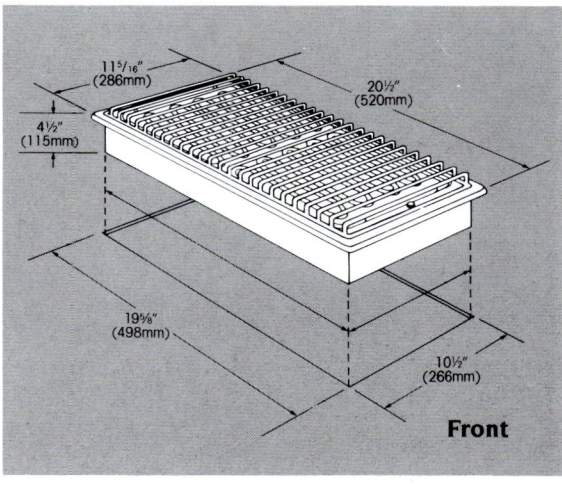

RBGF119E-Electric Grill.
240V/60 Hz.

Stainless steel unit • Lava rocks included • Stainless steel grilling grid • Two separately controlled swing-up heating elements each with numerous control settings.

Combines with CBEF2E Control Panel.

Optional covers available in White, Almond, Black, Gazelle and Stainless Steel.

Accessory item:
• Grill cover

NOTE: When installing multiple cooktops side-by-side, there should be a ¾″ countertop space between the units.

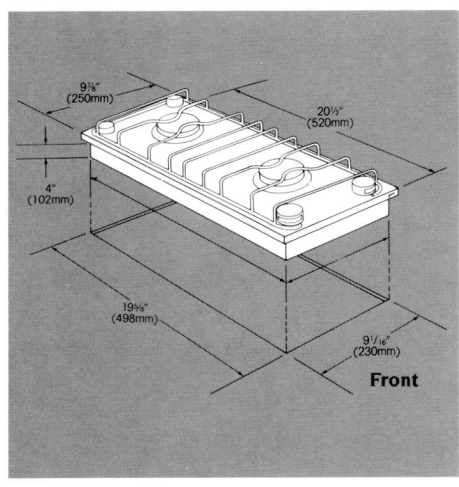

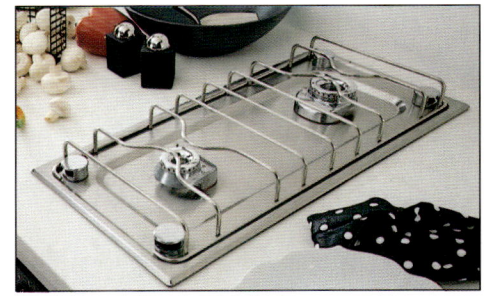

GBF117E-Gas Hob. 115V/60 Hz.

Two burner gas model • Electric ignition • Safety thermocouple • Equipped for natural gas • Convertible to LP • Pan support is stainless steel • Separate control panel included.

Available in White, Almond, Black, Gazelle and Stainless Steel.

Accessory item available:
• White face plate and control knobs

CAUTION: Consult installation instructions before making final cuts.

CBEF2E-Control Panel for RBSF117E Electric Hob or RBGF119E Electric Grill. 240V/60 Hz.

Control panel with indicator light for RBSF117E Electric Hob or RBGF119E Electric Grill • Two or more control panels can be interlocked together.

Shipped with black knobs and faceplates. Optional/white knobs and faceplates available.

Total Amps: 14.6.

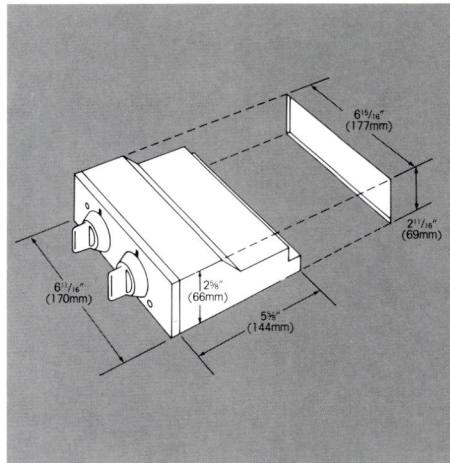

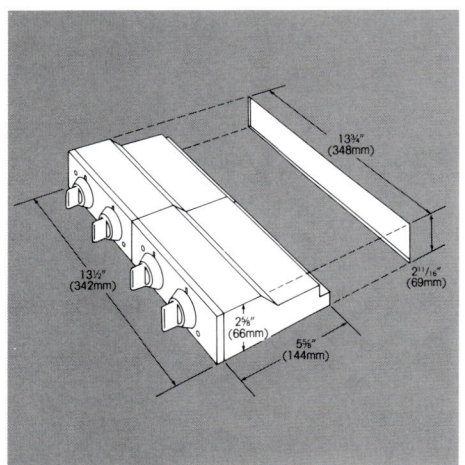

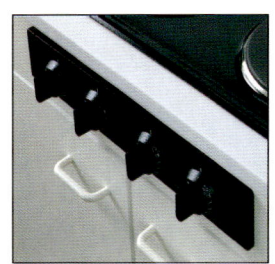

CBEF4E-Control Panel for RBF139CE Electric Glass-Ceramic Hob or RBSF129E Electric Hob. 240V/60 Hz.

Control panel with indicator lights for RBF139CE or RBSF129E hobs. Can be interlocked with CBEF2E.

Shipped with black knobs and faceplates. Optional/white knobs and faceplates available.

Total Amps: 33.8.

MCF899E Microwave Oven. 120V/60 Hz.

• Electronic touch controls, preprogrammed to cook 27 different items • Cook and defrost stages with 99-minute, 99-second timing capability in each stage • Ten power levels • Defrost & Hold setting • Two stage cooking • Automatic temperature probe • Reheat Times pad to short cut programming • Digital clock with handy 99-minute, 99-second timer • Digital prompt display • Removable molded glass cook & serve tray • Interior oven light • Under cabinet mounting kit available.

.8 cu. ft. capacity (22 liters).

Available in White.

Power Output: 700 Watts.

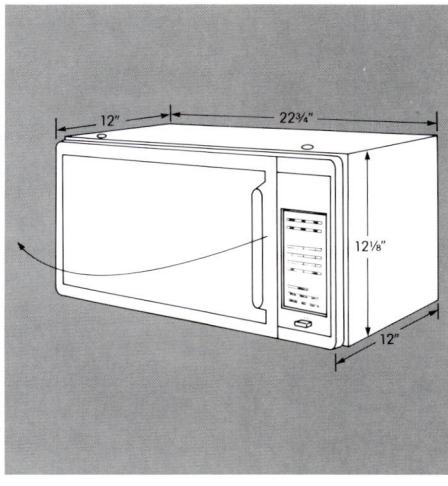

FCDF135E-Refrigerator. 115V/60 Hz.

Automatic defrost • ABS liner • Temperature control • Four adjustable feet • Reversible doors • Doors accept decorator panels up to ¼" thickness • Interior light • Adjustable shelf positions • Shutter for temperature adjustment in bottom compartment • See-through crispers.

Interior space: 13.1 cu. ft.

Available in White, Almond and Gazelle.

Total Amps: 1.7.

Wine cooler accessory kit available. Includes mirror door, and choice of brown coated wire shelves or wooden shelves, thermometer and snack drawer.

NOTE: All refrigeration models require a minimum of 3" (76mm) ventilation space above each unit.

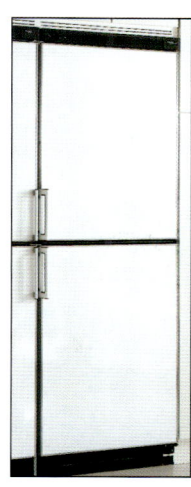

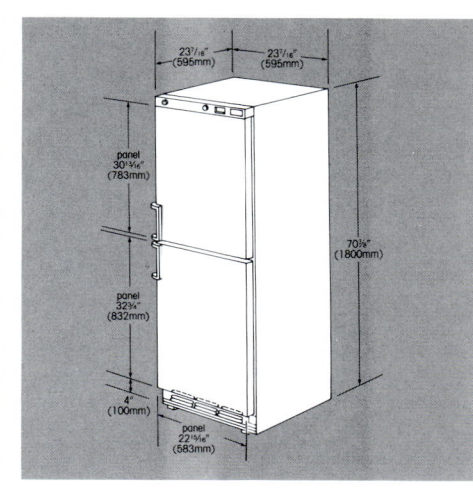

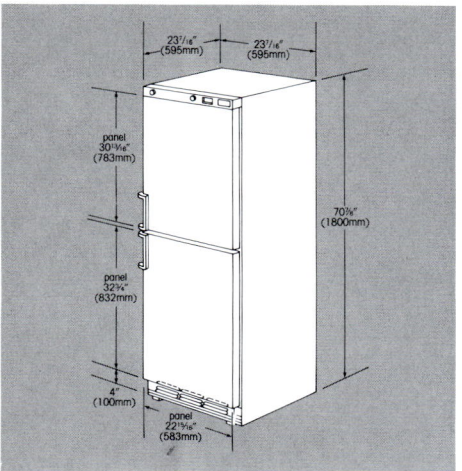

UFF1111E-Freezer. 115V/60 Hz.

Automatic icemaker • Manual defrost • Pull-out drawers with see-through fronts • Write-on storage cards • Built-in thermometer • Temperature control • Fast Freeze feature • Reversible doors • Doors accept decorator panels up to ¼" thickness • ABS liner • Four adjustable feet.

Interior space: 11.6 cu. ft.

Available in White, Almond and Gazelle.

Total Amps: 5.0.

UFPF101L-Frost-proof Freezer. 115V/60 Hz.

Automatic icemaker • Seven separate compartments with see-through fronts • Write-on storage cards • Built-in thermometer • Temperature control • Fast freeze feature • Reversible doors • Doors accept decorator panels up to ¼" thickness • ABS liner • Four adjustable feet.

Interior space: 9.6 cu. ft.

Available in White, Almond, and Gazelle.

Total Amps: 5.0.

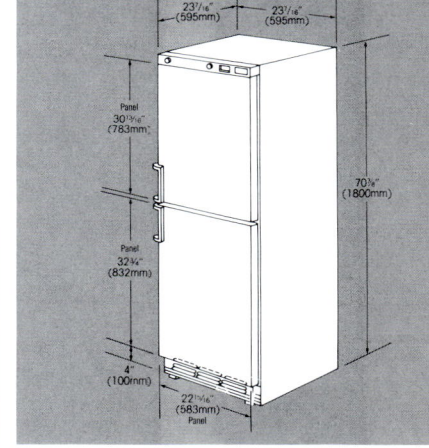

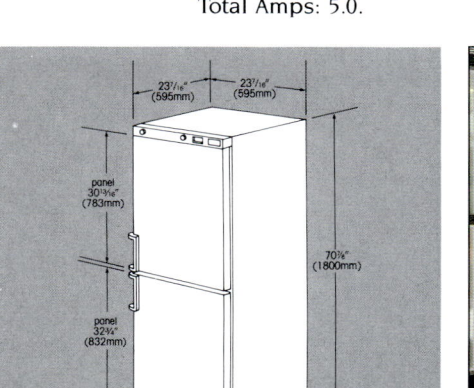

FPIF117BE-Refrigerator/Freezer. 115V/60 Hz.

Two fully-independent compartments with two compressors, two cooling circuits, and two temperature controls • Automatic defrost in top refrigerator compartment • Frost-Proof lower freezer compartment • ABS liner • Refrigerator has see-through crispers • Adjustable shelf positions • Interior light • Freezer has automatic icemaker • See-through storage fronts • Reversible doors • Doors accept decorator panels up to ¼" thickness • Energy Saver switch • Four adjustable feet.

Interior space: refrigerator 6.5 cu. ft., freezer 4.9 cu. ft.

Available in White, Almond and Gazelle.

Total Amps: 5.0.

Accessories available on all refrigeration models: • White coated wire shelves (standard shelves are chrome wire) • White door handles

FCDWF135EZ-Wine Cooler.
115V/60 Hz.

Two compartments for wine storage • Two temperature zone capability • Temperature control • Tinted glass doors • Two thermometers • ABS liner • Reversible doors • Ventilation valve in backwall for humidity • Adjustable shelves • Lock for security • Four Adjustable feet • Interior light • Gazelle cabinet color, however, the smoked glass doors with brushed stainless trim provide compatibility with all colors.

Total Amps: 1.7.

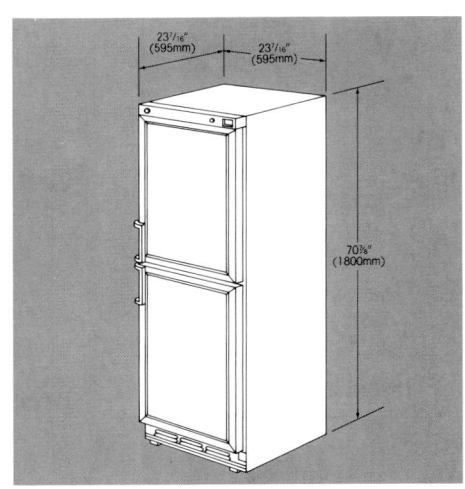

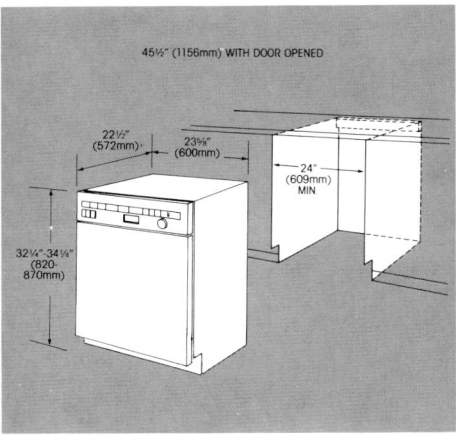

DWSF500E-Dishwasher (Integrated).
115V/60 Hz.

Stainless steel interior • 12 place setting capacity • 7 cycles (including Rinse and Hold) • Timer knob for cycle selection • Adjustable upper basket • Detergent dispenser • Rinse aid reservoir and dispenser • Three push buttons: 1) On/Off, 2) Water temp. 131°F or 149°F. 3) Economy dry.

Custom panel required to match cabinetry (not included).

Total Amps: 14.3.

DWF600E-Dishwasher (Panelable).
115V/60 Hz.

Porcelain enameled interior • Three-level wash action • Economy dry • Eleven push buttons • Delay start • Adjustable top rack • Detergent dispensers • Rinse aid dispenser • 14 place setting capacity • Color panels included. (Black, White, Almond and Brushed Chrome).

Total Amps: 12.2.

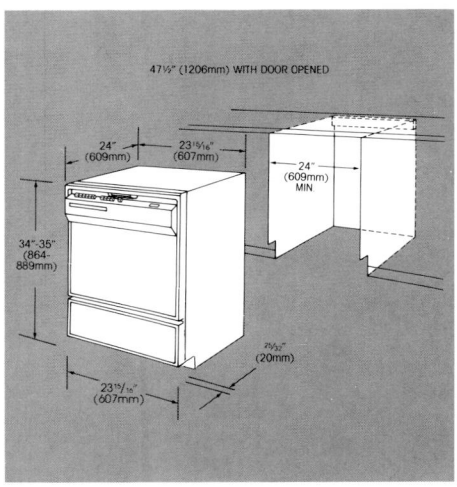

The high standards of Frigidaire quality results in continuing product improvements. We reserve the right to modify model specifications and features without notice or obligation.

Euroflair®
Imported by Frigidaire.

**Euroflair by Frigidaire
WCI Major Appliance Group
6000 Perimeter Drive
Dublin, Ohio 43017
(614) 792-4630**

White for the times.
Élite
from Frigidaire

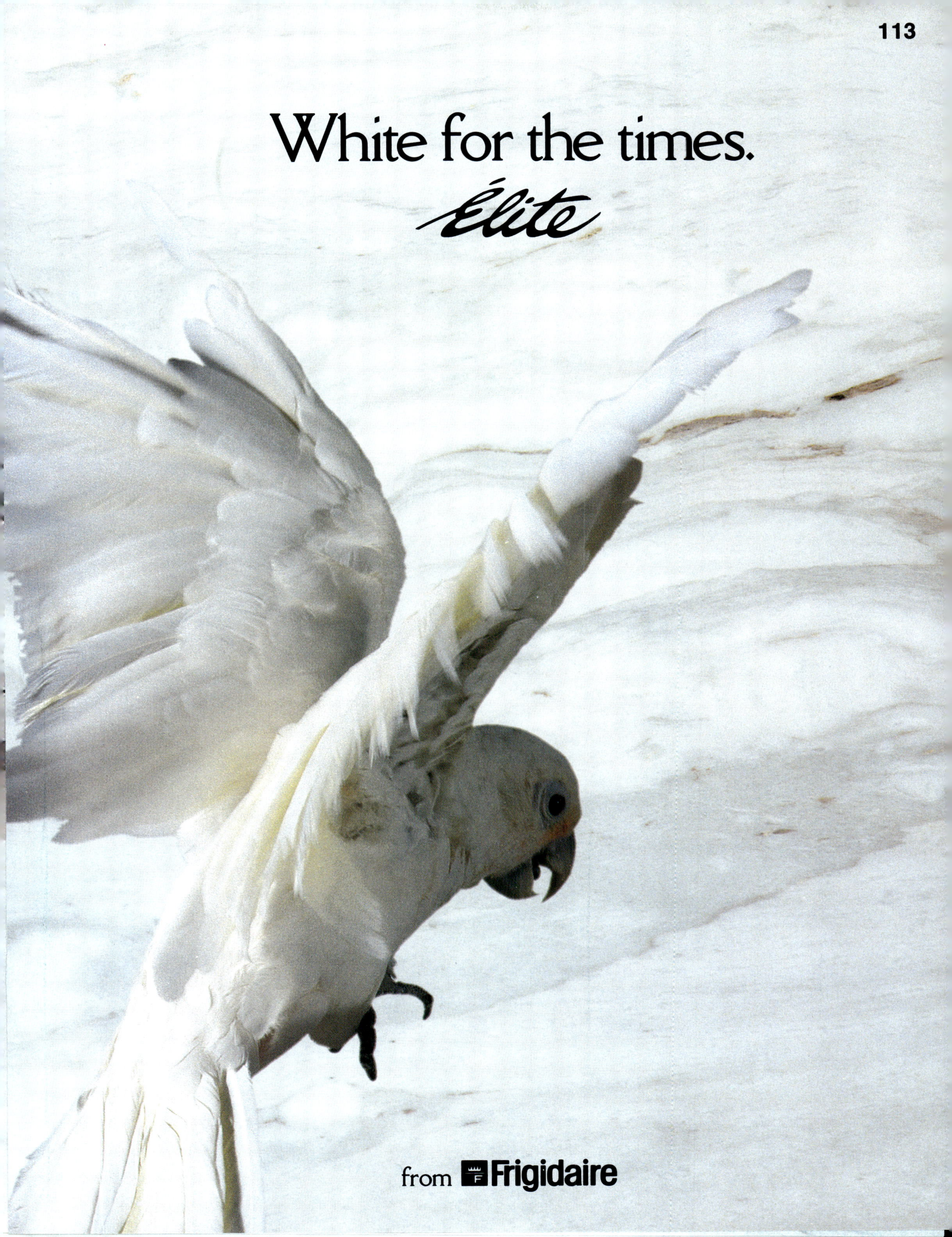

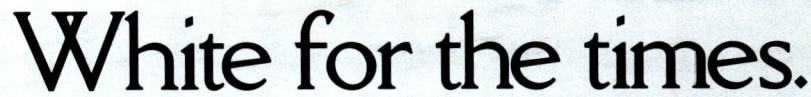

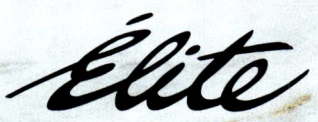

A beautifully-designed refrigerator,

Beauty that is more than skin deep,
especially when you look inside the *Elite*

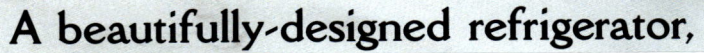

Form and function combine to make the Elite line the choice for discriminating homemakers. The soft, contemporary look, improved visibility and access, and little things like stay-up dairy doors, make your Elite a joy to own for years to come.

You'll love the automatic ice maker and the exclusive Fresh-Lok drawer, for keeping unwrapped foods from drying out. And there is a removable egg server in the Elite. In the Choose-A-Chill drawer, you can control temperature separately, to keep meats at the peak of freshness for days. And in the Vari-Fresh drawer, you can even adjust the humidity level, to keep produce fresher longer.

What you'll especially like about the Elite line is the design of its shelf space in both the freezer and refrigerator compartments. While the total space capacity is important, shelf area may be even more important, and Elite models maximize shelf space. Deep, adjustable door shelves can hold larger items, and also featured is a bottle retainer to hold smaller items firmly in place. Your Elite refrigerator also comes with a full width glide-out freezer basket, and handy Micro Serv dishes — for dual storage and microwave cooking use.

FPCE-21TILW

Powerful, quiet dishwashing, and with the distinction of *Elite*

The Elite dishwasher washes away even the toughest soils at the touch of a button, yet leaves all dishes and glasses immaculately spot-free. A Sani Wash/rinse water temperature booster can heat water to 150-degrees. And you have the option to select up to six wash cycles for optimum flexibility. Forced air drying means you don't have to wait long to unload. Other features include solid state controls and an adjustable upper rack. Of course, the Elite Ultra-Quiet dishwasher is Frigidaire's quietest model ever — the perfect complement to the way it blends with your kitchen decor.

DW-6700L

MCT-1375L

An understated design, with an abundance of microwave oven performance features.

The Elite microwave (MCT1375L) combines the conveniences you're looking for, with the elegant styling to match. Its 700 watts of quiet power and 1.3 cubic feet make it suitable for both large and small dishes. There's a built-in turntable for thorough cooking. The smaller, 0.8 cu. ft. (MCT-860L) model is designed so it may hang under a cabinet. Both Elite microwaves are fully programmable, with a defrost feature, and come with two removable trays.

MCT-860L

REGS-39WLW

A culinary classic, styled to make everyday cooking a pleasure.

There may never be an easier range to cook with, or to clean, than the beautiful, white, Elite Frigidaire. The Elite range incorporates the latest cooktop technology with electronic controls and self-cleaning oven. The Solid Surface Elements make for better cooking performance, and easier cleanup. Solid State Cookmaster Controls and Electronic Timer give accurate monitoring so you're free to make the most of your time.

If you're looking for the built-in simplicity of a cooktop, Elite gives you a beautiful white surface with solid heating

RBS-138L

elements that precisely maintain the temperatures you select. The Elite cooktop fits right into your countertop, and it's easy to clean.

Elite wall ovens that provide convenience and style.

Nothing beats the convenience of a beautiful Elite wall oven for baking, broiling or roasting in your modern kitchen. They can be positioned for easy access, and are styled to give your kitchen that clean, modern look. Whether you opt for a single wall oven or the double-oven Elite, you get white glass door windows, delay start cooking, electronic timers, self-cleaning convenience, and more even baking with the Dual-Radiant Baking System.

REG-78WL

REG-75WL

Elite completes your kitchen — right down to the range hood.

Even the range hood on the Frigidaire Elite line is styled for beauty and function. This slim white hood becomes an unobtrusive part of your kitchen decor, providing superior performance while quietly drawing unwanted air from your cooking area. Its solid-state speed control allows you to set the blower speed you wish. It includes a fluorescent light fixture and a filter system that is easy to clean.

RANGE HOOD		
FEATURES	**HV-30030W**	**HV-30036W**
COLOR SELECTION		
White	X	X
DIMENSIONS (Inches)		
Width	30"	36"
SPECIFICATIONS		
120 Volts	X	X
3.7 Amps	X	X
CFM-300	X	X
SONES-4.5	X	X
3¼" x 10" Vertical Duct	X	X

ELECTRIC RANGE	
FEATURES	**REGS-39WLW**
Infinitely Adj. Surface Unit Controls	Yes
6" Surface Units	2
8" Surface Unit	1 (Heat Minder)
9" Solid Heating Element	1
Dual-Radiant Baking System	Yes
Fluorescent Console Light	Yes
Cookmaster Control	Solid State
Clock w/Timer	Electronic
Dual Oven Controls	Yes
Oven Signal Light	Yes
Oven Light	Yes
Broiler Roaster Pan	Yes
2 Oven Racks w/Adj. Shelf Positions	Yes
Six Pass Broil Element	Yes
See Through Oven Door	Yes
White Glass Door	Yes
Full Width Storage Drawer	Yes
4 Leveling Legs	Yes
CLEANING CONVENIENCES	
Electri-clean Oven	Yes
Oven Clean Indicator Light	Yes
Automatic Oven Door lock	Yes
Porcelain Enamel Cooktop	Yes
Lift-off/Stand-up Door	Yes
Easy Clean Cooktop	Yes
Clean Sweep Design	Yes
COLOR SELECTION	
White	X
SPECIFICATIONS	
Oven interior width (in.)	23
Connected Load* (kW)	
@240 V	13.5
@208 V	10.1
Shipping Weight (approx. lb)	185

*Operates on 120/240V or 120/208V, 3-wire, 1 phase, 60-Hz circuit.

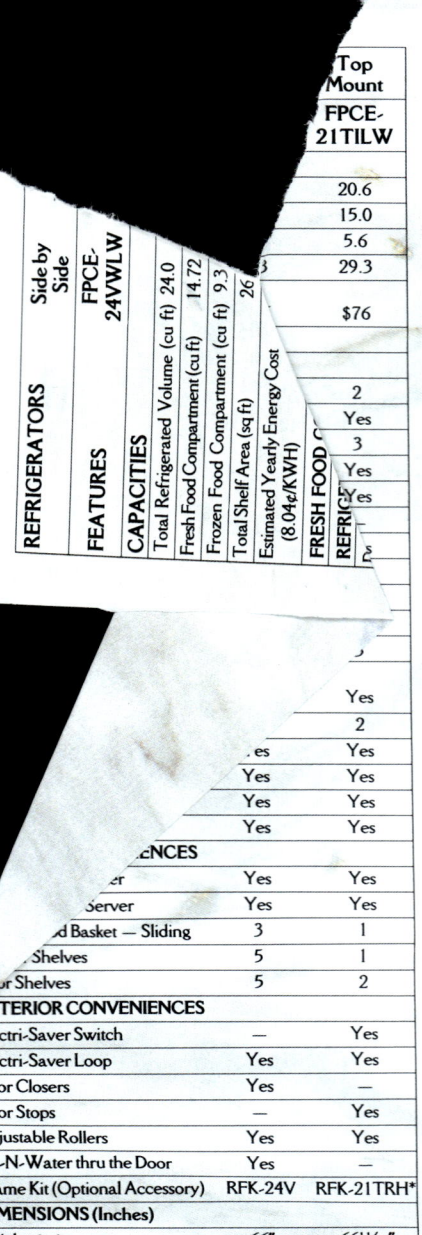

REFRIGERATORS

FEATURES	Side by Side FPCE-24VWLW	Top Mount FPCE-21TILW
CAPACITIES		
Total Refrigerated Volume (cu ft)	24.0	20.6
Fresh Food Compartment (cu ft)	14.72	15.0
Frozen Food Compartment (cu ft)	9.3	5.6
Total Shelf Area (sq ft)	26	29.3
Estimated Yearly Energy Cost (8.04¢/KWH)		$76

FRESH FOOD COMPARTMENT	2	2
	Yes	
	3	3
	Yes	Yes
	Yes	Yes

...ENCES		
...er	Yes	Yes
...Server	Yes	Yes
...d Basket — Sliding	3	1
... Shelves	5	1
...r Shelves	5	2

EXTERIOR CONVENIENCES		
Electri-Saver Switch	—	Yes
Electri-Saver Loop	Yes	Yes
Door Closers	Yes	—
Door Stops	—	Yes
Adjustable Rollers	Yes	Yes
Ice-N-Water thru the Door	Yes	—
Frame Kit (Optional Accessory)	RFK-24V	RFK-21TRH*
DIMENSIONS (Inches)		
Height + +	66″	66¹¹⁄₁₆″
Width **	35¾″	31″
Depth	31⅝″	30⅝″
COLOR SELECTION		
White	X	X
Shipping Weight in Pounds	321	236

+ + Condenser requires ventilation - allow 3″ height above refrigerator — 4″ for recessed installation.

** to facilitate installation in recessed area, add at least ½″ on each side.

* Order RFK-21TLH when changing door opening to left hand swing (hinges on left when facing refrigerator).

Dimensions shown are for planning purposes only. Always refer to the instructions packed with each product before making cuts.

With continuous product improvement a Frigidaire policy, specifications and models are subject to change without notice.

DISHWASHER

FEATURES	DW-6700L
Ultra-Quiet Sound Package	Yes
CYCLES	
Power Scrub-Pots & Pans	Yes
Crystal China	Yes
Short Wash	Yes
Normal Wash	Yes
Rinse / Hold	Yes
Rinse / Dry	Yes
OPTIONS	
Soil Level Selector	Yes
Power Dry-Heat On/Heat Off	Yes
Temp Assure 140°	Yes
Sani 150°	Yes
CONVENIENCES	
Wash Levels	3
Delay Start — Up to 12 Hrs.	Yes
Soft Food Pulverizer	Yes
Dura-Life Door Liner	Yes
Porcelain Enamel Tub	Yes
Full-Time Filter	Yes
Detergent Dispensers	3
Spots-Away Rinse Injector	Yes
Adjustable Upper Rack	Yes
Silverware Basket	Yes
Small Items Compartment	Yes
Forced Air Drying	Yes
Electronic Controls	Yes
Cancel/Reset	Yes
Drain Hose	Yes
SPECIFICATIONS	
Est. Yearly Energy Cost*	$33/$58
Electrical Requirements: Volts	115
Amperes**	12.2
Water Pressure, psi	16-125
Water Usage — Normal Cycle, Gal.	9.2
Shipping Weight, lbs.	106
DIMENSIONS (Inches)	
Height	35″ Max.
Width	24″
Depth	24″
Depth (Door open)	47½

* Gas/Electric Water Heater

** Separate 15-amp, 3-wire grounded circuit required.

COOKTOP

FEATURES	RBS-138L
Solid Heating Elements	+
Infinitely Adjustable Surface Unit Controls	Yes
Surface Unit Signal Light	Yes
CLEANING CONVENIENCES	
Easy-Clean Control Panel	Yes
Pull-Off Control Knobs	Yes
SPECIFICATIONS	
Connected Load* (kW) 240V/208V	7.0/5.2
Shipping Weight (approx lb)	45
DIMENSIONS (Inches)	
Width of Cooking Top	31¾
Depth of Cooking Top	20¾
Height of Cooking Top	3⁵⁄₁₆
Width of Opening	28⅜
Depth of Opening	19⅝
Minimum Counter Height Required	4 + +

+ 6″, 8″, 9″ solid heating elements. 8″ is Heat Minder Unit.

+ + Cable connection requires additional 1½″.

*Operates on 120/240V or 120/208V, 3-wire service.

MICROWAVE OVENS

FEATURES	MCT-860L	MCT-1375L
COOKING CONVENIENCES		
Cavity Size (cu. ft.)	0.8	1.3
Full Power Output (watts)	700	700
Auto-Defrost by Weight	Yes	Yes
Time of Day Clock	Yes	Yes
Timer	99′-99″	99′-99″
Turntable	Yes	Yes
Touch Controls	Yes	Yes
Power Settings	10	10
LED Display	Yes	Yes
Cycle End Signal	Yes	Yes
Cooking	Time	Time
Program Stages	3	3
Owner's Manual	Yes	Yes
Cookbook	Yes	Yes
Under-the-Cabinet Hang Kit	82-5816	—
Meal Rack Kit	—	88-9204
White Trim Kit	—	82-5609
Cooking Tray (Circular)	Yes	Yes
Cooking Tray (Rectangular)	Yes	Yes
Interior Oven Light	Yes	Yes
Reheat Control	Yes	Yes
SPECIFICATIONS		
Exterior Width w/Door Closed	22¾″	23⁷⁄₁₆″
Exterior Height	12⅛″	15½″
Exterior Depth w/Door Closed	12″	17¾″
Oven Interior Width	15½″	15½″
Oven Interior Height	8⅜″	10⅛″
Oven Interior Depth	11″	14½″
Shipping Wt. (approx. lbs.)	48	68

WALL OVENS

FEATURES	REG-78WL	REG-75WF	REG-75WL
Cookmaster Oven Control	Yes— Upper	Yes	Touch Pads
Clock & Minute Timer	Electronic	Electronic	Electronic
Interior Oven Light(s)	Both	Yes	Yes
Broiler-Roaster Pan	Yes	Yes	Yes
Glass Window in Door	Both	Yes	Yes
Vacation Safety Switch	—	Yes	Yes
CLEANING CONVENIENCES			
Electri-clean Oven	Upper	Yes	Yes
Electri-clean Door Lock	Auto	Auto	Auto
Porcelain Enamel Interior(s)	Yes	Yes	Yes
Lift-off Door	Yes	Yes	Yes
SPECIFICATIONS			
Connected Load* (kw)@ 240V/208V	7.4/5.8	5.6/4.2	5.6/4.2
Shipping Weight (approx. lb)	219	140	140
DIMENSIONS (Inches)			
Height of Wall Oven	50⁷⁄₁₆	30¾	30¾
Width of Wall Oven	26⅞	26⅞	26⅞
Depth of Wall Oven (w/o handle)	25⅜	25⅜	25⅜
Height of opening	48-min. 50-max.	28⅛-min. 30⅛-max.	28⅛-min. 30⅛-max.
Width of opening	24¾-min. 25¼-max.	24¾-min. 25¼-max.	24¾-min. 25¼-max.
Depth of opening	23½	23½	23½
Distance from Floor	11½	31	31

* Models operate on 120/240V or 120/208V, 3-wire, 1-phase, 60 Hz.

(UL) Listed by Underwriters' Laboratories, Inc.

FRIGIDAIRE ACTION LINE
Your Toll Free Information Center
1-800-451-7007

F **Frigidaire**

F89FL0602
Printed in the U.S.A.

6000 Perimeter Drive, Dublin, Ohio 43017

*The Monogram™
Component Cooktop System*

Infinite variations on a singular theme.

Welcome to Monogram,™ the most complete line of built-in appliances, all from GE. A single source ... with so many resources, all adding new dimensions of quality, efficiency and service to custom kitchen design. Like GE's nationwide network of factory-trained service professionals. And the helpful GE Answer Center® information service, (800.626.2000), which operates day and night to provide a wealth of Monogram product and installation information, including the location of Monogram dealers who can provide design assistance.

GE. A company which listens to the needs and desires of designers and homeowners alike, and responds with design literate, functional, innovative products. Like the Component Cooktop System ... infinite variations on a singular theme.

A Design Statement.

The elegant understated design of Monogram appliances. Accents of brushed aluminum or stainless in subtle counterpoint with the purity of milky glass. The confident compatibility of the entire product line. Versatility... gracefully at home in virtually any setting.

Each designer and every owner would probably interpret Monogram differently. But, one thing is clear. Since its introduction in 1987, as the first complete line of built-in appliances, Monogram has been embraced by the design community and its clientele.

This year, in response to the demand for more convenience and flexibility in the kitchen, Monogram proudly introduces the Monogram Component Cooktop System.

A versatile and space-conscious collection of cooking surfaces, incorporating efficient performance and a variety of cooking technologies into configurations limited only by imagination. We invite you to experience the "Kitchens of Monogram."

Monogram in the kitchen expresses a commitment to quality and detail that adds value to every other aspect of the home.

The Monogram component cooktop system.
Exceptional style, infinite variations.

Upon exploring the Monogram component cooktop system, you are likely to be astonished by the sheer abundance of choices it presents and inspires.

This highly versatile system accelerates the evolution of the modular cooktop. Five components are incorporated to fully accommodate individual cooking styles.

Homeowner and kitchen designer may select virtually any combination of components, for creation of a cooking surface that satisfies personal cooking preferences while allowing ample freedom of expression for design ingenuity.

The Monogram component cooktop system presents boundless opportunities to create a unique, personalized cooking resource.

You may wish to place a series of grills on an island, supplemented by gas and solid disk components on peripheral countertops.

Or you may prefer a pattern of gas components, arranged in a linear configuration.

Perhaps a mixture of components within an angular composition, to create a system of extraordinary versatility and visual appeal.

You may also choose to integrate your own countertop accessories: pastry boards, cutting surfaces, lift-out baskets, or other items to enhance convenience and efficiency.

We've designed the Monogram component cooktop system to complement virtually any custom kitchen decor. You will find it adaptable to a casual or formal setting, and perfectly compatible with the patterns, colors, textures, and architectural materials you have chosen for your kitchen.

Cooktop surfaces are crafted from high-quality stainless steel, brushed to a soft luster. And attractive control dials are designed for ease of operation: Simply press and rotate; the dial glides smoothly to the selected setting.

To assure proper channeling of excess heat and smoke to the out of doors, we've included the downdraft vent component as an integral element within the system.

Cleanup is practically effortless. Surface spots or spills may be gently whisked away. And, to renew the beauty of the porcelainized cast-iron grill and burner grates, all you need do is enlist the aid of your Monogram dishwasher.

Offering a stunning array of choices, the versatile, adaptable Monogram component cooktop system embodies personal expression of individual cooking style.

ZEW165N	*Downdraft grill cooktop component*
DIMENSIONS	*Height 19 7/8" (505 mm) Width 20 1/2" (521 mm) Length 21" (533 mm)*
ZEW135N	*Solid disk cooktop component*
DIMENSIONS	*Height 3 1/4" (83 mm) Width 15 1/2" (394 mm) Length 21" (533 mm)*
ZEW175N	*Downdraft vent component (shown with out-of-view remote mount control dial, accessory kit Pub. No. 3-A010)*
DIMENSIONS	*Height 19 7/8" (505 mm) Width 4 1/4" (108 mm) Length 21 1/4" (540 mm)*
ZGW125EN	*Gas cooktop component, controls on left*
DIMENSIONS	*Height 3 1/4" (83 mm) Width 15 1/2" (394 mm) Length 21" (533 mm)*

The Monogram component cooktop system: A variety of technologies; a limitless choice of modular configurations.

Gas and downdraft grill components.
A brilliant duet.

ZGW125EN   *Gas cooktop component,
            controls on left*

DIMENSIONS *Height 3 1/4" (83 mm)
            Width 15 1/2" (394 mm)
            Length 21" (533 mm)*

ZEW165N   *Downdraft grill
            cooktop component*

DIMENSIONS *Height 19 7/8" (505 mm)
            Width 20 1/2" (521 mm)
            Length 21" (533 mm)*

Should the flame even begin to falter, the automatic re-ignition device responds instantly, maintaining the selected level of heat.

We've equipped the gas component with spillproof burners and an attractive cast-iron grate, coated with smooth, tough porcelain.

The result: beauty, without the beastly chore of cleaning.

Downdraft grill component: attractive and versatile.

Complementing the gas component, the downdraft grill allows you to enjoy outdoor-style cooking in the comfort of your kitchen.

The porcelainized cast-iron grate creates a rhythmic visual accent, while offering a very practical advantage. It can be easily removed and transferred to your Monogram dishwasher for cleaning.

We've given each of the two heating elements of the grill a separate control dial. So you may heat only half the grilling surface, if you wish. Or use one section for grilling, the other for holding or warming foods.

The downdraft vent is automatically activated when the grill is turned on, and the fully variable control allows you to adjust fan speed to the level required.

For added convenience and safety, the control dial can be mounted beneath the countertop, within easy reach.

Gas component: the allure of function.

Refined appearance. Reliable performance. Durability and ease of cleaning.

The Monogram gas component incorporates all of these attributes.

To assure reliable operation, gas burners are controlled by a pilotless electronic ignition system. Press and turn the control dial, and the burner is immediately ignited.

Grill/griddle and solid disk components.
Variety, generously spiced with visual appeal.

116

The versatile grill component offers a tantalizing option, the griddle accessory.

You may use either cooking method within the same space. Or expand to include two grill components and a griddle accessory – a combination that doubles the cooking area, while allowing simultaneous use of grill and griddle.

A dedicated control assures even, overall heating of the griddle, which, of course, has a coated non-stick surface... because cleanup, though inevitable, need not be prolonged.

Solid disk component: a sensitive performance.

The accurate, sensitive solid disk component features dual cast-iron heating units. And, because these six- and eight-inch disks are sealed to the cooktop, you gain a dual benefit: attractive appearance and ease of cleaning.

Both disks are equipped with Sensi-Temp,™ which automatically maintains the temperature of the cooking utensil.

An additional advantage: The Monogram solid disk component, only 3 1/4 inches in height, doesn't preclude installation of a drawer beneath. So you gain a bit of extra space ... and a great deal more.

ZEW155N	*Updraft grill cooktop component*
DIMENSIONS	*Height 5 3/8" (137 mm) Width 16 3/8" (416 mm) Length 21" (533 mm)*
ZEW135N	*Solid disk cooktop component*
DIMENSIONS	*Height 3 1/4" (83 mm) Width 15 1/2" (394 mm) Length 21" (533 mm)*
JXDD43N	*Griddle accessory (shown in place on updraft grill)*

Such a multitude of choices
presents a rather delightful dilemma.

Variations on a theme.

Select the components ideally suited to your personal cooking style...and create a unique composition, one which perfectly accommodates your cooking needs and design preferences.

The freedom to exercise your

personal cooking preferences.

Monogram cooktop components...

in any arrangement.

ZEW135N   *Solid disk*
  cooktop component

DIMENSIONS   *Height 3 1/4" (83 mm)*
  Width 15 1/2" (394 mm)
  Length 21" (533 mm)

ZEW175N
Downdraft
vent component

DIMENSIONS   *Height 19 7/8"*
  (505 mm)
  *Width 4 1/4" ***
  (108 mm)
  Length 21 1/4"
  (540 mm)

Pub. No. 3-A010   *Optional remote*
  control accessory kit

ZGW124EN   *Gas cooktop component,*
  controls on right

DIMENSIONS   *Height 3 1/4" (83 mm)*
  Width 15 1/2" (394 mm)
  Length 21" (533 mm)

DIMENSIONS   *Control box:*
  Height 2 1/2" (64 mm)
  Width 3 9/16" (91 mm)
  Length 2 1/16" (52 mm)
  Escutcheon diameter
  2 11/16" (68 mm)

ZGW125EN   *Gas cooktop component,*
  controls on left

DIMENSIONS   *Height 3 1/4" (83 mm)*
  Width 15 1/2" (394 mm)
  Length 21" (533 mm)

Gas component
Two styles – one with control dials on the left, the other with right-side controls–assure convenience and safe placement of the downdraft vent.

Solid disk component
Durable cast-iron disks are sealed to the cooktop for attractive appearance and ease of cleaning.

Updraft grill/griddle component
Further extending the versatility of the system, the grill component offers the option of a griddle accessory.

Downdraft grill/griddle component
Downdraft venting unit and grill are combined in a single component; vent is automatically activated when grill is turned on.

Downdraft vent component
This unit may be paired with any component (except downdraft grill), enhancing the design and function of the cooktop. For convenient accessibility, the control may be remote-mounted on the countertop surface or cabinet front.

ZEW155N — *Updraft grill cooktop component*

DIMENSIONS — *Height 5 3/8" (137 mm)***
Width 16 3/8" (416 mm)
Depth 21" (533 mm)

JXDD43N — *Griddle accessory (shown in place on updraft grill)*

ZEW165N — *Downdraft grill cooktop component*

DIMENSIONS — *Height 19 7/8" (505 mm)***
Width 20 1/2" (521 mm)*
Length 21" (533 mm)

*Not including blower assembly
**Grease jar: 10" (254 mm)

An Invitation to Imagination.

Monogram offers a compelling array of choices, allowing you to create a visually enticing, highly functional cooking palette.

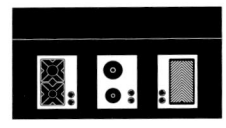

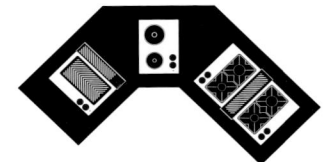

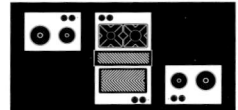

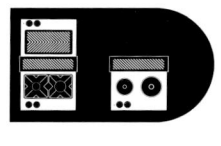
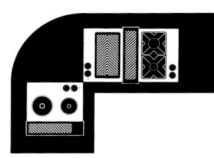
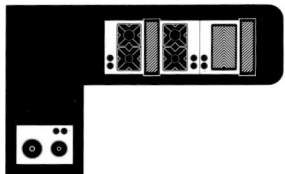

The illustrations shown here represent but a few of many possibilities you may wish to consider when designing your personalized cooktop system.

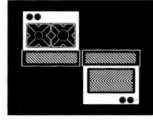

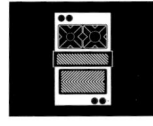

Monogram Kitchen Designer Planning Guide

With such myriad choices, perhaps the best place to begin is with the basics.

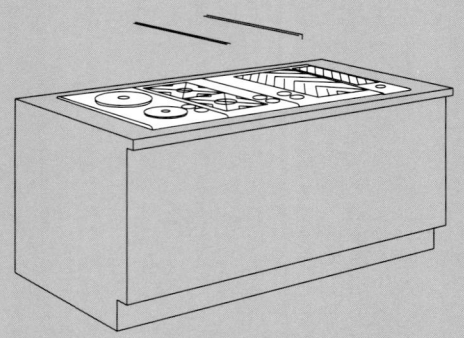

Component Cooktop System

NOTE: All multiple component installations require joiner strips between components. Appropriate joiners are shipped with each component product. When preplanning countertop cutout requirements, add $1/4''$ (6 mm) width for each downdraft joiner strip; add $3/4''$ (19 mm) width for each cooktop joiner strip.

For specific information regarding correct utilization of joiners, please refer to the Component Cooktop System Installation Instructions.

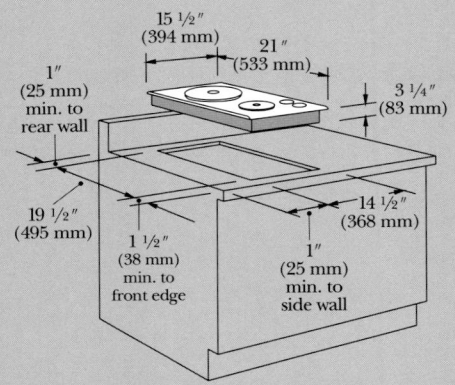

Solid Disk Cooktop Component

ZEW135N

Solid disk cooktop component

(Available in 208 volts as ZEW134N)

Features
- Dual cast iron heating units
- One 6″ disk and one 8″ disk, each equipped with Sensi-Temp™
- Sealed disks eliminate spill-through
- Only 3¼″ deep, leaving room for a drawer beneath
- UL approved
- Approximate shipping weight: 26 pounds.

Warranty
- *Full One-Year Warranty* For one year from date of original purchase, we will provide, at no additional charge, parts and service labor in client's home to repair or replace any part of the appliance that fails because of a manufacturing defect.
- Complete details available from your designer.

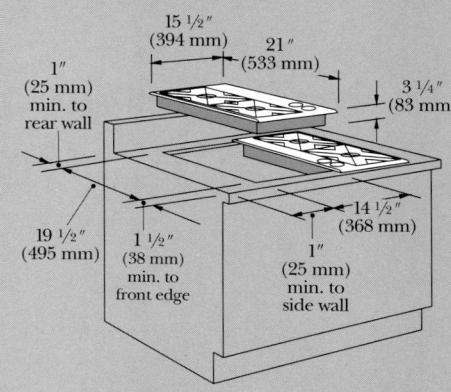

ZGW124EN

Gas cooktop
component,
controls on right

ZGW125EN

Gas cooktop
component,
controls on left

Features
- Available with controls
  on right or left side for
  ease of use and added
  safety
- One large 10,500 BTU
  burner and one
  smaller 6,000 BTU
  burner
- Reliable electronic
  ignition with auto-
  matic reignition
- Durable, porcelainized
  cast-iron grates with
  dynamic appearance
- AGA approved
- Approximate shipping
  weight: 26 pounds.

Warranty
- *Full One-Year Warranty*
  For one year from date
  of original purchase,
  we will provide, at no
  additional charge,
  parts and service labor
  in client's home to
  repair or replace any
  part of the appliance
  that fails because of a
  manufacturing defect.
- Complete details
  available from your
  designer.

Updraft Grill
Cooktop Component

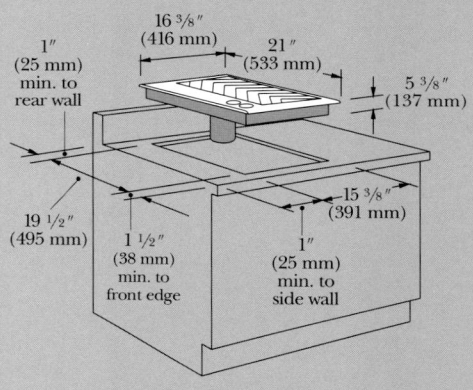

ZEW155N

Updraft grill
cooktop
component

(Available in
208 volts as
ZEW154N)

Features
- Rugged, porcelainized
  cast-iron grate (can be
  cleaned in Monogram
  dishwasher)
- Two heating elements
  with separate controls
- 1,750 watt heating
  element
- Optional griddle
  accessory kit available
- UL approved
- Approximate shipping
  weight: 42 pounds.

Warranty
- *Full One-Year Warranty*
  For one year from date
  of original purchase,
  we will provide, at no
  additional charge,
  parts and service labor
  in client's home to
  repair or replace any
  part of the appliance
  that fails because of a
  manufacturing defect.
- Complete details
  available from your
  designer.

JXDD43N
Griddle Accessory

Allows optional cooking
method in same space.
One piece design with
integrated heating ele-
ment simply plugs into
cooktop.

Converts control to
single dial, assuring even,
overall heating of the
griddle surface.

Downdraft Grill Cooktop Component

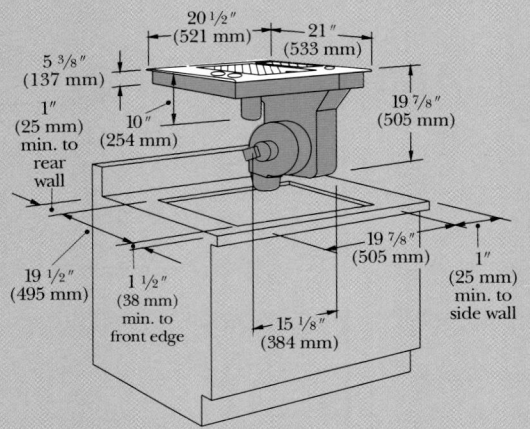

ZEW165N

Downdraft grill cooktop component

(Available in 208 volts as ZEW164N)

Features

- Outdoor-style cooking in the comfort of your kitchen
- Rugged, porcelainized cast-iron grate (can be cleaned in Monogram dishwasher)
- 2,800 watt heating element
- Two heating elements with separate controls
- Equipped with a downdraft vent which is automatically activated when the grill is turned on
- Optional griddle accessory kit available
- UL approved
- Approximate shipping weight: 80 pounds.

Warranty

- *Full One-Year Warranty*
  For one year from date of original purchase, we will provide, at no additional charge, parts and service labor in client's home to repair or replace any part of the appliance that fails because of a manufacturing defect.
- Complete details available from your designer.

**JXDD43N
Griddle Accessory**

Allows optional cooking method in same space. One piece design with integrated heating element simply plugs into cooktop.

Converts control to single dial, assuring even, overall heating of the griddle surface.

Downdraft Vent Component

ZEW175N

Downdraft vent component

Features

- Rugged, porcelainized cast-iron grate (can be cleaned in Monogram dishwasher)
- Removable, washable filter
- Equipped with variable-speed blower control
- Optional remote control accessory kit
- UL approved
- Approximate shipping weight: 44 pounds.

Warranty

- *Full One-Year Warranty*
  For one year from date of original purchase, we will provide, at no additional charge, parts and service labor in client's home to repair or replace any part of the appliance that fails because of a manufacturing defect.
- Complete details available from your designer.

**Pub. No. 3-A010
Accessory Kit**

Remote location of blower control, for added convenience and safety.

Monogram.™

Simplifying a complex process.

Monogram, a complete line of built-in appliances, was created to facilitate the often formidable process of designing and building a uniquely elegant, efficient custom kitchen.

An answer to the need for a simpler selection process. A response to the demand for impeccable styling, precise performance, fit and finish. Convenience, efficiency, and ease of use.

The Monogram line of built-in appliances embodies all of these elements. Thoughtfully planned, carefully engineered and executed, this quality line of built-in appliances is available to you from a single source.

That source is GE, a company that understands the needs of the designers and owners of today's finest custom kitchens.

GE invites you to take an inside look at Monogram.

If you wish to obtain a copy of the Monogram Designer Guide and Monogram Planning and Installation Information call 800.848.7722 (800.633.7173 in Kentucky).

To obtain specific information concerning any Monogram product or service, call GE Answer Center® consumer information service at 800.626.2000 – any time of day or night.

An inside look
at Monogram

The Monogram custom
side-by-side refrigerator.

This spacious refrigerator abandons tradition in favor of greater style and convenience. Measuring 42 inches in width, it can accommodate full-size party trays with ease, unlike standard 36-inch built-ins.

It's filled with delectable surprises, including advanced electronic controls, an ice-and-water dispenser, and a wine rack that will hold a full magnum of wine.

ZISW42EN
Custom side-by-side built-in refrigerator with white ice and water dispenser.

ZISB42EN
Custom side-by-side built-in refrigerator with black ice and water dispenser.

PRODUCT DIMENSIONS:
Height 84" (2134 mm)
Width 42" (1067 mm)
Depth 24" (610 mm)

CUTOUT DIMENSIONS:
Height 83 ¾" (2127 mm)
Width 41 ½" (1054 mm)
Depth 24" (610 mm)

Fresh food compartment

- Generous 15.6 cu. ft. capacity, 20 inches wide.
- Four adjustable tinted and tempered glass shelves.
- Quick Serve™ System: Handsome, durable dishes slide under shelves to save space (and can go directly into a conventional or microwave oven, then to the table).

- Food-Saver System. Sealed high-humidity bin, low-humidity bin and sealed snack tray.
- Large wine rack.
- Five adjustable door bins for storage flexibility.
- Removable egg bin.
- Dairy compartment with counter-balanced door for easy access.

Freezer compartment

- 10.1 cu. ft. capacity (9.8 cu. ft. in dispenser model).
- Automatic icemaker with removable bin that holds up to six pounds of ice.
- Five full-width shelves, completely adjustable (four shelves available in dispenser model).
- Five adjustable door bins (four bins in dispenser model).
- Slide-out utility basket for storage of bulk items.

The Monogram
custom side-by-side refrigerator.

ZIS42CN
*Custom side-by-side
built-in refrigerator*

PRODUCT DIMENSIONS:
*Height 84" (2134 mm)
Width 42" (1067 mm)
Depth 24" (610 mm)*

CUTOUT DIMENSIONS:
*Height 83 ¾" (2127 mm)
Width 41 ½" (1054 mm)
Depth 24" (610 mm)*

Monogram dispenser models offer other important features:

- Electronic through-the-door dispenser for ice cubes, crushed ice and chilled water.

- Audible signals, which automatically alert you when the temperature is too high, when a door has been left open, or when a power failure has occurred.

- Systems Monitor, ensuring accurate operation of electronic controls.

- Satin-finish shelf trim.

All models offer:

- Frozen food and fresh food compartments are operated by separate temperature controls.

- Rolls on wheels, for installation without damage to floor material.

- Simple, unique leveling capability assures true horizontal and vertical positioning.

- Protective door stops.

- Just 24 inches deep, flush with standard kitchen cabinets; accepts panels to match your cabinetry.

- Since there is no grill at the bottom, the refrigerator can be positioned to the toekick height of European or American cabinets, and a matching section of toekick material can be installed.

- Top-mounted grill can be easily removed for cleaning of grill and cooling unit.

The Monogram
double oven.

Monogram combines the sleek allure of a European built-in with the capacity and efficiency of a full-featured American oven. Solid-state electronic controls, an electronic meat thermometer and rotisserie, and self-cleaning capability offer an extra serving of convenience.

JKP40GK (model shown)
*White double oven,
rotary controls*

JKP47GK (model shown)
*Black double oven,
electronic controls*

JKP39GK
*Black double oven,
rotary controls*

JKP48GK
*White double oven,
electronic controls*

PRODUCT DIMENSIONS:
*Height 50 ⅜" (1280 mm)
Width 26" (660 mm)
Depth 24" (610 mm)
Depth with door open:
44 ½" (1130 mm)*

CUTOUT DIMENSIONS:
*Height 49 ⅝" (1260 mm)
Width 24 ¾" (629 mm)
Depth 24" (610 mm)*

- Solid-state electronic panel allows fingertip control of cooking times and temperatures.
- Both ovens are self-cleaning, eliminating a troublesome chore.
- Electronic meat thermometer in upper oven monitors internal temperature of meat as it cooks; signals when cooking is complete.

- Automatic rotisserie in upper oven expands cooking options, allowing meat to roast or broil while basting in its own natural juices.
- Programmed self-cleaning cycle.
- Variable broiling capability.
- Independent controls for cooking and cleaning – cook in one oven as the other cleans.
- Digital clock and reminder timer.
- Automatic oven timer.

The Monogram double oven is available with rotary controls for those who prefer the more traditional method of adjusting cooking time and temperature.

Additional features – all models

- Both ovens are large enough to accept virtually anything you may wish to prepare.
- Precision-designed controls respond accurately to exact settings selected.

The Monogram
single oven.

Contemporary styling…stunning performance.

The Monogram single oven complements your kitchen as beautifully as it fits your cooking requirements. This full-size, self-cleaning oven offers an automatic rotisserie and meat thermometer, and sensitive electronic cooking controls.

JKP19GK (model shown)
White single oven, electronic controls

JKP18GK
Black single oven, electronic controls

PRODUCT DIMENSIONS:
Height 29" (737 mm)
Width 26" (660 mm)
Depth 24" (610 mm)

CUTOUT DIMENSIONS:
Height 28 1/8" (714 mm)
Width 24 3/4" (629 mm)
Depth 24" (610 mm)

- Solid-state electronic touch controls assure ease of use and accurate control of cooking.
- Full-size interior meets American standards for cooking capacity.
- Electronic meat thermometer monitors the temperature of meat as it roasts or broils; signals when cooking is complete.

- Automatic rotisserie rotates meat slowly, allowing it to roast or broil in its own natural juices.
- Automatic oven timer; digital clock and reminder timer.
- Programmed self-cleaning cycle.
- Variable broiling capacity, for added flexibility.
- Oven door with window and matching control panel.

The Monogram
induction cooktop.

- Induction system heats utensils directly by magnetic friction rather than heat.
- Cooking surface remains relatively cool; spills are easily wiped clean.
- Solid-state electronic touch controls assure accuracy and ease of use.
- Responds instantly to selected setting.
- Illuminated panel provides clear display of cooking power level.
- Two 6″ and two 8″ cooking areas offer greater flexibility.
- Induction system is designed for use only with ferrous metal utensils, the choice of many professional chefs.
- No special wiring or venting is required.

Additional features
- Accessory kit JXDV69 provides optional downdraft venting, to direct heat and odors outside without the need for an overhead hood.

JP690K
Black induction cooktop with optional downdraft vent kit JXDV69

JP691K
White induction cooktop with optional downdraft vent kit JXDV69

PRODUCT DIMENSIONS:
*Height 6 3/8″ (162 mm)
Width 35″ (889 mm)
Depth 22″ (559 mm)*

CUTOUT DIMENSIONS:
*Height 6 3/8″ (162 mm)
Width 34 1/8″ (867 mm)
Depth 21 1/4″ (540 mm)*

The ultimate resource for surface cooking, the Monogram induction cooktop combines a dynamic appearance with fingertip ease of use, instantaneous response, and superb performance.

The Monogram gas downdraft cooktop.

- Requiring no overhead hood, the cooktop can be placed in a central island or incorporated into countertop.
- Tempered glass surface and sealed burner bowls assure ease of cleaning.
- Five pilotless burners – two large and three medium – assure energy-efficient operation.
- Reliable electronic ignition responds instantly and accurately.
- Cast-iron grates assure long-life durability.

Additional features

- Rotary-controlled downdraft venting system allows ventilator to be raised to variable height.
- Exhaust fan operates quietly; speed is fully variable.
- Rotary controls are positioned for ease of use as well as attractive appearance.

ZGU661EM
White gas downdraft cooktop with JXDV66 vent kit.

ZGU661EM
White gas downdraft cooktop with JXDV66 vent retracted.

ZGU660EM
Black gas downdraft cooktop with JXDV66 vent kit

NOTE: Both models can be converted to liquid propane gas operation.

PRODUCT DIMENSIONS:
*Height 22" (559 mm)
(including blower/plenum)
Vent height, raised position
8 3/8" (213 mm)
Width 36" (914 mm)
Depth 22 1/4" (565 mm)*

CUTOUT DIMENSIONS:
*Height 22" (559 mm)
Width 34 9/16" (877 mm)
Depth 21 3/8" (542 mm)*

The smooth, sparkling glass surface is equipped with five burners, offering extended cooking capability.

Sealed burner bowls, an automatic electronic ignition system, and a fully variable downdraft system further enhance the beauty and performance of this superb gas cooktop.

The Monogram gas
updraft cooktop.

- Easy-clean tempered glass surface.
- Sealed burner bowls, for ease of cleaning.
- Electronic ignition system responds instantly.
- Cooktop is only three inches deep, to fit over cabinets and drawers without intruding on storage space.
- High-efficiency burners: two large 11,000 BTU, three medium-sized 6,500 BTU.
- Reliable pilotless, spillproof, electronic ignition system.
- Individual porcelainized cast-iron burner grates.

Additional features

- Rotary controls offer ease of use and accurate response to selected settings.

ZGU650EM
Black gas updraft cooktop

ZGU651EM
White gas updraft cooktop

NOTE: *Both models can be converted to liquid propane gas operation.*

PRODUCT DIMENSIONS:
Height 3" (76 mm)
Width 36" (914 mm)
Depth 19 3/4" (502 mm)

CUTOUT DIMENSIONS:
Height 3" (76 mm)
Width 34 7/16" (875 mm)
Depth 18 5/16" (465 mm)

This sophisticated cooktop – clean, uncluttered, and remarkably efficient – includes sealed burner bowls, and a hidden, pilotless electronic ignition system.

The Monogram solid disk cooktop.

A splendid addition to the most elegant kitchen.

The distinguishing characteristics of this cooktop include sleek European styling, a lustrous finish, sealed disks, and highly sensitive electronic heat sensors.

ZEU633L
White solid disk cooktop

(Also available in 208 volts as ZEU634L.)

ZEU632L
Black solid disk cooktop

PRODUCT DIMENSIONS:
Height 3" (76 mm)
Width 35 1/2" (902 mm)
Depth 21" (533 mm)

CUTOUT DIMENSIONS:
Height 3" (76 mm)
Width 33 7/8" ± 1/8" (860 mm)
Depth 19 1/16" ± 1/8" (484 mm)

- Sealed disks eliminate spill-through.
- Seamless tempered glass surface can be wiped clean with ease.
- Solid cast-iron elements eliminate need for drip pans, further minimizing clean-up.
- Temperature selection controls allow choice of exact degree of heat desired.
- 9" rear and 8" front disks with sensors automatically maintain selected level of heat.
- 6" front and rear heating units have automatic temperature limiters to reduce heat if liquids should boil dry.
- Only 3" deep.

The Monogram
modular downdraft cooktop.

JP679BN
White modular downdraft cooktop with grill module

JP678BN
Black modular downdraft cooktop with grill module

PRODUCT DIMENSIONS:
Height 20 7/8" (530 mm) (including blower/plenum)
Width 36" (914 mm)
Depth 24 1/4" (616 mm)

CUTOUT DIMENSIONS:
Height 20 7/8" (530 mm)
Width 35 3/8" (899 mm)
Depth 23 15/16" (608 mm)

Meeting the most demanding cooking needs and design requirements, the Monogram modular downdraft cooktop can be installed virtually anywhere in your kitchen.

The modular system allows you to arrange the surface to meet your cooking needs... and change it as your require-ments change.

- Optional interchangeable modules include Calrod®, solid disk, grill, or griddle surface units.

- Solid-state electronic panel offers precision control of tem-perature and cooking func-tions.

- A fixed fifth burner expands cooking capacity.

- Sensi-Temp™ control, on the center-mounted solid disk, monitors temperature and automatically maintains the selected level of heat.

- Powerful downdraft venting system channels heat and odors to outside, keeping kitchen air fresh.

- Vent filter is removable and washable.

- For ease of cleaning, cooktop surface is finished in brushed chrome.

The Monogram modular down-draft cooktop, which includes standard grill cartridge, offers these optional modules available at extra cost to complete the cooktop:

JXDC41N Conventional electric cooktop module

JXDL44N Grill module

JXDD43N Griddle module

JXDS42N Solid disk cooktop module

Additional features

- Sensi-Temp™ has an audible boil detector which monitors cooking and signals when the contents of a utensil have reached the boiling point – so there is reduced danger of liquids overflowing or pans boiling dry.

- The solid disk module's cast-iron heating units seal to the cooktop for ease of cleaning.

- The griddle module is treated with a nonstick coating, so it can be simply wiped clean.

12

The Monogram
microwave oven.

- Generous .9 cu. ft. capacity – large enough to accept a leg of lamb or a 5-quart casserole.

- Electronic touch control panel allows pre-programming of Defrost, Hold, and Cook cycles in one operation.

- Control panel also provides step-by-step instructions for programming cooking functions.

- Choice of ten power levels.

- "Auto-roast" setting automatically monitors the temperature of meat as it cooks, and adjusts the heating as needed for a thoroughly-prepared meal.

- High-speed "cook 'n watch" setting automatically turns the oven off after three minutes.

- Minutes/seconds timer and clock.

Additional features

Accessory trim kit JX9HW available for built-in appearance

Microwave oven is shown suspended between two cabinet units, with trim molding to enhance the built-in appearance. This method of installation does not restrict airflow.

Designed for convenience, the Monogram microwave oven complements your custom kitchen – and multiplies your cooking options.

JEM32H
*White Electronic
Spacemaker II™
microwave oven*

PRODUCT DIMENSIONS:
*Height 11 ½" (292 mm)
Width 23 ½" (597 mm)
Depth 12 ⅝" (321 mm)*

CUTOUT DIMENSIONS:
*Height 15 1/16" (383 mm) max.
14 15/16" (379 mm) min.
Width 24 15/16" (633 mm) max.
24 13/16" (630 mm) min.
Depth 18" (457 mm) min.*

The Monogram
microwave/convection oven.

- Four ways to cook: microwave, convection, convection broiling and combination. Combine microwave and convection heating for speed and uniform browning.
- Large 1.4 cu. ft. capacity, large enough to accept a 12-pound turkey or a full crown roast.
- Electronic touch controls.
- Word prompting display provides step-by-step programming instructions.
- Automatic cooking settings: "auto-cook", combination "auto-roast" and "auto-defrost"; "auto-start" for delayed cooking.
- Ten microwave power levels.
- Minutes/seconds timer and clock.
- Accessory kit available for custom in-wall installation.

Additional features

Accessory trim kit JX14GW available for built-in appearance

JET343G
*White combination
microwave/convection oven*

PRODUCT DIMENSIONS:
*Height 15 1/4" (387 mm)
Width 23 13/16 " (605 mm)
Depth 18 1/2" (470 mm)
(excluding handle)*

CUTOUT DIMENSIONS:
*Height 18 3/4" ± 1/16" (476 mm)
Width 24 7/8 " ± 1/16" (682 mm)
Depth 23" (584 mm) max.
21" (533 mm) min.*

Designed for versatility, the Monogram microwave and convection oven combines the best of both worlds in food preparation — all the benefits of a conventional microwave oven, plus convection heating.

The Monogram dishwasher.

Quiet, intelligent and meticulous, the Monogram dishwasher is equipped with a touch control panel that gives you a choice of six settings. Electronic systems monitor internal activities and report them to you through digital readouts and an audible signal.

- Solid-state electronic touch controls.
- Five cycles/37 options:
  - POTSCRUBBER cycle cleans heavily soiled dishes and cooking utensils.
  - Normal Wash for every day dishloads.
  - Short Wash cleans lightly soiled dishes economically.
  - China/Crystal cycle for delicate items.
  - Rinse & Hold for partial loads.
  - Delayed Start option.
- Exclusive Multi-Orbit™ wash arm.
- Self-cleaning filter system

- Heavy sound insulation ensures quiet operation.
- Durable PermaTuf® tub and doorliner, covered by a full 10-year warranty, prevents leakage.
- Three-level wash system.
- Temperature Sensor system.
- Systems Monitor includes 11 performance-monitoring programs.
- Can be programmed to begin at a preset time.
- Upper rack provides ample room for tall glasses.
- Lower rack can comfortably accommodate large trays and utensils.

Additional features

Accessory kits are available for customizing the dishwasher to blend with your kitchen design:

GPF30
Trim strips for use with 24" deep cabinetry.

GPF31
Trim strips for use with 25" deep cabinetry, plus special access panel for use with toekicks higher than 4".

GPF32
Heavy-duty springs for use with decorative door panels weighing more than five pounds.

GPF33
Special brackets for installing dishwasher beneath countertop of granite or other impervious material.

GPF35
Installation kit provides smooth, continuous, trimless expanse of custom paneling.

GSD3000B
Black built-in dishwasher

GSD3000W
White built-in dishwasher

PRODUCT DIMENSIONS:
*Height 34" (864 mm) min. adjustable to 35" (889 mm)
Width 24" (610 mm)
Depth 25" (toekick) (635 mm)
(to door edge) 25 3/4" (654 mm)*

CUTOUT DIMENSIONS:
*Height 34 1/2" ± 1/8" (876 mm) from floor to underside of counter
Width 24 1/4" (616 mm) min.
Depth 24" (610 mm) min.*

The Monogram compactor.

- Drawer-type compactor accepts custom paneling to blend with cabinetry.
- Black/white reversible control panel offers design flexibility; control area will also accept custom panel.
- A removable key activates compactor, then locks it securely.
- Door latch prevents operation when drawer is open.
- Convenient bag storage area.
- Separate air freshener compartment.

Only 12 inches wide, the Monogram compactor offers design flexibility while conserving space in your kitchen. Compresses an average one-week accumulation of trash into a single easy-to-handle bag.

Listed by Underwriters Laboratories

All Monogram products are appropriately UL and AGA approved.

Product improvement is a continuing endeavor at General Electric, therefore, materials, appearance and specifications are subject to change without notice.

These dimensions are for planning purposes only. For more detailed dimensional and installation information, order the Monogram Designer Workbook.

GCG1000
Compactor with white/black reversible control panel.

PRODUCT DIMENSIONS:
Height 34 1/2" (876 mm)
Width 12" (305 mm)
Depth 20 1/4" (514 mm)

CUTOUT DIMENSIONS:
Height 34 1/2" ± 1/8"
(876 mm) from floor
to underside of counter
Width 12 1/4" (311 mm)
Depth 20 1/4" (514 mm)

If you wish to obtain a copy of the Monogram Designer Guide and Monogram Designer Workbook call 800.848.7722. (800.633.7173 in Kentucky).

Welcome to the Kitchens of Monogram
Designer Guide
Pub. No. 24-M010
Presents Monogram appliances in three beautiful kitchen settings. Covers appliance features, design planning information, dimensions and product warranties.
$7.00 each

Monogram 1990 Production Planning and Installation Information
Designer Workbook
Pub. No. 24-M020
Provides detailed information by trade category on the preparation and installation of Monogram built-in appliances.
$7.00 each

Welcome to the Kitchens of Monogram
Video introduction to Monogram.
Pub. No. 24-M040
Tour three beautifully designed kitchens: Tidewater, European Contemporary and English Country. Experience the complete Monogram line.
$10.00 each

To obtain specific information concerning any Monogram product or service call GE Answer Center® consumer information service at 800.626.2000 – any time of day or night.

Pub. No. 24-M030
©1990 GE Appliances
Printed in U.S.A.   Q. KY.

Monogram.™

GE Appliances
Louisville, KY 40225

JENN-AIR EXPRESSIONS™ COLLECTION: COOKTOPS

Triple cooktop Model C3400W,* optional Model AS130W solid element cartridge, optional Model AO310 griddle.

Jenn-Air redefines the standards again— in your favor.

A bold expanse of sleek glass-ceramic which nestles into your countertop. Design with poise: tastefully understated, classically contemporary. The Expressions™ Collection: the most versatile, flexible cooktop ever created. And you won't find this combination of modular options with flush-fitting design anywhere else.

It's Jenn-Air, now more than ever. And this totally new concept is all about choices: yours. Styling to express your personality. An array of sizes, colors and options to harmonize with your kitchen and meet your diverse cooking needs.

First things first: choose your size. Single, double or triple? We're ready with our world-famous PerimaVent™ downdraft ventilation system and indoor grilling.

Next, choose your controls (up to four different styles) and cooktop color at the same time (black, white or stainless steel). After you've chosen the basics, it's time for your options: cooktop cartridge choices (from halogen to conventional coils) and accessories.

When you say yes to the new style of Jenn-Air, you're saying "yes" to your own high standards. Does it get any easier—or any better?

Shown on cover, page two and page five: Avonite countertops; St. Charles cabinets

*Reference number only.

Triple cooktop Model C3400W,* optional Model AO345W grill covers (two sets)

The triple cooktop: possibilities times three.

Family gatherings, banquets with a panache: a Jenn-Air triple cooktop masters any important occasion. And Jenn-Air cartridge and accessory options can expand your horizons. Six-element cooking. Four elements and a grill. Two grills, two elements. Even three grills. Dual downdraft ventilation systems mean you can place your grill in any of the three cooking bays. More good things come in threes, too: your choices. Electronic or backlit controls, three cooktop colors—and the poised elegance of a bold, classic look.

Triple-cooktop color availabilities: electronic controls (black, white), backlit controls (black, white, stainless steel)

*Reference number only.

How many ways can you combine Jenn-Air cooktop choices? Let's see . . .

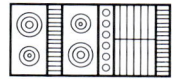 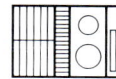 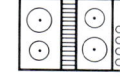  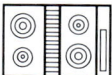 

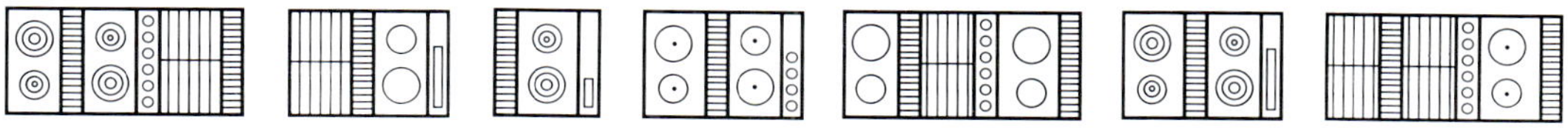

5

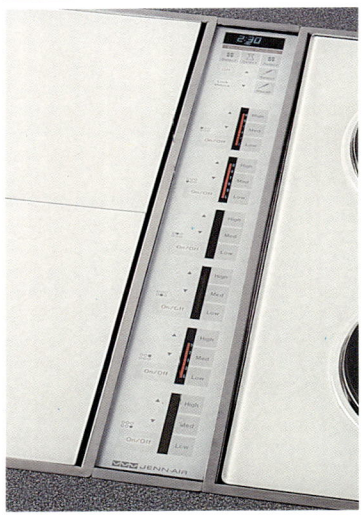

Technology in action—and it's easy to use. Jenn-Air electronic modules use touchpads to put all our advanced features at your fingertips. Including a countdown timer (displaying up to 99 minutes, 59 seconds) and individual control of cooking elements.

Triple-cooktop control module Model CP340W
(also available in black)

Jenn-Air electronic control modules provide advanced cooking capabilities in your choice of black or white. They're available for all three cooktop configurations: triple, double and single. And they offer some exciting advantages. A display to give you cooking information. Easy-to-read indicator lights to show you what's on. Touchpad control of eleven temperature levels and eight downdraft ventilation system fan speeds (preset for your convenience). A countdown timer. A probe which shows food temperature in 5° increments from 100° to 500°F right in the information display. It's high technology at your fingertips—and best of all, it's easy to use.

Jenn-Air electronic control modules respond to the touch of a fingertip. Indicator lights and an information display to tell you what's on and show you cooking-time count-down and food temperature. The look and performance? Definitely well done.

Double-cooktop control module Model CP240B
(also available in white)

Our electronic control modules include a temperature probe. Now you don't have to guess when your pork chops are cooked or your fudge is finished. When you hear the beep, you know your food has reached the selected temperature.

When there are children in your life, you can't watch their every move. That's another bonus of our electronic control modules: you don't have to. Just use the lock feature (press the touchpad twice and it's activated) and you don't have to worry about who's in the kitchen.

Single-cooktop control module Model CP140W
(also available in black)

The PerimaVent downdraft ventilation system is a key to Jenn-Air cooktop performance. With Jenn-Air electronic controls, choose from eight preset fan speeds at a touch. Triple cooktops include two fan controls to accommodate their dual downdraft ventilation systems.

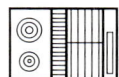

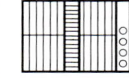
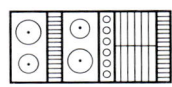
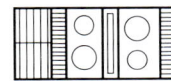

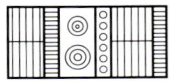

THE GLOW OF POWER: JENN-AIR BACKLIT AND SLIMLINE CONTROLS.

118

Jenn-Air backlit control modules are available in black, white and stainless steel for all three cooktop configurations (single, double, triple). They feature easy-to-use electromechanical control knobs. Triple cooktops include two fan-speed controls.

Triple-cooktop backlit control module Model CP320W (also available in black or stainless steel)

Turn on your grill and the PerimaVent downdraft ventilation system activates automatically. Or use the manual ventilation control at the rear of the control panel to set fan-speed level when you use Jenn-Air options (cooktop cartridges and accessories).

Double-cooktop backlit control module Model CP220B (also available in white or stainless steel)

An indicator ring around each backlit control knob glows when you activate the control.

Single-cooktop backlit control module Model CP120S (also available in black or white)

With Jenn-Air backlit control modules, it's easy to tell what's cooking. Press and turn a control knob. Instantly, the indicator ring around the knob glows and a cooking feature is activated.

Limited countertop area? Choose our remote control module for a double cooktop in black (Model CR220B) or white (Model CR220W). Installs under your cooktop at the front of your cabinet: an excellent option to remodeling plans with limited cutout space.

Another stylish space saver: our slimline control module (Model CP200B). Individual indicator lights glow when a surface element is on. Available in black (with black porcelain grill covers and standard grill element).

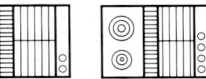
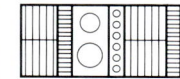

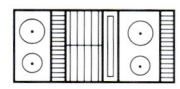
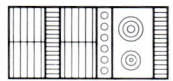
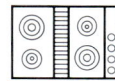
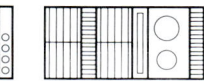
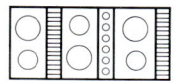

A. Model AH150B Halogen cartridge

B. Model AR140B Quick-Start™ radiant cartridge

C. Model AS130B solid element cartridge

D. Model AC110B conventional coil cartridge

Jenn-Air Cartridge Options.

A. Our *Halogen cartridge with Haloring™ elements* has a circular single-lamp infra-red heater which matches the round base of cooking utensils for optimum heat distribution. Turn it on and it lights immediately. Cartridge surface features wipe-clean glass-ceramic. Available in black. (Large element: 1800 watts. Small element: 1200 watts.)

B. Our *Quick-Start radiant cartridge* has two instant-on heating elements with unexposed coils. Wipe-clean glass-ceramic cartridge surface. Available in black. (Large element: 1700 watts. Small element: 1200 watts.)

C. *Cast-iron solid elements* provide even heat. Thermal limiter protects elements (see wearaway red dot). Wipe-clean glass-ceramic cartridge surface. Available in black or white. (Large element: 2000 watts. Small element: 1500 watts.)

D. *Conventional coils:* the dependable choice of generations. Unplug the large element and use our wok or "Big-Pot" canning element accessory options (see facing page). Available in black, white or stainless steel. (Large element: 2100 watts. Small element: 1250 watts.)

Jenn-Air cooktops change like magic when you change cooking methods. Our convertibility lets you switch from grilling to element cooking in seconds. Just remove the grill assembly and you're ready to insert a cartridge for four-element cooking. Or lift out one optional cooktop cartridge, plug in another, and presto: it's like having a completely different cooktop.

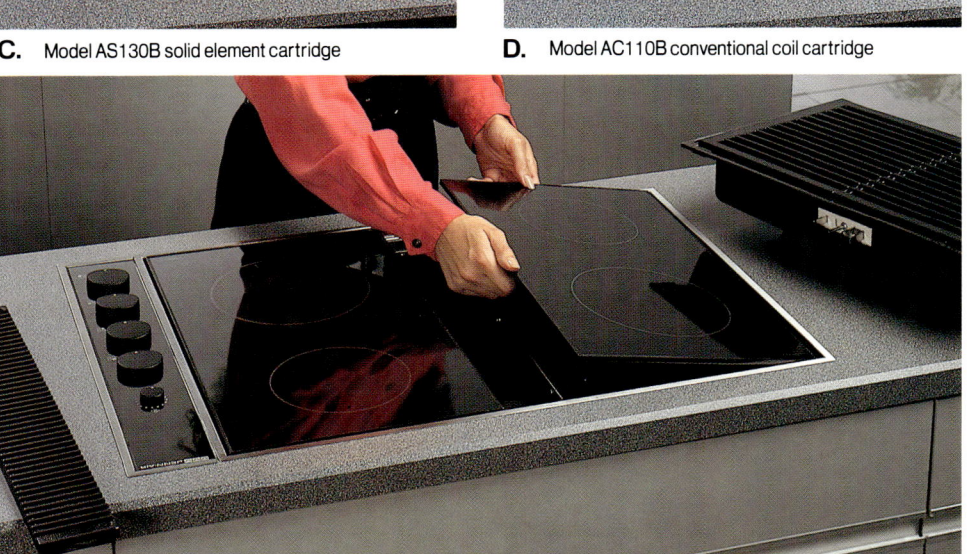

Haloring™ is a trademark of Ceramaspeed Limited.

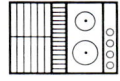
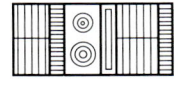
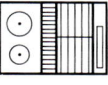
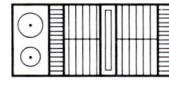
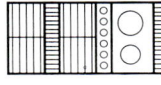
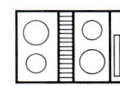
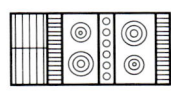
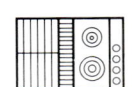

A. Model AO310 griddle

C. Model AO330 grill assembly

B. Model A141A wok

D. Model A145A "Big-Pot" canning element

Jenn-Air Accessory Options.

A. Our *griddle accessory* has a non-stick DuPont SilverStone SUPRA® finish and an integral 1300-watt heating element for even heat distribution.
B. Our *wok accessory* includes a heating element which replaces the large element in our optional conventional coil cartridge. Carbon steel bowl with nonstick finish. Lid, steaming rack and bamboo rice paddles are included. Great for steaming, stir frying, braising or stewing.
C. Our optional *grill* adds extra grilling capability to double and triple cooktops. Energy-Saver grill assembly comes complete with 2800-watt heating element, Savorizer™ pan and grill grates.
D. Cook your lobsters, pasta, corn and more with our optional *"Big-Pot" canning element*. This raised 2100-watt element plugs in place of the large coil in our optional Model AC110 conventional coil cartridge.

Choose our optional extra grill covers in three colors: white or black glass-ceramic, black porcelain and stainless steel. They cover your grill when it's not in use; glass-ceramic covers are tempered to resist high temperature.

Model AO345W white glass-ceramic grill covers

Model AO345B black glass-ceramic grill covers (AO340B black porcelain)

Model AO340S stainless steel grill covers

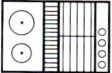
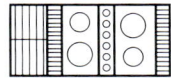
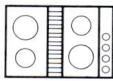

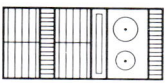
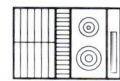

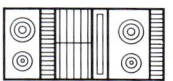
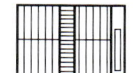

It almost cleans itself.

A Jenn-Air cooktop gives you convertible cooking flexibility—and another convertible plus: the cleaning ease of our take-apart grill design. All you have to do is remove the grill grates, air grille, filter and Savorizer™ liner pan, then wipe them clean in the sink or pop them in the dishwasher. In fact, every grill component is removable—even the basin pan. The grill element cleans itself as it cooks (and shouldn't be immersed in water). The basin pan wipes clean. Grill grates and Savorizer liner pan feature durable, high-quality nonstick finishes (Excalibur® and Duracoat) to keep food and spills from hanging on. And because grease drains into a two-cup remote container, there's even less to clean.

Top-notch Jenn-Air nonstick finishes turn most of your cooktop cleanup into wipe-up. Our griddle accessory is finished with DuPont SilverStone SUPRA®. Our special Savorizer™ liner pan (the heart of grilled tastes) includes a Duracoat finish. Our grill grates feature Excalibur® finish: a Jenn-Air exclusive for your cleaning ease.

Excalibur® is a registered trademark of Whitford Corporation.

 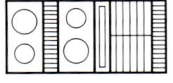 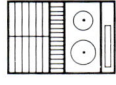 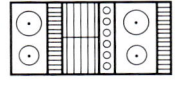 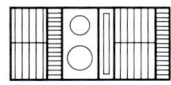 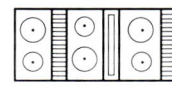 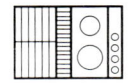 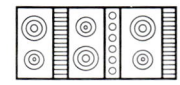

Redefining delicious: the inside story.

How do Jenn-Air cooktops cook up such delicious grilled foods? The secret's in our grill design. While your steaks cook on the grill grates, juices drip down to our Savorizer™ liner pan, where they're transformed into smoke, which rises back up to give your food that savor of savors, grilled flavor.

What happens to that savory smoke? Our PerimaVent downdraft ventilation system whisks it through your ductwork and out of your house.

And not only does Jenn-Air downdraft ventilation pull smoke and cooking vapors through the cooktop air grille: it also provides what's called perimeter ventilation. Wisps of smoke are captured and vented at the edges of the cooking area as well. The result: a cooler, cleaner kitchen and a tasty meal.

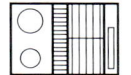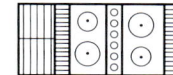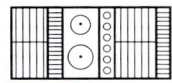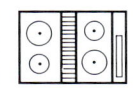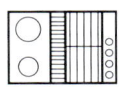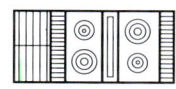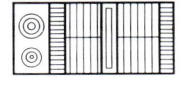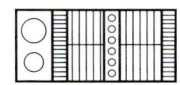

1

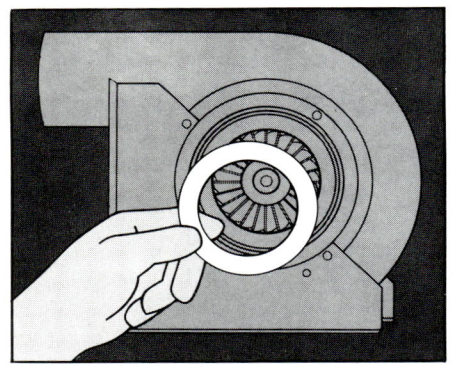

COOKTOP DUCTING DATA

	DUCT LENGTH RECOMMENDATIONS (Maximum)[1]	
	5" Diameter	6" Diameter or 3¼" x 10"[2]
All Electric	10'[3]	60'

[1]**IMPORTANT:** See installation instructions shipped with product before selecting island cabinetry, making cutouts or beginning installation. Use 6" or 3¼" x 10" duct on island or peninsula installations. For best performance, it is suggested that no more than three 90° elbows be used with 6" or 3¼" x 10" duct. Each foot of flex duct counts as two feet of metal duct. Each flex elbow counts as two metal elbows. For longer duct runs of 31' to 60', the restricter ring on the blower inlet housing must be removed. 6" round or 3¼" x 10" duct recommended for long duct run installations.

[2]Count each 90° elbow as 5' of duct.

[3]When venting electric cooktops, 5" diameter round duct may be used to vent straight out the back of the appliance and directly through the wall for 10' or less.

Failure to follow ducting recommendations or use recommended ducting accessories may result in substandard performance. Laundry-type wall caps never should be used.

For triple system installation use one duct system per blower.

Here's how it works.

For duct runs equivalent to 30' or less, install as received. For duct runs equivalent to 31' to 60', simply snap out the restricter ring on the blower inlet housing. Instantly, you have the power to vent up to the equivalent of 60' (using 6" round or 3¼" by 10" duct).

JENN-AIR COOKTOP DUCTING ACCESSORIES

Model A403 Surface Wall Cap—Single damper; down discharge. Fits 3¼" x 10" duct.

Model A405 Surface Wall Cap—Single spring-loaded damper; down discharge. Fits 5" diameter duct. Requires opening 5½" in diameter.

Model A406 Surface Wall Cap—Single spring-loaded damper; down discharge. Fits 6" diameter duct. Requires opening 6½" in diameter.

Model A453 Transition—5" round to 3¼" x 10" duct.

Model A456 Transition—5" to 6" round duct.

Model A463 Transition—6" round to 3¼" x 10" duct.

Model A495 Transition—90° angle for transition from 5" round to 3¼" x 10" duct.

Model A496 Transition—90° angle for transition from 6" round to 3¼" x 10" duct.

Part 708786 Thermal Break—Fits 5" (12.7 cm) round duct. Adds 2' to duct length calculation.

Part 715557 Thermal Break—Fits 6" (15.25 cm) round duct. Adds 2' to duct length calculation.

Part 701943 (Part 5950, Leigh Products) Roof Jack—10" x 10" (25.4 cm x 25.4 cm)

TYPICAL COOKTOP DUCT ARRANGEMENTS

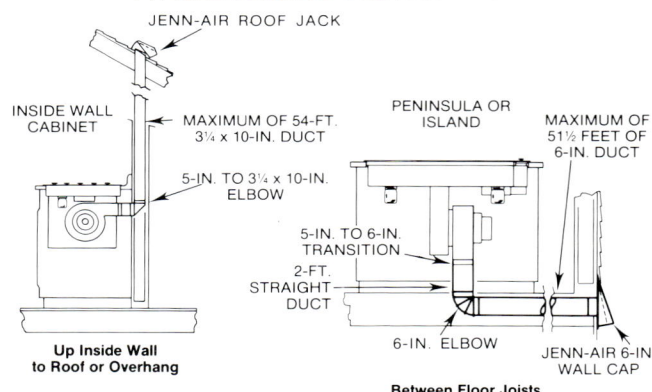

JENN-AIR ROOF JACK

INSIDE WALL CABINET — MAXIMUM OF 54-FT. 3¼ x 10-IN. DUCT

5-IN. TO 3¼ x 10-IN. ELBOW

PENINSULA OR ISLAND — MAXIMUM OF 51½ FEET OF 6-IN. DUCT

5-IN. TO 6-IN. TRANSITION

2-FT. STRAIGHT DUCT

6-IN. ELBOW — JENN-AIR 6-IN. WALL CAP

Up Inside Wall to Roof or Overhang

Between Floor Joists

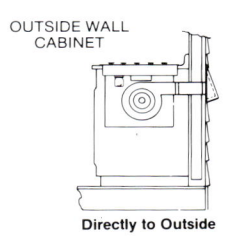

OUTSIDE WALL CABINET

Directly to Outside

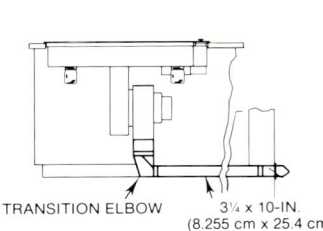

PENINSULA

TRANSITION ELBOW — 3¼ x 10-IN. (8.255 cm x 25.4 cm)

Thru Cabinet Toe Space

IMPORTANT: Dimensions Shown in Both Inches and Centimeters.

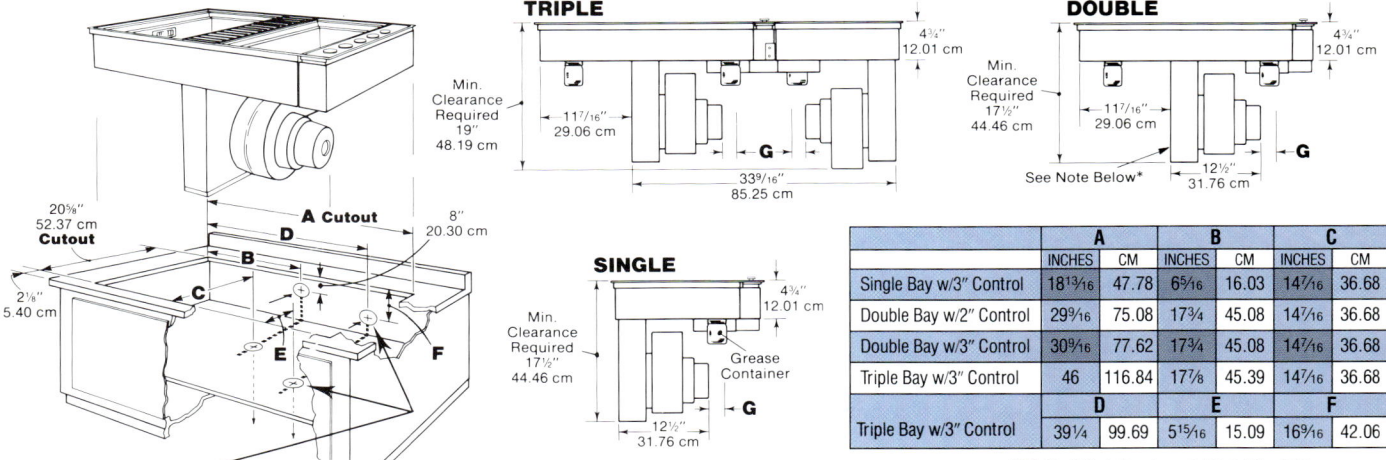

20⅝" 52.37 cm **Cutout**

2⅛" 5.40 cm

A Cutout

8" 20.30 cm

TRIPLE

4¾" 12.01 cm

Min. Clearance Required 19" 48.19 cm

11⁷⁄₁₆" 29.06 cm

33⁹⁄₁₆" 85.25 cm

G

DOUBLE

4¾" 12.01 cm

Min. Clearance Required 17½" 44.46 cm

11⁷⁄₁₆" 29.06 cm

See Note Below*

12½" 31.76 cm

G

SINGLE

4¾" 12.01 cm

Min. Clearance Required 17½" 44.46 cm

Grease Container

12½" 31.76 cm

G

	A		B		C	
	INCHES	CM	INCHES	CM	INCHES	CM
Single Bay w/3" Control	18¹³⁄₁₆	47.78	6⁵⁄₁₆	16.03	14⁷⁄₁₆	36.68
Double Bay w/2" Control	29⁹⁄₁₆	75.08	17¾	45.08	14⁷⁄₁₆	36.68
Double Bay w/3" Control	30⁹⁄₁₆	77.62	17¾	45.08	14⁷⁄₁₆	36.68
Triple Bay w/3" Control	46	116.84	17⅞	45.39	14⁷⁄₁₆	36.68
	D		E		F	
Triple Bay w/3" Control	39¼	99.69	5¹⁵⁄₁₆	15.09	16⁹⁄₁₆	42.06

NOTE: 2" or 3" Control denotes nominal Control Glass Width.

Tolerances ± ¹⁄₁₆ Inch OR ± .16 cm apply to dimensions A thru C only.

CONSULT DUCTING GUIDE FOR PROPER INSTRUCTION.

Triple only — Right hand duct openings

NOTE: Blower may be rotated for horizontal or vertical direction by loosening nuts around blower inlet.

IMPORTANT
Dimension "**G**"—Provide 2" min. (5.08 cm) cabinet clearance to motor for cooling purpose.

NOTE: Where possible, 6" (15.24 cm) is recommended for motor/blower service.

Side Clearance—Grills installed near a side wall must allow a minimum clearance of 6" (15.24 cm) between cooktop and sidewall for maximum ventilation performance.

IMPORTANT: Specifications subject to change without notice. See instructions shipped with product before installation or use.

FEATURES	COOKTOP REFERENCE NUMBERS							
COOKTOP[1]	C1200	C1400	C2000	C2200	C2400	CR2200	C3200	C3400
	COOKTOP COMPONENT MODEL NUMBERS							
CONTROL MODULE	CP120	CP140	CP200	CP220	CP240	CR220	CP320	CP340
BASE MODULE 1	CM100	CM100	CM200	CM200	CM200	CM200	CM200	CM200
BASE MODULE 2							CM100	CM100
Overall Width of Cooktop	19¼	19¼	29 15/16	30 15/16	30 15/16	27⅜	46¼	46¼
Overall Depth of Cooktop	21⅛	21⅛	21⅛	21⅛	21⅛	21⅛	21⅛	21⅛
Cutout Width	18 13/16	18 13/16	29 9/16	30 9/16	30 9/16	26⅞	46	46
Cutout Depth	20⅝	20⅝	20⅝	20⅝	20⅝	20⅝	20⅝	20⅝
Blower Assembly Clearance (below countertop)[2]	17½	17½	17½	17½	17½	17½	19	19
Total Connected Load[3] —KW —Amps (at 120/240 VAC)	3.75 16.66	3.75 16.66	7.25 31.25	7.25 31.25	7.25 31.25	7.25 31.25	11.00 47.91	11.00 47.91
Jenn-Air Golden Product Warranty	•	•	•	•	•	•	•	•
Long Duct Run Motor	•	•	•	•	•	•	•	•
Indoor Grilling	•	•	•	•	•	•	•	•
Energy-Saver Grill[4]	•	•		•	•	•	•	•
Standard Grill[4]			•					
Accepts Grill/Cooktop Accessories	•	•	•	•	•	•	•	•
Countertop/Island/Peninsula Installation	•	•	•	•	•	•	•	•
Single Cooktop	•	•						
Double Cooktop			•	•	•	•		
Triple Cooktop							•	•
PerimaVent™ Downdraft Ventilation System	•	•	•	•	•	•	•	•
Variable-Speed Ventilation Fan	•	•	•	•	•	•	2	2
Slimline Controls			•					
Backlit Controls	•			•		•	•	
Remote Controls						•		
Electronic Touch Controls		•			•			•
Temperature Probe		•			•			•
Color Availabilities (B=Black, W=White, S=Stainless steel)	B, W, S	B, W	B	B, W, S	B, W	B, W	B, W, S	B, W

NOTE: A control-module package (with color designation) and base module(s) must be selected to configure a cooktop. Use the control-module and base-module model numbers when ordering a cooktop configuration. One grill assembly is included in every control-module package. All cartridges and accessories are optional.

[1]Cooktop reference number only. A control-module package (with color designation) and base module(s) must be selected and ordered to configure a cooktop. One grill assembly is included in every control-module package. All cartridges and accessories are optional.

[2]Blower can be swiveled 90°.

[3]All models are U.L. listed for 3-wire 120/240 VAC.

[4]Energy-Saver grill has independent control of front and rear sections of grill (1400 watts each). Standard grill has unified control of entire grill element.

CUTOUT DIMENSIONS FOR REMOTE

IMPORTANT:

Dimensions Shown in Both Inches and Centimeters.

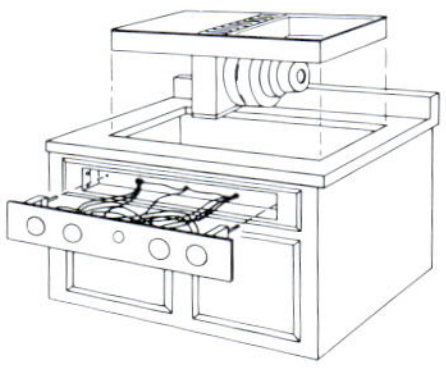

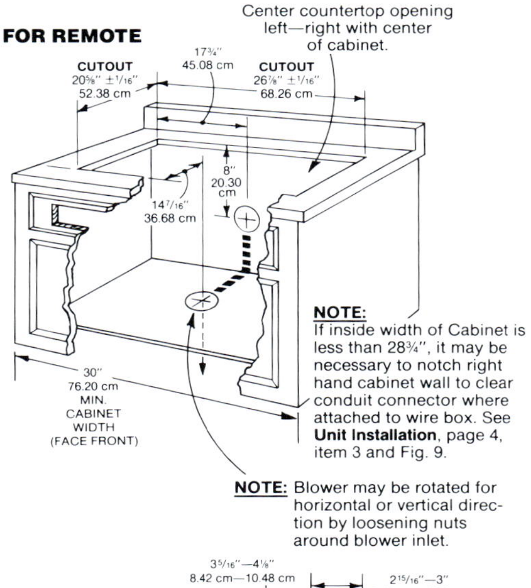

Center countertop opening left—right with center of cabinet.
CUTOUT
20⅝" ±1/16"
52.38 cm
17¾"
45.08 cm
CUTOUT
26⅞" ±1/16"
68.26 cm
8"
20.30 cm
14 7/16"
36.68 cm
30"
76.20 cm
MIN.
CABINET
WIDTH
(FACE FRONT)
NOTE: If inside width of Cabinet is less than 28¾", it may be necessary to notch right hand cabinet wall to clear conduit connector where attached to wire box. See Unit Installation, page 4, item 3 and Fig. 9.
NOTE: Blower may be rotated for horizontal or vertical direction by loosening nuts around blower inlet.

CABINET/FALSE FRONT CUTOUT

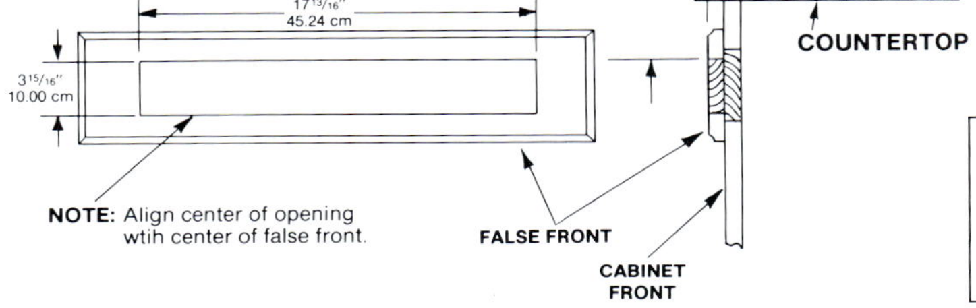

3 5/16"—4⅛"
8.42 cm—10.48 cm
2 15/16"—3"
7.46 cm—6.62 cm
COUNTERTOP
17 13/16"
45.24 cm
3 15/16"
10.00 cm
NOTE: Align center of opening wtih center of false front.
FALSE FRONT
CABINET FRONT

JENN-AIR COOKTOP CONTROL-MODULE PACKAGES

	ELECTRONIC			ELECTROMECHANICAL		
SIZE	SINGLE	DOUBLE	TRIPLE	SINGLE	DOUBLE	TRIPLE
CONTROL-MODULE	CP140	CP240	CP340	CP120	CP200 CP220 CR220	CP320
Savorizer™ Liner Pan	1	1	1	1	1	1
Grill Element[1]	1	1	1	1	1	1
Wipe-Away Excalibur® Grill Grates	2	2	2	2	2	2
Color-Coordinated Grill Covers[2]	2	2	2	2	2	2
Color-Coordinated Air Grille	1	1	2	1	1	2
Temperature Probe	1	1	1			

NOTE: A control-module package (with color designation) and base module or modules must be selected to configure a cooktop. One grill assembly is included in every control-module package. All cartridges and accessories are optional.

[1]All control-module packages include an Energy-Saver grill element, except for Model CP200B, which includes a standard element.

[2]All color-coordinated grill covers feature either stainless steel or tempered glass, except those included with control module Model CP200B, which feature black porcelain.

JENN-AIR COOKTOP BASE MODULES

SIZE	SINGLE	DOUBLE	TRIPLE
BASE MODULE	CM100	CM200	CM100 + CM200
Removable Basin Pan Included	1	2	3
Air Filter Included	1	1	2
Remote Drain Jars Included	1	2	3
Ventilation Systems Included[1]	1	1	2

NOTE: A control-module package (with color designation) and base module or modules must be selected to configure a cooktop. Use the base-module model numbers below when ordering a cooktop configuration. One grill assembly is included in every control-module package. All cartridges and accessories are optional.

[1]Single- and double-bay modules include one downdraft ventilation system (blower). Since the triple-bay configuration is composed of a single-bay module plus a double-bay module, it includes two ventilation systems (which must be vented separately).

JENN-AIR COOKTOP CARTRIDGE FEATURE CHART

COOKTOP CARTRIDGE TYPE[A]	COLOR AVAILABILITIES		
	BLACK	WHITE	STAINLESS STEEL
HALOGEN CARTRIDGE Model AH150B	•		
QUICK-START™ RADIANT CARTRIDGE Model AR140B	•		
SOLID ELEMENT CARTRIDGE Model AS130B	•		
Model AS130W		•	
CONVENTIONAL COIL CARTRIDGE Model AC110B	•		
Model AC110W		•	
Model AC110S			•

NOTE: All cartridges rated 240V.

JENN-AIR COOKTOP ACCESSORY FEATURE CHART

ACCESSORY TYPE[A]	MODEL NUMBER
WOK[B]	A141A
GRIDDLE[C]	A0310
GRILL ASSEMBLY[D]	A0330
COLOR-COORDINATED GRILL COVERS[E] Black glass-ceramic, White glass ceramic, Stainless steel, Black porcelain	A0345B, A0345W, A0340S, A0340B
"BIG-POT" CANNING ELEMENT[F]	A145A

[A]Plug-in accessories rated 240V.
[B]Wok can only be used with conventional coil cartridge.
[C]Griddle has integral 1300-watt heating element.
[D]Grill includes Savorizer™ pan, Energy-Saver grill element and grill grates.
[E]One set (2) included to cover grill when not in use.
[F]Raised 2100-watt element plugs in place of large conventional coil element.

IMPORTANT: Specifications subject to change without notice. See instructions shipped with product before installation or use.

IMPORTANT:
Specifications subject to change without notice. All dimensions listed in inches. Dimensional specifications are provided for comparison purposes only. Never use these figures for product installation. See installation instructions and ducting information shipped with product before selecting cabinetry, making cutouts or beginning installation.

Cover Photo
Designer Line Model CCG456W

Over-the-Range Microwave Oven Model M457B
Sealed Gas Cooktop Model CCG456B
Single Electric Wall Oven Model W130

Designer Line Model CCG456

A winning combination: the responsiveness and heat control of gas cooking—and the cleaning convenience of sealed burners. Automatic reignition relights burners after short interruptions. Porcelain-on-steel burner bowls are easy to clean. Durability features include porcelainized cast-iron burner caps and porcelain-on-steel grates. All indicator markings are protected by the ⁵⁄₁₆″-thick glass cooktop surface.

- 30″ width, 2⅝″ depth to accommodate installation over Jenn-Air single electric wall oven Model W130.

- Four burner ratings for cooking flexibility (large burners — 12,000 BTU, 10,000 BTU; small burners —9,500 BTU, 9,000 BTU. Natural gas only).

- ⁵⁄₁₆″-thick glass cooktop surface.

- Six fingers keep burner grates steady.

- AGA and CGA approved for natural gas.

MODEL CCG456 DESIGNER LINE SEALED GAS COOKTOP FEATURES AND SPECIFICATIONS[1]	
Overall Width	30″
Overall Depth	21″
Cutout Width	26⁹⁄₁₆″
Cutout Depth	20¹⁄₁₆″
BTUs (Natural only) Right Front Right Rear Left Front Left Rear	12,000 9,000 9,500 10,000
Jenn-Air Golden Product Warranty	•
Countertop/Island/Peninsula Installation	•
AGA/CGA Approved	•
Four-Burner Cooktop	•
Electronic Pilotless Ignition	•
Automatic Reignition	•
Designer Line Styling	•
Color Availabilities (B=black, W=white)	•

[1]Smoke and steam capture requires use of range hood or ventilation system in over-the-range microwave oven.

IMPORTANT: Specifications subject to change without notice. All dimensions listed in inches. Dimensional specifications are provided for comparison purposes only. Never use these figures for product installation. See installation instructions shipped with product before selecting cabinetry, making cutouts or beginning installation.

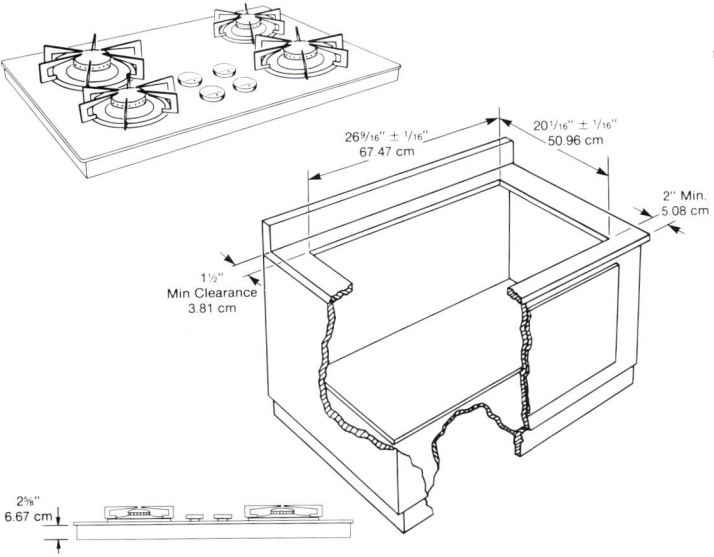

26⁹⁄₁₆″ ± ¹⁄₁₆″
67.47 cm

20¹⁄₁₆″ ± ¹⁄₁₆″
50.96 cm

2″ Min.
5.08 cm

1½″
Min Clearance
3.81 cm

2⅝″
6.67 cm

 **Jenn-Air**

3035 Shadeland
Indianapolis, Indiana 46226-0901
U.S. & Foreign Patents & Patents Pending
Specifications subject to change without notice.

Jenn-Air convertible grill-ranges and grill-range cooktops are right for the finest kitchens. Our cooktop cartridge and accessory options help you build a complete cooking system with the flexibility to make every meal a masterpiece.

Whether you choose electric or gas cooking, downdraft ventilation (we pioneered it) or an updraft configuration, Jenn-Air quality means complete cooking convenience—and enjoyment.

Conventional Electric Coils: Model A100
• Large element removes to accept wok or "big pot" canning element accessories
Model A100 (stainless steel, shown),
Model A100B (black porcelain, not shown),
Model A100W (white porcelain, not shown)

Glass-Ceramic Elements: Model A120*
• Easy-to-clean black surface

*Model A120 and Model A105 are rated 120/240V. Available with 120/208V rating (add -8 to end of model number).

Gas Two-Burner Module: Model AG200B
• Converts gas grill to two burners

Rotiss-Kebab: Model A31
• For electric grills only
• Motor-driven rotiss autom rotates food with minima attention
• Skewers for kebabs includ

See Page 25 for complete cooktop cartridge and accessory specifications and features.

2

Solid Elements: Model A105*

- Cast iron, easy-clean elements (no drip bowls) provide even heat
- Thermal limiter protects elements (see wearaway red dot)
- Easy-to-clean glass cartridge surface

Model A105 (black, shown), Model A105W (white, not shown)

Griddle Accessories: Models A302, AG302

- Self-draining, family-sized
- Featuring superior nonstick DuPont SilverStone® SUPRA

Model A302 (electric, shown), Model AG302 (gas, not shown). Models not interchangeable.

Wok Accessories:
Models A141A, AG340

- Carbon steel bowl with nonstick finish
- Lid, steaming rack, bamboo rice paddles included
- Use for stir frying or steaming
- Electric model for use with conventional coil elements only

Model A141A (electric, shown), Model AG340 (gas, not shown). Models not interchangeable.

Induction: Models A135, A130

- Applies magnetic field to cookware
- Pot gets hot, surface stays cool
- Instant response, gas-like heat control
- Indicate R for rear plug-in, F for front plug-in

Model A135 (black, shown), Model A130 (white, not shown)

Grill Cover: Model A341

- Covers electric grill while not in use

Model A341 (black, shown), Model A341W (white, not shown)

"Big Pot" Canning Element: Model A145A

- Use for canning or "big pot" cooking
- Replaces large Jenn-Air conventional coil element when using large pots (over 8″ diameter)

Grill Assembly: Model A158

- Includes plug-in Energy-Saver grill element, two grill-rocks, two grill grates, storage tray

Cooker-Steamer: Model A335

- For electric grills only
- Poach, blanch, steam, stew
- See-through cover, two position basket with handles

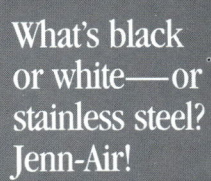

What's black or white—or stainless steel? Jenn-Air!

Select Jenn-Air grill-ranges and grill-range cooktops are available in color choices including white, black or stainless steel. For your white kitchen, our optional conventional coil and solid element cooktop cartridges are available in white. Select a white grill cover, too—and for your free-standing grill-range, our white deluxe lighted backsplash and white color side panels are the perfect optional finishing touches. Jenn-Air gives you complete cooking flexibility—in step with your style.

See Page 25 for complete cooktop cartridge and accessory specifications and features.

utdoor-grilled flavor: thanks to Jenn-Air, it's been an indoor pleasure for 28 years. We pioneered the downdraft ventilation system—and now we offer both downdraft and updraft grill-range models.

All Jenn-Air Designer Line electric grill-ranges provide the following performance quality features.

- Indoor grilling (high-performance updraft ventilation system required for updraft grill-range)
- Grill element: 2800 watts (downdraft) or 2500 watts (updraft)
- Accepts optional grill/cooktop cartridges and accessories
- Electronic clock with timer
- Self-cleaning bake-and-broil oven
- Clock-controlled cooking and self cleaning
- Variable temperature broil
- Formed oven rack guides
- Installation flexibility
- Long-duct-run option (downdraft models only)
- Overall dimensions: 35½" H, 29¹⁵⁄₁₆" W, 26³⁄₈" D (door handle adds 2" to depth)

Designer Line Model SEG196 Downdraft Dual-Fuel™ Grill-Range
All applicable Jenn-Air grill-range performance quality features plus the following:

- Convertible gas cooktop with E-ven Heat™ grill burner (total grill-side rating: 16,000 BTUs, natural or LP) and two surface burners (natural, 10,000 BTUs; LP, 9,000 BTUs)
- Electronic pilotless ignition
- Cooktop converts to four-burner cooking with optional two-burner module (Model AG200)
- Self-cleaning electric oven
- Selective-Use™ convection and bake/broil oven
- Frameless black glass oven door with window
- Free-standing or slide-in installation (shown)
- Convertible to LP gas

Designer Line Model S176W Downdraft Electric Grill-Range (shown with the following options: Model A105W solid element cooktop cartridge, Model A519W deluxe lighted backsplash)
All Jenn-Air grill-range performance quality features plus the following:

- Twin-convertible cooktop with Energy-Saver grill element
- User-friendly electronic touch controls
- Electronic oven controls with clock controlled cooking and cleaning
- Selective-Use™ convection and bake/broil oven
- Frameless glass oven door with window
- Automatic door-lock mechanism for self-cleaning function
- Free-standing or slide-in installation

Available in white (Model S176W, shown) and black (Model S176)

The right installation options.

Most Jenn-Air grill-ranges can be installed in a slide-in configuration. Our long-duct-run option (up to the equivalent of 60′) provides even more installation flexibility than ever. Most models also offer the option of free-standing placement (with optional custom or lighted deluxe backsplash and optional color side panels in white, black or almond). If you prefer to extend your cabinetry below the oven door of your grill-range, choose our "drop-in-look" Model D156, supported by four legs which extend to the floor. A cabinet front then provides the "drop-in" look.

Optional custom backsplash Model A507

See Page 26 for complete grill-range specifications and features.

4

Designer Line Model S156 Downdraft Electric Grill-Range (shown with optional Model A105 solid element cooktop cartridge)
All Jenn-Air grill-range performance quality features plus the following:
- Twin-convertible cooktop with Energy-Saver grill element
- Selective-Use™ convection and bake/broil oven
- Free-standing or slide-in installation

Designer Line Model D156 Downdraft Electric Grill-Range (shown with optional Model A105 solid element cooktop cartridge)
All Jenn-Air grill-range performance quality features plus the following:
- All the features of Model S176 but with "drop-in-look" installation
- Available in black

Designer Line Model S136 Downdraft Electric Grill-Range (shown with optional Model A105 solid element cooktop cartridge)
All Jenn-Air grill-range performance quality features plus the following:
- Twin-convertible cooktop with standard grill element
- Free-standing or slide-in installation

Designer Line Model SU146 Updraft Electric Grill-Range (shown with optional Model A100 conventional coil cooktop cartridge)
All Jenn-Air grill-range performance quality features plus the following:
- Convertible cooktop with Energy-Saver grill element
- User-friendly electronic touch controls
- Electronic oven controls with clock controlled cooking and cleaning
- Selective-Use™ convection and bake/broil oven
- Frameless glass oven door with window
- Automatic door-lock mechanism for self-cleaning function
- Free-standing or slide-in installation
High-performance range hood required for indoor grilling.

See Page 26 for complete grill-range specifications and features.

5

Jenn-Air electric grill-range cooktops can suit any cook and every décor. From tri-convertible flexibility to space-saving single-convertible convenience, here are the right choices—and colors.

All Designer Line Jenn-Air electric convertible grill-range cooktops with downdraft ventilation provide the following performance quality features.

- Indoor grilling
- 2800-watt grill element
- Accepts optional grill/cooktop cartridges and accessories
- Countertop or island/peninsula installation flexibility
- Long-duct-run option

Tri-Convertible (Downdraft Ventilation)

Mix optional cooktop cartridges and accessories to create the ultimate Jenn-Air grill-range cooktop. A delight for the gourmet cook.

Jenn-Air flexibility means cooking pleasure.

Jenn-Air twin- and tri-convertible grill-range cooktops offer you a versatile cooking system. Two optional twin-element cooktop cartridges (such as our cast iron solid elements, shown above) provide four-element convenience. A wide variety of grill/cooktop accessory options provides additional flexibility.

Designer Line Model C236B (shown with two optional Model A105 solid element cooktop cartridges)

Designer Line Model C316W (48" width; shown with two optional Model A105W solid element cooktop cartridges)
All Jenn-Air grill-range cooktop performance quality features plus the following:

- Tri-convertible grill-range cooktop with downdraft ventilation system and Energy-Saver grill element (far righthand cooking bay does not accept grill)
- Utensil storage with lift-up wooden cover
- Overall dimensions: 46³⁄₁₆" W, 21⁹⁄₁₆" D

Color availabilities: stainless steel with white accents (Model C316W, shown), stainless steel (Model C316, not shown)

Twin-Convertible and Convertible (Downdraft Ventilation)

Our most popular models. Choose from models featuring twin-convertible flexibility or permanently installed conventional coil elements paired with a grill.

Designer Line Model C206 (30″ width)
All Jenn-Air grill-range cooktop performance quality features plus the following:
- Single-convertible grill-range cooktop (left bay only) with downdraft ventilation system and standard grill element
- Two permanently installed conventional coil elements
- Overall dimensions: 29⅞″ W, 21½″ D
- Stainless steel finish

Designer Line Model C236B (30″ width; shown with optional Model A105 solid element cooktop cartridge)
All Jenn-Air grill-range cooktop performance quality features plus the following:
- Twin-convertible grill-range cooktop with downdraft ventilation system and Energy-Saver grill element
- Accepts optional grill/cooktop cartridges and accessories
- Overall dimensions: 29¹⁵⁄₁₆″ W, 21⁹⁄₁₆″ D
- Color availabilities: stainless steel (Model C236), white porcelain (Model C236W, shown), black porcelain (Model C236B, shown)

Model C236W

Jenn-Air features cleanability.

Our electric grill-range cooktops provide maximum cooking performance—and are designed for complete cleaning ease as well. Nonstick grill grates and cast-iron grill-rocks can be cleaned in the sink or go right in the dishwasher once any burned-on residue is removed. The porcelain grill basin features wipe-clean rounded corners and a convenient forward slope to aid cleanup. Use household cleaner and a sponge or plastic scrubber for easy removal of grill-basin soil. Since most grease and excess drippings drain into our remote grease containers, start-to-finish cleaning is quick and simple.

Single-Convertible (Downdraft Ventilation)

For smaller kitchen spaces—or as the ultimate convenience for your family room—choose a Jenn-Air single-convertible electric grill-range cooktop and put cooking flexibility where you want it.

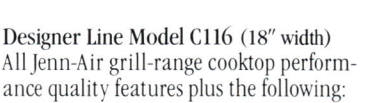

Designer Line Model C116 (18″ width)
All Jenn-Air grill-range cooktop performance quality features plus the following:
- Single-convertible grill-range cooktop with Energy-Saver grill element
- Accepts optional grill/cooktop cartridges and accessories
- Overall dimensions: 18⅝″ W, 21⁹⁄₁₆″ D
- Stainless steel finish

Kitchens which can't accommodate a downdraft ventilation system *can* have a Jenn-Air cooktop. Our updraft electric lineup includes four-element models (conventional coils or cast iron solid elements) and convertible models. For updraft grilling, choose a high-performance ventilation system (in ducted range hood or over-the-range microwave oven).

Jenn-Air Lanai™ Outdoor Grills are two ways to satisfy outdoor appetites. Especially designed for outdoor use, they add electric grilling pleasure to your lanai, patio, deck or porch.

Updraft Cooktops

Choose four permanently installed surface elements (conventional coils or cast iron solid elements). Or select an updraft grill-range cooktop with convertible flexibility and a 2500-watt grill element. Add an updraft ventilation system (in over-the-range microwave oven or range hood) for complete cooking performance.

Designer Line Model CU240 (30″ width; shown with optional Model A100 conventional coil cooktop cartridge)
- Convertible grill-range cooktop
- Indoor grilling with high-performance ducted range hood or over-the-range microwave oven
- 2500-watt Energy-Saver grill element
- Accepts optional grill/cooktop cartridges and accessories
- Overall dimensions: 29⅞″ W, 21½″ D

Perimeter colors: stainless steel (Model CU240, shown) or black porcelain (Model CU240B)

Designer Line Model CU230 (30″ width)
- Single-convertible grill-range cooktop (left bay only)
- Indoor grilling with high-performance ducted range hood or over-the-range microwave oven
- 2500-watt standard grill element (grills on left side only)
- Two permanently installed conventional coil elements
- Accepts optional grill/cooktop cartridges and accessories
- Overall dimensions: 29⅞″ W, 21½″ D

Stainless steel finish

8

See Pages 27-29 for complete electric cooktop specifications and features.

Designer Line Model CCS446 (30″ width)

- Four cast iron solid elements (two with Auto Temp sensor controls, two with Protect Temp thermal limiters with wearaway red dots)
- Individual solid-element indicator lights
- Attractive easy-clean glass cooktop surface
- Overall dimensions: 30″ W, 21″ D

Available in black glass (Model CCS446, shown) and white glass (Model CCS446W)

Designer Line Model CCR466B (30″ width)

- Four circular Quick-Start™ heating elements: two 8″ diameter (2100W), two 6″ diameter (1200W)
- Wipe-clean translucent black-glass ceramic finish
- No coils or drip pans to clean
- A surface indicator light indicates when an element is on
- Hot Surface light indicates cooktop is hot, stays lit till cooktop is cool
- Overall dimensions: 30″ W, 21″ D

Black Ceran surface

Designer Line Model CCE406 (33″ width)

- Four conventional coil elements
- Individual surface-element indicator lights
- Accepts optional accessories: Model A141A wok, Model A145A "big pot" canning element
- Overall dimensions: 33⅜″ W, 21⅜″ D

Perimeter colors (flush-mount edge): brushed chrome (Model CCE406, shown), black porcelain (Model CCE406B), almond porcelain (Model CCE406L)

Jenn-Air® Lanai™ Outdoor Grills (Downdraft Ventilation)

For cooking flexibility, each model accepts electric grill accessory options: Model A302 griddle, Model A335 Cooker-Steamer and Model A341 grill cover.

Designer Line Model G0106B (18″ width)

- U.L. approved for outdoor use
- Downdraft ventilation
- Non-convertible single grill
- 2800-watt standard grill element
- 30-minute timer
- Overall dimensions: 18¹⁄₁₆″ W, 21½″ D

Black porcelain finish

Designer Line Model G0206B (30″ width)

- U.L. approved for outdoor use
- Downdraft ventilation
- Non-convertible twin grill
- Two 2800-watt standard grill elements
- Overall dimensions: 29⅞″ W, 21½″ D

Black porcelain finish

See Pages 27-29 for complete electric cooktop specifications and features.

Gas cooktop precision *and* downdraft ventilation—or a four-burner updraft cooktop: Jenn-Air offers you the choices you want for your gas kitchen. Our gas grill-range cooktops offer you convertible flexibility. Our non-grilling gas cooktop gives you the convenience of four surface burners.

All Jenn-Air Designer Line gas cooktops provide the following performance quality features.

- Convertible cooktop (grill-range cooktop models only)
- Electronic pilotless ignition
- Convertible to LP gas
- Countertop or island/peninsula installation

Gas Cooktops

Designer Line Model CG106B/Downdraft Ventilation (18″ width)
All Jenn-Air gas cooktop performance quality features plus the following:
- Single-convertible grill-range cooktop
- Indoor grilling with downdraft ventilation
- Accepts gas grill/cooktop accessories
- E-ven Heat™ grill burner (total grill-side rating: 16,000 BTUs, natural or LP)
- Converts to two-burner cooktop with optional two-burner module (Model AG200)
- Overall dimensions: 18¹⁄₁₆″ W, 21½″ D

Perimeter colors: black porcelain (Model CG106B, shown) or stainless steel (Model CG106

Designer Line Model CG206B/Downdraft Ventilation (30″ width)
All Jenn-Air gas cooktop performance quality features plus the following:
- Convertible grill-range cooktop
- Indoor grilling with downdraft ventilation
- E-ven Heat™ grill burner (total grill-side rating: 16,000 BTUs, natural or LP)
- Two surface burners on right side (rating per burner: natural, 10,000 BTUs; LP, 9,000 BTUs)
- Accepts gas grill/cooktop accessories
- Converts to four-burner cooktop with optional two-burner module (Model AG200)
- Overall dimensions: 29⅞″ W, 21½″ D

Perimeter colors: black porcelain (Model CG206B, shown) or stainless steel (Model CG206)

Designer Line Model CG205W
All Jenn-Air gas cooktop performance quality features plus the following:
- Convertible grill-range cooktop
- Downdraft ventilation
- Four surface burners (rating per burner: natural, 10,000 BTUs; LP, 9,000 BTUs right side/natural, 8,000 BTUs; LP, 8,000 BTUs left side).
- Accepts gas grill/cooktop accessories
- Left side converts to grill with optional grill assembly (Model AG150 with E-ven Heat™ grill burner. Total grill-side rating: 16,000 BTUs, natural or LP)
- Overall dimensions: 29⅞″ W, 21½″ D)

White porcelain finish

Designer Line Model CCG406B/Updraft Ventilation (30″ width)
All Jenn-Air gas cooktop performance quality features plus the following:
- Four surface burners (rating per burner: natural, 10,000 BTUs; LP, 9,000 BTUs)
- Overall dimensions: 29⅞″ W, 21½″ D

Perimeter colors: black porcelain (Model CCG406B, shown) or stainless steel (Model CCG406)

10

See Pages 27-29 for complete gas cooktop specifications and features.

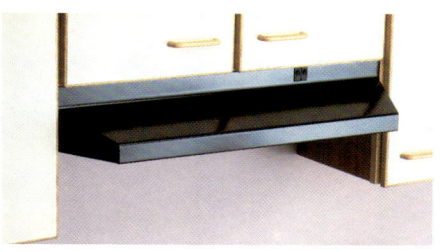

Model RH170*

- Two-speed fan
- One lighting level
- Vertical discharge on 7″ round duct
- Rated 180 CFM (vertical round)
- Overall dimensions: 5″ H, 30″ W, 17⅝″ D

Also available (not shown):

- **Model RH130** (vertical or horizontal discharge on 3¼″ x 10″ rectangular duct; rated 180 CFM)*
- **Model RH101*** (ductless installation with charcoal filter)

All above models available in black, almond, white enamel or stainless steel.

Model RH800B*

- Two lighting levels
- Vertical discharge on 7″ round duct
- Vertical or horizontal discharge on 3¼″ x 10″ rectangular duct
- Rated 350 CFM (vertical rectangular or horizontal rectangular)
- Pull-out Hidavent™ canopy telescopes out of under-cabinet compartment
- Automatic on/off fan control activates when hood is pulled out or retracted
- Remembers selected setting when pulled out
- Overall dimensions: 11³⁄₁₆″ H, 30″ W, 11″ D

Available in black or white

Model RH480

- High-performance design for use with updraft grill-range cooktops
- Touch-control operation
- Variable-speed fan
- Three lighting levels
- Vertical or horizontal discharge on 3¼″ x 10″ duct
- Adaptable to 7″ round duct
- Rated 440 CFM (vertical rectangular), 410 CFM (horizontal rectangular)
- Black-glass-look front panel
- Overall dimensions: 7″ H, 30″ W, 19¾″ D

Available in black, almond, white enamel and stainless steel

Model RH206W*

- Variable speed fan
- One lighting level
- Vertical discharge on 7″ round duct
- Vertical or horizontal discharge on 3¼″ x 10″ rectangular duct
- Ductless installation with charcoal filter
- Rated 300 CFM (vertical round), 200 CFM (vertical rectangular), 180 CFM (horizontal rectangular)
- White hood with gray controls, Dusty Rose accent stripe
- Overall dimensions: 7″ H, 30″ W, 19¾″ D

Also available (not shown):

Model RH200* with all the features of Model RH206W plus a black-glass-lock front panel. Available in almond, black enamel or stainless steel.

Model RH440

- High-performance design for use with updraft grill-range cooktops
- Variable-speed fan
- Two lighting levels
- Vertical or horizontal discharge on 3¼″ x 10″ duct
- Adaptable to 7″ round duct
- Rated 440 CFM (vertical rectangular), 410 CFM (horizontal rectangular)
- Black-glass-look front panel
- Overall dimensions: 7″ H, 30″ W, 18¹¹⁄₁₆″ D

Available in black, almond, white enamel or stainless steel

Model RH400 (not shown; installs under custom cabinetry)

- High-performance design for use with updraft grill-range cooktops
- Variable-speed fan
- Two lighting levels
- Vertical or horizontal discharge on 3¼″ x 10″ duct
- Adaptable to 7″ round duct
- Rated 440 CFM (vertical rectangular), 410 CFM (horizontal rectangular)
- Overall dimensions: 7″ H, 22″ W, 11¼″ D

*For use with non-grilling cooktops.

The perfect companion to your Jenn-Air updraft grill-range or cooktop: a Jenn-Air range hood. Our high-performance hoods (400 Series) are designed to accommodate updraft models' grilling capability. We offer you a wide range of ducting and installation choices, too.

See Page 34 for complete range hood specifications and features.

Which single wall oven is right for you? With 24", 27" and 30" models in black and white, Jenn-Air fits any kitchen. Most models include convection cooking for speedier preparation of many foods (often at lower temperatures). For gas kitchens, choose a wall oven with separate broiler compartment.

All Jenn-Air Designer Line single electric wall ovens provide the following performance quality features.

- Electronic clock with timer
- Self-cleaning bake-and-broil oven
- Clock-controlled cooking and self cleaning
- Catalytic smoke eliminator
- Formed rack guides
- Broiler pan included

Single Electric Wall Ovens

Designer Line Single Model W116 (24" width)
All Jenn-Air wall oven performance quality features.
- Overall dimensions: 29⅝" H, 23⅞" W, 25³⁄₁₆" D

Designer Line Single Model W136 (27" width)
All Jenn-Air wall oven performance quality features plus the following:
- Selective-Use™ convection and bake/broil oven
- Large capacity oven
- Temperature control broiling
- Overall dimensions: 28⅞" H, 26¾" W, 25" D

Designer Line Single Model W156W (27" width)
All Jenn-Air wall oven performance quality features plus the following:
- Selective-Use™ convection and bake/broil oven
- Large-capacity oven
- Temperature control broiling
- User-friendly electronic touch controls
- Electronic oven controls with clock controlled cooking and cleaning
- Memory programming/ programming recall
- Automatic door-lock mechanism for self-cleaning function
- Temperature probe
- Overall dimensions: 28⅞" H, 26¾" W, 25" D

Available in white (Model W156W, shown) and black (Model W156)

12

See Pages 30-32 for complete wall oven specifications and features.

Gas Wall Oven

Designer Line Single Model W130W (30″ width)
All Jenn-Air wall oven performance quality features plus the following:

- Large-capacity oven
- Memory programming/ programming recall
- Undercounter or in-wall installation
- Overall dimensions: 28″ H, 30½″ W, 24″ D

Available in white (Model W130W, shown) and black (Model W130)

Designer Line Gas Model WG206 with Separate Broiler Compartment (24″ width)

- Digital clock with timer
- Electronic pilotless ignition
- Convertible to LP gas
- 16,000 BTUs (natural or LP)
- Separate lower broiler compartment
- Broiler pan included
- Overall dimensions: 46⅝″ H, 23¾″ W, 25⅛″ D

Jenn-Air wall ovens: the right size *and* the right features.

Whether you're remodeling your kitchen, building a new home or replacing your current wall oven, Jenn-Air fits your plans. Our single wall ovens are available in 24″, 27″ and 30″ widths. Choose 24″ and 27″ Jenn-Air double ovens and 27″ double/ combination models. Choose the Jenn-Air wall oven you've always wanted—in the right size for *your* interior design.

See Pages 30-32 for complete wall oven specifications and features.

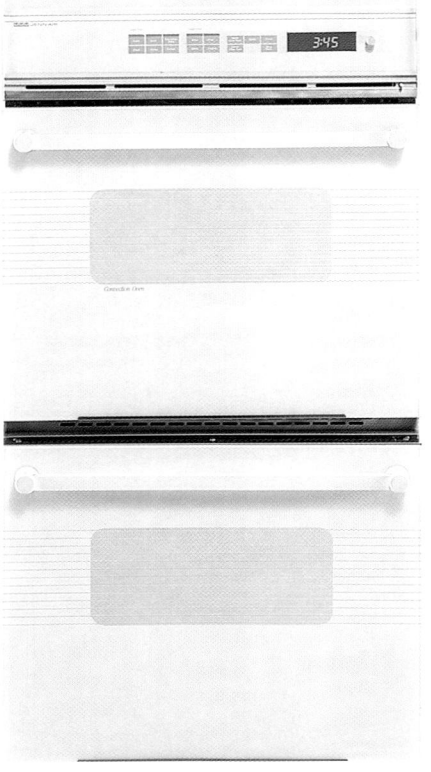

With Jenn-Air double ovens, it's easy to prepare varied dishes at the same time. Choose a 24″ or 27″ model to suit your kitchen design. Our 27″ double/combination wall ovens pair up microwave and radiant (conventional) cooking capabilities for complete kitchen mastery. Most models include a temperature probe and feature three-rack convection cooking.

All Jenn-Air Designer Line double and double/combination wall ovens provide the following performance quality features.

- Electronic clock with timer
- Self-cleaning bake-and-broil oven
- Clock-controlled cooking and self cleaning
- Catalytic smoke eliminator
- Formed rack guides
- Broiler pan included

Double Electric Wall Ovens

Designer Line Double Model W216 (24″ width)

All Jenn-Air wall oven performance quality features (upper oven) plus the following:

- Standard-clean lower oven (baking only)
- Overall dimensions: 46 5/16″ H, 23 7/8″ W, 25 3/16″ D

Designer Line Double Model W256W (27″ width)

All Jenn-Air wall oven performance quality features in upper and lower ovens, plus the following:

Both ovens

- User-friendly electronic touch controls
- Electronic oven controls with clock controlled cooking and cleaning
- Memory programming/programming recall
- Automatic door-lock mechanism for self-cleaning function
- Large capacity
- Overall dimensions: 51″ H, 26 3/4″ W, 25″ D

Upper oven

- Selective-Use™ convection and bake/broil oven
- Temperature probe

Available in white (Model W256W, shown) and black (Model W256)

See Pages 30-32 for complete wall oven specifications and features.

Double/Combination Wall Ovens

Designer Line Double/ Combination Model W236
(27″ width)
All Jenn-Air wall oven performance quality features (lower
oven) plus the following:

Both ovens
- Overall dimensions: 48⁷⁄₁₆″ H,
  26¾″ W, 25″ D

Upper oven (microwave)
- 625 watts of power
- Electronic clock with timer
- Electronic touch controls
- Ten power levels plus defrost
- Temperature probe
- Memory programming

Lower oven
- Selective-Use™ convection
  and bake/broil oven
- Large-capacity oven

Designer Line Double/ Combination Model W276W
(27″ width)
All Jenn-Air wall oven performance quality features (lower
oven) plus the following:

Both ovens
- Overall dimensions: 48⁷⁄₁₆″ H,
  26¾″ W, 25″ D

Upper oven (microwave)
- 625 watts of power
- Electronic clock with timer
- Ten power levels plus defrost
- Temperature probe
- Memory programming

Lower oven
- Selective-Use™ convection
  and bake/broil oven
- Large-capacity oven
- User-friendly electronic touch
  controls
- Electronic oven controls with
  clock controlled cooking and
  cleaning
- Memory programming/
  programming recall
- Automatic door-lock mechanism
  for self-cleaning function

Available in white (Model W276W,
shown) and black (Model W276)

Convection cooking: a Jenn-Air plus.

Convection cooking is featured on most Jenn-Air grill-
ranges (and many Jenn-Air
wall ovens). Fan-forced hot
air cooks many foods at
lower temperatures than are
required for radiant (conventional) cooking. Many foods
also cook in less time with
convection. Enjoy juicier
roasts, lighter bread textures,
beautifully golden-browned
baked goods, three-rack
baking and much more.

Built in or over the range: Jenn-Air microwave ovens go exactly where you need them—even on your countertop.

Pair up your Jenn-Air wall oven with a built-in microwave in black or white. For the built-in look, an optional trim kit adds the finishing touch. Or top off your Jenn-Air grill-range or cooktop with an over-the-range microwave, featuring below-oven work surface lighting (and a built-in ventilation system on some models). All our microwaves have the power—and programming features —you need.

Designer Line Built-In Model M166W (shown installed with optional trim kit Model A526W, over single wall oven Model W156W)

- 1.1-cubic-foot capacity
- 625 watts of power
- 10 power levels plus defrost
- Two-stage memory programming
- Electronic touch control
- Temperature probe/hold
- Preprogrammed cook code (probe)
- Oven rack
- Removable glass tray
- Suitable for countertop use
- Accepts optional built-in trim kits for installation of oven in 27" cabinet (18⅛" x 24½" opening) or 24" cabinet (15⅝" x 22¼" opening)
- Overall dimensions: 15¼" H, 21¾" W, 15¾" D

Available in white (Model M166W, shown) and black (Model M166)

Designer Line Model M166W

Designer Line Over-The-Range Model M416

- 1.0-cubic-foot capacity
- 625 watts of power
- 10 power levels plus defrost
- Two-stage memory programming
- Electronic touch control
- Preprogrammed defrost and cook codes
- Programming command prompts
- Delay start
- Designed for use above all gas and electric grill-ranges and grill-range cooktops with down-draft ventilation
- Below-oven work surface light fixture
- Nonventilated
- Overall dimensions: 14⅝" H (front), 16½" H (back), 30" W, 13" D

See Page 33 for complete microwave oven specifications and features.

Designer Line Over-The-Range Model M436W

- 1.0-cubic-foot capacity
- 625 watts of power
- 10 power levels plus defrost
- Two-stage memory programming
- Electronic touch control
- Preprogrammed defrost code
- Programming command prompts
- Delay start
- Built-in exterior exhaust system (convertible to recirculating ventilation with optional filter kit Model MF110)
- Designed for use above all non-grilling gas and electric updraft cooktops. (Not recommended over grill-ranges or cooktops with grilling capability unless grill-range or cooktop is equipped with downdraft ventilation.)
- Below-oven work surface light
- Overall dimensions: 14⅝″ H (front), 16½″ H (back), 30″ W, 13″ D

Available in white (Model M436W, shown) and black (Model M436)

Designer Line Over-The-Range Model M446

- 1.0-cubic-foot capacity
- 625 watts of power
- 10 power levels plus defrost
- Two-stage memory programming
- Electronic touch control
- Preprogrammed defrost code
- Programming command prompts
- Delay start
- Built-in high-performance exhaust system
- Designed for use above all updraft gas and electric cooktops including electric grill-ranges and grill-range cooktops which require updraft ventilation
- Smoke shield
- Below-oven work surface light
- Overall dimensions: 14⅝″ H (front), 16½″ H (back), 30″ W, 13″ D

See Page 33 for complete microwave oven specifications and features.

Jenn-Air side-by-side refrigerators offer flexible storage. All models accept custom door panels, to match wall treatments, cabinetry or other Jenn-Air appliances.

All Jenn-Air side-by-side refrigerators include the following performance quality features.

- Optional Black Door Panel Kit and Decorator Trim Kit available
- Accepts custom front panels
- White or almond textured steel doors
- Adjustable easy-roll wheels
- Freezer/refrigerator lights
- Two door stop positions
- Tri-Lock™ shelves
- Deep Storage freezer and refrigerator shelves
- Dairy Compartment with butter dish
- Wine Rack
- See-through Sealed Crisper
- Temp Control Drawer
- Refrigerator shelf tender
- Lift-out Egg Caddy

Model JRSD246

All Jenn-Air side-by-side refrigerator performance quality features plus the following:
- 24-cubic-foot total refrigerated volume
- Crystal White interior
- Glide-Trac™ roller drawer system for smooth movement
- Four Deep Storage freezer door shelves with easy-off fronts
- Four adjustable freezer shelves
- Bulk Storage wire basket (freezer)
- Always Ice™ Automatic Ice Maker with bin
- Lighted Convenience Center
- Temp Control Drawer
- Humidity-controlled Sealed Crisper
- Three Tri-Lock™ Shelves (adjustable/removable cantilever glass refrigerator shelves)
- Jenn-Air Premier Designer Line Styling
- Accepts optional white Decorator Trim Kit

Model JRSD246 (shown with optional Black Door Panel Kit Model BDS24D-02)

Model JRSD226

All Jenn-Air side-by-side refrigerator performance quality features plus the following:
- 22-cubic-foot total refrigerated volume
- Crystal Gray interior
- Four Deep Storage freezer door shelves with easy-off fronts
- Bulk Storage freezer drawer
- Always Ice™ Automatic Ice Maker with bin
- Lighted Convenience Center
- Temp Control Drawer
- Deli Drawer
- Four Tri-Lock™ Shelves (adjustable/removable cantilever glass refrigerator shelves)
- Jenn-Air Designer Line Styling
- Accepts optional white Decorator Trim Kit

Model JRSD226

See Page 35 for complete side-by-side refrigerator specifications and features.

del JRSD246

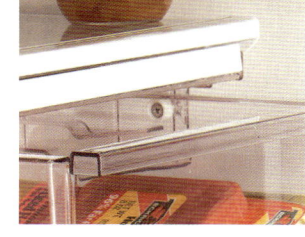

Jenn-Air Premier Designer Line refrigerators offer our Glide-Trac™ Roller Drawer System for smooth movement of all freezer and refrigerator drawers.

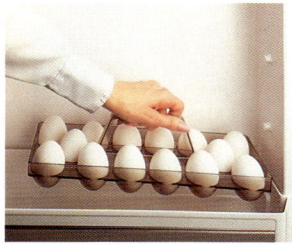

Our lift-out Egg Caddy makes it easy to carry eggs to your cooking area.

Our Temp Control Drawer provides adjustable cooling levels for extra-cool refrigerator storage without freezing.

Adjustable/Lift-off refrigerator door shelves easily adjust to meet your needs.

Model JRS226

All Jenn-Air side-by-side refrigerator performance quality features plus the following:

- 22-cubic-foot total refrigerated volume
- Crystal Gray interior
- Six Deep Storage freezer door shelves with easy-off fronts
- Bulk Storage freezer drawer
- Accepts optional Automatic Ice Maker
- Temp Control Drawer
- Deli Drawer
- Four Tri-Lock™ Shelves (adjustable/removable cantilever glass refrigerator shelves)
- Jenn-Air Designer Line Styling

Custom door panels: a Jenn-Air plus.

Easy-to-install Jenn-Air trim kit options: the finishing touch for your kitchen design. For an all-black color scheme (or to match other Jenn-Air appliances), choose an optional Black Door Panel Kit. To match refrigerator doors to wall treatments, cabinetry or other décor elements, choose an optional Decorator Trim Kit and install custom panels up to 0.25" thick.

Model JRS226

See Page 35 for complete side-by-side refrigerator specifications and features.

Your fine china and favorite cooking utensils deserve careful cleaning after a great meal. Select a Jenn-Air dishwasher and get the job done.

All Jenn-Air Designer Line dishwashers provide the following performance quality features.

- Heavy, Normal and Conserva Wash cycles
- Heated and Air Dry cycles
- Three-level wash system
- Deep upper rack
- Silverware basket with lidded small items basket
- Automatic rinse dispenser
- Rinse and Hold
- Accepts custom door panels

Designer Line Model DU466W

All Jenn-Air dishwasher performance quality features plus the following:

- Soft food disposer
- Durable plastic tub
- Double sound insulation
- Four front door panel colors available (see Page 37 for feature information)
- Overall dimensions: 34″ H (min.), 35″ H (max.), 24″ W, 23¼″ D (excluding door depth)

Available with white control panel (Model DU466W, shown) or black control panel (Model DU466)

Designer Line Model DU486

All Jenn-Air dishwasher performance quality features plus the following:

- High-velocity Jetstream™ cleaning system
- Metered fill
- Food disposer
- Porcelain enamel tub
- Triple insulation
- Deep upper rack with fold down dividers
- Ultra-Mesh™ filter
- Indicator light
- Four front door panel colors available (see Page 37 for feature information)
- Overall dimensions: 34″ H (min.), 35½″ H (max.), 24″ W, 24⅟₁₆″ D (excluding door depth)

See Page 37 for complete dishwasher specifications and features.

Designer Line Model DU506

All Jenn-Air dishwasher performance quality features plus the following:

- High-velocity Jetstream™ cleaning system
- Metered fill
- Food disposer
- Porcelain enamel tub
- Deep upper rack with fold down dividers
- Ultra-Mesh™ filter
- Indicator lights

- Sani-Scrub cycle
- Delay Wash
- Cancel Cycle
- Four front door panel colors available (see Page 37 for feature information)
- Overall dimensions: 34″ H (min.), 35½″ H (max.), 24″ W, 24¹⁄₁₆″ D (excluding door depth)

Designer Line Model DU598W

All Jenn-Air dishwasher performance quality features plus the following:

- Electronic touch controls
- High-velocity Jetstream™ cleaning system
- Metered fill
- Food disposer
- Deep upper rack with fold down dividers
- Ultra-Mesh™ filter
- Signal lights
- Sani-Scrub cycle
- Delay Wash

- Cancel Cycle
- Four front door panel colors available (see Page 37 for feature information)
- Overall dimensions: 34″ H (min.), 35½″ H (max.), 24″ W, 24¹⁄₁₆″ D (excluding door depth)

Available with white control panel (Model DU598W, shown) or black control panel (Model DU598)

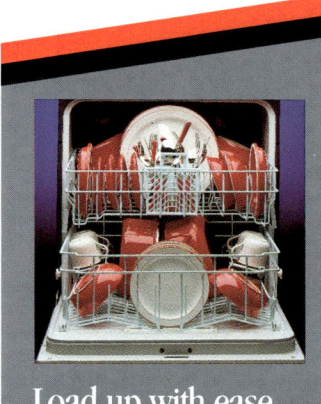

Load up with ease.

All Jenn-Air dishwashers include a deep upper rack to accommodate a variety of loading options. For additional flexibility, most models also offer fold down dividers to make the most of upper-rack space. Lower rack space also is configured for maximum flexibility, accepting large pots and odd-sized utensils with ease. For complete convenience, our silverware basket includes a lidded small items basket to keep utensils in place as they wash.

Cut kitchen litter down to size. Taking out the trash is nobody's favorite chore—but everyone will appreciate how easy it is with a Jenn-Air compactor.

Designer Line Model TC406

- Packs a week's trash from a family of four into one easy-carry package
- ⅓ h.p. motor with 2300 lbs. of ramforce (approx.); 120 VAC, 60 Hz, 6.5 amps
- Cycle time: 27 sec. (max.)
- Tilt-sensing anti-jam sensor
- Toe-release bar and fingertip handle
- Two reversible front panels included (black/white, almond/harvest gold)
- Accepts optional custom wood front panels
- Built-in solid air freshener compartment
- Overall dimensions: 34¹/₁₆" 15" W, 24" D. Cutout dimensions: 34¹¹/₃₂" H (±⁹/₃₂"), 1 24³/₁₆" D. Door panel insert dimensions (trim kit): 22¹⁵/₁₆" H, 14⅝" W, ¼" D.
- Uses Model TCB12 compac bags (12 per package)

Available with black control panel (Model TC406, shown) or white control panel (Model TC406W)

Disposer power: Jenn-Air powers away scraps and messes to help you keep your complete kitchen shining.

All Jenn-Air disposers provide the following performance quality features.

- Quick-mount collar
- ½ h.p. motor with manual reset
- Dishwasher drain connection
- Stainless steel sink flange
- Jam-resistant impeller arms

Deluxe Disposer Models GC440, GC460, GB460

All performance quality features plus the following:

- Continuous feed (Models GC440, GC460) or batch feed (Model GB460)
- Tough enough to grind-up nails
- Sound silencing non-corrosive grinding chamber
- Nicron shredder ring
- Positive pressure water sea

Model GC440 also features space-saver design.

Economy Disposer Models GC410, GC431

All performance quality features plus the following:

- Continuous-feed design
- Die-cast aluminum grinding chamber
- 2-360° swivel impellers

Model GC410 also features a galvanized steel shredder rin **Model GC431** offers a stainle steel shredder ring.

See Page 37 for complete disposer specifications and features.

Finishing touches: these accessories are the right extras for the complete Jenn-Air kitchen.

A—Model A910 5-Piece Cookware Set
- Enamel-on-steel construction
- Includes 9" skillet, 2½-quart au gratin pan, 2-quart saucepan
- Triple-fired white porcelain exteriors

B—Model A905 *Complete Cooking With Jenn-Air* Cookbook
- 192 pages of tested recipes and hints for electric cooking
- Hardbound with full-color illustrations

C—Model A913 Insulated Cookie Sheet
- Two layers of aluminum designed with inner air layer to help baked goods brown to perfection

D—Model A350 (shown), Model AG350 Storage Tray
- Holds one electric or gas grill-range/cooktop cartridge or accessory (except wok, Cooker-Steamer)

E—Model A911 Collo Electrol®
- Maintains matte black surface of cast iron solid elements

F—Model A912 Collo Luneta®
- Removes stains and heat discoloration from stainless steel cooktop, cartridge and cookware surfaces

Jenn-Air 190° Hot Water Dispenser

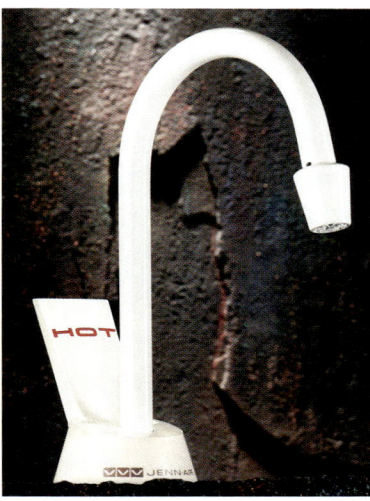

Model HW200W

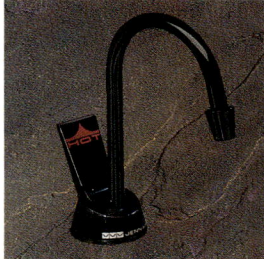

Model HW200B

Model HW100

- Delivers hot water at the touch, in seconds
- Capacity: Up to 60 cups of 190° water per hour
- Compact under-sink tank taps existing cold water supply
- 750 Watts, 6.5 amps, 115 VOLTS
- Heat-insulated operating controls
- 1/2-gallon instant heat reservoir
- Snap-action thermostat adjusts from 140° F to 200° F
- Self-closing instant valve
- 3-wire cord and 3-prong cord included (230)

Available in white (HW200W), black (HW200B) and low-profile chrome (HW100).

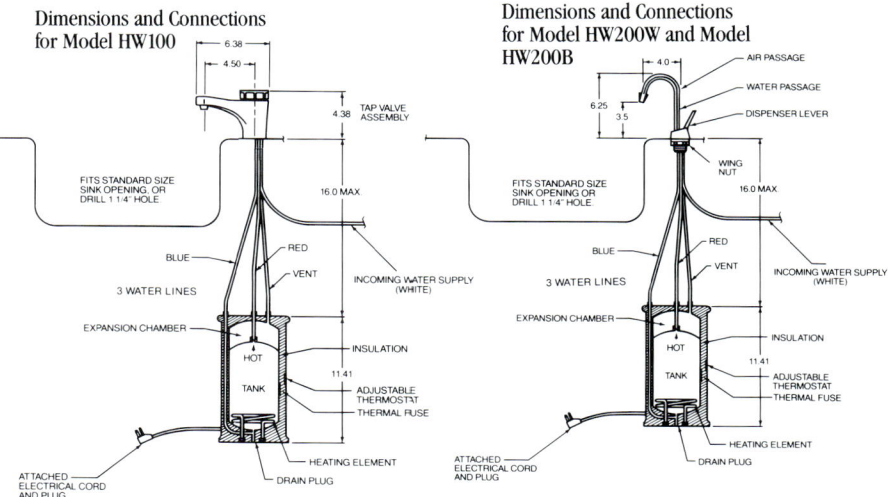

Dimensions and Connections for Model HW100

Dimensions and Connections for Model HW200W and Model HW200B

IMPORTANT Dimensional specifications are provided for comparison purposes only. Never use these figures for product installation. See installation instructions shipped with product before selecting sinks, making cutouts, or beginning installation.

Jenn-Air Grill-Range/Cooktop Cartridges and Module Feature Chart

Cooktop Cartridge Type	ELECTRIC									GAS[1]
	A100	A100B	A100W	A105[2]	A105W[2]	A120[2]	A130[2]	A135[2]	A158[3]	AG200B[4]
	Conventional Coils	Conventional Coils	Conventional Coils	Cast Iron Solid Elements	Cast Iron Solid Elements	Glass Ceramic	Induction[5]	Induction[5]	Energy-Saver Grill	2-Burner Module
Number of Elements/Burners	2	2	2	2	2	2	2	2	2	2
Color Availabilities (S=stainless steel, B=black, W=white)	S	B	W	B	W	B	W	B	B	B

[1]Cartridges designated "gas" are for use with gas convertible cooktops and Model SEG196 Dual-Fuel™ grill-range only.
[2]Rated 240V. Also available with 208V rating (add "-8" to end of model number). Models A130, A135 are dual rated 208/240V. Cartridges designated "electric" are for use with electric-powered grill-ranges and cooktops only and retrofit all Jenn-Air grill-ranges and cooktops manufactured since 1977.
[3]Model A158 has independent control of front and rear burners. Grill includes grill element, grates, grill-rocks and tray.
[4]48,000 BTUs per burner, natural or LP.
[5]Slide controls are front mounted on cartridge.
IMPORTANT: Electric and gas cartridges are not interchangeable. Specifications subject to change without notice. See instructions shipped with product before installation or use.

Jenn-Air Grill-Range/Cooktop Accessory Feature Chart

ACCESSORY TYPE	ELECTRIC[1]								GAS[2]		
	A141A[3]	A145A[4]	A302	A312	A335	A341	A341W	A350	AG302	AG340	AG350
	WOK	"BIG POT" CANNING ELEMENT	GRIDDLE	ROTISS-KEBAB	COOKER-STEAMER	BLACK GRILL COVER	WHITE GRILL COVER	STORAGE TRAY[5]	GRIDDLE	WOK	STORAGE TRAY[5]
For Use with Grill			•	•	•	•	•		•		
For Use on Gas Surface Burner										•	
For Use with Large Conventional Coil	•	•									

[1]Accessories designated "electric" are for use with electric-powered grill-range and cooktops only.
[2]Accessories designated "gas" are for use with gas convertible cooktops and Model SEG196 Dual-Fuel™ grill-range only.
[3]Electric wok cannot be used with glass-ceramic, solid element or induction cartridges.
[4]Raised element snaps in place of large conventional coil elements.
[5]Holds one cartridge or accessory. Fits all cartridges except induction; all accessories except wok, Cooker-Steamer.
ALSO AVAILABLE:
Model A905: Hardbound full-color cookbook, *Complete Cooking With Jenn-Air.* 192 pages of recipes and electric cooking tips.
Model A910: 5-piece cookware set. Enamel on steel with triple-fired white porcelain exteriors. Includes 9" skillet, 2½-qt. au gratin pan, 2-qt. saucepan. Recommended for use with all Jenn-Air grill-ranges, cooktops and cartridge elements except glass-ceramic and solid elements.
Model A911: Collo Electrol® maintains matte black surface of cast iron solid elements in cartridge or cooktop.
Model A912: Collo Luneta® removes stains, discoloration from stainless steel cooktop, cartridge and cookware surfaces.
Model A913: Jenn-Air insulated cookie sheet.
IMPORTANT: Electric and gas accessories are not interchangeable. Specifications subject to change without notice. See instructions shipped with product before installation or use.

Jenn-Air Grill-Range Feature Chart

JENN-AIR GRILL-RANGE FEATURES AND SPECIFICATIONS	DOWNDRAFT					UPDRAFT[1]
	ELECTRIC				DUAL-FUEL	ELECTRIC
	S136	S156	D156	S176	SEG196	SU146
Overall Height	35½	35½	35½	35½	35½	35½
Overall Width	29 15/16	29 15/16	29 15/16	29 15/16	29 15/16	29 15/16
Overall Depth[2]	26 3/8	26 3/8	26 3/8	26 3/8	26 3/8	26 3/8
Oven Interior Height	14¾	14¾	14¾	14¾	14¾	14¾
Oven Interior Width	21	21	21	21	21	21
Oven Interior Depth	18 9/16	18 9/16	18 9/16	18 9/16	18 9/16	18 9/16
Jenn-Air Golden Product Warranty	•	•	•	•	•	•
Long Duct Run Motor	•	•	•	•	•	
Indoor Grilling	•	•	•	•	•[3]	•[3]
Accepts Grill Accessories	•	•	•	•	•	•
Twin-Convertible Cooktop	•	•	•	•		
Convertible Cooktop					•	•
Energy-Saver Grill Element Included		•[4]	•[4]	•[4]		•[5]
Standard Grill Element Included	•[4]					
E-ven Heat™ Grill Burner Included					•	
Electronic Touch Control			•	•		•
Electronic Clock with Timer	•	•	•	•	•	•
Self-Cleaning Oven		•	•	•	•	•
Clock-Controlled Cook and Clean	•	•	•	•	•	•
Automatic Self-Clean Latch			•	•		•
Bake-and-Broil Oven	•	•	•	•	•	•
Convection Oven		•	•	•	•	•
3-Rack Baking		•	•	•	•	•
Variable Temperature Broil	•	•	•	•	•	•
Black Glass Oven Door with Window	•	•	•	•	•	•
Formed Rack Guides	•	•	•	•	•	•
Accepts Optional Backsplash[6]	•	•	•	•	•	•
Accepts Optional Base Trim Kits[7]	•	•		•	•	
Accepts Optional Color Side Panels[8]	•	•		•	•	•
Island/Peninsula Installation[9]	•	•	•	•	•	•
Slide-In Installation	•	•		•	•	•
Drop-In-Look Installation[10]			•			
Gas Cooktop/Electric Oven					•	
BTUs (Natural/LP)						
Surface burners (per burner)					10,000/9,000	
Grill burners (per burner)					8,000/8,000	
Electronic Pilotless Ignition					•	
Convertible to LP Gas					•	
U.L. Approved	•	•	•	•		•
A.G.A Design Certified					•	
Designer Line Styling	•	•	•	•	•	•
Color Availabilities (B=black, W=white)	B	B	B	B, W	B	B

1 High-performance range hood required (such as Jenn-Air Models RH400, RH440, RH480). See Page 10 for range hood specifications and features.

2 Add 2" for door handle.

3 On left side only.

4 2800-watt grill element.

5 2500-watt grill element.

6 Deluxe lighted backsplash Models A519 (black), A519W (white): add 10 9/16" to range height. Custom backsplash Model A507: add 5 1/4" to range height.

7 Custom accent panel slides in. Order Base Trim Kit Model A510.

8 Available in white (Model A501WT), black (Model A501BT) and almond (Model A501LT).

9 24" "double toe space" base cabinets will not accept grill-ranges in slide-in installation. Use 24" flush back design or 27" or deeper base cabinets.

10 "Drop-in-look" refers to a range supported by four legs which extend to the floor. Lower front section is recessed to allow installation of custom cabinetry panel.

Total connected load: All-electric models—50 amp minimum circuit protection required; Model SEG196—3[0] amp minimum circuit protection required. All models are U.L. listed. All electric models are dual rated for 3-w[ire] 120/240 VAC or 120/208 VAC, 60 Hz. For 120/208 VAC applications, appropriate electric grill element must b[e] substituted prior to installation. **All Jenn-Air electric grill-ranges are shipped complete with one grill assembly. Model SEG196 includes gas grill element and 2 surface burners. All cartridges, accessorie[s] backsplashes, base trim kits and side panels are optional.**

IMPORTANT: Specifications subject to change without notice. All dimensions listed in inches. Dimensional specifications are provided for comparison purposes only. Never use these figures for product installation. See installation instructions and ducting information shipped with product before selecting island cabinetry making cutouts or beginning installation.

Free-Standing Grill-Range Cutout
Models S136, S156, S176, SU146

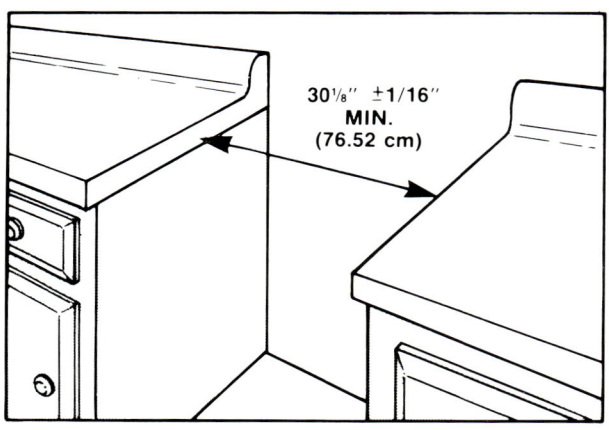

30 1/8" ±1/16"
MIN.
(76.52 cm)

Slide-In or "Drop-In-Look" Grill Range
Installation for All Grill-Range Models

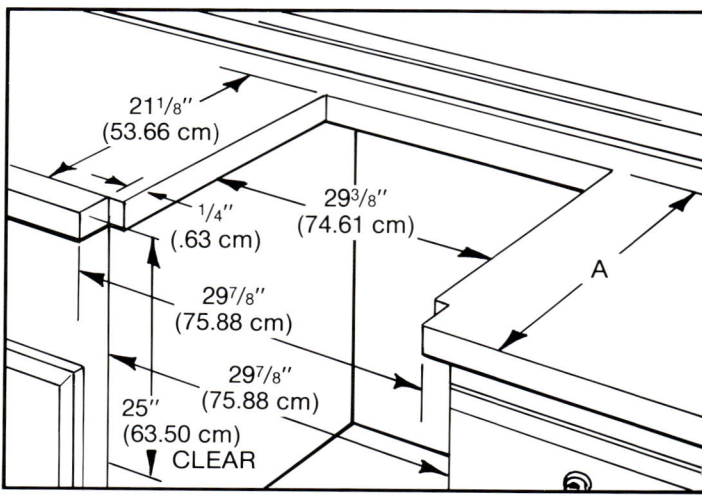

21 1/8" (53.66 cm)
1/4" (.63 cm)
29 3/8" (74.61 cm)
29 7/8" (75.88 cm)
29 7/8" (75.88 cm)
25" (63.50 cm) CLEAR
A

Overhang

If overhang is ½" to 1", dimension A=22 7/8". If overhang is 1" to 1¾", dimension A=23 3/16". Note: 25" height dimension does not include additional height of base and legs. See installation instructions shipped with product before selecting cabinetry, making cutouts or beginning installation.

Dimensional specifications are provided for comparison purposes only. Never use these figures for product installation. See installation instructions shipped with product before selecting cabinetry, making cutouts or beginning installation.

Jenn-Air Cooktop Feature Chart

JENN-AIR COOKTOP FEATURES AND SPECIFICATIONS	LANAI GRILLS GO106B	GO206B	ELECTRIC C116	C206	C236	C316	GAS CG106	CG205W	CG206	ELECTRIC CCE406	CCS446	CCR466B	CU230	CU240	GAS CCG406
	18"	30"	18"	30"	30"	48"	18"	30"	30"	33"	30"	30"	30"	30"	30"
Overall Width	18 1/16	29 7/8	18 5/8	29 7/8	29 15/16	46 13/16	18 1/16	29 7/8	29 7/8	33 5/8	30	30	29 7/8	29 7/8	29 7/8
Overall Depth	21 1/2	21 1/2	21 9/16	21 1/2	21 9/16	21 9/16	21 1/2	21 1/2	21 1/2	21 5/8	21	21	21 1/2	21 1/2	21 1/2
Cutout Width	17 1/8	28 7/8	17 1/8	28 7/8	28 7/8	45 3/4	17 1/8	28 7/8	28 7/8	33 1/16	26 5/8	29 7/16	28 7/8	28 7/8	28 7/8
Cutout Depth	20 15/16	20 15/16	20 15/16	20 15/16	20 15/16	20 15/16	20 15/16	20 15/16	20 15/16	21 1/16	20	20 7/8	20 15/16	20 15/16	20 15/16
Blower Assembly Clearance (below countertop)[2]	15 5/8	15 5/8	15 5/8	15 5/8	15 5/8	15 13/16	15 5/8	15 5/8	15 5/8						
Total Connected Load[3] —KW	3.05	5.85	3.6	6.87	6.87	10.2				6.7	6.7	7.0	6.7	6.7	
—Amps (at 120/240 VAC)	13.7	25.1	16.5	30.0	30.0	44.3				27.9	27.9	29.2	27.9	27.9	
BTUs (Natural/LP)[4] —Single unit, left side of double unit							8,000 8,000	8,000 8,000	8,000 10,000						10,000 9,000
—Right side of double unit								10,000 9,000	10,000 9,000						10,000 9,000
Jenn-Air Golden Product Warranty	•	•	•	•	•	•	•	•	•	•	•	•	•	•	•
Long Duct Run Motor	•	•	•	•	•	•	•	•	•				•	•	
Indoor Grilling			•	•	•	•[5]		•[5]	•[5]				•[5]	•[5]	
Accepts Grill/Cooktop Accessories[6]	•	•	•	•	•	•	•	•	•	•			•	•	•
Countertop Installation	•	•	•	•	•	•	•	•	•	•	•	•	•	•	•
Island/Peninsula Installation	•	•	•	•	•	•	•	•	•	•	•	•	•	•	•
U.L. Approved for Outdoor Installation	•	•													
Tri-Convertible Cooktop							•								
Twin-Convertible Cooktop					•										
Single-Convertible Cooktop			•	•			•						•		
Convertible Cooktop								•[7]	•[7]					•[7]	
Grill-Only Cooktop	•	•													
Energy-Saver Grill Element Included			•		•	•								•	
Standard Grill Element Included	•	2		•									•		
E-ven Heat™ Grill Burner Included							•								
Gas Surface Burners Included								4	2						4
Solid Elements Included											4[8]				
Conventional Coil Elements Included				2[8]						4[8]			2[8]		
Quick-Start™ Radiant Elements Included												4[8]			
Electronic Pilotless Ignition							•	•	•						•
Convertible to LP Gas							•	•	•						•
Designer Line Styling	•	•	•	•	•	•	•	•	•						
Color Availabilities (B = black porcelain, BC = brushed chrome, BG = black glass, L = almond porcelain, S = stainless steel, W = white)	B	B	S	S	B,S,W	S,W	B,S	W	B,S	B,BC,L	W,BG	BG[9]	S	B,S	B,S
Cooktop Perimeter Construction[10] (RF = roll formed, RFR = roll formed ring, ST = stamped)	ST	ST	RF	ST	ST, RF	RF	ST	ST	ST	RFR		RFR	ST	ST	ST

[1] Proper operation requires use of range hood (Models CU230, CU240 require a compatible high-performance ducted range hood such as Jenn-Air Models RH400, RH440, RH480). See Page 34 for Jenn-Air range hood specifications and features.

[2] Blower can be swiveled 90°.

[3] All electric models (except Models CCS446 and CCR466B) are U.L. listed and dual rated for 3-wire 120/240 VAC or 120/208 VAC, 60 Hz. For 120/208 VAC applications, appropriate grill element must be substituted prior to installation. Models CCS446, CCR466B are U.L. listed and rated for 3-wire 120/240 VAC only.

[4] Regulator connection 1/2" N.P.T. (male pipe). Electric supply for pilotless ignition: 120 VAC, 60 Hz. Power cord supplied.

[5] Model C316 does not accept grill in far righthand cooking bay. Models CU240, CU230, CG206 grill on left side only. Model CG205W accepts optional grill assembly Model AG150 on left side only.

[6] Optional two-burner module (Model AG200): 8,000 BTUs per burner (natural or LP). Electric grill accessories are designed for use ONLY with electric cooktops. Gas grill accessories are designed for use ONLY with gas cooktops. These accessories are not interchangeable. Model CCE406 accepts Model A141A wok and Model A145A "big pot" canning element only. Model CCG406 accepts Model A340 wok only. Models GO106B and GO206B accept Model A302 griddle, Model A341 grill cover and Model A335 Cooker-Steamer only. Model CG205W accepts Model A340 wok, Model AG150 grill assembly, and Model AG302 griddle (must be used in conjunction with Model AG150).

[7] Grills on left side only. Model CG205W accepts optional grill assembly Model AG150 on left side only.

[8] Permanently installed (conventional coil elements remove for cleaning). Conventional coil element wattage: 8" elements, 2100; 6" elements, 1250. Solid element wattage: 8" elements, 2000; 6" elements, 1500. Radiant element wattage: 8" elements, 2100; 6" elements, 1200.

[9] Ceran translucent ceramic surface.

[10] Stamped perimeter has rounded edge. Roll formed perimeter has square edge. Roll formed ring perimeter installs flush to countertop. Model CCS446 has perimeterless glass ceramic surface. Model C236 has roll formed perimeter. Models C236B, C236W have stamped perimeter.

IMPORTANT: Specifications subject to change without notice. All dimensions listed in inches. Dimensional specifications are provided for comparison purposes only. Never use these figures for product installation. See installation instructions and ducting information shipped with product before making cutouts or beginning installation.

Except as noted, all Jenn-Air cooktops are shipped complete with one grill assembly. All cartridges and accessories are optional.

Tri-Convertible Downdraft Cooktops

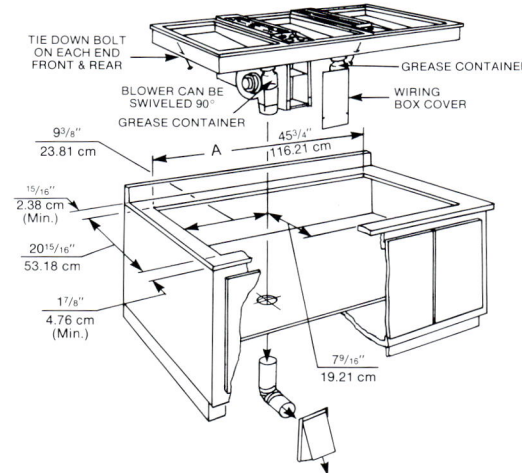

TIE DOWN BOLT ON EACH END FRONT & REAR
GREASE CONTAINER
BLOWER CAN BE SWIVELED 90°
GREASE CONTAINER
WIRING BOX COVER
9 3/8" 23.81 cm
A
45 3/4" 116.21 cm
15/16" 2.38 cm (Min.)
20 15/16" 53.18 cm
1 7/8" 4.76 cm (Min.)
7 9/16" 19.21 cm

Radiant Updraft Cooktop

Electric, Updraft: Model CCR466B

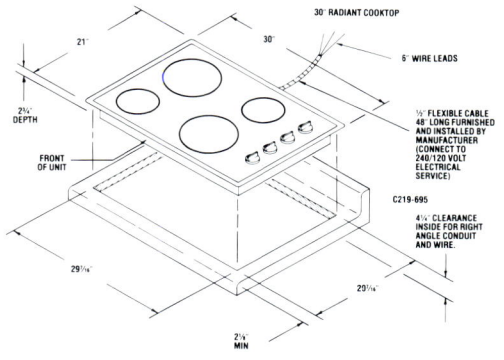

30" RADIANT COOKTOP
5" WIRE LEADS
21"
30"
2 1/4" DEPTH
FRONT OF UNIT
1/2" FLEXIBLE CABLE 48" LONG FURNISHED AND INSTALLED BY MANUFACTURER (CONNECT TO 240/120 VOLT ELECTRICAL SERVICE)
C219-695
4 1/4" CLEARANCE INSIDE FOR RIGHT ANGLE CONDUIT AND WIRE.
29 1/4"
20 1/4"
2 1/4" MIN

Dimensional specifications are provided for comparison purposes only. Never use these figures for product installation. See installation instructions shipped with product before selecting cabinetry, making cutouts or beginning installation.

Twin-Convertible and Single-Convertible Cooktops

Electric, Downdraft: **Models C206, C236, C236B, C236W**

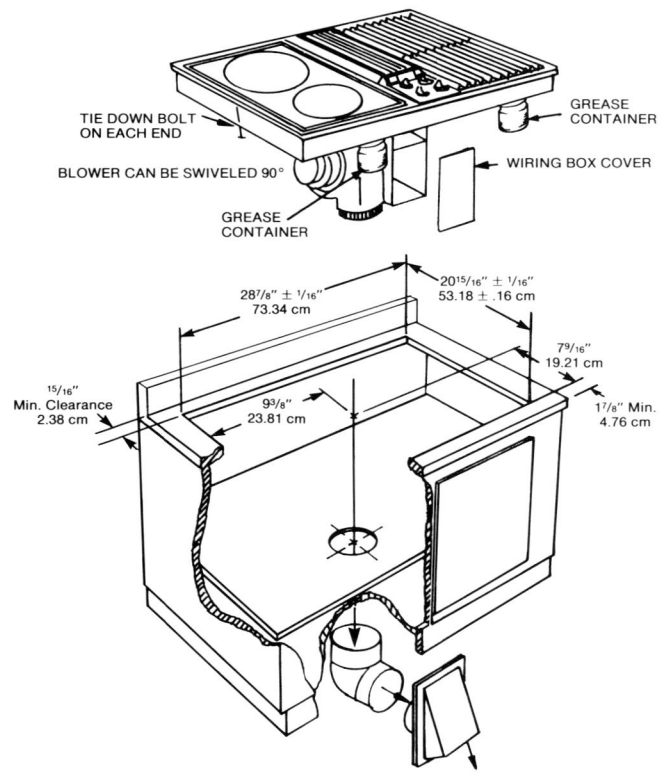

TIE DOWN BOLT ON EACH END

BLOWER CAN BE SWIVELED 90°

GREASE CONTAINER

GREASE CONTAINER

WIRING BOX COVER

$28^{7}/_{8}$" $\pm$ $^{1}/_{16}$"
73.34 cm

$20^{15}/_{16}$" $\pm$ $^{1}/_{16}$"
53.18 $\pm$ .16 cm

$7^{9}/_{16}$"
19.21 cm

$^{15}/_{16}$"
Min. Clearance
2.38 cm

$9^{3}/_{8}$"
23.81 cm

$1^{7}/_{8}$" Min.
4.76 cm

Single-Convertible Cooktop

Electric, Downdraft: **Model C116**
Gas, Downdraft: **Models CG106, CG106B**

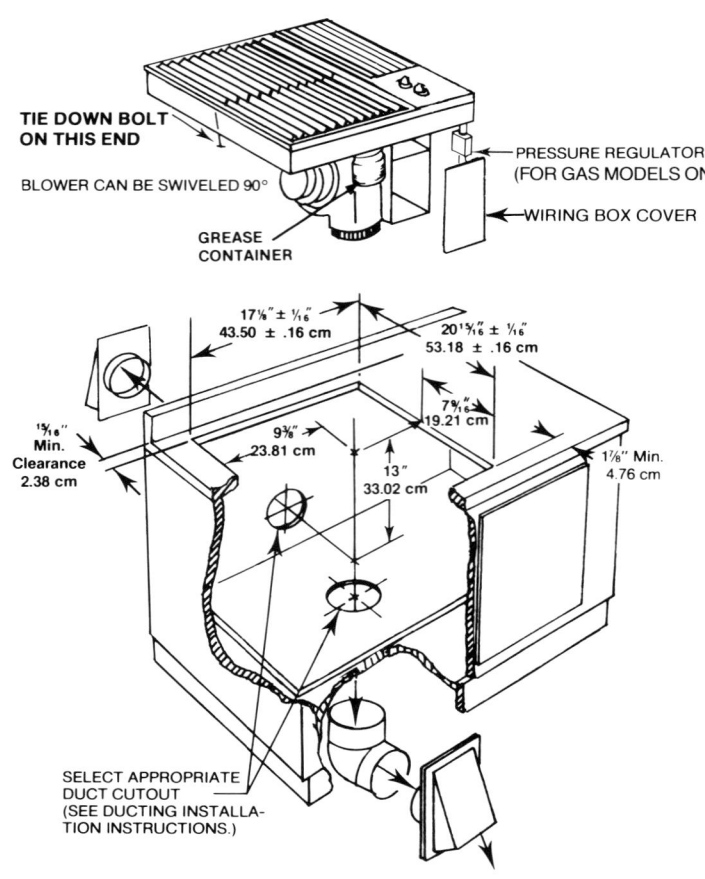

TIE DOWN BOLT ON THIS END

BLOWER CAN BE SWIVELED 90°

GREASE CONTAINER

PRESSURE REGULATOR (FOR GAS MODELS ONLY)

WIRING BOX COVER

$17^{1}/_{8}$" $\pm$ $^{1}/_{16}$"
43.50 $\pm$ .16 cm

$20^{15}/_{16}$" $\pm$ $^{1}/_{16}$"
53.18 $\pm$ .16 cm

$7^{9}/_{16}$"
19.21 cm

$^{15}/_{16}$"
Min. Clearance
2.38 cm

$9^{3}/_{8}$"
23.81 cm

13"
33.02 cm

$1^{7}/_{8}$" Min.
4.76 cm

SELECT APPROPRIATE DUCT CUTOUT (SEE DUCTING INSTALLATION INSTRUCTIONS.)

Convertible Cooktops

Gas, Downdraft: **Models CG206, CG206B, CG205W**

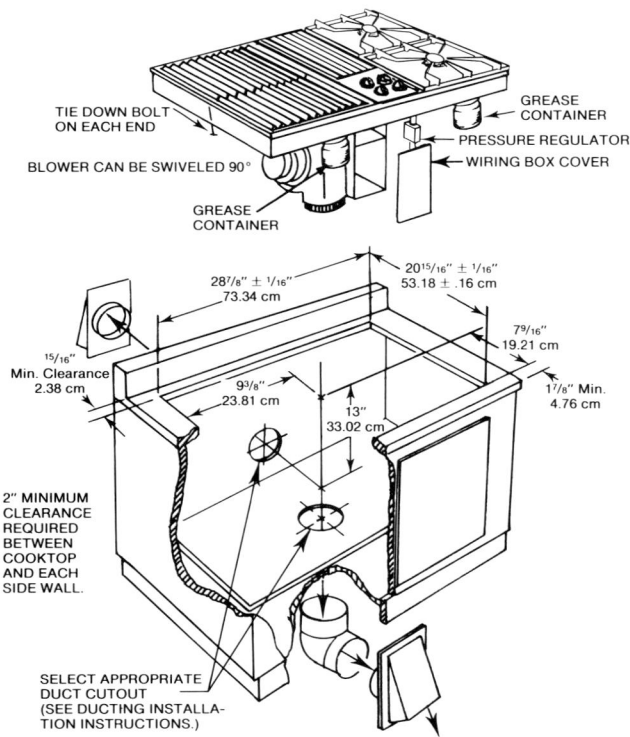

TIE DOWN BOLT ON EACH END

BLOWER CAN BE SWIVELED 90°

GREASE CONTAINER

GREASE CONTAINER

PRESSURE REGULATOR

WIRING BOX COVER

$28^{7}/_{8}$" $\pm$ $^{1}/_{16}$"
73.34 cm

$20^{15}/_{16}$" $\pm$ $^{1}/_{16}$"
53.18 $\pm$ .16 cm

$7^{9}/_{16}$"
19.21 cm

$^{15}/_{16}$"
Min. Clearance
2.38 cm

$9^{3}/_{8}$"
23.81 cm

13"
33.02 cm

$1^{7}/_{8}$" Min.
4.76 cm

2" MINIMUM CLEARANCE REQUIRED BETWEEN COOKTOP AND EACH SIDE WALL.

SELECT APPROPRIATE DUCT CUTOUT (SEE DUCTING INSTALLATION INSTRUCTIONS.)

Twin-Convertible and Convertible Cooktops

Electric, Updraft: **Models CU230, CU240, CU240B**

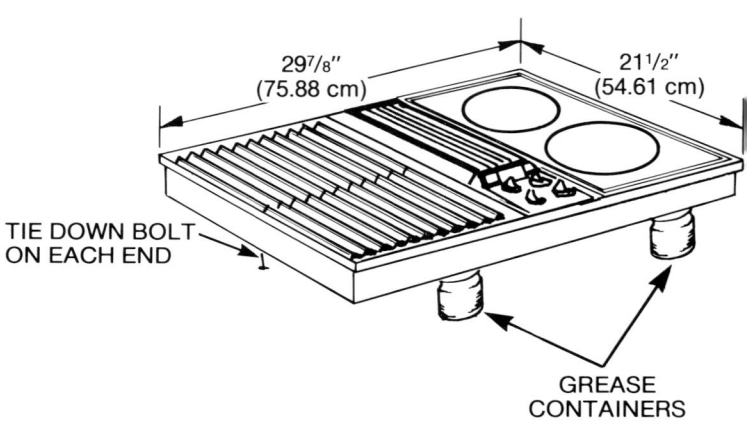

$29^{7}/_{8}$"
(75.88 cm)

$21^{1}/_{2}$"
(54.61 cm)

TIE DOWN BOLT ON EACH END

GREASE CONTAINERS

Dimensional specifications are provided for comparison purposes only. Never use these figures for product installation. See installation instructions shipped with product before selecting cabinetry, making cutouts or beginning installation.

Non-Convertible Solid Element Cooktops

Electric, Updraft: **Models CCS446, CCS446W**

Dimensional specifications are provided for comparison purposes only. Never use these figures for product installation. See installation instructions shipped with product before selecting cabinetry, making cutouts or beginning installation.

21" (53.3 cm)
2¾" DEPTH (7.0 cm)
30" (76.2 cm)
6" WIRE LEADS (15.2 cm)
FRONT OF UNIT
½" (1.2 cm) FLEXIBLE CABLE 48" (121.9 cm) LONG FURNISHED AND INSTALLED BY MANUFACTURER (CONNECT TO 240/120 VOLT ELECTRICAL SERVICE)
20" (50.8 cm)
3½" (9.0 cm) MIN. PLUS CLEARANCE INSIDE FOR RIGHT ANGLE CONDUIT AND WIRE
26⅝" (67.6 cm)
2⅛" MIN (5.4 cm)

Non-Convertible Conventional Coil Cooktops

Electric, Updraft: **Models CCE406, CCE406B, CCE406L**

MIN. ¾" 1.9 cm
33⅝" (85.4 cm)
21⅝" (54.9 cm)
3¹/₁₆" (7.8 cm)
MIN. 24" PLUS OVERHANG
21¹¹/₁₆" (53.5 cm)
MIN. 2³/₁₆" (5.6 cm)
33¹/₁₆" (84.0 cm)

Non-Convertible Gas Cooktops

Gas, Updraft: **Models CCG406, CCG406B**

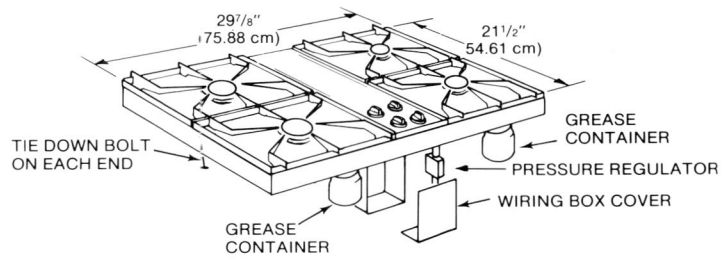

29⅞" (75.88 cm)
21½" 54.61 cm)
TIE DOWN BOLT ON EACH END
GREASE CONTAINER
PRESSURE REGULATOR
WIRING BOX COVER
GREASE CONTAINER

Lanai™ Outdoor Grills

Electric, Downdraft: **Models GO106B, GO206B**

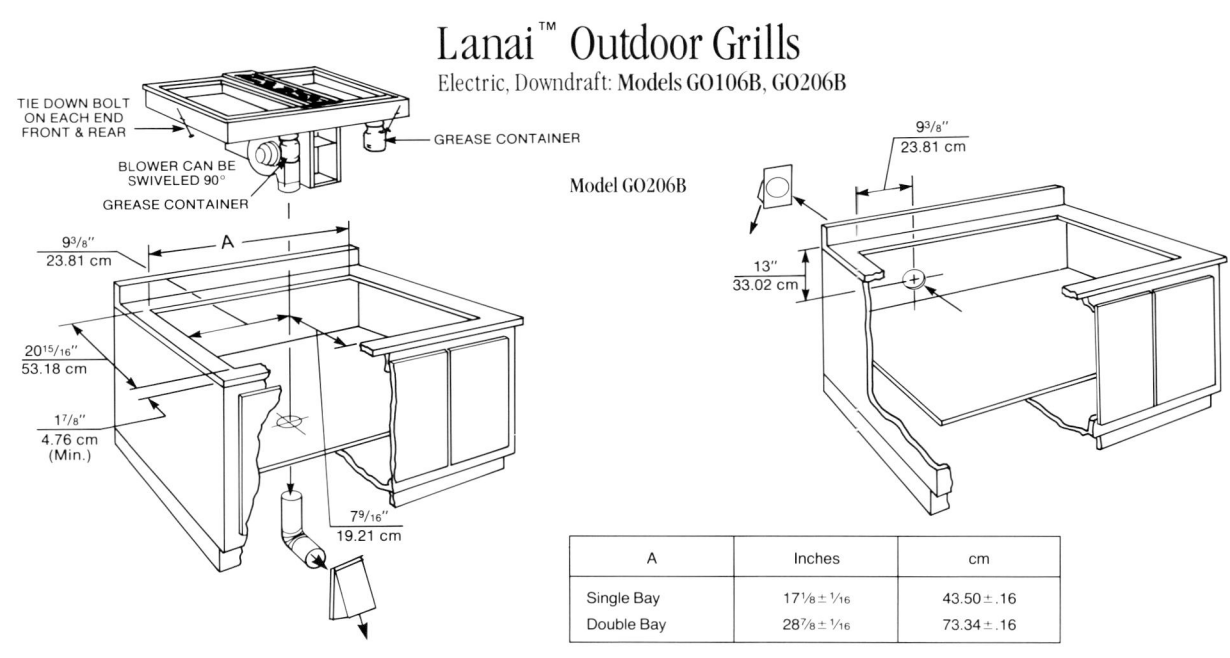

TIE DOWN BOLT ON EACH END FRONT & REAR
GREASE CONTAINER
BLOWER CAN BE SWIVELED 90°
GREASE CONTAINER
Model GO206B
9⅜" 23.81 cm
9⅜" 23.81 cm
A
13" 33.02 cm
20¹⁵/₁₆" 53.18 cm
1⅞" 4.76 cm (Min.)
7⁹/₁₆" 19.21 cm

A	Inches	cm
Single Bay	17⅛ ± ¹/₁₆	43.50 ± .16
Double Bay	28⅞ ± ¹/₁₆	73.34 ± .16

Jenn-Air Wall Oven Feature Chart

JENN-AIR WALL OVEN FEATURES AND SPECIFICATIONS	SINGLE ELECTRIC 24" W116	27" W136	27" W156	30" W130	DOUBLE ELECTRIC 24" W216	27" W256	DOUBLE/COMBINATION ELECTRIC 27" W2361	27" W2761	GAS 24" WG2062
Overall Height	29 5/8	28 7/8	28 7/8	28	46 5/16	51	48 7/16	48 7/16	46 5/16
Overall Width	23 7/8	26 3/4	26 3/4	30 1/2	23 7/8	26 3/4	26 3/4	26 3/4	23 3/4
Overall Depth3	25 3/16	25	25	24	25 3/16	25	25	25	25 1/8
Oven Interior Height	14	15	15	15	14U/12L	15 4	15 4	15 4	14U/12L
Oven Interior Width	18	19	19	22	18 4	19 4	19 4	19 4	18U/18L
Oven Interior Depth	19	18	18	18	19 4	18 4	18 4	18 4	19U/19L
Cutout Height	28 11/16	28 3/8	28 3/8	28 1/8	45 3/8	50 1/2	47 7/8	47 7/8	45 3/8
Cutout Width	22	25	25	30A	22	25	25	25	22
Cutout Depth	24	24	24	24	24	24	24	24	24
Total Connected Load —KW / —Amps (at 120/240 VAC)	3.6 / 15.0	5.7 / 24.2	5.7 / 24.2	3.5 / 14.6	6.5 / 27.1	11.4 / 48.4	7.1 / 35.3	7.1 / 35.3	
BTUs (Oven/Broiler; Natural/LP)6									16,000 / 16,000
Jenn-Air Golden Product Warranty	●	●	●	●	●	●	●	●	●
Catalytic Smoke Eliminator	●	●	●	●	●	●	●	●	
See-Through Oven Window	●	●	●	●	B	B	B	B	B
Formed Rack Guides	●	●	●	●	B	B	L	L	B
Large Capacity Oven		●	●	●		B	L	L	U
Temperature Control Broiling		●	●			B	L	L	
Clock-Controlled Baking	●	●	●	●	U	B	L	L	
Self-Cleaning Oven	●	●	●	●	U	B	L	L	
Automatic Self-Clean Lock			●			●	●	●	
Broiler Pan Included	●	●	●	●	U	U	L	L	L
3-Rack Convection Baking		●	●			U	L	L	
Temperature Probe			●			U	U	U	
Electronic Clock with Timer	●	●	●	●	●	●	B	B	
Digital Clock with Timer									●
Electronic Touch Control			●			●	U	B	
Memory Programming				●		B	U	B	
Programming Recall			●	●		B	U	B	
Microwave Oven							U	U	
Designer Line Styling	●	●	●	●	●	●	●	●	●
Color Availabilities (B = black, W = white)	B	B	B, W	B, W	B	B, W	B	B, W	B
Electronic Pilotless Ignition									●
Convertible to LP Gas									●
A.G.A. Design Certified									●
Undercounter Installation				●					

U = Upper, L = Lower, B = Both.

1 Order Trim Kit Model A517 to permit installation of wall oven Model W236 or W276 in cutout made for double wall oven Model W256. (Black models only).

2 Single wall oven with separate broiler compartment.

3 Add 2" for door handle (for Model WG206, add 1 3/4").

4 Both oven cavities (lower oven only on combination ovens).

A Minimum cutout width; 30 1/8" maximum.

6 Electric supply for pilotless ignition: 120 VAC, 60 Hz.

IMPORTANT: Specifications subject to change without notice. All dimensions listed in inches. Dimensional specifications are provided for comparison purposes only. Never use these figures for product installation. See installation instructions and ducting information shipped with product before making cutouts or beginning installation.

27" Double/Combination Wall Ovens
Models W236, W276, W276W

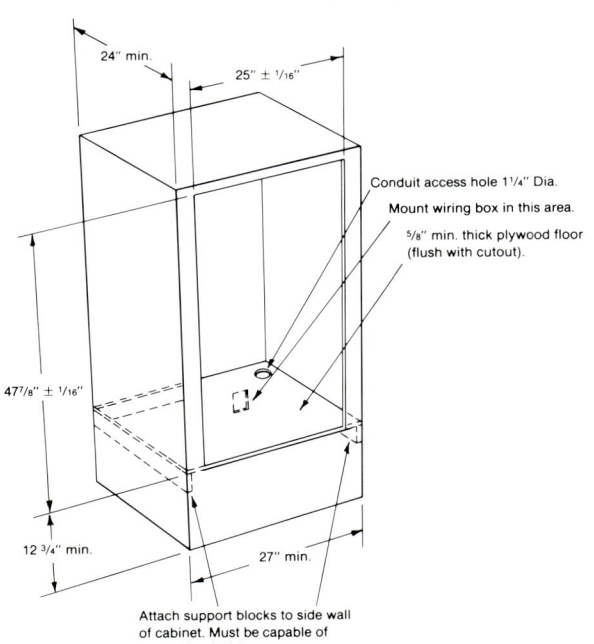

24" min.

25" ± 1/16"

Conduit access hole 1 1/4" Dia.

Mount wiring box in this area.

5/8" min. thick plywood floor (flush with cutout).

47 7/8" ± 1/16"

12 3/4" min.

27" min.

Attach support blocks to side wall of cabinet. Must be capable of supporting 240 lbs.

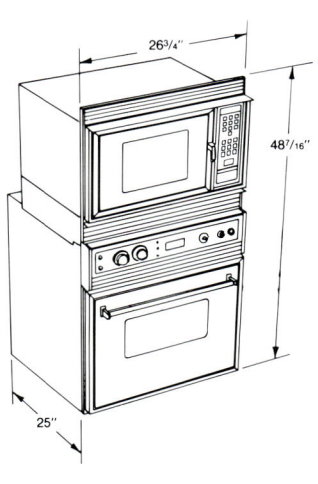

26 3/4"

48 7/16"

25"

Dimensional specifications are provided for comparison purposes. Never use these figures for product installation. See installation instructions shipped with product before selecting cabinetry, making cutouts or beginning installation.

27″ Double Wall Ovens
Models W256, W256W

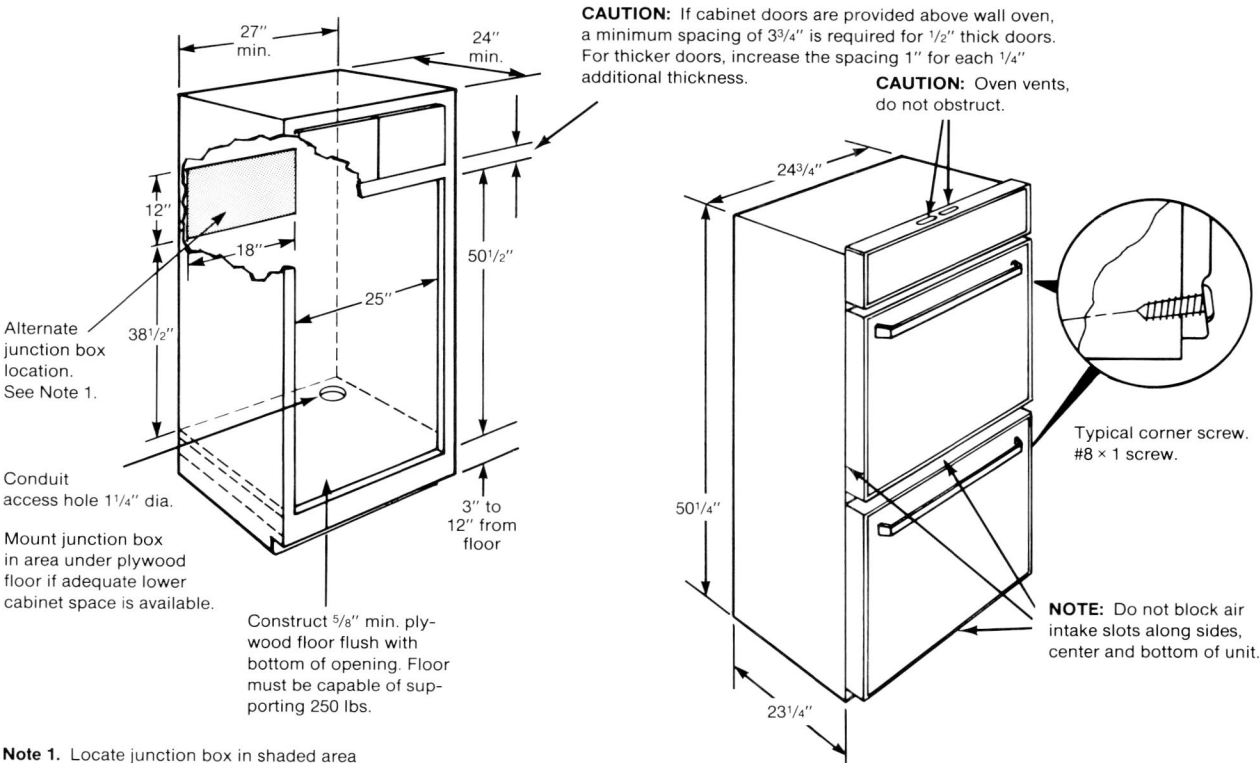

CAUTION: If cabinet doors are provided above wall oven, a minimum spacing of 3³/₄″ is required for ¹/₂″ thick doors. For thicker doors, increase the spacing 1″ for each ¹/₄″ additional thickness.

CAUTION: Oven vents, do not obstruct.

27″ min.

24″ min.

12″

18″

38¹/₂″

25″

50¹/₂″

Alternate junction box location. See Note 1.

Conduit access hole 1¹/₄″ dia.

Mount junction box in area under plywood floor if adequate lower cabinet space is available.

Construct ⁵/₈″ min. plywood floor flush with bottom of opening. Floor must be capable of supporting 250 lbs.

3″ to 12″ from floor

24³/₄″

50¹/₄″

23¹/₄″

Typical corner screw. #8 × 1 screw.

NOTE: Do not block air intake slots along sides, center and bottom of unit.

Note 1. Locate junction box in shaded area of rear wall so conduit will form a loop when oven is installed.

24″ Gas Wall Oven with Separate Broiler Compartment
Model WG206

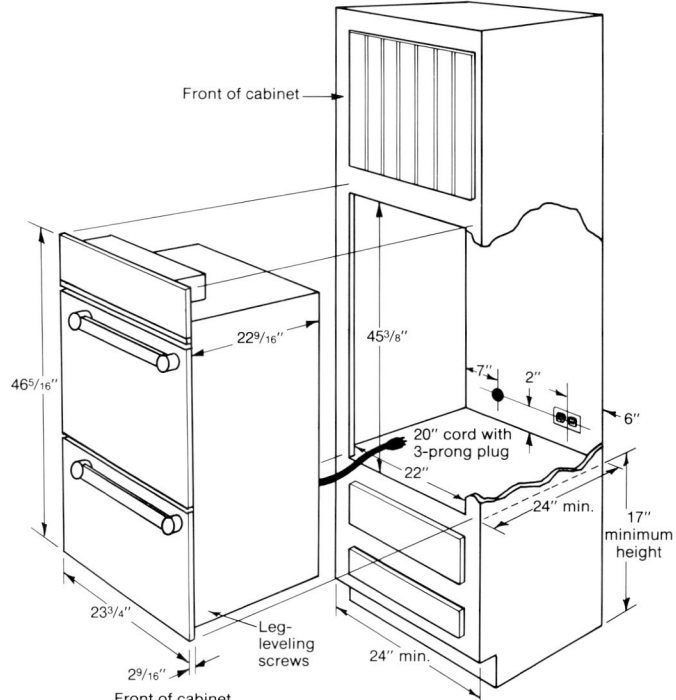

Front of cabinet

46⁵/₁₆″

22⁹/₁₆″

45³/₈″

7″

2″

6″

20″ cord with 3-prong plug

22″

24″ min.

17″ minimum height

23³/₄″

2⁹/₁₆″

Leg-leveling screws

24″ min.

Front of cabinet

Dimensional specifications are provided for comparison purposes only. Never use these figures for product installation. See installation instructions shipped with product before selecting cabinetry, making cutouts or beginning installation.

24" Double Wall Oven
Model W216

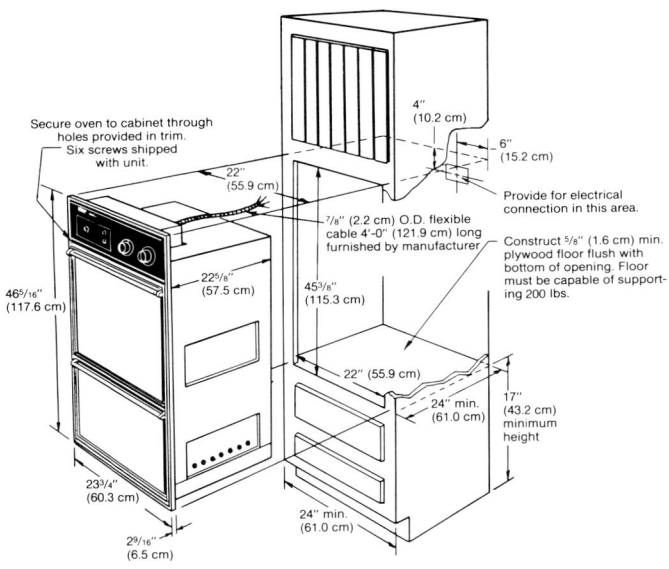

Secure oven to cabinet through holes provided in trim. Six screws shipped with unit.

22" (55.9 cm)

46⁵/₁₆" (117.6 cm)

22⁵/₈" (57.5 cm)

23³/₄" (60.3 cm)

2⁹/₁₆" (6.5 cm)

4" (10.2 cm)

6" (15.2 cm)

Provide for electrical connection in this area.

⁷/₈" (2.2 cm) O.D. flexible cable 4'-0" (121.9 cm) long furnished by manufacturer

45³/₈" (115.3 cm)

Construct ⁵/₈" (1.6 cm) min. plywood floor flush with bottom of opening. Floor must be capable of supporting 200 lbs.

22" (55.9 cm)

24" min. (61.0 cm)

17" (43.2 cm) minimum height

24" min. (61.0 cm)

30" Single Wall Ovens
Models W130, W130W

UNDERCOUNTER INSTALLATION

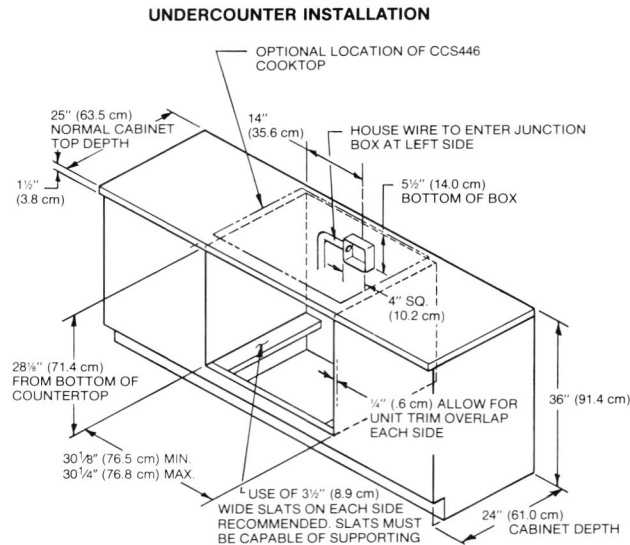

OPTIONAL LOCATION OF CCS446 COOKTOP

25" (63.5 cm) NORMAL CABINET TOP DEPTH

1½" (3.8 cm)

14" (35.6 cm)

HOUSE WIRE TO ENTER JUNCTION BOX AT LEFT SIDE

5½" (14.0 cm) BOTTOM OF BOX

4" SQ. (10.2 cm)

28⅛" (71.4 cm) FROM BOTTOM OF COUNTERTOP

¼" (.6 cm) ALLOW FOR UNIT TRIM OVERLAP EACH SIDE

36" (91.4 cm)

30⅛" (76.5 cm) MIN. 30¼" (76.8 cm) MAX.

USE OF 3½" (8.9 cm) WIDE SLATS ON EACH SIDE RECOMMENDED. SLATS MUST BE CAPABLE OF SUPPORTING 160 LBS.

24" (61.0 cm) CABINET DEPTH

24" Single Wall Oven
Model W116

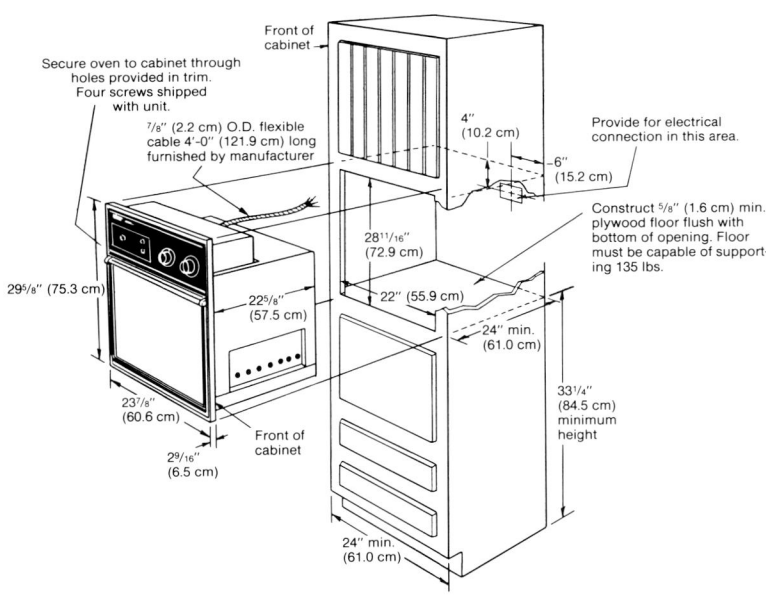

Front of cabinet

Secure oven to cabinet through holes provided in trim. Four screws shipped with unit.

⁷/₈" (2.2 cm) O.D. flexible cable 4'-0" (121.9 cm) long furnished by manufacturer

4" (10.2 cm)

6" (15.2 cm)

Provide for electrical connection in this area.

Construct ⁵/₈" (1.6 cm) min. plywood floor flush with bottom of opening. Floor must be capable of supporting 135 lbs.

29⅝" (75.3 cm)

22⅝" (57.5 cm)

28¹¹/₁₆" (72.9 cm)

22" (55.9 cm)

24" min. (61.0 cm)

23⅞" (60.6 cm)

2⁹/₁₆" (6.5 cm)

Front of cabinet

33¼" (84.5 cm) minimum height

24" min. (61.0 cm)

27" Single Wall Ovens
Models W136, W156, W156W

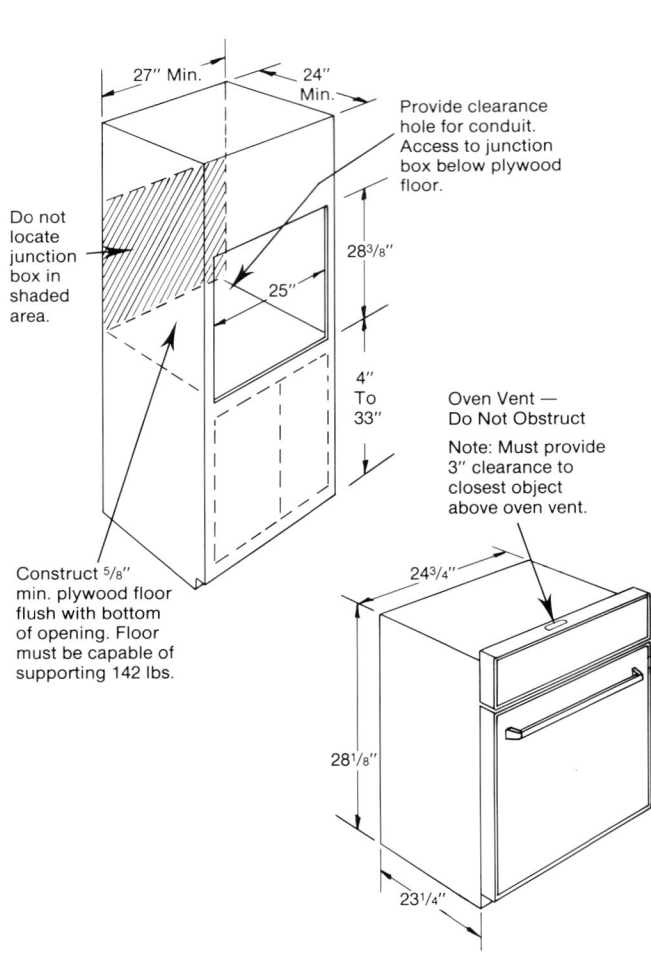

27" Min.

24" Min.

Provide clearance hole for conduit. Access to junction box below plywood floor.

Do not locate junction box in shaded area.

28³/₈"

25"

4" To 33"

Construct ⁵/₈" min. plywood floor flush with bottom of opening. Floor must be capable of supporting 142 lbs.

Oven Vent — Do Not Obstruct

Note: Must provide 3" clearance to closest object above oven vent.

24³/₄"

28⅛"

23¼"

Dimensional specifications are provided for comparison purposes only. Never use these figures for product installation. See installation instructions shipped with product before selecting cabinetry, making cutouts or beginning installation.

Jenn-Air Microwave Oven Feature Chart

JENN-AIR MICROWAVE OVEN FEATURES AND SPECIFICATIONS[1]	BUILT-IN M166	OVER-THE-RANGE M416	OVER-THE-RANGE M436	OVER-THE-RANGE M446
Overall Height (front)	15¼	14⅝	14⅝	14⅝
Overall Height (back)	15¼	16½	16½	16½
Overall Width	21¾	30	30	30
Overall Depth	15¾	13	13	13
Jenn-Air Golden Product Warranty	●	●	●	●
Oven Capacity (cu. ft.)	1.1	1.0	1.0	1.0
Black Glass Door with Window	●	●	●	●
Power Output (watts)	625	625	625	625
Power Levels	10	10	10	10
2-Stage Memory Programming	●	●	●	●
Electronic Touch Controls	●	●	●	●
Temperature Probe/Hold	●	●	●	●
Digital Display with Clock/Timer	●	●	●	●
Preprogrammed Defrost Code		●	●	●
Programming Command Prompts		●	●	●
Oven Rack	●	●		●
Preprogrammed Cook Code	●			
Preprogrammed Probe Code	●		●	●
Delay Start		●	●	●
Removable Glass Tray	●			
Designer Line Styling	●	●	●	●
Accepts Built-In Trim Kits[2]	●			
Below-Oven Work Surface Light		●	●	●
Built-In Exhaust System			●[3]	●
Provides Updraft Grilling Ventilation				●
Color Availabilities (B = black, W = white)	B, W	B	B, W	B

[1]Model M446 is designed for use above all updraft gas and electric grill-ranges and grill-range cooktops. Model M436 is designed for use above all non-grilling gas and electric updraft cooktops (Not recommended over grill-ranges or cooktops with grilling capability unless the range or cooktop is equipped with downdraft ventilation.) Model M416 is designed for use above all gas and electric grill-ranges and grill-range cooktops with downdraft ventilation. 2" clearance required between bottom of microwave oven and top of grill-range backsplash to permit access to below-oven work surface light fixture.

[2]Model M166 accepts Trim Kit Model A526 for microwave opening of 18⅛" x 24½" in 27" cabinet (order Trim Kit Model A526W for use with microwave Model M166W). Order Trim Kit Model A424 to install microwave oven in 24" cabinet where opening is 15⅝" x 22¼". With trim in place, microwave with trim dimensions are 17" height and 23¾" width for A424 installation; 19⅝" height and 26⅝" width for A526 installation.

[3]Models M436 and M436W—Charcoal Filter Kit available for recirculating ventilation. Order Filter Kit Model MF110.

IMPORTANT: Specifications subject to change without notice. All dimensions listed in inches. Dimensional specifications are provided for comparison purposes only. Never use these figures for product installation. See installation instructions and ducting information shipped with product before making cutouts or beginning installation.

Over-The-Range Microwave Ovens
Models M416, M436, M436W, M446

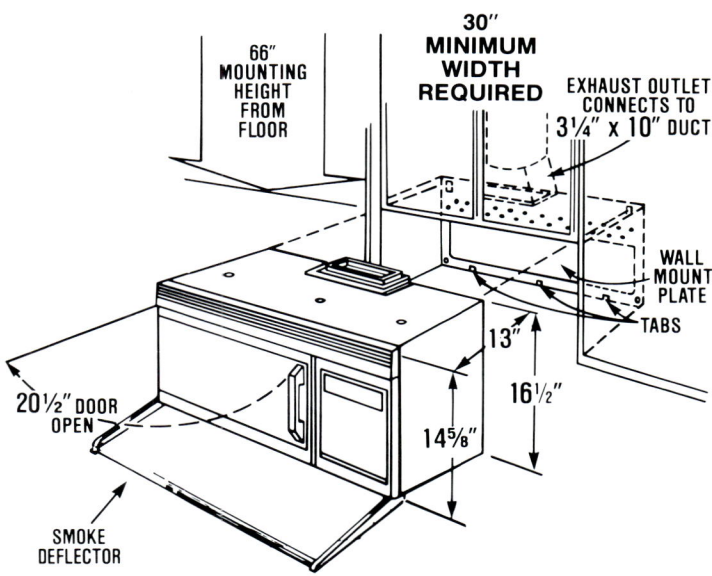

Note: Smoke Deflector On Model M446 Only

Microwave Oven Installation Above Single Wall Oven
Models M166, M166W

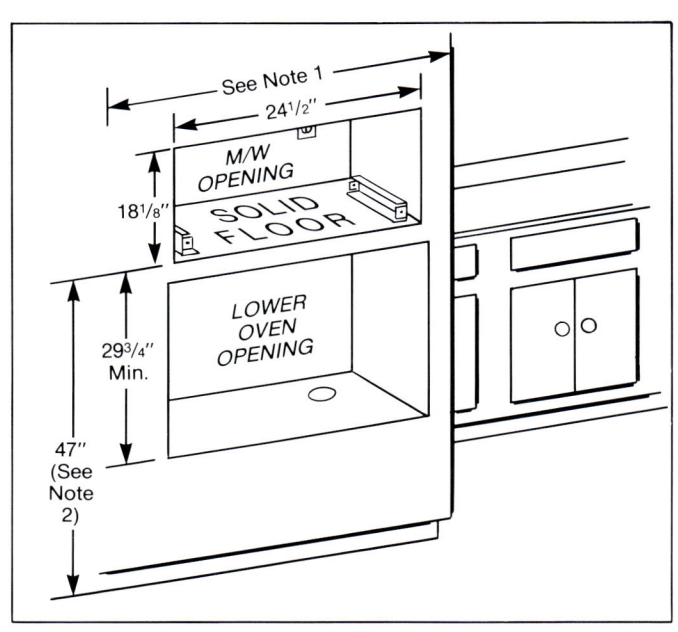

Note 1: When installing this Kit above a built-in oven, check built-in oven installation instructions to determine cutout dimensions for the (lower) wall oven.

Note 2: For a new installation, the 47" height dimension to the bottom of the cutout for the microwave oven is recommended. This places the microwave oven bottom at approximately 50" from the floor.

Dimensional specifications are provided for comparison purposes only. Never use these figures for product installation. See installation instructions shipped with product before selecting cabinetry, making cutouts or beginning installation.

Jenn-Air Range Hood Feature Chart

JENN-AIR RANGE HOOD FEATURES AND SPECIFICATIONS	RH101	RH130	RH170	RH200	RH206W	RH400	RH440	RH480	RH800
Overall Height	5	5	5	7	7	7	7	7	11 3/16
Overall Width	30	30	30	30	30	22	30	30	30
Overall Depth	17 5/8	17 5/8	17 5/8	19 3/4	19 3/4	11 1/4	18 11/16	19 3/4	11
Jenn-Air Golden Product Warranty	•	•	•	•	•	•	•	•	•
Touch Control Operation								•	
High-Performance Design[1]						•	•	•	
Variable-Speed Fan						•	•		•
2-Speed Fan	•	•	•	•	•				
Auto On-Off Fan Control									•
Telescoping Hidavent™ Canopy									•
Lighting Levels	1	1	1	1	1	2	2	3	2
Vertical or Horizontal Air Discharge on 3 1/4" x 10" Duct		•			•				
Vertical Discharge on 7" Round Duct			•	•	•				
Adaptable to 7" Round Duct[2]						•	•	•	
Ductless Installation	•3			•3	•3				
Rating (vertical rectangular, CFM)[4]		180		200	200	440	440	440	350
Rating (horizontal rectangular, CFM)[4]		180		180	180	410	410	410	350
Rating (vertical round, CFM)[4]			180	300	300				350
Cabinet Color Availabilities (B=black, L=almond, S=stainless steel, W=white)	B, L, S, W	B, L, S, W	B, L, S, W	B, L, S	W	B	B, L, S, W	B, L, S, W	B, W
Black-Glass-Look Front Panel				•	•		•		
Installs Under Custom Cabinetry					•				
For Use with Non-Grilling Cooktops	•	•	•	•	•				•

[1] High-performance range hood (such as Models RH400, RH440, RH480) is required for use above updraft cooktops with indoor grilling.

[2] Using transition; for vertical discharge only.

[3] Model RH101: ductless installation only. Order replacement charcoal filter Model RHF101. Models RH200 and RH206W convert to ductless installation. Order replacement charcoal filter Model RHF200.

[4] Ducting configuration and length can affect air flow rates. Ratings shown are based on range hoods with correctly installed ducting.

IMPORTANT: Specifications subject to change without notice. All dimensions listed in inches. Dimensional specifications are provided for comparison purposes only. Never use these figures for product installation. See installation instructions and ducting information shipped with product before making cutouts or beginning installation.

Models RH800B, RH800W

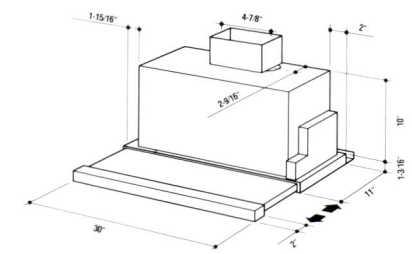

Model RH101

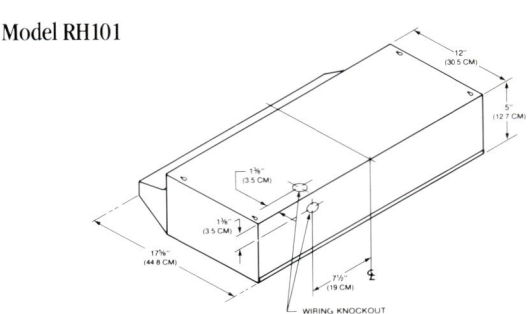

Model RH130

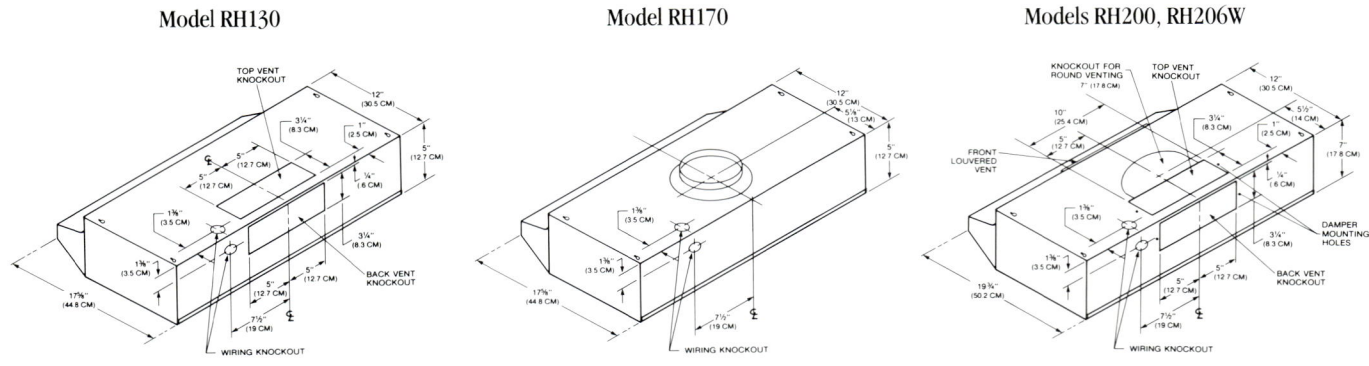

Model RH170

Models RH200, RH206W

Model RH400

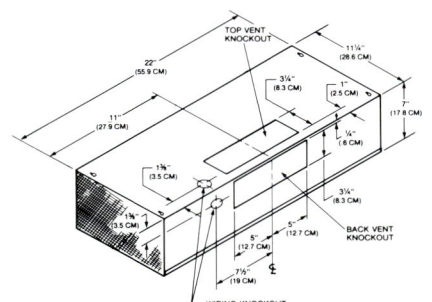

Model RH440

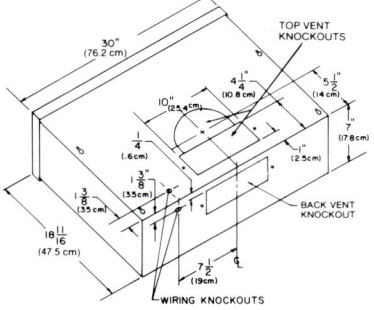

Model RH480

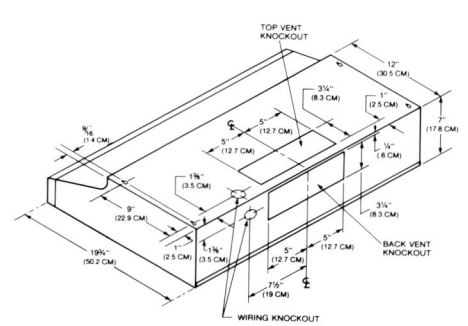

Dimensional specifications are provided for comparison purposes only. Never use these figures for product installation. See installation instructions shipped with product before selecting cabinetry, making cutouts or beginning installation.

Jenn-Air Side-By-Side Refrigerator Feature Chart

Exterior Overall Dimensions[1]	JRS226	JRSD226	JRSD246
Height (add 1/2" for door hinge and hinge cover)	66 3/8	66 3/8	66 3/8
Width (closed)	33 3/16	33 3/16	36
Width (doors open 90°; incl. handle)	36	36	38 3/4
Depth (closed; excl. handle)	29 1/4	29 1/4	29 1/4
Depth (doors open 90°)	48 27/32	48 27/32	48 27/32
Shipping Weight (approx. lbs.)	290	315	370

Interior Capacities (cu. ft. AHAM)

Total Refrigerated Volume	21.60	21.60	23.50
Fresh Food Compartment Volume	15.12	15.21	15.26
Freezer Compartment Volume	6.63	6.36	8.23
Total Shelf Area (sq. in.)	29.10	29.00	27.50

General Features

Jenn-Air Golden Product Warranty	•	•	•
White or Almond Textured Steel Doors[2]	•	•	•
Accepts Custom Front Panels[3]	•	•	•
Optional Black Door Panel Kit	BDS22-02	BDS22D-02	BDS24D-02
Optional Decorator Trim Kit[3]	DTS22-02	DTS22D-02	DTS24-02
Optional White Decorator Trim Kit[3]		RDK226	RDK246
Adjustable Easy-Roll Wheels	•	•	•
Foam Insulation	•	•	•
Freezer/Refrigerator Lights	•	•	•
2 Door Stop Positions	•	•	•
Tri-Lock™ Shelves	•	•	•
Glide-Trac™ Roller Drawer System[4]			•
Crystal Gray Interior	•	•	
Crystal White Interior			•
Jenn-Air Designer Line Styling	•	•	
Jenn-Air Premier Designer Line Styling			•

Freezer Features

Total Door Shelves	6	5	5
Deep Storage Door Shelves with Easy-Off Fronts	6	4	4
Removable Freezer Shelves (W=wire)	4W	4W	5W
Adjustable Freezer Shelves			4
Bulk Storage Drawer	•	•	•[5]
2 Mini Cube Trays with Ice Service Bin	•		
Accepts Optional Ice Maker[6]	•		
Always Ice™ Automatic Ice Maker with Bin		•	•
Lighted Convenience Center (Chilled Water/Ice Dispenser)		•	•

Refrigerator Features

Total Shelves	5	5	4
Fixed Position Glass Shelf	1	1	1
Adjustable Cantilever Glass Shelves	4	4	3
Dairy Compartment with Butter Dish	•	•	•
2-Bottle Foldaway Wine Rack	•	•	
Shelf-Mount Wine Rack			•
Humidity-Controlled Sealed Crisper			•
Sealed Crisper	•	•	
Temp Control Drawer	•	•	•
Deli Drawer	•	•	
Deep Storage Door Shelves with Easy-Off Fronts	2	2	2
Adjustable/Lift-Off Deep Storage Door Shelves	3	3	3
Shelf Tender	•	•	•
Lift-Out Egg Caddy	•	•	•
Door Shelf Cover		•	•

[1]**IMPORTANT: Specifications subject to change without notice. All dimensions listed in inches. Dimensional specifications are provided for comparison purposes only. Never use these figures for product installation. See installation instructions shipped with product before making cutouts or beginning installation.**

[2]Add "W" to end of model number to indicate white cabinet; "L" to end of model number to indicate almond cabinet.

[3]See facing page for door Trim Kit information. Optional White Refrigerator Trim Kit includes white tape for door handle inserts, white escutcheon and white Jenn-Air nameplate.

[4]For smooth movement of all freezer and refrigerator drawers.

[5]Wire basket.

[6]Order Model IMS105.

DOOR PANEL CHART–SIDE-BY-SIDE REFRIGERATOR MODELS

Custom Panel Dimensions with Existing Trim[1]
(All dimensions shown in inches)

These dimensions apply to panels included in the optional Black Door Panel Kit and to any optional door panels of 0.125" thickness.

Freezer Door Dimensions	JRS226	JRSD226	JRSD246
A1	11 11/16	–	–
A2	–	11 11/16	14 7/16
A3	–	11 11/16	14 7/16
B	61 3/16	–	–
C	–	17 3/16	17 3/16
D	–	31 11/16	31 11/16

Refrigerator Door Dimensions

E	20 15/16	20 15/16	20 15/16
F	61 3/16	61 3/16	61 3/16

Custom Panel Dimensions with Decorator Trim Kit[1]
(All dimensions shown in inches)

These dimensions apply to panels included in the optional Black Door Panel Kit and to any optional door panels of 0.125" thickness.

Freezer Door Dimensions	JRS226	JRSD226	JRSD246
A1	11 7/16	–	–
A2	–	11 7/16	14 3/16
A3	–	11 7/16	14 3/16
B	60 9/16	–	–
C	–	16 7/8	16 7/8
D	–	31 7/16	31 7/16

Refrigerator Door Dimensions

E	20 11/16	20 11/16	20 11/16
F	60 9/16	60 9/16	60 9/16

If a panel is more than 0.25" thick, its edges must be routed to 0.25" or less in thickness for installation.

When using a built-up or sculptured panel, an area adjacent to the door handles must be relieved to provide adequate clearance for fingers. The thicker the built-up panel, the more clearance is required.

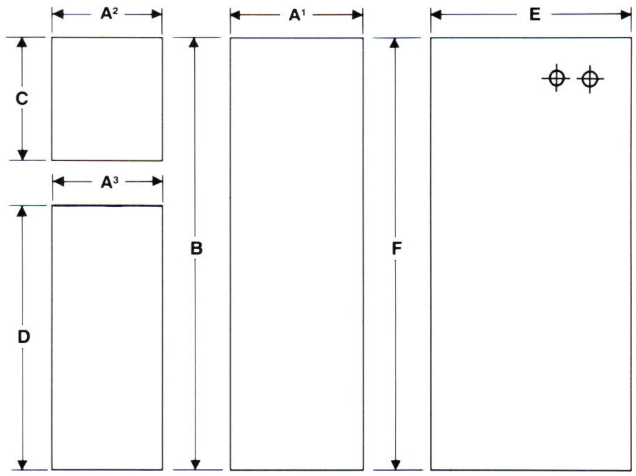

Dimensional specifications are provided for comparison purposes only. Never use these figures for product installation. See installation instructions shipped with product before selecting cabinetry, making cutouts or beginning installation.

Jenn-Air Top-Mount Refrigerator Feature Chart

Exterior Overall Dimensions[1]	JRT152	JRT172	JRT192	JRT196	JRT216	JRT236	JRTD226
Height (add ½" for door hinge and hinge cover)	60	64½	65½	65½	65½	65½	65½
Width (closed)	29	29	31½	31¹¹⁄₁₆	31¹¹⁄₁₆	33³⁄₁₆	33³⁄₁₆
Width (doors open 90° incl. handle)	30½	30½	33	33	33	34½	34½
Depth (closed; excl. handle)	27⅝	27⅝	27⅝	27⅞	30⅞	30⅞	30⅞
Depth (doors open 90°)	55¹⁵⁄₃₂	55¹⁵⁄₃₂	57³¹⁄₃₂	57³¹⁄₃₂	60³¹⁄₃₂	62¹⁵⁄₃₂	61¹⁵⁄₃₂
Shipping Weight (approx. lbs.)	215	230	245	250	270	285	310

Interior Capacities (cu. ft. AHAM)

Total Refrigerated Volume	14.60	16.50	18.60	18.50	20.90	22.50	22.00
Fresh Food Compartment Volume	10.43	11.71	12.90	12.83	14.54	15.61	15.15
Freezer Compartment Volume	4.14	4.82	5.67	5.67	6.39	6.80	6.36
Total Shelf Area (sq. in.)	18.40	23.00	25.40	26.20	29.70	31.80	33.10

General Features

Jenn-Air Golden Product Warranty	•	•	•	•	•	•	•
White or Almond Textured Steel Doors[2]	•	•	•	•	•	•	•
Lefthand Door Available[3]							•
Reversible Doors	•	•	•	•	•	•	
Accepts Custom Front Panels[4]				•	•	•	•
Optional Black Door Panel Kit[4]				BDT21-02	BDT21-02	BDT23-02	BDT22D-02
Optional Decorator Trim Kit[4]				DTT21-02	DTT21-02	DTT23-02	DTT22-02
Optional White Decorator Trim Kit[4]							RDK226
Adjustable Easy-Roll Wheels	•	•	•	•	•	•	•
Foam Insulation	•	•	•	•	•	•	•
Refrigerator Light	•	•	•	•	•	•	•
160° Door Stop Position	•	•	•	•	•	•	•
Tri-Lock™ Shelves			•	•	•	•	•
Glide-Track™ Roller Drawer System[5]							•
Crystal Gray Interior	•	•	•	•	•	•	
Crystal White Interior							•
Jenn-Air Designer Line Styling	•	•	•	•	•	•	
Jenn-Air Premier Designer Line Styling							•

Freezer Features

Deep Storage Door Shelves (F=full; S=split)	1+ 1 Can Rack	2	2	2	2	2	1F/2S
2-Position Shelf		•	•	•	•	•	•
Shelf Tender			•	•	•	•	•
2 Mini Cube Trays with Ice Service Bin	•	•	•	•	•	•	
Accepts Optional Ice Maker[6]	•	•	•	•	•	•	
Always Ice™ Automatic Ice Maker with Bin							•
Lighted Convenience Center (Chilled Water/Ice Dispenser)							•

Refrigerator Features	JRT152	JRT172	JRT192	JRT196	JRT216	JRT236	JRTD226
Total Shelves	3	4	5	5	5	5	5
Adjustable Wire Shelves (F=full; S=split)	2F	1F/2S					
Adjustable Cantilever Glass Shelves (S=split)			4S	4S	4S	4S	4S
Fixed Position Full Molded Shelf	1	1					
Fixed Position Glass Shelf			1	1	1	1	1
2-Bottle Foldaway Wine Rack						•	
Shelf-Mount Wine Rack							•
Sealed Crispers	2	2					1
Humidity-Controlled Sealed Crispers			2	2	2	2	1
Temp Control Drawer		•	•	•	•	•	•
Meat Drawer	•						
Energy Saver Switch	•	•	•	•	•	•	•
Dairy Compartment with Butter Dish	1	1	1	1	1	2[7]	1
Fixed Deep Storage Door Shelves	2½	3½	3½	1	1	1	1½
Adjustable/Lift-Off Deep Storage Door Shelves				5	5	4	3
Shelf Tender	•	•	•	•	•	•	•
Lift-Out Egg Storage (C=Caddy; R=Rack)	R	R	C	C	C	C	C
Door Shelf Cover						•	•

[1]**IMPORTANT: Specifications subject to change without notice. All dimensions listed in inches.Dimensional specifications are provided for comparison purposes only. Never use these figures for product installation. See installation instructions shipped with product before making cutouts or beginning installation.**

[2]Add "W" to end of model number to indicate white cabinet; "L" to end of model number to indicate almond cabinet.

[3]Add "L" to model number (before color indicator) to indicate lefthand door swing; "R" to indicate righthand door swing.

[4]See below for door Trim Kit information. The optional White Refrigerator Trim Kit includes white tape for door handle inserts, white escutcheon and white Jenn-Air nameplate.

[5]For smooth movement of all freezer and refrigerator drawers.

[6]Order Model IMT105.

[7]Includes 2 Dairy Compartments, 1 butter dish.

DOOR PANEL CHART—TOP-MOUNT REFRIGERATOR MODELS

Custom Panel Dimensions with Existing Trim.
(All dimensions shown in inches)

These dimensions apply to panels included in the optional Black Door Panel Kit and to any optional door panels of 0.125" thickness.

Freezer Door Dimensions	JRT196	JRT216	JRT236	JRTD226
A	31⁷⁄₁₆	31⁷⁄₁₆	32¹⁵⁄₁₆	32¹⁵⁄₁₆
B	19⅞	19⅞	19⅞	19⅞

Refrigerator Door Dimensions

C	31⁷⁄₁₆	31⁷⁄₁₆	32¹⁵⁄₁₆	32¹⁵⁄₁₆
D	39⅞	39⅞	39⅞	39¼
E	–	–	–	16½
F	–	–	–	14⅝*

*Dimension is 14⁵⁄₁₆ for lefthand refrigerator.

Custom Panel Dimensions with Decorator Trim Kit[1]
(All dimensions shown in inches)

Freezer Door Dimensions	JRT196	JRT216	JRT236	JRTD226
A	31³⁄₁₆	31³⁄₁₆	32¹¹⁄₁₆	32¹¹⁄₁₆
B	19¼	19¼	19¼	19¼

Refrigerator Door Dimensions

C	31³⁄₁₆	31³⁄₁₆	32¹¹⁄₁₆	32¹¹⁄₁₆
D	39¼	39¼	39¼	39¼
E	–	–	–	16³⁄₁₆
F	–	–	–	14⅝*

*Dimension is 14⁵⁄₁₆ for lefthand refrigerator.

If a panel is more than 0.25" thick, its edges must be routed to 0.25" or less in thickness for installation.

When using a built-up or sculptured panel, an area adjacent to the door handles must be relieved to provide adequate clearance for fingers. The thicker the built-up panel, the more clearance is required.

DOOR PANEL CHART — TOP MOUNTED REFRIGERATOR MODELS

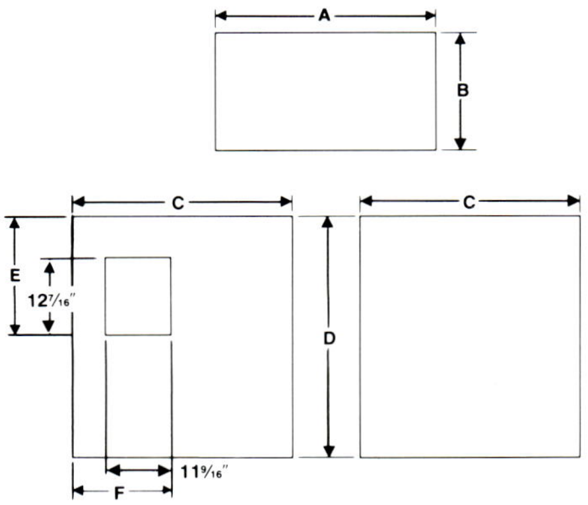

Dimensional specifications are provided for comparison purposes only. Never use these figures for product installation. See installation instructions shipped with product before selecting cabinetry, making cutouts or beginning installation.

Jenn-Air Dishwasher Feature Chart

JENN-AIR BUILT-IN DISHWASHER FEATURES AND SPECIFICATIONS	DU466	DU486	DU506	DU598
Overall Height (min./max.)	34 35	34 35 1/2	34 35 1/2	34 35 1/2
Overall Width	24	24	24	24
Overall Depth (excluding door depth)	23 1/4	24 1/16	24 1/16	24 1/16
Custom Door Panel Insert Height	19 1/8	18 3/8	18 3/8	18 3/8
Custom Door Panel Insert Width	23 9/16	23 11/16	23 11/16	23 11/16
Custom Door Panel Insert Depth	1/4	1/4	1/4	1/4
Accepts Custom Door Panels[1]	•	•	•	•
Access Panel Insert Height	3 11/16	4 15/16	4 15/16	4 15/16
Access Panel Insert Width	23 9/16	23 11/16	23 11/16	23 11/16
Access Panel Insert Depth	1/4	1/4	1/4	1/4
Fuse Requirements (amps)[2]	15	20	20	20
Water Supply[3] —p.s.i. —kg/sq. cm	15-120 1.06-8.44	15-120 1.06-8.44	15-120 1.06-8.44	15-120 1.06-8.44
Jenn-Air Golden Product Warranty	•	•	•	•
Heavy Wash Cycle	•	•	•	•
Normal Wash Cycle	•	•	•	•
Conserva Wash Cycle	•	•	•	•
Heated Dry	•	•	•	•
Air Dry	•	•	•	•
Soft Food Disposer	•			
Food Disposer		•	•	•
Ultra-Mesh™ Filter[4]		•	•	•
Folding Upper Rack Dividers		•	•	•
Deep Upper Rack	•	•	•	•
Silverware Basket (with Lidded Small Items Basket)	•	•	•	•
Metered Fill		•	•	•
Sound Insulation	•	•	•	•
Triple Sound Insulation		•	•	•
High Velocity Jetstream™ System		•	•	•
Porcelain Enamel Tub		•	•	•
Durable Plastic Tub	•			
Rinse & Hold	•	•	•	•
4 Front Door Panel Colors Available[5]	•	•	•	•
Automatic Rinse Dispenser	•	•	•	•
Signal Light(s)		•	•	•
Built-in Water Heating Element	•	•	•	•
Cancel Cycle			•	•
Sani-Scrub Cycle			•	•
Delay Start			•	•
Electronic Touch Controls				•
Designer Line Styling	•	•	•	•
Color Availabilities (B = black, W = white)	B, W[6]	B	B	B, W[7]

[1]Installing 1/4" custom door panels on Jenn-Air dishwasher Models DU466 and DU466W requires additional door panel trim kit. Product includes certificate for door panel trim kit (redeemable at no extra charge).

[2]Electric supply (all models): 115 VAC, 60 Hz. All models U.L. listed.

[3]3/8" female pipe thread connection is attached to water valve. Water should be at 140°F when it enters dishwasher.

[4]Only 100% filtered water is circulated over dishes.

[5]Models DU598W and DU466W include a reversible decorator front panel (black and white). Model DU466 includes a reversible panel (black and almond), plus a certificate which can be redeemed for a second reversible panel (white and harvest gold). All other models include four front door panel color options (black/white, almond/harvest gold).

[6]For black dishwasher, order Model DU466. For white dishwasher, order Model DU466W.

[7]For black dishwasher, order Model DU598. For white dishwasher, order Model DU598W.

Drain (all models): 1/2" I.D. flexible loop supplied (high drain loop on side).
Motor and Pump: Models DU486, DU506, DU598—1/3 h.p. reversible; direct-drive motor with high-efficiency pump. Model DU466—direct-drive motor with high-efficiency pump.

Compactor Models TC406 (black), TC406W (white)
Exterior Overall Dimensions: 34 1/16" H, 15" W, 24" D
Cutout Dimensions: 34 11/32" H (± 9/32"), 15" W, 24 3/16" D.
Door Panel Insert Dimensions (Trim Kit): 22 15/16" H, 14 5/8" W, 1/4" D.
Compactor Bags: Model TCB12 (package of 12).
1/3 h.p. motor with 2,300 lbs. ramforce (approx.).

IMPORTANT: Specifications subject to change without notice. All dimensions listed in inches. Dimensional specifications are provided for comparison purposes only. Never use these figures for product installation. See installation instructions shipped with product before making cutouts or beginning installation.

Jenn-Air Disposer Feature Chart

JENN-AIR DISPOSER FEATURES AND SPECIFICATIONS	DELUXE MODELS			ECONOMY MODELS	
	GC440	GC460	GB460	GC410	GC431
Jenn-Air Golden Product Warranty	•	•	•	•	•
Quick-Mount Collar	•	•	•	•	•
1/2 H.P. Motor with Manual Reset	•	•	•	•	•
Continuous-Feed Operation	•	•	•	•	•
Batch-Feed Operation			•		
Dishwasher Drain Connection	•	•	•	•	•
Stainless Steel Sink Flange	•	•	•	•	•
Sound Silencing Grinding Chamber	•	•	•		
Die-Cast Aluminum Grinding Chamber				•	•
Non-Corrosive Grinding Chamber	•	•	•		•
Nicron Shredder Ring	•	•	•		
Stainless Steel Shredder Ring					•
Galvanized Steel Shredder Ring				•	
Jam-Resistant Impeller Arms	•	•	•	•	•
2-360° Swivel Impellers				•	•
Positive Pressure Water Seal	•	•	•		
Space-Saver Design	•				

IMPORTANT: Specifications subject to change without notice. See installation instructions shipped with product before beginning installation.

Ducting Data (Grill-Ranges and Cooktops)

DUCT LENGTH RECOMMENDATIONS (Maximum)[1]		
	5" Diameter[2]	6" Diameter or 3¼" x 10"[3]
All Electric[4]	10'[5]	60'
All Gas[6]	10'	60'

[1]**IMPORTANT:** See installation instructions shipped with product before selecting island cabinetry, making cutouts or beginning installation. Use 6" or 3¼" x 10" duct on island or peninsula installations. For best performance, it is suggested that no more than one 90° elbow be used with 5" duct or three with 6" or 3¼" x 10" duct. Each foot of flex duct counts as two feet of metal duct. Each flex elbow counts as two metal elbows. For longer duct runs of 31' to 60', the restricter ring on the blower inlet housing must be removed. 6" round or 3¼" x 10" duct recommended for long duct run installations.

[2]Count each 90° elbow as 4' of duct.

[3]Count each 90° elbow as 5' of duct.

[4]Ducting recommendations for updraft grill-range and updraft grill-range cooktops are dependent upon ducting requirements of range hood selected for updraft ventilation.

[5]When venting electric grill-ranges or cooktops, 5" diameter round duct may be used to vent straight out the back of the appliance and directly through the wall for 10' or less.

[6]When venting Model SEG196 and gas grill-range cooktops, 5" diameter duct must be used for runs of 10' or less.

Jenn-Air Grill-Range Cooktop Ducting Accessories

Model A403 Surface Wall Cap—Single damper; down discharge. Fits 3¼" x 10" duct.

Model A405 Surface Wall Cap—Single spring-loaded damper; down discharge. Fits 5" diameter duct. Requires opening 5½" in diameter.

Model A406 Surface Wall Cap—Single spring-loaded damper; down discharge. Fits 6" diameter duct. Requires opening 6½" in diameter.

Model A453 Transition—5" round to 3¼" x 10" duct.

Model A456 Transition—5" to 6" round duct.

Model A463 Transition—6" round to 3¼" x 10" duct.

Model A495 Transition—90° angle for transition from 5" round to 3¼" x 10" duct.

Model A496 Transition—90° angle for transition from 6" round to 3¼" x 10" duct.

Model A403
Surface Wall Cap

Models A405/A406
Surface Wall Cap

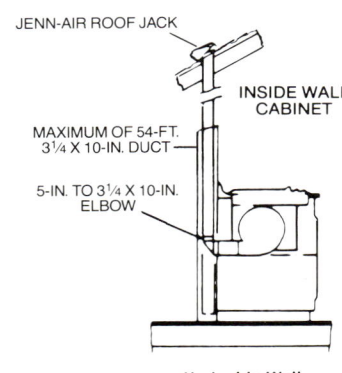

JENN-AIR ROOF JACK

INSIDE WALL CABINET

MAXIMUM OF 54-FT. 3¼ X 10-IN. DUCT

5-IN. TO 3¼ X 10-IN. ELBOW

Up Inside Wall to Roof or Overhang

Typical Grill-Range Cooktop Duct Arrangements

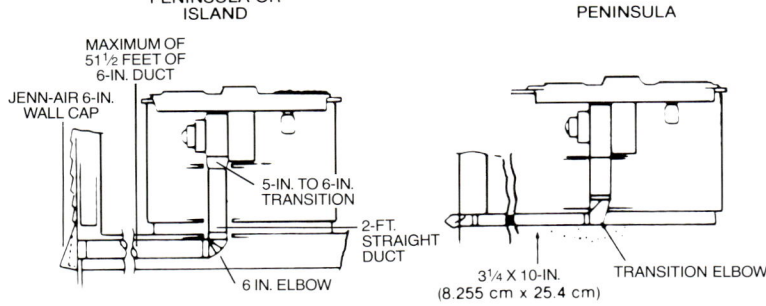

PENINSULA OR ISLAND

MAXIMUM OF 51½ FEET OF 6-IN. DUCT

JENN-AIR 6-IN. WALL CAP

5-IN. TO 6-IN. TRANSITION

2-FT. STRAIGHT DUCT

6 IN. ELBOW

Between Floor Joists

PENINSULA

3¼ X 10-IN. (8.255 cm x 25.4 cm)

TRANSITION ELBOW

Thru Cabinet Toe Space

For venting up to the equivalent of 60', use standard steel ducting and elbows.

OUTSIDE WALL CABINET

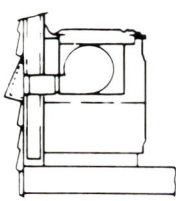

Directly to Outside

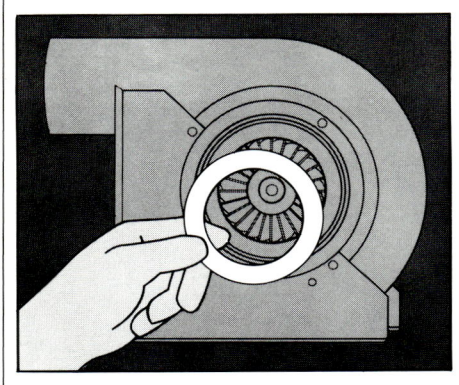

The Long Duct Run

With Jenn-Air's more powerful blower, Jenn-Air downdraft grill-ranges and grill-range cooktops can vent up to the equivalent of 60 feet.

Here's how it works.

For duct runs equivalent to 30' or less, install as received. For duct runs equivalent to 31' to 60', simply snap out the restricter ring on the blower inlet housing. Instantly, you have the power to vent up to the equivalent of 60' (using 6" round or 3¼" by 10" duct).

Typical Grill-Range Duct Arrangements

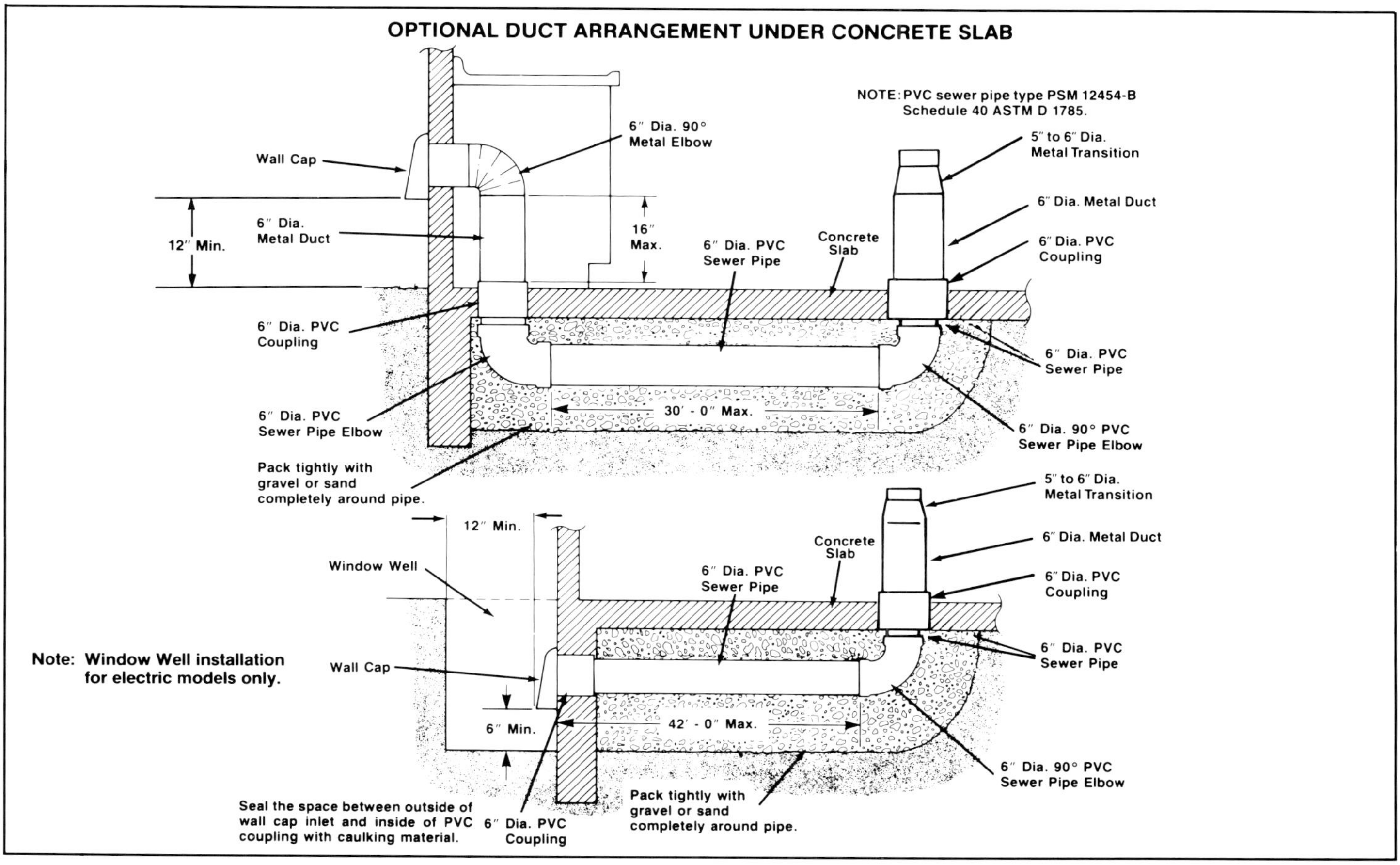

OPTIONAL DUCT ARRANGEMENT UNDER CONCRETE SLAB

NOTE: PVC sewer pipe type PSM 12454-B
Schedule 40 ASTM D 1785.

Wall Cap

6" Dia. 90°
Metal Elbow

5" to 6" Dia.
Metal Transition

6" Dia. Metal Duct

6" Dia. PVC
Coupling

6" Dia.
Metal Duct

12" Min.

16"
Max.

6" Dia. PVC
Sewer Pipe

Concrete
Slab

6" Dia. PVC
Coupling

6" Dia. PVC
Sewer Pipe

6" Dia. PVC
Sewer Pipe Elbow

30' - 0" Max.

6" Dia. 90° PVC
Sewer Pipe Elbow

Pack tightly with
gravel or sand
completely around pipe.

12" Min.

Window Well

6" Dia. PVC
Sewer Pipe

Concrete
Slab

5" to 6" Dia.
Metal Transition

6" Dia. Metal Duct

6" Dia. PVC
Coupling

6" Dia. PVC
Sewer Pipe

**Note: Window Well installation
for electric models only.**

Wall Cap

6" Min.

42' - 0" Max.

6" Dia. 90° PVC
Sewer Pipe Elbow

Pack tightly with
gravel or sand
completely around pipe.

Seal the space between outside of
wall cap inlet and inside of PVC
coupling with caulking material.

6" Dia. PVC
Coupling

Configuration shown above is applicable only to grill-range or
grill-range cooktop installation into slab construction.

Using PVC ducting (vs. metal ducting) will reduce the maximum duct
run recommendations to less than 60 equivalent feet.

DO	DON'T
Use 5" (12.7 cm), 6" (15.24 cm), or 3¼" x 10" (8.255 cm x 25.4 cm), pipe as recommended for your model	Use 4" (10.16 cm) dryer vent pipe or flex duct *
Use recommended wall caps.	Use laundry type wall cap.
Use no more than one 90° elbow with five inch (12.7 cm) duct or three 90° elbows with six inch (15.2 cm) or 3¼" x 10" (8.255 cm x 25.4 cm) duct.	Over run your system with too many bends and turns.
Duct system to the outside.	Vent into an attic or crawl space.
Mix 6" (15.24 cm) duct and 3¼" x 10" duct (8.255 cm x 25.4 cm) within the same system if necessary.	Reduce back to 5" (12.7 cm) system after using 6" (15.24 cm) or 3¼" x 10" (8.255 cm x 25.4 cm).
Tape all joints securely with several wraps of tape.	Butt joints, always use male-female connections in direction of flow.
Use one unit per duct system.	Exhaust more than one unit into a single system.

*Although not recommended, 5" or 6" metal flex duct may be used. Due to
the irregular surface of flexible ducting, each foot of flex duct counts as two (2)
feet of regular metal duct. Also, each elbow made in flex duct would count
twice as much as standard metal elbow. The best idea with flexible ducting
is to keep it as short and as straight as possible.

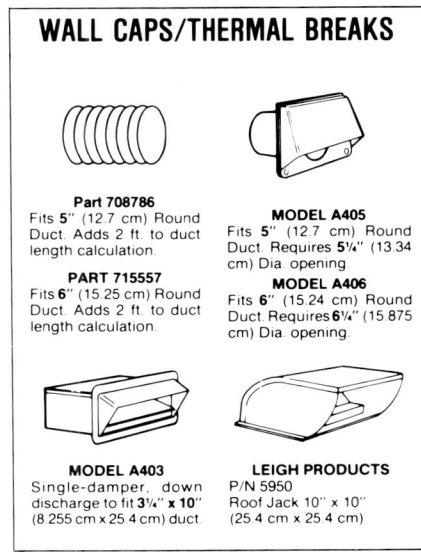

WALL CAPS/THERMAL BREAKS

Part 708786
Fits 5" (12.7 cm) Round
Duct. Adds 2 ft. to duct
length calculation.

PART 715557
Fits 6" (15.25 cm) Round
Duct. Adds 2 ft. to duct
length calculation.

MODEL A405
Fits 5" (12.7 cm) Round
Duct. Requires 5¼" (13.34
cm) Dia. opening.

MODEL A406
Fits 6" (15.24 cm) Round
Duct. Requires 6¼" (15.875
cm) Dia. opening.

MODEL A403
Single-damper, down
discharge to fit 3¼" x 10"
(8.255 cm x 25.4 cm) duct.

LEIGH PRODUCTS
P/N 5950
Roof Jack 10" x 10"
(25.4 cm x 25.4 cm)

Dimensional specifications are provided for comparison purposes only.
Never use these figures for product installation. See installation instructions shipped with product before selecting cabinetry, making cutouts
or beginning installation.

Jenn-Air
Golden Product Warranty Highlights

All Jenn-Air cooktops, grill-ranges, range hoods, ovens, grill and cooktop accessories, dishwashers, refrigerators and refrigerator accessories, compactors and disposers carry a minimum warranty of:

1ST Year
Full Warranty
Parts & Labor

2ND Year
Limited Warranty
Parts Only

. . . PLUS
an extended Warranty applies to these specific products:

Electronic Control Wall Ovens—2nd year parts and labor warranty on any part of the electronic control panel.

Electronic Control Grill-Ranges—2nd year parts and labor warranty on any part of the electronic control panel.

Built-in Oven/Microwave Combinations—2 years full warranty on parts and labor—plus microwave warranty (shown below) on microwave portion of oven.

Microwave Ovens—2 years full warranty on parts and labor—3rd through 5th years full warranty (parts and labor) on 9 major components of microwave oven.

Range Accessories—1 year full warranty on parts and labor—plus 2nd year limited warranty (parts only). 3rd year coverage of glass-ceramic used in cooktop cartridges (parts only) if it fails due to thermal breakage.

Induction Cooktop Cartridge—2 years full warranty on parts and labor—plus 3rd year (parts only) against thermal breakage of glass-ceramic.

Cast Iron Solid Elements (installed in Model A105 solid element cooktop cartridge and Model CCS446 updraft electric cooktop)—1 year full warranty on parts and labor—2nd through 5th years limited warranty (parts only).

Refrigerators—2nd through 5th years limited warranty on any part of the refrigeration system (compressor, evaporator, condenser, dryer or connecting tubing). Limited warranty covers repair of any break in interior liner excluding door liner. This extended warranty is limited to parts plus installation. Owner pays for service calls or trip charge to analyze system failure. Owner also is responsible for any shipping charges incurred (if applicable).

Dishwashers (All Models)—3rd through 5th years limited warranty (parts only).
- Power module cleaning system.
- Accessory panels on built-in models which rust.
3rd through 10th years limited warranty (parts only)
- Dishwasher tub and door liner if leak ever develops due to rust or corrosion.

Food Waste Disposers—1 year full warranty on parts and labor. 2nd through 5th years limited warranty on parts only (Models GB460, GC460, GC440). 2nd year limited warranty on parts only (Models GC431, GC410).

THE ABOVE ARE WARRANTY HIGHLIGHTS—FOR COMPLETE WARRANTY INFORMATION, SEE YOUR JENN-AIR DEALER.

Jenn-Air
COMPANY

3035 SHADELAND • INDIANAPOLIS, INDIANA 46226-0901
U.S. & Foreign Patents & Patents Pending
Specifications subject to change without notice.
Copyright 1990, Jenn-Air Company.
Printed in U.S.A.   11/90   Cat. 452L

King MINI-KITCHENS®

Refrigerator manufacturers for more than 50 years . . .

Compact Range · Sink · Refrigerator Combinations

King MINI-KITCHENS®
CAN SOLVE YOUR

COMPACT 30"

All-in-one kitchen center designed to meet minimum space areas

COMPACT OVEN

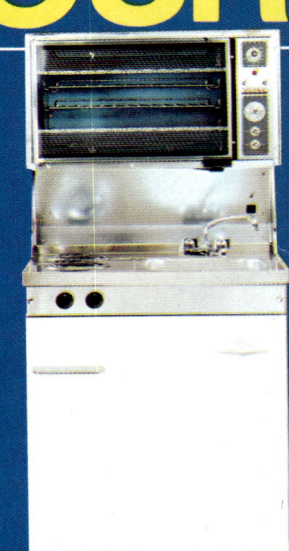

- Size: 30" wide x 36" high to countertop x 24" deep
- Refrigerator: 6 cu. ft. 30 lbs. frozen food capacity • Push button defrost refrigerator • Stainless steel range, sink and countertop • Also available without sink or burners

K30ES	Electric range-sink-refrigerator
K30GS	Gas range-sink-refrigerator
K30E	Electric range-refrigerator
K30G	Gas range-refrigerator
K30S	Sink-refrigerator

Overhead wall oven, microwave or conventional

- Size: 30½" wide x 18" deep, overall height 67" • Contains clock, light, glass door • Other features "same" as above
  K30ES/CO31E or **K30ES/MW31E**

COMPACT 39"

- Size: 39" wide x 36" high to countertop x 24" deep • Refrigerator: 6.5 cu. ft. 40 lbs. frozen food capacity • Push button defrost refrigerator • Stainless steel range, sink and countertop

K39ES	Electric range-sink-refrigerator-storage
K39GS	Gas range-sink-refrigerator-storage

COMPACT 42"

For recessed installations

- Size: 42" wide x 36" high x 24" deep • Integral end splashes • All other features and colors same as above

KR42E	Electric range-sink-refrigerator-storage
KR42G	Gas range-sink-refrigerator-storage

COMPACT 48"

All-in-one kitchen—in only four feet of space

- Size: 48" wide x 36" high to countertop x 24" deep • Refrigerator: 6 cu. ft. 30 lbs. frozen food capacity • 4 burner range • Oven with bake and broil element • Stainless steel range, sink and countertop • Push button defrost refrigerator • Cutlery drawer includes removable maple cutting board

KF48E	Electric range combination
KF48G	Gas range combination

COLOR CHOICE FOR ALL MODELS: White, Coppertone, Avocado, Harvest Gold, Almond

All-in-one kitchen center –

Compact Range·Sink·Refrigerator Combinations
SPACE PROBLEMS

COMPACT 51"

The perfect mini-kitchen® more features in less space

- Size: 51" wide x 36" high to countertop x 24" deep
- Refrigerator: 6.5 cu. ft. 40 lbs. frozen food capacity
- 4 burner range • Oven with bake and broil element
- Stainless steel range, sink and countertop • Push button defrost refrigerator • Cutlery drawer includes removable maple cutting board

KF51E Electric range combinations
KF51G Gas range combination

For recessed installations

- Size: 54" wide x 36" high to countertop x 24" deep. All specifications identical to unit described above
- Integral end splashes • All other features same as above

KR54E Electric range combination
KR54G Gas range combination

COMPACT 54"

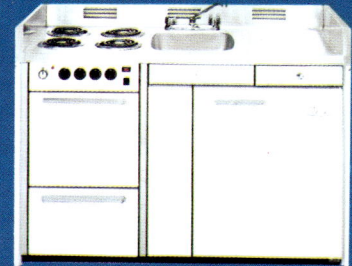

COMPACT 60"

- Size: 60" wide x 36" high to countertop x 24" deep
- Refrigerator: 6.5 cu. ft. 40 lbs. frozen food capacity
- 4 burner range • Oven with bake and broil element
- Stainless steel range, sink and countertop • Push button defrost refrigerator • Cutlery drawer includes removable maple cutting board

KF60E Electric range combination
KF60G Gas range combination

For recessed installations

- Size: 63" wide x 36" high x 24" deep • All specifications and colors same as above • Integral end splashes

KR63E Electric range combination
KR63G Gas range combination

COMPACT 63"

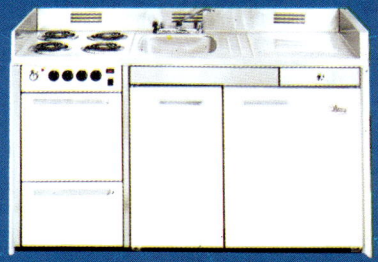

COMPACT 69"

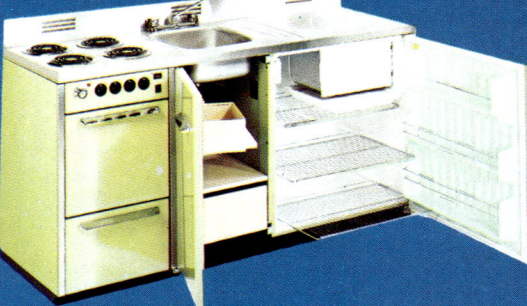

- Size: 69" wide x 36" high to countertop x 24" deep • Refrigerator: 9.2 cu. ft. 40 lbs. frozen food capacity • Stainless steel range, sink and countertop • 4 burner range
- Oven with bake and broil element
- Push button defrost refrigerator
- Cutlery tray mounted as above, includes removable maple cutting board

KF69E Electric range combination
KF69G Gas range combination

For recessed installations

- Size: 72"W x 36"H x 24"D
- Integral end splashes
- All other features and colors as above

KR72E Electric range combination
KR72G Gas range combination

COMPACT 72"

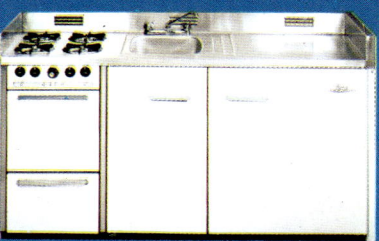

The maximum in utility, unsurpassed construction.

The popular REFRESH-ADE

It's a range . . . it's a sink It's a refrigerator

A complete refreshment center created in the tradition of fine furniture. Choose a contemporary or traditional cabinet style in decorator color or wood finishes to meet every planning requirement.

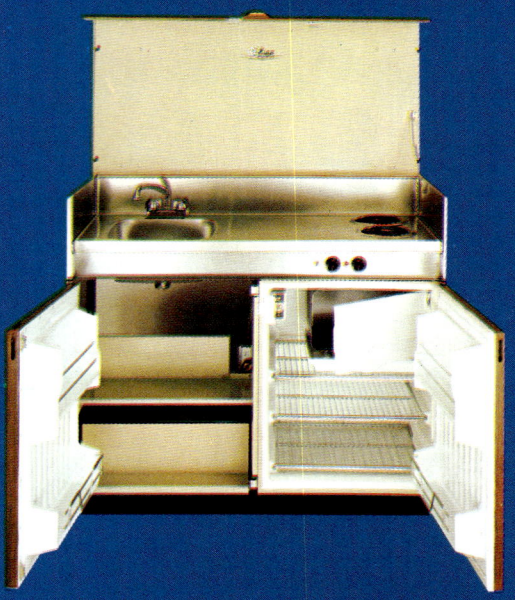

- Size: 48" wide x 36" high to countertop x 25½" deep
- Refrigerator: 6.5 cu. ft. 40 lbs. frozen food capacity • 6" high back and side splash board
- Stainless steel sink, range and countertop • Counter balanced top with fingertip lift
- Single lock closes all compartments

KT48E Finished in color
KT48EW Finished in walnut grain

CABINET CHOICE: Contemporary style or Traditional style.

The REFRESH-ADE JUNIOR, Hospitality Center

- Size: 29¼" wide x 36" high to countertop x 24" deep • Refrigerator: 6 cu. ft. 30 lbs. frozen food capacity
- 6" high back and side splash board
- Stainless sink, range and countertop • Counter balanced top cover with fingertip lift • Single lock closes all compartments

KT32EW Range-sink-refrigerator-walnut grain
KT32RW Range-refrigerator-walnut grain
KT32SW Sink-refrigerator-walnut grain
KT32E Range-sink-refrigerator-color
KT32R Range-refrigerator-color
KT32S Sink-refrigerator-color

 **MINI-KITCHENS**®

Manufactured by
KING REFRIGERATOR CORPORATION
76-02 Woodhaven Blvd., Glendale, N.Y. 11385
(718) 897-2200 • FAX: (718) 830-9440
TELEX 710-582-2364 • KING FRIGE NYK

King also manufactures a 24" wide **Compact, Under-Counter Refrigerator,** Model 777F. Send for details.

The following accessories are available: wall cabinets, microwave oven, range hood, disposer, wall guards, automatic defrost, icecube maker, light fixture.

Design, specifications and dimensions of equipment described herein subject to change without notice.

32M-4P90

KitchenAid®

*J*ust as it has for 40 years, you can be sure that the KitchenAid name on a product stands for performance, durability and quality. Many of the first KitchenAid dishwashers, introduced in 1949, are still providing dependable kitchen cleanup help. Now, that same high quality and durability are built into the full line of KitchenAid appliances you'll see here. Built-in and freestanding refrigerators; dishwashers and trash compactors; built-in ovens and cooktops; drop-in ranges; microwave ovens designed to be built-in; microwave hood combinations; laundry products; food waste disposers; and the INSTANT-HOT® water dispenser. All designed to give you the performance, durability and quality you have come to expect from KitchenAid appliances.

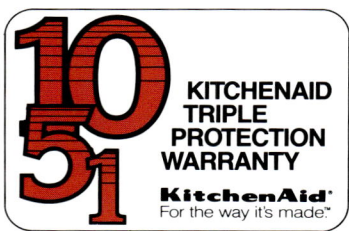

All KitchenAid home appliances are protected by liberal warranties. All are covered by at least a ONE-YEAR FULL WARRANTY on both parts and labor; many carry extended warranties. See back cover for product-specific warranties.

CONTENTS

The KitchenAid built-in refrigerator is a true built-in, with many features to help make installation and service easy. Only twenty-four inches deep, including doors, it installs flush with cabinet fronts. Eighty-four inches high, it can replace a freestanding refrigerator simply by removing the overhead cabinet. Available in three widths, 36, 42 and 48 inch.

Frost-Free Side-by-Side Refrigerator-Freezers

Model KSSS36DWX with Black Through-the-Door Ice and Water Dispenser

Model KSSS36DWW with White Through-the-Door Ice and Water Dispenser

Model KSSS36MWX with no Dispenser
• Overall Dimensions (in./cm): 36 (91.4) w × 24 (60.4) d × 84 (213.4) h.
• 20.1 cu. ft. capacity with 7.4 cu. ft. freezer.
• Approx. Shipping Weights (lbs./kg): KSSS36DWX, DWW – 522 (236.7); KSSS36MWX – 517 (234.4)

Model KSSS42DWX with Black Through-the-Door Ice and Water Dispenser

Model KSSS42DWW with White Through-the-Door Ice and Water Dispenser

Model KSSS42MWX with no Dispenser
• Overall Dimensions (in./cm): 42 (106.7) w × 24 (60.4) d × 84 (213.4) h.
• 24.3 cu. ft. capacity with 9.0 cu. ft. freezer.
• Approx. Shipping Weights (lbs./kg) – KSSS42DWX, DWW – 577 (261.7); KSSS42MWX – 572 (259.3).

Model KSSS48DWX with Black Through-the-Door Ice and Water Dispenser

Model KSSS48DWW with White Through-the-Door Ice and Water Dispenser

Model KSSS48MWX with no Dispenser

KSSS48 models available first quarter, 1991.
• Overall Dimensions (in./cm): 48 (121.9) w × 24 (60.4) d × 84 (213.4) h.
• 28.7 cu. ft. capacity with 10.6 cu. ft. freezer.
• Approx. Shipping Weights (lbs./kg) – KSSS48DWX, DWW – 677 (307.0); KSSS48MWX – 672 (304.8).

All models offer these convenience and performance features.

Refrigerator Food Storage Features
• Adjustable Crystal Frost shelves.
• ClearVue™ humidity controlled RollerTrac™ utility and crisper drawers with glass covers.
• RollerTrac™ WinterChill™ Meat Locker with glass cover. Air cooled, with temperature control.
• Wine/Egg rack.
• Four adjustable door bins.
• In-the-door utility compartment with butter dish.
• Brilliantly lighted interior.
• Separate front-mounted temperature controls for refrigerator and freezer sections; electronic air control for precise refrigerator section temperature.
• Dual magnet MagnaSeal™ door sealing system.
• Foam-insulated thin wall construction.
• Flat lower panels provide access to drawers when doors can be opened only 90°.
• Power interruption switch.

Frozen Food Storage Features
• Factory-installed automatic ice maker with roll-out ice bucket.
• One adjustable and two fixed heavy duty wire shelves.
• Two RollerTrac™ wire baskets.
• Two door bins in Dispenser models, four in others.

The true built-in

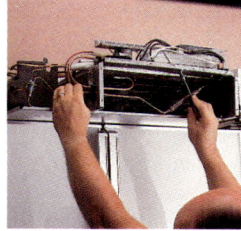

Slide-out refrigeration unit
The sealed refrigeration system unit is top mounted on tracks, so service can be performed without moving the refrigerator. Simply slide the unit out.

Adjustable door stops
Door stops, which are set at the factory for 137° swing, can easily be adjusted to 115° or 90° swing by the dealer or installer.

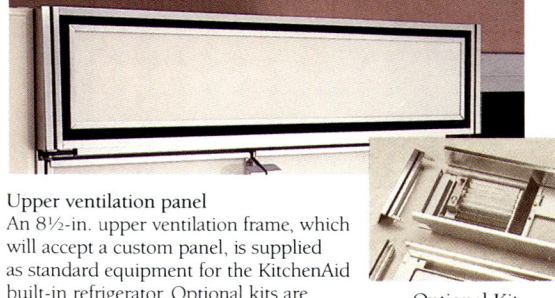

Optional Kit

Upper ventilation panel
An 8½-in. upper ventilation frame, which will accept a custom panel, is supplied as standard equipment for the KitchenAid built-in refrigerator. Optional kits are available to reduce the standard frame to 8 in. or 7½ in. (Optional 8-in., part no. 4318419, and 7½-in., part no. 4318418.)

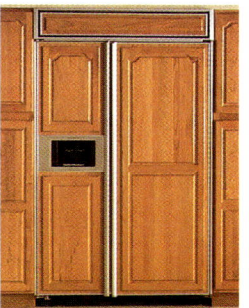

Custom door panels
KitchenAid built-in refrigerators are shipped ready for customizing with unfinished fronts and sides. From wood to match kitchen cabinets to metal or a glass look, panel choices are almost endless.

Color coordinated
Through-the-door dispenser models are available with White (shown) or Black dispenser. Combine the White dispenser with White door panels for complete color coordination.

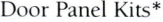

Door Panel Kits*

	Glass Look			Stainless Steel
	White	Almond	Black	
KSSS36DWX, DWW	4210464	4211168	4210469	4210593
KSSS36MWX	4318635	4318638	4318632	4318641
KSSS42DWX, DWW	4210570	4211160	4210569	4210594
KSSS42MWX	4318636	4318639	4318633	4318642
KSSS48DWX, DWW	4318424	4318425	4318423	4318426
KSSS48MWX	4318637	4318640	4318634	4318643

Panel Dimensions – Shown in inches (centimeters)

	KSSS36DW	KSSS36MW	KSSS42DW	KSSS42MW	KSSS48DW	KSSS48MW
Std. 8½-in. ventilation panel	6 (15.2) h × 32⅜ (82.3) w	6 (15.2) h × 32⅜ (82.3) w	6 (15.2) h × 38⅜ (97.5) w	6 (15.2) h × 38⅜ (97.5) w	6 (15.2) h × 44⅜ (112.7) w	6 (15.2) h × 44⅜ (112.7) w
Opt. 8-in. ventilation panel	5½ (14) h × 32⅜ (82.3) w Part No. 4318419	5½ (14) h × 32⅜ (82.3) w Part No. 4318419	5½ (14) h × 38⅜ (97.5) w Part No. 4318419	5½ (14) h × 38⅜ (97.5) w Part No. 4318419	5½ (14) h × 44⅜ (112.7) w Part No. 4318419	5½ (14) h × 44⅜ (112.7) w Part No. 4318419
Opt. 7½-in. ventilation panel	5 (12.7) h × 32⅜ (82.3) w Part No. 4318418	5 (12.7) h × 32⅜ (82.3) w Part No. 4318418	5 (12.7) h × 38⅜ (97.5) w Part No. 4318418	5 (12.7) h × 38⅜ (97.5) w Part No. 4318418	5 (12.7) h × 44⅜ (112.7) w Part No. 4318418	5 (12.7) h × 44⅜ (112.7) w Part No. 4318418
Freezer door panel	–	70⁷⁄₁₆ (178.9) h × 14¼ (36.2) w	–	70⁷⁄₁₆ (178.9) h × 16¾ (42.5) w	–	70⁷⁄₁₆ (178.9) h × 19¼ (48.9) w
Freezer upper door panel	26¼ (66.7) h × 14¼ (36.2) w	–	26¼ (66.7) h × 16¾ (42.5) w	–	26¼ (66.7) h × 19¼ (48.9) w	–
Freezer lower door panel	34⁷⁄₁₆ (87.5) h × 14¼ (36.2) w	–	34⁷⁄₁₆ (87.5) h × 16¾ (42.5) w	–	34⁷⁄₁₆ (87.5) h × 19¼ (48.9) w	–
Refrigerator door panel	70⁷⁄₁₆ (178.9) h × 19¼ (48.9) w	70⁷⁄₁₆ (178.9) h × 19¼ (48.9) w	70⁷⁄₁₆ (178.9) h × 22¾ (57.8) w	70⁷⁄₁₆ (178.9) h × 22¾ (57.8) w	70⁷⁄₁₆ (178.9) h × 26¼ (66.7) w	70⁷⁄₁₆ (178.9) h × 26¼ (66.7) w

All freestanding KitchenAid Refrigerator-Freezers share these Universal Quality Features

- Frost-Free operation.
- RollerTrac™ System for easy moving of heavily loaded crispers and drawers (except Model KTRI18KW).
- Adjustable Crystal Frost tempered glass shelves.
- Adjustable door storage bins.

- Removable wine/egg rack.
- Easy-to-clean one-piece liner.
- MagnaSeal™ door gaskets keep cold air in and warm air out.
- Power saver switch.

- Color-coordinated Almond or White cabinet with all-white interior.
- Textured-steel doors.
- Interior lights.
- Door stops.

Side-by-Side Refrigerator-Freezers
Model KSRS25QW (shown)
- 25.0 cu. ft. capacity with 9.8 cu. ft. freezer.
- Automatic ice maker with 10-lb. capacity ice bin.
- Crushed ice, ice crescents or chilled water through the door from illuminated dispenser.
- Fast Freeze shelf.
- Full-width Crystal Frost adjustable cantilever refrigerator shelves.
- Adjustable RollerTrac™ square-back crispers with humidity controls.
- Temperature-controlled WinterChill™ Meat Locker.
- Slide 'N' Lock refrigerator door bins.

Model KSRB25QW
(available 4th quarter 1990)
Identical to model KSRS25QW except:
- Comes with factory-installed trim kit and Black glass-look door panels.

Model KSRS22DW
Similar to model KSRS25QW except:
- 21.5 cu. ft. capacity with 7.1 cu. ft. freezer.
- Through-the-door dispenser delivers ice crescents or chilled water only.

Model KSRB22DW
(available 4th quarter 1990)
Identical to model KSRS22DW except:
- Comes with factory-installed trim kit and Black glass-look door panels.

Top-Freezer Refrigerator-Freezers
Model KTRS25KW
- 24.8 cu. ft. capacity with 7.7 cu. ft. freezer.
- Half-width Crystal Frost adjustable cantilever refrigerator shelves.
- RollerTrac™ crispers with humidity controls.
- ClearVue™ Meat Locker.
- Slide 'N' Lock refrigerator door bins hold gallon containers.
- Four ice trays and ice bucket standard; will accept optional ice maker kit KIMS8, part no. 1129312.

Model KTRS20KW
Identical to model KTRS22KW except:
- 19.8 cu. ft. capacity with 5.5 cu. ft. freezer.
- Bottom refrigerator door shelf has snap-in trim.

Model KTRS22KW (shown)
- 21.5 cu. ft. capacity with 6.0 cu. ft. freezer.
- Half-width Crystal Frost adjustable cantilever refrigerator shelves.
- RollerTrac™ square-back humidity-controlled crisper.
- ClearVue™ utility compartment.
- ClearVue™ Meat Locker.
- Slide 'N' Lock refrigerator door bins hold gallon containers.
- Four ice trays and ice bucket standard; will accept optional ice maker kit KIMS8, part no. 1129312.

Top-Freezer Refrigerator-Freezer
Model KTRI18KW (shown)
- Fits in a space only 30 in. wide.
- 18.0 cu. ft. capacity with 4.8 cu. ft. freezer.
- Half-width Crystal Frost adjustable cantilever refrigerator shelves.
- Humidity-sealed crispers.
- Adjustable Meat Locker.

- Adjustable refrigerator door bins…some hold gallon containers.
- Four ice trays and ice bucket standard; will accept optional ice maker kit KIMS8, part no. 1129312.

For complete feature summary, see page 6.

Bottom-Freezer Refrigerator-Freezer

Model KBRS22KW
(available 4th quarter 1990)

- 22.1 cu. ft. capacity with 7.4 cu. ft. freezer.
- Half-width Crystal Frost adjustable cantilever refrigerator shelves.
- RollerTrac™ square-back humidity-controlled crispers.
- ClearVue™ Meat Locker.
- Slide 'N' Lock refrigerator door bins... some hold gallon containers.
- Big bottom freezer with two slide-out baskets.
- Two ice trays and ice bucket standard; will accept optional ice maker kit KIMS8, part no. 1129312.

Trim kits, which accept custom or glass-look acrylic door panels (Black shown), are available for most models.

Trimless Black glass-look magnetic door panels are available for many models.

Panel Kit Part Nos.

Refrigerator Model	Trim Kit	Acrylic Panels for use with Trim Kit			Trimless Acrylic Panels			Door Handle Inserts		Black Base Grille
		Black	White	Almond	Black	White	Almond	Black	Woodgrain	Black
Side-by-Side KSRB25QW	Factory Installed	Factory Installed	NA	NA	NA	NA	NA	NA	NA	Factory Installed
KSRS25QW	4318336*	NA	4211148*	4211147*	NA	NA	NA	4318339	4318340	4318417
KSRB22DW	Factory Installed	Factory Installed	NA	NA	NA	NA	NA	NA	NA	Factory Installed
KSRS22DW	4318331*	NA	4211136*	4211135*	NA	NA	NA	4318334	4318335	4318416
Top Freezer KTRS25KW	4318317	4211276	4211280	4211284	4318318RH 4318433LH	4318314RH 4318434LH	4318315RH 4318435LH	4318322	4318323	4318415
KTRS22KW	4318303	819344	4318306	4318307	4318304RH 4318430LH	4318312RH 4318431LH	4318313RH 4318432LH	4318308	4318309	4318414
KTRS20KW	4318303	819344	4318306	4318307	4318304RH 4318430LH	4318312RH 4318431LH	4318313RH 4318432LH	4318308	4318309	4318414
KTRI18KW	NA	NA	NA	NA	4318300RH 4318427LH	4318310RH 4318428LH	4318311RH 4318429LH	4318301	4318302	4318413
Bottom Freezer KBRS22KW	4318324	4318326	4318327	4318328	4318325	4318316	4318412	4318329	4318330	4318414

NA – Not Available   RH – Righthand Door Swing   LH – Lefthand Door Swing

*Available 4th quarter 1990.

Dimensions for 1/4-Inch-Thick Custom Door Panels

All dimensions shown in inches.

Model	Refrigerator Door	Freezer Door	
		Upper	Lower
KSRS25QW	19 9/16 W × 63 3/8 H	14 13/16 W × 20 3/8 H	14 13/16 W × 28 7/16 H
KSRS22DW	19 9/16 W × 60 7/16 H	12 1/16 W × 17 3/8 H	12 1/16 W × 28 7/16 H
KTRS25KW	35 1/16 W × 40 7/16 H	35 1/16 W × 22 3/8 H	–
KTRS22KW	32 5/16 W × 40 7/16 H	32 5/16 W × 19 3/8 H	–
KTRS20KW	32 5/16 W × 40 7/16 H	32 5/16 W × 19 3/8 H	–
KBRS22KW	32 5/16 W × 36 7/8 H	–	32 5/16 W × 22 7/8 H
KTRI18KW	–	–	–

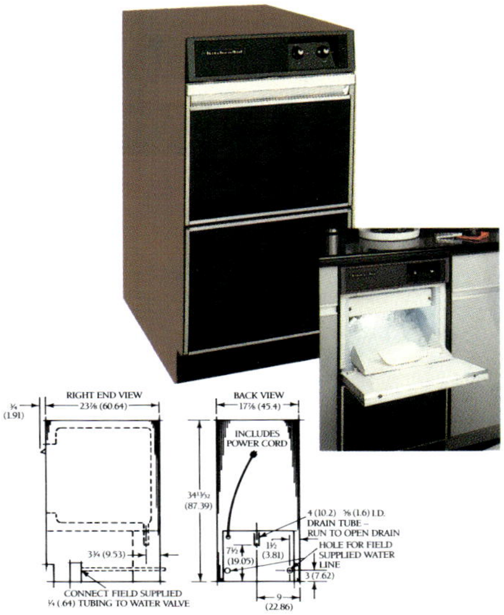

Automatic Ice Cube Maker

Model KUIS185S

- Makes up to 51 lbs. of ice cubes in 24 hrs. (50°F water and 70°F ambient).
- Cube thickness variable from 3/8 in. to 3/4 in.
- Ice production stops automatically when bin is full.
- Lighted storage bin holds 35 lbs. of ice.
- Standford Brown textured-steel cabinet can be installed built-in or freestanding.
- VARI-FRONT™ Panel Pack includes Almond, Harvest Wheat, Black and White. Metal frame can accommodate custom panels up to 1/4 in. thick. For information, see page 6.
- Optional stainless steel exterior trim, part no. 819421; stainless steel door panels, part no. 819419; hardwood top for freestanding installation, part no. 8178826; condensate pump, part no. 758840.
- Optional change-out control panels available: White, part no. 4210583; Almond, part no. 4210584.

KitchenAid Refrigerator Feature Comparison

	Side-by-Sides				Top Freezers				Bottom Freezer
	KSRB25QW	KSRS25QW	KSRB22DW	KSRS22DW	KTRS25KW	KTRS22KW	KTRS20KW	KTRI18KW	KBRS22KW
Total Vol. (Cu. Ft.)	25.0	25.0	21.5	21.5	24.8	21.5	19.8	18.0	22.1
Refrigerator Comp. Vol. (Cu. Ft.)	15.2	15.2	14.4	14.4	17.1	15.5	14.3	13.2	14.7
Freezer Comp. Vol. (Cu. Ft.)	9.8	9.8	7.1	7.1	7.7	6.0	5.5	4.8	7.4
Total Shelf Area (Sq. Ft.)	27.2	27.2	22.8	22.8	32.6	36.1	32.4	23.6	28.6
FREEZER									
Through-the-Door Ice & Water Dispenser	•	•	•	•	–	–	–	–	–
Automatic Ice Maker	•	•	•	•	Opt.*	Opt.*	Opt.*	Opt.*	Opt.*
Ice Bucket	•	•	•	•	•	•	•	•	•
Door Bins/Shelves	5/2	5/2	5/1	5/1	2/3	2/3	2/3	2/2	–/2
Slide-Out Basket	3	3	3	3	–	–	–	–	2
REFRIGERATOR									
Adjustable Crystal-Frost Shelves	3	3	3	3	3	3	3	3	2
RollerTrac™ Crispers	2	2	2	2	2	1	1	2**	2
RollerTrac™ WinterChill™ Meat Locker	•	•	•	•	–	–	–	–	–
RollerTrac™ Utility/Meat Drawer	–	–	–	–	•	•	•	–	•
Door Bins (Fixed and Adjustable)	4	4	4	4	5	5	5	5	4
Dairy Locker	•	•	•	•	•	•	•	50/50	•
Wine/Egg Rack	•	•	•	•	•	•	•	•	•
Power Saver Switch	•	•	•	•	•	•	•	•	•
REFRIGERATOR and FREEZER									
One-Piece Liner	•	•	•	•	•	•	•	•	•
Lighted Interior	•	•	•	•	•	•	•	Refrigerator Comp. Only	•
Textured Steel Doors	•	•	•	•	•	•	•	•	•
MagnaSeal™ Door Gaskets	•	•	•	•	•	•	•	•	•
Door Trim Kit	$\frac{1}{8}$-in. Std.	Opt.	$\frac{1}{8}$-in. Std.	Opt.	Opt.	Opt.	Opt.	–	Opt.
Door Stops	•	•	•	•	•	•	•	•	•
Automatic Door Closers	•	•	•	•	–	–	–	–	–
Reversible Door Swing	–	–	–	–	•	•	•	•	•
Height (In.)	$68\frac{7}{8}$	$68\frac{7}{8}$	$65\frac{7}{8}$	$65\frac{7}{8}$	$68\frac{7}{8}$	$65\frac{7}{8}$	$65\frac{7}{8}$	$65\frac{7}{8}$	$65\frac{7}{8}$
Width (In.)	$35\frac{1}{2}$	$35\frac{1}{2}$	$32\frac{3}{4}$	$32\frac{3}{4}$	$35\frac{1}{2}$	$32\frac{3}{4}$	$32\frac{3}{4}$	$29\frac{1}{2}$	$32\frac{3}{4}$
Depth (In.)	$29\frac{3}{4}$	$29\frac{3}{4}$	$29\frac{3}{4}$	$29\frac{3}{4}$	$29\frac{3}{4}$	$29\frac{3}{4}$	$27\frac{3}{4}$	$27\frac{3}{4}$	$29\frac{3}{4}$
Depth Incl. Handles (In.)	$32\frac{3}{16}$	$32\frac{3}{16}$	$32\frac{3}{16}$	$32\frac{3}{16}$	$32\frac{1}{8}$	$32\frac{1}{8}$	$30\frac{1}{8}$	$29\frac{11}{16}$	$31\frac{13}{16}$
Depth Extreme Swing of Door (In.)	$49\frac{1}{4}$	$49\frac{1}{4}$	$49\frac{1}{4}$	$49\frac{1}{4}$	$64\frac{3}{8}$	$61\frac{5}{8}$	$59\frac{5}{8}$	$55\frac{15}{16}$	$61\frac{5}{16}$
Electrical Requirements 115V, 60 Hz, AC	•	•	•	•	•	•	•	•	•
Approx. Shpg. Wgt. (Lbs.)	335	330	311	306	331	295	280	255	287

*4 ice cube trays included – Model KBRS22KW has 2 ice cube trays.
**Not RollerTrac.™

All dimensions shown in inches.

Specifications Model KUIS185S

Cube Size	($\frac{3}{8}$" to $\frac{3}{4}$") x $\frac{3}{4}$" x $\frac{3}{4}$"
Capacity per 24 Hrs.*	
Production	Up to 51 lbs.
Storage Rating	35 lbs.
Electrical Requirements	115 V., 60 Hz.
Water Supply	$\frac{1}{4}$" O.D. copper tube**
Drain	$\frac{5}{8}$" I.D. rubber tube**
Approximate Weights	
Net	103 lbs. (46.4 Kg)
Shipping	116 lbs. (52.2 Kg)

*Based on 70°F ambient and 50°F water temperatures.
**Subject to local codes.

Custom panel dimensions

	Width	Height
Upper	17"	$11\frac{1}{4}$"
Lower	17"	$11\frac{15}{16}$"

Specifications subject to change without notice.
Dimensions are for planning only. For complete details, see installation instructions packed with product.

Built-In Dishwashers

All KitchenAid Built-In Dishwashers share these Universal Quality Features

- SURE-SCRUB™ Multi-Level Washing System.
- Triple Filtration and Soil Collector System with Stainless Steel Hard Food Disposer.
- "Load-as-you-like" Random Loading.

- Completely usable upper and lower rack.
- FLO-THRU™ Drying System.
- TriDura® porcelain-on-steel tank and inner door.
- Rigidized steel frame.

- ENERGY SAVER NO-HEAT Dry Option.
- VARI-FRONT™ Panel Pack with reversible panel(s).
- All cycles safe for fine china and crystal.
- ½ hp. gold seal reversing motor.

 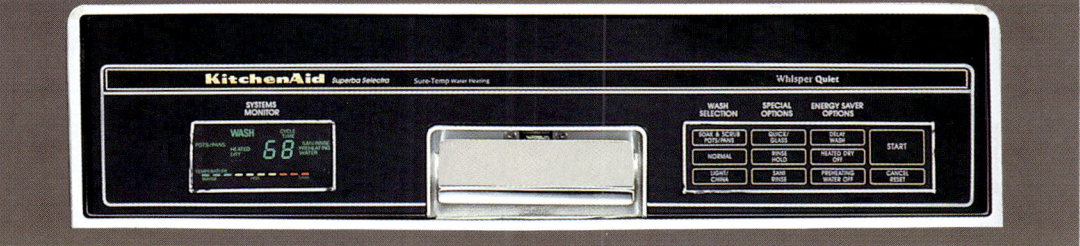

Model KUDA22ST

- 6-in. high console panel matches standard cabinet drawer depth.
- Solid-state electronic touch controls with three cycle selections: SOAK & SCRUB POTS/PANS, NORMAL, LIGHT/CHINA*.
- Special options: QUICK/GLASS, RINSE HOLD, SANI RINSE.

- Energy-saver options: DELAY WASH, HEATED DRY OFF, PREHEATING WATER OFF.
- START pad with memory repeats last cycle automatically.
- CANCEL/RESET pad.
- 16 Position Adjustable Rack with FLEX-O-DIVIDER™ System.

- CushionTip™ dish racks.
- DURAKOTE™ Nylon Racks with 3-Year Warranty.**
- Systems Monitor with Energy Use indication.
- SURE-TEMP™ System automatically heats water to approx. 140°F prior to circulation.
- WHISPER QUIET™ System for sound reduction.

Model KUDA220T

- 6-in. high console panel matches standard cabinet drawer depth.
- Instant-start pushbutton controls with five cycle selections: SOAK & SCRUB POTS/ PANS, NORMAL, LIGHT/CHINA*, QUICK GLASS and RINSE HOLD.
- Options: CANCEL/DRAIN, SANI RINSE, ENERGY SAVER DRY.

- 16 Position Adjustable Rack with FLEX-O-DIVIDER™ System.
- CushionTip™ dish racks.
- DURAKOTE™ Nylon Racks with 3-Year Warranty.**
- Cycle Monitor with indicators for HEATING WATER, WASH, RINSE, DRY, RINSE ONLY.

- SURE-TEMP™ System automatically heats water to approx. 140°F prior to circulation.
- WHISPER QUIET™ System for sound reduction.
- Available in White or Almond.
- Optional Brushed Stainless Steel control panel, part no. 4171389.

Superba™   Model KUDS220T

- Instant-start pushbutton controls with five cycle selections: SOAK & SCRUB POTS/ PANS, NORMAL, LIGHT/CHINA*, QUICK GLASS and RINSE HOLD.
- Options: CANCEL/DRAIN, SANI RINSE, ENERGY SAVER DRY.
- 16 Position Adjustable Rack with FLEX-O-DIVIDER™ System.

- CushionTip™ dish racks.
- DURAKOTE™ Nylon Racks with 3-Year Warranty.**
- Cycle Monitor with indicators for HEATING WATER, WASH, RINSE, DRY, RINSE ONLY.
- SURE-TEMP™ System automatically heats water to approx. 140°F prior to circulation.

- WHISPER QUIET™ System for sound reduction.

*All cycles are safe for fine china and crystal. For complete feature summary, see page 8.

**See Use & Care Guide for complete warranty information.

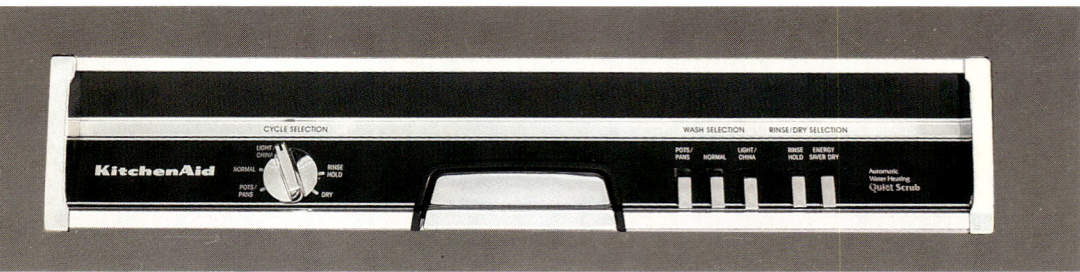

Model KUDI220T

- Easy to use rotary dial control with four cycle selections: POTS/PANS, NORMAL, LIGHT/CHINA*, and RINSE HOLD.
- ENERGY SAVER DRY.

- SURE-CLEAN™ automatic water heating heats circulating water.
- QUIET SCRUB™ Sound Reduction System.
- ChinaGuard™ protector.

- Automatic detergent and rinse agent dispensers.
- Available in Black or White (KUDI220WWH).

Model KUDC220T

- Easy to use rotary dial control with four cycle selections: POTS/PANS, NORMAL, LIGHT/CHINA*, AND RINSE HOLD.
- SURE-CLEAN™ automatic water heating.
- ENERGY SAVER NO-HEAT DRY and NO-HEAT WASH Options.
- Automatic detergent and rinse agent dispensers.
- High-density insulation.

Portable Dishwasher   Model KPDI620TA (not shown)

Control panel configuration identical to Model KUDI220T.

- Easy to use rotary dial control with four cycle selections: POTS/PANS, NORMAL, LIGHT/CHINA*, and RINSE HOLD.
- SURE-CLEAN™ automatic water heating.
- QUIET SCRUB™ Sound Reduction System.
- ChinaGuard™ protector.

- Automatic power cord reel.
- Heavy-duty casters with chromeplated caster guards.
- Unicoupler fill and faucet adapter for fill and drain hoses.
- Easy conversion to built-in – no extra-cost kit needed.
- All cycles are safe for fine china and crystal.

Dishwasher Feature Comparison

	KUDA220T	Electronic Control KUDA22ST	Superba™ Selectra KUDS22ST	Superba™ KUDS220T	KUDI220WWH KUDI220T	KUDC220T	Portable KPDI620T
SURE-SCRUB™ Multi-Level Washing	•	•	•	•	•	•	•
Triple Filtration and Soil Collector System	•	•	•	•	•	•	•
Automatic Detergent and Rinse Agent Dispensers	•	•	•	•	•	•	•
SOAK & SCRUB POTS/PANS Cycle	•	•	•	•	—	—	—
POTS & PANS Cycle	—	•	—	•	•	•	•
NORMAL Cycle	•	•	•	•	•	•	•
LIGHT/CHINA*·Cycle	•	•	•	•	•	•	•
QUICK GLASS Cycle	•	•	•	•	—	—	—
RINSE HOLD Cycle	•	•	•	•	•	•	•
SANI RINSE Option	•	•	•	•			
Energy Saver No-Heat Dry Option	•	•	•	•	•	•	•
Delay Wash		•	•				
Automatic Water Heating	SURE-TEMP	SURE-TEMP	SURE-TEMP	SURE-TEMP	SURE-CLEAN	SURE-CLEAN	SURE-CLEAN
14-Position FLEX-O-DIVIDERS™ Rack System	•	•	•	•	—	—	—
16-Position Adj. Upper Rack	•	•	•	•	•	•	•
CUSHION-TIP™ Dish Racks	•	•	•	•	•	•	•
DURAKOTE™ Nylon Racks (3-Year Warranty)	•	•	•	•	—	—	—
100% Usable Upper and Lower Rack	•	•	•	•	•	•	•
CHINAGUARD™ Protector	•				•	•	•
Sound Reduction Systems	WHISPER QUIET™	WHISPER QUIET™	WHISPER QUIET™	WHISPER QUIET™	QUIET SCRUB™	Fiber Glass	QUIET SCRUB™
FLO-THRU™ Drying System	•	•	•	•	•	•	•
TRIDURA® Tank and Inner Door	•	•	•	•	•	•	•
Solid-State Controls with Memory	—	•	•	—	—	—	—
½ HP Gold Seal Reversing Motor	•	•	•	•	•	•	•
VARI-FRONT™ Panel Pack	**	**	4 COLORS	4 COLORS	4 COLORS	Black/ Almond†	Black/ Almond
Portable Features††	—	—	—	—	—		•
Max. Watts	1475	1475	1475	1475	1360	1360	1360
Max. Amps Separate 15-amp., 3-wire grounded circuit required.	13.5	13.5	13.5	13.5	13.5	13.5	13.5
Weight (Lbs.) Shipping	151 (69 Kg)	151 (69 Kg)	151 (69 Kg)	151 (69 Kg)	123 (56 Kg)	121 (55 Kg)	183 (83 Kg)
Net	135 (61 Kg)	135 (61 Kg)	135 (61 Kg)	135 (61 Kg)	108 (49 Kg)	104 (47 Kg)	177 (81 Kg)
Warranty 10•5•1							

*All cycles are safe for fine china and crystal.
**Unit available in White or Almond.

†Free Mail-In Card for White/Harvest Wheat.
††Wood Top, Casters, Easy Conversion to Built-In.

Special Panel Option

Brushed Stainless Steel
Part No. 4169400
(Models KUDA220T and KUDA22ST, Part No. 4171198)

Basic Sizes for ¼" (.64 cm) Custom Front Panels – Shown in inches (centimeters)

	Width	Height
Door	23⅜/₁₆ (59.8)	18¹³/₁₆ (47.9)¹
Lower	23¹¹/₁₆ (60.2)	6⅝ (16.8)

Sides and top of door panel have ⁵/₁₆-in. edges; bottom has 1-in. edge.

¹Height of Door Panel for models KUDA220T and KUDA22ST is 17⁷/₁₆ (44.3).

Dimensions are for planning only. For complete details, see installation instructions packed with product.

Specifications subject to change without notice.

Trash Compactors

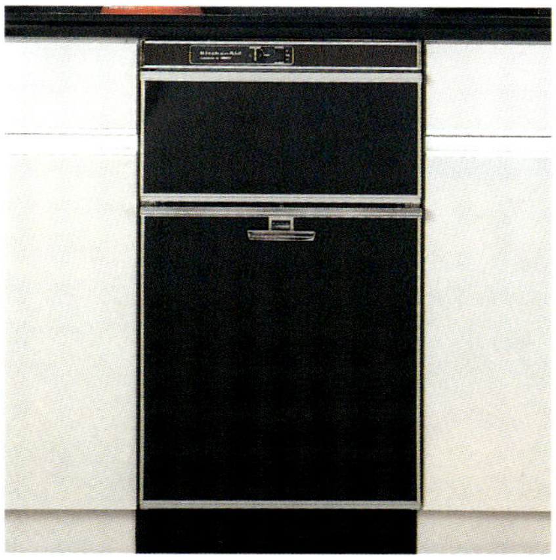

Built-In or Freestanding 18-Inch

Model KUCS181T

- Exclusive LITTER BIN® Door lets you load small items even while the compactor is operating.
- Large built-in storage compartment.
- Extra-large trash drawer.
- Exclusive Tilt-Away Trash Basket and basket release handle for easy trash removal.
- Exclusive activated charcoal air filter and odor control fan with ON/OFF switch.
- Exclusive ½ HP motor provides 3,000 lbs. of ram force to reduce trash to approx. ¼ volume in 35 sec. max.
- Exclusive Even-Pressure 3-Point Drive System helps prevent jams resulting from uneven loading.
- Exclusive 3-piece ram.
- Exclusive rigidized steel frame.
- VARI-FRONT™ Panel Pack (Almond, White, Black, Harvest Wheat).
- Converts to freestanding operation with optional maple wood top conversion kit no. 4164800.
- Optional change-out control panels available: White, part no. 4178062; Almond, part no. 4178063.
- Shipping weight (approx.) 210 lbs. (94.5 kg).

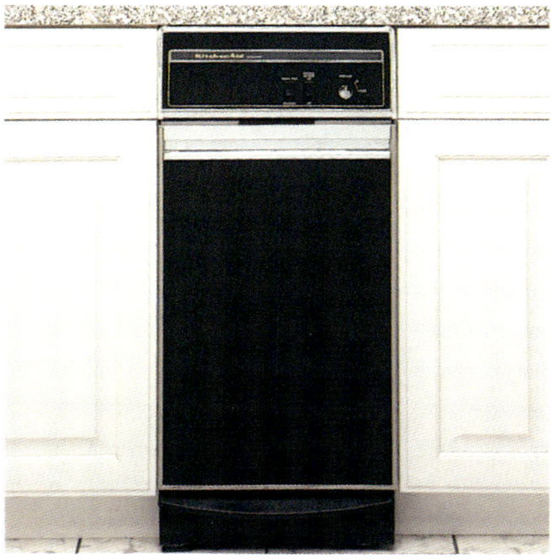

Built-In 15-Inch

Model KUCC151T

- SOLID PACK operation increases capacity up to 20%.
- Exclusive activated charcoal air filter and odor control fan with ON/OFF switch.
- Heavy gauge steel ram powered by ⅓ HP motor delivers 2,300 lbs. of force to crush trash in approx. 27 sec.
- Convenient Toe-Bar Drawer Opener.
- Designed for built-in undercounter installation.
- VARI-FRONT™ Panel Pack (Almond, White, Black, Harvest Wheat).
- Optional change-out control panels available: White, part no. 4151847; Almond, part no. 4151848; Brushed Stainless Steel, part no. 882681.
- Shipping weight (approx.) 150 lbs. (67.5 kg).

Electrical Requirements

	KUCS181T	KUCC151T
Volts (AC)	115	115
Hertz	60	60
Rated Load (Max. Amps)	9	6.5

Special 15 Amp. 3-Wire grounded circuit required.

Basic sizes for ¼-in. (.64 cm) Custom Front Panels

MODEL	WIDTH		HEIGHT	
	In.	cm	In.	cm
KUCS181T LITTER BIN® Door	17⁷⁄₁₆	44.3	7³¹⁄₃₂	20.2
Drawer	17⁷⁄₁₆	44.3	18¹⁵⁄₁₆	48.1
KUCC151T	14⅝	37.1	21⅞	55.6

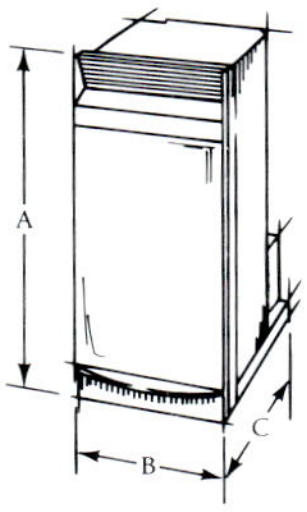

A
B
C

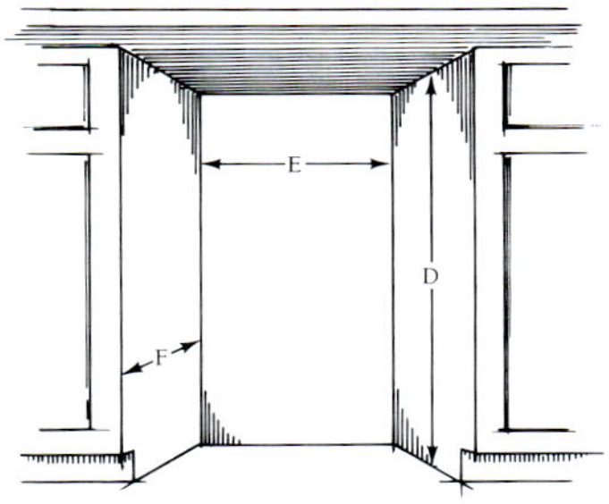

E
D
F

Compactor Dimensions

Model	A In.	A cm	B In.	B cm	C In.	C cm	D In.	D cm	E In.	E cm	F In.	F cm
KUCS181T	34⅛ to 35⅝	86.7 to 89.9*	17¾	45.1	24⅝ incl. door	62.5	34¼ min.	87	18	45.7	24 min.	61
KUCC151T	34¹⁄₁₆ to 34¾	86.5 to 88.3	14¹⁵⁄₁₆	37.9	24³⁄₁₆	61.4	34⅜ min.	87.3	15	38.1	24 min.	61

*Add 1½" (3.8 cm) when installed freestanding with maple wood optional top.

Dishwasher Dimensions

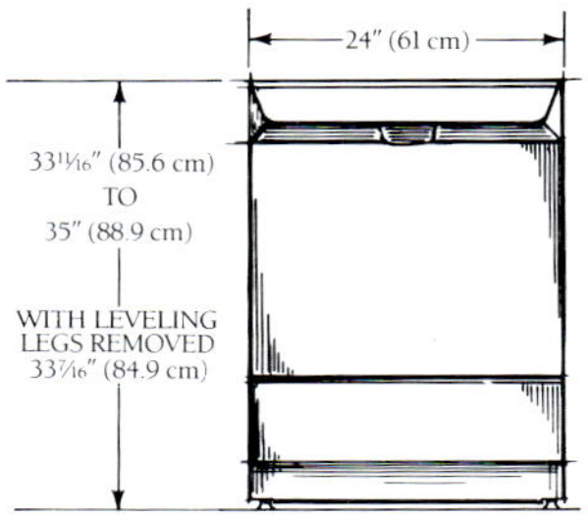

24" (61 cm)
33¹¹⁄₁₆" (85.6 cm)
TO
35" (88.9 cm)
WITH LEVELING
LEGS REMOVED
33⁷⁄₁₆" (84.9 cm)

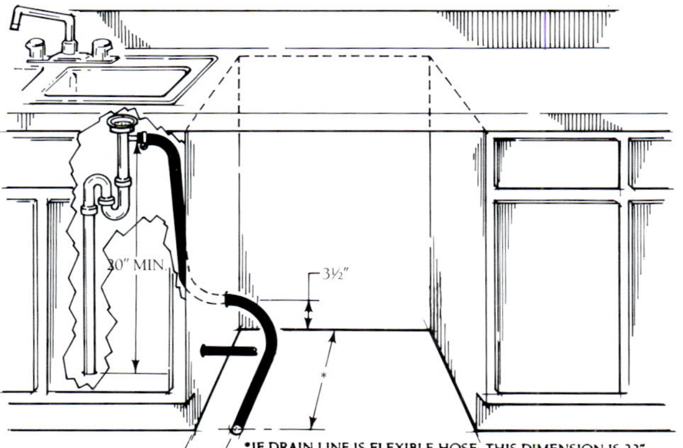

20" MIN.
3½"
6"
*IF DRAIN LINE IS FLEXIBLE HOSE, THIS DIMENSION IS 22"
ALTERNATE LOCATION
IF DRAIN LINE IS COPPER, THE COPPER SHOULD BE 12" PLUS A
12" LENGTH OF FLEXIBLE HOSE ATTACHED TO THE END

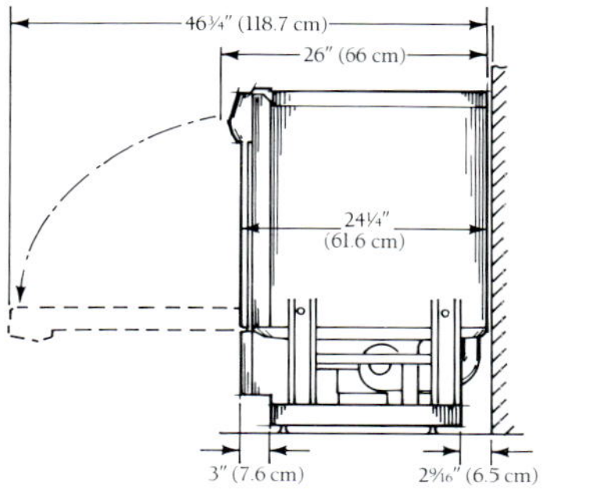

46¾" (118.7 cm)
26" (66 cm)
24¼"
(61.6 cm)
3" (7.6 cm)
2⁹⁄₁₆" (6.5 cm)

MIN. INLET WATER TEMPERATURE AT DISHWASHER 120° F (49° C).
INLET WATER PRESSURE OPERATING RANGE 10-120 psi (138-827 KPa).

INLET WATER TUBING ½" (1.27 cm) OD MIN.
DRAIN ⁹⁄₁₆" (1.43 cm) ID MIN. FLEXIBLE HOSE FROM CHECK VALVE.
⅝" (1.59 cm) OD MIN. COPPER TUBING MAY BE RUN FROM ⁹⁄₁₆" (1.43 cm) HOSE, IF NECESSARY.

Dimensions are for planning only. For complete details, see installation instructions packed with product.

Specifications subject to change without notice.

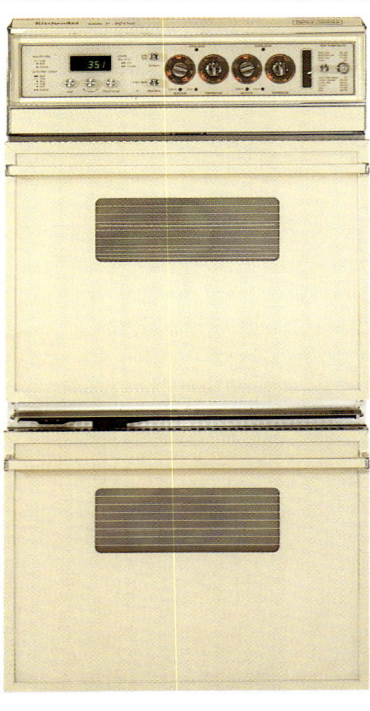

Microwave/Thermal Combination Oven

30-Inch Model KEMI300T

Microwave Oven
- 1.3 cu. ft. capacity.
- Easy-to-use solid-state touch controls provide up to 99 min., 99 sec. of cooking or defrosting time.
- One or two stage cooking.
- Temperature Probe.
- Variable Power Control.
- Automatic Rapid Defrost.
- Automatic Sensor Cooking with Cook/Reheat, Slow Cook/Simmer and Cook/Frozen settings.
- 12-Hr. Delay Start option.
- Whole Meal Cooking Rack.

Lower Oven
- Electronic Clock with lighted digital display.
- Two Element Balanced Baking and Roasting.
- Variable Temperature Broiling.
- Variable Self-Cleaning System.

Entire Unit
- Smoke eliminator…no outside venting.

Microwave/Thermal Combination Oven

27-Inch Model KEMI371T

Featured similarly to model KEMI300T but 27 inches wide.

Superba™ Microwave-Convection/ Thermal Combination Oven

27-Inch Model KEMS376T

Microwave-Convection Upper Oven
- 1.5 cu. ft. capacity.
- 100-min. timer with convection cooking temperatures and function indicators incorporated in lighted display.
- Solid-state touch controls.
- Five-level microwave variable power control.
- Ten convection temperature selections for Baking/Roasting, Broiling, and Slow Cooking.
- Low Mix/Bake and High Mix/Roast combination microwave-convection settings.
- One, two, three or four-stage cooking.
- Removable automatic turntable.

Lower Oven
All the quality features of model KEMI300T

PLUS
- Temperature Probe.
- Rotisserie.

Entire Unit
- Smoke eliminator…no outside venting.
- Available in White (shown), Almond or Black.

Superba™ Thermal-Convection™ Ovens

27-Inch Double Oven

Model KEBS277W

Upper Oven
- Convection or Thermal Balanced Baking and Roasting.
- Convection or Thermal Variable Temperature "Maxi" and "Econo" Broil.
- Convection Cooking/Defrosting/Dehydrating.
- Temperature Probe.

Lower Oven
- Two Element Balanced Baking and Roasting.
- Variable Temperature Broiling.

Entire Unit
- Electronic Clock with lighted digital display.
- Backlighted controls indicate power "ON."
- Variable Self-Cleaning System.
- Smoke eliminator…no outside venting.
- Available in White, Almond (shown) or Black.

27-Inch Single Oven

Model KEBS177W

Identical to the Upper Oven of model KEBS277W.

Superba™ Double Ovens

Model KEBS276W – 27-Inch
Model KEBS246W – 24-Inch
Upper Oven
- Electronic Clock with lighted display.
- Rotisserie.
- Temperature Probe.
- Two Element Balanced Baking and Roasting.
- Variable Temperature Broiling.
- Variable Self-Cleaning System.

Lower Oven
- Two Element Balanced Baking and Roasting.
- Variable Temperature Broiling.
- Variable Self-Cleaning System.

Entire Unit
- Oven "ON" light.
- Smoke eliminator…no outside venting.

Superba™ Single Ovens

Model KEBS176W – 27-Inch
Model KEBS146W – 24-Inch
Identical to the Upper Oven of models
KEBS276W and KEBS246W.

Double Ovens

Model KEBI271W – 27-Inch
Model KEBI241W – 24-Inch
Upper Oven
- Electronic Clock with lighted digital display.
- Two Element Baking and Roasting.
- Variable Temperature Broiling.
- Variable Self-Cleaning System.

Lower Oven
- Two Element Balanced Baking and Roasting.
- Broiling.
- Standard clean.

Entire Unit
- Oven "ON" light.
- Smoke eliminator…no outside venting.

Single Ovens

Model KEBI171W – 27-Inch
Model KEBI141W – 24-Inch
Identical to the Upper Oven of models
KEBI271W and KEBI241W.

30-Inch Double Oven

Model KEBI200V

Upper Oven
- Electronic Clock with lighted digital display.
- Two Element Balanced Baking and Roasting.
- Variable Temperature Broiling.
- Variable Self-Cleaning System.

Lower Oven
- Two Element Balanced Baking and Roasting.
- Broiling.
- Standard clean.

Entire Unit
- Oven "ON" lights.
- Smoke eliminator…no outside venting.

30-Inch Single Oven

Model KEBI100V
Identical to Upper Oven of model
KEBI200V.

Superba™ 24-Inch Double Oven
Model KGBS246S

Upper Oven
- Electronic Clock with lighted digital display.
- Rotisserie.
- Temperature Probe.
- Baking and Roasting/14,000 BTU natural or LP gas burner.
- Variable Temperature Broiling/12,000 BTU natural or LP gas burner.
- Standard clean.

Lower Oven
- Baking and Roasting/12,000 BTU natural or LP gas burner.
- Standard clean.

Entire Unit
- Power "ON" and Oven "ON" lights.
- No expensive outside venting.
- Shipped ready for use with natural gas; may be converted to LP gas — no kit required.
- Pilotless electric ignition.

Superba™ 24-Inch Single Oven
Model KGBS146S

Identical to Upper Oven of model KGBS246S.

Oven Door Panels in Color

Black glass doors are standard on all KitchenAid built-in ovens. Optional door panels, available for 24-in., 27-in. and 30-in. thermal ovens, make it possible to change oven door color. Please order door panels by part number.

Door Panel Part Nos.

Model No.	Glass		Porcelain					Brushed Chrome
	Almond	White	Almond	White	Fresh Avocado	Coffee	Harvest Wheat	
KEBI141W	3180224	3180226	NA	NA	NA	NA	NA	NA
KEBI141S	4169392	4169393	4164806	4164814	4164810	4164809	4164812	4164807
KEBS146W	3180224	3180226	NA	NA	NA	NA	NA	NA
KEBS146S	4169392	4169393	4164806	4164814	4164810	4164809	4164812	4164807
KEBI171W	3180225	3180227	NA	NA	NA	NA	NA	NA
KEBI171S	4169394	4169395	4164815	4164820	4169391	4164818	4164819	4164816
KEBS176W	3180225	3180227	NA	NA	NA	NA	NA	NA
KEBS176S	4169394	4169395	4164815	4164820	4169391	4164818	4164819	4164816
KEBS177W	3180225	3180227	NA	NA	NA	NA	NA	NA
KEBS177S	4169394	4169395	4164815	4164820	4169391	4164818	4164819	4164816
KEBI100V	814070	814069	NA	NA	NA	NA	NA	NA
*KEBI241W	3180224	3180226	NA	NA	NA	NA	NA	NA
*KEBI241S	4169392	4169393	4164806	4164814	4164810	4164809	4164812	4164807
*KEBS246W	3180224	3180226	NA	NA	NA	NA	NA	NA
*KEBS246S	4169392	4169393	4164806	4164814	4164810	4164809	4164812	4164807
*KEBI271W	3180225	3180227	NA	NA	NA	NA	NA	NA
*KEBI271S	4169394	4169395	4164815	4164820	4169391	4164818	4164819	4164816
*KEBS276W	3180225	3180227	NA	NA	NA	NA	NA	NA
*KEBS276S	4169394	4169395	4164815	4164820	4169391	4164818	4164819	4164816
*KEBS277W	3180225	3180227	NA	NA	NA	NA	NA	NA
*KEBS277S	4169394	4169395	4164815	4164820	4169391	4164818	4164819	4164816
*KEBI200V	814070	814069	NA	NA	NA	NA	NA	NA
KGBS146S	4169392	4169393	4164806	4164814	4164810	4164809	4164812	4164807
*KGBS246S	4169392	4169393	4164806	4164814	4164810	4164809	4164812	4164807

*Double ovens require two (2) door panels.

Oven Cavities
All dimensions in inches (centimeters)

	Width	Height	Depth (door closed)
24-in. Thermal Oven	17½ (44.5)	15 (38.1)	17¾ (45.1)
27-in. Thermal Oven	19½ (49.5)	15 (38.1)	17¾ (45.1)
27-in. Thermal-Convection Oven	19½ (49.5)	15 (38.1)	16⅛ (41.3)
30-in. Thermal Oven	22 (55.9)	16¾ (42.5)	18¼ (46.4)
Microwave Oven – 27-in. Combination	14¾ (37.5)	10⅛ (25.7)	16¼ (41.3)
Microwave Oven – 30-in. Combination	16⅞ (42.9)	9⅞ (25.1)	13⅞ (35.2)
Microwave/Convection Oven – 27-in. Combination	15½ (39.4)	10¼ (26)	16⅝ (42.2)

Built-In Ovens

	Electric															Gas	
Model No. Configuration	KEBI141W Single	KEBI171W Single	KEBI100V Single	KEBI241W Double	KEBI271W Double	KEBI200V Double	KEBS146W Single	KEBS176W Single	KEBS246W Double	KEBS276W Double	KEBS177W Single	KEBS277W Double	KEMI371T Comb.	KEMI300T Comb.	KEMS376T Comb.	KGBS146S Single	KGBS246S Double
Size	24″	27″	30″	24″	27″	30″	24″	27″	24″	27″	27″	27″	27″	30″	27″	24″	24″
Thermal	1	1	1	2	2	2	1	1	2	2	—	1	1	1	1	1	2
Thermal/Convection	—	—	—	—	—	—	—	—	—	—	1	1	—	—	—	—	—
Microwave-Convection	—	—	—	—	—	—	—	—	—	—	—	—	—	—	1	—	—
Microwave	—	—	—	—	—	—	—	—	—	—	—	—	1	1	—	—	—
Turntable	—	—	—	—	—	—	—	—	—	—	—	—	—	—	•	—	—
Whole Meat Cooking Rack	—	—	—	—	—	—	—	—	—	—	—	—	•	•	—	—	—
Two Element Balanced Baking/Roasting	•	•	•	•	•	•	•	•	•	•	•	•	•	•	•	—	—
Automatic Time Baking	•	•	•	Upper	Upper	Upper	•	•	•	•	•	•	•	•	•	•	•
Electronic Clock	•	•	•	•	•	•	•	•	•	•	•	•	•	•	•	•	•
Variable Temp. Broiling	•	•	•	Upper	Upper	•	•	•	•	•	•	•	•	•	•	•	•
Open or Closed Door Broiling	•	•	•	•	•	•	•	•	•	•	•	•	•	•	•	•	•
Porcelain Broiler Pan/ Chrome Grill	1	1	1	1	1	1	1	1	1	1	1	1	1	1	1	1	1
Variable Self-Cleaning Oven	•	•	•	Upper	Upper	Upper	•	•	Upper & Lower	Upper & Lower	•	Upper & Lower	Lower	Lower	Lower	—	—
Standard Clean Oven	—	—	—	Lower	Lower	Lower	—	—	—	—	—	—	—	—	—	•	Upper & Lower
Rotisserie	—	—	—	—	—	Upper	•	•	Upper	Upper	—	—	—	—	•	•	•
Temp. Probe	—	—	—	—	—	—	•	•	Upper	Upper	•	Upper	—	—	Lower	•	Upper
Racks	2	2	2	2 Upper 2 Lower	2 Upper 2 Lower	2 Upper 2 Lower	2	2	2 Upper 2 Lower	2 Upper 2 Lower	3	3 Upper 1 Lower	2 Lower	2 Lower	2 Upper 2 Lower	2	2 Upper 2 Lower
Molded in Rack Guides	•	•	•	•	•	•	•	•	•	•	•	•	Lower Only	Lower Only	Lower Only	•	•
Power "On" Light	—	—	—	—	—	—	•	•	•	•	•	•	—	—	•	•	•
Interior Light	•	•	•	•	•	•	•	•	•	•	•	•	•	•	•	•	•
Window	•	•	•	•	•	•	•	•	•	•	•	•	•	•	•	•	•
Minute Timer	•	•	•	•	•	•	•	•	•	•	•	•	•	•	•	•	•
Reinforced Porcelain Interior	•	•	•	•	•	•	•	•	•	•	•	•	Lower Only	Lower Only	Lower Only	•	•
High Density Insulation	•	•	•	•	•	•	•	•	•	•	•	•	•	•	•	•	•
Smoke Eliminator	•	•	•	•	•	•	•	•	•	•	•	•	•	•	•	—	—
Pilotless Electric Ignition	—	—	—	—	—	—	—	—	—	—	—	—	—	—	—	•	•
Weight (Approx.) Pounds Kilograms	136 (61.2)	141 (63.5)	136 (61.2)	219 (98.6)	227 (102.2)	220 (99)	144 (64.8)	147 (66.2)	245 (110.3)	253 (113.9)	152 (68.4)	260 (117)	253 (113.8)	228 (102.6)	272 (122.4)	168 (75.6)	258 (116.1)
Shipping Weight – Pounds Kilograms	156 (70.2)	162 (72.9)	156 (70.2)	246 (110.7)	257 (115.7)	250 (112.5)	164 (73.8)	168 (75.6)	272 (122.4)	283 (127.4)	173 (77.9)	290 (130.5)	283 (127.4)	258 (116.1)	302 (135.9)	188 (84.6)	287 (129.2)

Electric built-in ovens – Dimensions and Installation Data

All dimensions shown in inches (centimeters), weights in pounds (kilograms).

	Overall Dimensions					Cutout Dimensions			Electrical Data			Weights (approx.)	
			Depth (back to front)										
Model	Width (side to side)	Height (bottom to top)	Door Closed (to edge of door)	Door Closed (to edge of handle)	Door Open	Width (side to side)	Height (bottom to top)	Depth (min.) (back to front)	KW 240V	KW 208V	Circuit Amps (min.)	Net	Shipping
KEBI141W KEBS146W	24 (61)	29¾ (75.6)	26⅛ (66.4)	28¼ (71.8)	43¾ (111.1)	22½ (57.2)	28½ (72.4)	23⅝ (60.0)	3.1	2.3	30	131 (59) 136 (61.2)	150 (67.5) 155 (69.8)
KEBI171W KEBS176W	26 (66)	29¾ (75.6)	26⅛ (66.4)	28¼ (71.8)	43¾ (111.1)	24½ (62.2)	28½ (72.4)	23⅝ (60.0)	3.1	2.3	30	143 (64.4) 148 (66.6)	162 (72.9) 167 (75.2)
KEBS177W	26 (66)	29¾ (75.6)	26⅛ (66.4)	28¼ (71.8)	43¾ (111.1)	24½ (62.2)	28½ (72.4)	23⅝ (60.0)	3.1	2.3	30	153 (68.9)	172 (77.4)
KEBI100V	29⅝ (75.2)	32 7/16 (82.4)	25¼ (64.1)	27⅜ (69.5)	46½ (118.1)	28½ (72.4)	31⅝ (80.3)	23 (58.4)	5.6	4.2	30	136 (61.2)	156 (70.2)
KEBI241W KEBS246W	24 (61)	50⅞ (129.2)	26⅛ (66.4)	28¼ (71.8)	43¾ (111.1)	22½ (57.2)	49 (124.5)	23⅝ (60.0)	6.1	4.6	40	223 (100.4) 228 (102.6)	253 (113.9) 258 (116.1)
KEBI271W KEBS276W	26 (66)	50⅞ (129.2)	26⅛ (66.4)	28¼ (71.8)	43¾ (111.1)	24½ (62.2)	49 (124.5)	23⅝ (60.0)	6.1	4.6	40	235 (105.8) 244 (109.8)	265 (119.3) 274 (123.3)
KEBS277W	26 (66)	50⅞ (129.2)	26⅛ (66.4)	28¼ (71.8)	43¾ (111.1)	24½ (62.2)	49 (124.5)	23⅝ (60.0)	6.1	4.6	40	248 (111.6)	278 (125.1)
KEBI200V	29⅝ (75.8)	57⅜ (145.7)	25¼ (64.1)	27⅜ (69.5)	46½ (118.1)	28½ (72.4)	56 9/16 (143.7)	23 (58.4)	9.6	7.6	40	220 (99)	250 (112.5)
KEMI371T	26 (66)	50⅛ (127.3)	26½ (67.3)	28⅝ (72.7)	44½ (113)	24½ (62.2)	49 (124.5)	24 (61)	7.9	6.7	40	253 (113.8)	283 (127.4)
KEMS376T	26 (66)	50⅛ (127.3)	26½ (67.3)	28⅝ (72.7)	44½ (113)	24½ (62.2)	49 (124.5)	24 (61)	5.6	4.6	30	272 (122.4)	302 (135.9)
KEMI300T	29⅞ (75.9)	46 11/16 (118.6)	25¼ (64.1)	27⅜ (69.5)	46½ (118.1)	28½ (72.4)	46¼ (117.5)	23 (58.4)	8.3	6.9	40	228 (102.6)	258 (116.1)

Separate 3-wire with ground circuit required. 4 foot (121.9cm) flexible steel conduit with product. Dual Rated 240-208/120 Volts AC, 60 Hertz.
Minimum distance between cutout and cabinet doors: 24-in. and 27-in. models, 2½ in. (6.4 cm); 30-in models, 1¼ in. (3.2 cm).

Gas Built-In Ovens – Dimensions and Installation Data

All dimensions shown in inches (centimeters), weights in pounds (kilograms).

	Overall Dimensions					Cutout Dimensions			Electrical/Gas Data	Weights (approx.)	
			Depth (back to front)								
Model	Width* (side to side)	Height* (bottom to top)	Door Closed (to edge of door)	Door Closed (to edge of handle)	Door Open	Width (side to side)	Height (bottom to top)	Depth (min.) (back to front)	Circuit Amps (min.)	Net	Shipping
KGBS146S	24 (61)	31 7/16 (79.9)	26½ (67.3)	28⅝ (72.7)	44½ (113)	22½ (57.2)	31⅛ (79.1)	24 (61)	15	168 (75.6)	188 (84.6)
KGBS246S	24 (61)	52⅛ (132.4)	26½ (67.3)	28⅝ (72.7)	44½ (113)	22½ (57.2)	51¾ (131.4)	24 (61)	15	258 (116.1)	287(129.2)

Separate 2-wire with ground circuit required. 3½ foot (106.7cm) 120 Volts AC, 60 Hertz. 3-wire cord, 3-prong plug with product (for ignition).
Natural Gas – AS SHIPPED. LP Gas – convert to with STANDARD regulator.
*Add 1 inch (2.54 cm) to Width and ¾ inch (1.91 cm) to Height with exterior trim installed. Minimum distance between cutout and cabinet doors, 2½ in. (6.4).
Dimensions are for planning only. For complete details, see installation instructions packed with product. Specifications subject to change without notice.

KitchenAid microwave ovens are specially designed to be installed in combination with KitchenAid built-in electric ovens. So you can create a microwave/built-in oven combination custom made for the way *you* cook. Optional trim kits are available for installations above 24-inch, 27-inch and 30-inch KitchenAid built-in electric ovens. If you prefer, hang your KitchenAid microwave oven on a wall, using the Wall Mount Kit.

Model KCMS135S Microwave Oven shown installed above Thermal-Convection™ Single Oven

Model KCMS132S
- 1.3 cu. ft. capacity.
- Easy-to-use solid-state touch controls provide up to 100 min. of cooking or defrosting time.
- Temperature Probe cooks foods to preset internal temperature automatically.
- Variable Power Control delivers up to 700 watts.
- Automatic Rapid Defrost.
- WARM/HOLD setting.
- AUTO COOK Cycle with Cook/Reheat setting cooks foods automatically with no guessing at cooking times, no probes.
- Delay Start option.
- Interior light.
- Black glass see-through window; pewter grained wrapper.
- Whole Meal Cooking Rack optional.

Model KCMS135S
All the quality features of model KCMS132S PLUS
- AUTO COOK Cycle adds Slow Cook/ Simmer and Cook/Frozen settings.
- PAUSE setting.
- Whole Meal Cooking Rack standard.

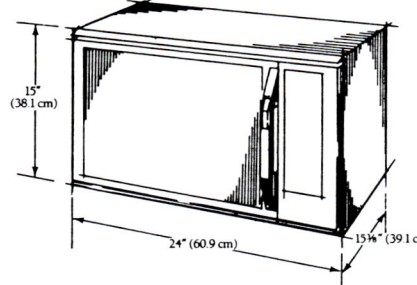

15" (38.1 cm)
24" (60.9 cm)
15⅜" (39.1 cm)

Dimensions and Installation Data
All dimensions shown in inches (centimeters), weights in pounds (kilograms)

| Model | Oven Cavity | | | Electrical Data | Weights (approx.) | |
	Width	Height	Depth	Circuit Amps (min.)	Net	Shipping
KCMS132S	16⅞ (42.9)	9⅞ (25.1)	13⅞ (35.2)	15	59 (26.6)	67 (30.2)
KCMS135S	16⅞ (42.9)	9⅞ (25.1)	13⅞ (35.2)	15	60 (27.0)	68 (30.6)

2-wire with ground circuit required. 4½ ft. (137.2 cm) 120 Volts AC, 60 Hertz. 3-wire cord, 3-prong plug. 700 watts.

Optional Kits

	Black	White	Almond
24-In. Built-In	832989	–	–
27-In. Built-In Trim	832991	815031	815032
30-In. Built-In Trim	832987	–	–
Wall Mount		832993	
Opt. Whole Meal Rack		832985	

Dimensions are for planning only. For complete details, see installation instructions packed with product.

Glass surface cooktops 30-Inch Electric
Model KECT305V

- Even-Heat Cast-Iron Elements – two 6-in. and two 7-in.
- Push-to-Turn Infinite-Heat Controls with Power Track Guides.
- "Lower-than-Low" Simmer.
- Built-in overheat protection.
- Tempered-glass top available in Black, White or Almond.
- Four Power "ON" lights.
- "Universal" overall/cutout size – fits virtually any 30-in. cutout.

Conventional cooktops 30-Inch Electric
Model KECS100S

- Two 6-in. and two 8-in. High-Speed Plug-In Elements; right front is 8-in. POWER™ Burner.
- Push-to-Turn Infinite-Heat Controls.
- Total Easy-Clean Design with exclusive Triple-Action Concealed Hinges.
- "Universal" overall/cutout size — fits virtually any 30-in. cutout.
- Available in Onyx Black, Almond or White Porcelain or Brushed Chrome.

30-Inch Gas
Model KGCS100S

Identical to model KECS100S except:
- Exclusive DAISY® Burners. Two rated 8,000 BTU Natural Gas/7,000 BTU LP; two are POWER™ Burners rated 12,000 BTU Natural Gas/10,000 BTU LP.
- Individual pilotless electric ignition for each burner.

Specifications subject to change without notice.

36-Inch Electric
Model KECT365V

Identical to model KECT305V except:
- Even-Heat Cast-Iron Elements – two 6-in., one 7-in., and one 9-in. POWER™ Burner.
- "Universal" overall/cutout size – fits virtually any 33-in. or 36-in. cutout.

30-Inch Gas
Model KGCT305T

- Four sealed burners – two POWER™ Burners.
- Push-to-Turn Infinite-Heat Controls with Power Track Guides.
- Tempered-glass top available in Black, White or Almond.
- Pilotless electronic ignition, automatic reignition. (120 volt electric service required.)
- "Universal" overall/cutout size – fits virtually any 30-in. cutout.
- LP gas converter, part no. 4175385.

36-Inch Gas
Model KGCT365T

Identical to model KGCT305V except:
- "Universal" overall/cutout size — fits virtually any 33-in. or 36-in. cutout.

36-Inch Electric
Model KECS160S

All the quality features of model KECS100S
PLUS
- Raised tempered-glass control panel.
- 144-sq.-in. wood work-surface insert.
- "Universal" overall/cutout size — fits virtually any 33-in. or 36-in. cutout.
- Optional Brushed Chrome work-surface-insert cover, part no. 4164377.

36-Inch Electric with Grill/Griddle
Model KECG260S

- Grill/Griddle has big 144-sq.-in. commercially finished grate for grilling. Griddle has same stick-resistant finish.
- Two 6-in. and two 8-in. High-Speed Plug-In Elements; right front is 8-in. POWER™ Burner.
- Push-to-Turn Infinite-Heat Controls.
- Total Easy-Clean Design with exclusive Triple-Action Concealed Hinges.
- "Universal" overall/cutout size — fits virtually any 33-in. or 36-in. cutout.

36-Inch.Gas with Grill/Griddle
Model KGCG260S

(Shown with optional Electric 5th element).

Identical to model KECG260S except:
- Exclusive DAISY® Burners. Two rated 8,000 BTU Natural Gas/7,000 BTU LP; two are POWER™ Burners rated 12,000 BTU Natural Gas/10,000 BTU LP.
- Individual pilotless electric ignition for each burner (120-volt electric service required).

Optional Cast-Iron 5th Element

Increase cooking capacity in KitchenAid built-in cooktops with grill/griddles using this optional cartridge that plugs into the grill area. 7-in. Cast-Iron Element is permanently sealed into the black tempered-glass surface.

Part No. 4173224 for use with KECG260S (requires 240 volt electric service).

Part No. 4173225 for use with KGCG260S (requires 120 volt electric service).

36-Inch Gas
Model KGCS160S

Identical to model KGCS100S except:
- Raised tempered-glass control panel.
- 144-sq.-in. wood work-surface insert.
- "Universal" overall/cutout size — fits virtually any 33-in. or 36-in. cutout.
- Optional Brushed Chrome work-surface-insert cover, part no. 4164377.

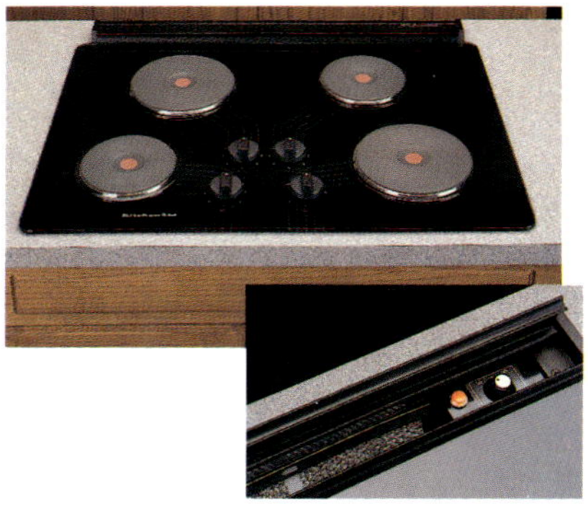

Add downdraft exhaust capability to any KitchenAid built-in cooktop, electric or gas, 30 in. or 36 in., with a Downdraft Vent System made up of an Intake/Plenum and a Power Unit. For example, equipping a KitchenAid 36-inch cooktop with

downdraft venting using an exterior power unit requires:

Intake/Plenum KIVD860T
Exterior Mount Power Unit KPED890T

The Power Unit can be mounted on the roof by adding Roof Mount Kit, part no. 4173296.

2 Intake/Plenums...match size to cooktop

Model KIVD800T
30-Inch Intake/Plenum (for 30-inch electric or gas cooktops)

Model KIVD860T
36-Inch Intake/Plenum (for 36-inch electric or gas cooktops)

- Air Intake Cover available in Black, White or Almond.
- Variable Speed Control.
- Power "ON" Light.
- 2 Removable Grease Filters can be washed in dishwasher or sink.
- Includes plenum support brackets.

2 Power Units...for interior or exterior mounting

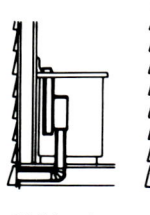

Model KPID850T
Interior/Cabinet Mount Power Unit
- Blower assembly with 6-in. Round Outlet.
- 6-in. Round Wall Cap.
- 6-in. Round or 3¼-in. x 10-in. Rectangular Ducting required. Maximum recommended duct run, 25 ft.
- 3-way vertical or horizontal venting capability.
- 450 CFM (approx.).

Model KPED 890T
Exterior Mount Power unit
- Blower assembly.
- 9-in. Round Take-Off.
- 9-in. Round In-Line Damper.
- 9-in. Round or 3¼-in. x 14-in. Rectangular Ducting required. Maximum recommended duct run, 55 ft.
- 180° venting capability.
- 900 CFM (approx.).

Roof Mount Kit

Part No. 4173296
If Exterior Power Unit is to be roof mounted, installation will require Roof Mount Kit in addition to Exterior Power Unit and appropriate Intake/Plenum. Kit includes protective cap and flashing.

Power Unit Electrical Requirements: 120-volt AC, 60 Hz. 15-amp. circuit for vent system only; cooktop requires separate circuit.

Power Unit installation methods

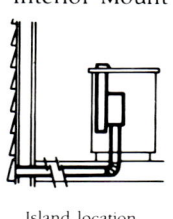

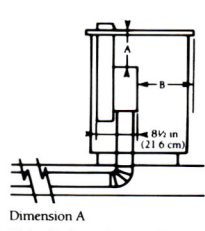

Interior Mount

Wall location   Island location

Dimension A
Right discharge 6 in. (15.2 cm)
Bottom discharge 7 in. (17.8 cm)
Left discharge 8 in. (20.3 cm)
Subtract 3¼ in. (8.3 cm) for burner box clearance with all KitchenAid cooktops.
Dimension B

| Electric | 16¾ in. (42.5 cm) |
| Gas | 16¼ in. (41.3 cm) |

Exterior Mount

Wall location   Island location   Roof location

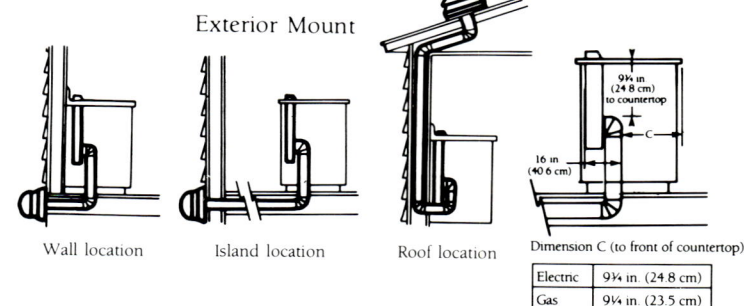

Dimension C (to front of countertop)

| Electric | 9¾ in. (24.8 cm) |
| Gas | 9¼ in. (23.5 cm) |

Basic dimensions and installation data
All dimensions shown in inches (centimeters), weights in pounds (kilograms).

Downdraft Vent Systems	OVERALL WIDTH Intake Only (Side to Side)	DEPTH Intake Only (Back to Front)	HEIGHT Intake/Plenum (Bottom to Top)	WIDTH with Cooktop (Side to Side)	DEPTH with Cooktop (Back to Front)	CUTOUT WIDTH with Cooktop (Side to Side)	DEPTH with Cooktop (Back to Front)	APPROX. WEIGHTS NET	SHIPPING
Intake/Plenum KIVD800T — 30-in. (for 30-in. KitchenAid electric and gas built-in cooktops)	28¾ (73.0)	2¼ (5.7)	23 (58.4)	30¾ (78.1)	24⅛ (61.3)	27 (68.5)	22¼ (56.5)	22 (9.9)	23 (10.4)
KIVD860T — 36-in. (for 36-in. KitchenAid electric and gas built-in cooktops)	35 (88.9)	2¼ (5.7)	23 (58.4)	36 (91.4)	24⅛ (61.3)	33¼ (84.5)	22¼ (56.5)	24 (10.8)	26 (11.7)
KPID850T — Interior	—	—	—	—	—	—	—	25 (11.3)	27 (12.2)
KPED890T — Exterior	—	—	—	—	—	—	—	22 (9.9)	24 (10.8)

Dimensions for planning only. For complete details, see installation instructions packed with product.   Specificiations subject to change without notice.

Modular Downdraft Cooktops

Model KECM860T with standard Griddle and optional Sealed Cast-Iron Element Plug-In Modules.

Model KECM860T with standard Grill and optional Open-Coil Element Plug-In Modules

Model KGCM860T with standard DAISY® Burner and Grill Modules.

36-Inch Electric Modular Downdraft Cooktop
Model KECM860T

- Plug-In Grill Module with Griddle for right or left side use. Both grill and griddle have non-stick finish. High-speed plug-in element, porcelain flavor generator plate, porcelain pan and removable grease pan.
- Tempered Glass Control panel with black trim.
- Push-to-Turn Infinite-Heat Controls.
- Power "ON" Light.
- Vent System Control with 2-speed fan.
- Center Vent System offers two-way (vertical or horizontal) venting capability. 6-in. round or ¾-in. x 10-in. rectangular ducting required.
- Total Easy-Clean Design – vent cover, twin filters, grills and grease well can be removed and washed in the dishwasher. Control panel and knobs are removable also. Raised edge all around helps keep spills on top of the cooktop where they're easy to wipe up.

Optional Accessories
Open-Coil Element Plug-In Module incorporates one 8-in. and one 6-in. high-speed plug-in element with removable chrome drip bowls in Black porcelain top. For right or left side use. Order model KECK80TBL.

Sealed Cast-Iron Element Plug-In Module includes one 7-in. and one 6-in. element in Black Glass top with Black porcelain trim. For right or left side installation. Order model KECK85TBL.

Plug-In Grill Module, identical to standard supplied module. Order part no. 4314994.

Accessory Griddle, identical to standard supplied griddle. Order part no. 786100.

Replacement Grease Filters, two to a package. Order part no. 786235.

36-Inch Gas Modular Downdraft Cooktop
Model KGCM860T

Featured similarly to electric downdraft model KECM860T except:

- Plug-In Grill module with Griddle for right side use only. Both Grill and Griddle have non-stick finish. Dual burners, rated 16,000 BTU natural gas/14,000 BTU LP gas. Heavy-duty black grates, porcelain pan and removable grease pan.
- DAISY® Burner module (for left side position only) incorporates one six-tower burner rated 11,000 BTU natural gas/ 9,000 BTU LP gas and one four-tower burner rated 8,000 BTU natural gas/7,000 BTU LP gas.
- Pilotless electric ignition (120 volt electric service required).
- Brushed Chrome finish with Black Trim.

Optional Accessories
DAISY® Burner Plug-In Module (for right side position only) includes two four-tower burners, each rated 8,000 BTU natural gas/7,000 BTU LP gas. Order model no. KGCK80TBL.

Accessory Griddle, identical to standard supplied griddle. Order part no. 786100.

Replacement Grease Filters, two to a package. Order part no. 786235.

How to determine venting system length

Add the equivalent length in feet of each fitting used in the system to the length of feet of straight duct used. The total, which should not exceed 26 ft., will be the calculated length of the venting system.

Downdrafts

Equivalent Lengths

Fitting	Equivalent Length (Ft.)
6″ Systems	
3¼″ x 10″ (12″) to 6″	4.5
3¼″ x 10″ (12″) to 6″ – 90° elbow	5
6″ to 3¼″ x 10″ (12″) – 90° elbow	9
90° elbow	5
6″ to 3¼″ x 10″ (12″)	1
45° elbow	2.5
6″ wall cap	0
3¼″ x 10″ Systems	
3¼″ x 10″ to 6″	4.5
6″ to 3¼″ x 10″ – 90° elbow	6
6″ to 3¼″ x 10″	1
3¼″ x 10″ – 90° elbow	5
3¼″ x 10″ – flat elbow	12
3¼″ x 10″ – wall cap	0
9″ Systems	
3¼″ x 14″ to 9″	4.5
3¼″ x 14″ to 9″ – 90° elbow	5.0
9″ to 3¼″ x 14″ – 90° elbow	9.0
90° elbow	5.0
9″ to 3¼″ x 14″	1.0
45° elbow	2.5

Index of recommended standard fittings

6″ Systems: Equivalent length of 6″ Duct

3¼″ x 10″ Systems: Equivalent length of 3¼″ x 10″ Duct

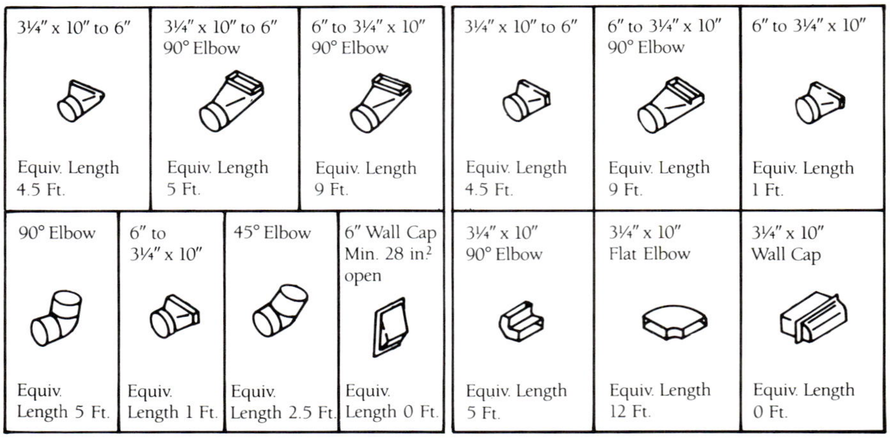

3¼″ x 10″ to 6″
Equiv. Length 4.5 Ft.
3¼″ x 10″ to 6″ 90° Elbow
Equiv. Length 5 Ft.
6″ to 3¼″ x 10″ 90° Elbow
Equiv. Length 9 Ft.
3¼″ x 10″ to 6″
Equiv. Length 4.5 Ft.
6″ to 3¼″ x 10″ 90° Elbow
Equiv. Length 9 Ft.
6″ to 3¼″ x 10″
Equiv. Length 1 Ft.
90° Elbow
Equiv. Length 5 Ft.
6″ to 3¼″ x 10″
Equiv. Length 1 Ft.
45° Elbow
Equiv. Length 2.5 Ft.
6″ Wall Cap Min. 28 in.² open
Equiv. Length 0 Ft.
3¼″ x 10″ 90° Elbow
Equiv. Length 5 Ft.
3¼″ x 10″ Flat Elbow
Equiv. Length 12 Ft.
3¼″ x 10″ Wall Cap
Equiv. Length 0 Ft.

Use 6″ or 3¼″ x 10″ duct on island or peninsula installations.
For best performance, it is suggested that no more than three 90° elbows with 6″ or 3¼″ x 10″ duct be used.

Electric and Gas Modular Downdraft Cooktops.
Basic Dimensions and Installation Data

All dimensions are shown in inches (centimeters), weights in pounds (kilograms).

BUILT-IN MODULAR DOWNDRAFT COOKTOPS	BASIC OVERALL DIMENSIONS: WIDTH (side to side)	DEPTH (back to front)	HEIGHT (bottom to top)	BASIC CUTOUT DIMENSIONS: WIDTH (side to side)	DEPTH (back to front)	ELECTRIC/GAS DATA: KW 240V	KW 208V	CIRCUIT AMPS (min.)	APPROX. WEIGHT: NET	SHIPPING
KECM860T – 36-in. Electric	36 (91.4)	21 (53.3)	16½ (41.9)	34¾ (88.3)	20⅛ (51.1)	7.0	—	40	73 (32.9)	77 (34.7)
KGCM860T – 36-in. Gas	36 (91.4)	21 (53.3)	16½ (41.9)	34¾ (88.3)	20⅜ (51.8)	—	—	15	102 (45.9)	106 (47.7)

Electric
- Separate 2-wire with ground circuit required – hard wired
- 240 Volts AC 60 Hertz

Gas
- Separate 2-wire with ground circuit required
- 120 Volts AC 60 Hertz (for ignition)
- Natural Gas – as shipped
- LP Gas – convert with standard regulator

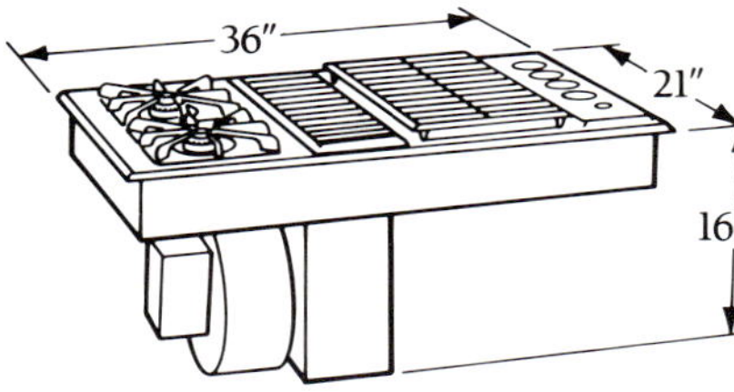

36″
21″
16½″

THROUGH-THE-FLOOR INSTALLATION
(PENINSULA OR ISLAND INSTALLATION SHOWN)

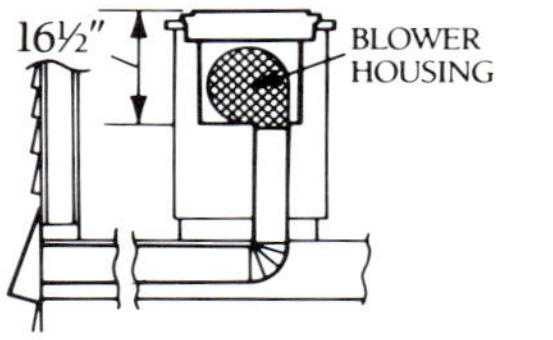

16½″
BLOWER HOUSING

THROUGH-THE-WALL INSTALLATION
(OUTSIDE WALL INSTALLATION SHOWN)

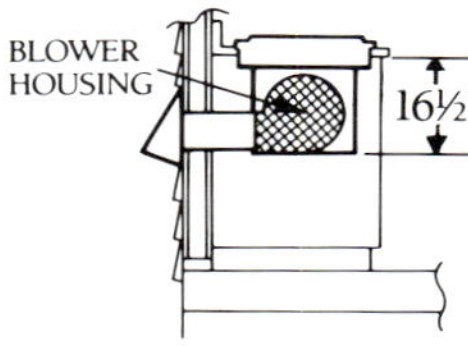

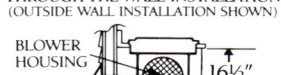

BLOWER HOUSING
16½″

Cooktop Dimensions

All dimensions in inches (centimeters), weights in pounds (kilograms).

Electric	OVERALL: Width (side to side)	Depth (back to front)	** Height	CUTOUT: Width (side to side)	Depth (back to front)	Height (min.)	ELECTRIC DATA: KW 240V	KW 208V	Circuit Amps (min.)	WEIGHTS (Approx.): Net	Shipping
KECS100S*	30¾ (78.1)	21¾ (55.2)	4 (10.2)	26½ (67.3) to 29⅝ (75.2)	18¾ (47.6) to 20⅝ (52.4)	3 (7.6)	7.2	5.4†	40	29 (13.1)	43 (19.4)
KECS160S*	36 (91.4)	21¾ (55.2)	4 (10.2)	33 (83.8) to 34⅞ (88.6)	18¾ (47.6) to 20⅝ (52.4)	3 (7.6)	7.2	5.4†	40	42 (18.9)	55 (24.8)
KECG260S*							9.0	6.8†	50	50 (22.5)	64 (28.8)
KECT305V*	30¾ (78.1)	21¾ (55.2)	4 (10.2)	26½ (67.3) to 29⅝ (75.2)	18¾ (47.6) to 20⅝ (52.4)	3 (7.6)	7.0	—	40	41 (18.5)	50 (22.5)
KECT365V*	36 (91.4)	21¾ (55.2)	4 (10.2)	33 (83.8) to 34⅞ (88.6)	18¾ (47.6) to 20⅝ (52.4)	3 (7.6)	8.1	—	40	52 (23.4)	64 (28.8)
Gas											
KGCS100S	30¾ (78.1)	21¾ (55.2)	4¼ (10.8)	26½ (67.3) to 29⅝ (75.2)	18¾ (47.6) to 20⅝ (52.4)	3¼ (8.3)	—	—	15***	44 (19.8)	64 (28.8)
KGCS160S	36 (91.4)	21¾ (55.2)	4¼ (10.8)	33 (83.8) to 34⅞ (88.6)	18¾ (47.6) to 20⅝ (52.4)	3¼ (8.3)	—	—	15***	60 (27.0)	76 (34.2)
KGCG260S							—	—	20***	70 (31.5)	86 (38.7)
KGCT305T	30¾ (78.1)	21¾ (55.2)	4½	26½ (67.3) to 29⅝ (75.2)	18¾ (47.6) to 20⅝ (52.4)	3¼ (8.3)	—	—	15***	62 (28.1)	71 (32.2)
KGCT365T	36 (91.4)	21¾ (55.2)	4½	33 (83.8) to 34⅞ (88.6)	18¾ (47.6) to 20⅝ (52.4)	3¼ (8.3)	—	—	15***	70 (31.5)	80 (36.3)

Separate 2-wire with ground circuit required. • Dual rated (open-coil element models) 240-208 Volts AC, 60 Hertz.

*4 foot (121.9 cm) flexible steel conduit with product.

**Power/Fuel supply connections extend below cooktop and are not included in Overall Height dimension.

***3½ ft. (106.7 cm) 120 Volts AC, 60 Hertz, 3 wire cord, 3 prong plug with product (for ignition).

†Special higher wattage 208V open-coil elements available:
- 6 in., Part No. 3177639
- 8 in., POWER™ Burner, Part No. 3177296
- 8 in., Part No. 3177292
- Grill (KECG260S only), Part No. 3177526

Dimensions are for planning only. For complete details, see installation instructions packed with product. Specifications subject to change without notice.

Model KHMC106W Microwave/Convection Hood installed above Model KEDT105V Electric Drop-In Range.

Dimensions are for planning only. For complete details see installation instructions packed with product. Specifications subject to change without notice.

Model KEDT105V (shown)
Cooktop Features
- Two 6-in. and two 7-in. Even-Heat Cast-Iron Elements with built-in overheat protection.
- Push-to-Turn Infinite-Heat Controls.
- "Lower-than-Low" Simmer.
- Four Power "ON" Lights.
- Total Easy-Clean Design with no drip bowls or drip pans.

Oven Features
- Two Element Balanced Baking and Roasting.
- Microcomputer Oven Control with lighted display.
- Variable Temperature Broiling.
- Variable Self-Cleaning System.
- Two racks/four rack positions.
- Oven "ON" and interior lights.
- Removable CONSTANT COOL door with see-through window.
- Smoke eliminator…no outside venting.

- Tempered-glass cooktop, control panel and oven door available in Almond, White or Black.

Model KEDS100V
Cooktop Features
- Two 6-in. and two 8-in. High-Speed Plug-In Elements.
- Push-to-Turn Infinite-Heat Controls.
- "Lower-than-Low" Simmer.
- Two Power "ON" Lights.
- Total Easy-Clean Design – raised control area; raised edge around cooktop to help keep spills from running onto countertops; and removable elements, control knobs, drip pans, and drip pan rings.

Oven Features
The Self-Cleaning Oven is identical to model KEDT105V.

- Tempered-glass control panel and door and porcelain cooktop available in Almond, White or Black.

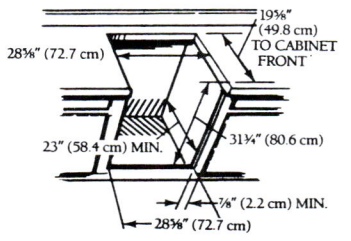

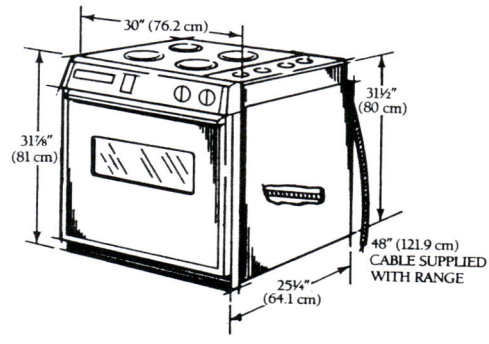

		Electrical Data			Approx. Weights – lbs. (kg)	
		KW 240V	KW 208V	Circuit Amps. (min.)	Net	Shipping
Drop-In	KEDS100V Open Coil	13.8	10.4	40	152 (68.4)	172 (77.4)
	KEDT105V Cast Iron	12.6	—	40	164 (73.8)	186 (83.7)

Drop-In models require separate 3-wire circuit with ground.

NOTE: When installing Drop-In Ranges in cabinet tops with formed front edge, shave raised section to clear 30-in. wide rim. (See sketch.) Cutout Depth is to front of cabinet, not edge of countertop.

Microwave/Hoods

Both models
- Built-in convertible ventilating system with 2-speed fan; vented or non-vented operation.
- Cooktop light.
- Easy to install.

Electrical Requirements – 120 volts, single phase, 60 Hz A.C. 15 or 20 amp. circuit.
Duct Outlet Size – 3¼ in. (8.0 cm) × 10 in. (24.5 cm).
Cooking Power – KHMS105W: 650 watts (2 liter load) @ 2450 MHz.
KHMC106W: 700 watts, microwave; 1350 watts, convection.

Microwave-Convection/Hood
Model KHMC106W (shown)
- 0.9 cu. ft. capacity.
- Solid-state microcomputer touch controls with 99-min., 99-sec. timer.
- Temperature Probe.
- Delay Start option.
- PAUSE setting.
- 5 microwave COOK cycles with preprogrammed power levels.
- EASY MINUTE setting.
- 5-selection CUSTOM DEFROST.
- 3 convection cycles…BAKE, BROIL, SLOW COOK…and 3 combination convection-microwave cycles…CUSTOM COOK, LOW MIX, HIGH MIX.
- Available in Almond, White or Black.

Microwave/Hood
Model KHMS105W
- 1.0 cu. ft. capacity.
- Solid-state microcomputer touch controls with 99-min., 99-sec. timer.
- Temperature Probe.
- Variable Power Control.
- Delay Start option.
- PAUSE setting.
- 2 COOK cycles.
- Automatic Rapid Defrost.
- AUTO SET cycle cooks foods just right without the bother of calculating time or using a Probe.
- WARM/HOLD setting.
- In-Use Reprogramming.
- Black cabinet with black-glass oven door.
- Available in Black or White.

Basic Installation Data All dimensions are shown in inches (centimeters), weights in pounds (kilograms).

	Dimensions			Approx. Weights	
	Width	Height	Depth	Net	Shipping
KHMS105W	29⅞ (75.9)	14¹³⁄₁₆ (36.3) Front; 16 (39.2) Rear	13⅞ (34.0) less handle	71 (32.0)	79 (35.6)
KHMC106W	29⅞ (75.9)	16½ (40.4)	15 (36.8)	74 (33.6)	87 (39.5)

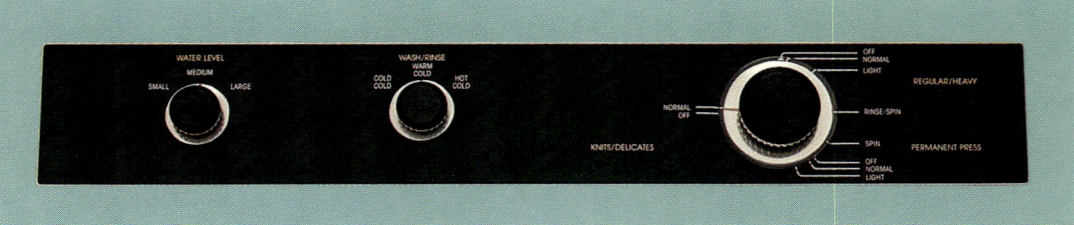

Washer
Model KAWE560W
- Easy-to-operate rotary controls.
- Extra capacity for extra-large loads of heavy fabrics.
- Three automatic cycles...HEAVY/ REGULAR, PERMANENT PRESS,

KNITS/DELICATES.
- Three wash/rinse water temperature selections...HOT/COLD, WARM/COLD, COLD/COLD.
- Three water level selections...LARGE, MEDIUM, SMALL.
- SURE-SCRUB™ Clothes Mover Agitator with Double Action Movement.

- SURE-CLEAN™ Self-Cleaning lint filter.
- Bleach and fabric softener dispensers.
- TriDura® porcelain-on-steel inner basket.
- Two spin speeds.
- QUIET SCRUB™ Sound Reduction System.
- Direct Drive wash system
- Galvanneal steel cabinet.

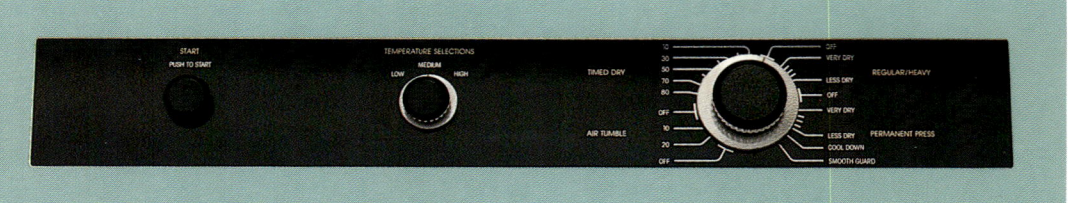

Dryer
Model KEYE660W (electric)
Model KGYE660W (gas)
- Easy to operate rotary control.
- Extra capacity, to match washer load for load.

- Four cycle selections...AUTOMATIC REGULAR, AUTOMATIC PERMANENT PRESS, TIME, AIR TUMBLE.
- SMOOTH GUARD™ clothes protection.
- Three temperature selections...HIGH, MEDIUM, LOW.

- CUSHIONED HEAT™ drying control.
- Porcelain work-surface top.
- 5,200-watt, 240/208 volt heavy duty premium alloy electric element or 22,000 BTU gas burner with pilotless electric ignition.

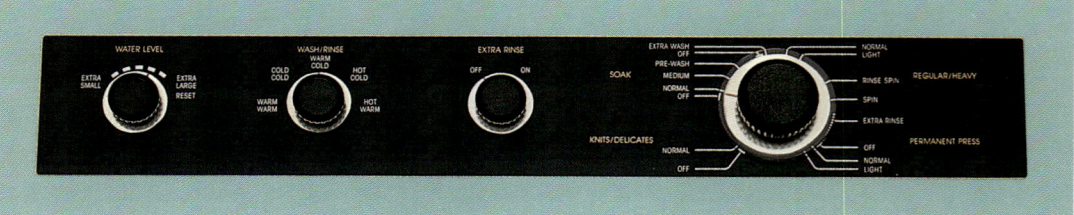

Superba™ Washer
Model KAWE860W
- Easy-to-operate rotary controls.
- Extra capacity, for extra-large loads of heavy fabrics.
- Six automatic cycles...HEAVY/REGULAR, EXTRA WASH, PERMANENT PRESS,

KNITS/DELICATES, PRE-WASH, SOAK.
- Five wash/rinse water temperature selections...HOT/WARM, HOT/COLD, WARM/WARM, WARM/COLD, COLD/COLD.
- Infinite water level control.
- EXTRA RINSE option.
- TriDura® porcelain-on-steel inner basket.

- SURE-SCRUB™ Clothes Mover Agitator with Double Action Movement.
- SURE-CLEAN™ Self-Cleaning lint filter.
- Bleach and fabric softener dispensers.
- Two wash and three spin speeds.
- WHISPER QUIET™ System.
- Direct Drive wash system.

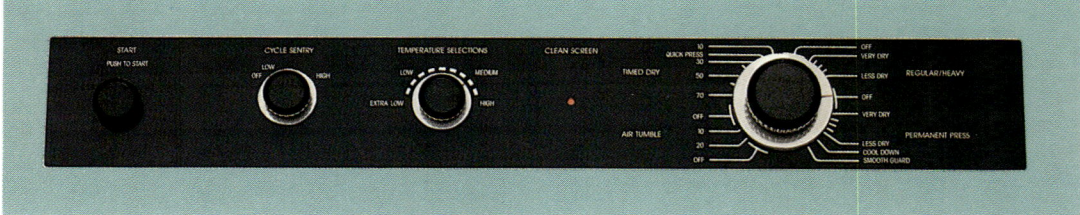

Superba™ Dryer
Model KEYE860W (electric)
Model KGYE860W (gas)
- Easy-to-operate rotary control.
- Five cycle selections...AUTOMATIC REGULAR, AUTOMATIC PERMANENT

PRESS, TIME, AIR TUMBLE, QUICK PRESS.
- Infinite temperature selection.
- CUSHIONED HEAT™ drying control.
- Adjustable CYCLE SENTRY signal.
- Visual Lint Alert signal.
- Fabric softener sheet dispenser.

- Lighted drum with drying rack.
- 5,200-watt, 240/208-volt heavy duty, premium alloy electric element or 22,000 BTU gas burner with pilotless electric ignition.

20

For information on KitchenAid Laundry Appliances not shown, see charts on page 21.

24-Inch LaundryCenter™ Washer/Dryer

Model KELC500W (electric)
Model KGLC500W (gas)
White (WH)
Almond (AL)
- Single hand-high control panel and single power cord.

Dryer
- Five cycles…AUTOMATIC REGULAR/HEAVY, AUTOMATIC PERMANENT PRESS, TIME DRY, AIR TUMBLE, QUICK PRESS.
- CUSTOM DRY Control.
- CUSHIONED HEAT™ System in Automatic cycles helps prevent overdrying.
- CYCLE SENTRY signal sounds when drying is complete.
- Electric: 3,600-watt, 240/208-volt heavy duty premium alloy element. Gas: 10,500-BTU burner with pilotless electric ignition.

Washer
- Seven automatic cycles…REGULAR, HEAVY, PERMANENT PRESS HEAVY, PERMANENT PRESS LIGHT, DELICATES, SOAK, PRE-WASH.
- Four wash/rinse water temperature selections…HOT/WARM, HOT/COLD, WARM/COLD, COLD/COLD.
- Four water level selections…EXTRA SMALL to EXTRA LARGE.

Easy to install, easy to service

Water inlet hoses, drain hose and dryer electrical connections can all be made from the front after the unit is in position. The control panel tilts out for easy access to electrical components. The unit can be vented through the floor, out the wall, or from either side. (For side exhaust, use part no. 694646.)

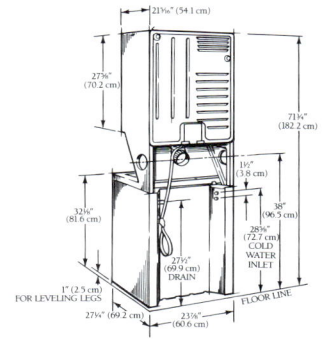

Clothes Washer Feature Comparison

	KAWE460W	KAWE560W	KAWE660W	Superba™ KAWE760W	Superba™ KAWE860W
Capacity	EXTRA 3.0 cu. ft.	EXTRA 3.0 cu. ft.	EXTRA 3.0 cu. ft.	EXTRA 3.0 cu. ft.	EXTRA 3.0 cu. ft.
Automatic Cycles	3	3	5	5	6
REGULAR/HEAVY	•	•	•	•	•
PERMANENT PRESS with Cool Down	•	•	•	•	•
KNITS/DELICATES	–	•	•	•	•
QUICK	•	–	–	–	–
PRE-WASH	–	–	•	•	•
EXTRA WASH	–	–	•	•	•
SOAK	–	–	–	–	•
EXTRA RINSE	–	–	–	–	•
Wash/Rinse Water Temp Combinations	3	3	3	4	5
Water Level Selections	3	3	4	INF	INF
Sound Reduction System	QUIET SCRUB™	QUIET SCRUB™	QUIET SCRUB™	WHISPER QUIET™	WHISPER QUIET™
Heavy-Duty Transmission & ½ HP Gold Seal Motor	1-SPEED	2-SPEED	3-SPEED	3-SPEED	3-SPEED
SURE-SCRUB™ Agitator	•	•	•	•	•
SURE-CLEAN™ Self-Cleaning Lint Filter	•	•	•	•	•
Galvanneal Steel Cabinet	•	•	•	•	•
Self-Leveling Rear Legs	•	•	•	•	•
Fabric Softener Dispenser	–	•	•	•	•
Bleach Dispenser	–	•	•	•	•
Porcelain Top/Lid	•	•	•	•	•
Water Consumption (REGULAR/HEAVY Cycle) Max. Fill – Gal. (liters)	46.2 (174.9)	46.2 (174.9)	46.2 (174.9)	46.2 (174.9)	46.2 (174.9)
Min. Fill – Gal. (liters)	31.6 (119.6)	31.6 (119.6)	31.6 (119.6)	31.6 (119.6)	31.6 (119.6)
Approx. Ship Wt. – Lbs. (kg)	179 (81.2)	179 (81.2)	179 (81.2)	179 (81.2)	179 (81.2)
10·5·2·1 Warranty	•	•	•	•	•

Clothes Dryer Feature Comparison

	KEYE560W KGYE560W	KEYE660W KGYE660W	Superba™ KEYE760W KGYE760W	Superba™ KEYE860W KGYE860W
Capacity	EXTRA 6.8 cu. ft.	EXTRA 6.8 cu. ft.	EXTRA 6.8 cu. ft.	EXTRA 6.8 cu. ft.
Cycle Selections	3	4	5	5
Automatic REGULAR/HEAVY	–	•	•	•
Automatic PERMANENT PRESS with Cool Down	–	•	•	•
REGULAR/HEAVY	•	–	–	–
PERMANENT PRESS with Cool Down	•	–	–	–
AIR TUMBLE	•	•	•	•
QUICK PRESS				
TIME DRY (Min)	0 – 110	0 – 80	0 – 70	0 – 70
Temperature Selections	2	3	4	INF
Cycle Time Display	–	–	–	•
CYCLE SENTRY™ End-of-Cycle Signal	–	•	•	Adjustable
CUSTOM DRY Control	–	Thermostatic	Electronic	Electronic
SMOOTH GUARD™ Control	–	•	•	•
CUSHIONED HEAT™ System	–	•	•	•
Porcelain Work Surface Top	•	•	•	•
Wide-Opening Hamper Door	•	•	•	•
Drum Light	–	–	•	•
CLEAN SCREEN Signal	–	–	Audible	Light
Fabric Softener Sheet Dispenser	Opt. Acc.	Opt. Acc.	Opt. Acc.	•
Dry Rack	Opt. Acc.	Opt. Acc.	Opt. Acc.	Opt. Acc.
Electric Element/Gas Burner	5,200 Watt 22,000 BTU	5,200 Watt 22,000 BTU	5,200 Watt 22,000 BTU	5,200 Watt 22,000 BTU
Approx. Ship. Wt. – Lbs. (kg)	140 (63.5)	140 (63.5)	140 (63.5)	140 (63.5)
10·5·2·1 Warranty	•	•	•	

Dimensions are for planning only. For complete details, see installation instructions packed with product.

Specifications subject to change without notice.

Washer
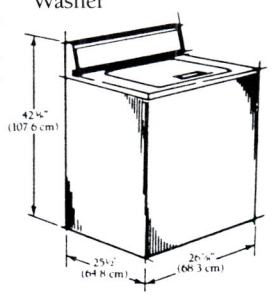

Dryer
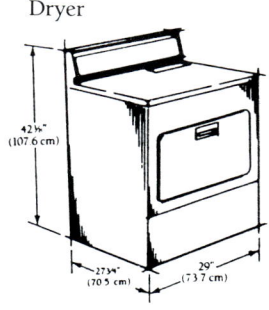

Model
KBDS250V

Model
KCDS250S

Model
KCDI250S

Model
KCDC250S

Model
KCDB250S

Model
KCDB150S

Superba™ Batch Feed Heavy-Duty Disposer
Model KBDS250V
- Easy twist fingertip control in two-piece stainless steel cover.
- Instant Energy 1 HP capacitor start motor.
- Anti-Jam automatic reversing action.
- Full Whisper Quiet polystyrene sound barrier.
- Stainless steel grind chamber and rotating shredder with two 360° swivel impellers.
- Cast high chrome shredder ring.
- Drain chamber with polypropylene corrosion resistant shield.
- Manual reset overload protector.
- 7-year full warranty.

Superba™ Continuous Feed Heavy-Duty Disposer
Model KCDS250S
- Instant Energy 1 HP capacitor start motor.
- Anti-Jam automatic reversing action.
- Full Whisper Quiet polystyrene sound barrier.
- Stainless steel grind chamber and rotating shredder with two 360° swivel impellers.
- Cash high chrome shredder ring.
- Drain chamber with polypropylene corrosion resistant shield.
- Manual reset overload protector.
- 7-year full warranty.

Imperial Continuous Feed Heavy-Duty Disposer
Model KCDI250S
- ¾ HP split phase motor
- Automatic reversing action.
- Whisper Quiet polystyrene sound barrier.
- Stainless steel grind chamber and rotating shredder with two 360° swivel impellers.
- Cast nickel chrome shredder ring.
- Drain chamber with polypropylene corrosion resistant shield.
- Manual reset overload protector.
- 5-year full warranty.

Custom Continuous Feed Disposer
Model KCDC250S
- ½ HP split phase motor.
- Stainless steel grind chamber, grind wheel, shredder ring, and sink flange.
- Two stainless steel 360° swivel impellers.
- Drain chamber with polypropylene corrosion resistant shield.
- 4-year full warranty.

Kadette Continuous Feed Disposers
Model KCDB250S (½ HP motor)
Model KCDB150S (⅓ HP motor)
- Split phase motor.
- Galvanized steel grind wheel, shredder ring, and die-cast aluminum grind chamber.
- Rotating steel shredder with two stainless steel 360° swivel impellers.
- Cast aluminum drain chamber.
- 1-year full warranty

Food Waste Disposer Specifications

	KBDS250V	KCDS250S	KCDI250S	KCDC250S	KCDB250S	KCDB150S
Type Feed	Batch	Continuous	Continuous	Continuous	Continuous	Continuous
Start Method	Cover Control	Wall Switch	Wall Switch	Wall Switch	Wall Switch	Wall Switch
Motor Type	Capacitor Start	Capacitor Start	Split Phase	Split Phase	Split Phase	Split Phase
Voltage/Cycles	120/60	120/60	120/60	115/60	115/60	115/60
Average Amps	9.0	9.0	7.6	6.7	6.7	6.1
Motor HP	1	1	¾	½	½	⅓
Motor RPM	1725	1725	1725	1725	1725	1725
Avg. Electrical Usage, KWH per Mo.	½	½	½	½	½	½
Avg. Water Usage, Gal. per Person per Day	1½	1½	1½	1½	1½	1½
Approx. Shipping Wt. – Lbs. (kg)	25 (11.3)	26 (11.7)	23 (10.4)	17 (7.7)	16 (7.2)	15 (6.8)
Drain Connection, Cushioned Slip Joint – In. (cm)	1½ (3.8)	1½ (3.8)	1½ (3.8)	1½ (3.8)	1½ (3.8)	1½ (3.8)
Dishwasher Connection	Yes	Yes	Yes	Yes	Yes	Yes

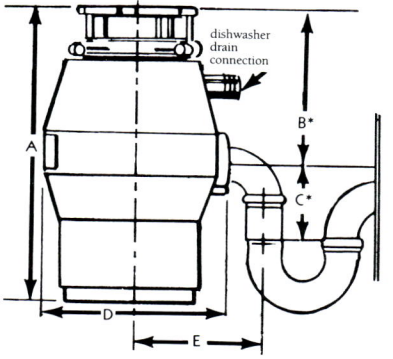

Drawing shows just one model type.

Garbage Disposer Dimensions

Model No.	A	B*	C*	D	E
KCDB150S	11⅜"	5¹⁵⁄₁₆"	4"	6⅝₁₆"	5"
KCDB250S	12⅝"	5¹⁵⁄₁₆"	4"	6⅝₁₆"	5"
KCDC250S	12¾"	6¹¹⁄₁₆"	4"	7²⁵⁄₃₂"	5¼"
KCDI250S	13⁷⁄₁₆"	6¹³⁄₁₆"	4"	9¹⁄₁₆"	5¼"
KCDS250S	13¹¹⁄₁₆"	6¹³⁄₁₆"	4"	10¹⁄₁₆"	7⅛"
KBDS250V	16¹⁄₁₆"	9⁷⁄₁₆"	4"	10¹⁄₁₆"	7⅛"

B* – Distance from bottom of sink to center line of disposer outlet. Add ½-inch when stainless steel sink is used.
C* – Length of waste line pipe from center line of disposer outlet to end of waste line pipe.
IMPORTANT: Plumb waste line to prevent standing water in the disposer motor housing.
Dimensions are for planning only. For complete details, see installation instructions packed with product.
Specifications subject to change without notice.

CHROME MODEL KHWS160VCR

ALMOND MODEL KHWS160VAL

WHITE MODEL KHWS160VWH

INSTANT-HOT® Water Dispenser MODEL KHWS160V

- Delivers 190° F water at the tap.
- Provides up to 60 cups of hot water per hour.
- Can be used in hard, soft, city or well-water areas.
- Exclusive anti-liming system helps minimize lime buildup.
- Easy to install…comes complete with everything needed for installation except length of ¼-in. O.D. copper tubing and two screws.
- 1-year full warranty.
- Approx. weight – net, 7½ lbs. (3.4 kg.); shipping, 9 lbs. (4.1 kg.).

Refrigerators and Ice Cube Maker

	10-Year Warranty LIMITED Parts Only	5-Year Warranty FULL Parts and Labor	1-Year Warranty FULL Parts and Labor
REFRIGERATORS	Sealed refrigeration system* (6th-10th year)	Sealed refrigeration system* Liner	●
BUILT-IN REFRIGERATORS	Sealed refrigeration system* (6th-10th year)	Sealed refrigeration system* Ice and water dispenser	●
ICE CUBE MAKER		Sealed refrigeration system*	●

*Sealed refrigeration system includes compressor, evaporator, condenser, drier, and connecting tubing.

Dishwashers, Trash Compactors and INSTANT-HOT® Water Dispenser

	10-Year Warranty LIMITED Parts Only (2nd-10th year)	5-Year Warranty LIMITED Parts Only (2nd-5th year)	3-Year Warranty LIMITED Parts Only (2nd-3rd year)	1-Year Warranty FULL Parts and Labor
DISHWASHERS	TRIDURA® tank and inner door	Motor	DuraKote™ nylon racks (KUDS and KUDA models)	●
TRASH COMPACTORS Model KUCS181T		Motor		●
Model KUCC151T				●
INSTANT-HOT® WATER DISPENSER				●

Built-In Ovens, Cooktops, Drop-In Ranges, Microwave Ovens and Hoods

	10-Year Warranty LIMITED Parts Only (2nd-10th year)	5-Year Warranty LIMITED Parts Only (2nd-5th year)	1-Year Warranty FULL Parts and Labor
BUILT-IN OVENS	Oven cavity and inner door	Electric elements or gas burners Magnetron tube	●
BUILT-IN COOKTOPS		Electric elements or gas burners	●
DROP-IN RANGES	Oven cavity and inner door	Electric elements	●
COUNTERTOP MICROWAVE OVENS	Magnetron tube	Electronic control	●
HOODS		Magnetron tube Convection element	●

Laundry Appliances

	10-Year Warranty LIMITED Parts Only (2nd-10th year)	5-Year Warranty LIMITED Parts Only (2nd-5th year)	2-Year Warranty LIMITED Parts Only (2nd year)	1-Year Warranty FULL Parts and Labor
CLOTHES WASHERS	Outer tub Gearcase assembly	Cabinet Electronic controls	●	●
CLOTHES DRYERS	Drum	Cabinet Electric element or gas burner Electronic controls	●	●
LAUNDRY CENTER™ WASHER/DRYER	Dryer drum Washer outer tub Washer gearcase assembly	Cabinet Electric element or gas burner	●	●

Food Waste Disposers

All KitchenAid® Food Waste Disposers carry FULL Warranties, Parts and Labor. Length of warranty varies with model.
Superba™ – 7 years. Imperial – 5 years. Custom – 4 years. Kadette – 1 year.

See Use & Care Guide for complete warranty details.

For the way it's made.™

KitchenAid • St. Joseph, Michigan 49085 U.S.A.
For more information call:
1-800-422-1230
®Registered trademark of KitchenAid
©1990 KitchenAid

KSX247

(Rev. 1090)
(CAT589) Printed in U.S.A.

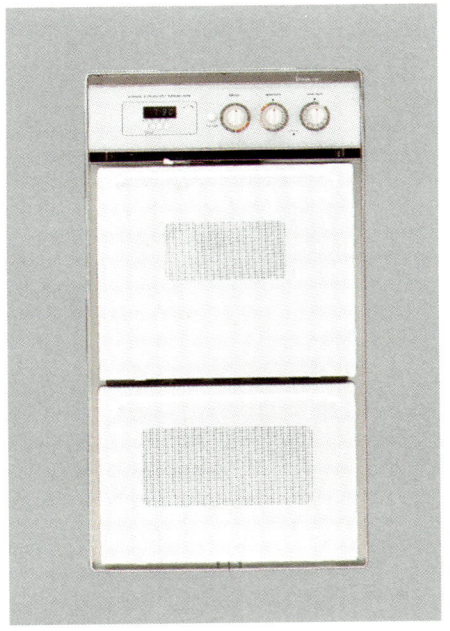

77N-5EVWW—27" Electric double oven with thin profile design for flush installation.

77N-5EVWM—27" Electric wall oven/microwave.

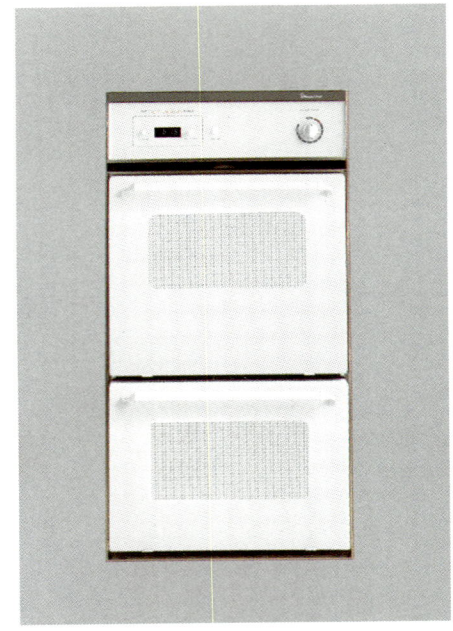

91N-4KLVW—24" Gas with continuous-clean oven (also available with standard oven—91N-4KVW).

BUILT-IN CONVENIENCE

Thin profile design
- White glass oven doors
- Self-cleaning oven
- Electronic clock
- Thin profile design for flush installation

Magic Chef®

79N-5EVW—27" Single Self-cleaning Electric with thin profile design for flush installation.

59N-5TVW—Two 30" Electric full-size ovens with electronic touch controls/thermostat; one-touch self-cleaning.

COOKTOPS

- Glass surface beauty
- Sealed burners and DuraGrates™ (Gas)
- Solid disc elements (Electric)
- Optional downdraft vent (HV30) available for electric cooktops
- Thin profile design for flush installation

82N-3K—30" Thin Profile Glass Gas Cooktop with Sealed burners/DuraGrates.™

88N-2/HV30—30" Thin Profile Glass Electric Cooktop with Solid disc heating elements (88N-2) shown with optional downdraft vent (HV30).

38N-6TVW-EV—30" Smoothtop Electric Range with electronic controls and one-touch self-cleaning oven.

34N-5TKVW-EV—30" Sealed Burner Gas Range with electronic controls and one-touch self-cleaning oven.

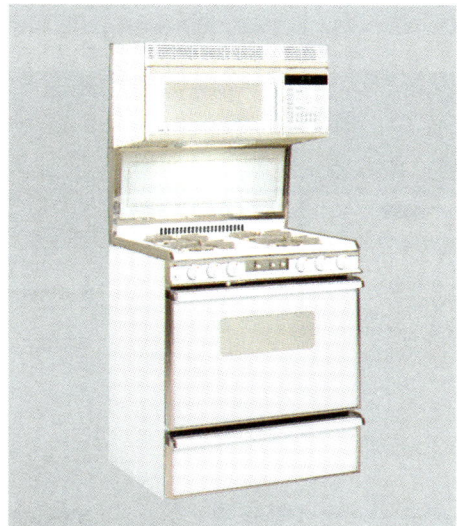

24N-7CKVWV8-EV—Eye-Level Range with full-size self-cleaning oven, cooktop with sealed burners and deluxe touch control microwave oven.

Smoothtop
- Fast-as-a-coil element
- Uses regular pots and pans
- High quality—5 year limited warranty on elements
- Easy to clean
- Electronic clock/ thermostat
- Electronic controls/ one-touch self-cleaning

Sealed Burners
- Sealed burners with 5 year warranty
- Burners are sealed to cooktop for easy cleaning
- Deluxe control knobs with infinite flame control
- High quality DuraGrates™

Infinite Flame Control

Electronic Controls
- Unique cooktop design overlays counter on both sides (does not overlap at back)
- Self-cleaning oven
- Electronic clock and oven control
- Slanted easy-to-read control panel with recessed knobs

64N-4TKVW—Gas Slide-in with electronic controls, one-touch self-cleaning oven and sealed burners.

68N-4TVW—Electric Slide-in with electronic controls, one-touch self-cleaning oven and solid disc elements.

58N-4TVW—Electric Drop-in with electronic controls, one-touch self-cleaning oven and solid disc elements.

SPECIFICATIONS

FREESTANDING RANGES

	34-Series		38-Series		Double Oven			64-Series		68/58-Series	
	Range	Oven	Range	Oven	Range	Microwave Oven	Lower Oven	Range	Oven	Range	Oven
Width	30″	22″	30″	22″	30″	18″	22″	30″	22″	30″	22″
Height	46″	15″	46″	15″	65¾″	8″	15″	36½″	15″	36½″	15″
Depth (not incl'd. Handle)	25⅝″	18″	25½″	18″	Pot Clearance 25½″	13½″ max. 12½″	18″	26½″	18″	26½″	18″
Approx. Shipping Weight	215 lbs.		195 lbs.		300 lbs.			180 lbs.		205 lbs. (68) 175 lbs. (58)	
Total Connected Load—			12.6 @ 240V							12.6 @ 240V	
KW Rating—			9.5 @ 208V							9.5 @ 208V	

WALL OVENS

	Upper Oven			Lower Oven			Cutout			Total Connected 120/240V	Load (KW) 120/208V	Approx. Ship. Wt. (lbs.)
Series	W	H	D	W	H	D	W	H	D			
77-M9	14½″	10⁷⁄₁₆″	13⅛″	18″	14″	19″	24¾″	46⅛″	24″ min.	6.4	5.1	220
91	18″	14″	19″	18″	12″	19″	22″	45⅜″	24″ min.	—	—	195
79	18″	14″	19″	—	—	—	24¾″	28⅛″	24″ min.	3.6	2.7	140
59T	22″	15″	18″	—	—	—	30⅛″	28⅛″	24″ min.	5.9	4.4	160
77	18″	14″	19″	18″	12″	19″	24¾″	46⅛″	24″ min.	6.5	4.9	215

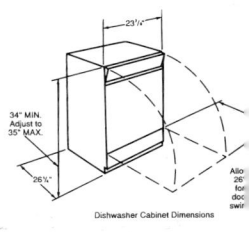

Dishwasher Cabinet Dimensions

COOKTOPS

	Exterior		Cutout		Approx. Shipping Weight	Total Connected Load	
Series	W	D	W	D	Lbs.	120/240V	120/208V
88-2	30″	21″	26⅝″	20″	40	7	5.3
82-3	30″	21″	28³⁄₁₆″	19¹³⁄₁₆″	40	—	—

DISHWASHER

	OUTSIDE DIMENSIONS			APPROX. SHIP. WT.
Model	H*	W	D	Pounds
DU96	34½″	23¾″	26¼″	100

*Adjustable from 34″ to 35″.
Drain hose included with each model.
Only 9 amps connected load.

MICROWAVE OVENS

	M46 Series	M16	M15 Series	VM11
Height (Exterior)	15¼″	12¾″	12¾″	16¼″
Width (Exterior)	21⅞″	20⅜″	20⅜″	30″
Depth (Exterior)	15¹¹⁄₁₆″	14″	13¼″**	13″*
Volume Inside (cu. ft.)	1.2	0.8	0.8	1.0
Approximate Shipping Weight	70 lbs.	46 lbs.	42 lbs.	97 lbs.
Total Connected Load (for 120 volts)	11.5 Amps	10.5 Amps	10 Amps	12 Amps
Output Power (Watts)	700**	600**	600**	600**

* Excluding handle   ** Liters water

DRYER

APPROX. SHIPPING WEIGHT 135 lbs.

TOTAL CONNECTED LOAD		
Amps	Volt (3-wire)	Hz.
15	120	60

Gas dryers work with natural or LP gas (with available kit).

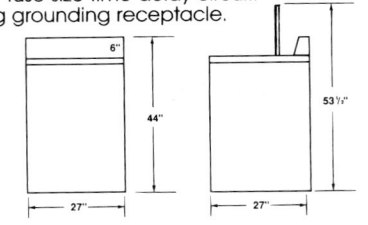

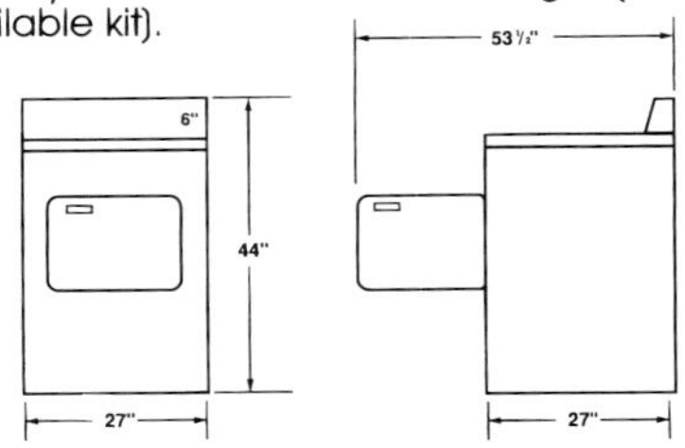

REFRIGERATORS

	Outside Dimensions		Depth Dimensions		Total Volume (cu. ft.)		AHAM Shelf Area (sq. ft.)		Approx. Shipping Weight
Models	H	W	w/handle	w/door open	Total	Refrig.	Frz.	AHAM	Pounds
BDNS24L9	66⅜″	35¾″	29¼″	48¾″	23.6	15.14	8.41	28.1	324
RC24-3AW	66⅜″	35¾″	29¼″	48¾″	23.6	15.14	8.49	28.1	322
RC22-3AW	66⅜″	33″	29¼″	48¾″	21.7	15.17	6.46	26.2	304
RB23-4AW	65½″	33″	30⅝″	62⅜″	22.0	15.17	6.89	29.9	288
RB23-4A	65½″	33″	30⅝″	62⅜″	22.5	15.58	6.89	32.3	269
RB21-4A	65½″	31½″	30⅝″	60⅝″	20.9	14.50	6.39	30.2	262
RB18-4AW	65½″	31½″	27⅞″	57⅝″	18.0	12.36	5.67	24.2	256
RB19-4A	65½″	31½″	27⅞″	57⅝″	18.5	12.80	5.67	26.5	246

WASHER

APPROX. SHIPPING WEIGHT 185 LBS.

TOTAL CONNECTED LOAD		
Amps	Volts	Hz.
11.5	120	60

15 AMP fuse size time delay circuit.
3 prong grounding receptacle.

Magic Chef®
Cleveland, TN 37311

Design certified by the American Gas Association. Listed by Underwriters' Laboratories. Specifications subject to change at manufacturer's option.

Dimensional information for reference only. For actual installation, refer to instructions packed with product.

WALL OVENS & COOKTOPS

Built-in beauty! Nothing adds more contemporary appeal to a kitchen than a wall oven. And no wall oven offers quite the styling, convenience features and dependability of a Maytag.

A wide range of models lets you choose the unit that most fits your cooking needs, kitchen decor and budget. And now, Maytag's new Deco-White™ selection of wall ovens for the ultimate in contemporary styling!

Model CWE1000 — The top of the Maytag line! Features include a self-cleaning radiant oven that automatically converts to a convection oven at the touch of a button. It also offers full computer touch control, an electronic digital clock, timer and a temperature probe to ensure precise cooking. In addition, there's a "delay- start" cook control, automatic oven light, see-through oven window and a porcelain broiler pan and insert.

Model CWE900 — Designed for under-the-counter installations, features include a self-cleaning oven, electronic digital clock, timer and a "delay-start" cook control. It also offers an automatic oven light, see-through oven window and a porcelain broiler pan and insert. Also available in Deco-White.™

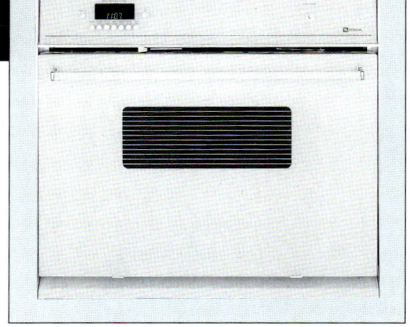

Deco-White™ Model ECWE900

Model CWE701 — Features include a self-cleaning oven, electronic digital clock, timer and a temperature probe to ensure precise cooking. It also offers a "delay-start" cook control, automatic oven light, see-through oven window and a porcelain broiler pan and insert.

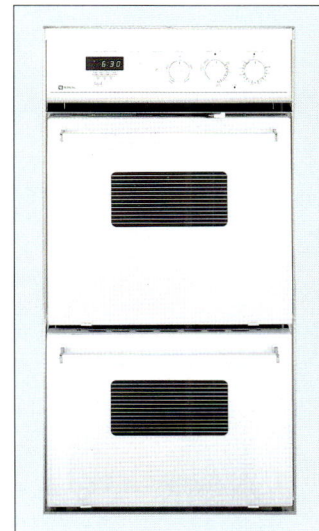

Deco-White™ Model ECWE550

Model CCE701 — Combines the advantages of both radiant and microwave cooking! Features include a self-cleaning oven with an electronic digital clock, timer and a temperature probe. It also offers a "delay-start" cook control, automatic oven light and a see-through oven window. Plus! A deluxe, programmable Maytag microwave oven on top.

Model CWE550 — Double the dependability! Features include a self-cleaning upper oven, electronic clock, timer and a "delay-start" cook control. It also offers an oven light switch, see-through oven window and a porcelain broiler pan and insert. Also available in Deco-White.™

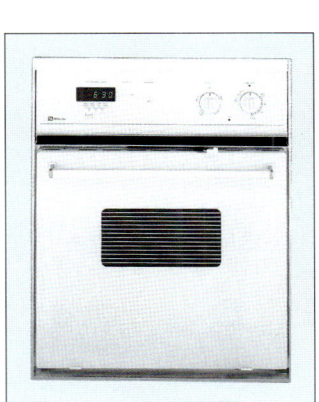

Deco-White™ Model ECWE470

Model CWE601 — Features include a self-cleaning oven, rotary clock, timer and a "delay-start" cook control. It also offers an automatic oven light, see-through oven window and a porcelain broiler pan and insert.

Model CWE470 — Features include a self-cleaning oven, electronic clock, timer and a "delay-start" cook control. It also offers an oven light switch, see-through oven window and a porcelain broiler pan and insert. Also available in Deco-White.™

MAYTAG 24″ ELECTRIC WALL OVENS

Model CWE402 — Features include an electronic clock, timer and a "delay-start" cook control. It also offers an oven light switch, see-through oven window and a porcelain broiler pan and insert. Lift-off oven doors make cleaning the oven as easy and convenient as possible!

Model CWE502 — Economy and dependability! Maytag's standard-clean double wall oven features an electronic clock, timer and a "delay-start" cook control. It also offers an oven light switch, see-through oven window and a porcelain broiler pan and insert.

ELECTRIC WALL OVEN FEATURES	CWE1000	ECWE900* CWE900	CWE701	CCE701	CWE601	ECWE550* CWE550	CWE502	ECWE470* CWE470	CWE402
Wall Oven Size	27″	30″	27″	27″	27″	24″	24″	24″	24″
Microwave Oven				X					
Convection/Radiant Oven	X								
Radiant Oven		X	X	X	X	2	2	X	X
Self-Clean Oven	X	X	X	X	X	Upper		X	
Standard-Clean Oven						Lower	X		X
3 Heavy-Duty Racks, Multi-Levels	X					X	X		
2 Heavy-Duty Racks, Multi-Levels		X	X	X	X			X	X
Electronic Clock & 99 Minute Timer	X	X	X	X		X	X	X	X
Rotary Clock & 60 Minute Timer					X				
"Delay-Start" Cook Control	X	X	X	X	X	X	X	X	X
Oven Window(s)	X	X	X	X	X	X	X	X	X
Oven Light	X	X	X	X	X	2	2	X	X
Pull-Off Control Knobs			X	X	X	X	X	X	X
Porcelain Broiler Pan & Insert	X	X	X	X	X	X	X	X	X
Black Glass Front	X	X	X	X	X	X	X	X	X
Temperature Probe	X		X	X					
Computer Touch Control	X			X					

*Deco-White™ models feature white control panels and white glass fronts.

MAYTAG 24″ GAS WALL OVENS

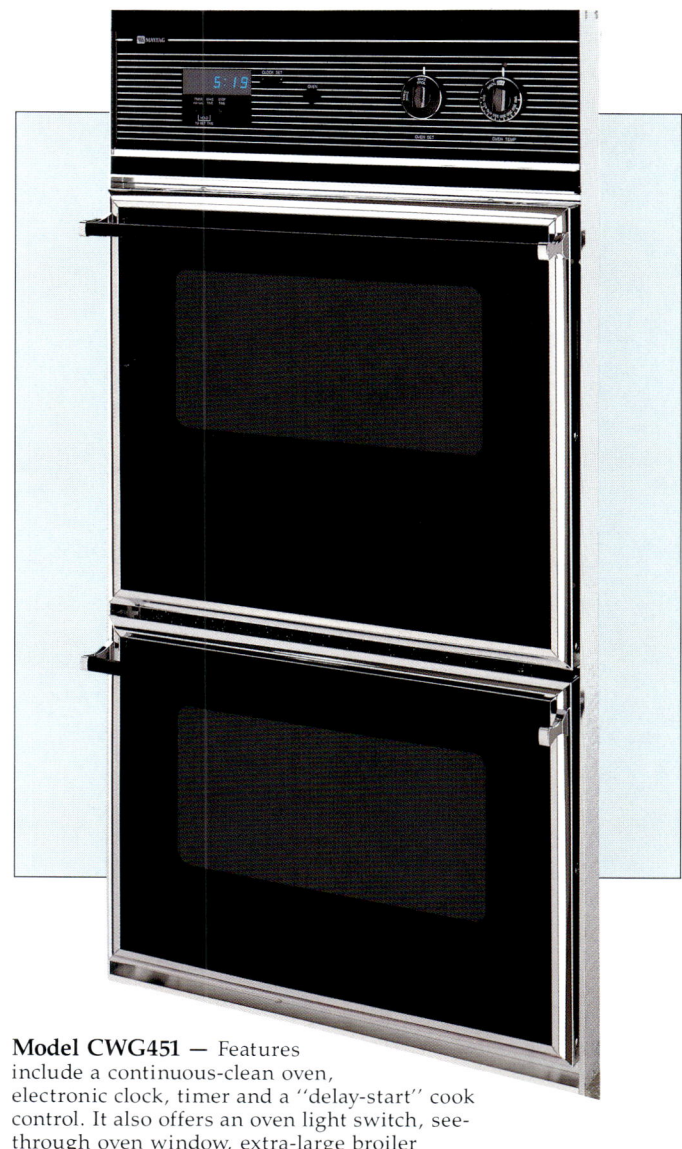

Model CWG402 — Features include a continuous-clean oven, electronic clock, timer and a ''delay-start'' cook control. It also offers an oven light switch, see-through oven window and a porcelain broiler pan and insert. *Also available in the standard-clean model CWG302.*

Model CWG451 — Features include a continuous-clean oven, electronic clock, timer and a ''delay-start'' cook control. It also offers an oven light switch, see-through oven window, extra-large broiler compartment with window and a porcelain broiler pan and insert. *Also available in the standard-clean model CWG351.*

GAS WALL OVEN FEATURES	CWG451	CWG402	CWG351	CWG302
Wall Oven Size	24″	24″	24″	24″
Continuous-Clean Oven	X	X		
Standard-Clean Oven			X	X
Electronic Clock & 99 Minute Timer	X	X	X	X
''Delay-Start'' Cook Control	X	X	X	X
2 Heavy-Duty Racks, Multi-Level	X	X	X	X
Oven Window & Oven Light	X	X	X	X
Even-Heat Broiler	X	X	X	X
Broiler Compartment Window & Light	X		X	
Black Glass Front	X	X	X	X
Solid State Pilotless Ignition	X	X	X	X
Built-In LP Conversion	X	X	X	X

The perfect complement to your Maytag wall oven is a sleek, contemporary Maytag cooktop. An array of models to choose from, each is designed with the quality construction, attractive good looks and superior performance that typify all Maytag appliances.

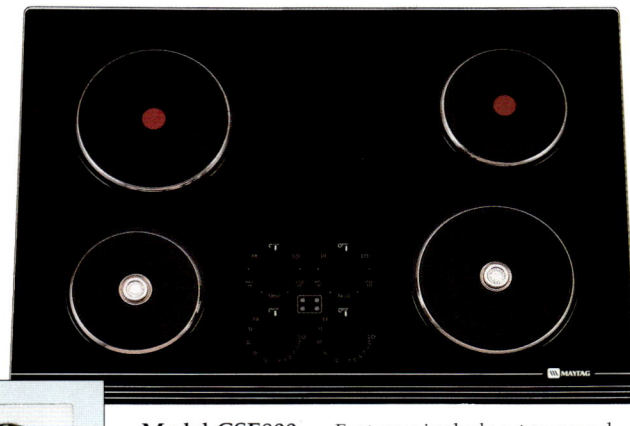

Deco-White™ Model ECSE800

Model CSE800 — Features include a tempered glass surface with solid disc surface elements for uniform, consistent heat. The elements are sealed right into the cooktop surface for easy cleaning, and two are equipped with sensors that monitor pan temperatures to minimize boil-overs. Indicator lights show the elements in use. Also available in Deco-White.™

Maytag's new top-of-the-line cooktop offers the utmost in cooking convenience and clean-up ease! Its smooth cooktop surface, elegant black styling and flush-to-counter installation makes it perfect for today's modern kitchen.

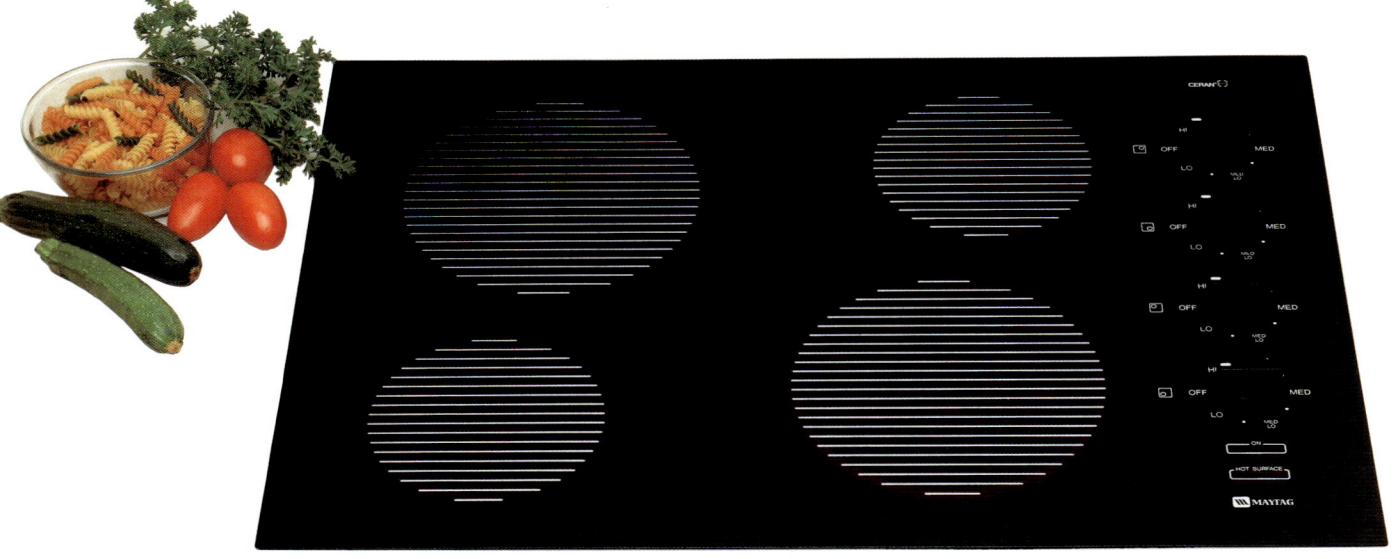

Model CSE900 — Pots and pans slide easily from burner to burner! Features include four high-speed radiant surface elements in a black glass Ceran® top. It also offers element-in-use indicator light, infinite set element controls and a "Hot Surface" light. It's smooth cooktop surface and pull-off knobs make cleaning simple!

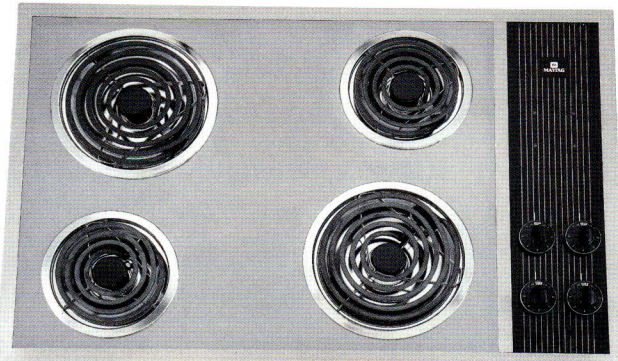

Model CSE601 — Features include a drip-retainer top with four removable, heavy-duty coil elements. It also offers a tempered glass control panel, surface indicator lights, chrome reflector bowls, pull-off knobs and a stainless steel trim. *Please note the cutout and product dimensions of this model on back of brochure.*

Model CSE400 — Features include a drip-retainer top with four removable, heavy-duty coil elements. It also offers a tempered glass control panel, infinite set element controls, chrome reflector bowls and pull-off knobs for easy cleaning.

MAYTAG EASY-CLEAN GAS COOKTOPS

Model CSG600 — The convenience of a fifth burner or griddle! Features include a solid state pilotless ignition, heavy porcelain enamel burner grates and removable, scratch-resistant burners. A lift-up surface and drip-retainer top mean quick, easy cleaning!

Model CSG560 — Features include a solid state pilotless ignition, sealed burners and square porcelain enamel burner grates. It also offers removable, precision click-set burner controls and a drip-retainer top.

Model CSG501 — Features include a solid state pilotless ignition, square porcelain enamel grates and removable, scratch-resistant burners. It also offers precision click-set burner controls, a lift-up surface and drip-retainer top.

COOKTOP FEATURES	ECSE*/ CSE 900	CSE 800	CSE 601	CSE 400	CSG 600	CSG 560	CSG 501
Cooktop Size	30"	30"	36"	30"	36"	30"	30"
Black Tempered Glass Surface	X	X					
Radiant Surface Elements in Ceramic Glass	X						
Solid Disc Elements		X					
Temp Sensor Control (2 Front Elements)		X					
Heavy-Duty Coil Surface Elements			X	X			
Tempered Glass Control Panel	X	X	X	X	X	X	X
Pull-Off Control Knobs	X	X	X	X	X	X	X
White/Almond/Brushed Chrome			X	X	X	X	X
Sealed Burners						X	
Removable Burners					X		X
Drip-Retainer Top			X	X	X	X	X
Lift-Up Cooktop					X		X
Precision Click-Set Burner Control					X	X	X
LP Convertible					X	X	X
Solid State Pilotless Ignition					X	X	X

*Deco-White™ model features a white control panel and white tempered glass surface.

MAYTAG DEPENDABILITY WARRANTY

Maytag wall ovens and cooktops come with a complete warranty that covers replacement and labor on all parts for one full year from date of purchase. In addition, a limited warranty provides free parts for two years.

Unlike most warranties, your Maytag warranty moves with you and is valid anywhere in the United States and Canada. See your Maytag dealer for complete warranty details.

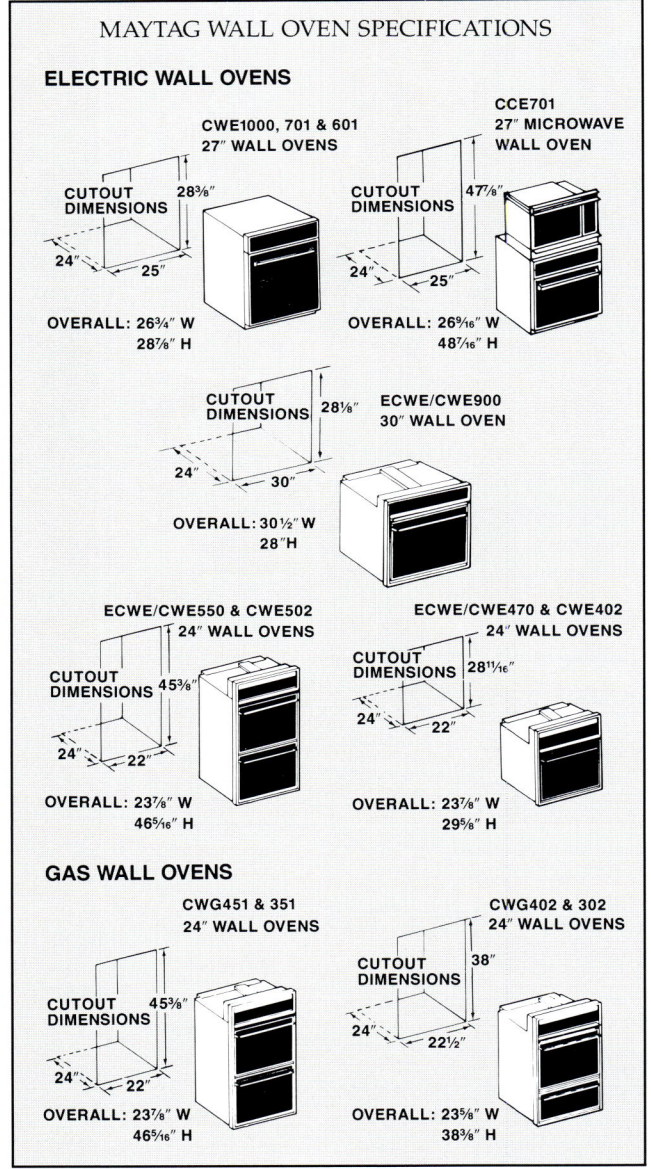

MAYTAG WALL OVEN SPECIFICATIONS

ELECTRIC WALL OVENS

CWE1000, 701 & 601
27″ WALL OVENS

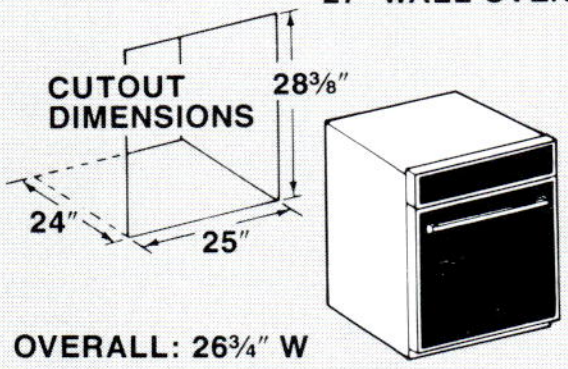
CUTOUT DIMENSIONS
28⅜″
24″
25″

OVERALL: 26¾″ W
28⅞″ H

CCE701
27″ MICROWAVE WALL OVEN

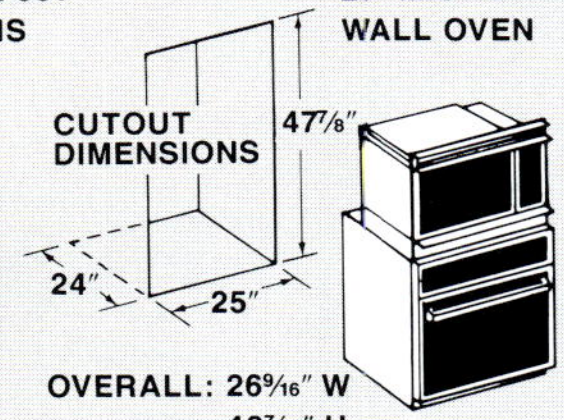
CUTOUT DIMENSIONS
47⅞″
24″
25″

OVERALL: 26⁹⁄₁₆″ W
48⁷⁄₁₆″ H

ECWE/CWE900
30″ WALL OVEN

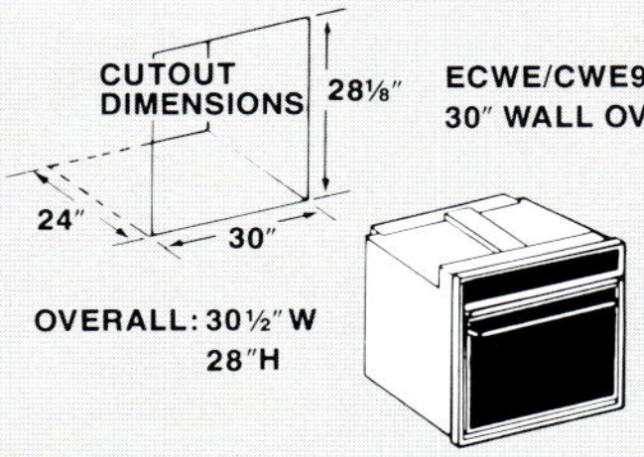
CUTOUT DIMENSIONS
28⅛″
24″
30″

OVERALL: 30½″ W
28″ H

ECWE/CWE550 & CWE502
24″ WALL OVENS

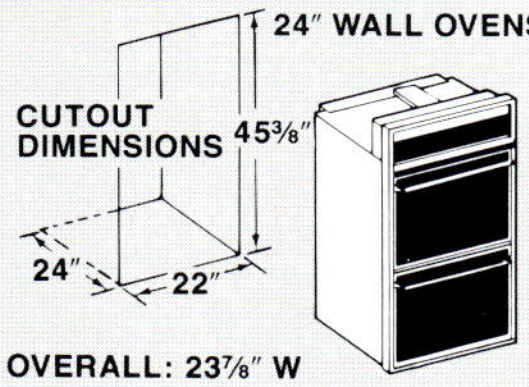
CUTOUT DIMENSIONS
45⅜″
24″
22″

OVERALL: 23⅞″ W
46⁵⁄₁₆″ H

ECWE/CWE470 & CWE402
24″ WALL OVENS

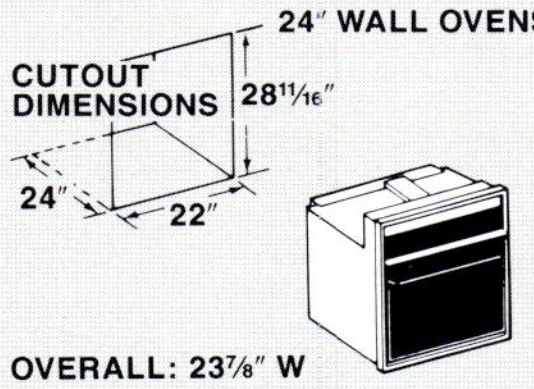
CUTOUT DIMENSIONS
28¹¹⁄₁₆″
24″
22″

OVERALL: 23⅞″ W
29⅝″ H

GAS WALL OVENS

CWG451 & 351
24″ WALL OVENS

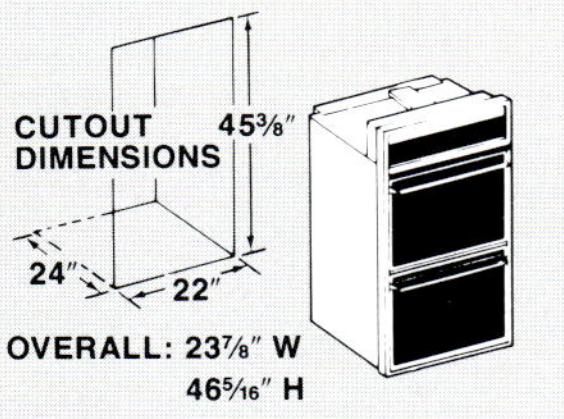
CUTOUT DIMENSIONS
45⅜″
24″
22″

OVERALL: 23⅞″ W
46⁵⁄₁₆″ H

CWG402 & 302
24″ WALL OVENS

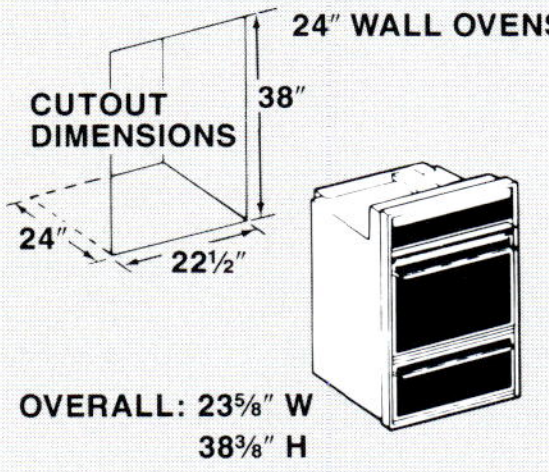
CUTOUT DIMENSIONS
38″
24″
22½″

OVERALL: 23⅝″ W
38⅜″ H

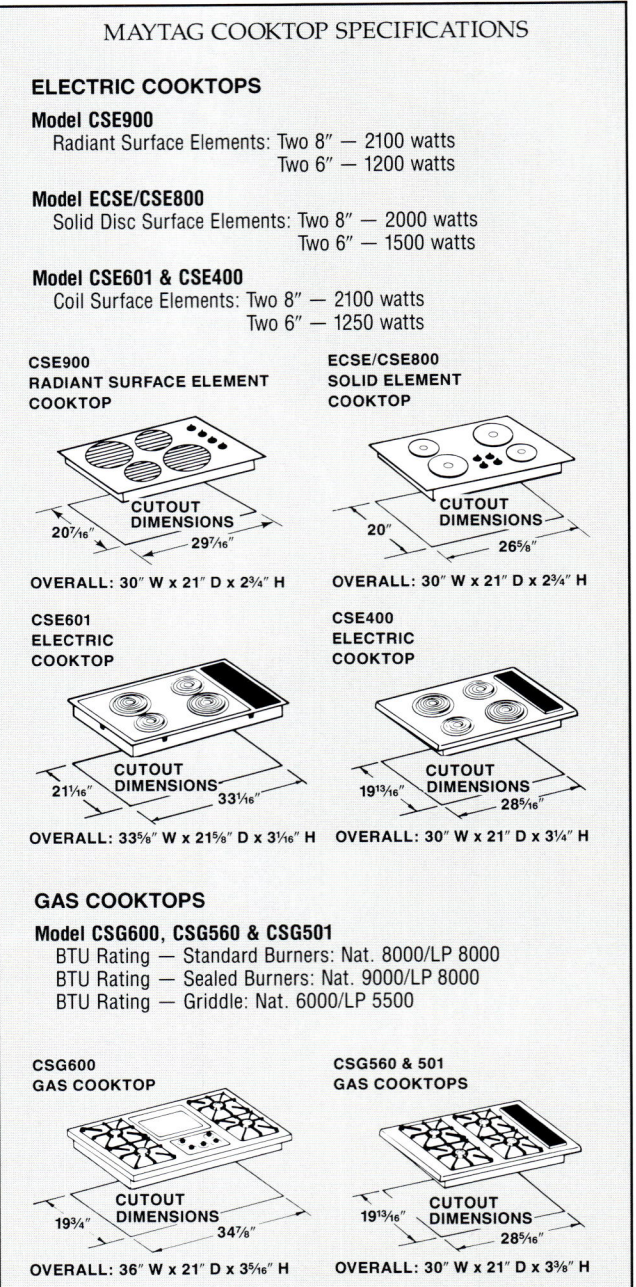

MAYTAG COOKTOP SPECIFICATIONS

ELECTRIC COOKTOPS

Model CSE900
Radiant Surface Elements: Two 8″ — 2100 watts
Two 6″ — 1200 watts

Model ECSE/CSE800
Solid Disc Surface Elements: Two 8″ — 2000 watts
Two 6″ — 1500 watts

Model CSE601 & CSE400
Coil Surface Elements: Two 8″ — 2100 watts
Two 6″ — 1250 watts

CSE900
RADIANT SURFACE ELEMENT COOKTOP

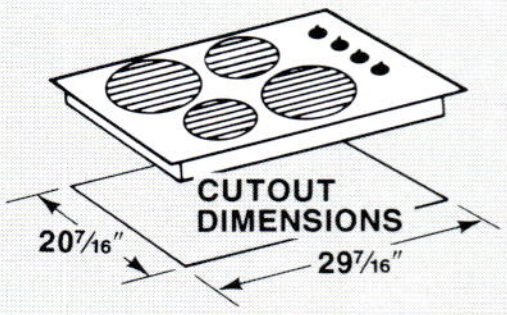
CUTOUT DIMENSIONS
20⁷⁄₁₆″
29⁷⁄₁₆″

OVERALL: 30″ W x 21″ D x 2¾″ H

ECSE/CSE800
SOLID ELEMENT COOKTOP

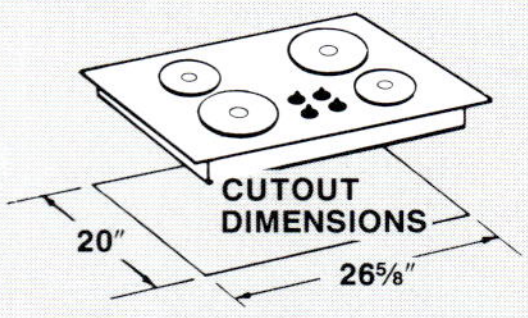
CUTOUT DIMENSIONS
20″
26⅝″

OVERALL: 30″ W x 21″ D x 2¾″ H

CSE601
ELECTRIC COOKTOP

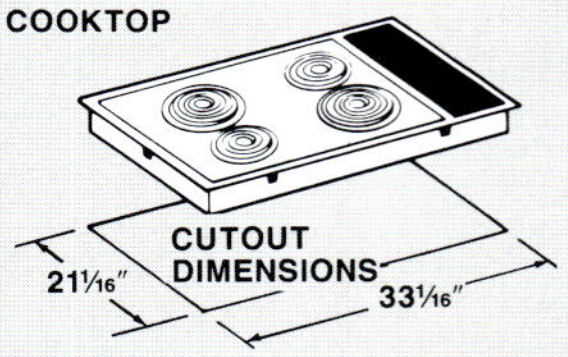
CUTOUT DIMENSIONS
21¹⁄₁₆″
33¹⁄₁₆″

OVERALL: 33⅝″ W x 21⅝″ D x 3¹⁄₁₆″ H

CSE400
ELECTRIC COOKTOP

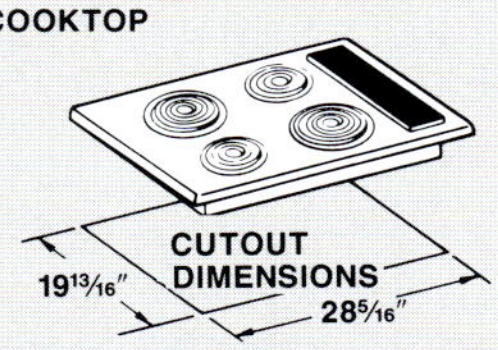
CUTOUT DIMENSIONS
19¹³⁄₁₆″
28⁵⁄₁₆″

OVERALL: 30″ W x 21″ D x 3¼″ H

GAS COOKTOPS

Model CSG600, CSG560 & CSG501
BTU Rating — Standard Burners: Nat. 8000/LP 8000
BTU Rating — Sealed Burners: Nat. 9000/LP 8000
BTU Rating — Griddle: Nat. 6000/LP 5500

CSG600
GAS COOKTOP

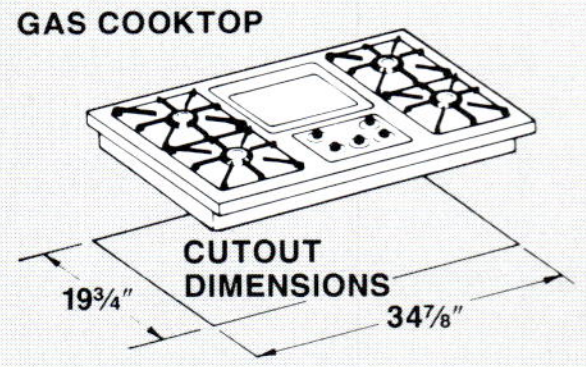
CUTOUT DIMENSIONS
19¾″
34⅞″

OVERALL: 36″ W x 21″ D x 3⁵⁄₁₆″ H

CSG560 & 501
GAS COOKTOPS

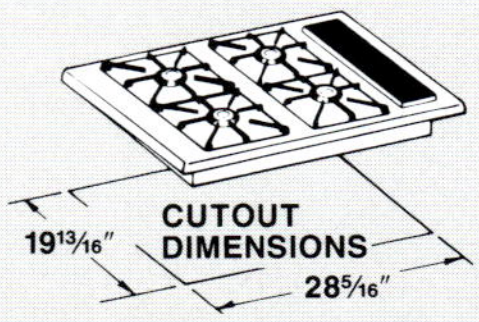
CUTOUT DIMENSIONS
19¹³⁄₁₆″
28⁵⁄₁₆″

OVERALL: 30″ W x 21″ D x 3⅜″ H

All dimensions shown are for planning purposes only. Consult the Installation Instructions that accompany each product before cutting cabinets or countertops.

Because of continuing product improvement, Maytag reserves the right to change specifications without notice.

787L-ADV JN1/91 175 Printed in U.S.A.

MAYTAG COMPANY, One Dependability Square, Newton, Iowa 50208

JETCLEAN™ DISHWASHERS

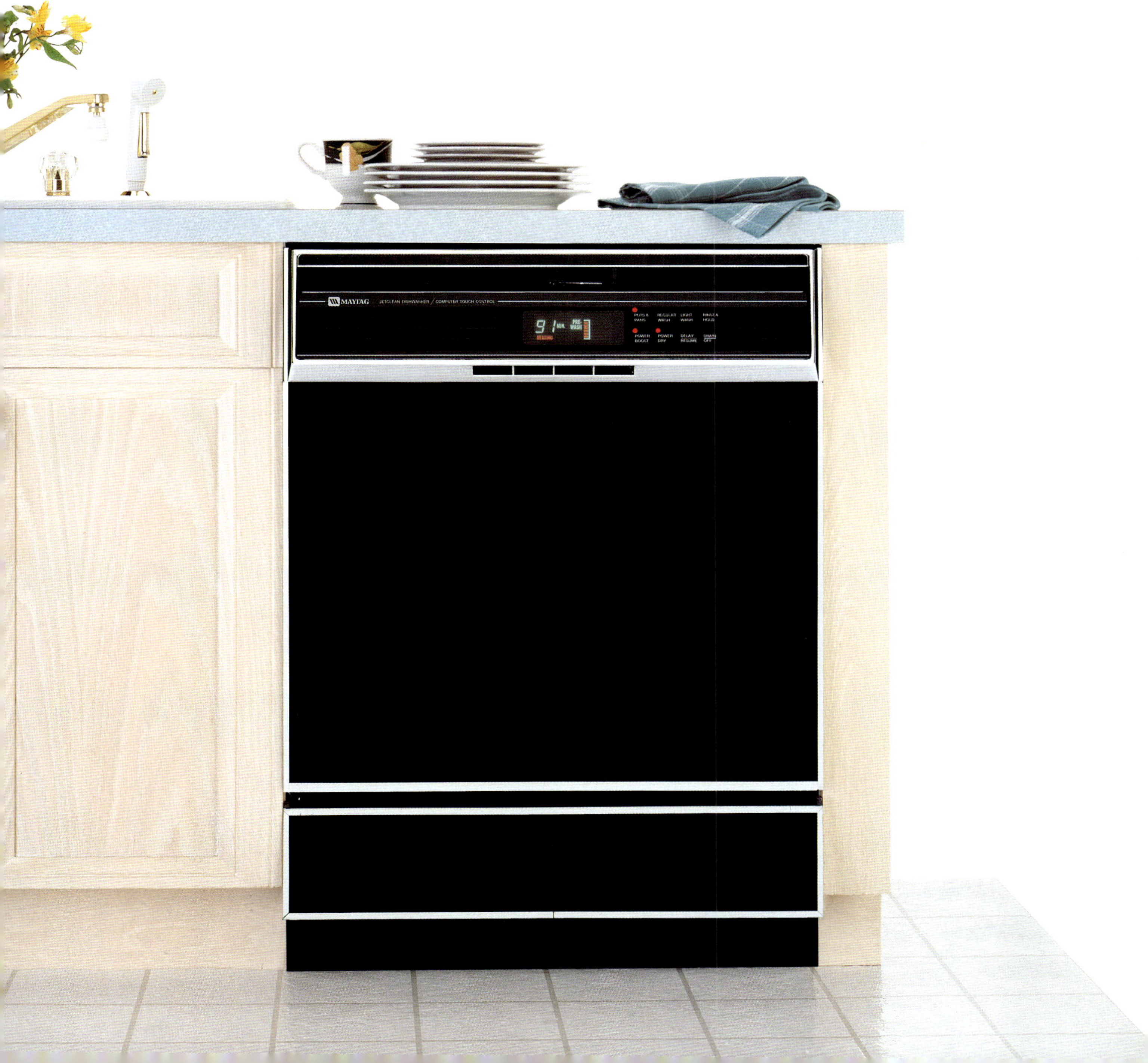

Today's Maytag Jetclean™ Dishwashers are more than just upgraded and improved versions of the standard dishwasher. They're loaded with the performance features and convenience extras that do practically everything but clear the table!

Maytag dishwashers are designed with wash cycle settings for a full range of cleaning jobs. There's a Regular Wash cycle for normal loads and a Pots & Pans cycle for tough cleaning jobs. For even added scrubbing power, water heating options are available on many models, along with a Light Wash cycle and a convenient Rinse & Hold cycle.

Every Maytag dishwasher gives you two fan dry settings. You can select either Power Dry heat or Energy Saver no-heat.

Both settings employ a highly efficient dryer fan system in which air is continuously circulated throughout the dishwasher.

Maytag dishwashers are unsurpassed in capacity, loading flexibility and cleaning power. And whichever Maytag dishwasher model you choose, each is designed for super-quiet operation.

Best of all, because they're Maytag dishwashers, you can depend on that quiet cleaning power load after load, day after day, year after year.

You can also depend on your new Maytag to add a touch of class to your kitchen. Dishwasher front panels include a full selection of today's most popular decorator colors. They can also be customized with wood panels in the same finish as the rest of your kitchen cabinets. In addition, you can select from two new Deco-White™ models. These dishwashers feature all-white front panels and control panels for the ultimate in contemporary styling!

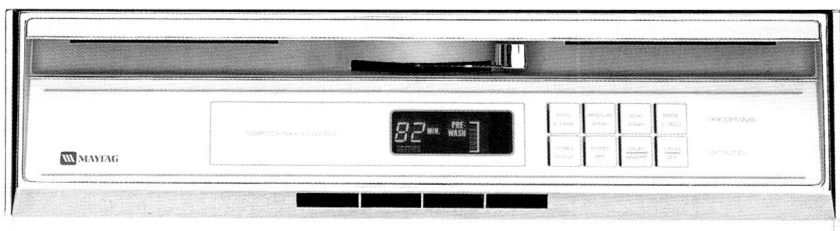

Deco-White™ Model EWU1005

Deluxe features include Computer Touch Control, a display readout of the cycle time remaining, and a delay start function. It also offers a Power Boost option in addition to the three standard wash cycles, "Clean", "Heating" and "Rinsed Only" indicators, folding upper rack dividers and a rinse dispenser.

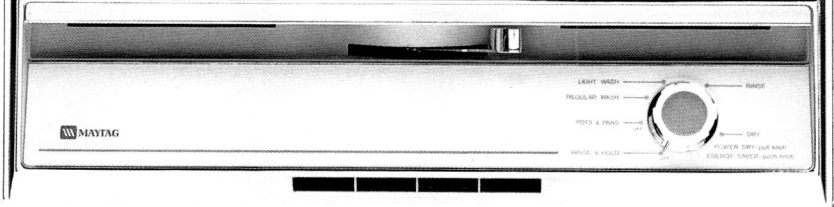

Deco-White™ Model EWU304

Features include a convenient Rinse & Hold cycle in addition to the three standard wash cycles. It also offers Power Dry heat and Energy Saver no-heat dry settings and the same long-life motor, power module, porcelain enamel tub and sound insulation standard to all Maytags.

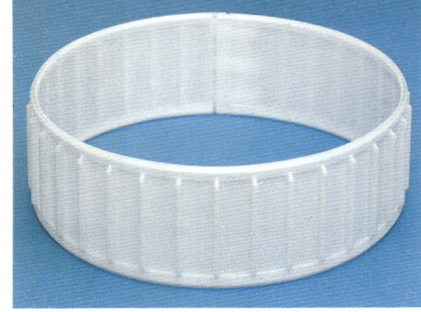

The Maytag wash system, along with the Maytag filter and internal food disposer, simply means that you don't have to wash your dishes *before* you wash your dishes!

No other dishwasher on the market is more spacious than a Maytag, or better designed for easy loading. Dual deep racking lets you place pots, casseroles and serving dishes on either rack. And folding upper rack dividers on some models offer even greater loading flexibility.

The tub and door of every Maytag dishwasher are finished with two coats of specially-formulated, protective porcelain enamel. Heavy-gauge steel dish racks are coated with vinyl to cushion and protect dishes. And rack guides are stainless steel to resist rust and corrosion.

Our Micro-Mesh Filter® continuously traps and removes tiny food particles. Every dish is washed and rinsed in 100% filter-cleaned water.

The patented, stainless steel "internal food disposer" handles both hard and soft foods.

47 cleaning jets fill the entire dishwasher cavity with high-velocity jets of water. Maytag's three level wash system forces water down from the top, out from the center and up from the bottom. Dishes, utensils and cookware are power-cleaned from every direction.

Every dishwasher model has "forced air" fan drying. Air is gently circulated throughout the dishwasher and exchanged every 30 seconds, drying dishes quickly and efficiently. After all, dishwashers are supposed to both wash *and* dry!

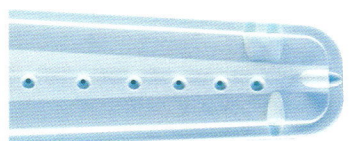

The compact power module filters, recirculates and drains the water. This simple, efficient motor and pump design is so dependable that Maytag warrants it, as well as all other wash system components, for five full years.

Dependably quiet Maytag dishwashers are equipped with an exclusive triple-insulation system. It consists of a thick fiberglass blanket, sound-absorbing pads, and a fiber mesh aluminum covering.

Smaller spray holes in the Maytag spray arm result in a finer, more vigorous spray for greater scrubbing power. So much power, in fact, that normally it is not necessary to rinse or prewash your dishes. Only burned-on foods may need extra attention.

Don't put off enjoying your dream dishwasher until you have your dream kitchen! Maytag's convertible/portable models WC704, WC504 and WC204 have the same features as the corresponding built-in models. With the Maytag Conversion Kit, each can be easily converted when you're ready for a built-in.

MAYTAG DEPENDABILITY WARRANTY

Maytag dishwashers come with a complete warranty that covers replacement and labor on all parts for one full year from date of purchase. A limited warranty provides free parts for two years. And for five years, there are free parts on replacements related to computer touch controls, cabinet rust and all Jetclean™ system components.

In addition, there are free parts for ten years on the porcelain enamel tub and inner door liner against leaks due to rust and corrosion.

Unlike most warranties, your Maytag warranty moves with you and is valid anywhere in the United States or Canada. See your Maytag dealer for complete warranty details.

MAYTAG DISHWASHER SPECIFICATIONS

ELECTRIC SUPPLY: 115 Volt; 60 Hz; 20 amp fuse required on EWU1005, WU1005, WU904, WU805, WU704 and WU504; all other models require 15 amp fuse. On portable models, 3-prong plug must be connected to properly grounded outlet.

WATER SUPPLY: Water pressure should be 15-120 p.s.i. (1.06-8.44 kg/sg. cm.)
Water temperature should be 140°F. when it enters the dishwasher.

DRAIN (Built-in Models): ½ I.D. flexible drain hose furnished. High drain loop positioned on side of dishwasher.

MOTOR AND PUMP: ⅓ H.P. reversible; two-stage pump for circulation and draining.

POWER CORD LENGTH (PORTABLES ONLY): 6½ Ft. (1.98 m).

HOSE LENGTH (PORTABLES ONLY): 4 ft. (1.22 m).

WEIGHT: Crated — convertible 200 lbs. (91 kg), built-in 132 lbs. (60 kg). Uncrated — convertible 173 lbs. (79 kg,), built-in 110 lbs. (50 kg).

BUILT-IN:

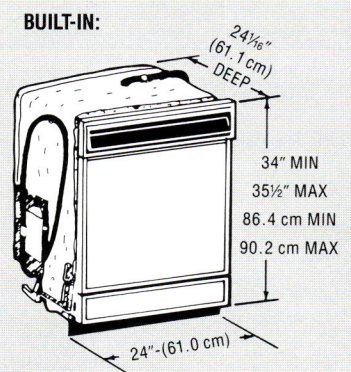

24¹⁄₁₆" (61.1 cm) DEEP

34" MIN
35½" MAX
86.4 cm MIN
90.2 cm MAX

24"-(61.0 cm)

Trim Kit:
Door Panel Insert:
¼" x 18¹⁷⁄₃₂" x 23¾"
(.64 cm x 47.1 cm x 60.3 cm)
Access Panel Insert:
¼" x 4¹⁵⁄₁₆" x 23¾"
(.64 cm x 12.5 cm x 60.3 cm)

Dimensions for the convertible dishwasher:
36½" x 24" x 27"
(92.7 cm x 61.0 cm x 68.6 cm).

"QuickConnect" Disposers

The perfect complement to your new Maytag dishwasher is a quality Maytag food waste disposer!

Every model features "QuickConnect" mounting for simple installation. A large, powerful motor and heavy duty, rust-resistant shredders grind all types of food waste, from celery to chicken bones. Jam-resistant impeller arms, made of high strength stainless steel, are swivel mounted so they swing away from food wastes that could cause jamming.

Our Batch Feed models feature Maytag's exclusive Auto-Start lid which turns on the unit when put into place. This prevents items from dropping into the disposer while it's operating. When the lid is removed, the disposer turns off.

Our Continuous Feed models are activated with a wall switch and feature an easy-load opening with a splash guard covering.

For more details, ask for a complete Maytag Food Waste Disposer specification sheet.

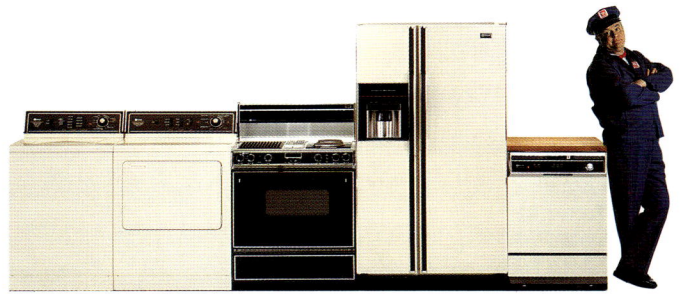

782L-ADV   JN 10/90 350 Printed in U.S.A.

MAYTAG COMPANY   One Dependability Square, Newton, Iowa 50208

FULL-SIZE STACKED
WASHERS & DRYERS

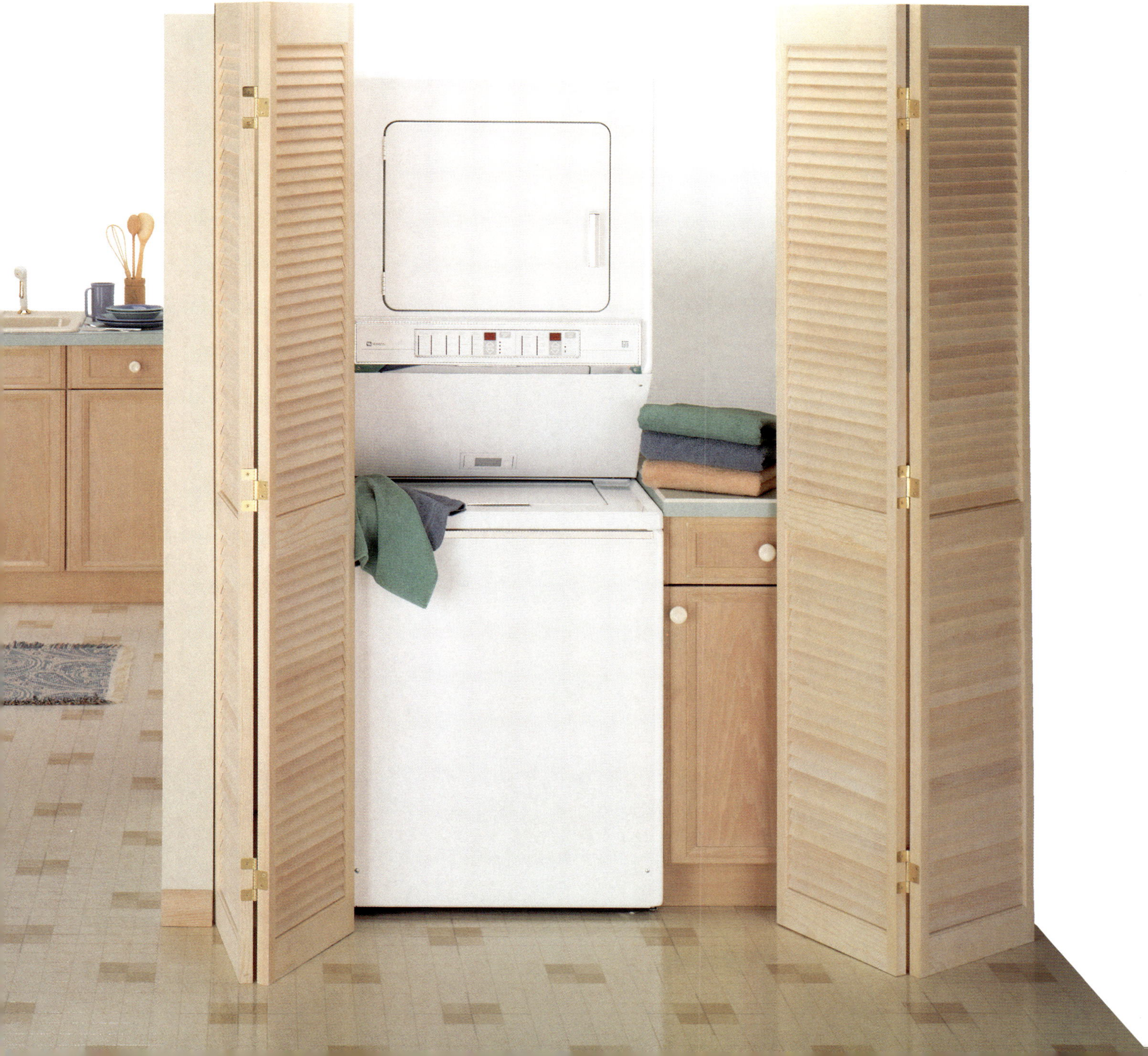

At first glance, you might not even recognize a Maytag stacked washer & dryer as laundry equipment. With its sleek, contemporary styling and clean, unobtrusive design, it's more like a work of art!

Because just one, incredibly compact unit incorporates both a *full-size* Maytag washer and a *full-size* Maytag dryer.

Designed to fit small areas, the Maytag stacked washer & dryer lets you bring the laundry room up from the basement and into the kitchen, the bath, the bedroom — even the hall closet. Wherever there are a few square feet to spare. Wherever laundry piles up! That's where your laundry equipment makes the most sense.

Model S9900

Computer Touch Controls on our model S9900 and Deco-White™ model ES9900 make operation easy. Simply select the desired wash or dry cycle with the touch of a finger! The computer automatically selects the most often used wash and rinse temperature, wash time and

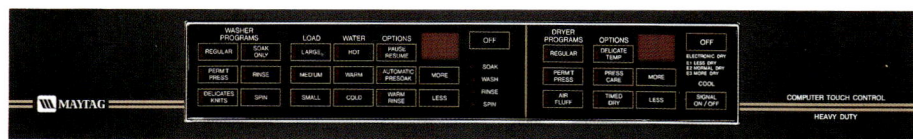

water level. And the most popular drying temperature, drying time and drying level. A digital display lets you know what those selections are. Yet, each selection can be changed to match your laundry loads.

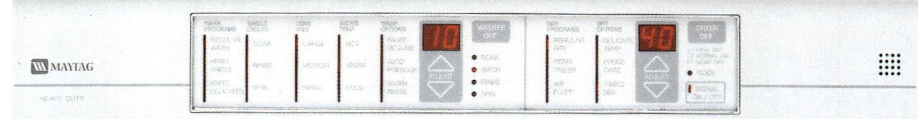

Rotary Controls on our model S7800 are simple to use. The washer dial lets you select from Regular, Permanent Press or Delicate wash cycles. The

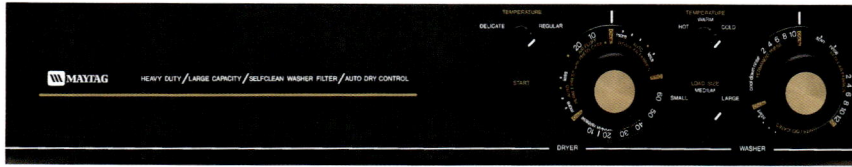

dryer dial lets you choose from Regular, Permanent Press, Delicate and Air Fluff dry cycles. In addition, Timed-Dry and Press Care options offer even greater flexibility and drying control.

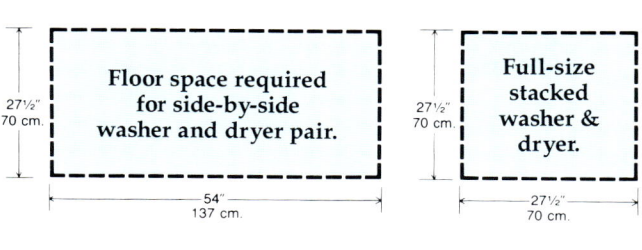

Model S7800

The same dependable features, which have made Maytag washers and dryers America's *most preferred brand* in consumer surveys, are the same features you'll find in a Maytag stacked washer & dryer.

A full range of wash cycles assures you the right water temperature and agitation for all kinds of fabrics. Our all-fabric drying is made possible by a high-capacity blower that produces a diagonal air flow for fast, even drying at temperatures that are gentle to your clothes.

And like all Maytag appliances, the Maytag stacked washer & dryer is built to last longer and need fewer repairs.

MAYTAG DEPENDABILITY WARRANTY

Maytag stacked washers & dryers come with a complete warranty that covers replacement and labor on all parts for one full year from date of purchase. A limited warranty provides free parts for two years. And for five years, there are free parts on replacements related to cabinet rust, dryer drum and touch controls on computer models.

In addition, there are free parts for ten years on the Dependable Drive™ Transmission in our washers.

Unlike most warranties, your Maytag warranty moves with you and is valid anywhere in the United States or Canada. See your Maytag dealer for complete warranty details.

DRYER FEATURES	ES/S9900	S7800
Controls	Computer Touch	Rotary
Drying Control	Electronic	Auto
Temperature Selections	3	3
Adjustable Degree Of Dryness	X	X
Delicate Temperature Setting	X	X
Press Care	X	X
Air Fluff	X	X
Permanent Press Cycle	X	X
Cycle Signal	Adjustable	X
Eye-Level Loading	X	X
Cool-Down Indicator Light	X	
Self-Diagnostics	X	
Up-Front Lint Filter	X	X

All models available with either gas or electric dryers.

WASHER FEATURES	ES/S9900	S7800
Controls	Computer Touch	Rotary
Warm Rinse Option	X	
Automatic Presoak/Soak Only Cycle	X	
Delicate/Knits Cycle	X	X
Permanent Press Cycle	X	X
Temperature Selections	5	3
Water Levels	3	3
Bleach Dispenser	X	X
Self-Cleaning Lint Filter	X	X
Fabric Softener Dispenser	X	X
Cycle Sequence Lights	X	
Surface Light	X	
Lid Lock	X	X
Self-Diagnostics	X	
White Porcelain Tub	X	X

Colors: Models S9900 and S7800 are both available in white or almond.
Deco-White™ model ES9900 (white control panel) is available in white only.

Because of continuing product improvement, Maytag reserves the right to change specifications without notice.

MAYTAG DRYER SPECIFICATIONS

Air Flow: 180 CFM
Exhaust: 4" duct permits a maximum of 50 feet rigid aluminum ductwork. Subtract 8 feet for each 90° elbow, 8 feet for an exhaust hood. Dryer vented out the back.
Motor: ¼ H.P.; 115 volt; 60 Hz thermoprotected against overload; auto reset.
Heat Source:
　Electric — Nichrome helix coil, 240 volt 3-wire, 4600 watts, 30 amp fuse.
　Gas — Single port burner 18,000 BTU/hr.; electric ignition; automatic shut-off.

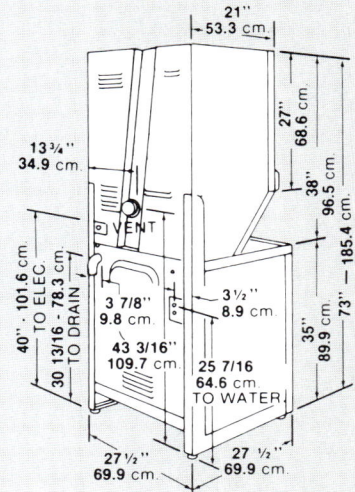

MAYTAG WASHER SPECIFICATIONS

Capacity: Large 16 (13 Imp.) gal; 60.6 lit.
Water Usage: (regular full cycle) —
　36 (30 Imp.) gal; 136 lit. — large
　28 (23 Imp.) gal; 106 lit. — medium
　24 (20 Imp.) gal; 91 lit. — small
Motor: ⅓ H.P., 115 volt; 60 Hz; reversible, thermoprotected against overload; automatic reset.
Power: 1-.17 kwh depending on cycle
Hose Lengths: Inlet 5 feet, 152 cm.; drain 4 feet, 122 cm.
Installation: Hot and cold connections with water pressure within 30-120 PSI range. At least 140°F. hot water; a drain; 115 volt electrical outlet properly grounded. Use standard 15 amp fuse.

Uncrated weight: Approximately 340 lbs. (154 kg.)

Adequate clearance is necessary for proper installation. Please consult product installation instructions.

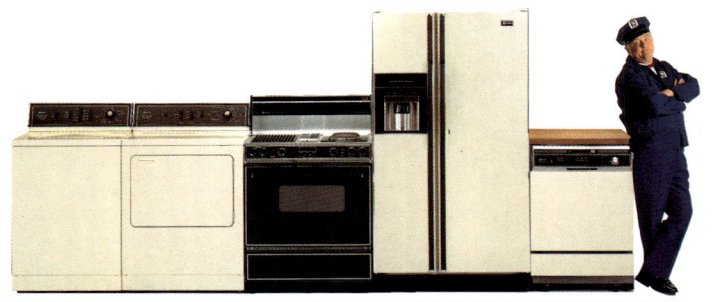

MAYTAG COMPANY One Dependability Square, Newton, Iowa 50208

783L-ADV JN 11/90 175M Printed in U.S.A.

REFRIGERATORS

RSD24A

The ultimate in side by side refrigeration is expressed in Model RSD24A, pictured at left, and the RSW24A with ice and water dispenser (page opposite). Both models even have a convenient rollout drawer which contains four sealed storage dishes that may be used in your microwave or oven.

Along with the other sizes of refrigerators with the deluxe package of features, such as Model RSD20A, seen at center left, you will find a double-walled meat keeper with temperature adjustment. Your fresh meats receive undivided attention as temperature and humidity are optimized, and the double wall helps prevent dry air from entering the chamber.

Maytag refrigerators reflect the architectural tenet of maximizing the use of space, as demonstrated by the efficient placement of the wine rack. And the flexibility of adjustable shelves and bins throughout all Maytag refrigerators.

Supporting this sophisticated design is the solid sense of adjustable cantilevered shelving, in every model, such as RSC20A, lower left. The sturdier construction of this design helps eliminate the rattle and shakes associated with ordinary refrigerators.

RSD20A shown, RSD22A is similar

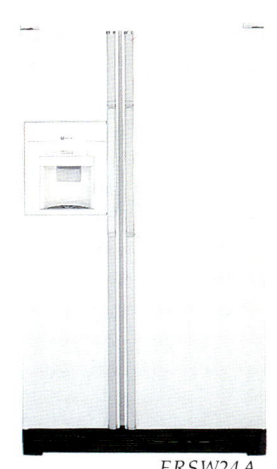

ERSW24A

ERSW22A

RSC20A

For the utmost in contemporary design and convenience, we point out our Deco-White™ models ERSW22A and ERSW24A in the two photographs above. (Also available in white and almond.)

Equipped with Maytag's Thirst Aid™ Station ice and water dispenser, it offers many advantages over similar systems available from other manufacturers.

The large fountain opening allows you to collect ice or water into pitchers or other large containers. Our molded foam insulation eliminates freezing in the water line and "sweating" from the opening. And our unique design virtually eliminates ice jams, which in turn reduces service calls.

Every Maytag refrigerator boasts a highlight you would never hear about on your own, our Whisper Cold™ compressor. We secure this high capacity compressor on quieting rubber cushion with weld nuts, rather than simple metal tabs, so they won't break during shipment. This is an excellent example of Maytag's unending commitment to dependable construction.

*Maytag Refrigerators Reflect the
Architectural Tenet of Maximizing the Use of Space.*

RSW24A

Upon closer inspection, you will discover that every side by side Maytag refrigerator boasts two slidable package dividers, refrigerator door closers, pull out freezer basket and freezer light. Note also the two sealed crispers, one of which is humidity selectable. Thus you can tailor the different moisture needs of fruits and vegetables, such as apples and lettuce, in their own preserving environments.

MAYTAG REFRIGERATORS WITH TOP MOUNT FREEZERS.

RTW22A

Every possible convenience has been designed into the top freezer model refrigerator RTW22A, pictured at left. Of particular interest is the superior design of the ice maker.

The Maytag icemaker detects when ice cubes have frozen, then flash-heats them. Thus loosened, the ice is effortlessly swept into the ice dispenser container.

Even Maytag refrigerators that are not factory-equipped with this ice maker will accept it at a later date. The necessary internal elements are included in every model.

RTS19A s

RTD21A shown
Models RTD23A and RTD19A are similar

Many capacity choices are available with the deluxe feature package, such as Model RTD21A, seen at left. Every facet of design enhances your use, such as the inclusion of a freezer light and the Sure-lock™ door bins. Flexible, in that they adjust and conform to your needs.

Every Maytag refrigerator keeps food fresh in ways you can't easily see. We do not insulate doors with the traditional fiberglass used by many other manufacturers. We prefer foam insulation that better presses itself into refrigerator and door cavities. Thus your Maytag refrigerator delivers a more even temperature throughout the insulated interior.

*You'll be comforted to know that every cubic
foot is stocked with famous Maytag dependability.*

The features are well illustrated in Model RTC19A at right, with its full length handle trim and chrome door caps. These models also feature deep-door shelves and a Keeper™ which tightens up to condiments to stop them from tipping.

You will appreciate the two dairy compartments, as they maintain the proper temperature, so that butter stays spreadable. The split wire shelves enhance your flexibility in arrangement. Plus this particular model adds an extra adjustable shelf in the freezer.

RTC19A shown, RTC17A is similar

A is similar

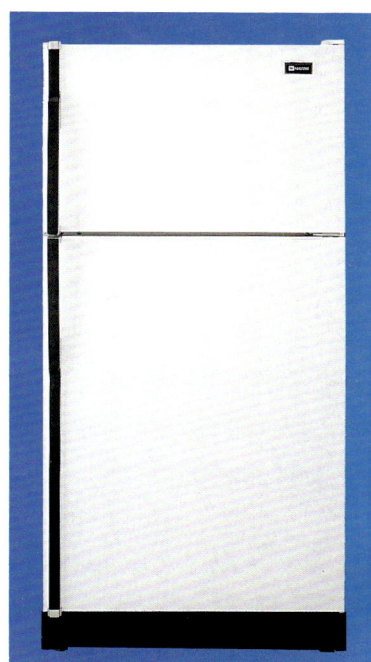

As for standard featured models such as RTS19A at center, you will be comforted to know that every cubic foot is stocked with famous Maytag dependability. The two adjustable cantilevered shelves are made of thicker wire, with the wires closer together than the spacing used by other manufacturers, to eliminate tipping. And of course the wires are coated with a white epoxy finish, to preserve shelf life.

You can count on finding long life protection like this in a Maytag refrigerator, which brings to mind the truism that dependability is in the details.

Our egg cradle holds well more than a dozen, and can be removed to the kitchen counter. The deep pockets of our bins, fixed into the door, always swing into use. Plus, with two sealed crispers and a covered dairy compartment, these models sacrifice no necessity to achieve economy.

Attention to detail and painstaking craftsmanship describe every model of top mount refrigerator. Whatever your selection, you'll find an energy saver switch, to save you money as your seasonal climate turns cooler and less humid. Also included are deep door bins fixed into the freezer, and a butter dish.

RTD17A

RTC15A

Model RTD17A, pictured left, shines with tempered glass shelves and crisper tops. You also receive the double wall meat drawer with temperature adjustment, as previously discussed. Note that this meat drawer is accepted in three different positions in the refrigerators. Again, adjustable shelves allow you to create space to best suit your needs.

As in the larger capacity models, you will still find slidable package "keepers" in both the refrigerator and freezer of Model RTC15A, as shown below. And of course, the second crisper drawer is humidity controlled by you.

Regardless of which size or feature package catches your eye, your new refrigerator is solidly built on Maytag innovation. Our high-impact liner is an excellent example of using superior material to help prevent even hairline cracks to the refrigerator interior.

Even though there are several model and capacity choices with varying features, there are still a good many features that are basic to every Maytag refrigerator. These include the temperature adjustable meat drawer, covered dairy compartment, removable egg tray, no-frost freezer, adjustable freezer shelves, ice storage container, and a choice of either almond or white for color. Also as an option on some models is a decorator front.

Every Maytag refrigerator measures up to certain standards of construction, which exceed those of other manufacturers. Throughout the appliance are examples of Maytag's straightforward belief in not cutting corners. We use galvanized steel, where others are content with plastic or cardboard. We use welds, where others use screws. We use screws, where others use nothing.

Easy Ice

Tempered Glass Shelves

Thirst Aid Station

No-Break Bins

Strongbox Hinges

Adjustable Door Bins

Roll-a-Drawers

*What best sets these refrig-
erators apart from others is
famous Maytag dependability.
While we cannot guarantee that
our lonely repairman will never
visit your home, we still feel your
best chance of seeing him is in our
television commercials.*

Easy Clean Access

Heavy Duty Wire Shelves

High Impact Liner

Sure-Lock Shelves

Create-a-Space System

Reinforced Airlock Seal

Textured Reversible Doors

Thirst Aid Station

Tempered Glass Shelves

Easy Ice

Adjustable Door Bins

Strongbox Hinges

No-Break Bins

Easy Clean Access

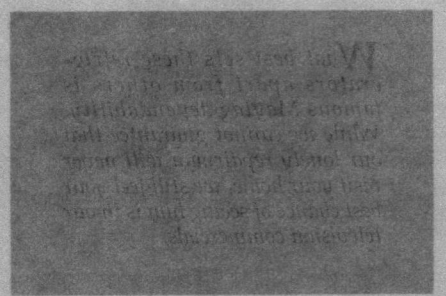

Roll-a-Drawers

Sure-Lock Shelves

High Impact Liner

Heavy Duty Wire Shelves

Textured Reversible Doors

Reinforced Airlock Seal

Create-a-Space System

*Maytag furnishes gliding rollers
on every drawer in every refrigerator*

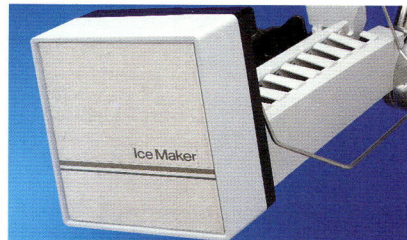

Easy Ice™. Every Maytag refrigerator is prepped to easily accept our ice maker, at your discretion.

Heavy Duty Tempered Glass Shelves. Sturdier steel and cantilevered brackets eliminate twisting under heavy loads.

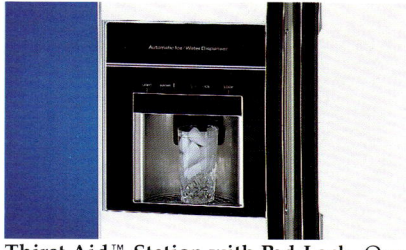

Thirst Aid™ **Station with Pad-Lock.** Our unique design allows you to easily fill large containers.

No-Break™ **Bins.** Practically indestructible and found throughout every Maytag refrigerator.

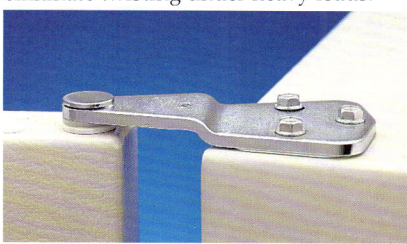

Strongbox™ **Hinges.** Stronger and heavier than regular hinges, to prevent doors from sagging.

Adjustable Door Bin with Keeper. Easily handles condiments from the refrigerator to your lunch table.

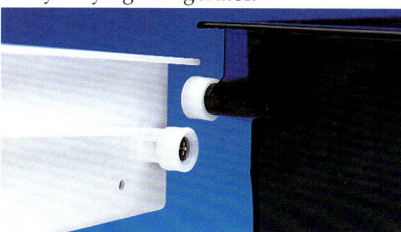

Roll-a-Drawers™. Maytag furnishes gliding rollers on every drawer in every refrigerator.

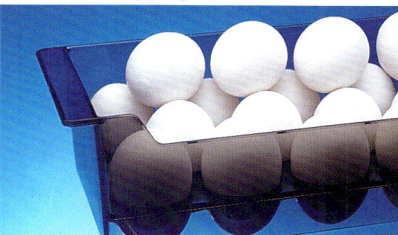

Egg Cradle. Nestles more than a dozen, and removes to your cooking area.

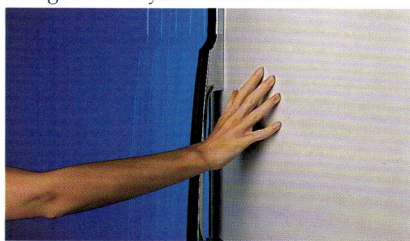

Easy Clean Access. Maytag's wide front wheels and metal bearings make light work of moving the refrigerator.

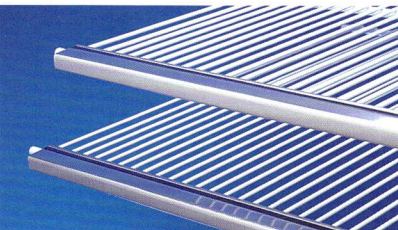

Heavy Duty Wire Shelves. No other refrigerator has sturdier shelves.

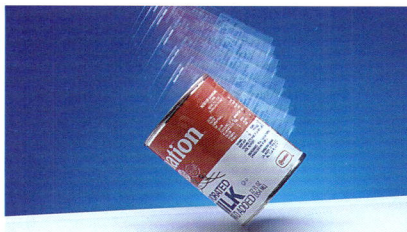

High Impact Liner. Maytag uses a liner material, which helps prevent even hairline cracks.

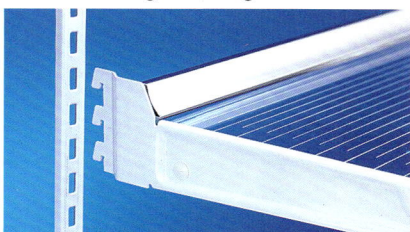

Sure-Lock™ **Shelves.** Only Maytag uses a triple-pronged locking design, to insure stability.

Create-a-Space™ **System.** Allows you to be the interior designer, shelves relocate at your discretion.

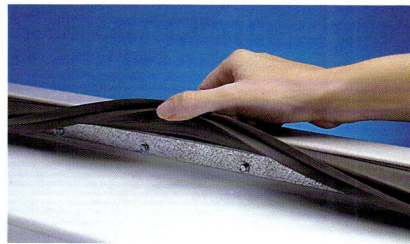

Reinforced Airlock™ **Seal.** Strengthened with steel, to prevent the door gasket from leaking.

Textured Steel Reversible Doors. Hides hand and fingerprints, a cleaner look for your kitchen.

Maytag Warranty

It is comforting to know that Maytag backs up dependability in writing. Every appliance comes with a full warranty which offers free labor and free repair or replacement of all parts on the complete refrigerator during the first year. Additionally, a limited warranty provides free parts on the complete appliance for the second year, and on some major components for the third through fifth years. (Please see refrigerator warranty for complete details.) And unlike other items in your home, you can never lose this warranty if you move. Any authorized Maytag servicer within the United States or Canada will be happy to honor it.

FEATURES	TOP MOUNTS										SIDE BY SIDE					
REFRIGERATORS	RTD23A	RTW22A	RTD21A	RTD19A	RTC19A	RTS19A	RTD17A	RTC17A	RTS17A	RTC15A	RSW24A	RSD24A	RSW22A	RSD22A	RSD20A	RSC20A
Heavy Duty Adjustable Wire Shelf					3 split	2		3 split	2	2						2
Heavy Duty Adjustable Tempered Glass Shelf	4 split	4 split	4 split	4 split	1 split		4 split	1 split			3	3	3	3	3	1
Fixed Crisper Shelf (Glass/Opaque)	G	G	G	G	O	O	G	O	O	O	G	G	G	G	G	O
Temp. Adj. Meat Drawer (Double/Single) Wall	D	D	D	D	S	S	D	S	S	S	D	D	D	D	D	S
Crisper Drawers (Sealed/Moisture Control)	S/M	S/M	S/M	S/M	S/M	2S	S/M	S/M	2S	S/M	S/M	S/M	S/M	S/M	S/M	S/M
Wine Rack	•	•									•	•	•	•	•	
Microwave/Utility Drawer											•	•				
Covered Dairy Compartment	2	1	2	2	2	1	2	2	1	1	1	1	1	1	1	1
Deep Fixed Door Bins	1	1	1	1	3	3½	3	3	3½	2½	1	1	1	1	1	5
Deep Adjustable Door Bins	4	4	4	4							4	4	4	4	4	
Keepers	2	2	2	2	2		2	2		1	2	2	2	2	2	2
Energy Saver Switch	•	•	•	•	•	•	•	•	•	•	auto	auto	auto	auto	auto	auto
NO FROST FREEZER																
Freezer Light	•	•	•	•							•	•	•	•	•	•
Heavy Duty Adjustable Wire Shelf	2	2	2	2	2	1	1	1	1	1	4	5	4	5	5	5
Deep Fixed Door Bins	2	2	2	2	2	2	2	2	2	2	5	6	5	6	6	6
Freezer Keeper	1	1	1	1	1		1	1		1						
Ice Cube Trays	4		4	4	4	2	2	2	2	2		4		4	4	4
Automatic Icemaker	option	yes	option	option	option	option	option	option	option	option	yes	option	yes	option	option	option
EXTERIOR FEATURES																
Ice and Water Dispenser		•									•		•			
Reversible Doors	•	Special Order	•	•	•	•	•	•	•	•						
Front Adjustable Wheels with Locks	•	•	•	•	•	•	•	•	•	•	•	•	•	•	•	•
Door Stops	2	2	2	2	2	2	2	2	2	2	2	2	2	2	2	2
Door Trim Kit "Option"	option	option	option	option	option						option	option	option	option		
Foam Door Insulation	•	•	•	•	•	•	•	•	•	•	•	•	•	•	•	•
Available in White and Almond	•	•	•	•	•	•	•	•	•	•	•	•	•	•	•	•
Shipping Weight (Lbs./Kg.)	314/142	328/149	306/139	282/128	270/122	268/121	260/118	254/115	249/113	240/109	373/169	358/162	345/156	330/150	321/146	310/141
Height (In./Cm.) *	65½/166	65½/166	65½/166	65½/166	65½/166	65½/166	64½/164	64½/164	64½/164	60/152	66⅜/169	66⅜/169	66⅜/169	66⅜/169	66⅜/169	66⅜/169
Width (In./Cm.)	33/84	33/84	31½/80	31½/80	31½/80	31½/80	29/74	29/74	29/74	29/74	35¾/91	35¾/91	33/84	33/84	31/79	31/79
Depth (In./Cm.) Including Handle	33/84	33/84	33/84	30/76	30/76	30/76	30/76	30/76	30/76	30/76	31⅓/79	31⅓/79	31⅓/79	31⅓/79	31⅓/79	31⅓/79
Depth (In./Cm.) with Door Open 90 Degrees	62⅜/158	62⅜/158	60⅞/155	57⅞/147	57⅞/147	57⅞/147	55⅜/141	55⅜/141	55⅜/141	55⅜/141	48¾/124	48¾/124	48¾/124	48¾/124	46¾/119	46¾/119
Total Shelf Area (Sq. Ft./Sq. M)	34.5/3.2	32.8/3.0	32.3/3.0	28.3/2.6	28.5/2.6	26.2/2.4	24.1/2.2	24.1/2.2	23.7/2.2	22.5/2.1	29.0/2.7	30.4/2.8	25.1/2.3	26.3/2.4	24.3/2.3	24.3/2.3
Total Volume (Cu. Ft./M)	22.5/.64	21.9/.62	21.0/.59	18.5/.52	18.6/.53	18.6/.53	16.5/.47	16.5/.47	16.5/.47	14.6/.41	23.5/.67	23.8/.67	21.6/.61	21.8/.62	20.2/.57	20.2/.57
Fresh Food Volume (Cu. Ft./M)	15.5/.44	15.0/.42	14.6/.41	12.8/.36	12.9/.37	12.9/.37	11.7/.33	11.7/.33	11.7/.33	10.5/.30	15.2/.43	15.2/.43	15.2/.43	15.2/.43	13.6/.38	13.6/.38
Freezer Volume (Cu. Ft./M)	7.0/.20	6.9/.20	6.4/.18	5.7/.16	5.7/.16	5.7/.16	4.8/.14	4.8/.14	4.8/.14	4.1/.12	8.3/.23	8.6/.24	6.4/.18	6.6/.19	6.6/.19	6.6/.19

All models listed in this brochure may not be available from every Maytag dealer. Because of continuing product improvements, Maytag reserves the right to change specifications without notice.

Deco white models available in ERSW24A and ERSW22A.

*NOTE: Does not include door hinge cover.
  For ease of installation, allow ½" clearance on sides and top.

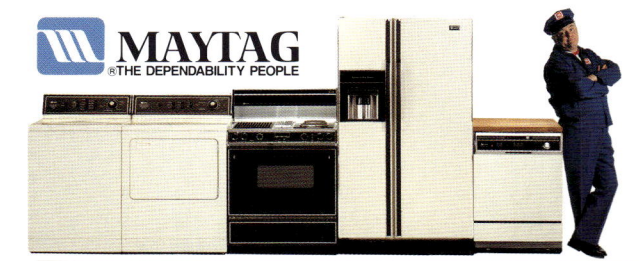

MAYTAG THE DEPENDABILITY PEOPLE

768L-ADV 12-90 225M   Printed in U.S.A.

MAYTAG COMPANY One Dependability Square, Newton, Iowa 50208

Miele built-in appliances

The new Miele family of built-in appliances

Miele built-in appliances

Technological advancements make today's kitchen ever more sophisticated. Indeed, the increasing emphasis placed on the professional kitchen design illustrates the enduring importance of the kitchen as a workplace. At Miele, we believe that a kitchen should be functional and practical, as well as visually attractive. Of course, this should also apply to the appliances.

The new generation of built-in appliances from Miele.
Too often appliances are obtrusive in the kitchen setting. Designed and manufactured to uncompromising standards, Miele appliances are intended to blend in with any well-made kitchen. And even where unusual installations are required, more often than not Miele appliances can be perfectly accomodated.

Miele built-in appliances – adaptable in appearance.
Perfection in any kitchen can only be achieved by selecting truly built-in appliances.
Many Miele appliances can be fitted with decor panels to correspond with the kitchen design. Dishwashers can even be fitted with a solid door front without trim kit. Washing machines, tumble dryers and dishwashers have a variable toekick height and recess depth.
Most appliances are available in a selection of finishes, including dark brown, white and black. Either of these choices will combine harmoniously with laminate or solid wood kitchens.

Miele built-in appliances – renown for uncompromising quality.

Since its inception in 1899, Miele has believed that long-term success is dependent upon product quality. By combining the best materials, the highest standards of workmanship and many years of experience, Miele ensures that it's appliances will be the source of pleasure for many years.

Miele built-in appliances – the ultimate in technologically advanced kitchen appliances.

Built-in appliances are the heart of any kitchen. Their timesaving features have revolutionized the way we live.
But today's appliances from Miele are designed to be more than merely functional. Apart from performing perfectly, they are quiet, reliable, low in energy and/or water consumption and a delight to look at.
From cooking and baking to dishwashing, from grilling and frying to venting, and from washing to drying, Miele has a wide selection of appliances to choose from. Browse through this brochure or visit your Miele dealer and see for yourself why we at Miele believe in our motto; "Miele – anything else is a compromise".

Ceramic cooktops

The advantages of ceramic cooktops
Ceramic cooktops not only look good, but have many practical day-to-day uses. For example,
- The smooth surface is very easy to keep clean.
- Pots and pans are in no danger of tipping over since the surface is perfectly flat.
- Two of the four burners are variable in size to allow for smaller or larger pots.
- When not in use the cooktop doubles up as additional countertop space, a practical feature particularly in smaller homes.
- The surface of the cooktop is made of a glass-type, heat-resistant and easily cleanable material. Its durability is far superior to many other similar looking cooktops – both past and present!
- During use, small red indicator lights appear at the front of the cooktop. These indicators will stay on even after the cooktop is switched off, so long as the surface is still too hot to touch.

Combiset program

The Miele combiset program gives you options. It lets you cook with gas or electricity or both, deep fry, barbecue, steam cook, vent or just have a place to rest hot pots and pans.
Identical in width and length, they can be arranged in any configuration you wish. They also come with a choice of control panel color, including black, white or stainless steel.

The largest item in the combiset program is the four burner gas unit. Identical in design with the smaller combiset units, this product can be easily added to a configuration of other combiset units.

It can also be installed on its own, even above the Miele combination oven H 818 B. But wherever installed, the Miele four burner gas fits right in – not just because of its design, but the choice of control panel colors helps your appliances be color coordinated with the kitchen cabinetry.

A first from Miele –
the dishwasher with the removeable cutlery tray

Miele dishwashing technology: advantages without compromise.
A combination of technological achievement and experience. Europe's first dishwasher was manufactured in 1929 by Miele. Since that time Miele has had a considerable influence on the development of the dishwasher. For example, Miele built the world's first microcomputer controlled dishwasher with touch control in 1978. Today's new dishwasher generation represents the latest in this long history of innovative successes.

The new generation is best characterized by the improved quality and performance. The new dishwasher succeeds an extremely successful series, which was in production for nearly 10 years. All the good features from the past have been retained, namely: strong circulation pump, stainless steel interior, automatic spray pressure and a practical selection of washing programs. And, of course, the very high standards of workmanship always associated with Miele.

However, in many respects the new dishwasher signifies a totally new development in appliances. The expanded washing cabinet with the third washing level, the turbo-thermic drying system, the even lower water and energy consumption figures and expanded program selection are the main features of this new concept. A concept that gives you advantages without compromise.

Clean and economical: The triple filter system.
In order to have excellent washing results with the lowest possible water usage, Miele dishwashers are equipped with a triple filter system. The large, fine and microfine filters ensure that the re-circulated water remains micro-filtered clean. Therefore, once removed from the dishes the dirt doesn't come into contact with them again.

Automatic spray pressure.
All Miele dishwashers are fitted with three spray arms. Not only are various spray nozzles angled so that every item receives a direct spray, but the water pressure of the spray arm is different from layer to layer. The lower arm provides a powerful spray for the washing of pots, pans and plates in the lower basket; the middle and top arms ensure that a gentler spray washes the cups and glasses in the top basket.

Built-in water heating booster.
Usually the hot water entering most dishwashers is both too hot and too cold! Since different wash programs require different washing temperatures, dishwashers without a built-in water heating booster can not be really effective.

Miele dishwashers are all equipped with this water heating capability, allowing you to turn your water boiler temperature a little lower. For programs that require higher temperatures, the internal heating booster raises the incoming water temperatures to the prescribed level. This not only ensures excellent washing results, but saves on your water heating costs.

More capacity and flexibility: Miele introduces the world's first dishwasher with separate cutlery tray.

Increased capacity: A larger top basket.
The expanded internal size of the washing cabinet, together with the height-adjustable top basket and practical layout of the lower basket, makes dishwashing more economical than ever before.

In the top basket of the dishwasher models without cutlery tray, two layers of cups and glasses can be washed, still allowing the lower layer to accomodate items of almost 5 inches in height.

Those models without cutlery tray are equipped with a larger, better designed cutlery basket. Note how even the teaspoons get a separate wash and that the basket handle will help in unloading.

Increased capacity: The third washing level.
The cutlery tray or third washing level was invented by Miele. In fact Miele is the only manufacturer of this washing system, which was all made possible by increasing the internal size of the washing cabinet by 11%.

Washing cutlery has now reached new heights. The increased space above the top basket allowed for the insertion of the specially designed cutlery tray. Located directly beneath the top spray arm (Miele dishwashers all have three), the cutlery is always ensured an excellent, hygienic wash. Moreover, by separating the cutlery during loading, the scratching of even your finest silverware is avoided. Since the tray can be totally removed, even loading is made easier. And finally, having dispensed with the traditional cutlery basket, more capacity exists in the lower basket for pots, pans and plates.

The top models allow the configuration of the lower basket to be changed at any time. By removing the inserts, large, awkward shaped items, such as casserole dishes or woks, can be easily accomodated. Acquiring the optional glassware insert allows long-stemmed wine glasses (to $9\frac{1}{2}''$) to be washed in the lower basket. Who else gives you this type of flexibility?

The standard configuration of the lower basket accomodates large plates on the left and pots, pans and other items on the right.

Capacity exists for the comfortable loading of 12 place settings. Dishwashers without the cutlery tray will accomodate plates of up to $11\frac{3}{4}''$ in diameter.

Washing, drying and ironing

Miele has been manufacturing top quality washing machines for more than 80 years. Miele engineers are continuously striving to achieve the highest possible quality and reliability of Miele products. Of course, this does not make Miele appliances cheaper, but extremely good and, in the long, run a far better buy.

Miele's laundry products are designed not only to wash, dry and iron, but also to take perfect care of your wash. For example, different fabrics should be washed according to their fabric group. That is why Miele washing machines have a wide selection of programs to suit all fabrics, including woolens and delicates.

Tumble dryers from Miele do away with many inconveniences. Simply transfer the load from the washing machine to the tumble dryer, it all goes in! Just as the washing machine should take care of the fabric type, so should the dryer. With programs for extra dry and non-iron, normal, machine and hand iron, the tumble dryer does just that. The electronic sensor system controls the machine and switches off the heating as soon as the desired degree of dryness has been reached.

Unlike many other brands, Miele dryers have a gentler drying action. This prevents the fabrics from losing their shape and becoming limp. After all, Miele thinks it makes a lot of sense to protect your laundry.

The washing machine and tumble dryer can be installed under a countertop or stacked. Miele's unique condenser drying system allows dryers to be located almost anywhere. A choice of door hinging is a practical advantage which, together with the insertable decor panels, allows laundry products to be designed into any kitchen or laundry room.

And a well-equipped laundry room would not be complete without the Miele rotary iron. Comfortably seated, it is a pleasure to watch one perfectly ironed piece of laundry after another glide out of the machine.

A more detailed description of Miele laundry products is available in a separate brochure. See your Miele dealer or call Miele Appliances, Inc. for a copy.

Miele Appliances, Inc.
22 D Worlds Fair Drive
Somerset
New Jersey 08873
Tel. 201/560-0899
800/843-7231
Telex 751730
Telefax 201/560-9649

Miele Appliances, Inc.
1900 South Norfolk Street
Suite 101
San Mateo, California 94403
Telephone: (415) 571-9074
Telefax: (415) 571-9188

NUTONE RANGE HOODS

NuTone Decorator Range Hoods help keep kitchens fresh, clean and beautiful!

With NuTone, there's no reason to put up with lingering cooking odors, smoke, heat, humidity or excessive grease in your kitchen.

You can keep it fresh and clean every day with a NuTone Range Hood. Mounted directly above your cooking surface, it collects and filters out airborne cooking by-products.

NuTone offers more styles than ever before to provide powerful air movement — tested and certified by the Home Ventilating Institute.

NuTone Range Hoods. Designer styling plus proven power and performance — *guaranteed!*

New P9100S 400 CFM Twin Blower Range Hood

P9100S Powerful 400 CFM Twin Blower Range Hood with heat sensor and night light.
Superb new styling with easy-to-use sliding switches. Infinite speed switch for just the air delivery needed...up to 400 CFM! Three sizes: 30", 36", 42". Baked enamel finishes in All White, Almond, Black, White with black trim–plus Stainless Steel. Vents horizontally or vertically.

SH-2000 Slide-Away Range Hoods
Eliminates the need for a cabinet. You simply face the hood body with doors or a panel to match your cabinets. Only the slim, squared-off Hood 'visor' is visible —a thin line underscoring your beautiful cabinetry.

To remove smoke, steam or cooking odors, just pull out the tempered glass visor. This turns on an exceptionally efficient dual-centrifugal blower to keep your kitchen fresh.

Easily accessible sliding controls operate variable speed fan, bright cooking light or night light. 320 CFM, 5.0 sones.
SH-2024WH 24" wide. **SH-2030WH** 30" wide. **SH-2036WH** 36" wide.

SH-1000 Slide-Away Range Hoods
Easily installed in a standard cabinet above range or cooktop. Ideal for remodeling an existing kitchen, as well as for new homes. Like the SH-2000, the SH-1000 features a pull-out see-through tempered glass 'visor' that acti-vates a powerful blower. Variable speed fan, bright cooking light, night light. Available in All White or Black finish.
SH-1024WH 24" wide. **SH-1030WH** 30" wide. **SH-1036WH** 36" wide.

TH-500 Tilt-Away Range Hoods
The range hood that isn't there until you need it! TH-500 mounts to the wall above your range or cooktop. The pivoting front of the hood is faced with a panel or doors to match your adjacent cabinets. Closed, it seems there is no hood at all. But when you pull the front panel forward, it becomes a great collection canopy for smoke, heat and kitchen odors. Set the fan at a nominal speed, so when you pull out the canopy the dual centrifugal blower is immediately activated. For more air movement, adjust the easy-to-reach switch under the canopy. Fan automatically shuts off when you push the canopy in. A second sliding switch lets you turn the light up for cooking or down as a night light when not using the blower. 320 CFM, 5.0 sones.
TH-524 24" wide. **TH-530** 30" wide. **TH-536 36"** wide.

TH-500-SO Tilt-Away Shells
Complete with solid-state controls and light assemblies. Use with Exterior Mounted Fans shown at right. All motor noise stays outside your home.

NN8300 Convertible Twin Blower Hood with night light.
Right up to the time of installation you can decide to use it with 3¼" x 10" ducting...or as a Non-Duct. *And no special kit is needed!* Powerful, but quiet. Solid-state controls. Activated charcoal filters combined with grease filters included. 30" and 36" sizes in four enamel finishes plus stainless steel.

MM6500 Convertible Decorator Hood One beautiful hood—three ducting options! Infinite speed control for quiet, efficient operation. Right up to the time of installation, you can decide to use it with 3¼" x 10" duct horizontally or vertically...7" round duct...or as a non-duct. 30", 36", 42" sizes. Four enamel finishes plus stainless steel.

TH-500 Tilt-Away Range Hood, open

TH-500 Tilt-Away Range Hood, closed

NN8300 Convertible Twin Blower Hood

SH-1000 Series Slide-Away Range Hood

Slim, sliding visor of the SH-1000WH is virtually invisible...until things get cooking!

MM Series Decorator Range Hood

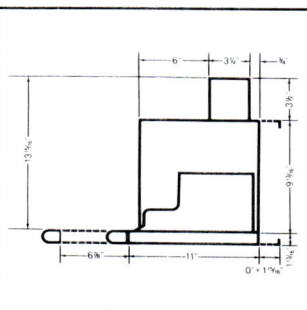

SH-1000 is easily installed in a standard cabinet above the range or cooktop

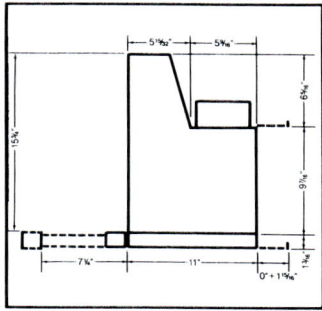

SH-2000 eliminates need for a cabinet. Front of hood is faced with matching doors or panel

SH-2000WH Slide-Away Range Hood

SO-9100S Series Range Hood Shells Same as P9100S except has no power unit. Sliding switches for fan and lights. Use Exterior Mounted Fans shown below. Available in three sizes, three finishes.

For extra quiet inside use Hood Shells with NuTone Exterior-Mounted Fans.

RF-35 Roof Fan Strong centrifugal blower, 270 CFM. Uses 7" round duct. Aluminum damper opens and closes automatically.

WF-35 Wall Fan Housing is baked enamel on zinc-coated steel. Similar to RF-35.

RF-1N Roof Fan ⅛ HP motor, 620 CFM. Aluminum housing with 24" sq. self-flashing flange.

WF-1N Wall Fan All aluminum housing with stainless steel fittings, rainshield included. 650 CFM.

RF-35 Roof Fan

WF-35 Wall Fan

WF-1N Wall Fan

RF-1N Roof Fan

For complete information on the full line of NuTone Range Hoods, see Catalog HF-300.

NuTone products add comfort, convenience, security and entertainment to your home

Radio-Intercoms *mpp*

You can be in two places at once! NuTone Radio-Intercom gives you room-to-room intercom ... the security of answering your front door without opening it ... lets you listen-in on the baby or to a sick room ... enjoy FM/AM radio in any room, poolside or on the patio!

Central Vacs *mpp*

Imagine vacuum cleaning so thorough you have to dust less often! So quiet you can vacuum while baby naps or the family watches TV. So convenient you don't have to lug around a heavy motor. All you carry is a lightweight hose and cleaning tool. Cleaning room-to-room, up and down stairs, basement, garage is easier. No wonder NuTone Central Vac is one of today's most-wanted features.

The power unit is built-in. NuTone offers six different systems. Sanitary, fully disposable soil bag models, and bagless units with the revolutionary NuTone Draw-down™ Cyclonic patented technology. Easy to install, they add value to any home.

Door Chimes *mpp*

Express your personal decorating touch with a traditional or contemporary NuTone Chime. Chime tones range from two-note to chordtone to the beloved Westminster chime sequence ... or even one you can program to play any tune you can whistle, sing or hum!
There are even wireless extension chimes and a new visual door signal for the hearing impaired!

Paddle Fans Add comfort and energy efficiency with an elegant NuTone contemporary or traditional fan. Light Kits are also available. *mpp*

mpp This symbol identifies NuTone Maximum Performance Products - *guaranteed for as long as you own your home.*

For the name of your nearby NuTone sales outlet, **DIAL FREE 1-800-543-8687** in the contiguous U.S., except in Ohio call 1-800-582-2030.

Send for FREE catalog

NuTone Inc., Dept. KBS-3
P.O. Box 1580, Cincinnati, Ohio 45201

Name		Title
Company		
Address		
City	State	Zip
Phone		9220

Form 9220, printed in U.S.A 1/91   Product specifications subject to change without notice.

NuTone

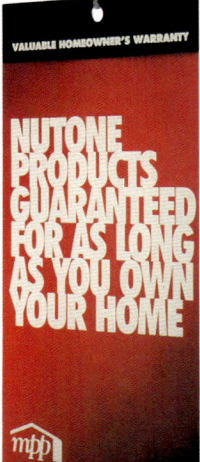

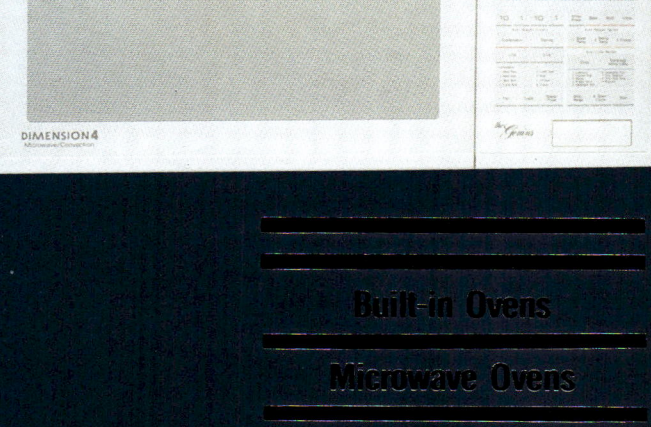

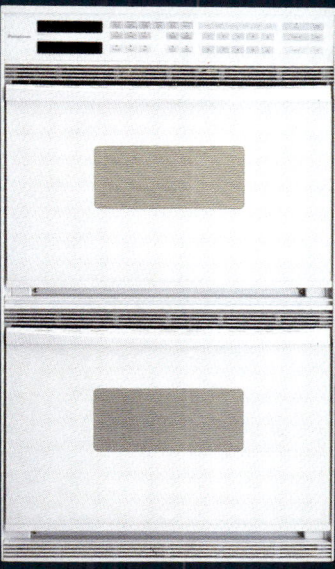

Built-in Ovens

Microwave Ovens

Electric Cook Tops

Panasonic

Contents

Continuing the Tradition

Over the past three decades Panasonic has been committed to improving people's lives through advanced technology. And we're proving it again with our innovative lineup of cooking appliances. Whether it's our exciting Cuisine III built-in ovens, over-the-range microwave ovens, built-in microwave ovens, cooktops or downdrafts, Panasonic is defining today's modern kitchen with an accent on form as well as function.

Designed For Excellence

Panasonic realizes that your kitchen is more than just a place where food is prepared--it's a statement of style! Which is why we've designed a lineup of built-in cooking appliances that are as beautiful as they are brilliant. And since each appliance is finely crafted with a close attention to detail, you can depend on the same quality that has made Panasonic a trusted name throughout the world.

Panasonic technology

NN-ED750H

BUILT-IN OVENS

Panasonic Cuisine III built-in ovens combine microwave, thermal and convection heat to create an oven that performs up to eight different cooking functions! And with these versatile ovens you'll also enjoy convenient features such as illuminated user-friendly touch controls, a self-cleaning preset with an automatic locking door system and a concealed lower heating element. Plus, with its flush-mounted Euro-style design, Cuisine III built-in ovens are a tasteful blend of style and technology!

1. MICROWAVE

Cuisine III ovens offer microwave convenience and the ability to easily accomodate family-sized meals. Its uniform microwave distribution is designed for even cooking. And with Auto Weight Defrost, simply enter the weight of most frozen foods and press START--the oven will automatically calculate the power levels and defrosting times!

2. CONVECTION

Cuisine III ovens produce outstanding browning results. A fan constantly circulates hot air within the oven cavity for uniform temperatures and even browning results for many of your favorite recipes.

3. BAKE

Thorough cooking and browning of your foods are possible when selecting BAKE. And thanks to the three-shelf baking capability you can use one, two or three racks at a time!

NN-ES750H

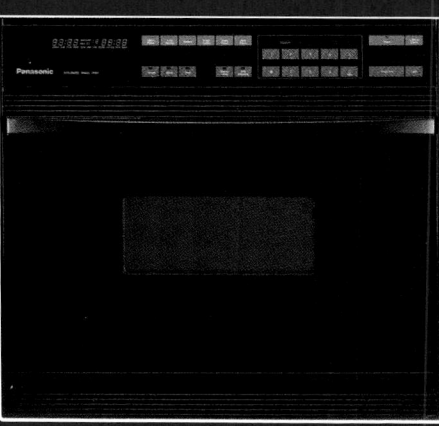

NN-ES750B

NN-ED750B

4. BROIL

Cuisine III ovens are designed to let you enjoy many of your favorite foods without the smoke that's normally associated with broiling. A catalytic converter allows you to broil with the door closed so you can keep your kitchen clean!

5. MICROWAVE/ROAST COMBINATION

Roast Combination is ideal for roasting meats, poultry and casseroles. Combination cooking automatically alternates between convection and microwave cooking for browned foods with microwave quickness.

6. MICROWAVE/BAKE COMBINATION

Bake combination combines radiant heat with microwave convenience to cook cakes, pies, vegetables and appetizers. Foods will bake quickly while retaining an attractive golden-brown appearance.

7. MICROWAVE/BROIL COMBINATION

Broil Combination provides the best of two popular cooking methods. You'll be able to quickly prepare meats and poultry that are tender on the inside, crispy on the outside.

8. SIMMER

The Simmer feature cooks you food by using low heat for slow cooking. This allows you to tenderize tough foods like pot roast or to protect delicate foods such as casseroles. The simmer feature also produces excellent soups and stews!

NN-2959

OVER-THE-RANGE MICROWAVE OVENS

Panasonic has put its advanced technology into a stylish lineup of over-the-range microwave ovens. Selected models allow you to cook by four different methods -- microwave, bake, combination microwave/convection or broil. While other models provide one-touch sensor cooking that eliminates the need to calculate cooking times or power levels for many of your favorite receipes.

With so many fabulous features such as three-stage memory, Auto Start and variable power levels, there's cooking versatility throughout the entire lineup! Plus, each of the ovens offers a three-way ventilation system that allows for installation in virtually any kitchen. At Panasonic we've helped to make cooking one of life's simple pleasures!

Three-Way Ventilation System

The 3-way ventilation system allows for installation in almost any kind of kitchen! The three ventilation options allow the user to send the air out of the kitchen through a top or back ventilation duct. Or, for houses without an exhaust duct, the oven will circulate clean, filtered air back into the room. A replaceable filter is also included.

Rotating Wave Guide

A special rotating wave guide beneath the oven floor helps to distribute microwaves evenly throughout the oven cavity. This design eliminates the need to interrupt the cooking process to manually rotate foods.

Easy Installation

Panasonic over-the-range ovens can be easily installed with a slide-in installation kit. Simply secure the hanger brackets in place and then slide in the oven. Once installed, your oven can also operate as a two-speed exhaust fan and range light.

FOUR COOKING METHODS IN ONE OVEN (NN-2959, NN-2909)

Microwave: Panasonic over-the-range ovens offer microwave convenience with variable power levels of 80-700 watts. So you'll be able to defrost foods quickly, reheat left-overs in seconds and prepare a wide variety of your favorite foods!

Bake: Convection cooking utilizes the constant circulation of dry, heated air throughout the oven and around foods to help produce excellent baking and browning results. **Microwave/Convection Combination:** Combination cooking allows you to roast meats and poultry that are tender and juicy on the inside, thoroughly browned on the outside. Best of all, you can enjoy delicious foods in a fraction of the time it takes to cook them in a conventional oven.

Broiling: Broiling seems to bring out the best in foods like steaks and chops. With convection broiling, heat is forced into the food, quickly cooking the outside to seal in natural juices and flavor.

Genius Auto Sensor (NN-2959, NN-2909, NN-2808)

The Genius Auto Sensor control utilizes a humidity sensor to provide one-touch cooking. As steam is released from food, a sensor will detect the changing levels of moisture in the oven. When a significant change in steam occurs, the oven will signal its microprocessor computer to calculate an appropriate amount of time to complete the cooking process.

Auto Sensor Cook With One-Touch Convenience (NN-2959, NN-2909, NN-2808)

Auto Sensor Cook allows you to automatically cook many of your favorite foods. Simply select the appropriate food category and let the oven do the rest!

Auto Sensor Reheat (NN-2959, NN-2909, NN-2808)

With Auto Sensor Reheat you can accurately reheat foods in accordance with their current state of preparation. So, you can set the oven to reheat: 1) Room temperature foods, 2) Refrigerated foods, or 3) Frozen foods at the appropriate power levels and times with just a touch of a button!

Auto Weight Combination Cook (NN-2959, NN-2909)

This automatic cooking program lets you combination-cook meats and poultry by weight, without manually setting the cooking times and power levels. Just select the proper food category, enter the weight of the food and touch START!

Auto Weight Defrost

Thanks to Auto Weight Defrost there's no need to calculate defrosting times or power levels. Simply touch the Defrost pad, enter the weight of your frozen food and press START. The oven does the rest automatically!

Doneness Control (NN-2959, NN-2909, NN-2808)

The Doneness Control adds flexibility to the Auto Sensor program. By touching either the More or Less Doneness control pad you can increase or decrease the cooking time for any recipe. This allows you to tailor the cooking program to your own personal taste!

Auto Start

This handy feature allows you to preset the oven to begin cooking up to 12 hours in advance! It's a great way to have a fully cooked meal waiting for you whenever you wish!

Variable Power Levels

Panasonic over-the-range ovens have variable power levels for enhanced versatility. The power levels can be adjusted from Warm at 80 watts, to a High setting of 700 watts for fast cooking!

NN-2909

NN-2808

NN-2408

MICROWAVE OVENS AND BUILT-IN TRIM KITS

NN-9850

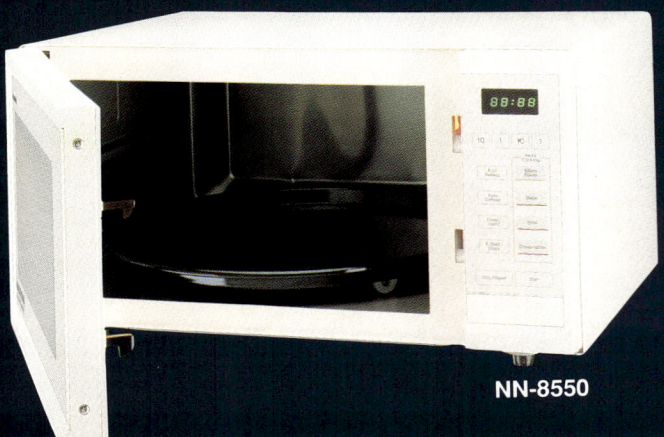

NN-8550

MICROWAVE OVENS AND BUILT-IN TRIM KITS

The Panasonic lineup of microwave ovens offers incredible versatility and performance. Each of these microwave ovens offer four popular cooking methods for unlimited cooking possibilities -- microwave, bake, combination microwave/convection, and broil. And since our ovens come equipped with an automatic turntable there's no need to interrupt the cooking process in order to manually rotate your food.

Panasonic microwave ovens are designed to suit any taste. One model has a built-in bread bakery which allows you to make delicious homemade bread with minimal effort! And selected models offer such outstanding features as Turbo Reheat, Turbo Defrost and one-touch cooking. Plus, with one of the optional built-in trim kits, you can neatly and securely position your oven into an open area of kitchen cabinet space for a custom finished look. When your kitchen calls for variety, the answer is Panasonic!

Microwave: The standard microwave funtions allow you to defrost foods in a flash, reheat leftovers in seconds and quickly prepare delicious meats, vegetables, fish, casseroles and more!

Bake: Thanks to the combination of our flat heater system plus convection heat, you can bake scrumptious cakes, pies, breads, pastries and casseroles with outstanding results.

Microwave/Convection Combination: Combination cooking allows you to combine the best properties of microwaving and baking. So, with microwave quickness, you'll also be able to enjoy foods that are tender on the inside, evenly browned on the outside.

Broiling: Broiling seems to bring out the best in foods like steaks and chops. With convection broiling, heat is forced into the food, quickly cooking the outside to seal in natural juices and flavor.

Automatic Turntable

The Panasonic Cook-A-Round Automatic Turntable continously rotates food to help promote even cooking, while accomodating most three-quart dishes. And for added convenience the round tray and roller ring are easily removed for cleaning.

One-Touch Sensor Cooking
(NN-9850, NN-3959)

The Sensor Cook feature brings one-touch simplicity to everyday cooking. With a single touch of one of the sensor keys, cooking begins automatically. There's no need to calculate time or power levels!

Turbo Defrost

You can defrost meats, fish and poultry according to the food's weight. By using the weight keys, simply enter the food's weight and touch START. It's that easy!

Turbo Reheat

The Turbo Reheat feature allows you to quickly reheat foods from room or refrigerator temperatures. Simply press the Auto Reheat Key and enter up to as many as 4 servings. It's an easy way to enjoy one of the most popular functions of the microwave oven.

Auto Start

This handy feature allows you to preset the oven to begin cooking up to 12 hours in advance! It's a great way to have a fully cooked meal waiting for you whenever you wish!

Bread Bakery Functions
(NN-3959)

Loaf Setting: The Loaf setting allows you to make delicious home made bread. Simply combine the ingredients in the special teflon coated pan and touch the Bread Key. The oven will knead and bake the dough automatically. You simply remove a tasty loaf of bread in four hours!

Dough Setting: Using the Dough setting stops the bread-making process after the kneading has been completed. This allows you to remove and shape the dough into delectable foods like rolls or croissants and then bake as desired.

12-Hour Timer: A convenient timer lets you pre-program the oven to bake bread up to 12 hours in advance. It's a great way to wake up to the wonderful aroma of fresh-baked bread!

NN-3959

DOWNDRAFT COOKTOPS

ELECTRIC DOWNDRAFT COOKTOPS AND SOLID DISC COOKTOPS

Electric Downdraft Cooktops

Panasonic puts style and versatility into a remarkable appliance that's ready for any of your cooking needs! With the Pansonic electric downdraft cooktop, you have the option of using up to five different optional interchangeable cartridges- grille, griddle, coil elements, solid-disc elements or ceramic glass. So, whether you're looking for the great taste of an outdoor grille or the cooking ease of a teflon coated griddle, Panasonic lets you create the appliance of your choice!

36" Downdraft Cooktop : NN-EC630B

- Convenient vent system
- Five optional interchangeable cartridges :
    1. NN-AC620 - Coil
    2. NN-AC630 - Solid element
    3. NN-AC640 - Smooth top
    4. NN-AC610 - Griddle
    5. NN-AC600 - Grille
- Raised outer edges
- Side mounted controls
- Easy-to-remove control panels
- Two-piece lift out filter
- Independent vent switch
- Self-ventilating motor
- Countertop or island installation

Solid Disc Element Cooktops

Panasonic solid disc cooktops are designed to make an elegant statement in any kitchen. Handsomely styled, these tempered glass cooktops feature heavy cast iron elements that provide outstanding uniform heat distribution. And since the smooth cooktop surface eliminates the need for drip pans, cleanup is fast and easy. Panasonic solid disc cooktops...performance that's matched by beauty.

36" Solid Disc Glass Cooktops : NN-EC620B, NN-EC620H
- Tempered glass cooktop surface
- Two 8" and two 6" sealed solid disc elements
- Non-slide element surfaces
- Euro-style design
- Allows for installation of a drawer or cabinet underneath

30" Solid Disc Glass Cooktops : NN-EC020B, NN-EC020H
- Tempered glass cooktop surface
- Two 8" and two 6" sealed solid disc elements
- Non-slide element surfaces
- Euro-style design
- Allows for installation of a drawer or cabinet underneath

Panasonic technology

DOUBLE OVEN

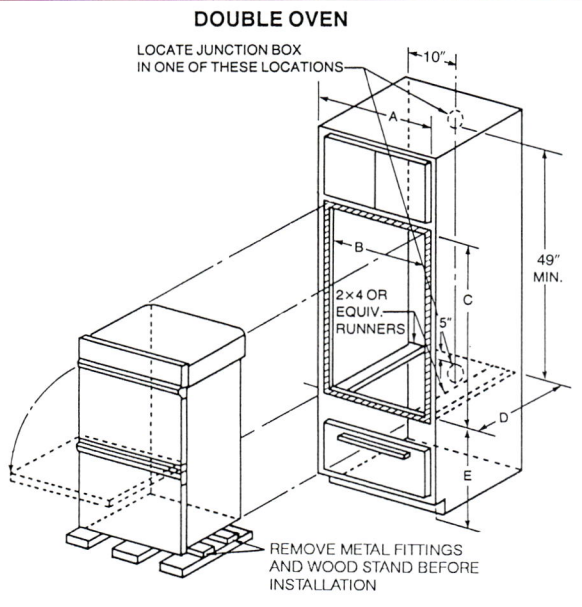

LOCATE JUNCTION BOX
IN ONE OF THESE LOCATIONS

←10"→

A

B

2×4 OR
EQUIV.
RUNNERS

5"

C

D

E

49"
MIN.

REMOVE METAL FITTINGS
AND WOOD STAND BEFORE
INSTALLATION

A Cabinet Width   27"
B Cabinet Cutout   24" min.   24-5/8" max.
C Cutout Height   43-3/4"
D Cutout Depth   23-1/2" min.
E Cutout Location   16" min.

SINGLE OVEN

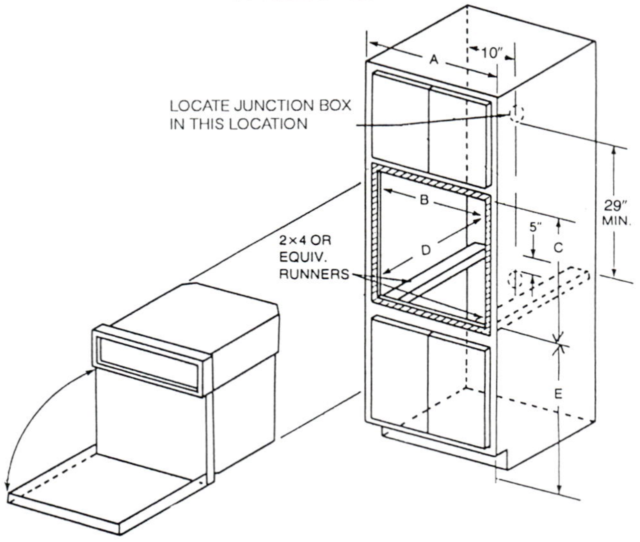

LOCATE JUNCTION BOX
IN THIS LOCATION

A ←10"→

B

D

5"

C

E

29"
MIN.

2×4 OR
EQUIV.
RUNNERS

A Cabinet Width   27"
B Cabinet Cutout   24" min.   24-5/8" max.
C Cutout Height   24-1/8"
D Cutout Depth   23-1/2" min.
E Cutout Location   36" min.

NOTE: The entire weight of the oven(s) are supported by the 2″ × 4″ or equivalent runners. Make sure these runners are level and rigidly mounted.

		NN-ES750H	NN-ES750B	NN-ED750H	NN-ED750B
Single oven		●	●		
Double oven				●	●
Self-cleaning oven		● 890°F	● 890°F	Upper & Lower 890°F	Upper & Lower 890°F
Overall dimensions (W × H × D)	inch	26½ × 25¼ × 22¹³⁄₁₆		26½ × 44¹⁵⁄₁₆ × 22¹⁵⁄₁₆	
	metric	673 × 641 × 580		673 × 1141 × 582	
Overall oven interior dimensions	Inch	18⅜ × 13¼ × 15⅜		18⅜ × 13¼ × 15⅜	
(W × H × D)	metric	466 × 335 × 390		466 × 335 × 390	
Cutout dimensions (W × D)	min	24 × 23½		24 × 23½	
Cutout dimensions (W × H)	max	24⅝ × 24⅛		24⅝ × 43¾	
Oven cabinet width required		27	27	27	27
Oven shelves		3	3	4	4
Broiler pan/rack		●	●	●	●
Oven door with window		●	●	●	●
Glass door		White	Black	White	Black
Electronic oven timer		●	●	●	●
Cleaning time (3hr. pre-set) (1hr. 30min.–4hr. 30min.)		Variable	Variable	Variable	Variable
MICROWAVE FEATURES					
Microwave power		700W	700W	700W	700W
Auto weight defrosting		●	●	●	●
Electronic digital display		●	●	●	●
Clock timer		●	●	●	●
Time-controlled microwave cooking		●	●	●	●
Temperature Probe Cook		●	●	●	●
Electronic MWO touch controls		●	●	●	●
Microwave cooking timer		99min. 99sec.	99min. 99sec.	99min. 99sec.	99min. 99sec.
Microwave power levels		10	10	10	10
Microwave oven cavity		2.1 cft	2.1 cft	2.1 cft	2.1 cft
CONVENTIONAL OVEN FEATURES					
Convection		500°F	500°F	500°F	500°F
Bake		500°F	500°F	500°F	500°F
Broil		●	●	●	●
Bake combination		300°–450°F	300°–450°F	300°–450°F	300°–450°F
Roast combination		300°–425°F	300°–425°F	300°–425°F	300°–425°F
Simmer		300°F	300°F	300°F	300°F
Broil combination		●	●	●	●
Three rack baking		●	●	●	●
GENERAL FEATURES					
Catalytic converter		●	●	●	●
Oven interior light		●	●	●	●
Stand timer		●	●	●	●
European styling		●	●	●	●
One year warranty (parts & labor)		●	●	●	●
KW rating	120/240V	6.3	6.3	9.4	9.4
Approx. shipping weight (lbs)		170 LBS	170 LBS	288 LBS	288 LBS

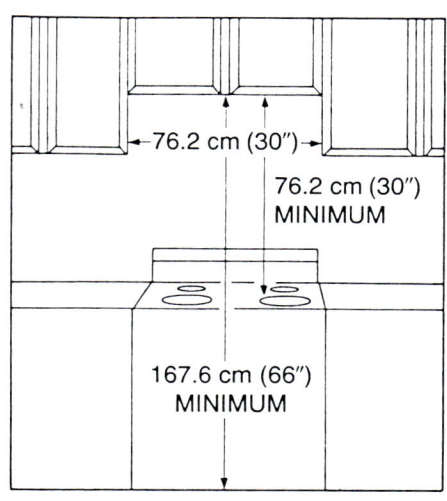

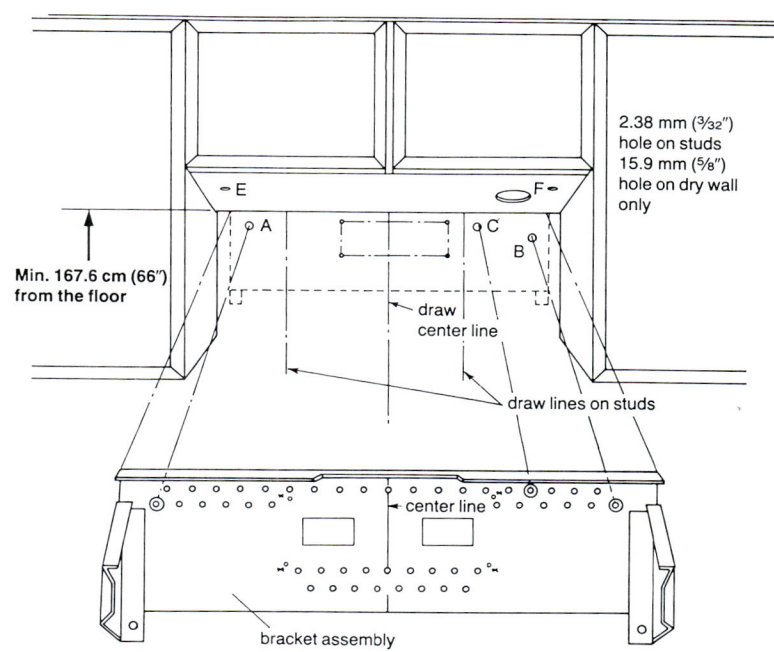

76.2 cm (30″)

76.2 cm (30″)
MINIMUM

167.6 cm (66″)
MINIMUM

2.38 mm (³⁄₃₂″)
hole on studs
15.9 mm (⁵⁄₈″)
hole on dry wall
only

Min. 167.6 cm (66″)
from the floor

E

A

F

C

B

draw center line

draw lines on studs

center line

bracket assembly

Specifications

The Panasonic Line up		NN-2959	NN-2909	NN-2808	NN-2408
Cooking Power		700 W	700 W	700 W	700 W
Cavity Size		1.0 cft.	1.0 cft.	1.0 cft.	1.0 cft.
Convection Bake (Oven Temp)		Yes (200−450°F) Auto Preheat	Yes (200−450°F) Auto Preheat		
Broil		Yes	Yes		
Combination		Yes	Yes		
Auto Weight Combination		Yes	Yes		
Auto Sensor Control	Cook	Yes	Yes	Yes	
	Doneness Control	Yes	Yes	Yes	
Auto Reheat/Sensor Reheat		Sensor Reheat	Sensor Reheat	Sensor Reheat	Auto Reheat
Auto Weight Defrost		Yes	Yes	Yes	Yes
Auto Start		Yes	Yes	Yes	Yes
Memory Stages		3	3	3	3
Auto Count-up		Yes	Yes	Yes	Yes
Defrost Function		Yes	Yes	Yes	Yes
Delay Start/Stand		Yes (up to 99 min. 99 sec.)	Yes (up to 99 min. 99 sec.)	Yes (up to 99 min. 99 sec.)	Yes (up to 99 min. 99 sec.)
Timer		99 min. 99 sec.	99 min. 99 sec.	99 min. 99 sec.	99 min. 99 sec.
Digital Clock/Read Out Display		Yes	Yes	Yes	Yes
Touch Control		Yes	Yes	Yes	Yes
Oven Interior		Stainless	Stainless	Epoxy	Epoxy
Oven Dimension (H × W × D)		8³⁄₁₆″ × 18⁵⁄₁₆″ × 11″ (208mm × 465mm × 280mm)	8³⁄₁₆″ × 18⁵⁄₁₆″ × 11″ (208mm × 465mm × 280mm)	8³⁄₁₆″ × 18⁵⁄₁₆″ × 11″ (208mm × 465mm × 280mm)	8³⁄₁₆″ × 18⁵⁄₁₆″ × 11″ (208mm × 465mm × 280mm)
Outside Dimension (H × W × D)		16⁷⁄₈″ × 29¹⁵⁄₁₆″ × 14³⁄₁₆″ (429mm × 760mm × 360mm)	16⁷⁄₈″ × 29¹⁵⁄₁₆″ × 14³⁄₁₆″ (429mm × 760mm × 360mm)	16⁷⁄₈″ × 29¹⁵⁄₁₆″ × 14³⁄₁₆″ (416mm × 760mm × 360mm)	16⁷⁄₈″ × 29¹⁵⁄₁₆″ × 14³⁄₁₆″ (416mm × 760mm × 360mm)
Power Requirements		120 V. 60 Hz, 13 A, 1,500 W, AC only	120 V. 60 Hz, 13 A, 1,500 W, AC only	120 V. 60 Hz, 13 A, 1,500 W, AC only	120 V. 60 Hz, 13 A, 1,500 W, AC only
Shipping Weight		Aprox. 80.3 lbs.	Approx. 80.3 lbs.	Approx. 67 lbs.	Approx. 67 lbs.

MICROWAVE OVENS & BUILT-IN TRIM KITS
(DETAILS)

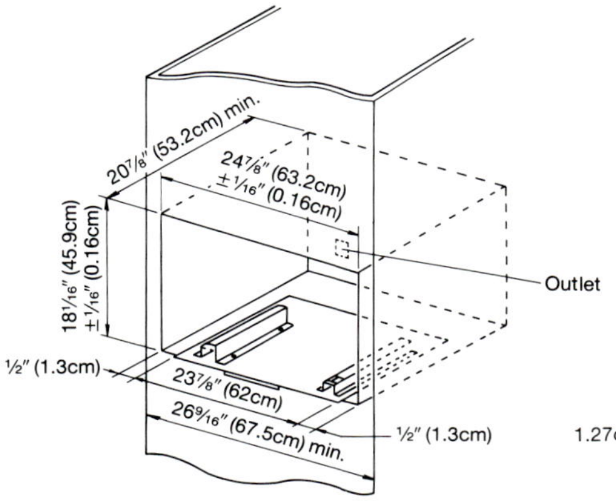

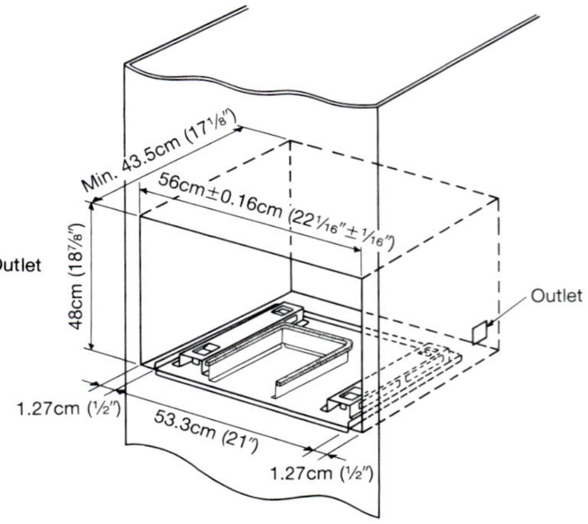

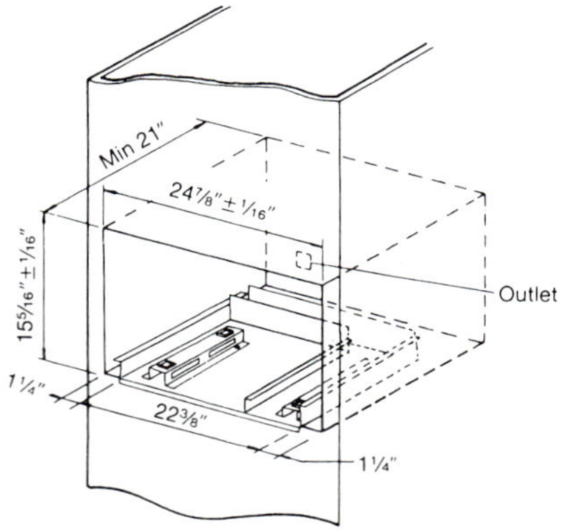

Specifications

The Panasonic Line up		NN-9850 (white)
Cook-A-Round Automatic Turntable		Yes
Cooking Power		700 W
Cavity Size		1.5 cft.
Convection/Bake (Oven Temp)		Yes (200–450°F) Auto Preheat
Broil		Yes
Combination		Yes
One Touch Features	Reheat	Yes
	Casserole	Yes
	Vegetables	Yes
	Frozen Convenience Foods	Yes
	Meat	Yes
	Poultry	Yes
	Cake	Yes
	Pie	Yes
More/Less Control		Yes
Auto Reheat		Sensor
Auto Defrost		Turbo
Auto Start		Yes
Memory Stages		3
Auto Count-up		Yes
Defrost Function		Yes
Delay Start/Stand		Yes (up to 99min. 99sec.)
Timer		99 min. 99 sec.
Digital Clock/Read Out Display		Yes
Touch Control		Yes
Oven Interior		Stainless
Oven Dimension (H × W × D)		9½″ × 16¼″ × 16 13/16″ (242 × 412 × 426mm)
Outside Dimension (H × W × D)		14 13/16″ × 23 7/8″ × 18 7/8″ (376 × 606 × 481mm)
Power Requirements		120 V. 60 Hz, 12.5 A, 1,500 W, AC only
Shipping Weight		Approx. 64 lbs.
Trim Kit Installation		TK909 (W)

The Panasonic Line up		NN-3959 (white) (Lighted Key Pads)
Cook-A-Round Automatic Turntable		Yes
Cooking Power		700 W
Cavity Size		1.1 cft.
Bread Bakery	Loaf Settings	Yes
	Dough Settings	Yes
Convection/Bake (Oven Temp)		Yes (105, 200–450°F) Auto Preheat
Broil		Yes
Combination		Yes
Weight Combination		Yes
One Touch Features (Lighted Keys)	Defrost	Yes
	Reheat	Yes
	Roast (Well, Med, Rare)	Yes
	Poultry	Yes
	Vegetable (Soft,Root)	Yes
	Seafood	Yes
	Cake (2 kinds)	Yes
	Frozen Convenience Foods	Yes
Large User Friendly Display		Yes
Auto Reheat		Sensor
Memory Stages		3
Auto Start		Yes
Defrost Function		Yes
Auto Count-up		Yes
Delay Start/Stand		Yes (up to 99min. 99sec.)
Timer		99 min. 99 sec.
Touch Control		Yes
Oven Interior		Easy cleaning materia
Oven Dimension (H × W × D)		9½″ × 14 7/16″ × 14 5/8″ (232 × 367 × 372mm)
Outside Dimension (H × W × D)		15 3/16″ × 22″ × 17¾″ (385 × 558 × 450mm)
Power Requirements		120 V. 60 Hz, 12.5 A, 1,500 W, AC only
Shipping Weight		Approx 69 lbs.
Trim Kit Installation		TK359

The Panasonic Line up	NN-8550 (white)
Cook-A-Round Automatic Turntable	Yes
Cooking Power	800 W
Cavity Size	1.1 cft.
Convection/Bake (Oven Temp)	Yes (200–450°F) Auto Preheat
Broil	Yes
Combination	Yes
Auto Weight Combination	
Auto Sensor Cook	
Doneness Control	
Auto Reheat	Programmed
Auto Defrost	Turbo
Auto Start	Yes
Memory Stages	3
Auto Count-up	Yes
Defrost Function	Yes
Delay Start/Stand	Yes (up to 99min. 99sec.)
Timer	99 min. 99 sec.
Digital Clock/Read Out Display	Yes
Touch Control	Yes
Oven Interior	Stainless
Oven Dimension (H × W × D)	7 7/8″ × 14 13/16″ × 15 9/16″ (201 × 375 × 395mm)
Outside Dimension (H × W × D)	12 1/16″ × 21 7/8″ × 16 11/16″ (306 × 555 × 425mm)
Power Requirements	120 V. 60 Hz, 12.5 A, 1,500 W, AC only
Shipping Weight	Approx 48 lbs.
Trim Kit Installation	TK800 (W)

Downdraft Cooktop NN-EC630

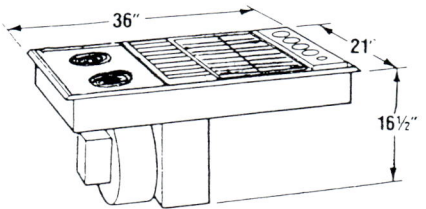

Accessory Specifications for NN-EC630

NN-AC620
240 Volt, 14.0 Amps.. 60 Hz.
8" Element . . . . 2100 Watts
6" Element . . . . 1250 Watts
Approximate Shipping Weight; 10 lbs.

Grille NN-AC600: 240 Volts, 2400 Watts, 10 Amps., 60 Hz.
Approximate Shipping Weight: 10 lbs.

Black Glass NN-AC640
240 Volts, 2400 Watts, 10 Amps., 60 Hz.
Approximate Shipping Weight: 15 lbs.

Solid Disc Elements NN-AC630
204 Volts, 14.5 Amps., 60 Hz.
8" Element . . . . 2000 Watts
6" Element . . . . 1500 Watts
Approximate Shipping Weight: 20 lbs.

THROUGH-THE-FLOOR INSTALLATION
(PENINSULA OR ISLAND INSTALLATION SHOWN)

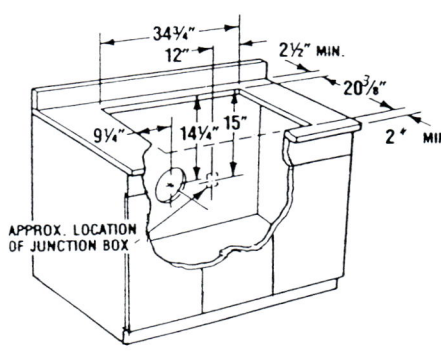

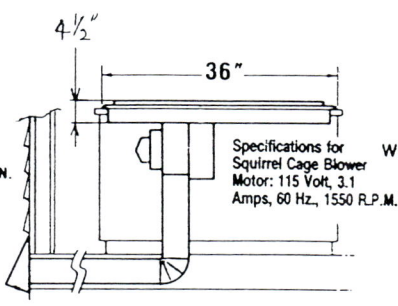

Specifications for Squirrel Cage Blower
Motor: 115 Volt, 3.1 Amps, 60 Hz., 1550 R.P.M.

NN-EC630 Specifications
120/240 Volts, 30 Amps, 60 Hz, Grounded Power Supply
Approximate Shipping Weight NN-EC630: 75 lbs.

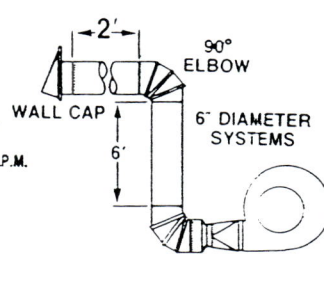

Duct Length Recommendations: 6" Diameter or 3¼" x 10". Recommended 26' Maximum Calculated Length

THROUGH-THE-WALL INSTALLATION
(OUTSIDE WALL INSTALLATION SHOWN)

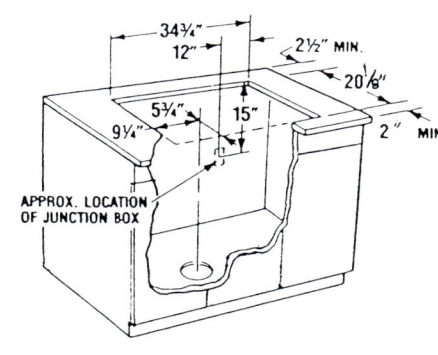

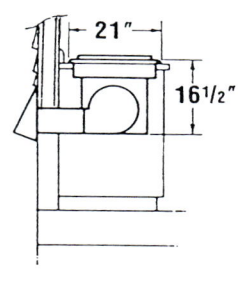

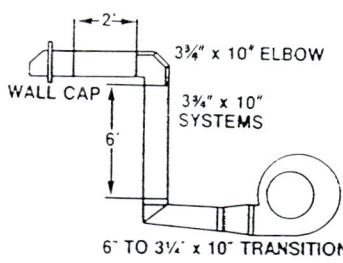

Important: It is suggested that no more than three 6", 90° Elbows or 3¼" x 10" Elbows be used.

Solid Disk Cooktop

NN-EC620
NN-EC520

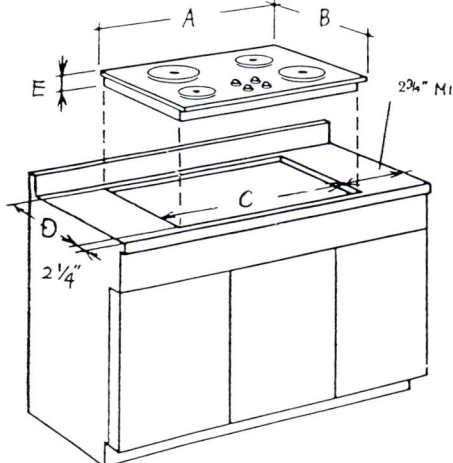

Dimensions:

	A	B	C	D	E
NN-EC620	36"	21"	30¾"	20"	4¼"
NN-EC520	30"	21"	26¾"	20"	4¼"

NN-EC620 Specifications:
7.0 Kilowatt Rating/240 V.A.C./60 Hz./30 Amps.
8" Element . . . . 2000 Watts
6" Element . . . . 1500 Watts
Approximate Shipping Weight: 50 lbs.

NN-EC520 Specifications:
7.0 Kilowatt Rating/240 V.A.C./60 Hz./30 Amps.
8" Element . . . . 2000 Watts
6" Element . . . . 1500 Watts
Approximate Shipping Weight: 40 lbs.

Panasonic

Panasonic Company
Division of Matsushita Electric Corporation of America
Executive Offices
One Panasonic Way, Secaucus, NJ 07094 (201) 348-7000

NORTHEAST GROUP
Panasonic New York:
50 Meadowlands Parkway, Secaucus, NJ 07094 (201) 348-7000
Panasonic Boston:
1 Dedham Place, Dedham, MA 02026 (617) 326-4000

MID-ATLANTIC GROUP
Panasonic Baltimore:
Baymeadows Industrial Park, 6749 Baymeadow Drive, Glen Burnie, MD 21061 (301) 761-1900
Panasonic Philadelphia:
Pike Industrial Park, 400 Pike Road, Huntingdon Valley, PA 19006 (215) 364-8300

MID-WEST GROUP
Panasonic Chicago:
425 East Algonquin Road, Arlington Heights, IL 60005 (708) 364-7900
Panasonic Minneapolis:
7900 International Drive, Suite 100, Bloomington, MN 55425 (612) 854-2412

SOUTHERN GROUP
Panasonic Atlanta:
1854 Shackleford Court, Norcross, GA 30093 (404) 717-6700
Panasonic Dallas:
4500 Amon Carter Blvd., Fort Worth, TX 76155 (817) 571-1895

WESTERN GROUP
Panasonic Los Angeles:
6550 Katella Avenue, Cypress, CA 90630 (714) 373-7200
Panasonic Hawaii:
99-859 Iwaiwa Street, P.O. Box 774, Honolulu, HI 96808-0774 (808) 488-7779
Panasonic Seattle:
14220 Inter Urban Avenue So., Seattle, WA 98168-4662 (206) 246-2383
Panasonic San Francisco:
3825 Hopyard Road, Suite 124, Pleasanton, CA 94588 (415) 463-2922

Panasonic Sales Company:
San Gabriel Industrial Park, State Road PR-3 KM 9.5, 65th Infantry Avenue, Carolina, PR 00628 (809) 750-4300

RUSSELL
RANGE

THE ORIGINAL.

INNOVATION

RUSSELL RANGE leads the field in design innovation. We pioneered the domestic appliance industry as the **first** manufacturer to produce and market the unique ''Safe-Slide''™ top grate system. Each grate is designed to cover only one burner making the size and weight of each grate manageable. Our clean construction eliminates the exposure of unsightly hardware. RUSSELL RANGE manufactures the **only** commercial-style domestic cooktops that **fit flush** into standard 24" cabinetry...

STANDARDS

RUSSELL RANGE has a commitment to quality that is unsurpassed in our industry. By employing master craftsmen on the cutting edge of modern technology, we achieve the most intricate detail and precise fit. The result is timeless beauty and complete satisfaction for the most demanding users. All RUSSELL RANGE products are setting the standards for quality and excellence now and for years to come...

VERSATILITY

RUSSELL RANGE blends innovation with bold styling to offer great flexibility in kitchen design. Along with A.G.A. certification for ''zero clearance'' installation, our cooktops are offered with either a square or bullnose front to create a clean, flush line with your choice of counter edges. Our dramatic stainless and black finish will enhance every kitchen design from Classic Country to Contemporary European to Hi-Tech Professional...

ELEGANCE Solid Brass Edition

THREE TOP FINISHERS

Russell Range offers a choice of three beautiful finish combinations to compliment any kitchen style or design.

- The *CLASSIC* has the durability and style of brushed stainless for a slick professional look.

- The *CONTEMPO* adds the drama of black porcelain in harmony with stainless. Its enduring, smooth, shiny surface will stand up to years of use and cleaning.

- The *ELEGANCE* series, another in the long list of Russell Range design achievements, features a solid brass front polished to a gleaming mirror finish for the elegance, sophistication and warmth of solid brass.

- All Russell Ranges feature precision welding with no visible assembly hardware. The *ultimate* cooking experience is also the *ultimate* in beautiful furniture for your kitchen.

PRECISION DESIGN & CRAFTSMANSHIP

RUSSELL RANGE cooktops represent superior accomplishments in design and workmanship. Our exacting specifications and strict quality control ensure a perfect installation and a perfect fit.

Notice the softened edges and lack of visible assembly hardware or seams. Notice the use of fine-grained, non-magnetic, surgical, 18/8 stainless steel. We make *smart-looking and smart-cooking* appliances.

Stainless/Black   *All Stainless*   *Brass/Black*

Mounts flush

INNOVATIVE DESIGN...PROFESSIONAL PE

Optional, easy to clean, stainless steel backsplash; required only for installation against combustible type wall.

Pilotless, high-power commercial stainless steel burners are rated up to 15,000 BTU's to satisfy a full range of cooking needs.

Versatile bullnose or square front designed to be compatible with your choice of counter edges.

Safe A.G.A. approved "push-to-turn" control

Modula
ed, cast

Optional custom-fitted, nickel plated wok ring locks into place over any burner.

Modular stainless steel or black porcelain support pans with removable drip bowls will fit any dishwasher.

A.G.A. certified for "zero clearance" and mounts **flush** into any standard 24" deep cabinet.

ain coat-
fe-
e system
iginal.

Stainless steel leg-cover apron conceals leveling legs and creates a "built-in" appearance.

Ultra low simmer

Black porcelain finis

POWER ON DEMAND

PROBLEM:

Standard residential ranges cannot achieve the same professional cooking results in the home that can be achieved in restaurants (i.e. cajun blackening, veal or chicken searing, stir-frying, quick browning, or carmelizing).

Standard, residential ranges *can* heat some pans to the desired temperatures. However, when food is added to the pan, the pan's surface cools considerably and temperature recovery is too slow to produce the desired result.

SOLUTION:

RUSSELL RANGE'S burners, putting out up to 15,000 BTUs, can power through this cool-down period producing the perfect result. Ultra-high output maintains sizzling-hot temperatures on the surface of the pan even when cold food is added.

PROBLEM:

Hot spots occur over residential type burners even with the use of high quality, professional cookware.

SOLUTION:

RUSSELL RANGE's ultra-high output flame wraps around the entire bottom of the pan, not just the center. This prevents hot spots even if the bottom of the pan is not perfectly flat.

PROBLEM:

Sauces and chocolate can break down, scorch and separate due to lack of constantly controlled low heat.

SOLUTION:

RUSSELL RANGE's ultra-low setting spreads the flame over a larger diameter burner. This low, even flame diffusion will "hold" your sauces and chocolate without scorching. When using quality cookware, your Russell Range will outperform any other cooktop on the market.

PROBLEM:

Standard residential cooktops typically offer within a 36" measurement, 4 burners of which only one is "higher rated." This is inadequate for the serious or professional style cook.

SOLUTION:

RUSSELL RANGE 6-burner cooktops efficiently offer six full-size, full-power range burners in a 36" measurement.

PROBLEM:

Homeowners whose kitchens have space limitations would like a professional style, high output cooktop.

SOLUTION:

RUSSELL RANGE is the only manufacturer to offer a full-size, full-feature, high-output cooktop in a 4-burner, 24" wide model. This size is perfect for a small kitchen or a second cooking station.

REVERSIBLE GRIDDLE/GRILL ACCESSORY

- Covers two burners with a total output of up to 30,000 BTUs and gives a broad choice of temperature settings
- Reversible for greater cooking flexibility
- Removable for easy cleaning and storage
- Solid, matte finish, cast iron plate conducts and diffuses heat quickly and evenly
- The grill side lifts foods out of their own fats for low-fat, healthier grilling
- Subtle slope channels cooking oils or fats away from food and into the grease well
- Baked-on coating is rust-resistant
- Nickel plated frame locks securely into place over any two front-to-back burners

Grill

Griddle

PERFORMANCE

RUSSELL RANGE's infinite flame control combines, high-power with ultra low simmer to take restaurant style cooking one step further. Our exclusive ''Safe-Slide''™ top grate system blends the grace of sweeping curves with the durability of porcelain enameled cast iron. Our simple and comfortable ''push-to-turn'' knobs along with pilotless ignition, make operation safe and easy. The innovative modular design makes cleaning a snap...

Four burner model FSC 24-4

PRESTIGE

RUSSELL RANGE products are the gourmet's choice for outfitting a first class kitchen. Available solely through the most exclusive dealers nationwide, our cooktops are specified by top architects and kitchen designers. A RUSSELL RANGE cooktop will complete the most prestigious kitchen and please the most discerning homeowner. It is a source of pride and a symbol of quality and exclusivity...

RUSSELL RANGE COOKTOPS...

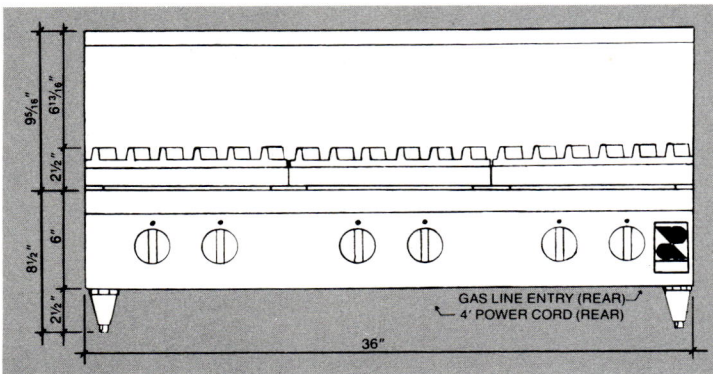

MODEL FSC 36-6

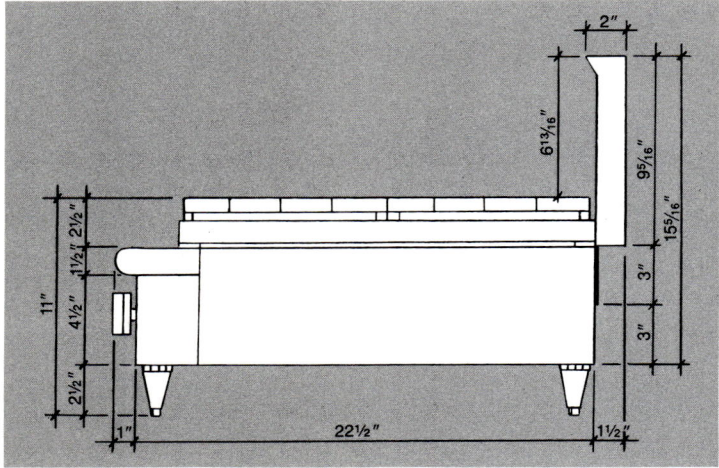

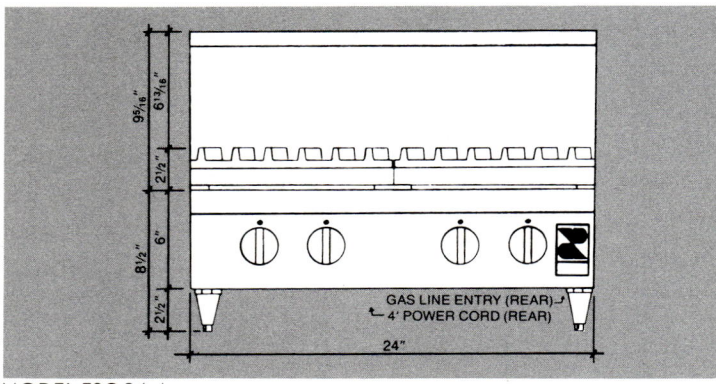

MODEL FSC 24-4

SPECIFICATIONS

- Electrical requirements: 1 amp, 120 volts, A.C. 60Hz

- 4-foot cord and 3-prong plug provided

- Shipping weight approx. 110 lbs. (FSC 36-6), 85 lbs. (FSC 24-4)

- Gas entry: bottom, right-rear corner

- All models are A.G.A. certified for ''zero clearance'' installation

- All models convert from natural gas to propane in the field with no additional parts

- Adjustable legs

- Pilotless electronic spark ignitors

- Stainless steel or black porcelain support pans and drip bowls available

- Black finish, heavy-duty, reversible cast iron griddle/grill optional

- All units must be vented properly

- Specifications subject to change without notice

SERVICE

All RUSSELL RANGE products come with a five year warranty on parts and one year warranty on labor and the support of a nationwide service team. We strive to insure that every customer has a reliable product with years of creative, worry-free cooking...

GAS LINE 1/2"
Gas Pressure
4" W.C. Nat.
10" W.C. L.P.

RUSSELL RANGE, INC.
325 SOUTH MAPLE AVE. #5
SOUTH SAN FRANCISCO, CA 94080

RUSSELL RANGE ® © 1990

SHARP

CAR**O**USEL® II
MICROWAVE OVENS

R-1831, R-1830

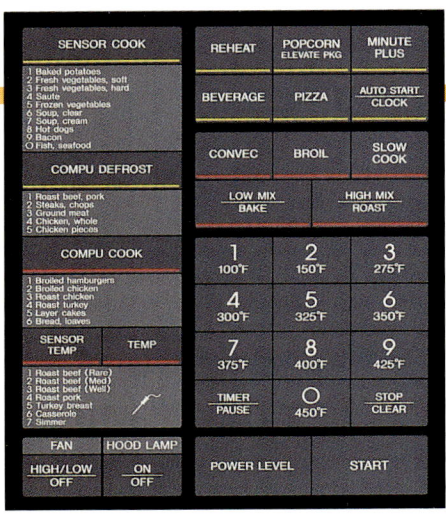

- New ESP Sensor Cook automatically cooks favorite foods

- Microwave Pizza key plus Popcorn, Beverage and Reheat keys are one-touch easy!

- Auto-Touch controls with 2-color display, 99 minute 99 second timer, Auto Start, clock, Timer/Pause and Minute Plus

- Programmable 4-stage cooking; 10 Variable Power levels

- Two combination settings with convection temperature control from 100°F to 450°F; Broil preheats oven and signals when ready

- Slow Cook expands timer up to 4 hours for slow cook recipes

- CompuDefrost is an easy, no-fail defrost for meat, poultry

Carousel II Over The Range Convection Microwave Ovens leave the counter free and install with ease. Each is equipped with work-saving ideas that make home cooking as quick and easy as eating out. R-1831 is designed in striking all white. R-1830 is available in black.

Generous 0.9 cu. ft. interior has a 13" diameter porcelain enamel turntable. Each unit features Sharp's advanced electronic controls for the hood lamp and powerful, built-in dual speed exhaust system; 310 cfm horizontal discharge, 300 cfm vertical discharge.

New ESP Sensor Cook determines microwave cooking times/power levels for automatic cooking of many favorite food categories. Popcorn, Reheat, Pizza and Beverage keys offer Instant Start convenience. Microwave, convection, combination and broil options make it easy to prepare beautiful breads, tender cakes, and moist, flavorful meat and poultry. Sensor Temp simplifies automatic temperature probe cooking so food is cooked to the desired degree of doneness.

CompuCook computes convection and combination times/temperatures for perfect broiling, roasting and baking.

Each oven installs ducted or non-ducted without needing recirculating kit and extra space. Optional RK-250 Filler Panel Kit with two 3" black panels for installation in spaces wider than 30". RK-210 Charcoal Filter for non-ducted installations. When mounted, oven top must be minimum of 66" from floor, 30" from cooking surface. Output power: 800 watts.*

LIMITED WARRANTY
7 years on magnetron tube
2 years on all other parts
2 years on related labor and in-home service
See Operation Manual for complete details

* IEC-705 Test Procedure.

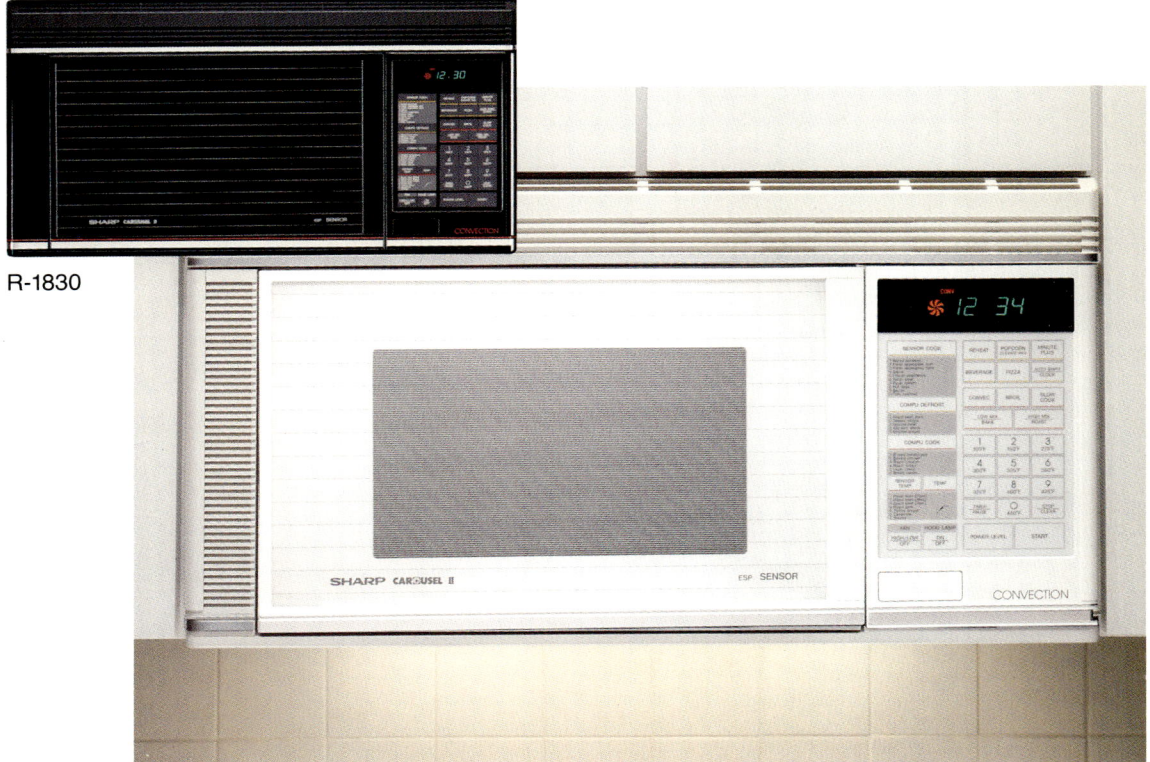

R-1830

R-1831

OVER THE RANGE

R-1420B

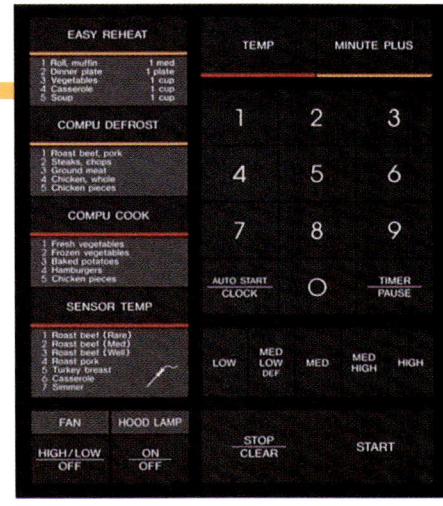

Carousel II Over The Range Microwave Oven in a streamlined black cabinet design leaves your counter open for maximum work space. Its 0.9 cu. ft. interior with 12¾" diameter turntable is a comfortable fit for family size meals. Installation is simple, offering versatility for remodeling projects or new homes.

Easy Reheat™ is a quick, no-work way to reheat a roll or muffin, dinner plate, vegetables, individual casserole or soup. CompuCook has 5 settings for automatic cooking of fresh or frozen vegetables, baked potatoes, hamburgers or chicken pieces. CompuDefrost is a no-mistakes defrost by weight for meat and poultry; step-by-step instructions in the display indicate when to cover, turn over, break apart or rearrange food.

Sensor Temp makes sure roasts, poultry and casseroles are cooked to the temperature of your choice; the 7 preset food temperatures make temperature probe cooking easy. The 5 Variable Power levels are always-ready for successful results with a variety of foods.

Oven installs ducted or non-ducted without needing recirculating kit and extra space. Optional RK-250 Filler Panel Kit with two 3" black panels for installation in spaces wider than 30". RK-210 Charcoal Filter for non-ducted installations. When mounted, oven top must be minimum of 66" from floor, 30" from cooking surface. Output power: 800 watts.*

- Space-efficient Over The Range design leaves counter free

- Electronic controls for hood lamp and powerful 2-speed fan; built-in exhaust system features 310 cfm horizontal discharge, 300 cfm vertical discharge

- Precise 10-key Auto-Touch with 99 minute 99 second timer, clock and Auto Start; Minute Plus sets one minute of time per touch

- Timer/Pause can be used as a kitchen timer or as a pause between stages to check food, add ingredients or stir

- Easy Reheat is ideal for snacks and single servings

- Programmable for 3-stage cooking

LIMITED WARRANTY
7 years on magnetron tube
1 year on all other parts
1 year on related labor and in-home service
See Operation Manual for complete details

*IEC-705 Test Procedure.

OVER THE RANGE

R-9H81B, R-9H91B

DELUXE SENSOR		
REHEAT	POPCORN ELEVATE PKG	MINUTE PLUS

SENSOR TEMP	SENSOR COOK
1 Roast beef (Rare)	1 Baked potatoes
2 Roast beef (Med.)	2 Fresh vegetables, soft
3 Roast beef (Well)	3 Fresh vegetables, hard
4 Roast pork	4 Saute
5 Turkey breast	5 Frozen vegetables
6 Casserole	6 Soup, clear
7 Simmer	7 Soup, cream
	8 Hot dogs
	9 Bacon
	0 Fish, sea/food

COMPU COOK	COMPU DEFROST
1 Broiled hamburgers	1 Roast beef, pork
2 Broiled chicken	2 Steaks, chops
3 Roast chicken	3 Ground meat
4 Roast turkey	4 Chicken, whole
5 Layer cakes	5 Chicken pieces
6 Bread, loaves	

CONVEC	1	100°F
LOW MIX BAKE	2	150°F
HIGH MIX ROAST	3	275°F
BROIL	4	300°F
SLOW COOK	5	325°F
TEMP	6	350°F
TIMER PAUSE	7	375°F
AUTO START CLOCK	8	400°F
POWER LEVEL	9	425°F
MEMORY PLUS	O	450°F
STOP CLEAR		START

- Browns, bakes, broils and crisps with 4-way cooking

- One-touch Reheat and Popcorn Sensor keys — no guesswork!

- Deluxe ESP senses when a variety of foods are done

- CompuCook computes times/ temperature settings for automatic combination and convection cooking

- CompuDefrost defrosts meat and poultry quickly, safely

- Accessories: broiling trivet and rack for 2-level baking

- Optional Built-in Kits RK-66W (aluminum) and RK-66A (black) for wall oven installation

LIMITED WARRANTY
7 years on magnetron tube
2 years on all other parts
2 years on related labor and in-home service
See Operation Manual for complete details

*IEC-705 Test Procedure.

Carousel II Convection Microwave Ovens offer a versatile 4-way cooking team in a choice of white pinstripe cabinet (R-9H91B) or charcoal pinstripe cabinet (R-9H81B). Brown, bake, broil or crisp with the microwave, convection, combination and broil options. Sharp's advanced convection system circulates super-heated air...moisture and flavor are sealed in, while the outer surface is quickly cooked. Meats stay juicy; breads bake golden brown.

Two timesaving combination cycles are perfect for roasting or baking. Convection temperature control ranges from 100°F for proofing bread to 450°F for broiling. Broil key automatically preheats oven and signals when ready. Slow Cook expands timer capacity up to 4 hours for baked beans, marinated meats and stews. Programmable for up to 4 cooking stages.

Popcorn Sensor key makes microwave popcorn one-touch easy! There's no guesswork or mistakes. Deluxe ESP™ Sensor Cook senses when 10 categories of food are done for automatic cooking. Sensor Temp uses preprogrammed temperature probe settings for combination and microwave cooking — meats are cooked to the desired degree of doneness. Memory Plus™ stores your most often used cooking time for quick recall. Features Auto-Touch® controls with 99 minute 99 second timer, Timer/Pause key, 2-color digital display, Auto Start, clock, 5 Variable Power levels and Minute Plus. Large 1.5 cu. ft. capacity with 15⅜" porcelain enamel turntable, stainless steel interior. Output power: 800 watts.*

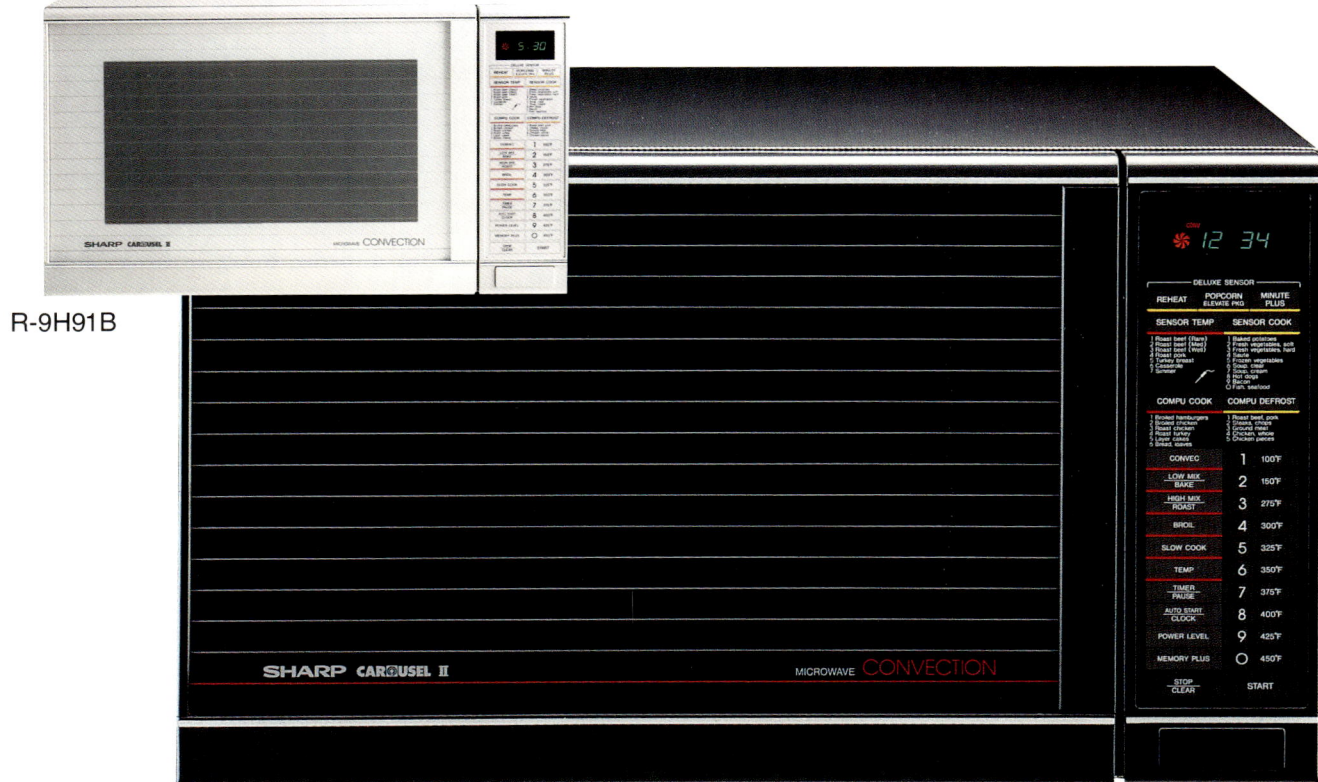

R-9H91B

R-9H81B

CONVECTION

R-8R71B

Carousel II Rotisserie Convection Microwave Oven is a true innovator. The Rotisserie automatically slow turns meats, poultry and seafood for deliciously browned food. Cooking times are kept to a minimum and juices are sealed in for added flavor. The movable heater makes it easy to brown foods on the outside and keep them juicy and tender on the inside. A "down-up" key puts the heater where you need it for easy cleaning. Touch the Broil key to select one of 3 positions for perfect broiling.

Features 4-way cooking: microwave, convection, automatic convection/microwave and broil options. Combination cycles save time for roasting and baking. Convection temperature control ranges from 100°F to 450°F.

Deluxe ESP Sensor Cook senses when favorite microwave foods are done. One-touch Popcorn, Reheat and Pizza Sensor keys mean no guesswork and no mistakes. CompuCook automatically computes times/temperatures for automatic cooking and broiling. CompuDefrost is a no-fail defrost based on weight for meat and poultry.

Auto-Touch controls with 99 minute 99 second timer, deluxe 2-color display with symbols, Memory Plus, Auto Start, clock, Timer/Pause, 5 Variable Power levels, Minute Plus. 1.3 cu. ft. capacity; 14½" porcelain enamel turntable. Includes broiling trivet, rack for 2-level baking, skewer support, skewer, 2 prongs. Charcoal pinstripe cabinet. Output power: 800 watts.*

- Remarkable new Rotisserie is ideal for boneless roasts, chicken, Cornish hens, sea scallops, shrimp or kabobs

- Browns, bakes, broils and crisps with 4-way cooking

- Movable heater for easy browning, quick cleanups

- 2-color display with words, numbers and symbols

- Popcorn, Pizza and Reheat Sensor keys are one-touch easy

- Programmable 4-stage cooking

- Slow Cook expands timer up to 4 hours for baked beans, marinated meats, stews

- Optional Built-in Kit RK-67 for wall oven installation

LIMITED WARRANTY
7 years on magnetron tube
2 years on all other parts
2 years on related labor and in-home service
See Operation Manual for complete details

*IEC-705 Test Procedure.

ROTISSERIE
CONVECTION

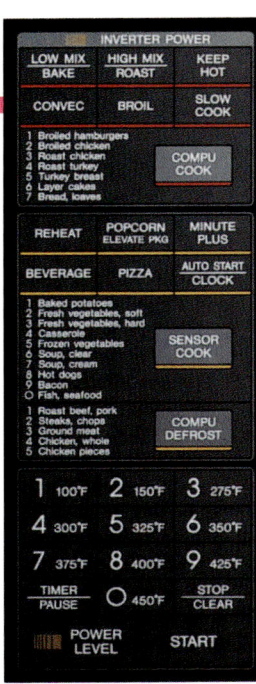

R-700H

- Inverter power offers precise cooking control for great results

- 4-way cooking: microwave, convection, convection/microwave and broil options

- Reheat half a mug of coffee or tea with convenient one-touch Beverage key

- New microwave Pizza Sensor key

- Programmable 4-stage cooking

- Auto-Touch controls with 99 minute 99 second timer, clock, Auto Start, Timer/Pause key and Minute Plus features

- Accessories: broiling trivet and rack for 2-level baking

- Optional Built-in Kit RK-56 for wall oven installation

LIMITED WARRANTY
7 years on magnetron tube
2 years on all other parts
2 years on related labor and in-home service
See Operation Manual for complete details

Carousel II Convection Microwave Oven With Inverter Power offers an engineering breakthrough. The speed of microwave heating can now be precisely controlled for excellent results with delicate sauces and seafood. The Inverter produces continuous power at reduced power levels, working like a dimmer on a chandelier. It also enhances microwave energy and convection heat combination cooking. Defrosting yields more even results with less shielding. One-touch "Keep Hot" key keeps food hot up to 30 minutes without drying out or overcooking.

Sharp's 4-way cooking team: microwave, convection, combination (2 settings) and broil options offer unsurpassed versatility. Convection temperature control ranges from 100°F to 450°F. Broil setting preheats oven to 450°F and signals when ready. Slow Cook expands timer capacity up to 4 hours. CompuCook computes convection and combination times/temperatures for broiling, roasting and baking.

Deluxe ESP Sensor Cook automatically senses when favorite microwave foods are cooked. Instant Start Popcorn, Pizza, Reheat and Beverage keys are everyday time-savers. CompuDefrost is a safe, efficient defrost based on weight for meat and poultry. 100 Variable Power levels from 0% to 100%. New 1.0 cu. ft. design with 13" porcelain enamel turntable; charcoal pinstripe cabinet. Output power: 720 watts.

INVERTER
CONVECTION

R-7A82, R-7A92

Carousel II Convection Microwave Ovens are designed for value-conscious families who want more options and timesaving features. These 1.0 cu. ft. models offer family size capacity, high output wattage, 4-way cooking and a choice of colors. R-7A92 is sleekly styled in all white; R-7A82 is available in charcoal pinstripe.

Brown, bake, broil and crisp with the microwave, convection, combination and broil team. One-touch Popcorn, Beverage and Dinner Plate keys offer Instant Start convenience. CompuCook has 7 settings to compute convection and combination times/temperatures for automatic cooking. CompuDefrost is the fast, safe and easy way to defrost meat and poultry by weight.

Two combination settings, 10 Variable Power levels and a Slow Cook setting offer added versatility. Convection temperature control ranges from 100°F to 450°F. Broil key preheats oven to 450°F and signals when ready.

Easy-to-set Auto-Touch controls include 99 minute 99 second timer, clock, Auto Start and Minute Plus. Timer/Pause can be used as a kitchen timer or as a pause between cooking stages. Optional Built-in Kits RK-56W (white) or RK-56 (black) for wall oven installation. Output power: 800 watts.*

- Family size 1.0 cu. ft. capacity with 13" diameter porcelain enamel turntable and choice of cabinet colors

- 4-way cooking lets you brown, bake, broil or crisp

- Programmable 4-stage cooking

- Popcorn, Beverage and Dinner Plate keys for one-touch ease

- Special combination settings for roasting and baking

- Accessories: broiling trivet and rack for 2-level baking

- Optional Built-in Kits RK-56W (white) and RK-56 (black) for wall oven installation

LIMITED WARRANTY
7 years on magnetron tube
2 years on all other parts
2 years on related labor and in-home service
See Operation Manual for complete details

* IEC-705 Test Procedure.

R-7A92

R-7A82

CONVECTION

SHARP®

Your Sharp Microwave Oven can be built into your kitchen wall or cabinet using the appropriate Sharp Built-in Kit. Complete hardware and easy-to-follow instructions are included. Prepare cabinet or wall opening according to the illustration below, providing access to a separate 3-pronged, 115-120v AC outlet, 15 amps or larger.

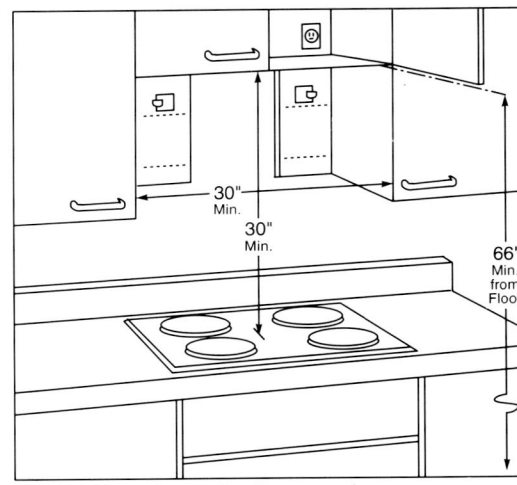

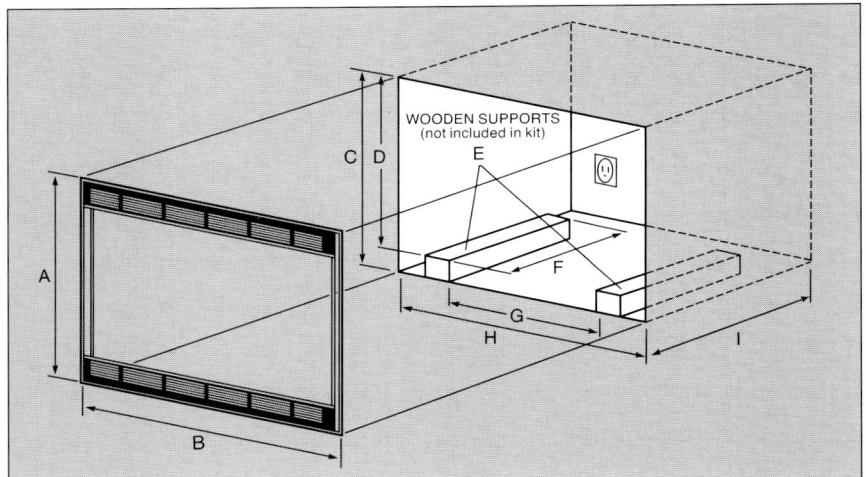

WOODEN SUPPORTS
(not included in kit)

Each Sharp Over The Range microwave can be easily adapted for either outside ventilation (vertical or horizontal) or non-vented, ductless recirculation.

Make sure top of oven will be at least 66" from the floor and at least 30" from the cooking surface. A separate 15 amp or more electrical receptacle must be located in the cabinet directly above the microwave oven.

	A	B	C	D	E	F	G	H	I
RK-66W, RK-66A	19⅞"	26½"	17⅛" (+ height of wood)	17⅛"	nominal 2"×2" actual 1⅝"×2"×15"	15"	18⅜"±⅛"	25¼"±⅛"	min. 19½"
RK-56, RK-56W	18⅜"	23½"	17⁵⁄₁₆"±³⁄₁₆"	15¹¹⁄₁₆"±³⁄₁₆"	nominal 2"×2" actual 1⅝"×2"×16½"	16½"	14"±½"	22"±½"	19¹¹⁄₁₆"±⁷⁄₁₆"
RK-67	17⅛"	23⅜"	16¼"±⅛" (+ height of wood)	16¼"±⅛"	nominal 2"×2" actual ¾"×1⁹⁄₁₆"×18½"	18½"	18⅞"±⅛"	22⅝"±⅛"	21¼"±⅜"

SPECIFICATIONS	R-1831, R-1830	R-1420B	R-9H91B, R-9H81B	R-8R71B	R-700H	R-7A82, R-7A92
Oven Capacity:	0.9 cu. ft.	0.9 cu. ft.	1.5 cu. ft.	1.3 cu. ft.	1.0 cu. ft.	1.0 cu. ft.
Display:	2-color lighted digital display	Lighted digital display	2-color lighted digital display	Deluxe lighted with symbols; 2-color	Lighted digital display	Lighted digital display
Control:	Solid state, touch sensitive, audible entry tone, programmable to 4 sequences	Solid state, touch sensitive, audible entry tone, programmable to 3 sequences	Solid state, touch sensitive, audible entry tone, programmable to 4 sequences	Solid state, touch sensitive, audible entry tone, programmable to 4 sequences	Solid state, touch sensitive, audible entry tone, programmable to 4 sequences	Solid state, touch sensitive, audible entry tone, programmable to 4 sequences
Convection Control:	100°F, 150°, 275° - 450°F in 25° increments		100°F, 150°, 275° - 450°F in 25° increments	100°F, 150°, 275° - 450°F in 25° increments	100°F, 150°, 275° - 450°F in 25° increments	100°F, 150°, 275° - 450°F in 25° increments
Automatic Temperature Probe:	90°F - 200°F settings with Sensor Temp	90°F - 200°F settings with Sensor Temp	90°F - 200°F settings with Sensor Temp			
Cabinet:	R-1831: White painted R-1830: Black painted	Black painted	R-9H91: White pinstripe R-9H81: Charcoal pinstripe	Charcoal pinstripe	Charcoal pinstripe	R-7A92: White R-7A82: Charcoal pinstripe
Output Power:	Conv: 1350W Micro: 800W*	Micro: 800W*	Conv: 1450W Micro: 800W*	Conv: 1450W Micro: 800W*	Conv: 1400W Micro: 720W	Conv: 1400W Micro: 800W*
Outside Dimensions:	29⅞" × 16½" × 15" (WHD)	29⅞" × 16½" × 15" (WHD)	24⅝" × 14¾" × 18⅜" (WHD)	21⅞" × 14⅞" × 20⅜" (WHD)	20½" × 13¼" × 18½" (WHD)	20½" × 13¼" × 18½" (WHD)
Oven Dimensions:	13⅝" × 8⅜" × 13½" (WHD)	13⅝" × 8½" × 13½" (WHD)	16⅛" × 9⅝" × 16⅛" (WHD)	14¾" × 9⅞" × 15⅛" (WHD)	13⅝" × 8¾" × 13¾" (WHD)	13⅝" × 8¾" × 13¾" (WHD)
Oven Interior:	Stainless steel with light	Acrylic painted with light	Stainless steel with light	Stainless steel with light	Stainless steel with light	Stainless steel with light
Approximate Weight:	Net: 74 lbs. Shipping: 87 lbs.	Net: 68 lbs. Shipping: 81 lbs.	Net: 58 lbs. Shipping: 65 lbs.	Net: 60 lbs. Shipping: 68 lbs.	Net: 44 lbs. Shipping: 49 lbs.	Net: 48 lbs. Shipping: 53 lbs.
AC Line Voltage:	120V, single phase, 60Hz, AC only	120V, single phase, 60Hz, AC only	120V, single phase, 60Hz, AC only	120V, single phase, 60Hz, AC only	120V, single phase, 60Hz, AC only	120V, single phase, 60Hz, AC only
AC Power Required:	Conv: 1.6kW, 13.3A Micro: 1.6kW, 13.3A	Micro: 1.6kW, 13.3A	Conv: 1.55kW, 13.0A Micro: 1.47kW, 12.3A	Conv: 1.55kW, 12.9A Micro: 1.47kW, 12.3A	Conv: 1.5kW, 12.5A Micro: 1.42kW, 12.2A	Conv: 1.5kW, 12.5A Micro: 1.42kW, 12.2A
Safety Compliance:	FCC, DHHS, UL listed	FCC, DHHS, UL listed	FCC, DHHS, UL listed	FCC, DHHS, UL listed	FCC, DHHS, UL listed	FCC, DHHS, UL listed
Supplied Accessories:	Broiling trivet, baking rack, temperature probe	Temperature probe	Broiling trivet, baking rack, temperature probe	Broiling trivet, baking rack, ceramic skewer support, skewer, 2 prongs	Broiling trivet, baking rack	Broiling trivet, baking rack
Optional Accessories: (Available at extra cost)	RK-250 Filler Panel Kit (two 3" black panels); RK-210 Charcoal Filter required for non-ducted installations	RK-250 Filler Panel Kit (two 3" black panels); RK-210 Charcoal Filter required for non-ducted installations	Built-in Kit RK-66W (aluminum) or RK-66A (black) for in-the-wall installation**	Built-in Kit RK-67 for in-the-wall installation**	Built-in Kit RK-56 for in-the-wall installation**	Built-in Kit RK-56W (white) or RK-56 (black) for in-the-wall installation**

*IEC-705-1988 Test Procedure. **Refer to Operation Manual or Installation Instructions for installation recommendations. Specifications subject to change without notice. U.S. patents 4,341,409; 4,149,056; 4,547,643; 4,542,270; 4,036,151.

Sharp Electronics Corporation

Corporate Headquarters and Executive Offices
Sharp Plaza, Mahwah, New Jersey 07430-2135   Phone: (201) 529-8200
Regional Sales Offices and Distribution Centers
Northeast: Sharp Plaza, Mahwah, New Jersey 07430-2135   Phone: (201) 529-8200
Midwest: 1300 Naperville Dr., Romeoville, Illinois 60441   Phone: (708) 759-8555
Western: 20600 One Sharp Plaza, South Alameda St., Carson, California 90810
Phone: (213) 637-9488
Southeastern: 725 Old Norcross Road, Lawrenceville, Georgia 30245
Phone: (404) 995-0717

Printed in U.S.A.   **MW-06-022**

STERLING

XCELLENCE BUILT-IN

36"
FOUR BURNER
UPDRAFT
GLASS SURFACED
GAS COOKTOP

Only 2" deep, this cooktop can be fitted above drawers and appliances.

The sealed spillage bowls keep the interior of the cooktop spill-free (a major advantage over most other designs). Deep enough to contain most spills, they are carefully shaped for easy cleaning.

There are 2 high speed burners and 2 medium burners, each capable of the fiercest boil or gentlest simmer. The gapped design of the burner grates means that the flame keeps clear of the prongs, ensuring long-life.

Each burner is ignited automatically as the control is turned on. The electrode is hidden within the burner and protected against spills for reliable operation.

GCT 360
BLACK

GCT 361
WHITE

GCT 362
ALMOND

2yr Warranty

PRODUCT FEATURES

Longer lasting, energy saving cast iron burner grates which keep clear of the flame.

Fully controllable high efficiency burners, from rapid boil to gentle simmer.

Solid brass flame spreader for extra durability.

Pilotless electronic ignition protected from spills for extra reliability.

Only 2 inches deep to fit over cabinet drawers or other appliances.

In stunning white, dramatic black, or subtle almond with elegant European styling.

AMERICA'S BIGGEST SELLING GAS COOKTOP

STERLING
EXCELLENCE BUILT-IN

GAS CONVECTION WALL **OVEN/ BROILER**

Brings refined European design and unique cooking and cleaning features to North American kitchens.

The full-width broiler and oven doors open down to reveal amazingly large full-width cooking compartments. This remarkable cooking capacity is all-usable space, made possible by the unique STERLING smokeless Sola® broiler and the unique STERLING gas convection Gyroflo® oven system which eliminates transfer of food flavor allowing 'full menu' cooking.

The oven's unique STERLING *low temperature self-clean* system combines the sterilizing action of an open gas flame with special linings to destroy almost all grease, fumes and smoke during cooking. This means the large viewing glass and door seals stay cleaner, and the *energy* and *time* needed by standard high temperature self-clean systems is saved. Because there are no complicated parts to malfunction, service costs are reduced. The system is so good, we back it with a money back satisfaction warranty.

GBI 240
BLACK

GBI 24I
WHITE

GBI 242
ALMOND

The automatic microprocessor programmer is easy to use. Simply set 'finish time', 'cooking time', turn knob to auto and oven control to the desired setting. A time-of-day clock and minute-minder are also incorporated.

ELEGANT EUROPEAN

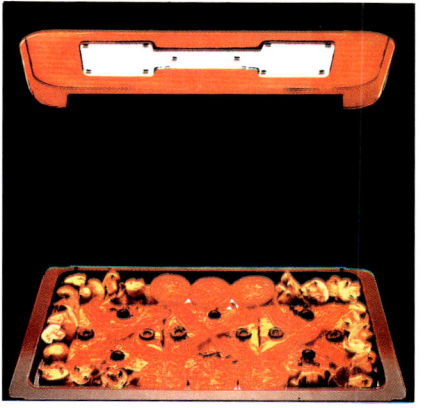

THE UNIQUE STERLING SOLA® BROILER

- **Fast, even heat** from side to side and front to rear
- **Consistent, controlled results** with thinnest toast to thickest steak
- Smokeless Broiler, **no mess, no fumes**
- Automatic re-ignition – **safe and dependable**

THE UNIQUE STERLING GAS CONVECTION GYROFLO® OVEN

- **Natural Gas Convection** (GYROFLO ®) full menu cooking
- **More usable cooking space,** floor to ceiling, wall to wall
- **Consistent,** controlled results every time
- Automatic re-ignition – **safe and dependable**
- **No preheat,** no taste transfer
- **No mess, no fumes**

140A

Unique Gyroflo® gas convection 'full menu' cooking.

Unique Sola® broiling – fast, even and smokeless.

Unique low temperature self-cleaning system with money back satisfaction warranty.

Automatic electronic ignition and re-ignition.

Automatic microprocessor programmer/clock.

Spacious oven and broiler compartments.

Full-width glass door with large viewing panel and interior lights.

Elegant European styling.

In dramatic black, stunning white or subtle almond.

STYLING

STERLING

EXCELLENCE BUILT-IN

Sterling is Europe's largest manufacturer of gas cooking appliances, with a distinguished heritage – one hundred years experience of craftsmanship and quality.

These cooktops are leading examples of **STERLING** design and innovation in action.

THE GBI 240 BUILT-IN OVEN AND GCT 360/5 COOKTOP ▶

ELEGANT EUROPEAN
STYLING

NEW 30" UPDRAFT GLASS SURFACED GAS COOKTOP

This cooktop is slim enough to fit right into the countertop and can accommodate another appliance or drawer right underneath it – true space saving.

The sealed hotplate spillage bowls keep the interior of the cooktop spill-free (a major advantage over most other designs). Deep enough to contain most spills, they are carefully shaped for easy cleaning.

There are 4 versatile burners, each capable of the fiercest boil or gentlest simmer.

Each burner is ignited by a simple push button control and is re-ignited should the flame be extinguished. The electrode is hidden within the burner and protected against spills for reliable operation.

GCT 300
BLACK

GCT 301
WHITE

2yr Warranty

PRODUCT FEATURES

Automatic re-ignition.

Longer lasting, energy saving heavy duty burner grates.

Fully controllable high efficiency burners, from rapid boil to gentle simmer.

Pilotless electronic ignition protected from spills for extra reliability.

In stunning white or dramatic black with elegant European styling.

NEW 36" FIVE BURNER UPDRAFT GLASS SURFACED GAS COOKTOP

Only 2³/₁₆" deep, this cooktop can even be fitted above drawers or other appliances.

The sealed hotplate spillage bowls keep the interior of the cooktop spill-free (a major advantage over most other designs). Deep enough to contain most spills, they are carefully shaped for easy cleaning.

This new cooktop has five burners – 2 rapid burners and 3 semi-rapid burners, each capable of the fiercest boil or gentlest simmer. The gapped design of the burner grates means that the flame stays clear of the prongs, ensuring long-life.

Each burner is ignited automatically as the control is turned on. The electrode is hidden within the burner and protected against spills for reliable operation.

GCT 360/5
BLACK

GCT 361/5
WHITE

GCT 362/5
ALMOND

PRODUCT FEATURES

Automatic re-ignition and sealed burners.

Longer lasting, energy saving cast iron burner grates which are clear of the flame.

Fully controllable high efficiency burners, from rapid boil to gentle simmer.

Pilotless electronic ignition protected from spills for extra reliability.

Only 2 inches deep to fit over cabinet drawers or other appliances.

In stunning white or dramatic black and now available in almond. With elegant European styling.

EXCELLENCE BUILT-IN

36" FIVE BURNER GLASS SURFACE
GAS COOKTOP WITH DOWNDRAFT EXTRACTOR

Advanced, practical features and refined European styling, designed to suit North American kitchens.

The sealed hotplate spillage bowls keep the interior of the cooktop spill-free (a major advantage over most other designs). Deep enough to contain most spills, they are carefully shaped for easy cleaning.

This cooktop has five burners – two rapid and three semi-rapid, each capable of the fiercest boil or gentlest simmer. The gapped design of the burner grates means that the flame stays clear of the prongs, ensuring long-life.

Each burner is ignited automatically as the gas control is turned on. The electrode is hidden within the burner and protected against spills for reliable operation.

Using the latest electronic control technology gives reliable and positive ignition and also provides re-ignition should the flame accidentally blow out.

5 burner glass cooktop with downdraft extractor.

GCT 360/5/D
BLACK

GCT 361/5/D
WHITE

2yr Warranty

140A

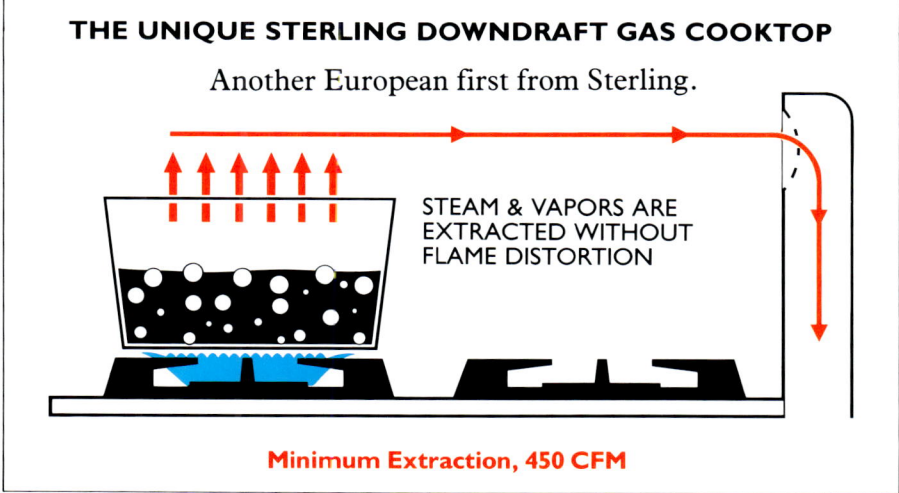

THE UNIQUE STERLING DOWNDRAFT GAS COOKTOP

Another European first from Sterling.

STEAM & VAPORS ARE EXTRACTED WITHOUT FLAME DISTORTION

Minimum Extraction, 450 CFM

The revolutionary STERLING downdraft extractor is raised and lowered by a control mounted centrally on the cooktop, and cleanly extracts the steam and vapors produced when cooking, without distorting the flame. The speed of the fan is infinitely variable from zero to its full power setting. Since the glass surfaced gas cooktop is only 2³⁄₁₆″ deep when fitted, a half drawer or half shelf may be accommodated underneath even with the extractor in the lowered position.

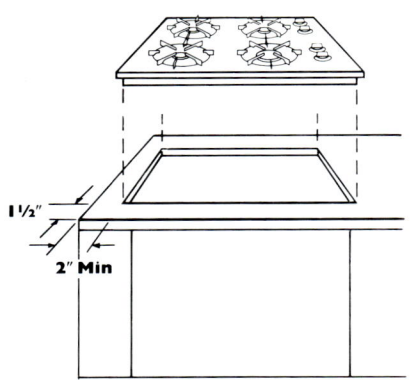

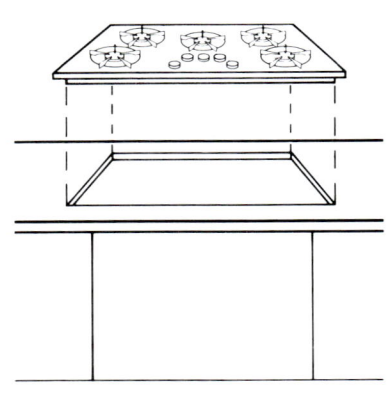

1½"

2" Min

GCT 300/301	Width Ins	Depth Ins	Height from Top of Worktop
Overall Cooktop	30	21	2½
Counter Top Cut-Out	28 9/16	19½	

GCT 360/361/362/5	Width Ins	Depth Ins	Height from Top of Worktop
Overall Cooktop	36	19 11/16	2 3/16
Counter Top Cut-Out	34 7/16	18 5/16	

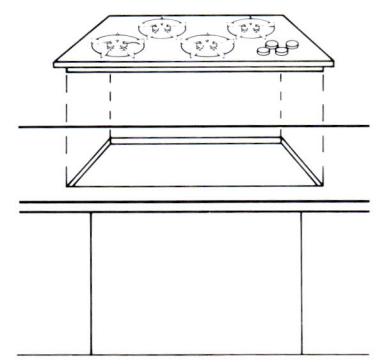

GCT 360/361/362	Width Ins	Depth Ins	Height from Top of Worktop
Overall Cooktop	36	19¼	2
Counter Top Cut-Out	32¼	16¾	

GCT 360/361/5/D	Width Ins	Depth Ins	Height from Top of Worktop
Overall Cooktop	36	22¼	2 3/16
Counter Top Cut-Out	34 7/16	21⅛	

PRODUCT FEATURES

DOWNDRAFT EXTRACTOR
Steam and vapors are extracted without flame distortion.

Fan speed infinitely variable.

In white or black.

COOKTOP
Easy clean, tempered glass surface with sealed spillage wells.

Automatic re-ignition.

Longer lasting, energy saving cast iron burner grates.

Fully controllable high efficiency burners, from rapid boil to gentle simmer.

Pilotless electronic ignition protected from spills for extra reliability.

In stunning white or dramatic black with elegant European styling.

Warranty
Sterling appliances are guaranteed against faulty material or workmanship for a full two year period from the date of original purchase. If any part is found to be defective within the warranty period, we or our Service Agents will replace or at our option, repair that part free of charge for materials and labor.

Our policy is one of constant development and improvement. Whilst the leaflet is accurate at the date of printing, specification/appearance may be changed in the interest of continued improvement.

EXCELLENCE BUILT-IN
STERLING DOMESTIC APPLIANCES INC.
89 ACCESS ROAD NORWOOD
MASSACHUSETTS 02062
SERVICE CENTER PHONE: 617 784 1900
SALES PHONE: 617 255-9909/9910
FACSIMILE: 617 255 9911

Built-in Home Refrigeration Designed for Beauty and Performance

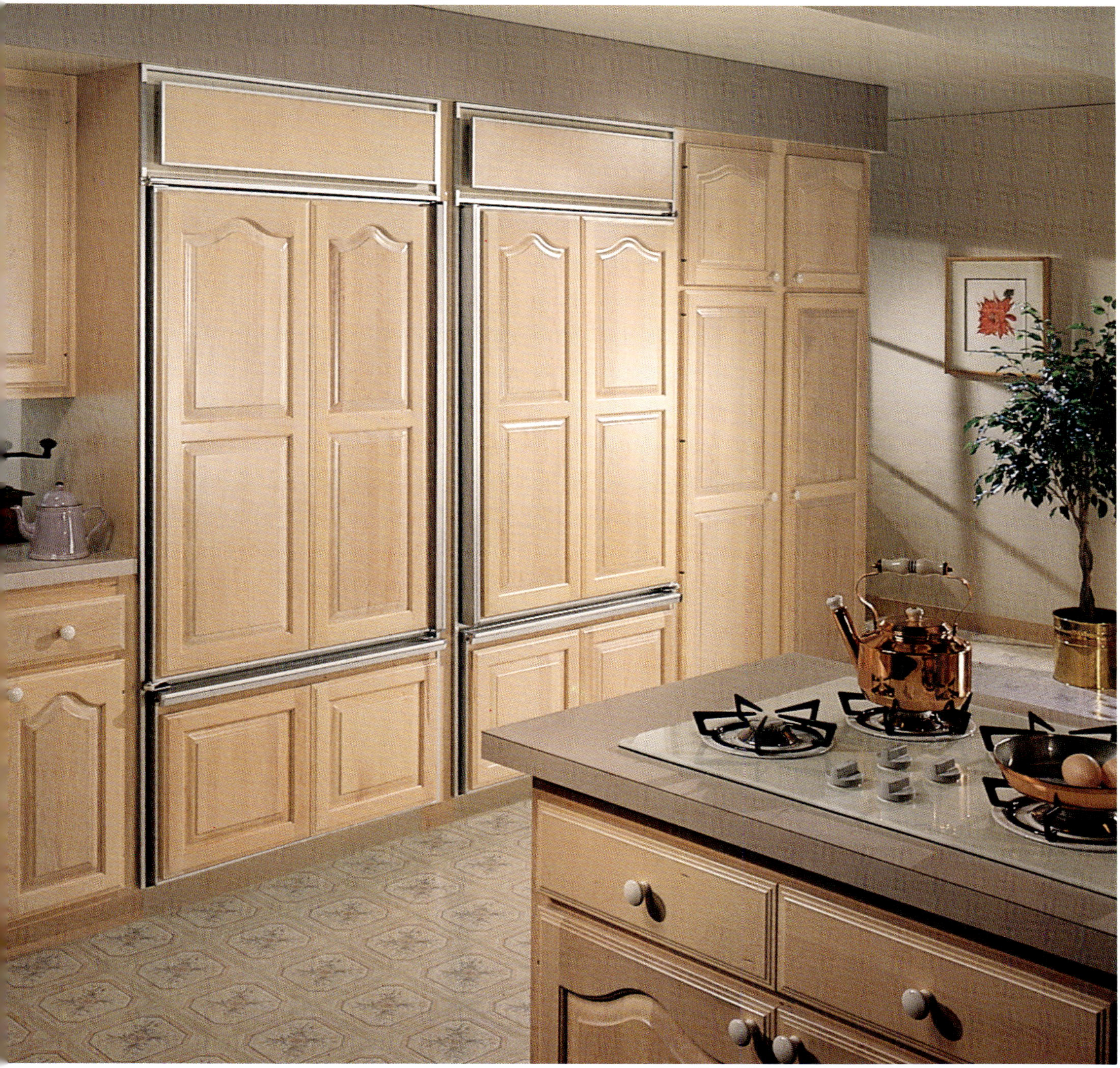

SUB-ZERO

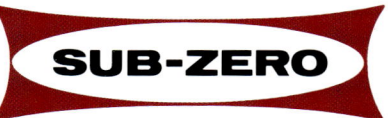

The first choice in Kitchens of distinction

In remodeling and new construction, the look of distinction in kitchens begins with the beauty of built-in appliances and built-in refrigeration by Sub-Zero. That's why leading custom kitchen designers choose Sub-Zero first. Classic in styling and unequaled for storage, convenience and quality, Sub-Zero true built-ins are the ultimate in elegant home refrigeration.

Enjoy the elegance of Built-in refrigeration

Sub-Zero home refrigeration is designed to enhance the beauty of any decor by blending compatibly with other kitchen furnishings. This is possible because of its simple design. . .removable decorative panels and the fact it is the same 24″ depth as most base kitchen cabinets. A Sub-Zero is designed with a minimum of external hardware, making it hardly noticeable when built into a kitchen. It also has an exclusive toe-base feature, important in kitchen appliances, which lines up with kitchen cabinets.

All units are constructed with the 24″ depth which enables the face to fit flush with most standard base cabinets. A typical free-standing refrigerator protrudes into the room 4 to 6 inches beyond cabinets, creating an unsightly appearance and takes up valuable space in the room.

Sub-Zero built-ins are designed to accept removable exterior panels of any material on the front and sides. In doing so, the unit practically disappears into the overall kitchen, blending completely into the decor instead of dominating the kitchen appearance, as a free-standing unit does. And, because the panels are removable, they can be changed, should the room decor change.

These true built-in features mean your home refrigeration need not be an unattractive standout but can now complement the over-all style of the kitchen and function as an integral part of the total kitchen design. They allow individual styling and expression of your personal taste.

Built-in work savers

Truly an accent to the kitchen of distinction, Sub-Zero built-in refrigeration offers all of the time and work saving features that today's lifestyles require…like convenient usable storage, easy up-keep, simplified cleaning, automatic defrosting and automatic ice maker.

The shallow depth makes it easier to find what you are looking for, eliminating the need to search for items that have found their way to the back shelf area (as in other refrigerators). This, along with the fact that all shelves are fully adjustable, gives even greater flexibility for storage arrangements.

Easy up-keep is achieved because of the quality materials and craftsmanship used in the construction of a Sub-Zero …interior, exterior and mechanical.

Cleaning is simplified because of two reasons: First the unit's built-in feature eliminates cracks and crevices that would normally collect dust and also eliminates the chore of pulling the refrigerator out to clean behind it.

Secondly, all shelves in Sub-Zero full-size units are removable to allow for ease of cleaning.

The automatic defrost feature is standard on all full-size models as well as the undercounter models (except

Model 550

249R). This eliminates the need to shut down the refrigerator to defrost and clean the unit.

Another standard feature of the full-size units is the automatic ice maker which produces an adequate supply of ice automatically without the need to handle awkward ice trays.

Many models to choose from

Whatever your space or usage requirements, Sub-Zero offers a selection of over 12 models to fit your needs and specifications. Choose from the popular side-by-side, the over-n-under (freezer on the bottom), the all-freezer and all-refrigerator units, compact undercounter refrigerators and ice makers. Ranging in width from 12″ to 48″, Sub-Zero units offer capacities to 30.0 cubic feet. The combination all-refrigerator and all-freezer together provide as much as 40.0 cubic feet of food storage.

New twelve-year maximum protection

Sub-Zero has always backed what it has manufactured, and now offers even more protection with its new twelve-year "Protection Plan". From the day your Sub-Zero is installed, you have a full five-year (parts and labor) warranty and limited sixth through twelfth-year (parts) warranty on the sealed system, consisting of the compressor, condenser, evaporator, drier and all connecting tubing. You also have a full three-year (parts and labor) warranty on mechanical parts (i.e., timer, motor, control, icemaker) defective because of materials or workmanship, and a full one-year (parts and labor) warranty on the entire product. (See warranty for non-residential use and other exceptions.) Sub-Zero stands behind every refrigerator and freezer they manufacture, ensuring you of the finest in service and trouble-free maintenance.

Outstanding performance and craftsmanship

Sub-Zero is a leader in the industry in engineering functional refrigeration. Because Sub-Zero full-size units use a refrigerant in both the refrigerator and freezer compartments, proper and even temperatures are maintained more consistently throughout. This is the same type system used in some commercial refrigerators and is a standard feature in Sub-Zero home units, to insure top performance and operation.

Complete factory testing of every Sub-Zero unit is your assurance of quality workmanship.

More than just refrigeration, Sub-Zero quality craftsmanship is a tradition, custom designed to enhance the value and elegance of your home for years to come.

Maximum storage with the 500 SERIES Models 501R and 501F

For large families or those people who need maximum storage, Sub-Zero offers the convenience of its new Eurostyled all-refrigerator (Model 501R) and all-freezer (Model 501F) with a total storage capacity of 40 cubic feet. The "all-refrigerator's" 20 cubic foot capacity makes this exclusive unit the largest built-in all-refrigerator on the market. One of the advantages of these units is the flexibility of planning your kitchen. The units can be installed side-by-side or with a convenient counter between them or at opposite ends of the room, depending on your kitchen layout. Adjustable shelving in both the refrigerator and freezer gives even more storage versatility. The 501F has an automatic ice maker. The "all-refrigerator" Model 501R is also ideal for people who have existing freezer storage. **Separate detailed specification sheets on models 501R and 501F available upon request.**

501F   501R

ALL FREEZER
Model 501F—Automatic defrost. Freezer is equipped with automatic ice maker.
ALL REFRIGERATOR
Model 501R—Automatic defrost refrigerator.

Model	501F	501R
Capacity	20.0 cu. ft.	20.0 cu. ft.
Dimensions	Height 73″ Width 36″ Depth 24″	Height 73″ Width 36″ Depth 24″
Finished Roughing-In Dimensions	35¹/₂″x72³/₄″	35¹/₂″x72³/₄″
Weight (lbs.)	363 crated	376 crated

* Additional shelves available at extra cost.

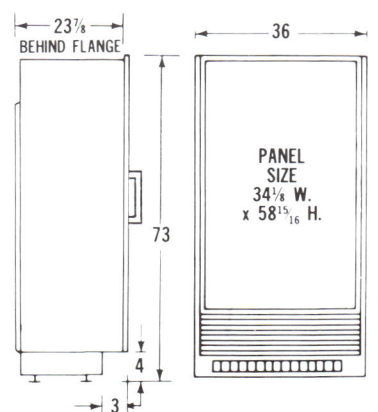

23⅞ BEHIND FLANGE

36

PANEL SIZE 34⅛ W. x 58¹⁵/₁₆ H.

73

4

3

Minimum height required (when levelers in) is 72⁷/₁₆″

NOTE: Roughing-in width is 71½″ when these models are installed side by side. If mullion is used to separate cabinets, add mullion width to 71½″ dimension. Filler must be used when installed hinge to hinge.

One 115 volt, 60 cycle single phase, 15 amp. A.C. wall outlet for each unit, must be provided.

Refer to 500 series "Installation Instruction" booklet for detailed installation and panel requirements.

Model 561

Model 561 Interior

SUB-ZERO

Side by Side Combination
Models 561 and 532

The new 500 series incorporates exciting engineering innovations, with built-in beauty and elegant Eurostyled interiors. This series also features the new satin-brushed aluminum exterior trim and simplicity of design. The elegant combination of white and clear interiors, together with the built-in appearance, offers breathtaking beauty.

Sub-Zero's model 561 features an 8.9 cu. ft. freezer and 12.5 cu. ft. refrigeration in convenient top-to-bottom, side-by-side storage. Its two compressors provide independent temperature control of the freezer and refrigerator compartments. The freezer compartment has four pull-out storage baskets, automatic ice maker with removable ice storage drawer and adjustable door storage.

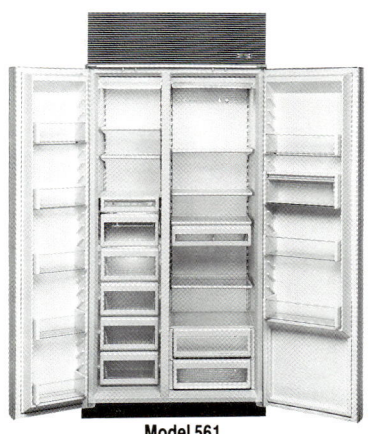

Model 561

COMBINATION REFRIGERATOR-FREEZER
Model 561 — Automatic defrost model. Freezer compartment equipped with automatic ice maker.

Capacity:	12.5 cu. ft. Refrigerator 8.9 cu. ft. Freezer
Dimensions:	Height 84″ Width 36″ Depth 24″
Finished Rough-In Dimensions	35½″ x 83¾″
Weight (lbs.):	480 lbs. crated

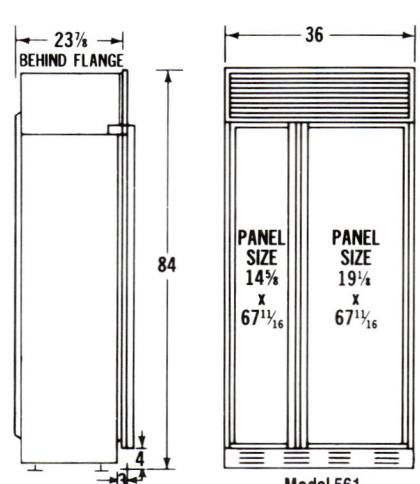

← 23⅞ →
BEHIND FLANGE

84

4
3

← 36 →

PANEL SIZE 14⅜ x 67¹¹⁄₁₆

PANEL SIZE 19¼ x 67¹¹⁄₁₆

Model 561

One 115 volt, 60 cycle, single phase 15 amp. A.C. wall outlet must be provided.

Minimum height required (when levelers in) is 82⅞″

Refer to "Installation Instruction" booklet for detailed installation and panel requirements.

Model 532

Model 532 Interior

Sub-Zero's huge 30 cu. ft. combination refrigerator/freezer model 532 is one of the largest home built-in units made. It incorporates new engineering innovations and Eurostyled interior. It has an 11.2 cu. ft. freezer and 18.8 cu. ft. refrigerator with convenient top-to-bottom storage.

The freezer compartment has four pull-out storage baskets, an automatic ice maker with roll-out removable ice storage drawer and adjustable door storage. The refrigerator has four self-sealing crispers, each with independent humidity control. It also features an adjustable roll-out utility drawer, adjustable door storage shelves and adjustable glass

shelves. This model also has two compressors to provide independent temperature control in both the freezer and refrigerator compartments.

Detailed specification sheets on model 532 and 561 are available on request.

Optional solid panel grilles that accept matching panels also available for both units. Detailed specification sheets on both units and grilles available upon request.

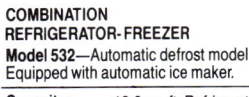

Model 532

COMBINATION REFRIGERATOR-FREEZER
Model 532—Automatic defrost model Equipped with automatic ice maker.

Capacity:	18.8 cu. ft. Refrigerator 11.2 cu. ft. Freezer
Dimensions:	Height 84" Width 48" Depth 24"
Finished Rough-In Dimensions:	47 1/2" x 83 3/4"
Weight (lbs.):	563 crated

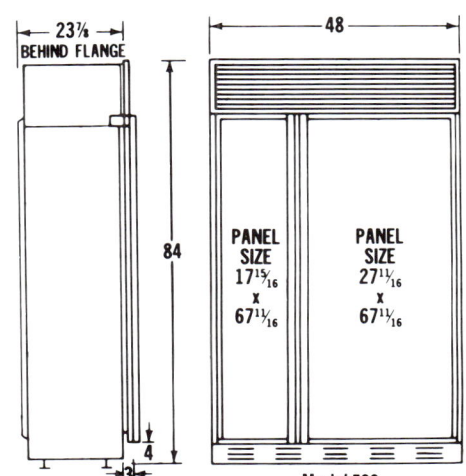

23 7/8 BEHIND FLANGE

48

PANEL SIZE 17 15/16 x 67 11/16

PANEL SIZE 27 11/16 x 67 11/16

84

4

3

Model 532

One 115 volt, 60 cycle, single phase 15 amp. A.C. wall outlet must be provided.

Minimum height required (when levelers in) is 82 7/8"

Refer to 500 series "Installation Instruction" booklet for detailed installation and panel requirements.

Model 550

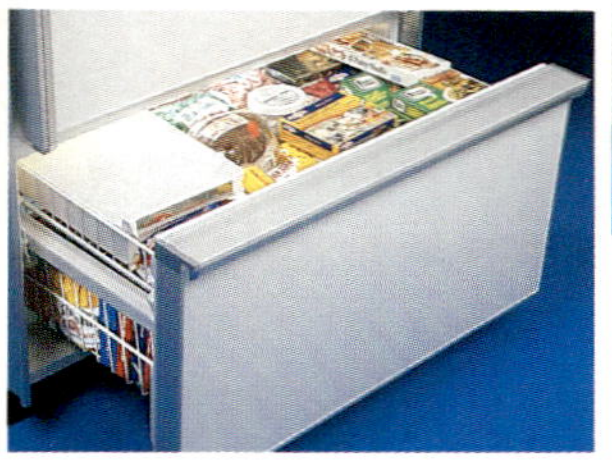

Model 550 Interior

Over-N-Under (freezer on bottom)
Models 550 and 511

For those who prefer, Sub-Zero offers a convenient arrangement with freezer on the bottom. This design was prompted by the fact that the refrigerator section is used more often than the freezer, thereby providing the greatest convenience and best accessibility. The refrigerated top half offers full width storage on adjustable shelves while frozen foods below are easily accessible with a pull-out drawer.

The over-n-under units in the 500 series also incorporate exciting engineering innovations with built-in beauty and elegant Eurostyled interiors. These units also feature the new satin-brushed aluminum exterior trim and simplicity of design.

Sub-Zero's 22.1 cu. ft. model 550 over-n-under combination unit has a 6.4 cu. ft. slide-out, double-tier freezer drawer in the

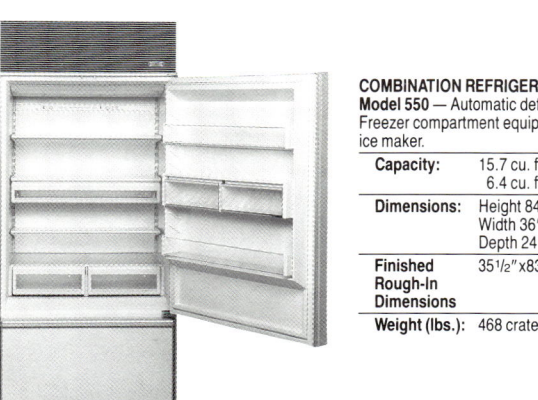

Model 550

COMBINATION REFRIGERATOR-FREEZER
Model 550 — Automatic defrost model.
Freezer compartment equipped with automatic ice maker.

Capacity:	15.7 cu. ft. Refrigerator 6.4 cu. ft. Freezer
Dimensions:	Height 84" Width 36" Depth 24"
Finished Rough-In Dimensions	35½" x 83¾"
Weight (lbs.):	468 crated

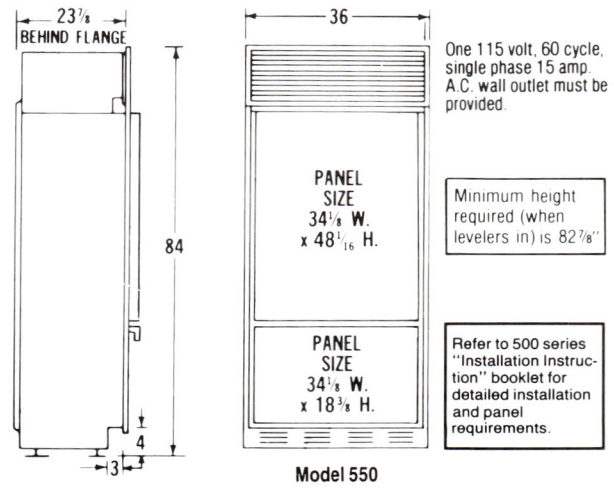

23⅞"
BEHIND FLANGE

36

84

4

3

One 115 volt, 60 cycle, single phase 15 amp. A.C. wall outlet must be provided.

PANEL SIZE
34⅛" W.
x 48¹/₁₆ H.

PANEL SIZE
34⅛" W.
x 18⅜ H.

Minimum height required (when levelers in) is 82⅞"

Refer to 500 series "Installation Instruction" booklet for detailed installation and panel requirements.

Model 550

(Optional panel grille shown)   Model 511

Model 511 Interior

bottom. The freezer has an automatic ice maker with removable ice storage container. The top pull freezer handle and double-tier design provide easy access. The refrigerator has two self-sealing crispers, each with independent humidity control. It has a roll-out utility drawer, adjustable glass shelves and fully adjustable door storage.

The model 511 features a 5.2 cu. ft. slide-out double-tier freezer drawer and a 12.7 cu. ft. refrigerator compartment. Again the freezer has an automatic ice maker with removable ice storage container. Like the model 550, easy freezer access is provided by top pull handle and roll-out double-tier design.

These over-n-under models are extremely versatile for kitchen designs used alone or in various combinations, such as the kitchen shown on the cover of this brochure.

Both units have two compressors which provides independent temperature control in both the refrigerator and freezer compartments. These units are backed by Sub-Zero's exclusive Twelve-Year Protection Plan.

Optional solid panel grilles that accept matching panels also available. Specification sheet available upon request. Detailed specification sheets on models 550 and 511 are available upon request.

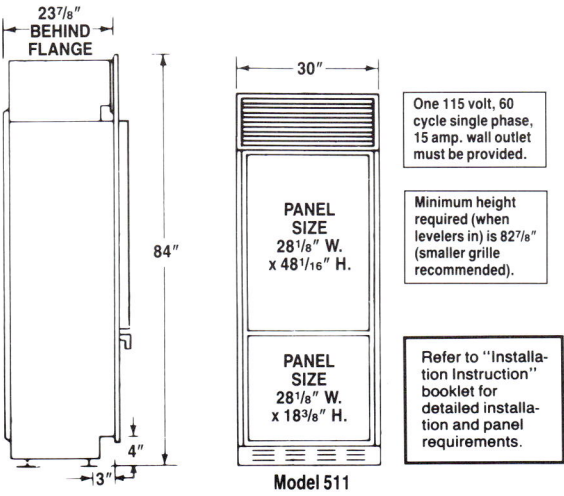

23⁷/₈″ BEHIND FLANGE

84″

4″

3″

30″

One 115 volt, 60 cycle single phase, 15 amp. wall outlet must be provided.

PANEL SIZE 28¹/₈″ W. x 48¹/₁₆″ H.

Minimum height required (when levelers in) is 82⁷/₈″ (smaller grille recommended).

PANEL SIZE 28¹/₈″ W. x 18³/₈″ H.

Refer to "Installation Instruction" booklet for detailed installation and panel requirements.

Model 511

COMBINATION REFRIGERATOR-FREEZER
Model 511 — Automatic defrost model. Freezer compartment equipped with automatic ice maker.

Capacity:	12.7 cu. ft. Refrigerator 5.2 cu. ft. Freezer
Dimensions:	Height 84″ Width 30″ Depth 24″
Finished Rough-In Dimensions	29¹/₂″ x 83³/₄″
Weight (lbs.):	375 crated

Model 511

SUB-ZERO

Features of full-size, built-in units

1. Convenient Storage

All Sub-Zero units are 24″ in depth to conform to most kitchen base cabinet units. This not only improves appearance of finished installation but provides more accessible storage on interior shelves.

2. 12-Year Sub-Zero Protection Plan

Full five-year (parts and labor) warranty and limited sixth through twelfth-year (parts) warranty on the sealed system, consisting of the compressor, condenser, evaporator, drier and all connecting tubing; a full three-year (parts and labor) warranty on mechanical parts (i.e., timer, motor, controls, ice maker) defective because of materials or workmanship; and a full one-year (parts and labor) warranty on the entire product from the date of installation. (Does not include installation.) (See warranty for non-residential use and other exceptions.)

3. Automatic Ice Maker

Makes and stores crescent-shaped ice pieces. Although several conditions affect the amount of ice that is produced in a given period of time, an adequate supply is provided. (Model 532 and 561 icemaker shown)

4. Automatic Defrosting

Automatically eliminates frost accumulation in both refrigerator and freezer sections.

5. Accepts Removable Decorative Door Panels

Front panels of virtually any material, not exceeding 1/4″ in thickness are easily installed. Raised panels may also be used when perimeter edge does not exceed 1/4″. **(We recommend routing, recessing or optional extended handles for finger clearance when using raised panels.) Refer to Installation Instruction Guide for detailed information. Only colored and stainless steel panels are available from the factory. (50# per door panel weight limit.)**

6. Side Panels

Unit is made to accept side panels if sides are exposed. Only colored and stainless steel panels are available from the factory.

7. Front-Vented

Allows for true built-in installation and eliminates over heating.

8. Removable and Adjustable Shelves

Cantilever type glass shelves in the refrigerator and wire shelves in the freezer for easy cleaning and flexible storage.

9. Deluxe Crispers

Spacious, self-sealing crispers have easy-glide roller design and adjustable, independent humidity control to assure food freshness.

10. Interiors

Award-winning Eurostyled white and clear interior.

11. Magnetic Door Gasket

Surrounds entire door with a pull that assures a positive seal. **NOTE** — Because of a perfect seal, allow a slight delay before reopening door.

12. Right or Left Door Swing

Available, when specified, on all over-n-under and single door units (all side-by-side units are hinged on outside). Doors are not reversible.

13. Portable Egg Trays

Convenient and versatile, they may be carried to the table or preparation area.

14. Adjustable Dairy Compartment

Versatile, positive sealing compartment for dairy items.

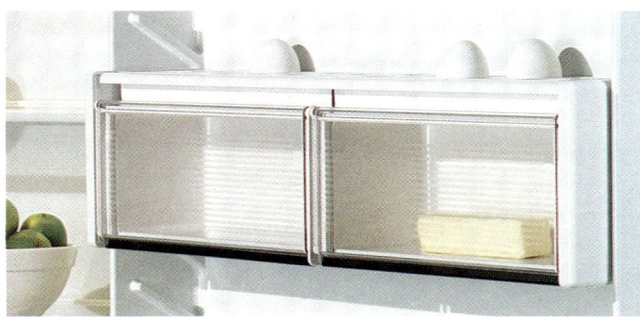

15. Adjustable Utility Basket

Adjustable roll-out refrigeration basket offers handy storage for small items.

16. Clean Trim

No visible screws.

17. Colored Panels

Decorator front and side steel panels are available from Sub-Zero in the following colors: Harvest Gold, Almond, Avocado, Coffee, Stainless Steel and White.

18. Grilles

Standard grille height is 11″. Other available grille heights range from 10″ to 15″ in 1″ increments. Optional decorative, solid panel grilles that accept matching panels also available in these sizes.

Panel grille

19. Toe Space Base

Integral part of cabinet. Inset is 4″ high by 3″ deep — meeting specifications of American Institute of Architects and conforming with most bases of kitchen cabinets.

20. Door Handles

Standard as shown in photographs throughout this literature.

21. Door Closers

All models equipped with door closers.

22. Door Stops

Although most installations do not require a door stop (door opens to 130°), an optional kit is available if needed. The Door Stop Kit allows the door to open to 90°.

23. Rollers

Unit has rollers and convenient leveling system for ease of installation.

24. Additional Shelves

Available at additional cost.

> **IMPORTANT:** For proper operation and use, the door must open at least a full 90°. A minimum 2″ filler should be used in corner installations to assure a 90° door opening. Remember to allow enough clearance in front of unit for full door swing.

Undercounter models

Sub-Zero undercounter refrigerators, freezers, combinations and ice makers are ideal for the bar, den, family room, yacht or office. They are designed to be installed under a counter. However, some may also be used as free-standing units.

All under-counter models are self-venting, have foamed-in-place insulation, have durable ABS easy to clean interiors and accept front door panels of practically any material to harmonize with cabinets or other equipment. They also have right to left door swings which are interchangeable in the field (kit required except model 245). All of these features and more are backed by Sub-Zero's New 12-Year Protection Plan—Providing a full five-year (parts and labor) warranty and limited sixth through twelfth year (parts) warranty on the sealed system, consisting of the compressor, condenser, evaporator, drier and all connecting tubing; a full three-year (parts and labor) warranty on mechanical parts (i.e., timer, motor, controls, icemaker) defective because of materials or workmanship; and a full one-year (parts and labor) warranty on the entire product from the date of installation. (Does not include installation.) (See warranty for non-residential use and other exceptions.)

The Sub-Zero combination models 245 and 801 provide automatic defrost, refrigerator storage, freezer storage and automatic ice making.

Sub-Zero also offers "all-refrigerator" and "all-freezer" undercounter units. The model 249RP "all-refrigerator" features automatic defrost, door storage and adjustable compartment shelving. Our model 249FF "all-freezer" features automatic defrost, adjustable compartment shelving and can be equipped with an automatic ice maker.

A unit for those who desire primarily refrigerator storage with some freezer storage is the model 249R. This unit is a manual defrost, with a small full-width freezer, door storage and adjustable compartment shelving.

We also offer built-in ice makers for those who entertain in style. For those cases where a smaller unit is desired or use of a drain is prohibitive, the model 221M "slimline automatic ice maker" is available. This unit is only 12" wide, has "easy-tilt" door and automatic shut-off so it makes ice only as you use it. A true built-in, it has front-venting, requires no drain, is 24" in depth and accepts front panels to complement virtually any decor. Requirements for clear ice can be satisfied with the new model 506, which provides an abundance of crystal-clear cubes in a unit that requires only an 18" width. Featuring a drop-down hopper-type door, this unit stores up to 35 pounds of 3/4" cubes. *This unit requires a drain or pump.*

Separate specification sheet on each undercounter model is available upon request.

Undercounter Model	249R	249RP	249FF	245	506	221M	801
Capacity	4.4 cu. ft. Refrigerator .7 cu. ft. Freezer	4.9 cu. ft. Refrigerator	4.6 cu. ft. Freezer	3.0 cu. ft. Refrigerator 1.9 cu. ft. Freezer	Stores 35 lbs. of ice	Stores 600 pieces of ice	2.9 cu. ft. Refrigerator 2.6 cu. ft. Freezer
Unit Dimensions [Levelers in] (H × W × D in inches)	$33^{13}/_{16}$ × $23^{7}/_8$ × 24	$33^{13}/_{16}$ × $23^{7}/_8$ × 24	$33^{13}/_{16}$ × $23^{7}/_8$ × 24	34 × $23^{7}/_8$ × 24	$34^{13}/_{32}$ × $17^{7}/_8$ × $23^{7}/_8$	$33^{15}/_{32}$ × 12 × 24	$33^{5}/_8$ × 36 × $23^{7}/_8$
Weight (lbs.)	120 crated	117 crated	135 crated	139 crated	110 crated	122 crated	265 crated

Note: Refer to "Installation Instruction" booklet for detailed water, electrical and other installation requirements.

Model 249R

Model 249RP

Model 249FF
(ICEMAKER OPTIONAL)

Model 245

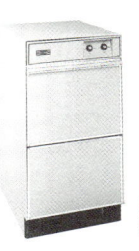

Model 506

Model 801

Model 221M
(caution, this unit must be built-in)

Installation specifications

Following are the installation specifications for all Sub-Zero full-size and undercounter models. The dimensions shown in the chart correlate with the schematic drawings. For further details refer to the **Installation Instruction Booklet.**

Schematic drawing

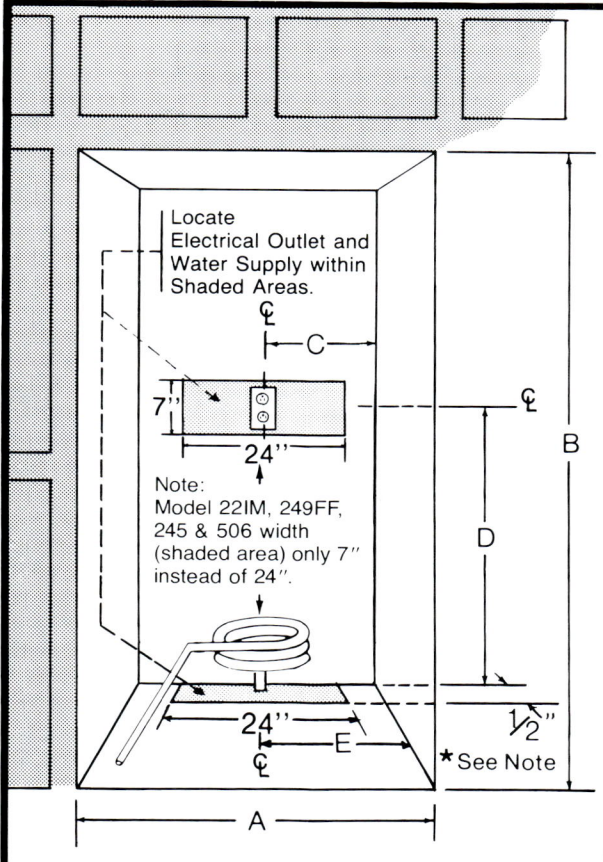

Locate Electrical Outlet and Water Supply within Shaded Areas.

Note:
Model 22IM, 249FF, 245 & 506 width (shaded area) only 7″ instead of 24″.

* See Note

Door Clearance Schematic Drawing Top View

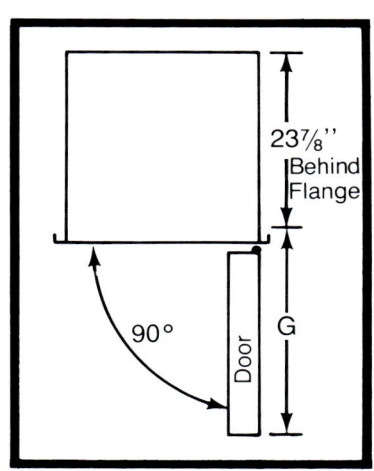

23⅞″ Behind Flange

90°

Door

G

Wood grille not available from Sub Zero.

Model No.	Finished Rough Opening Dimensions		Recommended Electrical Outlet Location		Water Supply Location	Door Panel Dimensions (width x height)	Minimum Door Clearance Requirement at 90°
	A	B	C	D	E		G
550	35½″	83¾″	18″	79″	18″	34⅛″ x 48 1/16″ & 34⅛″ x 18⅜″	36 1/16″
511	29½″	83¾″	15″	79″	15″	28⅛″ x 48 1/16″ & 28⅛″ x 18⅜″	30⅛″
561	35½″	83¾″	18″	79″	18″	14⅝″ x 67 11/16″ & 19⅛″ x 67 11/16″	20¾″
532	47½″	83¾″	18″	79″	18″	17 15/16″ x 67 11/16″ & 27 11/16″ x 67 11/16″	29¼″
501R	35½″	72¾″	18″	7″		34⅛″ x 58 15/16″	36 1/16″
501F	35½″	72¾″	18″	7″	18″	34⅛″ x 58 15/16″	36 1/16″
801	35½″	34½″	18″	3½″	18″	16⅞″ x 22⅞″ (both)	18½″
245	24″	34½″	5½″	4½″	12″	23½″ x 28⅛″	25 13/16″
249R	24″	34½″	12″	14″		23⅝″ x 30″	25⅜″
249RP	24″	34½″	12″	14″		23⅝″ x 30″	25⅜″
249FF	24″	34½″	5″	14″	18″	23⅝″ x 30″	25⅜″
22IM	12″	34½″	6″	6″	6″	11 9/16″ x 30″	27 13/16″
506	18″	34½″	6″	6″	11″	17″ x 13 3/16″ & 17″ x 11 15/16″	11¾″

*NOTE: Water line may come directly thru wall, not higher than 3″ from floor.

(Optional panel grille shown)

How to buy

Sub-Zero home refrigeration can be seen and purchased at top custom kitchen dealers and appliance stores in all major cities across the United States and many Canadian cities. If not available in your area, feel free to contact Sub-Zero direct for the distributor nearest you. (Canada residents use 608-271-2233/ U.S. residents 800-222-7820.)

Service

There are hundreds of authorized service centers throughout the country to provide warranty service and perform other service functions. These centers maintain a stock of Sub-Zero approved parts and a staff of qualified repair technicians. The service center nearest you may be found in the yellow pages or by contacting the dealer you purchased the unit from. If service cannot be found, contact Sub-Zero direct: Canada residents 608-271-2233/ U.S. residents 800-356-5826.

SUB-ZERO FREEZER CO., INC.

Post Office Box 4130
Madison, Wisconsin 53711
608/271-2233

141A

Tappan Built-In Ovens & Cooktops

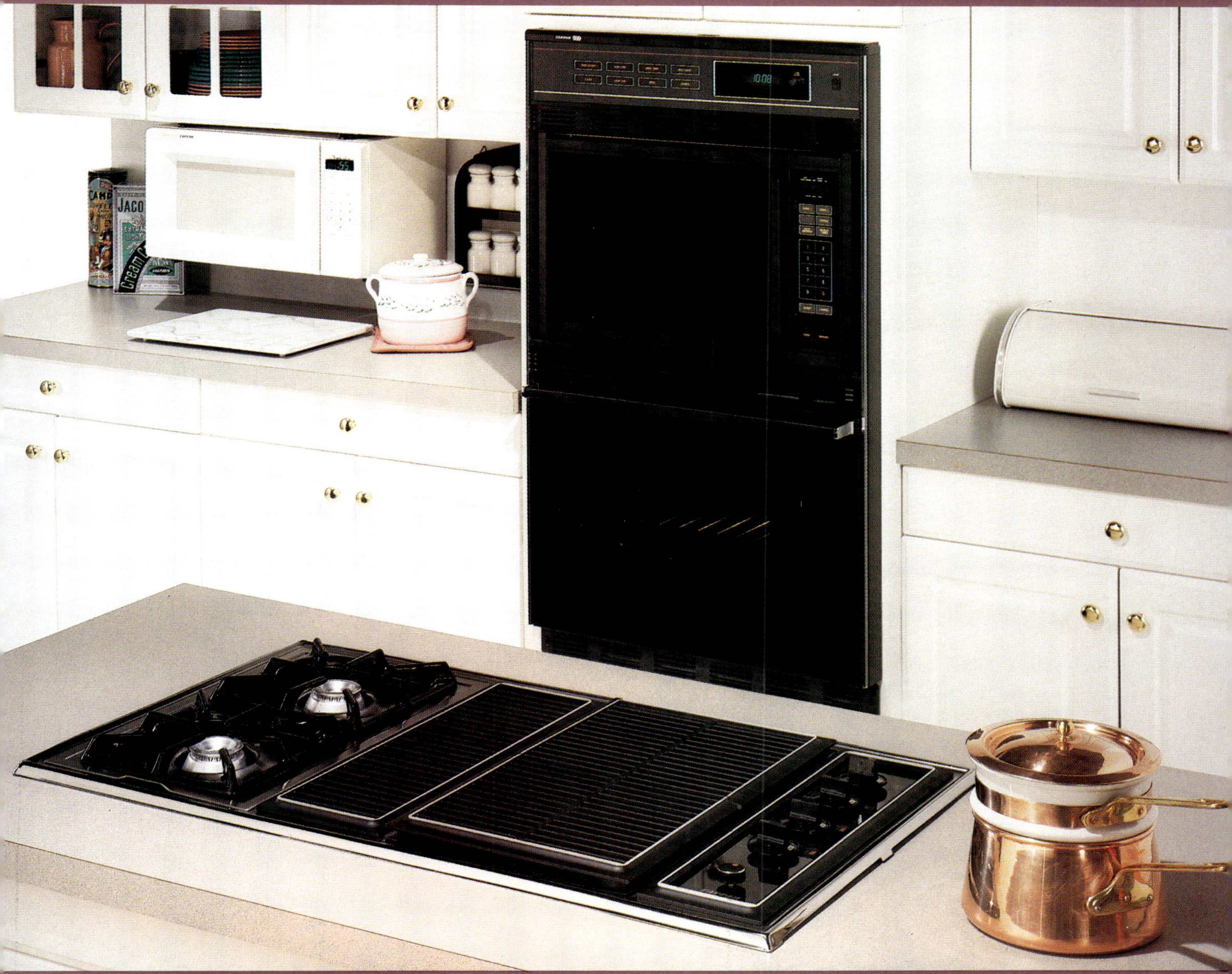

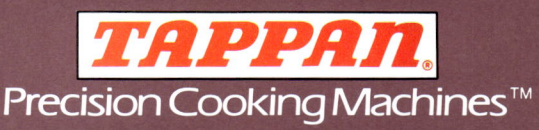

TAPPAN®

Precision Cooking Machines™

Gas Wall Ovens

For style and performance, nothing beats a Tappan Built-In Gas Oven. Whether you choose one of our revolutionary self-cleaning ovens or a fully featured continuous-cleaning model, you're making legendary Tappan quality a permanent fixture in the kitchen of your dreams. And, since Tappan Built-In Ovens fit beautifully in more than 90% of existing cavities, they're the right choice whether you're building or remodeling.

MODEL 12-4990

24" oven ■ Automatic self-cleaning oven ■ Electronic oven controls with time and temperature display ■ Removable white glass Visualite® door ■ Electronic digital clock ■ Electronic ignition ■ Eye-level broiler ■ Storage drawer with white glass door ■ Automatic oven light ■ Two chrome oven racks ■ Oven interior size: 17" W x 18½"D x 16"H ■ White-on-White graphics ■ Available in white only

MODEL 12-4980

24" oven ■ Automatic self-cleaning oven ■ Electronic oven controls with time and temperature display ■ Removable black glass Visualite® door ■ Electronic digital clock ■ Electronic ignition ■ Eye-level broiler ■ Storage drawer with black glass door ■ Automatic oven light ■ Two chrome oven racks ■ Oven interior size: 17" W x 18½"D x 16"H

MODEL 12-3699

24" oven ■ Continuous-cleaning oven ■ Backlit dials on control panel ■ Black glass Visualite® door on oven and broiler ■ Automatic oven start/stop ■ Electronic digital clock ■ Electronic ignition ■ Lower compartment broiler with 3-position rack ■ Oven interior size: 18½" W x 18½"D x 16"H ■ Broiler interior size: 18½" W x 18½"D x 16"H

MODEL 12-2299

24" oven ■ Standard porcelain oven
■ Electronic ignition ■ Glide-out broiler
■ Clock with 4-hour timer ■ Oven interior size: 18½" W x 18½"D x 16"H
■ Broiler interior size: 19¾" W x 19"D x 8⅛"H

NOTE: All features not available on all models.

GAS WALL OVEN FEATURES	12-4990	12-4980	12-3699	12-2299
Automatic self-cleaning oven	X	X		
Continuous cleaning oven			X	
Porcelain oven				X
Continuous Cleaning Broiler			X	
Electronic ignition	X	X	X	X
Decorative glass control panel	X	X	X	X
Electronic oven controls	X	X		
Clock/4 hr. timer				X
Electronic clock-cook start/off	X	X	X	
Backlit controls			X	
Lift-off doors	X	X	X	X
Two chrome oven racks (adjustable)	X	X	X	X
Glide-out broilers				X
Lower broiler compartment			X	
Closed-door broiling	X	X	X	X
Broiler pan and insert	X	X	X	X
Keep-warm oven thermostat			X	X
Interior oven light	X	X	X	X
Storage drawer w/black glass		X		
Storage drawer w/white glass	X			
Black Glass Visualite® Door		X	X	X
White Glass Visualite® Door	X			
White on White Graphics	X			
Approx. Ship. Wt. (lbs.)	147	147	196	153
DIMENSIONS				
Depth	25⅜"	25⅜"	25⅜"	25⅜"
Width	23⅞"	23⅞"	23⅞"	23⅞"
Height	38⁷⁄₁₆"	38⁷⁄₁₆"	50¹¹⁄₁₆"	38⁷⁄₁₆"

Backlit Controls For Easy Reading
Large, backlit dials for accurate reading of settings is a Tappan bright idea.

Automatic Electronic Clock
Easy-to-set digital controls start and stop the oven automatically.

Glide-Out Broiler
Rolls out for easy access. Specially designed pan and grid reduce smoke and splatters.

Electronic Oven Control.
Sophisticated electronics give you accurate control of baking and broiling. Two display windows let you set cooking time and temperature.

Gas Cooktops

The perfect complement to a Tappan Built-In oven, Tappan Gas Cooktops offer built-in style and convenience which fit beautifully in nine out of ten existing cutouts. Choose from 26", 30", or 36" models, designed for cooks who insist on appliances that look fantastic and perform just as well.

MODEL 14-3089

30" Cooktop ■ Electronic ignition ■ Three 10,000 BTU and one 7,000 BTU sealed European-style burners with lock-type valves ■ Square burner grates ■ Natural gas only ■ White-on-White graphics ■ Available in white only

MODEL 14-3088

30" Cooktop ■ Electronic ignition ■ Three 10,000 BTU and one 7,000 BTU sealed European-style burners with lock-type valves ■ Square burner grates ■ Natural gas only ■ Available in white, almond, black, chrome

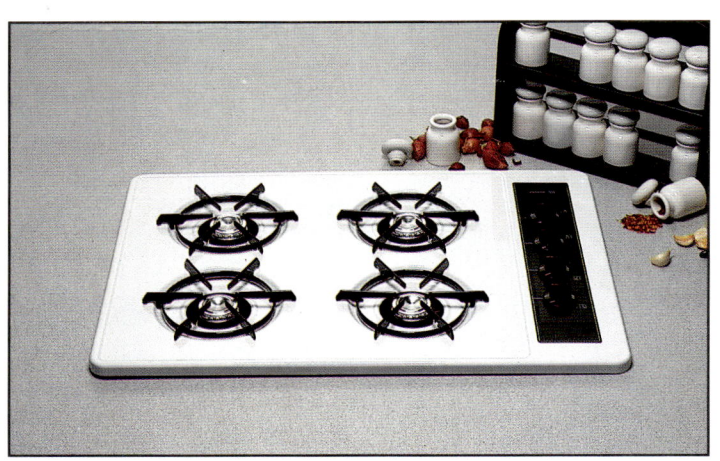

MODEL 14-3038

30" Cooktop ■ Electronic ignition ■ Four preadjusted burners ■ Lift-up top ■ Lock-type valves ■ Convertible pressure regulator ■ Also available with pilot ignition as model 14-3028 ■ Available in white, almond, chrome

MODEL 14-3632

36" Cooktop ■ Electronic ignition ■ Four preadjusted burners ■ Chrome pans ■ Lift-up top ■ Lock-type valves ■ Convertible pressure regulator ■ Also available with pilot ignition as model 14-3622 ■ Available in white, almond, chrome

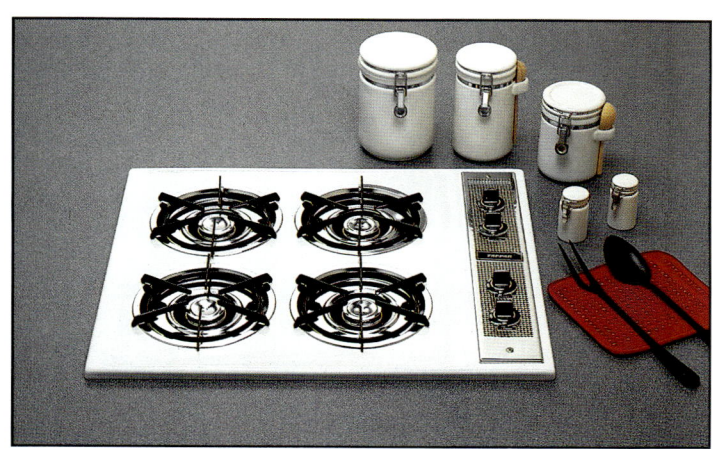

MODEL 14-2639

26" Cooktop ■ Electronic ignition ■ Four preadjusted burners ■ Chrome pans ■ Lift-up top ■ Lock-type valves ■ Convertible pressure regulator ■ Also available with pilot ignition as model 14-2629 ■ Available in white, chrome, almond

NOTE: All features not available on all models.

GAS COOKTOP FEATURES	14-3632	14-3622	14-3089	14-3088	14-3038	14-3028	14-2639	14-2629
Four burners	X	X	X	X	X	X	X	X
Sealed burners			X	X				
Square grates			X	X				
Lift-up top	X	X			X	X	X	X
Chrome spillover bowls	X	X					X	X
Lock-type valves	X	X	X	X	X	X	X	X
Pressure regulators	X	X	X	X	X	X	X	X
Pre-adjusted burners	X	X	X	X	X	X	X	X
Electronic ignition	X		X	X	X		X	
Pilot ignition		X					X	X
Colors: White	X	X	X	X	X	X	X	X
Almond	X	X		X	X	X	X	X
Brushed Chrome	X	X		X	X	X	X	X
White-on-White Graphics			X					
Approx. ship. wt. (lbs.)	32	32	35	35	32	32	30	30
DIMENSIONS								
Depth	3⁵⁄₃₂	3⁵⁄₃₂	3½	3½	4	3½	3½	3½
Width	18⅝	18⅝	21½	21½	21½	21½	21⁹⁄₁₆	21⁹⁄₁₆
Length	36	36	30	30	30	30	25¾	25¾

Square Grates and Sealed Burners
Make it easy to slide pots from one burner to another. Sealed burners keep spills from leaking through the top.

Lift-Up Top
Makes cleaning below the surface quick and easy.

Lock-Type Controls
Knobs must be pushed in to turn, an important safety feature, especially for families with children.

27" Electric Wall Ovens

When built-in appliances are in the blueprints, Tappan has the right all-electric ovens to fill the cut-outs. Choose single ovens, dual oven models or even a microwave combination for extra capacity and convenience. With Tappan, the value and style are built right in.

MODEL 57-2729

27" oven ■ 1.3 cu. ft. microwave upper oven with browning element and Turn-about® turntable ■ Automatic self-cleaning lower oven ■ Electronic touch controls for both ovens with time and temperature display ■ Vari-broil control ■ White glass Visualite® lower door lifts off ■ Electronic clock with timer ■ White-on-White graphics ■ Available in white only ■ Microwave oven interior size: 15½" W x 14½"D x 9⅜"H ■ Lower oven interior size: 18½" W x 18½"D x 16"H

■ MODEL 57-2709

27" oven ■ 1.3 cu. ft. microwave upper oven with browning element and Turn-about® turntable ■ Automatic self-cleaning lower oven ■ Electronic touch controls for both ovens with time and temperature display ■ Vari-broil control ■ Black glass Visualite® lower door lifts off ■ Electronic clock with timer ■ Microwave oven interior size: 15½" W x 14½"D x 9⅜"H ■ Lower oven interior size: 18½" W x 18½"D x 16"H

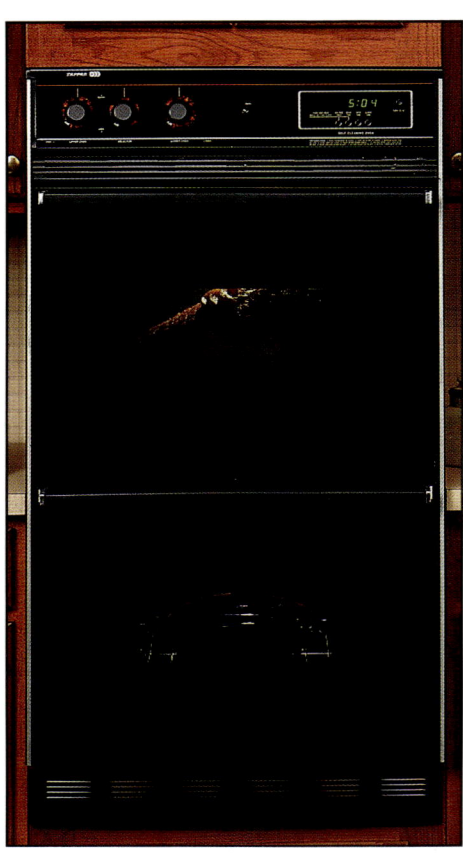

MODEL 11-5969

27" oven ■ Automatic self-cleaning upper oven ■ Standard porcelain lower oven ■ Vari-broil control ■ Double oven broiling and baking ■ Electronic clock with automatic start/stop ■ Black glass Visualite® oven doors lift off ■ Back-lit controls ■ Upper oven interior size 18½" W x 18½"D x 16"H ■ Lower oven interior size 18½" W x 18½"D x 16"H

MODEL 11-4989

27" oven ■ Automatic self-cleaning oven ■ Vari-broil control ■ Electronic clock with automatic start/stop ■ White glass Visualite® oven door lifts off ■ Back-lit controls ■ White-on-White graphics ■ Available in white only ■ Oven interior size 18½" W x 18½"H x 16"H

MODEL 11-4969

27" oven ■ Automatic self-cleaning oven ■ Vari-broil control ■ Electronic clock with automatic start/stop ■ Black glass Visualite® oven door lifts off ■ Back-lit controls ■ Oven interior size 18½" W x 18½"H x 16"H

NOTE: All features not available on all models.

27" ELECTRIC OVEN FEATURES	57-2729	57-2109	11-5969	11-4989	11-4969
Touch controls	X	X			
Microwave upper oven	X	X			
Turnabout® Microwave turntable	X	X			
Browning element in microwave	X	X			
Self-cleaning oven	X	X	upper	X	X
Porcelain oven			lower		
Double-oven convenience	X	X	X		
Electronic clock-cook start/off	X	X	X	X	X
Lift-off oven door	lower	lower	both	X	X
Broiler pan with insert	X	X	upper	X	X
Vari-broil control	X	X	X	X	X
Double oven broiling & baking			X		
Interior oven light/peek switch	X	X	X	X	X
Clean & lock indicator light	X	X	X	X	X
Oven "on" indicator light	X	X	X	X	X
Two oven racks	X	X	X	X	X
One oven rack (lower)			X		
Tempered glass control panel	Touch	Touch	X	X	X
Black glass Visualite® door		X	X		X
White glass Visualite® door	X			X	
White-on-White Graphics	X			X	
Backlit control dials			X	X	X
Approx. Ship. Wt. (lbs.)	235	235	219	140	140
DIMENSIONS					
Depth	25⅜"	25⅜"	25⅜"	25⅜"	25⅜"
Width	26⅞"	26⅞"	26⅞"	26⅞"	26⅞"
Height	48¹³⁄₁₆"	48¹³⁄₁₆"	50⁷⁄₁₆"	30¾"	30¾"

Automatic Electronic Clock.
Make it easy to set the oven to automatically start and stop cooking at any time.

Extra Large Ovens.
Banquet-sized capacity easily handles everything from holiday feasts to big-screen TV dinners. Standard on all Tappan built-in ovens

Automatic Self-Cleaning Ovens.
Clean themselves at the touch of a button, eliminating your worst kitchen chore.

24" Electric Ovens

MODEL 11-1969

24" oven ■ Automatic self-cleaning oven ■ Vari-broil control ■ Electronic clock with automatic start/stop ■ Black glass Visualite® door lifts off ■ Backlit controls ■ Oven interior size 17" W x 18½"D x 16"H

MODEL 11-2969

24" oven ■ Automatic self-cleaning upper oven ■ Standard porcelain lower oven ■ Double oven broiling and baking ■ Vari-broil control ■ Electronic clock with automatic start/stop ■ Backlit controls ■ Black glass Visualite® doors lift off ■ Upper oven interior size 17" W x 18½"D x 16"H ■ Lower oven interior size 17" W x 18½"D x 16"H

MODEL 11-2439

24" oven ■ Continuous-cleaning upper oven ■ Continuous-cleaning lower oven ■ Double oven broiling and baking ■ Vari-broil control ■ Clock with 60-minute timer ■ Black glass Visualite® doors lift off ■ Upper oven interior size 18½" W x 18½"D x 16"H ■ Lower oven interior size 18½" W x 18½"D x 16"H

4-Position Broiler.
Gives you precise control when you broil. Rack glides out easily, fits securely.

Backlit Controls For Easy Reading. Large, backlit dials for accurate reading of settings is a Tappan bright idea.

MODEL 11-1559

24" oven ■ Continuous-cleaning oven ■ Vari-control broiler ■ Clock with 60-minute timer ■ Black glass Visualite® door lifts off ■ Oven interior size 18½" W x 18½"D x 16"H (Also available with standard porcelain oven as Model 11-1159)

NOTE: All features not available on all models.

24" ELECTRIC OVEN FEATURES	11-2969	11-2439	11-1969	11-1559	11-1159
Self-cleaning oven	upper		X		
Continous cleaning oven		X		X	
Porcelain oven	lower				X
Double oven convenience	X	X			
Electronic clock-cook start/off	X		X		
Automatic clock/timer		X		X	X
Lift-off oven door	both	both	X	X	X
Broiler pan with insert	upper	upper	X	X	X
Vari-broil control	X	X	X	X	X
Double oven broiling & baking	X	X			
Interior oven light	X	X	X	X	X
Clean & lock indicator light	X		X		
Two oven racks	upper	X	X	X	X
One oven rack (lower oven)	X	X			
Tempered glass control panel	X	X	X	X	X
Black glass Visualite® door	X	X	X	X	X
Backlit controls	X		X		
Approx. ship. wt. (lbs.)	193	182	124	117	117
DIMENSIONS					
Depth	25⅜"	25⅜"	25⅜"	25⅜"	25⅜"
Width	23⅞"	23⅞"	23⅞"	23⅞"	23⅞"
Height	50⁷/₁₆"	50⁷/₁₆"	30¾"	30¾"	30¾"

Electric Cooktops

The finishing touch in the ideal all-electric kitchen is a Tappan Built-In Cooktop. Available in 26", 30" and 36" models, Tappan Cooktops are easy to use and easy to clean. And because they're from Tappan, they're every bit as stylish as they are functional.

MODEL 13-3099

30" cooktop ■ White glass cooktop ■ Two 6", one 8" and one 9" infinite heat solid disc elements (Automatic temperature-maintaining heat-sensor element available on 8" elements) ■ Surface indicator light ■ Push-to-turn control knobs ■ White-on-White-graphics ■ Available in white only

MODEL 13-3087

30" Cooktop ■ One 9", one 8" and two 6" infinite heat solid disc elements (8" includes automatic heat sensor) ■ Black glass top ■ Available in black only

MODEL 13-3078

30" Cooktop ■ Two 8" and two 6" infinite heat solid disc elements ■ Surface indicator light ■ Available in white, almond and black

MODEL 13-3069

30" cooktop ■ Black Glass Ceran™ Cooktop ■ Avant-garde black glass Ceran™ surface with elegant black trim ■ Completely smooth surface cleans with a wipe ■ Doubles as extra counter space when not in use ■ Red indicator light stays lit until surface is safe to touch ■ Infinite heat controls located on right side ■ Two 8" and two 6" burners ■ One piece knob and skirt ■ Available in black only

MODEL 13-3028

30" Cooktop ■ Two 8" and 6" deluxe top elements with chrome pans ■ Lift-up top ■ Surface indicator light ■ Available in white, almond and brushed chrome

MODEL 13-3008

30" Cooktop ■ One 8" and three 6" standard top elements with chrome pans ■ Lift-up top ■ Surface indicator light ■ Available in white, almond and brushed chrome

MODEL 13-3628

36" Cooktop ■ Two 8" and two 6" deluxe top elements with chrome pans ■ Lift-up top ■ Surface indicator light ■ Available in almond and brushed chrome

MODEL 13-3620

36" Cooktop ■ Two 8" and Two 6" standard top elements with chrome pans ■ Lift-up top ■ Surface indicator light ■ Available in white, almond and brushed chrome

MODEL 13-2620

26" Cooktop ■ One 8" and Three 6" standard top elements with chrome pans ■ Lift-up top ■ Surface indicator light ■ Available in white, almond and brushed chrome

Solid Heating Elements
Simplify electric range clean-up with solid top elements. Keep spills on top where they can be wiped up.

Heat-Sensor Element (inset)
Available on some solid-element electric ranges. Automatically adjusts the heat to maintain the set cooking temperature.

ELECTRIC COOKTOP FEATURES	36"		30"						26"
	13-3628	13-3620	13-3099	13-3087	13-3078	13-3069	13-3028	13-3008	13-2620
Hinged lift-up top	X	X					X	X	X
Solid disc elements			X	X	X				
Surface indicator light	X	X	X	X	X	X	X	X	X
Push-to-turn controls	X	X	X	X	X	X	X	X	X
Chrome spillover bowls	X	X					X	X	X
6" 1250W elements		2				2 (1200W)	2	3	3
6" 1500W elements	2		2	2	2				
8" 2000W elements			1	1	2	1 (1700W)			
8" 2100W elements		2					2	1	1
8" 2600W elements	2								
9" 2600W elements			1	1		1 (2100W)			
Colors: White	X	X				X	X	X	X
Almond	X	X				X	X	X	X
Brushed chrome	X	X					X	X	X
Black				X	X				
Black Glass Ceran™						X			
White Glass			X						
White-on-White Graphics			X						
KW Rating @ 240v	8.2	6.7	7.6	7.6	7.0	6.2	6.7	5.9	5.9
KW Rating @ 208v	6.2	5.0	5.7	5.7	5.3	—	5.1	4.4	4.4
Approx. ship. wt. (lbs.)	41	28	48	48	37	42	31	30	28
DIMENSIONS									
Depth of Cooktop*	3"	3⁵/₃₂"	3¾"	3¾"	3"	3¾"	3"	3"	3½"
Width of Cooktop*	21½"	18"	21"	21"	21½"	21"	21½"	21½"	21⁹/₁₆"
Height of Cooktop*	36"	36"	30"	30"	30"	30⅜"	30"	30"	25¾"

*NOTE: These are *not* cutout dimensions.

"Over-the-Range" Microwave Ovens

Tappan built-in microwave ovens offer full-sized performance in a convenient, out-of-the-way package that frees counter space and complements any kitchen design.

MODEL 56-2990 SPACESAVER®

1.1 cu. ft. oven ■ 650 watts of microwave cooking power ■ Touch controls ■ Ten power levels ■ Automatic defrost ■ Automatic temperature probe ■ White see-thru oven window ■ Built-in exhaust fan ■ White-on-white graphics

MODEL 56-2890 SPACESAVER®

1.1 cu. ft. oven ■ 650 watts of microwave cooking power ■ Touch controls ■ Ten power levels ■ Automatic defrost ■ Automatic temperature probe ■ Black see-thru oven window ■ Built-in exhaust fan

Installation Diagram Section

Gas Wall Ovens

MODELS   12-3699 ▶

Electrical Requirements:
115/120V, 15 Amps. Comes equipped with electrical cord.

CUTOUT DIMENSIONS			
MODELS FOR		A	B
24" 2 Cavity	MAX	51¾"	14"
	MIN	50¼"	10"

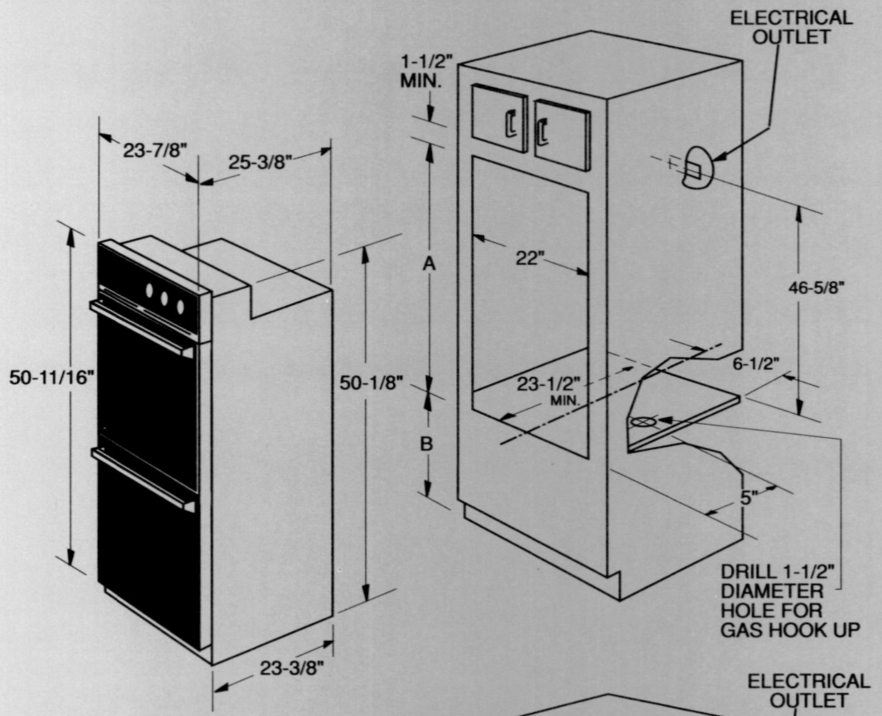

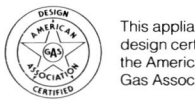

This appliance is design certified by the American Gas Association

MODEL   12-4990 ▶
12-4980
12-2299

CUTOUT DIMENSIONS			
MODELS FOR		A	B
24" 1½ Cavity	MAX	39"	27½"
	MIN	37½"	10"

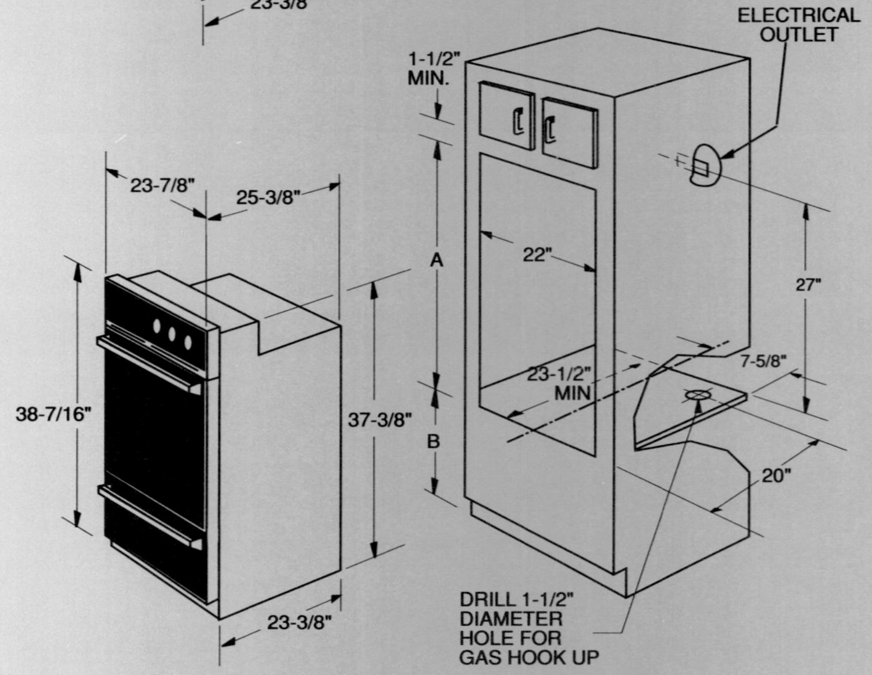

Gas Cooktops

MODELS   14-3089 ▶
14-3088
14-3038

Electrical Requirements:
115/120V, 15 Amps. Comes equipped with electrical cord.

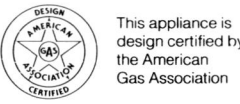

This appliance is design certified by the American Gas Association

ELECTRICAL OUTLET

1-1/2" MIN.

23-7/8"   25-3/8"

22"

46-5/8"

6-1/2"

50-11/16"   50-1/8"   A   B   23-1/2" MIN.

5"

23-3/8"

DRILL 1-1/2" DIAMETER HOLE FOR GAS HOOK UP

ELECTRICAL OUTLET

1-1/2" MIN.

23-7/8"   25-3/8"

22"

27"

7-5/8"

38-7/16"   37-3/8"   A   B   23-1/2" MIN.

20"

23-3/8"

DRILL 1-1/2" DIAMETER HOLE FOR GAS HOOK UP

30"   21 ½"

2 ½" Measured down from countertop edge

19"

26 ⅝"

MIN. 3"

MIN. 2 ¼"

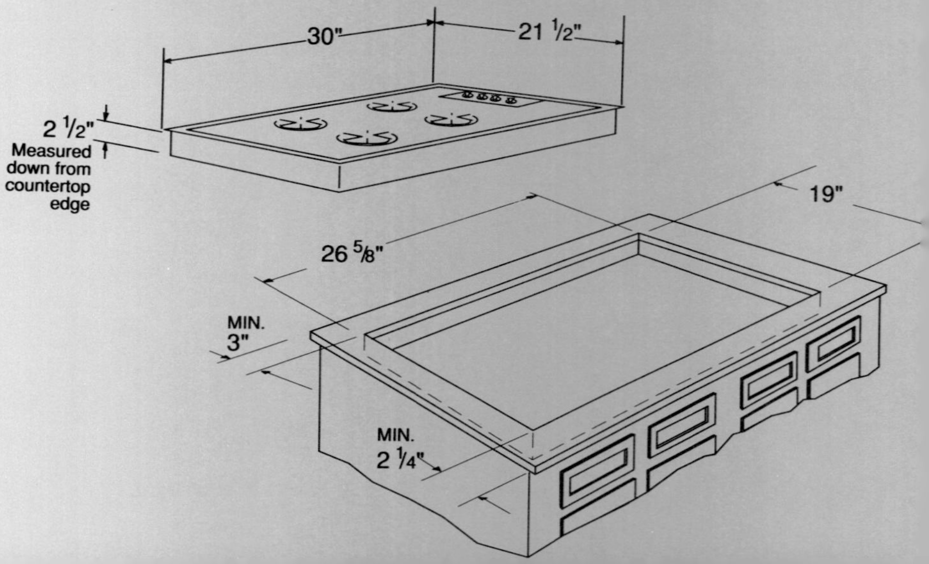

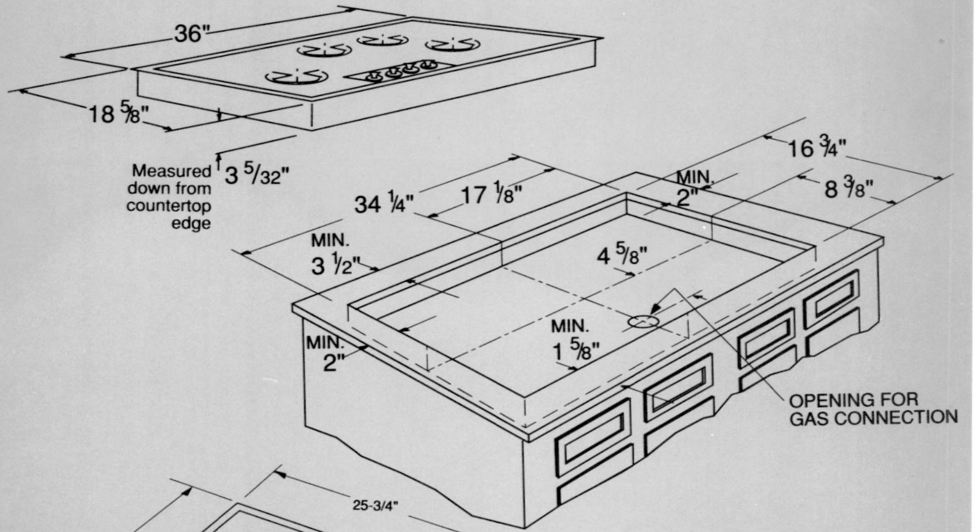

36"

18 5/8"

Measured down from countertop edge 3 5/32"

16 3/4"

MIN. 2"

8 3/8"

34 1/4"   17 1/8"

MIN. 3 1/2"

4 5/8"

MIN. 2"

MIN. 1 5/8"

OPENING FOR GAS CONNECTION

MODELS 14-3632
14-3622

◄

Electrical Requirements:
115/120V, 15 Amps. Comes equipped with electrical cord.

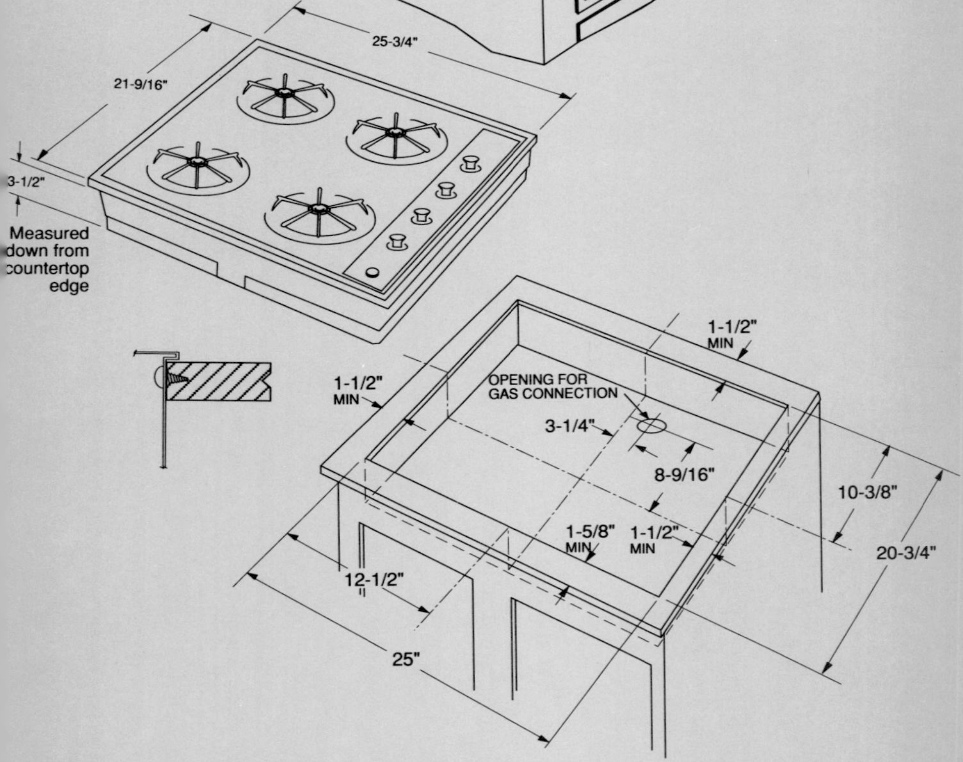

25-3/4"

21-9/16"

3-1/2"

Measured down from countertop edge

MODELS 14-2639
14-2629

◄

This appliance is design certified by the American Gas Association

1-1/2" MIN

1-1/2" MIN

OPENING FOR GAS CONNECTION

3-1/4"

8-9/16"

10-3/8"

1-5/8" MIN   1-1/2" MIN

20-3/4"

12-1/2"

25"

27" MIN.

1-1/2" MIN.

D   E

HOLE FOR CABLE

3" MAX.

23-1/2"

24-11/16"

48-7/8"

46"

18"

1-7/8" MIN.

ELECTRICAL JUNCTION BOX

26-7/8"   25-3/8"

6' CABLE

27" Electric Wall Ovens

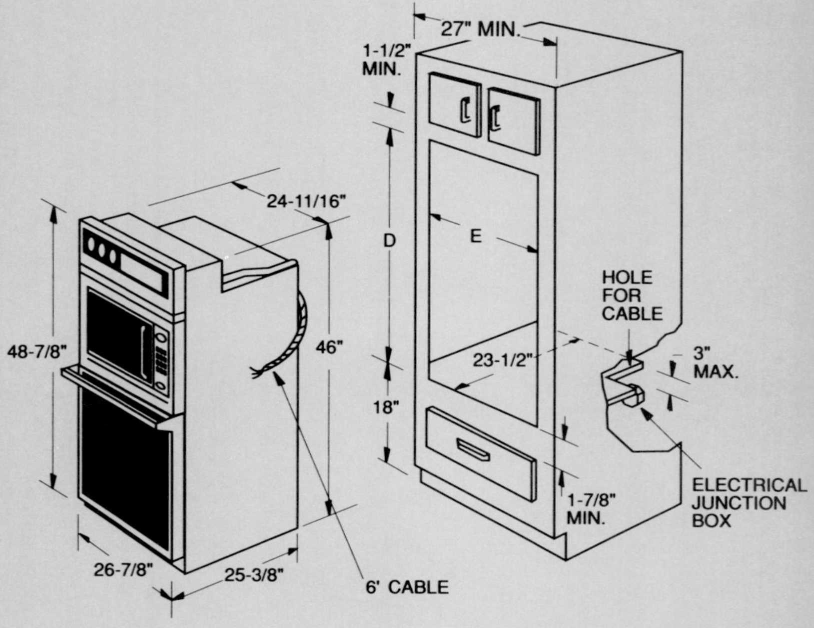

MODELS 57-2729
57-2709

◄

Electrical Requirements:
240/208V. Comes equipped with electrical conduit.

CUTOUT DIMENSIONS			
MODELS FOR		D	E
27" Micro Oven	MAX	48 1/4"	25 1/4"
	MIN	46 1/4"	24 3/4"

27" Electric Wall Ovens

MODEL 11-5969 ▶

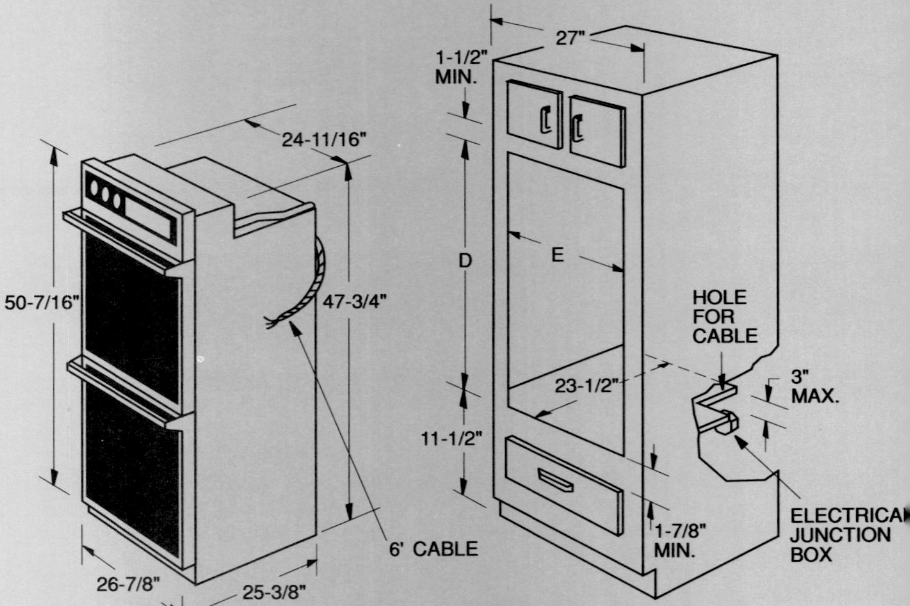

Electrical Requirements:
240/208V. Comes equipped with electrical conduit.

CUTOUT DIMENSIONS			
MODELS FOR		D	E
27" Double Oven	MAX	50"	25¼"
	MIN	48"	24¾"

MODELS 11-4989 ▶
11-4969

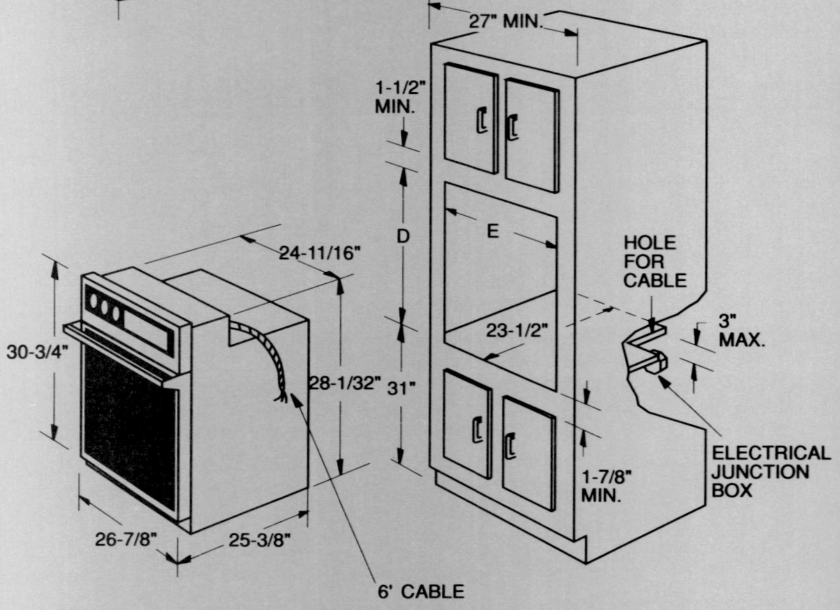

CUTOUT DIMENSIONS			
MODELS FOR		D	E
27" Single	MAX	30⅛"	25¼"
	MIN	28⅛"	24¾"

Listed by Underwriters' Laboratories, Inc.

24" Electric Wall Ovens

MODELS 11-2969 ▶
11-2439

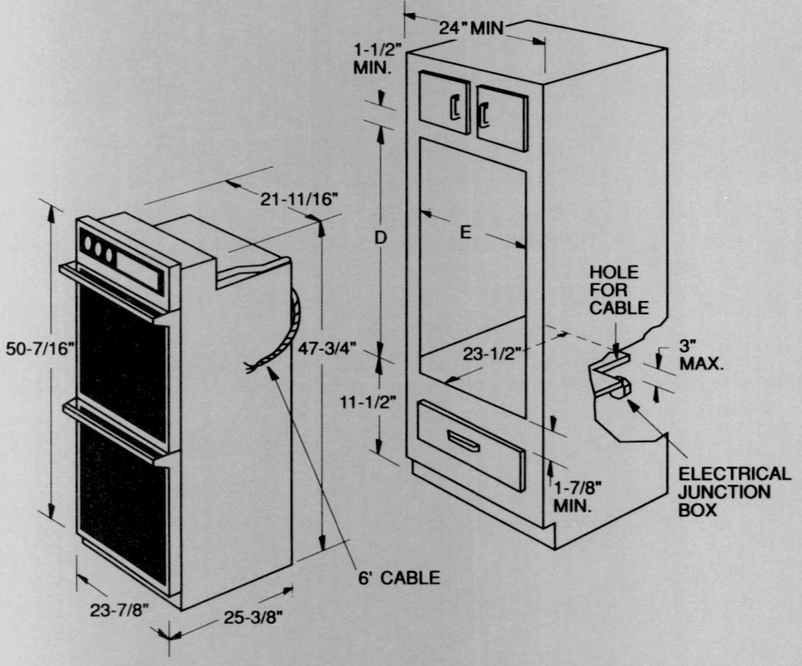

Electrical Requirements:
240/208V. Comes equipped with electrical conduit.

CUTOUT DIMENSIONS			
MODELS FOR		D	E
24" Double Oven	MAX	50"	22¼"
	MIN	48"	22"

27" Double Oven diagram:
27", 1-1/2" MIN., D, E, 24-11/16", 50-7/16", 47-3/4", HOLE FOR CABLE, 3" MAX., 23-1/2", 11-1/2", 1-7/8" MIN., ELECTRICAL JUNCTION BOX, 6' CABLE, 26-7/8", 25-3/8"

27" Single Oven diagram:
27" MIN., 1-1/2" MIN., D, E, 24-11/16", 30-3/4", 28-1/32", 31", HOLE FOR CABLE, 3" MAX., 23-1/2", 1-7/8" MIN., ELECTRICAL JUNCTION BOX, 26-7/8", 25-3/8", 6' CABLE

24" Double Oven diagram:
24" MIN, 1-1/2" MIN., D, E, 21-11/16", 50-7/16", 47-3/4", HOLE FOR CABLE, 3" MAX., 23-1/2", 11-1/2", 1-7/8" MIN., ELECTRICAL JUNCTION BOX, 23-7/8", 25-3/8", 6' CABLE

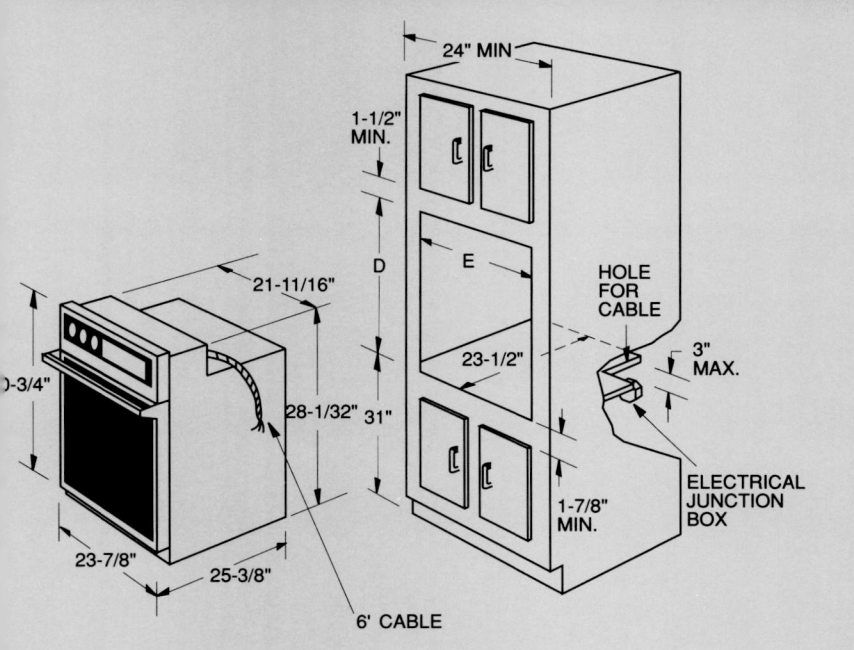

24" MIN

1-1/2" MIN.

D

E

HOLE FOR CABLE

3" MAX.

ELECTRICAL JUNCTION BOX

21-11/16"

0-3/4"

28-1/32"

31"

23-1/2"

1-7/8" MIN.

23-7/8"

25-3/8"

6' CABLE

MODELS
11-1969
11-1559
11-1159

CUTOUT DIMENSIONS			
MODELS FOR		D	E
24" Single Oven	MAX	30⅛"	22¼"
	MIN	28⅛"	22"

Electric Cooktops

MODELS
13-3099
13-3087
13-3078
13-3028
13-3008
13-3628

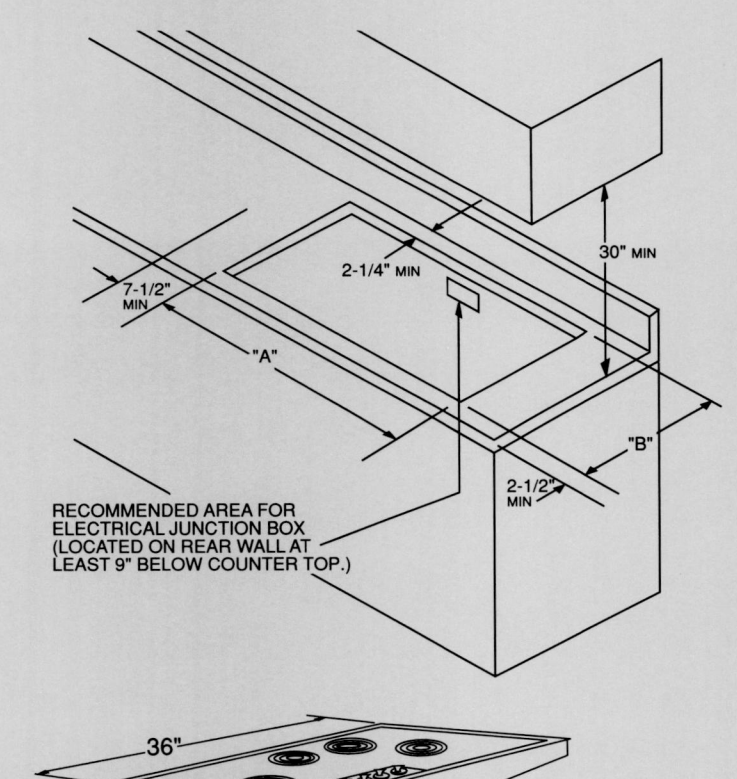

30" MIN

2-1/4" MIN

7-1/2" MIN

"A"

"B"

2-1/2" MIN

RECOMMENDED AREA FOR ELECTRICAL JUNCTION BOX (LOCATED ON REAR WALL AT LEAST 9" BELOW COUNTER TOP.)

CUTOUT DIMENSIONS			
MODELS FOR		A	B
30"	MAX	29¼"	21"
	MIN	26⅝"	19"
36"	MAX	35¼"	21"
	MIN	32⅝"	19"

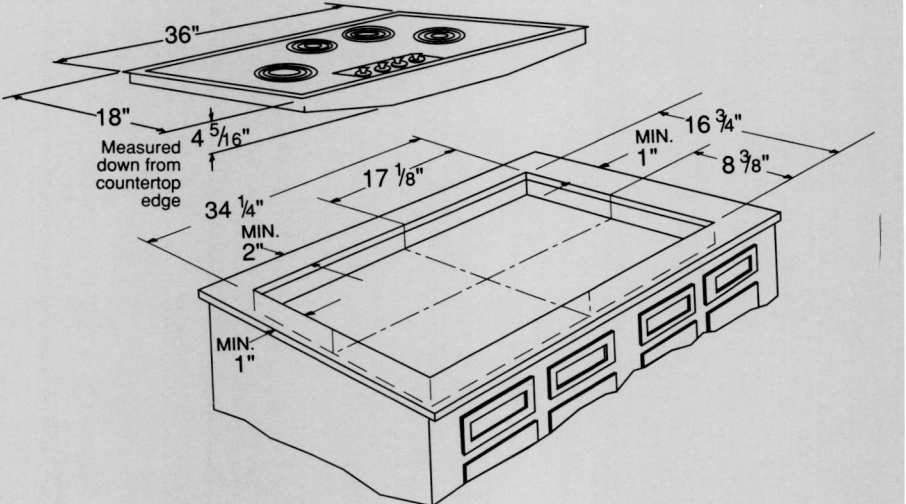

36"

18"
Measured down from countertop edge

4 5/16"

16 ¾"
MIN. 1"

8 ⅜"

17 ⅛"

34 ¼"
MIN. 2"

MIN. 1"

MODEL 13-3620

141A
Electric Cooktops

MODEL 13-2620

Electrical Requirements:
240/208V. Comes equipped with electrical conduit.

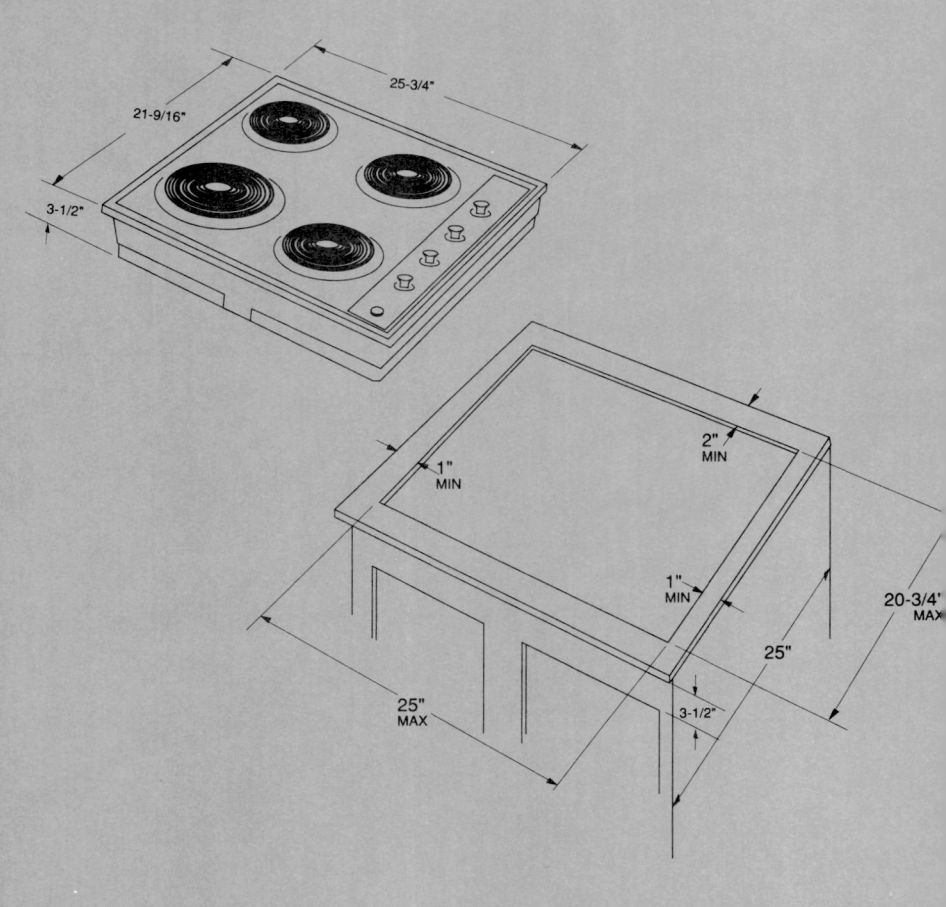

Built-In Microwave Ovens

MODELS 56-2990
56-2980

Exterior Dimensions: 30"W x 13"D x 14-5/8"H (in front) and 16-1/4"H (in rear)

Interior Oven Dimensions: 18"W x 12-1/2"D x 7-5/8"H

Approximate Shipping Weight: 96 lbs.

Optional Accessories:
82-5012-10 Recirculating Filter kit for inside venting
82-5014-10 Side Filler kit when replacing 36" or 42" hood (Model 56-2890) Note: Two kits required for 42" hood replacement.
82-5010-10 Side Filler kit for model 56-2990

Listed by
Underwriters'
Laboratories,
Inc.

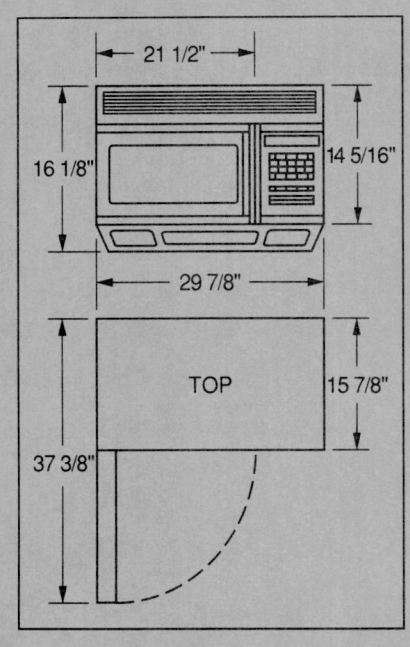

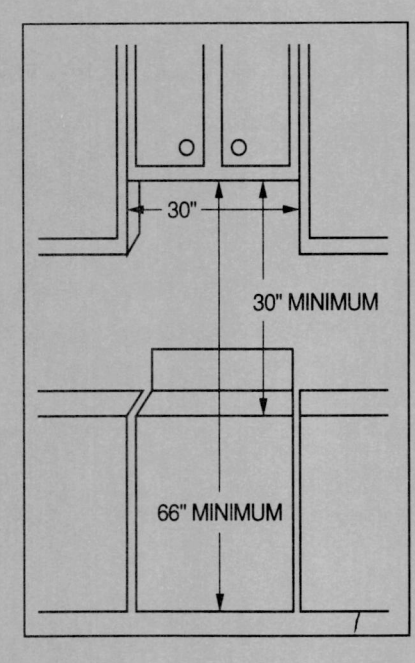

Tappan Warranty

With Tappan, you'll enjoy a full one-year warranty covering both parts and labor. Our goal is to build products that work for years with little or no service, but if something should require attention, help is as close as your telephone. More than 5,000 service professionals nationwide ensure quick, expert response to your call. Which is why so many people insist on Tappan — the brand backed by more than 100 years of customer satisfaction.

See your Tappan retailer or call the toll-free number listed below for a copy of the complete warranty.

For the name of the Tappan dealer nearest you, call the toll-free Tappan 24-hour "Rapid Response" line: 1-800-537-5530.

Precision Cooking Machines

6000 Perimeter Drive, Dublin, OH 43017

142

ULTRA® WINE REFRIGERATORS
HE BEST WAY TO IMPROVE BOTTLED POETRY

Ultra from Traulsen represents a half century of leadership in the manufacture of commercial refrigerators and freezers. It assures you of the perfect environment for the development and storage of wine. Ultra's balanced air circulation provides ideal temperatures and desirable humidity for aging wine. And our unique wine rack controls sedimentation by minimizing vibration. Experience the incomparable quality and durability of Traulsen's stainless steel construction. Let the Ultra Wine Refrigerator protect your valuable investment, while you enjoy the poetry of fine wine.

⊓ TRAULSEN

TRAULSEN'S ULTRA® WINE REFRIGERATORS CREATE THE BEST CONDITIONS FOR THE FLOURISHING OF FINE WINE.

Model UR 48 WT—shown with optional 4 glass doors and laminated KoolKlad® exterior.

Model UR 30 WT—shown with optional glass door and laminated KoolKlad® exterior.

Model UC 27 WT—undercounter model shown with optional stainless steel top.

DISTINCTIVE ULTRA FEATURES ASSURE YOU THAT YOUR WINE WILL REACH ITS FULL BOUQUET.

• Stainless steel construction, magnetic door seal and foamed-in-place polyurethane insulation shield wine from light and temperature changes that can affect its flavor.

• Vertical storage design maximizes capacity when space is at a premium.

• Compressor mounting allows all models to be "built-in".

• Exclusive Digitraul® exterior digital readout keeps you aware of consistent temperature range of 53°–57°. If other temperatures are required we can set them at your choice.

• Specially designed adjustable wine racks hold bottles tilted to keep the cork moist while providing easy-access and reading of labels. This design prevents bottle slippage.

• Interior lighting (except Model UC 27 WT) permits immediate check of wine stock for inventory control.

• Locks supplied for the protection of wine investment.

OPTIONS

• Triple pane clear tempered glass doors offer visibility for short term storage and display purposes.

• KoolKlad® customized exterior treatment of plastic laminate bonded at the factory for room decor coordination.

• Legs are available for commercial applications when specified.

• Left door hinging available upon specification.

• All models are available as self-contained or remote to meet the wide variety of customers' needs.

Means Daily Energy Consumption per ASHRAE 117-1986	MODEL		
	UR 48 WT	UR 30 WT	UC 27 WT
	KWH-4.8	KWH-3.8	KWH-2.7

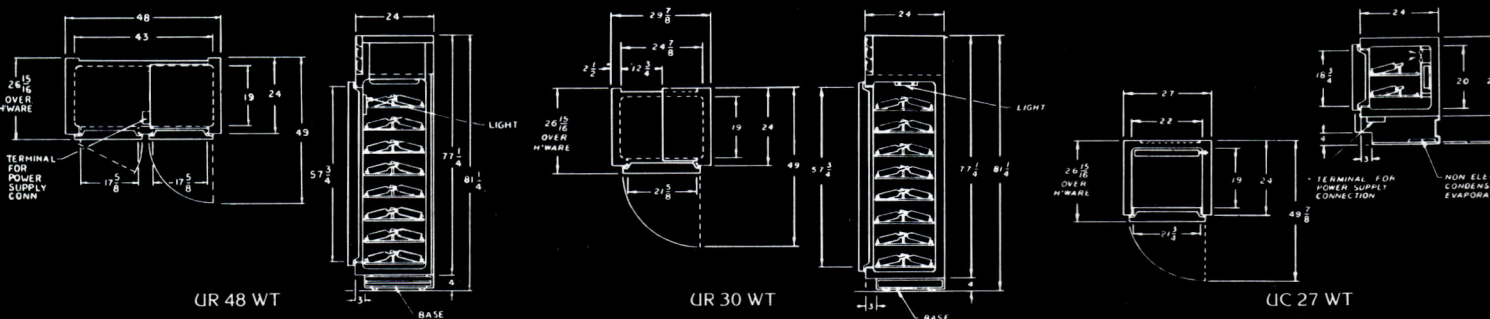

UR 48 WT   UR 30 WT   UC 27 WT

SPECIFICATIONS & DIMENSIONS

MODEL	DESCRIPTION	CAPACITY APPROX.	DIMENSIONS (in.)	CONVENIENCES	ELECTRICAL DATA	UNCRATED WEIGHT
UR 48 WT	48" wide wine refrigerator	31.6 cu. ft. ea./16 cases	48"W, 81-1/4"H, 24"D	2 doors, 16 wine racks, locks	115–1–60	450 lbs.
UR 30 WT	30" wide wine refrigerator	17.9 cu. ft. ea./8 cases	29-7/8"W, 81-1/4"H, 24"D	1 door, 8 wine racks, lock	115–1–60	320 lbs.
UC 27 WT	27" wide undercounter wine refrigerator	5.1 cu. ft. ea./2 cases	27"W, 34"H, 24"D	1 door, 2 wine racks, lock	115–1–60	154 lbs.

+ Extra wine racks available for all units.
+ + Fluorescent lighting available for model UR 48 WT only.
+ + + Stainless steel top available for model UC 27 WT when used free standing.

Traulsen's Ultra® line of wine refrigerators can be purchased from leading commercial and residential dealers across the country.
For further information, please call our toll free number (1-800-542-4022). In New York State, please call (718) 463-9000 or write Traulsen & Co., Inc., Ultra Division, 114-02 15th Avenue, College Point, New York 11356.

Due to a continuous improvement program, all models & specifications are subject to change without notice:

Traulsen & Co., Inc.
Ultra Division
114-02 15th Avenue
College Point, N.Y. 11356
(718) 463-9000

Rev. 11/90

Announcing the Whirlpool DesignerWhite Collection…all-white appliances that will make your kitchen as colorful as you like. Because white is the perfect neutral, DesignerWhite appliances fit into any kitchen decorating or color scheme.

Color-on-color…bold or pastel. Monochromatic or multi. Pattern-on-pattern. Complex textures. Wood…stained, bleached or painted. Satiny metals. Whirlpool DesignerWhite™ home appliances coordinate beautifully with any of them. And you can change the look anytime without changing your appliances.

The full line of DesignerWhite home appliances includes a wide selection of all-white cooking, refrigeration, laundry and kitchen cleanup products, to satisfy the requirements of builders and remodelers as well as homeowners. For a truly distinctive kitchen, choose appliances from the Whirlpool DesignerWhite Collection. The rest of the color is up to you.

Whirlpool®

DesignerWhite™
Home Appliances

DesignerWhite ™
Home Appliances

***DesignerWhite Set-In
Electric Range
Model RS676PXV***
Built-in look without
built-in cost is only one
of the beauties of this
Whirlpool set-in range
with self-cleaning oven.
The solid-element glass
cooktop wipes clean in
a minute, while the
electronic MEALTIMER™
clock automates oven
cooking and cleaning.

***DesignerWhite Electric Range
Model RF361PXX***   The bright-white styling of this
Whirlpool electric range looks at home in any
kitchen. Add to its automatic MEALTIMER™ clock
high-speed plug-in elements with hold-down clips and
self-cleaning oven plus many other easy-cleaning
features and you have a range that's a real joy to use.
Versatile all-white styling. Cooking flexibility.
Cleaning ease. They're all yours with this Whirlpool
DesignerWhite™ 30-inch electric range, for the
look you want, the good cooking and convenience
you deserve.

***DesignerWhite
Electric Range
Model RF391PXXW***
The electronic
MEALTIMER™ clock
that automates oven
cooking and cleaning in
this Whirlpool 30-inch
electric range can be
a great help to today's
busy family. A self-
cleaning oven and high-
speed surface elements
add still more convenience,
while gleaming white
styling looks smart in
just about any kitchen.

DesignerWhite Gas Range
Model SF376PEW The waist-high broiler of this Whirlpool 30-inch gas range lets you enjoy "charbroiled" outdoor flavor any day of the year. Add an electronic MEALTIMER™ clock, self-cleaning oven, and a host of features designed to make cleanup easy and you have the gas range you've always dreamed of in the gleaming all-white styling you want.

DesignerWhite Gas Range
Model SF386PEW This Whirlpool 30-inch gas range with self-cleaning oven adds the beauty of sealed burners so you'll never have drip pans or burner box to clean. The electronic MEALTIMER™ clock incorporates oven controls for automatic cooking and the broiler is at waist height, for still more convenience. Electronic ignition helps save energy. And the white look is a standout in any kitchen.

DesignerWhite™
Home Appliances

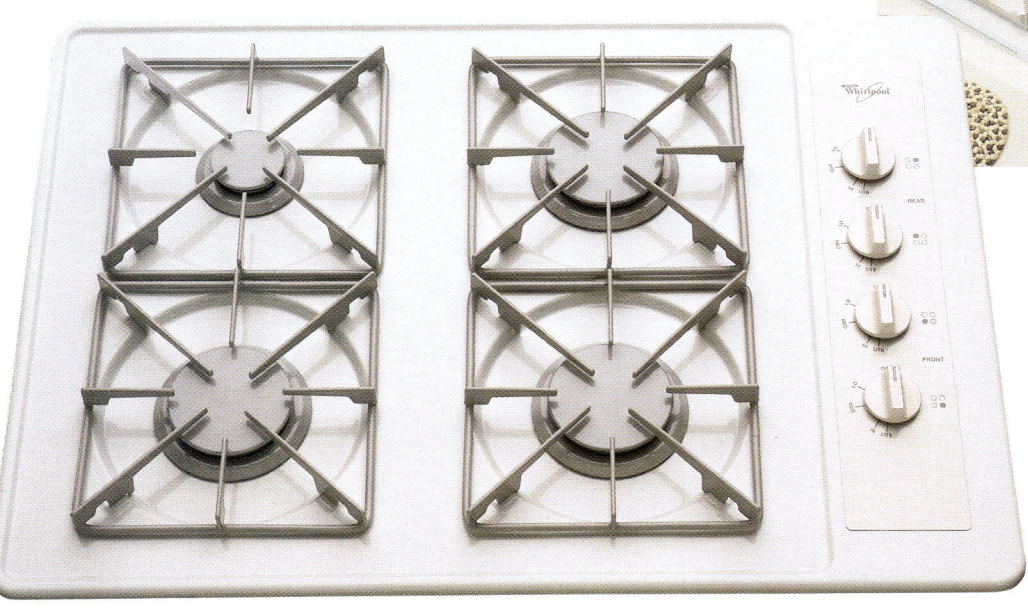

DesignerWhite Gas Cooktop
Model SC8630EWW Sealed burners in this Whirlpool 30-inch gas cooktop make cleanup easier than ever. There are no drip bowls and no hard-to-reach burner box to struggle with and spills wipe away from the white porcelain-enamel SPILLGUARD™ cooktop in a minute. Easy-to-use controls let you "fine tune" heats for precision cooking. Cooktop, controls, burners and grates are color coordinated for today's wanted all-white look.

DesignerWhite
Gas Cooktop
Model SC8536EWW
The convenience of a built-in griddle is yours in this Whirlpool 36-inch gas cooktop whose DesignerWhite styling complements today's popular light, bright kitchen. The white porcelain-enamel cooktop surface wipes clean easily, as does the porcelain-enamel burner box. White griddle cover, white controls, pearl-gray grates and porcelain burner caps complete the white look.

DesignerWhite Gas Modular
Downdraft Cooktop
Model SC8900EXW You'll need no exhaust hood when you install this self-ventilating Whirlpool 36-inch cooktop which comes complete with two-burner module and plug-in steak grill module. Cooktop, modules and controls are all bright white. And you can tailor the cooktop to the way you cook with optional accessory modules.

Non-Stick Accessory
Griddle
Part No. 786100

Surface Burner
Accessory Module
Part No. 4320716

Motorized
Accessory Rotisserie
Part No. 786225

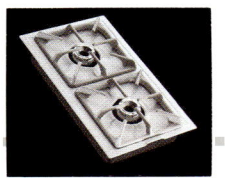

DesignerWhite Electric Modular Downdraft Cooktop Model RC8900XXW This Whirlpool 36-inch cooktop with built-in ventilating system is an inspired choice for installation where islands or cathedral ceilings make an exhaust hood impractical. The plug-in steak grill module is standard, with other modules available as optional accessories. The all-white styling is a standout in harmonizing or contrasting countertops.

Non-Stick Accessory Griddle
Part No. 786100

Coil Element Accessory Module
Part No. 4320712

Solid Surface-Unit Accessory Module
Part No. 4320713

Ceramic Smooth-Top Accessory Module
Part No. 4320714

Accessory Grill
Part No. 4320711

DesignerStyle Slide-Out Exhaust Hoods Models RH7730XXS (30-in.) and RH7736XXS (36-in.) Slide it out, it's a trim, efficient hood that whisks away kitchen smoke and odors. Slide it in and this Whirlpool exhaust hood with three-speed fan practically "disappears" into cabinet fronts. An optional White Trim Kit is available to convert the standard brushed-aluminum front panel to the white look (30-inch, part no. 883144; 36-inch, part no. 883145). Can be installed vented or non-vented.

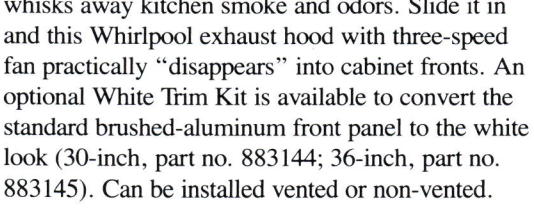

DesignerWhite Exhaust Hoods Models RH4931XW (30-in.) and RH4936XW (36-in.) When the Whirlpool DesignerWhite cooktop you choose requires an exhaust hood, this is the perfect solution. Variable speed electronic touch controls make operation easy and effective and installation can be either vented or non-vented.

DesignerWhite Glass-Surface Electric Cooktops Models RC8430XTW (30-in.), RC8330XTW (30-in., for 208V installation) and RC8436XTW (36-in.) A dazzling combination of high style and high performance, these Whirlpool DesignerWhite cooktops have solid elements that transfer heat evenly for uniform cooking. Elements are sealed into the white tempered-glass cooktop so spills wipe away easily... no reflector bowls or burner box to clean.

DesignerWhite™
Home Appliances

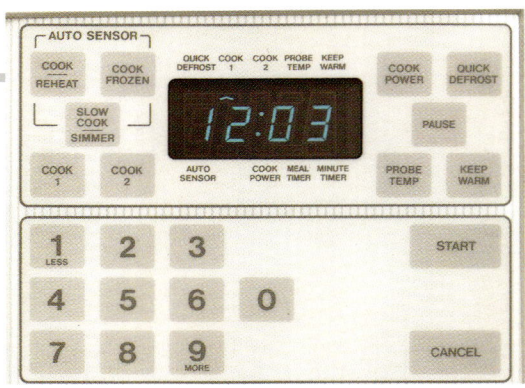

Electronic MEALTIMER™ *Clock*
Easiest to use timer ever! Simply touch the button for the wanted function...BAKE HOURS, STOP TIME, SELF-CLEAN or MIN/SEC TIMER... and set the time. The oven does the rest, automatically.

DesignerWhite Built-In Microwave Oven Combination
Model RM286PXV The best of both worlds, this Whirlpool DesignerWhite built-in oven delivers the speed of microwave cooking and versatility of thermal baking and broiling in a single unit that fits in a space only 30 in. wide. The AUTO SENSOR cycle of the 1.3 cu. ft. capacity touch-control microwave oven cooks foods without the bother of determining time or cook power. An electronic MEALTIMER™ clock, which controls both automatic cooking and the self-clean cycle of the lower thermal oven, is integrated with the microwave oven control system, for still greater convenience. All-white styling is the crowning touch for this ultimate cooking appliance.

DesignerWhite Built-In Electric Double Ovens
Model RB270PXXW (30-in.)   Every good cook knows there's no substitute for two ovens when it comes to meal preparation convenience. This Whirlpool 30-inch model gives you the capacity you need plus the versatility to handle most oven-cooking assignments. An electronic MEALTIMER™ clock controls cooking and cleaning in the self-cleaning upper oven; the lower oven offers many easy-cleaning features. The clock's easy-to-read blue display accents the white look.
DesignerWhite Models RB770PXXW (27-in.) and RB170PXXW (24-in.)
These Whirlpool built-in double ovens offer the same features as model RB270PXXW in sizes to fit 27-in. and 24-in. cutouts.

DesignerWhite Built-In Electric Single Oven
Model RB260PXXW (30-in.)   Do your plans call for a single oven? This DesignerWhite 30-inch built-in oven gives you the consistent cooking performance and easy cleaning you want. An electronic MEALTIMER™ clock controls cooking and cleaning while the Balanced Cooking System gives you all-around cooking for dependable results. The self-cleaning system eliminates one of homemaking's worst jobs. And the all-white styling complements any kitchen decorating scheme.
DesignerWhite Models RB760PXXW (27-in.) and RB160PXXW (24-in.)   These Whirlpool built-in single ovens offer the same features as model RB260PXXW in sizes to fit 27-in. and 24-in. cutouts.

Temperature Probe
It's easy to cook foods to an exact degree of doneness with a Whirlpool microwave oven. Just insert the probe and set the desired internal temperature of the food. The oven turns off automatically when that temperature is reached.

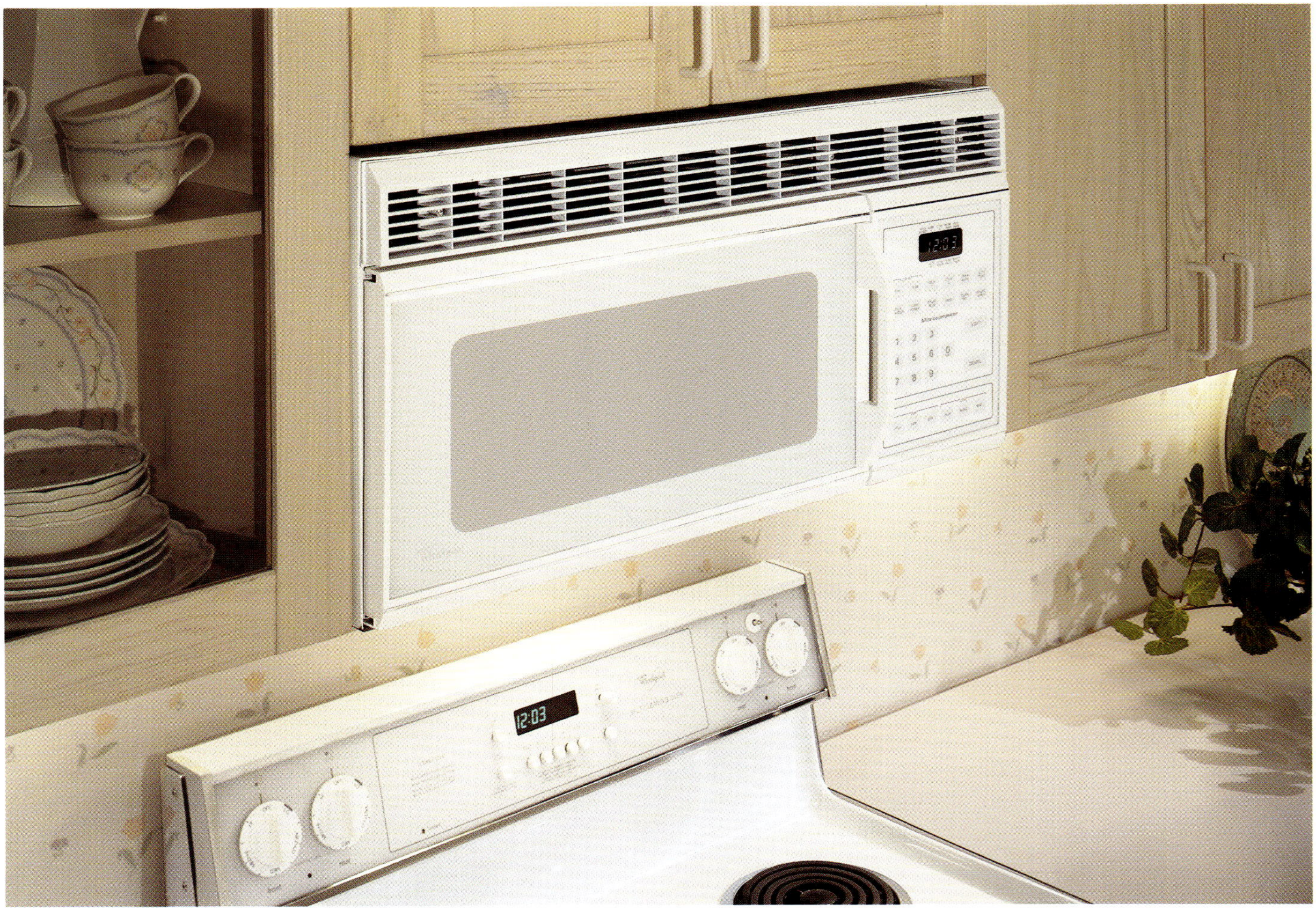

DesignerWhite Microwave Oven/Hood Combination
Model MH6701XW Imagine! A microwave oven *and* an efficient ventilating system in a single unit! That's what you get when you choose the Whirlpool DesignerWhite TimeMaster™ microwave oven/hood combination for your kitchen. All-white styling makes this versatile appliance at home in just about any setting. AUTO SET, QUICK DEFROST and KEEP WARM cycles are only a few of the time savers built into the 1.0 cu. ft. capacity touch control microwave oven. The exhaust system can be installed either vented or non-vented.

DesignerWhite Microwave Ovens
Full-Size Model MT6901XW Versatility is the middle name of this 1.2 cu. ft. capacity DesignerWhite TimeMaster™ microwave oven. POPCORN, BEVERAGE and DINNER PLATE cycles provide the correct timing and cook power for these tasks at a touch. Or touch the ADD MINUTE pad for an extra minute of cooking time. A removable glass turntable helps ensure even cooking. Optional built-in kits are available.

Full-Size Model MW8901XS A compelling style statement in any kitchen, this Whirlpool DesignerWhite TimeMaster™ 1.3 cu. ft. capacity microwave oven is big enough to roast a turkey. Microcomputer controls provide the convenience of AUTO SENSOR, AUTO START, QUICK DEFROST and KEEP WARM cycles at a touch. There's even a temperature probe, to cook foods to precise internal temperatures. Optional built-in kits available.

Mid-Size Model MT1851XW A removable glass turntable in this DesignerWhite TimeMaster™ 0.8 cu. ft. microwave oven rotates automatically to cook foods uniformly. AUTO SET, QUICK DEFROST and KEEP WARM cycles add cooking convenience.

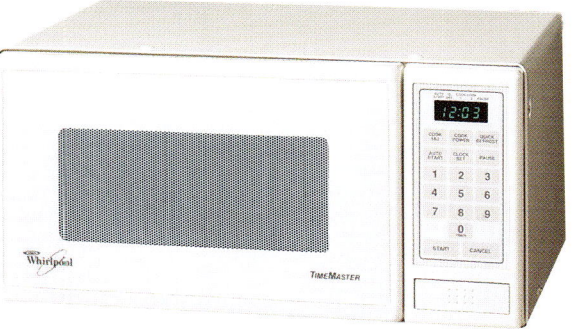

Compact Model MS1451XW
This 0.4 cu. ft. model gives you cooking speed and flexibility in minimum space…a perfect choice for your second microwave oven. Removable glass tray bottom shelf is easy to clean. An under-cabinet mounting kit is available.

DesignerWhite™
Home Appliances

DesignerWhite Top-Freezer No-Frost Refrigerator-Freezer Model ET25RKXYW The room and convenience you need are all yours in this big-capacity 25.1 cu. ft. No-Frost refrigerator. If you've had it with stubborn ice trays, opt for the optional ICEMAGIC® automatic ice maker and you'll get a continuous supply of ice without trays to fill and spill. Large humidity-controlled sealed crispers, adjustable meat pan with see-through cover, adjustable tempered-glass shelves, and easy-to-move button-mount bins in both refrigerator and freezer doors are just a few of the ways this Whirlpool refrigerator helps you keep things organized. And it's all white inside and out for the clean, modern look you want in your kitchen.

DesignerWhite Top-Freezer No-Frost Refrigerator-Freezer

Model ET22RMXYW The ICEMAGIC® automatic ice maker which delivers ice with no trays to fill and spill is standard in this 21.7 cu. ft. DesignerWhite refrigerator. Up-front controls make temperature adjustments easy. Up-front lighting makes foods easy to locate while it shows off the gleaming all-white interior with its tempered-glass shelves. Sealed crispers are humidity controlled, the meat pan can be positioned where it's most convenient for you, and the button-mount door bins hold gallon containers and beverage-packs.

DesignerWhite Top-Freezer No-Frost Refrigerator-Freezer

Model ET22RKXYW All the quality features of model ET22RMXYW except its ICEMAGIC® automatic ice maker is optional. Four ice cube trays and an ice bucket are standard.

DesignerWhite Top-Freezer No-Frost Refrigerator-Freezer

Model ET20RKXYW Family-size 19.9 cu. ft. capacity is only the beginning of the convenience that's built into this Whirlpool DesignerWhite refrigerator. Adjustable tempered-glass shelves can be positioned to accommodate foods of all shapes and sizes. Humidity-controlled sealed crispers hold lots of vegetables and fruits. Button-mount door bins can be moved easily, provide handy storage for gallon containers and beverage-packs. There's even a portable utility bin for eggs or other small items.

DesignerWhite Top-Freezer No-Frost Refrigerator-Freezer

Model ET18RKXYW If you think today's popular all-white look is available only for kitchens where space is unlimited, think again. This Whirlpool DesignerWhite refrigerator can be installed in a space only 30 in. wide, yet provides more than 18 cu. ft. of food storage room. Its top freezer accepts an optional ICEMAGIC® automatic ice maker and its super storage door has easy-to-move button-mount bins that can hold gallon containers and beverage-packs. Adjustable tempered-glass shelves, humidity-controlled sealed crispers, and adjustable meat pan are just a few more of its many conveniences.

DesignerWhite Bottom-Freezer No-Frost Refrigerator-Freezer

Model EB22RKXXW If you prefer a refrigerator with a bottom freezer, it's now yours in an all-white version. The big 7.4 cu. ft. lighted freezer of this 22.1 cu. ft. capacity refrigerator is equipped to accept an optional ICEMAGIC® automatic ice maker. Two full-width slide-out baskets make frozen foods of all sizes and shapes easily accessible. The refrigerator section is equally as convenient, with humidity-controlled sealed crispers, adjustable meat pan, and adjustable tempered-glass shelves. Button-mount bins in the door are big enough for gallon containers and beverage-packs.

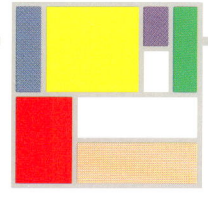

DesignerWhite
Home Appliances

DesignerWhite Side-by-Side No-Frost Refrigerator-Freezer Model ED27RQXXW All the room you want, all the convenience you need, all-white styling. You get it all in this 26.7 cu. ft. capacity No-Frost side-by-side Whirlpool DesignerWhite refrigerator with ThirstCrusher™ thru-the-door ice and water dispenser that delivers crescent or crushed ice or chilled water at a touch. Large, humidity-controlled crispers, temperature-controlled meat pan, adjustable SPILLGUARD™ glass shelves, and adjustable button-mount gallon door storage bins provide lots of room for all kinds of foods, while the snack bin and wine rack add still more storage convenience. Slide-out freezer baskets make the most of freezer space and the quick-freeze compartment hurries up molded salads and desserts.

**DesignerWhite Side-by-Side
No-Frost Refrigerator-Freezer
Model ED25RQXXW**   Inside, the convenience and space you need. Outside, clean, contemporary all-white styling. What else do you want? This 25.0 cu. ft. Whirlpool DesignerWhite refrigerator has it all. ThirstCrusher™ thru-the-door ice and water dispenser. Button-mount gallon-size door storage bins. Slide-out SPILLGUARD™ glass shelves. Snack bin. Slide-out freezer baskets. Quick-freeze compartment. And the all-white doors are leather-look textured steel that literally sheds fingerprints and cleans like a dream.

**DesignerWhite Side-by-Side
No-Frost Refrigerator-Freezer
Model ED22RQXXW**   This roomy 21.6 cu. ft. capacity model offers many of the conveniences found in other Whirlpool DesignerWhite refrigerators. ThirstCrusher™ thru-the-door ice and water dispenser. Adjustable SPILLGUARD™ glass shelves. Button-mount storage bins in both refrigerator and freezer doors. Slide-out freezer baskets. You get the capacity and storage space you need, the all-white styling you want, and the quality you've a right to expect when you choose any Whirlpool DesignerWhite refrigerator.

**Automatic Ice Maker with Glacial Water Dispenser
Model EC5150WV (shown with optional DesignerWhite Trim Kit #4317849)
Automatic Ice Maker Model EC5100XT**   The last word in convenience for your kitchen or recreation room, these versatile Whirlpool appliances which can be installed in a space only 18 in. wide produce clear, hard ice and store it in a lighted bin. Model EC5150WV makes up to 25.5 lbs. of ice every 24 hours and stores approx. 17 lbs. The Glacial Ice Water System collects a portion of the clear ice supply and converts it naturally to ice-cold water. The result is chilled water that is cleaner than the water it was originally made from. Model EC5100XT freezes up to 51 lbs. of ice a day and can store up to 35 lbs. in its roomy bin. The optional DesignerWhite trim kit (part no. 4317849) includes a white control panel, knobs, decal, grille and chrome trim…everything you need for a true DesignerWhite look.

Glacial Ice Water Dispenser
Simply press your glass against the handy dispenser bar to enjoy refreshing, ice-cold water. There's always a supply on tap, with no jugs to carry home and return.

DesignerWhite™
Home Appliances

DesignerWhite Undercounter Dishwasher
Model DU8550XX This Whirlpool DesignerWhite New Generation dishwasher with three-level POWER CLEAN™ system washes clean without prerinsing. HI-TEMP Washing is preprogrammed; if you don't want it, simply select LOW ENERGY WASH, one of this model's four automatic cycles. The CLEAN TOUCH™ console completes the flush, streamlined look that begins with all-white New Generation styling.

CLEAN TOUCH™ Console
Designed to provide the look and feel of electronics without the cost, the sleek CLEAN TOUCH console incorporates easy-to-operate controls mounted on a smooth, flush-to-cabinet surface that wipes clean in a minute. The "hidden" door latch contributes to the streamlined look.

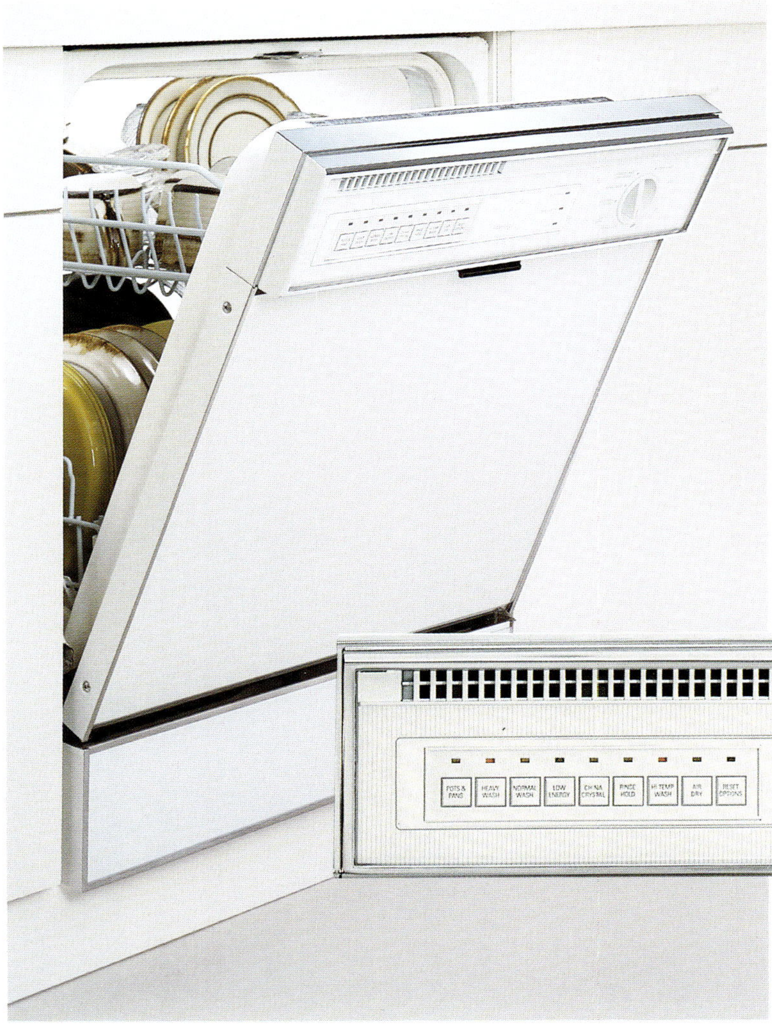

DesignerWhite Dishwasher

Model DU8950XT Modern design and technology join forces in this Whirlpool DesignerWhite Dishwasher where clean-lined all-white styling echoes the clean-dishes-with-no-prerinsing performance of its POWER CLEAN™ System. QUIET WASH™ System makes noisy dishwasher operation a thing of the past. And HI-TEMP option ensures water hot enough to get even the greasiest dishes clean.

New Generation
DesignerWhite Dishwasher

Model DU8950XX – Available Spring, 1991

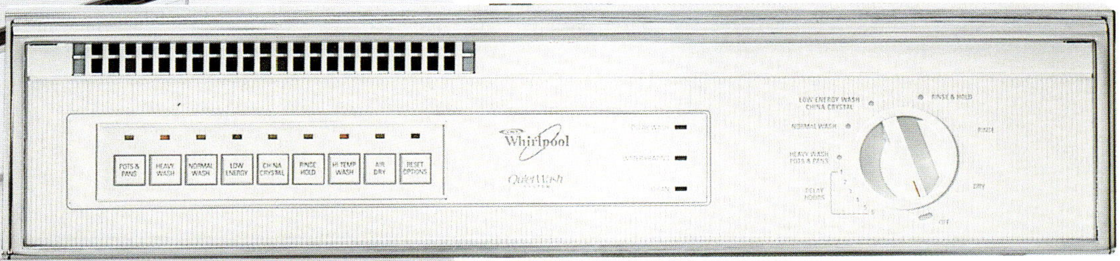

DesignerWhite Compactor

Model TU8150XT Add a matching Whirlpool DesignerWhite compactor to complete kitchen cleanup convenience. This invaluable Whirlpool appliance reduces a week's worth of trash for an average family of four to one easy-to-carry bag. QUIET PACK sound conditioning helps keep operation quiet, while EASY ROLLERS™ wheels make installation quick and easy.

TOUCH-TOE™ Bar
A toe tap on the handy foot pedal and the compactor drawer glides open, ready to load. A big convenience when both hands are full of trash.

Designer White™
Home Appliances

DesignerWhite Automatic Washer
Model LA9320XT
DesignerWhite Clothes Dryers
Models LE9520XT (electric) and LG9521XT (gas)   All-white styling for the laundry. What could be more appropriate? This Whirlpool DesignerWhite laundry pair gets clothes clean while it gives fabrics the care that keeps them looking their best. **The washer:** Eight automatic cycles wash everything from dirty denims to filmy synthetics correctly. The MAGIC CLEAN® lint filter never needs cleaning and an automatic dispenser adds bleach at the right time for optimum results. **The dryer:** Electronic DRY-MISER® control dries to a selected degree of dryness automatically. The Gentle Heat System provides extra fabric care by helping prevent overdrying. And, the CLEAN TOUCH On and Off end-of-cycle signal, wide-opening hamper door and FINISH GUARD® control add to the conveniences you expect come laundry day.

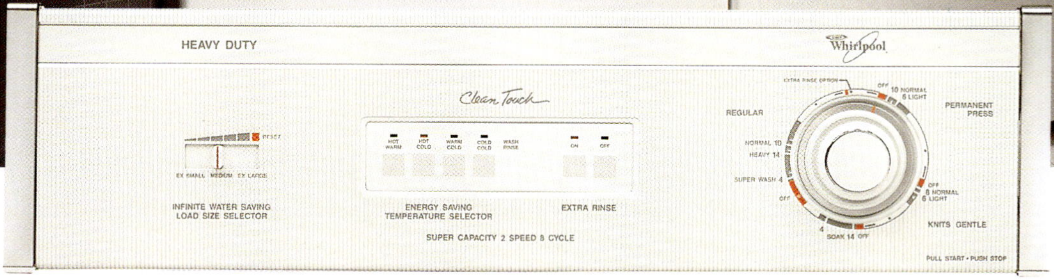

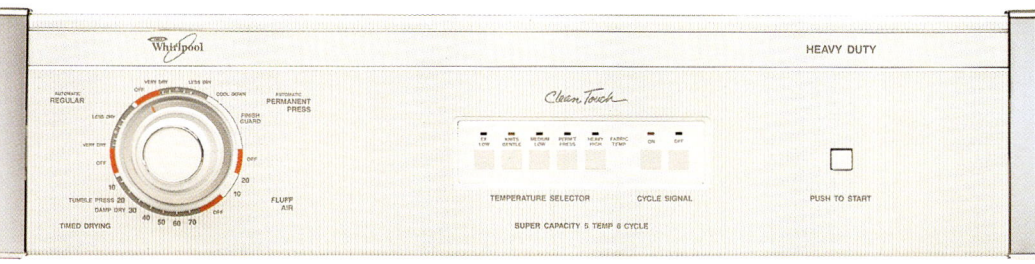

CLEAN TOUCH™
Consoles
No dust or dirt catching seams and corners on the control consoles of these DesignerWhite laundry products! The smooth, easy-to-use flush console surfaces wipe clean easily.

**DesignerWhite
Thin Twin®
Laundry System
Models LT7000XVW
(electric) and
LT7100XVW (gas)**
This Whirlpool
DesignerWhite 27-Inch
Thin Twin® Laundry
System gets your big
loads clean. The large-
capacity five-cycle
top dryer offers infinite
temperature control
for "fine-tuning" dryer
heat to fabric, electronic
DRY-MISER® control,
an end-of-cycle signal,
wide-opening 180°
side-swing door with
window and interior
drum light. The large-
capacity washer has six
automatic cycles, two
wash and spin speeds,
and Gentle Wash
System for cleaning
power and fabric care.
MAGIC CLEAN® self-
cleaning lint filter and
an automatic bleach
dispenser help save time
and work.

**DesignerWhite Thin Twin® Laundry System
Models LT5000XVW (electric) and LT5100XVW
(gas)** This space-saving DesignerWhite
Thin Twin® Laundry System fits in a space only
24 in. wide, for just about limitless installation
possibilities…in the kitchen or bathroom, under
the stairs, in a closet, to mention a few. The top
dryer has five cycles, DRY-MISER® control to dry
from LESS DRY to VERY DRY automatically,
and Gentle Heat System. The six-cycle, two-speed
washer is equipped with an easy-clean lint filter and
Gentle Wash System, to give all fabrics proper care.

Form No. 9SH11

Quality you can count on...today.
Benton Harbor, MI 49022 U.S.A.

2/91
Printed in U.S.A.

Now that you've decided to buy a restaurant range for your home buy the *real* restaurant range.

Buy a Wolf.

Introducing The Wolf Gourmet Series

THE GOURMET SERIES

Quite frankly, we're a little embarrassed by our success in the home range market. You see, for the last 60 years The Wolf Range Company has manufactured gas-fired cooking ranges for the world's finest hotels, restaurants and institutions.

However, it seems that a lot of homeowners and designers have been ignoring our warning labels: FOR COMMERCIAL USE ONLY.

A lot of Wolf's are cooking in a *lot* of home kitchens. Ok, you win.

The Wolf Range Company is now manufacturing The Gourmet Series, designed specifically for home use. We've got both Counter Top and Free Standing models in configurations to match your cooking needs and in sizes for "real life" home kitchens. No matter how big your kitchen is,

The new Gourmet Series has TREMENDOUS cooking power. Naturally, it's a Wolf.

The Gourmet Series features heavy duty, "spider-design" burner grates for strength and the maximum heat transfer possible, an inside-the-oven electric broiler, instant-on electronic ignition, cool touch knobs and handles, mirror-polished griddle finishes, easy to clean charbroiler grates, chefs-size porcelain interior ovens and more.

Check out our specs. We encourage you to compare The Gourmet Series to those other "restaurant-style" appliances that have recently been rushed to market.

Beware of sheepish ranges in Wolf's clothing.

Learn more about
Wolf's Gourmet Series, call
Stan Waldman, President,
The Wolf Range Company
800-366-WOLF
or
FAX 213-637-7931
or write
19600 South Alameda Street
Compton, California 90221-6291

ISE IN-SINK-ERATOR

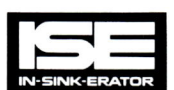

New Classic® Supreme 2000

State-of-the-art electronics... convenient touch-pad cycle selection.

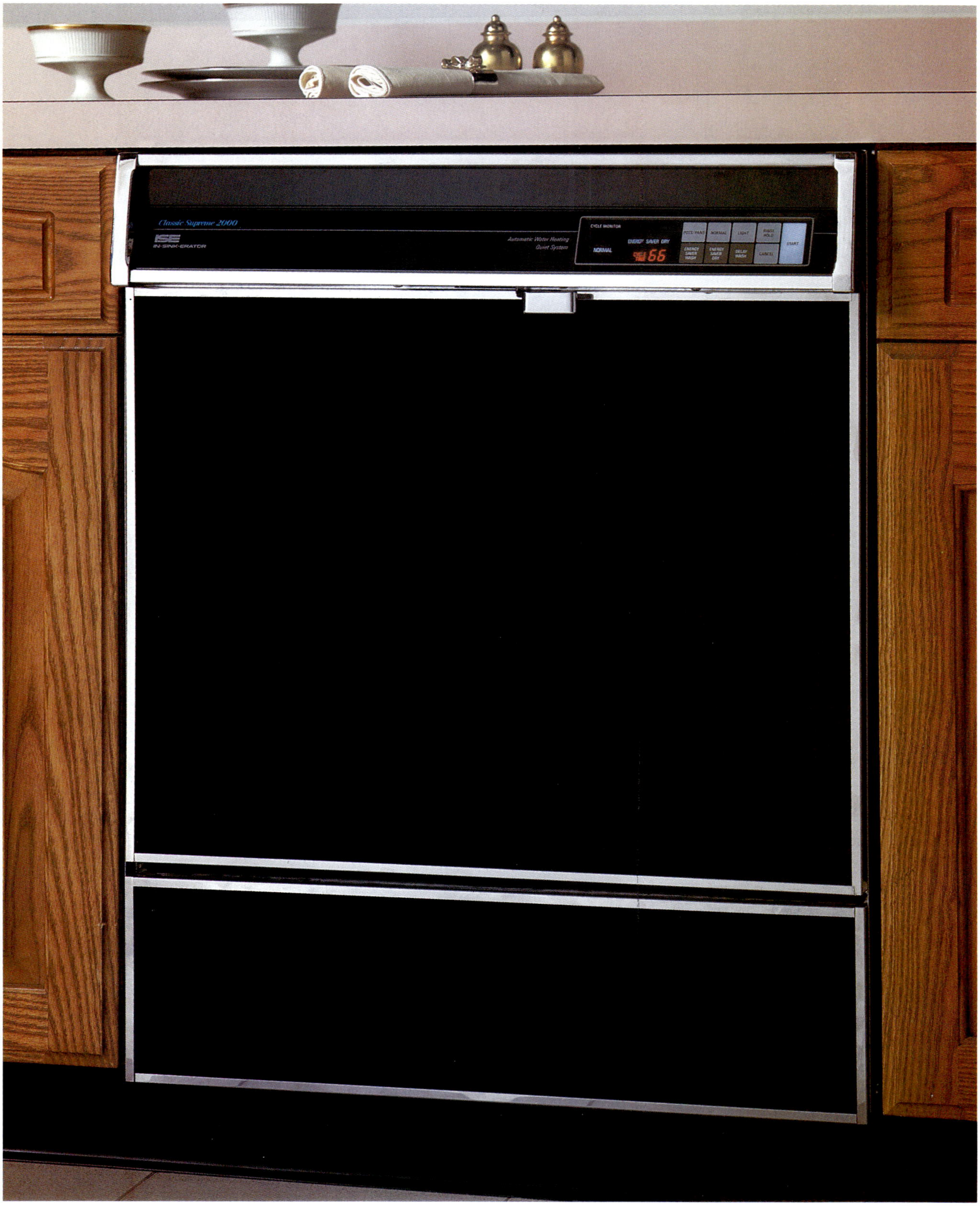

Presenting The New Classic® Supreme 2000 by In-Sink-Erator.

A solid-state electronic-control dishwasher that has all the quality features of the Classic Supreme. Plus a lot more. More convenience. More accuracy. And proven dependability. Here is a dishwasher whose efficiency speaks for itself, quietly.

At the heart of this high-tech wonder is an ingenious sensor system. A precision vacuum fluorescent digital display panel features large, illuminated words and numbers that are easily viewed, even in the brightest room. And this control panel has no buttons, grooves or recessed areas for dirt to collect.

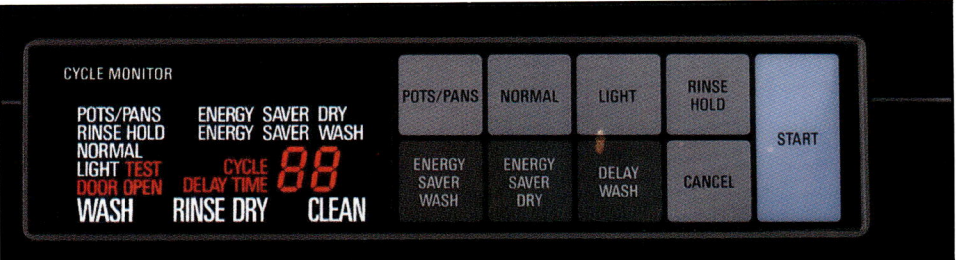

Solid-state electronics make the Classic Supreme 2000 one of the easiest, most efficient and user-friendly dishwashers today.

User-Friendly Communications

Imagine…a dishwasher that tells you what cycle or option you've selected, how many minutes remain until the end of the cycle, then flashes the word CLEAN once a wash cycle is completed. If you interrupt a cycle to add dishes, simply close and lock the door and the machine restarts automatically. There's even a diagnostics feature with nine independent test sequences to assist a service technician.

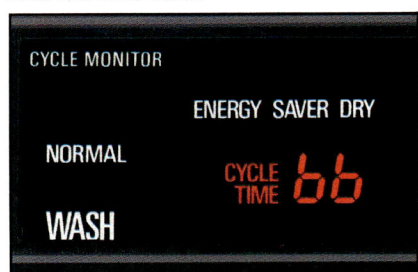

Cycle Scheduling Flexibility

The Classic Supreme 2000 has four regular cycles: Pots & Pans, Normal Wash, Light Wash and Rinse & Hold. A special DELAY WASH feature allows you to load the dishwasher, program it, then delay the start of any wash cycle for up to nine hours to take advantage of economical, non-peak utility rates. The delay wash feature can also be programmed for delay periods of less than a full hour.

There is also a CYCLE MEMORY feature. The Supreme 2000 remembers the last cycle used and repeats it each time you press START. This eliminates the need to reprogram every time, especially convenient for daily routine dishwashing cycles.

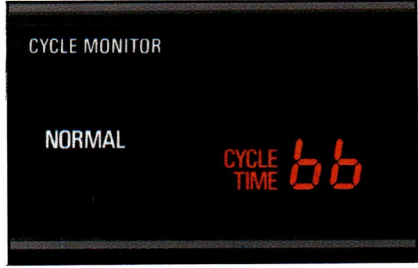

Quiet Cleaning Power

The 2000, like all Classic Supreme dishwashers incorporates the exclusive QUIET SYSTEM™ sound package making it one of the quietest operating dishwashers available. Plus, a highly efficient wash system, unique three-stage filtration and automatic water heating for maximum cleaning power and consistently clean dishware.

Here is a dishwasher that's extremely quiet. A dishwasher that delivers beautiful results. A dishwasher that's the ultimate in electronic efficiency and ease. Here is the Classic Supreme 2000.

Specifications*

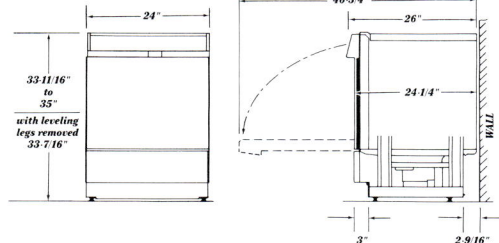

Dimensions are for reference only. Check Installation Guide packed with each model.

Basic sizes for ¼" Custom Front Panels:
Door Panel Width 23⁹/₁₆″
Door Panel Height 18¹³/₁₆″
Lower Panel Width 23¹¹/₁₆″
Lower Panel Height 6⁵/₈″

Basic Plumbing Data:
Water Supply—
• Inlet Water Temperature— 120°F (49°C) minimum at the dishwasher.
• Inlet Water Pressure Operating Range— 20 to 120 psi.
• Inlet Water Tubing Size—½″ OD minimum.

Basic Electrical Data:
• 115 volts AC, 60 Hertz.
• Maximum Amps—13.5; separate 15 amp 3-wire grounded circuit required.

Drain:
• ⁹/₁₆″ ID minimum flexible hose from check valve; ⁵/₈″ OD minimum copper tubing may be run from ⁹/₁₆″ hose if necessary.

Built to be Best.™

4700-21st Street, Racine, WI 53406-5093

ISE IN-SINK-ERATOR *Classic® Supreme 3000*

New excitement in a color-drenched world.

Presenting the New Classic Supreme® 3000 by In-Sink-Erator.

No artificial colors. No chrome additives.

The new Classic Supreme 3000 gives you the undiluted, undeniable impact of all-white. Bold. Powerful. Pure. And exclusively from In-Sink-Erator.

With styling that's truly contemporary. And a look that compliments any cabinetry, from traditional to Euro-style.

Quality features you want.

The Classic Supreme 3000 offers exceptional wash-ability, loading versatility and quiet operation. The special Quiet System™ sound package makes it one of the quietest dishwashers on the market today.

There are four highly efficient cycles—Pots and Pans, Normal, Light, Rinse and Hold. Plus Energy Saver and Dry options.

The Supreme 3000 has four lower and two upper stainless steel wash arms that deliver powerful scrubbing action to all parts of the wash chamber.

There's also automatic water heating and a unique three-stage filtration system with a built-in food disposer. We even added a "clean" light indicator that glows when the dishes are done.

And a multiple position upper rack can be raised, lowered or tilted for maximum loading convenience and flexibility.

The new Classic Supreme 3000. Another beautiful kitchen appliance from In-Sink-Erator.

Specifications*

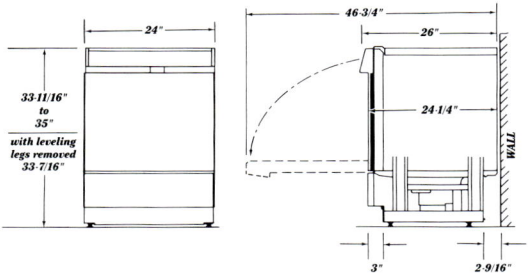

*Dimensions are for reference only. Check Installation Guide packed with each model.

Basic sizes for ¼" Custom Front Panels
Door Panel Width 23⁹⁄₁₆″
Door Panel Height 18¹³⁄₁₆″
Lower Panel Width 23¹¹⁄₁₆″
Lower Panel Height 6⅝″

Basic Plumbing Data
Water Supply—
- Inlet Water Temperature—120°F (49°C) minimum at the dishwasher
- Inlet Water Pressure Operating Range—20 to 120 psi
- Inlet Water Tubing size—½″ OD minimum

Basic Electrical Data
- 115 volts AC, 60 Hertz
- Maximum Amps—13.5; separate 15 amp 3-wire grounded circuit required

Drain
- ⁹⁄₁₆″ ID minimum flexible hose from check valve; ⅝″ OD minimum copper tubing may be run from ⁹⁄₁₆″ hose if necessary

IN-SINK-ERATOR

Built to be Best.™
4700 21st Street
Racine, WI 53406-5093

 **GN-3 Dispenser Systems**

New Steamin' Hot® Water Colors from In-Sink-Erator.

Model GN-3W-in White

Presenting the GN Dispenser Series in Designer Colors

Model GN-3A

Model GN-3B

Model GN-3

The extra touch of color that takes kitchens out of the ordinary!

Crisp alpine white. Creamy-rich almond. New midnight black. Three beautiful colors that make Steamin' Hot dispensers one of the most up-to-the-minute features in kitchens today.

Colors that blend effortlessly, elegantly into any decor. Completing the mood, never conflicting with it. And that's very important to those who always want what's new. What's best. And what's extra in kitchens.

The extra touch of convenience.
The creative uses are unlimited. This super-heated water system and dispenser delivers 190° cooking-hot water instantly. For soups to sauces, to fresh-ground filter drip coffee. Or any recipe that calls for boiling water. Pure function. Pure style. It's why 94% of the people who own one wouldn't do without it.

In addition to the new GN-3 Designer Series, we offer a complete line of other quality hot water dispensers...from the economical HOT-1 to the popular H-770 and HC (hot/cold) dual purpose models.

How a dispenser works.
A super-heated water system and dispenser-in-one. Compact tank fits neatly under the sink. Connects to the kitchen's cold water line. Plugs into standard household outlet.

As the water in the tank is heated, some expands and enters the expansion chamber. When you press the handle, unheated water enters the tank at the bottom forcing 190° hot water out of the spout from the tank and expansion chamber.

Both the tank and expansion chamber are open to the atmosphere and are not under pressure.

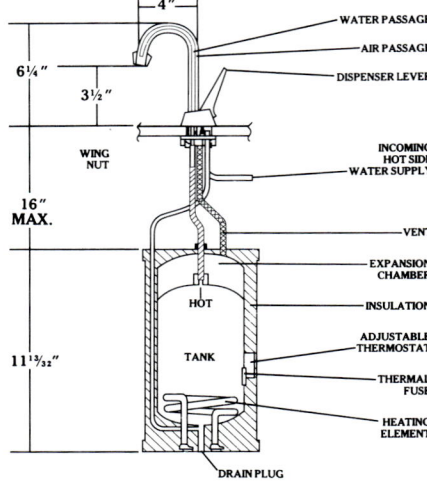

Specifications:
Capacity:
½ gallon, up to 60 cups of 190° F. water per hour.
Electrical:
750 watts, 6.5 amps, 115 volts A.C. U.L. listed—3-wire cord and 3-prong plug provided. (230)
Thermostat:
Snap-action, adjustable from 140°F. to 200°F. (factory pre-set at 190° F.)
Warranty:
1 year full parts and labor.

Insulation:
Meets U.L. 94HF-1 flammability specification.
Valve:
Instant, self-closing.
Shipping wt.:
9 lbs.

Model HC Steamin' Hot® dispensers offer two conveniences in one.
The versatile, dual-purpose HC dispenser model features two levers. One for 190° cooking hot water instantly. The other for tap water for drinking or cooking. The cold water supply line can be connected to water filters, purifiers, chillers or other drinking water accessories (not available from In-Sink-Erator).
Available in white, almond and black.

IN-SINK-ERATOR

Built to be Best.™

*4700 21st Street,
Racine, WI 53406-5093*

ISE IN-SINK-ERATOR *Food Waste Disposers by In-Sink-Erator*

The finishing touch of convenience for today's kitchens.

America's preferred choice.

High performance, superb quality and outstanding warranties. All reasons why In-Sink-Erator is the first choice of builders, kitchen remodelers, plumbing contractors, architects, designers...and families nationwide. Disposers found in three out of four homes are made by In-Sink-Erator.

Making the best product possible.
In-Sink-Erator disposers have the best quality record of any kitchen appliance. Less than one out of 2,000 disposers ever require service during the warranty period. And if a problem should ever arise, the in-home service warranty is backed by over 2,500 factory-authorized service centers.

Compatible with septic tanks.
A big misconception about food waste disposers is that they can't be used in homes serviced by septic systems. Not so. You can enjoy the convenience of an In-Sink-Erator disposer in your home with the properly sized septic tank.

In-Sink-Erator. Simply the best food waste disposer money can buy.

Classic® Series

Classic Features:
- Available in continuous-feed (Classic) or batch-feed (Classic LC) models.
- Powerful 1 H.P. motor offers maximum grinding efficiency.
- Full 7-year parts and in-home service warranty is one of the best available.
- Automatic reversing action offers anti-jam, trouble-free operation.

- Thick, upper shell contains sound-deadening insulation for extra quiet operation.
- Large cast nickel chrome shredder ring can handle the toughest grinding jobs.
- Large capacity, stainless steel grind chamber offers maximum resistance to corrosion.

Performance Plus® Series

Model 77 and 17 Features:
- Available in continuous-feed (77) and batch-feed (17) operation.
- Heavy-duty ¾ H.P. motor offers the right level of power for efficient grinding.
- Full 5-year parts and in-home service warranty assures long-term protection.
- Exclusive automatic reversing action offers anti-jam, trouble-free operation.
- Sound-insulated upper shell provides quiet operation (Model 77).
- Stainless steel shredder ring offers maximum grinding efficiency.
- Stainless steel grind chamber resists corrosion for longer life.

Better Model 333/SS Features:
- Rugged ½ H.P. motor offers excellent grinding power.
- Full 4-year parts and in-home service warranty provided.
- Large stainless steel grind chamber offers increased grinding capacity.

Good Model 333 Features:
- ½ H.P. motor is tough against any food waste.
- Full 3-year parts and in-home service warranty provides long-term protection.
- Long-life corrosion-resistant grind chamber.

Badger Models

Badger 5 Features:
- Full one-year parts and in-home service warranty.
- ½ H.P. motor for good grinding efficiency.
- Galvanized steel shredder ring for reliable grinding ability.
- Corrosion-resistant grind chamber.

Badger 1 Features:
- ⅓ H.P. motor.
- One-year full parts and in-home service warranty.

IN-SINK-ERATOR

Built to be Best.™

4700 21st Street,
Racine, WI 53406-5093

NUTONE KITCHEN GUIDE

The NuTone Food Center: One powerful built-in motor operates 10 appliances ... makes cooking and storage easier!

The powerful, yet compact Food Center Power Unit installs easily *beneath* your countertop ... operates 10 of your most-used kitchen appliances!

You see only the flush Surface-Plate in Decorator White porcelain or Classic Stainless Steel. It's always conveniently there when you need it, but you have complete use of your counter when not using it.

Solid-State Infinite Speed Control assures the correct speed for each lightweight, full size appliance - every one beautifully designed to handle food prep jobs with ease.

With no heavy, bulky motors, they're easy to put away in a cabinet when you are not using them. And instead of 10 cords to plug in and get tangled up, you have none!

Blender – 272, shown on Power Unit 251 with classic stainless steel surface-plate.

Food Processor – 256N, shown on Power Unit 251WH with handsome white porcelain finish surface-plate.

For complete information on the NuTone Food Center, see Catalog FC-200.

Mixer – 271

Fruit Juicer – 173N

Knife Sharpener – 274

Ice Crusher – 281

Juice Extractor – 231

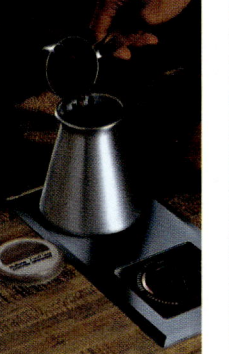

Coffee Grinder – 276

Can Opener – 279

Shredder-Slicer – 278N

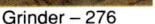

The NuTone Ironing Center 'hides' in the wall until you need it!

A NuTone Ironing Center organizes all your ironing needs in one place, and looks great in any room.

To use it, just open the cabinet door, pull down the ironing board and you're ready to iron! The board swivels 180° and adjusts up and down. Plus there's a safety timer, automatic electric cut-off when closed, handy work light, storage shelf and garment hook. Steel cabinet fits between standard studs.

Choice of three decorator door styles. Wood doors can be painted or stained to match your decor. *mpp*

For complete information on the full line of NuTone Ironing Centers, see Catalog IC-800.

Board folds up into cabinet for storage

AVC-40 Deluxe Built-in Ironing Center

Surface Mount Frame Kit AVC-SM is genuine wood and easy to install in existing homes

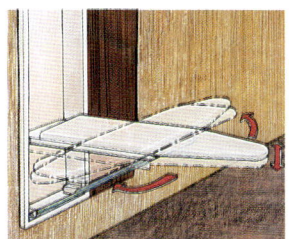

Board swivels 180° to face any direction

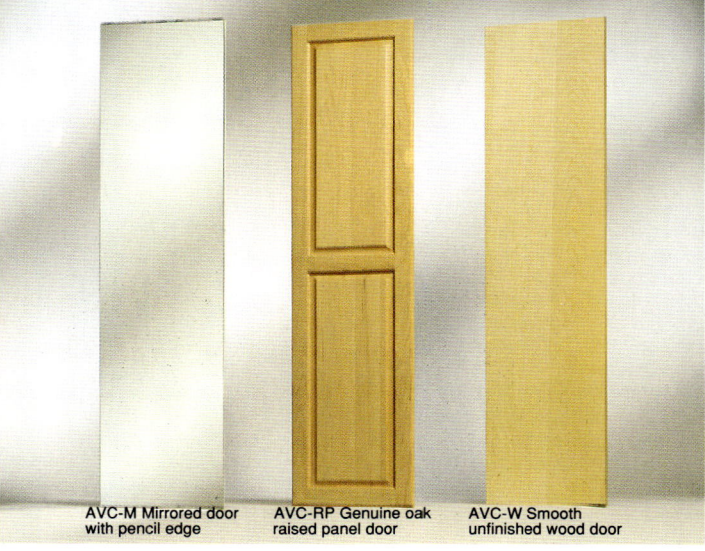

AVC-M Mirrored door with pencil edge

AVC-RP Genuine oak raised panel door

AVC-W Smooth unfinished wood door

NuTone Hot Water Dispenser

Perfect for right-now instant food preparation: coffee, soups and more. Faster than a microwave! Warm baby bottles and loosen jar lids, too. *Really* gives you 190° cooking-hot water every time, up to 60 cups an hour. No splash, no splatter. Automatic turn-off, too! Easy to install - no soldering - plugs into conventional 3-prong outlet.

For complete information on NuTone Hot Water Dispensers, see Catalog HW-100.

EH-190WH Hot Water Dispenser in Classic White ... brings time-saving convenience to kitchen, wet bar, office, RV, boat! Also available: EH-190 Black and Chrome finish.

NuTone products add comfort, convenience, security and entertainment to your home

Radio-Intercoms *mpp*

You can be in two places at once! NuTone Radio-Intercom gives you room-to-room intercom ... the security of answering your front door without opening it ... lets you listen-in on the baby or to a sick room ... enjoy FM/AM radio in any room, poolside or on the patio!

Central Vacs *mpp*

Imagine vacuum cleaning so thorough you have to dust less often! So quiet you can vacuum while baby naps or the family watches TV. So convenient you don't have to lug around a heavy motor. All you carry is a lightweight hose and cleaning tool. Cleaning room-to-room, up and down stairs, basement, garage is easier. No wonder NuTone Central Vac is one of today's most-wanted features.

The power unit is built-in. NuTone offers six different systems. Sanitary, fully disposable soil bag models, and bagless units with the revolutionary NuTone Draw-down™ Cyclonic patented technology. Easy to install, they add value to any home.

Door Chimes *mpp*

Express your personal decorating touch with a traditional or contemporary NuTone Chime. Chime tones range from two-note to chordtone to the beloved Westminster chime sequence ... or even one you can program to play any tune you can whistle, sing or hum!
There are even wireless extension chimes and a new visual door signal for the hearing impaired!

Paddle Fans
Add comfort and energy efficiency with an elegant NuTone contemporary or traditional fan. Light Kits are also available. *mpp*

mpp This symbol identifies NuTone Maximum Performance Products - *guaranteed for as long as you own your home.*

For the name of your nearby NuTone sales outlet, **DIAL FREE 1-800-543-8687** in the contiguous U.S., except in Ohio call 1-800-582-2030.

Send for FREE catalog

NuTone Inc., Dept. KBS-3
P.O. Box 1580, Cincinnati, Ohio 45201

Name	Title
Company	
Address	
City	State Zip
Phone	9220

Form 9220, printed in U.S.A 1/91   Product specifications subject to change without notice.

NuTone

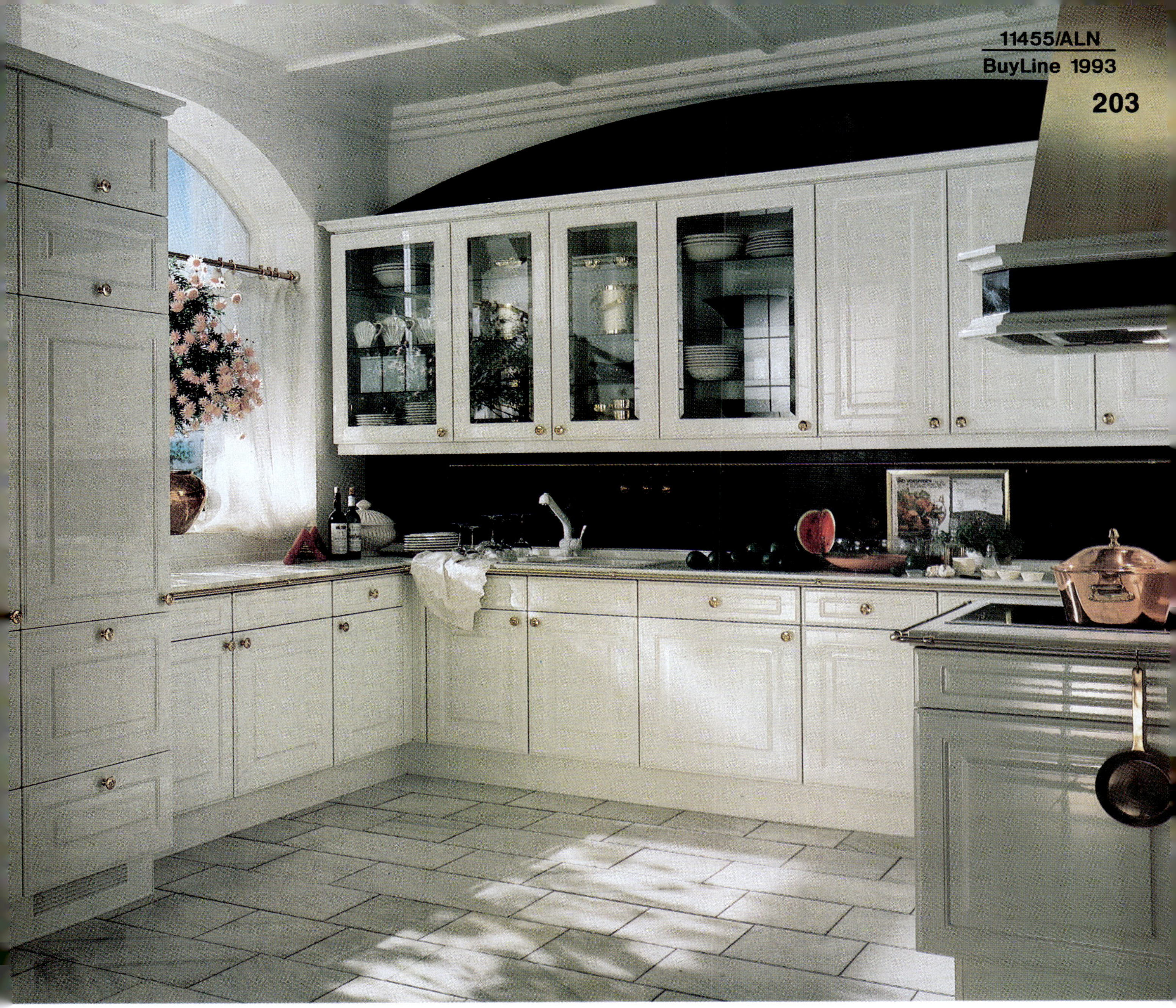

ALNO®
...the world's kitchen

USA Collection 1991

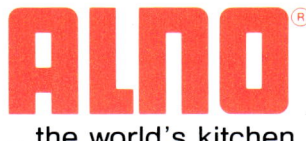

60 Years of ALNO-
From a Workshop to an
Industrial Concern

ALNO Kitchen
Cabinets Inc.
New Castle,
Delaware
▼

A computer ►
controlled plant
finishes the
individual parts
according to
order
requirements.

It is no coin- ►
cidence that
ALNO kitchens
enjoy a long
life. All parts
have to stand
up to many
tests which are
far more
demanding
than any wear
and tear in the
household.

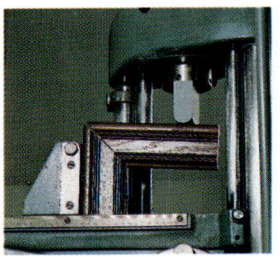

▲ ALNO Moebelwerke GmbH & Co. KG, Pfullendorf, aerial photograph authorized by Reg.
Präs. Tübingen.

ALNO Kitchen Cabinets, Inc., a wholly owned subsidiary of Alno Moebelwerke, GmbH & Co. KG., supplies a full range of products for the U.S. market. The 48,000 square foot New Castle, Delaware facility is a full service organization, providing production, product training, design, installation and shipping to ensure customer satisfaction. ALNO has a wide range of cabinet styles and types, available through a national network of dealers.

ALNO Moebelwerke, GmbH & Co., located in Pfullendorf, West Germany recently celebrated its sixtieth anniversary. The company was founded in 1927 by Albert Nothdurft, in Wangen near Göppingen. His craftsmanship and uncompromising quality standards became increasingly renowned, and are the main reasons for the very positive development of the company. Today the factory covers more than 74 acres where over 1,800 highly qualified employees produce quality kitchen furniture for the quality-conscious consumer.

Most Modern Production Technology

ALNO built-in kitchens are manufactured to the highest quality standards by optimal computerization, work processors, high tech machinery to cope with the volume of orders and free ALNO employees from routine and physical effort.

ALNO Product

To satisfy the demands of the market, continuous quality controls take place.

Incoming raw materials are rigorously checked and tested in the factory laboratory. Final control after assembly ensures all products leave the factory in perfect condition.

ALNO gives a 5-year limited guarantee on materials and craftsmanship.

Modern overhead and floor transport systems and highly trained employees make sure that ALNO built-in kitchens and appliances arrive punctually and trouble-free in the hands of ALNO appointed dealers.

To optimize deliveries, ALNO kitchens are shipped by company owned trucks.

ALNOCHROM — *charcoal*

Laminates

Alno laminate doors come in high and low pressure laminates. Styles vary from simple flat doors to postformed doors with wood or chrome trims. The range of finishes includes matte, high gloss, and wood grains in a wide range of colors.

Wood

Alno wood doors are constructed from the finest hardwoods and veneers available, in Oak, Spruce, or Ash. They are available in a variety of finishes including natural stains, pigmented washes, to pearlized lacquers.

ALNOTANN - Reprinted from METROPCLITAN HOME Magazine ©Copyright, Meredith Corp., 1989. All rights reserved.

ALNOTESS — *jasmine*

Lacquer

Alno lacquered doors are manufactured from shaped high density fiberboard, finished with repeated coats of catalytic lacquer in matte or high gloss, to a flawless finish. Colors available are white, light grey, jasmine, or graphite grey.

Cover photo: Alnoflair, white high gloss

Technical Description

ALNO built-in kitchens are renowned for their high quality. To maintain this standard stringent measures are taken from the quality control of materials delivered and the manufacturing of parts to final assembly. Fully trained personnel, exact statistical testing methods and a laboratory ensure this quality. ALNO built-in kitchens fulfill all the requirements of the official kitchen standard DIN 18022 and the requirements on emission of formaldehyde 0.1 ppm (E1). ALNO's fully developed technology is protected by various patents.

Toe-kick   1

Each cabinet stands on 4 stable toe kick feet made of scratch resistant plastic, which can be adjusted by up to 30 mm (1-1/8'') by means of adjustable screws, to compensate for uneven floors. Adjustments to the front feet are made from the front. Those at the back are made from above through holes in the base of the cabinet. The toe kick feet are concealed at the front and sides by a continuous toe kick panel. The panel may be removed by means of brackets and the bottom edge is protected by a flexible PVC sealer strip. A toe kick drawer or step ladder is also available.

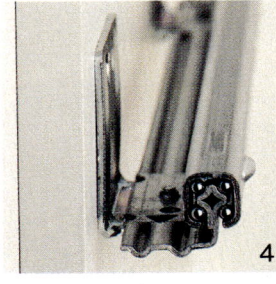

Shelves   2

These are 16 mm (5/8'') thick, melamine covered on both sides and surrounded by glued-on edges. Shelf heights are adjustable by means of a series of brackets set 35 mm (1-3/8'') apart, and the design prevents the possibility of their being pulled out unintentionally.

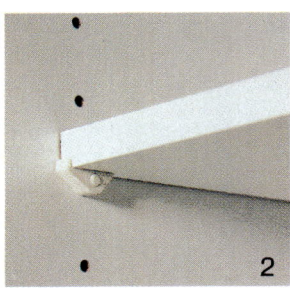

Hinges   3

The self-closing, all metal hinges are particularly strong. As all hinges, they are continually subjected to hard durability tests. The opening angle of 108° gives unhindered access to the cabinet. The built-in automatic spring-closing allows free movement of the open door, closing softly by the spring mechanism in the last stage. The hinges can be adjusted in three directions to adjust the door.

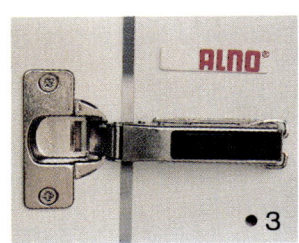

Box

Cabinet sides and visible bases are made from particleboard, 16 mm (5/8'') thick, and covered on both sides in melamine.

Interior: beige, white or jasmine. The front laminate edges match the exterior. The construction of the tall and base cabinet is by tongue and grooved corner joint and in wall cabinets by a mitred joint. Heated liquid polyamide is injected into the corner joint under high pressure. The strength of the corner with this process is twice that with the usual dowel joint. The system of holes 35 mm (1-3/8'') apart allows easy adjustment of shelves and various accessories.

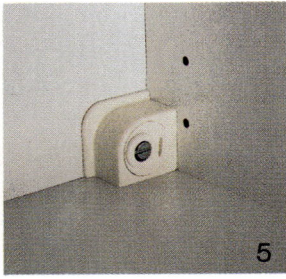

Shallow drawers   4

Covered inside and out with hygienic synthetic material. The base is grooved all around and fits tightly to the frame by means of synthetic lips. The drawer runs on concealed Quadro tracks which provide complete stability in all directions and smooth running (load up to 55 lbs.). Height and sideways adjustments are possible. The front can be exchanged if damaged and the drawers have stops to prevent them from falling out.

Deep drawers

They glide on easy running, quiet roller tracks with guides at the side, which prevents sideways play. Sides, track and fixing for front and back is a single uncomplicated and strong piece. Stable edge supports and adjustable dividers ensure that the drawers may be used to their full capacity. Stops prevent the drawers from falling out accidentally. The front can be adjusted for height and if damaged can be easily exchanged. (Max. load 66 lbs.)

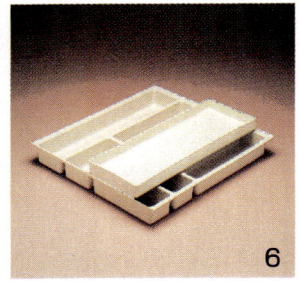

Hanging wall cabinets   5

Very easy and safe installation by means of hardwood batten and a special cam in the cabinet. Adjustment in 3 directions is possible without taking down the cabinet. (Max. load per cam 132 lbs.)

Accessories   6

An extensive program of accessories complete the program. These may be included when the kitchen is first planned or added at a later date. All the interior accessories like drawers and synthetic material parts are off-white to match our jasmine, beige and white interior box colors.

Cornice

Used to add visual effect to tall and wall cabinets, and available in various colors and styles. Over end shelves the cornice is rounded off. Shelves, windows and doorways may be fitted with cornice shelves to complete the overall effect.

ALNO ®

ALNO Kitchen Cabinets, Inc.
196 Quigley Boulevard
New Castle, DE 19720
Telephone: (302) 323-1246
Telefax: (302) 323-0421
Telex: 905007

CORNERSTONES

Excellence in European-design cabinetry

UltraCraft®
division of Alside®

mILAN

Dive into a world of beauty with Milan lacquer cabinets. Hand-buffed to perfection, the luminance complements the curved 90° radius edges. Its 32-color spectrum of solids and metallics is offered exclusively by UltraCraft.

fORM & fUNCTION

UltraCraft cabinetry embodies all the virtues of European-design, yet is manufactured right here in the U.S.A. You get impeccable styles, colors and finishes, coupled with the expertise of America's finest cabinetmakers. Every cabinet is made with a personal touch from one of our craftsmen. UltraCraft. Integrating form and function — for perfection.

gENEVA II

Geneva. A graphic display of luxury. Sophisticated high-pressure laminate surfaces in satiny colors unite with the sleek lines of the custom-coordinated c-channel for a keen contemporary presentation. Curved 180° radius edges eliminate the need for hardware.

wINDSOR

Inspired by nature, Windsor's golden oak finish illuminates a kitchen with the splendor of sunset. Warm honey hues accent the grain of the beautiful solid oak, while a contoured outline adds a touch of grandeur.

SUSSEX II

A splash of color. A dab of detail. Sussex II, with its resilient high-pressure laminate surface, rounded 90° radius edges and palette of colors is a true reflection of today's simple pleasures and carefree lifestyles.

aSPEN

Aspen. A soothing blend of contemporary color and traditional design. The impeccable style of this solid door with its charming raised panel and lustrous white-painted finish tickles the senses.

UltraCraft®
division of Alside®

Vanities

UltraCraft in the bath is a subtle statement of style. Our cabinetry offers you unlimited design potential as well as carefree maintenance.

accessories

A myriad of accessories accompanies the UltraCraft line to fully complement and enhance any kitchen.

Range Hood & Appliance Garage

Base Lazy Susan

Pull-Out Tray

Glass Door

Pantry Cabinet

Microwave Cabinet

Cutlery Divider

Specifications

CABINETS

UltraCraft cabinets feature frameless construction and design, with vertical borings at increments of 32mm. Except backs, cabinet connections are doweled and glued and constructed of ⅝″-thick furniture grade, ANSI-approved medium density particleboard. Interior features fully adjustable shelves. Cabinets carry KCMA certification and seal and comply with the ANSI A161.1-1985 standard.

DOORS

A combination of 78 different door styles and finishes is available. All door styles are of full-overlay design. Contemporary doors feature core material of furniture-grade particleboard or fiberboard covered with either high-pressure laminate, melamine, lacquer or painted finish. Door thickness ranges from ⅝″ to ¾″; exposed edges are fully banded. Traditional door styles are constructed of kiln-dried, select grade oak, maximum thickness ¾″.

DRAWERS

Drawer heads feature the same material and construction as doors. Doweled and glued at connections, the front, sides and back of drawer box are ⅝″ thick; bottom is ¼″ thick. Both sides of the drawer ride on quiet nylon rollers encased in epoxy-coated steel tracks. Load-carrying capacity is 75 lbs. per pair; drawers are removable when fully extended.

HINGES

Hinges are spring-loaded and produced from tempered steel. They're engineered to open at least 110°, six-way adjustable, fully concealed. Corner base cabinet hinges open 170° for full access into cabinet.

division of *Alside*®

A LIMITED WARRANTY TO CONSUMERS
Good Housekeeping PROMISES
REPLACEMENT OR REFUND IF DEFECTIVE

2109 N. Greensboro Street
Liberty, North Carolina 27298
(919) 622-4281   (800) 262-4046

KITCHEN CABINET
KCMA
MANUFACTURERS ASSOCIATION

Kabinart™

Centennial Oak

Centennial Oak

Beautifully finished Centennial Oak Cabinets give a beautiful finish to any kitchen. Classic straight lines frame the painstaking craftsmanship of man and nature for a look of uninterrupted harmony.

Like all Kabinart Cabinets, the Centennial Oak line is constructed solely of wood and wood products, with doors and face frames shaped from solid oak. To ensure that the natural beauty enhances your home's

warm environment for years to come, the cabinets are protected with a durable, detergent-resistant finish. The stain is first applied, then hand wiped and sealed by an electrostatic process. It is then hand sanded and coated electrostatically with a catalytic varnish. Exterior ends and complete interiors have our exclusive easy to clean *Kabinex*™ finish. And now, when you choose Kabinart *Deluxe* Cabinets, with genuine ply-

wood sides, you can choose our optional *solid wood drawers*.

Centennial Oak offers you incomparable value. The richness and beauty of real wood. Styling that enhances any decor. Features that maximize space and convenience. And the quality and craftsmanship that distinguish all Kabinart Cabinets — and the homes that have them.

Wheat

Glacial

Honeywood

Chestnut

◁ When you choose Kabinart, you can coordinate your cabinetry, with designs so functional and distinctive, they're equally at home in your kitchen, baths or family room.

Adjustable shelves on wall cabinets

Whisper smooth Kabin-glide™ *epoxy drawer guides*

Easy to clean Kabinex™ *interiors*

Solid oak doors with self closing hinges

Beauty that's more than skin deep

Doors are sanded and finished to protect and enhance the wood's natural beauty. Standard bevels or finger dips allow easy opening, and eliminate the need for handles which would distract from the integrity of the design and make the cabinets hard to clean. Self-closing hinges ensure that doors close silently and easily. Side mounted *Kabin-glide*™ epoxy drawer guides provide dual support and assure that drawers glide silently and smoothly, with the touch of a finger. All wall cabinets feature adjustable shelves and easy to clean *Kabinex*™ interiors, making cleanup and storage go smoothly. Fix your shelves to fit your needs. Shaped edges are smooth to the touch. ½" thick shelves are standard on all cabinets.

Kabinart™
United Cabinet Corporation
3650 Trousdale Drive • P.O. Box 110774
Nashville, TN 37211 • Phone (615) 833-1961

Kabinart™

Windsor Oak

Windsor Oak

Windsor Oak Cabinets have the look of understated elegance. As beveled glass highlights the beauty of a mirror, the softly sculpted, gently curved lines of Windsor Oak Cabinets quietly enhance the wood's natural beauty.

Like all Kabinart Cabinets, the Windsor Oak line is constructed solely of wood and wood products, with doors and face frames shaped from solid oak. To ensure that the natural beauty enhances your home's warm environment for years to come, the cabinets are protected with a durable, detergent-resistant finish. The stain is first applied, then hand wiped and sealed by an electrostatic process. It is then hand sanded and coated electrostatically with a catalytic varnish. Exterior ends and complete interiors have our exclusive easy to clean *Kabinex*™ finish. And now, when you choose Kabinart *Deluxe* Cabinets, with genuine plywood sides, you can choose our optional *solid wood drawers.*

Windsor Oak offers you incomparable value. The richness and beauty of real wood. Styling that enhances any decor. Features that maximize space and convenience. And the quality and craftsmanship that distinguish all Kabinart Cabinets — and the homes that have them.

Wheat

Glacial

Honeywood

Chestnut

◁ When you choose Kabinart, you can coordinate your cabinetry, with designs so functional and distinctive, they're equally at home in your kitchen, baths or family room.

Adjustable shelves on wall cabinets

Whisper smooth Kabin-glide™ *epoxy drawer guides*

Easy to clean Kabinex™ *finish*

Solid oak cathedral doors with self-closing doors

Beauty that's more than skin deep

Doors are sanded and finished to protect and enhance the wood's natural beauty. Standard bevels or finger dips allow easy opening, and eliminate the need for handles which would distract from the integrity of the design and make the cabinets hard to keep clean. Self-closing hinges ensure that doors close silently and easily. Side mounted *Kabin-glide*™ epoxy drawer guides provide dual support and assure that drawers glide silently and smoothly, with the touch of a finger. All wall cabinets feature adjustable shelves and easy to clean *Kabinex*™ interiors, making cleanup and storage go smoothly. Fix your shelves to fit your needs. Shaped edges are smooth to the touch. ½" thick shelves are standard on all cabinets.

Kabinart™

United Cabinet Corporation
3650 Trousdale Drive • P.O. Box 110774
Nashville, TN 37211 • Phone (615) 833-1961

CERTIFIED NKCA CABINET

Kabinart™

Oxford

Oxford

Oxford Cabinets features the clean profile so popular in European cabinetry. The simplicity of design lets you choose accents that express your individuality and imagination, to make any room truly your own.

Like all Kabinart Cabinets, the Oxford line is constructed solely of wood and wood products. To ensure that the natural beauty enhances your home's warm environment for years to come, the cabinets are protected with a durable, detergent-resistant finish. The stain is first applied, then hand wiped and sealed by an electrostatic process. It is then hand sanded and coated electrostatically with a catalytic varnish. Exterior ends and complete interiors have our exclusive easy to clean Kabinex™ finish. And now, when you choose Kabinart *Deluxe* Cabinets, with genuine plywood sides, you can choose our optional *solid wood drawers*.

Oxford offers you incomparable value. The richness and beauty of real wood. Styling that enhances any decor. Features that maximize space and convenience. And the quality and craftsmanship that distinguish all Kabinart Cabinets — and the homes that have them.

*Glacial**

Honeywood

◁ When you choose Kabinart, you can coordinate your cabinetry, with designs so functional and distinctive, they're equally at home in your kitchen, baths or family room.

Adjustable shelves on wall cabinets

Whisper smooth Kabin-glide™ epoxy drawer guides (Shown here in Ivory)

Easy to clean Kabinex™ interiors

*Choose Almond or Ivory melamine veneer doors with self closing hinges**

Beauty that's more than skin deep

Doors close silently and easily. All wall cabinets feature adjustable shelves and easy to clean Kabinex™ interiors, making cleanup and storage go smoothly. Fix shelves to fit your needs. Shaped edges are smooth to the touch. ½" thick shelves are standard in all cabinets. Side mounted Kabin-glide™ epoxy drawer guides provide dual support and assure that drawers glide silently and smoothly, with the touch of a finger.

*Glacial finish available in Ivory melamine only

Kabinart™

United Cabinet Corporation
3650 Trousdale Drive • P.O. Box 110774
Nashville, TN 37211 • Phone (615) 833-1961

CERTIFIED NKCA CABINET

Kabinart™

Valley Oak

Valley Oak

The classic straight lines of Valley Oak Cabinets emphasize the artistry and symmetry of real wood to complement any decor — without dominating it.

Like all Kabinart Cabinets, the Valley Oak line is constructed solely of wood and wood products, with face frames shaped from solid oak. To ensure that the natural beauty enhances your home's warm environment for years to come, the cabinets are protected with a durable, detergent-resistant finish. The stain is first applied, then hand wiped and sealed by an electrostatic process. It is then hand sanded and coated electrostatically with a catalytic varnish. Exterior ends and complete interiors have our exclusive easy to clean Kabinex™ finish. And now, when you choose Kabinart *Deluxe* Cabinets, with genuine plywood sides, you can choose our optional *solid wood drawers.*

Valley Oak offers you incomparable value. The richness and beauty of real wood. Styling that enhances any decor. Features that maximize space and convenience. And the quality and craftsmanship that distinguish all Kabinart Cabinets — and the homes that have them.

Wheat

Honeywood

Chestnut

◁ When you choose Kabinart, you can coordinate your cabinetry, with designs so functional and distinctive, they're equally at home in your kitchen, baths or family room.

Adjustable shelves on wall cabinets

Whisper smooth Kabin-glide™ epoxy drawer guides

Easy to clean Kabinex™ interiors

Solid oak frame and oak veneer panel doors with self-closing hinges

Beauty that's more than skin deep

Doors are sanded and finished to protect and enhance the wood's natural beauty. Standard bevels or finger dips allow easy opening, and eliminate the need for handles which would distract from the integrity of the design and make the cabinets hard to keep clean. Self-closing hinges ensure that doors close silently and easily. Side mounted *Kabin-glide™* epoxy drawer guides provide dual support and assure that drawers glide silently and smoothly, with the touch of a finger. All wall cabinets feature adjustable shelves and easy to clean *Kabinex™* interiors, making cleanup and storage go smoothly. Fix your shelves to fit your needs. Shaped edges are smooth to the touch. ½" thick shelves are standard on all cabinets.

Kabinart™

United Cabinet Corporation
3650 Trousdale Drive • P.O. Box 110774
Nashville, TN 37211 • Phone (615) 833-1961

THE KITCHEN & BATH CABINETRY OF MERILLAT

TABLE OF CONTENTS

Merillat
AMERICA'S CABINETMAKER ™

KITCHENS

1. **WHITEBAY** White vinyl laminate with raised-panel doors.

2. **AVIA** Frameless white laminate cabinetry. Also available with oak or gray trim.

3. **RUTLAND** Economy-priced white laminate cabinetry.

4. **ARTIQUE** White laminate cabinetry with natural light oak finish handle.

5. **CIRRUS** Economy-priced white laminate cabinetry.

6. **OMNI** Almond laminate cabinetry with medium oak finish handle.

7. **NOUVEAU** Economy-priced textured almond laminate cabinetry.

8. **BISQUE OAK** Washed-parchment finish with recessed panel doors.

9. **HEATHER OAK** With washed-parchment finish. Shown with cathedral-style doors.

10. **SPRINGBROOK** Natural light oak finish with recessed-panel doors.

11. **SUMMERHILL CATHEDRAL** Natural light oak finish with raised-panel doors.

12. **HOMESTEAD OAK** Medium oak finish with recessed-panel doors.

13. **MEADOW OAK CATHEDRAL** Medium oak finish with raised-panel cathedral-style doors.

14. **WYNDTREE OAK** Medium oak finish with planked country-style doors.

15. **HORIZON** Economy-priced cabinetry with wood-grain laminate finish.

16. **BURNWYCK OAK** Dark oak finish with recessed-panel doors.

17. **ASHLEY OAK CATHEDRAL** Dark oak finish with traditional raised-panel doors.

18. **AMHERST CHERRY CATHEDRAL** Cherry finish with cathedral-style raised-panel doors.

1

2

3

4

5

6

7

8

9

10

11

12

13

14

15

16

17

18

BATHS

1. **NOUVEAU** Economy-priced textured almond laminate cabinetry.

2. **OMNI** Almond laminate cabinetry with medium oak finish handle.

3. **SPRINGBROOK** Natural light oak finish with recessed-panel doors.

4. **SUMMERHILL** Natural light oak finish with raised-panel doors.

5. **HOMESTEAD OAK** Medium oak finish with recessed panel doors.

6. **MEADOW OAK** Medium oak finish with raised-panel doors.

7. **WYNDTREE OAK** Medium oak finish with planked country-style doors.

8. **HORIZON** Economy-priced cabinetry with wood-grain laminate surface.

9. **BURNWYCK OAK** Dark oak finish with recessed-panel doors.

10. **ASHLEY OAK** Dark oak finish with raised-panel doors.

ADDITIONAL BATH STYLES
(NOT SHOWN)
(Refer to back cover for door styles.)

WHITEBAY White vinyl laminate with raised-panel doors.

RUTLAND Economy-priced white laminate cabinetry.

AVIA Frameless white laminate cabinetry. Also available with oak or gray trim.

ARTIQUE White laminate cabinetry with natural light oak finish handle.

CIRRUS Economy-priced white laminate cabinetry.

HEATHER OAK Raised panels with washed-parchment finish.

BISQUE OAK Recessed panels with washed-parchment finish.

AMHERST CHERRY Cherry cabinetry with raised-panel doors.

1

2

3

4

5

6

7

8

9

10

KITCHEN ACCESSORIES

1

2

1. SPACIOUS PANTRIES With two solid oak swing-out units, two door-shelf units, 46 adjustable shelves, seven fixed shelves, and up to 32 cubic feet of storage.

2. WIRE PANTRY RACK White, adjustable wire racks make many pantry storage combinations possible.

3. LAZY SUSAN CABINETS The 28" diameter tray keeps stored items within reach. Frameless tray diameter is 32".

4. APPLIANCE GARAGE Fits under wall cabinets to provide hidden storage for small appliances. Also available in double width for extra capacity.

5. MICROWAVE OVEN SHELF Accommodates free-standing and built-in units.

6. BASE WASTEBASKET Mounts on roll-out tray for easy use in recycling or disposal of refuse.

7. BASE SWING-OUT SHELF Provides easy access to canned goods.

8. REVOLVING SHELF KIT With three sturdy revolving shelves.

9. CUTTING BOARD AND KNIFE TRAY KIT Roll-out cutlery tray with solid maple cutting board mounts in place of drawer on WhisperGlide® guides.

10. STEMWARE RACK Decoratively displays stemmed glassware. Available only in natural oak.

11. LEADED GLASS DOORS Available in rectangular or cathedral styles.

12. RANGE HOOD Available in oak or cherry finish, almond or white laminate. Avia and Whitebay range hood tilts out. A 350 CFM blower or range light unit can be added.

13. MODULAR SHELVING SYSTEM Provides attractive and practical storage for any room in the house. Available in oak, cherry and white laminate.

14. GALLERY PLATE RAILING Keeps decorative pieces in order. Valances and decorative molding are also available.

15. GLASS DOOR UNIT An attractive way to display collectibles. (Available in Avia only.)

16. TILT-OUT SINK TRAY Provides handy storage for cleaning supplies.

OAK DRAWER CORE (Not shown) Now available for kitchen cabinets. Half-inch thick solid red oak with rounded edges creates a furniture-quality look. Equipped with WhisperGlide® Drawer & Tray Guide System.

BATH ACCESSORIES

17. VANITY HAMPER Creates easy access with a tilt-out removable wire basket.

18. VANITY LIGHT BAR Brightens up a vanity area.

19. MEDICINE CABINET Provides organized storage for bath accessories. NOTE: Some items may not be available in all styles and finishes. See specifications for details.

3

4

5

6

7

8

9

10

11

12

13

14

15

16

BATH ACCESSORIES

17

18

19

▲ FEATURES

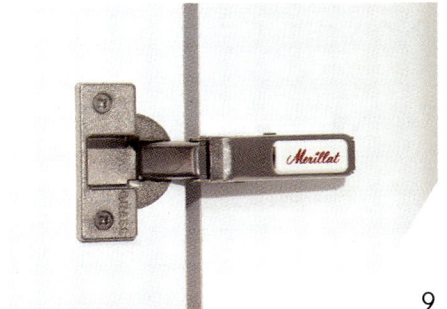

These features are available on all Merillat cabinet lines, except where noted.

1. SELF-CLOSING HINGES For framed cabinetry. Closes the door when it's within 30 degrees of the cabinet front for convenience and safety.

2. DURABLE FURNITURE-QUALITY FINISH Provides protection from moisture, spills, scratching and aging.

3. ROLL-OUT TRAYS Standard in most lines. Maximizes the storage area while providing convenient access to often-used items. Equipped with WhisperGlide® Drawer & Tray Guide System.

4. EASY-CLEAN INTERIORS Interiors are finished with a surface that stands up to water, spilled foods and household chemicals.

5. Half-inch ADJUSTABLE SHELVES Single-door wall cabinets have ½" thick extra-sturdy adjustable shelves to make storing tall and short items easy.

6. WHISPERGLIDE® DRAWER & TRAY GUIDE SYSTEM Rubber-cushioned nylon rollers and epoxy-coated steel channels provide smooth operation and durability.

7. SOLID OAK FRAMES AND TRU-SQUARE CORNER GUSSETS High-quality oak stiles and rails are double-dowelled, then glued and aligned in precision air clamps to form rigid front frames. The corner gussets, where countertops are attached, add strength and keep cabinets true and square.

8. REVERSE BEVEL Creates easy to open doors and drawers, makes surface hardware optional.

9. SELF-CLOSING/CONCEALED HINGES For frameless cabinetry. Concealed hinges close the door when it's within 10 degrees of the cabinet front.

10. MELAMINE INTERIOR (FRAMELESS CABINETRY) A durable interior that stands up to moisture, spills and household chemicals.

MATCHING WALL CORNER CABINET

WALL CABINET

UTILITY CABINET

LAZY SUSAN BASE CABINET

BASE CABINET

OVEN CABINET

Merillat offers a number of standard and accessory cabinets that add flair and function to any kitchen plan. Most are available in both framed and frameless styles, designed to make the most of the available storage space. Most Merillat base cabinets utilize roll-out trays for convenient access, and some wall cabinets have adjustable shelves. Both wall and base cabinets are available with single or double doors. We also offer double-faced cabinets that allow access from two sides, perfect for island or peninsula installation. Our vanity cabinets, utility cabinets and base lazy Susan cabinets add specialized, organized storage space.

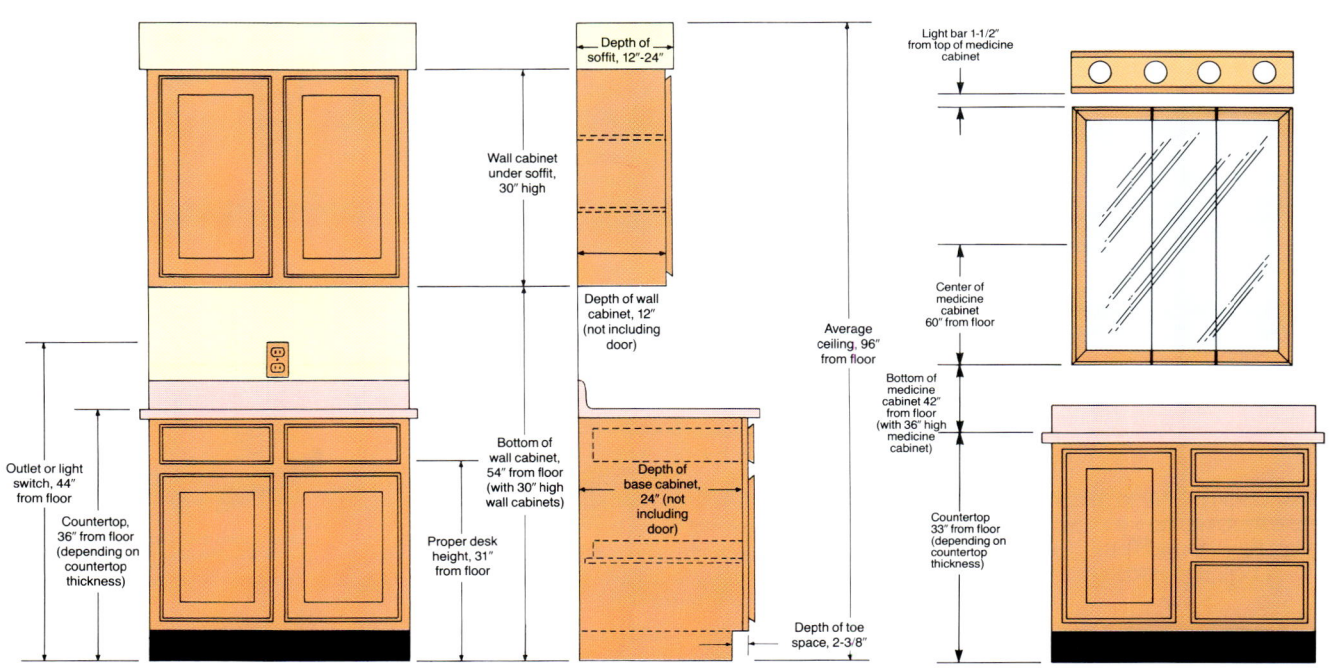

Outlet or light switch, 44" from floor

Countertop, 36" from floor (depending on countertop thickness)

Wall cabinet under soffit, 30" high

Depth of wall cabinet, 12" (not including door)

Bottom of wall cabinet, 54" from floor (with 30" high wall cabinets)

Proper desk height, 31" from floor

Depth of soffit, 12"-24"

Depth of base cabinet, 24" (not including door)

Depth of toe space, 2-3/8"

Average ceiling, 96" from floor

Light bar 1-1/2" from top of medicine cabinet

Center of medicine cabinet 60" from floor

Bottom of medicine cabinet 42" from floor (with 36" high medicine cabinet)

Countertop 33" from floor (depending on countertop thickness)

◢ FRAMED SPECIFICATIONS

1.   GENERAL

1.01   Scope

1.01.01 The scope of this specification is to cover the design, construction and installation of all kitchen and bath cabinetry.

1.03   Submittals

1.03.01 Supplier will furnish shop drawings, which are taken from the architect's drawings, specifically calling out the cabinet nomenclature and sizes. Supplier shall also submit floor plans and elevations for the cabinets showing layout, dimensions and details of installation.

1.03.02 Submit cabinet door samples with manufacturer's range of colors for selection by the architect.

1.03.03 Submit manufacturer's literature on cabinets.

2.   PRODUCT

2.01   Cabinets shall be "   " (specify door style) as manufactured by Merillat Industries, P.O. Box 1946, Adrian, MI 49221. Size and type as required to meet configuration indicated on drawings.

2.02   Certification

2.02.01 All cabinetry shall carry the National Kitchen Cabinet Association (NKCA) certified cabinet seal; the Kitchen Cabinet Manufacturers Association (KCMA) certified cabinet seal; and meet or exceed the "recommended minimum construction and performance standards for kitchen cabinets" outlined in the American National Standards Institute (ANSI) ANSI/NKCA A161.1-1985.

2.03   Materials — Case Construction
Depending on the door style selected, all Merillat cabinet frames shall be constructed of solid red oak or solid cherry. All veneered components shall be selected architectural grade sliced red oak or cherry, depending on style selected. "Solid hardwood" in these specifications refers to either solid oak or solid cherry, depending on cabinet line. No similar wood species such as ash or maple shall be substituted in any component or accessory.

2.03.01 Cabinet frames shall have ¾" thick x 1⅝" wide solid hardwood rail and stile members. Center stiles shall be ¾" thick x 3¼" or 6¼" wide solid hardwood. All frame joints shall be reinforced and precisely aligned with two ⅜" diameter birch dowels bonded with adhesive.

2.03.02 End panels shall be ⅜" thick — 48 lb. industrial grade particleboard laminated inside and out with a water and household chemical resistant 2 mil rigid reverse printed vinyl. End panels shall be machined to accept tops, bottoms, and backs and on double-door wall cabinets they shall be also machined to accept shelves.

2.03.03 Wall cabinet tops and bottoms shall be ½" thick — 48 lb. industrial grade particleboard for extra strength and rigidity. These components shall be laminated on two sides with a water and household chemical resistant 2 mil rigid reverse printed vinyl. A dado joint and adhesive shall be used to join the tops and bottoms to the end panels.

2.03.04 Base cabinet bottoms shall be ⅜" thick — 48 lb. industrial grade particleboard laminated with a water and household chemical resistant 2 mil rigid reverse printed vinyl on the interior side. The bottoms shall be joined to the end panels with dado joints and adhesive. Glue blocks shall be used to reinforce the bottoms of cabinets 27" or wider. The upper portion of base cabinets shall be strengthened with ½" thick gussets which maintain squareness.

2.03.05 All backs shall be ¼" thick — 50 lb. density particleboard with a water and household chemical resistant 2 mil rigid reverse printed vinyl laminated to the interior side. Wall cabinet backs shall be reinforced with ¼" thick particleboard screw rails at the top and bottom. Wall cabinet backs shall be retained by a groove in the end panels; and glued and stapled to the tops and

bottoms and to the shelves on 27" wide and larger sizes. Base cabinet backs shall be attached in the same manner, but the top of the cabinet shall have an 11/16" x 2¼" pine screw rail securing the back to the top of the cabinet.

2.03.06 All 30" high wall cabinets 24" wide and under shall have adjustable shelves made of ½" thick — 48 lb. density industrial grade particleboard. The shelves shall be laminated with a water and household chemical resistant 2 mil rigid reverse printed vinyl. The front edge of the shelf shall be filled and printed with a simulated oak grain. Cabinet sides shall be drilled for durable locking shelf supports adjustable on 2½" increments.

2.03.07 All double-door wall cabinets 24" and over in height shall have fixed shelves. These ½" thick shelves shall have the same specs as the adjustable shelves, but they shall be fixed to the end panels with dado joints and glue, and on all 27" wide or larger shelves they shall be stapled through the back to assure rigidity.

2.03.08 All Nouveau, Cirrus and Horizon base cabinets, except sink bases, shall have half depth fixed shelves. The shelves shall be ½" thick — 48 lb. density industrial grade particle board with a water and household chemical resistant 2 mil rigid reverse printed vinyl laminated to the top surface. They shall be supported on the ends with shelf clips, but are not adjustable. The backs of the shelves shall be supported with staples driven through the cabinet backs. All shelves in base cabinets 27" or wider shall have a support apron under the shelf for additional strength.

2.03.09 The toe board shall be ⅜"-48 lb. density industrial grade particleboard and extend from the floor to the cabinet bottom. This not only supports the bottom but also effectively seals the toe space against vermin and insects. The toe board shall be covered with a ⅜" black vinyl covered particleboard strip which provides an easy cleaning, mop resistant finish.

2.03.10 Base lazy Susan cabinets shall have two 28" diameter revolving plastic shelves with reinforced bottoms, to provide 7.5 square feet of storage, with finger-tip accessibility.

2.04   Drawer Construction (Horizon, Cirrus and Nouveau only)

2.04.01 All Horizon, Cirrus and Nouveau shall have ⅜" thick — 48 lb. density particleboard drawer sides, which shall be rabbeted to accept ½" thick fronts and backs. All drawer components shall be laminated on the exterior side with a water and household chemical resistant 2 mil rigid reverse-printed vinyl. The interior faces of the drawer sides shall be laminated with a water and household chemical resistant 4 mil semi-rigid reverse printed vinyl and the ends shall be wrapped around radiused edges of the drawer components.

2.04.02 Fronts and backs shall be ½" thick — 48 lb. density industrial grade particleboard with a water and household chemical resistant 2 mil rigid reverse printed vinyl on the outside and a water and household chemical resistant 4 mil semi-rigid reverse printed vinyl on the inside. Top edges shall be radiused and wrapped with vinyl.
The drawer box shall be assembled with white glue and staples at each corner. The drawer core shall be secured to the drawer front with two to four screws.

2.04.03 All Horizon, Cirrus and Nouveau drawer bottoms shall be ¼" thick — 50 lb. density particleboard with a water and household chemical resistant 2 mil rigid reverse printed vinyl laminated to the interior side. Bottom shall be retained in the side panels by a ¼" groove, and secured with a bead of white glue. The drawer bottom shall be secured at the front and back with staples.

2.04.04 Horizon, Cirrus and Nouveau drawer slides shall be exclusive Merillat designed, with 4-point suspension, consisting of two 6063 T-5 tempered aluminum extrusions with U-shaped cross-

sections. The larger of the two extrusions shall be the case member which is fastened to the front frame with a molded nylon positive stop and a screw. The back of the guide shall have a slotted adjustment hole and shall be fastened to a wood support block with a screw. The support block shall be bonded and stapled to the cabinet back. The smaller of the two extrusions shall be fastened to the drawer front with a screw. The rear of the guide shall be retained with a molded nylon guide/stop and secured to the drawer back with a screw. The drawer guide shall also serve to strengthen and support the drawer bottom. The drawer core shall be supported by two "L" shaped nylon glides, which act as bearing surfaces and are fastened to the cabinet front frame cross rail with staples.
NOTE: Horizon R and Nouveau R base cabinet drawers are fitted with an epoxy-coated side-mounted captive roller drawer system. The system consists of a pair of epoxy-coated 1.25 mm steel slides that roll on close-tolerance nylon rollers.

2.C4.05 All other style drawer cores use the Merillat WhisperGlide® System and shall have ⅜" thick — 48 lb. density particleboard sides that are attached to the ½" particleboard front and back. The drawer sides shall be laminated with a water and household chemical resistant 4 mil semi-rigid reverse printed vinyl on the interior and a water and chemical resistant 2 mil rigid reverse printed vinyl on the exterior surfaces. The top edges of the drawer sides, back and front shall be radiused and wrapped with a water and household chemical resistant 4 mil semi-rigid reverse printed vinyl. The corners of the drawer core shall be lap joined and bonded with adhesive and staples.

2.04.06 The drawer bottom shall be ¼" thick — 50 lb. density particleboard with 2 mil reverse printed wood-grained vinyl on the interior face. The bottom shall be attached to the sides, back and front with adhesive and staples. The drawer slide "L" shaped lip shall be bent around the bottom to reinforce the joints. The powder-coated steel WhisperGlide® core member supports the drawer to a maximum capacity of a 50 lb. load.

2.04.07 All base cabinets except Cirrus, Horizon R and Nouveau R shall have roll-out trays consisting of ⅜" thick — 48 lb. density particleboard sides which are laminated on the outside with a water and household chemical resistant 2 mil rigid reverse printed vinyl. The inside surface shall be laminated with a water and household chemical resistant 4 mil semi-rigid reverse printed vinyl and wrapped around the radiused top edge. The ends shall be rabbeted to received the front and back. The tray front shall be ¾" thick solid red oak finished with a tough coating of heat activated conversion varnish which is impervious to household chemicals.
The tray front shall be rabbeted at the bottom edge to receive the bottom. The tray back shall be ½" thick — 48 lb. density particleboard with a water and household chemical resistant 4 mil semi-rigid reverse printed vinyl on the interior and a water and household chemical resistant 2 mil rigid reverse printed vinyl on the exterior. The water and household chemical resistant 4 mil semi-rigid reverse printed vinyl shall be wrapped around the radiused top edge of the tray back. All four corners of the tray shall be attached with staples. The tray bottom shall be ¼" thick — 50 lb. density particleboard with a water and household chemical resistant 2 mil rigid reverse printed vinyl on the interior face. The bottom shall be attached with adhesive and staples. The formed lip of the WhisperGlide® reinforces this joint.

2.04.08 The exclusive Merillat WhisperGlide® side-mounted roller drawer system shall be mounted on all drawer and tray cores with the exception of Horizon, Nouveau, Cirrus, Horizon R and Nouveau R. This system shall consist of a pair of epoxy coated 1.25 mm steel slides that roll on close-tolerance nylon wheels. The wheels shall be isolated from the metal slides with a pliable "O" ring tire which dampens the noise normally associated with most roller slide systems. The support channel half of the Merillat Whisper-Glide® shall be mounted to the oak front frame of the cabinet with a screw and shall snap into an adjustable plastic adapter on the inside back of the cabinet. The drawer and tray core half of the Merillat WhisperGlide® shall be attached to the front and back of the core with screws. The "L" shaped bottom of this member wraps around the core to reinforce it and provide a finished edge.

2.05 Door and Drawer Front Construction

2.05.01 Horizon doors shall be ⅝" thick — 48 lb. density industrial grade particleboard laminated on two sides with wood-grained pattern low pressure melamine for balanced construction to prevent warpage. The melamine laminate is bonded to the particleboard and provides a water and household chemical proof surface. The vertical edges of the doors shall be edgebanded with a .4mm thick melamine wood-grained design edge-banding.

The horizontal door edges shall be machined with a coved/reverse bevel and banded with a soft-formed melamine wood-grained design edgebanding to form a finger pull. Horizon doors shall be mounted on exclusive Merillat designed self-closing concealed hinges. Hinges shall have horizontal and vertical adjustments. Doors shall have pliable rubber bumpers to dampen noise.

2.05.02 Horizon drawer fronts have the same construction as Horizon doors.

2.05.03 Nouveau doors and drawer fronts shall be constructed the same as Horizon. However, Nouveau shall have an almond-colored textured melamine surface with an abstract tan-colored horizontal textured pattern. Nouveau shall have the same wood-gained melamine edgebanding and soft-formed handle as Horizon. Nouveau shall also utilize the same self-closing hinge as Horizon.

2.05.04 Cirrus doors and drawer fronts shall be constructed the same as Horizon. However, Cirrus shall have a white melamine surface. Cirrus shall have a natural finish wood-grained melamine edgebanding and soft-formed handle. Cirrus shall also utilize the same self-closing hinge as Horizon.
NOTE: Horizon, Cirrus and Nouveau cabinets have "full-overlay" contemporary styling where the doors and drawers conceal the cabinet front frame. Extra attention must be given to clearances in corners and near appliances when planning a kitchen with these cabinets.

2.05.05 Springbrook, Homestead and Bisque doors shall have ¾" thick and 2⁵⁄₁₆" wide solid red oak stiles and rails joined at the four corners with tongue-and-groove joints. The joints shall be bonded with adhesive. The frame shall be molded with a double-bead detail on the inside and a coved/reverse bevel shall be machined on the outside perimeter to serve as a finger grip. A ⁵⁄₃₂" thick plain-sliced veneered red oak plywood center panel shall be retained by a groove machined in the frame.

2.05.06 Omni doors shall be ⅝" thick — 48 lb. density particleboard with almond-colored melamine surfaces on both sides for balanced construction to prevent warpage. Three sides of the door shall be edged with a .4mm thick melamine banding. The fourth edge shall be capped with a ¾" x 1½" solid oak handle with integral finger grip. The oak shall be selected to ensure a consistent horizontal grain pattern on all handles. The handle shall be attached to the door with ⁵⁄₁₆" x 1¾" hardwood dowels and bonded permanently with adhesive. Omni doors shall be mounted on fully concealed self-closing hinges.

These hinges feature strong three-point mounting and shall be adjustable in both the vertical and horizontal directions. Doors shall have pliable rubber bumpers to dampen noise.

2.05.07 Omni drawer fronts shall be constructed the same as the doors.

2.05.08 Artique doors and drawer fronts shall be constructed the same as Omni. However, Artique shall have a white melamine surface. Artique shall also utilize the same self-closing hinge as Omni.
NOTE: Omni and Artique cabinets have contemporary styling in which the doors and drawers conceal the cabinet front frames. Several of the cabinets, i.e., blind corner and BLS 36, have overlay panels on them to provide continuity. Extra attention must be given to clearances in corners and near appliances when planning a kitchen with these cabinets.

2.05.09 Summerhill, Meadow, Heather and Amherst doors shall have ¾" thick x 2⁵⁄₁₆" wide frame components hand selected for uniform and pleasing grain patterns. These solid hardwood stiles and rails shall be joined at the four corners with tongue-and-groove joints. The joints shall be bonded with adhesive. The frame shall be molded with a double-bead detail on the inside; and a coved/reverse bevel is machined on the outside perimeter to serve as a finger grip. The raised center panel shall consist of a 48 lb. density particleboard core with its edges machined in a coved shape. The front and back of the panel shall be covered with select hardwood veneers.

The veneer shall be bonded to the substrate using adhesive, heat and pressure. The resulting panel has the appearance of solid hardwood without the inherent problems of shrinkage and splitting. The panel is retained by a groove machined in the edge of the door frame.

This construction shall provide a strong door that resists the expansion, shrinkage and splitting associated with other types of raised panels. The veneered center panel shall provide the uniformity of grain and finish found in fine furniture. Doors shall have pliable rubber bumpers to dampen noise.

2.05.10 Summerhill, Homestead, Meadow, Bisque, Springbrook, Heather, Wyndtree and Amherst drawer fronts shall be ¾" thick glued-up, solid hardwood lumber. The front and back of the panel shall be veneered with select furniture grade veneers. This technique combines the strength of solid hardwood with the uniform grain pattern of fine veneers.
NOTE: Summerhill, Meadow, Heather and Amherst cathedral-styled wall cabinets can be used with square raised panel base cabinets to design a more elegant, formal kitchen.

The cathedral doors are constructed the same as the square raised panel doors except for a wide ¾" thick x 4⅛" top rail which is shaped in a cathedral arch. The raised center panel is machined to match.

2.05.11 Wyndtree Oak doors shall have ¾" thick red oak boards edge glued side-by-side to produce a solid oak panel. The panel shall be V-grooved on the front for a decorative effect. At the bottom of the V-groove shall be a saw kerf that allows the panel to expand and contract without splitting. There shall be identical saw kerfs on the back of the door adjacent to the face kerfs. Oak battens ⅝" thick x 1½" wide shall be fastened to the back of the door with countersunk screws. These battens shall reinforce the door and prevent it from cupping. The outside edges of the door shall be machined with a reverse bevel finger grip and decorative cove shape.

2.06 Hinges

2.06.1 All Merillat doors shall be mounted on antique English, brass plated finish self-closing hinges, which automatically close the cabinet door when it is within 30 degrees of the face frame.

The safety feature helps prevent accidents caused by people bumping into cabinet doors that are left open inadvertently. Doors shall have pliable rubber bumpers to dampen noise. Horizon, Cirrus and Nouveau shall have semi-concealed hinges. Omni and Artique shall have fully concealed hinges.

2.07 Finishes

2.07.01 Merillat oak cabinets are available in light, medium and dark parchment stain finishes. All contain pigments that accentuate the grain.
Merillat oak components shall be sanded to prepare the surface for staining. The penetrating stain shall be applied with a variety of specially designed electrostatic spray equipment (door and drawer fronts), mechanical spray devices (frames) or hand-spray equipment (accessories) tailored specifically to the type of part being finished. The stain shall be wiped to move it into the pores of the oak and to remove excess finish. A vinyl sealer coat shall be applied to prevent the oak from taking on or giving up moisture, which could cause warping and cracking. The sealer also helps to bond the top coat to the product. The sealer shall be lightly sanded to prepare the surface for top coating. The high-solids, heat activated conversion varnish top coat shall create a durable envelope protecting the oak wood from chemicals, abrasion and detergents.

2.07.02 Merillat Heather Oak and Bisque Oak cabinets are available in a white-pigmented stain.
Merillat Heather Oak and Bisque Oak shall be sanded to prepare the surface for staining. The stain shall be applied with automatic mechanical spray equipment (doors, drawer fronts and front frames, and accessory components). The stain shall be brushed into the pores of the wood to provide grain definition and remove excess finish. A vinyl sealer coat shall be applied to prevent the oak from taking on or giving up moisture, which could cause warping and cracking. The sealer provides a bonding base for the top coat. The sealer shall be lightly sanded to prepare the surface for top coating. The high-solids, heat activated conversion top coat shall create a durable envelope which protects the oak from chemical abrasion and detergents. The conversion top coat shall contain blocking agents to retard the effects of ultraviolet light on the finish.

2.07.03 Merillat cherry cabinets are available only in a medium-toned dye stain finish. Merillat cherry components shall be sanded to prepare the surface for staining. The dye stain shall be applied with mechanical spray equipment (doors, drawer fronts and front frames, and accessory components). The dye stain shall be brushed into the pores of the wood to provide grain definition and remove excess finish. A vinyl sealer coat shall be applied to prevent the cherry from giving up or taking on moisture, which could cause warping and cracking. The sealer also helps to bond the top coat to the product. The sealer shall be lightly sanded to prepare the surface for top coating. The high-solids, heat activated conversion top coat shall create a durable envelope protecting the cherry from chemicals, abrasion and detergents.

2.07.04 Some Merillat accessory items shall be top coated with lacquer.

3. RUTLAND/WHITEBAY SPECIFICATIONS

3.01 Cabinet Frames

3.01.01 Cabinet frames shall have ¾" thick x 1⅛" wide hardwood rail and stile members. Center stiles shall be ¾" thick x 2¼", 5¾" or 8¼" wide solid hardwood. All frame joints shall be reinforced and precisely aligned with two ¼" diameter birch dowels and bonded with precisely metered adhesive. Cabinet stiles and rails are

FRAMED SPECIFICATIONS

grooved with a ⅛" deep groove to accept end panels and both top and bottom panels. Cabinet frames extend ¼" beyond the end panels for trimability in the field. Merillat cabinets are within 1/32" of tolerance to specified height and width.

3.02 End Panels

3.02.01 Merillat end panels shall be ⅜" thick — 48 lb. density industrial grade particleboard laminated inside and out with a water and household chemical resistant 2.5 mil rigid solid color vinyl. End panels shall be machined to accept tops, bottoms and cabinet backs.

3.03 Cabinet Tops and Bottoms

3.03.01 Wall cabinet tops and bottoms shall be ½" thick — 48 lb. density industrial grade particleboard for extra strength and rigidity. These components shall be laminated on two sides with a water and household chemical resistant 2.5 mil rigid solid color vinyl. A dado joint and adhesive shall be used to join the tops and bottoms to the end panels and cabinet front frame, creating a stronger, more stable cabinet.

3.03.02 Base cabinet bottoms shall be ½" thick — 48 lb. density industrial grade particleboard laminated with a water and household chemical resistant 2.5 mil rigid solid color vinyl on the interior side. The bottoms shall be joined to the end panels and cabinet front frame with dado joints and adhesive. Glue blocks shall be used to reinforce the bottoms of cabinets 27" and wider. The upper portion of base cabinets shall be strengthened with ½" thick gussets dadoed into front frame, back rail and end panels. Gussets maintain squareness.

3.03.03 All cabinet backs shall be ¼" thick — 50 lb. density particleboard laminated with a water and household chemical resistant 2.5 mil rigid solid color vinyl on the interior side. Wall cabinet backs shall be retained by a groove in the end panels. Base cabinet backs shall be attached in the same manner, but the top of the cabinet shall have an 11/16" x 2¼" pine screw rail securing the back to the cabinet. Base cabinet backs extend to the floor to provide added strength.

3.04 Shelves

3.04.01 All wall cabinets 24" high and taller, under 42" in width, have adjustable shelves made of ½" thick — 48 lb. density industrial grade particleboard. All wall cabinets 42" and wider have fixed shelves dadoed into the end panels. The shelves shall be laminated with a water and household chemical resistant 2.5 mil rigid solid color vinyl. The front edge of the shelf shall be covered with a melamine edgebanding. Cabinet sides, for those cabinets with adjustable shelves, are precision drilled for durable locking shelf supports adjustable to (three) locations on 2½" increments. The shelf is supported in the center with adjustable supports in corresponding locations on the back of cabinet frame center stile.

3.04.02 All Rutland base cabinets shall have half depth fixed shelves. The shelves shall be ½" thick — 48 lb. density industrial grade particleboard with a water and household chemical resistant 2.5 mil rigid solid color vinyl laminated to the top surface. Exposed shelf edge is laminated with melamine edgebanding. Shelves shall be supported on the ends with shelf clips, but are not adjustable. All shelves in base cabinets 27" and wider shall have a support apron under shelf.

3.05 Rutland Drawer and Drawer Cores

3.05.01 All Rutland drawer sides, fronts and backs shall be ½" thick — 48 lb. density industrial grade particleboard rabbeted to accept front and back. All drawer components shall be laminated on the exterior side with a water and household chemical resistant 2.5 mil rigid solid color vinyl. The interior faces of the drawer sides, fronts and backs shall be laminated with a water and household chemical resistant 4 mil semi-rigid solid color vinyl and wrapped around the top radiused edges of the drawer components.

3.05.02 The corners of the drawer core shall be lapjointed and bonded with adhesive and staples. The drawer core bonded with adhesive and staples shall be secured to the drawer front with two or four screws depending on the drawer size.

3.05.03 Bottoms shall be ¼" thick — 50 lb. density particleboard, 4 mil vinyl laminated to the interior side. The bottom shall be attached to the sides, back and front with adhesive and staples. The drawer slide "L" shaped lip wraps the drawer bottom and reinforces drawer construction. The epoxy coated steel roller guide core member supports the drawer to a maximum capacity of a 50 lb. load.

3.05.09 Drawers in base cabinets 30" wide and over use a ⅜" thick particleboard bottom for additional support.

3.06 Drawer Slides

3.06.01 The Merillat Rutland drawer guide system is a side-mounted captive roller drawer system. The system consists of a pair of epoxy coated 1.25 mm steel slides that roll on close-tolerance nylon rollers. The support channel half of the Merillat roller glide shall be mounted to the front frame of the cabinet with a screw. The rear of the channel snaps into an adjustable plastic adapter on the inside back of the cabinet. The drawer core half of the Merillat roller guide shall be attached to the front and back of the core with screws. The "L" shaped bottom of this member wraps around the core to reinforce it and provide a finished edge.

3.07 Whitebay Drawer Core and Tray Construction

3.07.01 All Whitebay drawer cores use the exclusive Merillat WhisperGlide® System and shall have ½" thick — 48 lb. density particleboard sides that are attached to the ½" particleboard front and back. The drawer sides shall be laminated with a water and household chemical resistant 4 mil semi-rigid solid color vinyl on the interior and a water and chemical resistant 2.5 mil rigid solid color vinyl on the exterior surfaces. The top edges of the drawer sides, backs and fronts shall be radiused and wrapped with a water and household chemical resistant 4 mil semi-rigid solid color vinyl. The corners of the drawer core shall be lapjointed and bonded with adhesive and staples.

3.07.02 The drawer bottom shall be ¼" thick — 50 lb. density particleboard with 2.5 mil solid color vinyl on the interior face. The bottom shall be attached to the sides, back and front with drawer bottom to reinforce drawer construction. The epoxy-coated steel WhisperGlide® core member supports the drawer to a maximum capacity of a 50 lb. load.

3.07.03 Drawers in base cabinets 30" wide and over use a ⅜" thick particleboard bottom for additional support.

3.07.04 All base cabinets shall have roll-out trays mounted with adapters attached to cabinet back. Trays are standard with all base cabinets (except 9" wide). Optional add-on trays for base cabinets available.

3.07.05 Lapjointed assembly consisting of ½" thick — 48 lb. density industrial grade particleboard with 4 mil semi-rigid solid color vinyl wrapped around the radiused top edge to help prevent marring and chipping. The tray front shall be ¾" solid hardwood with a triple coating of heat activated conversion paint.

3.07.06 Quarter-inch thick 50 lb. density particleboard laminated with 4 mil vinyl on the interior sides. The bottom is attached with adhesive and staples. The formed lip of the WhisperGlide® reinforces these joints.

3.08 Toe Space

3.08.01 The toeboard shall be ⅜"-48 lb. density particleboard and extend from the floor to the cabinet bottom. This adds support to the bottom and effectively seals the toe space against vermin and insects. The toeboard shall be covered with a ⅜" white vinyl covered particleboard strip.

3.09 Rutland Door and Drawer Front Construction

3.09.01 All shall be ⅝" thick — 48 lb. density industrial grade particleboard laminated with water and household chemical/abrasion resistant white low pressure melamine. The white color has been developed specifically to provide maximum opacity and match the white used for most major appliances and countertop materials. The edges of doors and drawer fronts are edgebanded with a .4mm thick melamine edgebanding, custom color matched to the front.

3.10 Whitebay Door and Drawer Front Construction

3.10.01 All shall be ¾" thick — 48 lb. density furniture grade medium density fiberboard. The one-piece medium density fiberboard is precision machined to exact tolerances. The component is laminated on the front side with a 16 mil vinyl that is thermo-formed to the door face. The back of the component is laminated with water and abrasion resistant white melamine. Both front surface and back are color matched and have been developed to provide the maximum opacity and resistance to abrasion, water and household chemicals and yellowing.

3.11 Hinges

3.11.01 Rutland doors are mounted on exclusive Merillat designed self-closing, nickel-plated semi-concealed hinges and open to 110 degrees. Hinges shall have horizontal and vertical adjustments. Whitebay doors are mounted on fully concealed, self-closing, nickel-plated hinges and open to 120 degrees. The hinges feature dowelled mounting and four-way adjustability.

4. FIRE RESISTANCE

4.01 Face frame and case has been tested in accordance with Underwriters Labs, Inc. (UL) flame spread test: Building Materials Section 40J8.5.7.

5. FORMALDEHYDE EMISSION LEVELS

5.01 Formaldehyde emissions conform to ANSI A208.1 1987 specifications and HUD rule on Manufactured Home Construction and Safety Standards, 24CFR part 3280 (August 9, 1984).

5.02 Formaldehyde emissions for raw particleboard is restricted to 0.3 parts per million.

6. INSTALLATION

6.01 Contractor shall verify all on-site dimensions and notify supplier of any variances or changes.

6.02 Install cabinets as indicated on the drawings. Install plumb and level, with all joints tight, in accordance with instructions shipped with cabinets.

6.03 Shim cabinets as required and trim with molding to match cabinets.

6.04 Secure to walls with screws embedded one inch minimum in solid wood framing or blocking.

6.05 Install miscellaneous hardware and accessories as indicated on the drawings.

6.06 Clean cabinets and leave in perfect operating order with all doors, shelves and drawers aligned and plumb.

For further information, send to Merillat for a full product specification guide. Merillat Industries, Inc., P.O. Box 1946, Adrian, MI 49221.

In keeping with our policy of continuous refinement, Merillat Industries reserves the right to alter specifications and styles without general notice or obligation to make similar changes in products previously produced.

CORONADO
by QuakerMaid

As the latest introduction to the Quaker Maid product lineup—

Coronado provides a combination of superior quality workmanship, custom features and excellent market value.

Streamlined manufacturing technology and proce-dures enable Quaker Maid to provide Coronado with a shorter lead time, while supplying a large variety of product selections. Glass inserts, finished interiors and curved cabinets are just some of the features that make Coronado an attractive option for new construction or remodeling markets.

Quaker Maid   A Division of WCI, Inc.   State Route 61   Leesport, PA 19533   215/926-7217

QuakerMaid

Your Partners For Success.

Since 1950, more than 500 dealers have come to rely on Quaker Maid's experience and commitment to quality.

Quaker Maid has been known for superior workmanship and excellence in design. Each cabinet selection is custom crafted; designed and built to your customers' specific needs and satisfaction.

Design Innovations.

As industry leaders, Quaker Maid is continuously updating its lines to meet changing market demands.

With Classic, Q2000 and Coronado, Quaker Maid provides a full spectrum of product choices. Ultra custom, frameless, limited custom, woods, laminates, leadership door styles and superior finishes ensure your client needs will be met.

For more information on Quaker Maid's fine quality products, call us today at 215/926-7217.

Appliances courtesy of Euroflair by Frigidaire, WCI Appliance Group, a division of WCI, Inc.

QuakerMaid
WCI CABINET GROUP

State Route 61   Leesport, PA 19533   215/926-7217

K&BSB/1991

Elite Series

Monaco

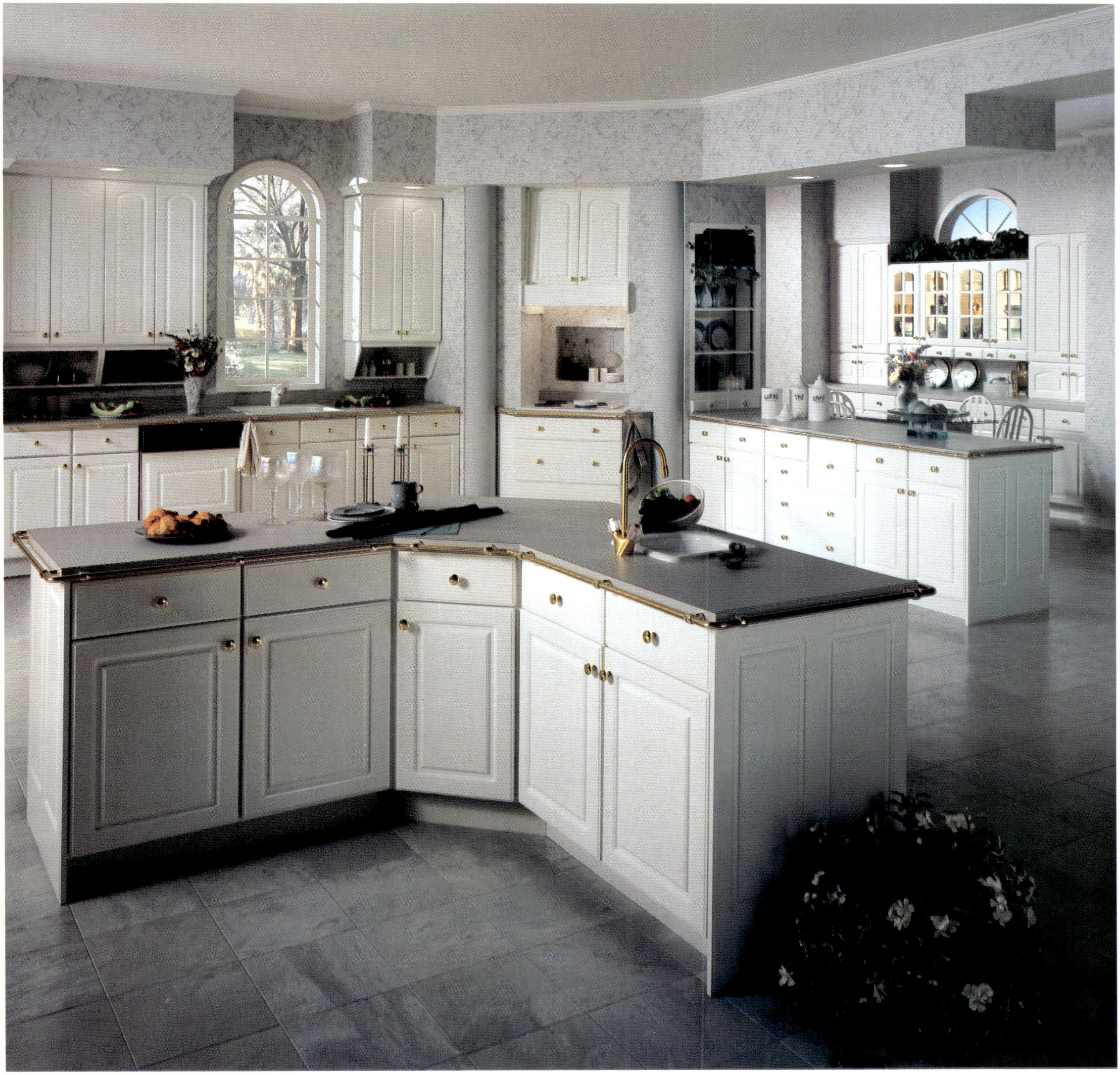

White

WELLBORN CABINET, INC.

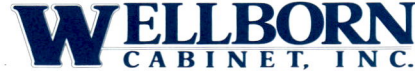

Clean lines, a Roman arched design and sleek styling . . . all with a hint of traditional elegance. These elements combine to create Monaco, our top-of-the-line cabinetry.

The ultimate in design elegance is created with Monaco. On the outside, Monaco features ³⁄₄″ thick full overlay doors and drawer fronts of HDF, High Density Fiberboard, layered in a gleaming white enamel finish for long-lasting durability. The soft Roman arch and detailed door and drawer edge profile give Monaco a fashion look all its own. On the inside, discriminating buyers will be pleased to find the cabinet interior is covered in a white laminate for easy cleaning with a fresh look. Drawers glide smoothly with epoxy coated drawer guides. Plus, our cabinets are equipped with sturdy ⁵⁄₈″ thick shelves.

This beautiful bathroom features 84″ high linen cabinets for covenient storage. And matching tri-view medicine cabinets have adjustable shelves. To create a unique style, the bathroom is accented with a radius moulding on cabinet tops and wall treatments.

Matching **Wall End Panels** mount easily on your cabinets and have left and right reversibility.

A **Raised Panel Dishwasher Front** matches your cabinetry and customizes your kitchen.

Full Overlay Crown Moulding adds a final touch to your kitchen.

Monaco has a white laminate interior. The drawers have epoxy drawer slides with positive open and close features.

White

Traditional Side Lights complement your tri-view mirrors and cabinetry.

Slide out this adjustable pantry for spacious storage in a 24″ wide **Utility Storage Cabinet**.

A **Pull Out Wastebasket** and **Sink Basket** make excellent use of space under your sink.

Bookcases display your favorite items and are available in 24″, 30″ and 36″ widths.

A **Contemporary Wood Hood** is available in 30″ and 36″ widths. Matching doors are available to decorate your hood.

24″, 30″ and 36″ **Contemporary Shelves** add style and a convenient display for your accessories.

White

Wellborn cabinetry can be designed in other rooms of the home for elegance and convenience. With our Accessory Collection, you'll find everything you need to make items easily accessible and be able to customize your designs.

This dining room displays your most cherished pieces through crafted mullion doors and adds an extra design touch with cassette drawers. Sliding shelves in the base cabinets give easy access to your china. In addition, all accessory kits are white to complement the cabinet color.

So remember, with Wellborn you can count on quality and style because our cabinetry is made by "People Who Care."

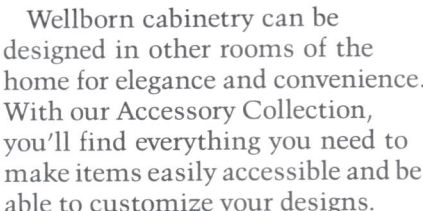

These handy **Tilt-Out Trays** provide easy reach for sponges and soaps.

A **Spice Rack** matches the white cabinet interior and mounts in a 18" wide base drawer.

Three Drawer Range Base has shallow top drawer for cooktop allowance, 30" and 36" widths.

Matching Base End Panels distinguish your cabinet ends and have left and right reversibility.

WELLBORN
People Who Care

Wellborn Cabinet, Inc.
Route One
Ashland, Alabama 36251
(205) 354-7151

It is characteristic of white painted cabinetry to age over time when exposed to sunlight and general household chemicals.
Due to this aging process, minor differences may develop with color match when replacing doors on existing cabinetry or adding additional cabinetry at a later date.

YORKTOWNE
KITCHEN
C A B I N E T S

Cabinets shown with
optional decorative hardware.

Yorktowne
CABINETS®

PREMIER SERIES

AVAILABLE COLORS

ALMOND
AUTUMN
CHESTNUT
FROSTED
WHEAT
WHITE

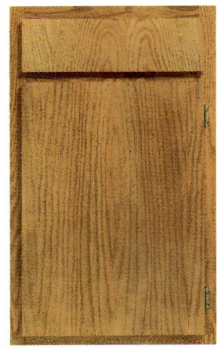

MONTEREY
CHESTNUT
WHEAT

DORSET
CHESTNUT
FROSTED
WHEAT

OAKRIDGE
AUTUMN
CHESTNUT
FROSTED
WHEAT

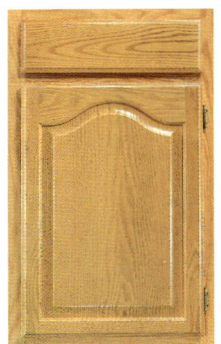

WINDSOR CATHEDRAL
AUTUMN
CHESTNUT
FROSTED
WHEAT

WINDSOR SQUARE
AUTUMN
CHESTNUT
FROSTED
WHEAT

CLASSIC SERIES

AVAILABLE COLORS

AUTUMN
CHESTNUT
FROSTED
WHEAT

COUNTRY MANOR
CHESTNUT
WHEAT

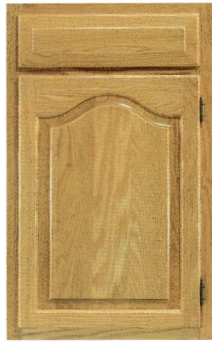

CHAPELLE
AUTUMN
CHESTNUT
FROSTED
WHEAT

COVENTRY
AUTUMN
CHESTNUT
FROSTED
WHEAT

WILLIAMSBURG
AUTUMN
CHESTNUT
FROSTED
WHEAT

ARLINGTON CATHEDRAL
AUTUMN
CHESTNUT
FROSTED
WHEAT

SIGNATURE SERIES

AVAILABLE COLORS

AUTUMN
CHAMPAGNE
CHERRY
CHESTNUT
CINNAMON
FROSTED
NATURAL
SPICE
TOFFEE
WHEAT

YORKSHIRE CATHEDRAL
CHERRY
CINNAMON
SPICE

YORKSHIRE SQUARE
CHERRY
CINNAMON
SPICE

CANTERBURY
TOFFEE

HERMITAGE
TOFFEE

HEIRLOOM
CHAMPAGNE
CHERRY
NATURAL
SPICE

CONTEMPRA SERIES

AVAILABLE COLORS

ALMOND
AUTUMN
CHERRY
CHESTNUT
FROSTED
GRAY
WHEAT
WHITE

NORMANDY
ALMOND
GRAY
WHITE

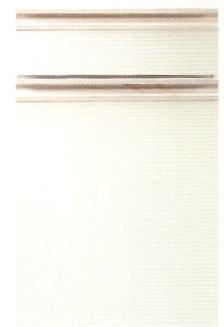

VISTA
ALMOND
FROSTED
WHITE

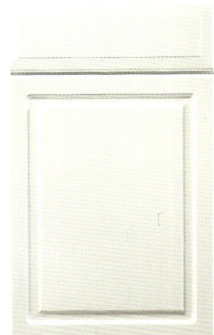

PRELUDE
WHITE

CENTURY HILL CATHEDRAL
AUTUMN • CHESTNUT
FROSTED • WHEAT

CENTURY HILL SQUARE
AUTUMN • CHESTNUT
FROSTED • WHEAT

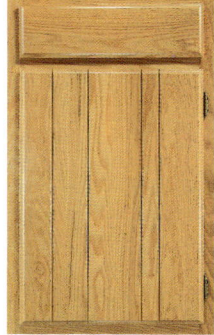

JAMESTOWN
AUTUMN
CHESTNUT
FROSTED
WHEAT

BISCAYNE DELUXE
ALMOND
FROSTED
WHITE

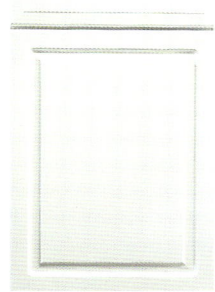

WHITEHALL
WHITE

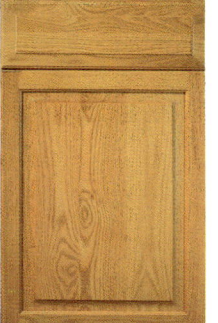

ARLINGTON SQUARE
AUTUMN
CHESTNUT
FROSTED
WHEAT

YORKTOWNE
KITCHEN
C A B I N E T S

ASBURY
CHAMPAGNE
CHERRY
NATURAL
SPICE

LANCASTER CATHEDRAL
AUTUMN
CHESTNUT
FROSTED
WHEAT

LANCASTER SQUARE
AUTUMN
CHESTNUT
FROSTED
WHEAT

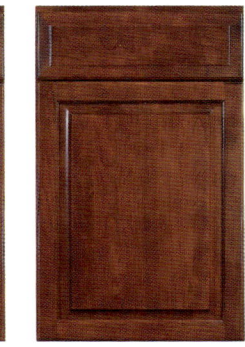

**ROYALE CHERRY
CATHEDRAL**
CHERRY

**ROYALE CHERRY
SQUARE**
CHERRY

Due to the chemical differences between printing inks and the pigments used in our manufacturing process, we cannot guarantee exact color reproduction of cabinet finishes.

Ultimate selection should be made from actual samples.

The closer you look, the better it gets!

Excellent design and quality construction are hallmarks of Yorktowne cabinetry. Yorktowne cabinets are constructed by skilled craftsmen to rigid quality standards and bear the certification label of the Kitchen Cabinet Manufacturers Association, your assurance that the kitchen you select will withstand the rigors of everyday use.

Convenience and function are equally important, and with Yorktowne's wide selection of specialty storage cabinets you can customize your kitchen, bath, den or other rooms to satisfy every personal need and desire.

Value, Quality, Dependability. You'll find all three in a large selection of over 80 cabinet style and color combinations in oak, maple, hickory and cherry wood, or solid color laminate in traditional, country or contemporary styling.

Yorktowne kitchen and bath cabinets. Always the latest in advanced technology plus the beauty, look and feel of old world charm and craftsmanship.

Please note that the complete selection of Yorktowne kitchen cabinet styles, colors and finishes is also available for bath vanity cabinets.

AVAILABLE COLORS

ALMOND

AUTUMN

CHAMPAGNE

CHERRY

CHESTNUT

CINNAMON

FROSTED

GRAY

NATURAL

SPICE

TOFFEE

WHEAT

WHITE

YORKTOWNE KITCHEN CABINETS

29 CABINET STYLES
88 STYLE AND COLOR COMBINATIONS
FOR KITCHEN AND BATH VANITY CABINETS

AVAILABLE COLORS

	STYLES	AUTUMN	WHEAT	CHESTNUT	FROSTED	WHITE	ALMOND	GRAY	TOFFEE	CHERRY	CHAMPAGNE	SPICE	NATURAL	CINNAMON
PREMIER	MONTEREY		■	■										
	DORSET		■	■	■									
PREMIER DELUXE	OAKRIDGE	■	■	■	■									
	WINDSOR CATHEDRAL	■	■	■	■									
	WINDSOR SQUARE	■	■	■	■									
	JAMESTOWN	■	■	■	■									
	BISCAYNE DELUXE					■	■	■						
	WHITEHALL					■								
CLASSIC	COUNTRY MANOR		■	■										
	CHAPELLE	■	■	■	■									
	COVENTRY	■	■	■	■									
	WILLIAMSBURG	■	■	■										
	ARLINGTON CATHEDRAL	■	■	■	■									
	ARLINGTON SQUARE	■	■	■	■									
SIGNATURE	YORKSHIRE CATHEDRAL									■		■		■
	YORKSHIRE SQUARE									■		■		■
	CANTERBURY								■					
	HERMITAGE								■					
	HEIRLOOM									■	■	■	■	
	ASBURY									■	■	■		
	LANCASTER CATHEDRAL	■	■	■	■									
	LANCASTER SQUARE	■	■	■	■									
CONTEMPRA	NORMANDY					■	■	■						
	VISTA				■	■	■							
	PRELUDE					■								
	CENTURY HILL CATHEDRAL	■	■	■	■									
	CENTURY HILL SQUARE	■	■	■	■									
	ROYALE CHERRY CATHEDRAL									■				
	ROYALE CHERRY SQUARE									■				

INC.

P.O. Box 2231, Red Lion, PA 17356
(717) 244-4011

CERTIFIED
KCMA
CABINET
KITCHEN CABINET
MANUFACTURERS
ASSOCIATION
ANSI/KCMA A161-1

Please note that the complete selection of Yorktowne kitchen cabinet styles, colors and finishes is also available for bath vanity cabinets.

Form No. CB032

Printed in U.S.A.

CLOSET
MAID®

Clairson
International

STORAGE
SYSTEMS

Brand use study shows 55% of builders chose CLOSET MAID®

General Specifications:

Furnish and install in all closets Closet Maid® vinyl-coated, steel-rod, ventilated shelving and storage products manufactured by Clairson International, Ocala, Florida.

Materials

All shelving and storage products shall be constructed of Grade C-1008 bright basic cold drawn steel wire with average tensile strength of 100,000 PSI. All steel rods shall be resistance welded at intersection of cross deck wires. Deck rod spacing shall be on 1" increments. Cross deck wires shall be trimmed smooth to longitudinal wires.

Finish

Metal shall be cleaned and primed prior to coating to ensure a proper bond of coating material. Vinyl-coating shall be of a non-exudating formula PVC, applied by fluidized bed process to a thickness of 7-11 mils. Vinyl-coating shall bridge intersections of the welded cross wires to provide a continuous protective coating. Elasticity of the protective coating shall be sufficient to prevent chipping and cracking of the protective finish.

Mounting Hardware/Instructions

Components provide for Closet Maid shelving installation to drywall *without requiring mounting to wall studs.*

Wall Mounting:

Place wall clips 12" apart on a level line where shelves will be attached to wall.

Drywall:

Drill 1/4" hole. Insert #174 XBA Back Clip Anchor. Use #10 screw to expand the clip's anchor behind drywall to secure shelving.

Wood:

Attach #199 Anchorless Fin Back Clip to wood or stud with #8 or #10 screw.

Concrete:

Drill 3/16" hole. Insert #175 Fin Back Clip. Use #8 screw to secure the anchor.

Shelf Support:

Use Closet Maid Series #160 XSB Support Brackets, #117 or #118 poles, or #120 Corner Support Bracket to support all shelves. Place these supports approximately 36" apart (24" recommended for areas designed for heavy use). Closet Maid Shelf Spanner™ #176 for 16" shelf, or #178 for 20" shelf, is recommended every 30" for heavy duty applications.

Wall to Wall Installations:

Cut shelves to a length of 1" shorter than the actual wall-to-wall measurement.

Use #170 XEB End Bracket to support shelf front rods. For drywall installation, drill 1/4" hole and use #250 Grey Anchor with #10 screw. For concrete installation, drill 3/16" hole and use #207 Anchor with #8 screw.

Open End Installations:

Secure shelving to wall above each XSB Support Bracket installation with a #202 Down Clip using a #250 Anchor and #10 screw.

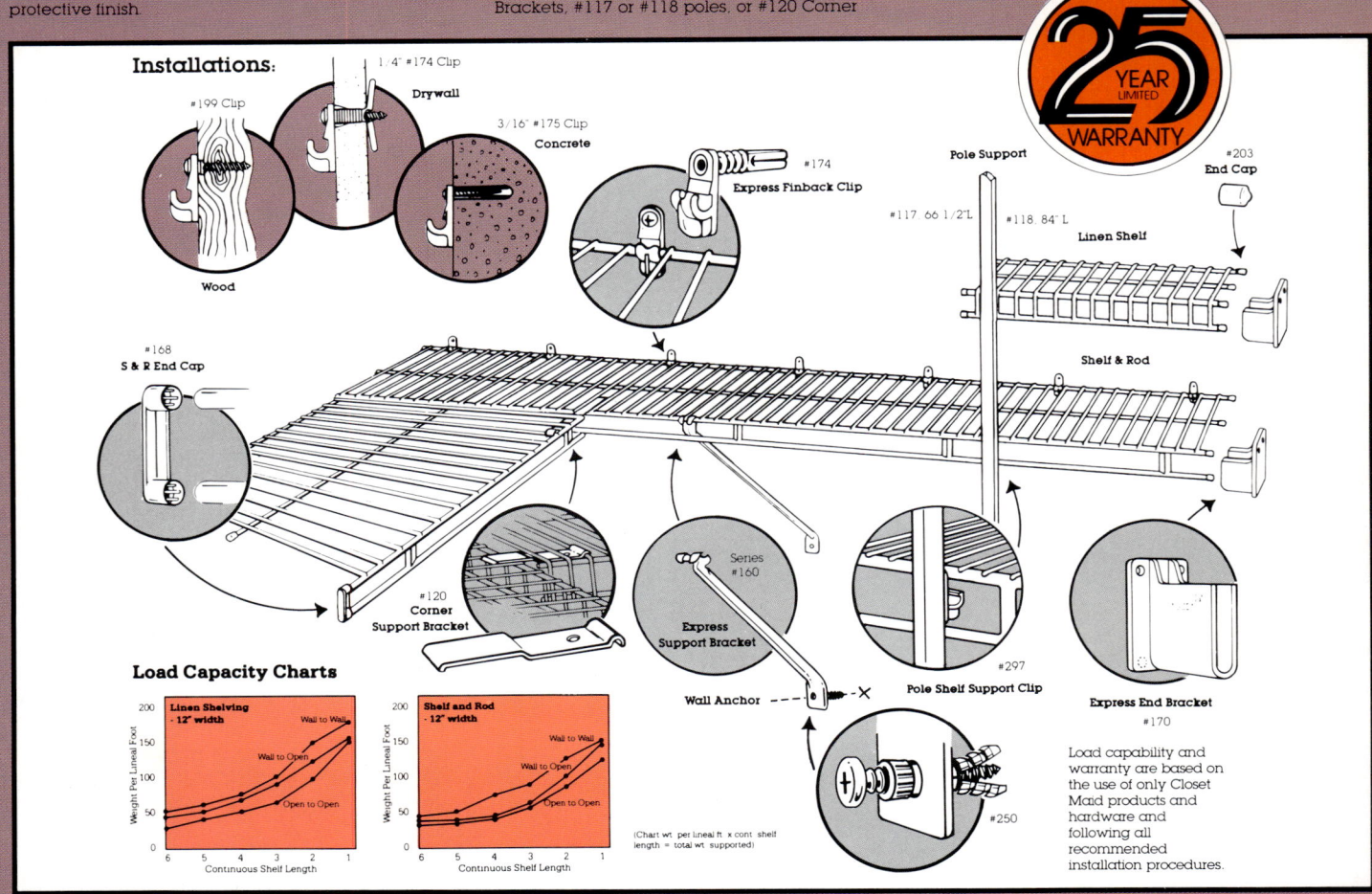

Installations:

#199 Clip — Wood — 1/4" #174 Clip — Drywall — 3/16" #175 Clip — Concrete

#174 Express Finback Clip

#168 S & R End Cap

#120 Corner Support Bracket

Series #160 Express Support Bracket — Wall Anchor

Pole Support — #117 .66 1/2"L — #118 .84" L — Linen Shelf — Shelf & Rod — #203 End Cap

#297 Pole Shelf Support Clip

Express End Bracket #170

#250

Load capability and warranty are based on the use of only Closet Maid products and hardware and following all recommended installation procedures.

Load Capacity Charts

Linen Shelving - 12" width — Weight Per Lineal Foot — Wall to Wall — Wall to Open — Open to Open — Continuous Shelf Length

Shelf and Rod - 12" width — Weight Per Lineal Foot — Wall to Wall — Wall to Open — Open to Open — Continuous Shelf Length

(Chart wt. per lineal ft × cont shelf length = total wt supported)

Engineered for Quality

Wire

Our wire is drawn from continuous cast steel rods and is produced in a controlled cooling process with continual in-line testing to ensure our demanding specifications for weldability, ductability and consistent tensile strength.

Coatings

Clairson International's vinyl coating is a proprietary Polyvinyl Chloride Resin (PVC), with an exclusive mixture of ingredients including plasticizers, stabilizers, pigments and other additives — none of which are listed as hazardous materials in OSHA 29CFR1910.1017.

Clairson's GLIDEKOTE™ is an exclusive, high performance hybrid polyester that is exceptionally strong and durable. GlideKote has an additive that creates a very low coefficient of friction, adding years of performance and ease in sliding. Our in-line four-stage coating process, with "state of the art" equipment, includes washing, chemical pretreatment to ensure good adhesion, and automatic electrostatic powder coating. The thermosetting powder is cross linked and cured in ovens at 400° F, resulting in the highest quality coated products in the industry.

Plastics

Clairson International's patented plastic components are manufactured to high performance standards and meet rigid material requirements. Various parts are specified with high impact styrene to prevent cracking, while others are made of nylon 66 when it is critical to eliminate any possibility of stretching. When pliability is needed, a performance-tested PVC is specified.

Design

With over 20 years of design experience in storage and organization, Clairson International has accumulated an impressive list of patents, maintains an ongoing in-house testing facility, and continues to be the leader in new product innovation. These patent rights exclude others from making, using or selling these exact items throughout the USA. We have been granted the title to the following patents:

Patent No.:

3,765,634, 3,859,002, 4,316,593, 4,548,327, 4,708,552, D295,472, D295,182, 4,629,077, 4,646,998, 4,693,380, 4,735,325, 4,732,284, 74,369, 4,783,035, 4,781,349.

The decision to purchase a new home is often made in a CLOSET MAID® closet.

Basic

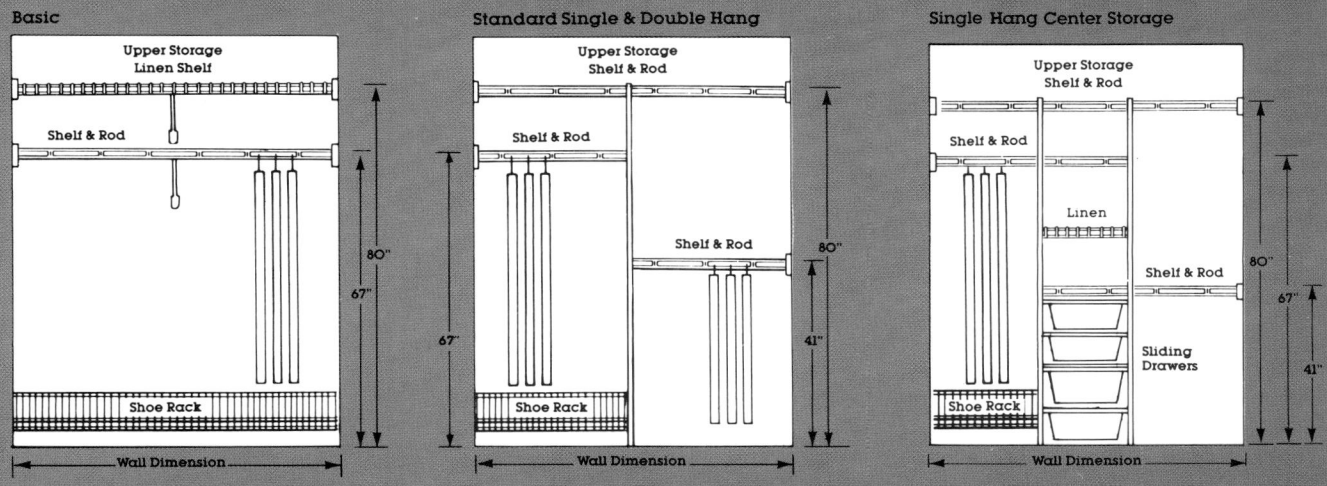

Standard Single & Double Hang

Single Hang Center Storage

His & Hers

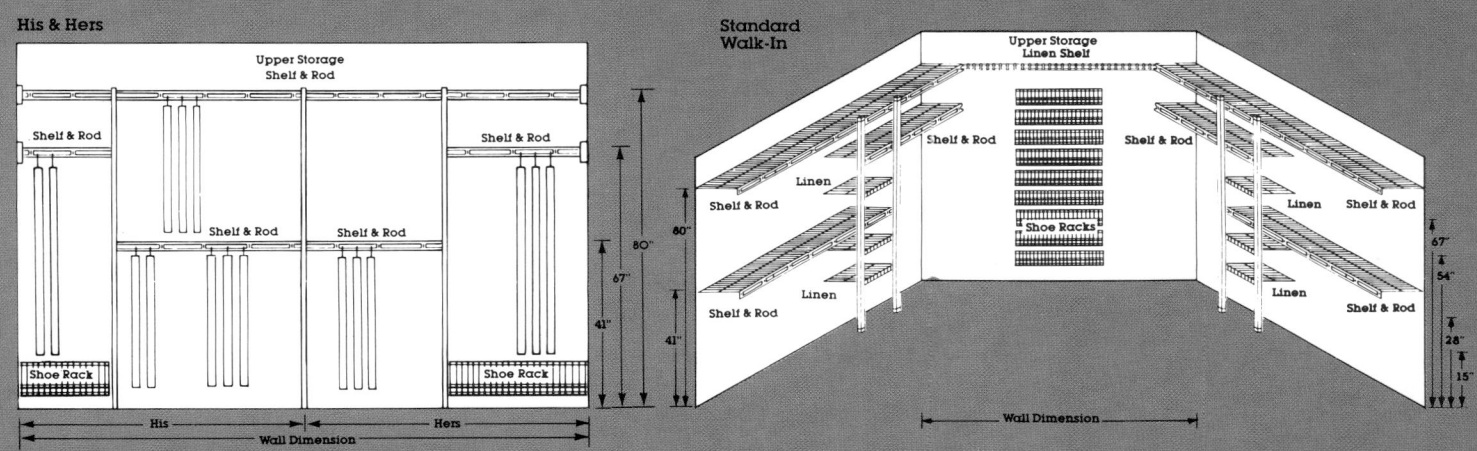

Standard Walk-In

LAMINATE SYSTEM

Laminate Wall Mount

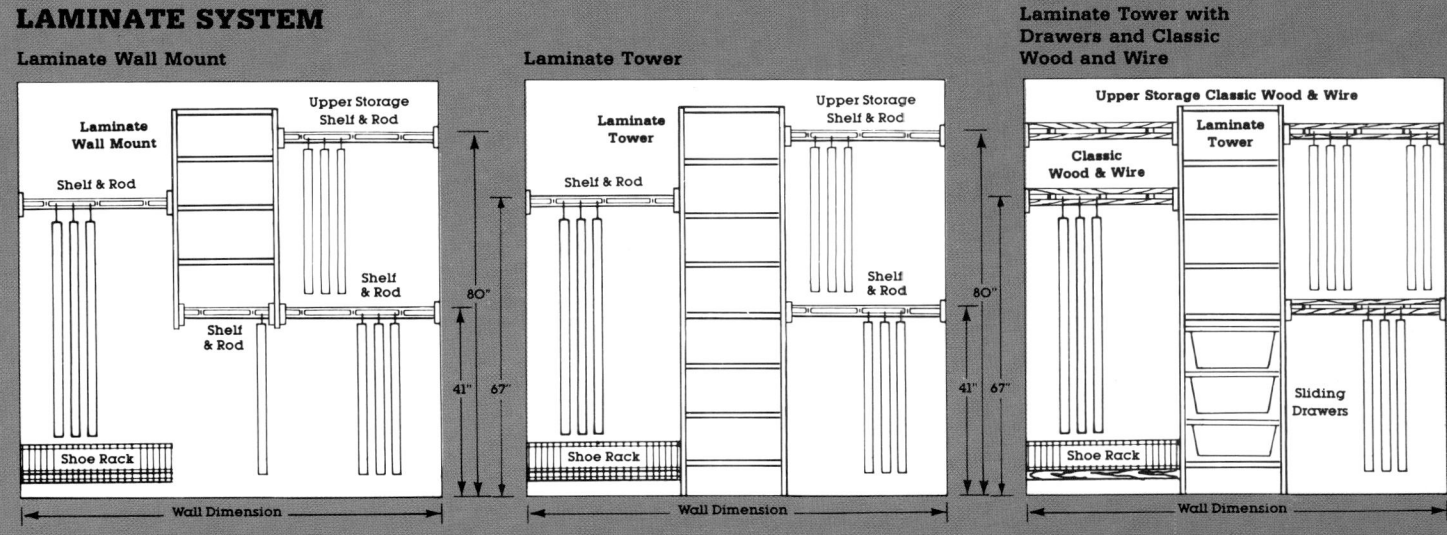

Laminate Tower

Laminate Tower with Drawers and Classic Wood and Wire

STORAGE SYSTEMS

just say **ELKAY**

STAINLESS STEEL SINKS

STAINLESS STEEL SINKS

just say ELKAY

GOURMET COLLECTION
WITH SOUND GUARD INSULATION
GOURMET CUISINE CENTRÉ
18 GAUGE • TYPE 302 • SELF RIM

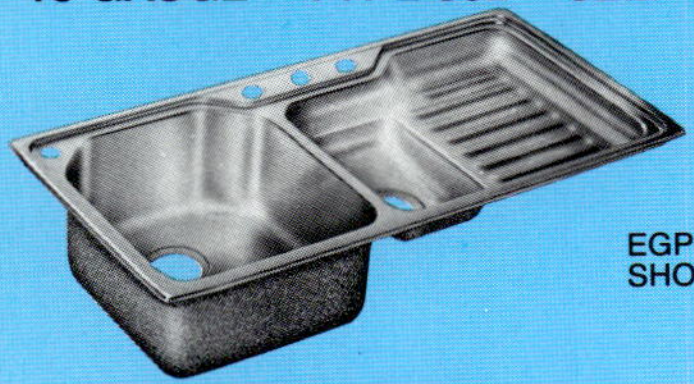

EGPI-4322-L4 SHOWN

CONTEMPORARY

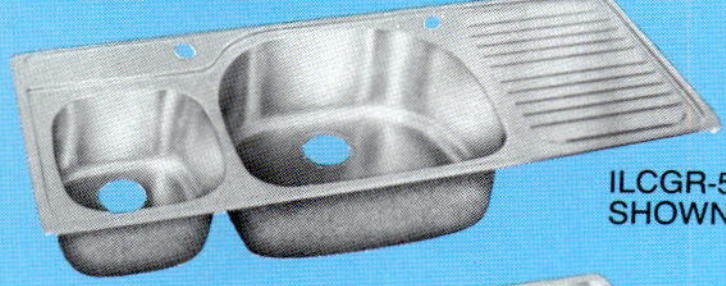

ILCGR-5322-LS2 SHOWN

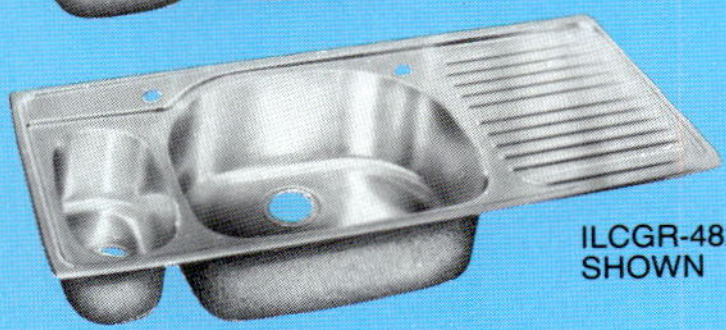

ILCGR-4822-LS2 SHOWN

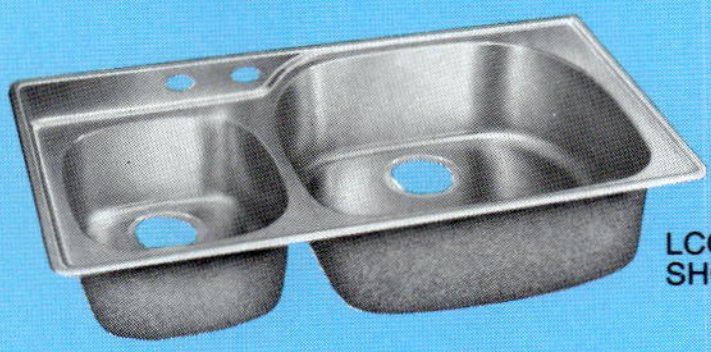

LCGR-3822-L-2 SHOWN

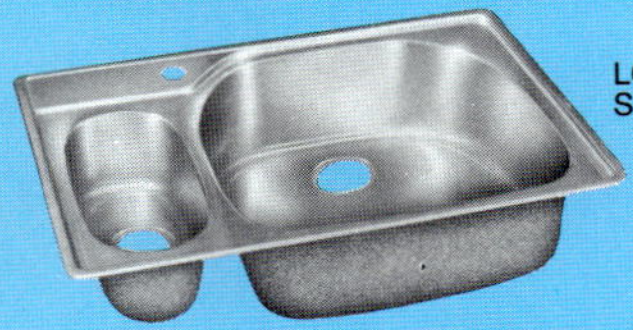

LCGR-3322-L-1 SHOWN

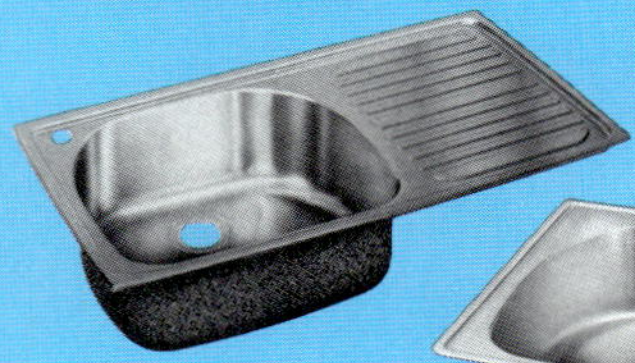

ILCGR-4022-L-1 SHOWN

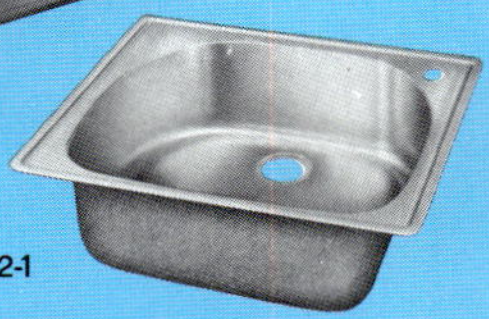

LCGR-2522-1 SHOWN

MODEL NUMBER	OVERALL SIZE		INSIDE EACH COMPARTMENT LEFT			RIGHT			DRAINBOARD LENGTH
	L	W	L	W	D	L	W	D	
DOUBLE COMPARTMENT WITH DRAINBOARD									
•EGPI-4322-L	43	22	16	18	10	7½	12⅞	6½	12⅞
•EGPI-4322-R	43	22	7½	12⅞	6½	16	18	10	12⅞
ILCGR-5322-L	53	22	11¾	13¼	6 7/16	21	18⅝	8	17⅛
ILCGR-5322-R	53	22	21	18⅝	8	11¾	13¼	6 7/16	17⅛
ILCGR-4822-L	48	22	7	14⅛	16 1/16	21	18⅝	8	16 15/16
ILCGR-4822-R	48	22	21	18⅝	8	7	14⅛	6 1/16	16 15/16
DOUBLE COMPARTMENT									
LCGR-3822-L	38	22	11¾	13¼	6 7/16	21	18⅝	8	—
LCGR-3822-R	38	22	21	18⅝	8	11¾	13¼	6 7/16	—
LCGR-3322-L	33	22	7	14⅛	6 1/16	21	18⅝	8	—
LCGR-3322-R	33	22	21	18⅝	8	7	14⅛	6 1/16	—

•INCLUDES CBP-1116 CUTTING SURFACE.

MODEL NUMBER	OVERALL SIZE		COMPARTMENT SIZE			DRAINBOARD LENGTH
	L	W	L	W	D	
SINGLE COMPARTMENT WITH DRAINBOARD						
ILCGR-4022-L	40	22	21	18⅝	8	17
ILCGR-4022-R	40	22	21	18⅝	8	17
SINGLE COMPARTMENT						
LCGR-2522	25	22	21	18⅝	8	—

SUFFIX "L" OR "R" DENOTES SINK COMPARTMENT IS LOCATED LEFT OR RIGHT OF DRAINBOARD.

GOURMET COLLECTION
WITH SOUND GUARD INSULATION
TRADITIONAL
18 GAUGE • TYPE 302 • SELF RIM

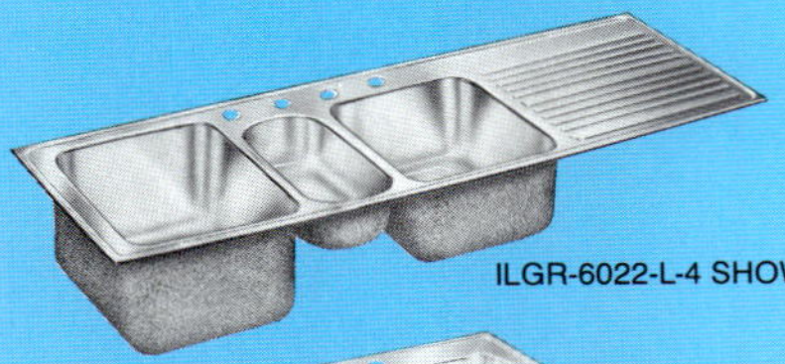

ILGR-6022-L-4 SHOWN

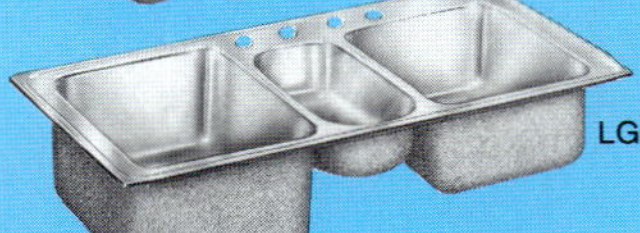

LGR-4322-4 SHOWN

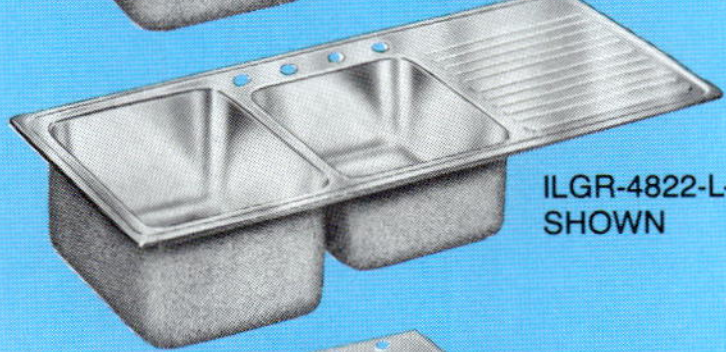

ILGR-4822-L-4 SHOWN

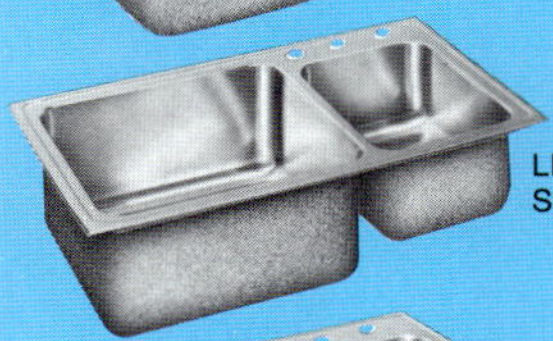

LFGR-3722-3 SHOWN

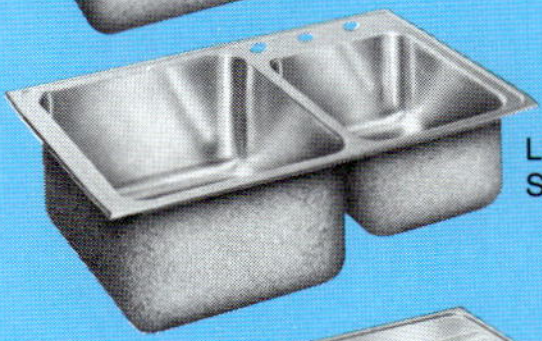

LFGR-3322-3 SHOWN

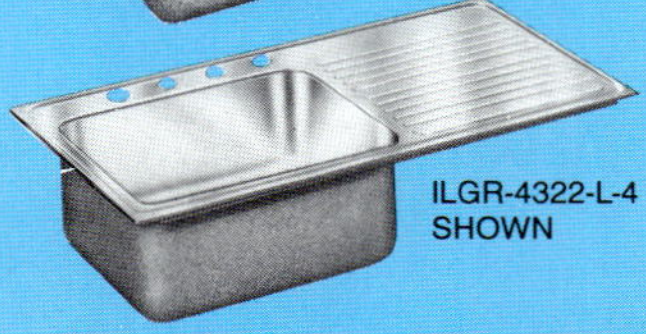

ILGR-4322-L-4 SHOWN

MODEL NUMBER	OVERALL SIZE		INSIDE EACH COMPARTMENT LEFT			CENTER			RIGHT			DRAINBOARD LENGTH
	L	W	L	W	D	L	W	D	L	W	D	
TRIPLE COMPARTMENT WITH DRAINBOARD												
ILGR-6022-L-4	60	22	14	18	10	7½	15¾	5⅛	13½	16	8	19¾
ILGR-6022-R-4	60	22	13½	16	8	7½	15¾	5⅛	14	18	10	19¾
TRIPLE COMPARTMENT												
LGR-4322	43	22	14	18	10	7½	15¾	5⅛	13½	16	8	—

MODEL NUMBER	OVERALL SIZE		INSIDE EACH COMPARTMENT LEFT			RIGHT			DRAINBOARD LENGTH
	L	W	L	W	D	L	W	D	
DOUBLE COMPARTMENT WITH DRAINBOARD									
ILFGR-5422-L	54	22	20	18	10	11½	16	8	19¾
ILFGR-5422-R	54	22	11½	16	8	20	18	10	19¾
ILFGR-4822-L	48	22	16	19	10	11½	16	8	17½
ILFGR-4822-R	48	22	11½	16	8	16	19	10	17½
ILGR-5422-L	54	22	14	18	10	16	16	8	19⅞
ILGR-5422-R	54	22	16	16	8	14	18	10	19⅞
ILGR-4822-L	48	22	14	18	10	13½	16	8	17⅛
ILGR-4822-R	48	22	13½	16	8	14	18	10	17⅛
DOUBLE COMPARTMENT									
LFGR-3722	37	22	20	18	10	11½	16	8	—
LFGR-3322	33	22	16	19	10	11½	16	8	—
LGR-3722	37	22	14	18	10	16	16	8	—
LGR-3322	33	22	14	18	10	13½	16	8	—

MODEL NUMBER	OVERALL SIZE		COMPARTMENT SIZE			DRAINBOARD LENGTH
	L	W	L	W	D	
SINGLE COMPARTMENT WITH DRAINBOARD						
ILGR-4322-L	43	22	21	15¾	10	20
ILGR-4322-R	43	22	21	15¾	10	20

ALL DIMENSIONS IN INCHES
L (LENGTH, LEFT TO RIGHT) W (WIDTH, FRONT TO BACK) D (BOWL DEPTH)

Lustertone® HIGHEST QUALITY
18 GAUGE • TYPE 302 • SELF RIM

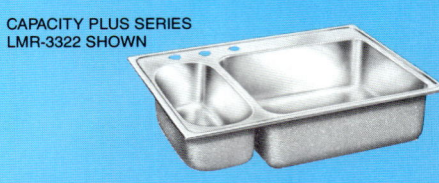

CAPACITY PLUS SERIES
LMR-3322 SHOWN

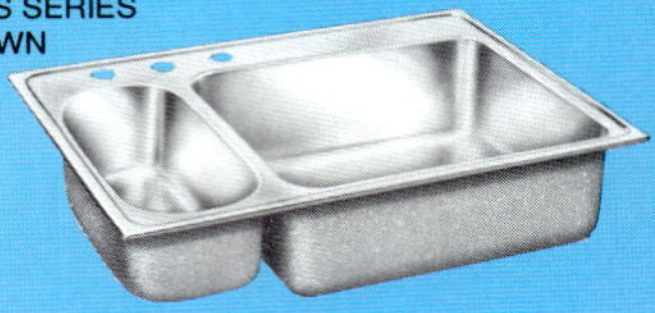

TWO FIFTY PLUS SERIES
LR-250 SHOWN

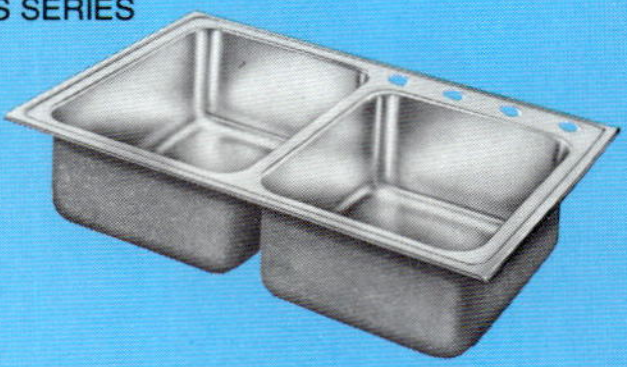

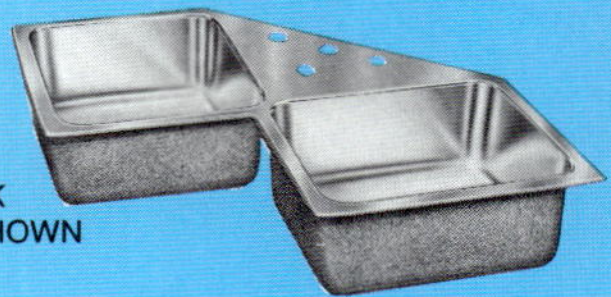

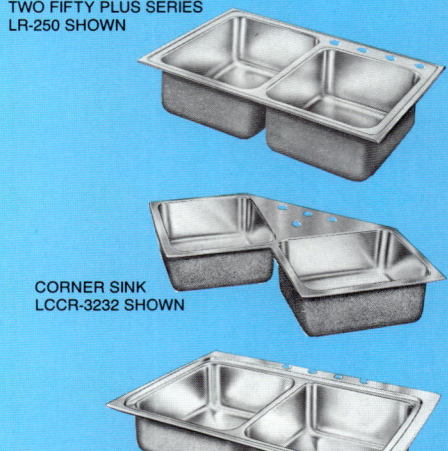

CORNER SINK
LCCR-3232 SHOWN

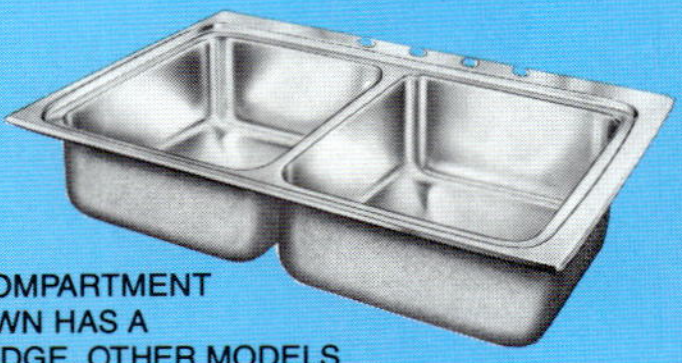

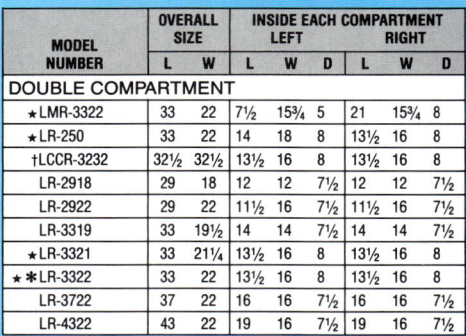

✱DOUBLE COMPARTMENT LR-3322 SHOWN HAS A 7/16″ DROP LEDGE. OTHER MODELS HAVE A 3/16″ DROP LEDGE.

✱SINGLE COMPARTMENT LR-2522 SHOWN HAS A 7/16″ DROP LEDGE. OTHER MODELS HAVE 3/16″ DROP LEDGE.

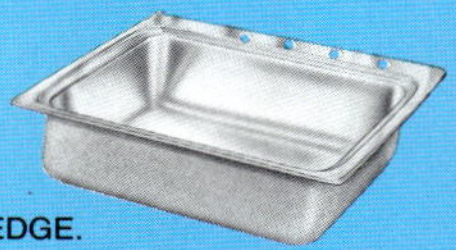

MODEL NUMBER	OVERALL SIZE		INSIDE EACH COMPARTMENT LEFT			RIGHT		
	L	W	L	W	D	L	W	D
DOUBLE COMPARTMENT								
★LMR-3322	33	22	7½	15¾	5	21	15¾	8
★LR-250	33	22	14	18	8	13½	16	8
†LCCR-3232	32½	32½	13½	16	8	13½	16	8
LR-2918	29	18	12	12	7½	12	12	7½
LR-2922	29	22	11½	16	7½	11½	16	7½
LR-3319	33	19½	14	14	7½	14	14	7½
★LR-3321	33	21¼	13½	16	8	13½	16	8
★✱LR-3322	33	22	13½	16	8	13½	16	8
LR-3722	37	22	16	16	7½	16	16	7½
LR-4322	43	22	19	16	7½	19	16	7½

†No Drop Ledge

MODEL NUMBER	OVERALL SIZE		INSIDE COMPARTMENT SIZE		
	L	W	L	W	D
SINGLE COMPARTMENT					
LR-1517	15	17½	12	12	7½
LR-1522	15	22	11½	16	7½
LR-1716	17	16	14	10	7½
LR-1720	17	20	14	14	7½
LR-1722	17	22	13½	16	7½
LR-1918	19	18	16	11½	7½
LR-1922	19	22	16	16	7½
LR-2219	22	19½	18	14	7½
LR-2222	22	22	19	16	7½
★LR-2521	25	21¼	21	15¾	8
★✱LR-2522	25	22	21	15¾	8
LR-3122	31	22	28	16	7½

★Sound Guard Insulation

STAINLESS STEEL SINKS

just say ELKAY

Pacemaker Starlite® FINE QUALITY
20 GAUGE • TYPE 302 • SELF RIM

TRIPLE COMPARTMENT
PSMR-4322 SHOWN

CAPACITY PLUS
PSMR-3322-R SHOWN

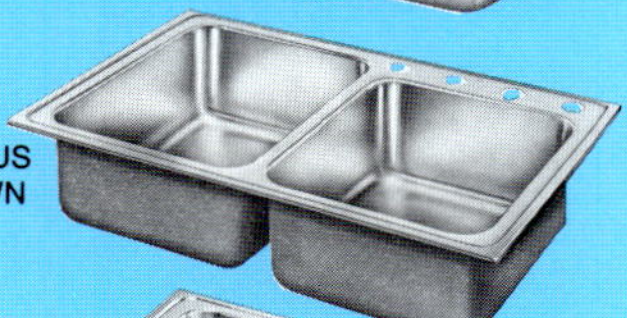

TWO FIFTY PLUS
PSR-250 SHOWN

WITHOUT FAUCET LEDGE-NARROW
PSFR-3319 SHOWN

DOUBLE COMPARTMENT
✱PSR-3322 SHOWN HAS A 7/16″ DROP LEDGE. OTHER MODELS HAVE A 3/16″ DROP LEDGE.

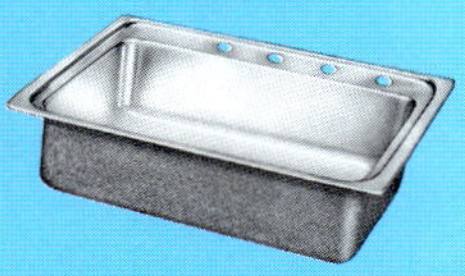

SINGLE COMPARTMENT
✱PSR-2522 SHOWN HAS A 7/16″ DROP LEDGE OTHER MODELS HAVE A 3/16″ DROP LEDGE.

MODEL NUMBER	OVERALL SIZE L	OVERALL SIZE W	INSIDE EACH COMPARTMENT LEFT L	LEFT W	LEFT D	CENTER L	CENTER W	CENTER D	RIGHT L	RIGHT W	RIGHT D
TRIPLE COMPARTMENT											
★PSMR-4322	43	22	14	18	7¼	9¼	12	5	14	18	7¼

MODEL NUMBER	OVERALL SIZE L	OVERALL SIZE W	INSIDE EACH COMPARTMENT LEFT L	LEFT W	LEFT D	RIGHT L	RIGHT W	RIGHT D
DOUBLE COMPARTMENT								
★PSMR-3322	33	22	7½	15¾	5	21	15¾	7¼
★PSMR-3322-R	33	22	21	15¾	7¼	7½	15¾	5
★PSR-250	33	22	14	18	7¼	13½	16	7¼
PSFR-3319	33	19½	13½	16	7¼	13½	16	7¼
PSR-3319	33	19½	14	14	7¼	14	14	7¼
★PSR-3321	33	21¼	13½	16	7½	13½	16	7½
✱★PSR-3322	33	22	13½	16	7½	13½	16	7½
PSR-4322	43	22	19	16	7¼	19	16	7¼

MODEL NUMBER	OVERALL SIZE L	OVERALL SIZE W	INSIDE COMPARTMENT SIZE L	W	D
SINGLE COMPARTMENT					
PSR-1517	15	17½	12	12	7¼
PSR-1716	17	16	14	10	7¼
PSR-1720	17	20	14	14	7¼
PSR-1722	17	22	13½	16	7¼
PSR-1918	19	18	16	11½	7¼
PSR-2219	22	19½	18	14	7¼
PSR-2222	22	22	19	16	7¼
★PSR-2521	25	21¼	21	15¾	7½
★✱PSR-2522	25	22	21	15¾	7½
PSR-3122	31	22	28	16	7¼
PSRS-3322	33	22	28	16	7¼

★Sound Guard Insulation

CELEBRITY® GOOD QUALITY
20 GAUGE • TYPE 302 • SELF RIM

TRIPLE COMPARTMENT
CMR-4322 SHOWN

CAPACITY PLUS
CMR-3322 SHOWN

TWO FIFTY PLUS
CR-250 SHOWN

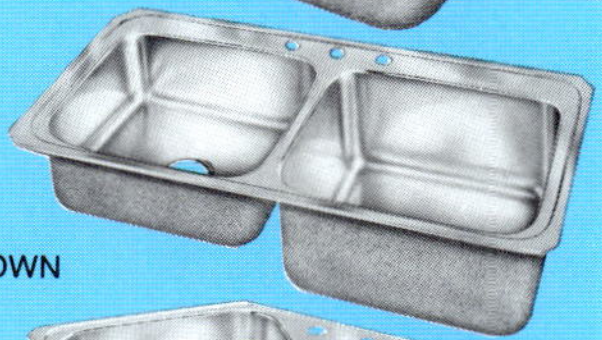

SINK AND TRAY
STCR-3322-R SHOWN

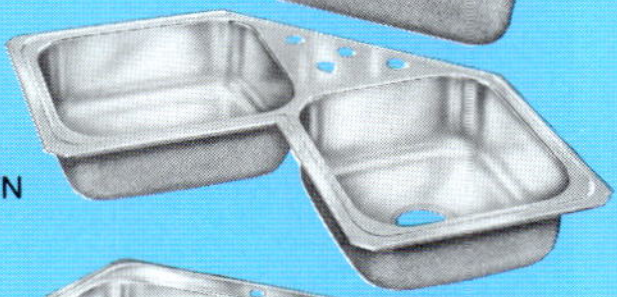

CORNER SINK
CCR-3232 SHOWN

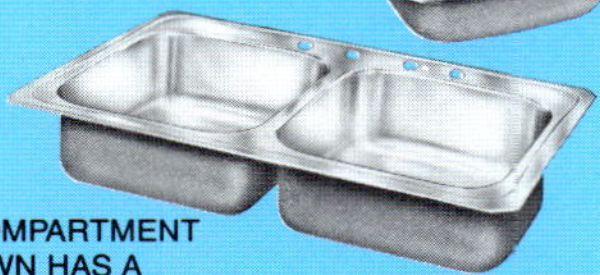

✱DOUBLE COMPARTMENT CR-3322 SHOWN HAS A 1/4″ DROP LEDGE. OTHER MODELS HAVE A 3/16″ DROP LEDGE

✱SINGLE COMPARTMENT CR-2522 SHOWN HAS A 1/4″ DROP LEDGE. OTHER MODELS HAVE A 3/16″ DROP LEDGE.

MODEL NUMBER	OVERALL SIZE L	OVERALL SIZE W	INSIDE EACH COMPARTMENT LEFT L	LEFT W	LEFT D	CENTER L	CENTER W	CENTER D	RIGHT L	RIGHT W	RIGHT D
TRIPLE COMPARTMENT											
CMR-4322	43	22	13½	18	7	10	12	5	13½	18	7

MODEL NUMBER	OVERALL SIZE L	OVERALL SIZE W	INSIDE EACH COMPARTMENT LEFT L	LEFT W	LEFT D	RIGHT L	RIGHT W	RIGHT D
DOUBLE COMPARTMENT								
CMR-3322	33	22	7½	15¾	5	21	15¾	7
CR-250	33	22	13½	18	7	14	15¾	7
STCR-3322-L	33	22	14	15¾	10	14	15¾	7
STCR-3322-R	33	22	14	15¾	7	14	15¾	10
CCR-3232	31⅞	31⅞	15¾	14	7	15¾	14	7
CR-3321	33	21¼	14	15¾	7	14	15¾	7
✱CR-3322	33	22	14	15¾	7	14	15¾	7
CR-4322	43	22	19	15¾	7	19	15¾	7
†GECR-3321	33	21¼	14	15¾	5⅜	14	15¾	5⅜

MODEL NUMBER	OVERALL SIZE L	OVERALL SIZE W	INSIDE COMPARTMENT SIZE L	W	D
SINGLE COMPARTMENT					
CR-1721	17	21¼	14	15¾	7
CR-2521	25	21¼	21	15¾	7
✱CR-2522	25	22	21	15¾	7
CR-3122	31	22	28	15¾	7
CRS-3322	33	22	28	15¾	7
†GECR-2521-L	25	21¼	21	15¾	5⅜
†GECR-2522-R	25	21¼	21	15¾	5⅜

†L (upper left) or R (upper right) denotes drain hole location

BAR SINKS
GOURMET BAR SINKS
WITH SOUND GUARD INSULATION

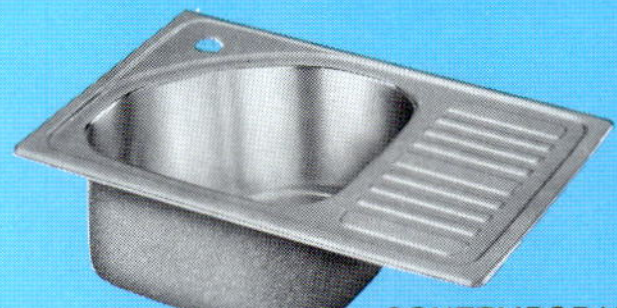

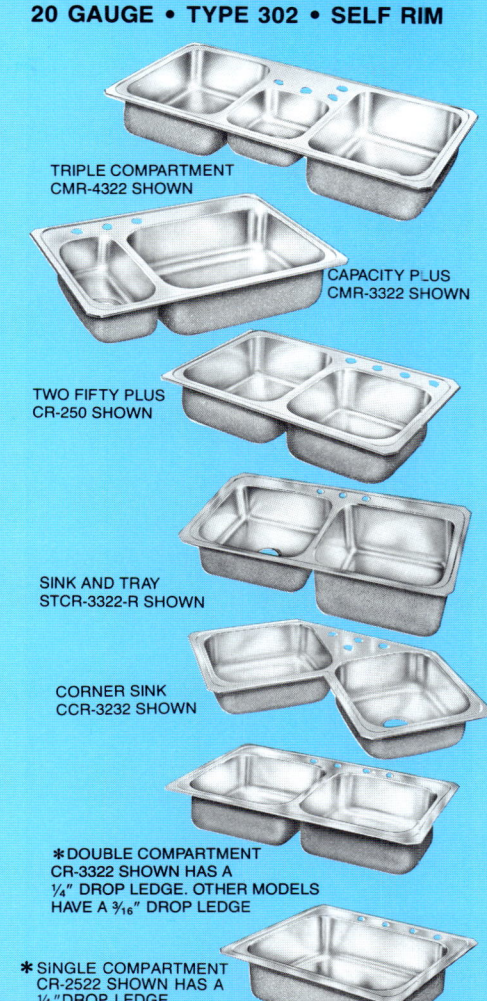

CONTEMPORARY
GOURMET WITH DRAINBOARD
BILGR-2115-L SHOWN

BLGR-1515 SHOWN

Lustertone® BAR SINKS

BLR-15 SHOWN

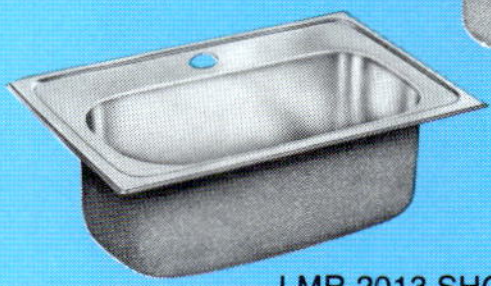

LMR-2013 SHOWN

Pacemaker Starlite® BAR SINK

BPSR-2317 SHOWN

CELEBRITY® BAR SINK

BCR-15 SHOWN

MODEL NUMBER	OVERALL SIZE L	OVERALL SIZE W	INSIDE COMPARTMENT SIZE L	W	D	DRAIN-BOARD LENGTH
GOURMET COLLECTION						
BILGR-2115-L	21	15	11½	11½	6½	7¾
BILGR-2115-R	21	15	11½	11½	6½	7¾
BLGR-1515	15	15	11½	11½	6½	—
Suffix L (left) or R (right) denote sink compartment is to left or right of drainboard						
LUSTERTONE						
BLR-15	15	15	12	9¼	7	—
LMR-2013	19½	13	15¾	7½	6	—
PACEMAKER/STARLITE						
BPSR-2317	23	17	9¼	12 (each compartment)	6	—
CELEBRITY						
BCR-15	15	15	12	10	6	—

ALL DIMENSIONS IN INCHES
L (LENGTH, LEFT TO RIGHT), W (WIDTH, FRONT TO BACK), D (BOWL DEPTH)

STAINLESS STEEL SINKS

Lustertone® HIGHEST QUALITY
18 GAUGE • TYPE 302 • SELF RIM

SINKETTE SELECTION

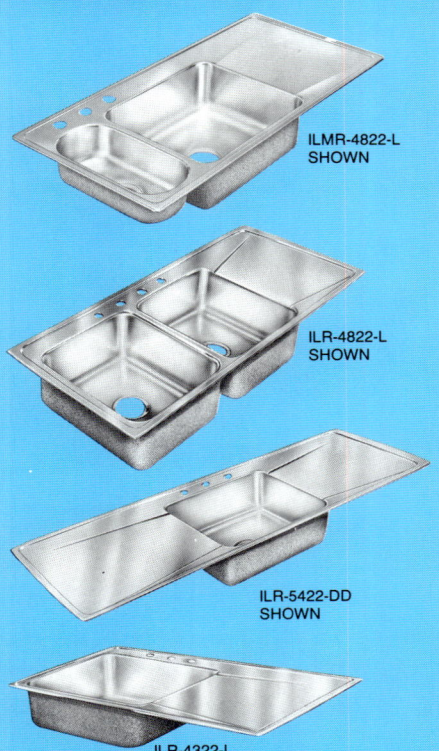

ILMR-4822-L SHOWN

ILR-4822-L SHOWN

ILR-5422-DD SHOWN

ILR-4322-L SHOWN

SINK TOP SELECTION

D-6029 SHOWN

S-4819-L SHOWN

Lustertone® HIGHEST QUALITY
18 GAUGE • TYPE 302 • SELF RIM

CLASSROOM DRINKING FOUNTAIN WITH SINK SELECTION

DRKR-3717-R-C SHOWN

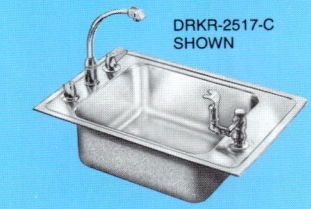

DRKR-2517-C SHOWN

DEEP SINK SELECTION

DLR-2522-10 SHOWN

DLFR-2519-10 SHOWN NO FAUCET LEDGE

Lustertone® HIGHEST QUALITY
18 GAUGE • TYPE 302 • SELF RIM

LAVATORY SELECTION

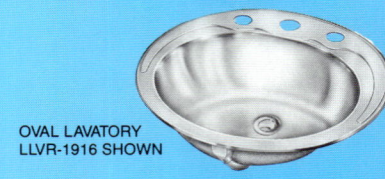

OVAL LAVATORY LLVR-1916 SHOWN

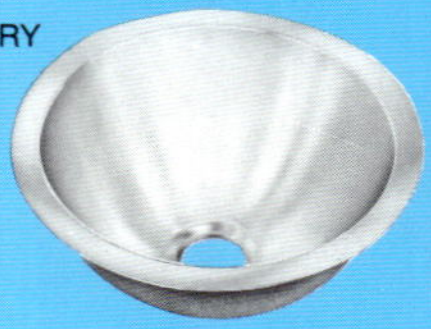

ROUND LAVATORY RLR-9 SHOWN

Pacemaker Starlite® FINE QUALITY
20 GAUGE • TYPE 302 • SELF RIM

LAVATORY SELECTION

RECTANGULAR LAVATORY PSLVR-1917-CS SHOWN

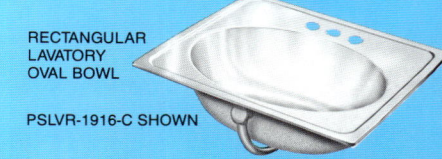

RECTANGULAR LAVATORY OVAL BOWL PSLVR-1916-C SHOWN

MODEL NUMBER	OVERALL SIZE		INSIDE EACH COMPARTMENT						DRAIN-BOARD LENGTH
			LEFT			RIGHT			
	L	W	L	W	D	L	W	D	
SINKETTE—DOUBLE COMPARTMENT									
ILMR-4822-L	48	22	7½	15¾	5	19	16	7½	18⅝
ILR-4822-L	48	22	13½	16	7½	13½	16	7½	17⅞
ILR-4822-R	48	22	13½	16	7½	13½	16	7½	17⅞
SINKTOP—DOUBLE COMPARTMENT									
D-6029	60	22	16	16	7½	16	16	7½	15⁷⁄₁₆

MODEL NUMBER	OVERALL SIZE		INSIDE COMPARTMENT SIZE			DRAIN-BOARD LENGTH
	L	W	L	W	D	
SINKETTE—SINGLE COMPARTMENT						
ILR-5422-DD	54	22	22	16	7½	16
ILR-4322-L	43	22	22	16	7½	19½
ILR-4322-R	43	22	22	16	7½	19½
ILR-3322-L	33	22	16	16	7½	15
ILR-3322-R	33	22	16	16	7½	15
SINKTOP—SINGLE COMPARTMENT						
S-4819-L	48	25	19	16	7½	26
S-4819-R	48	25	19	16	7½	26

NOTE: MODELS WITH SUFFIX "L" OR "R" DENOTES SINK COMPARTMENT IS TO LEFT OR RIGHT OF DRAINBOARD.

MODEL NUMBER	OVERALL SIZE		INSIDE EACH COMPARTMENT					
			LEFT			RIGHT		
	L	W	L	W	D	L	W	D
•FOUNTAIN WITH SINK—DOUBLE COMPARTMENT								
DRKR-3717-L-C	37¼	17	9¼	12	3½	16	11½	7½
DRKR-3717-R-C	37¼	17	16	11	7½	9¼	12	3½
SUFFIX "L" OR "R" DENOTES FOUNTAIN BOWL LOCATION								

MODEL NUMBER	OVERALL SIZE		INSIDE COMPARTMENT SIZE		
	L	W	L	W	D
• FOUNTAIN WITH SINK—SINGLE COMPARTMENT					
DRKR-2517-C	25	17	16	13½	7½
DEEP SINKS—WITH FAUCET LEDGE					
DLR-1722-10	17	22	13½	16	10
★ DLR-1919-10	19½	19	16	13½	10
DLR-2222-10	22	22	19	16	10
DLR-2222-12	22	22	19	16	12
DLR-2522-10	25	22	21	15¾	10
DLR-2522-12	25	22	21	15¾	12
DLR-3122-12	31	22	28	16	11½
DEEP SINKS—WITHOUT FAUCET LEDGE					
DLFR-1917-10	19	17	16	13½	10
DLFR-2519-10	25	19½	21	15¾	10
DLFR-2519-12	25	19½	21	15¾	12

•Classroom sinks available with or without fittings
★ Sound Guard Insulation

In keeping with our policy of continuing product improvement, Elkay reserves the right to change product specifications without notice.

MODEL NUMBER	OVERALL SIZE		INSIDE BOWL SIZE		
	L	W	L	W	D
LUSTERTONE • OVAL LAVATORY					
LLVR-1916	19⅝	16¾	15½	11⅜	6
LLVR-1916-CS*	19⅝	16¾	15½	11⅜	6
LUSTERTONE • ROUND LAVATORY					
RLR-9	11⅜ Dia.		9 Diameter x 4 Deep		
RLR-12	14⅜ Dia.		12 Diameter x 6 Deep		
PACEMAKER/STARLIGHT RECTANGULAR LAVATORY					
PSLVR-1917	19	17	16	11½	6
PSLVR-1917-CS*	19	17	16	11½	6
RECTANGULAR LAVATORY • OVAL BOWL					
PSLVR-1916	19	17	15½	11⅜	6
PSLVR-1916-CS*	19	17	15½	11⅜	6

*Faucet holes are on 2 inch centers

ALL DIMENSIONS IN INCHES
L (LENGTH, LEFT TO RIGHT), W (WIDTH, FRONT TO BACK), D (BOWL DEPTH).

FOR COMPLETE INFORMATION ON ELKAY STAINLESS STEEL SINKS AND FAUCETS SEE CATALOG NO CS-11.

ELKAY MANUFACTURING COMPANY
2222 CAMDEN COURT • OAKBROOK, IL 60521
PHONE: 708/574-8484 • TELEX: RCA 289234
DIRECT CUSTOMER SERVICE NUMBER:
708/572-3192

(REV. 9/90) F-2035

■■■ Franke Elements™ undermount sink components

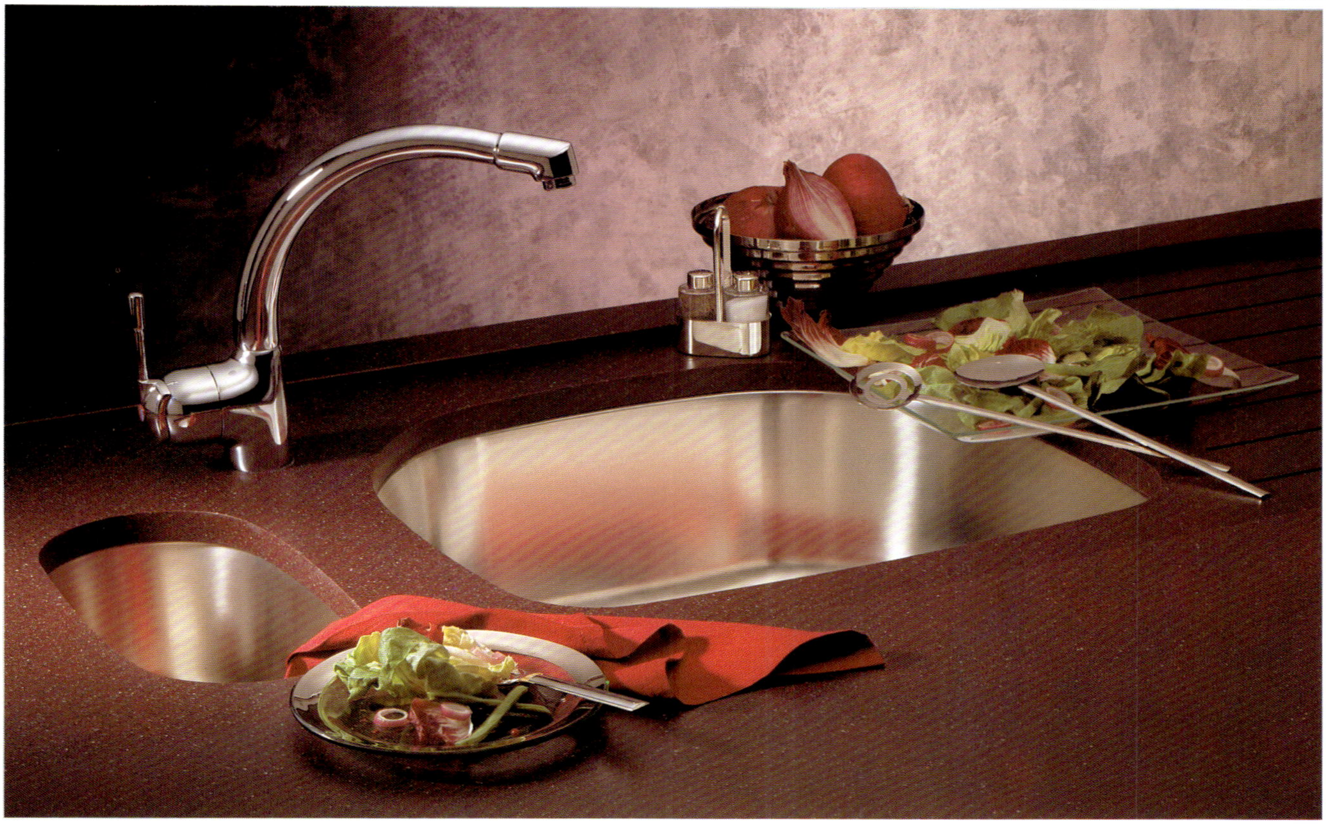

■■■ Modern times, modern methods. The contemporary appeal of granite, marble, and man-made solid surfacing materials inspired Franke to develop a line of stainless steel sink components that mount below these countertop surfaces, in any desired configuration.

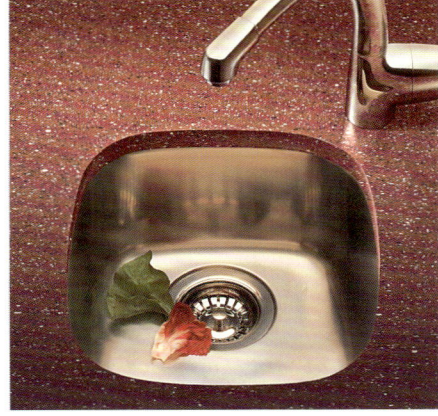

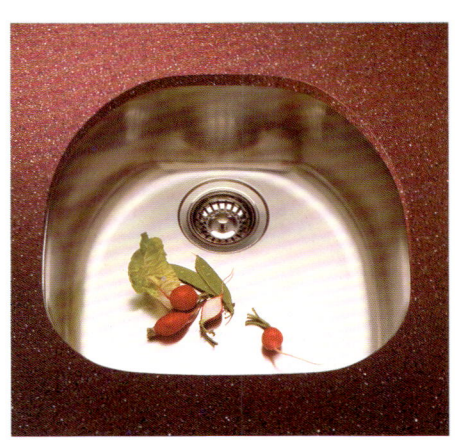

Franke, Inc.
Kitchen Systems Division
P.O. Box 428
Hatfield, PA 19440

FRANKE®

Kitchen Sinks
Faucets
Accessories
Hot Water Dispensers

■ Technology ■ Quality ■ Design

■■■ Elements.™ Components, accessories.

■■■ **ER 110** Highly polished, sculptural salad sink. Large enough for kitchen chores— stunning on an island—yet a perfect size for bar installations, too. Beautiful in pairs, or in combination with other Element components.
Overall dimensions: 16⅛″ diameter

■■■ Opposite page: Prestige™ Element components.
PR 110-21 Main sink compartment
Overall dimensions: 21¼″ x 18¾″
PR 110-7 Elliptical side compartment
Overall dimensions: 7⅛″ x 14³⁄₁₆″
EO 110 Square side compartment
Overall dimensions: 11¾″ x 13⅜″
NA 110 Nobel™ component
Overall dimensions: 16½″ x 16½″

■■■ **EP 110-13** Square bowl with a hi-tech look that blends decorously with stainless appliances. Optional stainless accessories complete the look.
Overall dimensions: 13⅜″ x 15¾″

■■■ **EP 110-6** Rectangular scrap sink to team with EP 110-13 or place individually— perhaps next to your chopping block?
Overall dimensions: 6¼″ x 11¹³⁄₁₆″

■■■ The accessory options
For **ER 110**
ER 30W White grid drainer
ER 50W White drain basket
ER 40S Teak cutting board
ER 40W White synthetic cutting board
　　　(not shown)
For **EP 110-13**
EP 30 Stainless grid drainer
EP 50 Stainless drain basket
EP 40W White synthetic cutting board
EP 40S Teak cutting board
　　　(not shown)
For **EP 110-6**
EP 70 Stainless colander

Standard Prestige™ accessories may be ordered for Prestige undermount Elements.

Standard Nobel™ accessories may be ordered for NA 110 undermount.

Elements photographed in Avonite®

monARCH TiLE®

Because well-dressed homes are back in tile.™

1991

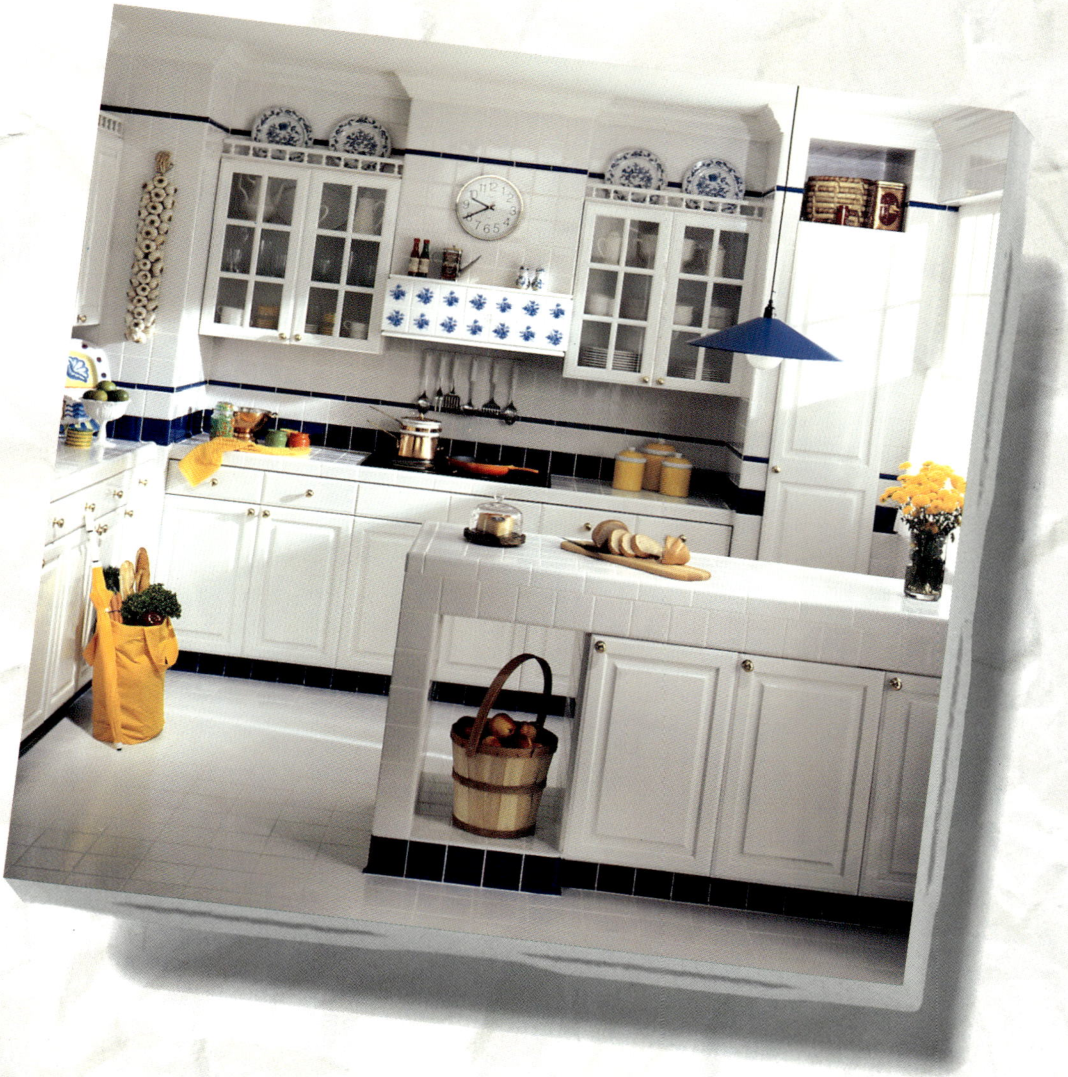

As interior design trends come and go, one material remains at the height of style — ceramic tile. Tile is versatile, durable and attractive; and as architects, designers, builders, homeowners, contractors and remodelers, the decision falls to you on color, finish, pattern and materials. Monarch Tile, Inc. is the name behind some of the most popular ceramic tiles available today. Our products are used for residential and commercial applications ranging from the most luxurious private bath, to heavily used, high traffic commercial areas.

We recognize that our past growth and future success depend on our ability to understand current trends and anticipate the future needs of our customers. We believe that the most important objective we have is to provide excellent quality in our product and in our service.

We design, test and manufacture our tile to the most exacting requirements, and our products meet or exceed every applicable industry standard. This is important to our customers. They know they receive only the best quality tile from Monarch. Tile that will retain its beauty for years to come.

We are continually developing new products, colors, and textures to meet the demands of the marketplace. In fact, we have become the choice of many demanding designers, architects, remodelers and homeowners because of our ability to anticipate market trends and coordinate with other manufacturers' products.

Monarch Tile has been manufacturing and distributing quality ceramic tile products for 45 years. We are one of the fastest growing tile manufacturers in our industry, with worldwide facilities. We will maintain our growth by continuing to make customer commitment our primary objective.

We have representatives and distributor locations nationwide, ready to serve you. So if you need any information, just look in the back of this catalog for the sales representative in your area.

On the cover: Designers depend on us to carry just the right shade of that new, hot color. This year, that new color is white, and on the cover you'll see one of our contributions to this year's designs — Ice, from the Brite Glaze line.

©1991, Monarch Tile, Inc.

Specifications

Series Name	Use	Sizes Available	Finish	Water Absorption	Breaking Strength	Thermal Shock	Frost Resistant	Thickness	Glaze Hardness	Rating**	Pg.
Vision™	Walls Floors	Nom. 8" x 8" Act. 7³/₄" x 7³/₄" Nom. 12" x 12" Act. 11³/₄" x 11³/₄"	Matte Polished*	Impervious .5% Max. ASTM C-373	Avg. 250 PSI ASTM C-648		Yes ASTM C-1026	⁵/₁₆"		ABCDE	3
Safari Series®	Walls	4" x 4" 6" x 6"**	Glazed Matte Impressed	Non-vitreous Avg. 13% ASTM C-373	Avg.130 Lbs. ASTM C-648	Resistant ASTM C-484	No ASTM C-1026	Nominal ³/₈" ASTM C-499	Avg. 6.5-7.0† Moh's scale	E	4-5
Candlelight®	Floors	6" x 6"	Glazed Matte	Non-vitreous Avg. 13% ASTM C-373	Avg.130 Lbs. ASTM C-648	Resistant ASTM C-484	No ASTM C-1026	Nominal ⁵/₁₆" ASTM C-499	Avg. 6.5-7.0† Moh's scale	DE	6
Shadows®	Walls	4¹/₄" x 4¹/₄" 6" x 6"	Glazed Glossy	Non-vitreous Avg. 13% ASTM C-373	Avg. 130 Lbs. ASTM C-648	Resistant ASTM C-484	No ASTM C-1026	Nominal ⁵/₁₆" ASTM C-499	Avg. 5.5-6.0† Moh's scale	E	7
Millstone®	Walls Floors	4¹/₄" x 4¹/₄" 6" x 6" 1" x 6" Liner	Glazed Matte Rock-faced	Non-vitreous Avg. 13% ASTM C-373	Avg.130 Lbs. ASTM C-648	Resistant ASTM C-484	No ASTM C-1026	Nominal ⁵/₁₆" ASTM C-499	Avg. 6.5-7.0† Moh's scale	E	8
Millbrite®	Walls	4¹/₄" x 4¹/₄" 1" x 6" Liner	Glazed Glossy Rock-faced	Non-vitreous Avg. 13% ASTM C-373	Avg.130 Lbs. ASTM C-648	Resistant ASTM C-484	No ASTM C-1026	Nominal ⁵/₁₆" ASTM C-499	Avg. 6.0-6.5† Moh's scale	E	9
Brite Glaze®	Walls	4¹/₄" x 4¹/₄"	Glazed Glossy	Non-vitreous Avg. 13% ASTM C-373	Avg.130 Lbs. ASTM C-648	Resistant ASTM C-484	No ASTM C-1026	Nominal ⁵/₁₆" ASTM C-499	Avg. 6.0-6.5† Moh's scale	E	10
Kristaline®	Walls Floors	4¹/₄" x 4¹/₄" 4" Hexagon 6" x 6"	Glazed Textured	Non-vitreous Avg. 13% ASTM C-373	Avg.130 Lbs. ASTM C-648	Resistant ASTM C-484	No ASTM C-1026	Nominal ⁵/₁₆" ASTM C-499	Avg. 6.0-6.5† Moh's scale	E	11
Monticello®	Walls	4¹/₄" x 4¹/₄" 6" x 6"	Glazed Hammered	Non-vitreous Avg. 13% ASTM C-373	Avg.130 Lbs. ASTM C-648	Resistant ASTM C-484	No ASTM C-1026	Nominal ⁵/₁₆" ASTM C-499	Avg. 6.0-6.5† Moh's scale	E	11
Sparklers™	Walls	1" x 6" Rope Molding ¹/₂" x 6" Liner	Glazed Glossy	Non-vitreous Avg. 13% ASTM C-373	Avg.130 Lbs. ASTM C-648	Resistant ASTM C-484	No ASTM C-1026	Nominal ⁵/₁₆" ASTM C-499	Avg. 6.0-6.5† Moh's scale	E	12
Pizzazz Accents®	Walls	4¹/₄" x 4¹/₄" 1" x 6" Liner	Glazed Glossy	Non-vitreous Avg. 13% ASTM C-373	Avg.130 Lbs. ASTM C-648	Resistant ASTM C-484	No ASTM C-1026	Nominal ⁵/₁₆" ASTM C-499	Avg. 6.0-6.5† Moh's scale	E	13
Regatta Series®	Walls	4" x 4"	Glazed Glossy Impressed	Non-vitreous Avg. 13% ASTM C-373	Avg.130 Lbs. ASTM C-648	Resistant ASTM C-484	No ASTM C-1026	Nominal ³/₈" ASTM C-499	Avg. 5.0-5.5† Moh's scale	E	14
Matte Glaze®	Walls	4¹/₄" x 4¹/₄" 6" x 6"	Glazed Matte	Non-vitreous Avg. 13% ASTM C-373	Avg.130 Lbs. ASTM C-648	Resistant ASTM C-484	No ASTM C-1026	Nominal ⁵/₁₆" ASTM C-499	Avg. 6.0-6.5† Moh's scale	E	15
Lunar®	Walls	4¹/₄" x 4¹/₄" 6" x 6"	Glazed Mottled	Non-vitreous Avg. 13% ASTM	Avg.130 Lbs. ASTM C-648	Resistant ASTM C-484	No ASTM C-1026	Nominal ⁵/₁₆" ASTM C-499	Avg. 6.0-6.5† Moh's scale	E	15
Gallery Designs™	Walls	4¹/₄" x 4¹/₄" 6" x 6"	Glazed Matte and Glossy Decorated	Non-vitreous Avg. 13% ASTM C-373	Avg. 130 Lbs. ASTM C-648	Resistant ASTM C-484	No	See Specific Series	See Specific Series	E	16-19
Ceramic Mosaics®	Walls Floors	1" x 1" 2" x 2" Medley Patterns, Border Patterns	Unglazed Porcelain Ceramic Mosaics	Impervious ASTM C-373	Avg. 250 PSI ASTM C-648		Yes ASTM C-1026	Nominal ¹/₄"		ABCDE	20

*Special Order
**Rating
A Extra heavy use, intensive foot traffic and 300 lb. loads on rubber wheels.
B Heavy use or intensive foot traffic.
C Normal use or heavy indoor/outdoor traffic.
D Moderate use or light indoor domestic traffic.
E Very moderate use or light indoor traffic without abrasion.

†Monarch Tile Specification

All Monarch products meet or exceed the American National Standard Specification for Ceramic Tile, ANSI A137.1-1988, and are certified as meeting the highest quality standards. A Master Grade certificate is available upon request. Shade variation is inherent in all fired clay products. Refer to actual samples prior to specification. For detailed specifications or technical information, contact your nearest sales representative.

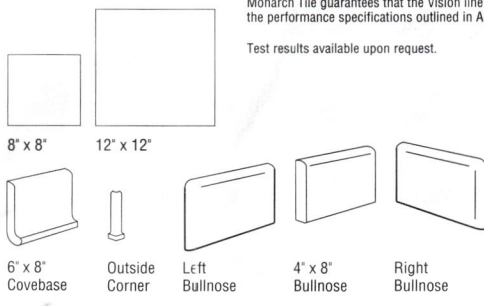

Residential entryway. Floor tile: Vision Series, 4031 Llama.

4010 Angora

4000 Raven

4076 Colonial Blue

4026 Cameo

4034 Cinnabar

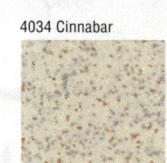

4075 Sapphire

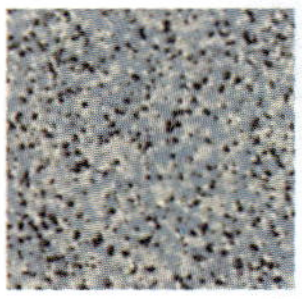

4031 Llama

NEW! VISION

Monarch has taken another step forward and landed on Vision, our new porcelain floor tile. Vision, a sophisticated addition to any room, is stronger than natural granite. Independent testing has proved Vision to be the toughest, most durable and most perfectly formed porcelain available. It is, by far, more resistant to abrasion than glazed tile or unglazed pavers.

Carefully controlled processes, special porcelain body and stringent quality control measures ensure a fully vitrified porcelain tile with through-bodied color that never fades. Also, because Vision is virtually impervious to moisture, it naturally resists stains.

Available in matte and polished finishes*, Vision is recommended for interior and exterior walls and interior floors. Any place you'd like to add some refinement, put down Vision… and step on it!

*Polished finishes available on special order only.

Performance Data	Requirements	VISION™	ASTM Testing
Abrasive Wear	100 Min.	244	C501
Bond Strength	50 psi Min.	154 psi	C482
Coefficient of Friction (Unpol shed)	.5 Min.	.86*	C2018
Facial Dimension (Range)	1.5% Max.	.13%	C499
Range of Thickness	.040" Max.	±.011"	C499
Warpage (Diagonal)	±.75% Max.	.11%	C485
Wedging	1.00% Max.	.37%	C502

* Like any material, Monarch porcelain tends to become slippery when wet; we recommend that care to be taken to keep the surface dry.

Monarch Tile guarantees that the Vision line meets or exceeds the performance specifications outlined in ANSI A137-1-1980.

Test results available upon request.

8" x 8"

12" x 12"

6" x 8" Covebase

Outside Corner

Left Bullnose

4" x 8" Bullnose

Right Bullnose

913 Almond Bark

983 Gray Dawn

934 Gazelle

912 White Tiger

936 African Sand

SAFARI

From the jungles of Africa to the counters of your kitchen. The Safari Series brings in the colors of the wild — the neutrals of the windblown plains, the white of cool linen. The glazed matte, rolling surface of the tile hints of the natural texture of the land.

The Safari Series was designed for use as residential counters and backsplashes, but is tough enough for commercial walls.

Residential kitchen, San Antonio, Texas.
Countertop and backsplash: 4"x 4"
Safari Series, 913 Almond Bark.

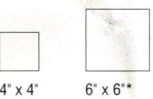

4" x 4"   6" x 6"**

*Special order only. Inquire for availability.

NEW SAFARI COLORS

Now you can explore the wonder of tile with some exciting *new* colors from the Safari Series. With the same glazed matte finish and rolling surface, the new Safari colors coordinate well with the original Safari colors, as well as with appliances and other products. When you're on the hunt for just the right tile, outfit yourself with the Safari Series.

Five new Safari Series colors, clockwise from top left: 923 Apple Blossom, 963 Abyss, 992 Honeysuckle, 974 Riviera, 926 Savannah.

963 Abyss-New

974 Riviera-New

926 Savannah-New

992 Honeysuckle-New

923 Apple Blossom-New

823 Pale Mauve

831 Almond

836 Wet Sand

885 Sterling

878 Blue Cloud

826 Coral Dust

CANDLELIGHT

You're lying in the bath, relaxed, almost asleep. Bubbles cover the water's surface the length of the bathtub. You open your eyes slightly and you've been transported to a beach at sunset. But then you realize you're really at home, surrounded by beautiful Candlelight tile.

In Candlelight, you'll find the same colors as in the Shadows Series, but with a matte finish, increasing your coordination options. Candlelight is a good choice for commercial walls and residential applications — bathroom walls, tub and shower surrounds, countertops, and even light residential flooring.

Residential bath and dressing room, Las Vegas, Nevada. Tub surround and floor: 6"x 6" Candlelight, 836 Wet Sand. Walls: 6"x 6" Shadows, 436 Wet Sand.

6" x 6"

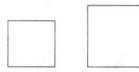

SHADOWS

They may be experts at ice cream, but this store also knows its tile. They chose the Shadows line — a wise decision. Shadows is great for interior walls, entryways, lobbies, counter fronts and countertops. Or use Shadows for residential kitchen and bath countertops, entryway walls and other vertical applications.

The Shadows line and the Candlelight Series are Monarch's most distinctive tile groups. These products work together in total coordination through their colors and design.

Baskin-Robbins, Sarasota, Florida.
Walls: 6"x 6" Shadows, 423 Pale Mauve.

4¹/₄" x 4¹/₄"   6" x 6"

485 Sterling

478 Blue Cloud

423 Pale Mauve

431 Almond

436 Wet Sand

426 Coral Dust

727-S Santa Rosa Mauve

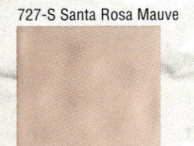

777-S Sierra Plains

772-S Sandia Blue

723-S Desert Shell

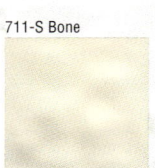

711-S Bone

710-S White

Painted Desert Sky

Painted Desert Terra

726-S Peach Bluff

736-S Mexican Sand

737-S Sandalwood

784-S Gray

MILLSTONE

We've taken the majestic shades of the Painted Desert at dawn, the natural tones of old Indian pottery, and the beautiful colors of handwoven blankets, and combined them in our top quality Millstone Series.

Millstone was designed for interior walls, countertops, vanity tops and residential floors. It coordinates well with the Millbrite Series, so your design options are greatly increased. In addition, two 1"x 6" diagonally striped multicolored liners add a touch of energy and even more color coordination possibilities.

Commercial Office Building. Walls: 4¼" x 4¼" Millstone 772-S Sandia Blue, 777-S Sierra Plains, 723-S Desert Shell, 727-S Santa Rosa Mauve with 1" x 6" Painted Desert Sky liner.

4¼" x 4¼"   6" x 6"

1" x 6" Available in Painted Desert Sky and Painted Desert Terra Only

MILLBRITE

The Southwest is alive in the Millbrite Series. Not the rustic roughness of the barren desert, but the contemporary, artistic spirit of the people. The wonderful colors of Millbrite combine with a high gloss finish, allowing more light to reflect and creating a polished look.

Bring the warmth of Millbrite to entryway walls, countertops, vanity tops, and commercial walls. Millbrite coordinates with Millstone for countless design options. Add the Painted Desert accent liners for an individualized design.

Residence. Bathroom walls, bathtub surround and countertop: 4¼" x 4¼" Millbrite, 183-S Tonto 172-S Sandia Blue, 123-S Desert Shell.

4¼" x 4¼"   1" x 6" Available in Painted Desert Sky and Painted Desert Terra Only

183-S Tonto

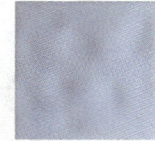
172-S Sandia Blue

123-S Desert Shell

113-S Almond

112-S Bone

Painted Desert Sky

Painted Desert Terra

127-S Santa Rosa Mauve

110-S White

126-S Peach Bluff

136-S Mexican Sand

BRITE GLAZE

197 Yellow

148 Butternut

185 Sterling**

117 Antique

110* White**

113 Almond

143 Gold Dust

172 Light Blue

111 Frost White

123 Pale Mauve

142 Pepper

124 Venetian Pink

114* Bone White

137 Sandalwood

126 Georgia Peach

136 Mexican Sand

178 Winter Blue

177 Regency Blue

119 Ice

BRITE GLAZE

Brighten up your space with Brite Glaze. Brite Glaze, an extensive collection of pastel colors with rich gloss, adds a light, airy feel to any setting. Designed for any interior vertical surfaces in commercial, institutional and residential settings, Brite Glaze is the standard, perfect for any application.

Brite Glaze, one of our top-of-the-line tiles, works well in both contemporary and traditional decor. It cleans up well, and coordinates with many other products.

4¹/₄" x 4¹/₄"   MS-1 Scored Tile

* 110 and 114 Mono-Score Pattern MS-1 are stocking items. No minimum order is required. All other Brite Glaze colors are offered in our Mono-Score Pattern MS-1 as special order with a 4500 square foot minimum requirement.

** Available in 1" x 6" liners

Good Shepherd Retirement Facility, Sun City, Arizona. Atrium planters: 4¹/₄" x 4¹/₄" Brite Glaze, 113 Almond and 136 Mexican Sand.

KRISTALINE

272 Light Blue 248 Butternut

237 Sandalwood 213 Almond

285 Sterling 243 Gold Dust

210 White 214 Bone White

278 Winter Blue 228 Sugar Plum

219 Ice 226 Georgia Peach

KRISTALINE

Here's a tile that will do it all — Kristaline. The glazed textured look can dress up a residential countertop, but it can also take the wear of most commercial and institutional vertical uses. In fact, Kristaline is a smart choice for everything from residential walls to light-duty commercial floors.

Kristaline is available in a variety of colors, sizes and shapes, so you can use your creativity to coordinate trim and accent pieces. Or use it to complement our Brite Glaze Series. Flexibility is your advantage with Kristaline.

Commercial Restroom. Walls: Kristaline 210 White with A106 and A107 Kristaline 272 Light Blue Accent trim.

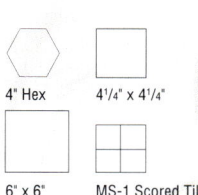

4" Hex 4¼" x 4¼"

6" x 6" MS-1 Scored Tile†

†All of our Kristaline colors are offered in our Mono-Score Pattern MS-1 as special order with a 4500 square foot minimum requirement.

MONTICELLO

You're looking for that classical, refined quality, but with a contemporary flair. You'll find it in the beautiful patterns of the Monticello line.

Monticello's colors and design create a certain tranquility, with its hammered texture and double-glazed finish. Use Monticello on your walls, countertops and vanity tops for a classic look.

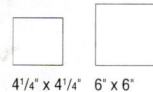

4¼" x 4¼" 6" x 6"

MONTICELLO

314 Linen

323 Peach 383 London Fog

336 Caramel 334 Maple

SPARKLERS

You can light up an entire room with just a few Sparklers. Sparklers are ceramic tile accent liners and rope moldings that mix and match to coordinate with your tile, fixtures, wallpaper and paint. Let the designer in you take over as you add color, dimension and style to your room.

Easy to install Sparklers come in 10 accent liner colors and 5 rope molding colors. Sparklers are recommended for interior installation on backsplashes, tub surrounds, showers, and other vertical surfaces. They are also a great way to cost effectively add color and luster to commercial surfaces.

Residential kitchen. Wall: 4¹/₄" x 4¹/₄" Brite Glaze Background, 110 White; Sparklers accent liners, DS11 Navy Blue and DS8 White; Sparklers rope molding, DS3 Hunter Green.

1" x 6" Rope Moldings — 5 colors; 3 pieces per pack

¹/₂" x 6" Liners — 10 colors; 10 pieces per pack

DS3 Hunter Green

DS8 White

DS9 Black

DS11 Navy Blue

DS17 Dusty Rose

DS2 Almond

DS4 Peach

DS18 Thunder Gray

DS1 Pastel Blue

DS51 Rose

DS3 Hunter Green

DS8 White

DS9 Black

DS17 Dusty Rose

DS11 Navy Blue

627 Burgundy°

600 Black Magic•

677 Royal Blue°

667 Hunter Green°

PIZZAZZ ACCENTS

These bold characters really pack a powerful punch. Whether you're going for high fashion or high tech, Pizzazz Accents are always high profile. The bright colors and glossy finish add a spark of excitement to any application.

Designed for residential and commercial interior walls and light-duty countertops, Pizzazz Accents take an ordinary wall and make it fun. The 1"x 6" liners* offer even more opportunities for design. Pizzazz Accents — because every wall needs a little pizzazz.

1" x 6"   4¼" x 4¼"

Price Group
• Group 1
° Group 2

*1" x 6" liners are also available in Brite Glaze colors 110 White and 185 Sterling.

Please note that care should be taken when using sanded grout with this tile, since abrasion of the glaze surface is possible.

Majestic Gyros, St. Peters, Missouri. Walls: 4¼" x 4¼" Pizzazz Accents, 677 Royal Blue; Brite Glaze 110 White.

627 Burgundy

600 Black Magic

677 Royal Blue

667 Hunter Green

625 African Violet

675 Teal

638 High Society Brown

623 Quince Blossom

BRITE GLAZE

110 White

185 Sterling

625 African Violet°

675 Teal°

638 High Society Brown°

623 Quince Blossom°

13

So, you've got the plans laid out for your tiled wall, and you know it will look great, but you wish there were some way to personalize it, to add an element of visual interest. That's what interesting trim or a feature design to exhibit your artistic talent.

Gallery Designs are a group of six collections of beautifully decorated tiles: the Country the Nature Scenes Collection, the Southwestern Collection, and the Borders Collection. Each group contains several designs, from single tiles to 12-tile murals.

The designs were carefully work in contemporary and traditional decor, and the colors coordinate with most interior settings. So add a touch of artistic beauty to your tile applications.

Center Insert

Outside Border Corner

Inside Border Corner

Straight Border

Straight Border with Bow
Background color: 110
Roses N' Ribbons also available on 710-S

TRELLIS 4¼" x 4¼"

Center Insert

Outside Border Corner

Inside Border Corner   Straight Border
Background color: 710-S Trellis also available on 110

COUNTRY DUCKS 4¼" x 4¼"

Insert B, Single Duck

Version A Trio Border

Two Ducks, Insert D (L)

Two Ducks, Insert C (R)
Background color: 110
Country Ducks also available on 710-S

COUNTRY COLLECTION

You don't have to have a white picket fence and blue shutters to enjoy the Country Collection tiles, but you may be reminded of a country cottage with these designs.

The Country Collection includes three groups of designs, each with border and insert pieces. This charming Series was designed to adorn walls and countertops.

Residence. Bathroom Walls: 4¼" x 4¼" Gallery Designs, 110 Roses N' Ribbons. Field Tile: 4¼" x 4¼" 110 Brite White. Floor: 1" Hex Monarch Ceramic Mosaics, 1806 White.

MUSHROOMS 4¼" x 4¼"

Background color: 711-S
Mushrooms also available on 110 and 113

BOTANICAL BERRIES 4¼" x 4¼"

Background color: 110
Botanical Berries also available on 711-S and 712

STILL LIFE 4¼" x 4¼"

Background color: 711-S
Still Life also available on 110 and 113

BERRIES 4¼" x 4¼"

Background color: 110
Berries also available on 711-S and 712

FRUIT BASKET DELIGHT 4¼" x 4¼"

Peach   Pear

Peach-Multi-Grapes   Peach Trio

Apple

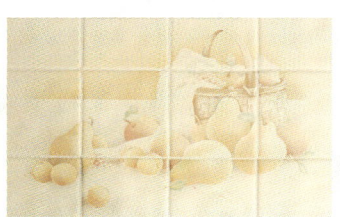

Fruit Basket Delight Mural Background color: 711-S
Individual Fruit Basket Delight and Mural are also
available on 110 and 712

DELICIOUS FRUITS 4¼" x 4¼"

Background color: 711-S
Delicious Fruits also available on 110 and 712

Take a walk through a farmers' market in the summer, and you'll see the inspiration for the Life Styles Collection. This Series brings in the best of a fresh garden to commercial and residential tile applications.

These beautifully illustrated tiles are ideal for kitchen and bathroom walls. Choose from six groups of designs, all of which coordinate with almost any setting.

Residence. Kitchen Countertop: 4¼" x 4¼" Gallery Designs, 711-S Fruit Basket Delight Mural and matching decorative inserts. Field Tile: 4¼" x 4¼" Millstone, 711-S Bone.

FLORAL COLLECTION

Here's proof that wallflowers can be fun. These delicately hand-decorated floral designs will enhance a kitchen back-splash, countertop or shower wall — any place a bright spot is needed.

The Floral Collection is six groups of designs, from the contemporary Spring Poppies in three color combinations, to the traditional Field Flowers single tile designs. Bring a touch of spring into the room with the Floral Collection.

FIELD FLOWERS 6" x 6"

Background color: 711-S

BLUE DELFT ROSES 4¼" x 4¼"

Background color: 110
Blue Delft Roses also available on 710-S

SUMMER STRAW FLOWERS 4¼" x 4¼"

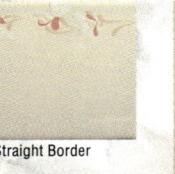 

Straight Border

Minimural

Outside Border, Right

Center Insert
Background color: 113
Summer Straw Flowers also available on 711-5

WILD ROSES 6" x 6"

Background color: 712

SPRING POPPIES - BLUE 4¼" x 4¼"

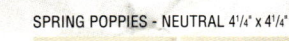

Background color: 110
Spring Poppies-Blue also available on 113

SPRING POPPIES - NEUTRAL 4¼" x 4¼"

Background color: 113
Spring Poppies-Neutral also available on 110

SPRING POPPIES - PINK 4¼" x 4¼"

Background color: 110
Spring Poppies-Pink also available on 113

LILIES OF THE FIELD 4¼" x 4¼"

Background color: 113
Lilies of the field also available on 713

NATURE SCENES COLLECTION

Just imagine a tranquil seascape at dusk, or a mountainous landscape in summer. Now imagine them on a beautiful entryway wall. The Nature Scenes Collection consists of four delicately illustrated seascapes and landscapes.

The Nature Scenes Collection is great for residential and commercial applications. The next time you want to create a light, relaxing atmosphere, try the Nature Scenes Collection.

DUNES 6" x 6"

Background color: 710-S
Dunes also available
on 711-S

SAILING 6" x 6"

Background color: 710-S
Sailing also available
on 711-S

CLIFFS 6" x 6"

Background color: 710-S
Cliffs also available
on 711-S

SEAGULLS 6" x 6"

Background color: 710-S
Seagulls also available
on 711-S

SOUTHWESTERN COLLECTION

One of the oldest symbols in American art is once again the rage. This flame stitch pattern has adorned Indian blankets for many years, and now it is available on tile.

This patterned wall and countertop tile is called Taos, and is available in center insert and straight border tiles.

Residence. Foyer: 4¼" x 4¼" Gallery Designs, 110 Taos, Center Insert.

BORDERS COLLECTION

White is hot this year, so you want to use it. But you also want it to have a little personality. Well, you've got to draw the line somewhere, so do it with the Borders Collection.

Two beautiful border groups will add dramatic highlights to walls, countertops and backsplashes. Choose from the Marble Borders or California Poppies.

Residence. Bathroom Walls: 6" x 6" Gallery Designs, California Poppies 712, Pink. Field Tile: 6" x 6" Matte Glaze, 712 Matte White. Floor Tile: 6" x 6" Candlelight, 823 Pale Mauve.

SOUTHWESTERN COLLECTION

TAOS 4¼" x 4¼"

Center Insert | Straight Border
Background color: 110
Taos also available on 113 and 711-S

BORDERS COLLECTION

CALIFORNIA POPPIES 6" x 6"

Insert, Blue | Insert, Pink

Straight Border, Blue | Straight Border, Pink

Straight Border, Blue, Flower | Straight Border, Pink, Flower
Background color: 712

MARBLE BORDERS 4¼" x 4¼"

Blue | Black

Rust | Gray
Background color: 110
Marble Borders also available on 712

Checkerboard Pattern
B-1, B-1A Field

Indian Blanket
B-2, B-2A Field

Greek Key
B-3, B-3A Field

Stripes-n-More
B-4, B-4A Field

1415 Blush* 2" X 2"

90 Destin 1" X 1"

1806 White* 2" x 2", 1" x 1"

1817 Silver Lining 2" x 2"

1730 Light Dove Gray* 2" x 2"

1740 Dark Dove Gray* 2" x 2"

1808 Bone* 2" x 2", 1" x 1"

1017 Regatta* 2" x 2"

1661 Parchment 2" x 2"

1001 Light Winter Blue 2" x 2"

1051 Midnight Blue* 2" x 2"

70 Platinum Gray 1" x 1"

1340 Creme D'Brim* 2" x 2"

48 Sea Shell 1" x 1"

1550 Pale Mauve* 2" x 2"

30 Corn Tassel 1" x 1"

1840 Black Pearl* 2" x 2"

68 Pewter 1" x 1"

1220 Seagull 2" x 2"

66 Thistle 1" x 1"

683 Tamara Range* 2" x 2"

1806 White* 1" Hex

10 Cayman 1" x 1"

2481 (681/683) 2" x 2"

1686 Pearl White 2" x 2"

1694 Mushroom 2" x 2"

1680 London Fog 2" x 2"

1692 Panama Beach 2" x 2"

1688 Malibu Sand* 2" X 2"

1440 Bisque 2" X 2"

CERAMIC MOSAICS

Remember the friendly neighborhood restaurant and bar, with the rich wood paneling and shiny brass accents? Where the pressure of the day disappeared as soon as you walked through the door. Now you can recreate that feel with Ceramic Mosaics.

Ceramic Mosaics are the most durable and versatile ceramic surfacing available — 20 colors, 8 medleys and 4 border patterns make them a great choice for custom work. Try a pastel pattern for a light, contemporary look. Designed for commercial, institutional and residential interior and exterior walls and floors, Ceramic Mosaics are stainproof, frostproof, fireproof, sanitary and impervious to moisture.

☐ 1" x 1"   ☐ 2" x 2"   ⬡ 1" Hex*

* Stocking colors; all other colors are special order.

Wayward Lady Restaurant, Corpus Christi, Texas. Field: 1" Hex Unglazed Ceramic Mosaics, 1806 White. Logo Style: 1" Hex, 1806 White, 1730 Light Dove Gray and 1740 Dark Dove Gray.

MTM 2010 Ceramic Tile Mastic. MTM 2010 is a multipurpose, synthetic, Type 1, acrylic latex-based mastic, manufactured for the interior installation of all types of vitreous and non-vitreous ceramic wall and floor tile on vertical or horizontal surfaces. Complies with ANSI A136. 1-1967.

MTM 4400 Type II Adhesive Ceramic Wall Tile Mastic. A non-flammable, latex-based ceramic wall tile mastic, manufactured for the interior installation of ceramic tile. Complies with ANSI A136. 1-1967.

MONARCH TILE TRIM AND ANGLE CHART

Number	Dimensions	Shadows	Candlelight	Pizzazz Accents	Regatta	Matte Glaze	Millstone	Brite Glaze	Kristaline	Mono-Score	Monticello	Millbrite	Safari	Lunar
Bullnose — For Conventional Mortar Installations														
A-3602	6" H x 6" L Cap					•	•	•	•		•	•		•
AN-3602	6" H x 6" L Out Angle					•	•	•	•		•	•		•
A-4200	2" H x 6" L Cap	•	•			•	•	•	•		•	•		•
AM-4200	2" H x 2" L Angle	•	•			•	•	•	•		•	•		•
AN-4200	2" H x 2" L Angle	•	•			•	•	•	•		•	•		•
A-4402	4¼" H x 4¼" L Cap			•		•	•	•	•	•	•	•		•
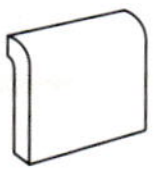 AM-4402	4¼" H x 4¼" L Angle			•		•	•	•	•	•	•	•		•
AN-4402	4¼" H x 4¼" L Angle			•		•	•	•	•	•	•	•		•
ABR/L-4402	4¼" H x 4¼" L Round in Angle					•	•	•	•		•	•		•
Bullnose — For Thin-Setting Bed Installations														
S-4249	2" H x 4" L Cap					•								•
S-4269	2" H x 4" L Cap					•	•		•		•	•		•
SM-4269	2" H x 2" L Angle					•	•		•		•	•		•
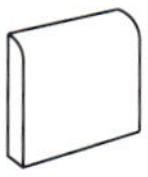 SN-4269	2" H x 2" L Angle					•	•	•	•		•	•		•
SMX-4269	2" H x 4¼" L Wrap Around					•	•		•		•	•		•
S-4449	4¼" H x 4¼" L Cap			•	•	•	•	•	•		•	•	•	•
SM-4449	4¼" H x 4¼" L Angle			•	•	•	•	•	•		•	•	•	•
SN-4449	4¼" H x 4¼" L Angle			•	•	•	•	•	•		•	•	•	•
S-4669	6" H x 6" L Cap	•	•			•	•	•	•		•	•		•
SM-4669	6" H x 6" L In Angle	•	•			•	•	•	•		•	•		•
SN-4669	6" H x 6" L Out Angle	•	•			•	•	•	•		•	•		•
Coves — For Conventional Mortar Installations														
A-3401	4¼" H x 4¼" L Cove Base			•		•	•	•	•	•	•	•		•
ACR/L-3401	4¼" H x 4¼" L Rad. Angle			•		•	•	•	•	•	•	•		•
AB-3401	4¼" H x 4¼" L Angle			•		•	•	•	•	•	•	•		•
A-3461	4¼" H x 6" L Cove Base	•	•			•	•	•	•		•	•		•
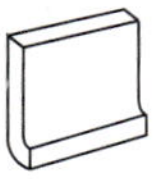 ACR/L-3461	4¼" H x 6" L Rad. Angle					•	•	•	•		•	•		•

Number	Dimensions	Shadows	Candlelight	Pizzazz Accents	Regatta	Matte Glaze	Millstone	Brite Glaze	Kristaline	Mono-Score	Monticello	Millbrite	Safari	Lunar
Coves — For Thin-Setting Bed Installations														
SCR/L-3401	4¼" H x 4¼" L Surface Angle			•		•	•	•	•		•	•		•
SCR/L-3461	4¼" H x 6" L Surface Angle	•				•	•		•		•	•		•
SCR/L-3601	6" H x 6" L Surf. Angle	•				•	•	•	•		•	•		•
Bases (Sanitary) Thin-Set														
S-3419	4¼" H x 6" L Rd. Top Cove		•			•	•	•	•		•	•	•	•
SCR/L-3419	4¼" H x 6" L		•			•	•	•	•		•	•		•
SB-3419	Block Angle					•	•	•	•		•	•		•
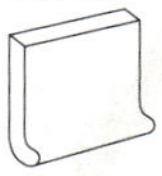 S3619	6" H x 6" L Rd. Top Cove					•	•	•	•		•	•		•
SCR/L-3619	6" H x 6" L Surf. Angle					•	•	•	•		•	•		•
SB-3619	¾" x ¾" x 6" In Angle					•	•	•	•		•	•		•
Curb Tile Double Bullnose														
A-7250	2½" H x 6" L Double Bullnose					•	•	•	•		•	•		•
ACR/L-7250	2½" H x 6" L Angle					•	•	•	•		•	•		•
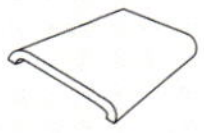 AKC-7250	2½" H x 6" L Angle					•	•	•	•		•	•		•
Quarter Round Beads														
A-104	1" W x 4" L Out Round		•				•							•
AC-104	1" W x 4" L Out Angle		•				•							
 A-106	1" W x 6" L Out Round	•	•	•		•	•	•	•		•	•		•
AC-106	1" W x 6" L Out Angle	•	•	•		•	•	•	•		•	•		•
AK-106	1" W x 1" L In Angle	•	•	•		•	•	•	•		•	•		•
AU-106	Sink Angle	•	•	•		•	•	•	•		•	•		•
Counter Trim														
A-8242	2⅜" x 2½" x 4 V Cap						•					•		•
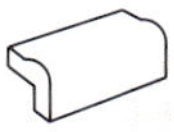 A-8262	2⅜" x 2½" x 6 V Cap	•	•	•		•	•	•	•		•	•		•
AM-8262	2½" H x 2½" L In Angle	•	•	•		•	•	•	•		•	•		•
AN-8262	2½" H x 2½" L Out Angle	•	•	•		•	•	•	•		•	•		•

POLISHED BRASS
CHROME

AMBASSADOR

areslux

ETCHED CRYSTAL
WITH MAHOGANY
BRACKETS
POLISHED BRASS
CHROME
WHITE
BLACK
GREY
RED
PINK
GARNET
BLUE
TEAL
NATURAL

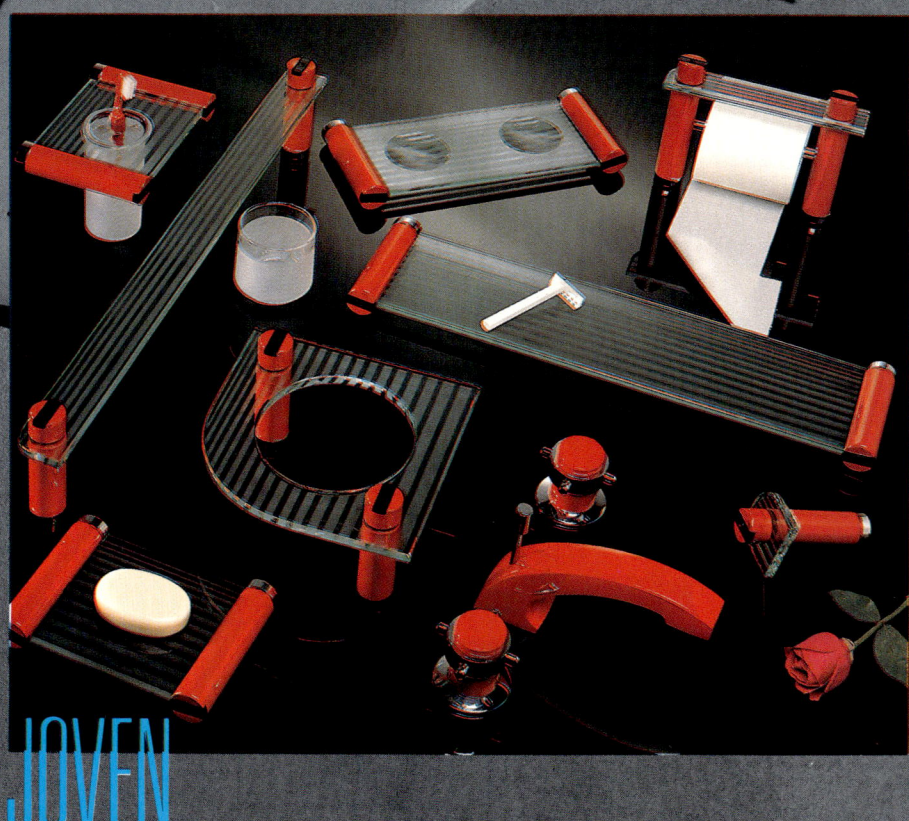

JOVEN

POLISHED BRASS
CHROME
CLEAR OR BRONZE
1/2" CRYSTAL

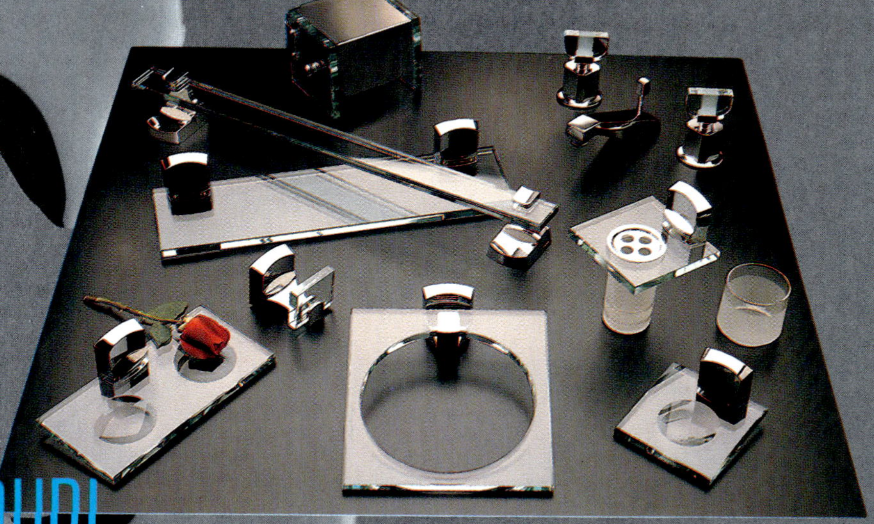

RUBI

areslux

POLISHED BRASS
CHROME
CLEAR OR BRONZE
3/8" CRYSTAL

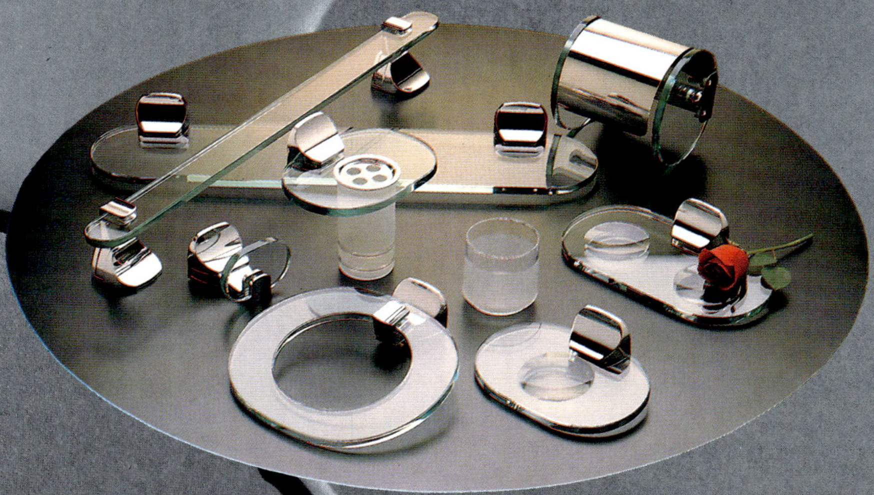

CRYSTALUX

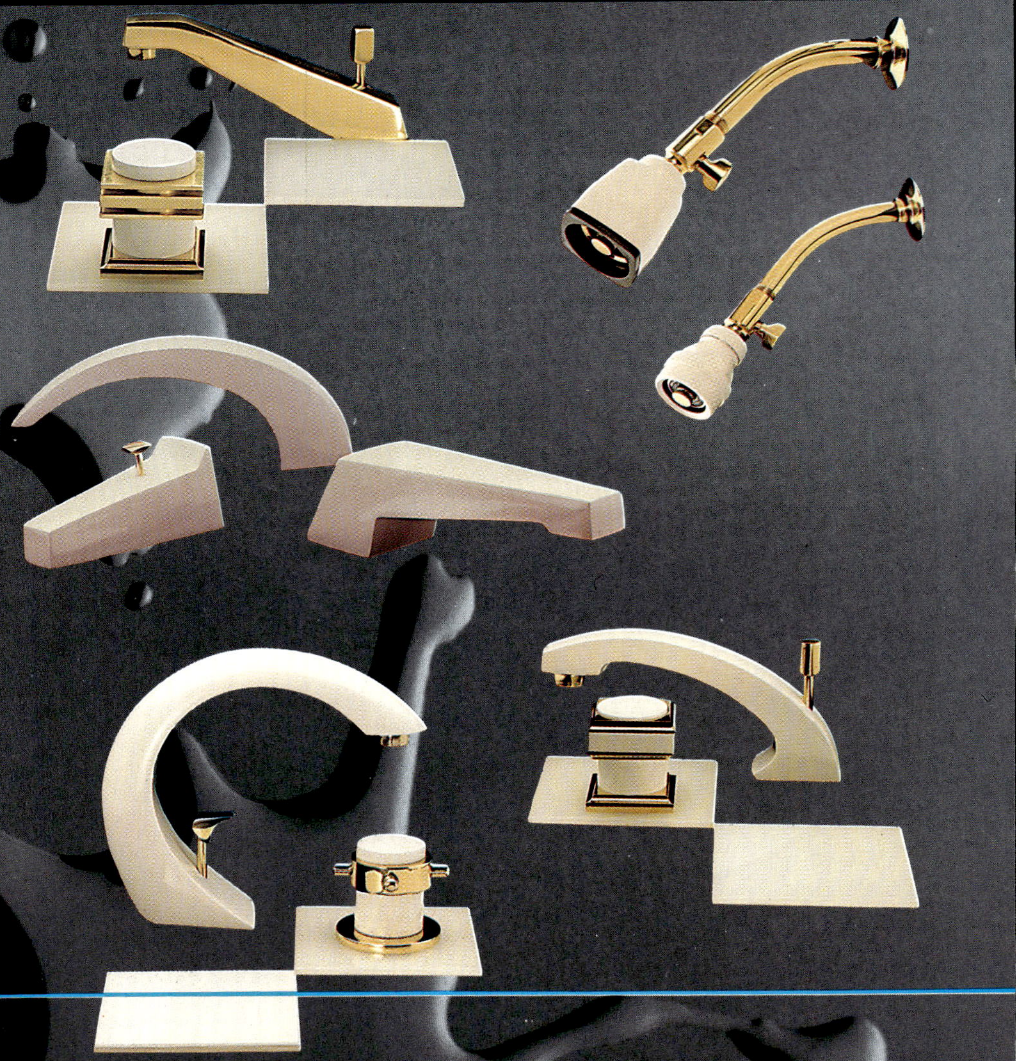

areslux

SPOUTS
HANDLES
ROMAN TUB SPOUT
SHOWERS
WALL SPOUT
POLISHED BRASS
CHROME
WHITE
BLACK
GREY
RED
PINK
GARNET
BLUE
NATURAL

8229 N.W. 66 ST. MIAMI, FL. 33166 TELE (800) 523-1564 (305) 5926126 TELEX 4948699 FAX 47775155

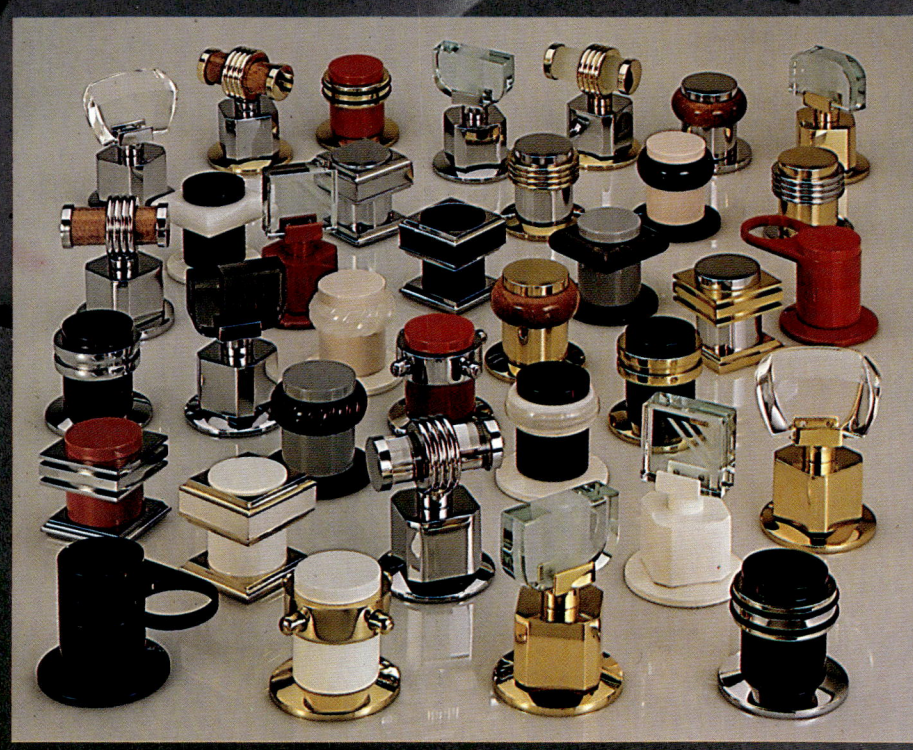

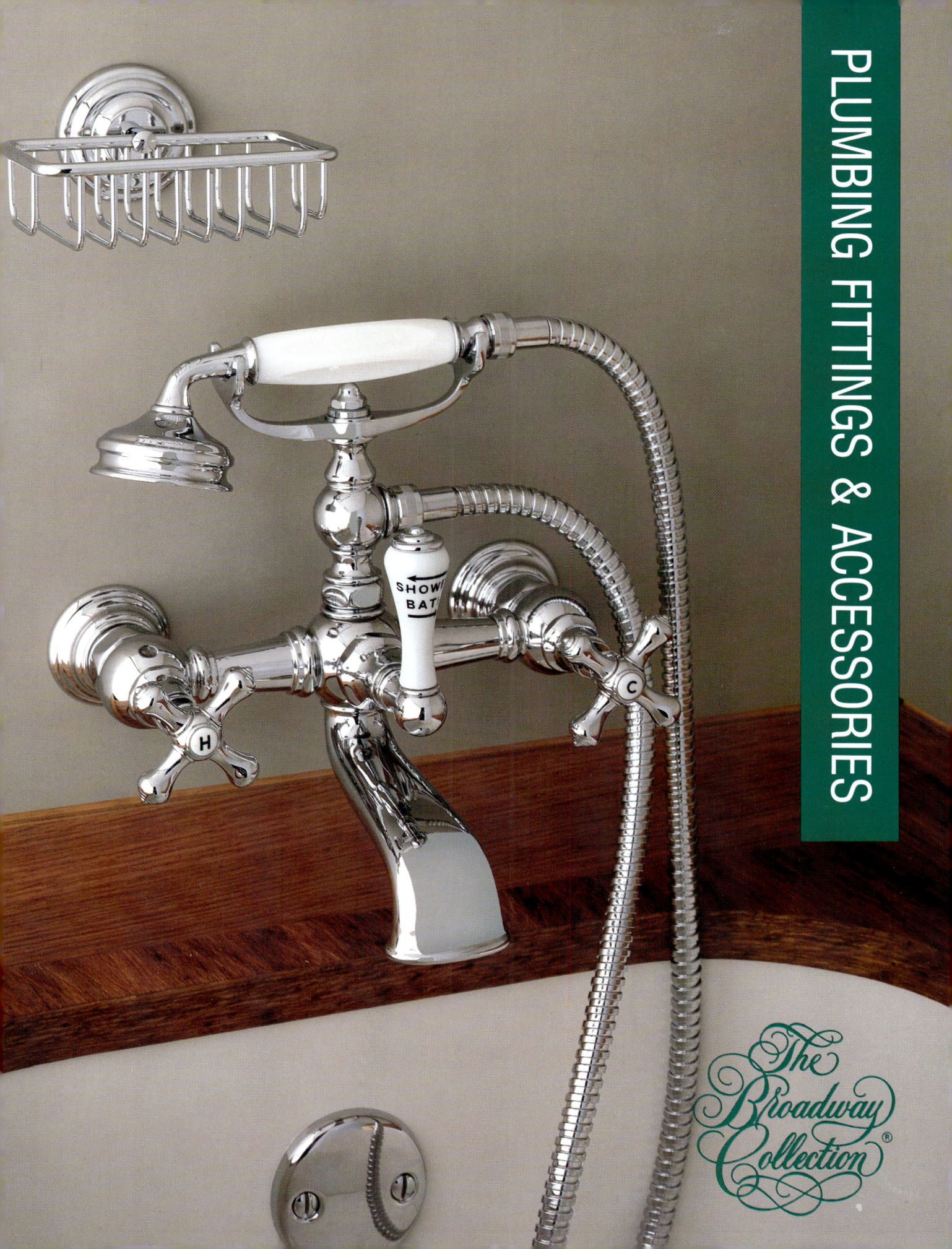

The Broadway Collection®

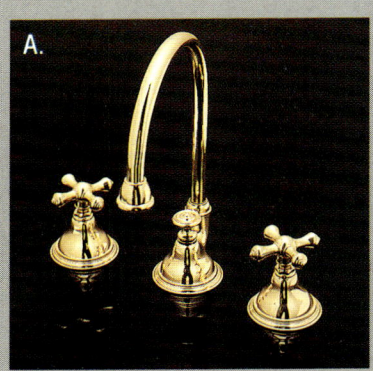
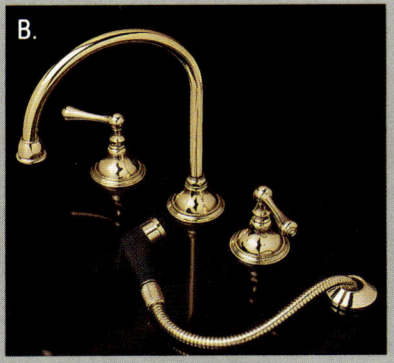

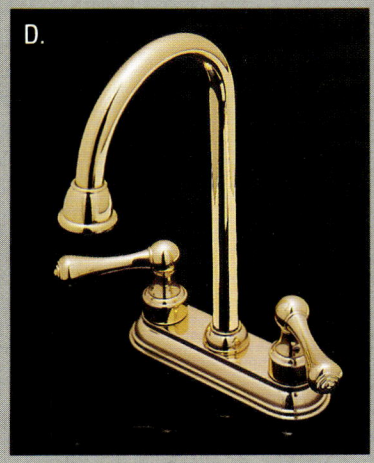

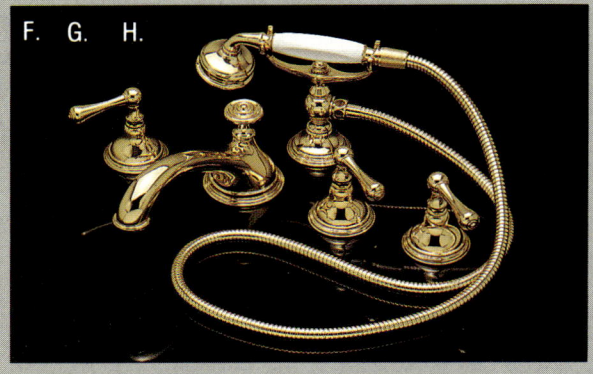

Old Dominion Suite®

A. 26.10254   Gooseneck Spreadset Faucet[1]

B. 26.10368   Kitchen Swivel Faucet with Hand Spray

C. 26.10047   Centerset Faucet[1]

D. 26.10296   Bar Faucet[1]

E. 26.10146   Spreadset Faucet[1]

F. 26.11090   Roman Tub Set, $3/4''$ [1,2]

G. 26.12144 $1/2''$ Diverter Valve

H. 38.10062   Deck Mount Cradle Hand Shower Set

I. 26.11629   Deck Mount Bidet Fitting for Kohler Fixture

    26.11650   for American Standard Fixture

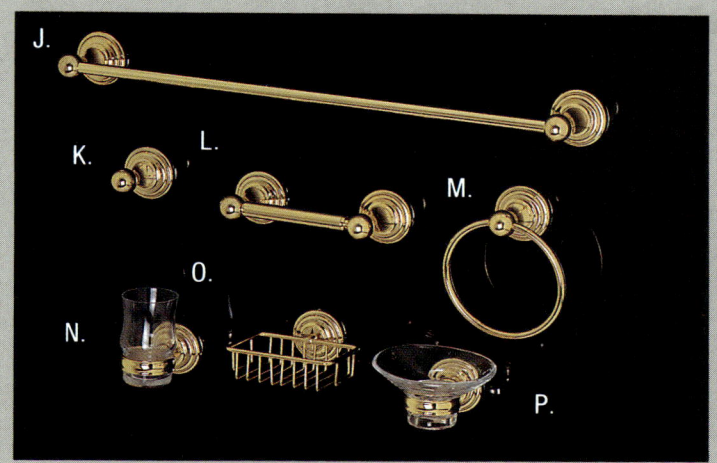

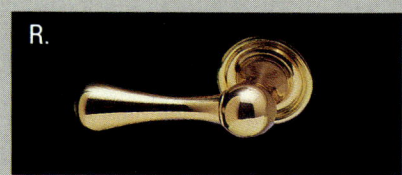

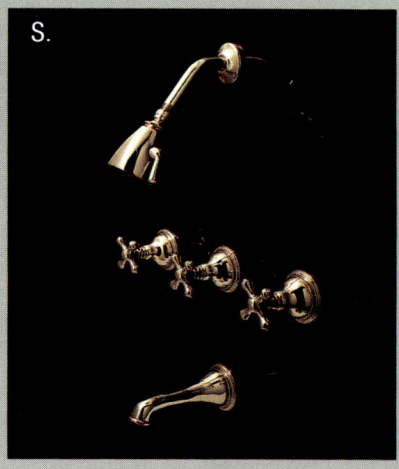

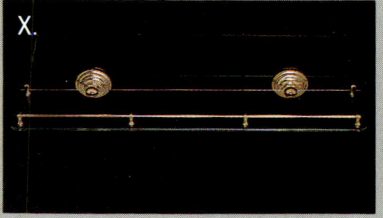

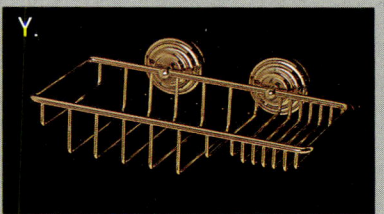

Old Dominion Suite®

J.	10.10031	18″ Towel Bar
	10.10032	24″ Towel Bar
	10.10033	30″ Towel Bar
K.	10.10111	Robe Hook
L.	10.10079	Paper Holder
M.	10.10096	Towel Ring
N.	10.10182	Tumbler with Holder
O.	10.10155	Soap Basket
P.	10.10135	Soap Dish with Holder
Q.	10.10255	Three Tier Towel Shelf
R.	10.10204	Tank Lever
S.	26.10768	Three Valve Tub & Shower[1]
T.	26.11550	Balance Pressure Tub & Shower[1]
U.	22.10074	1 $\frac{1}{2}$″ Right Hand Grab Bar
V.	22.10061	1″x 18″ Grab Bar
W.	22.10068	1 $\frac{1}{2}$″ x 18″ Grab Bar
X.	10.10193	Vanity Shelf
Y.	10.10156	Soap and Sponge Basket
Z.	10.10187	Recessed Tissue Holder

Finishes available: 031, 509, 605, 620, 625, 626.
[1]CSA criterion met. See Page 23.
[2]Available with $\frac{1}{2}$″ Valves.

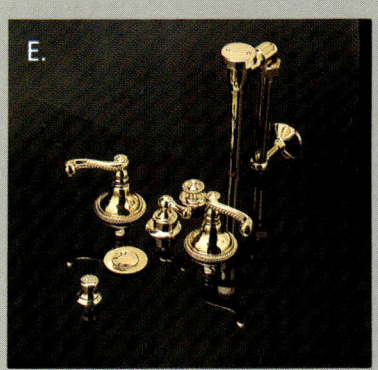

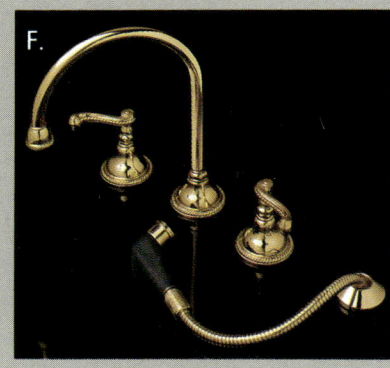

English Rope Suite®

A. 26.10023   Centerset Faucet[1]
B. 26.10230   Gooseneck Spreadset Faucet[1]
C. 26.10282   Bar Faucet[1]
D. 26.10110   Spreadset Faucet[1]
E. 26.11623   Deck Mount Bidet Fitting for Kohler Fixture
    26.11644   for American Standard Fixture
F. 26.10362   Kitchen Swivel Faucet with Hand Spray

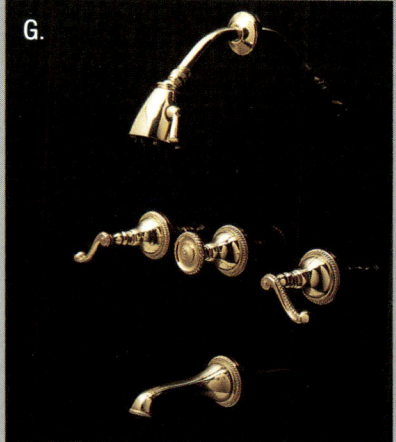

G.

H.

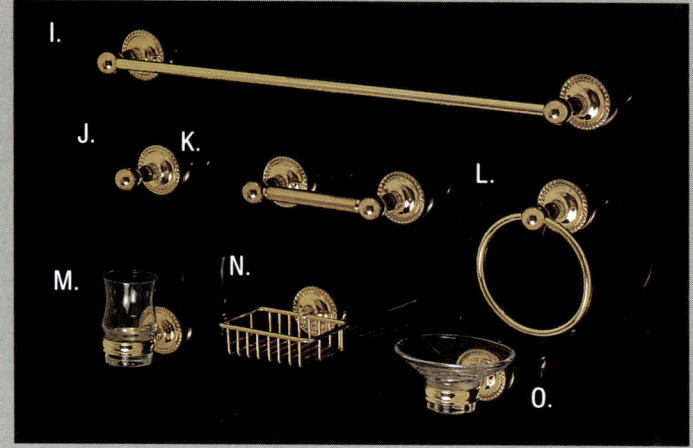

I.

J. K.

L.

M. N.

O.

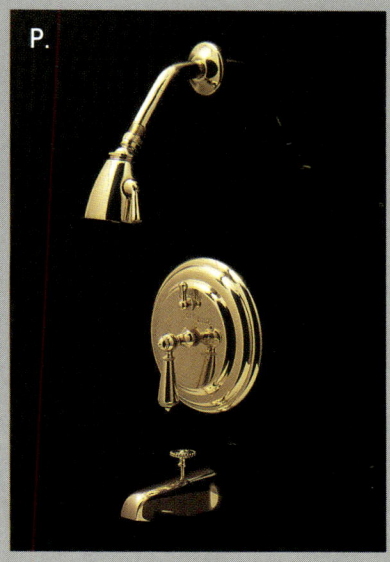

P.

Q. R. S.

T.

U.

English Rope Suite®

G.	26.10747	Three Valve Tub & Shower[1]
H.	26.11083	Roman Tub Set,$3/_4$" [1, 2]
I.	10.10311	18″ Towel Bar[3]
	10.10312	24″ Towel Bar[3]
	10.10313	30″ Towel Bar[3]
J.	10.10315	Robe Hook[3]
K.	10.10314	Paper Holder[3]
L.	10.10316	Towel Ring[3]
M.	10.10308	Tumbler w/tumbler Holder[3]
N.	10.10318	Soap Basket[3]
O.	10.10306	Soap Dish w/dish Holder[3]
P.	26.11538	Balance Pressure Tub & Shower[1]
Q.	22.10046	1 $1/_2$″ Right Hand Grab Bar
R.	22.10033	1″ x 18″ Grab Bar
S.	22.10040	1 $1/_2$″ x 18″ Grab Bar
T.	10.10199	Tank Lever
U.	10.10317	Vanity Shelf [3]

(Not Shown)

10.10319	Soap and Sponge Basket

Finishes available: 509, 605, 620, 625.
[1]CSA criterion met. See Page 23.
[2]Also available with $1/_2$″ Valves.
[3]Patent Pending.

A. B. C.

D.

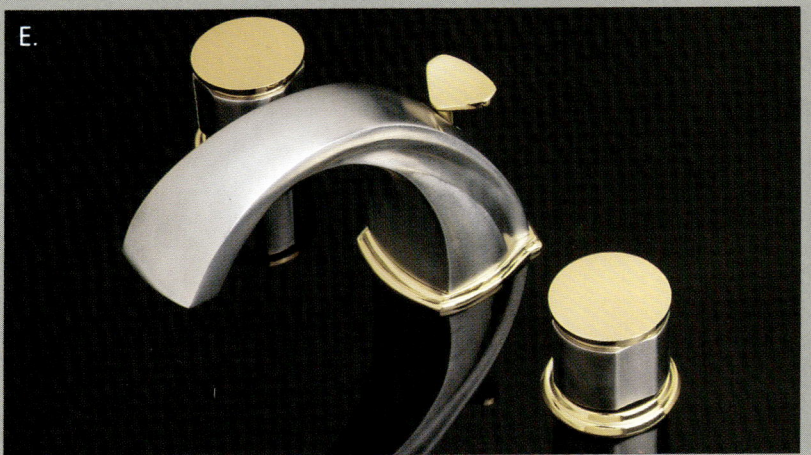

E.

F.

G.

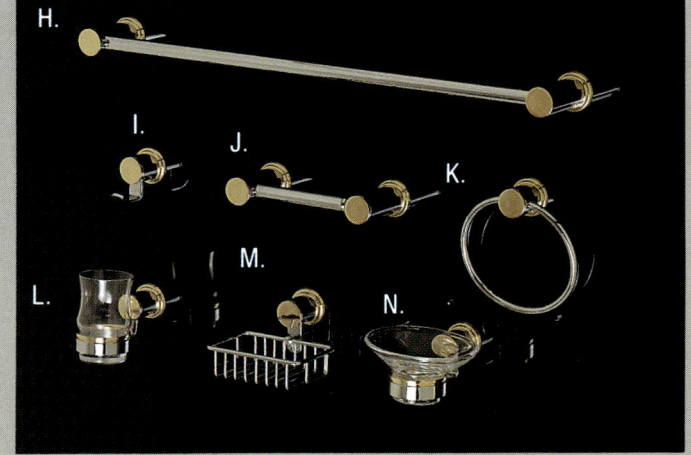

H.

I.

J.

K.

L.

M.

N.

Beau Monde Suite®

A.	26.11074	Roman Tub Set, $^3/_4''$ [1, 2]
B.	26.12131	$^1/_2''$ Diverter Valve
C.	38.10078	Deck Mount Hand Shower
D.	26.12167	Mono Block Faucet
E.	26.10071	Spreadset Faucet[1, 3]
F.	26.10721	Three Valve Tub & Shower[1]
G.	26.12168	Mono Block Bidet Fitting
H.	10.10296	18″ Towel Bar
	10.10297	24″ Towel Bar
	10.10298	30″ Towel Bar
I.	10.10300	Robe Hook
J.	10.10299	Paper Holder

K.	10.10301	Towel Ring	(Not Shown)		
L.	10.10293	Tumbler with tumbler Holder		10.10322	Soap and Sponge Basket
M.	10.10321	Soap Basket		10.10328	Vanity Shelf
N.	10.10291	Soap Dish with dish Holder			

Finishes available: 518, 519, 605, 625, 626.
[1]CSA criterion met. See Page 23.
[2]Also available with $^1/_2''$ Valves.
[3]Patent Pending.

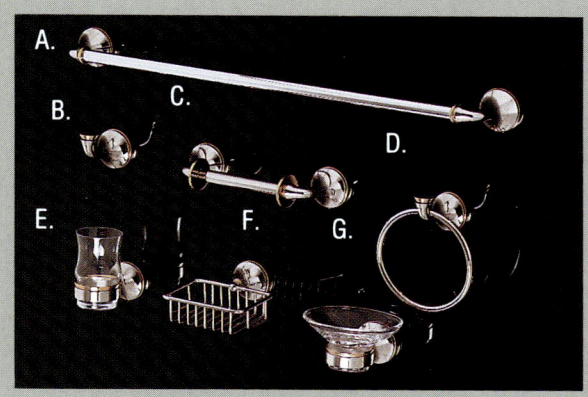

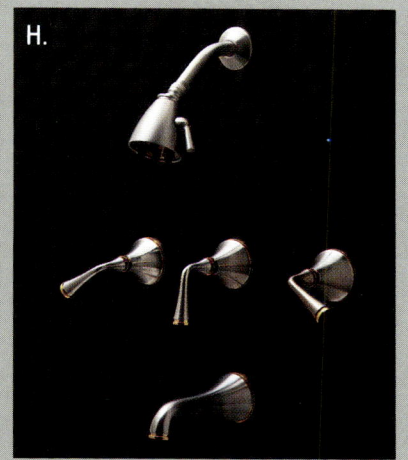

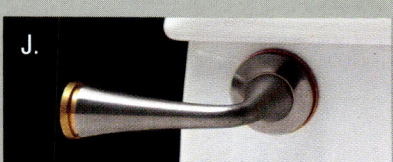

Taliesen Suite®

A.	10.10040	18″ Towel Bar
	10.10041	24″ Towel Bar
	10.10042	30″ Towel Bar
B.	10.10113	Robe Hook
C.	10.10082	Paper Holder
D.	10.10098	Towel Ring
E.	10.10184	Tumbler with Holder
F.	10.10324	Soap Basket
G.	10.10140	Soap Dish with Holder

H.	26.10781	Three Valve Tub & Shower[1]
I.	26.10175	Spreadset Faucet[1]
J.	10.10206	Tank Lever
K.	26.11556	Balance Pressure Tub & Shower[1]
L.	26.11095	Roman Tub Set,$\frac{3}{4}$″ [1,2]
M.	26.12149	$\frac{1}{2}$″ Diverter Valve
N.	38.10078	Deck Mount Hand Shower

(Not Shown)		
	10.10325	Soap and Sponge Basket
	10.10326	Vanity Shelf

Finishes available: 518, 519, 605, 625, 626.
[1]CSA criterion met. See Page 23.
[2]Also available with $\frac{1}{2}$″ Valves.

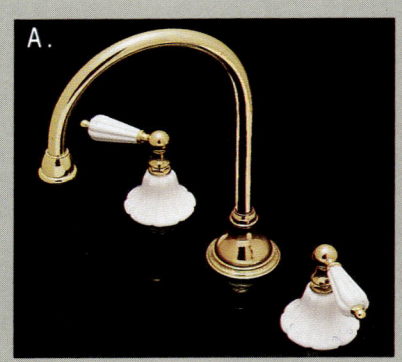

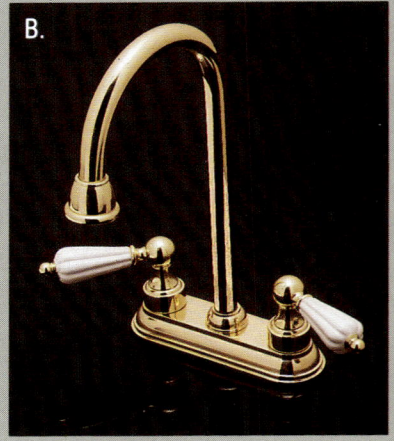

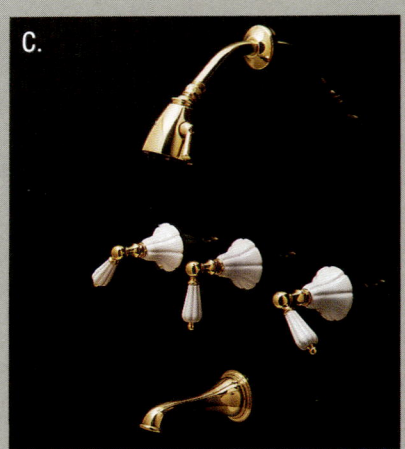

La Coquille Petite Suite

A.	26.10332	Kitchen Swivel Faucet[1]
B.	26.10290	Bar Faucet[1]
C.	26.10754	Three Valve Tub & Shower[1]
D.	26.10126	Spreadset Faucet[1]
E.	10.10213	Porcelain Oval Mirror 19 $\frac{1}{2}$" x 24 $\frac{1}{2}$"
F.	10.10191	Vanity Shelf
G.	26.11086	Roman Tub Set, $\frac{3}{4}$"[1,2]
H.	26.12140	$\frac{1}{2}$" Diverter Valve
I.	38.10062	Deck Mount Cradle Hand Shower Set
J.	10.10201	Tank Lever
K.	26.10035	Centerset Faucet[1]

Finishes available: 509, 605, 620, 625.
[1]CSA criterion met. See Page 23.
[2]Available with $\frac{1}{2}$" Valves.

A.

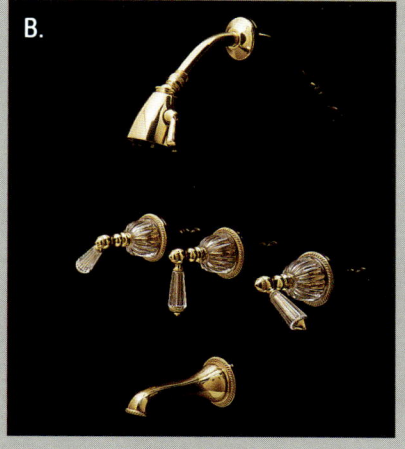
B.

C.

D.

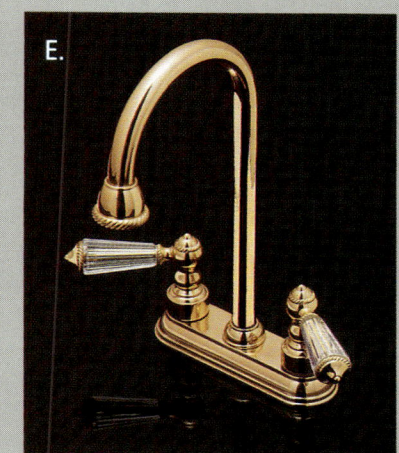
E.

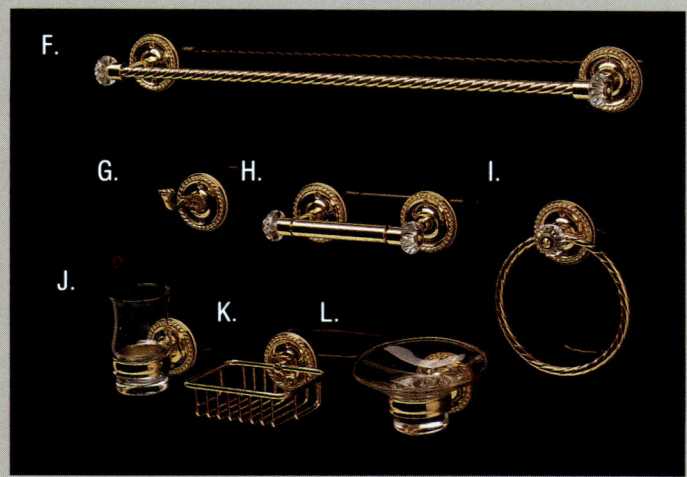
F. G. H. I. J. K. L.

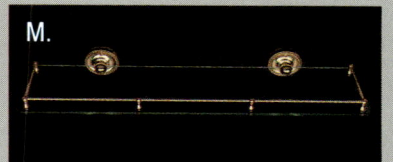
M.

N.

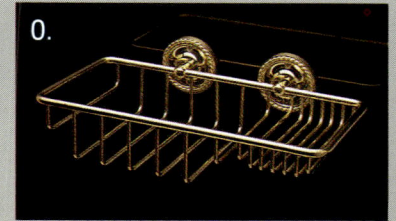
O.

Clarie Crystal Suite®

A. 26.10001   Centerset Faucet[1]
B. 26.10724   Three Valve Tub & Shower[1]
C. 26.11075   Roman Tub Set, $\frac{3}{4}$" [1, 2]
D. 26.10077   Spreadset Faucet[1]
E. 26.10272   Bar Faucet[1]
F. 10.10001   18" Towel Bar
   10.10002   24" Towel Bar
   10.10003   30" Towel Bar
G. 10.10103   Robe Hook

H. 10.10064   Paper Holder
I. 10.10088   Towel Ring
J. 10.10171   Tumbler with Holder
K. 10.10145   Soap Basket
L. 10.10116   Soap Dish with Holder
M. 10.10231   Vanity Shelf
N. 10.10196   Tank Lever
O. 10.10146   Soap and Sponge Basket

Finishes available: 509, 605, 620, 625.
[1]CSA criterion met. See Page 23.
[2]Available with $\frac{1}{2}$" Valves.

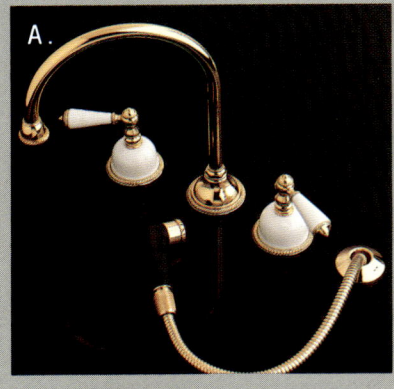

Colony White Suite

A. 26.10356   Kitchen Swivel Faucet with Hand Spray

B. 26.10005   Centerset Faucet[1]

C. 26.10274   Bar Faucet[1]

D. 26.10086   Spreadset Faucet[1]

E. 26.10214   Gooseneck Spreadset Faucet[1]

F. 26.11619   Deck Mount Bidet Fitting for Kohler Fixture

     26.11640   for American Standard Fixture

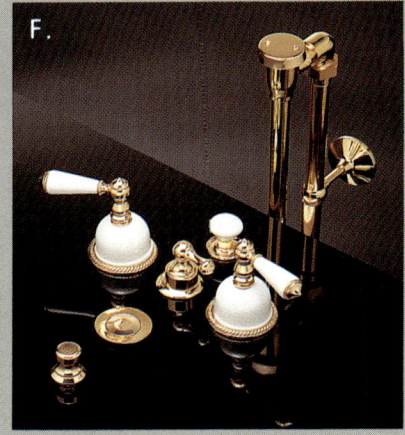

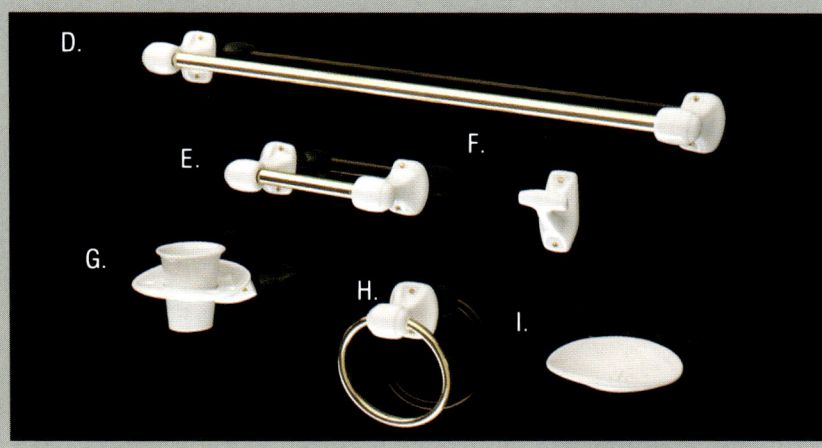

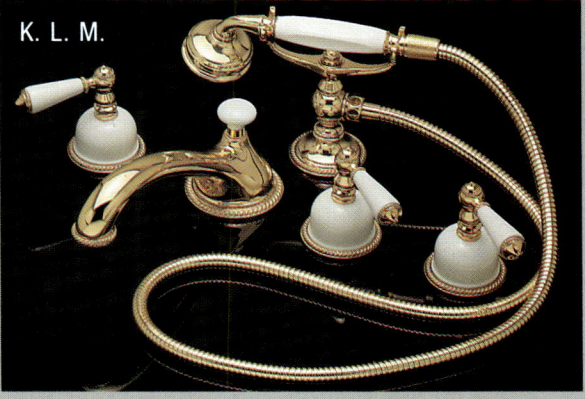

Colony White Suite

A.	10.10208	Porcelain Mirror 30″ x 24″
B.	26.10730	Three Valve Tub & Shower
C.	10.10197	Tank Lever
D.	10.10005	18″ Towel Bar
	10.10006	24″ Towel Bar
	10.10007	30″ Towel Bar
E.	10.10066	Paper Holder
F.	10.10104	Robe Hook
G.	10.10227	Toothbrush & Tumbler Holder with Tumbler
H.	10.10089	Towel Ring
I.	10.10117	Soap Dish
J.	26.11533	Balance Pressure Tub & Shower[1]
K.	26.11077	Roman Tub Set, $^3/_4$″ [1,2]
L.	26.12133	$^1/_2$″ Diverter Valve
M.	38.10063	Deck Mount Cradle Hand Shower Set

Finishes available: 509, 605, 620, 625.
[1]CSA criterion met. See Page 23.
[2]Available with $^1/_2$″ Valves.

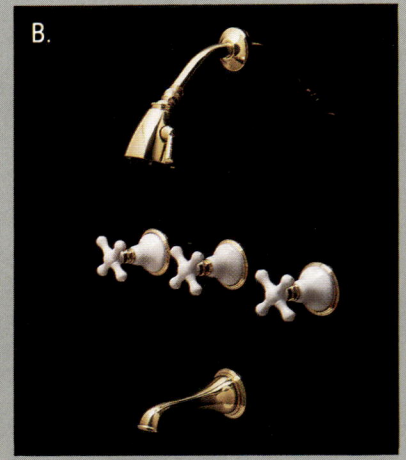

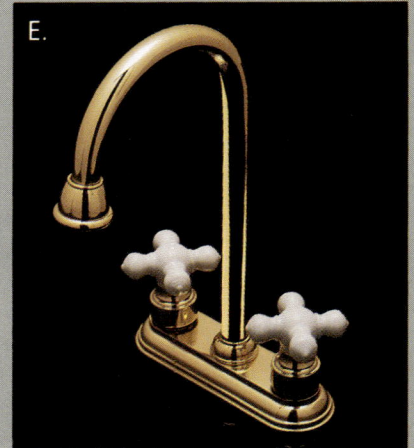

Colony White Suite

A. 26.10007 Centerset Faucet[1]
 26.10009 Centerset Faucet with
   ''Hot'' & ''Cold'' Trim[1]
B. 26.10732 Three Valve Tub & Shower[1]
 26.10734 Three Valve Tub & Shower
   with ''Hot'' & ''Cold'' Trim[1]
C. 26.10216 Gooseneck Spreadset
   Faucet[1]
 26.10218 Gooseneck Spreadset with
   ''Hot'' & ''Cold'' Trim[1]
D. 26.10090 Spreadset Faucet with
   ''Hot'' & ''Cold'' Trim[1]
E. 26.10275 Bar Faucet[1]
 26.10276 Bar Faucet with
   ''Hot'' & ''Cold'' Trim[1]

F. 26.11078 Roman Tub Set $^3/_4''$ [1,2]
 26.11079 Roman Tub Set with
   ''Hot'' & ''Cold'' Trim, $^3/_4''$ [1,2]
G. 26.10088 Spreadset Faucet[1]

Finishes available: 509, 605, 620, 625.
[1]CSA criterion met. See Page 23.
[2]Available with $^1/_2''$ Valves.

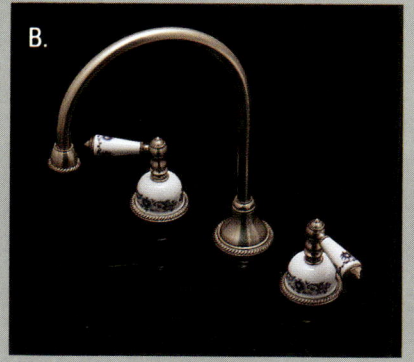

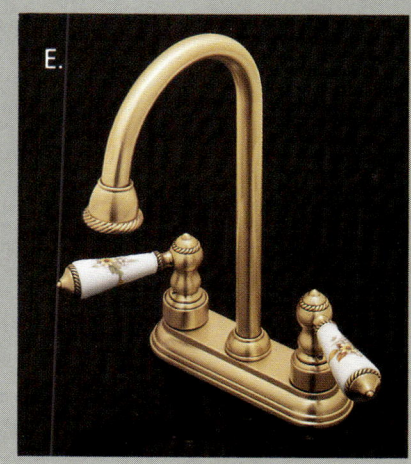

Decorated Porcelain Suites

A. 26.10039   Meadow Flower® Centerset Faucet[1]
B. 26.10350   Village Blue® Kitchen Swivel Faucet[1]
C. 10.10205   Summer Bouquet® Tank Lever
D. 26.10183   Village Blue® Spreadset Faucet[1]
E. 26.10302   Summer Bouquet® Bar Faucet[1]
F. 10.10044   Village Blue® 18″ Towel Bar
   10.10045   Village Blue® 24″ Towel Bar
   10.10046   Village Blue® 30″ Towel Bar
G. 10.10084   Village Blue® Paper Holder
H. 10.10114   Village Blue® Robe Hook
I. 10.10229   Village Blue® Toothbrush and Tumbler
              Holder with Tumbler
J. 10.10099   Village Blue® Towel Ring
K. 10.10142   Village Blue® Soap Dish

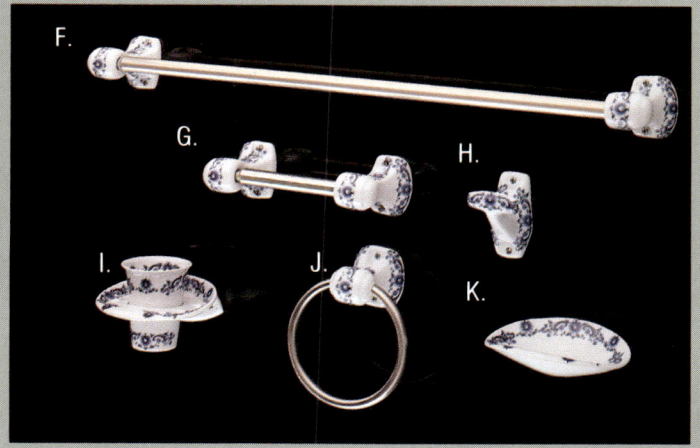

Finishes available: 509, 605, 620, 625.
[1]CSA criterion met. See Page 23.

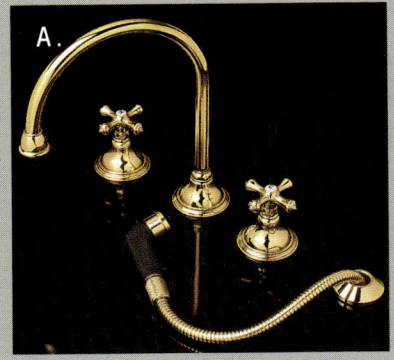

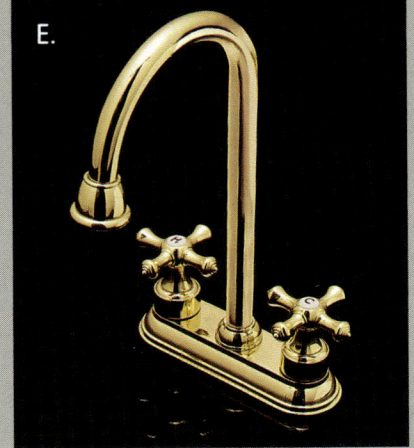

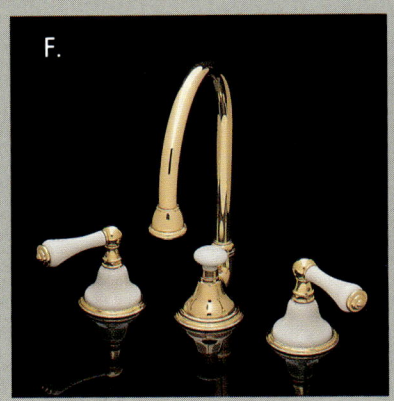

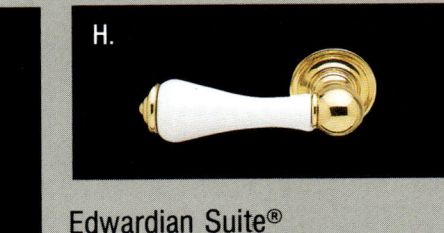

Edwardian Suite®

A.	26.10361	Kitchen Swivel Faucet with Hand Spray
B.	26.10383	Deck Mount Kitchen Swivel Faucet[1]
C.	26.12170	Mono Block Bidet Fitting
D.	26.10103	Spreadset Faucet[1]
E.	26.10280	Bar Faucet[1]
F.	26.10224	Gooseneck Spreadset Faucet[1]
G.	26.12169	Mono Block Faucet
H.	10.10198	Tank Lever
I.	26.11658	Exposed Tub and Shower, Wall Mount

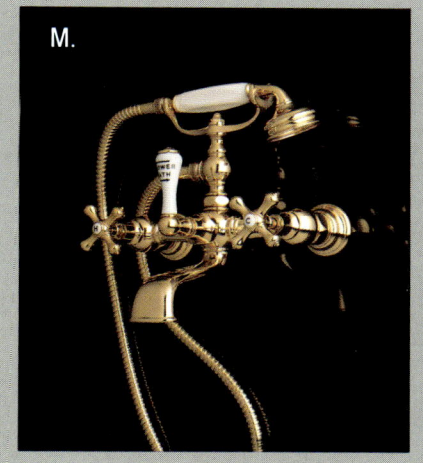

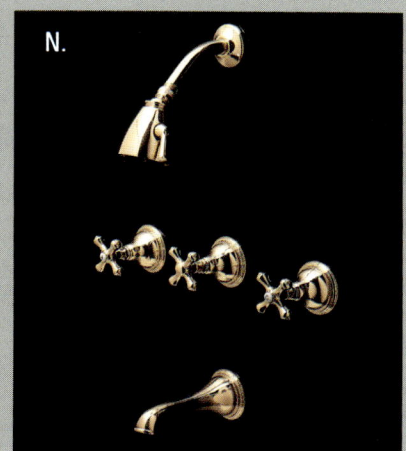

Edwardian Suite®

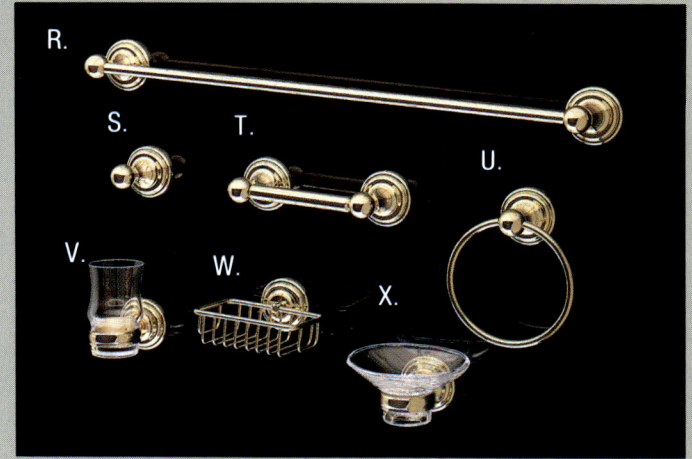

J.	26.10018	Centerset Faucet[1]
K.	26.12028	Basin Cock Faucet, "Hot"[1]
L.	26.12029	Basin Cock Faucet, "Cold"[1]
M.	26.11663	Exposed Tub and Hand Shower, Wall Mount
N.	26.10741	Three Valve Tub & Shower[1]
O.	26.11082	Roman Tub Set, $3/_4$" [1, 2]
P.	26.12137	$1/_2$" Diverter Valve
Q.	38.10067	Deck Mount Cradle Hand Shower Set
R.	10.10031	18" Towel Bar*
	10.10032	24" Towel Bar*
	10.10033	30" Towel Bar*
S.	10.10111	Robe Hook*
T.	10.10079	Paper Holder*
U.	10.10096	Towel Ring*
V.	10.10182	Tumbler with Holder*
W.	10.10155	Soap Basket*
X.	10.10135	Soap Dish with Holder*

Finishes available: 031, 605, 625.
*Also Available in 509, 620, 626.
[1]CSA criterion met. See Page 23.
[2]Available with $1/_2$" Valves.

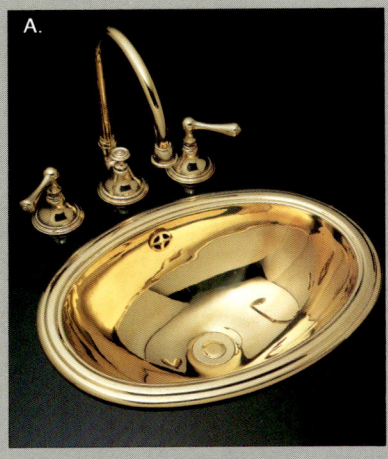

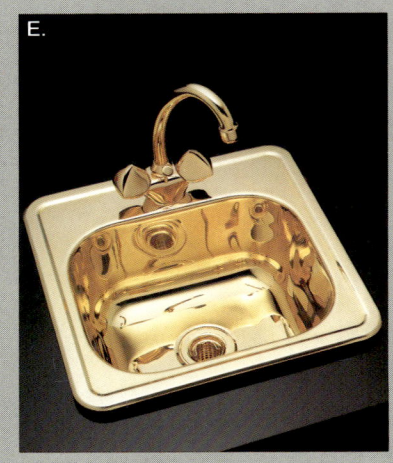

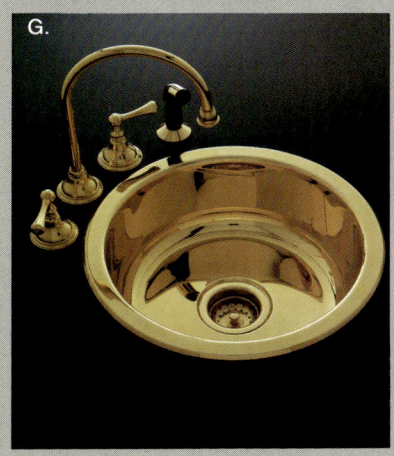

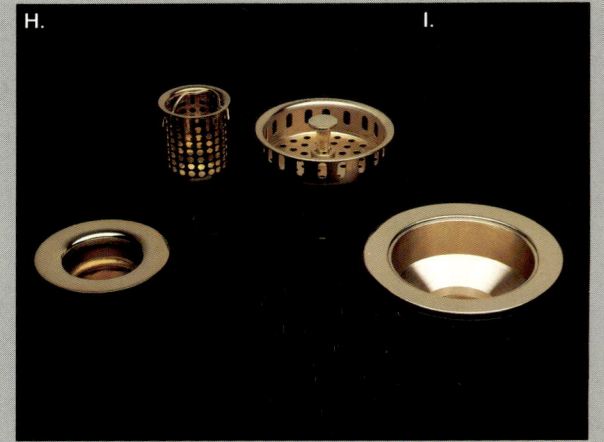

Brass Bowls

A. 30.10237   Over the Counter Bowl
13 $^1/_2$" x 18"
^{w}/Overflow System

B. 30.10238   Under the Counter Bowl
13 $^1/_2$" x 18"
^{w}/Overflow System

C. 30.10232   Rectangular Bar Sink
11" x 13"

D. 30.10236   Bar Sink
15" x 15"
4" C-C Mounting

E. 30.10241   Bar Sink
15" x 15"
Sinlge Hole Mounting

F. 30.10242   Round Bar Sink
15" Diameter

G. 30.10243   Round Kitchen Sink
18" Diameter

H. 40.10060   2" Basket Strainer
for Bar Sinks[1]

I. 40.10120   3" Basket Strainer
for Kitchen Sinks[2]

Broadway's brass bowls, made of solid brass are available in 031 - Polished Brass, Uncoated, providing years of quality service.

[1]Sold separately, for use with 30.10232, 30.10236, 30.10241 and 30.10242.

[2]Sold Separately, for use with 30.10243

Old Dominion Suite®

Accord Concealed Mount

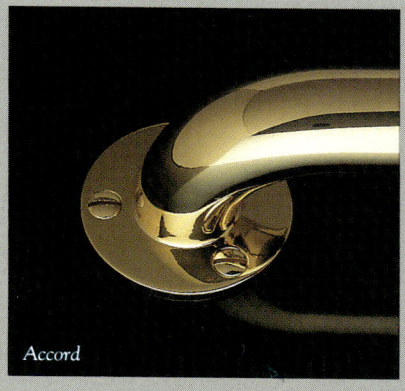

Accord

Edwardian Suite®

The Broadway Collection® offers grab bars in an array of quality finishes: Uncoated Polished Brass · 031, French Bronze · 509, Clear Coated Polished Brass · 605, Pewter · 620, Polished Chrome · 625, and Brushed Chrome · 626.

The Broadway Collection® grab bars come in a variety of suited styles, and functional designs, with diameters and finishes to satisfy your needs.

English Rope Suite®

French Scroll Suite®

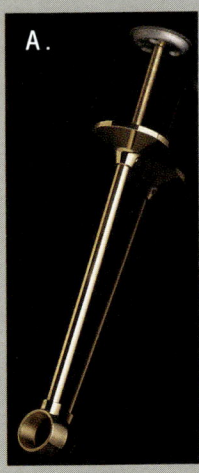

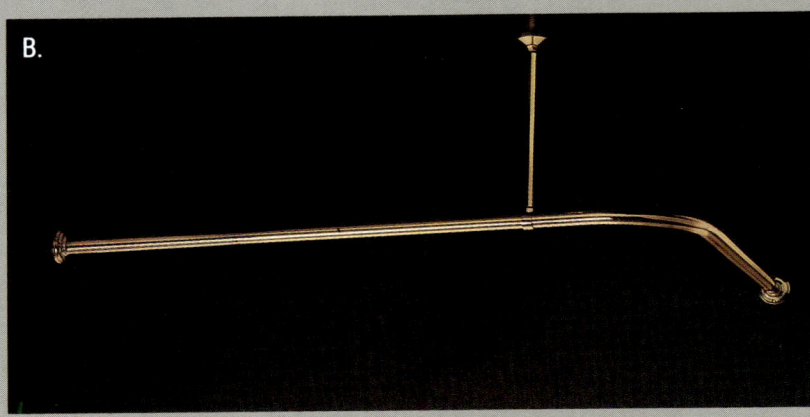

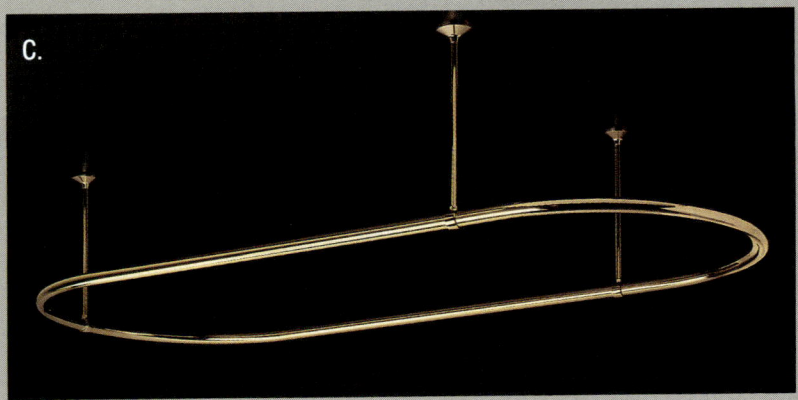

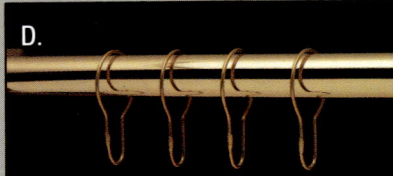

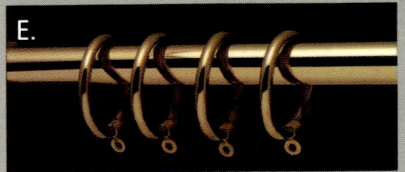

Bath Accessories

A.	10.10221	12" Ceiling Bracket (Can be reduced to 2")
	10.10223	36" Ceiling Bracket
B.	10.10215	90º Shower Rod* 66" x 28 1/2" x 1" O.D.
C.	10.10214	Oval Shower Rod* 58" x 26" x 1" O.D.
D.	10.10224	1 3/8" Shower Curtain Ring
E.	32.10137	1 1/2" Curtain Ring
	32.10138	2" Curtain Ring
F.	10.10219	Old Dominion Brackets Exposed Mount for 1" Shower Rod
G.	10.10252	Old Dominion Brackets Concealed Mount for 1" Shower Rod
H.	10.10320	English Rope Brackets Concealed Mount for 1" Shower Rod
I.	10.10220	Adjustable Brackets for 1" Shower Rod
J.	10.10216	1" x 60" Shower Rod*
	10.10217	1" x 72" Shower Rod*

Finishes available: 031, 509, 605, 620, 626.
*Brackets Not Included.

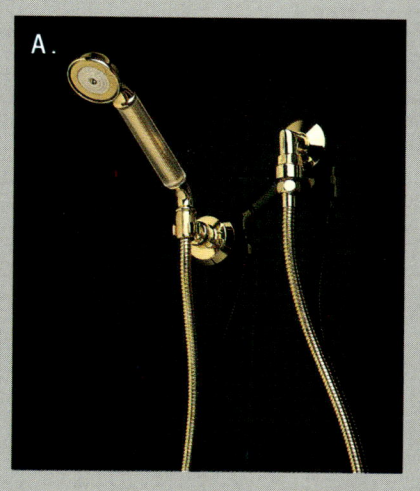

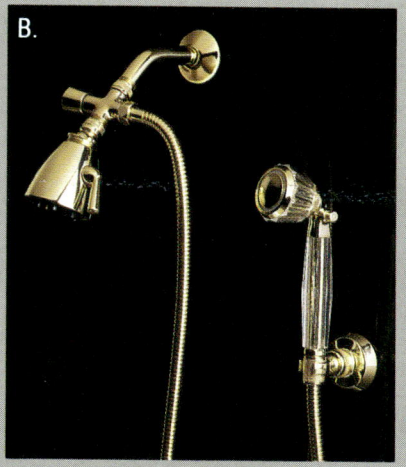

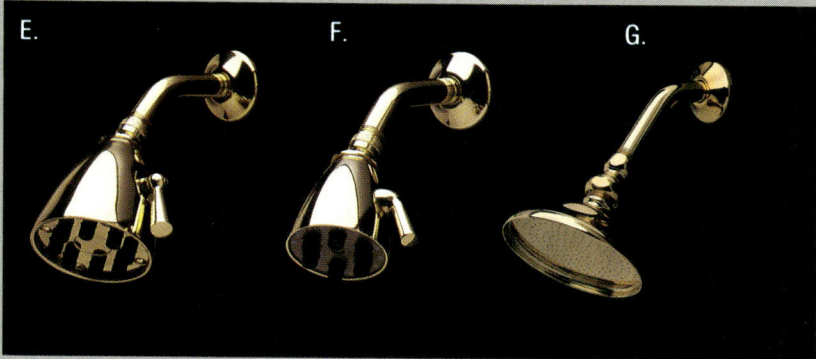

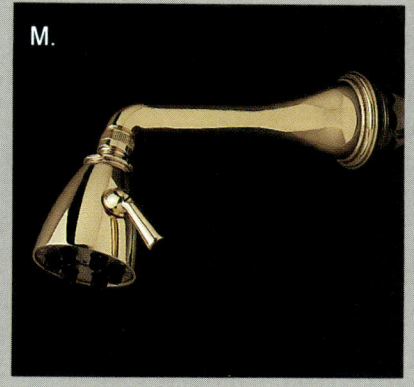

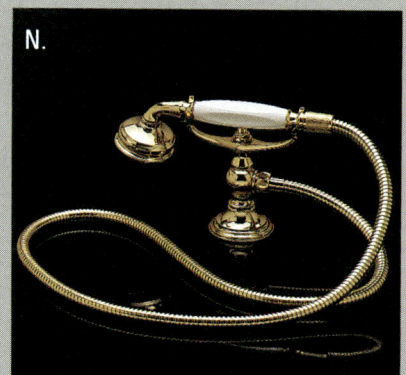

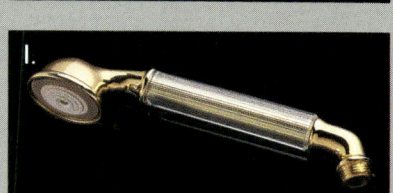

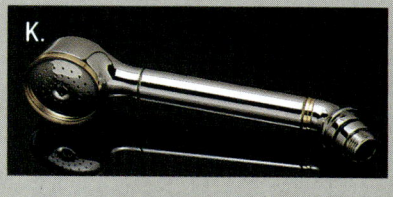

Shower Systems

A. 38.10029 Model 20 Wall Mount Hand Shower Set

B. 38.10030 Model 30 Wall Mount Hand Shower Set Shown with 38.10018 Diverter Valve

C. 26.12144 Old Dominion Suite® $1/_2''$ Diverter Valve

D. 26.11073 $3/_4''$ Diverter Valve

E. 38.10036 $3\,^5/_8''$ Face Shower Head, Arm, and Flange

F. 38.10034 $2\,^3/_4''$ Face Shower Head,[1] Arm, and Flange

G. 38.10055 5″ Face Shower Head, Arm, and Flange

H. 38.10010 Model 30 Hand Set

I. 38.10009 Model 20 Hand Set

J. 38.10011 Model 40 Hand Set

K. 38.10074 Model 50 Hand Set

L. 38.10075 Model 60 Hand Set

M. 38.10070 Old Dominion Suite® One Piece Shower Arm

N. 38.10062 Old Dominion Suite® Deck Mount Cradle Hand Shower Set

Finishes available: 031, 509, 605, 620, 625, 626.
[1]CSA criterion met. See Page 23..

Ceramic Disc Valve

Proven Advantages:

- Smooth operation and positive indexing.

- Non-rising Spindle.

- Quarter turn operation

- Forged, Precision Brass Body. (250% greater tensile strength than cast brass)

- The Ceramic Discs are proven at one million cycles and are surrounded by a solid brass housing.

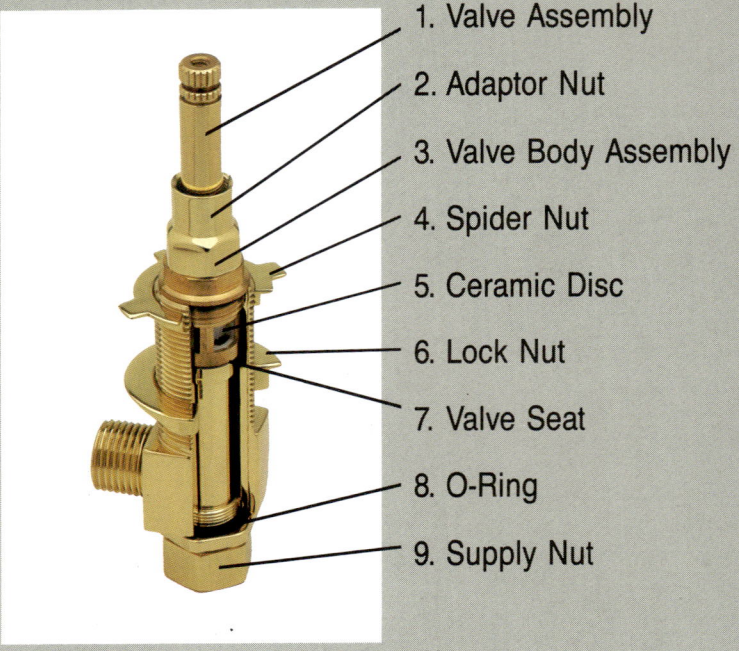

1. Valve Assembly

2. Adaptor Nut

3. Valve Body Assembly

4. Spider Nut

5. Ceramic Disc

6. Lock Nut

7. Valve Seat

8. O-Ring

9. Supply Nut

Balance Pressure Valve

Proven Advantages:

- The desired temperature can be selected and maintained without interruption from changes in water pressure. This system eliminates bursts of "scalding hot" or "freezing cold" water.

- The "balance pressure module" is engineered to be "self-cleaning" of the contaminents often found in water systems, particularly new ones.

- Servicing of valve is simplified by the use of modular valve components and the accessing of the valve through the front.

- The same rough-in is used for both tub and shower combinations and showers only, simplifying multiple installations.

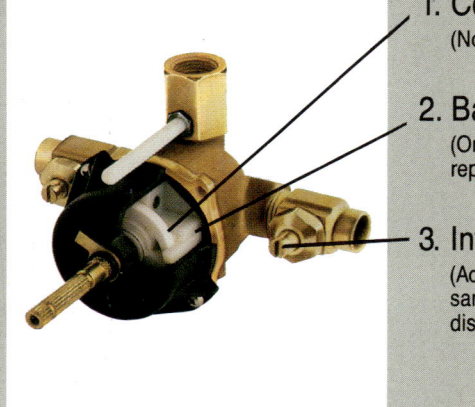

1. Ceramic Disk
   (Non-scoring surface)

2. Balance Pressure Module
   (One piece for quick and easy replacement)

3. Integral Stops
   (Additional plumbing fittings on the same water source are not disturbed when water is shut off)

The Broadway Collection®

Division of Broadway Industries, Inc.
250 N. Troost
Olathe, Ks 66061 USA
TOLL FREE (USA & Canada)
1-800-766-1966
TELEX: 6875014

Warnock Hersey

MEMBER PLUMBING MANUFACTURERS INSTITUTE

Printed in U.S.A.

96.10033/0990

Precious Metal
Collection

Precious Metals and Liquid Assets for the Kitchen.

In your kitchen everything has its place. Everything has a purpose. It all works together in perfect unison, as does your faucet by Central Brass.

3

0122-WSA24*C02
Chrome Kitchen Faucet
with Hi-rise spout, wood
lever handles on 8″ centers.

Central BRASS

Precious Metal Collection

0289-A80*C09
*Polished Brass Bar
Faucet with rigid goose-
neck spout and Silver-Crown acrylic
handles. Single hole mount.*

0287-GSAELS*C09
*Polished Brass Bar Faucet with 4" swivel gooseneck
spout and 4" color-coded wrist blade handles.
Single hole mount.*

Precious Metals. Entertaining ideas for the bar.

Central Brass adds a splash and twist to drinks you serve in your bar. Shown here, gleaming high-rise spouts, reflective of a fine taste for entertaining at home.

Central BRASS

Precious Metal Collection

A/B

Drinks on the house. Cheers!

Central Brass at the bar mixes perfectly with any decor in sleek, high-rise lines. Shown here, our three cordial styles.

A 0284-A*C02 — Top Left
Chrome Bar Faucet with
6½" rigid gooseneck
spout and wing handles.
Single hole mount.

B 0285-A*C02 — Top Right
Chrome Bar Faucet with
6-½" swivel gooseneck
spout and wing handles.
Single hole mount.

C 0084-GSA23*C02
Chrome Bar Faucet with
4" swivel gooseneck
spout and porcelain lever
handles on 4" centers.

C

Central
BRASS

Precious Metal Collection

A

Precious Metals. More shower power.

Elegance at your fingertips with a perfect handle on temperature control. Shown here, Central Brass classics: two-handled and single-handled shower valves.

C/D

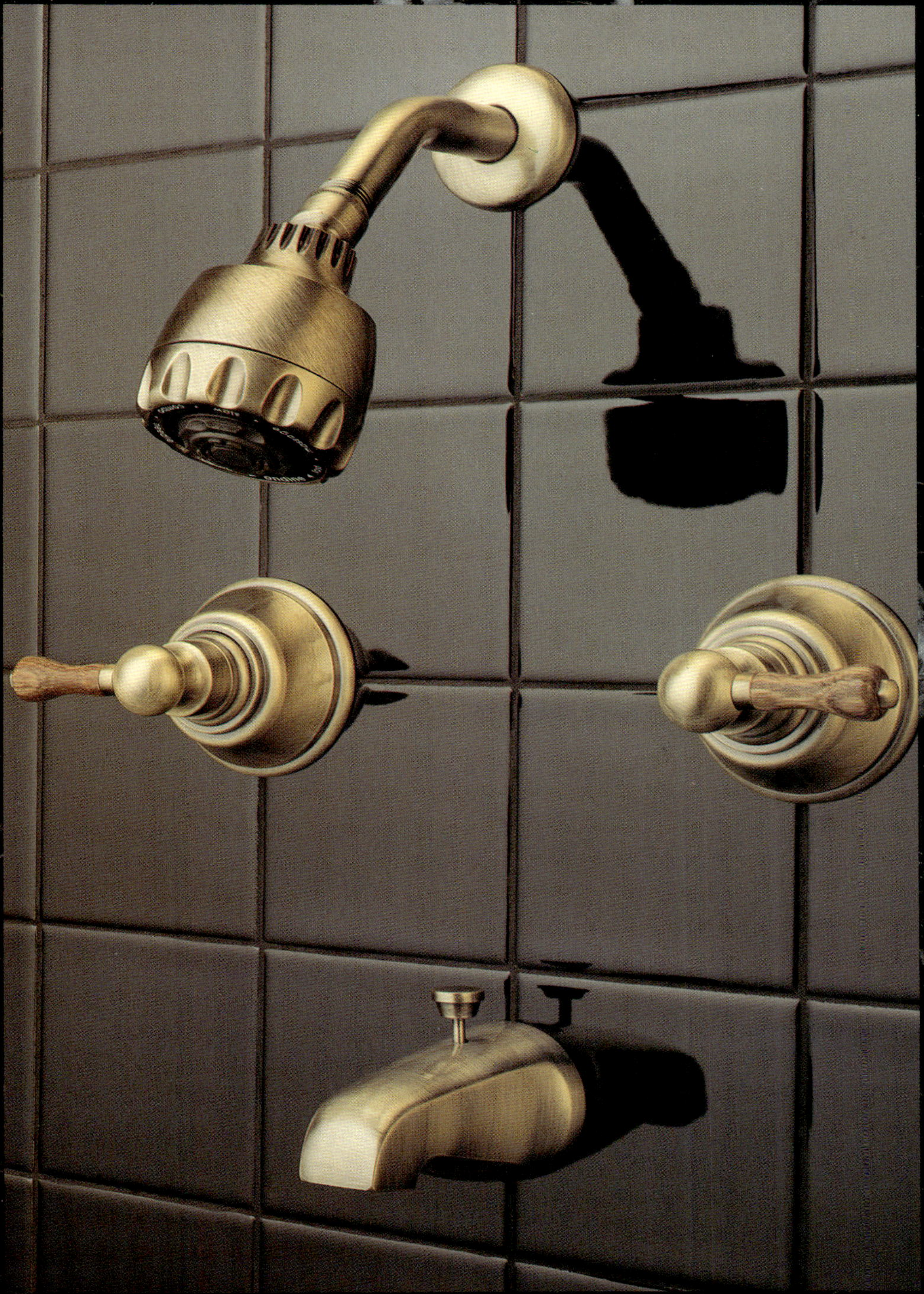

A 0971-93*C09
Polished Brass three-valve
tub and shower with
porcelain lever handles on
11″ centers.

B 0997-84*C08
Antique Brass two-valve
tub and shower with wood
lever handles on 8″
centers.

C 0100*002
Central Gard Pressure
Balanced Tub and Shower
— Chrome.

D 0100*008
Central Gard Pressure
Balanced Tub and Shower
— Antique Brass.

Also available in
polished brass
0100*009

B

Precious Metal Collection

22

Precious Metals. *A perfect reflection of you.*

For the pure luxury of the bath, designed especially with you in mind, Central Brass adds just the touch you need. Polished. Elegant. Classic. Your choice is crystal clear.

1181-009
Polished Brass Roman Tub
Deck Mount with silver-
crown acrylic handles.

Central BRASS

Precious Metal Collection

A

B

Precious Metals for the Whirlpool.

The ultimate luxury: a touch of Central Brass for the hot tub. Inviting you in for a dip with a splash of style.

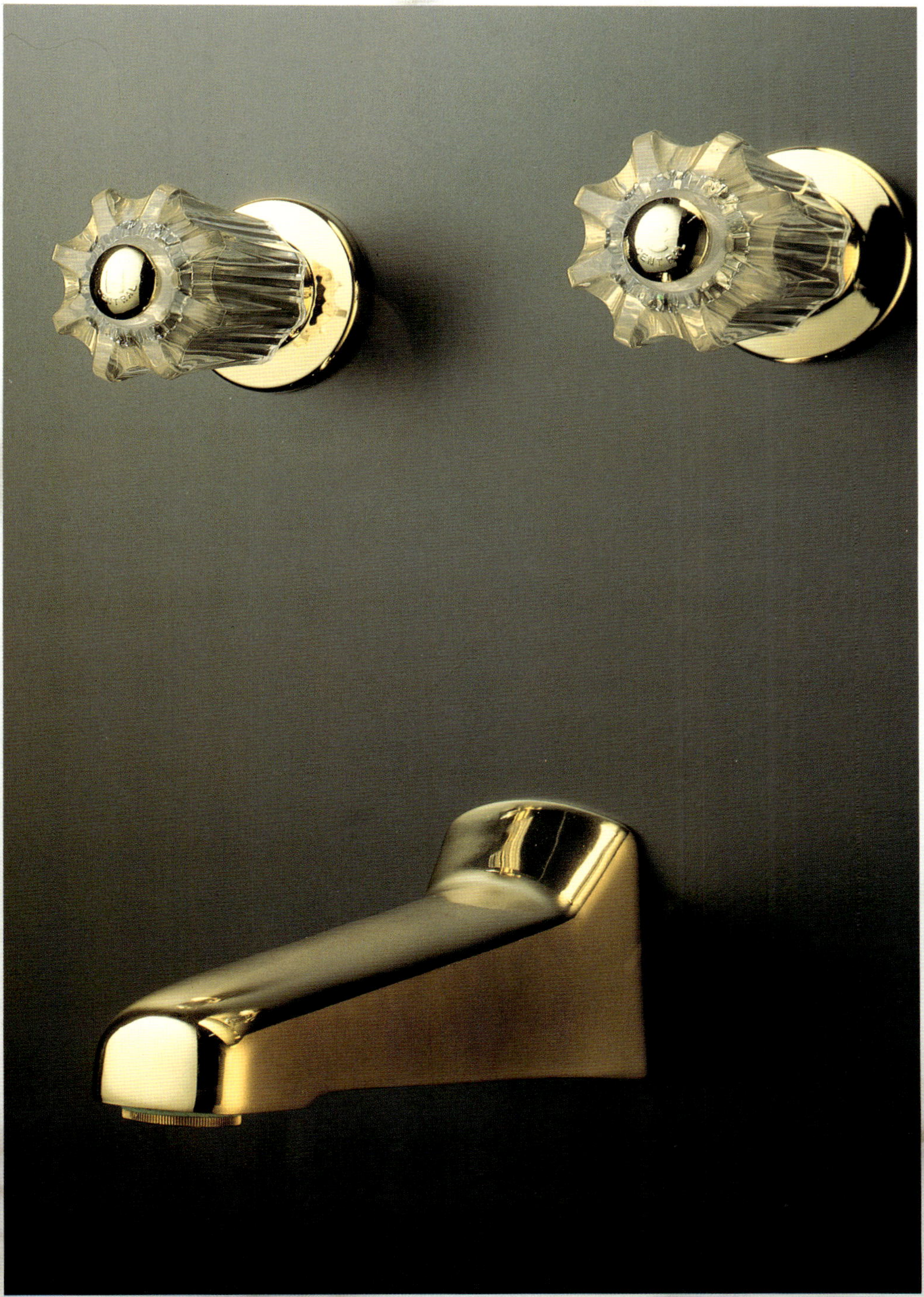

D/E

C

A 1181*008
Antique Brass Roman Tub
Deck Mount with acrylic
handles.

B 1181
Polished Chrome Roman
Tub Deck Mount with
acrylic handles.

C 3146*009 with
0905-80*C09
Polished Brass Wall
Mount Roman Tub filler.

D 3146*002
Polished Chrome Wall
Mount Roman Tub Spout.

E 3146*008
Antique Brass Wall Mount
Roman Tub Spout.

Precious Metal Collection

2950 East 55th Street, Cleveland, Ohio 44127 (216) 883-0220

CBPMC 1088

CHICAGO FAUCETS®

Decorative Products

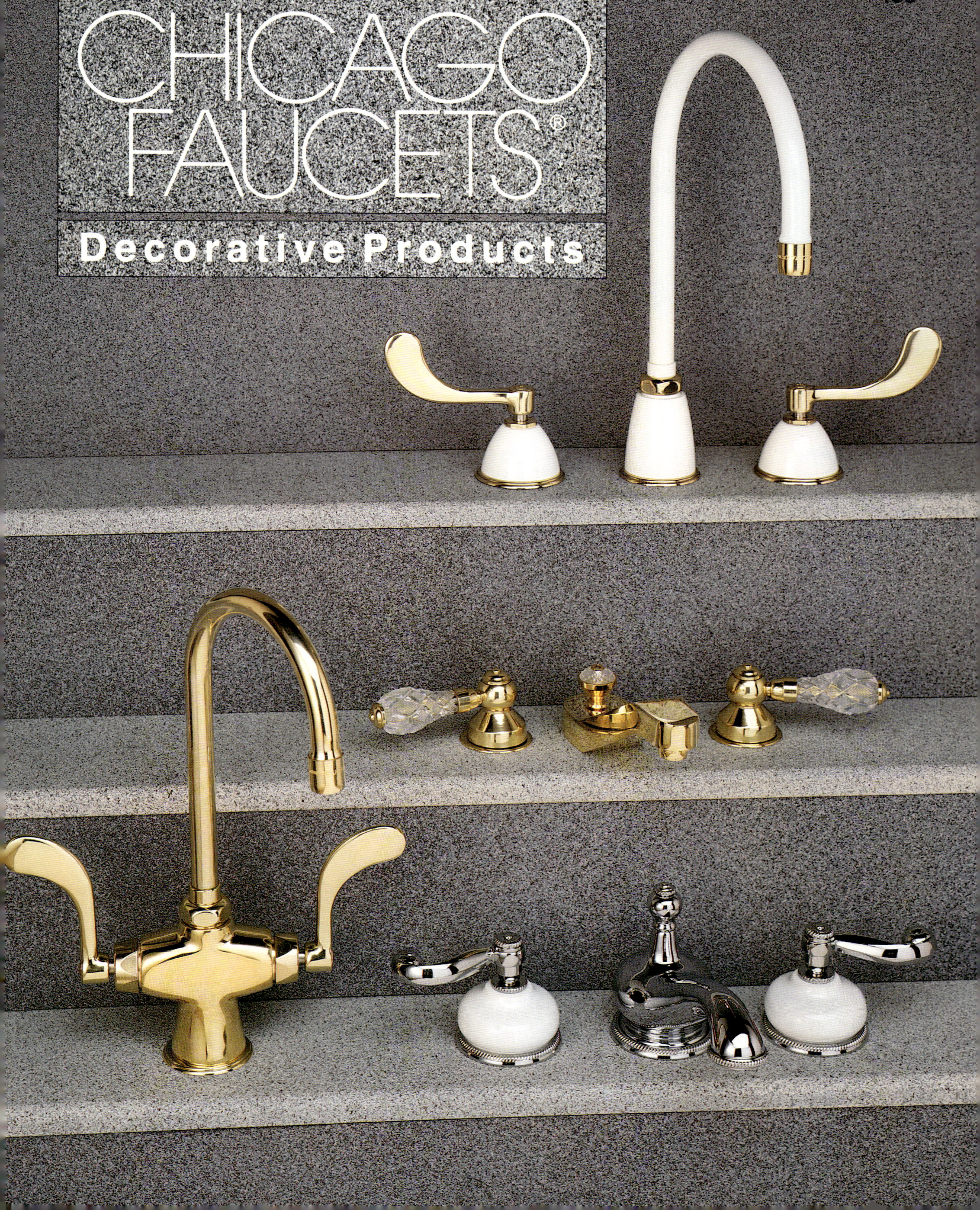

The Renaissance Collection®
Twenty pages of full-color photos of Chicago Faucet's beautiful Renaissance Collection of kitchen, bath and bar faucets. This information brochure also includes detailed ordering information and roughing-in dimensions.

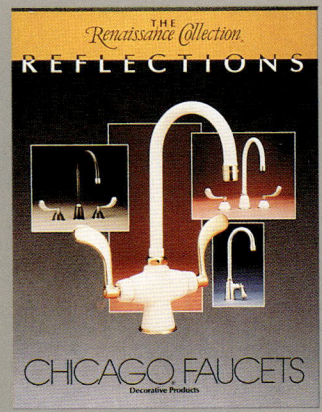

Reflections of Renaissance®
The Reflections Series of the Renaissance Collection introduces kitchen and bar faucets in new white, chrome and charcoal finishes accented with polished brass or chrome trim. Reflections Euro-style high profile spouts and distinctive blade handles are presented in this full-color brochure.

The Legacy Collection®
This colorful brochure features the elegant bath faucets of Chicago Faucet's exciting Legacy Collection. Choose from six distinctive styles with metal or ceramic escutcheons accented in braided or plain trim.

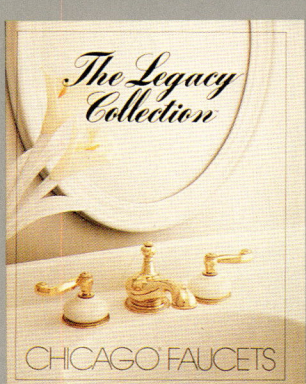

The Chalyce Collection®
Chicago Faucet's elegant Chalyce Collection of contemporary bath faucets in beautiful polished brass and spectacular chrome finishes is illustrated in this full-color brochure.

For more complete information about Chicago Faucet's Decorative Products, ask for our full line product brochures.

CHICAGO FAUCETS®

Decorative Products

THE CHICAGO FAUCET COMPANY

2100 South Nuclear Drive, Des Plaines, IL 60018
Phone: 312-694-4400   Fax: 708-298-3101
Telex: 282528 CGO FAUCET DSP

Dec Prod 8/90   Printed in U.S.A.

Replacement, remodeling or new construction — Grohe manufactures an impressive collection of fine solid brass plumbing fixtures for the kitchen, bath or spa.

Grohe products are priced for your profitability — and your customer's budget.

Unequalled in design, style and quality . . . there is no substitute for Grohe . . . the Original European.

GROHE MOVES WATER

GROHE AMERICA

THE UP-SCALE™ COLLECTION

Grohe's Up-Scale™ Collection…with color accents…adds elegance to the kitchen, bath and spa.

The Up-Scale™ Collection is available in Chrome, 23-Karat Gold, Polished Brass, White, Black, Bone and Nu-Silver™ finishes.

Unequalled in design, style and quality…there is no substitute for Grohe…the Original European.

GROHE
MOVES WATER

Shower heads, interchangeable personal hand showers, body sprays, a shower/body massage, and the all important Grohmix™ Thermostat Valves . . . to maintain your desired water temperature. Grohe has it all for your custom dream shower.

Replacement, remodeling or new construction — Grohe manufactures an impressive collection of fine solid brass plumbing fixtures for the kitchen, bath or spa.

Unequalled in design, style and quality . . . there is no substitute for Grohe . . . the Original European.

Write or call for Grohe's complete Product Literature File.

HANSA AMERICA

HANSA. The High Watermark for Faucets.

Who says a masterpiece of faucet engineering has to look like a piece of machinary? The evolution of our single lever ceramic disc kitchen faucet offers convenience and gratifying performance.

**The Ronda faucets and shower systems are the flagship of
the Hansa marque.** They constitute a series that defines the
standards for the upper most stratum of the lavatory.

The Hansa thermostat concealed mixer is the most advanced and accurate shower system available. It provides the ultimate in function by protecting you from sudden fluctuations in temperature. And beyond the norm, Hansa allows you to select the exact temperature you wish to shower or bathe in, and maintain that temperature under the most demanding conditions.

The most decorative and advanced shower system has been painstakingly engineered to support your every whim. A Hansa shower system can provide either an invigorating shower or a serene and soothing one.

We have only one quality standard . . . the best.

Only one faucet looks and performs like this: Hansa. A Hansa
faucet is engineered and built like no other in the world.
Recognized as the world's leader in ceramic disc and thermostatic
technology, Hansa has been manufacturing and engineering
classics decade after decade.

**At Hansa we incorporate the most brilliant and advanced
engineering yet applied to faucet manufacturing.** Our exhalted
engineering standards are renewed each and every day by the
most demanding testing conditions: in homes around the world.

**At Hansa each product is manufactured to excel in every way
possible.** Engineering excellence and an alluring design is an apt
description of what every Hansa product is bred to accomplish.
The Hansa difference is one you can see and feel for years
and years.

HANSA·AMERICA·

931 W. 19th Street
Chicago, IL. 60608
Telephone: 312-733-0025
Telefax: 312-733-4220
Telex: 209417

JADO

PLUMBING FITTINGS & ACCESSORIES

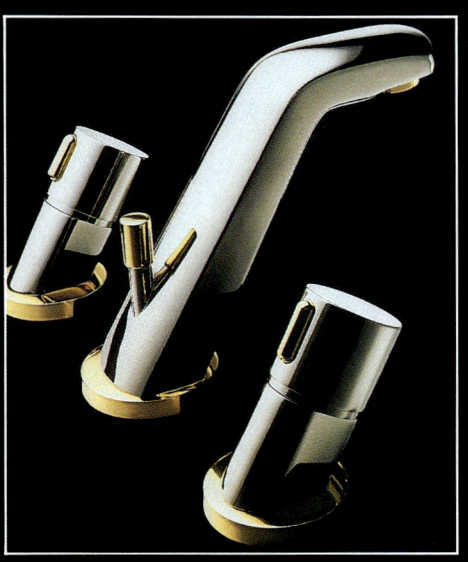

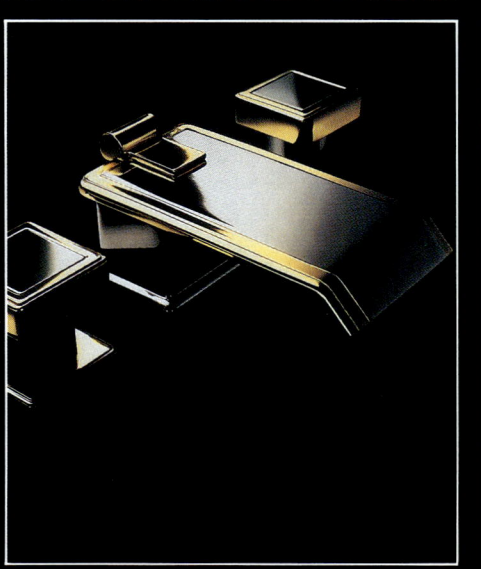

WORKS OF ART IN BRASS

JADO

SERIES JETLINE

Widespread Lavatory Set-Lever Handle...848/901

Finishes Available

- **Polished Chrome**
- **Silver Nickel/Gold**

Roman Tub Set with Hand Shower-Knob Handle...849/912

Single Control Thermostatic Shower Set...875/942

24" x 32" Mirror...512/608

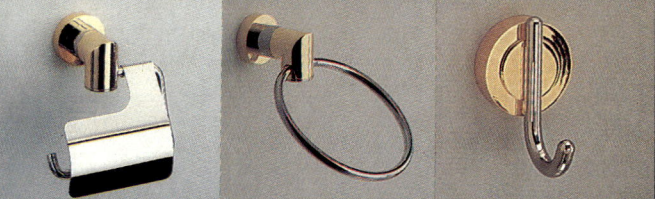

Hooded Tissue Holder...512/145   6" Ring...512/150   Robe Hook...512/010

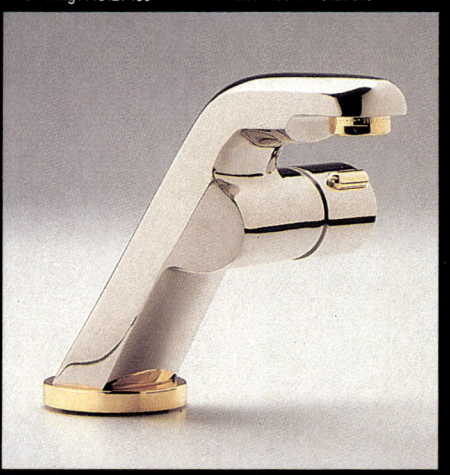

Single Hole "Cold" Water Tap...846/012

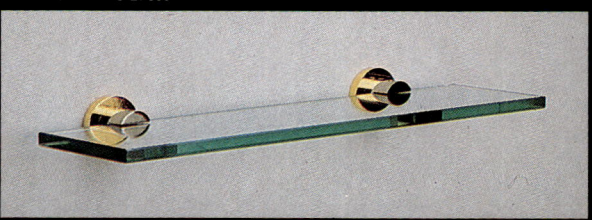

30" Towel Bar...512/800

Shelf...512/612

JADO

SERIES GOLDEN GATE

Finishes Available

- ■ Silver Nickel/Gold
- ■ Black Chrome/Gold
- ■ Brushed Nickel/Diamond Cut
- ■ Black Chrome/Diamond Cut

Widespread Lavatory Set-Flat Spout. . .843 / 912

Roman Tub Set-Flat Spout-with Hand Shower. . .844 / 932

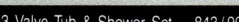

3 Valve Tub & Shower Set. . .843 / 992

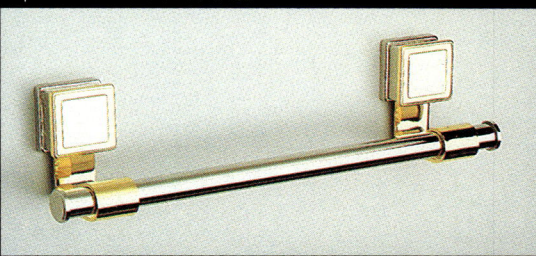

18" Towel Bar. . .031 / 460

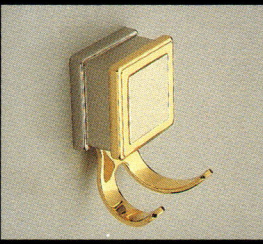

Robe Hooks. . .031 / 010

Hooded Tissue Holder. . .031 / 145

24" x 24" Mirror. . .031 / 616

Widespread Lavatory Set-"C" Spout. . .843 / 902

For further information call:
National: (800) 227-2734
California: (800) 238-8345
FAX: (800) 552-5236

JADO

PO BOX 1329 ● Camarillo, California 93011

JADO

SERIES GALLERIA

Finishes Available

- ■ **Silver Nickel/Gold**
- ■ **Brushed Chrome/Polished Chrome**
- ■ **Black Chrome/Gold**

Widespread Lavatory Set. . .823 / 903

Roman Tub Set with Hand Shower. . .823 / 922

3 Valve Tub & Shower Set. . .823 / 917

24'' x 24'' Mirror. . .033 / 606

Robe Hook. . .032 / 010

Hooded Tissue Holder. . .032 / 145

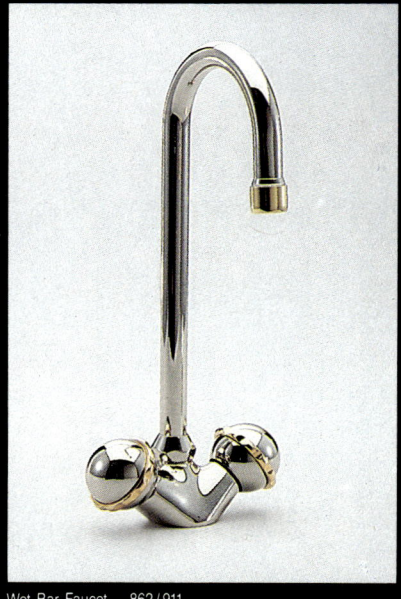

Wet Bar Faucet. . .862 / 911

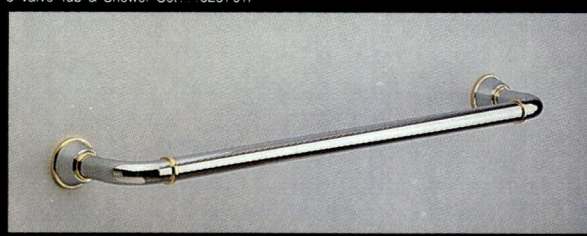

30'' Towel Bar. . .032 / 800

For further information call:
National: (800) 227-2734
California: (800) 238-8345
FAX: (800) 552-5236

JADO

PO BOX 1329 ● Camarillo, California 9301

JADO

500

SERIES ORIENTAL

Finishes Available

- **Polished Brass**
- **Polished Chrome**
- **Polished Gold**
- **Silver Nickel/Gold**

Widespread Lavatory Set...893/933

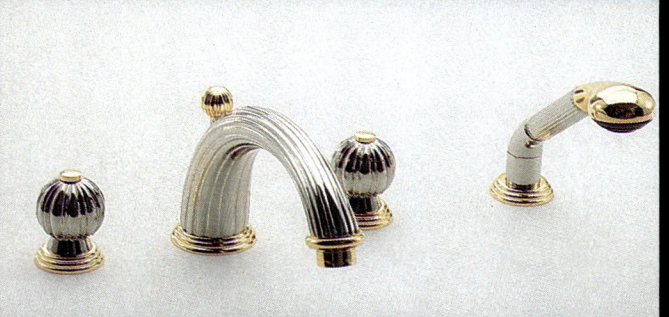

Roman Tub Set with Hand Shower...894/933

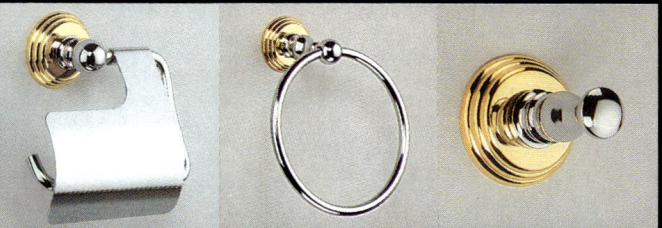

Hooded Tissue Holder...033/145   6'' Towel Ring...033/150   Robe Hook...033/010

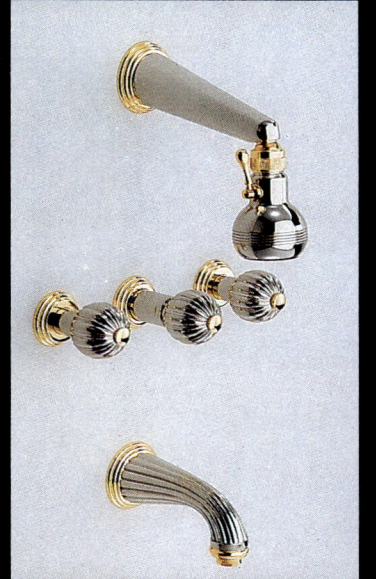

3 Valve Tub & Shower Set...855/931

24'' x 24'' Mirror...033/606

Single Hole Lavatory Set...891/903

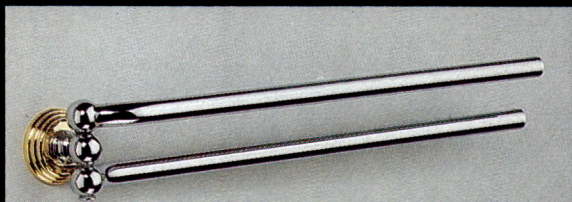

24'' Double Towel Bar...033/452

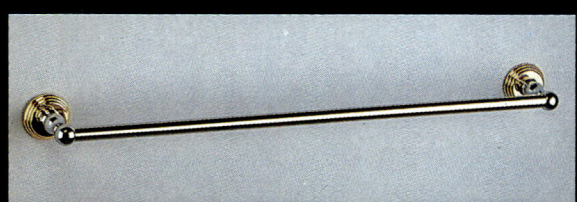

24'' Towel Bar...033/601

For further information call:
National: (800) 227-2734
California: (800) 238-8345
FAX: (800) 552-5236

JADO

PO BOX 1329 ● Camarillo, California 9301

JADO

SERIES EVERGREEN

Finishes Available

- Silver Nickel/Gold
- Brushed Nickel/Gold

Widespread Lavatory Set...853/907

Roman Tub Set with Hand Shower...855/927

Hooded Tissue Holder...021/145   6" Towel Ring...021/150   Robe Hook...021/002

Single Control Thermostatic Shower Set...875/907

3 Valve Tub and Shower Set...855/917

24" x 32" Mirror...021/608

Tumbler...021/161

Soap Dish...021/171

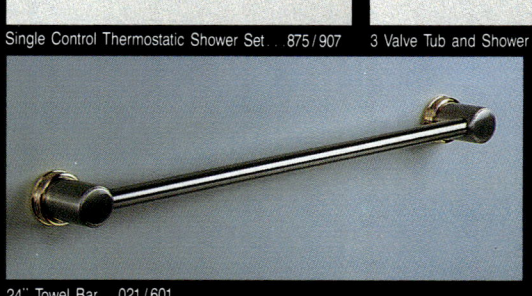

24" Towel Bar...021/601

Shelf...021/612

For further information call:
National: (800) 227-2734
California: (800) 238-8345
FAX: (800) 552-5236

JADO

PO BOX 1329 ● Camarillo, California 93011

JADO

SERIES CLASSIC

Finishes Available

- ■ **Brushed Nickel**
- ■ **Polished Chrome**
- ■ **Polished Brass**

Widespread Lavatory Set-Cross Handle. . .853 / 938

Roman Tub Set with Hand Shower-Cross Handle. . .855 / 990

Hooded Tissue Holder. . .033 / 145   6" Towel Ring. . .033 / 150

3 Valve Tub & Shower Set. . .855 / 948

24" Towel Bar. . .033 / 601

Widespread Lavatory Set-Straight Lever Handle. . .853 / 948

For further information call:
National: (800) 227-2734
California: (800) 238-8345
FAX: (800) 552-5236

JADO

PO BOX 1329 ● Camarillo, California 9301

LUXURY FORGED BRASS FROM GERMANY

PRODUCTS AVAILABLE

Single hole LAV sets
Widespread LAV sets
Wet bar Faucets
Single hole Bidet sets
3-hole Bidet sets
Roman tub sets
Roman tub with hand shower
3 valve tub and shower sets
2 valve shower sets
2 valve tub sets
Single control thermostatic shower sets
Tub and shower thermostatic sets
3/4" thermostatic mixing valve sets
5-port diverters
4-port diverters
1/2" and 3/4" wall valves
Body sprays
Wall angle stops

Hand shower systems
Robe Hooks
6" and 8" towel rings
12" towel bars
18" towel bars
24" towel bars
30" towel bars
24" double towel bars
Tissue holders
Tumbler holders
Soap dish holders
24" shelves
Mirrors
Toilet brush holders
Facial tissue box
Waste paper baskets
Wire soap trays

1/4 Turn Ceramic Disc Cartridge - **LIFETIME WARRANTY**

For further information call our Architectural Consultants
National: (800) 227-2734
California: (800) 238-8345
FAX: (800) 552-5236

PO BOX 1329 ● Camarillo, California 93011

SPEAKMAN DECORATIVE SENSORFLO™ FAUCETS[1]

- Style/Flair
- Color/Finish
- Simplicity of Operation
- Quality Trouble-Free Designs
- Designed for the Environment

SPEAKMAN'S Decorative Designed for the Nineties

The Speakman Decorative SENSORFLO Faucets have been designed for the nineties upscale decorator markets. The simplicity of operation, style and flair adds to the overall quality of the product.

See, feel, and compare the craftsmanship and beauty — engineered like no other faucet in the world.

Style/Flair
These ergonomically designed electronic faucets offer the ultimate in style and flair. The simplistic eyecatching shapes have contemporary and classical appeal.

Color/Finish
The colors and finishes have been developed for the designer in mind. White, black, polished chrome, and polished brass allow the designer/decorator many choices to integrate the product with the interior surroundings. Exquisite, lustrous finishes add beauty and softness to the product.

Simplicity of Operation
The Speakman Decorative SENSORFLO barrier-free products have been thoughtfully designed for all in mind.

The SENSORFLO products require no handles to turn on the flow of water. Simply place one's hands under the faucet as shown and the water flows. **The faucet of the nineties.**

SD-8075-A

SD-8058

SD-8061

SPEAKMAN
The Quality Leader Since 1869
P.O. Box 191, Wilmington, DE 19899-0191
1-302/764-9100, FAX: 1-302/764-1956

[1]Patent Pending
SENSORFLO™ — T.M. Speakman Company
©Copyright, Speakman Company, 1990
#92-0332   2/90

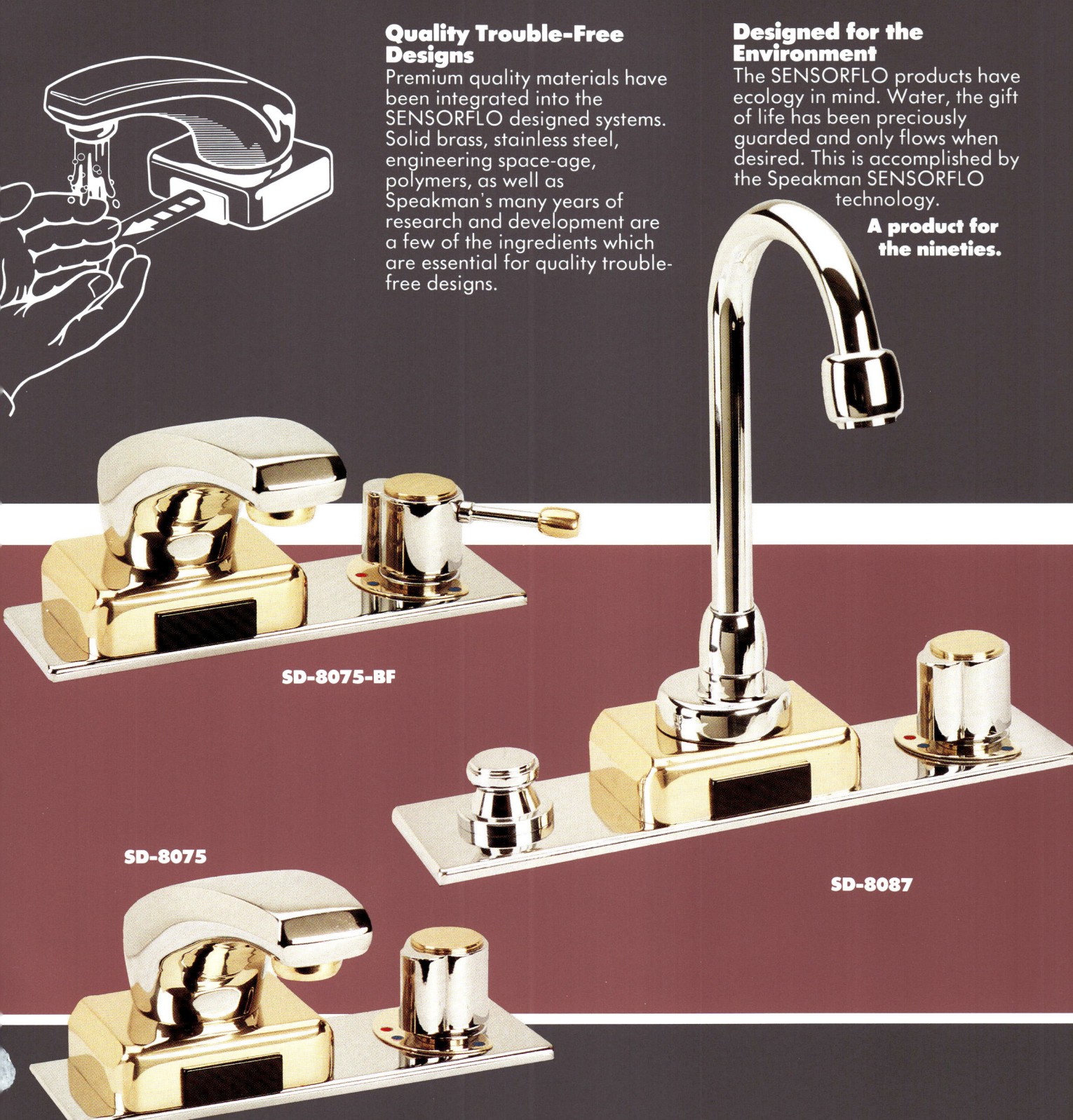

Quality Trouble-Free Designs

Premium quality materials have been integrated into the SENSORFLO designed systems. Solid brass, stainless steel, engineering space-age, polymers, as well as Speakman's many years of research and development are a few of the ingredients which are essential for quality trouble-free designs.

Designed for the Environment

The SENSORFLO products have ecology in mind. Water, the gift of life has been preciously guarded and only flows when desired. This is accomplished by the Speakman SENSORFLO technology.

A product for the nineties.

SD-8075-BF

SD-8075

SD-8087

Exciting New Finishes

The finishes offered include the deep luster of polished chrome, a blending of the durability of polished chrome and the beauty of brass accents, the contemporary look of polished chrome with black accents, and a touch of today's demand for color by using white epoxy.

Models range from the basics to include soap dispensers, temperature selection or under counter mixers, barrier-free design, and unique new drain operations.

Decorative SENSORFLO Electronic Sensor Faucets Product Line

Polished Chrome Design
SD-8000, SD-8005, SD-8007, SD-8008, SD-8010, SD-8015, SD-8017, SD-8018

White Design
SD-8030, SD-8035, SD-8037, SD-8038, SD-8040, SD-8045, SD-8047, SD-8048

Black/Chrome Design
SD-8051, SD-8055, SD-8057, SD-8058, SD-8061, SD-8065, SD-8067, SD-8068

Polished Chrome/Polished Brass Design
SD-8075, SD-8077, SD-8078, SD-8085, SD-8087, SD-8088

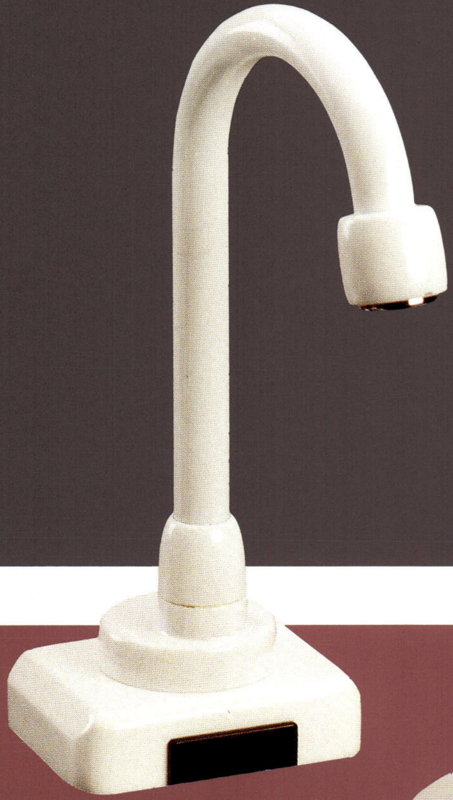

SD-8040

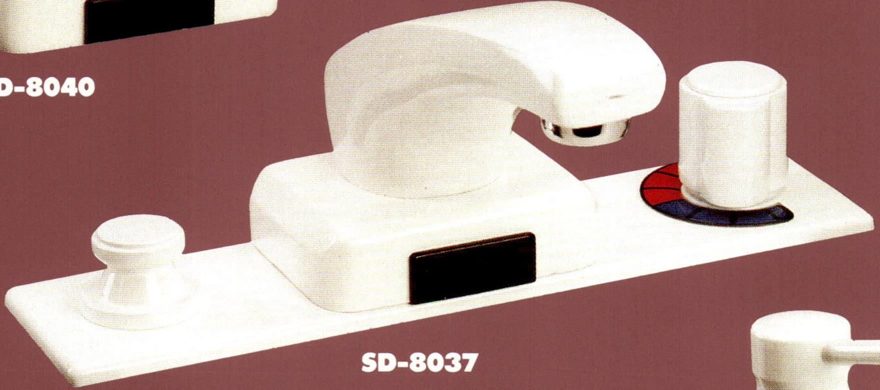

SD-8037

SD-8048

SPEAKMAN
The Quality Leader Since 1869
P.O. Box 191, Wilmington, DE 19899-0191
1-302/764-9100, FAX: 1-302/764-1956

MEMBER
PLUMBING
MANUFACTURERS
INSTITUTE

PERSONAL...

Hand Showers
Shower Systems
Shower Heads
Deck Mounts
Glide Bar Units
Accessories

Create a magnificent bathing atmosphere that reflects your own personal style.

Alsons ™

Alsons has been making innovative shower and bath products for over thirty years and has become the bathing preference for today's active and fitness-minded people.

For added bathing pleasure and the convenience of a hand-held shower, Alsons offers a complete selection to personalize any bath.

Alsons showers are available in eight beautiful finishes.

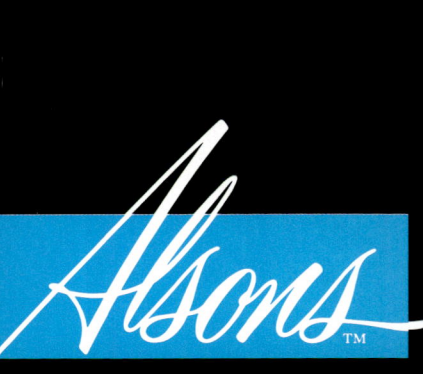

525 East Edna Place P.O. Box 31
Covina, California 91723
Phone: (818) 966-1668

Designer Faucets by ALTMANS

Ribbon Waterfiller

BAR FAUCET
With Pink Crystal Rope Rings

Paris Lavset

Dolphin Lavset

Monterey Waterfiller

Saucer Waterfiller

SUITE 80 Deckset

SUITE 20 LAVSET Melon Handles

This brochure is only
our enormous variet
faucets.

For full set of Catal
send $5.

If you are a specifie
please write to us on yo
For a complimentary C

C LAVSET With Line

F LAVSET With Crystal Swirl.

THERMOSTAT With Paris Handles

Antibes Waterfiller

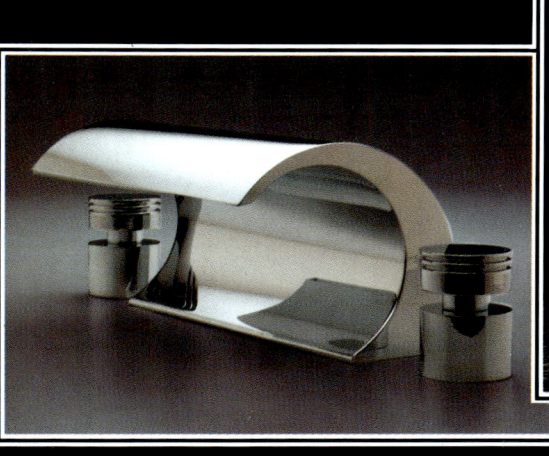

Atlantis Waterfiller

J LAVSET With Bordeaux Levers

...ling of
...quality

...please

...Dealer
...rhead
...ue.

E LAVSET With Opaque Crystal Rings

SUITE 50 Harmony Lavset.

ALTMAN FAUCETS ARE MODULAR.
ANY HANDLE CAN BE COMBINED
WITH ANY SPOUT. OVER 36,000
VARIATIONS.

J LAVSET With Canne Handles

G LAVSET With Bordeaux Cross Handles

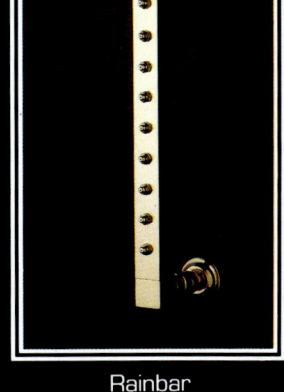

Rainbar

SUITE 10

by **ALTMANS**

C LAVSET LAQUER DE CHINE
Black/Gold With Turban Rings

G LAVSET With Wave Rings

F DECKSET With Line Cylinders and Rings

We use "State Of The Art" gem-hard carbide-ceramic disk valves that NEVER WEAR OUT! In fact, we guarantee FREE REPLACEMENT FOR THE LIFE OF THE FAUCET. A ¼ turn closes the valve with an absolute precision you can actually feel and they are 20% quieter than conventional valves.

B LAVSET With Riverstone Handles

Aquaduct Deck Spout

FOR THE NAME OF YOUR LOCAL ALTMANS
DISTRIBUTOR PLEASE CALL.
1-800-678-NINE (213) 859-0126

ALTMANS DISTRIBUTION / 655 n. lapeer, los angeles, california 90069

ARTISTIC BRASS™

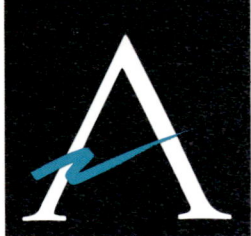

rtistic Brass first introduced decorative, solid brass fittings for the bath over 30 years ago. Today, we are recognized for our reputation for producing unparalleled quality and distinctive design.

We provide the assurance of solid brass construction and our handcrafted quality. Each brass component is polished, assembled, and tested by hand. Our exclusive Marine™ Protective Finish and ceramic disc valves ensure years of trouble-free service, backed by our 5-year limited warranty.

Artistic Brass offers a wide selection of contemporary and traditional styles. Classics · Colonial · Architectural Accents · España · Eclectic

Each series has a complete range of matching accessories, tub and shower fittings, and Roman tub sets, as shown on the two illustrated pages in this brochure.

Our many innovative decorative finishes will enable you to create a coordinated ensemble of faucets and accessories for your home.

Shown are the three decorative metal finish options for the Classics and Colonial collections and selected Eclectic series. España styles are available in Polished Brass. In addition, the 12 contemporary dual metal finishes and color combinations are pictured with the Architectural Accents collection.

Welcome to the world of Artistic Brass, a company created on a bedrock of design, uncompromising quality and a dedication to the design needs of the most discriminating homeowners.

Polished Brass

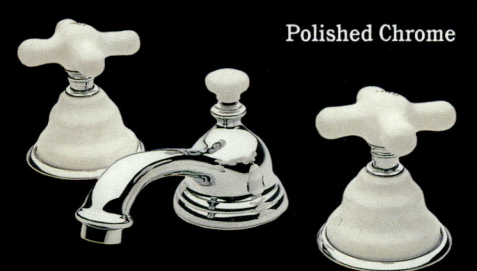

Polished Chrome

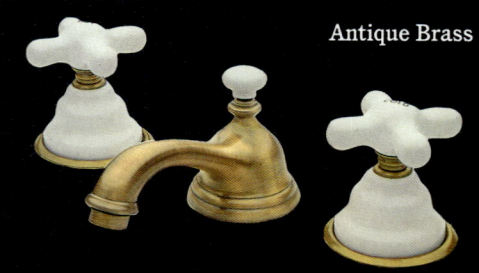

Antique Brass

605-L
4" Centerset

65-L
Widespread Lavatory Fitting

Clarion/65 Series

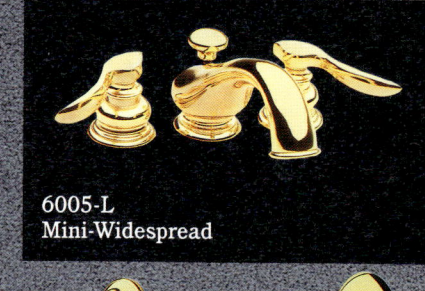

6005-L
Mini-Widespread

6046
Towel Ring

5046
Towel Ring

2246
Towel Ring

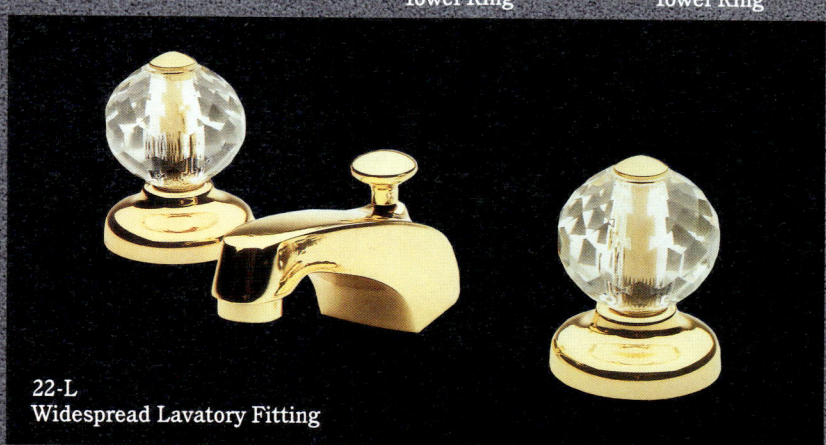

22-L
Widespread Lavatory Fitting

Regency/22 Series

208-L
4" Centerset

26-L
Widespread Lavatory Fitting

Classic/26 Series

2646
Towel Ring

22-3D51
3-Handle Tub/ Shower
Combination

512-RTS
Roman Tub Spout

342-L
4″ Centerset

3006-L
Mini-Widespread

3446
Towel Ring

340-L
Widespread Lavatory Fitting

Winchester/340 Series

5046
Towel Ring

6046
Towel Ring

407-L
4″ Centerset

47-L
Widespread Lavatory Fitting

Fredericksburg/47 Series

604-L
4″ Centerset

64-L
Widespread Lavatory Fitting

Lexington/64 Series

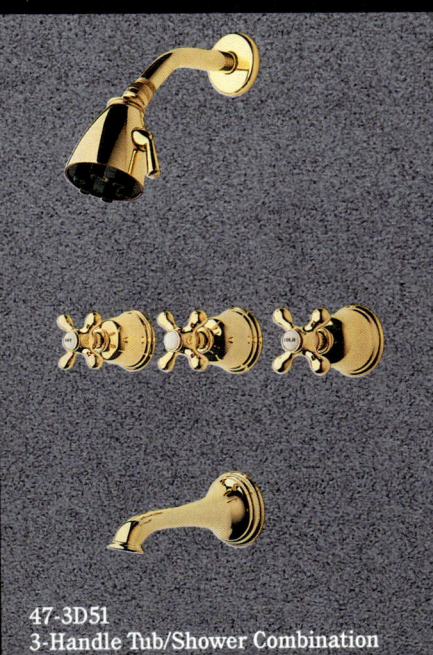

47-3D51
3-Handle Tub/Shower Combination

6004-L
Mini-Widespread

ARTISTIC BRASS FAUCETS AND ACCESSORIES
CLASSICS, COLONIAL, ESPAÑA, AND ECLECTIC SERIES

Artistic Brass offers a wide range of fittings and accessories, featuring our exclusive Marine™ Protective Finish (MPF) and ceramic disc valves.

Please see your showroom representative for more details.

LAVATORY FAUCETS

Widespread Lavatory Fitting

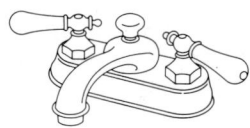
4" Centerset

Mini-Widespread
Styles available: 3002-L, 3004-L, 3006-L, 6003-L , 6004-L, 6005-L

TUB AND SHOWER FITTINGS

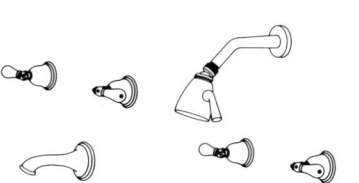
Tub Fitting   **Shower Fitting**

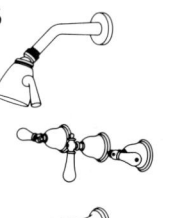
3-Handle Tub/Shower Combination

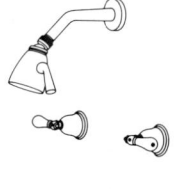
2-Handle Tub/Shower Combination

Single Control Shower Fitting with Pressure Balance Valve

Single Control Tub/Shower Combination Fitting with Pressure Balance Valve

---

DECK MOUNT ROMAN TUB FITTINGS

Roman Tub Spout   **Quick Connect Roman Tub Spout 3211-RTS Only**

Roman Tub Set Deck Mount

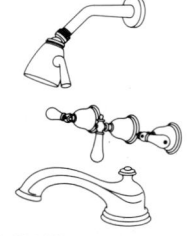
3-Handle Tub/Shower Combination with Roman Tub Spout

Roman Tub Set and Personal Shower with Retractable Hose

Roman Tub Set and Personal Shower with Cradle Bracket

*Bidet
Specify wall or deck mount.

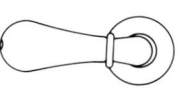
**Trip Waste and Overflow

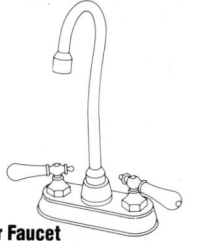
Tank Lever Handle

Wet Bar Faucet

Minispread Wet Bar Faucet
Styles available: 3002-WBF, 3004-WBF, 3006-WBF, 6003-WBF, 6004-WBF, 6005-WBF

ACCESSORIES

18" Towel Bar   24" Towel Bar   30" Towel Bar

Robe Hook

Towel Ring

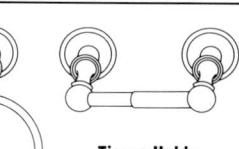
Tissue Holder

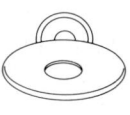
Wall Soap Dish

Toothbrush and Tumbler Holder

MARINE™ PROTECTIVE FINISH
An Artistic Brass Exclusive

The lustrous finish of each Artistic Brass fitting and accessory is protected by our exclusive Marine™ Protective Finish (MPF).

MPF is a crystal clear protective coating, 4 times thicker than conventional coatings, that protects the brass even in harsh salt air or hard water environments.

MPF's durability and resistance to corrosion not only meet and exceed industry standards but are backed by our 5 year limited warranty.

CERAMIC VALVES
- Quarter-turn, positive stop
- Non-rising stem
- Ceramic Disc
    Washerless
    Solid Brass Construction
    Guaranteed Long Life

MINI-WIDESPREADS
- Elegant alternative to 4" centerset
- Styling of a widespread faucet
- Proportioned and engineered to fit 4" drilled vanities
- Quick connect spout and one-piece valve body for easy installations

*Bidet: If required by local code, order vacuum breaker 5504.
**Trip Waste and Overflow: Shipped standard with grid-type drain. If local code requires pop-up stopper-type drain, specify when ordering.
Certified by manufacturer: Complies with California Energy Standards and other states' standards of 3.0 gpm maximum.

Architectural Accents features 7 dual-metal finish combinations plus white, almond, and black color finishes with a choice of polished brass or polished chrome trim.

The decorative metal finishes are hand polished in an 8-step process and are protected by Artistic Brass' exclusive Marine™ Protective Finish.

The color finishes are high impact polymer resins which are bonded to solid brass, under high temperatures, in Artistic Brass' state-of-the-art infrared ovens. This thermoset process produces durable color finishes that are highly resistant to chipping and scratching.

PC/PB
Polished Chrome/
Polished Brass

PB/PC
Polished Brass/
Polished Chrome

PB/PC
Polished Brass/
Polished Chrome

SC/PB
Satin Chrome/
Polished Brass

SC/PB
Satin Chrome/
Polished Brass

SC/PC
Satin Chrome/
Polished Chrome

SB/PB
Satin Brass/
Polished Brass

AL/PB
Almond/
Polished Brass

BK/PB
Black/
Polished Brass

BK/PC
Black/
Polished Chrome

WH/PB
White/
Polished Brass

WH/PC
White/
Polished Chrome

PB
Polished Brass

PC
Polished Chrome

Architectural Accents I/Finishes

PC/PB
Polished Chrome/
Polished Brass

PB/PC
Polished Brass/
Polished Chrome

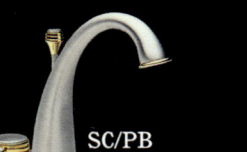
SC/PB
Satin Chrome/
Polished Brass

SC/PC
Satin Chrome/
Polished Chrome

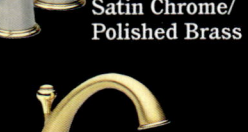
SB/PB
Satin Brass/
Polished Brass

AL/PB
Almond/
Polished Brass

BK/PB
Black/
Polished Brass

BK/PC
Black/
Polished Chrome

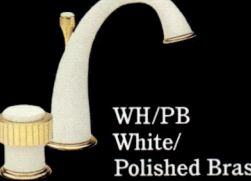
WH/PB
White/
Polished Brass

WH/PC
White/
Polished Chrome

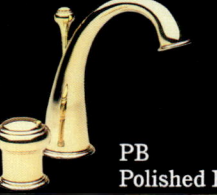
PB
Polished Brass

PC
Polished Chrome

80-L
Widespread Lavatory Fitting

Wave/80 Series/Architectural Accents II

8046
Towel Ring

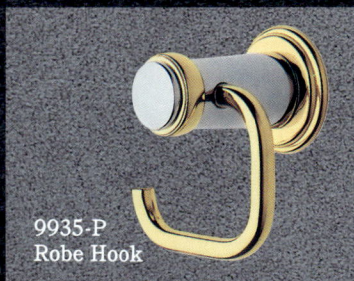

9935-P
Robe Hook

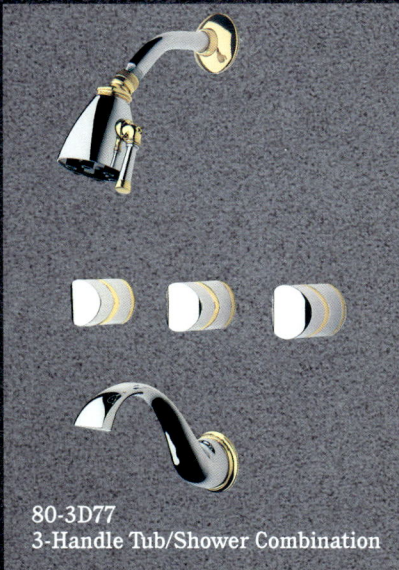

80-3D77
3-Handle Tub/Shower Combination

87-L
Widespread Lavatory Fitting

Ionic/87 Series/Architectural Accents II

3800-RTS
Quick Connect
Roman Tub Spout

9346
Towel Ring

9346
Towel Ring
Black Marble

93-L
Widespread Lavatory Fitting
White Onyx

93-L
Widespread Lavatory Fitting
Polished Chrome/Polished Brass Finish

Cubist/93 Series/Architectural Accents III

Polished Brass/Polished Chrome Finish

Travertine

Black Marble

2246
Towel Ring

91-L
Widespread Lavatory Fitting

Crystal/91 Series/Architectural Accents II

9446
Towel Ring

94-L
Widespread Lavatory Fitting

Robie/94 Series/Architectural Accents III

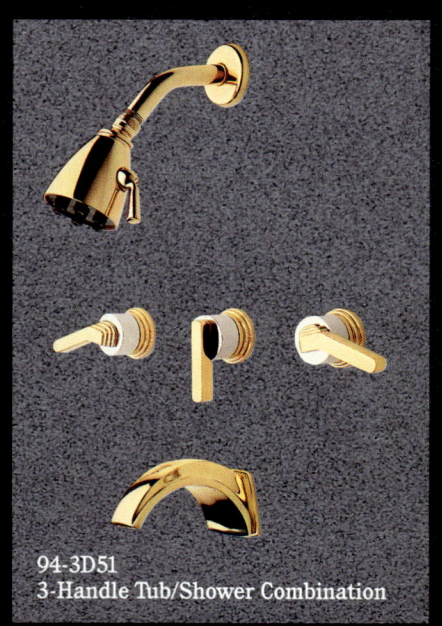

94-3D51
3-Handle Tub/Shower Combination

Onyx, marble, and travertine are products of nature.
The veining and color may vary from those shown.

3955-P
Wall Soap Dish

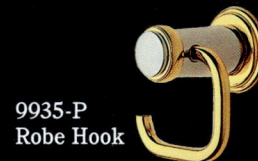

9935-P
Robe Hook

95-L
Widespread Lavatory Fitting

Doric/95 Series/Architectural Accents II

97-L
Widespread Lavatory Fitting

Ionic/97 Series/Architectural Accents II

92-L
Widespread Lavatory Fitting

Diamond Cut/92 Series/Architectural Accents II

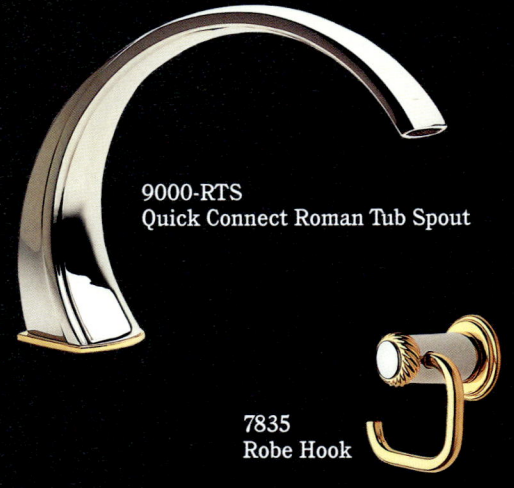

9000-RTS
Quick Connect Roman Tub Spout

7835
Robe Hook

98-L
Widespread Lavatory Fitting

Hellenistic/98 Series/Architectural Accents II

Espańa

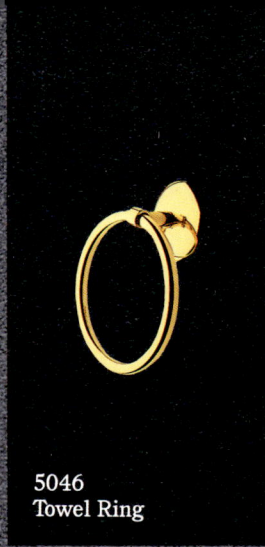

48-L
Widespread Lavatory Fitting

Swan/48 Series

480-RTS
Roman Tub Spout

5046
Towel Ring

400-RTS
Roman Tub Spout

4046
Towel Ring

400-L
Widespread Lavatory Fitting

Barcelona/400 Series

450-L
Widespread Lavatory Fitting

La Reina/450 Series

4500-RTS
Roman Tub Spout

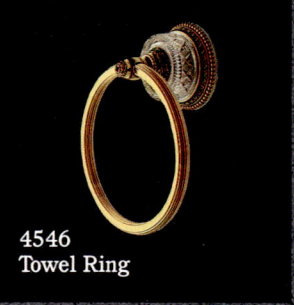

4546
Towel Ring

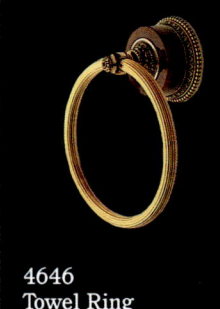

4646
Towel Ring
Brown Onyx

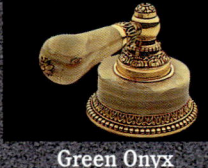

Green Onyx

Black Onyx

460-L
Widespread Lavatory Fitting
Brown Onyx

Onyx/460 Series

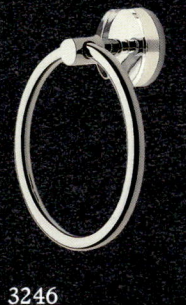

3246
Towel Ring

322-L
4" Centerset

320-L
Widespread Lavatory Fitting

Reflections/320 Series

312-L
4" Centerset

310-L
Widespread Lavatory Fitting

Delicious/310 Series

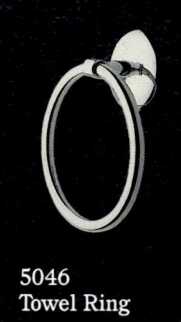
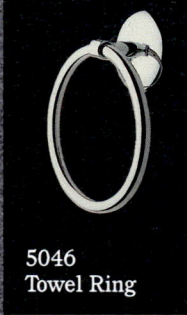

5046
Towel Ring

740-L
Widespread Lavatory Fitting

Wedgwood/740 Series

7446
Towel Ring

590-L
Widespread Lavatory Fitting

580-L
Widespread Lavatory Fitting

Grand Tour/Flanders & Picardy/580 & 590 Series

570-L
Widespread Lavatory Fitting

Grand Tour/Verona/570 Series

5846
Towel Ring

5946
Towel Ring

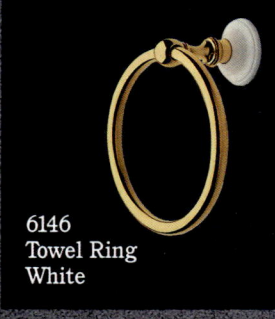

6146
Towel Ring
White

ARTISTIC BRASS FAUCETS AND ACCESSORIES
ARCHITECTURAL ACCENTS

Artistic Brass offers a wide range of Architectural Accents fittings and accessories, featuring our exclusive Marine™ Protective Finish (MPF) and ceramic disc valves.

Please see your showroom representative for more details.

LAVATORY FAUCETS

Widespread Lavatory Fitting

Mini-Widespread
Style available: 7006-L

TUB AND SHOWER FITTINGS

Tub Fitting

Shower Fitting

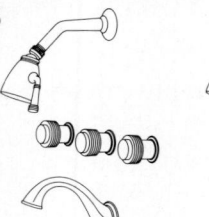
3-Handle Tub/Shower Combination

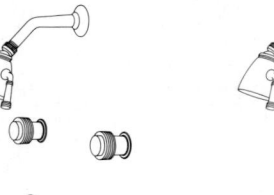
2-Handle Tub/Shower Combination

Single Control Shower Fitting with Pressure Balance Valve

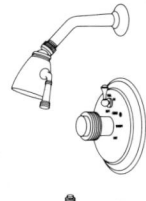
Single Control Tub/Shower Combination Fitting with Pressure Balance Valve

DECK MOUNT ROMAN TUB FITTINGS

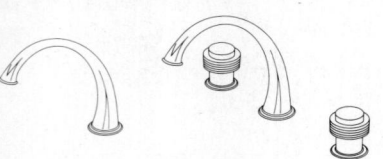
Quick Connect Roman Tub Spout

Roman Tub Set Deck Mount

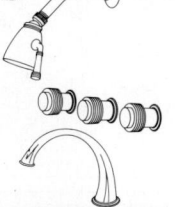
3-Handle Tub/Shower Combination with Roman Tub Spout

Roman Tub Set and Personal Shower with Retractable Hose

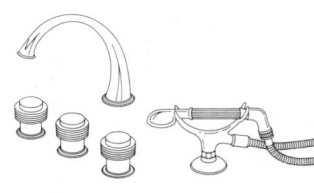
Roman Tub Set and Personal Shower with Cradle Bracket

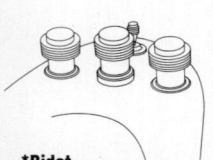
***Bidet**
Specify wall or deck mount

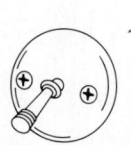
****Trip Waste and Overflow**

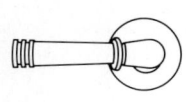
Tank Lever Handle

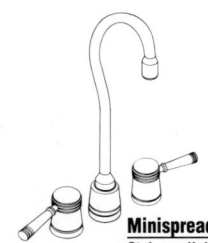
Minispread Wet Bar Faucet
Style available: 7006-WBF

ACCESSORIES

18″ Towel Bar   **24″ Towel Bar**   **30″ Towel Bar**

Robe Hook

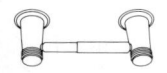
Towel Ring

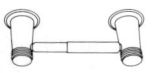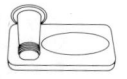
Tissue Holder

Wall Soap Dish

Toothbrush and Tumbler Holder

18″ Shelf

LONG BROACH STEMS

Architectural Accents tub and shower fittings are shipped standard with long broach stems for easy installation without critical tolerances.

ROMAN TUB VALVES AND QUICK CONNECT SPOUTS

- Easy rough-ahead installation of clamp-type valves and spout connector allows installation of handle trim and snap-on decorative spout after deck is finished.
- High flow capacity 3/4″ valves

ANTI-SCALD PRESSURE BALANCE VALVES

- Maintains constant water temperature.
- Eliminates sudden bursts of scalding hot or freezing cold water.
- Automatically compensates for changes in water pressure.
- Meets code requirements.

---

*Bidet: If required by local code, order vacuum breaker 5504.
**Trip Waste and Overflow: Shipped standard with grid-type drain. If local code requires pop-up stopper-type drain, specify when ordering.
 Certified by manufacturer: Complies with California Energy Standards and other states' standards of 3.0 gpm maximum.
 Patents pending on all Architectural Accents products.

CPA-105 9/89 150M

ARTISTIC BRASS™   A Masco Company
4100 Ardmore Avenue South Gate, California 90280
©1989 Masco Building Products Corporation Printed in U.S.A.

EDITION DORNBRACHT

Designer Fittings and Accessories for the Bathroom

DORNBRACHT

...water has never flowed more beautifully

Top design, inspired ideas, ideal solutions. The key to the bathroom of your dreams.
Exclusive creations, naturally combined with technical perfection.
Available in a wide variety of combinations for those who seek the out-of-the-ordinary.
The latest example is our Edition Fino.
Circle vs. straight line. Dieter Sieger's contribution to aesthetic geometry.
The circle as basis of the exciting contrast to the straight line reaches its aesthetic realization in the Fino collection.

An uncompromisingly modern design, whose character lies in its conical and cylindrical forms.
Its most striking feature is the high-tech lever, available in various finishes to create an interesting contrast with the base.
Edition Point — the epitome of modern design.

EDITION DOMANI

560

Futuristic in design and technology, the fitting and accessories are modern without being trendy.
The excitingly clear, functional design conceals the most advanced ceramic disc cartridge technology.

The fascination of this Edition lies in its geometric forms:
the cylindrical base and the hemispherical heads.
In addition, these two elements are available in various finishes which can be individually selected to offer further contrast.
Exciting, clear design for a totally modern bathroom concept.

EDITION MADISON 360

The great classic with its own nostalgic charm.
Its character lies in the cross-head handles inlaid with porcelain and the hexagonal outlets.
Fittings and accessories that combine style with function.

EDITION MADISON FLAIR

An elegant variation of our classic.
The surfaces of the lever inlays can be combined to contrast with those of the fittings.
With matching accessories to give your bathroom a certain flair.

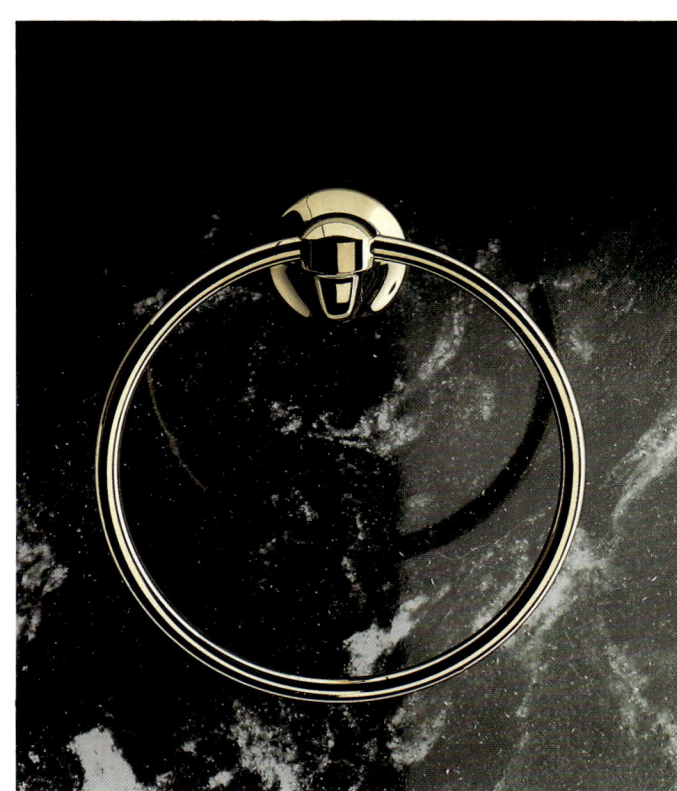

A continuation in design of the popular Edition Bel Air.
The outlet is perfection in form with its flowing, harmonious lines.
The handles are styled to unite beauty with function.
Fittings and accessories — in perfect harmony.

Almost a classic among modern designer fittings.
The practical square handles form an appealing contrast to the graceful lines of the curved outlets.
For timeless beauty in the bathroom. With the matching accessories, even more beautiful.

The distinguishing artistic features are the spherical handles.
An exciting "touch" of design.
Fitting and accessories — perfect for bathrooms in which geometric forms predominate.

EDITION BEL AIR

The popular fittings and accessories in perfect harmony.
With various ring-types, to give the bathroom of your dreams a more individual touch.
Bathroom design with personality.

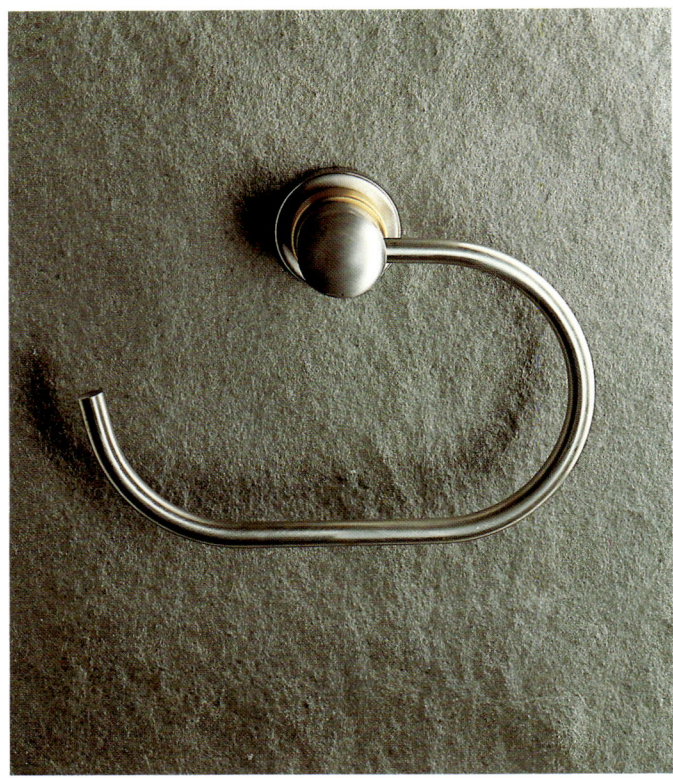

EDITION RIVIERA

Fittings and accessories serve as graceful adornments for the luxury bathroom.
Classic Italian design — reflected in the perfectly formed outlet and exquisitely styled handles — for an atmosphere of elegance.

EDITION ATHEN

A design inspired by the forms of classical antiquity.
This Grecian style particularly comes into
its own in the luxury bathroom.

EDITION 5000

Created to harmonize with the "Toboga" line from Villeroy and Boch.
Organically formed with striking design features.
For harmony in bathroom design.

The character of this Edition derives from the graceful lines of the outlet.
A point of decorative interest is created by the beaded edging of the handles, which catches and reflects the light.
A royal design — in fittings and accessories.

VARIETY IN DESIGN

Dornbracht offers a variety of design for the bathroom; a wide choice of elegant Editions and a multitude of variations. A wide range of fine surface treatment and trend-setting colours offer a choice for every taste.
Let your imagination run free: Some additions give you the option to realize your own personal design ideas.

Trend-setters: our editions Bel Air and Bellevue, with their myriad possibilities to combine different ring types and ring finishes. A wide range of design variations with the high-tech lever and ring in the edition Point.
Create your vision — rich in contrast with the clearly defined half-sphere of the edition Polaris. And — brand new — the finish combinations of the "Sieger" edition Fino.

The modern bathroom as a reflection of personal life-style is becoming an ever-increasing trend. With this in mind, we have rejected rigid and restricting programmes and instead offer our customers Editions to meet with individual tastes. That is what we mean by variety in design.

chrome .00

gold plated .01

bronze .02

dull chrome .05

dull nickel .06

silver nickel .08

Durabrass .09

white .12

black .13

red .15

turquoise .19

smoke grey metallic .30

black metallic .31

mat black .33

Our wide range encompasses fittings for wash-basin, bath-tub, shower and bidet, in all technical variations. Whatever plans you have for improving your bathroom — Dornbracht design offers unlimited possibilities.

For your wash-basin you may decide on the practical single lever mixer with multi-function handle, allowing you to control the water flow and hot and cold with one hand.

You might prefer the classic three hole basin mixer — central outlet with separate handles for hot and cold water. Or perhaps the compact and convenient form of the single hole basin mixer, in which the handles are incorporated into the base of the fitting, holds more appeal for your. It's all a question of style.

Individuality in design is also available for the bath — from the four hole bath/shower mixer set with deck-mounted outlet, handles and hand shower, to wall-mounted and in-wall fittings, where all supply pipes are concealed — everything is possible.

Our shower programme is equally versatile and varied — for example, our shower heads and body sprays, available with separate volume controls if desired. We also offer a variety of alternatives for the bidet — you can choose from single hole, three hole or single lever bidet mixer sets. The most modern technology is incorporated into our thermostats for baths, showers and bidets — for perfect temperature control at your finger tips. Whatever your wishes for the bathroom of your dreams, there are no technical limitations with Dornbracht.

The real beauty of Dornbracht Design is that it runs true to form — right to the end. Matching accessories give harmony to the corresponding editions. A complete range, starting with mirrors and extending to towel rings and holders, soap dishes and mouthwash glasses — perfection in form and function.

Our collection incorporates top design for the kitchen. A number of our Editions include a selection of stylish sink fittings, specially designed with function in mind. Your specialist dealer has comprehensive brochure material to help your select your desired Edition. Or simply write to us. Dornbracht brings design into the bathroom.

DORNBRACHT

...water has never flowed more beautifully

DORNBRACHT

...water has never flowed more beautifully

Dornbracht, D-5860 Iserlohn, W.-Germany

Represented exclusively by

International Corporation

1201 West Loop North, Suite 170
Houston, Texas 77055
Phone 713/688–1862   Fax 713/688–9025

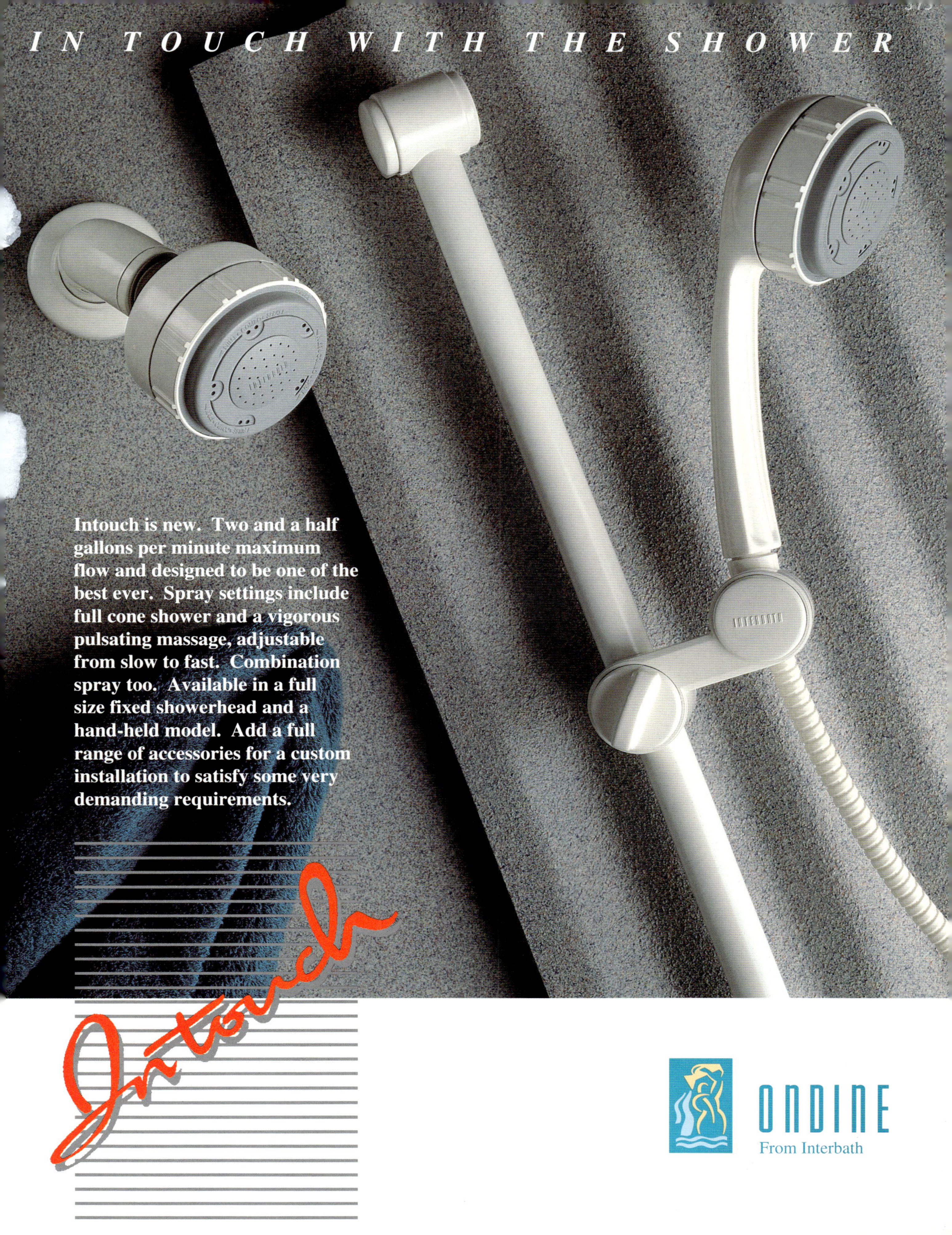

IN TOUCH WITH THE SHOWER

Intouch is new. Two and a half gallons per minute maximum flow and designed to be one of the best ever. Spray settings include full cone shower and a vigorous pulsating massage, adjustable from slow to fast. Combination spray too. Available in a full size fixed showerhead and a hand-held model. Add a full range of accessories for a custom installation to satisfy some very demanding requirements.

Intouch

ONDINE
From Interbath

Spray settings are easily selected by the turn of a dial. Gradually move from a full cone spray to a combination with pulsating massage and to slow and fast massage sprays.

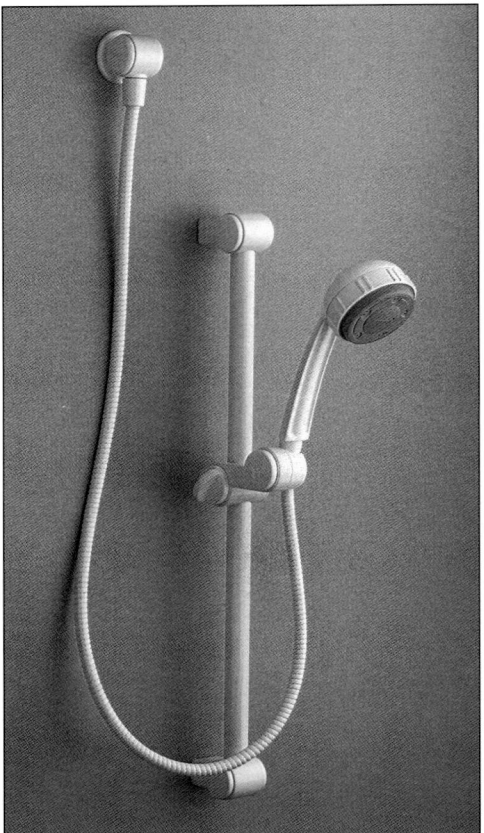 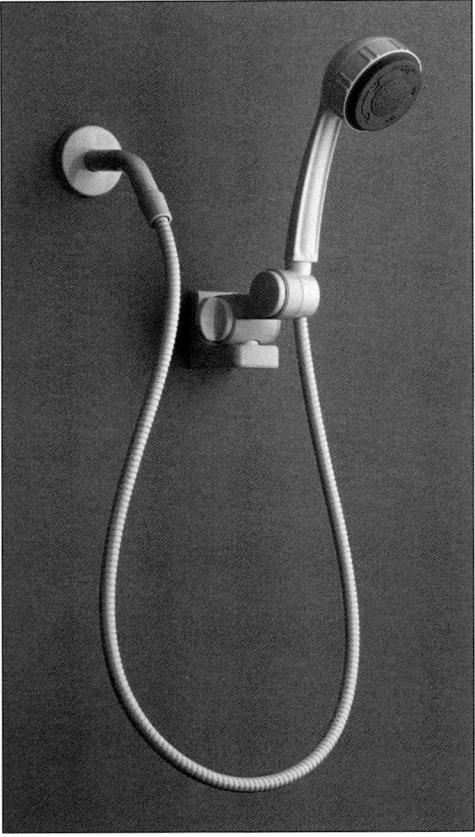

The right accessories are important. A 24 inch slide bar (#28600) allows instant height adjustment as well as horizontal and vertical spray angle positioning.
To specify the complete unit use model No. I 313 AWW.

A similar wall mount having 1/2 inch NPT connections (see part # I713ACWW) may be used for installation directly to a water supply outlet.
To specify the complete unit use model No. I 513AWW.

Intouch™ slide bar, 24 inch long. White
Model No. 28600 WW

Intouch™ Hand-held Shower.
White. Model No.26100WW

Intouch™ Showerhead.
White. Model No.26600WW

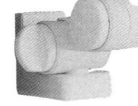

Intouch™ Wall Mount.
White. Model No. 28010WW

Shower Arm Mount.
White. Model No. 28083

Intouch™ Supply Elbow.
1/2 in. x 1/2 in. White. Model No.27430WW

Intouch™ Shower Arm.
Adjustable inlet, 1/2 in. White. Model No.27422WW

Metaflex™ Hose.
White. 1/2 in. x 1/2 in. Model No.28213WW

Intouch™ Wall Mount.
With 1/2 inch hose outlet. White. Model No. 27431WW

Refer to ONDINE full line catalog for accessories not shown. All specifications subject to change without notice.

ONDINE
From Interbath

IB 500   © 1991, Interbath, Inc.   Interbath Inc.   427 N. Baldwin Park Blvd., City of Industry, CA 91746   Phone: 818 369 1841   Fax: 818 961 353

Spray adjustment.

Elite II™ shower sprays adjust gradually from a fine needle to full flow. There are pulsating massage spray settings and a combination spray. Specially selected materials and innovative mechanical design help prevent clogging and corrosion.

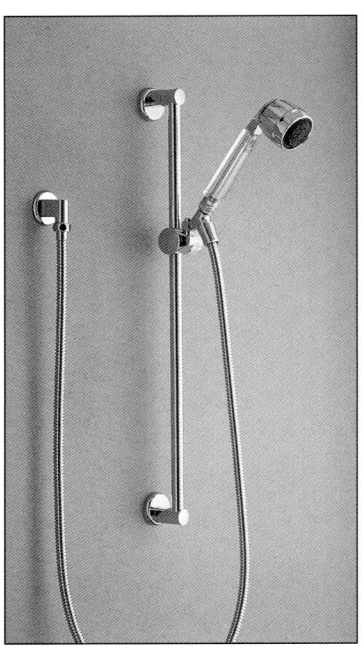

Model No. 773

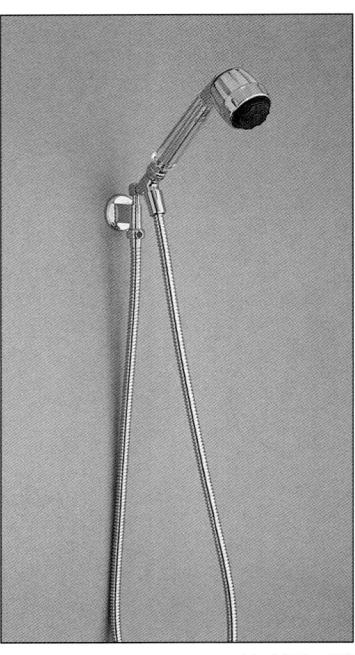

Model No. 573

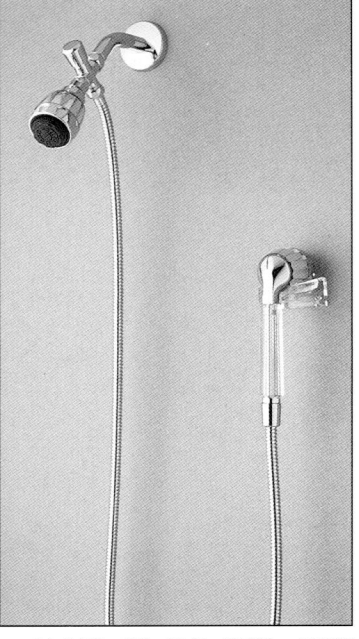

Model No. 173 with No. 28490 and 28719

Model No. 773 includes a 24 inch slide bar for instant shower height adjustment.

Model No. 573 installs to a 1/2 inch NPT outlet. Includes supply elbow, handset adaptor and 59 inch interlock hose.

Model No. 173 comes with acrylic wall hanger, Elite II™ handset and 59 inch interlock hose.

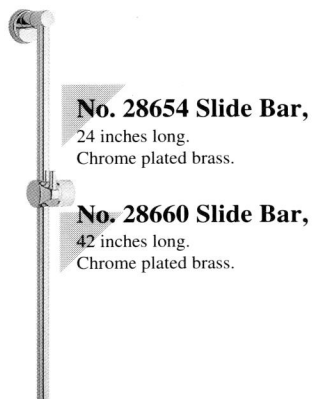

No. 28654 Slide Bar,
24 inches long.
Chrome plated brass.

No. 28660 Slide Bar,
42 inches long.
Chrome plated brass.

No. 28320 Wall Hanger
Clear acrylic.

No. 28490 Elite II™ Showerhead
1/2 inch inlet, chrome plated brass and clear acrylic.

No. 286313/657 Wall Mount and Swivel Adaptor.
1/2 inch x 1/2 inch, chrome plated brass.

No. 228719 Diverter Valve
For shower arm. 1/2 inch inlet, 1/2 inch outlets for fixed and hand-held showers. Chrome plated brass.

No. 28195 Shower Hose
59 inches long, interlock profile design, chrome plated brass. 1/2 inch x 1/2 inch.

No. 28090 Elite II™ Handset
Chrome plated brass and clear acrylic.

No. 28430 Tub Spout
3/4 inch inlet with 1/2 inch adaptor. Side outlet for hand-held shower. Chrome plated brass.

All items listed are chrome plated unless designer finishes are specifically requested.
Refer to Ondine® full line catalog for accesories not shown.
Ondine® showers comply with all code requirements as currently written. All specifications subject to change without notice.

From Interbath

IB 503   © 1991, Interbath, Inc.   Interbath Inc.   427 N. Baldwin Park Blvd., City of Industry, CA 91746   Phone: 818 369 1841   Fax: 818 961 353

IN TOUCH WITH THE SHOWER

Exceptional performance. Advanced design. Old fashioned value.

Regent showerheads are made of solid brass. They come in two sizes, both engineered to show what a shower can do at a flow rate of just 2.5 gallons per minute.

A lever control allows for convenient spray adjustment, full flow to fine needle.

Regent

ONDINE
From Interbath

All Ondine® showerheads shown below are equipped with a flow controller that limits water use to 2.5 US gallons per minute at 80 psi. Ondine® flow controllers automatically adjust to lower water pressure for superior performance. Symbols shown identify specific feautures:

||| Adjustable Spray ≡ Pulsating Massage Spray |‖| Combination Adjustable/Massage Spray
⬤ Temporary Shut-Off Control ♣ Saves Water and Energy.

No.28446
Watersaver Showerhead.
Adjustable spray. Designed to prevent clogging and corrosion. Chrome plated ABS and brass.

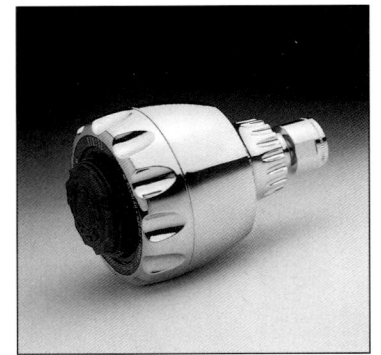

No.28410 ELITE MASSAGE™.
Continuous adjustment of shower spray from full flow to fine needle and further on to combination massage and full massage. Specially selected materials and innovative mechanical design help prevent clogging and corrosion. Chrome plated ABS and brass.

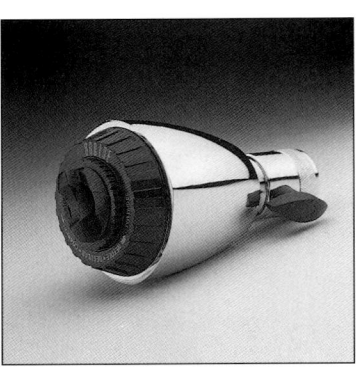

No. 29446
Super Watersaver Showerhead.
Same as No.28446 above. Includes manual flow controller.

NO. 28490 Elite II™ Showerhead.
Same feature as NO. 28410 above. Chrome plated brass and clear acrylic.

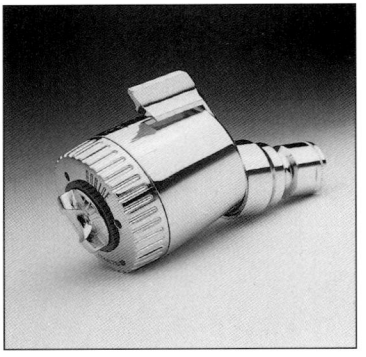

No. 28405
Watersaver Massage.
Lever switches to three different settings, including temporary shut-off. Sprays include pulsating massage and a fully adjustable shower flow, fine to coarse. Chrome plated ABS and brass.

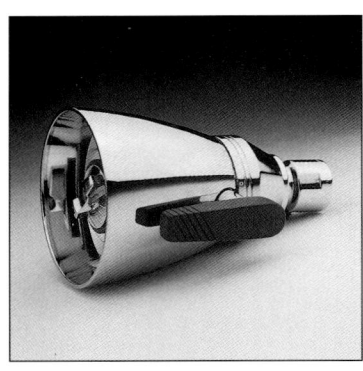

No. 28455 REGENT™ Showerhead.
Large lever controls two concentric spray rings, both independently adjustable from fine needle to full flow.
Specially selected materials for spray forming components help prevent clogging and corrosion. Solid brass, chrome plated.

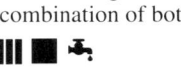

No. 28303 Deluxe Watersaver.
Spray settings are a fully adjustable outer, strong center flow and a combination of both. Lever control.

No. 28454 REGENT™ Showerhead.
Large lever controls full cone spray from fine needle to regular and coarse flows. Invigorating center spray. Designed to help prevent clogging and corrosion. Solid brass, chrome plated.

All items listed are chrome plated unless designer finishes are specifically requested.
Refer to Ondine® full line catalog for accesories not shown.
Ondine® showers comply with all code requirements as currently written. All specifications subject to change without notice.

ONDINE
From Interbath

IB 502   © 1991 Interbath, Inc.   Interbath Inc. 427 N. Baldwin Park Blvd., City of Industry, CA 91746   Phone: 818 369 1841 Fax: 818 961 353

The Greatest Advance In Bathing Since Hot Water.

The UltraValve™ Sho

It Just May Be The Most Intelligent

The Shower with a Brain.

This is what the future will be. A water delivery system that thinks before you do–because its integrated microprocessor adjusts the temperature of the water before it even touches your body. A system that automatically balances water pressure and gives you double protection against scalding. Only one such system exists today. The UltraValve System. That's why the U.S. government granted us a patent.*

So Safe It's Fail Safe.

Scalding hot water can give you third degree burns in one second. With UltraValve, that can never happen. Its reliable, mircroprocessor protects you from inadvertently setting the temperature above 112°F.
And if it ever does go above that, an ingenious memory valve** instantly shuts the water off.

Nirvana at Your Fingertip.

UltraValve turns on with a touch of your finger and automatically mixes hot and cold water to 98°F. Want it higher? Just set it to the temperature you want. UtraValve responds in seconds, then constantly maintains the temperature you selected. Warning: indulgences of this magnitude are habit-forming.

Install It Anywhere.

Because it has a mind of its own, you can put UltraValve wherever you want it. Inside the shower–or on an outside wall, where you can turn on the water before you step in.

*patent applied for and approved
**contains Memrysafe® technology

The Greatest Advance In Bathing Since Hot Water.

UltraValve™

er Control System. 585

ter Delivery System Ever Invented.

Whatever Your Bathroom Decor,
UltraValve™ Looks Right At Home.

What's Behind The UltraValve Shower Control System?

Sheer Genius.

Ultravalve: Model No.: V-210-132

Physical Dimensions:
- Control Module – 5.75 x 5.75 x 1.5 inches
- Valve Body – 6.0 x 4.5 x 3.5 inches

Approximate Weight: 6.5 Lbs.

Connections:
- Electric – 115 Volt GFI
- Inlet – ½" x 14 NPT Female
- Discharge – ½" x 14 NPT Female

Operating Characteristics:
- Key Actuated Microprocessor control
- Operating Voltage – 9 Volts with Auxiliary 9Volt Alkaline Battery
- Control Temperature Range – 70°F to 112°F
- Inlet Water Temperature Range
  - Cold = 45°F Min. to 83°F Max.
  - Hot = 165°F Max.
- Maximum Rated Operating Pressure–125 PSIG
- MEMRYSAFE® Activation Temperatures –118° to 120° F
- Flow Range = 3.0–6.0 GPM

Materials of Construction:
- Valve Body–Cast Brass
- Valve Components
  - Fused Silica – Acetal Copolymer
  - Buna "N" Rubber – CDA 260 Brass
  - 304 Stainless Steel – 70/30 CTRG, Brass
  - Glass Filled Polymer
- Memrysafe® Actuator
  - Acetal Copolymer
  - 303 Stainless Steel
  - Copper, Zinc, Aluminum Alloy

Patent Applied for and Allowed.

Memry Plumbing Products • 69 Armory St. • Worcester, MA 01603 • (508) 799-9931

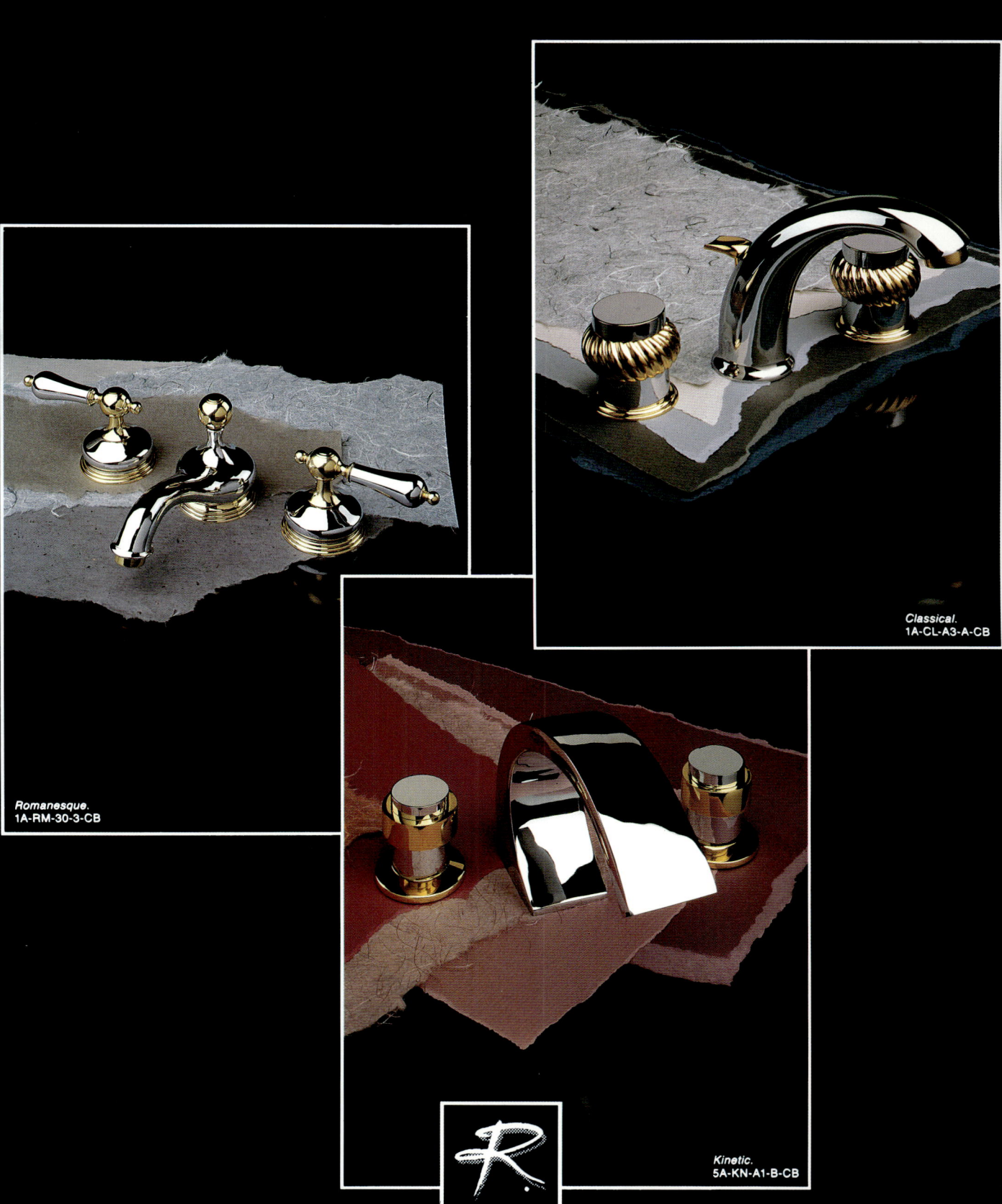

R A P H A E L
The Essence of Elegance

Classical.
1A-CL-A3-A-CB

Romanesque.
1A-RM-30-3-CB

Kinetic.
5A-KN-A1-B-CB

RAPHAEL

The genius of Raphael. The ability to create a work of art at once lyrical and dramatic, pictorially rich and sculpturally solid. Raphael, the company, is committed to perpetuating the style of Raphael, the artist, by seeking to provide its customers with an extensive selection of dramatically rich, uniquely styled faucets.

As a Nortek company, Raphael is backed by the strength of a $1 billion, *Fortune* 500 American company committed to supplying products of the highest quality. Every Raphael faucet is cast from the finest brass and protected with a polish-free protective coating. The ¼-turn washerless ceramic disk valves carry a lifetime limited warranty. Raphael's complete line of faucets and accessories is available in a variety of luxurious finishes to complement any decor. The essence of elegance ... from Raphael.

Byzantine.
5A-BZ-30-3-BB

Impressionist.
1A-IM-A2-B-CB

Front Cover Photos:

Romanesque. Picturesque ... timeless.
Classical. Delicate lines and sensual curves.
Kinetic. Rakishly contemporary ... at home with the latest trends.

Left Photos:

Byzantine. Exotically different ... wonderfully ornate.
Impressionist. Gracefully reflected impressions of color and light.

Bauhaus.
1A-BA-A8-C-CB

Moderne.
1A-MO-A8-C-CB

Gothic.
1A-GO-40-3-BB

Bauhaus. Balanced symmetry . . . precise execution.

Moderne. Strikingly different . . . a dramatic blend of subtle curves and tapered angles.

Gothic. Decidedly European . . . elegant simplicity to inspire traditional themes.

Venetian.
1A-VE-10-1-BB

Neoclassic.
1A-NC-C4-B-CB

Flemish.
1A-FM-15-2-BB

Venetian. Graceful ... subtle ...
enduring.
Neoclassic. A lyric touch for
modern decor ... setting the standard for tomorrow's classic.
Flemish. Tranquil ... idyllic ...
quietly elegant.

Raphael Ltd.
A Nortek Company

P. O. Box 386
Brookfield, Wisconsin 53008
1-800-RAPHAEL
414-786-5336

Aqua-Pure®
Drinking Water Systems

Because water is what we're made of.

Aqua-Pure Drinking Water Systems — A Step Beyond Filtration

Improving water quality has been CUNO's business for over 75 years. CUNO is the world leader in filtration, providing Aqua-Pure systems for millions of homes to prevent staining from dirt and rust, as well as controlling typical taste and odor problems. However, in many areas of the world people are becoming increasingly concerned over the threat of contamination in drinking water. If you're the person seeking that extra high quality water for drinking and cooking, Aqua-Pure offers two types of specialty systems to suit your needs — the **Aqua-Pure Chemical Removal Filter and Aqua-Pure Reverse Osmosis Systems**.

The Aqua-Pure Chemical Removal Filter

The threat of contamination in drinking water can take many forms. The most common chemicals of concern are "volatile organic chemicals" (VOCs) and "Trihalomethanes" (THMs). The sources of VOCs can be from leaking underground gasoline storage tanks or industrial solvents that seep through the ground. THMs are the byproducts from chlorination, the most dangerous

one being chloroform. Our biggest problem is that studies show thousands of organic chemicals can be detected in drinking water, but only a few have been regulated by the EPA. The EPA (Environmental Protection Agency) establishes "Maximum Contaminant Levels," the "safe level," for these tasteless and odorless chemicals.

The question most people ask is, "Is there such a thing as a 'safe level' for harmful chemicals?".

Because of the widespread problem, EPA testing has established that Granular Activated Carbon is the Best Available Technology for removing VOCs and THMs. However, just because a filter contains activated carbon, doesn't mean it has the ability to remove these compounds, although it can make the water taste better. The APCRF Chemical Removal Filter combines a special grade of Granular Activated Carbon with a design that allows for prolonged contact with the

carbon to assure effective reduction of THMs and VOCs — of course, it makes the water taste great, too!

The APCRF is independently tested and validated by the National Sanitation Foundation (NSF) for the specific reduction of these compounds. That's confidence you can rely on.

The Aqua-Pure Reverse Osmosis System

In addition to organic chemical contaminants, some people are concerned over the possibility of metals and salts that can be in drinking water — lead from solder in the plumbing, aluminum from the municipal treatment plant, and even sodium which is a concern for people on low sodium diets.

The process of Reverse Osmosis effectively and efficiently reducing metals and salts. Reverse Osmosis uses a semi-permeable membrane that allows water molecules to pass through, but rejects the metals and salts which are washed down the drain. To be effective, the system processes water very slowly, so it comes with a 2 to 3 gallon (7.6 to 11.4 liter) storage tank to hold the processed water until you need it.

The Aqua-Pure Reverse Osmosis System goes beyond just reverse osmosis. The Aqua-Pure Reverse Osmosis System synergistically combines the technologies of reverse osmosis for removing metals and salts with activated carbon filtration to reduce the VOCs and THMs. In effect, the Aqua-Pure Reverse Osmosis System can reduce the entire spectrum of contaminants that can be found in drinking water! No ordinary filter system can make this claim.

At your fingertips, the water is conveniently dispensed by a special faucet mounted on your sink. Discover the difference clean water makes for everything — coffee, tea, soups, juices, cooking, ice cubes, baby formula, pets, or just a refreshing glass of clean drinking water!

Whether you use the Aqua-Pure Chemical Removal Filter or the Aqua-Pure Reverse Osmosis System, you'll have the peace of mind knowing that you are using a truly quality water system for all your drinking and cooking needs.

Aqua-Pure Drinking Water Systems — more convenient than bottled water at a fraction of the cost. The quality that fits your health-conscious lifestyle.

Aqua-Pure Chemical Removal Filter

The APCRF Chemical Removal System uses the APC77 Cartridge that has been specifically designed to reduce hazardous volatile organic chemicals.

Chemical Removal Filter Cartridges
Water first passes through a 5 micron filter which filters microscopic particulate contaminants. It then passes through a large depth bed of granular activated carbon to adsorb hazardous chemicals, i.e., make them adhere to the surface of the carbon granules. Adsorption is the most effective method for reducing organic chemical contaminants.

Flow Regulator
Controls flow through the activated carbon depth bed along an extra long flow-path which maximizes water contact time in the carbon bed.

Space Requirements:
Unit measures 13-1/4" height x 4-11/16" width (336.5mm x 119.1mm)

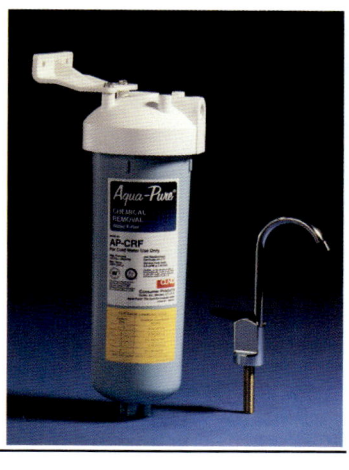

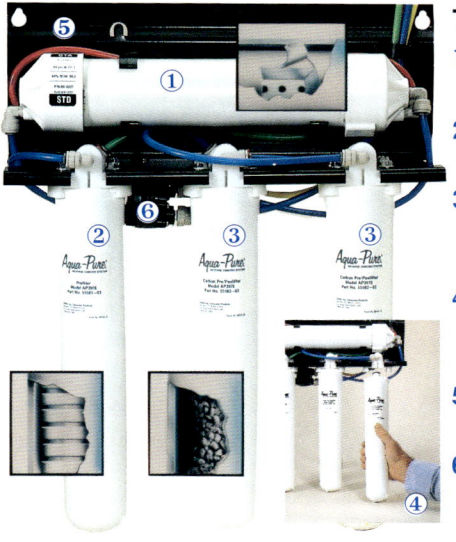

The Aqua-Pure Reverse Osmosis System

1. **Reverse Osmosis Membrane:** Represents the heart of the system. The spiral wound membrane removes up to 95% of the dissolved solids (i.e. salts, metals, etc.)

2. **Sediment Cartridge.** Graded density cellulose fiber prefilter provides increased dirt and rust removal capabilities.

3. **Chemical Reduction/Taste and Odor Filter Cartridge:** Aqua-Pure's double carbon filtration system provides large activated carbon capacity and maximum contact time for better chemical, chlorine and taste/odor reduction.

4. **Quick-Change Cartridge:** Streamlined design minimizes space requirements under the sink. The patented bayonet design allows quick and easy sanitary cartridge changeouts, with no water spillage.

5. **Unitized System:** Pre-assembled onto a metal wall bracket, for easy installation. Only 5 simple connections are needed, and you're ready to use your RO system.

6. **Automatic Shutoff Valve:** Conserves water by shutting off inlet water when the storage tank is full.

Space Requirements:
a. Unit (wall mounted): 19" Height x 15" Width x 5" Depth (483mm x 381mm x 127mm).
b. Storage Tank: 19-11/16" Height x 9-1/16" Diameter.

Optional Accessories:
ROMNTR — In-line water quality monitor for measuring TDS level in R/O product water.

Drinking Water System Application Chart
Impurities Reduced

Parameter	Taste/Odor Filter	Aqua-Pure Chemical Removal Filter	Aqua-Pure Reverse Osmosis System
Aluminum			•
Barium			•
Cadmium			•
Chloramines		•	•
Chlorine	•	•	•
Chromium			•
Copper			•
Flouride			•
Lead			•
Silver			•
Tastes/Odors	•	•	•
TCE		•	•
THMs		•	•
Sediment	•	•	•
VOCs		•	•
Zinc			•

Note: The performance of any system depends on proper application, installation, maintenance, and the degree of severity and/or combination of water problems

Decorator Faucets

PRODUCT PERFORMANCE DATA
AQUA-PURE CHEMICAL REMOVAL FILTER

Recognized Volatile Organic Chemical (VOC) Contaminants	Challenge Levels Parts Per Billion (PPB)	Minimum Percent Reduction Throughout Cartridge Life
cis-l, 3-Dichloropropene	80	95%
Chlorobenzene	80	95%
Ethylbenzene	80	95%
Hexachlorobutadiene	40	95%
ortho-Xylene	80	95%
Tetrachloroethylene	80	95%
Toluene	80	95%
trans-1 2-Dichloroethylene	80	95%
1, 1 2,2-Tetrachloroethane	80	95%
1, 2-Dichlorobenzene	80	95%
1, 2-Dichloropropane	80	95%
1, 2-Dichloroethane	80	95%

USEPA Regulated Volatile Organic Chemical (VOC) Contaminants	Challenge Levels Parts Per Billion (PPB)	Contaminant Reduced To Below This USEPA Max Allowable Contaminant Level Parts Per Billion (PPB)
Benzene	30	5
Carbon Tetrachloride	40	5
p-Dichlorobenzene	80	5
Trichloroethylene	300	5
Trihalomethanes(THMs)	300	15
1,1-Dichloroethylene	50	7
1,1,1-Trichloroethane	80	5
1 2-Dichloroethane	100	5

MODEL NO.	CONNECTION SIZE	DIMENSIONS HEIGHT	DIMENSIONS MAX. DIAMETER	SERVICE FLOW RATE	MAX. WATER TEMP.	MAX. WATER PRES.	REPLACEMENT CTG. NO.	REPLACE-MENT CTG. QTY.	CAPACITY
APCRF	3/8"NPT	13-1/4" (336.5mm)	4-11/16" (119.1mm)	0.5 gpm (1.9 lpm)	100° F (38° C)	125 psi (8.62 bar)	APC77	1	200 gallons (757 liters for VOC reduction)

These charts set forth allowable claims which can be made for drinking water treatment units that have met NSF requirements for chloroform reduction.

THMs are a family ot hazardous compounds formed by the reaction of chlorine (used to disinfect public water supplies) with natural organic substances in the water.

Other listed VOCs are chemical compounds frequently used in industrial applications. These chemicals are used as metal degreasers, paint and coating solvents, dry cleaning solvents, aerosol vapor depressants, and additives in gasoline.

The APCRF is also highly effective for the reduction of common disinfection agents, such as chloramines and chlorine (99%).

AQUA-PURE REVERSE OSMOSIS SYSTEM

USEPA Regulated Inorganic Chemicals	CTA Membrane Average Influent	CTA Membrane Average Effluent	CTA Membrane Average Rejection	TFC Membrane Average Influent	TFC Membrane Average Effluent	TFC Membrane Average Rejection	MCL[2] (Mg/1)
Barium[4]	10.33	0.07	99%	10.48	0.148	99%	1.0
Cadmium	0.036	0.0002	99%	0.033	0.0002	99%	0.01
Hexavalent Chromium[4]	0.162	0.003	98%	0.148	0.001	98%	0.05
Trivalent Chromium[4]	0.05	N.D.1	99%	0.12	0.001	99%	0.05
Fluoride	8.4	.45	95%	8.4	0.22	97%	4.0
Lead	0.11	0.003	97%	0.063	0.005	92%	0.05
Mercury	0.0091	0.0002	98%	0.0082	0.0002	98%	10.0
Nitrate[4,5]	Not Recommended			30.5	1.58	95%	10.0
Radium	—	—	80%+3	—	—	80%+3	5PCi/1
Selenium	0.98	0.003	97%	0.098	0.002	98%	0.01

MODEL	APRO3-CTA APRO3-CTAS	APRO3-TFC APRO3-TFCS	APRO3/TFC APRO3/TFCS
Application	For use on chlorinated water, or most municipally-treated waters.	For use on non-chlorinated water, such as well water.	For use on chlorinated water with a pH of 9 or above
Membrane	CTA	TFC	TFC
Water Pressure	40-100 psi (2.8-6.9 bar)	40-100 psi (2.8-6.9 bar)	40-100 psi (2.8-6.9 bar)
Water Temp	40°-85° F (4°-29° C)	40°-100° F (4°-29° C)	40°-100° F (4°-29° C)
Daily System Capacity2	5-8 gallons (19-30 liters)	6-10 gallons (22.7-38 liters)	6-10 gallons 22.7-38 liters)
pH Range	5.5-9.0	3-11	3-11
Maximum TDS level	1500 ppm	2000 ppm	2000 ppm
TDS Rejection (typical)3	up to 94%	up to 97%	up to 97%
Storage Capacity4	2-3 gallons (7.6-11.4 liters)	2-3 gallons (7.6-11.4 liters)	2-3 gallons (7.6-11.4 liters)
Warranty	1 year on module 3 years on unit		

The values shown above represent the average percent rejection on Aqua-Pure Reverse Osmosis Systems when tested in accordance to NSF Standard 58 protocol.
1 N.D. = Not Detectable
2 National Primary Drinking Water Regulations (U.S.EPA)
3 The reduction of radium was verified by using barium as a surrogate under NSF Standard 58 protocol.
4 Barium. Chromium. Nitrate tested at 750 mg/l TDS.
5 Nitrate reduction Is acceptable for treatment or Influent concentrations up to 30 mg/l; additional Treatment or Individual design shall be required for higher influent levels.

Recognized Inorganic Chemicals	CTA Average Rejection	TFC Average Rejection
Aluminum	85-95%	88-98%
Chloride	80-90%	83-95%
Copper	85-95%	88-98%
Iron	85-95%	88-98%
Magnesium	85-95%	88-98%
Manganese	85-95%	88-98%
Nickel	85-95%	88-98%
Phosphate	85-95%	88-98%
Silver	75-85%	88-98%
Sodium	80-90%	83-95%
Sulfate	85-95%	88-98%
Zinc	85-95%	88-98%

The values shown above represent typical rejection rate ranges for the listed inorganic compounds. Data has been derived from a variety of sources, including third party testing organizations, as well as academic and industry studies. The Aqua-Pure Reverse Osmosis System also reduces the organic contaminants as listed above under the APCRF performance chart.

NOTE: Products using activated carbon filters are not intended for use where water is microbiologically unsafe or unknown quality.

FORM NO. LITDWSBRO Rev. 12/90
©CUNO, Inc., 1990

Model APCRF has been tested and listed under NSF Standard 53 for the reduction of volatile organic chemicals (VOCs).

If you suspect that your water supply may contain any of the above referenced contaminants, we recommend having your water analyzed. Refer to your local health department for approved testing facilities.

CUNO

Consumer Products
A unit of Commercial Intertech Corp.

CUNO, Inc.
Consumer Products
400 Research Parkway, Meriden, Connecticut 06450, USA
Telex: 221083, Telefax: 203-238-8701
Toll Free: 1-800-243-6894
In Connecticut or worldwide 203-237-5541, Ext. 770.
Printed in U.S.A.

Marble Series

- Hand sculptured from 100% marble
- 8 beautiful styles
- Available in 12 marble colors and patterns
- Call factory for details

Marble and China Lavatories from

American China

OCOTILLO 17½" x 14"
STEPPE 17¼" x 14⅛"

FLOWER 18½" x 14½"
ARROYO 18¼" x 15"

CANYON 19½" x 15¼"
BELLE EPOQUE 17½" x 14"

BELLE TERRA 17⅜" x 14¼"
PLATEAU 17½" x 14⅛"

LIBERTY W/S 23¾" x 21"
SEDONA 22" x 16¼"

SEDONA W/S 22" x 19¾"

LIBERTY 22¾" x 18½"

BELLE EPOQUE GRANDE
20¾" x 16½"

SEDONA UNDER COUNTER
21" x 15¾"

BELLE TERRA GRANDE
20¾" x 16½"

CORTEZ SHELF

AVONDALE SHELF

CORTEZ PEDESTAL

AVONDALE PEDESTAL

CODES	COLOR LIST	CATEGORIES	COLOR MATCH	CODES	COLOR LIST	CATEGORIES	COLOR MATCH
01	WHITE	I		31	SHELL	III	AS
02	BONE	II	AS	32	MANHATTAN	III	VB
03	PARCHMENT	II	K	33	DRESDEN BLUE	III	AS
04	ALMOND	II	K	34	CERULEAN BLUE	III	K
05	COUNTRY GREY	III	K	35	EXPRESSO	IV	K
06	BLACK	IV		36	PEACH BISQUE	III	E
07	FRENCH VANILLA	II	K	37	ASPEN GREEN	III	K
08	MEXICAN SAND	III	K	38	CREAMY YELLOW	III	E
09	WILD ROSE	III	K	39	NATURAL	II	E
10	STERLING SILVER	III	AS	40	HERON BLUE	III	K
11	NEW ORLEANS BLUE	III	K	41	INNOCENT BLUSH	III	K
12	SUNSET	III	VB	42	HONEYDEW	III	AS
13	BEIGE	III	VB	43	SAFFRON YELLOW	III	AS
14	CHAMPAGNE	II	VB	44	RUBY	IV	E
15	CARAMEL	III	VB	45	TEAL	IV	K
16	JASMINE	IV	VB	46	TWILIGHT BLUE	III	E
17	STELLA	IV	VB	47	DUSTY ROSE	III	E
18	CROCUS	IV	VB	48	CONCORD GRAPE	IV	AC
19	ANEMONE	IV	VB	49	GLACIER BLUE	III	K
20	SWISS CHOCOLATE	IV	K	50	SEAFOAM GREEN	III	K
21	NAVY	IV	K	51	CLASSIC GREY	III	E
22	RASPBERRY PUREE	IV	K	52	BLONDE	III	AS
23	EVERGREEN	III	K	53	JERSEY CREAM	III	K
24	BLUEBERRY	IV	K	54	OPALESCENCE***	IV	AC
25	TAUPE	IV	K	55	AMERICANA BROWN	IV	AS
26	TENDER GREY	III	K	56	MATTE WHITE	IV	VB
27	THUNDER GREY	III	K	57	DESERT BLOOM	IV	E
28	FAWN BEIGE	III	AS	58	VERDE GREEN	IV	E
29	MAGNOLIA	IV	VB	59	MATTE BLACK	IV	AC
30	HEATHER	III	AS				

Pedestal Lavatories

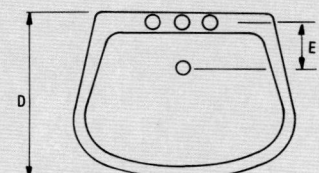

PEDESTALS

	OVERALL DIMENSIONS		OUTSIDE DEPTH	INSIDE DEPTH	FAUCET TO DRAIN	BOLT SPREAD	ANCHOR HEIGHT	ROUGH-IN DIMENSIONS		
	A × B		C	D	E	F	G	DRAIN	HOT/COLD	SUPPLY SPACING
AVONDALE ✱	24½"	34"	9"	20½"	5"	11"	32¾"	19"- 21"	24"- 26"	8"
CORTEZ ✱	20"	34½"	8"	17"	4½"	8½"	32½"	21"- 23"	26"- 28"	8"

✱ AVAILABLE IN 8" WIDE SPREAD, 4" CENTER SPREAD AND KNOCKOUTS TO MEET DESIRABLE FAUCET SET.

ALL DIMENSIONS LISTED HEREIN ARE NOMINAL.

Shelves

AVONDALE SHELF

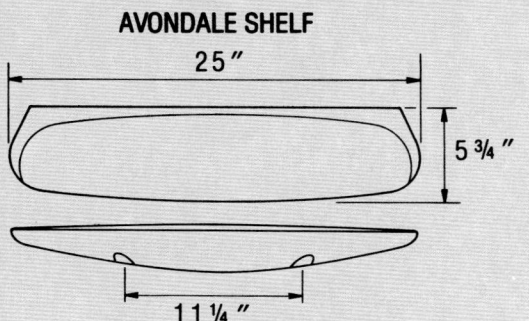

25"

5 ¾ "

11 ¼ "

CORTEZ SHELF

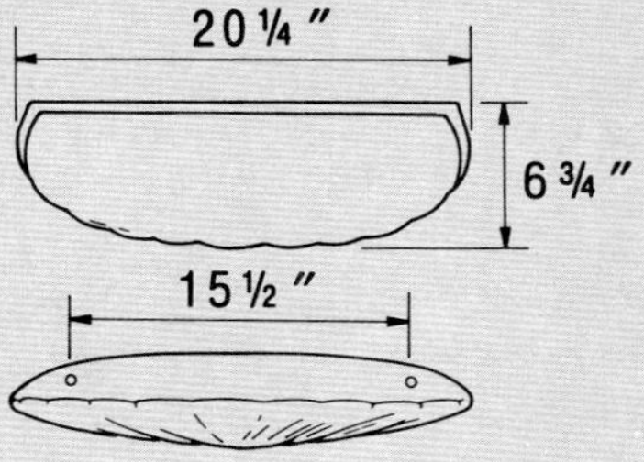

20 ¼ "

6 ¾ "

15 ½ "

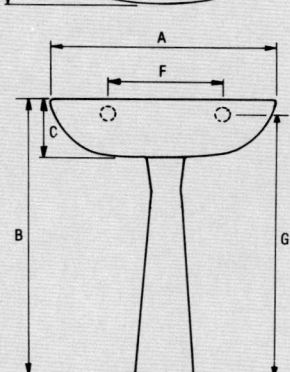

Countertop Lavatories

	OVERALL DIMENSIONS	OUTSIDE DEPTH	INSIDE DEPTH	INSIDE WIDTH	BACK RM TO DRAIN	LIP DEPTH	KNOCK OUT ONLY	SELF RIMMING	UNDER COUNTER
	A × B	C	D	E	F	G	H		
ARROYO	18¼"×15"	7¼"	5½"	15¾"	7¼"	3/4"		X	
PLATEAU	17½"×14⅛"	7⅛"	5½"	15¾"	6¾"	1/2"		X	X
OCOTILLO	17½"×14"	7"	5¼"	15½"	7¼"	1/2"		X	
STEPPE	17¼"×14⅛"	7"	5¼"	15½"	7¼"	1/2"		X	
FLOWER	18½"×14½"	7⅛"	5½"	15¾"	7½"	5/8"		X	
CANYON	19½"×15¼"	7"	5¼"	15¼"	7½"	1/2"		X	
SEDONA	22"×16¼"	9"	6¾"	18¾"	4¾"	7/8"		X	
SEDONA UNDER COUNTER	21"×15¾"	9¼"	7¼"	18½"	4¼"	3/4"			X
SEDONA KNOCK OUT ✱	22"×19¾"	9"	6¾"	18"	7½"	5/8"	5¼"	X	
LIBERTY	22¾"×18½"	8½"	6¼"	17¾"	9¼"	5/8"		X	
LIBERTY KNOCK OUT ✱	23¾"×21"	8½"	6¼"	17¾"	12"	5/8"	9½"	X	
BELLE TERRA	17⅜"×14¼"	7⅛"	5½"	15½"	6⅞"	3/4"		X	
BELLE TERRA GRANDE	20¾"×16½"	7⅝"	6"	18"	8¼"	3/4"		X	
BELLE EPOQUE	17½"×14"	7¼"	5½"	15¾"	7"	5/8"		X	
BELLE EPOQUE GRANDE	20¾"×16½"	8"	6"	18¼"	8½"	5/8"		X	

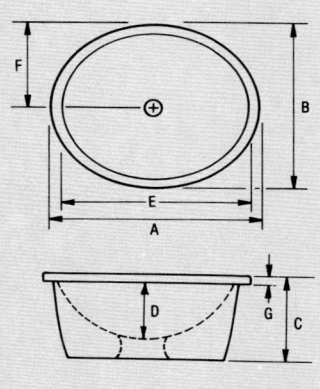

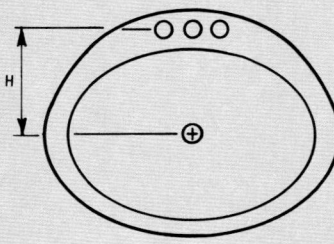

American China manufactures high quality china wash basins. We specialize in innovative designs, a wide array of colors, dependability and fast delivery.

We are the only company in the country to offer 59 colors, custom color mixing for special orders, 15 bowl designs, two pedestal designs and hand-painting to your specifications. Our Designer Series is unsurpassed for beauty and uniqueness.

When you order from American China, you can count on a beautiful product, quality workmanship and unsurpassed customer service.

Designer hand painted drop in lavatories or pedestal lavs.
Logo and decaling available.

Solid gold, platinum or embellishment available in
drop in lavs or pedestal lavs.

Hand painted lavatories with matching tile available.

Gold, platinum or color pinstriping available in
all drop in lavs or pedestal lavs.

Opalescent colors available.

Things of Beauty Collection ™

from

American China

(602) 470-1005

3618 E. La Salle • Phoenix, Arizona 85040
800-359-3261, Fax # 602-470-0684

4

American Standard

FIXTURES

TABLE OF CONTENTS

EXPLORING THE EXTRAORDINARY

American Standard invites you to explore the extraordinary. Beautiful fixtures that open up a world of possibilities for the bathroom. The most daring innovations. The newest styles. And the latest technology.

Select the bathroom suite of your dreams. Choose from one of our design-matched collections, each with its own distinctive personality based on shape, proportion, and line. Find the lavatory, whirlpool or bathtub, toilet or bidet you have been looking for. Or investigate a world of complementary accessories. Then devise a color strategy to make it all a perfect match.

American Standard has dreamed of untold ways to express yourself. So let American Standard nourish your imagination. Why settle for the ordinary? Set your sights on the extraordinary.

SENSORIUM AND AMBIANCE: A TOTAL BATHING ENVIRONMENT

Behold the ultimate bathing experience. The luxurious Sensorium™ whirlpool equipped with Ambiance™, a computerized whirlpool and environment control system that brings to life a total bathing environment.

Ambiance allows you to preset the time and temperature of your whirlpool up to twenty-four hours in advance. When you are ready to bathe, it lets you dim the lights. Turn on some music. Or telephone a friend. You can even unlock the front door. All with the mere touch of a button.

Why step out of the bath? Indulge yourself to the fullest. With the ultimate bathing experience. Sensorium with Ambiance.

 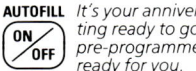

 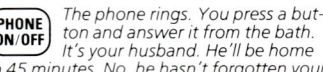

AMBIANCE: STEP BY STEP

By operating the hand-held remote control you can close the drain, dim the lights, turn on your Ambiance stereo system, or talk on the phone. In addition, you can control five additional appliances, including your television. With the help of the wall-mounted console and integral video monitor, you can even greet visitors at the front door. And let them in.

But that's not all. A quick phone call to Ambiance's computer and you can trigger your whirlpool to fill itself at the time and temperature of your choice.

What was once impossible is now the ultimate in bathroom technology. Ambiance. From American Standard.

AMBIANCE 2500
3760.002 Chrome trim
3760.021 Bone trim
3760.094 Gold trim

Micro-processor control system for Sensorium with a TV/intercom/video camera surveillance system, remote control for 5 appliances and room light. Touch tone speaker telephone system with incoming call signal-call hold-15 telephone number storage with auto dial-redial last number called feature, system interface with supplied stereo system. Automatic system mute for intercom or telephone use.

Visual displays of low-medium-high water depth setting and control, programmed time for auto-fill, programmed water temperature setting, clock with alarm feature, on/off status of pool light and 5 remote control appliances and integral fiber optic pool light, electro-mechanical drain open or closed status and control. Featuring American Standard factory installed whirlpool system including six color-matched multi-directional, flow-adjustable jets, two air volume controls, color-matched anti-vortex suction fitting, ¾ h.p. self-draining 2-speed pump and motor with 24 hour dry run seal, Champagne air pump, low water level cut-off, integral electro-mechanical pressure balanced filler valve with manual override. All features can be operated from bathroom and one other room. Factory installed trim in Chrome, Bone or Gold finish, (two built-in grab bars, two air volume controls, bath waste and overflow, and aerator).

AMBIANCE 2000
3760.202 Chrome trim
3760.221 Bone trim
3760.294 Gold trim

Same as above less TV/intercom/video camera surveillance system. With door intercom system.

Optional components: TV controller with on/off, volume, channel selector (3761.300). Additional hand-held remote control (3761.200). Separate charger unit (3761.400) for hand-held remote control.

SENSORIUM WHIRLPOOL
3560.116 Chrome trim
3560.117 Bone Trim
3560.118 Gold trim

Acrylic. Center drain outlet. Integral headrests and lumbar supports. Two built-in grab bars. Slip-resistant surface. Bath waste and overflow. Integral pressure balanced bath filler. Suitable for two bather use. Featuring American Standard factory installed whirlpool system including six color-matched, multi-directional, flow-adjustable jets, two brass air volume controls, color-matched anti-vortex suction fitting, ¾ h.p. self-draining pump and motor, and bath-mounted ULTRA-SENSE PLUS™ electronic whirlpool on/off control with low water cut-off. Available with factory installed trim in a choice of Chrome, Bone or 24K Gold finish consisting of two built-in grab bars, two air volume controls, bath waste and overflow, and aerator.

SENSORIUM BATHING POOL
3060.116 Chrome trim
3060.117 Bone trim
3060.118 Gold trim
Same as above less whirlpool system.

SENSORIUM WHIRLPOOL/AMBIANCE
3760.002 Ambiance 2500 Chrome trim
3760.021 Ambiance 2500 Bone trim
3760.094 Ambiance 2500 Gold trim
3760.202 Ambiance 2000 Chrome trim
3760.221 Ambiance 2000 Bone trim
3760.294 Ambiance 2000 Gold trim

72" L x 44" W x 18" D

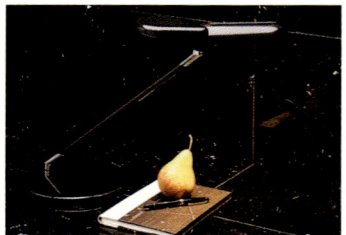

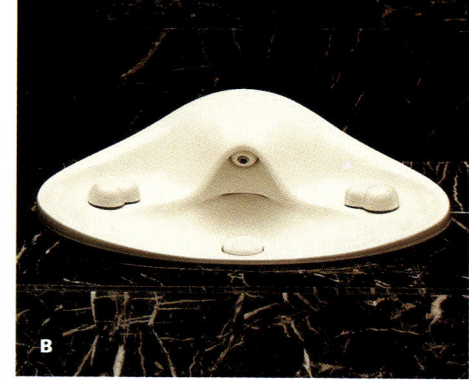

THE BREATHTAKING ORIGINALITY OF THE WARREN PLATNER COLLECTION

Behold the stunning achievement of master architect Warren Platner. Subtly evoking the contours of the human body. With fluid lines, graceful curves, and sensuous shapes.

Craftsmen take as long as ten days and as many as thirty individual steps to make each piece. Handles and spouts are made of the same pure vitreous china as the fixtures, resulting in remarkable unity of design.

The breathtaking originality of the Warren Platner Collection. A majestic celebration of natural forms. Available exclusively in Bone.

A – PEDESTAL LAVATORY 0099.605
Vitreous china with china faucet handles and china drain plug. Factory installed integral faucet with trajectory spout. Rear overflow. Provided with two handle variations: shell-shaped and twist-shaped. Mounting kit supplied.
    31 3/8" H x 40" W x 23" L

B – COUNTERTOP LAVATORY 0469.610
Vitreous china with china faucet handles and china drain plug. Factory installed integral faucet with trajectory spout. Rear overflow. Self-rimming. Provided with two handle variations: shell-shaped and twist-shaped. Mounting kit supplied.
    30" x 20"

C – TOILET 2029.600
Vitreous china, one-piece construction. Side-mounted china push-button flush actuator and concealed china bolt caps. Design-matched toilet seat. Elongated toilet bowl. Siphon vortex flush action.
    26 1/2" H x 22" W x 32 1/2" L

D – BIDET 5029.615
Vitreous china with china faucet handles and china drain plug. Integral flushing rim and overflow. Color-matched douche spray. Concealed vacuum breaker. Factory installed integral fitting. Provided with two handle variations: shell-shaped and twist-shaped.
    24" H x 17 1/8" W x 32" L

E – The Platner Collection comes with both shell-shaped and twist-shaped handles, so you can choose or change your luxury.

The Warren Platner Collection and Sensorium are available exclusively in Bone.

5

THE LINEAR CLARITY OF GALLERIA

The Galleria™ Suite. A thrilling direction for the future of bathroom design. The perfect complement to the home of today. Captured here in Light Turquoise.

Crisp lines. Faceted shapes. A fresh profile. The linear clarity of Galleria. The last word in bathroom design.

A – PEDESTAL LAVATORY
8" spread faucet holes 0180.054 (shown)
4" center faucet holes 0180.042
Center hole only 0180.068
Vitreous china. Lavatory with pedestal. Rear overflow.
Mounting kit supplied.
   31" H x 30½" W x 19¾" L

B – COUNTERTOP LAVATORY
8" spread faucet holes 0177.012 (shown)
4" center faucet holes 0177.034
Center hole only 0177.023
Vitreous china. Front overflow. Self-rimming.
Mounting kit supplied.
   26" x 20"

C – TOILET 2014.013
Vitreous china. One-piece construction. Top-mounted, push-button flush actuator. Design-matched integrated toilet seat and tank cover. Elongated toilet bowl. Concealed bolt caps. Siphon vortex flush action. Efficient water saver (3½ gals. per flush cycle). Requires a minimum working pressure to ensure adequate performance (30 P.S.I. at the inlet valve).
   17" H x 19" W x 30¾" L

D – BIDET
For deck mounted fitting 5021.015 (shown)
For wall mounted fitting 5019.017
For over-the-rim fitting 5021.047
Vitreous china. Integral flushing rim (except 5021.047). Douche spray (except 5021.047). Concealed floor mounting. Suitable for above-the-floor roughing. Order fittings separately.
   16¼" H x 16¼" W x 26" L

E – WHIRLPOOL 2718.013
Acrylic. Center drain outlet. Integral lumbar support and armrests. Slip-resistant surface. Universal design for left or right hand, island or sunken installations. Suitable for two bather use. Featuring American Standard factory installed whirlpool system including six color-matched multi-directional, flow-adjustable jets, color-matched anti-vortex suction fitting, rigid P.V.C. harness, ¾ h.p. self-draining pump and motor with 24 hour dry run seal, and bath-mounted ULTRA-SENSE PLUS™ electronic whirlpool on/off control with low water cut-off.

BATHING POOL 2718.002
Same as above less whirlpool system.
   72" L x 36" W x 20" D

Whirlpools and bathing pools come untrimmed. Trim kits available in Chrome, Polished Brass, White, Bone, 24K Gold, Classic Mink, or Classic Turquoise.

Galleria shown here in Black with Amarilis™ Lexington New Wave spouts and Roma™ clear acrylic lever handles in 24K Gold finish. Also available in the complete line of American Standard colors.

THE CLASSICAL
APPEAL OF ROMA

The striking Roma™ Suite. In a dazzling Black. Injecting dramatic flavor into an American classic.

A myriad of fixture options make each suite an original. Choose from exquisite whirlpool models. A selection of three different toilets. Decide between a countertop or pedestal lavatory.

The classical appeal of Roma. Irresistible to even the most discriminating tastes.

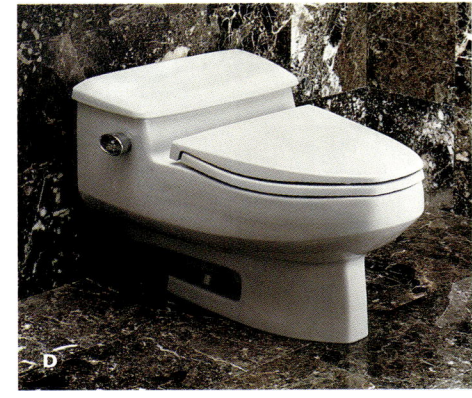

THE ROMA SUITE

A – COUNTERTOP LAVATORY
8" spread faucet holes 0177.012
4" center faucet holes 0177.034 (shown)
Center hole only 0177.023
Vitreous china. Front overflow. Self-rimming.
Mounting kit supplied.
 26" x 20"

B – ROMA GOLD™
Pedestal lavatory 0176.235 (shown)
Countertop lavatory 0177.175
One-piece toilet with Vent-Away 2009.115
One-piece toilet less Vent-Away 2009.125
Bidet 5014.055
22K Gold in-glaze for the Roma Suite.
See page 42 for details.

C – PEDESTAL LAVATORY
8" spread faucet holes 0176.017
4" center faucet holes 0176.068 (shown)
Center hole only 0176.041
Vitreous china. Lavatory with pedestal. Rear overflow.
Mounting kit supplied.
 31" H x 30" W x 20½" L

D – VENT-AWAY™ TOILET 2009.017
Vitreous china. One-piece construction. Chrome
plated, side-mounted push/pull flush/vent actuator.
Design-matched toilet seat. Elongated contoured toilet
bowl. Water operated built-in ventilator. Siphon vortex
flush action. Requires a minimum working pressure to
ensure adequate performance (30 P.S.I. at the inlet
valve).
TOILET 2009.026
Same as above less Vent-Away ventilator.
 19¾" H x 20½" W x 30½" L

E – TWO-PIECE TOILET 2080.018
Vitreous china. Chrome plated, side-mounted push-
button flush actuator. Close coupled elongated siphon
jet flush action bowl and tank. Efficient water saver
(3½ gals. per flush cycle).
 29½" H x 16" W x 29¾" L

F – ROMA II TOILET 2012.014
Vitreous china. One-piece construction. Chrome plated, side-mounted push-button flush actuator. Elongated toilet bowl. Siphon vortex flush action. Efficient
water saver (3½ gals. per flush cycle).
 22" H x 20⅛" W x 29½" L

G – BIDET
For deck mounted fitting 5014.030
For wall mounted fitting 5013.032
For over-the-rim fitting 5014.049 (shown)
Vitreous china. Integral flushing rim (except 5014.049).
Douche spray (except 5014.049). Suitable for above-
the-floor roughing. Order fittings separately.
 15¾" H x 14⅛" W x 25⅞" L

H — 5½' WHIRLPOOL 2645.013
Acrylic. End drain outlet. Integral lumbar support. Beveled headrest. Slip-resistant surface. Universal design for left or right hand, island or sunken installations. Oval bathing well. Featuring American Standard factory installed whirlpool system including six color-matched multi-directional, flow-adjustable jets, color-matched anti-vortex suction fitting, rigid P.V.C. harness, ¾ h.p. self-draining pump and motor with 24 hour dry run seal, and bath-mounted ULTRASENSE PLUS™ electronic whirlpool on/off control with low water cut-off.

5½' BATHING POOL 2645.002
Same as above less whirlpool system.
　　66" L x 36" W x 18" D

I — 5' WHIRLPOOL 2640.013
Enameled cast iron. End drain outlet. Integral lumbar support. Beveled headrest. Slip-resistant surface. Universal design for left or right hand, island or sunken installations. Oval bathing well. Featuring American Standard factory installed whirlpool system including four color-matched multi-directional, flow-adjustable jets, color-matched anti-vortex suction fitting, rigid P.V.C. harness, ½ h.p. self-draining pump and motor with 24 hour dry run seal, and bath-mounted ULTRA-SENSE PLUS™ electronic whirlpool on/off control with low water cut-off.

5' BATHING POOL 2640.002
Same as above less whirlpool system.
　　60" L x 42" W x 16" D

5' WHIRLPOOL 2643.014 (not shown)
Acrylic. End drain outlet. Integral lumbar support. Beveled headrest. Slip-resistant surface. Universal design for left or right hand, island or sunken installations. Optional detachable apron available (0602.850). Featuring American Standard factory installed whirlpool system including four color-matched multi-directional, flow-adjustable jets, color-matched anti-vortex suction fitting, rigid P.V.C. harness, ½ h.p. self-draining pump and motor with 24 hour dry run seal, and 0-30 minute mechanical timer. Available with optional bath-mounted ULTRASENSE PLUS™ electronic whirlpool on/off control with low water cut-off (2643.013).
　　60" L x 42" W x 18" D

J — SOAKING WHIRLPOOL 2710.013
Acrylic. Center drain outlet. Integral seat. Slip-resistant surface. Universal design for left or right hand, island or sunken installations. Oval bathing well. Suitable for two bather use. Featuring American Standard factory installed whirlpool system including six color-matched multi-directional, flow-adjustable jets, color-matched anti-vortex suction fitting, rigid P.V.C. harness, ¾ h.p. self-draining pump and motor with 24 hour dry run seal, and bath-mounted ULTRASENSE PLUS™ electronic whirlpool on/off control with low water cut-off.

SOAKING POOL 2710.002
Same as above less whirlpool system.
　　54" L x 42" W x 32½" D

Whirlpools and bathing pools come untrimmed. Trim kits available in Chrome, Polished Brass, White, Bone, 24K Gold, Classic Turquoise, or Classic Mink.

Roma Vent-Away, Roma and Roma II toilet flush actuators also available in Polished Brass, White, Bone or 24K Gold finish.

Roma shown here in Silver with Ceramix™ and Amarilis™ faucets. Also available in the complete line of American Standard colors, except the Roma Soaking Whirlpool (2710.013) and Roma Soaking Pool (2710.002) which are available in White, Dresden Blue, Bone and Silver.

THE TRADITIONAL BEAUTY OF HERITAGE

The traditional beauty of the Heritage™ Suite. A nostalgic interpretation of turn-of-the-century style. In a pristine White.

Follow the detailing on each individual fixture. Admire the exquisite quality of line.

Create an air of authenticity in your bathroom with the Heritage Suite. Celebrate the richness of America's past — with American Standard.

THE HERITAGE SUITE

A — PEDESTAL LAVATORY 0191.024
8" spread faucet holes only.
Vitreous china. Lavatory with pedestal. Rear overflow.
Mounting kit supplied.
    31" H x 30" W x 20" L

B — COUNTERTOP LAVATORY 0456.017
8" spread faucet holes only.
Vitreous china. Front overflow. Self-rimming.
Mounting kit supplied.
    26" x 19½"

C — TOILET 2031.016
Vitreous china. One-piece construction. Chrome plated, side-mounted trip lever. Insulated tank. Solid brass water control valve. Design-matched toilet seat. Elongated toilet bowl. Siphon vortex flush action. Efficient water saver (3½ gals. per flush cycle).
    23⅛" H x 20" W x 28½" L

D — BIDET 5032.026
For deck mounted fitting only. Vitreous china. Integral flushing rim. Douche spray. Integral overflow. For below-the-floor roughing. Concealed mounting bracket. Order fittings separately.
    14¼" H x 13¾" W x 25¾" L

THE GLAMOROUS LOOK
OF PLAZA SUITE

A sophisticated suite for sophisticated tastes. The Plaza Suite™ has a flair for the dramatic. What a way to showcase American Standard's demure shade of Bone.

Notice the smoothed edges. The breathtaking balance. The purity of line.

The glamorous look of the Plaza Suite. Penthouse perfect. For those who choose to make a statement with their bathroom.

THE PLAZA SUITE

A — PEDESTAL LAVATORY
8" spread faucet holes 0184.017 (shown)
4" center faucet holes 0184.038
Center hole only 0184.053
Vitreous china. Lavatory with pedestal. Rear overflow.
Mounting kit supplied.
   31" H x 30" W x 19" L

B — COUNTERTOP LAVATORY
8" spread faucet holes 0187.010 (shown)
4" center faucet holes 0187.021
Center hole only 0187.132
Vitreous china. Front overflow. Self-rimming.
Mounting kit supplied.
   26" x 18"

C — PLAZA PETITE COUNTERTOP LAVATORY
8" spread faucet holes 0409.037 (shown)
4" center faucet holes 0408.023
Center hole only 0409.045
Vitreous china. Front overflow. Self-rimming.
Mounting kit supplied.
   24" x 18"

D — TOILET 2016.019
Vitreous china. One-piece construction. Chrome
plated, side-mounted push-button flush actuator.
Design-matched toilet seat. Elongated contoured toilet
bowl. Siphon vortex flush action. Efficient water saver
(3½ gals. per flush cycle).
   22⅞" H x 20" W x 30" L

E — BIDET
For deck mounted fitting 5027.037 (shown)
For wall mounted fitting 5025.032
For over-the-rim fitting 5027.048
Vitreous china. Integral flushing rim (except 5027.048).
Integral overflow. Douche spray (except 5027.048).
Order fittings separately.
   14½" H x 15⅞" W x 25½" L

F – WHIRLPOOL 2728.013
Acrylic. End drain outlet. Integral lumbar support and two armrests. Slip-resistant surface. Universal design for left or right hand, island or sunken installations. Featuring American Standard factory installed whirlpool system including six color-matched multi-directional, flow-adjustable jets, color-matched anti-vortex suction fitting, rigid P.V.C. harness, ¾ h.p. self-draining pump and motor with 24 hour dry run seal, and bath-mounted ULTRASENSE PLUS™ electronic whirlpool on/off control with low water cut-off.

BATHING POOL 2728.002
Same as above less whirlpool system.
   72" L x 36" W x 20" D

Whirlpools and bathing pools come untrimmed. Trim kits available in Chrome, Polished Brass, White, Bone, 24K Gold, Classic Turquoise, or Classic Mink.

Toilet flush actuator also available in Polished Brass, White, Bone or 24K Gold finish.

THE GRACEFUL CHARM
OF ELLISSE

American Standard's contribution to the Museum of Modern Art's permanent collection. A triumph of design.

The graceful charm of the Ellisse™ Suite. An undeniably elegant addition to any home. Especially as it appears here in refreshing White.

Looking for something different? Consider Whisper Patterns™. Thanks to a unique process, one of three original designs can be fired ''in-glaze'' on the Ellisse Suite of fixtures, creating a subtle three-dimensional effect. Heather in soft lines. Shell in a zigzag. Silver in a pinstripe. An artistic alternative to the usual route. Available only with Ellisse.

THE ELLISSE SUITE

Ellisse is the only American Standard suite that may be ordered in Whisper Patterns. Choose from three original designs. Heather in soft lines. Shell in a zigzag. Or Silver in a pinstripe. Ellisse is also available in the complete selection of American Standard colors.

A – COUNTERTOP LAVATORY
8" spread faucet holes 0076.013
4" center faucet holes 0076.027
Center hole only 0076.033
Vitreous china. Rear overflow. Self-rimming. Mounting kit supplied.
   24" x 20"

COUNTERTOP LAVATORY – WHISPER PATTERNS
Shell 8" spread faucet holes 0076.054 (shown)
   4" center faucet holes 0076.074
   Center hole only 0076.183
Heather 8" spread faucet holes 0076.065
   4" center faucet holes 0076.085
   Center hole only 0076.195
Silver 8" spread faucet holes 0076.042
   4" center faucet holes 0076.062
   Center hole only 0076.174

B – TOILET 2008.019
Vitreous china. One-piece construction. Chrome plated, side-mounted push-button flush actuator. Design-matched contoured seat. Elongated contoured toilet bowl. Siphon vortex flush action. Efficient water saver (3½ gals. per flush cycle).
   22¾" H x 21½" W x 30½" L

TOILET – WHISPER PATTERNS
Shell 2008.127 (shown)
Heather 2008.146
Silver 2008.073

C – PEDESTAL LAVATORY
8" spread faucet holes 0075.010
4" center faucet holes 0071.010
Center hole only 0075.037
Vitreous china. Lavatory with pedestal. Rear overflow. Mounting kit supplied.
   31" H x 26¾" W x 22½" L

PEDESTAL LAVATORY – WHISPER PATTERNS
Shell 8" spread faucet holes 0075.074 (shown)
   4" center faucet holes 0071.074
   Center hole only 0075.563
Heather 8" spread faucet holes 0075.085
   4" center faucet holes 0071.085
   Center hole only 0075.579
Silver 8" spread faucet holes 0075.062
   4" center faucet holes 0071.062
   Center hole only 0075.547

D — BIDET

For deck mounted fitting 5054.015
For wall mounted fitting 5055.029
For over-the-rim fitting 5005.021
Vitreous china. Integral flushing rim (except 5005.021).
Douche spray (except 5005.021). Rear overflow.
Suitable for above-the-floor roughing. Order fittings
separately.
   5005 15½" H x 14⅝" W x 22⅜" L
   5054/5055 15⅝" H x 14¾" W x 25½" L

BIDET — WHISPER PATTERNS

Shell For deck mounted fitting 5054.458
     For wall mounted fitting 5055.429
     For over-the-rim fitting 5005.079 (shown)
Heather For deck mounted fitting 5054.464
     For wall mounted fitting 5055.436
     For over-the-rim fitting 5005.085
Silver For deck mounted fitting 5054.445
     For wall mounted fitting 5055.417
     For over-the-rim fitting 5005.064

E — ELLISSE GRANDE™ WHIRLPOOL 2708.013

Acrylic. Center drain outlet. Slip-resistant surface. Universal design for island or sunken installations. Oval bathing well. Suitable for two bather use. Two integral soap dishes. Featuring American Standard factory installed whirlpool system including eight color-matched multi-directional, flow-adjustable jets, color-matched anti-vortex suction fitting, rigid P.V.C. harness, 1 h.p. self-draining pump and motor with 24 hour dry run seal, and bath-mounted ULTRASENSE PLUS™ electronic whirlpool on/off control with low water cut-off.

ELLISSE GRANDE BATHING POOL 2708.002

Same as above less whirlpool system.
   72" L x 60" W x 20" D

F — WHIRLPOOL 2706.013

Acrylic. Center drain outlet. Slip-resistant surface. Universal design for island or sunken installations. Oval bathing well. Suitable for two bather use. Two integral soap dishes. Featuring American Standard factory installed whirlpool system including six color-matched multi-directional, flow-adjustable jets, color-matched anti-vortex suction fitting, rigid P.V.C. harness, ¾ h.p. self-draining pump and motor with 24 hour dry run seal, and bath-mounted ULTRASENSE PLUS™ electronic whirlpool on/off control with low water cut-off.

BATHING POOL 2706.002

Same as above less whirlpool system.
   72" L x 44" W x 18" D

Whirlpools and bathing pools come untrimmed. Trim kits available in Chrome, Polished Brass, White, Bone, 24K Gold, Classic Turquoise or Classic Mink.

Toilet flush actuator also available in Polished Brass, White, Bone or 24K Gold finish.

THE UNDERSTATED ELEGANCE OF ELLISSE PETITE

The Ellisse Petite™ Suite: a perfectly-proportioned edition of the original — only drawn to a reduced scale. A space-saving success. Particularly enchanting in Classic Mink.

The understated elegance of the Ellisse Petite Suite. Delicate. Daring. A quiet reminder that good things still come in small packages.

THE ELLISSE
PETITE SUITE

A – PEDESTAL LAVATORY
8″ spread faucet holes 0078.025 (shown)
4″ center faucet holes 0079.013
Center hole only 0079.138
Vitreous china. Lavatory with pedestal. Rear overflow.
Mounting kit supplied.
    31½″ H x 24½″ W x 21″ L

B – TWO-PIECE TOILET 2085.019
Vitreous china. Chrome plated flush actuator. Close
coupled elongated siphon jet flush action bowl and
tank. Efficient water saver (3½ gals. per flush cycle).
    26¾″ H x 19″ W x 29⅞″ L

C – BIDET
For deck mounted fitting 5054.015 (shown)
For wall mounted fitting 5055.029
For over-the-rim fitting 5005.021
Vitreous china. Integral flushing rim (except 5005.021).
Douche spray (except 5005.021). Rear overflow.
Suitable for above-the-floor roughing. Order fittings
separately.
    5005 15½″ H x 14⅝″ W x 22⅜″ L
    5054/5055 15⅝″ H x 14¾″ W x 25½″ L

D – COUNTERTOP LAVATORY
8″ spread faucet holes 0411.039 (shown)
4″ center faucet holes 0410.021
Center hole only 0411.047
Vitreous china. Rear overflow. Self-rimming. Mounting
kit supplied.
    24″ x 18¼″

E – WHIRLPOOL/BATH APRON 0602.850
Apron order number only. Available for Roma 5′ Acrylic
Whirlpools 2643.013, 2643.014, Lexington 5′ Whirlpools 2715.013, 2715.014 and Lexington 5′ Bath
2715.002.

*Toilet flush actuator also available in Polished Brass,
White, Bone or 24K Gold finish.*

*Ellisse Petite Suite shown here in Orchid with Amarilis
Fabian spouts and handles in 24K Gold finish. Also
available in the complete line of American Standard
colors.*

THE REFRESHING SIMPLICITY
OF LEXINGTON

The refreshing simplicity of the Lexington™ Suite.
Compact elegance that adds a beautiful dimension
to any home.

And Blond is the perfect color for Lexington.
Quiet but memorable. Subdued but strong.

Create a serene bathroom environment. With one of
American Standard's true accomplishments in design.
The luxurious Lexington Suite.

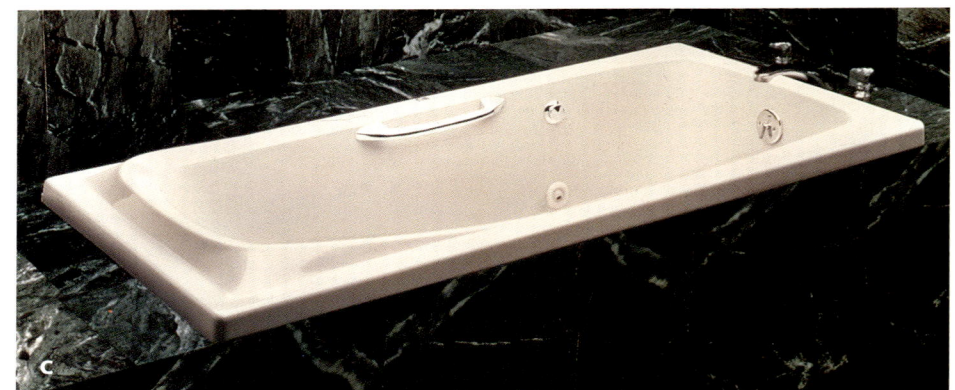

THE LEXINGTON
SUITE

A – PEDESTAL LAVATORY
8" spread faucet holes 0178.014 (shown)
4" center faucet holes 0179.015
Center hole only 0178.136
Vitreous china. Lavatory with pedestal. Rear overflow.
Mounting kit supplied.
   31" H x 24" W x 18" L

B – COUNTERTOP LAVATORY
8" spread faucet holes 0492.207 (shown)
4" center faucet holes 0493.015
Center hole only 0492.176
Vitreous china. Dual front overflows. Self-rimming.
Mounting kit supplied.
   22" x 19"

C – 5½' WHIRLPOOL 2729.014
Acrylic. End drain outlet. Integral lumbar support.
Slip-resistant surface. Universal design for left or right
hand, island or sunken installations. Optional detachable apron available (0660.855). Featuring American
Standard factory installed whirlpool system including
six color-matched multi-directional, flow-adjustable
jets, color-matched anti-vortex suction fitting, rigid
P.V.C. harness, ¾ h.p. self-draining pump and motor
with 24 hour dry run seal, and 0-30 minute mechanical timer. Available with optional bath-mounted
ULTRASENSE PLUS™ electronic whirlpool on/off
control with low water cut-off (2729.013).

5½' BATHING POOL 2729.002
Same as above less whirlpool system.
   66" L x 32" W x 18" D

D — 5' WHIRLPOOL 2715.014

Acrylic. End drain outlet. Integral lumbar support. Slip-resistant surface. Universal design for left or right hand, island or sunken installations. Optional detachable aprons available (2715.900, 0602.850 and 0603.850). Featuring American Standard factory installed whirlpool system including four color-matched multi-directional, flow-adjustable jets, color-matched anti-vortex suction fitting, rigid P.V.C. harness, ½ h.p. self-draining pump and motor with 24 hour dry run seal, and 0-30 minute mechanical timer. Available with optional bath-mounted ULTRASENSE PLUS™ electronic whirlpool on/off control with low water cut-off (2715.013).

5' BATHING POOL 2715.002
Same as above less whirlpool system.
  60" L x 32" W x 18" D

E — SOAKING WHIRLPOOL 2720.014

Acrylic. Center drain outlet. Integral lumbar support. Slip-resistant surface. Universal design for left or right hand, island or sunken installations. Optional detachable aprons available (2720.900, 0602.250 and 0603.250). Featuring American Standard factory installed whirlpool system including four color-matched multi-directional, flow-adjustable jets, color-matched anti-vortex suction fitting, rigid P.V.C. harness, ½ h.p. self-draining pump and motor with 24 hour dry run seal, and 0-30 minute mechanical timer. Available with optional bath-mounted ULTRASENSE PLUS™ electronic whirlpool on/off control with low water cut-off (2720.013).

SOAKING BATH 2720.002
Same as above less whirlpool system.
  60" L x 36" W x 20" D

F — ELONGATED TOILET 2006.014
Vitreous china. One-piece construction. Chrome plated flush actuator. Siphon vortex flush action. Efficient water saver (3½ gals. per flush cycle).
  22¼" H x 20¾" W x 29⅝" L

G — ROUND FRONT TOILET 2007.012
Vitreous china. One-piece construction. Chrome plated flush actuator. Siphon vortex flush action. Efficient water saver (3½ gals. per flush cycle).
  22¼" H x 20¾" W x 27⅝" L

H — BIDET
For deck mounted fitting 5007.014 (shown)
For wall mounted fitting 5006.201
For over-the-rim fitting 5007.041
Vitreous china. Integral flushing rim (except 5007.041). Douche spray (except 5007.041). Integral overflow. Order fittings separately.
  15" H x 14" W x 25¾" L

Whirlpools and bathing pools come untrimmed. Trim kits also available in Chrome, Polished Brass, White, Bone, 24K Gold, Classic Turquoise, or Classic Mink.

Toilet flush actuators also available in Polished Brass, White, Bone or 24K Gold finish.

Lexington shown here in Heather with Amarilis Conventional and Amarilis Lexington spouts and Roma clear acrylic triangle handles in Chrome finish. Also available in the complete line of American Standard colors.

THE LINE BY AMERICAN STANDARD: A TOUCH OF CLASS

Give your fixtures a touch of class. The Line™ is an elegant way to add continuity to your bathroom look. A unique process is used to decorate some of our most popular fixtures with an "in-glazed," textured stripe that you can actually feel. White with a Blue line. Bone with a Rust line. Or Silver with a Plum line. Select a stripe that will point your bathroom in a contemporary direction.

Take your coordinated look one step further with matching tiles. American Olean's accent wall tiles provide an exciting extension to your choice of bathroom decor.

The Line by American Standard. Another stroke of genius.

A

B

C

D

A — THE LINE ACCENT WALL TILES FROM AMERICAN OLEAN
Providing an exciting extension of your choice of line.

B — WHITE WITH BLUE LINE
Inglazed textured stripe that you can actually feel.

C — BONE WITH RUST LINE

D — SILVER WITH PLUM LINE

THE LINE PRODUCTS

A – THE LINE TILCHE PEDESTAL LAVATORY
White 8" spread faucet holes 0082.264
       4" center faucet holes 0083.226
       Center hole only 0082.242
Bone 8" spread faucet holes 0082.285
       4" center faucet holes 0083.271
       Center hole only 0082.219
Silver 8" spread faucet holes 0082.297 (shown)
       4" center faucet holes 0083.253
       Center hole only 0082.238
Vitreous china. Lavatory with pedestal. Rear overflow.
Mounting kit supplied.
    31½" H x 22¼" W x 20¾" L

B – THE LINE AQUALYN COUNTERTOP LAVATORY
White 8" spread faucet holes 0475.279
       4" center faucet holes 0476.283
       Center hole only 0475.246
Bone 8" spread faucet holes 0475.262
       4" center faucet holes 0476.291
       Center hole only 0475.235
Silver 8" spread faucet holes 0475.258 (shown)
       4" center faucet holes 0476.224
       Center hole only 0475.217
Vitreous china. Front overflow. Self-rimming.
Mounting kit supplied.
    20" x 17"

C – THE LINE TOILET, ELONGATED 12" Rough
White 2812.283
Bone 2812.274
Silver 2812.267 (shown)
Vitreous china. Close coupled elongated bowl and
tank. Chrome plated flush actuator. Siphon jet flush
action. Efficient water saver (3½ gals. per flush cycle).
Speed Connect tank connection system.
    26⅞" H x 20⅜" W x 29⅞" L

D – THE LINE TOILET, ROUND FRONT 12" Rough
White 2312.215
Bone 2312.237
Silver 2312.242 (shown)
Vitreous china. Close coupled round front bowl and
tank. Chrome plated flush actuator. Siphon jet flush
action. Efficient water saver (3½ gals. per flush cycle).
Speed Connect tank connection system.
    26⅞" H x 20⅜" W x 28¼" L

E – THE LINE MADVAL BIDET
White For deck mounted fitting 5002.236
      For wall mounted fitting 5004.202
      For over-the-rim fitting 5002.261
Bone For deck mounted fitting 5002.225
      For wall mounted fitting 5004.289
      For over-the-rim fitting 5002.258
Silver For deck mounted fitting 5002.213 (shown)
      For wall mounted fitting 5004.274
      For over-the-rim fitting 5002.247
Vitreous china. Integral flushing rim (except 5002.261,
5002.258 and 5002.247). Vertical douche spray
(except 5002.261, 5002.258 and 5002.247).
Order fittings separately.
    15" H x 13¾" W x 25⅜" L

COMPLETING THE LOOK: THE LAVATORIES

American Standard has the lavatory to complete your bathroom look. Pedestal, countertop, and wall-hung models in the most elegant styles. Each a combination of flawless craftsmanship and superior design.

This Tilche™ pedestal lavatory is a perfect example. An arresting presence in any bathroom. Especially as it is shown here in striking Black.

Give your bathroom a clean, contemporary look. With an American Standard lavatory.

THE LAVATORIES

A – HEXALYN™ COUNTERTOP LAVATORY
8" spread faucet holes 0485.013 (shown)
4" center faucet holes 0485.027
Center hole only 0485.033
Vitreous china. Front overflow. Self-rimming.
Mounting kit supplied.
  22" x 19"

B – OVALYN™ COUNTERTOP LAVATORY
Vitreous china. Front overflow.
With unglazed rim 19¼" x 16¼" 0470.013
With unglazed rim 21¼" x 17¼" 0470.039
With glazed rim 19¼" x 16¼" 0470.021
With glazed rim 21¼" x 17¼" 0470.047
Requires mounting frame by others.

C – AQUALYN™ COUNTERTOP LAVATORY
8" spread faucet holes 0475.020 (shown)
4" center faucet holes 0476.028
Center hole only 0475.047
Vitreous china. Front overflow. Self-rimming.
Mounting kit supplied.
  20" x 17"

D – RONDALYN™ COUNTERTOP LAVATORY
8" spread faucet holes 0490.011 (shown)
4" center faucet holes 0491.019
Center hole only 0490.156
Vitreous china. Front overflow. Self-rimming.
Mounting kit supplied.
  19" DIA.

E – TILCHE PEDESTAL LAVATORY
8" spread faucet holes 0082.016 (shown)
4" center faucet holes 0083.014
Center hole only 0082.135
Vitreous china. Lavatory with pedestal. Rear overflow.
Mounting kit supplied.
  31½" H x 22¼" W x 20¾" L

**F – CORNER MINETTE™ WALL HUNG
LAVATORY** 0451.021
Vitreous china. Front overflow. Supplied with wall
hangers. For 4" center faucets only.
  11" x 16¼"

G – HIGHLYN™ COUNTERTOP LAVATORY
8" spread faucet holes 3000.015
4" center faucet holes 3001.013 (shown)
Acid-resistant enameled cast iron. Front overflow. Dual
soap depressions. Requires mounting frame by others.
  20" x 18"

H – CIRCLYN™ COUNTERTOP LAVATORY
8" spread faucet holes 3200.011
4" center faucet holes 3201.035 (shown)
Acid-resistant enameled cast iron. Front overflow.
Requires mounting frame by others.
   18" DIA.

I – HORIZON™ COUNTERTOP LAVATORY 3301.025
Acid-resistant enameled cast iron. Front overflow.
Self-rimming. For 4" center faucets only.
   19" DIA.

J – OVAL HORIZON™ COUNTERTOP LAVATORY
8" spread faucet holes 3302.015 (shown)
4" center faucet holes 3303.013
Acid-resistant enameled cast iron. Front overflow.
Self-rimming.
   20" x 17"

33

THE LAVATORIES

A – FAIRLYN™ COUNTERTOP LAVATORY
8" spread faucet holes 3150.059 (shown)
4" center faucet holes 3151.016
Acid-resistant enameled cast iron. Front overflow.
Requires mounting frame by others.
   26" x 18"

B – LEDGELYN™ COUNTERTOP LAVATORY
8" spread faucet holes 3210.044
4" center faucet holes 3211.059 (shown)
Acid-resistant enameled cast iron. Front overflow.
Requires mounting frame by others.
   19" x 16"

C – SPACELYN™ COUNTERTOP LAVATORY
Faucet ledge on right 3220.019
Faucet ledge on left 3222.015 (shown)
Acid-resistant enameled cast iron. Front overflow.
Requires mounting frame by others.
For 4" center faucets only.
   20" x 12"

D – VANETTE™ COUNTERTOP LAVATORY
3003.605
Acid-resistant enameled steel. Front overflow. Self-rimming. Dual soap depressions with mounting kit supplied. For 4" center faucets only.
   19" DIA.

E – OVATION™ COUNTERTOP LAVATORY
3004.207
Acid-resistant enameled steel. Front overflow. Self-rimming. Dual soap depressions with mounting kit supplied. For 4" center faucets only.
   20" x 17"

F – COMRADE™ WALL HUNG LAVATORY
With wall hanger 0124.024
For concealed arms 0124.131
Vitreous china. Rear overflow. Soap depression.
For 4" center faucets only.
   20" x 18"

G – DECLYN™ WALL HUNG LAVATORY
With wall hanger 0321.026
For concealed arms 0321.075
Vitreous china. Rear overflow. Soap depression.
For 4" center faucets only.
   19" x 17"

THE TOILETS

American Standard toilets are the perfect combination of form and function. In styles that bring beauty to your bathroom. And in colors that never fail to impress.

Consider the New Cadet — an updated edition of the model that has been a best-seller for over fifty years. "Speed Connect" coupling assures that your New Cadet will be installed quickly and easily. And thanks to an improved flushing system, you actually save water.

All American Standard toilets are guaranteed to live up to the highest performance standards. Striking design, practicality and performance — a quality promise from American Standard.

THE TOILETS

A – ELONGATED GLENWALL™ TOILET
2093.631
Vitreous china. Close coupled elongated wall hung bowl and tank. Chrome plated flush actuator. Siphon jet flush action.
29" H x 18⅞" W x 28½" L

B – NEW CADET™ ELONGATED TOILET
2812.053
Vitreous china. Close coupled elongated bowl and tank. Speed Connect tank/bowl coupling system. Chrome plated flush actuator. Siphon jet flush action. Efficient water saver (3½ gals. per flush cycle).
26⅞" H x 20⅜" W x 29⅞" L

C – NEW CADET TOILET
12" rough 2312.038
Vitreous china. Close coupled round front bowl and tank. Speed Connect tank/bowl coupling system. Chrome plated flush actuator. Siphon jet flush action. Efficient water saver (3½ gals. per flush cycle).
26⅞" H x 20⅜" W x 28¼" L

D – PLEBE™ TOILET 2131.175
Vitreous china. Close coupled round front bowl and tank. Color-matched flush actuator. Siphon action reverse trap flush. Efficient water saver (3½ gals. per flush cycle).
28⅛" H x 18⅞" W x 27⅝" L

ELONGATED PLEBE TOILET 2138.012 (not shown)
Vitreous china. Close coupled elongated bowl and tank. Color-matched flush actuator. Siphon action reverse trap flush. Efficient water saver (3½ gals. per flush cycle).
28⅛" H x 18⅞" W x 29⅝" L

E – YORKVILLE™ TOILET 2128.115
Vitreous china. Close coupled round front back outlet bowl and tank. Chrome plated flush actuator. Siphon jet flush action. Efficient water saver (3½ gals. per flush cycle).
28½" H x 18⅞" W x 26½" L

ELONGATED YORKVILLE TOILET 2130.151 (not shown)
Vitreous china. Close coupled elongated back outlet bowl and tank. Chrome plated flush actuator. Siphon jet flush action. Efficient water saver (3½ gals. per flush cycle).
28½" H x 18⅞" W x 28½" L

F – NEW CADET AQUAMETER™ TOILET
2172.123
Vitreous china. Close coupled round front bowl and tank. Chrome plated flush actuator. Siphon action reverse trap flush. Pressure-assisted 1.5 g.p.f. water saver. Speed Connect tank/bowl coupling system.
27¼" H x 20⅜" W x 29⅛" L

G – ELONGATED NEW CADET AQUAMETER TOILET 2292.203
Vitreous china. Close coupled elongated bowl and tank. Chrome plated flush actuator. Siphon action reverse trap flush. Pressure assisted 1.5 g.p.f. water saver. Speed Connect tank/bowl coupling system.
27¼" H x 20⅜" W x 31⅛" L

H – PLEBE AQUAMETER 2139.116
Vitreous china. Close coupled round front bowl and tank. Color-matched flush actuator. Siphon action. 1.5 g.p.f. water saver.
30" H x 18⅞" W x 27¼" L

THE BIDETS

The air of mystery that once surrounded the bidet is rapidly disappearing. And no wonder. Personal hygiene has become a concern of the nineties.

Simply by sitting astride the bidet, you are afforded a quick and convenient method of washing. You control the temperature and intensity of the water for your own cleansing comfort.

All American Standard bidets come in a variety of colors and elegant designs to match your selection of toilet. The bidet: the sophisticated way to raise the level of your family's hygiene.

THE BIDETS

A – ROMA BIDET
For deck mounted fitting 5014.030
For wall mounted fitting 5013.032
For over-the-rim fitting 5014.049 (shown)
Vitreous china. Integral flushing rim (except 5014.049).
Douche spray (except 5014.049). Suitable for above-the-floor roughing. Order fittings separately.
 15¾" H x 14⅛" W x 25⅞" L

B – PLAZA BIDET
For deck mounted fitting 5027.037 (shown)
For wall mounted fitting 5025.032
For over-the-rim fitting 5027.048
Vitreous china. Integral flushing rim (except 5027.048).
Integral overflow. Douche spray (except 5027.048).
Order fittings separately.
 14½" H x 15⅞" W x 25½" L

C – HERITAGE BIDET 5032.026
For deck mounted fitting only. Vitreous china. Integral flushing rim. Douche spray. Integral overflow. For below-the-floor roughing. Concealed mounting bracket. Order fittings separately.
 14¼" H x 13¾" W x 25¾" L

D – ELLISSE BIDET
For deck mounted fitting 5054.015
For wall mounted fitting 5055.029
For over-the-rim fitting 5005.021

Vitreous china. Integral flushing rim (except 5005.021).
Douche spray (except 5005.021). Rear overflow.
Suitable for above-the-floor roughing. Order fittings separately.
 5005 15½" H x 14⅝" W x 22⅜" L
 5054/5055 15⅝" H x 14¾" W x 25½" L

ELLISSE BIDET – WHISPER PATTERNS
Shell For deck mounted fitting 5054.458
 For wall mounted fitting 5055.429
 For over-the-rim fitting 5005.079 (shown)
Heather For deck mounted fitting 5054.464
 For wall mounted fitting 5055.436
 For over-the-rim fitting 5005.085
Silver For deck mounted fitting 5054.445
 For wall mounted fitting 5055.417
 For over-the-rim fitting 5005.064

E – ELLISSE PETITE BIDET
For deck mounted fitting 5054.015 (shown)
For wall mounted fitting 5055.029
For over-the-rim fitting 5005.021
Vitreous china. Integral flushing rim (except 5005.021).
Douche spray (except 5005.021). Rear overflow. Suitable for above-the-floor roughing. Order fittings separately.
 5005 15½" H x 14⅝" W x 22⅜" L
 5054/5055 15⅝" H x 14¾" W x 25½" L

F – LEXINGTON BIDET
For deck mounted fitting 5007.014 (shown)
For wall mounted fitting 5006.201
For over-the-rim fitting 5007.041

Vitreous china. Integral flushing rim (except 5007.041).
Douche spray (except 5007.041). Integral overflow.
Order fittings separately.
 15" H x 14" W x 25¾" L

G – THE LINE MADVAL BIDET
White For deck mounted fitting 5002.236
 For wall mounted fitting 5004.202
 For over-the-rim fitting 5002.261
Bone For deck mounted fitting 5002.225
 For wall mounted fitting 5004.289
 For over-the-rim fitting 5002.258
Silver For deck mounted fitting 5002.213 (shown)
 For wall mounted fitting 5004.274
 For over-the-rim fitting 5002.247
Vitreous china. Integral flushing rim (except 5002.261, 5002.258 and 5002.247). Vertical douche spray (except 5002.261, 5002.258 and 5002.247).
Order fittings separately.
 15" H x 13¾" W x 25⅜" L

H – MADVAL BIDET
For deck mounted fitting 5002.035 (shown)
For wall mounted fitting 5004.023
For over-the-rim fitting 5002.062
Vitreous china. Integral flushing rim (except 5002.062). Vertical douche spray (except 5002.062).
Order fittings separately.
 15" H x 13¾" W x 25⅜" L

BATHS AND WHIRLPOOLS: A BATHING SENSATION

Test the waters at American Standard — where the bath and whirlpool have been raised to unprecedented levels of quality, comfort, and ergonomically-contoured design.

Savor the uncompromising elegance of the Ellisse whirlpool in Light Mink — the embodiment of relaxation in both color and form. All American Standard whirlpools have the benefit of the latest technology. Including color-matched, multi-directional, flow-adjustable jets which provide soothing hydro-massage. And the fabulous ULTRASENSE PLUS™ system, an electronic control which allows you to operate the whirlpool system without leaving the comfort of your bath.

American Standard baths and whirlpools. Combining the finest materials with the most beautiful designs. A bathing sensation.

THE BEAUTY OF STRENGTH:
STRATFORD AND PRINCETON WITH AMERICAST

A – STRATFORD™ WHIRLPOOL 2470.013
Acid-resistant porcelain enameled **Americast™**. End drain outlet. Integral lumbar support. Beveled head rest. Slip-resistant surface. Universal design for left or right hand, island or sunken installations. Featuring American Standard factory installed whirlpool system including six color-matched multi-directional, flow-adjustable jets, two brass air volume controls, color-matched anti-vortex suction fitting, rigid P.V.C. harness, ¾ h.p. self-draining pump and motor with 24 hour dry run seal, and bath-mounted ULTRASENSE PLUS™ electronic whirlpool on/off control with low-water cut-off.

BATHING POOL 2470.002
Same as above less whirlpool system.
   66" L x 32" W x 18" D

B – PRINCETON™ RECESS BATH
Right outlet 2391.202 Left outlet 2390.202
Acid-resistant porcelain enameled **Americast**. Integral tiling ledge, apron, and lumbar support. Beveled head rest. Slip-resistant surface.
   60" L x 30" W x 14" D
Also available for above floor rough installations –
2392.202 for left outlet; 2393.202 for right.
   60" L x 30" W x 16¾" D

PRINCETON RECESS BATH WITH LUXURY LEDGE (shown)
Right outlet 2395.202 Left outlet 2394.202
Acid-resistant porcelain enameled **Americast**. Integral tiling ledge, apron, and lumbar support. Beveled head rest. Extended ledge for added shoulder and elbow room, and storage convenience. Slip-resistant surface.
   60" L x 34" W x 14" D
Also available for above floor rough installations –
2396.202 for left outlet; 2397.202 for right.
   60" L x 34" W x 16¾" D

C – SALEM™ BATH
Right outlet 0135.137 Left outlet 0137.133
Acid-resistant enameled steel. Slip-resistant surface. Straight tiling bead. Sound deadening styrofoam pad under tub. (Less slip-resistant surface in White only: Right outlet 0135.129; Left outlet 0137.125).
   60" L x 30" W x 15" D
Also available for above floor rough installations –
0136.135 for left outlet; 0134.130 for right.
   60" L x 30" W x 16¼" D

D – CONTOUR™ RECESS BATHING POOL
Right outlet 2185.403 Left outlet 2187.409
Acid-resistant enameled cast iron. Slip-resistant surface. Wide rim seat. Extra long and wide bathing area.
   66" L x 32" W x 16" D

E – FONTAINE™ 6' WHIRLPOOL 2650.013
Acid-resistant enameled cast iron. Integral lumbar support. Beveled headrest. Slip-resistant surface. Universal design for left or right hand, island or sunken installations. Featuring American Standard factory installed whirlpool system including six color-matched multi-directional, flow-adjustable jets, color-matched anti-vortex suction fitting, rigid P.V.C. harness, ¾ h.p. self-draining pump and motor with 24 hour dry run seal, and bath-mounted ULTRASENSE PLUS™ electronic whirlpool on/off control with low water cut-off.

FONTAINE BATHING POOL 2650.002
Same as above less whirlpool system.
    72" L x 36" W x 18" D

F – SPECTRA™ WHIRLPOOL
Right outlet 2605.014 Left outlet 2607.014
Acid-resistant enameled cast iron. Integral lumbar support. Slip-resistant surface. Wide bathing area. Featuring American Standard factory installed whirlpool system including four color-matched multi-directional, flow-adjustable jets, brass air volume control, color-matched anti-vortex suction fitting, rigid P.V.C. harness, ½ h.p. self-draining pump and motor with 24 hour dry run seal, and 0-30 minute mechanical timer. Available with optional bath-mounted ULTRASENSE PLUS™ electronic whirlpool on/off control with low water cut-off (2605.013, 2607.013).

SPECTRA BATHING POOL
Right outlet 2605.002 Left outlet 2607.002
Same as above less whirlpool system. (Available less grab bars: Right outlet 2605.103; Left outlet 2607.109).
    60" L x 32" W x 16" D

G – FONTAINE 5' 2637.013
Acid-resistant enameled cast iron. End drain outlet. Integral lumbar support. Beveled headrest. Slip-resistant surface. Featuring American Standard factory installed whirlpool system including four color-matched multi-directional, flow-adjustable jets, two brass air volume controls, color-matched anti-vortex suction fitting, rigid P.V.C. harness, ½ h.p. self-draining pump and motor with 24 hour dry run seal, bath-mounted ULTRASENSE PLUS™ on/off control with low water cut-off.

FONTAINE 5' BATHING POOL 2637.002
Same as above less whirlpool system.
    60" L x 36" W x 20" D

H – FONTAINE 5½' 2183.013
Acid-resistant enameled cast iron. End drain outlet. Integral lumbar support. Beveled headrest. Slip-resistant surface. Featuring American Standard factory installed whirlpool system including six color-matched multi-directional, flow-adjustable jets, two brass air volume controls, color-matched anti-vortex suction fitting, rigid P.V.C. harness, ¾ h.p. self-draining pump and motor with 24 hour dry run seal, and bath-mounted ULTRASENSE PLUS™ electronic whirlpool on/off control with low water cut-off.

FONTAINE 5½' BATHING POOL 2183.002
Same as above less whirpool system.
    66" L x 32" W x 18" D

Whirlpools and bathing pools come untrimmed. Trim kits available in Chrome, Polished Brass, White, Bone, 24K Gold, Classic Turquoise, or Classic Mink.

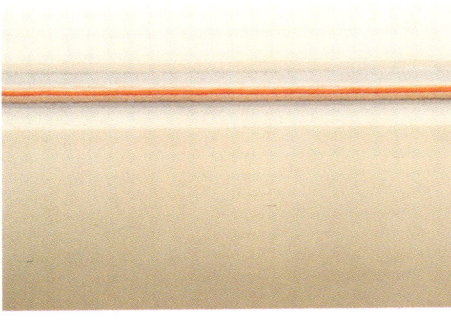

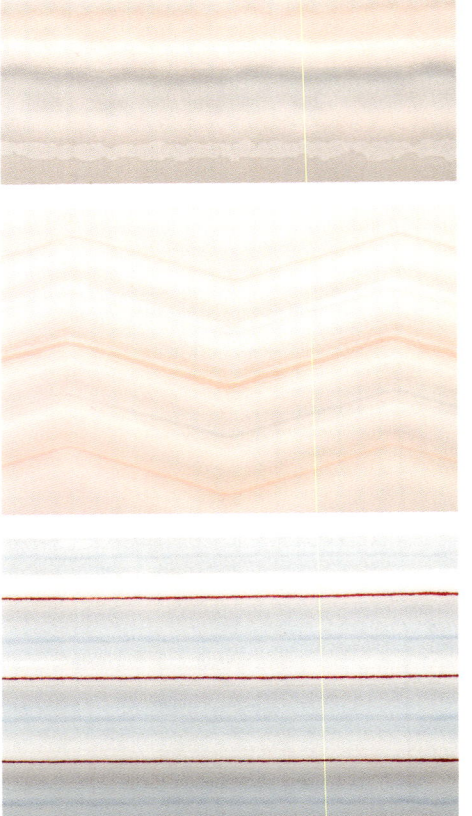

UNFORGETTABLE TOUCHES: PATTERNS, LINES, AND TEXTURES

Those unforgettable touches. American Standard knows many ways to add a special dimension to your bathroom decor.

WHISPER PATTERNS

Complement your choice of color with one of our **Whisper Patterns**. Thanks to a unique process, one of three original designs can be fired "in glaze" on American Standard's elegant Ellisse Suite, creating a subtle three-dimensional effect. Heather in soft lines. Shell in a zigzag. Silver in a pinstripe. An artistic alternative to the usual route.

THE LINE

Perhaps your tastes gravitate towards geometric design. **The Line** is American Standard's newest way of adding continuity to your bathroom look. Choose White with a Blue line. Bone with a Rust line. Or Silver with a Plum line. Select a stripe which points your bathroom in a contemporary direction.

Take your coordinated look one step further with designer tiles — companions to our Whisper Colors, Whisper Patterns, and to The Line. American Olean's accent wall tiles provide a beautiful extension to any style you choose.

ROMA GOLD

For a richly dramatic effect, choose Roma Gold, a special process which fires 22K Gold into the fixtures of our stylish Roma Suite. Treat your eyes to a dazzling display — give your bathroom the Midas touch. With Roma Gold.

AN ACCENT FOR BATHROOMS: AMERICAN STANDARD COLORS

American Standard puts the proper accent on your bathroom. With an exciting array of alluring colors. The best way to guarantee an absolutely beautiful bathroom decor.

Whether it be a striking color from The Tones™ Collection like Classic Turquoise or a delicate Whisper Color™ like Shell, American Standard's colors are always in fashion. Venture beyond the ordinary. With American Standard.

CHIANTI 170

FRENCH BLUE 196

AQUAMARINE 197

SUNSHINE 200

WHITE 020

DRESDEN BLUE 163

ORCHID 179

FAWN BEIGE 045

BONE 021

BLACK 178

SILVER 165

SHELL 173

HEATHER 174

BLOND 176

HONEYDEW 177

LIGHT TURQUOISE 191

CLASSIC TURQUOISE 193

LIGHT MINK 190

CLASSIC MINK 192

COLOR SELECTION CHART

	WHITE 020	DRESDEN BLUE 163	ORCHID 179	FAWN BEIGE 045	BONE 021	BLACK 178	SILVER 165	SHELL 173	HEATHER 174	BLOND 176	HONEYDEW 177	LIGHT TURQUOISE 191	CLASSIC TURQUOISE 193	LIGHT MINK 190	CLASSIC MINK 192
WHIRLPOOLS – ACRYLIC															
SENSORIUM – 3560/3760 Series					•										
ELLISSE GRANDE – 2708 Series	•	•	•	•	•	•	•	•	•	•	•	•	•	•	•
ELLISSE – 2706 Series	•	•	•	•	•	•	•	•	•	•	•	•	•	•	•
GALLERIA – 2718 Series	•	•	•	•		•	•	•	•	•	•				
PLAZA SUITE – 2728 Series	•	•	•	•		•	•	•	•	•	•	•	•	•	•
ROMA SOAKING POOL – 2710 Series	•					•									
ROMA 5½ – 2645 Series	•	•	•	•	•	•	•	•	•	•	•	•	•	•	•
ROMA 5 – 2643 Series	•	•	•	•	•	•	•	•	•	•	•	•	•	•	•
LEXINGTON 5½ – 2729 Series	•	•	•	•	•	•	•	•	•	•	•	•	•	•	•
LEXINGTON SOAKING POOL – 2720 Series	•	•	•	•	•	•	•	•	•	•	•	•	•	•	•
LEXINGTON 5 – 2715 Series	•	•	•	•	•	•	•	•	•	•	•	•	•	•	•
WHIRLPOOLS – AMERICAST™															
STRATFORD – 2470 Series	•	•	•	•	•	•	•	•	•	•	•	•	•	•	•
WHIRLPOOLS – ENAMELED CAST IRON															
FONTAINE 6 – 2650 Series	•	•	•	•	•	•	•	•	•	•	•	•	•	•	•
FONTAINE 5½ – 2183 Series	•	•	•	•	•	•	•	•	•	•	•	•	•	•	•
FONTAINE 5 – 2637 Series	•	•	•	•	•	•	•	•	•	•	•	•	•	•	•
ROMA 5 – 2640 Series	•	•	•	•	•	•	•	•	•	•	•	•	•	•	•
SPECTRA – 2605/2607 Series	•	•	•	•	•	•	•	•	•	•	•	•	•	•	•
BATHING POOLS – ACRYLIC															
SENSORIUM – 3060 Series					•										
ELLISSE GRANDE – 2708 Series	•	•	•	•	•	•	•	•	•	•	•	•	•	•	•
ELLISSE – 2706 Series	•	•	•	•	•	•	•	•	•	•	•	•	•	•	•
GALLERIA – 2718 Series	•	•	•	•	•	•	•	•	•	•	•	•	•	•	•
PLAZA SUITE – 2728 Series	•	•	•	•		•	•	•	•	•	•	•	•	•	•
ROMA SOAKING POOL – 2710 Series	•					•									
ROMA 5½ – 2645 Series	•	•	•	•	•	•	•	•	•	•	•	•	•	•	•
LEXINGTON 5½ – 2729 Series	•	•	•	•	•	•	•	•	•	•	•	•	•	•	•
LEXINGTON SOAKING POOL – 2720 Series	•	•	•	•	•	•	•	•	•	•	•	•	•	•	•
LEXINGTON 5 – 2715 Series	•	•	•	•	•	•	•	•	•	•	•	•	•	•	•
BATHING POOLS – AMERICAST™															
STRATFORD – 2470 Series	•	•	•	•	•	•	•	•	•	•	•	•	•	•	•
PRINCETON – 2390/2393 Series	•	•	•	•	•	•	•	•	•	•	•				
PRINCETON LUXURY LEDGE – 2394/2396 Series	•	•	•	•	•	•	•	•	•	•	•				
BATHING POOLS – ENAMELED CAST IRON															
FONTAINE 6 – 2650 Series	•	•	•	•	•	•	•	•	•	•	•	•	•	•	•
FONTAINE 5½ – 2183 Series	•	•	•	•	•	•	•	•	•	•	•	•	•	•	•
FONTAINE 5 – 2637 Series	•	•	•	•	•	•	•	•	•	•	•	•	•	•	•
ROMA 5 – 2640 Series	•	•	•	•	•	•	•	•	•	•	•	•	•	•	•
SPECTRA – 2605/2607 Series	•	•	•	•	•	•	•	•	•	•	•	•	•	•	•
CONTOUR – 2185/2187 Series	•	•	•	•	•	•	•	•	•	•	•	•	•		
BATHING POOLS – ENAMELED STEEL															
SALEM – 0135.137/0137.133 Series	•	•		•	•		•	•							
SALEM – 0135.129/0137.125 Series	•														
LAVATORIES – VITREOUS CHINA															
PLATNER PEDESTAL – 0099.605 Series					•										
GALLERIA PEDESTAL – 0180 Series	•	•	•	•	•	•	•	•	•	•	•	•	•	•	•
ROMA PEDESTAL – 0176 Series	•	•	•	•	•	•	•	•	•	•	•	•	•	•	•
ROMA GOLD PEDESTAL – 0716 Series	•														
ELLISSE PEDESTAL – 0075 Series	•	•	•	•	•	•	•	•	•	•	•	•	•	•	•
ELLISSE WHISPER PATTERNS PEDESTAL – 0075 Series							•	•	•	•	•				
ELLISSE PETITE PEDESTAL – 0079 Series	•	•	•	•	•	•	•	•	•	•	•	•	•	•	•
HERITAGE PEDESTAL – 0191.024 Series	•														
PLAZA SUITE PEDESTAL – 0184 Series	•	•	•	•	•	•	•	•	•	•	•	•	•	•	•
THE LINE TILCHE PEDESTAL – 0082/0083 Series	•					•	•								
TILCHE PEDESTAL – 0082/0083 Series	•	•	•	•	•	•	•	•	•	•	•	•	•	•	•
LEXINGTON PEDESTAL – 0178/0179 Series	•	•	•	•	•	•	•	•	•	•	•	•	•	•	•
PLATNER COUNTERTOP – 0469.610					•										
ROMA/GALLERIA COUNTERTOP – 0177 Series	•	•	•	•	•	•	•	•	•	•	•	•	•	•	•
ROMA GOLD COUNTERTOP – 0177 Series	•														
ELLISSE COUNTERTOP – 0076 Series	•	•	•	•	•	•	•	•	•	•	•	•	•	•	•
ELLISSE WHISPER PATTERN COUNTERTOP – 0076 Series							•	•	•	•	•				
ELLISSE PETITE COUNTERTOP – 0410/0411 Series	•	•	•	•	•	•	•	•	•	•	•	•	•	•	•
HERITAGE COUNTERTOP – 0456.017	•														
PLAZA SUITE COUNTERTOP – 0187 Series	•	•		•	•		•	•	•	•	•	•	•	•	•
PLAZA SUITE PETITE COUNTERTOP – 0408/0409 Series	•	•		•	•		•	•	•	•	•	•	•	•	•
LEXINGTON COUNTERTOP – 0492/0493 Series	•	•	•	•	•	•	•	•	•	•	•	•	•	•	•

Product	WHITE 020	DRESDEN BLUE 163	ORCHID 179	FAWN BEIGE 045	BONE 021	BLACK 178	SILVER 165	SHELL 173	HEATHER 174	BLOND 176	HONEYDEW 177	LIGHT TURQUOISE 191	CLASSIC TURQUOISE 193	LIGHT MINK 190	CLASSIC MINK 192
LAVATORIES — VITREOUS CHINA															
OVALYN COUNTERTOP – 0470 Series	●	●	●	●	●	●	●	●	●	●	●	●	●	●	●
HEXALYN COUNTERTOP – 0485 Series	●	●	●	●	●	●	●	●	●	●	●				
THE LINE AQUALYN COUNTERTOP – 0475/0476 Series	●				●	●	●								
AQUALYN COUNTERTOP – 0475/0476 Series	●	●	●	●	●	●	●	●	●	●	●				
RONDALYN COUNTERTOP – 0490/0491 Series	●	●	●	●	●	●	●	●	●	●	●				
COMRADE WALL HUNG – 0124 Series	●	●		●	●	●	●	●	●	●	●				
CORNER MINETTE WALL HUNG – 0451.021	●	●		●	●		●	●	●	●	●				
LAVATORIES — ENAMELED CAST IRON															
HIGHLYN COUNTERTOP – 3000/3001 Series	●	●		●	●		●	●	●	●	●				
CIRCLYN COUNTERTOP – 3200/3201 Series	●	●		●	●		●	●	●	●	●				
FAIRLYN COUNTERTOP – 3150/3151 Series	●	●		●	●		●	●	●	●	●				
LEDGELYN COUNTERTOP – 3210/3211 Series	●	●		●	●		●	●	●	●	●				
SPACELYN COUNTERTOP – 3220/3222 Series	●	●		●	●		●	●	●	●	●				
HORIZON COUNTERTOP – 3301.025*	●	●	●	●	●	●	●	●	●	●	●				
OVAL HORIZON COUNTERTOP – 3302/3303 Series*	●	●	●	●	●	●	●	●	●	●	●				
LAVATORIES — ENAMELED STEEL															
VANETTE COUNTERTOP – 3003 Series	●	●		●	●		●	●							
OVATION COUNTERTOP – 3004 Series	●	●		●	●		●	●							
BIDETS															
PLATNER – 5029.615						●									
GALLERIA – 5019/5021 Series	●	●	●	●	●	●	●	●	●	●	●	●	●	●	●
ROMA – 5013/5014 Series	●	●	●	●	●	●	●	●	●	●	●	●	●	●	●
ROMA GOLD – 5013/5014 Series	●														
THE LINE MADVAL – 5002/5004 Series	●				●		●								
MADVAL – 5002/5004 Series	●	●	●	●	●		●	●	●	●	●	●	●	●	●
ELLISSE – 5005/5054/5055 Series	●	●	●	●	●		●	●	●	●	●	●	●	●	●
ELLISSE WHISPER PATTERN – 5005/5054/5055 Series					●			●	●						
HERITAGE – 5032.026	●														
PLAZA SUITE – 5025/5027 Series	●	●		●	●		●	●	●	●	●	●	●	●	●
LEXINGTON – 5006/5007 Series	●	●	●	●	●	●	●	●	●	●	●			●	●
TOILETS — RESIDENTIAL															
PLATNER – 2029.600						●									
GALLERIA ONE-PIECE – 2014.013	●	●	●	●	●	●	●	●	●	●	●	●	●	●	●
ELLISSE ONE-PIECE – 2008.019	●	●	●	●	●	●	●	●	●	●	●	●	●	●	●
ELLISSE WHISPER PATTERN ONE-PIECE – 2008 Series					●			●	●						
ROMA GOLD ONE-PIECE – 2009 Series	●														
ROMA ONE-PIECE – 2009 Series	●	●	●	●	●	●	●	●	●	●	●	●	●	●	●
HERITAGE ONE-PIECE – 2031.016	●														
PLAZA SUITE ONE-PIECE – 2016.019	●	●		●	●		●	●	●	●	●	●	●	●	●
ROMA II ONE-PIECE – 2012.014	●	●		●	●	●	●	●	●	●	●	●	●	●	●
LEXINGTON ONE-PIECE – 2006.014/2007.012	●	●	●	●	●	●	●	●	●	●	●			●	●
ROMA TWO-PIECE – 2080.018	●	●		●	●	●	●	●	●	●	●	●	●	●	●
ELLISSE PETITE TWO-PIECE – 2085.019	●	●	●	●	●	●	●	●	●	●	●	●	●	●	●
GLENWALL ELONGATED WALL HUNG – 2093 Series	●	●	●	●	●	●	●	●	●	●	●	●		●	●
CADET ELONGATED 18" – 2108 Series	●	●	●	●	●	●	●	●	●	●	●				
THE LINE ELONGATED TWO-PIECE – 2812 Series	●				●		●								
THE LINE ROUND FRONT TWO-PIECE – 2312 Series	●				●		●								
NEW CADET ELONGATED – 2812 Series	●	●	●	●	●	●	●	●	●	●	●				
NEW CADET AQUAMETER ELONGATED – 2292.203	●	●	●	●	●	●	●	●	●	●	●				
CADET ROUND FRONT – 2120/2124 Series	●	●	●	●	●	●	●	●	●	●	●				
NEW CADET ROUND FRONT – 2312 Series	●	●	●	●	●	●	●	●	●	●	●				
NEW CADET AQUAMETER ROUND FRONT 2172.123	●	●	●	●	●	●	●	●	●	●	●				
ELDERLY NEW CADET AQUAMETER 18" – 2168.128	●	●	●	●	●	●	●	●	●	●	●				
PLEBE ELONGATED – 2138.012	●	●	●	●	●		●								
PLEBE ROUND FRONT – 2131.175	●	●	●	●	●		●								
PLEBE AQUAMETER ROUND FRONT – 2139.116	●	●	●	●	●		●								
YORKVILLE ROUND FRONT – 2128.115	●	●	●	●	●	●	●	●	●	●	●				
YORKVILLE ELONGATED – 2130.151/2134.129	●	●	●	●	●	●	●	●	●	●	●				

*also available in Chianti, French Blue, Aquamarine and Sunshine.

47

Living up to a higher standard.

A Natural Wonder

DECO

Design, Quality and Service

AND BATES

3699 INDUSTRY AVENUE • LAKEWOOD, CALIFORNIA 90712 • (213) 595-8824 • (800) 726-7680 • FAX (213) 988-0764

Timeless

MBS 1012

Design, Quality and Service

AND BATES

3699 INDUSTRY AVENUE • LAKEWOOD, CALIFORNIA 90712 • (213) 595-8824 • (800) 726-7680 • FAX (213) 988-0764

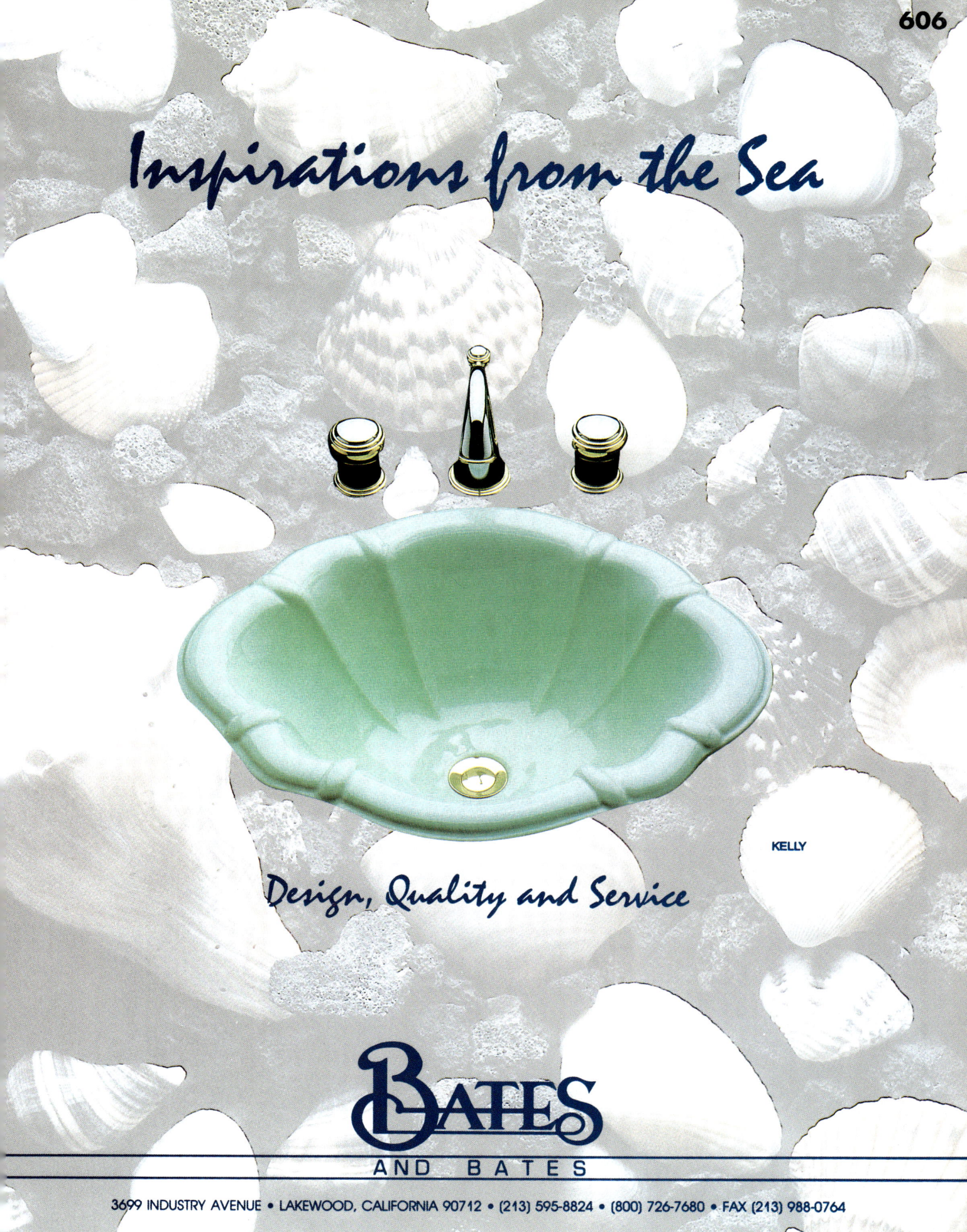

Reaching for the Sky

CONSUL

Design, Quality and Service

BATES
AND BATES

3699 INDUSTRY AVENUE • LAKEWOOD, CALIFORNIA 90712 • (213) 595-8824 • (800) 726-7680 • FAX (213) 988-0764

BARCLAY PRODUCTS LIMITED

1991 Edition

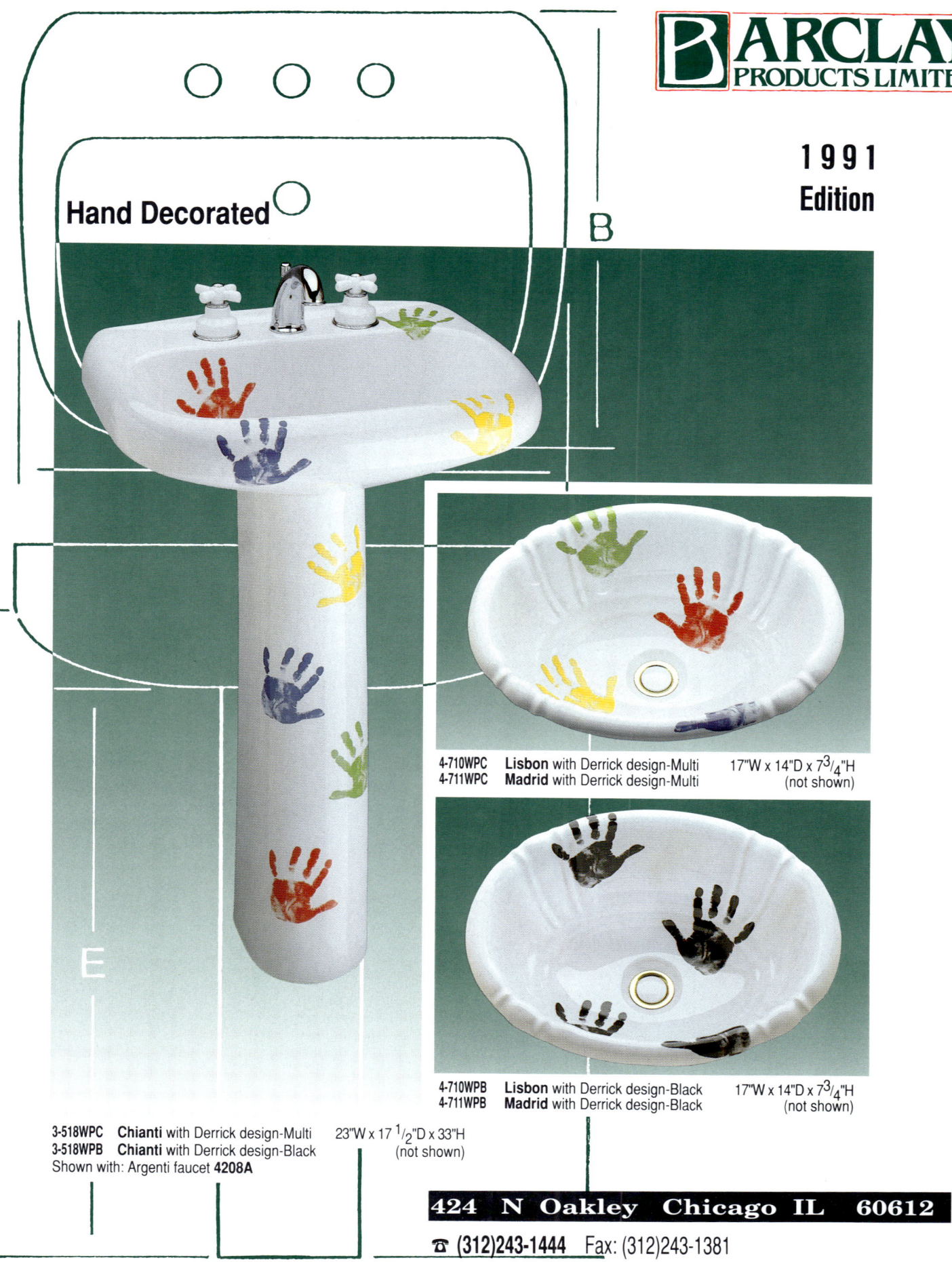

Hand Decorated

4-710WPC   **Lisbon** with Derrick design-Multi   17"W x 14"D x 7³/₄"H
4-711WPC   **Madrid** with Derrick design-Multi   (not shown)

4-710WPB   **Lisbon** with Derrick design-Black   17"W x 14"D x 7³/₄"H
4-711WPB   **Madrid** with Derrick design-Black   (not shown)

3-518WPC   **Chianti** with Derrick design-Multi   23"W x 17 ¹/₂"D x 33"H
3-518WPB   **Chianti** with Derrick design-Black   (not shown)
Shown with: Argenti faucet **4208A**

424 N Oakley Chicago IL 60612

☎ (312)243-1444   Fax: (312)243-1381

Decorated Victoria

3-458WO **Victoria** with Olivia design   25"W x 20$\frac{1}{2}$"D x 32"H
Shown with: Argenti faucet **4202L**

3-458WK **Victoria** with Kimberly design   25"W x 20$\frac{1}{2}$"D x 32"H
Shown with: Argenti faucet **4202L**

3-458W **Victoria** white pedestal   25"W x 20$\frac{1}{2}$"D x 32"H
Shown with: Argenti faucet **4202L**

3-458WV **Victoria** with Violet design   25"W x 20$\frac{1}{2}$"D x 32"H
Shown with: Argenti faucet **4202L**

3-458 Decorated **Victoria** is available in 8" drillings only.

Also available in undecorated:

3-458W	**Victoria** white pedestal 8" faucet drillings	25"W x 20$\frac{1}{2}$"D x 32"H
3-458B	**Victoria** bone pedestal 8" faucet drillings	(not shown)
3-454W	**Victoria** white pedestal 4" faucet drillings	(not shown)
3-454B	**Victoria** bone pedestal 4" faucet drillings	(not shown)

424 N Oakley Chicago IL 60612

☎ **(312)243-1444**   Fax: (312)243-1381

Decorated Shells

3-508WL　**Shell** with Limoges design　　19"W x 16$\frac{3}{4}$"D x 35"H
Shown with: Argenti faucet **4202L**

3-508WE　**Shell** with Evelyn design　　19"W x 16$\frac{3}{4}$"D x 35"H
Shown with: Argenti faucet **4202L**

3-508W　**Shell** white pedestal　　19"W x 16$\frac{3}{4}$"D x 35"H
　　　　8" faucet drillings
Shown with: Argenti faucet **4202L**

3-508WM　**Shell** with Marie design　　19"W x 16$\frac{3}{4}$"D x 35"H
Shown with: Argenti faucet **4202L**

Also available in undecorated:

3-508B	**Shell** bone pedestal	(not shown)
	8" faucet drillings	
3-504W	**Shell** white pedestal	(not shown)
	4" faucet drillings	
3-504B	**Shell** bone pedestal	(not shown)
	4" faucet drillings	

424 N Oakley Chicago IL 60612

☎ **(312)243-1444**　Fax: (312)243-1381

Hand Decorated
Lavatory Basins

4-710WPC   **Lisbon** with Derrick design-Multi   17"W x 14"D x 7^3/$_4$"H
4-711WPC   **Madrid** with Derrick design-Multi   (not shown)
Available with Black handprints

4-710WH   **Lisbon** White   17"W x 14"D x 7^3/$_4$"H
4-711WH   **Madrid** White   (not shown)

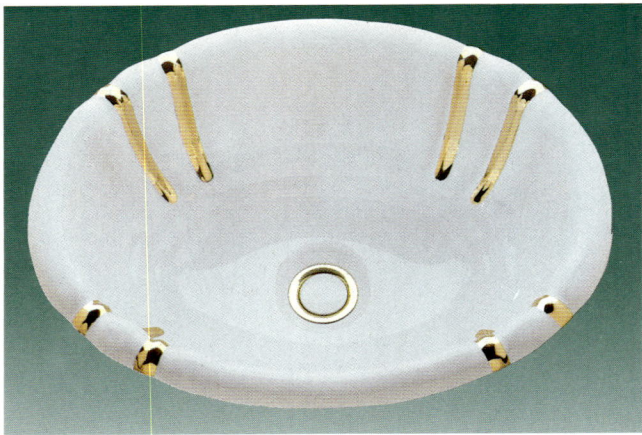

4-710WG   **Lisbon** with Gold design   17"W x 14"D x 7^3/$_4$"H
4-711WG   **Madrid** with Gold design   (not shown)
Available with Silver design

4-710WN   **Lisbon** with Nicole design   17"W x 14"D x 7^3/$_4$"H
4-711WN   **Madrid** with Nicole design   (not shown)

4-710WA   **Lisbon** with Adrienne design   17"W x 14"D x 7^3/$_4$"H
4-711WA   **Madrid** with Adrienne design   (not shown)

4-710WI   **Lisbon** with Iris design   17"W x 14"D x 7^3/$_4$"H
4-711WI   **Madrid** with Iris design   (not shown)

Barclay © 1990

424 N Oakley Chicago IL 60612
☎ **(312)243-1444**   Fax: (312)243-1381

Hand Decorated
Lavatory Basins

| 4-710WO | **Lisbon** with Olivia design | 17"W x 14"D x 7$^3/_4$"H |
| 4-711WO | **Madrid** with Olivia design | (not shown) |

| 4-710WD | **Lisbon** with Danielle design | 17"W x 14"D x 7$^3/_4$"H |
| 4-711WD | **Madrid** with Danielle design | (not shown) |

| 4-710WC | **Lisbon** with Collette design | 17"W x 14"D x 7$^3/_4$"H |
| 4-711WC | **Madrid** with Collette design | (not shown) |

| 4-710WB | **Lisbon** with Brigitte design | 17"W x 14"D x 7$^3/_4$"H |
| 4-711WB | **Madrid** with Brigitte design | (not shown) |

| 4-710WK | **Lisbon** with Kimberly design | 17"W x 14"D x 7$^3/_4$"H |
| 4-711WK | **Madrid** with Kimberly design | (not shown) |

| 4-710WE | **Lisbon** with Evelyn design | 17"W x 14"D x 7$^3/_4$"H |
| 4-711WE | **Madrid** with Evelyn design | (not shown) |

424 N Oakley   Chicago IL   60612

☎ **(312)243-1444**   Fax: (312)243-1381

Pedestal Lavatories

4-648 Antique   **4-649 Antique shelf**
Shown with: Argenti faucet **4202L**

3-818 Windsor
Shown with: Argenti faucet **4202L**

4-648WH	**Antique** white pedestal 8" faucet drillings	26½"W x 21½"D x 33½"H
4-641WH	**Antique** white pedestal with 1 hole drilling	(not shown)
4-649WH	**Antique** white shelf	27"W x 5"D x 3"H
3-818WH	**Windsor** pedestal lavatory	24½"W x 20"D x 32½"H
4-618WH	**Classic** pedestal 8" faucet drillings	28"W x 21"D x 32"H
4-619WH	**Classic** shelf	27½"W x 6"D x 5½"H

4-618 Classic   **4-619 Classic shelf**
Shown with: Argenti faucet **4206A**

424 N Oakley Chicago IL 60612

☎ (312)243-1444   Fax: (312)243-1381

Pedestal Lavatories

3-204 Chelsea
Shown with: Argenti faucet **4706L**

3-314 Hartford/3-324 Oxford
Shown with: Argenti faucet **4706L**

3-518 Chianti
Shown with: Argenti faucet **4208A**

3-204W	**Chelsea** white pedestal 4" faucet drillings	$18^3/_4$"W x 14"D x 30"H
3-204B	**Chelsea** bone pedestal 4" faucet drillings	(not shown)
3-314W	**Hartford** white pedestal 4" faucet drillings	$22^1/_2$"W x $17^1/_2$"D x 32"H
3-314B	**Hartford** bone pedestal 4" faucet drillings	(not shown)
3-318W	**Hartford** white pedestal 8" faucet drillings	(not shown)
3-318B	**Hartford** bone pedestal 8" faucet drillings	(not shown)
3-324W	**Oxford** white pedestal 4" faucet drillings	$24^3/_4$"W x 19"D x 32"H
3-324B	**Oxford** bone pedestal 4" faucet drillings	(not shown)
3-328W	**Oxford** white pedestal 8" faucet drillings	(not show
3-328B	**Oxford** bone pedestal 8" faucet drillings	(not sho
3-518W	**Chianti** pedestal	23"W x $17^1/_2$"D x

424 N Oakley Chicago IL

☎ **(312)243-1444**   Fax: (312)243-1381

Victoria Water Closets

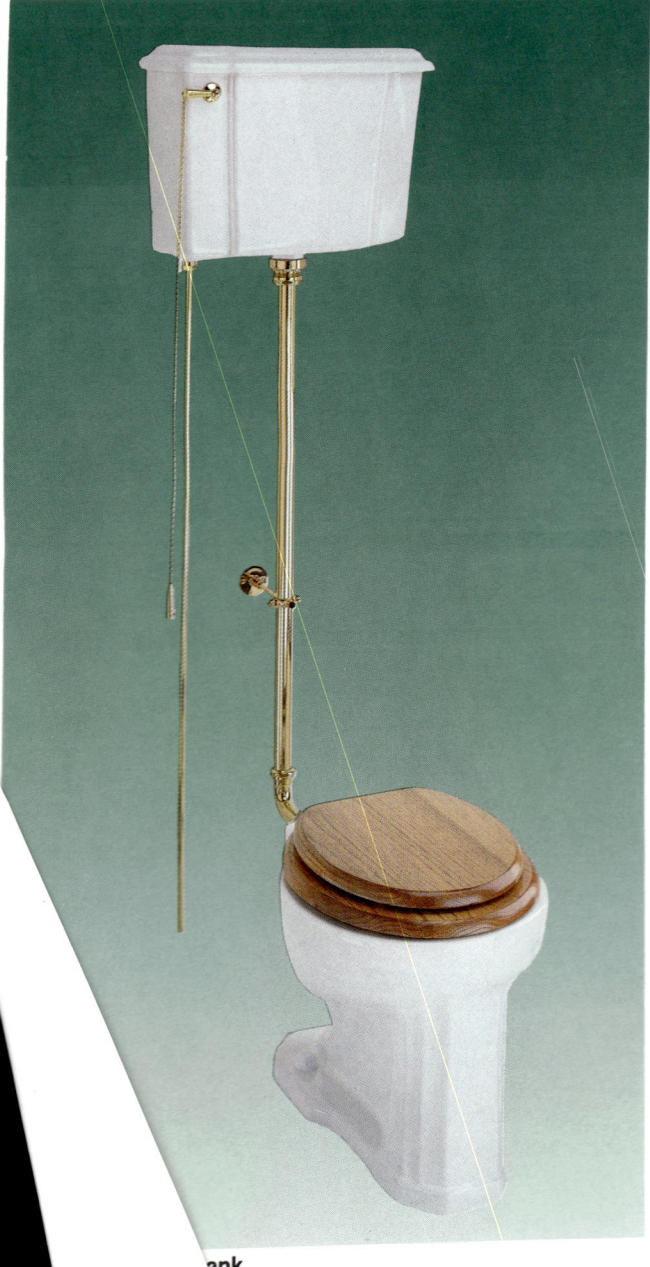

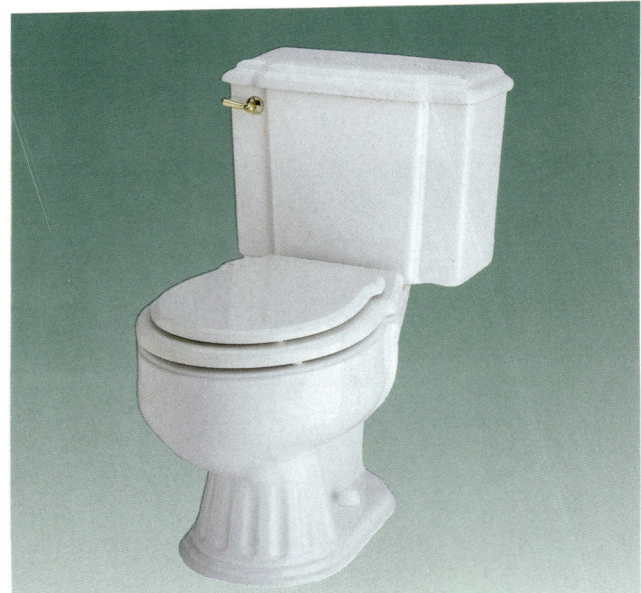

2-422 Victoria wall hung

2-402 Victoria water closet

...ank

....ank with brass trim
...with brass trim
...k with chrome trim   (not shown)
...ith chrome trim   (not shown)

...th brass trim
...ass trim
........chrome trim   (not shown)
........me trim   (not shown)

33"H

2-402WB	**Victoria** white water closet	
9-402WB	**Victoria** white closet seat	
2-402BB	**Victoria** bone water closet	(not shown)
9-402BB	**Victoria** bone closet seat	(not shown)
	All the above have brass trim	
2-402WC	**Victoria** white water closet	(not shown)
9-402WC	**Victoria** white closet seat	(not shown)
2-402BC	**Victoria** bone water closet	(not shown)
9-402BC	**Victoria** bone closet seat	(not shown)
	All the above have chrome trim	

424 N Oakley   Chicago IL   60612

☎ **(312)243-1444**   Fax: (312)243-1381

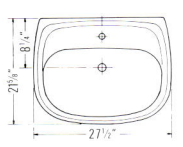

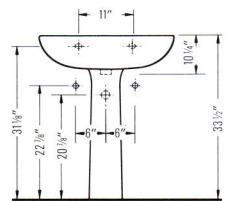

Pedestal:	# 857.50
Basin:	# 420.70
Stock Colors:	White, Black
Accommodates:	Single Hole, Widespread

Non-stocked colors: Manhattan – 11, Amber – 41, Fogo – 47, Rose-Perle – 54, Jasmin – 72, Edelweiss – 78, Flannel – 79, Opaline-Blue – 15, Opaline-Grey – 43, Opaline-Beige – 45, Opaline-Rose – 55.

Edition Giamo

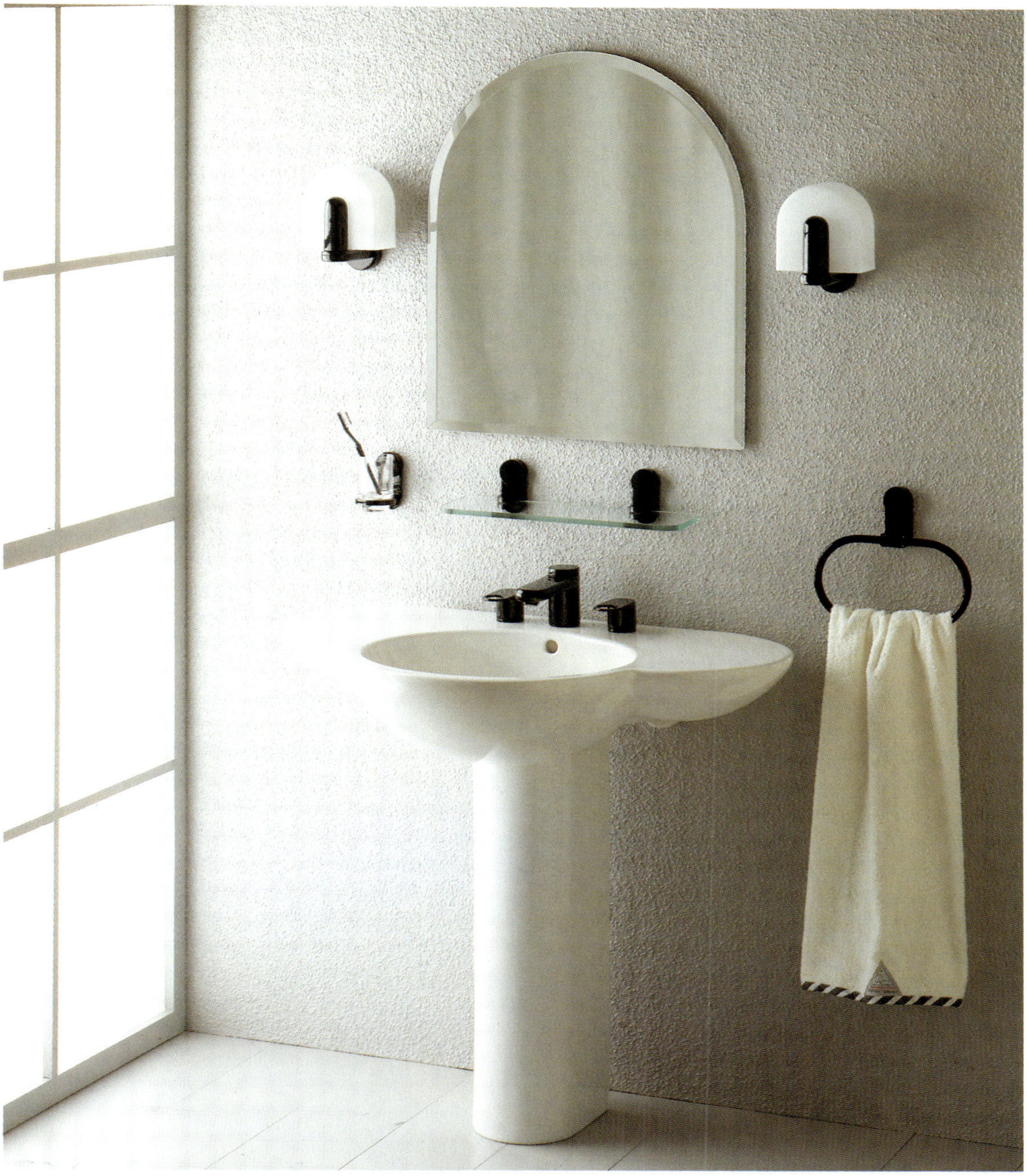

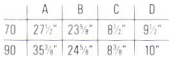

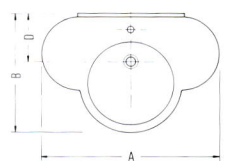

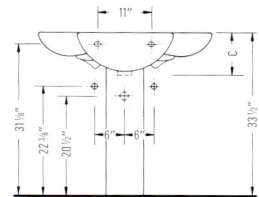

	A	B	C	D
70	27½"	23⅝"	8½"	9½"
90	35⅜"	24⅝"	8⅜"	10"

Pedestal:	# 857.40
Basin:	70, # 430.70
	90, # 430.90
Stock Color:	White
Accommodates:	Single Hole, Widespread

Non-stocked colors: Manhattan – 11, Royal-Turquoise – 17, Royal-Rose – 53, Jasmin – 72, Edelweiss – 78, Flannel – 79.

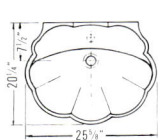

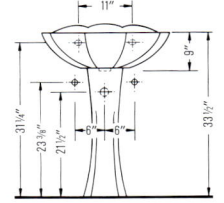

Pedestal:	# 858.00
Basin:	# 436.65
Stock Colors:	White, Black
Accommodates:	Single Hole, Widespread

Non-stocked colors: Manhattan – 11, Amber – 41, Jasmin – 72, Edelweiss – 78, Flannel – 79, Opaline-Grey – 43, Opaline-Beige – 45.

Edition Orchidee

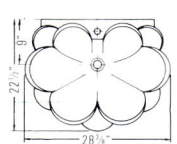

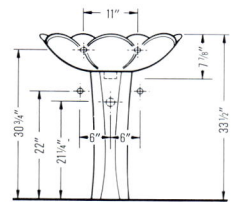

Pedestal:	# 2622.00
Basin:	# 2613.70
Stock Colors:	White, Black
Accommodates:	Single Hole

Non-stocked colors: Rose-Perle – 54, Jasmin – 72, Edelweiss – 78, Flannel – 79, Opaline-Blue – 15, Opaline-Grey – 43, Opaline-Beige – 45, Opaline-Rose – 55.

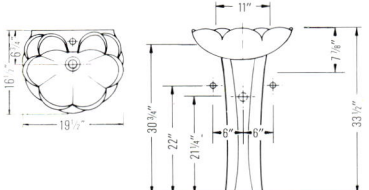

Pedestal:	# 2622.00
Hand-Rinse-Basin:	# 2614.50
Stock Colors:	White, Black
Accommodates:	Single Hole

Non-stocked colors: Rose-Perle – 54, Jasmin – 72, Edelweiss – 78, Flannel – 79, Opaline-Blue – 15, Opaline-Grey – 43, Opaline-Beige – 45, Opaline-Rose – 55.

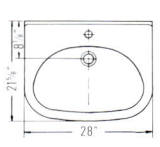

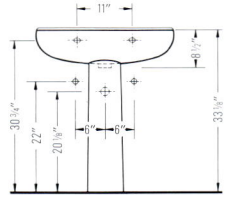

Pedestal: # 2122.00
Basin: # 2113.70
Stock Colors: White, Black
Accommodates: Single Hole,
Widespread

Non-stocked colors: Manhattan – 11, Rose-Perle – 54, Jasmin – 72, Edelweiss – 78, Flannel – 79.

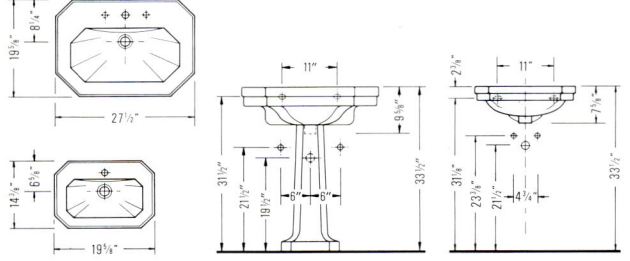

Non-stocked colors: Manhattan – 11, Edelweiss – 78, Flannel – 79.

Pedestal:	# 857.90
Basin:	# 438.70
Hand-Rinse-Basin:	# 785.50
Stock Color:	White
Accommodates:	Single Hole, Widespread

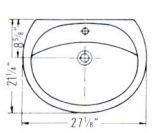 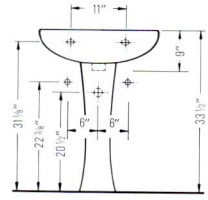

Pedestal:	# 2222.00
Basin:	# 2213.70
Stock Colors:	White, Black
Accommodates:	Single Hole, Widespread

Non-stocked colors: Manhattan – 11, Amber – 41, Rose-Perle – 54, Jasmin – 72, Edelweiss – 78, Flannel – 79, Opaline-Blue – 15, Opaline-Grey – 43, Opaline-Beige – 45, Opaline-Rose – 55.

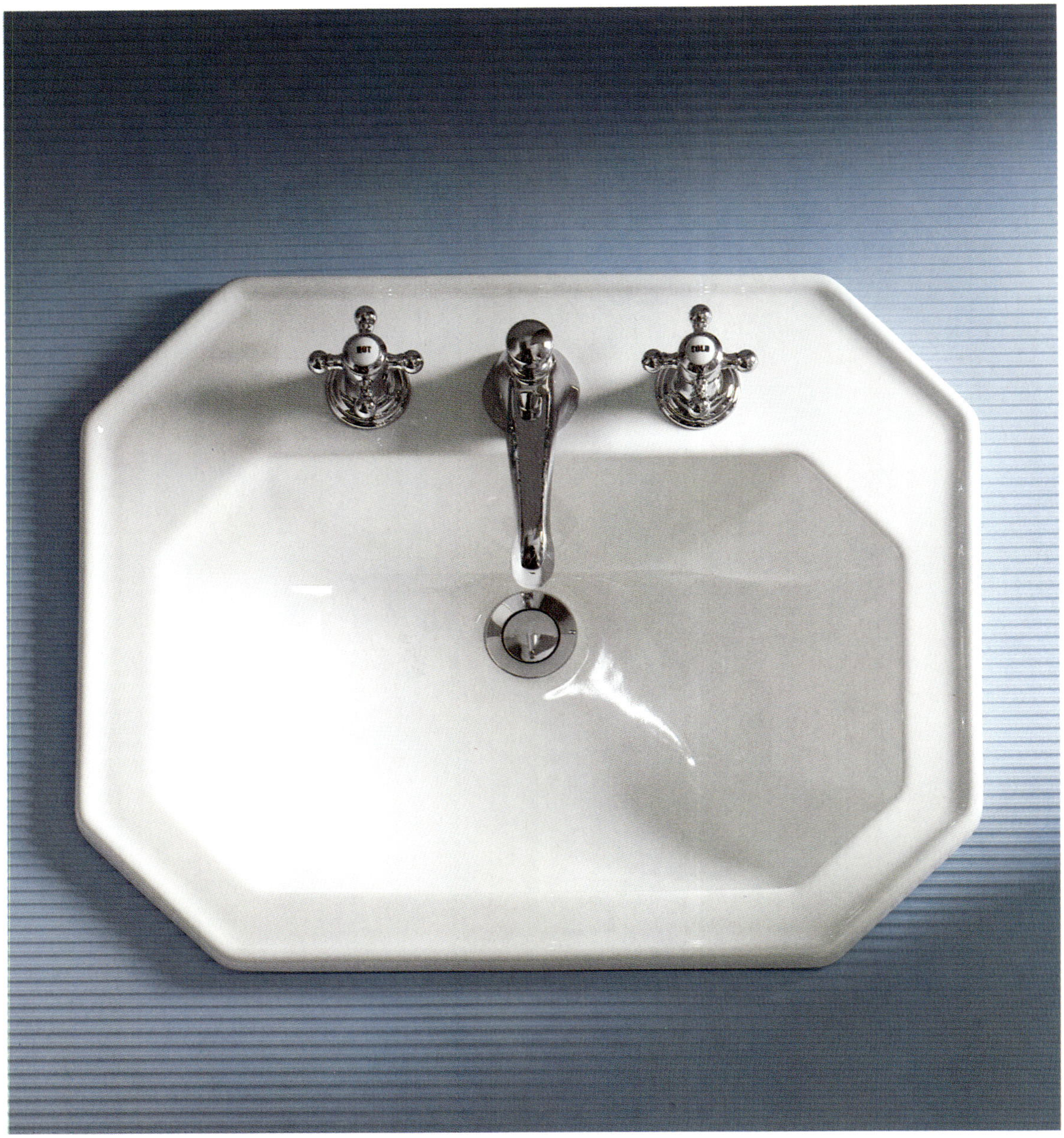

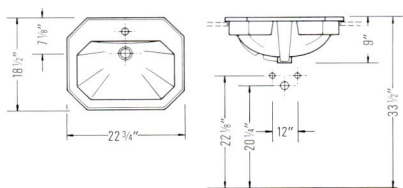

Vanity basin:	# 476.58
Stock Color:	White
Accommodates:	Single Hole, Widespread

Vanity basins

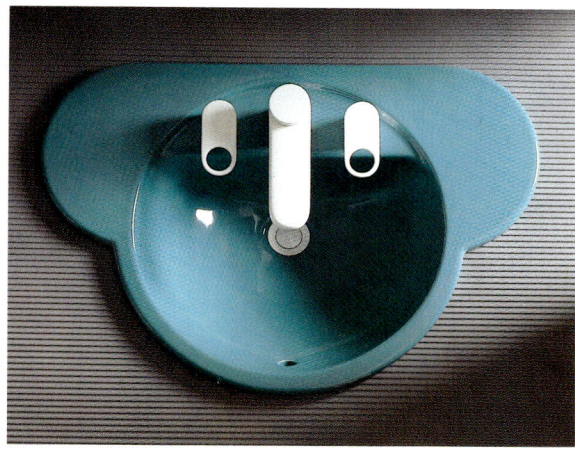

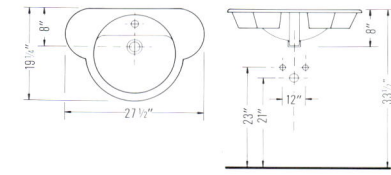

Vanity basin:	# 469.70
Stock Color:	White
Accommodates:	Single Hole, Widespread

Non-stocked colors: Manhattan – 11, Royal-Turquoise – 17, Royal-Rose – 53, Jasmin – 72, Edelweiss – 78, Flannel – 79.

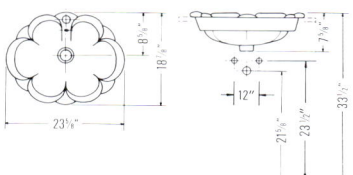

Vanity basin:	# 477.60
Stock Colors:	White, Black
Accommodates:	Single Hole

Non-stocked colors: Rose-Perle – 54, Jasmin – 72, Edelweiss – 78, Flannel – 79, Opaline-Blue – 15, Opaline-Grey – 43, Opaline-Beige – 45, Opaline-Rose – 55.

The Colors

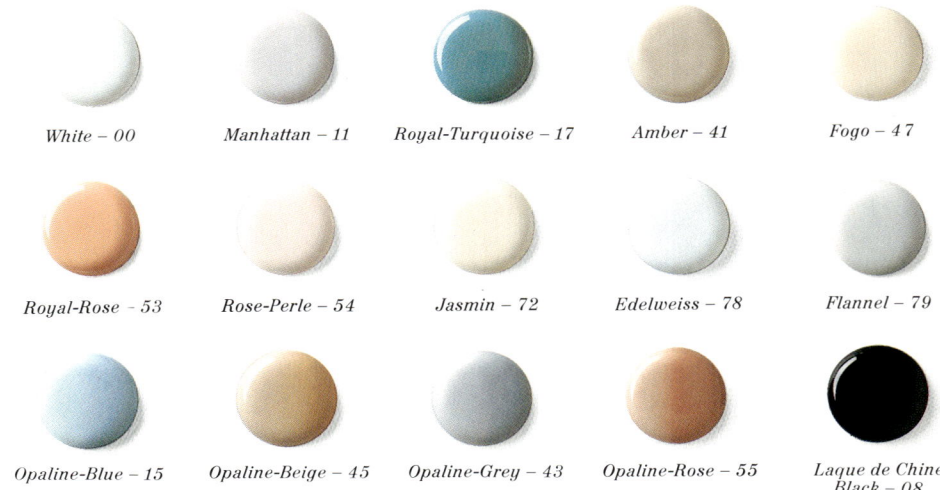

White – 00 Manhattan – 11 Royal-Turquoise – 17 Amber – 41 Fogo – 47

Royal-Rose – 53 Rose-Perle – 54 Jasmin – 72 Edelweiss – 78 Flannel – 79

Opaline-Blue – 15 Opaline-Beige – 45 Opaline-Grey – 43 Opaline-Rose – 55 Laque de Chine Black – 08

White and black only stocked colors. Please contact Santile International Corporation for other color availability.

U.S. Representatives:

Santile
International Corporation
1201 West Loop North, Suite 170, Houston, Texas, 77055
713/688 - 1862

Exportdivision: DURAVIT B.P. 10 · France 67240 Bischwiller · Phone 88 90 61 00 · Telex 890502 · Telefax 88 90 61 01
DURAVIT AG · P.O.B. 240 · Federal Republic of Germany W-7746 Hornberg · Phone 078 33/70-0 · Teletex 783321 · Telex (17) 783321 · Telefax 078 33/70 2 89

The Gerber DecorLine® Collection

615

Decorator Faucets and Fittings

Finishes
The unique home is created through attention to detail. First, select a finish that compliments and enhances the color and decor of each room.

Polished Brass

Chrome & Polished Brass

Antique Brass

Black Pearl

GERBER

Chrome

Colours

Colours: *Almond, Red, White, Jet, Gray*

Handles

Ultamira™ modular handles allow a choice of style with three different rings; facet, triple and rope. Mix or match finishes for the distinctive look you want for your faucet or fitting.

& Handles

Additional choices for the faucets and fittings in this catalog.

Crystalite™ (Clear or Charcoal)

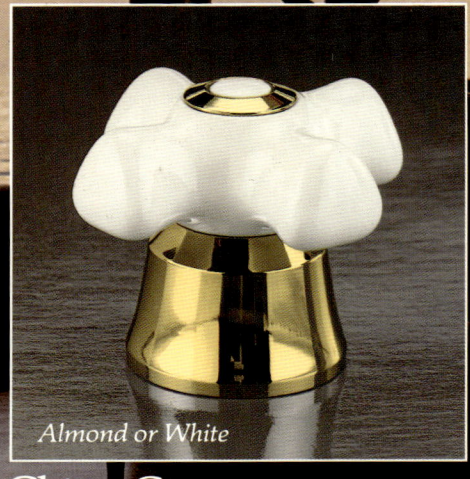
Almond or White

Tru-Wood™

Wrist Handle   China Cross   Lever

China (Almond or White)

Metal

Clear Brass, Clear Chrome, or Charcoal

ever

Crystaline™

Bar Faucets

Gerber faucets feature Ceramaflow™ ceramic disc cartridges with 10 year warranty for years of trouble free operation. Custom design your faucet to its surroundings through the choice of finish and handles.

Goose Neck Bar Faucet In Chrome And Polished Brass
With Metal Lever Handles

Goose Neck Bar Faucet In Red With Brass Trim
And Metal Lever Handles

Faucet With
Filler™ Spout
lished Brass With
Crystaline™ Handles

8

Polished Brass With Matching Ultamira™ Handles

Antique Brass With Tru-Wood™ Lever Handles

Concept Four™ Lavatory Faucet in Gray
and Black Pearl With Matching Ultamira Handles

GERBER

INTARSIA *Sea Spout*™ *Lavatory Faucet*
in Convergence Motif

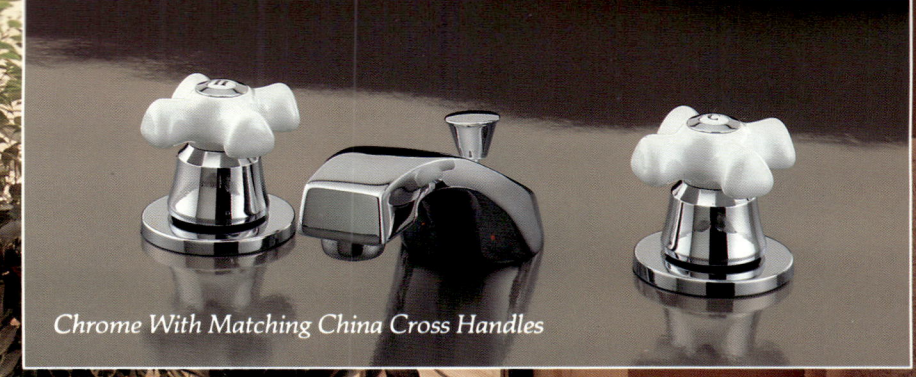

Chrome With Matching China Cross Handles

Widespread Lavatory Faucets

Enhance the ambiance. Define the luxury. Choose the finish and handle design that fit. All of these Gerber faucets feature Ceramaflow™ ceramic disc cartridges.

Handles

Tub and Shower Fittings

Detail the decorator look down to the tub and shower in matching finish and handle styles.

GERBE

Two Handle Tub And Shower In Polished Brass With Ultamira™ Handles

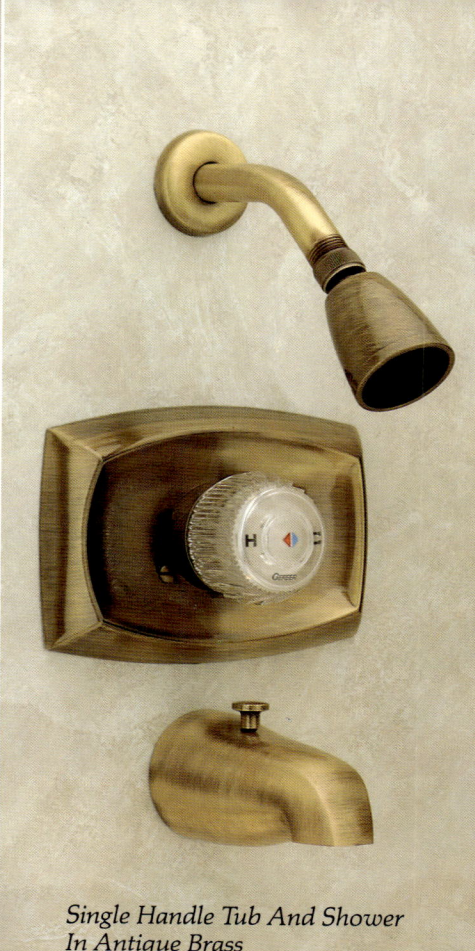

Single Handle Tub And Shower In Antique Brass

Two Handle Tub And Shower In Polished Brass With Clear Crystaline™ Handles

Three Handle Tub And Shower In Chrome And Polished Brass With Metal Lever Handles

Safe-Temp™ Pressure Balance Tub And Shower In Polished Brass

Two Handle Tub And Shower In Black Pearl With Charcoal Crystaline™ Handles

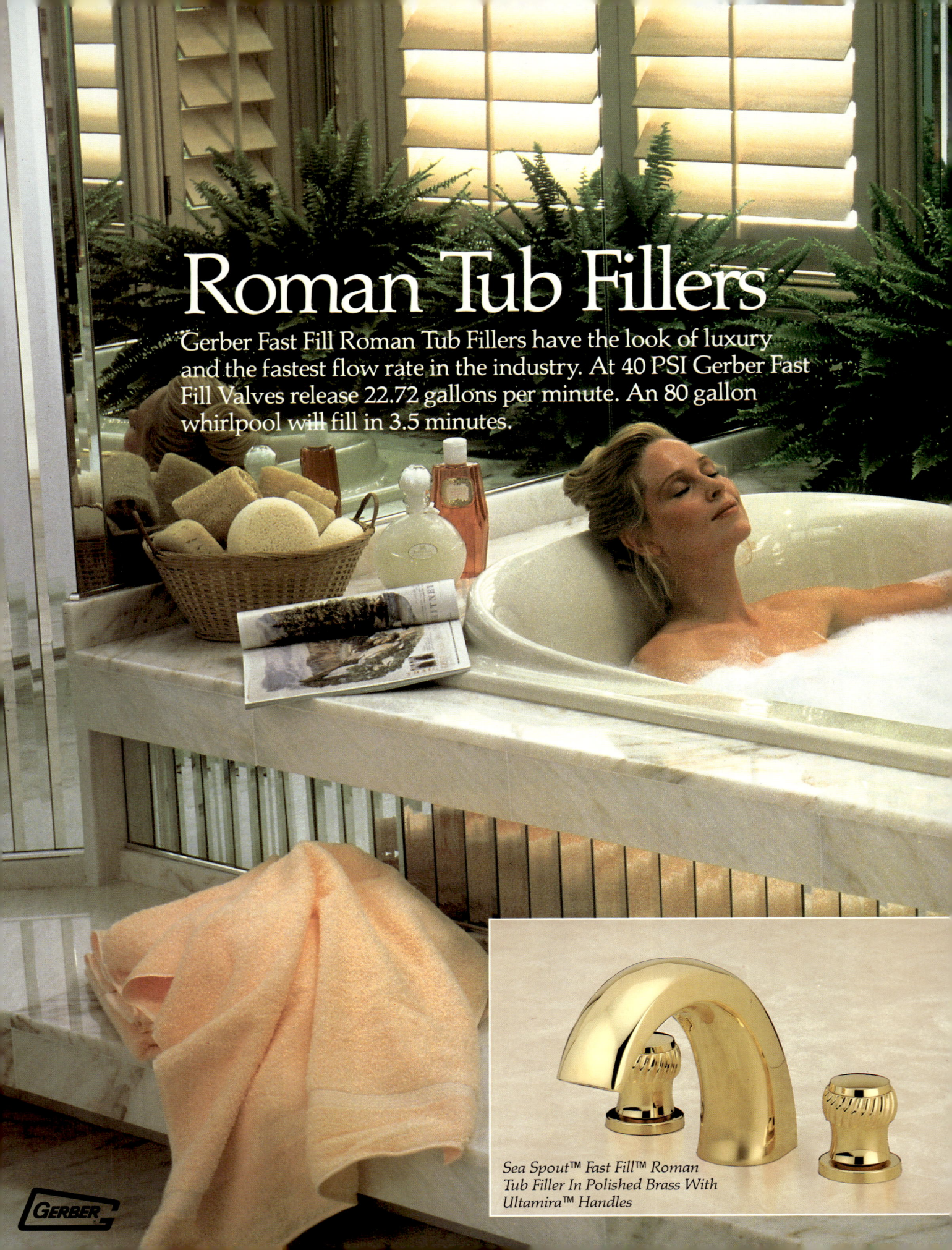

Roman Tub Fillers

Gerber Fast Fill Roman Tub Fillers have the look of luxury and the fastest flow rate in the industry. At 40 PSI Gerber Fast Fill Valves release 22.72 gallons per minute. An 80 gallon whirlpool will fill in 3.5 minutes.

Sea Spout™ Fast Fill™ Roman Tub Filler In Polished Brass With Ultamira™ Handles

Large Roman Wall Spout In White

Roman Wall Spout In Antique Brass

Fast Fill™ Roman Tub Filler In Chrome
And Polished Brass With Metal Lever Handles

Concept Four™ FINAL FIT, Fast Fill Roman Tub Filler
in Polished Brass with White China Cross Handles.

20

Tank Levers, Pop-up Rods and Bidet Fittings

Accessorize your bath down to the last detail.

Tank Levers

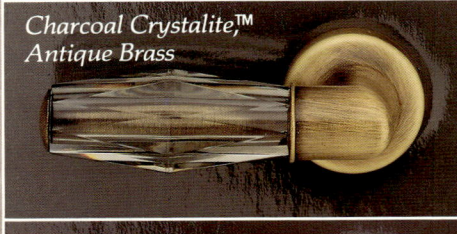
Charcoal Crystalite,™ Antique Brass

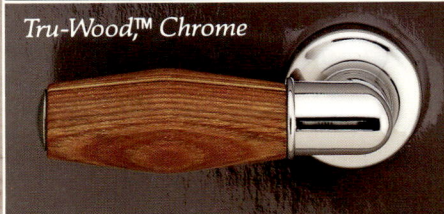
Tru-Wood,™ Chrome

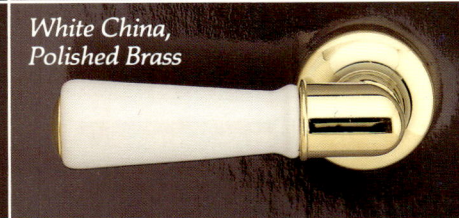
White China, Polished Brass

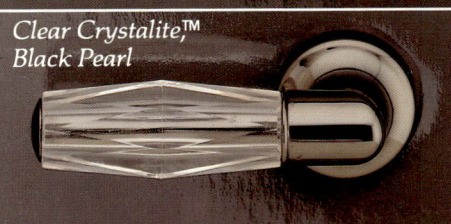
Clear Crystalite,™ Black Pearl

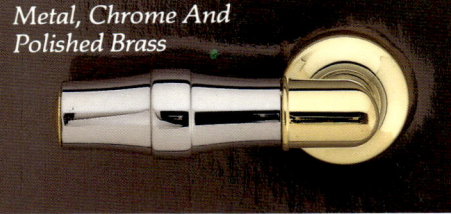
Metal, Chrome And Polished Brass

Pop-Up Rods

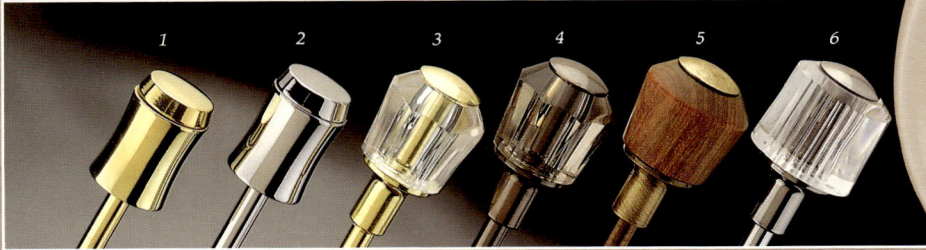

*1. Ultamira,™ Polished Brass 2. Ultamira,™ Chrome 3. Clear Crystalite™ Polished Brass
4. Charcoal Crystalite,™ Black Pearl 5. Tru-Wood,™ Antique Brass 6. Clear Crystaline,™ Chrome*

Bidet Fittings:
Choose from any of the handles
and finishes in this catalog for the bidet.

*Mirage® Low Profile
Toilet In Blush With
Metal Tank Lever In
Chrome And
Polished Brass*

*Three Handle
Adjustable Bidet
Fitting In Chrome
And Polished Brass
With Crystaline™
Handles*

*La Mer® Lavatory
In Blush With
Widespread Lavatory
Faucet In Polished
Brass With
Clear Crystalite™
Lever Handles*

GERBER

Write or call for our Chrome Plated Faucets and Fittings Catalog; Genuine Vitreous China Catalog; and Colours Catalog of Decorator Faucets and Fittings.

PROFESSIONALLY MADE.  PROFESSIONALLY SOLD.

Gerber Plumbing Fixtures Corp., 4656 West Touhy Avenue, Lincolnwood, IL 60646
(708) 675-6570, FAX (708) 675-5192

INTARSIA™

Pattern shown:
Convergence in
brushed nickel with
polished brass accents

Faucet Artistry

G E R B E R

INTARSIA™

Intarsia Fine jewelry-like designs are made possible by new Gerber technology that provides two separate lasting finishes on a single metal surface. The result is spectacular. Additionally, lavatory faucets feature Ceramaflow™ ceramic disc cartridges and the Roman tub fillers feature "fast fill" valves.

Pattern shown:
Infinity in brushed brass with polished brass accents

Contact your Gerber dealer for full information on the designs and finishes for Intarsia faucets.

 Gerber Plumbing Fixtures Corporation, 4656 W. Touhy Ave., Lincolnwood, IL 60646 • (708) 675-6570, FAX (708) 675-5192

© 1990 GPF   Made in U.S.A.   Printed in U.S.A.   Catalog INT49-10M

Washmobil

A unique collection of contemporary bathroom fixtures and accessories constructed from tubular steel finished with a highly durable epoxy enamel finish. All Chrome fixtures are constructed from tubular brass.

Designed by Philippe Starck.

Hastings

TILE & IL BAGNO COLLECTION

AQUARELLO

A space saving wall hung basin with 2 shelves, soap & tumbler holder, and 14″ round pivoting mirror. Towels can be hung from support bars. Available in Red, Yellow, White or Matte Black. 50 lbs.

WASHMOBIL S

Free-standing washbasin with arched mirror, shelf, towel bars, soap & tumbler holder. Available in Red, Yellow, White, Matte Black or Chrome with stainless steel basin. 75 lbs.

WASHMOBIL P

Same feature as model "S" but wall hung without legs. Available in color only. 66 lbs.

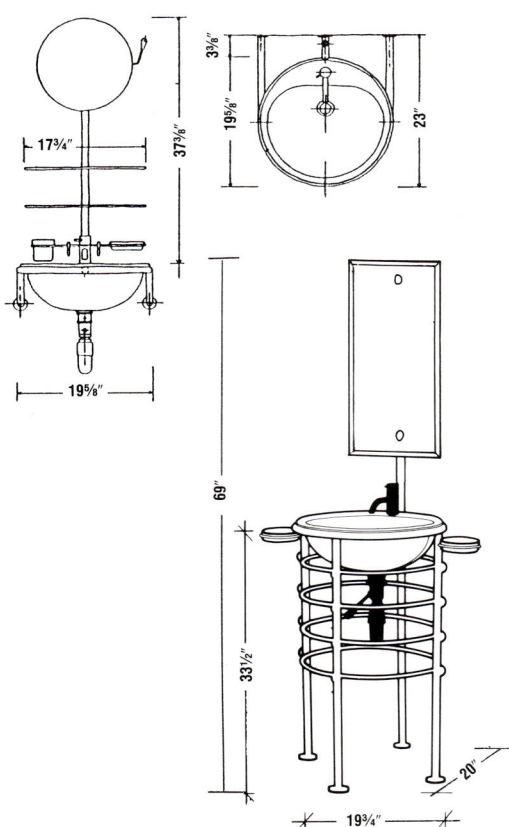

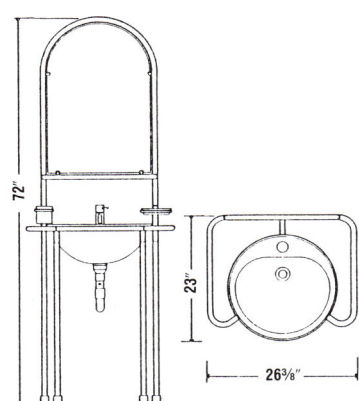

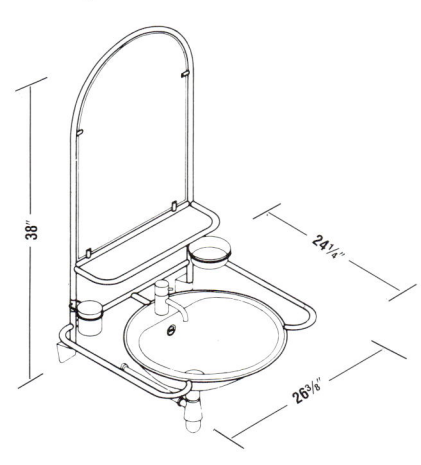

STARCK: (Cover Page)

A free-standing basin with post mounted mirror incorporating 4 towel hoops, swinging side mounted soap & tumbler holders. Available in Matte Black or Chrome with stainless steel basin. 40 lbs.

STARCK II

Same as above without mirror and post. 35 lbs.

Washmobil Collection Color Choices:

- ■ White
- ■ Red
- ■ Yellow
- ■ Matte Black

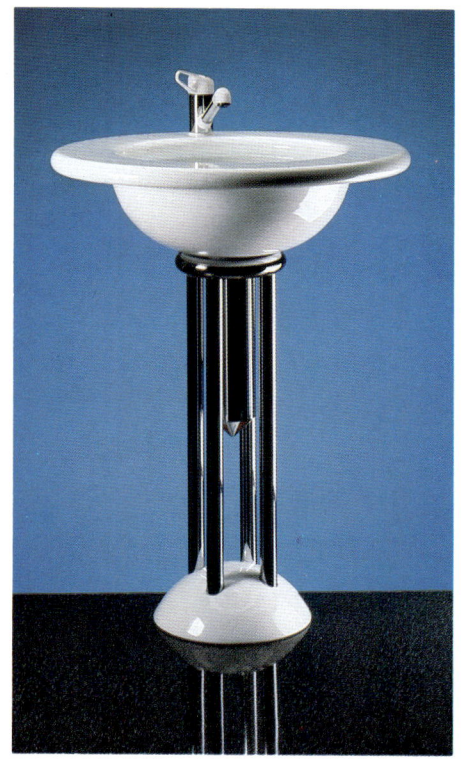

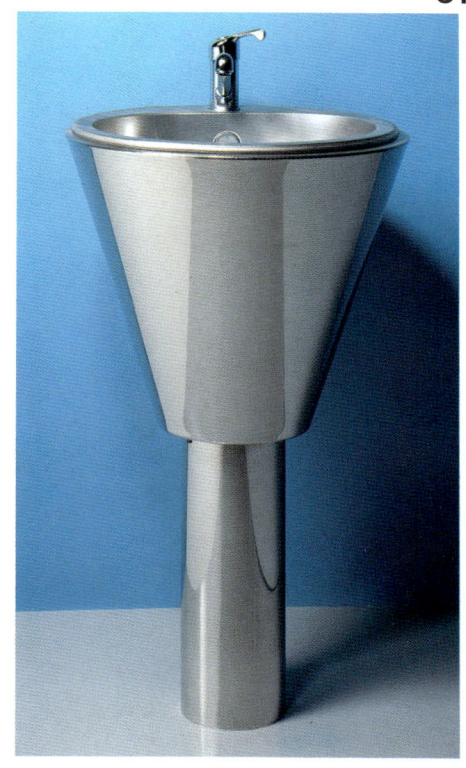

DELPHI

Ultra modern standing basin with wide rolling rim. 4 leg column supports basin and conceals trap assembly. Unit is secured to wall with bracket mounted behind basin. Available in White and Chrome only with 1 hole basin. 45 lbs.

EWA BASIN

A great space saver—tubular wall hung frame with 3 mounting posts for quick installation. The color coordinated basin is enameled on both sides. Towels can be hung from support bars. 30 lbs.

RIFLESSO

For use with the Ewa wall basin or by itself, this arched mirror incorporates a full length shelf. Mirror attaches to wall using 2 mounting posts located behind shelf. 35 lbs.

EUCLIDE

A free-standing ultra modern conical pedestal with matching basin and faucet. The unit is floor mounted with internal 3 bolt floor flange. Available in all colors and Chrome. 50 lbs.

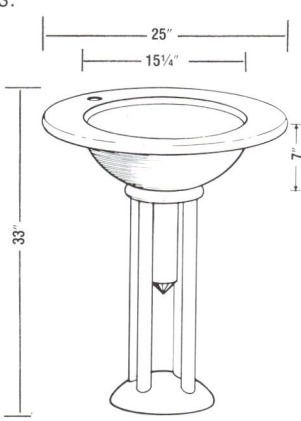

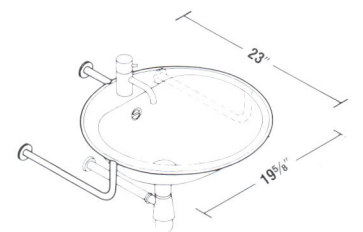

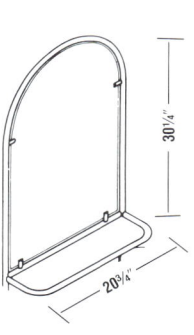

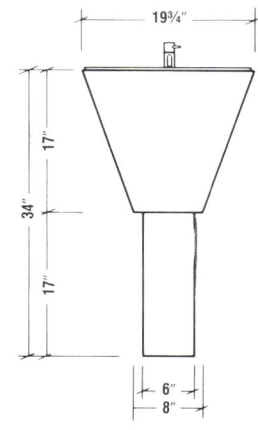

TECHNICAL CHARACTERISTICS:

- Color Washmobil frames are made of tubular steel coated with epoxy enamel. Basins are steel, color-enameled on both sides. Chrome frames are made of tubular brass. Stainless steel basins are hand-polished inside and out.
- Hastings will interchange basin color with Washmobil frame if you desire a 2 color effect.
- All units include matching color Hi-Fi single lever faucets with pop-up drain and trap assembly.
- All free-standing units are secured to the floor with screws

mounted through adjustable leveling feet.
- All wall hung units are installed with sturdy 3 point mounting posts, concealed by the tubular frame. Walls must be constructed with adequate support to accept weight of unit. If installing on tile over sheetrock, we recommend crosscats be fitted behind wall at mounting bracket locations.
- All units are shipped KD in one box and are easy to assemble with all interconnecting parts and mounting hardware provided. 1½" color-matched drain trap assembly is included.

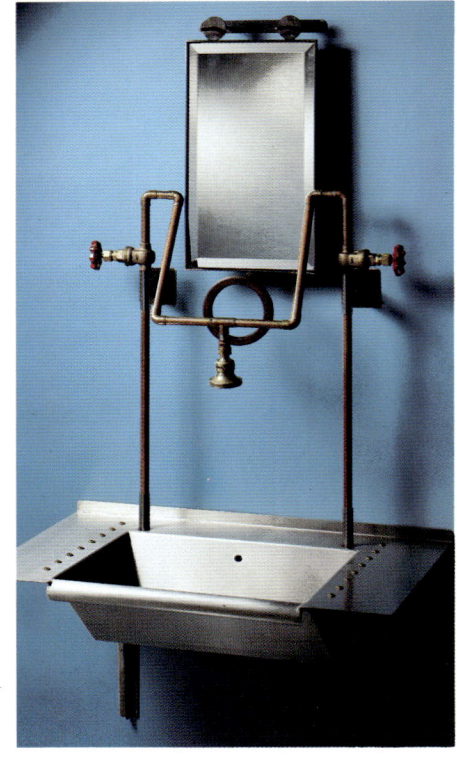

RAPSODY

Rapsody is a sleek floating wall mounted basin with a contoured glass countertop. Aluminum support brackets suspend basin 3" from wall. Glass countertop available in 32" width. Other sizes available by special order. Rapsody can also be installed without glass countertop.

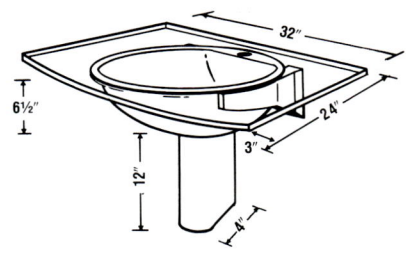

SERIE LM

Serie LM is a clean lined contemporary wash basin in minimalist style. There are convenient swing out towel bars. Stainless steel basin is secured with 4 brass accent screws. The frame is solid tubular stainless steel.

PROLOGUE 2000

Prologue 2000 wash basin reflects the industrial look as designed by David Zelman, made from stainless steel with exposed copper tubing and brass fittings. Factory styled knobs and spout create a structural framework. Included is a rectangular mirror with patina finish frame and round towel holder.

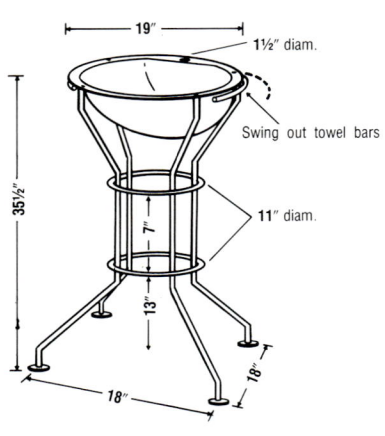

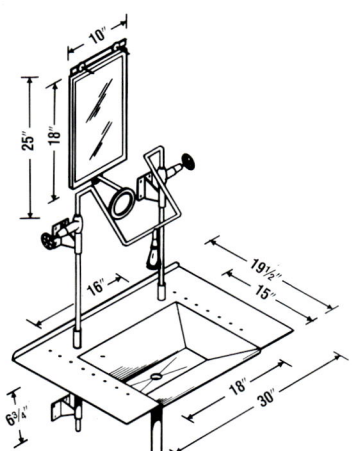

Hastings

TILE & IL BAGNO COLLECTION

GENERAL OFFICES 30 COMMERCIAL STREET / FREEPORT, NY 11520 / 516-379-3500 / FAX 516-379-3187
SHOWROOMS 230 PARK AVENUE SO. / NEW YORK, NY 10003 / 212-674-9700 / FAX 212-674-8083
404 NORTHERN BLVD. / GREAT NECK, NY 11021 / 516-482-1840 / FAX 516-482-5350
1296-1298 MDSE. MART / CHICAGO, IL 60654 / 312-527-0565 / FAX 312-527-2537

Printed in U.S.A.

The integrated, flexible, reliable faucet system

Form and function come full circle in Concentrix, the revolutionary new faucet system from Moen. This bold departure in faucet design combines the ability to coordinate the look of your faucets throughout a room or the entire house, with Moen reliability you can depend on.

Integrated Styling

The Moen Concentrix system allows you to match a variety of faucet types, single-handle or two-handle, in the kitchen, lavatory, roman tub or tub/shower, with the same decorator look. Coordinate the convenience and safety of a single-handle pressure-balanced tub/shower with an elegant two-handle widespread lavatory faucet. Or capture the same classic feeling of your bathroom in your kitchen as well.

Flexible Design

Concentrix' revolutionary modular system of interchangeable handle inserts allows you the flexibility to select your personal decorator look for every faucet. The interchangeable handle inserts are available in a variety of contemporary shapes — round, grooved and square — and finishes — chrome, polished brass, chrome/polished brass and glacier. Design it yourself. Just choose the faucet style and finish you want, then select the handle insert of your choice, to create just the right look. Concentrix gives you hundreds of options to choose from, and new shapes, colors and styles will continually be introduced in the future.

Moen Reliability

Concentrix features a variety of beautiful designs to give you a perfectly coordinated decor, wherever your decorating scheme requires it. All backed by the features that make the Moen difference. Lifetime Limited Warranty against leaks and drips. Moen quality and engineering, built with uncompromising excellence. Patented washerless cartridge design. Water and energy-saving flow-control aerator standard on every model. Extra-wide temperature selection comfort zone and our unique Temperature Memory system on single-handle faucets. The result is a faucet you can be proud of and depend on for years.

Concentrix by Moen

A new concept in faucet decorating to satisfy both your aesthetic preferences and long-term functional demands.

Concentrix

5971-P/H-202-P

5971/H-202

5973/H-202

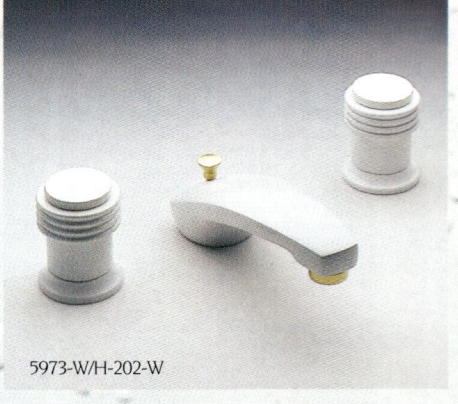

5973-W/H-202-W

Mood and motion take shape in Grooved Concentrix handles. This grooved insert provides an enticing high-tech look that's slightly daring, yet classically tasteful.

Concentrix. A modular faucet system that combines the best in styling and reliability for the bath and kitchen. In Chrome, Glacier and Polished Brass finishes.

GROOVED

4221/H-102-W

4923-W/H-202-W

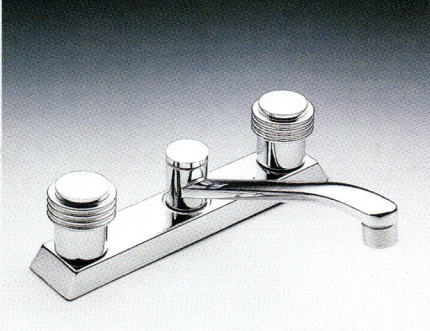

7970/H-202

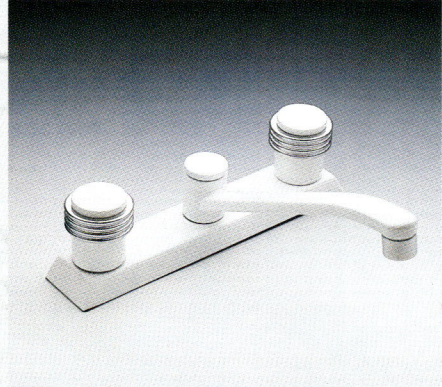

7970-W/H-202

4921-P/H-202-P

2253/H-102

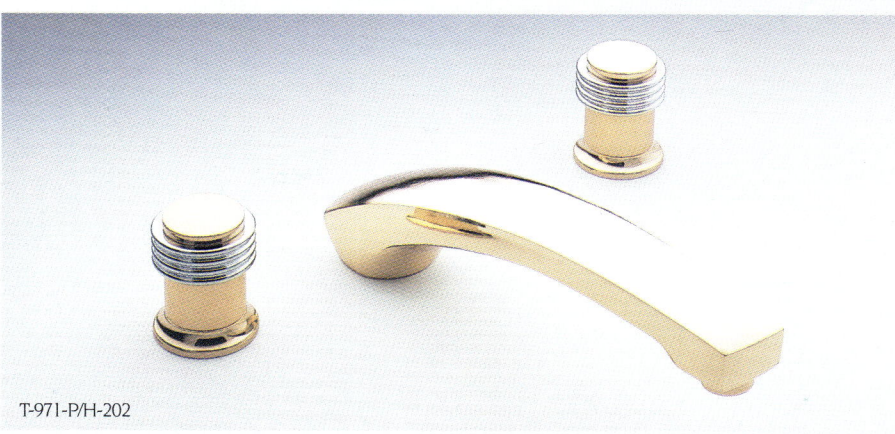

T-971-P/H-202

5981-P/H-202-W

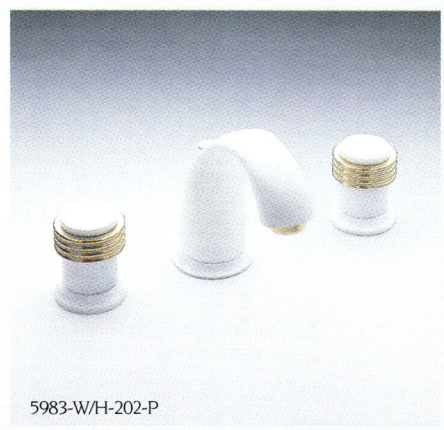

5983-W/H-202-P

GROOVED

Concentrix

5973/H-200

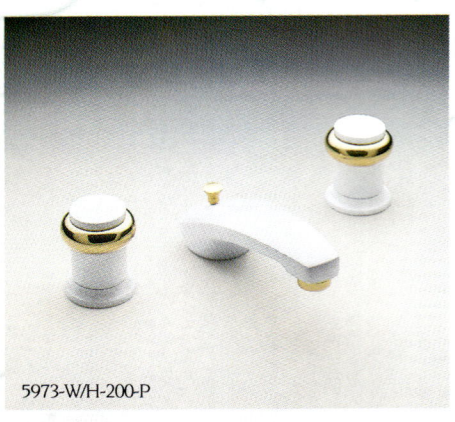

5973-W/H-200-P

Grace and grandeur take shape in Round Concentrix handles. These cool, smooth circular inserts provide the sleek, elegant lines demanded by many contemporary interiors.

Concentrix. A modular faucet system that combines the best in styling and reliability for the bath and kitchen. In Chrome, Glacier and Polished Brass finishes.

ROUND

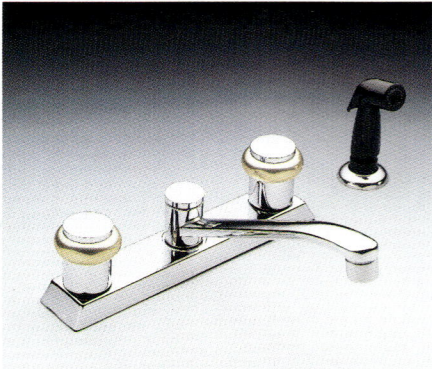

7980/H-200-P

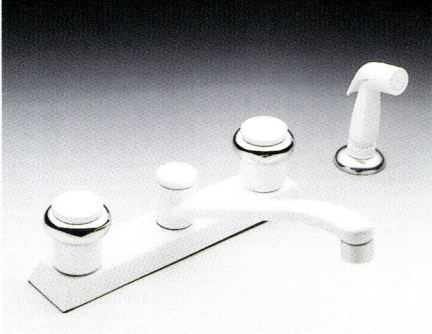

7980-W/H-200

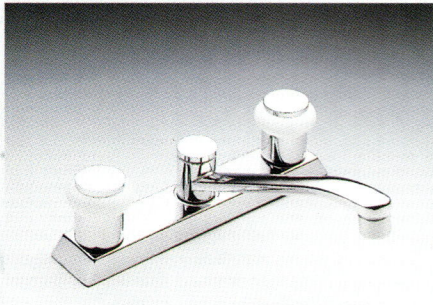

7970/H-200-W

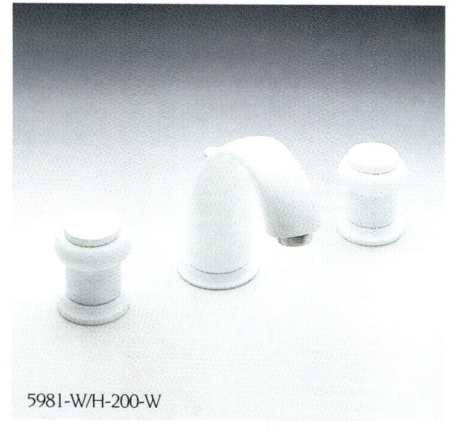

5981-W/H-200-W

5983/H-200

4221/H-100-P

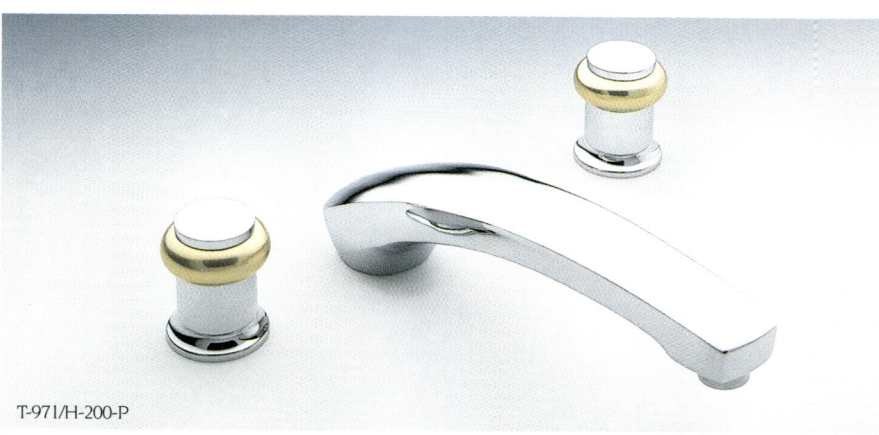

T-971/H-200-P

3103-W/H-100-P

ROUND

Concentrix

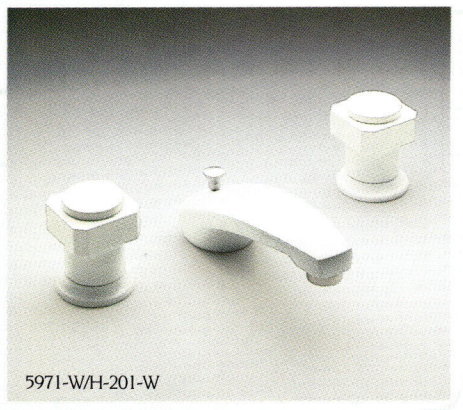

5971-W/H-201-W

5973/H-201

5971-P/H-201-W

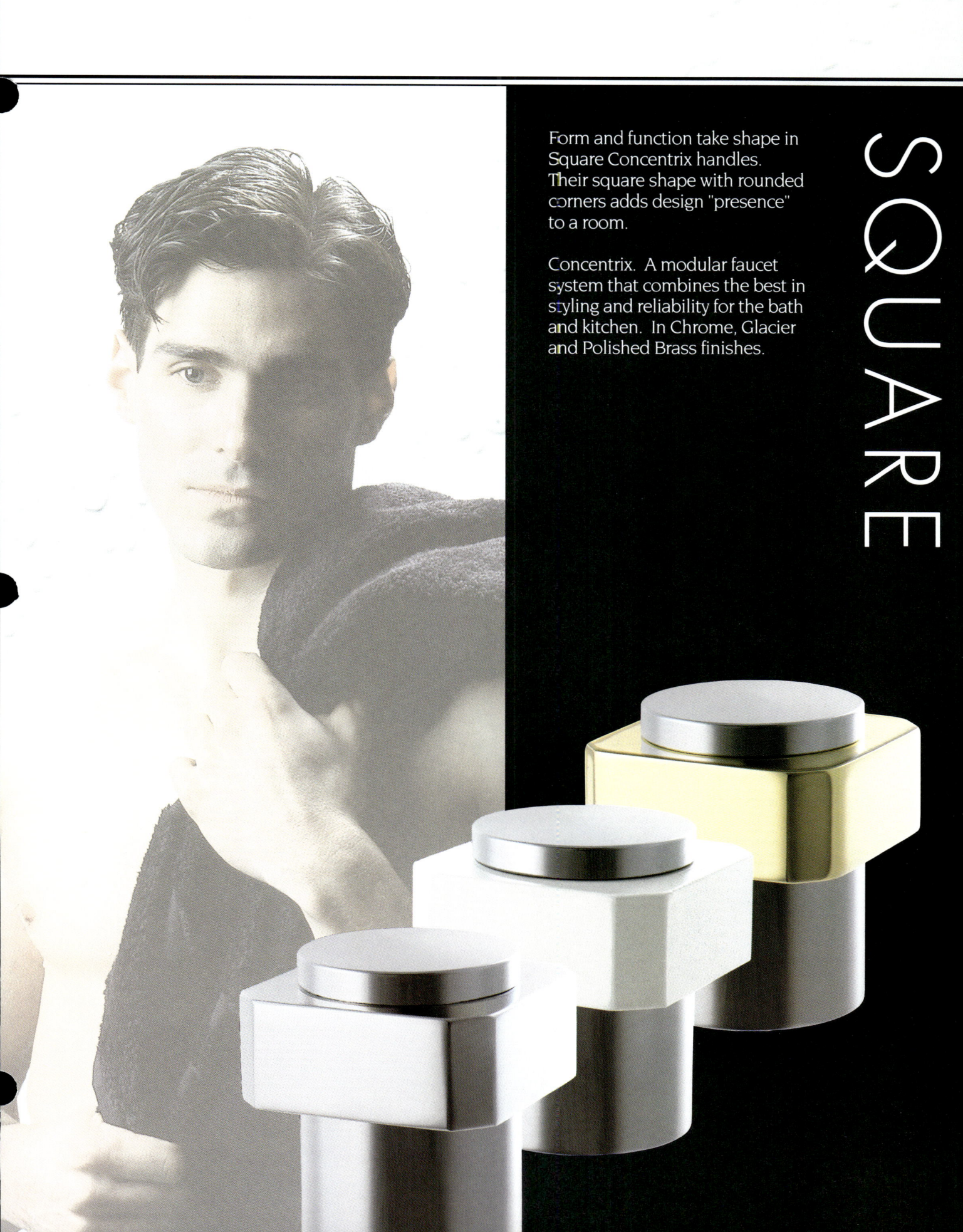

Form and function take shape in Square Concentrix handles. Their square shape with rounded corners adds design "presence" to a room.

Concentrix. A modular faucet system that combines the best in styling and reliability for the bath and kitchen. In Chrome, Glacier and Polished Brass finishes.

SQUARE

2251/H-101

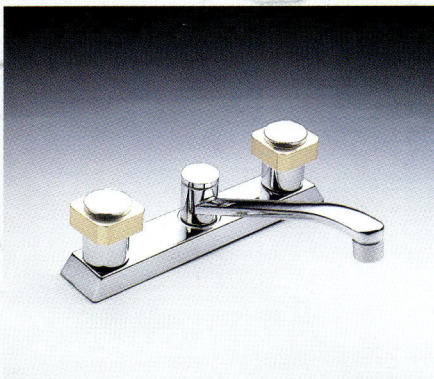

7970/H-201-P

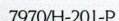

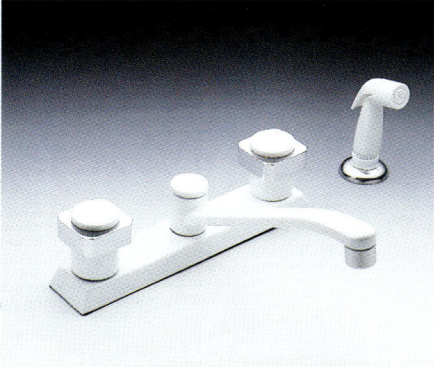

7980-W/H-201

4221-P/H-101-W

4223/H-101

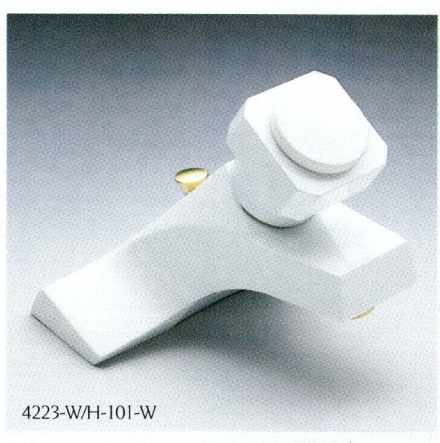

4223-W/H-101-W

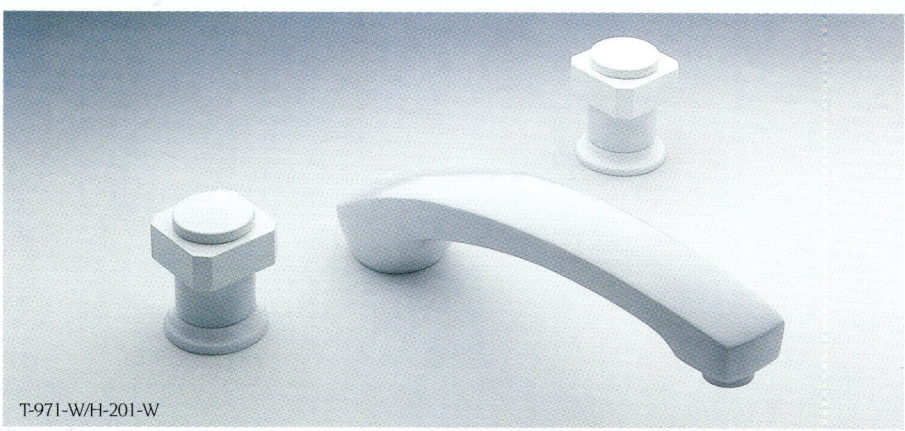

T-971-W/H-201-W

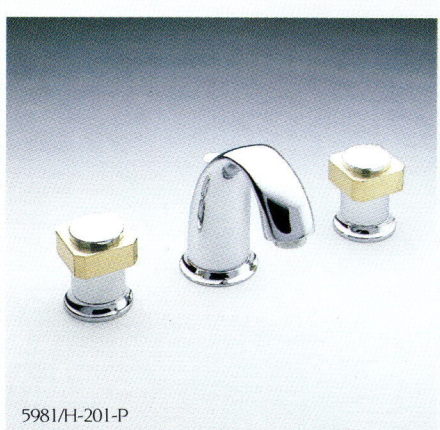

5981/H-201-P

SQUARE

Concentrix — *How to Order*

1. Choose the faucet style and model number from Chart 1.
   This model number includes everything except the Concentrix handle inserts.
2. Choose the Concentrix handle insert style and model number from Chart 2.
3. Combine the two model numbers, starting with the faucet number first, followed by the insert number.

CHART 1	Lavatory, Roman Tub, Shower & Kitchen Faucets without Inserts				
	Chrome	Glacier/Chrome	Glacier/Polished Brass	Polished Brass	Chrome/Polished Brass
Single-Handle Lavatory	4221	4221-W	4223-W	4221-P	4223
Two-Handle Lavatory	4921	4921-W	4923-W	4921-P	4923
Two-Handle Widespread Lavatory	5971	5971-W	5973-W	5971-P	5973
Two-Handle Widespread Lav. with High-Arc Spout	5981	5981-W	5983-W	5981-P	5983
Roman Tub*	T-971*	T-971-W*	T-973-W*	T-971-P*	T-973*
Single-Handle Shower (Pressure-Balanced listed in parenthesis)	2241 (3101)	2241-W (3101-W)	2243-W (3103-W)	2241-P (3101-P)	2243 (3103)
Single-Handle Tub/Shower Combination (Pressure-Balanced listed in parenthesis)	2251 (3111)	2251-W (3111-W)	2253-W (3113-W)	2251-P (3111-P)	2253 (3113)
Two-Handle Kitchen	7970 (7980 w/Hose Spray)	7970-W (7980-W w/ Hose Spray)			

* Separate #4999 rough-in valve required.

Concentrix Handle System

CHART 2	Concentrix Inserts		
	Chrome	Glacier	Polished Brass
Round	H-100 (H-200 pair)	H-100-W (H-200-W pair)	H-100-P (H-200-P pair)
Square	H-101 (H-201 pair)	H-101-W (H-201-W pair)	H-101-P (H-201-P pair)
Grooved	H-102 (H-202 pair)	H-102-W (H-202-W pair)	H-102-P (H-202-P pair)

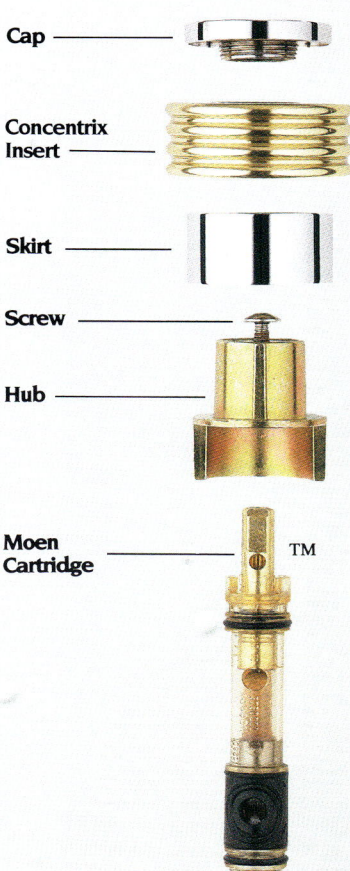

Cap

Concentrix Insert

Skirt

Screw

Hub

Moen Cartridge ™

For example:
1. You choose a Single-Handle Chrome Lavatory Faucet from Chart 1 — Model 4221.
2. You choose a Grooved Polished Brass insert from Chart 2 — Model H-102-P.
3. Your easy-order number is 4221/H-102-P.

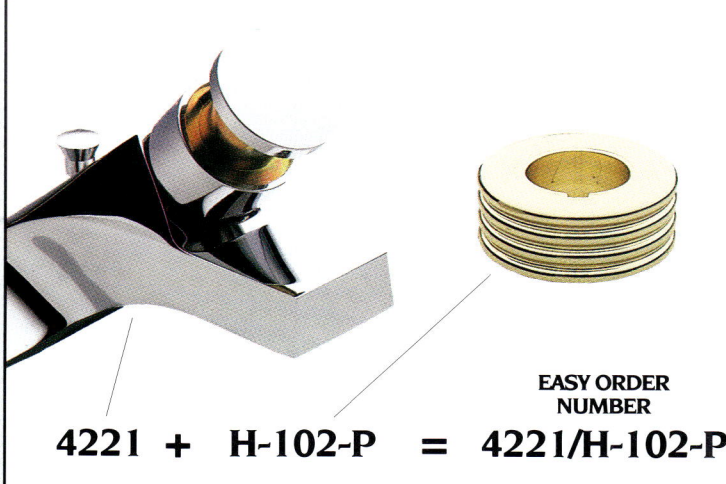

EASY ORDER NUMBER

4221 + H-102-P = 4221/H-102-P

Display System
For more information about Concentrix displays, call 1-800-347-6636 or your local Moen representative.

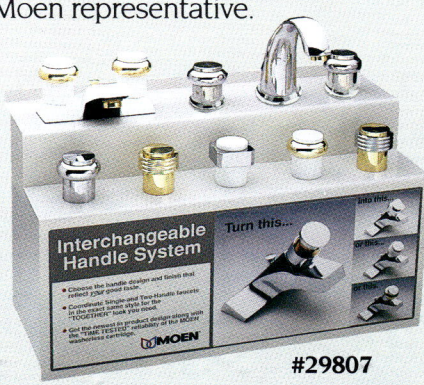

#29807

Concentrix™

The integrated, flexible, reliable faucet system

Moen. Faucets for a lifetime. Moen's Lifetime Limited Warranty protects against leaks and drips for as long as you own the product. Moen faucets have a Lifetime Limited Warranty behind them because they have our exclusive patented cartridges inside them.

Washerless. Moen faucets feature a patented washerless cartridge. Its washerless design means there are fewer parts to cause problems.

Temperature Preselection. Moen single-handle faucets have this feature. **Widest Comfort Zone.** Finding the right mix of hot and cold is easy with Moen.

Easy Operation. A feather-light touch will turn Moen faucets on and off. **Flow Control.** Flow-Rator® limits water flow for maximum water and energy savings.

Professional's Choice. Moen is rated number one in best product quality and fewest callbacks in independent surveys of professional plumbers and home builders.

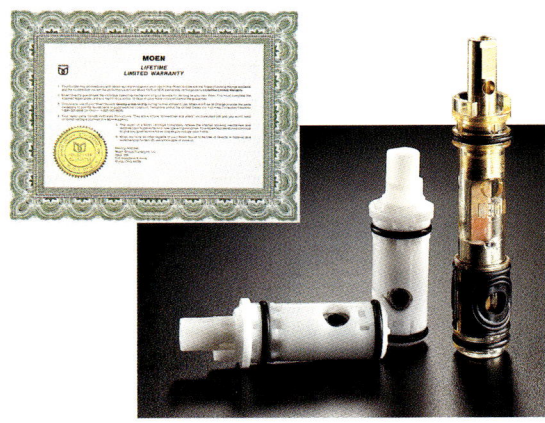

Please refer to Moen's warranty card enclosed with each Moen product for specific warranty details.

Moen Incorporated
377 Woodland Avenue
Elyria, OH 44036-2011

Madison

Porcher sets the trends with the creation of Madison. Entirely conceived by Porcher's progressive design team, Madison epitomizes geometric inspiration. Madison. A collection for the 90's distinguished by graphic lines that are simple, elegant. Immediately recognizable — always unmistakably French. Porcher leads the way in the art of bath design with Madison, by incorporating the best international design trends into an exquisite, contemporary collection.

Porcher faucets shown.

The spirit of Madison is characterized by European design identity that has revolutionized the plumbing industry. The bath has gained overdue prominence as an area for design expression with the entry of European products into the American market. Madison offers that sophisticated attitude toward water and bath. The "art du bain."

Madison

captures the spirit of the 90's.

Misty Gray — AX   **Rose Pearl — AN**   **Creme — 48**   **White — 11**

Madison

captures the aesthetic spirit...

with a single design motif that allows so many combinations for bathrooms, large or small, simple or grand, with cabinetry or without. Two sizes of pedestal lavatories, two interpretations of counter top lavatories, three possibilities of wall-hung lavatories, a 1.6-gallon toilet and an acrylic tub, the Madison collection offers limitless design potential to create a unified design that will fit the most demanding space requirements.

Porcher faucets shown.

Madison

UNE LIGNE DES ANNÉES 90

PORCHER™

CORPORATE HEADQUARTERS:
13-160 MERCHANDISE MART
CHICAGO, ILLINOIS 60654
PHONE: 312.923.0995
         800.338.1756
FAX: 312.923.1184

WESTERN REGION:
650 MAPLE AVENUE
TORRANCE, CA 90503
PHONE: 213.212.6112
FAX: 213.212.6775

Available through:

"Quality Pumps Since 1939"

ZOELLER CO.

3280 Old Millers Lane
P.O. Box 16347 • Louisville, Kentucky 40216
(502) 778-2731 • FAX (502) 774-3624

QWIK JON SEWAGE REMOVAL SYSTEMS

SERIES 100/102* - Standard, economical system designed for built in or free standing installation.

MODELS:
Model 100 (Patent Pending)
Model 102* (Patent Pending)

TYPICAL INSTALLATIONS

Versatile installation enables the pump compartment and piping to be concealed by the installation of a wall. **NOTE:** Access must be maintained to the pump compartment. **NOTE:** The Qwik Jon is designed to fit flush with any elevated floor made of standard 2″ x 6″ material (actual dimensions 1½″ x 5½″). And you can add a Lavatory-Bathtub-Shower with the installation of the 2″ adapt-a-flex seal (provided). Tub or shower requires built in installation. See Installation Instructions.

INSTALL A QWIK JON JUST ABOUT ANYWHERE

- Designed to accommodate a toilet, lavatory and a bathtub
- Use with a variety of toilet styles (1.6 Gallon residential flush (other installations use over 3 gallon flush)
- Perfect for basements, family rooms, warehouse, factories, room additions
- No need to destroy concrete floors
- Reduces construction costs
- Pumps any direction
- Fits just about anywhere

*Includes UL Listed WM267 Pump unit

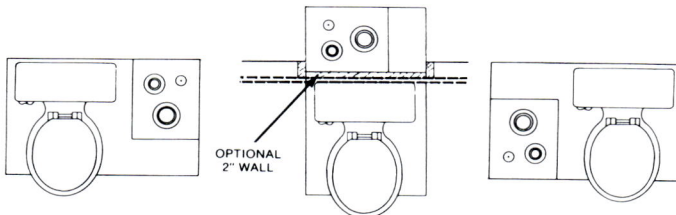

OPTIONAL 2″ WALL

Code approved (Consult factory)

Basic Installation
Toilet, Fixtures and Piping Not Included

Built In Installation
Toilet, Fixtures and Piping Not Included

TECHNICAL INFORMATION

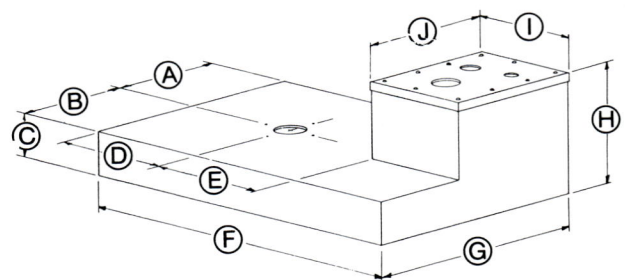

QWIK JON SYSTEMS INCLUDE:

Sewage Pumps

MODEL 100
Pump: Model WM 262
1/2 HP 115V 12 amps
Shaded pole
Weight: 25 lbs.

MODEL 102
Model WM 267
1/2 HP 115V 10.4 amps
Split phase
51 lbs.
UL Listed

NOTE:
Sewage Pumps WM262 & WM267 are designed
for use in Qwik Jon units only. They are not
designed for use in any other application.

- Automatic preset mercury float switch
- Thermal overload protected motor
- Stainless steel screws, bolts & handle
- Non-clogging vortex impeller
- Passes 2″ solids (sphere)
- UL listed 3-wire neoprene 10 ft. cord & plug
- Maximum temperature rating -130° F
  (54 deg. C)

Tank

MODEL 100/102 (Pat. Pend.)
- Polyethylene
- Lt. gray finish
- Lightweight
- Wt. 26 lbs.

2″ Back Flow Device and Union

- 2″ back flow device (check local codes) required
  to prevent backflow of water and sewer gas
- No threading of pipe required
- Fits ABS, PVC and steel pipe
- Rated at 25 PSI
- Weight: 2 lbs.

ALL IN ONE CARTON

- Tank, lid & gasket
- ½ HP sewage pump
- Back flow device (check local codes)
- 2″ Discharge & 3″ Vent with adapt-a-flex seals
- 2″ adapt-a-flex seal for additional fixtures
- Hardware pack and floor anchor kit
- Installation instructions
- Shipping weight:
    100 System - 63 lbs.
    102 System - 89 lbs.

ITEMS NEEDED BY INSTALLER

- Supply fittings, toilet gasket & waste pipe
- Toilet fixture
- Electrical source with ground fault interrupter
  protected receptacle
- Water source
- Tools
- Floor Flange seal extender kit for built in installations
  Part Number 100-0050 for ¾″ floors
  Part Number 100-0051 for ½″ floors

TANK DIMENSIONS

MODEL NO.	A	B	C	D	E
100/102	12¼	12¼	5½	12¼	14⅛
	F	**G**	**H**	**I**	**J**
100/102	41	25	16¼	14	17

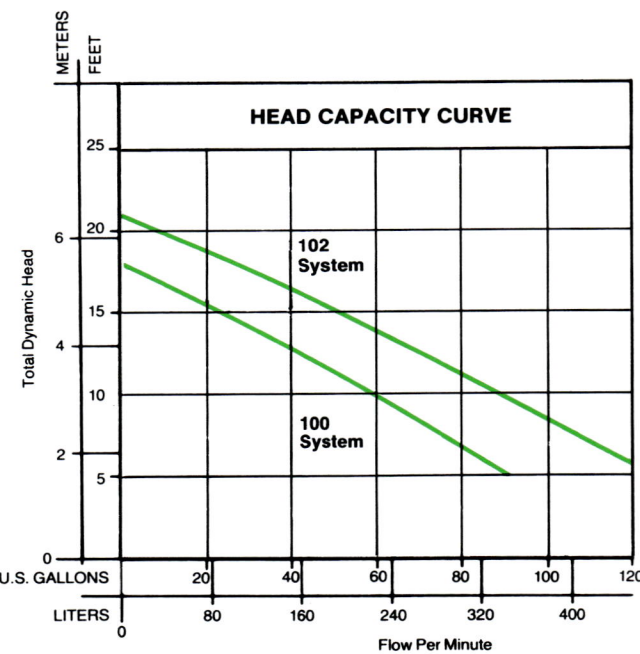

Model	262(100)		267(102)	
Ft.	**Meters**	**Gal.**	**Ltrs.**	**Gal.**	**Ltrs.**
5	1.52	90	341	128	484
10	3.05	60	227	89	337
15	4.57	22.5	85	50	189
Lock Valve:		18 Ft.		21.5 ft.	

NOTE: Recommended for installations up to 16′
total dynamic head. Consult factory if installation is
above 15′ vertical height in 2″ pipe.

CAUTION
All installation of controls, protection devices and wiring should be done by a qualified
licensed electrician. All electrical and safety codes should be followed including the
most recent National Electric Code (NEC) and the Occupational Safety and Health Act
(OSHA).

Colorfloors™ and ColorWalls™
630

The Industry Leaders

SB6034
A large Colorfloor™ for a spacious shower or possibly to replace a bathtub.

- The most models
- The most colors
- 10 year warranty
- Drain assembly included

SB6034

SB3838C
Our most demanded neo-angle corner unit, or the slightly smaller **SB3636C**.

SB3838C • SB3636C

SB3636DT
This corner model, with two thresholds, allows entry from either side.

SB3636DT

Great Bathrooms begin with Clarke

Clarke Products Inc.

SB3442

SB3442
Designed to fit at either end of
the common 42″ wide bathtub
or whirlpool.

Introduction to Colorfloors™

Our Colorfloors™ offer you a durable and
colorful alternative to tile, molded plastic,
cultured marble, gel coat fiberglass and terrazzo shower bases. Clarke Colorfloors™ are
made to provide you with a shower base that
does not fade, mildew, stain, crack or leak.
Our 10 year limited warranty provides
assurance of performance.

Available in 30 colors. We offer a model for
every bath and color scheme. All have our exclusive slip-resistant bottom for safety; most are
IAPMO listed. Some models include integral seats.

Colorfloors™

Beautiful now. Beautiful years from now.

SB4234
A 42″ wide entrance/threshold with
34″ of depth makes this Colorfloors™
very roomy or the larger **SB4834** that
is 48″ wide and 34″ deep.

SB4234 • SB4834

SB4242C

SB4242C
This oversized
Colorfloors™ Neo Angle
provides ample space.

New from Clarke . . . Colorwalls™

ColorWalls™ are acrylic wall panels that provide a superb alternative to tile and slab panel materials. Because ColorWalls™ eliminate grout lines, they are easy to clean and maintain. They give a finished dimension to your shower, yet have the practicality of three integrally molded soap and shampoo shelves and the safety of an assistance bar. Designed to fit Clarke Colorfloors™, they are available in all our 30 colors.

Clarke Products Inc.

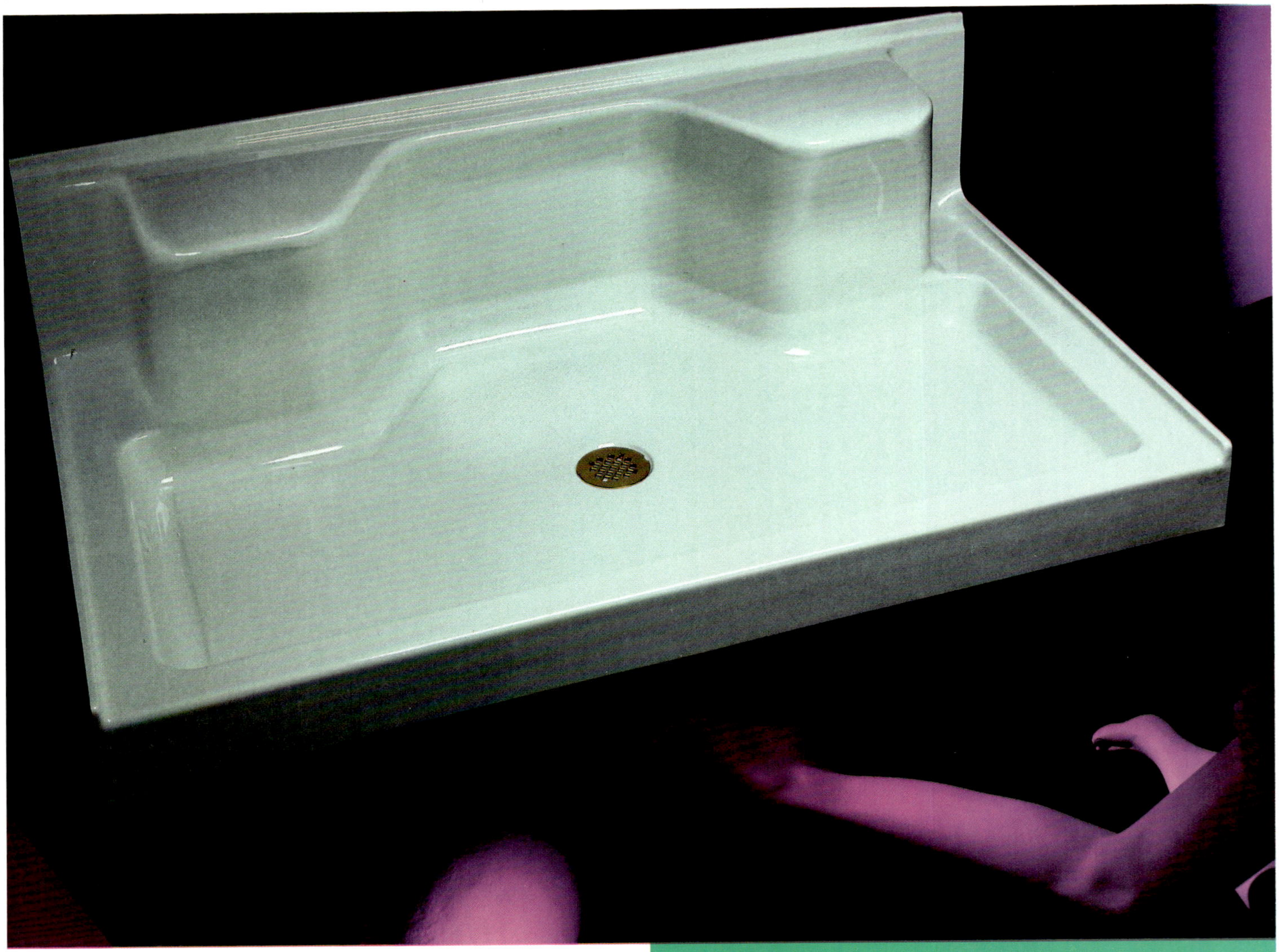

SB6O34DS
For the ultimate in showers, this Colorfloor™ features two integral seats. Ideal for the disabled or a steam bath.

SB6O34DS

SB3636 • SB3232 • SB4242

SB3636
A perfect size for most homes. Our most popular model, or **SB3232**, same shape, but 4″ shorter on all sides.
SB4242 . . . This large shower base can fit at either end of a 42″ wide bathtub . . . beautifully.

Clarke Products Inc.

Niagara™

Elisa™

Whirlpool – W4272
Soaking Tub – T4272

SB3838RC This rounded front Colorfloor™ with its attractive style lines is the perfect match for an elegant bathroom.

Clarke Products

Design • Safety • Value

We are manufacturers of acrylic plumbing fixtures and offer 18 different whirlpool and soaking tub models, 16 choices of Colorfloors™ (our shower bases), 8 modular showers and tub/shower choices and our newest product, ColorWalls™ (acrylic wall panels). Choose from 30 colors.

Acrylic . . . the perfect material for bath and shower fixtures. Clarke uses ICI-Perspex™, cell-cast acrylic known for its high gloss, ease of maintenance and durability. The mirror-like finish and brilliant gloss can be beautifully maintained for years.

The Concentra I™

The Concentra I™
An elegant oval with distinctive concentric
design lines, adaptable for any interior. Fits
neatly into a five foot space or corner.
Available as a whirlpool (as shown —
W3858C) or as a soaking bath only (T3858C).

- Length: 58" (1473.2 mm)
- Width: 38" (965.2 mm)
- Depth: 19" (482.6 mm)
- Operating capacity: 40 gallons (151.6 L)
- To overflow level: 50 gallons (189.5L)

Whirlpool features:
- 5 Jets
- ¾ HP Pump/Motor
- 2 Air Volume Controls
- On/Off Air Controls

Clarke Products Inc.

The Stellar™

This deep oval tub is designed with both comfort and safety in mind. There is room for two people. Includes armrests and an underwater safety light that comes with five standard lens colors. Four assistance bars are added for safety along with comfortable, molded headrests. Available as a whirlpool (as shown — W4472) or as a soaking tub (T4472).

- Length: 72″ (1828.8 mm)
- Width: 44″ (1117.6 mm)
- Depth: 23″ (584.2 mm)
- Operating capacity: 80 gallons (303.2 L)
- To overflow level: 90 gallons (341.1L)

Whirlpool features:
- 8 Jets
- 1 HP Pump/Motor
- 2 Air Volume Controls
- Four Function On/Off Air Control
- Light with 5 Lens Colors
- 4 Assistance Bars

The Stellar™

Reasons to Buy Clarke Products:

Slip-Resistant Bottoms.
We have developed a superior slip-resistant bottom to improve your foot traction. An added safety feature.

Soaking Bathtubs.
All of our bathtubs are available without whirlpool systems. Many of our customers prefer the design, 30 color choices and enjoyment of a roomy and deep soaking tub.

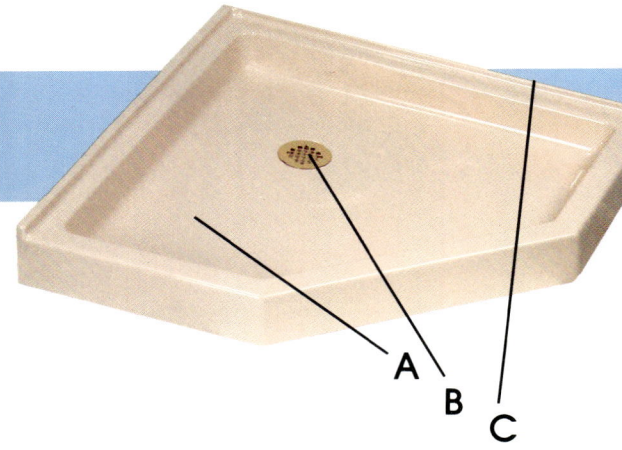

Colorfloors™
ACRYLIC SHOWER BASES

A. – Slip-resistant bottom for your safety.
B. – Complete drain assembly comes standard with every Colorfloors™.
C. – Water barrier/tile line is permanently vacuum-formed and prevents water damage.
D. – Most models are IAPMO listed.
E. – Available in 16 models that fit most showers. 30 colors.
F. – Warranty. All Colorfloors™ have a limited 10-year warranty.

• All 18 **Clarke Whirlpool Bath** choices are UL and IAPMO listed and available in all 30 colors. Many are standard with assistance bars, slip-resistant bottoms and all are standard with pneumatic air controls. We offer a wide color choice in trim as well as chrome, polished brass, antique brass and gold. Some have molded-in tile flanges. All Clarke whirlpools use our "Direct-Flow" system for superb hydrotherapy performance and noise reduction.
• Our **Colorfloors™** offer you a durable and colorful alternative to tile, molded plastic, cultured marble, gel coat fiberglass and terrazzo shower bases. **Clarke Colorfloors™** are made to provide you with a shower base

that does not fade, mildew, stain, crack or leak. Our 10 Year Limited Warranty provides assurance of performance.

Clarke Colors:
• Jasmine 06 (Matte) • Natural 05 • Almond 03 • Bone 04 • Tender Grey 08 • Sterling Silver 07 • Country Grey 09 • Ice Grey 24 • Graphite 10 (Matte) • Shell 12 • Wild Rose 16 • Dusty Rose 17 • Raspberry 18 • Ruby 28 • Innocent Blush 13 • Desert Bloom 14 • Peach Bisque 15 • White 01 • Edelweiss 02 (Matte) • Seafoam Green 21 • Teal 20 • Black 11 • Ebony 27 (Matte) • Glacier Blue 22 • Navy 23 • Light Mink 25 • Light Turquoise 26 • Red 19 • Verde

---

All product specifications and features are subject to change without prior notification.

Sizes are nominal. See individual specification sheets for exact sizes.

© 1991 Clarke Products Inc.

Listed
27E7

Write or Call for our complete 1991 brochure.

Designed by AD IDEAS • Arlington, TX

Clarke Products Inc.
Great Bathrooms begin with Clarke

1202 Avenue J East, Grand Prairie, Texas 75050
(214) 660-1992 • FAX 214-660-2259
• Customer Service 1-800-426-8964

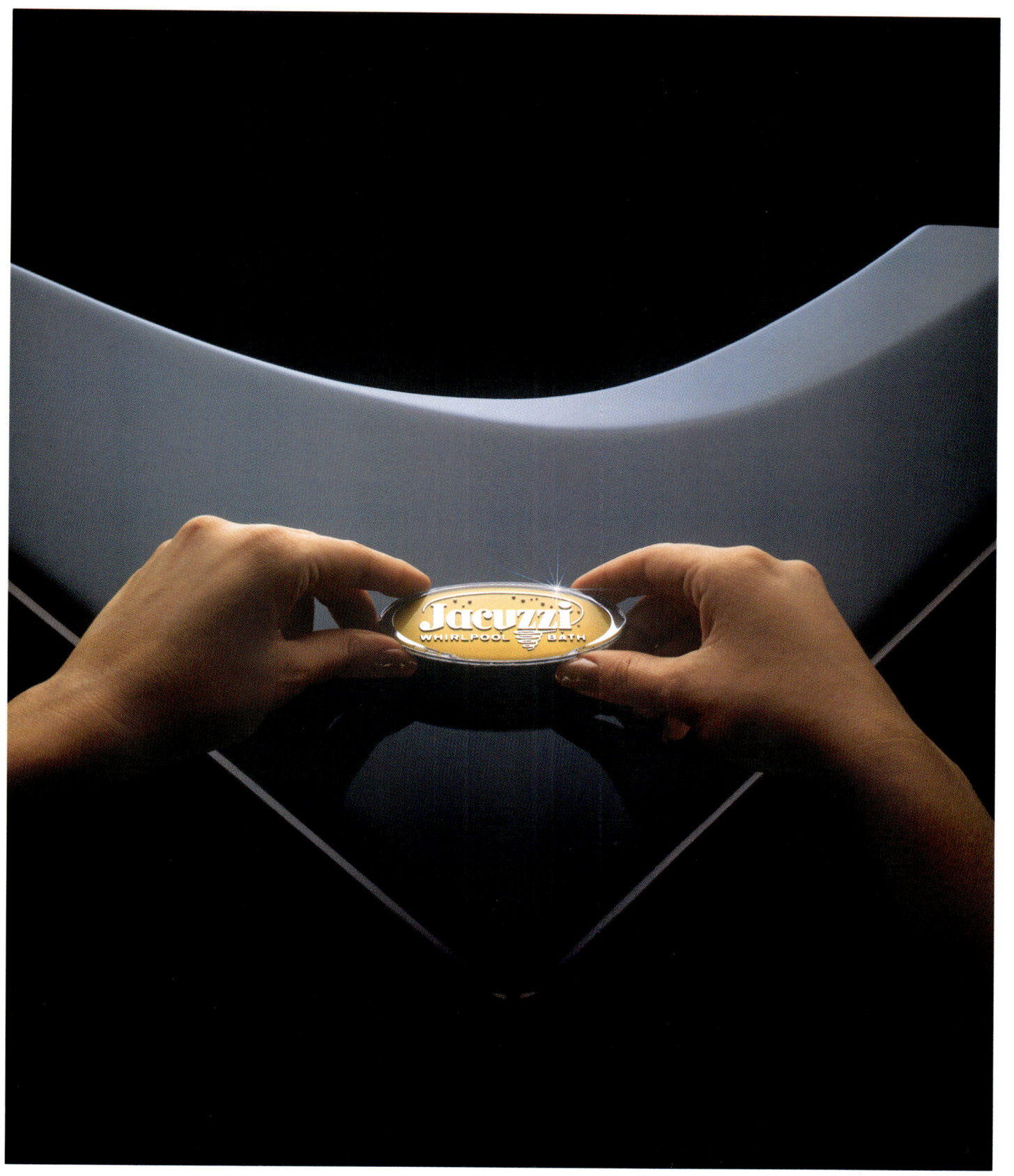

The International Designer Collection
1991

You can see the dramatic difference.

Inch for inch, no other whirlpool can match the power—or the pleasure—of PowerPro® jets by Jacuzzi Whirlpool Bath.

You can feel the luxurious difference.

The result is powerful—but gentle—hydrotherapy for the whole body.

Our patented PowerPro jets make the difference.

Only Jacuzzi whirlpool baths have more of what you really buy a whirlpool for.

Jacuzzi jets turn a whirlpool bath into the luxurious, relaxing experience it is meant to be. But as you can see, not every jet is built the same. Some are too weak to do an effective job.

Only Jacuzzi PowerPro jets have the power to be gentle. They combine air and water from all directions, creating a broad, massaging circular pattern of bubbles. PowerPro jets are fully adjustable to focus on body areas that need special attention. You feel the soothing, penetrating, therapeutic difference every time you bathe. It's the complete relaxation experience you expect—and deserve—from your Jacuzzi whirlpool bath.

Manufacturer A

Manufacturer B

Manufacturer C

Manufacturer D

Jacuzzi Whirlpool Bath

PowerPro jet

The Originator. The Innovator.

Major jet systems in the whirlpool bath and spa industry were tested under identical conditions to evaluate the performance of each system's jet action. test protocol was the same for each jet, and the photography, as shown, represents air/water travel and volume as actually occurred in the test.

12   18   24   30   36   42   48

JACUZZI WHIRLPOOL BATH. WHER

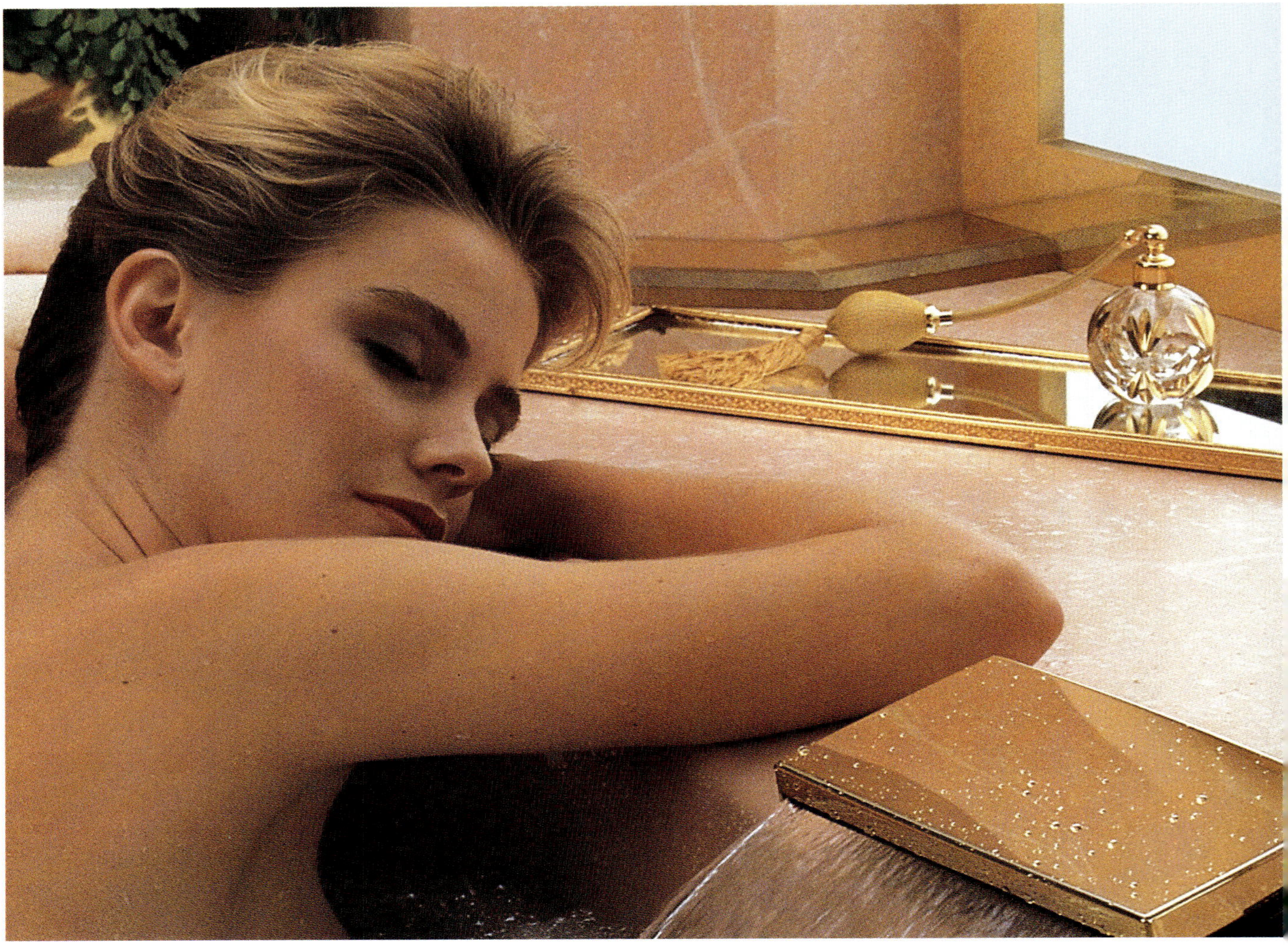

The ultimate in hydrotherapy. Any whirlpool bath can make bubbles. But only a Jacuzzi® whirlpool bath has the patented Power Pro® jet system that soothes and refreshes your entire body with high-volume, low-pressure hydrotherapy. The result is the complete relaxation experience and your own customized massage.

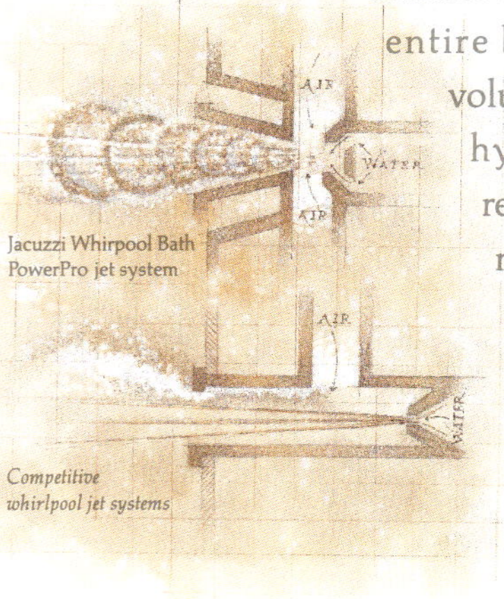

Jacuzzi Whirpool Bath PowerPro jet system

Competitive whirlpool jet systems

The components of pleasure. The total experience of enjoyment in a Jacuzzi whirlpool bath is the

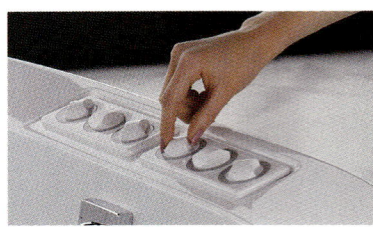

UXURY IS A STANDARD FEATURE.

sum of many intelligently designed parts: ergonomic seating, the soothing sounds of the Water Rainbow® fill spout,

why we back up each one of our baths with an extensive warranty program and nationwide service network.

Whether the criterion is innovative design and technology or quality manufacturing, Jacuzzi® whirlpool baths provide the standard by which all other whirlpool baths are judged.

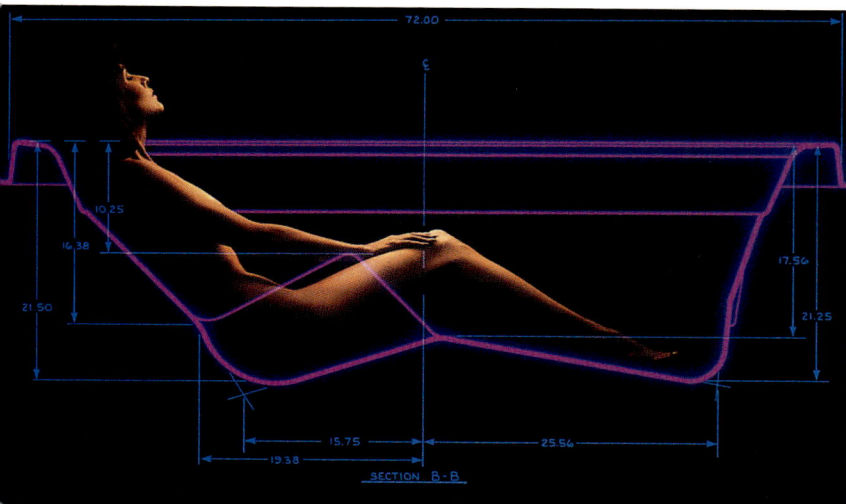

the Magic Touch® on/off switch, and the patented Silent Air induction system. Jacuzzi Whirlpool Bath has thought of everything, so you don't have to think of anything except unwinding.

So reliable, it's relaxing.

Your whirlpool bath should be a soothing experience. That's why our first priority is building a dependable, quality product every time. It is also

A tradition of trust.

At Jacuzzi Whirlpool Bath we're very proud that we invented the whirlpool bath

The original Jacuzzi Brothers

back in 1968. But we are even more proud of the reputation we've built since that time.

An international bestseller.
Jacuzzi Inc. is the world leader in whirlpool baths, with 250 international patents and 10 factories worldwide. Now in Europe, Asia, North and South America, Jacuzzi Inc. provides a universal way to relax and retreat.

It's a good feeling to know that our hard work is leading to a very relaxing end—a luxurious bathing experience for each and every one of our customers.

Roy Jacuzzi
President and
Chief Executive Officer,
Jacuzzi Inc.

The Originator. The Innovator.

FONTANA

■ The ultimate luxury is the one you share, which is why Jacuzzi Whirlpool Bath created the dramatic Fontana™ whirlpool bath for two. The Fontana is as roomy as it is beautiful, with every detail designed with your pleasure in mind: the cascading waterfall, the European-style hand-held shower and the conveniently placed Magic Touch® fingertip jet control. Put them together and you have a special environment all your own, the ultimate refuge from a stressful world.

SPECIFICATIONS:

- *DIMENSIONS:* 72" long x 54" wide x 28" high.
- *MATERIAL:* High-gloss acrylic, fiberglass reinforced.
- *CONSTRUCTION:* Self-contained, completely preplumbed.
- *INSTALLATION:* Recessed in floor or platform.
- *WHIRLPOOL MOTOR/PUMP:* 1½ HP, 115V 20 AMP service required.
- *WATER CAPACITY:* 110 U.S. gallons.
- *FLOOR LOADING:* 58 lbs./sq. ft.
- *SHIPPING WEIGHT:* 298 lbs.
- *CERTIFICATIONS:* UL and IAPMO listed, factory pretested.

Product specifications subject to change without notice.

FEATURES:

- Four patented, fully-adjustable PowerPro® jets.
- Scalloped bath rim crests in a spectacular stairstep waterfall with built-in WaterRainbow.®
- An acrylic panel reveals a second Water Rainbow fill spout, for a dual cascade effect. The panel also houses a hand-held European-style shower.
- Roomy interior provides dual bathing comfort and ease.

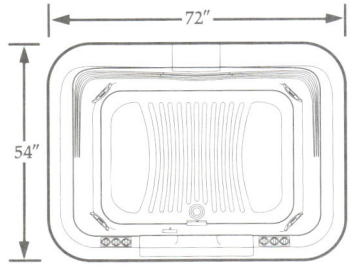

EURA • MIRA

■ Even at first glance, you can see that this is a vision in whirlpool bath design. Select the two-person Eura™ or the Mira™ for one. The fluid lines and uplifted contours set them apart from the ordinary. Both baths offer ample width and raised backrests for the ultimate in contoured comfort. And to enhance your bathing experience even further, you'll find luxurious features such as our Magic Touch® control and PowerPro® jet system. With the Eura and Mira, you can truly escape from it all.

SPECIFICATIONS:

- *DIMENSIONS:* EURA: 72" long x 42" wide x 19½" high. MIRA: 72" long x 36" wide x 19" high.
- *MATERIAL:* High-gloss acrylic, fiberglass reinforced.
- *CONSTRUCTION:* Self-contained, completely preplumbed.
- *INSTALLATIONS:* Recessed in floor or platform, or with optional matching skirt.
- *WHIRLPOOL MOTOR/PUMP:* ¾ HP, 115V 20 AMP service required.
- *WATER CAPACITY:* EURA: 75 U.S. gallons. MIRA: 65 U.S. gallons.
- *FLOOR LOADING:* EURA: 44 lbs./sq. ft. MIRA: 45 lbs./sq. ft.
- *SHIPPING WEIGHT:* EURA: 171 lbs. MIRA: 153 lbs.
- *CERTIFICATIONS:* UL and IAPMO listed, factory pretested.

Product specifications subject to change without notice.

FEATURES:

- Fully-adjustable PowerPro jets
- Raised backrest at each end
- Optional Water Rainbow® spout

EURA

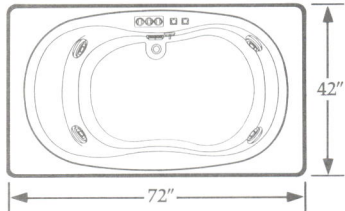

MIRA

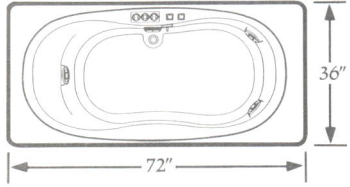

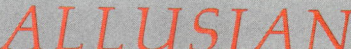

ALLUSIAN

■ Every once in a while, things change. And all of a sudden there's a new way to look at things. The Allusian™ is a change on that order. A new shape, fresh lines and a level of design excellence that makes the Allusian the ultimate statement in whirlpool bathing.

SPECIFICATIONS:

- *DIMENSIONS:* 84" long x 84" wide x 25" high.
- *MATERIAL:* High-gloss acrylic, fiberglass reinforced.
- *CONSTRUCTION:* Self-contained, completely preplumbed
- *INSTALLATIONS:* Recessed in floor or platform. (Must provide service access to both pumps)
- *WHIRLPOOL MOTOR/PUMP:* Two 1 HP, 2-speed motors/pumps. Two dedicated 115V 20 AMP circuits required.
- *WATER CAPACITY:* 150 U.S. gallons.
- *RECOMMENDED WATER HEATER:* 100 gallons
- *FLOOR LOADING:* 46 lbs./sq. ft.
- *SHIPPING WEIGHT:* 649 lbs.
- *CERTIFICATIONS:*
  UL and IAPMO listed, factory pretested.

Product specifications subject to change without notice.

FEATURES:

- Six fully-adjustable PowerPro® jets
- Two Water Rainbow spouts: one to fill, the other to recirculate
- Two 12-volt interior lights with a choice of colored lenses
- Two acrylic covers with mirrored interiors and accessory area

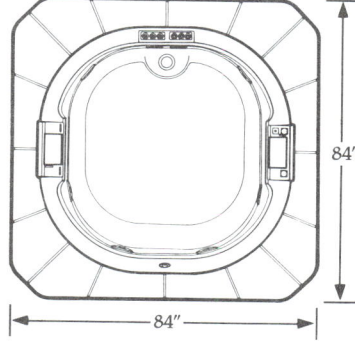

84"

84"

VIANTE · VIANTE GRANDE

■ Classic, spacious whirlpool baths with beautiful swirling lines, the Viante™ and Viante Grande™ are fashioned for comfort as well as for style. Patented PowerPro® jets make for a bathing experience that's more than just relaxing—it's therapeutic.

SPECIFICATIONS:

- *DIMENSIONS:* VIANTE GRANDE: 60" long x 42" wide x 20" high. VIANTE: 60" long x 36" wide x 20" high, available May 1991.
- *MATERIAL:* High-gloss acrylic, fiberglass reinforced.
- *CONSTRUCTION:* Self-contained, completely preplumbed.
- *INSTALLATION:* Recessed in floor or platform, or with optional matching skirt.
- *WHIRLPOOL MOTOR/PUMP:* ¾ HP, 115V, 20 AMP service required.
- *WATER CAPACITY:* VIANTE GRANDE: 70 U.S. gallons.
- *FLOOR LOADING:* VIANTE GRANDE: 49 lbs./sq. ft.
- *SHIPPING WEIGHT:* VIANTE GRANDE: 155 lbs.
- *CERTIFICATIONS:* UL and IAPMO listed, factory pretested. ⓊⓁ ⓟ
  Product specifications subject to change without notice.

FEATURES:

- VIANTE GRANDE: Four patented, fully-adjustable PowerPro jets
  VIANTE: Three patented, fully-ajustable PowerPro jets
- Unique scalloped European design
- Provides the luxury and style of a larger tub in a five-foot space
- Optional faucet and handles

VIANTE

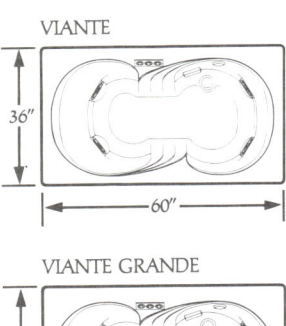

36"
60"

VIANTE GRANDE

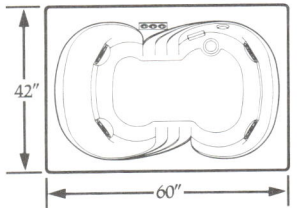

42"
60"

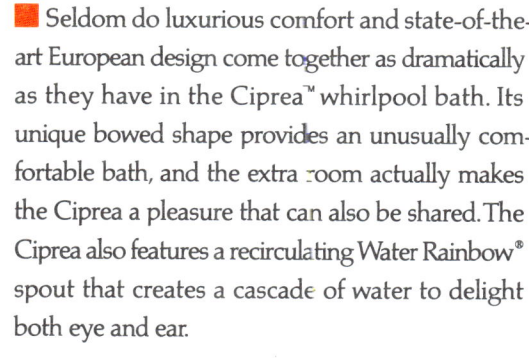

■ Seldom do luxurious comfort and state-of-the-art European design come together as dramatically as they have in the Ciprea™ whirlpool bath. Its unique bowed shape provides an unusually comfortable bath, and the extra room actually makes the Ciprea a pleasure that can also be shared. The Ciprea also features a recirculating Water Rainbow® spout that creates a cascade of water to delight both eye and ear.

SPECIFICATIONS:

- *DIMENSIONS:* CIPREA: 72" long x 48" wide x 20" high. MYA: 60" long x 38" wide x 20" high.
- *MATERIAL:* High-gloss acrylic, fiberglass reinforced.
- *CONSTRUCTION:* Self-contained, completely preplumbed.
- *INSTALLATION:* Factory installed matching skirt.
- *WHIRLPOOL MOTOR/PUMP:* ¾ HP, 115V 20 AMP service required.
- *WATER CAPACITY:* CIPREA: 75 U.S. gallons. MYA: 65 U.S. gallons.
- *FLOOR LOADING:* CIPREA: 46.5 lbs./sq. ft. MYA: 53.5 lbs./sq. ft.
- *SHIPPING WEIGHT:* CIPREA: 207 lbs. MYA: 141 lbs.
- *CERTIFICATIONS:* UL and IAPMO listed, factory pretested.

Product specifications subject to change without notice.

FEATURES:

- Fully-adjustable PowerPro® jets
- Unique bowed interior and matching skirt for extra bathing space
- Water Rainbow spout mounted on side wall of bath to create a cascade of water (Ciprea only)
- Built-in armrests
- Side drain/overflow

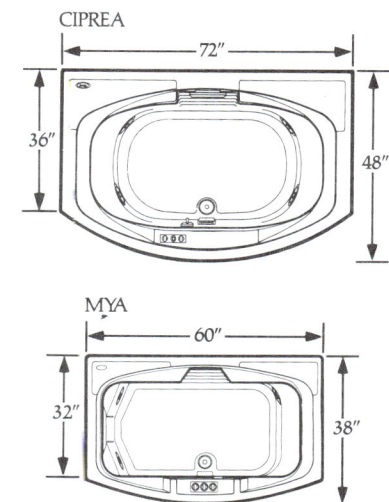

CIPREA

72"
36"
48"

MYA

60"
32"
38"

■ Leave it to the innovators at Jacuzzi Whirlpool Bath to create an entirely new concept in whirlpool bathing. Thanks to its revolutionary shape, the elegantly—and intelligently—designed Maurea™ whirlpool bath is as sleek and sophisticated as it is comfortable and functional. Not only does the Maurea easily accommodate two bathers side by side, it also features a contoured backrest and built-in armrests for complete relaxation. In addition, there is a special side seat for bathside grooming as well as a tastefully concealed vanity with mirror and accessory area. Top it off with the peaceful sounds of the cascading Water Rainbow® fill spout, and you have an environment that's nothing short of pure pleasure.

SPECIFICATIONS:

- *DIMENSIONS:* 72" long x 63" wide x 22" high.
- *MATERIAL:* High-gloss acrylic, fiberglass reinforced.
- *CONSTRUCTION:* Self-contained, completely preplumbed.
- *INSTALLATION:* Recessed in floor or platform.
- *WHIRLPOOL MOTOR/PUMP:* ¾ HP, 115V 20 AMP service required.
- *WATER CAPACITY:* 80 U.S. gallons.
- *FLOOR LOADING:* 51.5 lbs./sq. ft.
- *SHIPPING WEIGHT:* 320 lbs.
- *CERTIFICATIONS:* UL and IAPMO listed, factory pretested.

Product specifications subject to change without notice.

FEATURES:

- Four fully-adjustable PowerPro® jets
- Contoured backrest and built-in armrests for added comfort
- Integral seat for bathside grooming
- Water Rainbow fill spout with matching acrylic cover
- Built-in hot and cold water faucets

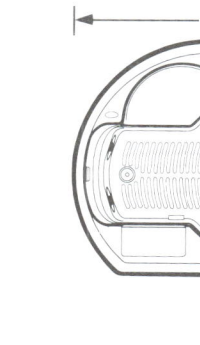

■ When can a totally new design be considered a classic? When it is the Opalia,™ a whirlpool bath so elegantly simple and gracefully shaped it transcends the merely fashionable. You won't find a single straight line in the Opalia, from its superb oval shaping and asymmetrically curved rim to its etched detailing and shell bottom design. The Opalia is the essence of comfort as well as beauty, with a spacious six-foot size and built-in armrests perfectly suited to luxuriant bathing for two.

SPECIFICATIONS:

- *DIMENSIONS:* 72" long x 44" wide x 22" high.
- *MATERIAL:* High-gloss acrylic, fiberglass reinforced.
- *CONSTRUCTION:* Self-contained, completely preplumbed.
- *INSTALLATION:* Recessed in floor or platform.
- *WHIRLPOOL MOTOR/PUMP:* ¾ HP, 115V 20 AMP service required.
- *WATER CAPACITY:* 98 U.S. gallons.
- *FLOOR LOADING:* 53 lbs./sq. ft.
- *SHIPPING WEIGHT:* 175 lbs.
- *CERTIFICATIONS:* UL and IAPMO listed, factory pretested.

Product specifications subject to change without notice.

FEATURES:

- Four fully-adjustable PowerPro® jets
- Interior contours with built-in armrests
- Attractive ribbed pattern on slip-resistant shell bottom
- Optional faucet and handles

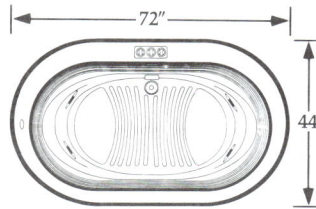

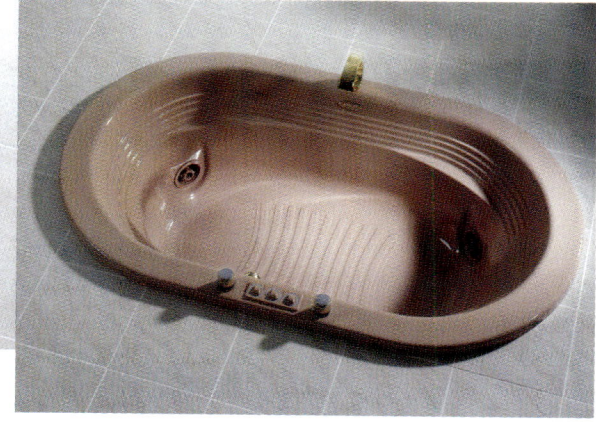

AURA

■ As the originator of whirlpool bathing you would expect Jacuzzi Whirlpool Bath to lead in innovative design. With the Aura,™ this tradition continues. A new level of comfort, extraordinary features and stunning design make the Aura the ultimate two-person lounger bath.

SPECIFICATIONS:

- *DIMENSIONS:* 72" long x 60" wide x 20" high.
- *MATERIAL:* High-gloss acrylic, fiberglass reinforced.
- *CONSTRUCTION:* Self-contained, completely preplumbed.
- *INSTALLATIONS:* Recessed in floor or platform.
- *WHIRLPOOL MOTOR/PUMP:* 1.5 HP, 115V 20 AMP service required.
- *WATER CAPACITY:* 125 U.S. gallons.
- *FLOOR LOADING:* 52 lbs./sq. ft.
- *SHIPPING WEIGHT:* 348 lbs.
- *CERTIFICATIONS:* UL and IAPMO listed, factory pretested.

Product specifications subject to change without notice.

FEATURES:

- Four fully-adjustable PowerPro® jets
- Two Water Rainbow spouts: one to fill, the other to recirculate
- Built-in hot & cold water faucets
- Two acrylic covers with mirrored interiors, concealing the controls and providing an accessory area for bathing items
- Two interior lights with a selection of colored lenses
- Two individual loungers

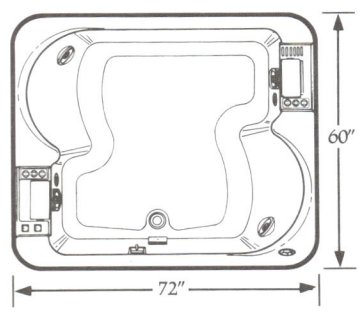

60"

72"

■ One of the most exciting designs we have ever introduced, the Amea™ whirlpool bath combines the distinctive lines of European style with the kind of practical innovations that have made Jacuzzi Whirlpool Bath the leader in whirlpool bathing. Its integral headrest and sloping backrest provide an extraordinary degree of comfort. The unique seat allows for bath-side grooming, or a convenient place to store bathing items.

SPECIFICATIONS:

- *DIMENSIONS:* AMEA 5.5: 66" long x 36" wide x 20" high. AMEA 6: 72" long x 36" wide x 28" high.
- *MATERIAL:* High-gloss acrylic, fiberglass reinforced.
- *CONSTRUCTION:* Self-contained, completely preplumbed.
- *INSTALLATION:* Recessed in floor or platform, or with optional matching skirt.
- *WHIRLPOOL MOTOR/PUMP:* ¾ HP, 115V, 20 AMP service required.
- *WATER CAPACITY:* AMEA 5.5: 55 U.S. gallons. AMEA 6: 65 U.S. gallons.
- *FLOOR LOADING:* AMEA 5.5: 44 lbs./sq. ft. AMEA 6: 45 lbs./sq. ft.
- *SHIPPING WEIGHT:* AMEA 5.5: 147 lbs. AMEA 6: 145 lbs.
- *CERTIFICATIONS:* UL and IAPMO listed, factory pretested.

Product specifications subject to change without notice.

FEATURES:

- Fully-adjustable PowerPro® jets
- Integral headrest for added comfort
- Integral seat for bath-side grooming or a convenient shelf to store bathing items
- Side drain/overflow
- Optional Water Rainbow® spout

AMEA 6

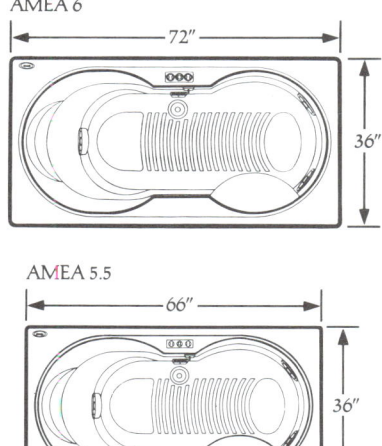

AMEA 5.5

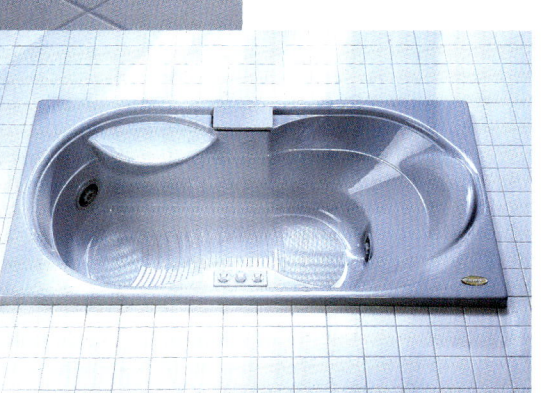

BIANCA

■ The Bianca™ provides a perfect place for just the two of you. A place to be alone—together. And to be away from it all. Of course, you'll find the Bianca just as enjoyable when you bathe by yourself. Our whirlpool system is famous for creating a very special experience. And with the Bianca, it's an experience that can bring two people together.

SPECIFICATIONS:
- *DIMENSIONS:* 72" long x 48" wide x 20" high.
- *MATERIAL:* High-gloss acrylic, fiberglass reinforced.
- *CONSTRUCTION:* Self-contained, completely preplumbed.
- *INSTALLATIONS:* Recessed in floor or platform, or by constructing a skirt.
- *WHIRLPOOL MOTOR/PUMP:* 1½ HP, 115V 20 AMP service required.
- *WATER CAPACITY:* 85 U.S. gallons.
- *FLOOR LOADING:* 48 lbs./sq. ft.
- *SHIPPING WEIGHT:* 179 lbs.
- *CERTIFICATIONS:* UL and IAPMO listed, factory pretested.

Product specifications subject to change without notice.

FEATURES:
- Four fully-adjustable PowerPro® jets
- Contoured backrest
- Side-by-side bathing space
- Optional faucet and handles.

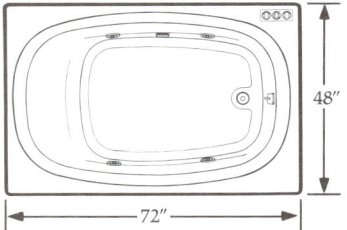

48"

72"

PRIMA II

■ The dramatic Prima II™ will dazzle your senses. It's a work of art, with contours as captivating as fine sculpture. And the luxury standard features of Prima II make it an equally captivating experience. Once you are inside, the Magic Touch® on/off switch enables you to activate the whirlpool with just a touch of your finger. The entire system is adjustable, to suit your every mood. The Prima II by Jacuzzi Whirlpool Bath—it'll take you to another world.

SPECIFICATIONS:

- *DIMENSIONS:* 72″ long x 36″ wide x 18″ high.
- *MATERIAL:* High-gloss acrylic, fiberglass reinforced.
- *CONSTRUCTION:* Self-contained, completely preplumbed.
- *INSTALLATIONS:* Recessed in floor or platform, or with optional matching skirt.
- *WHIRLPOOL MOTOR/PUMP:* ¾ HP, 115V 20 AMP service required.
- *WATER CAPACITY:* 65 U.S. gallons.
- *FLOOR LOADING:* 46 lbs./sq. ft.
- *SHIPPING WEIGHT:* 161 lbs.
- *CERTIFICATIONS:* UL and IAPMO listed, factory pretested.

Product specifications subject to change without notice.

FEATURES:

- Three fully-adjustable PowerPro® jets
- Sloped backrest for reclining
- Optional Water Rainbow fill spout & faucet knobs

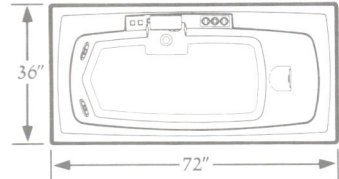

■ *WATER RAINBOW ULTRA*
Larger, bolder and more luxurious, the oval Water Rainbow® ultra fill spout offers the same soothing murmur of cascading water as our classic Water Rainbow fill spout. It also fills faster than conventional fill spouts, with a ¾" opening instead of the standard ½" variety. Choose from chrome or brass metallic finishes with Rope, Ring or Band handles.

ROPE

RING

BAND

■ *WATER RAINBOW*
Like the Jacuzzi® whirlpool bath itself, our Water Rainbow® fill spout has become synonymous with pure pleasure and relaxation. This private waterfall is equipped with flow control and shower diverter, and can be color-coordinated to complement your Jacuzzi whirlpool bath. Choose from lustrous chrome, gold or bright brass metallic finishes, or any one of fourteen color-matched Designer shades. Also available with Rope, Ring or Band handles.

■ *SUPER METRO*
Designed specifically for larger tubs, this impressive faucet is the essence of sleek and modern bathroom elegance. The Super Metro is fashioned of solid brass and finished in chrome or brass. Available with Rope, Ring or Band handles.

■ *SEA CREST*

The Sea Crest faucet is at once graceful and dramatic. It is also quite practical, as it delivers hot water quickly to the tub or lavatory. Fashioned of solid brass and finished in lustrous brass or chrome with your choice of Rope, Ring or Band handles.

ROPE

RING

BAND

CROSS

LEVER

RENAISSANCE

With its handsome shape and sculpted lines, the Renaissance faucet will remain a classic for generations. Choose from lever or cross grip handles. Available in chip-resistant white, silver or almond, as well as chrome or brass finishes. Constructed from solid brass.

METRO

Like a fine work of modern art, the Metro faucet is both bold and innovative. Fashioned of solid brass and finished in chrome, brass, white or almond, Metro faucets are available for both bath and basin.

8-PORT

6-PORT

JACUZZI® SHOWER HEADS

Choose a gentle rain or an invigorating spray—quality is evident in every detail of the Jacuzzi® shower heads. These solid brass fixtures, with your choice of brass or chrome finishes, match Jacuzzi® faucets for coordinated appeal. Choose between two different sizes.

OPTIONS

BRASS

CHROME

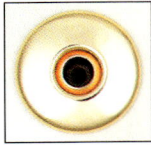
GOLD

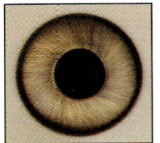
ANTIQUE BRASS

SATIN BRASS

Metal Finish Jets
Swirl-way offers as an option, metal finish jets in brass, chrome, gold, antique brass and satin brass.

Variable Speed Pump
This pump has six different flow settings which allow you to adjust the whirlpool action to your comfort level.

Touch Sensor
The touch sensor provides sensitive finger tip on/off control as well as a built-in, 20-minute timer and a low-water level cut-off that ensures proper pump operation.

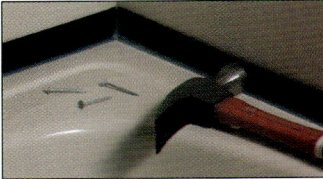

Nailing Flange
Swirl-way can provide a factory installed nailing flange for special installation needs. (The nailing flange will slightly alter the dimensions of the unit.)

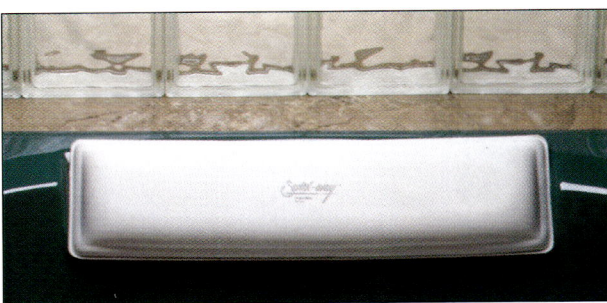

Pillows
In addition to providing comfort, Swirl-way pillows are stain resistant and can be easily removed for cleaning.

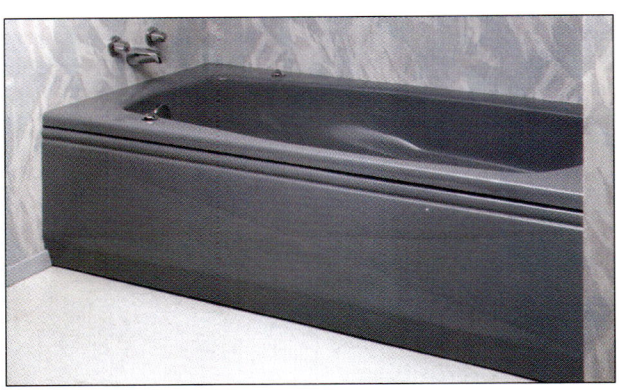

Tub Skirts
Our skirt panels provide easy access to the underside of the tub and are perfectly matched to the whirlpool bath color. (Tub skirts are not available on all models.)

In-line Heater
Our heater is thermostatically controlled to maintain water temperature and increase your bathing comfort.

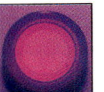 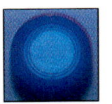   

Mood Lights
Swirl-way offers five different color filters for our mood lights. With front access, it's simple to change the bulb and filter.

Heat Transfer Unit
This efficient non-electrical system takes excess heat energy from the pump motor and distributes it into the water. The heat transfer unit is not available on all Swirl-way models.

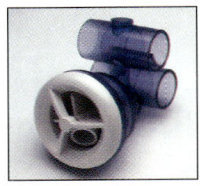

Micro'ssage™ Jet
This unique rotating jet enhances your relaxation pleasure with its circular hydromassage whirlpool action.

CODE COMPLIANCE

 Listed No. 2719

 Listed No. SP-1179

 UL® Listed 47E6 hydromassage bathtub

CSA® Listed S.259 hydromassage bathtub

 State of Ohio and various other state and local approvals

 When tested for compliance to the require-ments of ANSI A112.19.7M and A112.19.8M for "Whirlpool Bath Appliances" and ANSI Z124.1 for "Plastic Bathtub Units" the tested units are found to comply and are acceptable for listing under the Terralab Engineers, Inc. follow-up service. Listed No. 15197

Swirl-way®
Plumbing Group

For Dealer Locations, Call Toll Free: 1-800-999-1459
1505 Industrial Drive ■ P.O. Box 210 ■ Henderson, Texas, USA 75653-0210 ■ FAX: 903-657-3450

Take A Stand

Demand The Finest Quality— Ask For A Swirl-way Shower Base

Swirl-way has developed a superior line of acrylic shower bases with the same beauty and durability our whirlpool baths are known for.

Our designs include a versatile combination of shapes and sizes to accommodate the installation demands of new construction and remodeling.

Now it's easy to achieve a designer look when you include our shower bases in your bathroom plans.

Remember, all Swirl-way products are manufactured to our exacting standards, insuring years of trouble-free service and lasting beauty.

We also offer a 10-year limited warranty backed by Swirl-way service. Our warranty gives you peace of mind, and our 800 number gives you quick response to any questions that might arise.

1-800-999-1459

Swirl-way ®

Plumbing Group

Faucet by Hansgrohe
Shower Enclosure by Glass Products International, Ltd.

S P E C I F I C A T I O N S

A Step Up In Quality

Swirl-way shower bases are a step up from the ordinary. We've combined beauty and design with a quality material—acrylic, to produce a shower base that provides years of trouble-free performance and easy maintenance.

The Practical Choice

- *Acrylic maintains its luster and is easy to clean.*

- *Our extensive designs give you the flexibility to meet the most demanding installation requirements.*

- *Swirl-way shower bases are engineered to be compatible with today's most popular shower door enclosures allowing you maximum choices in completing your bathroom decor. And choosing a Swirl-way base will give you the safety of a skid-resistant shower floor.*

- *Colors enhance the decor in any bathroom. Swirl-way's extensive color options give you the ability to create that special look.*

Design, beauty, engineering, and value. Swirl-way shower bases are the practical choice for new construction or remodeling.

Plumbing Group

For Dealer Locations, Call Toll Free:
1-800-999-1459
FAX: 903-657-3450
1505 Industrial Drive
P.O. Box 210
Henderson, Texas
75653-0210

36" x 36"
Single Threshold
Length O.D. .... 35½"
Width O.D. .... 35½"
Approx. Ship. Wt. ... 35 lbs.
#3636-ST

32" x 32"
Single Threshold
Length O.D. .... 32"
Width O.D. .... 32"
Approx. Ship. Wt. ... 30 lbs.
#3232-ST

36" x 36"
Double Threshold
Length O.D. .... 35½"
Width O.D. .... 35½"
Approx. Ship. Wt. .... 35 lbs.
#3636-DT

36" x 42"
Single Threshold Short Side
Length O.D. .... 36"
Width O.D. .... 42"
Approx. Ship. Wt. .... 35 lbs.
#3642-STSS

38" x 38"
Neo-Angle
Length O.D. .... 37½"
Width O.D. .... 37½"
Approx. Ship. Wt. ... 32 lbs.
#3838-TTNA

36" x 36"
Neo-Angle
Length O.D. .... 36"
Width O.D. .... 36"
Approx. Ship. Wt. ... 30 lbs.
#3636-TTNA

42" x 36"
Single Threshold Long Side
Length O.D. .... 42"
Width O.D. .... 36"
Approx. Ship. Wt. .... 35 lbs.
#4236-STLS

48" x 32"
Single Threshold Long Side
Length O.D. .... 48"
Width O.D. .... 32"
Approx. Ship. Wt. .... 35 lbs.
#4832-STLS

48" x 34"
Single Threshold Long Side
Length O.D. .... 48"
Width O.D. .... 34"
Approx. Ship. Wt. .... 35 lbs.
#4834-STLS

60" x 34"
Single Threshold Long Side
Length O.D. .... 60"
Width O.D. .... 34"
Approx. Ship. Wt. .... 40 lbs.
#6034-STLS

Century Shower Door

Manufacturing Continual advances in our manufacturing techniques assure the highest quality craftsmanship at the greatest value possible.

Inventory To ensure prompt delivery we maintain an extensive inventory of raw materials, as well as finished units.

At Century we focus on customer service. Our professional staff is fully trained to answer all your design, delivery and pricing questions.
800 524 2578

Shipping In order to provide our customers with rapid delivery without damage, we engineer our cartons and inserts product by product.

For more than 40 years Century Shower Door has represented the highest product quality, innovative design and superior service. With the growing trend in custom designed enclosures, Century continues to lead the way by working closely with their dealers to achieve the finest results. For the ultimate in design and service, Century is the answer.

Tile By Villeroy & Boch

Century offers a broad choice of glass options and painted finishes. We feature 12 standard colors or we will custom match the finish to your color scheme.

Centec Frameless Series offers an elegant, open design for contemporary bathrooms.

Lucette Series of deluxe framed enclosures provides the highest quality and the widest range of design options. It is available in all finishes.

Park Ridge Estates, "A Pouliot Community"

Custom Capabilities We maintain a large inventory of custom metal profiles that allow us to respond to virtually any design challenge.

Century, the innovators in design & service.

Century Shower Door, Inc. ▪ 250 Lackawanna Avenue ▪ West Paterson, NJ 07424 ▪ 201 785 4290 ▪ 800 524 2578

Centec Series
Frameless

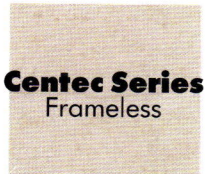

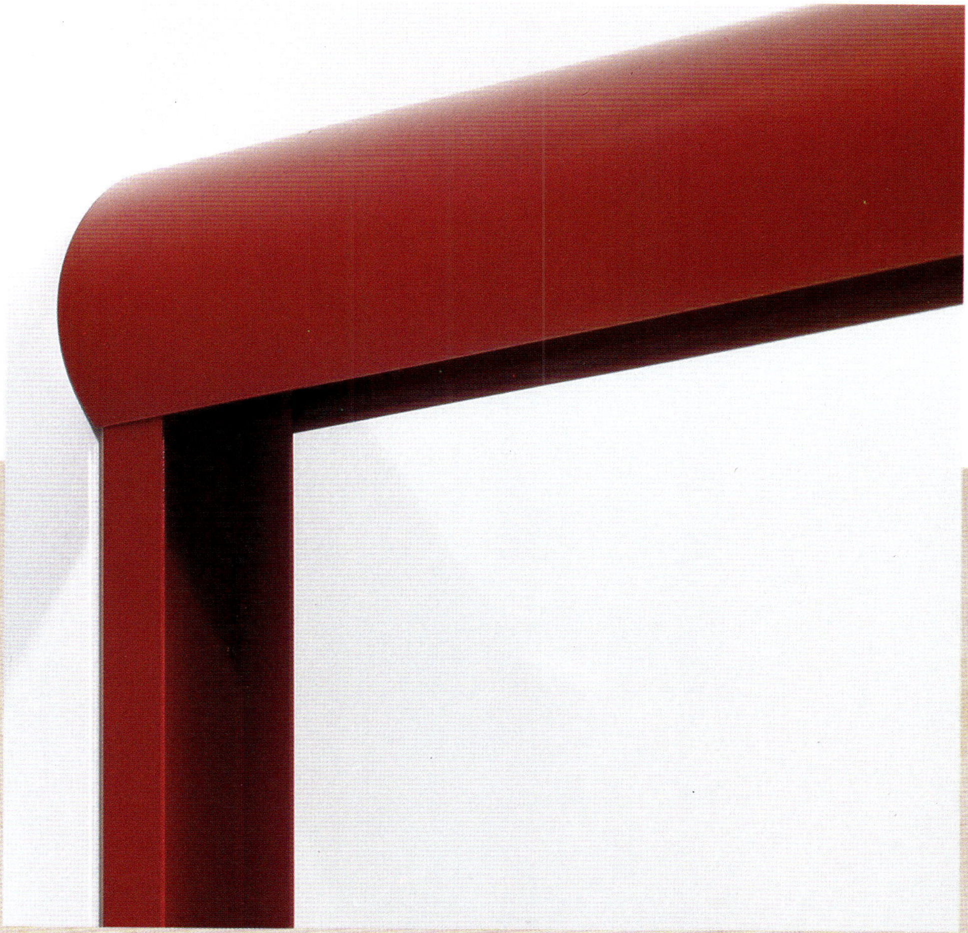

CENTURY

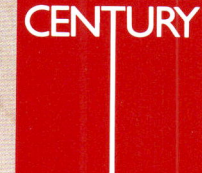

Centec is truly an innovation in design and engineering. Its unmistakable header & virtually invisible doors make the most of your bathroom. Available in all standard sliding door configurations for bath or shower, Centec frameless enclosures make a simple, elegant statement in any environment.

Centec comes in all standard applications and a wide range of custom sizes. We also feature 12 standard colors or will custom match to fit your color scheme.

The unique frameless design of Centec complements any bathroom. Its distinctive radial header design provides stability and friction-free door movement. The tempered glass doors have polished & radiused edges for added safety, and feature pass-through tubular towel bars. An extra wide polypropylene centerguide and rubber side bumpers provide years of smooth, maintenance-free operation.

Tile by Villeroy & Boch

The **quality and design** of the Centec sets it apart from traditional enclosures. The distinctive header is made of heavy gauge, highly polished aluminum. The glass is ¼ inch clear tempered with polished edges all around for added safety. The bottom track features twin caulking channels and a three inch center guide to assure smooth movement and carefree maintenance. Century is the innovator in shower enclosures.

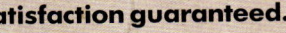

atisfaction guaranteed.

Century Shower Door, Inc. ■ 250 Lackawanna Avenue ■ West Paterson, NJ 07424 ■ 201 785 4290 ■ 800 524 2578 ■ FAX 201 785 0777

Lucette Series
Deluxe Framed

CENTURY

Limitless possibilities for limited spaces. Lucette is available in a wide range of standard & custom configurations to match any decor or space requirement. Three of our most popular styles are shown here, the standard tub enclosure, the neo-angle, for limited spaces and the hinged door with grill. Century stocks virtually any configuration for immediate delivery.

Lucette Gold Tub L-158 clear glass

Lucette Black NeoAngle L-1669 clear glass

Lucette Silver Hinged Door L-71 obscure glass

Lucette is available in a broad choice of glass options and painted finishes. We feature 12 standard colors or we will custom match the finish to your color scheme.

Lucette deluxe enclosures combine classic design, easy installation and carefree maintenance with the highest quality workmanship. Our enclosures fit perfectly even in difficult situations. Extrusions are designed for maintenance-free operation and easy cleaning through years of use. All Century products are engineered to the toughest specifications.

Lucette Silver Buttress Tub Enclosure L-636B clear glass

Painted or anodized, standard or custom, Century works closely with dealers to achieve the finest results. Every Lucette extrusion is inspected by hand to guarantee perfect fit, finish and maintenance free operation. For high quality, classic design and limitless possibilities, Lucette is the answer.

Top: Lucette, Red Door and Panel L-1627 with clear glass
Bottom: Lucette, Gray Stall Shower L-4670 with clear glass

Top: Lucette Silver Tub L-158 with gray designer glass
Bottom: Lucette Gold Corner Enclosure L-1631B with clear glass

Satisfaction guaranteed.

Century Shower Door, Inc. ■ 250 Lackawanna Avenue ■ West Paterson, NJ 07424 ■ 201 785 4290 ■ 800 524 2578 ■ FAX 201 785 0777

COLOR

Subtle or bold. Pastel or bright. It's your choice. Our finest framed and frameless shower doors are available in 12 designer colors, including white, almond, grey, black and red. Custom color adds a contemporary European look to Century's top quality materials and construction. Let us match your color scheme. For more than 40 years, Century has designed and produced shower and bath enclosures that reflect quality from start to finish.

Choose your color to match tile, high-light fixtures or just add a splash of color with Century top quality painted finishes.

Century Standard Colors were carefully chosen to match the fixture colors of most major manufacturers.

Dusty Rose

Teal Green

BronzeTone

Cobalt Blue

Royal Red

Almondtone

Cameo Cream

Caramel

Linen White

Platinum Gray

Powder Gray

Black Onyx

Satisfaction guaranteed.

Century Shower Door, Inc. ■ **250 Lackawanna Avenue** ■ **West Paterson, NJ 07424** ■ **201 785 4290** ■ **800 524 2578** ■ **FAX 201 785 0777**

Custom Enclosures

Century responds to your **custom design** needs with products that combine quality, innovation and creativity. With the growing trend in custom enclosures, Century leads the way by working closely with dealers to achieve the finest results with top-of-the-line craftsmanship. We provide accurate layouts and precise fabrication to assure a perfect fit every time. With our wide inventory of custom profiles production is fast and the design possibilities are endless.

Gold Lucette with angled buttress

Gold Lucette with steam release transom at Park Ridge Estates, A Pouliot Community

Our wide inventory of custom metal profiles enables us to quickly produce the highest quality enclosures in virtually any configuration. With Century the design possibilities are endless and the delivery is the best in the business.

Dusty Rose oversized Lucette

Gold Lucette with steam release transom and custom designed roof

For 40 years Century shower enclosures have represented the highest product quality, innovative design and superior service. For the ultimate in custom design and service, Century is the answer.

Satisfaction guaranteed.

Custom bronzetone finish Lucette

Gold anodized Lucette with buttress

White Centec with buttress return

Century Shower Door, Inc. ▪ 250 Lackawanna Avenue ▪ West Paterson, NJ 07424 ▪ 201 785 4290 ▪ 800 524 2578 ▪ FAX 201 785 0777

ShowerTech GL

K-8 Towel Warmer, Delphi Pedestal, T50 Mirror, ShowerTech Series 2000, Rondo and Colonna Tile

Hastings
BATH COLLECTION

Series 2000

Curved frameless shower enclosure in sizes from 32-40 inches. The radius clear tempered glass doors are 6 millimeters and the stationary panels are 8 millimeters thick. The patented extruded aluminum hinge assemblies have a baked on enamel powder finish. Watertight seams exist between the radius doors by use of patented snap-on magnetic seals. Vacuum formed acrylic bases are available in colors with an anti-skid surface. Hardware comes in black, white, yellow, red, chrome or brass. Custom sizes are available.

Series 2100

Neo Angle frameless shower enclosure in sizes from 34-42 inches. The 135° angled clear tempered glass door and panels are 8 millimeters thick. The patented adjustable extruded aluminum hinge assemblies have a baked on enamel powder finish. Watertight seams exist between the hinged door and panels by the use of patented snap-on magnetic seals. The door is reversible for left or right operation. Vacuum formed acrylic bases are available in colors with an anti-skid surface. Hardware comes in black, white, yellow, red, chrome or brass. Custom sizes are available.

Model: S2000
Background Tile: Hastings Traccia Series

Model: S2100
Background Tile: Hastings Maschere Series

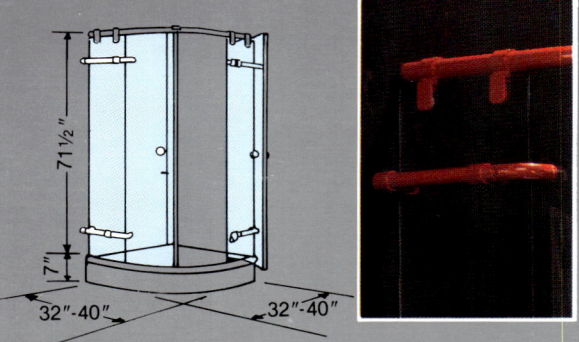

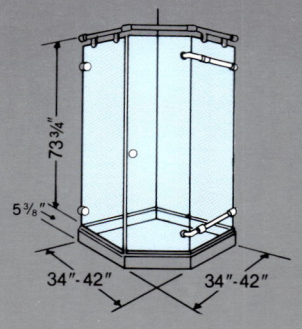

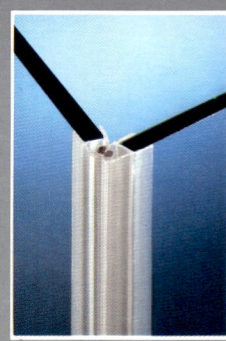

Magnetic Seals

Series 2200

Frameless door and panel enclosure made of 8 millimeters thick clear tempered glass. A patented snap-on magnetic seal creates a watertight seam. Extruded aluminum hinge assemblies have a baked on enamel powder finish. Interconnecting patented hinge fittings and nylon cams make adjustments simple. The door and panel are reversible for left or right installations. Vacuum formed acrylic bases are available in colors with an anti-skid surface. Hardware comes in black, white, yellow, red, chrome or brass. Custom sizes are available.

Series 2300

Frameless sliding door shower enclosure. The series configurations are wall to wall, 90 degree door and panel, 90 degree door and panel with adjacent tub, and "U" shaped shower enclosures. Door and panels are 8 millimeters thick, clear tempered glass. Watertight seams exist between sliding doors by use of patented snap-on magnetic seals. Vacuum formed acrylic bases are available in colors with an anti-skid surface. Hardware comes in black, white, yellow, red, chrome or brass. Custom sizes are available.

Model: S2200
Background Tile: Hastings Maschere Series

Model: S2323

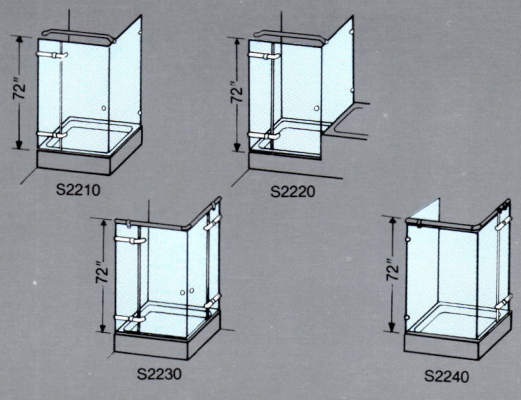

S2210 S2220
S2230 S2240

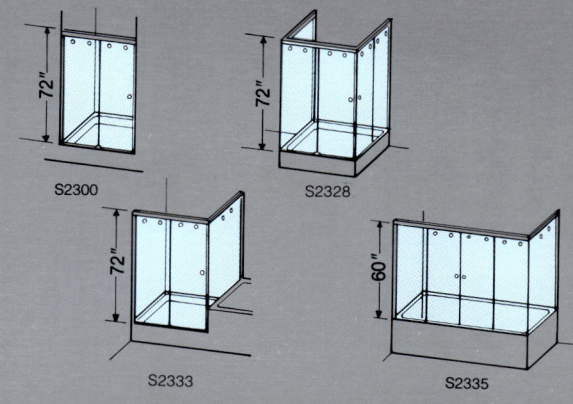

S2300 S2328
S2333 S2335

Series 782

Bi-folding doors are 8 millimeters thick of clear tempered glass. A horizontal rubber seal makes the unit watertight. The frame is extruded aluminum with a baked on enamel powder finish. The unit attaches to existing ceramic tile walls with masonry anchors and is leveled by adjustable set screws with 3/4" tolerance. The folding doors are reversible for left or right installations. Available in white, bone, black, chrome or brass.

Hastings
IL BAGNO COLLECTION

Hastings IL Bagno Collection has a complete line of bathroom fixtures and accessories in matching colors, including 1/4 turn ceramic disc faucets, basins, vanities, whirlpool baths and ceramic tile.

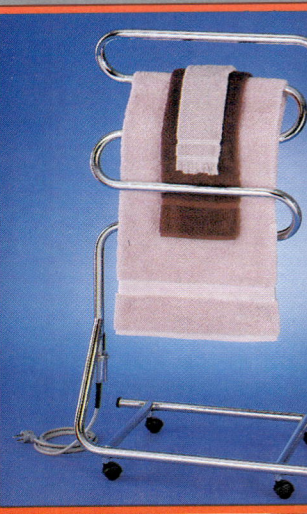

Model: SC782
Background Tile: Hastings Maschere Series

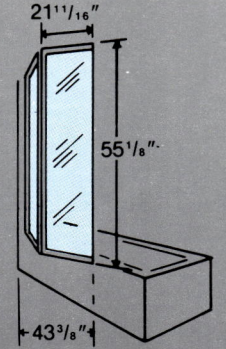

21¹¹/₁₆"

55¹/₈"

43³/₈"

GENERAL OFFICES
30 Commercial Street, Freeport, NY 11520
(516) 379-3500   FAX: (516) 379-3187

SHOWROOMS
230 Park Avenue South, New York, NY 10003
(212) 674-9700   FAX: (212) 674-8083

404 Northern Boulevard, Great Neck, NY 11201
(516) 482-1840   FAX: (516) 482-5350

1296-1298 Merchandise Mart, Chicago, IL 60654
(312) 527-0565   FAX: (312) 527-2537

680

TUB-MASTER®
Folding Shower Doors

Beauty and Convenience

TUB-MASTER...
The shower door your family will love.

TUB-MASTER folding shower door forever ends blowing shower curtains and keeps the floors dry.

BT 60

By-Passing and Folding Tub Enclosure

This uniquely designed folding door is the only by-passing tub enclosure that offers access to the tub. Simply unhook the outside and inside towel bar and TUB-MASTER's special panel-hinge design allows the doors to fold neatly to both sides. The Model BT's wide-open access makes bathing children and cleaning exceptionally easy. The high impact plastic makes it a safe and convenient alternate to standard glass by-pass doors.

By-Passing and Folding Shower Door

This Folding Door is designed expressly for large shower openings. Its unique design provides a "wide-open" access to the shower which makes cleaning easier and allows the shower to dry out faster, helping to prevent scale and mildew build-up on the tile. When the doors are closed, water stays in and the floors stay dry.

BS 60

Open, TUB-MASTER gives a more spacious feeling to the bathroom.

Lifetime Warranty

TUB-MASTER products are warranted against failure resulting from defects in material in its manufacture as long as you own the home where it was originally installed. TUB-MASTER has a one year commercial warranty.

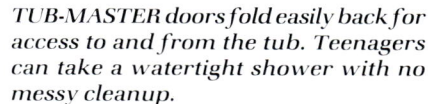

TUB-MASTER doors fold easily back for access to and from the tub. Teenagers can take a watertight shower with no messy cleanup.

Children enjoy the openness of the tub for playful bathing. These shower doors are completely safe and shatterproof.

FT 60

TUB-MASTER Space Saving Shower Doors

Open, the shower dries out quickly. The shower door folds back and doesn't re-quire a swing-radius of floor space as glass doors do.

FS 34

Doors available in contemporary bath decorator colors with polished gold, silver, antique, white, almond or gray frames.

Continuous Folding Tub Enclosure

The exclusive panel-hinge design allows the door to fold completely to either side, providing full access to the tub, making it both convenient and safe. An outstanding feature of this tub enclosure is a specially designed en-closed track that keeps the door securely "on track." Another feature is folding drying arms for mess-free drying in the tub.

Continuous Folding Shower Door

Known as the "space saver," this Continuous Folding Shower Door offers exceptional advantages over old fashioned blowing shower curtains and swinging glass doors. When the door is closed for showering the water stays in and the floor stays dry — alleviating the nuisance of old fashioned blowing shower curtains and mopping up wet floors. No extra floor space is required for a swing radius, making it ideal for smaller bathrooms.

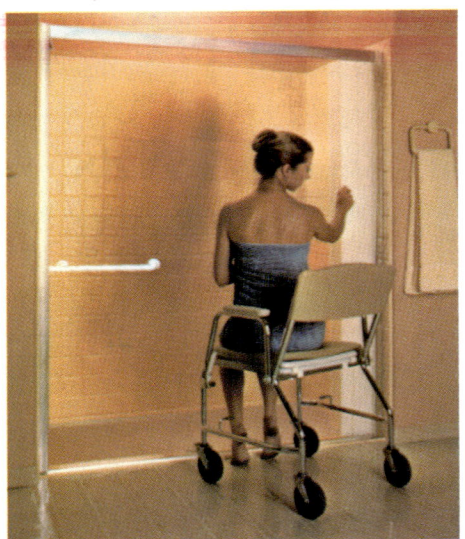

Barrier Free Shower Doors

Barrier Free shower doors are specially designed to allow totally unobstructed access to the tub or shower and still provide a shower door that keeps the water in and the bathroom floor dry. Barrier Free doors are available to fit any size tub or shower opening.

Shower Stall Shower Doors

Designed for installation in metal or plastic shower stalls and showers with small openings up to 36 inches. The FSI Model installs on the inside wall of the shower instead of between jambs. The door folds neatly behind the returns and thus does not take up needed space in small shower openings or require extra floor space for a swing radius.

Custom Shower Doors

All bathrooms are not created equal and TUB-MASTER rises to the challenge by providing custom shower and tub enclosures designed to fit your specifications. TUB-MASTER's extensive engineering and manufacturing capabilities can produce shower and tub enclosures to fit any need — without overextending your budget.

IMPORTANT

The wide variety of shower door sizes offered by TUB-MASTER to fit the different tub and shower opening sizes make it necessary for you to measure the opening carefully…to insure prompt, efficient handling of your orders.

HOW TO ORDER TUB-MASTER DOORS

1. Indicate TUB-MASTER style — "B" deluxe or "F" standard.
2. Whether for tub "T" or shower "S."
3. Check opening size — width and height for accuracy.
4. Select frame color — gold, silver, antique, white, almond or gray.
5. Choose panel and hinge color.
6. When ordering doors for Fiberglass tub/shower modules, please list manufacturer's name, model number, **width and height of opening.**

WHERE TO MEASURE

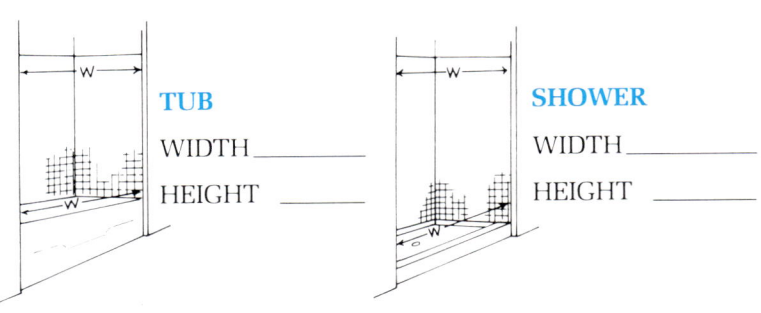

TUB
WIDTH _____
HEIGHT _____

SHOWER
WIDTH _____
HEIGHT _____

BEAUTIFUL DECORATOR COLOR HINGES AND PANELS*

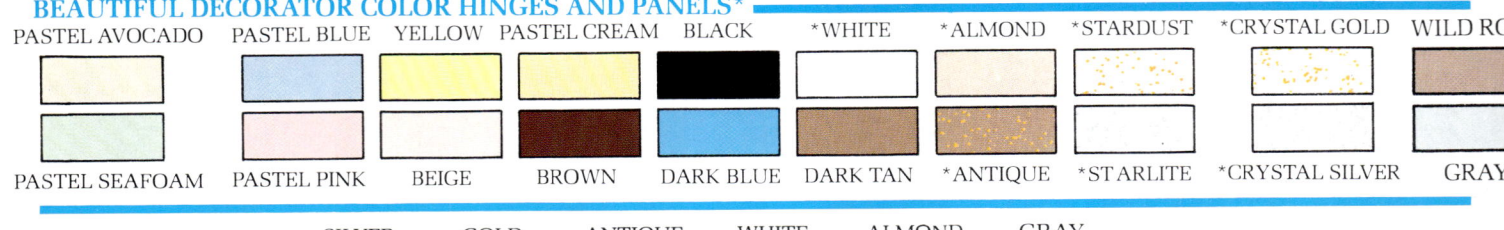

| PASTEL AVOCADO | PASTEL BLUE | YELLOW | PASTEL CREAM | BLACK | *WHITE | *ALMOND | *STARDUST | *CRYSTAL GOLD | WILD RO |
| PASTEL SEAFOAM | PASTEL PINK | BEIGE | BROWN | DARK BLUE | DARK TAN | *ANTIQUE | *STARLITE | *CRYSTAL SILVER | GRAY |

FRAME COLORS

| SILVER | GOLD | ANTIQUE | WHITE | ALMOND | GRAY |

TUB-MASTER Corp.

Made in the USA

Home Office: 413 Virginia Drive, Orlando, Florida 32803, 1-407-898-2881
Branch Plant: 1866 Lake Place, Ontario, California 91761, 1-714-947-0777

TMCP PP 25M 11/90

The Fine Art Of Showering

WORK RIGHT

MASTER DESIGNED SHOWER ENVIRONMENTS

Where Beauty And Comfort Combine

At last . . . a shower environment as refreshing to the eye as it is to the body. From the master shower designers at Work Right, innovators in frameless design, comes the Work Right shower environment: the ultimate combination of beauty and functionality.

Work Right master designed shower environments offer the finest in modern shower design. Space-opening frameless doors. Butted glass corners. Glass that's sparkling clear, warmly bronzed or coolly frosted. High Light™ finishes that coordinate with today's dramatic fixtures. A range of shapes limited only by your imagination. With Work Right you can enclose a tub, turn a shower into a steam room, even create a central showerscape as a focus for your master bath.

Traditional and contemporary, large and small — Work Right showers highlight over one million of the finest hotel and home bathrooms around the world.

"It took Work Right to turn the shower from a basic plumbing fixture into a sophisticated design element with flexibility that keeps my bath designs fresh and invigorating. Once my clients have seen a Work Right shower environment, they won't settle for anything else." — Interior designer

Quality Craftsmanship Brings Pleasure To All Your Senses

A glance at this book will show you that a Work Right shower environment is beautiful from the outside. But the real beauty can't be shown here . . . because it lies in the precision

engineering that makes every Work Right shower a delight to the senses.

We start with the best materials: heavy extruded aluminum frames, tempered safety glass, vinyl seals, nylon latches and rollers. Then we add precision-engineered details developed over nearly two decades. Smooth-moving, extra-quiet doors. No-drip sloping drain bars. Vinyl-sealed door jambs to keep the water inside where it belongs. A patented latch system. Adjustable jambs for out-of-plumb walls. Even extra-deep towel bars for your fluffiest towels.

For the final touch, we add a High Light™ finish as unique and beautiful as your bathroom: buffed and bright dipped metals or powder-coated paints, color-coordinated to today's dramatic fixtures. And these three steps — materials plus engineering plus finishes — add up to quality.

It's care like this that makes the Work Right shower environment more than just another pretty space — that creates a luxurious environment for a daily retreat into refreshment.

A Lifetime Of Easy, Worry-Free Enjoyment

I t's your shower's job to keep you clean . . . not the other way around.

Our frameless swinging, sliding and pivot doors eliminate dirt-gathering edges and corners — and for extra maintenance ease, we've even developed a unique open track design that lets you clean the base of a sliding door with a single wipe.

And your Work Right shower is as safe as it is clean. Heavy extruded aluminum frames and 3/16″ tempered safety glass exceed required safety codes to maximize your home and family's well-being.

"You don't even have to explain to buyers that Work Right showers are safe and easy to maintain. Just the clean, open look and the solid 'feel' of the doors and fixtures are enough to tell the story — and make the sale." — Homebuilder

Courtesy American Olean

Frameless Sliding Panels

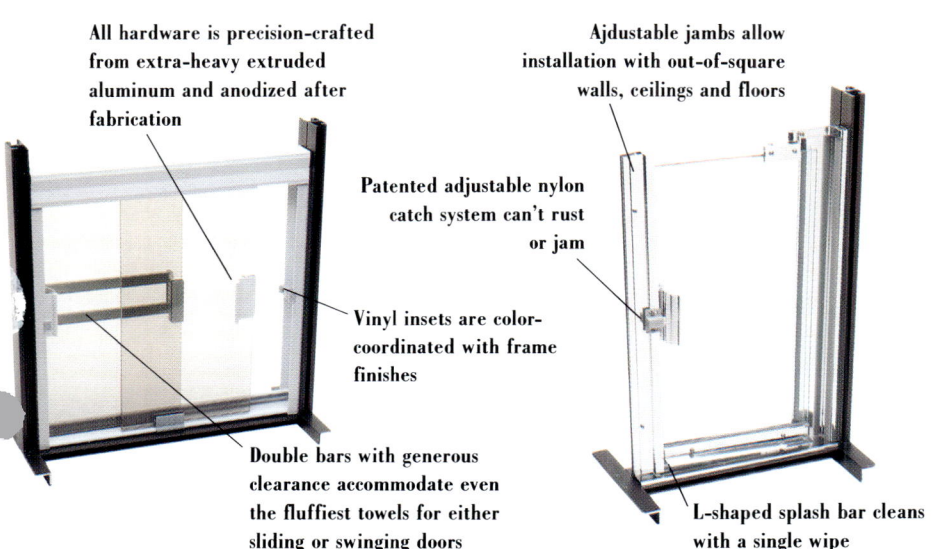

All hardware is precision-crafted from extra-heavy extruded aluminum and anodized after fabrication

Vinyl insets are color-coordinated with frame finishes

Double bars with generous clearance accommodate even the fluffiest towels for either sliding or swinging doors

Frameless Pivot Door

Ajdustable jambs allow installation with out-of-square walls, ceilings and floors

Patented adjustable nylon catch system can't rust or jam

L-shaped splash bar cleans with a single wipe

Frameless Shower Door

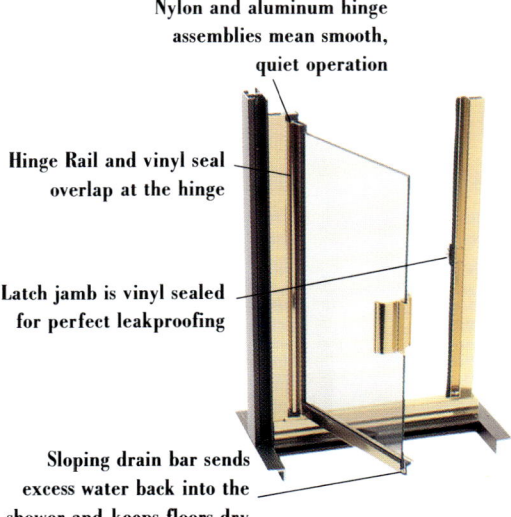

Nylon and aluminum hinge assemblies mean smooth, quiet operation

Hinge Rail and vinyl seal overlap at the hinge

Latch jamb is vinyl sealed for perfect leakproofing

Sloping drain bar sends excess water back into the shower and keeps floors dry

A Pleasure To Install

Your installer doesn't have to be an artist to create a Work Right shower environment.

All Work Right showers feature modular construction for easy component availability — no more waiting weeks for parts from the factory. Each model is precut, drilled and packaged complete at our factory for easy job site installation. We've even developed a patented adjustable frame for out-of-level or out-of-plumb wall openings.

Best of all, each of our 200-plus certified dealer/installers nationwide is factory-trained, required to maintain stock on hand, and backed by one of the industry's most comprehensive systems of technical support. We'll provide your installer — and you — with color chips, specification sheets, line drawings, installation instructions and application suggestions.

We offer everything to help you get a great-looking, well-installed shower every time.

FULL HEIGHT SHOWER DOOR MODEL D-1000		
FOR OPENINGS	HEIGHT	USE MODEL
20" to 21"	66⅝"	D-1000-20
21" to 22"	66⅝"	D-1000-21
		........THROUGH
34" to 35"	66⅝"	D-1000-34
1" adjustable jambs, header and curb available as option		

STALL SHOWER MODEL SS-1190-34		
FOR OPENINGS	HEIGHT	USE MODEL
Up to 34" x 34"	69"	SS-1190-34
panel and full height door at 90°		

PIVOT DOOR MODEL D-2000P		
FOR OPENINGS	HEIGHT	USE MODEL
24½" to 26½"	67¼"	D-2000P-24 to 26
26½" to 28½"	67¼"	D-2000P-26 to 28
28½" to 30½"	67¼"	D-2000P-28 to 30
30½" to 32½"	67¼"	D-2000P-30 to 32
32½" to 34½"	67¼"	D-2000P-32 to 34
34½" to 36½"	67¼"	D-2000P-34 to 36
2" adjustable jambs, no header, with full curb		

STALL SHOWER MODEL SS-1190-38		
FOR OPENINGS	HEIGHT	USE MODEL
Up to 38" x 38"	69"	SS-1190-38
Up to 48" x 48"	69"	SS-1190-48
two panels and full height door at 90°		

STALL SHOWER MODEL SS-11180		
FOR OPENINGS	HEIGHT	USE MODEL
34" to 42"	69"	SS-11180-42
43" to 48"	69"	SS-11180-48
49" to 60"	69"	SS-11180-60
60" to 72"	69"	SS-11180-72*
panel and full height door in line		
* door centered between two side panels		

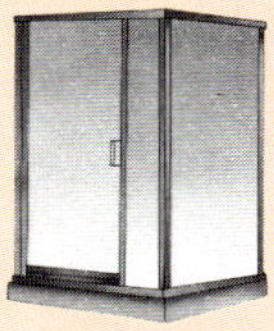

STALL SHOWER MODEL SS-11135		
FOR OPENINGS	HEIGHT	USE MODEL
Up to		
24" x 27" x 24"	69"	SS-11135-38
two panels and full height door — neo angle		

Create Your Own Work Of Art

With Work Right, now the highlight of your day — your shower — can be the highlight of your home as well.

Start with the knowledge that you've chosen a shower environment that's been master-designed for the ultimate in beauty and functionality. Then select the functions, shapes and finishes that complement the decor in each bathroom in your home.

And when you're through, you'll have something very special. A treat for the eye, a treat for the body. A Work Right master designed shower environment.

For complete design information, or the location of your nearest Work Right dealer/installer, call 800/358-9064 (800/862-4995 from California).

"I've been a Work Right dealer for four years now. It's the easiest product in my showroom to sell and service — and it's also a real attention-getter."

— Bathroom fixtures showroom owner

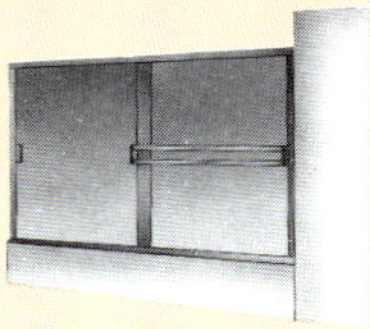

SLIDING TUB/SHOWER ENCLOSURE 1400 SERIES

FOR OPENINGS	USE MODEL	
	Tub 57⅜" HT	Shower 70⅜" HT
Up to 42"	TE-1400-42	SE-1400-42
42" to 48"	TE-1400-48	SE-1400-48
48" to 54"	TE-1400-54	SE-1400-54
54" to 60"	TE-1400-60	SE-1400-60
60" to 66"	TE-1400-66	SE-1400-66

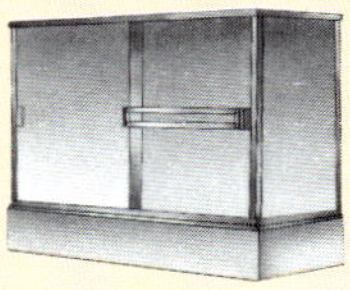

SLIDING TUB/SHOWER ENCLOSURE 1400 SERIES

FOR OPENINGS	USE MODEL	
SLIDERS up to 60" with 12" in-line panel	Tub 57⅜" HT TE-1400-1-72	Shower 70⅜" HT SE-1400-1-72
SLIDERS Up to 60" with 24" in-line panel	Tub 57⅜" HT TE-1400-1-84	Shower 70⅜" HT SE-1400-1-84

SLIDING TUB/SHOWER ENCLOSURE 1400 SERIES

FOR OPENINGS	USE MODEL	
SLIDERS up to 60" with two 12" in-line panels	Tub 57⅜" HT TE-1400-2-84	Shower 70⅜" HT SE-1400-2-84

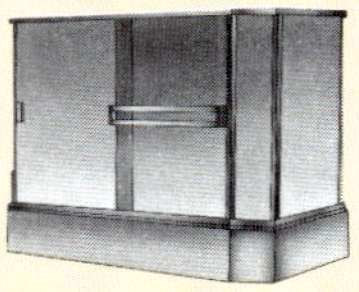

SLIDING TUB/SHOWER ENCLOSURE 1400 SERIES

SLIDERS up to 60" with 36" end panel	Tub 57⅜" HT TE-1400-3	Shower 70⅜" HT SE-1400-3
with 90° end panel		

SLIDING TUB/SHOWER ENCLOSURE 1400 SERIES

FOR OPENINGS	USE MODEL	
SLIDERS up to 60" with 12" & 24" end panels	Tub 57⅜" HT TE-1400-4	Shower 70⅜" HT SE-1400-4
with neo-angle end panels		

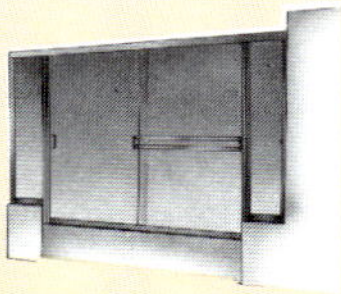

Options

Tracks: 1400 Series ships with open tracks. To order a "W" track use a 1200 Series designation. All resulting heights will be 3/8" less than the 1400 Series listings.

Towel bars: Available on any system
Finishes: Silver, gold, heritage brass, black, white, red or custom.
Glass: Clear, obscure, bronze, or custom etched.

Guide Specifications

Part 1 General

1.1 Work included: Provide shower doors as needed for a complete and proper installation

1.2 Related work by others

  a. Shower receptor base (specify one — tile shower pan, pre-fab shower pan, bathtub)

  b. Wall surface (specify one — tile, marble, cultured marble, fiberglass/plastic, non-porous watertight material

  c. Sealants and caulking (specify a compatible sealant for aluminum and glass)

1.3 Quality assurance

  a. Mock up/sample installation Factory approved mock up sample will represent minimum quality for the work

  b. Source quality control Factory tests for metal hardness, finish and dimensional tolerance

  c. Code compliance
    ANSI 297.1
    CPSC 16CFR1201
    ASTM C1048-85
    USFS DD-G-1403B

1.4 Delivery, storage and handling by others

  a. Deliver to job site door(s) assembled and ready for installation

  b. Store off ground, under cover, protected from weather and construction activities

  c. Do not lay glass flat either in transport or storage

1.5 Sequencing/Scheduling
  Shower door(s) are to be installed only after related work 1.2a and 1.2b is completed

Part 2 Systems

2.1 Specified system or equal
  Work Right Products, Inc.
  Oakland, CA
  (specify one: D-1000, D-2000-P, TE-1200, TE-1400, SE-1200, SE-1400, SS-11180, SS-1190, SS-11135)

2.2 Materials

  a. Shower door(s) shall be constructed of (specify clear, obscure, bronzed or custom etched) 3/16" tempered safety glass with all exposed edges polished and rounded.

  b. Aluminum sections shall be 6463 T5 aluminum alloy with a minimum thickness of .062"

  c. Aluminum sections shall be buffed and bright dipped anodized or powder coat painted (specify finish or color)

  d. Swinging shower door(s) shall have vinyl seal at both the latch jamb and hinge jamb side of door

  e. Sliding shower enclosures shall have patented roller brackets at the top of each sliding panel

2.3 Fabrication

  a. Shop assembly of doors and sliding panels shall be completed prior to delivery to job site

  b. Fabrication of metal for out-of-plumb or out-of-level conditions exceeding normal adjustments shall be done prior to installation

  c. Roller brackets for clear glass sliding panels shall be bonded to glass with silicone sealant 24 hours prior to installation

  d. Handles shall be secured by means of pressure fitting (Options) System shall include (choose) towel bars, anti-splash bar or adjustable sloping drain bar

  e. Sliding shower enclosures shall have one piece, pressure fitted handles and roller brackets

Part 3 Execution

3.1 Surface preparation
  Prior to installation of unit, installer shall be sure that surface is free from foreign matter that could compromise the watertight bond of unit to surface (e.g., rust, dirt, grease, paint, mastic, taping compound, etc.)

3.2 Installation
  Unit(s) shall be installed consistent with current manufacturer's guidelines and instructions

3.3 Field quality control
  Installer shall be responsible to test that door operates smoothly and that at no time does the glass come into contact with metal during normal operation

3.4 Adjusting and cleaning
  Installer shall be responsible for adjusting door operation and for securing the owner care and maintenance card to unit

WORK RIGHT

MASTER DESIGNED SHOWER ENVIRONMENTS

Oakland, CA
Call (800) 358-9064
California (800) 862-4995
Intl. (707) 263-0290
FAX (707) 263-4048

U.S. Pat. No. 3,827,737; 3,796,405; 3,787,936; 4,484,411

Member
NGA
National Glass Association

NATIONAL KITCHEN & BATH ASSOCIATION
NKBA
MANUFACTURER
COUNCIL

bema
BATH ENCLOSURE
MANUFACTURERS
ASSOCIATION

Geberit Bath Waste and Overflow

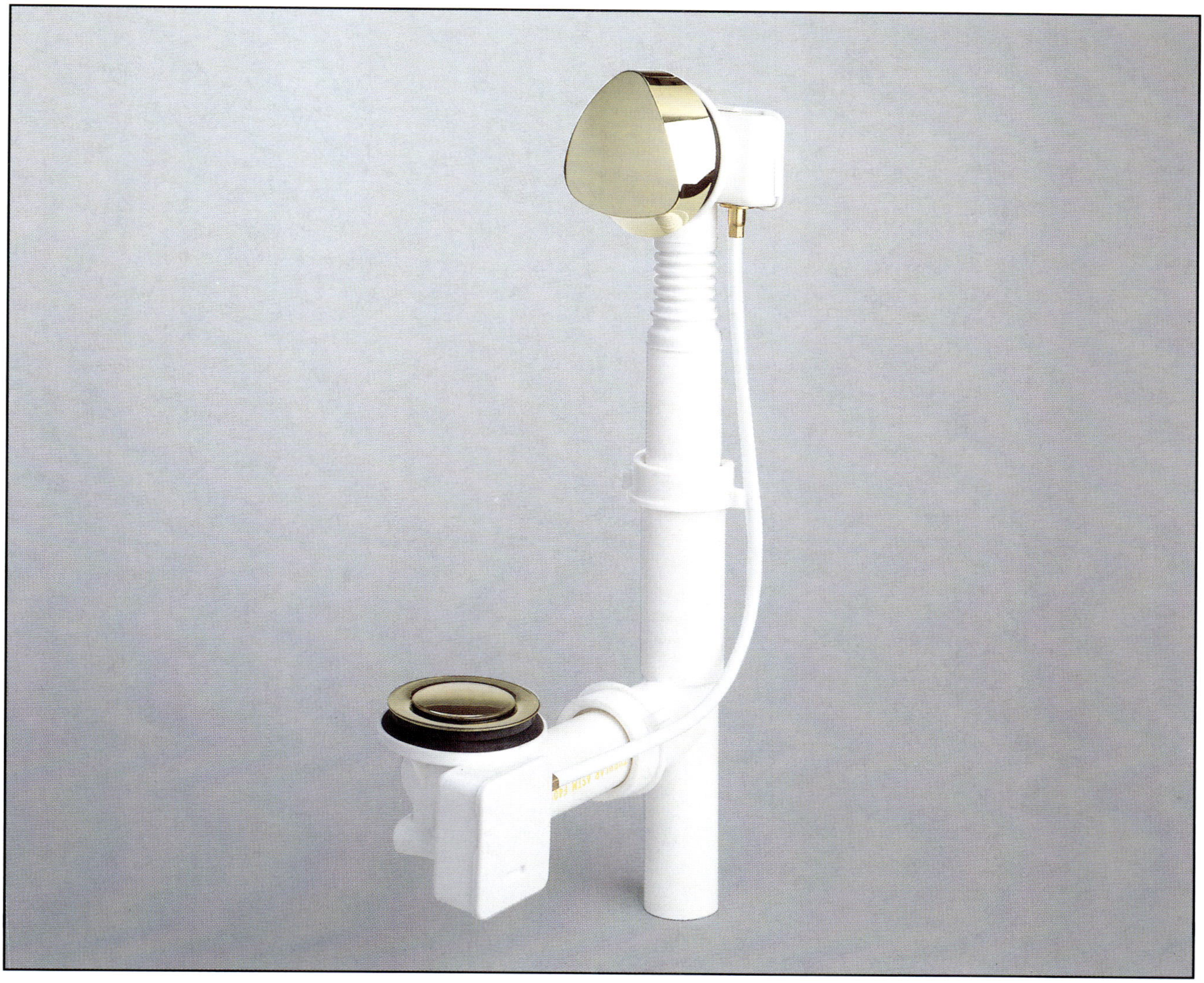

Now European styling for demanding Americans with the elegance and performance that's perfect for up-graded bath designs.

GEBERIT

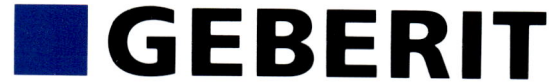

Your best bath designs deserve the Geberit finishing touch.

Complement the artistry of the finest bath decor with the most appropriate trim for tub or whirlpool. Finishes are now available to match popular faucet treatments. A quarter turn of the distinctively contoured Geberit handle provides a beautiful and smooth drain function.

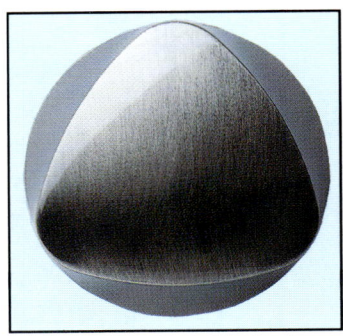
Old Silver (Pewter)

Bright Brass

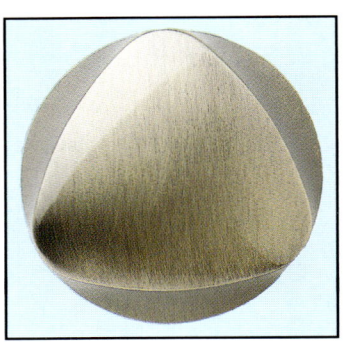
Antique Brass

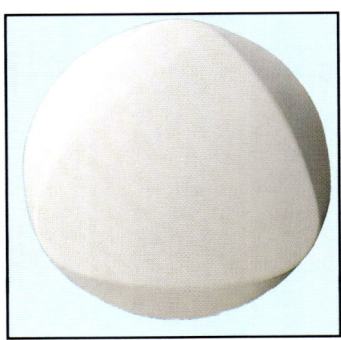
Chrome

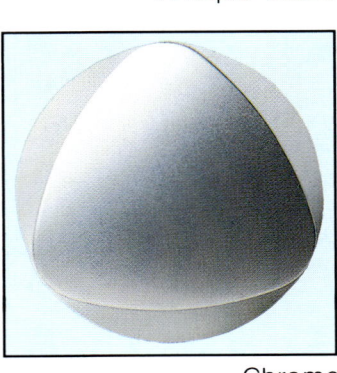
Bone

Gold

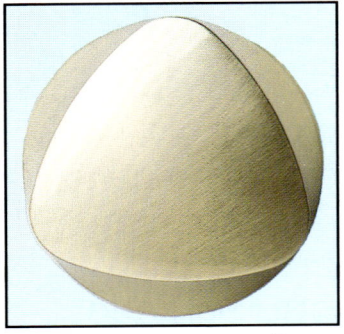
Satin Brass

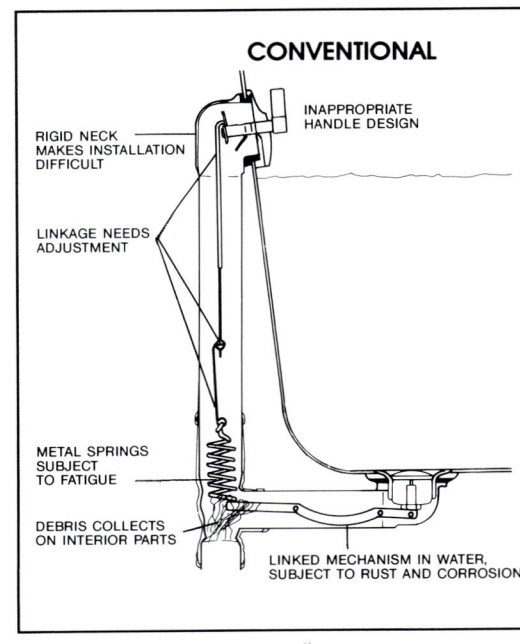
CONVENTIONAL

RIGID NECK MAKES INSTALLATION DIFFICULT

INAPPROPRIATE HANDLE DESIGN

LINKAGE NEEDS ADJUSTMENT

METAL SPRINGS SUBJECT TO FATIGUE

DEBRIS COLLECTS ON INTERIOR PARTS

LINKED MECHANISM IN WATER, SUBJECT TO RUST AND CORROSION

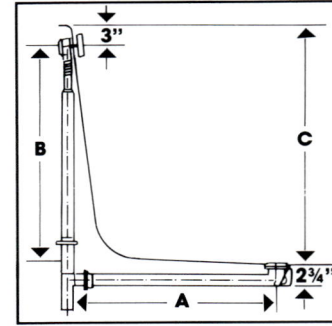

Engineered for years of trouble-free performance.

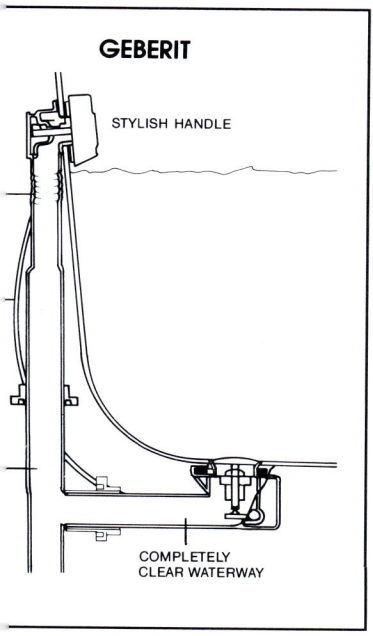

GEBERIT

STYLISH HANDLE

COMPLETELY
CLEAR WATERWAY

Compare! The conventional design has always been a trouble-maker. Waste entangles with the inside mechanism, slowing the flow and eventually clogging the drain. Metal parts corrode, weaken, separate and leak!

The time is right for a truly reliable design! Geberit puts critical working parts outside, away from the water! Waste flows freely through sturdy, non-corrosive PVC tubing. The drain plug is actuated by a rigidly mounted encased Bowden cable made of nickel chromium steel. It never needs adjustment, assuring perfect performance every time.

Geberit's exclusive flexible neck adjusts to an exact fit in all tubs, acrylic, fiberglass, cast iron, steel, marble. The PVC slip tee and 1½″ tailpiece make installation easy. For drain connection, use solvent weld or 1½″ slip joint.

There's no doubt. When you specify Geberit, you've selected the very best bath waste and overflow in the business!

Geberit Bath Waste and Overflow Specifications

MODEL NO. SERIES	A MAXIMUM	B MAXIMUM	C MAXIMUM TOTAL DEPTH
150.165	6″	14″	16″
150.156	8″	19″	22″
150.157	12″	24″	27″
150.158	20″	26″	29″

Custom sizes available on request
In Compliance with: **ASTM F409**

CAN/CSA · B125 · M89

L 11327
B125

White

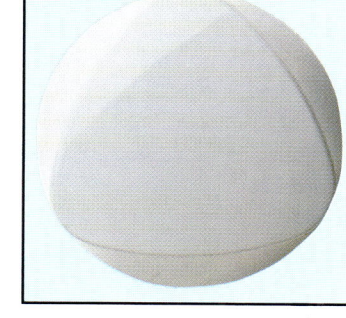

Grey

Geberit Bath Waste and Overflow Ordering Guide

Bath Waste and Overflow with Trim Kit for Acrylic, Fiberglass, Cast Iron or Steel Tubs and Whirlpools				
FINISH	12" - 16" DEPTH	16'' - 22'' DEPTH	22'' - 27'' DEPTH	22'' - 29'' DEPTH
Chrome	150.165.21	150.156.21	150.157.21	150.158.21
Gold	150.165.45	150.156.45	150.157.45	150.158.45
Antique Brass	150.165.97	150.156.97	150.157.97	150.158.97
Old Silver (Pewter)	150.165.98	150.156.98	150.157.98	150.158.98
Satin Brass	150.165.CH	150.156.CH	150.157.CH	150.158.CH
Bright Brass	150.165.CL	150.156.CL	150.157.CL	150.158.CL
White	150.165.DY	150.156.DY	150.157.DY	150.158.DY
Bone	150.165.AA	150.156.AA	150.157.AA	150.158.AA
Grey	150.165.DX	150.156.DX	150.157.DX	150.158.DX
Solid Brass Chrome	150.185.21	150.176.21	150.177.21	150.178.21
Solid Brass Gold	150.185.45	150.176.45	150.177.45	150.178.45
Solid Brass Polished	150.185.85	150.176.85	150.177.85	150.178.85
Solid Brass Antique	150.185.97	150.176.97	150.177.97	150.178.97

For Acrylic, Fiberglass, Cast Iron or Steel Tubs and Whirlpools

Bath Waste and Overflow without Trim Kits	
MODEL NO.	TUB DEPTH
150.165.00	12" - 16"
150.156.00	16'' - 22''
150.157.00	22'' - 27''
150.158.00	22'' - 29''
Trim Kits	
FINISH	MODEL NO.
Chrome	254.809.21
Gold	254.809.45
Antique Brass	254.809.97
Old Silver (Pewter)	254.809.98
Satin Brass	254.809.CH
Bright Brass	254.809.CL
White	240.725.DY
Bone	240.725.AA
Grey	240.725.DX
Solid Brass Chrome	240.722.21
Solid Brass Gold	240.722.45
Solid Brass Polished	240.722.85
Solid Brass Antique	240.722.97

For Cultured Marble Tubs and Whirlpools

Bath Waste and Overflow without Trim Kits	
MODEL NO.	TUB DEPTH
150.186.00	12" - 16"
150.172.00	16'' - 22''
150.173.00	22'' - 27''
150.174.00	22'' - 29''
Trim Kits	
FINISH	MODEL NO.
Chrome	240.706.21
Gold	240.706.45
Antique Brass	240.706.97
Old Silver (Pewter)	240.706.98
Satin Brass	240.706.CH
Bright Brass	240.706.CL
White	240.726.DY
Bone	240.726.AA
Grey	240.726.DX
Solid Brass Chrome	240.707.21
Solid Brass Gold	240.707.45
Solid Brass Polished	240.707.85
Solid Brass Antique	240.707.97

1 year limited warranty
Warranty on finishes other than chrome is 90 days.

Geberit Manufacturing, Inc.
P.O. Box 2008, 1100 Boone Drive
Michigan City, IN 46360

Toll Free: 1 (800) 225-7217
(219) 879-4466
Fax: (219) 872-8003

 **GEBERIT**

Form #1364 - 1190 - 20M

Geberit Remote Control Kitchen Drain.

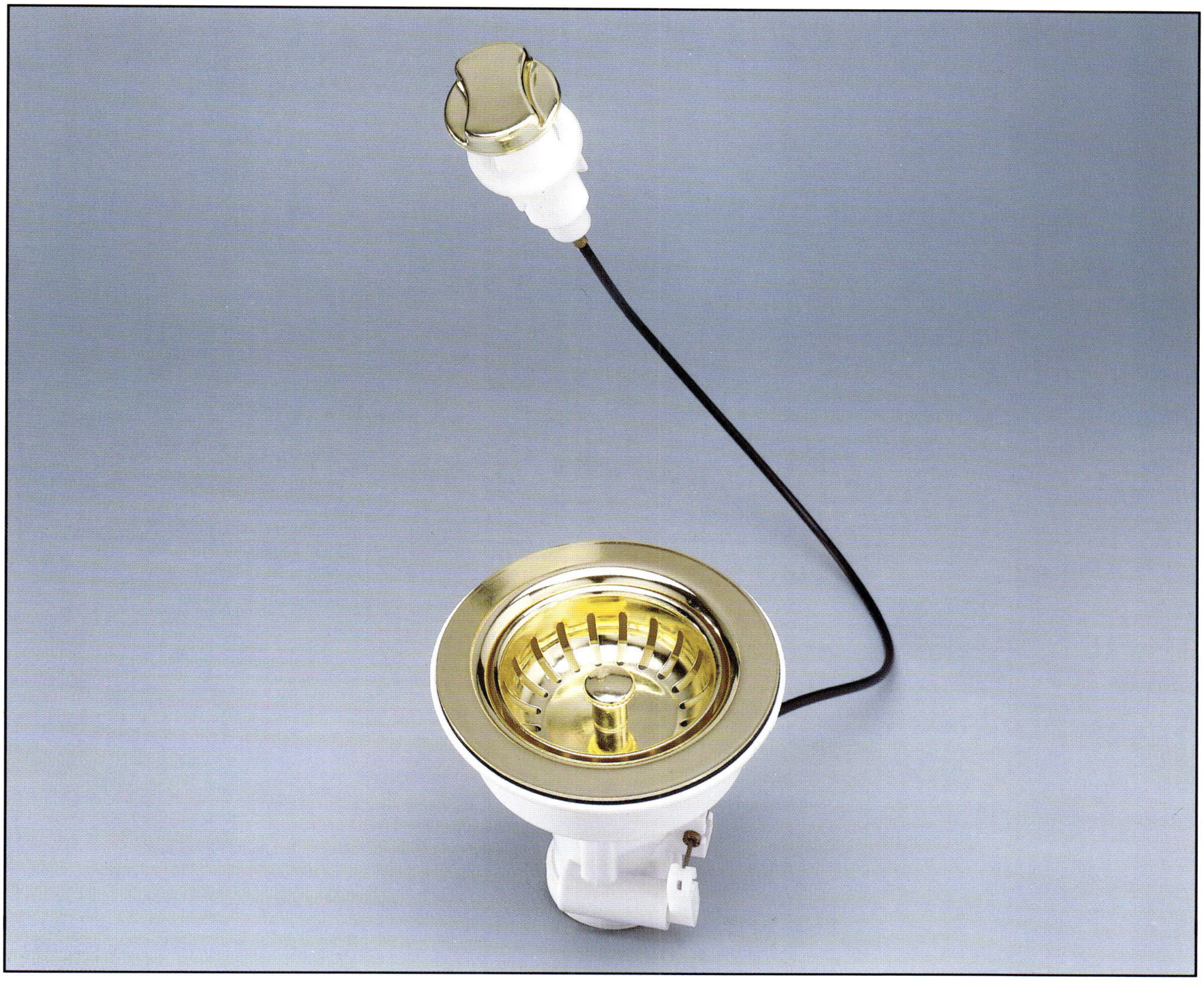

Here's the latest convenience for the kitchen sink, styled to match the popular European look. This up-grade opens and closes with an easy turn of its deck-mounted knob.

GEBERIT

Precision designed and quality built... so it always works like a charm!

Now, there's no need to move dishes, pans, or put hands in the water to lift the basket strainer.

The easy to operate drain is actuated by a rigidly mounted encased Bowden cable made of nickel chromium steel. It never needs adjustment, assuring perfect performance every time. A positive drain seal prevents leakage. The unit delivers trouble-free service with no maintenance.

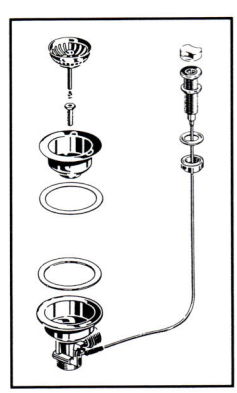

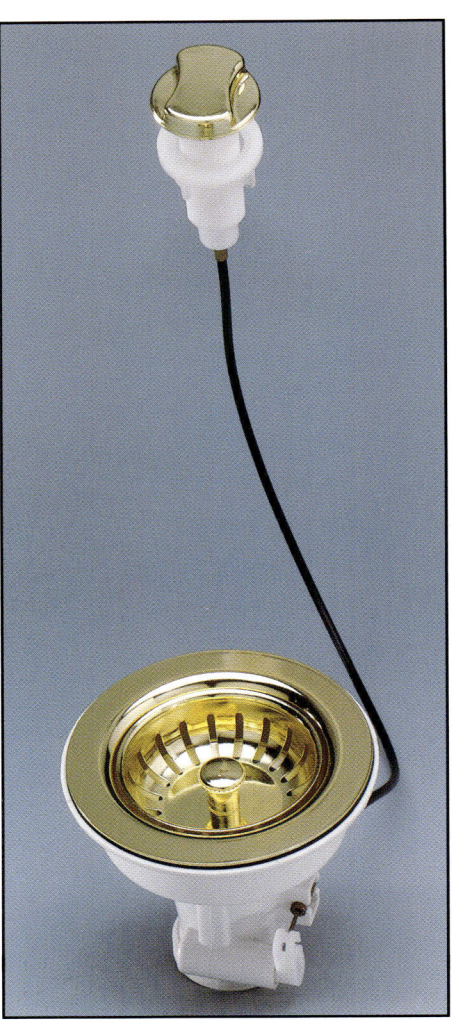

The Geberit Remote Control Kitchen Drain includes a stainless steel basket strainer and flange. Its non-corrosive drain fits into the standard 3½'' opening in all stainless, cast iron, enameled steel, and composite sinks. A normal deck hole accomodates the control knob. That's an easy-to-install kitchen up-grade!

FINISH	MODEL NO.
Chrome	152.106.21
Bright Brass	152.106.CL
White	152.106.DY
Almond	152.106.EJ
Black	152.106.EK
Grey	152.106.DX

Geberit Manufacturing, Inc.
P.O. Box 2008, 1100 Boone Drive
Michigan City, IN 46360

Toll Free: 1 (800) 225-7217
(219) 879-4466
Fax: (219) 872-8003

BALDWIN® BATH

EPIC™ ACCESSORIES

BALDWIN —
Where Design and Quality Create an American Tradition

For over forty years, Baldwin has been building a worldwide position of leadership in solid brass products for the home: architectural hardware, lighting and home furnishing accessories that are unmatched for design integrity and brilliance of finish. Now this same excellence of design, of uncompromising quality, comes to the bath... from the most classic to the most contemporary.

BALDWIN BATH/EPIC ACCESSORIES — UNCOMPROMISING QUALITY

Baldwin Bath/Epic Accessories are produced in the U.S.A. from solid brass through a Forging Process to yield a denser, stronger, heavier product. The smooth, blemish-free surface of each piece is meticulously polished to a brilliant luster and carefully protected by a clear baked-on coating for durability and ease of maintenance. All designs feature concealed mounting to eliminate visible fasteners and provide a tamper-proof installation.

Every imaginable detail including distinctively designed packaging has been considered to offer the highest standard of service. Each box includes all required fasteners for any condition, installation tools and simple step by step instructions.

Elegant Designs. Uncompromising Quality. Reliable Performance.

Baldwin Bath/Epic Accessories... a new tradition for the most exciting baths in residential and commercial installations.

LEXINGTON®

Warm. Inviting. The open, generous styling of Lexington accessories creates a charm that is notably American.

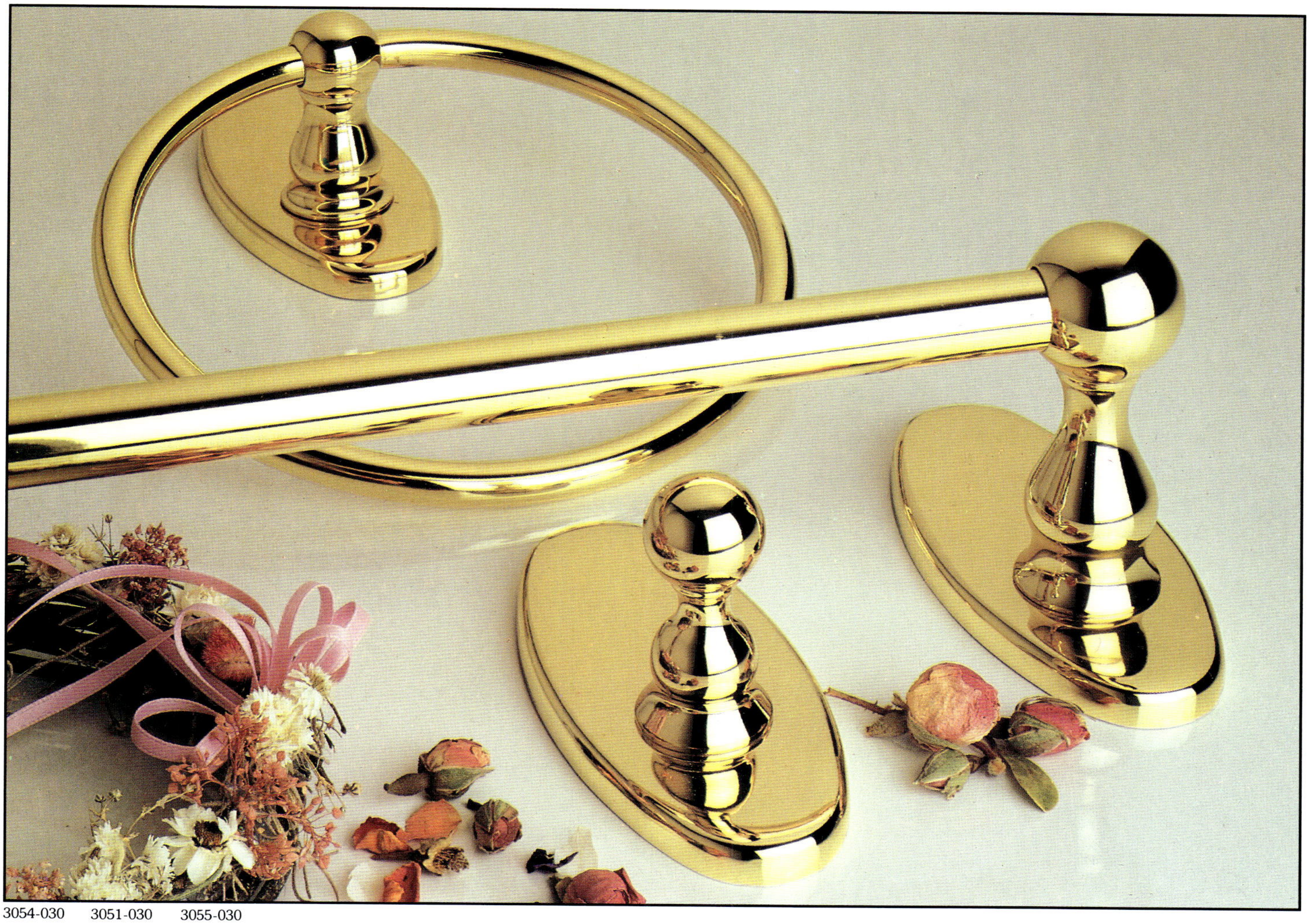

3054-030 3051-030 3055-030

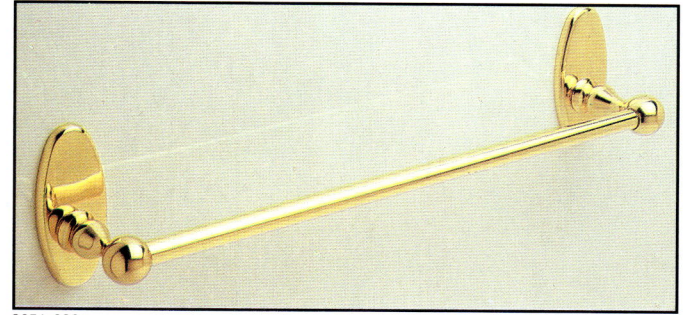

3051-030

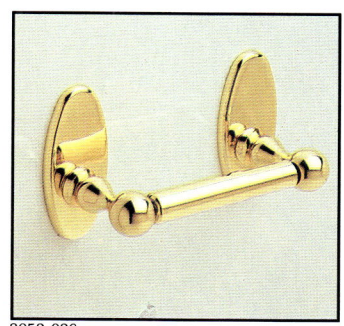

3053-030

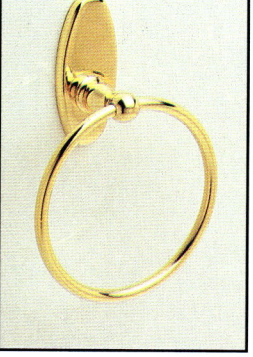

3054-030

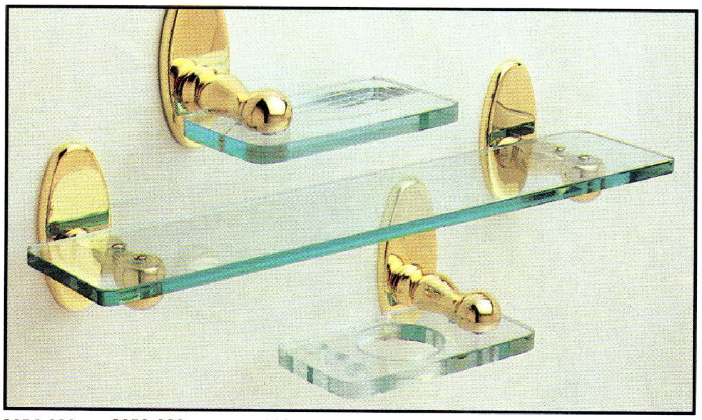

3056-030 3058-030 3057-030

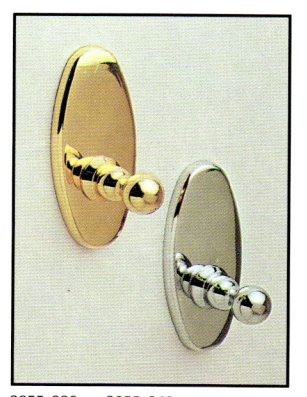

3055-030 3055-260

PARAGON®

Distinguished. Masterful. Polished metal on metal
makes a commanding architectural statement in the Paragon bath.

3274-253   3271-253

3271-326   3271-253   3271-256

3274-253

3275-253

3273-253

3276-253   3278-253   3277-253

GEORGETOWN®

Grace. Charm. Understated elegance reflected in the
traditional style of Georgetown bath appointments.

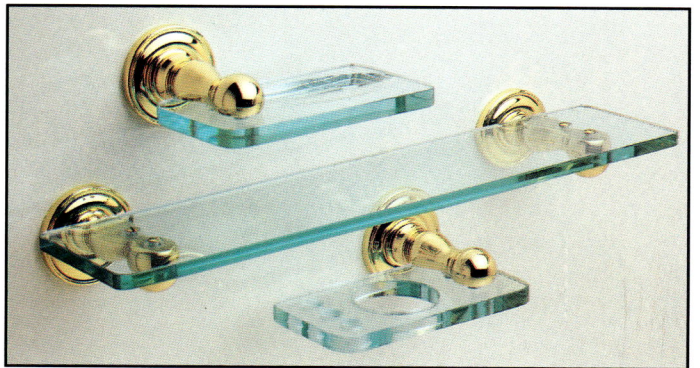

3011-030   3014-030

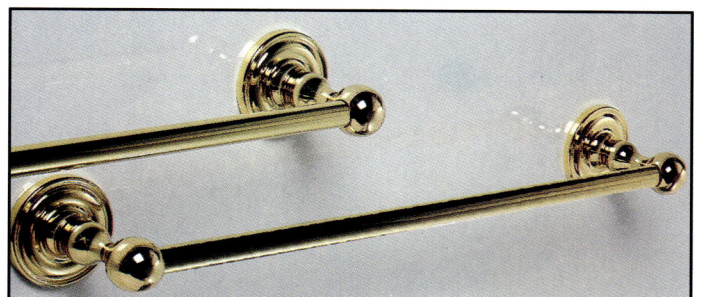

3011-030

3013-030   3013-030-BP

3015-030

3016-030   3018-030   3017-030

D A L L A S ®

Bold. New. Far reaching. Where baths are ample and boldly designed
for fresh contemporary Dallas elegance.

3221-030-A   3221-030

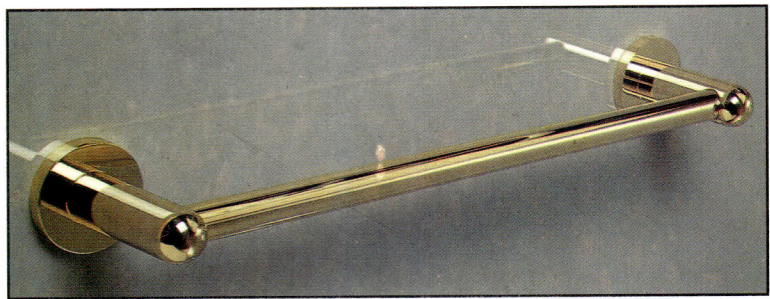

3221-030

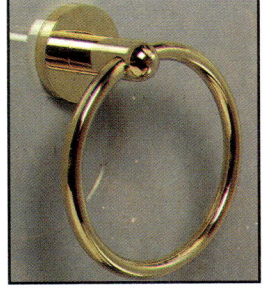

3224-030

3224-030-A

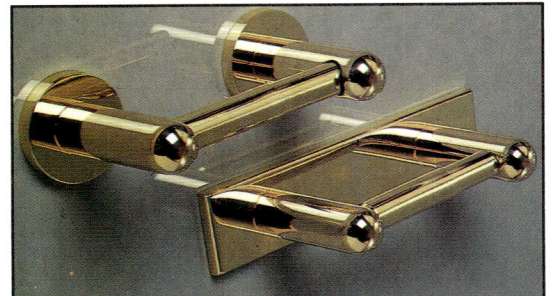

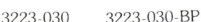

3223-030   3223-030-BP

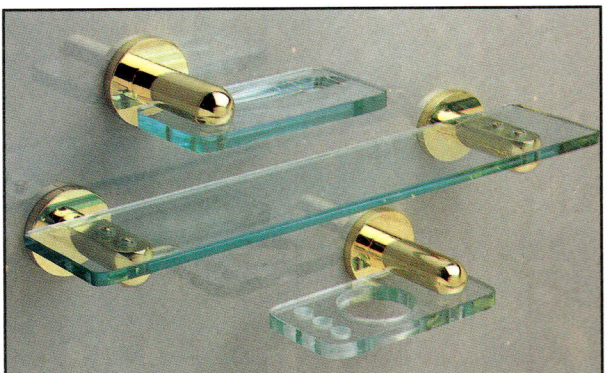

3226-030   3228-030   3227-030

3225-030

VICTORIA®/ HAMPTON®

Refined. Gracious. The dignified elegance of a bygone era is reflected in timeless Limoges porcelain.
Hampton is designed with black and Victoria with white Limoges porcelain.

3111-260   3101-030   3105-030

3111-030   3101-030

3113-030   3103-030

3115-030   3105-030

3114-030

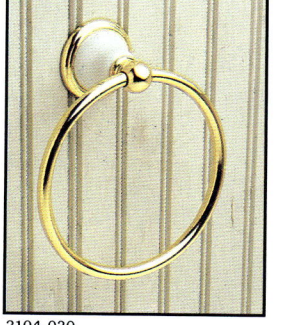

3104-030

3116-030   3117-030   3106-030   3107-030

PALM BEACH®

Fashionable. International. Easy going luxury and impeccable taste are
reflected in traditionally styled Palm Beach bath interiors.

3035-030   3031-030

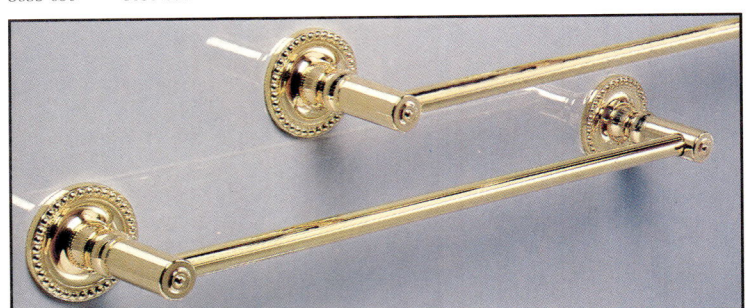

3031-030

3034-030

3033-030   3033-030-BP

3036-030   3038-030   3037-030

A T L A N T A ®

Antebellum heritage. Towers of chrome and glass. In home and bath there are contrasts
as well, further accented by the brilliant Atlanta contemporary design.

3245-326   3244-326

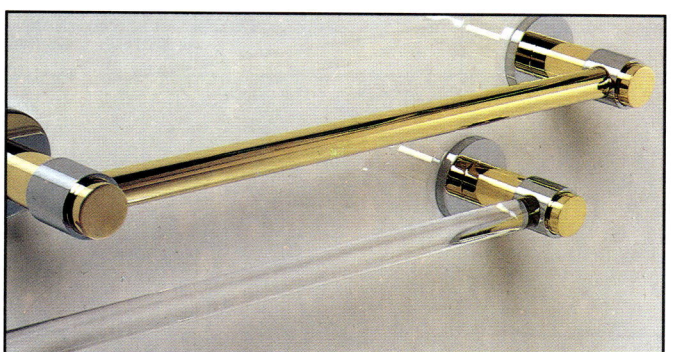

3241-326   3241-326-A

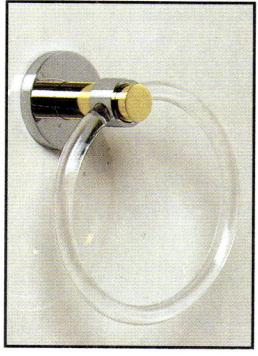

3244-326-A

3245-326

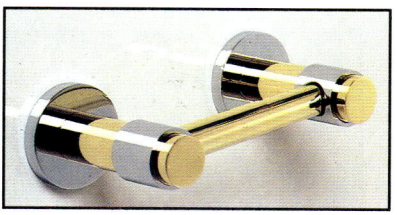

3243-326

3243-326-BP

3266-030   3268-030   3267-030

AVAILABLE FINISHES AND COORDINATES

Series	Lexington	Paragon	Dallas	Victoria	Hampton	Palm Beach	Atlanta	Georgetown	Cambridge	New York	New Orleans	Manhattan	Palm Springs	Solid Towel Bars
Finishes														
Polished Brass (030)	•		•	•	•	•	•	•	•	•	•	•	•	•
Polished Chrome (260)	•		•	•	•		•	•	•	•		•	•	•
Antique Brass (060)								•	•					
Polished Brass/ Polished Chrome (326)		•					•							
Polished Black Nickel/ Polished Brass (253)		•												
Polished Black Nickel/ Polished Chrome (256)		•												
Polished Chrome/ Polished Brass (263)												•		
Polished Black Nickel (250)													•	
Satin Nickel/ Polished Brass (153)							•							

COORDINATE OPTIONS

	Lexington	Paragon	Dallas	Victoria	Hampton	Palm Beach	Atlanta	Georgetown	Cambridge	New York	New Orleans	Manhattan	Palm Springs	Solid Towel Bars
18″ Towel Bar	•	•	•	•	•	•	•	•	•	•	•	•	•	
24″ Towel Bar	•	•	•	•	•	•	•	•	•	•	•	•	•	
30″ Towel Bar	•	•	•	•	•	•	•	•	•	•	•	•	•	
Acrylic Towel Rod			•				•					•	•	
Acrylic Towel Ring			•				•					•	•	
Large Backplate for Tissue Holder			•			•	•	•				•	•	

- All Baldwin Accessories in brass finishes are protected with a unique, clear enamel coating.
- All Baldwin Accessories have concealed mounting. All mounting devices are supplied.

Baldwin Bath/Epic Accessories are the perfect companions for Epic Faucets from the Epic Corporation.
Designed with an unerring eye for form and function, Epic Faucets are available through select distributors nationwide.
For information and availability, call 1-800-543-4634.

Items in this brochure are covered by one or more of the following patents 293,867; 294,905; 296,006; 296,175; 296,637; 298,710; 299,096, 299,097; 299,098; 301,293; 303,333. Other patents pending.

**Where Design and Quality
Create an American Tradition**

BALDWIN HARDWARE CORP. • 841 E. WYOMISSING BLVD. • READING, PA 19612, U.S.A. • PHONE (215) 777-7811 • FAX (215) 777-7256

M A N H A T T A N®

Bigger. Brighter. Faster paced. These qualities are clearly defined
by the clean cut tastes of Manhattan in Polished Chrome and Brass.

3251-263-A   3251-263

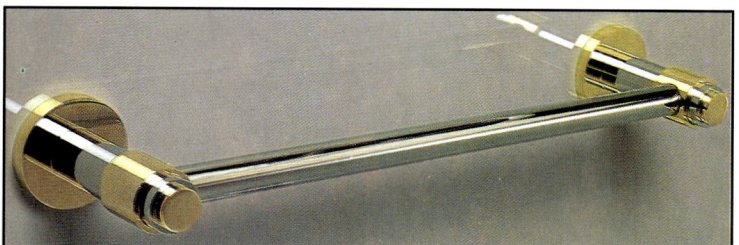

3251-263

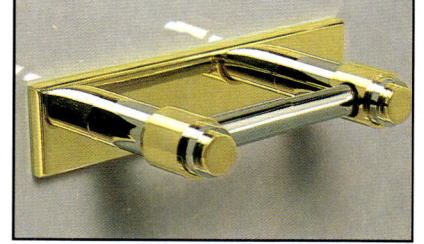

3253-263-BP

3255-263

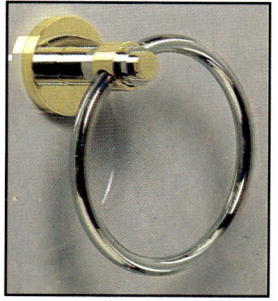

3254-263

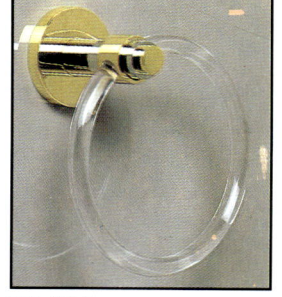

3254-263-A

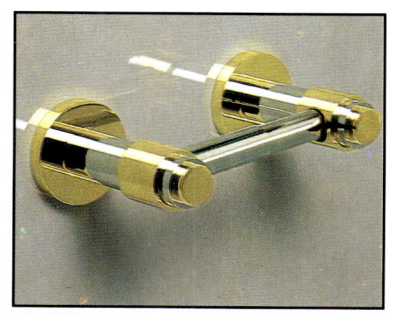

3253-263

PALM SPRINGS®

Informality in entertainment and dress creates an atmosphere of contemporary living.
Stylish and sophisticated down to the finest details of Palm Springs bath decor.

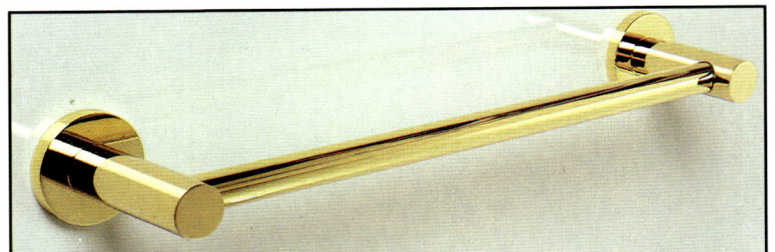

3211-030   3211-260   3211-250

3211-030

3214-030

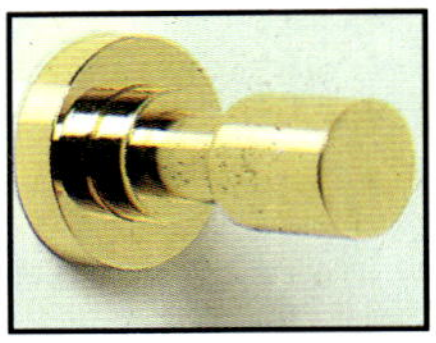

3215-030

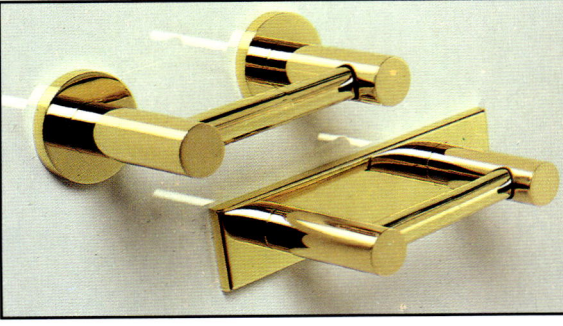

3213-030   3213-030-BP

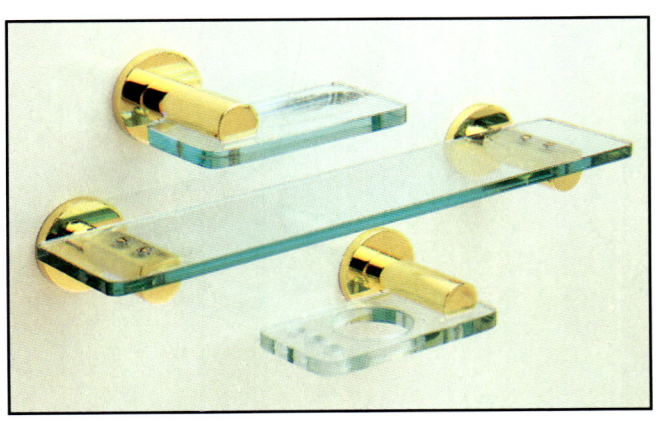

3216-030   3218-030   3217-030

ACCESSORIES

Complementary accessories include solid brass Towel Bars, 16″ or 24″ lengths.

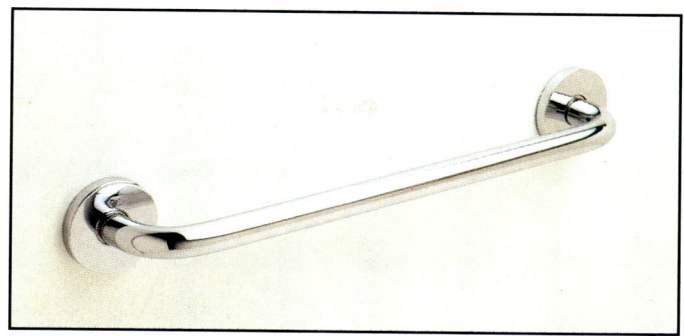

3421-260

FINISHES

Highly Polished Brass. Subtle Antique Brass. Sparkling Chrome, Polished Brass and Chrome Combined. Contemporary Polished Black Nickel. The richest, most requested finishes are available from Baldwin.

The first step to the perfect finish of Baldwin Bath/Epic Accessories is Baldwin's manufacturing process. Formed by Hot Forging, each piece of brass has a surface superior to those produced by casting. Free from the blemishes inherent in cast products, the smooth sur-face of Baldwin brass bath accessories is carefully polished by skilled craftsmen to bring out the deep warm luster of the brass and to create a mirror-like brilliance.

With respect for your investment, Baldwin has protected each brass piece with a unique, clear enamel. Using the latest technology, the enamel is bonded onto Baldwin Bath/Epic Accessories to provide a lasting beauty with minimum care.

030 Polished Brass

060 Antique Brass

153 Satin Nickel
Polished Brass

250 Polished Black Nickel

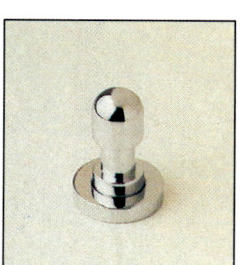

260 Polished Chrome

253 Polished Black Nickel
Polished Brass

256 Polished Black Nickel
Polished Chrome

263 Polished Chrome
Polished Brass

326 Polished Brass
Polished Chrome

AVAILABLE FINISHES AND COORDINATES

Series	Lexington	Paragon	Dallas	Victoria	Hampton	Palm Beach	Atlanta	Georgetown	Cambridge	New York	New Orleans	Manhattan	Palm Springs	Solid Towel Bars
Finishes														
Polished Brass (030)	●		●	●	●	●	●	●	●	●	●	●	●	●
Polished Chrome (260)	●		●	●	●		●	●	●	●		●	●	●
Antique Brass (060)								●	●					
Polished Brass/ Polished Chrome (326)		●					●							
Polished Black Nickel/ Polished Brass (253)		●												
Polished Black Nickel/ Polished Chrome (256)		●												
Polished Chrome/ Polished Brass (263)												●		
Polished Black Nickel (250)													●	
Satin Nickel/ Polished Brass (153)							●							

COORDINATE OPTIONS

	Lexington	Paragon	Dallas	Victoria	Hampton	Palm Beach	Atlanta	Georgetown	Cambridge	New York	New Orleans	Manhattan	Palm Springs	Solid Towel Bars
18″ Towel Bar	●	●	●	●	●	●	●	●	●	●	●	●	●	
24″ Towel Bar	●	●	●	●	●	●	●	●	●	●	●	●	●	
30″ Towel Bar	●	●	●	●	●	●	●	●	●	●	●	●	●	
Acrylic Towel Rod			●				●					●	●	
Acrylic Towel Ring			●				●					●	●	
Large Backplate for Tissue Holder			●			●	●	●				●	●	

● All Baldwin Accessories in brass finishes are protected with a unique, clear enamel coating.

● All Baldwin Accessories have concealed mounting. All mounting devices are supplied.

Baldwin Bath/Epic Accessories are the perfect companions for Epic Faucets from the Epic Corporation.
Designed with an unerring eye for form and function, Epic Faucets are available through select distributors nationwide.
For information and availability, call 1-800-543-4634.

Items in this brochure are covered by one or more of the following patents 293,867; 294,905; 296,006; 296,175; 296,637; 298,710; 299,096, 299,097; 299,098; 301,293; 303,333. Other patents pending.

**Where Design and Quality
Create an American Tradition**

BALDWIN HARDWARE CORP. • 841 E. WYOMISSING BLVD. • READING, PA 19612, U.S.A. • PHONE (215) 777-7811 • FAX (215) 777-7256

Discover The Luxury That Europeans Have Savored For Generations.

Myson Towel Warmers. A Trad

S6 CHROME (hydronic)

This tasteful refinement which English country inns and Europe's discerning homes have treasured for generations is now yours to discover on this side of the Pond. A marvelous blend of practicality and beauty, Myson towel warmers have been designed to complement any decor—from the most traditional to the ultra-modern. Our finely crafted tubular towel warmers feature finishes in polished brass, gleaming chrome or lustrous gold plate. And our sleek multirail towel warmers can be colour coordinated to match your bathroom colour precisely.

Available in a variety of shapes

...ition Of Elegance Comes Home.

and sizes, Myson towel warmers can be mounted on the wall or floor. Choose from electric or hot water versions. And if you so desire, you can even select one of our convenient portable units.

Meticulously fashioned in England to the most exacting standards, Myson towel warmers use only the finest materials to ensure countless years of enjoyment. In fact, every single towel warmer we make is individually tested by our technicians before it receives our stamp of approval. So, why not add a touch of luxury to your bath? Myson towel warmers. A fine European tradition is now yours to savor.

B26 REGAL GOLD
(hydronic)

MRS 6 ENAMEL
(hydronic)

Add The Finishing Touch To Your Home.

Myson towel warmers are yours to enjoy in every style—from traditional to contemporary. For more information, contact your Myson dealer.

EO 140 POLISHED BRASS
(electric)

B26 REGAL GOLD (hydronic)

CYG 5/1 POLISHED BRASS (hydronic)

EMR 750 ENAMEL (electric)

MYSON   P.O. Box 7789 • Fredericksburg, VA 22404 • Phone: 703/371-4331 • Fax: 703/371-7455

normbau

A Newman Tonks Company

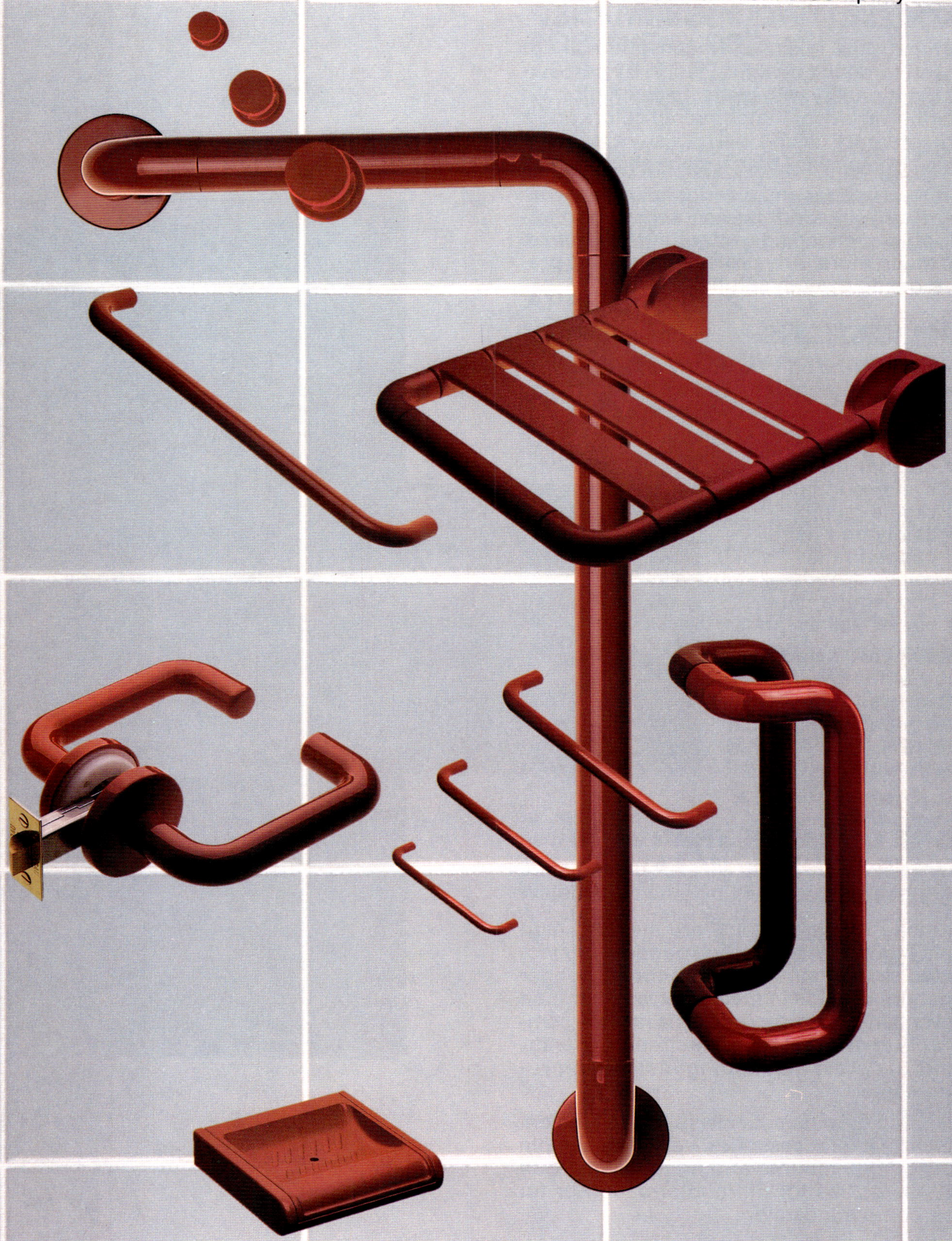

BATH HARDWARE

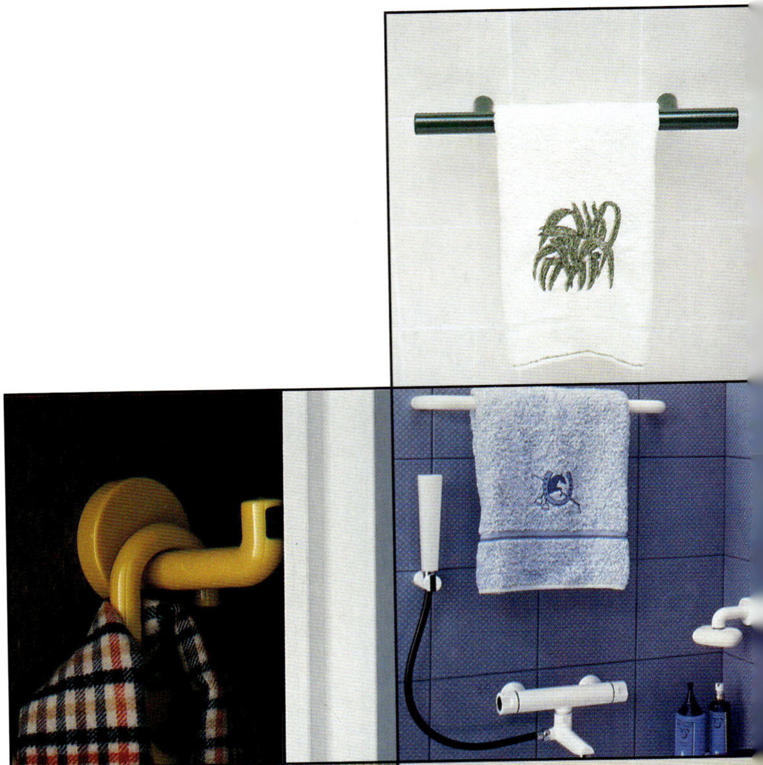

DESIGN INSPIRATION

With Normbau's extensive line of bath hardware and accessories, in an array of vibrant contemporary colors, the design possibilities are endless.

APPLICATIONS

Our entire ensemble of bath hardware is ideally suited for residential, commercial and institutional installations and handicapped requirements. (See our special section on handicapped systems, page 3.)

- towel bars, holders and hooks
- towel rods
- grab bars
- toilet tissue holders, pilfer-proof holders, spare tissue holders
- paper towel holders
- toilet brush and holders
- symbols
- bath shelf and mirror supports
- soap holders
- shower head holders, curtain rods
- hooks and hangers
- ventilation grills
- accessories

COLORFUL TEXTURE, DURABLE DESIGN

Normbau bath hardware is fabricated from the finest quality injection molded nylon. Due to the natural elasticity of the material, Normbau products are virtually unbreakable and scratch-proof for years of service.

The striking colors are a result of the molding process itself. Guaranteed to be fade resistant, Normbau bath systems will maintain their uniform and vibrant colors.

Our complete catalog shows all bath hardware elements and accessories including sample applications, mounts and attachments. Call 1-800-356-2920 for more information or for your complete catalog.

CONSIDER THE POSSIBLILITES

Like architecture, any hardware design is limited by the imagination of its creator. But Normbau expands the limits with its unconventional line of door locks, levers and knobs.

And Normbau makes each product with practicality in mind. The result: hardware that inspires the designer and serves the user as well.

APPLICATIONS

Consider the possibilities wih Normbau's line of colorful, contemporary-styled door hardware. UL approved, Normbau door locks, levers and knobs are suitable for both interior and exterior applications and are available in any of 12 decorator colors.

- lever handles for passage or privacy doors
- door knobs for passage doors
- knob-lever sets for passage doors
- lever handles for mortise locks
- lever trim set for mortise locks
- dummy lever handle door hardware
- accessories

FUNCTION WITH A PLEASING APPEARANCE

Normbau locks, levers and knobs are made of top-quality sturdy materials and are UL approved. Normbau elements can be designed in virtually any combination to meet any door installation requirement.

Our complete catalog shows all hardware elements and accessories including sample applications and attachments. Call 1-800-356-2920 for more information or for your complete catalog.

Available in 12 Exciting
Decorator Colors

PUSH-PULL HANDLES

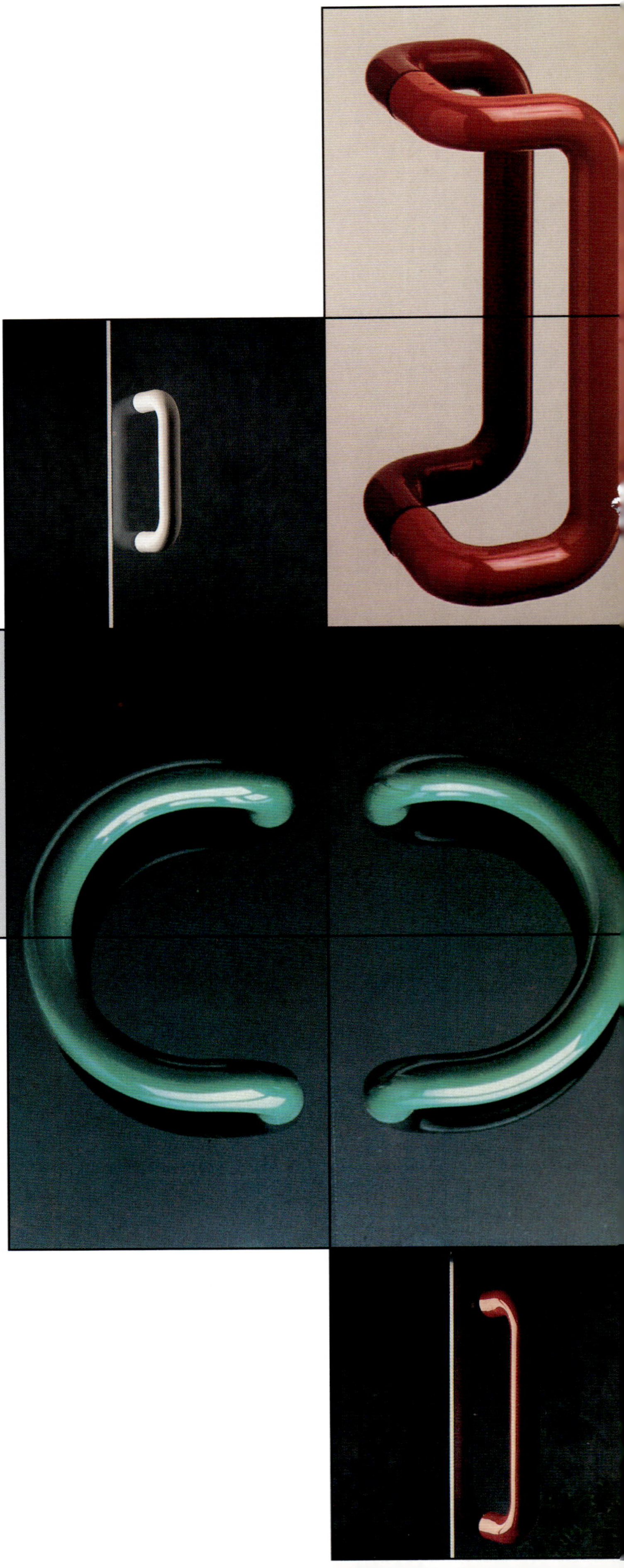

EXPANDING THE LIMITS OF CONVENTIONAL DESIGN

Fine architecture is a window into the designers imagination. And fine hardware is an integral part of any design, sometimes inspiring an entire spacial concept. And Normbau breaks the bonds of conventional design with an innovative, contemporary line of push-pull handles.

APPLICATIONS

Normbau push-pull handles have a wide range of industrial and commercial uses--from schools and gymnasiums to hospitals, shopping centers and restaurants.

- push-pull handles 34mm (1-5/16")
- push-pull handles 40mm (1-9/16")
- through-bolt installation
- surface installation
- back-to-back installation

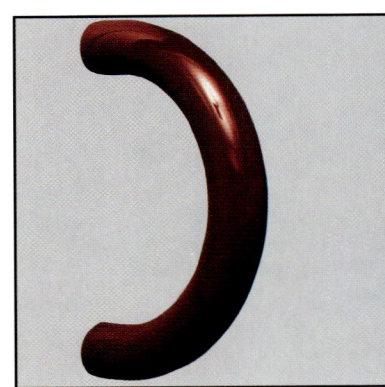

CREATIVE VERSATILITY

Normbau push-pull handles are made of the highest quality durable nylon. And they have the versatility to meet virtually any installation requirement. Normbau also offers custom designs and sizes on request.

Our complete catalog shows all push-pull system elements and attachments including sample applications. Call 1-800-356-2920 for more information or for your complete catalog.

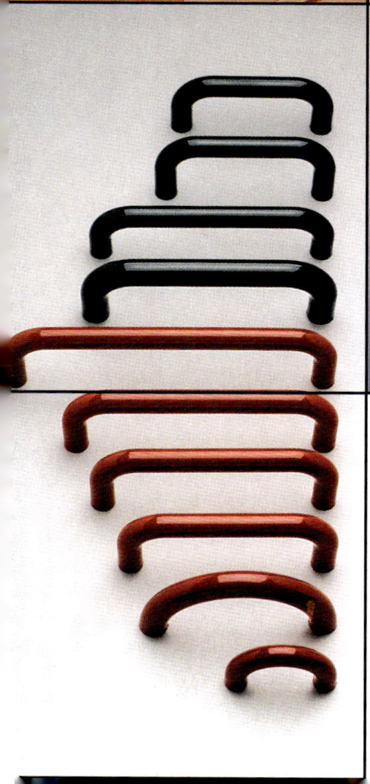

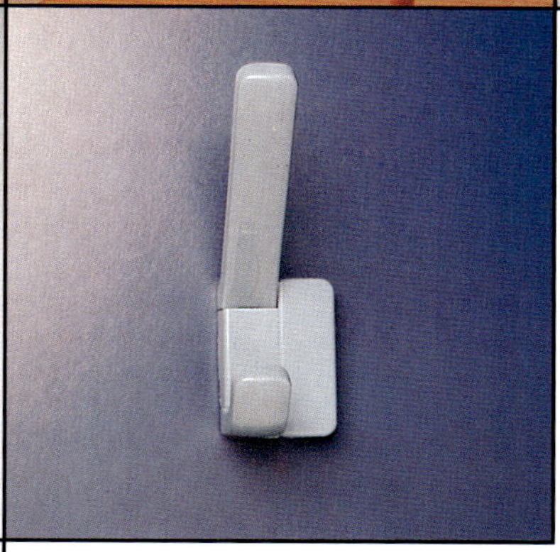

IDEAS WITH NO LIMITS

Consider the possibilities. With a splash of color, a contemporary design, Normbau adds distinction and excitement to residential and commercial cabinetry.

CABINET HARDWARE APPLICATIONS

From bath and kitchen cabinetry in the home, to commercial applications, Normbau has an extensive line of hardware in shapes and sizes to fit virtually any need--available in 12 exciting decorator colors to carry your design through to the last detail.

PULLS AND ACCESSORIES

- cabinet handles and knobs
- multi-use handles
- flush door pulls
- push- and kickplates
- doorstops
- mail slots
- letter boxes
- ventilation grills
- hooks and hangers

DURABILITY AND STYLE

Normbau cabinet hardware, made of high-quality, sturdy nylon, is fade and scratch resistant for long-lasting beauty and wear. And each design is available in 12 decorator colors.

Our complete catalog shows all cabinet hardware elements and accessories, including sample applications and attachments. Call 1-800-356-2920 for more information or for your free catalog.

Available in 12 Exciting
Decorator Colors

EXCEPTIONAL DURABILITY

Normbau strikes a perfect balance between imaginative design and dependable composition. Our products are made of nylon, an extremely durable material, consisting of the highest quality thermoplastic polyamide.

Nylon is highly elastic, virtually unbreakable, and can be molded in both smooth and knurled finishes for a sure and comfortable grip.

Precision snap fittings allow Normbau components to be mounted via concealed attachments to further enhance the clean and fluid lines of the Normbau systems you create.

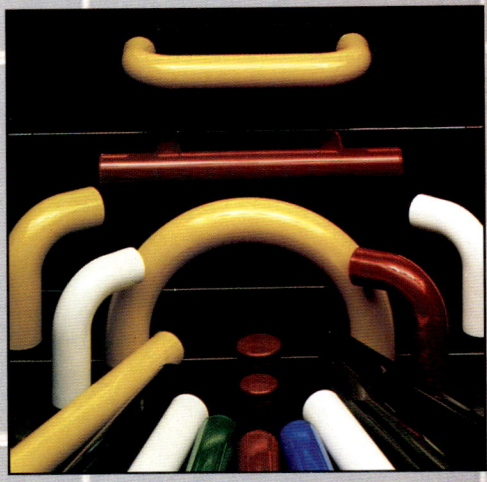

REINFORCED STEEL CORE

Normbau components are available with a reinforced zinc-coated steel core for added safety and durability.

The sturdy structure and composition of Normbau systems can endure the most severe application, succeeding where conventional metal, plastic and other materials fail. The unique properties of nylon give it the ability to:

- resist stress cracking from cleaning solvents and detergents
- endure fatigue under severe environmental conditions, including temperatures as high as 794° and as low as -4°.

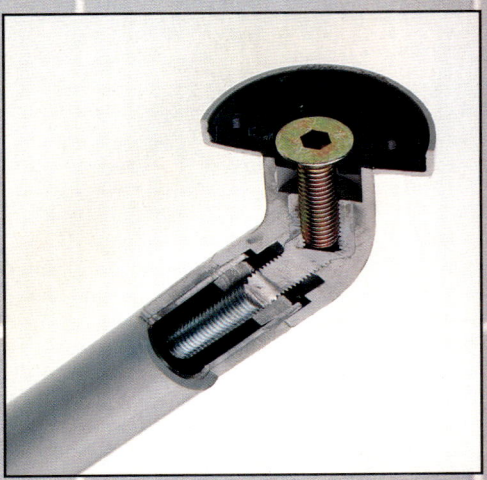

12 EXCITING COLORS

Color makes the difference. And with Normbau systems, the color you order is the color you'll get, now and for years to come.

That's because Normbau pigments are added during the injection molding process, to ensure the color will never fade, scratch or chip.

For more information about Normbau products or for your complete catalog, call 1-800-356-2920.

A Newman Tonks Company

P.O. Box 548 • Shepherdsville, KY 40165
Rt. 4 Branham Way • Mt. Washington, KY 40047
Phone (502) 538-7386 • FAX (502) 538-6400
WATS 800-356-2920 • Telex #466712

Available in red, yellow, blue, white, dark gray, ivory, light gray, black, slate blue, brown, almond, and green.

NUTONE
BATH
GUIDE

NuTone offers functional Bath Cabinet design options with enduring beauty, for every decor

3031PB Broadway TriVista

DT-50 Vision (two) M-3036-P Mirror Creates illusion of a mirrored wall, but with storage. Each unframed Vision beveled edge mirror door is 16" x 36" x ³/₄" and conceals a 14" x 34" cabinet. Center mirror is 30" x 36".

D-119 Portrait The special look of cherry wood frames a beautiful oval shape mirror. Or, choose genuine Dark Oak or Honey Oak. Overall size: 20" x 36".

D-142 Reflections Clear "looking-glass" and bronze framing mirror, each beveled a full 1". Overall size: 16 ¹/₂" x 26".

D-144 Reflections Oval clear mirrors on beveled bronze mirror. Bevel is full 1". 16 ¹/₂" x 26".

D-146 Reflections Distinctive octagonal beveled mirror-on-beveled-mirror creates three-tiered illusion. Size: 18" x 28".

D-169N Deauville Polished brass finish seamless aluminum tubing outlines graceful arched beveled mirror. Size: 17³/₄" x 29³/₄".

D-171 Continental Cabinet DL-171 Continental Top Light Polished Brass half-round frame adds rich detail to rectangular mirror door. Matching Toplight features mirror-chrome backplate. Cabinet 16" x 26", Toplight 16" x 5".

D-172 Bravo Hand-crafted arched mirror in rich gold-finished frame! Inlaid mirror strips have mitered corners. Overall size: 19" x 30".

D-960 Hollywood Radius corner bevel-edge mirror door topped with a row of built-in lights creates dramatic impact. Surface mounts, includes convenience outlet. Overall size: 18" x 33¹/₈" x 4³/₄".

D-980 Encore Smart squared-corner beveled edge mirror door and toplights. Surface mounts, features a convenience outlet. Overall size: 18" x 33¹/₈" x 4³/₄".

3030PB Continental TriVista Polished Brass half-round frame surrounds three hinged mirror doors for all-round viewing. Built-in light has mirrored chrome backplate. "Invisible" door hardware, magnetic snap-lock catches. Surface mounted. Overall size: 29¹/₂" x 29" x 5".

3031PB Broadway TriVista Beveled mirror doors with bold polished brass finish frame offer convenient all-round viewing. Built-in lights are set against a beveled mirror panel. Surface-mount cabinet has beveled mirror sidepanels. Overall size: 29¹/₂" x 29" x 5".

For complete information on the full line of NuTone Bath Cabinets, see Catalog BC-900.

D-119 Portrait

DT-50 Vision (two) with M-3036-P Mirror

D-960 Hollywood

D-171 Continental Cabinet
DL-171 Continental Top Light

D-172 Bravo

D-144 Reflections

D-142 Reflections

D-980 Encore

D-169N Deauville

D-146 Reflections

3030PB Continental TriVista

NuTone products add comfort, convenience, security and entertainment to your home

Radio-Intercoms ℗

You can be in two places at once! NuTone Radio-Intercom gives you room-to-room intercom ... the security of answering your front door without opening it ... lets you listen-in on the baby or to a sick room ... enjoy FM/AM radio in any room, poolside or on the patio!

Central Vacs ℗

Imagine vacuum cleaning so thorough you have to dust less often! So quiet you can vacuum while baby naps or the family watches TV. So convenient you don't have to lug around a heavy motor. All you carry is a lightweight hose and cleaning tool. Cleaning room-to-room, up and down stairs, basement, garage is easier. No wonder NuTone Central Vac is one of today's most-wanted features.

The power unit is built-in. NuTone offers six different systems. Sanitary, fully disposable soil bag models, and bagless units with the revolutionary NuTone Draw-down™ Cyclonic patented technology. Easy to install, they add value to any home.

Door Chimes ℗

Express your personal decorating touch with a traditional or contemporary NuTone Chime. Chime tones range from two-note to chordtone to the beloved Westminster chime sequence ... or even one you can program to play any tune you can whistle, sing or hum!
There are even wireless extension chimes and a new visual door signal for the hearing impaired!

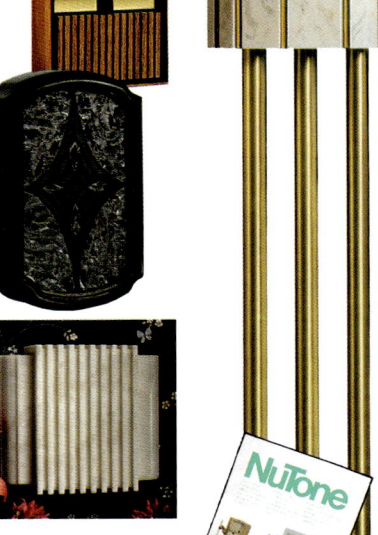

Paddle Fans
Add comfort and energy efficiency with an elegant NuTone contemporary or traditional fan. Light Kits are also available. ℗

℗ This symbol identifies NuTone Maximum Performance Products - *guaranteed for as long as you own your home.*

For the name of your nearby NuTone sales outlet, **DIAL FREE 1-800-543-8687** in the contiguous U.S., except in Ohio call 1-800-582-2030.

NuTone

VALUABLE HOMEOWNER'S WARRANTY

NUTONE PRODUCTS GUARANTEED FOR AS LONG AS YOU OWN YOUR HOME

℗

Omnipanel By Runtal

Imagine the possibilities.....

Omnipanel *By Runtal*

The Omnipanel by Runtal has long been considered an essential in the finest European Homes and Hotels. Now offered in North America, the Omnipanel may be used in bathrooms, kitchens, foyers, laundry rooms, or any other room where decorative drying, warming, or heating is a must. Imagine the possibilities the Omnipanel has in your home, office, or distinctive project.

Available in a wide variety of designer colors and finishes, the Omnipanel may be ordered in either electric (both UL & CSA listed) or hydronic models. In addition, model types and sizes allow for variations in BTU output from low (warming and drying items such as towels) to high (heating entire rooms).

Experience one of the world's great lifestyle refinements.

Call or write for your nearest Runtal Representative, or displaying showroom.

JUST IMAGINE!

Runtal North America, Inc.
187 Neck Road
Ward Hill, MA 01835
1-800-526-2621

runtal ®
RADIATORS

ACCENT THE BEAUTIFUL BATHROOM.

Bemis Toilet Seats offer distinctive ways to accent or color coordinate your bath designs. Designed for quality and long life, you can choose seats with exclusive sculptured lids, soft seats, embroidered seats, lustrous solid plastic seats or genuine solid wood seats. What's more, Bemis seats are available in every fixture manufacturers' colors. Bemis also offers a complete line of durable solid plastic seats for commercial and institutional use. For the name of your nearest representative call 1-800-558-7651, now.

BEMIS

SEATS TO MATCH OR ACCENT FIXTURES.

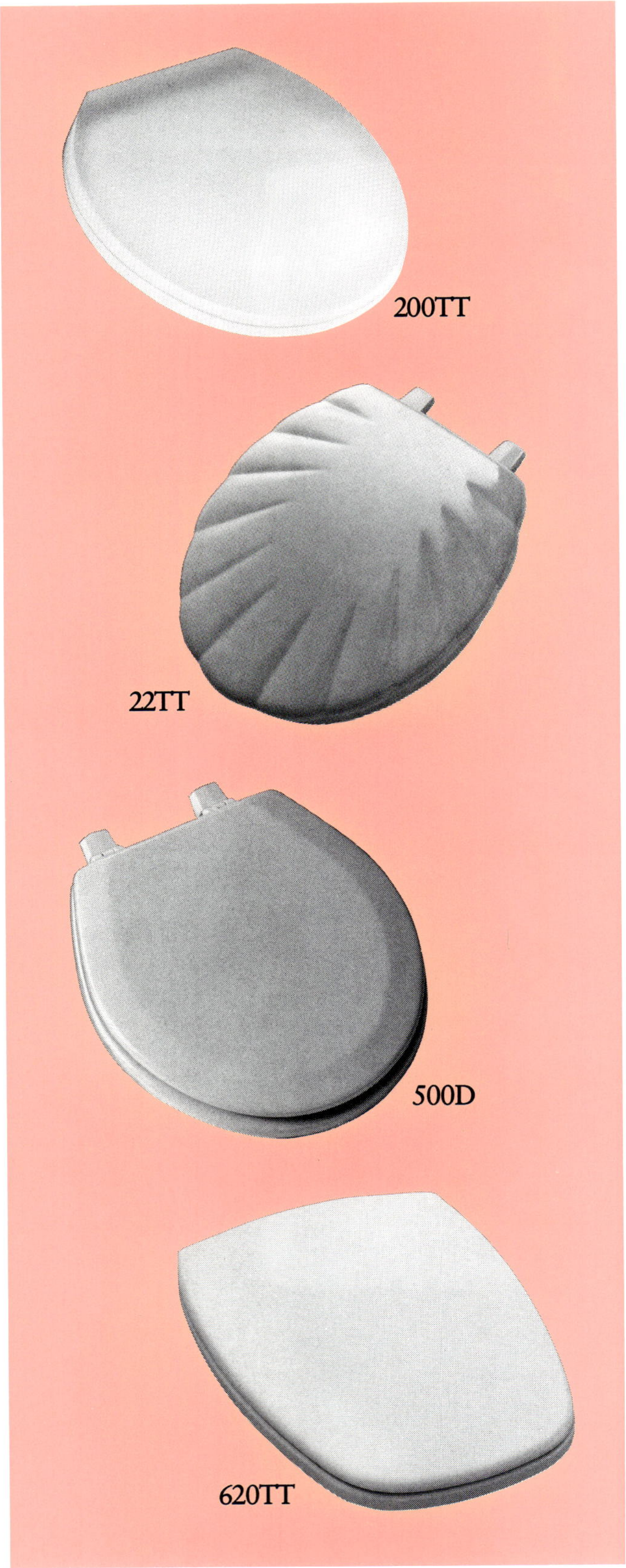

200TT Regular Bowl
Sleek, solid plastic seat molded of heavy-weight Duraloy. Molded-in bumpers on seat and cover are easy to clean, never need replacement. Top-tightening, color-matched hinges are locked-in with stainless steel pintles to prevent wobbling. Available in black, white and fixture manufacturers' colors.

1200TT Same seat for elongated bowl.

22TT Regular Bowl
Graceful, molded wood seat with sculptured shell design cover. Features durable color-matched bumpers on seat and cover. Color-matched hinges are top-tightening, easy to install from above the bowl. Available in a range of pastel colors.

122TT Same seat for elongated bowl.

500D Regular Bowl
Durable, molded wood seat with tapered cover features color-matched bumpers on seat and cover. Color-matched, molded plastic **Dial-on** hinge installs from above the bowl. Dials off for easy cleaning. Multi-coat baked enamel finish is available in white, black and fixture manufacturers' colors.

1500D Same seat for elongated bowl.

620TT Regular Bowl
Trim, squared-back design to fit Eljer Emblem bowls. Molded of Duraloy® solid plastic with built-in bumpers that are easy to clean, never need replacement. Color-matched, locked-in hinges with stainless steel pintles are top-tightening. Available in Eljer fixture colors.

1620TT Same seat for elongated bowl.

200TT

22TT

500D

620TT

Bemis Manufacturing Company, Sheboygan Falls, WI 53085   414-467-4621 or 1-800-558-7651 FAX: 414-467-8573

Olsonite®

The Specifiers' Choice

DECORATIVE WOODS

Make a strong fashion statement while complimenting any decor with Olsonite's woodflour seats. Select from our elegant sea shell design, or decorative marbles, granites and burlwood. Olsonite's woodflour seats make a beautiful difference. Color matched top mount hinge simplifies installation.

SEA SHELLS

520 Distinctive sea shell sculptured cover adds an elegant accent to the baked enamel durability of Olsonite's classic design wood composition seat. Available in many decorative colors.

FASHION

570 Vogue, contemporary look with stunning white and black marble, grey and brown granite and burlwood designer covers. Hinges are top mounted and color coordinated.

TOILET SEATS
Matching Towels and Scales

OLSONITE CORPORATION   8801 CONANT   DETROIT, MICHIGAN 48211   (313) 875-5831   1-800-521-8266   FAX (313) 874-2846

BATH COLLECTION

Complete bathroom ensembles with sensational new three dimensional embroidery on an extremely durable soft touch seat co-ordinated with matching towels and scales. Towel sets include bath, hand and fingertip in one easy-hang package. Scales in convenient hang-up carton for effective storage/merchandising.

SPRINGTIME

EMD 18 Two well accepted patterns combined in Olsonite's Springtime. Butterfly and rose with padded satin-like inlay lend a luxurious three dimensional look. Complete bathroom ensemble with matching towels and scales.

TWIN DUCKS

EMD 44 Lovable country ducks with accent color bills and feet and charming, colorful bows comprise Olsonite's Twin Ducks pattern. Coordinate the entire room with matching towels and scales.

SOFT SHELLS

EMD 17 Unique three dimentional embroidery compliment this beautiful sea shell pattern with matching towel sets and scale. Available in a popular range of colors this soft touch seat features improved squared ring and full cover lid engineered for durability.

SWANS

EMD 9 Graceful pair of swans in white satin embroidered with just the right accent color in Olsonite's striking and attractive Swan pattern. Follow the theme with matching towels and padded scale.

OLSONITE CORPORATION   8801 CONANT   DETROIT, MICHIGAN 48211   (313) 875-5831   1-800-521-8266   FAX (313) 874-2846

Expressions

By Beneke®

Model 6150

The Bathroom Seat As

Model 1000/1000E

T he bathroom. A key element in contemporary home design. Accentuated with marbleized fixtures or warm country woods, the bath has become a showplace for fixtures, cabinetry, tile and, now, bathroom seats. Expressions by Beneke is a line of exquisitely styled seats crafted to complement the

An Element Of Design.

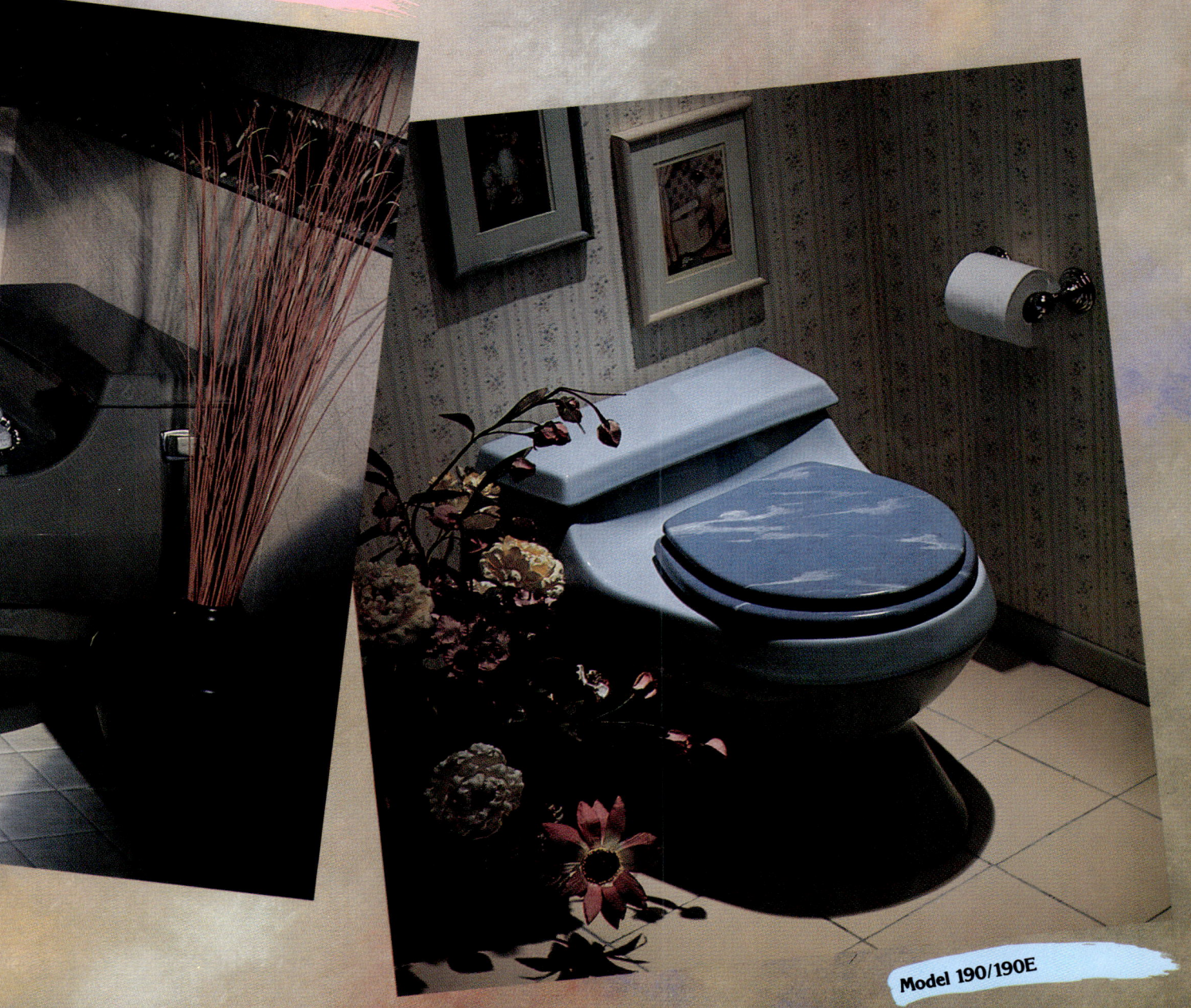

Model 180/180E

Model 190/190E

materials and colors that are part of today's bathroom designs.

Beneath the contemporary style lies traditional Beneke quality. With smooth color, fine woodworking detail and unique designs, Expressions by Beneke represents the finest in bathroom appointments.

Model 420/520

Model 550

Model 6150
Marbleized Seashell in Black
A unique design available in a wide range of colors as a round front model (Model 6150). This seat coordinates with the fashionable china prevalent in luxury bath designs.

Model 190/190E
Faux Marble in Dark Blue
High style and bold strokes of creativity. This seat has both. Fashion colors and chrome-plated hinges carry the look of luxurious fixtures and marble countertops. Available for round (Model 190) and elongated bowls (Model 190E), this seat provides a unique point of interest for the bath.

Model 1000/1000E
Bleached Oak
Hand-rubbed Southern oak extends the look of bleached oak cabinetry and vanities. Our special moisture-resistant sealer, chrome-plated hinge and attention to fine woodworking detail creates a seat that's durable, long-lasting and comfortable. For bathrooms using golden oak or a "weathered wood" look, we also offer seats with these finishes. All our oak seats are available for round (Model 1000) or elongated bowls (Model 1000E).

Model 550
Marbleized in Parchment
Sleek, European styling in the bath. Designed to coordinate with today's marbleized countertops, the 550 creates a bath of drama, distinction and comfort.

Model 420/520
in Teal
Today's bathroom is a symphony of color. Now the bathroom seat is in perfect harmony. Available in an array of high fashion and fixture matched colors, this seat is a statement of luxury and sophistication. Available for regular (Model 420) and elongated bowls (Model 520).

Model 180/180E
Stone Look in Black
A bold statement in texture, this seat provides new flexibility in working with today's stone look countertops. With a rich, sophisticated look, it fits contemporary designs. Available for regular (Model 180) or elongated bowls (Model 180E).

*F*or a color reference chart, pricing information and the name of the representative in your area, contact our Customer Service department at 1-800-647-1042.

A division of Sanderson Plumbing Products Inc., P.O. Box 1367, Columbus, Mississippi 39703, (601) 328-4000 FAX: (601) 329-4362

Expressions™
By Beneke®
An Element Of Bath Design

280 Carlingview Dr., Toronto, Canada M9W5GI, (416) 675-7177 FAX: (416) 675-4644

Du Pont's technological innovation combines a patented blend of natural minerals and high performance acrylics to form CORIAN®. This extraordinary material combines the elegance of marble and the permanence of stone, and adds the feature of repairability.

CORIAN is a solid, homogeneous, filled material containing methyl methacrylate. Developed by Du Pont to meet the needs of the architectural, building and design market, CORIAN is used in both commercial and residential applications. These include countertops, work surfaces, sinks, vanities and lavatories, tub and shower surrounds, walls, partitions, wainscoting, windowsills, molding, baseboards and thresholds.

Proven in commercial installations for over 15 years, CORIAN has been specified and successfully used in a wide range of new construction and remodeling projects including hotels, motels, universities, healthcare and food service facilities, as well as residential kitchens and baths. It is a unique surfacing material available worldwide only from Du Pont.

CORIAN can be purchased through Du Pont's worldwide network of distributors. For the name of the nearest CORIAN distributor and CORIAN sales representative, or to receive additional technical information, literature or samples, contact the nearest location listed on the back cover. In the U.S.A., call Du Pont toll-free at 1-800-4-CORIAN or write Du Pont Co., CORIAN Products, G-50902, Wilmington, DE 19801.

SHEET AND SHAPE

CORIAN is readily available from distributors in both sheet and pre-cast shapes. Sheet sizes range up to 30" x 145" (760 x 3680 mm) in thicknesses of ¼" (6 mm), ½" (13 mm), and ¾" (19 mm). Shaped products include one-piece vanity tops and bowls, countertops and sinks, and lavatories.

ENDURING BEAUTY

Unlike plastic laminates and gel-coated polyester materials that offer only a thin, decorated surface, CORIAN is solid. Its color and pattern run through its entire thickness. Thus, minor surface scratches or cuts can be easily repaired using fine abrasives. Because of its proven durability, Du Pont confidently backs CORIAN with an unprecedented 10 year warranty program.

10 Year Limited Warranty For CORIAN® Products

Du Pont warrants to the original purchaser of any Du Pont CORIAN solid surface product for commercial or residential use that Du Pont will repair or replace, without charge, such product if it fails due to a Du Pont manufacturing defect during the first ten years after initial installation. This includes reasonable labor charges needed to repair or replace the product. *(Details available from your CORIAN distributor or representative.)*

EASY CARE

Because CORIAN is non-porous, most stains wipe right off. More stubborn stains—even cigarette burns—rub off with abrasive household cleanser or fine sandpaper (a procedure not normally recommended with laminates or cultured marble products).

DESIGN FLEXIBILITY

CORIAN can be cut, shaped, routed, drilled and sanded like fine hardwood to create exciting shapes, edge details or surface effects. CORIAN may also be combined and blended with wood, brass, tile, acrylics, and other CORIAN colors for truly unique designs and edge treatments. Design possibilities are further enhanced with the natural stone look of Sierra, the most recent additions to the CORIAN line. In addition, CORIAN resin inlays, available in a wide range of colors, can be used to create distinctly original effects.

READY INFORMATION

Check the phone numbers and addresses listed on the back cover. A Spec-Data® Sheet is also available.

TABLE 1 Technical Data - CORIAN® Solid Surface Products

PROPERTY	TYPICAL RESULT	TEST
Tensile Strength	6000 psi	ASTM-D-638
Tensile Modulus	1.5×10^6 psi	ASTM-D-638
Elongation	0.4% min.	ASTM-D-638
Hardness	94	Rockwell "M" Scale
	56	Barcol Impressor
Thermal Expansion	3.02×10^{-5} in./in./°C	ASTM-D-696
Gloss (60° Gardner)	5-20	ANSI-Z124 HUD Bulletin UM 73
Color Stability	No change-200 hrs.	NEMA-LD-3
Wear & Cleanability	Passes	ANSI-Z124 HUD Bulletin UM 73
Boiling Water Surface Resistance	No visible change	NEMA-LD-3
High Temperature Resistance	No change	NEMA-LD-3
Izod Impact	0.28 ft.-lbs./in. of notch	ASTM-D-256 (Method A)
Stain Resistance Sheets	Passes	ANSI-Z124 HUD Bulletin UM 73
Impact Resistance:	No Fracture	NEMA-LD-3
	¼" slab-36" drop ½ lb. ball ½" slab-36" drop 1 lb. ball ¾" slab-36" drop 2 lb. ball	
Point Impact: Bowls	No cracks or chips	ANSI-Z124 HUD Bulletin UM 73
Weatherability	No change-1000 hrs.	ASTM-D-1499
Specific Gravity*	1.8 Standard Color 1.69 Sierra Colors	
Water Absorption	24 hrs. 0.04 0.09	Long Term 0.4 (¾") 0.8 (¼") ASTM-D-570
Flammability		ASTM-E-84

	STANDARD COLORS				SIERRA COLORS	
	¼"**		½"	¾"	½"	¾"
Flammability	Masonry	Gypsum	Sheet	Sheet	Sheet	Sheet
Flame Spread	15	25	5	5	15	15
Smoke Developed	20	25	10	15	25	30
Class	I	I	I	I	I	I

*Approximate weight per square foot for standard colors: ¼" (6 mm) 2.35 lbs. ● ½" (13 mm) 4.7 lbs. ● ¾" (19 mm) 7.0 lbs.

**¼" (6 mm) results reflect material adhered to both masonry surfaces and standard grade ½" (13 mm) thick Gypsum Board using Panel Adhesive for Du Pont CORIAN® and tested as a composite.

CORIAN®
SOLID SURFACE PRODUCTS

*CORIAN is Du Pont's registered trademark for its premium quality brand of solid surface products. Only Du Pont makes CORIAN.

Integral Vanity Top and Bowl

The molded one-piece construction combines the smooth, continuous surface of the vanity and bowl, thus eliminating hard-to-clean dirt catching crevices. Single or double bowl units can be ordered with a variety of bowl positions. A separate 2⅞" (78 mm) backsplash is included. Many can be ordered with standard pre-drilled faucet holes. Custom top configurations can be supplied to meet nearly every design need.

Lavatories. CORIAN lavatories are available in four styles and are an excellent choice in combination with CORIAN sheet vanity tops or conventional vanity top material. (Offers maximum flexibility of bowl positions). Lavatories include models for topmounting, undermounting or fabricating a seamed undermount bowl to give the appearance of an integral vanity top and bowl.

Integral Kitchen Top and Sink. Available in single or double bowl, one-piece kitchen top and sink vanities. Single or double bowl designs measure 10' (3050 mm) long, 25" (630 mm) wide and ¾" (19 mm) thick. All units come with 4⅞" x ¾" (124 mm x 19 mm) backsplash.

Sinks. These sinks, in single or double-bowl units, offer complete flexibility of color and placement. They work well in residential or commercial applications as kitchen, wet bar or small wash-up sinks. Top mount, bevel mount, undermount or seamed undermount installations may be used. A series of Eurostyle, double-bowl drainboard sinks, which are functional as well as elegant, is also available.

Accessories. CORIAN Joint Adhesive–for bonding CORIAN to CORIAN. Available in Bone, Cameo White, Dawn Beige, Taupe, Peach, Misty Green, Pearl Gray, Dusty Rose and Glacier White.

Silicone Sealant for CORIAN–for installing backsplashes, reveal edges, sealing tub and shower seams. Available in Translucent White, Dawn Beige, Bone, Taupe, Peach, Misty Green, Pearl Gray, Dusty Rose, Glacier White and Clear.

Panel Adhesive for Du Pont CORIAN–bone colored, neoprene-based adhesive for adhering vertical wall panels.

Other–Accessories include undermount hardware for bowls and sinks (individually or bulk packaged), Scotch-Brite® wiping pads for cleaning and heat conductive tape to line cooktop cutout for heat dispersion.

Color. CORIAN is available in classic and versatile neutral colors to complement any interior:

Cameo White, an opalescent white; Dawn Beige, a soft white with delicate beige veining throughout; Almond, a subtle almond tone; Satin Gray, a light, solid gray; Bone, a warm pleasing color with no pattern; and Dusty Rose, a shaded pink. The CORIAN Designer Collection features the natural stone look of Sierra Midnight, a dramatic dark gray; Sierra Dusk, a subtle gray; Sierra Sandstone, a wood-coordinating shade; and Pink Coral, a dramatic rose-quartz shade. And the five newest CORIAN colors: Taupe, a soft grayed brown; Peach, a warm blush of color; Misty Green, a light minty hue; Pearl Gray, a translucent blue-gray; and Glacier White, a bright white with a subtle translucency.

For custom effects, shades of CORIAN can be blended together or combined with other materials for a dramatic statement. Other materials such as wood, acrylics, metal and tile can also be inlaid to provide unique edge treatments or design appeal.

CORIAN Inlay Colors. Inlay Colors, made of acrylic resin-based material, can be used to add decorative elements by routing out the desired design, filling with inlay color, and sanding and finishing the area. Colors include chocolate, raspberry, red, blue, green, yellow and black. In addition, the standard joint adhesive colors can be used.

Standard Vanity Top and Bowl Sizes

Sizes Single Bowl Inches	mm	Bowl Position* Inches	mm
19½" x 25"	500 x 630	C	
19½" x 31"	500 x 790	C	
19½" x 37"	500 x 940	C	
22" x 25"	560 x 630	C	
22" x 31"	560 x 790	C	
22" x 37"	560 x 940	C	
22" x 43"	560 x 1090	C	
22" x 49"	560 x 1240	15"-LCR-15"	380
22" x 61"	560 x 1550	15"-LCR-15"	380
22" x 73"	560 x 1850	18"-LCR-18"	460
Double Bowl			
22" x 49"	560 x 1240	12½"-LCR-12½"	320
22" x 61"	560 x 1550	15½"-LCR-15½"	390
22" x 73"	560 x 1850	18½"-LCR-18½"	470

*C-Center, L-Left, R-Right. For non-centered bowls, bowl positions are shown in inches (mm) from edge of top to center of drain.
Note: Please contact Du Pont where minimum tolerance(s) is critical.

AVAILABLE WORLDWIDE

USA
Du Pont Co.
PPD Dept.
Wilmington, DE 19898
1-800-4-CORIAN

CANADA
Du Pont Canada, Inc.
CORIAN Products
P.O. Box 2300 Streetsville
Mississauga, Ontario
L5M 2H3
416-821-3300

EUROPE
Du Pont de Nemours
International S.A.
P.O. Box CH-1211
Geneva 24
Switzerland
TLX No. 22512

AUSTRALIA
Du Pont Australia Ltd.
Northside Gardens
168 Walker Street
P.O. Box 930
North Sydney,
N.S.W. 2060
TLX AA20685

JAPAN
MRC Du Pont Co., Ltd.
No. 30 Kowa Bldg. 6F
Tokyo 106, Japan

CENTRAL ASIA PACIFIC
Du Pont Asia Pacific Ltd.
1122 New World Office Bldg.
(East Wing)
Salisbury Road, Tsin Sha Tsui
Kowloon, Hong Kong
TLX 76296 DPTHK HX

CORIAN®
SOLID SURFACE PRODUCTS

AVRON
SOLID SURFACE MATERIALS
NOW, YOU CAN DREAM IN COLOR

Avron®

Anti-Staining Properties

This table indicates the degrees of cleaning action necessary to remove various stains from Avron. The household products and foods listed below were in contact with work surfaces of Avron sheet for 16 hours or more. We treated the resulting marks or stains with the cleansing agents marked. In the cleansing agent column:

1 is warm water.
2 is a mild detergent, such as diluted dish washing liquid or a proprietary disinfectant cleanser.
3 is a non-abrasive, cream cleanser.
4 is a scouring powder.

CLEANSING AGENT: 1 2 3 4

HOUSEHOLD PRODUCT/FOOD: Soap bar, Beet juice, Biological washing powder, Bleach, Blood, Blue food coloring, Coffee, Dishwasher rinse, Dishwasher powder, Domestic detergent, Emulsion paint, English mustard, Green food coloring, Lemon juice, Lipstick, Malt vinegar, Nail polish, Nail polish remover, Neat orange cordial, Red food coloring, Red wine, Shoe polish, Tea, Typewriter correction fluid, Tomato ketchup, Vegetable oil, Dish washing liquid, Water-based ink

Chemical Resistance

This table shows Avron's resistance to a variety of chemicals. The agents listed were in contact with work surfaces of Avron sheet for 16 hours or more. We then washed the Avron surface with warm water and noted the results. In the effect column:

1 indicates no effect.
2 indicates slight whitening.
3 indicates a removable stain.
4 indicates repairable surface damage, restored by light sanding.

EFFECT: 1 2 3 4

CHEMICAL:
Acids — 30% acetic, 20% hydrochloric, 33% sulfuric
Alkalis — 28% ammonium hydroxide, 10% sodium hydroxide
Salts — 2% potassium permanganate, 1% silver nitrate
Solvents — acetone, ethyl acetate, 1,1,1-trichloroethane, Petroleum ether, Toluene, Chloroform

TECHNICAL DATA FOR AVRON SOLID SURFACE PRODUCTS

PROPERTY	TYPICAL RESULT	TEST
Tensile Strength	4300 psi	ASTM D638
Tensile Modulus	2.19 x 10^6 psi	ASTM D638
Elongation	0.30%	ASTM D638
Hardness	55	Barcol Impressor
Thermal Expansion	3.24 x 10^{-5} in/in °F	ASTM D696
Gloss (60 Gardner)	5-20	ANSI Z124 HUD Bulletin UM73
Color Stability	No Change—200 hrs	NEMA LD-3
Wear & Cleanability	Passes	ANSI Z124 HUD Bulletin UM73
Boiling Water Surface Resistance	No Change	NEMA LD-3
High Temperature Resistance (500°F)	No Change	NEMA LD-3
Izod Impact	0.26 ft.-lb./in. of notch	ASTM D256 (Method A)
Stain Resistance	Passes	ANSI Z124 HUD Bulletin UM73
Impact Resistance: Sheets / Point Impact: Bowls	½ lb. ball @ 36" No Fracture No Cracks or Chips	NEMA LD-3 ANSI Z124 HUD Bulletin UM73
Weatherability	1000 hrs Class 3-4	ASTM D1499
Specific Gravity	1.74	
Water Absorption	Sheet Thickness: ½" 24 Hrs. 0.03%	ASTM D570
Canadian Standards	Pass	CAN/SCA-B 45.0-88 CAN/SCA-B 45.5-88

All tests were completed by United States Testing Company, Inc.

Values quoted for properties of Avron result from tests on representative sheet samples, and do not constitute specifications.

FLAMMABILITY	ASTM E84		
	¼" Sheet	½" Sheet	¾" Sheet
Flame Spread	40	20	15
Smoke Developed	25	15	5
Class	11	1	1

PRODUCT IDENTIFICATION

AVRON Solid Surfacing Material, A product of ICI

MANUFACTURER

ICI/KSH Inc., 10091 Manchester Road, St. Louis, Missouri 63122
314-966-3111

PRODUCT DESCRIPTION

COMPOSITION & MATERIALS: Avron is composed of tough, water-resistant, non-porous acrylic, with double its weight of a special inorganic mineral.

BASIC USES: Avron is a premium quality, solid surface material for counter tops in kitchens, bathrooms, laboratories, work stations, bar tops, and similar applications; and for wall coverings in foyers and other locations where you are seeking an elegant and stately appearance. Signs and logos, as well as a variety of other fabricated products, can be fabricated or engraved into Avron.

LIMITATIONS: Avron has been developed for interior applications. Where exposure to weather is contemplated, consult the manufacturer as to the suitability of the material. Do not expose Avron to temperatures above 350°F, or constant temperatures above 212°F, for extended periods of time.

Do not cement Avron in temperatures below 60°F, and take care not to install Avron where moisture may be trapped behind it.

Avron is suitable for horizontal or vertical applications. Avron is not a load bearing material, except on short spans (usually less than 2 feet) and must be structurally supported. Overhangs in excess of 3 inches for 1/2 inch Avron should be avoided, as well as sharp, angled notches or sharp corners, where cracks may start.

WARRANTY: Avron solid surface material carries a 10 year warranty when properly fabricated and installed by a Certified Avron Craftsman. Full copies of the warranty are available from your Certified Avron Craftsman.

SIZE & THICKNESS: Avron sheets are manufactured in 3 thicknesses, 6mm, 12mm and 18mm (nominal ¼", ½" and ¾"). Sheet goods are available in stock sizes of 760mm x 3600mm (30" x 142") in all three thicknesses.

COLORS: More than 20 designer pastel and solid colors are available. Custom colors can be developed for specific applications.

FINISH: Avron is available from the manufacturer with a fine matte finish, ready to install. It can be sanded and polished to anything from a flat matte finish to a marble-like sheen.

INSTALLATION: Avron should be installed by specially-trained fabricators. A network of Avron Craftsmen is available nationwide. For the Avron Craftsman nearest you, contact ICI.

No special tools are required for fabricating Avron. General woodworking tools can be used for almost all fabrication operations, with little or no modification.

Avron should be installed on a lumber frame if used on horizontal applications. Avron can be routed, sanded, cut formed and bonded.

CEMENTING & BONDING: Avron color-matched, 2-part cements are available for making seams and for mounting sinks and bowls.

Avron silicone sealants, color-matched to the Avron colors, are available for flexible seams.

Avron vanity bowls, in all the Avron colors, are available for surface- and under-mounting. Asterite acrylic composite sinks are recommended for kitchen applications.

AVAILABILITY & COST: Avron is available through Avron Craftsmen and distributors nationwide. Contact ICI for the nearest location. Cost will vary according to the thickness and sheet size. Your local Avron representative will be able to provide pricing information.

MAINTENANCE: Avron solid surface products can be cleaned easily with soap and water or common household cleansers. For more stubborn stains or light scratches or burns, use 320 to 420 grit sand paper, and then surface polish back to the original gloss. For complete care and maintenance information, ask your Avron Craftsman or distributor, or call ICI for the Avron care and maintenance booklet.

AVRON
ICI Acrylics • KSH Inc.
10091 Manchester Road
St. Louis, MO 63122
(800) 325-9577
(800) 444-0803 (FAX)
(314) 966-3111

DECORATIVE LAMINATE PRODUCTS ASSOCIATION

NATIONAL KITCHEN & BATH ASSOCIATION
NKBA
MANUFACTURER
COUNCIL

Avron, ICI, Asterite and *KSH* are trademarks of companies within the ICI Group.

Manufactured under U.S. Patent No. 4251576.

NEVAMAR®
DECORATIVE
SURFACES

Leading Design.
Lasting Performance.

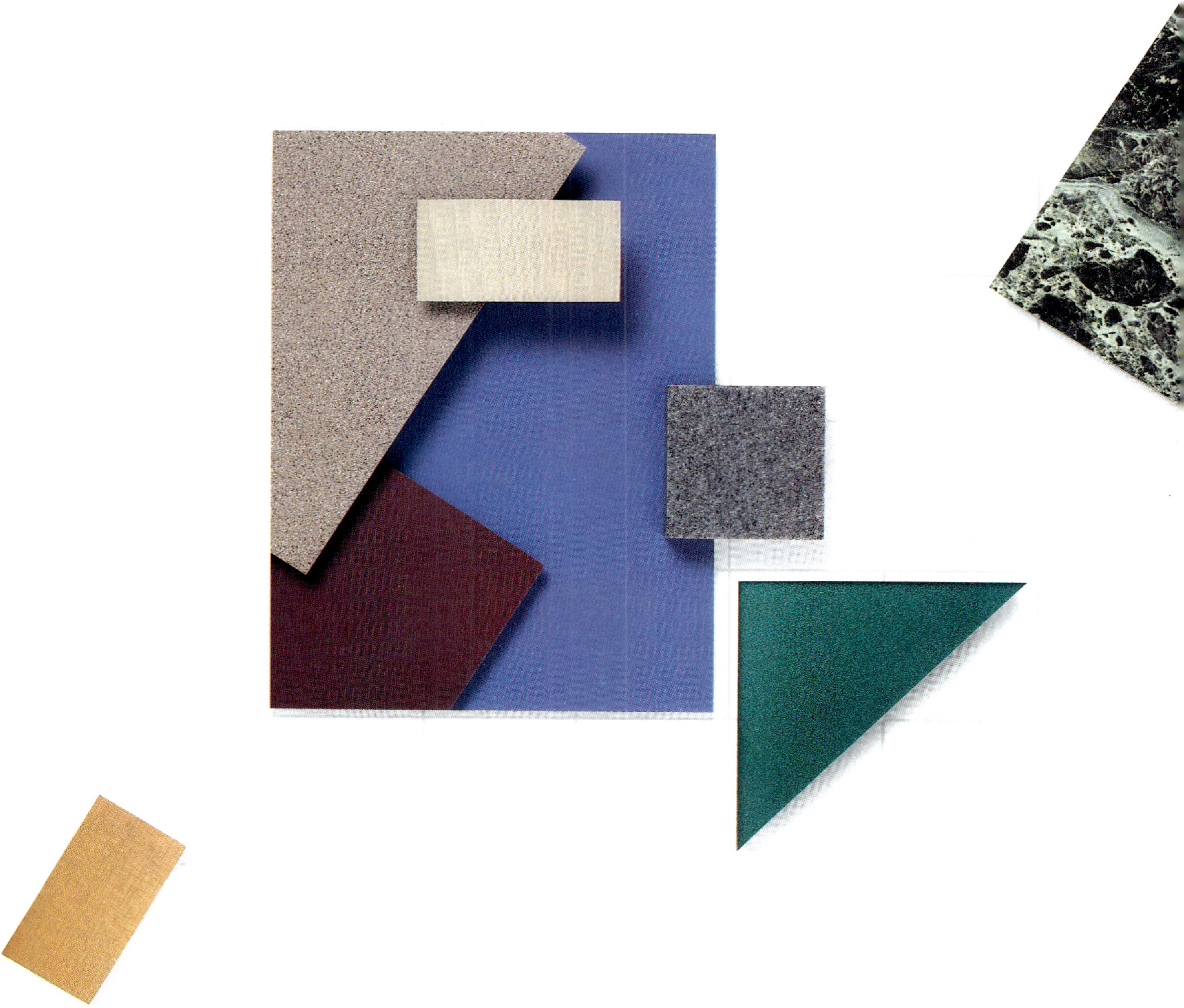

SURFACING MATERIALS

Innovation is the key to Nevamar surfaces...from decorative and functional plastic laminates to exciting and unique, new materials you won't find anywhere else. A full line featuring the colors, patterns and finishes today's designers look for. So for the latest in surface design, and technology, look to the industry's leader in innovation. Look to Nevamar.

ARP SURFACE®

A revolutionary technical development in laminate durability, the ARP SURFACE keeps Nevamar laminates looking new longer. It provides superior resistance to sliding wear and scuffing with significantly better NEMA Wear Value than conventional laminates.

The ARP SURFACE is standard on Nevamar solid color laminates, patterns and woodgrains with Textured Finish as well as all solid colors in Glossie Finish.

LAMINATES

Nevamar offers one of the broadest, most innovative lines of standard laminate surfaces in the industry, including:
Patterns—soft, subtle designs with a European flair.
Stone-Looks—contemporary and classic designs in Mirror Finish.
Woodgrains—life-like reproductions capturing the natural beauty of fine wood veneers.
Dimensionals—exclusive stipple, grid and line dimen-

sional finishes for solid colors.
Solid Colors—an extensive line of colors from which to choose...today's most wanted solids, carefully chosen with designer input, and periodically updated to reflect your current needs. Nevamar's exclusive ARP SURFACE is standard on all Textured Finish and Glossie Finish solids.

Designed by: John Landy,
    AIA–Landy Associates
Photography by: © Norman McGrath (1989)

Fabricated by:
    Murphy-Catton
Photography by:
    Bender & Bender

Photo courtesy of:
    Hayman-Chaffey

Designed by: John Landy, AIA
    –Landy Associates
Photography by:
    © Norman McGrath (1989)

Fabricated by: Murphy-Catton
Photography by: Bender & Bender

Nevamar Corporation…innovation in decorative surfacing for almost 50 years.

Fabricated by:
Dimensional Design, Inc.
Photography by:
Foto-Graphics

Photography by:
Foto-Graphics

Designed by:
Michael Anderson/
Fred Goodwin
Fabricated by:
Ben Benson &
Associates
Photography by:
Blakeslee-Lane

Designed by:
Linda Lissman,
LSK Design
Associates, LTD
Fabricated by:
Custom Wall Systems
Photography by:
John McManus

NEVAMAR®
DECORATIVE SURFACES

Nevamar Corporation
Odenton, Maryland 21113

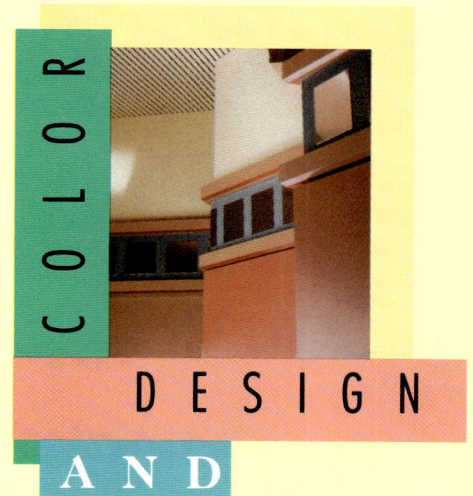

COLOR

DESIGN

AND

WILSONART®
BRAND DECORATIVE LAMINATE

Adventurous designers are driving the dull kitchen and the tepid bath into extinction, and WILSONART surfacing products are some of the most formidable weapons in their arsenal. Well-known for North America's best-selling decorative laminates, we've expanded our offering to include just about any surfacing option around — each one designed to work in coordination with the others. This total surfacing concept means we can provide what it takes to express most any design idea. Like these . . . A guided tour of the Southwest. The kitchen designed by Wayne Williams

Wayne Williams, CKD

won the 1990 Certified Kitchen Designer Excellence in Kitchen Design

competition, sponsored by Ralph Wilson Plastics Company and the Maytag

Company. ■ The ultimate bathroom. That's the only way to describe

this lesson in fluent English country designed by Martha Kerr. ■

We'll be happy to provide you with complete product specifications, plans

and detail drawings for Wayne Williams' kitchen and Martha Kerr's bath.

See the back cover for details.

Martha Kerr, CKD/CBD, CR

4   Here's a virtual catalogue of **WILSONART** products in one setting. Total coordination is evident throughout this kitchen — from the countertop pattern to the solid color on the cabinets, the linear accents added by the edge moldings and tambours — even the color wash of the veneer on the ceiling beams.

Take a quick visual tour of this spicy southwestern kitchen.

The sights include an uncompromising color palette, ingenious

ideas and unique architectural details. It all comes together for

a look as hot as Santa Fe red sauce.

Conceived as the centerpiece of a Lake Tahoe vacation

home, the room combines great livability, unquestionable style

and a festive, entertaining atmosphere. It's well-equipped for

large-scale gourmet cooking, and laid out so two busy cooks can

prepare a formal dinner simultaneously — without stepping all

over each other. Yet its casual, warm character makes it equally

appropriate for just hanging out on Saturday morning.

Inspired by the classic Palladian window, this treatment of laminate and Decorative Tambours, with a Decorative Metals accent, is a crowning touch for the built-in wine rack.

WILSONART Surfacing Products:

Countertops: Mocha Glace decorative laminate (4141-6)

Cabinets: Mesa Red decorative laminate (D398-6)

Perma-Edge® Bevel Moldings clad with Cayenne and Adobe laminates (SE A. D306-6 B. D394-6)

Decorative Tambours in Mocha Glace (Type 802/4141-6)

Backsplash: Inlaid SOLICOR® Colorthrough Laminate in Adobe (D394-6), Cayenne (D306-6) and Clear Teal (D378-6)

Ceiling Frieze: Clear Teal SOLICOR (D378-6), with Decorative Metals in Polished Natural Aluminum (6251)

Ceiling Beams: Craftwood® Tinted Veneer with the Light Beige washed tint (1531-CG))

Maytag Appliances:

Refrigerator: (RSW24 A with trim kit)

Microwave: (CME800 W with trim kit)

Dishwasher: (WU1000 with trim kit)

Freestanding Range: (CDE851 Black)

Wall Oven: (CME1000 Black)

American Standard Plumbing Fixtures:

Kitchen Sink: Hostess Double Square Bowl in Fawn Beige (7165.018)

Faucet: Dualux Kitchen Faucet in Chrome Finish (1825.049)

Island Sink: Manhattan Party Pak Bar Sink in Fawn Beige (7055.025)

Faucet: Dualux Faucet in Chrome Finish (4320.024)

Coordinating PVC Edgebanding: CANPLAST

Decorative Hardware: Strothmann

Functional Hardware: Julius Blum, Inc.

Unique details, like the door insert of pierced SOLICOR Colorthrough Laminate in Clear Teal, punctuate the entire room.

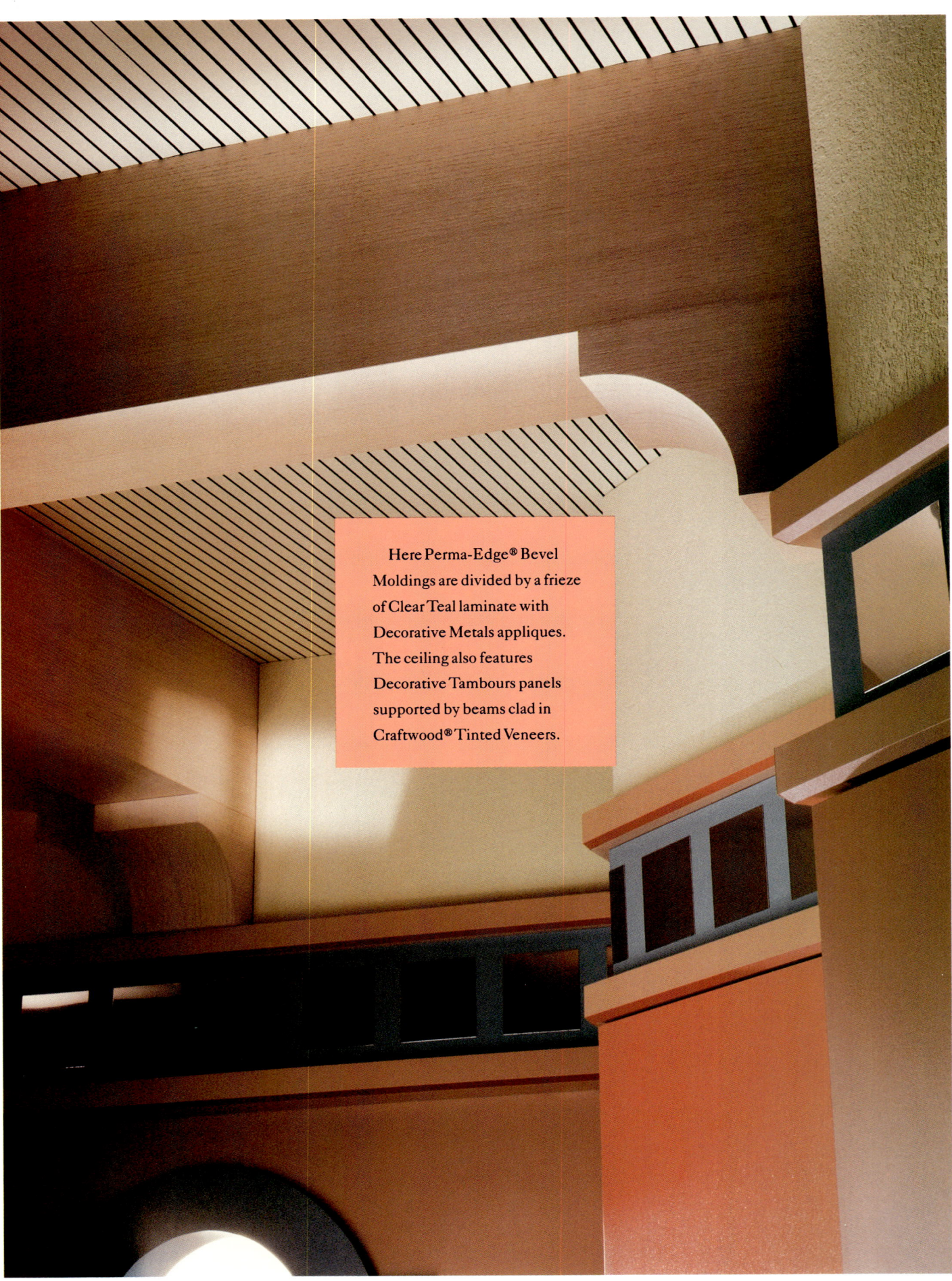

Here Perma-Edge® Bevel Moldings are divided by a frieze of Clear Teal laminate with Decorative Metals appliques. The ceiling also features Decorative Tambours panels supported by beams clad in Craftwood® Tinted Veneers.

Here Decorative Tambours, Perma-Edge Bevel Moldings and standard laminates coexist beautifully on a two-level island.

Throughout the kitchen traditional southwestern touches, like the quatrefoil window treatment and Native American backsplash motif, balance the contemporary, highly functional design of the overall room. And laminates in just the right southwestern shades bring off the effect to perfection.

This is a great example of how wonderful ideas and WILSONART products have been combined to create a true domestic *tour de force*.

The total coordination of our product line can pull together a color palette even this adventurous.

The backsplash motif is achieved with inlaid SOLICOR Colorthrough Laminates in three colors.

Functional touches like sliding tambour doors and pull-out work surfaces add an interest of their own.

Decorative Tambours, washed to match the floor tile, lift the soft green accent color from floor to ceiling. This is the man's lavatory area.

Here floor tile, edge moldings, laminate and washed wood tambours all work together in perfect visual harmony.

The theme of new ideas in a traditional context continues to every corner of the room. One example is the open shower area, complete with multiple heads, and featuring a convenient seating area.

In this room, ingenious ideas for shared relaxation and enjoyment, and an accent on total WILSONART coordination, make for an environment that combines the best of the old and new. Can modern surfacing products work in a soft, romantic atmosphere? The answer is an emphatic yes, spoken here in perfect English.

Throughout the bath, a wealth of WILSONART surfacing products provides direct surface transportation to the English countryside.

For more information, complete product specifications

and working drawings for the Williams kitchen and Kerr

bath, just call:

1-800-433-3222

In Texas: 1-800-792-6000

WILSONART®
BRAND DECORATIVE LAMINATE

Bringing new solutions to the surface™

Corporate Headquarters
Ralph Wilson Plastics Co.
600 General Bruce Drive
Temple, TX 76504
Phone: (817) 778-2711
Fax: (817) 770-2384 (24 hours)

HOTLINE
When you need immediate response to a question, or quick delivery of
product samples and literature (within 24 hours), call toll-free:
1-800-433-3222
In Texas: 1-800-792-6000

outer dome
inner diffuser

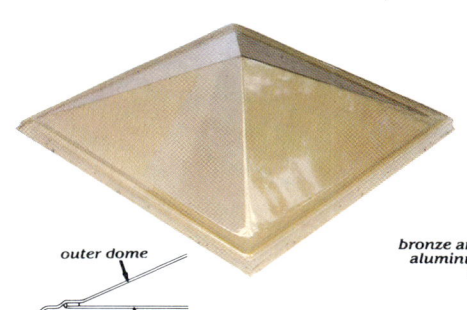

outer dome
diffuser

bronze anodized aluminum cap · tempered glass

Lexan® inner diffuser

DOME LENS

Domed skylight lens offers strength and durability. The G.E. LEXAN® material is actually stronger than the roofing material it replaces. Double dome construction gives excellent insulating qualities. Bronze or clear outer domes, clear or white diffusers.

PYRAMID LENS

A double domed skylight with a different look. The architecturally exciting skylight is sure to be an attention getter. It is made of exceptionally strong G.E. LEXAN® Bronze or clear outer domes, clear or white diffusers.

GLASS LENS

This new Glass/LEXAN lens offers benefits not available with an all glass lens. ⅛" tempered glass on the outside and an unbreakable patented G.E. LEXAN® polycarbonate inner diffuser on the inside with over one inch of dead air space between for excellent insulation and safety.

Pat #4823525

gasket
flashing
curb

gasket · hatch
flashing
curb · crank · screen

WOOD CURB

These insulated curbs are ready to install. Top quality cedar frame with hand wrapped and soldered flashing and neoprene gasket. Flashings are available in painted galvanized metal, copper or stainless steel.

WOOD HATCH

Combine the advantages of a skylight with the features of a window. Hand wrapped and soldered flashing of galvanized metal, copper or stainless steel over top quality insulated cedar curb and frame for lasting service. Screen is included.

R and U Values Compared

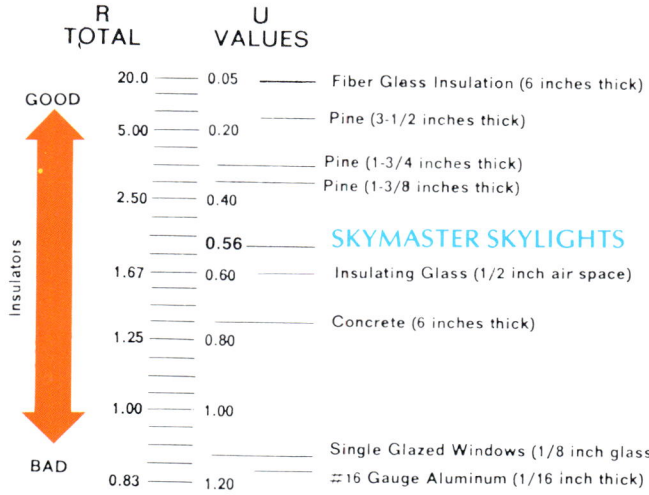

R TOTAL	U VALUES	
GOOD		
20.0	0.05	Fiber Glass Insulation (6 inches thick)
5.00	0.20	Pine (3-1/2 inches thick)
		Pine (1-3/4 inches thick)
2.50	0.40	Pine (1-3/8 inches thick)
	0.56	**SKYMASTER SKYLIGHTS**
1.67	0.60	Insulating Glass (1/2 inch air space)
1.25	0.80	Concrete (6 inches thick)
1.00	1.00	
BAD		Single Glazed Windows (1/8 inch glass)
0.83	1.20	#16 Gauge Aluminum (1/16 inch thick)

Insulators

Open the skylight for natural air flow ventilation. A convenient handle is supplied. An extension crank or electric operator is also available.

Ultra-Violet Stability
Skylights made from LEXAN sheet, block the transmission of damaging ultra-violet light but provides the solar energy transmission necessary for illumination and plant growth.

SELF-FLASHING SKYLIGHTS

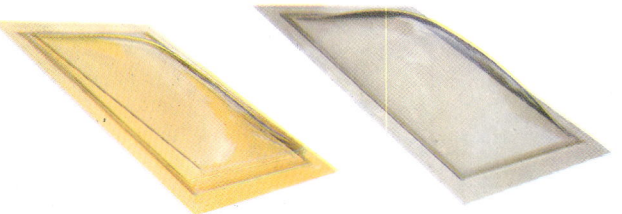

SURFACE WEDGE LENS

This patented skylight has unique channel ribs to promote the flow of water over the skylight allowing it to naturally run off the end. This low cost, energy efficient unit really is special. Bronze or clear outer domes with clear or white diffusers.
Pat #4548006

SURFACE DOME LENS

The low silhouette of this skylight and the self-flashing installation makes it become part of the roof's plane. The air space between the double domes creates a thermal insulation barrier. Bronze or clear outer domes, with clear or white diffusers.

SURFACE ROUND LENS

Use it in a wall or on a roof. Wherever you use the Sunbubble it will be visually exciting. Made of strong G.E. LEXAN® for durability, double domed for insulation, created to be different.

SURFACE WEDGE CLUSTER LENS

The surface wedge cluster lens can cover 2, 3 or 4 roof truss openings with no loss of truss support by cutting. A seamless and patented self-flashing design can be used near the peak of the roof or in any other location.

CUSTOM   ACCESSORIES

CUSTOM SKYLIGHTS

Special sizes and shapes are available for your unique application. SKYMASTER will custom design and build that special unit. Contact SKY-MASTER's Engineering Department.

Extension Crank

The Extension Crank is made of sturdy aluminum with an attractive satin-finish and non-corrosive handle. Equipped with a choice of 4 levels of reach, from 6 to 10 feet.

Electric Operator

This Power Operator is designed to open and close Skymaster's Wood Curb Hatch Skylights. This compact, weatherproof motor is designed to fit all Skymaster Hatches, new or already installed.

Gasket

This factory assembled gasket makes installing skylights on homemade curbs much easier. Instead of globs of caulk, the gasket gives a clean effective finished seal.

Aluminum Cap

This aluminum trim is bronze anodized for a long lasting finish. It is available for all the sizes of SKYMASTER skylights.

Skymaster Limited Lifetime Warranty (Abbreviated)

All Skymaster Skylights are warrantied against defects in material and workmanship when the unit is properly installed and maintained according to the instructions. If a problem occurs within the first five (5) years, another skylight will be furnished. After five (5) years a replacement may be purchased for fifty percent off current list price. For complete warranty information contact TUB-MASTER Corporation.

A DIVISION OF TUB-MASTER CORP.

MADE IN USA

Home Office: 413 Virginia Drive, Orlando, Florida 32803, 1-407-898-2881
Branch Plant: 1866 Lake Place, Ontario, California 91761, 1-714-947-0777

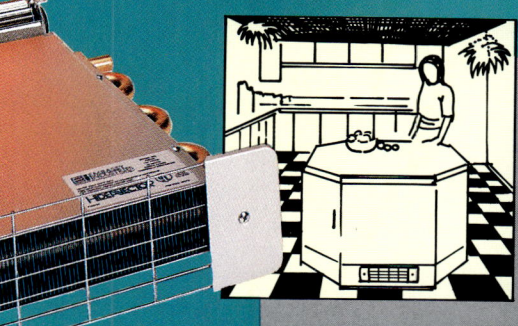

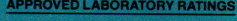
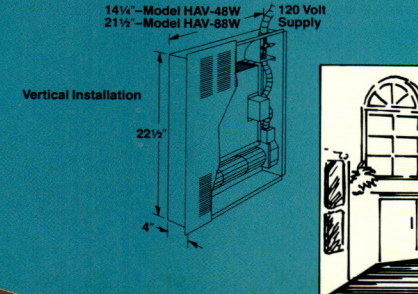
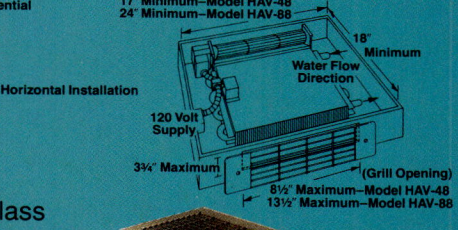

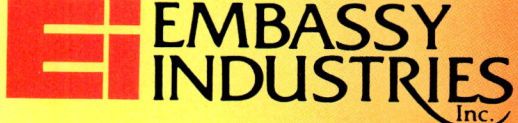

Which Formica® Brand surface to choose?

When it comes to countertops, there are only three possibilities. Each has its own special advantages. And Formica Corporation is the only company that makes them all.

1

LAMINATE. There's only one Formica brand laminate. Although other people now make laminate, we invented it, and we're still the best at it. Which you'll realize when you see the amazing variety of patterns, colors and textures we offer. You can be wildly—or even not so wildly—creative with it. If you're planning on doing a kitchen or bath and quality is important, ask for Formica brand laminate by name and accept no substitutes.

2

COLORCORE®. For a customized look, you should look into ColorCore surfacing material. Color is what ColorCore is all about—color that goes all the way through, so its beauty isn't interrupted by the dark edge of regular laminate. ColorCore gives you the look of a solid surface at less cost, as well as the option to do distinctive custom edge treatments like the one shown. And there are over a hundred ColorCore colors to choose from.

3

SURELL™. The newest and unquestionably the most exciting solid ever introduced, SURELL solid surfacing material has a timeless, sculpted look. It gives you the beauty and elegance of marble and granite in a choice of countertops, vanities with molded backsplashes, lavatory bowls and showers, all with the assurance of Formica brand quality. Solid color choices are available, as well as several remarkably realistic granites. If you're doing a kitchen or bath to match a lifestyle that's here to stay, SURELL solid surfacing material is your design solution.

For the name of the kitchen and bath dealer nearest you, call 1-800-FORMICA.

FORMICA® BRAND
products

The Name Brand in Surfacing.

450 Ways To Please
All The People, All The Time.

The key to being successful is finding your niche. At Siro, we make decorative hardware that's beautiful, durable, and moreover, unique. We create trend-setting designs using distinguished coating techniques like simulated stone, suede, pickled wood and marble – to name a few.

Kitchen and Bath Dealers — Designers and Cabinet Shops

Put simply, Siro gives you 450 ways to compliment any cabinet design and laminate. If you haven't already become part of the Siro National Distributor Network, we want you to learn about and benefit from our uncompromising customer commitment which includes free 4-color literature, a comprehensive merchandising kit, a dramatic point-of-purchase display system and our prompt 24-Hour Quick-Ship Service. Call 1-800-537-7476 today (305-968-0104 in Florida) and we'll provide you with a free presentation brochure and our national distributor list.

We're not another hardware company. We draw on over 40 years of experience in the international market and from patented technologies that *work* to give you a consistently high standard of quality and innovation. C'mon. Step up to Siro today.

Step Up To **SIRO** DeSigns   *A New Generation Of Decorative Hardware*

SIRO DESIGNS, Inc., 2010 NW 55th Avenue, Margate, FL 33063
1-800-537-7476 (OUTSIDE FL), 305/968-0104, FAX 305/968-0106

CATALOGERS'
BRANCH OFFICES & REPRESENTATIVES
INDEX

AFEEL CORPORATION

Please Contact Home Office:

Afeel Corporation
15240 Transistor Lane
Huntington Beach, CA 92649

| | 714-373-2788 |
| Fax: | 714-373-2791 |

ALNO KITCHEN CABINETS, INC.

DEALER LISTINGS
ALABAMA
Kitchen Potential
Homewood   205-870-8467
CALIFORNIA
Axis Kitchen Gallery
Laguna Beach   714-494-2442
Deluxe Kitchen and Bath
San Francisco   415-753-8850
European Woodworks
Santa Rosa   707-528-0422
Kitchen Fair
San Carlos   415-595-3559
COLORADO
Cabinet Group International, Inc.
Vail   303-476-1942
Modern Kitchen Center
Glenwood Springs   303-945-9191
CONNECTICUT
Form Limited
Greenwich   203-869-6880
DELAWARE
Evergreen Propery Services LTD.
Bethany Beach   302-537-9508
ILLINOIS
Cabinet Group International
Lyons   708-442-5244
IOWA
Kitchen, Bath & Home
Ames   515-233-2604
MAINE
Indisco
Scarboro   207-883-5562
MARYLAND
The Kitchenry
Owing Mills   301-356-3044
MASSACHUSETTS
Dalia Kitchen Designs
Boston   617-482-2566

MICHIGAN
Kitchens International
Grand Rapids   616-956-1196
MONTANA
Cutter's Custom Kitchens and Bath, Inc.
Des Peres   314-965-5700
NEW JERSEY
Bondi's World of Kitchens
Ramsey   201-327-6260
Classic Kitchen & Bath
Cherry Hill   609-429-1492
Custom Creations, Inc.
Livingston   201-740-9771
Euro-Line Design
Ocean City   609-645-0888
Kitchen Ideas Inc.
N. Plainfield   201-753-4141
Studio "C" Creative Cabinetry, Inc.
Monmouth Junction   201-329-0580
NEW YORK
A.G.N. LTD.
Manhasset   516-365-5211
Igal's ALNO Kitchen
Huntington   516-424-4949
Kuhale Corp.
Forest Hills   718-997-7004
PENNSYLVANIA
Creative Nook
Downingtown   215-269-6585
SOUTH CAROLINA
Designs in Wood
Charleston   803-795-7959
VIRGINIA
Courthouse Kitchen & Baths
Fairfax   703-352-3001
Roanoke Kitchen Center
Roanoke   703-772-3961
WISCONSIN
Junge & Associates, Inc.
Glendale   414-228-7300

ALSONS CORPORATION

ALABAMA
McCain Sales Company
Birmingham   205-967-4095
ALASKA
Almex Alaska
Anchorage   907-561-2324
ARIZONA
The Marketing Pros
Phoenix   602-582-6870

ARKANSAS
Jack Rich Sales
Little Rock   501-224-1711
CALIFORNIA (Northern)
Weber Associates
Sonoma   707-938-3000
CALIFORNIA (Southern)
Great Western Sales Inc.
Gardena   213-323-7900
COLORADO
Tom Brady, Inc.
Denver   303-722-2893
CONNECTICUT
Don Regan Sales Corp.
Waterbury   203-575-9443
DELAWARE
See Pennsylvania (Eastern)
DISTRICT OF COLUMBIA
See Maryland
FLORIDA
Tom Kleppe & Assoc., Inc.
Orlando   407-679-7044
FLORIDA (Panhandle)
See Alabama
GEORGIA
Oliver-Williams-Davis, Inc.
Roswell   404-475-8569
HAWAII/GUAM
Crown Sales, Inc.
Honolulu   808-845-7881
IDAHO
See Utah
ILLINOIS (Central)
R.K. Ray Sales Inc.
Decatur   217-423-2544
ILLINOIS (Northern)
Landsman & Associates, Ltd.
Bensenville   708-860-0989
ILLINOIS (Southern)
See Missouri (St. Louis)
INDIANA
Ashworth-Train & Assoc. Inc.
Indianapolis   317-849-9936
IOWA
Mack McClain & Assoc., Inc.
Des Moines   515-288-0184
KANSAS
McClain & Assoc. Inc.
Olathe   913-339-6677
KENTUCKY
See Ohio
LOUISIANA
See Mississippi
MAINE
See Massachusetts (Eastern)

MARYLAND
Soter-Martin & Associates, Inc.
Millersville   301-987-5115
MASSACHUSETTS (Eastern)
Adelson Bros., Inc.
Billerica   508-667-9300
MASSACHUSETTS (Western)
See Connecticut
MICHIGAN
Sales Plus, Inc.
Ferndale   313-544-3777
MICHIGAN (Upper Peninsula)
See Wisconsin
MINNESOTA
S.D. McCullough & Assoc., Inc.
Minneapolis   612-827-5544
MISSISSIPPI
Don Bass Co., Inc.
Jackson   601-982-3754
MISSOURI
Mechanical Reps
St. Louis   314-427-1300
MISSOURI (Western)
See Kansas
MONTANA
See Colorado
NEBRASKA
See Iowa
NEVADA (Northern-Reno)
See California (Northern)
NEVADA (Southern-Las Vegas)
See Arizona
NEW HAMPSHIRE
See Massachusetts (Eastern)
NEW JERSEY (Northern)
Payson & Schechter
Bluefield   201-743-6570
NEW JERSEY (Southern)
See Pennsylvania (Eastern)
NEW MEXICO (El Paso, TX)
See Colorado
NEW YORK
Meyer-Bressen, Inc.
Albany   518-465-0066
NEW YORK (New York City, Long Island)
Chasco Plbg. & Htg. Corp.
Cedarhurst   516-374-4884
NORTH CAROLINA
R.L. Robinson & Assoc. Inc.
Raleigh   919-847-4501
NORTH DAKOTA
See Minnesota

OHIO
The Gambill Co., Inc.
Moscow   513-553-2048

OKLAHOMA
See Texas (Northern)

OREGON
See Washington

PENNSYLVANIA (Eastern)
Wayne R. Peden Inc.
West Chester   215-431-2254

PENNSYLVANIA (Western)
Keystone Mountainer Sls.
Washington   412-228-5770

RHODE ISLAND
See Massachusetts (Eastern)

SOUTH CAROLINA
See North Carolina

SOUTH DAKOTA
See Minnesota

TENNESSEE (Eastern)
See Georgia

TENNESSEE (Western)
See Alabama

TEXAS (Northern)
Jim Roemer & Assoc.
Dallas   214-956-9988

TEXAS (Southern)
Ron Henson Mfgrs., Reps., Inc.
Houston   713-691-5103

UTAH
R.E. Fitzpatrick Sales, Inc.
Midvale   801-566-7156

VERMONT
See Massachusette (Eastern)

VIRGINIA
Soter-Martin & Associates, Inc.
Richmond   804-550-2164

WASHINGTON
Burke West Sales
Kent   206-395-0112

WEST VIRGINIA
See Pennsylvania (Western)

WISCONSIN
Burton-Anderson & Assoc.
New Berlin   414-782-2870
See Minnesota

WYOMING
See Colorado

CANADA
R.G. Dobbins Sales, Ltd.
Downsview, Ontario   416-663-5465

PUERTO RICO/U.S. Virgin Islands
Inter American Builders Agencies Co., Inc.
Carolina   809-752-0200
Marketing Headquarters:
Tom Leonard, Sr. VP
Bob Michaluk, Mktng.
Alsons Corporation
525 E. Edna Place
Covina, CA 91723   818-966-1668
Raymond E. Miller, VP Sales
12724 Diamond Drive
Burnsville, MN 55337 612-882-0115

ALTMAN DISTRIBUTION INC.

Please Contact Home Office:

Altman Distribution Inc.
Sidney Altman
655 N. LaPeter Drive
Los Angeles, CA 90069   213-859-0126
Fax: 213-859-1266
Telex: 3775762 ALTMAN DIST.

AMANA REFRIGERATION, INC.

Please Contact Home Office:

Amana Refrigeration, Inc.
Amana, IA 52204   800-843-0304

AMERICAN CHINA

ALABAMA
See Georgia

ALASKA
See Washington

ARIZONA
Progressive Marketing
Bill Osborn
Phoenix   602-841-8056

ARKANSAS
See Oklahoma

CALIFORNIA (Northern)
Thomas Ramos, Inc.
Thomas Ramos
Santa Cruz   408-429-9506

CALIFORNIA (Southern)
Associated Sales
Thomas J. Clarke
San Diego   619-546-4418

COLORADO
Design Sales
Craig Iverson
Icehouse Design Center
Denver   303-294-0041

CONNECTICUT
See Massachusetts

DELAWARE
See New Jersey

FLORIDA
Titus Associates
Jerry Titus
Ft. Lauderdale   305-733-9930

GEORGIA
Fletcher Sales & Marketing
Dean Paul Fletcher
Marietta   404-427-7105

IDAHO
See Colorado

ILLINOIS
Schroeder & Associates
James W. Schroeder
Evanston   708-869-0202

INDIANA
See Illinois

KANSAS
Berger Sales, Inc.
Zane Berger
Prairie Village   913-649-2006

KENTUCKY
See Michigan

MAINE
See Massachusetts

MASSACHUSETTS
Snyder-Nygren Co., Inc.
Steve Nygren
Norwood   617-551-0516

MICHIGAN
Pete A. Theisen
Pontiac   313-682-7770

MISSOURI (Western)
See Kansas

MONTANA
See Colorado

NEVADA (Las Vegas)
See Arizona

NEVADA (Las Vegas, Sparks)
See California

NEW HAMPSHIRE
See Massachusetts

NEW JERSEY
World Traders, Inc.
Dan O'Brien
Metuchen   201-494-9510
                      201-727-9102

NEW MEXICO
See Arizona

NEW YORK (Metro)
See New Jersey

NEW YORK (Northern)
See Massachusetts

NORTH CAROLINA
See Georgia

OHIO
See Michigan

OKLAHOMA
Hardware & Plumbing Fashions
Monty Irons
Ponca City   405-765-4686

OREGON
See Washington

PENNSYLVANIA (Eastern)
See New Jersey

PENNSYLVANIA (Pittsburgh)
See Michigan

RHODE ISLAND
Massachusetts

SOUTH CAROLINA
See Georgia

TENNESSEE
See Georgia

TEXAS
See Oklahoma

UTAH
Colorado

VERMONT
See Massachusetts

WASHINGTON
Mitchell & Associates
Bill Mitchell
Everett   206-365-9712

WYOMING
See Colorado

AMERICAN STANDARD, INC.

CALIFORNIA
Los Angeles District/Showplace
Los Angeles   213-657-7600
Montebello
Montebello   213-725-6573
San Francisco District
San Ramon   415-837-6488

FLORIDA
Orlando District
Maitland   407-660-9330

GEORGIA
Atlanta District
Roswell   404-992-9531

ILLINOIS
Chicago District/Showplace
Rolling Meadows   708-506-0800

KANSAS
Kansas City District
Leawood   913-341-4800

MARYLAND
Capital District
Kensington   301-946-9331

MASSACHUSETTS
Boston District
Wellesley   617-237-3121

NEW YORK
IDCNY/Center One
Long Island City   718-482-0190

PENNSYLVANIA
Philadelphia District
West Conshohocken   215-941-9172
Pittsburgh District/Showplace
Pittsburgh   412-471-8200

TEXAS
Dallas District/Showplace
Dallas   214-991-0841

WASHINGTON
Seattle District
Renton   206-255-0700

ARESLUX

Please Contact Home Office:

Areslux
Myra Levi
8229 NW 66th Street
Miami, FL 33166   800-523-1564
Fax: 305-477-5155
Telex: 494-8699

ARTISTIC BRASS

Please Contact Home Office:

Artistic Brass
Customer Service
4100 Ardmore Ave.
South Gate, CA 90280 213-564-1100
Fax: 213-563-8501

REPRESENTATIVES

ALABAMA
See Georgia

ALASKA
See Washington

ARIZONA
MCA & Associates
Phoeniz   602-943-6927
Fax: 602-943-4850
Tempe   602-968-1655

CALIFORNIA
Ray Arenson
Los Angeles   213-553-7364

CALIFORNIA (Northern, above San Luis Obispo)
Tjader Sales
Mountain View   415-969-9626
Fax: 415-969-0221

CALIFORNIA (Southern, Imperial, Orange, Riverside, San Bernardino, & San Diego counties)
Coker Sales
Newport Beach   714-722-5587

CALIFORNIA (Southern, Los Angeles county North to San Luis Obisbo)
Rob Kuhlman, Inc.
Thousand Oaks   805-523-9619
Fax: 805-523-0201

COLORADO
C & D Sales
Lakewood   303-988-0176
Fax: 303-980-1910

CONNECTICUT
See New York (NYC & The Five Boroughs)

DELAWARE
See Maryland
See Virginia

DISTRICT OF COLUMBIA
See Maryland
See Virginia

FLORIDA
C.T. Rittberger, Inc.
Stuart   407-287-0581
Fax: 407-283-7030

GEORGIA
John Roebuck & Associates
Doraville   404-237-0426
Fax: 404-458-1620

HAWAII
Elin Teichner Associates
Kamuela   808-885-8026
Fax: 808-885-5717
(Fax Service, not direct)

IDAHO (Northern Panhandle)
See Washington

IDAHO
See Colorado

ILLINOIS (Southern)
See Kansas
See Missouri

ILLINOIS (Northern)
Ronald T. Scala Co., Inc.
Chicago   312-685-6719
Fax: 312-685-2469

INDIANA
Hitchcock Sales Company
Indianapolis   317-872-4335
Fax: 317-872-6875

IOWA
See Minnesota

KANSAS
Ramsay/Harrison, Inc.
Lenexa   913-492-5887
Fax: 913-492-0019
See Missouri

KENTUCKY
See Indiana

LOUISIANA
See Mississippi

MAINE
See New Hampshire

MARYLAND
Dans Company, Inc.,The
Brandywine   301-782-7881
Fax: 301-372-6061

MASSACHUSETTS
See New Hampshire

MICHIGAN (Metropolitan Detroit area)
Robus Sales
Birmingham   313-646-8339
Fax: 313-646-7876

MINNESOTA
Granse Corporation
Lakeville   612-469-2193
Fax: 612-469-2196
Priorlake   612-435-7097
Apple Valley   612-432-9254

MISSISSIPPI
Jim Davis Associates
Florence   601-939-4808
Fax: 601-939-4808
(Fax # same as phone #; fax is automatically rolled over to fax machine.)

MISSOURI
Ramsay/Harrison, Inc.
Chesterfield   314-532-9189
Fax: 314-537-0188
See Kansas

MONTANA (Butte only)
See Minnesota

NEBRASKA
See Minnesota

NEBRASKA (Western)
See Colorado

NEVADA (Northern)
See California (Northern, above San Luis Obispo)

NEVADA (Las Vegas)
See Arizona

NEW HAMPSHIRE
Sales Partners
Barnstead   603-664-5711
Fax: 603-664-5725

NEW JERSEY
See New York (NYC & The Five Boroughs)

NEW MEXICO (Albuquerque)
See Colorado

NEW MEXICO (Southern)
See Arizona

NEW YORK (NYC & The Five Boroughs)
Philip Brill & Associates
Port Washington   516-944-7720
Fax: 516-944-7743

NEW YORK (Western & Upper State)
See New Hampshire

NORTH CAROLINA
Ecford Enterprises, Inc.
Charlotte   704-377-4774
Fax: 704-343-9034

NORTH DAKOTA
See Minnesota

OHIO
Paul Kern Associates
Mayfield Heights   216-442-3007
Fax: 216-461-3630

OKLAHOMA
See Texas

OREGON
See Washington

PENNSYLVANIA (Eastern)
See Maryland
See Virginia

PENNSYLVANIA (Western)
See Ohio

RHODE ISLAND
See New Hampshire

SOUTH CAROLINA
See North Carolina

SOUTH DAKOTA
See Minnesota

TENNESSEE (Except Memphis)
See Georgia

TEXAS (El Paso)
See Arizona

TEXAS (Except El Paso)
North Texas Marketing
Dallas   214-340-7712
Fax: 214-340-0128

UTAH
See Colorado

VERMONT
See New Hampshire

VIRGINIA
Dans Company, Inc., The
Mechanicsville   804-550-2308
Fax: 804-288-9104

WASHINGTON
Pinnacle Marketing
Woodinville   206-487-6525
Fax: 206-487-6527

WEST VIRGINIA
See Ohio

WISCONSIN (North West)
See Minnesota

WISCONSIN (Southeastern)
See Illinois (Northern)

WYOMING (Southern)
See Colorado

ASKO INC.

Asko Inc.
903 N Bowser, Suite 170
Richardson, TX 75081   214-644-8595
Fax: 214-644-8593

ARIZONA
Salmi Distributing Corporation
Scottsdale   602-949-7300
   800-777-2564
Tucson   602-327-7491

CALIFORNIA
Sues, Young & Brown, Inc.
Baldwin Park   818-338-3800
Purcell-Murray Co., Inc.
Brisbane   415-468-6620

COLORADO
Meadow Creek Sales Corp.
Denver   303-934-2317
   800-777-6702

FLORIDA
Major Appliances, Inc.
Ft. Lauderdale   305-979-4700

ILLINOIS
Leeland International Dist.
Elmhurst   708-834-0888

INDIANA
Robco Distributing Co.
Indianapolis   317-788-0853

KANSAS
T.H. Rogers Distributing
Lenexa   913-599-1132

LOUISIANA
Louis W. Howat & Son, Inc.
New Orleans   504-947-6601

MARYLAND
The Zamoiski Co.
Baltimore   301-539-3000

MASSACHUSETTS
New Hearth
Norwood   617-769-6222
   800-356-3803

MICHIGAN
Trevarrow Inc.
Auburn Hills   313-377-2300
   800-482-1948

MISSOURI
Brightman Distributors
St. Louis   314-993-6666

NEBRASKA
T.H. Rogers Distributing
Omaha   402-558-0988
   800-888-0988

NEW JERSEY
Carl Schaedel and Co., Inc.
West Caldwell   201-228-4300

NORTH CAROLINA
Peerless
Charlotte   704-375-0255

OHIO
Top Brands, Division of Trevarrow Inc.
Maple Heights   216-587-2233

OREGON
Electrical Distributing Inc.
Portland   503-226-4044

PENNSYLVANIA
C&F Distributors
Columbia   717-684-3814
S.S. Fretz, Jr., Inc.
Philadelphia   215-671-8300

SOUTH DAKOTA
T.H. Rogers Distributing
Sioux Falls   605-336-3760

TENNESSEE
King Kitchens Distributing Company
Memphis   901-362-9651

TEXAS
VAH Distributors
Richardson   214-235-5201
Houston   713-682-0688

WASHINGTON
Electrical Distributing Inc.
Kent   206-395-7874

BRITISH COLUMBIA
Canwest Wholesale LTD
Surrey, British Columbia   604-594-1688

CANADA
Like Distributing Company
Scarborough, Ontario ... 416-291-2143
Dajon Electromenagers Inc.
Laval, Quebec ... 514-381-8013

BALDWIN HARDWARE CORPORATION

Please Contact Home Office:

Baldwin Hardware Corporation
841 East Wyomissing Boulevard
P.O. Box 15048
Reading, PA 19612 ... 215-777-7811
Fax: ... 215-777-7256

BARCLAY PRODUCTS LTD.

Please Contact Home Office:

Barclay Products Ltd.
Sales Lead Department
424 N. Oakley Blvd.
Chicago, IL 60612 ... 312-243-1444
Fax: ... 312-243-1381
Telex: ... 4330371 STERL UI

BATES & BATES

Please Contact Home Office:

Bates & Bates
3699 Industry Avenue
Lakewood, CA, 90712 ... 213-595-8824
... 800-726-7680
Fax: ... 213-988-0764

BEMIS MANUFACTURING COMPANY

ALABAMA
Will & Pierce Agency
Fairhope ... 205-928-1520
ALASKA
See Oregon
ARIZONA
The Marketing Pros
Scottsdale ... 602-863-4302
ARKANSAS
See Texas
CALIFORNIA
Buffington & Associates
Hayward ... 415-786-1600
Sales Support Inc.
Tustin ... 714-259-8744
COLORADO
J.N. Marshall Inc.
Denver ... 303-399-1050

CONNECTICUT
Pendleton Associates
Manchester ... 203-646-4411
DELAWARE
See Virginia
DISTRICT OF COLUMBIA
See Virginia
FLORIDA
Carr Co.
Boca Raton ... 407-997-0999
GEORGIA
McKee-Nix
Tucker ... 404-934-8061
HAWAII
Keyline Sales of Hawaii
Honolulu ... 808-833-3558
IDAHO
See Colorado
ILLINOIS
Broderick & Associates
Chicago ... 312-286-5577
R.K. Ray Sales Inc.
Decatur ... 217-423-2545
See Missouri (St. Louis)
INDIANA
The Brown Company
Zionsville ... 317-873-4564
See Illinois (Chicago)
IOWA
PRI, Inc.
Des Moines ... 515-276-0749
KANSAS
Hebco
Overland Park ... 913-491-0797
KENTUCKY
Jebco
Louisville ... 502-459-2782
See Missouri (St. Louis)
LOUISIANA
Landers & Associates
Kenner ... 504-466-9376
MAINE
See Massachusetts (Avon)
MARYLAND
See Virginia
MASSACHUSETTS
W.P. Haney Company Inc.
Avon ... 617-588-6464
See Connecticut
MICHIGAN
Dave Lozuaway & Assoc.
Flint ... 313-234-1635
See Wisconsin (Milwaukee)
MINNESOTA
Soderholm & Associates
Anoka ... 612-427-9635
MISSISSIPPI
See Louisiana
MISSOURI
J.W. Sullivan Company
St. Louis ... 314-644-5454
See Kansas
MONTANA
See Colorado
NEBRASKA
See Colorado
See Iowa
NEVADA
See Arizona
See California (Hayward)

NEW HAMPSHIRE
See Massachusetts (Avon)
NEW JERSEY
Ward/Kahn Company
S. Orange ... 201-763-1420
See Pennsylvania (Huntingdon)
NEW MEXICO
See Colorado
NEW YORK
Twin D & Associates
Latham ... 518-783-0634
Wm. K. Near & Assoc.
Bronxville ... 212-295-1409
NORTH CAROLINA
Ballantyne-Ludwig Smith
Charlotte ... 704-525-7805
NORTH DAKOTA
See Minnesota
OHIO
Curnayn Sales Company
Medina ... 216-722-4192
Libb Company
Columbus ... 614-451-1433
OKLAHOMA
H.W. France Company
Tulsa ... 918-664-5642
OREGON
Dahlquist-Rush- Shepherd
Portland ... 503-285-2832
PENNSYLVANIA
Keystone-Mountaineer Sales
Washington ... 412-228-5770
Henny-McLaren, Inc.
Huntingdon ... 215-947-0850
RHODE ISLAND
See Massachusetts (Avon)
SOUTH CAROLINA
See North Carolina
SOUTH DAKOTA
See Minnesota
TENNESSEE
Ray Patton & Associates
Nashville ... 615-383-9657
TEXAS
Wingard Corporation
Ft. Worth ... 817-335-4802
UTAH
See Colorado
VERMONT
See Connecticut
VIRGINIA
Duhart Associates
Richmond ... 804-379-0150
WASHINGTON
See Oregon
WEST VIRGINIA
See Pennsylvania (Washington)
WISCONSIN
Burton-Anderson & Assoc.
New Berlin ... 414-782-2870
See Minnesota
WYOMING
See Colorado

BENEKE/DIVISION SANDERSON PLUMBING

REPRESENTATIVES:
ALABAMA
Cruse & Associates
Alabaster ... 205-663-9642
Fairhope ... 205-928-9311
Jemison ... 205-688-2479
Saginaw ... 205-663-8662
ALASKA
See Washington
ARKANSAS
See Tennessee
CALIFORNIA (Southern)
Pro Line Sales
Rancho Santa Fe ... 619-756-4993
Van Nuys ... 818-906-8687
Woodland Hills ... 818-883-1113
CONNECTICUT
Omni Marketing, Inc.
Southington ... 203-224-8827
DELAWARE
See Pennsylvania (Eastern)
FLORIDA
Charles H. Liphart & Son
Jacksonville ... 904-731-7777
FLORIDA (Northwest)
See Alabama
GEORGIA
All Season's Marketing
Marietta ... 404-565-2397
IDAHO
See Washington
ILLINOIS
Added Sales Co.
Elk Grove Village ... 708-640-0123
INDIANA
Aspinall Assoc., Inc.
Indianapolis ... 317-325-2583
Lebanon ... 317-325-2583
INDIANA (Lake County only)
See Illinois
KENTUCKY (Eastern)
Disney-McLane, Inc.
Fort Thomas ... 606-781-3571
Independence ... 606-356-5473
KENTUCKY (Western)
See Indiana
MAINE
See Connecticut
MARYLAND
See Pennsylvania
MASSACHUSETTS
See Connecticut
MINNESOTA
Granse & Associates
Lakeville ... 612-469-2191
NEVADA
See California (Southern)
NEW HAMPSHIRE
See Connecticut
NEW JERSEY (Northern)
BMC Manufacturer's Reps, Inc.
Springfield ... 800-777-6262
NEW JERSEY (Southern)
See Pennsylvania (Eastern)
NEW MEXICO
Foster Sales Co.
Artesia ... 505-292-9098

NEW YORK (New York City)
Robert Shwab Assoc., Inc.

Amityville	516-691-5052
Armonk	914-273-5935
Hauppage	516-234-5668
Larchmont	914-834-6800
White Plains	914-997-6167

NEW YORK
K.C. Mets Sales Co.

Fayetteville	315-637-3660

NORTH CAROLINA
See Georgia

NORTH DAKOTA
See Minnesota

OHIO
Disney-McLane, Inc.

Cincinnati	513-541-1682

OKLAHOMA
See Texas (Northern)

OREGON
See Washington

PENNSYLVANIA
Giorgio Sales

Rehrersburg	717-933-5866

RHODE ISLAND
See Connecticut

SOUTH CAROLINA
See Georgia

SOUTH DAKOTA
See Minnesota

TENNESSEE
Ford & Associates

Bartlett	901-385-8121
Brentwood	615-371-9346
Cordova	901-756-5525
Memphis	901-324-6154

TEXAS (Northern)
Jim Roemer & Associates

Dallas	214-956-9988

TEXAS (Other)
See New Mexico

VERMONT
See Connecticut

WASHINGTON
Stone, Drew/Ashe & Jones, Inc.

Bellevue	206-455-4462
Seattle	206-763-2850

WISCONSIN
See Minnesota

ALL OTHER STATES

Beneke Customer Service	800-647-1042

BERLONI, THE CONTINENTAL KITCHEN GROUP

Please Contact Home Office:

Berloni, The Continental Kitchen Group
727 East Ave.
Pawtucket, RI 02860

	800-695-4824
Fax:	401-726-5755

BLANCO

Please Contact Home Office:

Blanco
James S. Tomaksky
1001 Lower Landing Road, Suite 607
Blackwood, NJ 08012   609-228-3500
Fax: 609-228-7956

BROADWAY COLLECTION, THE

Please Contact Home Office:

The Broadway Collection
Gerald Holscher, Sales Manager
1010 W. Santa Fe

Olathe, KS 66061-3125	913-782-6244
Toll Free:	800-766-1661
Fax:	913-782-0647

CENTRAL BRASS MANUFACTURING COMPANY

Please Contact Home Office:

Central Brass Manufacturing Company
John Raleigh
2930 East 55th Street
Cleveland, OH 44127   216-883-0220

CENTURY SHOWER DOOR INCORPORATED

Please Contact Home Office:

Century Shower Door Incorporated
250 Lackawanna Ave.

West Paterson, NJ	201-785-4290
Fax:	201-785-0777

THE CHICAGO FAUCET COMPANY

ALABAMA
Nel-Mac Sales, Inc.

Birmingham	205-942-9757

ALASKA
Roth and Company

Anchorage	907-344-9962

ARIZONA
R.D. Wager Company

Phoenix	602-968-8586

ARKANSAS
Fred Smith Co.

North Little Rock	501-753-7400

CALIFORNIA (Northern)
R.V. & Associates

Benicia	707-745-3655

CALIFORNIA (Southern)
Alno, Inc. (Decorative Only)

Chatsworth	818-882-6028

Renco Sales

Buena Park	714-521-8550

COLORADO
Edward F. Vance

Denver	303-433-0517

CONNECTICUT
Croft & Smith, Inc.

Niantic	203-739-4488

FLORIDA
The Seabridge Company

West Palm Beach	407-585-3606

GEORGIA
Bradford Sales Co.

Atlanta	404-448-3400

HAWAII
Hawaii Sales Assocs.

Honolulu	808-847-1547

IDAHO (Northern)
See Washington

IDAHO (Southern)
See Utah

ILLINOIS (Northern)
Brown-Miller Ltd.

Hillside	312-544-7500

ILLINOIS (Southern)
Ziel Co.

Molline	309-762-3700

INDIANA
The Stafford Company

Carmel	317-844-7706

IOWA (Western)
See Nebraska

IOWA (Eastern)
See Illinois (Southern)

KANSAS
RIVARD & Associates Inc.

Shawnee	913-262-3090

KENTUCKY (Central
See Indiana

KENTUCKY (Eastern)
See Ohio (Southwest and Northwest)

KENTUCKY (Western)
See Missouri (Eastern)

LOUISIANA
Grant & Associates, Inc.

New Orleans	504-733-2999

MAINE
See Massachusetts (Eastern)

MARYLAND
E.J. Dwyer Co.

Laurel	301-792-9307

MASSACHUSETTS (Eastern)
Stratford Associates

W. Roxbury	617-445-3410

MASSACHUSETTS (Western)
See Connecticut

MICHIGAN
The Taggart Company

Farmington Hills	313-553-4388

MINNESOTA
John Hamel Co.

Minneapolis	613-339-4696

MISSISSIPPI
Butler Sales, Inc.

Pearl	601-939-2804

MISSOURI (Eastern)
Heinkel Sales, Inc.

St. Louis	314-842-3500

MISSOURI (Western)
See Kansas

MONTANA
Vemco Sales

Great Falls	406-727-5335
Billings	406-248-8373
Missoula	406-549-6113

NEBRASKA
Service Reps

Omaha	402-571-5404

NEVADA (Northern)
See California (Benicia)

NEVADA (Southern)
Korner Company

Las Vegas	702-362-8503

NEW HAMPSHIRE
See Massachusetts (Eastern)

NEW JERSEY (Northern)
Sales Assoc. Mfg. Mktg.

Kenilworth	201-245-8400

NEW JERSEY (Southern)
See Pennsylvania (Eastern)

NEW MEXICO
Massey-Johnson Assoc.

Albuquerque	505-345-7908

NEW YORK (NYC Area)
Agnew Associates, Inc.

Long Island City	718-786-3180

NEW YORK (Eastern)
Kolstad Associates

Latham	518-785-5654

NEW YORK (Central)
Kolstad Associates

Rochester	716-288-2080

NEW YORK (Western)
Kolstad Associates

Buffalo	716-834-1445

NORTH CAROLINA
Bradford Sales Co., Inc.

Charlotte	704-588-6262
Raleigh	919-872-5190

NORTH DAKOTA
See Minnesota

OHIO (Northeast)
J.A. Bastl & Associates

Westlake	216-871-2827

OHIO (Central & Northwest)
The BWA Co., Inc.

Hilliard	614-876-2477

OHIO (Southwest)
The BWA Co., Inc.

Cincinnati	513-921-4343

OKLAHOMA
BDH Inc.

Oklahoma City	405-232-2940
Tulsa	918-664-4800

OREGON
See Washington

PENNSYLVANIA (Eastern)
Rinear Associates

Warminster	215-674-5450

PENNSYLVANIA (Western)
Fitzgerald Associates

Verona	412-241-7770

RHODE ISLAND
See Massachusetts (Eastern)

SOUTH CAROLINA
Bradford Sales Co., Inc.
Irmo   803-772-5342

SOUTH DAKOTA
See Minnesota

TENNESSEE (Central)
Fox Sales
Nashville   615-254-7732

TENNESSEE (Eastern)
Ben O'Neal Company, Inc.
Chattanooga   615-624-3359

TENNESSEE (Western)
Jim Cook Sales
Memphis   901-345-1231

TEXAS (Northern)
Thompson Company
Richardson   214-437-9193

TEXAS (Southern)
Paul Harmon & Associates
Houston   713-521-0350

TEXAS (Western)
Massey-Johnson Assoc.
El Paso   915-532-9270

UTAH
Woodruff Sales
Salt Lake City   801-972-3023

VERMONT
See Massachusetts (Eastern)

VIRGINIA (DC Area)
See Maryland

VIRGINIA
Central Sales Inc.
Newport News   804-244-3333

WASHINGTON
J. Wm. Jones Sls. Agency
Bellevue   206-747-4447

WEST VIRGINIA
See Pennsylvania (Western)

WISCONSIN
Advanced Ind'l. Marketing
Sun Prairie   608-837-5005

WYOMING (Northern)
See Montana

WYOMING (Southern)
See Colorado

CANADA
R.G. Dobbin Sales Ltd.
Downsview, Ontario   416-663-5465

CLAIRSON INTERNATIONAL CORPORATION

Please Contact Home Office:

Clairson International Corp.
720 S.W. 17th Street
Ocala, FL 32674
  904-351-6100
  800-874-0008
Fax: 904-867-8583

CLARKE PRODUCTS INC.

Contact Home Office Please:

Clarke Products Inc
Don Clark
1202 Ave. J East
Grand Prairie, TX 75050
  214-660-1992
  800-426-8964
Fax: 214-660-2259

CLOSET MAID

Contact Home Office Please:

Closet Maid
720 S.W. 17th Street
Ocala, FL 32674
  904-351-6100
  800-874-0008
Fax: 904-867-8583

CREDA LIMITED

North American Headquarters:
ILLINOIS
Creda Inc.
Mr. J. Tackenberg
Chicago, IL 60648   312-647-8024
Fax: 312-647-6917
Distributors: USA
ARIZONA
National Brands Inc.
Phoenix   602-269-3201
CALIFORNIA
Purcell Murray Co. Inc.
Brisbane   415-468-6620
Schreiber Distributing
South Gate   213-564-1801
  714-739-5363
HAWAII
Admor Distributors Corp.
Honolulu   808-537-4501
INDIANA
Robco Distributing
Indianapolis   317-788-0853
KENTUCKY
Birch Wholesale Inc.
Ashland   606-329-9117
MASSACHUSETTS
Appliance Dist. of Mass.
Franklin   617-528-4796
NEW JERSEY
Cooper Distributing Co. Inc.
Newark   201-643-2680
NORTH CAROLINA
Warren Distributing Company
Raleigh   919-828-9100
OREGON
Amco Distributing, Inc.
Milwaukee   503-659-2623
TENNESSEE
Consumers
Knoxville   615-523-7135

TEXAS
Seneca Dist.
Houston   713-827-1639
WASHINGTON
Domestic Supply Company
Seattle   206-575-1900
CANADA
Canwest Wholesale
Surrey, B.C.   604-594-1688
Like Distributors Limited
Scarborough, Ontario   416-291-9651
Los Distributing Amiel Ltcc
Chomoday, Laval, Quebec   514-381-8013

CUNO INCORPORATED/ CONSUMER PRODUCTS

Please Contact Home Office:

CUNO Incorporated
Consumer Products
Bruce Hafner
400 Research Parkway
Meriden, CT 06480   203-238-8715
Fax: 203-238-8701

DACOR CORPORATION

ARIZONA
Interwest Appliance Dist
Phoenix   602-271-0100
CALIFORNIA
Dacor
Pasadena   818-799-1000
Sierra Electronics Dist.
Sacramento   916-483-9295
COLORADO
Meadow Creek Sales
Denver   303-934-2317
CONNECTICUT
New Hearth
North Haven   203-288-3821
FLORIDA
Gulf Central Corporation
Tampa   813-985-3185
GEORGIA
Dacor
Atlanta   404-979-2897
HAWAII
Kitchen Distribution Center
Honolulu   808-531-9827
ILLINOIS
Leeland International Dist., Inc.
Elmhurst   708—834-0888
MARYLAND
Colonial Distributing
Beltsville   301-595-7300
MICHIGAN
Appliance Distributors, Inc.
Whitmore Lake   313-443-0080
MISSOURI
G.W. Ryan Dist. Co.
Kansas City   816-241-3100

NEW JERSEY
Cooper Distributing
Newark   201-643-2680
NEW MEXICO
Interwest Appliance Dist.
Albuquerque   505-345-9001
NEW YORK
Wittenberg Distributors
Syracuse   315-475-1395
NORTH CAROLINA
Warren Distributing Corp.
Raleigh   919-828-9100
OKLAHOMA
OK Distributing Co., Inc.
Oklahoma City   405-751-8833
OREGON
Moore Company
Portland   503-234-5000
PENNSYLVANIA
Peirce-Phelps, Inc.
Philadelphia   215-879-7070
TEXAS
Texas Sales & Marketing
Houston   713-460-2400
The Jarrell Company
Dallas   214-363-7211
WASHINGTON
Dacor
Seattle   206-840-5640
WEST VIRGINIA
Cabinet Supplier, Inc.
Huntington   304-429-1395
WISCONSIN
Morley-Murphy Company
Milwaukee   414-357-7900

DORNBRACHT/ SANTILE INTERNATIONAL CORPORATION

U.S.A. Headquarters/Importer:
1201 West Loop North, Suite 170
Houston, TX 77055   713-688-1862
Toll Free   800-344-1434
Fax: 713-688-9025
Sales Representatives:
ALABAMA
See Georgia
ALASKA
See California (Northern)
ARIZONA
See California (Southern)
ARKANSAS
See Texas
CALIFORNIA (Northern)
Nicholaas Marketing
Stockton   209-473-1161
CALIFORNIA (Southern)
Eurosource LTD
La Crescenta   818-249-2000
COLORADO
Design Sales
Aurora   303-671-8391
CONNECTICUT
See Massachusetts
DELAWARE
See Maryland

DISTRICT OF COLUMBIA
See Maryland
FLORIDA
Whitehead & Associates
Plantation   305-424-6529
GEORGIA
Whitehead & Associates
Newnan   404-254-0834
HAWAII
See California (Southern)
IDAHO
See Colorado
ILLINOIS
Schroeder & Associates
Evanston   708-869-0202
INDIANA
See Illinois
IOWA
See Wisconsin
KANSAS
Mega Marketing
Overland Park   913-381-6014
KENTUCKY (Eastern)
See Ohio
KENTUCKY (Western)
See Illinois
LOUISIANA
See Texas
MAINE
See Massachusetts
MARYLAND
J D L Associates
Ellicott City   301-750-2225
MASSACHUSETTS
Jon Spector & Associates
Cambridge   617-484-7700
MICHIGAN
See Ohio
MINNESOTA
The Stabeck Company
Wayzata   612-475-0900
MISSISSIPPI
See Texas
MISSOURI
See Kansas
MONTANA
See Texas
NEBRASKA
See Kansas
NEVADA (Northern)
See California (Northern)
NEVADA (Southern)
See California (Southern)
NEW HAMPSHIRE
See Massachusetts
NEW JERSEY (Northern
See Massachusetts
NEW JERSEY (Southern)
See Maryland
NEW MEXICO
See Colorado
NEW YORK
See Massachusetts
NORTH CAROLINA
See Georgia
NORTH DAKOTA
See Minnesota
OHIO
R D Scott & Associates
Chagrin Falls   216-247-7368

OKLAHOMA
See Texas
OREGON
See California (Northern)
PENNSYLVANIA (Eastern)
See Maryland
PENNSYLVANIA (Western)
See Ohio
RHODE ISLAND
See Massachusetts
SOUTH CAROLINA
See Georgia
SOUTH DAKOTA
See Minnesota
TENNESSEE
See Georgia
TEXAS
William Smyth
Dallas   214-691-6803
UTAH
See Colorado
VERMONT
See Massachusetts
VIRGINIA
See Maryland
WASHINGTON
See California (Northern)
WEST VIRGINIA
See Ohio
WISCONSIN
Supply Source Inc.
Middleton   608-836-6955
WYOMING
See Colorado

DUPONT CORIAN

Corian Customer Response Center
G-52050
P.O. Box 80010
Wilmington, DE 19880-0010
                          1-800-4CORIAN

DURAVIT/SANTILE INTERNATIONAL CORPORATION

U.S.A. Headquarters/Importer
1201 West Loop North, Suite 170
Houston, TX 77055   713-688-1862
Toll Free: 800-344-1434
Fax: 713-688-9025
Sales Representatives:
ALABAMA
See Georgia
ALASKA
See California (Northern)
ARIZONA
See California (Southern)
ARKANSAS
See Texas
CALIFORNIA (Northern)
Nicholaas Marketing
Stockton   209-473-1161

CALIFORNIA (Southern)
Eurosource LTD
La Crescenta   818-249-2000
COLORADO
Design Sales
Aurora   303-671-8391
CONNECTICUT
See Massachusetts
DELAWARE
See Maryland
DISTRICT OF COLUMBIA
See Maryland
FLORIDA
Whitehead & Associates
Plantation   305-424-6529
GEORGIA
Whitehead & Associates
Newnan   404-254-0834
HAWAII
See California (Southern)
IDAHO
See Colorado
ILLINOIS
Schroeder & Associates
Evanston   708-869-0202
INDIANA
See Illinois
IOWA
See Wisconsin
KANSAS
Mega Marketing
Overland Park   913-381-6014
KENTUCKY (Eastern)
See Ohio
KENTUCKY (Western)
See Illinois
LOUISIANA
See Texas
MAINE
See Massachusetts
MARYLAND
J D L Associates
Ellicott City   301-750-2225
MASSACHUSETTS
Jon Spector & Associates
Cambridge   617-484-7700
MICHIGAN
See Ohio
MINNESOTA
The Stabeck Company
Wayzata   612-475-0900
MISSISSIPPI
See Texas
MISSOURI
See Kansas
MONTANA
See Texas
NEBRASKA
See Kansas
NEVADA (Northern)
See California (Northern)
NEVADA (Southern)
See California (Southern)
NEW HAMPSHIRE
See Massachusetts
NEW JERSEY (Northern)
See Massachusetts
NEW JERSEY (Southern)
See Maryland

NEW MEXICO
See Colorado
NEW YORK
See Massachusetts
NORTH CAROLINA
See Georgia
NORTH DAKOTA
See Minnesota
OHIO
R D Scott & Associates
Chagrin Falls   216-247-7368
OKLAHOMA
See Texas
OREGON
See California
PENNSYLVANIA (Eastern)
See Maryland
PENNSYLVANIA (Western)
See Ohio
RHODE ISLAND
See Massachusetts
SOUTH CAROLINA
See Georgia
SOUTH DAKOTA
See Minnesota
TENNESSEE
See Georgia
TEXAS
William Smyth
Dallas   214-691-6803
UTAH
See Colorado
VERMONT
See Massachusetts
VIRGINIA
See Maryland
WASHINGTON
See California (Northern)
WEST VIRGINIA
See Ohio
WISCONSIN
Supply Source Inc.
Middleton   608-836-6955
WYOMING
See Colorado

ELKAY MANUFACTURING COMPANY

ALABAMA
Nel-Mac Sales Inc.
Birmingham   205-942-9757
ARIZONA
R.D. Wager Co.
Tempe   602-968-8586
ARKANSAS
Fred Smith Co.
North Little Rock   501-753-7400
CALIFORNIA (Northern)
Pacific Sales
Campbell   408-379-3300
CALIFORNIA (Southern)
Renco Sales Inc.
Buena Park   714-521-8550
COLORADO
Priest-Zimmerman Inc.
Denver   303-657-0663

CONNECTICUT
Davenport Associates
Wallingford — 203-265-2389

DELAWARE
See New Jersey (Southern)

DISTRICT OF COLUMBIA
See Maryland

FLORIDA (Southern)
Maco of Florida, Inc.
Pompano Beach — 305-960-0220

FLORIDA (West Central)
Maco of Florida, Inc.
Temple Terrace — 813-989-2474

FLORIDA (East Central)
Maco of Florida, Inc.
Orlando — 407-295-5832

FLORIDA
Maco of Florida, Inc.
Jacksonville — 904-396-7586

FLORIDA (Pensacola Area)
See Alabama

GEORGIA
Repco Sales of Georgia
Woodstock — 404-591-2100

HAWAII
Crown Sales, Inc.
Honolulu — 808-845-7881

IDAHO (Northern)
See Washington

IDAHO (Southern)
See Utah

IDAHO (Southwestern)
See Oregon

ILLINOIS (Northern)
Broderick & Assocs. Inc.
Chicago — 708-439-5070

ILLINOIS (Mid-Central)
Fassett Sales Co.
Bloomington — 309-663-8451

INDIANA (Northern & Southern)
Shadco, Inc.
Indianapolis — 317-251-9045

IOWA
RB Associates, Inc.
Ames — 515-232-3338

KANSAS
See Missouri

KENTUCKY
Shadco, Inc.
Louisville — 502-426-9615

LOUISIANA (Northern)
Agent Service Inc.
Shreveport — 318-869-1626

LOUISIANA (Southern)
Bremermann Co., Inc.
New Orleans — 504-899-3415

MAINE
See Massachusetts

MARYLAND
Chesapeake Marketing Inc
Hyattsville — 301-577-2164

MASSACHUSETTS
Adelson Brothers Inc.
Billerica — 508-667-9300

MICHIGAN (Eastern)
Balfrey & Johnston Inc.
Detroit — 313-864-2800

MICHIGAN (Western)
Van R. Kipka Sales
Grand Rapids — 616-458-2266

MICHIGAN (Upper Peninsula)
See Wisconsin

MINNESOTA
Bongard Corp.
St. Paul — 612-483-3452

MISSISSIPPI (Northern)
Butler Sales Inc.
Pearl — 601-939-2804

MISSISSIPPI (Southern)
See Louisiana (Southern)

MISSOURI (Eastern)
M/R & Associates Inc.
St. Louis — 314-962-8960

MISSOURI (Western)
McQueeny-Lock Company
Kansas City — 816-221-0700

MONTANA
Clapper Company Inc.
Billings — 406-252-9385

NEBRASKA
R.B. Associates Inc
Omaha — 402-895-3340

NEVADA (Las Vegas)
Korner Company
Las Vegas — 702-362-8503

NEVADA (Western-Reno)
See California

NEW HAMPSHIRE
See Massachusetts

NEW JERSEY (Northern)
Maloney & Curcio
Summit — 201-277-6400

NEW JERSEY (Southern)
Cope-Wardell Assocs. Inc.
Runnemede — 609-939-0800
In Philadelphia — 215-923-3045

NEW MEXICO
M & M Sales
Albuquerque — 505-884-1733

NEW YORK (Eastern)
Robco Specialties, Inc.
Albany — 518-463-6607

NEW YORK (Central)
Repco Sales
Syracuse — 315-422-7555

NEW YORK (West Central)
Minic Sales & Service
Rochester — 716-442-0606

NEW YORK (Western)
Edward C. Oldach
Buffalo — 716-634-0024

NEW YORK (NYC Area)
Robert Shwab Associates
Larchmont — 914-834-6800

NORTH CAROLINA (Northern)
See Virginia

NORTH CAROLINA (Southern)
Strickland Sales Co.
Charlotte — 704-525-3043

NORTH DAKOTA (Eastern)
See Minnesota

NORTH DAKOTA (Western)
See South Dakota

OHIO (Central)
The BWA South Company
Hilliard — 614-876-2477

OHIO (Southwest)
The BWA South Company
Cincinnati — 513-921-4343

OHIO (Northeast)
The BWA Company, Inc.
Cleveland — 216-781-4040

OKLAHOMA
Brazeal, Dilbeck, Hoevelman, Inc.
Oklahoma City — 405-232-2940
Tulsa — 918-664-4800

OREGON
Curry/Wiebe Sales
Portland — 503-289-1851

PENNSYLVANIA (Eastern)
See New Jersey

PENNSYLVANIA (Western)
Fitzgerald Assoc. Inc.
Verona — 412-241-7770

PENNSYLVANIA (Central)
Martin & Smith Inc.
Huntington Valley — 215-355-7676
Linglestown — 717-652-4021

RHODE ISLAND
See Massachusetts

SOUTH CAROLINA
See North Carolina

SOUTH DAKOTA (Eastern)
See Minnesota

SOUTH DAKOTA (Western)
Dakota Repco, Inc.
Rapid City — 605-341-7931

TENNESSEE (Eastern)
Ford & Associates
Brentwood — 615-371-9346

TENNESSEE (Western)
Ford & Associates
Memphis — 901-324-6154

TEXAS (Southeastern)
Sarco of Texas
Houston — 713-680-1116

TEXAS (Southwestern)
Jim Martin & Assocs.
San Antonio — 512-734-7064

TEXAS (Northern)
Braswell and Associates
Dallas — 214-239-7465

TEXAS (El Paso Area)
M & M Sales
El Paso — 915-772-0393

UTAH
The Lovell/Williams Company
Salt Lake City — 801-975-7053

VERMONT
See Massachusetts

VIRGINIA
Joseph H. Keller Assoc.
Richmond — 804-288-7004

WASHINGTON (Eastern)
O'Conner-Shrope Sales
Spokane — 509-534-1516

WASHINGTON (Western)
Stone-Drew/Ashe & Jones
Seattle — 206-763-2850

WASHINGTON (Southern)
See Oregon

WEST VIRGINIA
See Pennsylvania (Western)

WISCONSIN
Stickler & Assoc. Inc.
Milwaukee — 414-771-0400

WYOMING (Northern)
See Montana

WYOMING (Southern)
See Colorado

PUERTO RICO
Bruno Rodriguez
Puerta de Terra — 809-724-8865

EMBASSY INDUSTRIES, INC.

RESIDENTAL REPRESENTATIVES

ALASKA
See Washington

CALIFORNIA (Northern)
RKR Sales Company
Pleasanton, — 415-426-5060
Fax: — 415-426-0880

COLORADO
MPD Inc.
Denver — 303-322-0169
Fax: — 303-322-0374

CONNECTICUT
See Massachusetts

DELAWARE (New Castle)
See Pennsylvania (Eastern)

DELAWARE (Including the counties of: Kent and Sussex.)
See Maryland

DISTRICT OF COLUMBIA
See Maryland

FLORIDA (Panhandle)
See Georgia

IDAHO (Panhandle)
See Washington

ILLINOIS (Northern, including the counties of: Lake, Porter and Springfield)
Lyall-Thresher Associates
Glenview — 708-483-1414
Fax: — 708-483-1424

ILLINOIS (Southern, north to and including the following counties: Hancock, Brawn, Cass, Menard, Sangamon, Macon, Piat, Champaign and Edgar.)
See Missouri (Eastern)

INDIANA (Including the following counties: Wayne, Franklin, Union, Dearborn and Switzerland)
See Kentucky

INDIANA (Excluding the following counties: Lake, Porter, Wayne, Franklin, Dearborn and Switzerland.)
P & H Marketing
Indianapolis — 317-244-6888
Fax: — 317-244-6889
Bristol
Syracuse

INDIANA
See G.W. Berkheimer Company and all branches.
See Illinois (Northern)

IOWA (Except the river cities from Dubuque, south to and including Bettendorf and Davenport)
See Minnesota

IOWA (Including the river cities from Dubuque, south to Bettendorf and Davenport)
See Illinois (Northern)

KANSAS
Hydronics Heating Distributors
Topeka   913-234-5332
R.C. Neuer Company
Overland Park   913-341-6556

KENTUCKY
See Ohio

MAINE
See Massachusetts (Eastern)

MARYLAND
Taylor Sales
Randallstown   301-922-0592
               301-922-1554
Fax: 301-922-6472

MASSACHUSETTS
Metro Sales
Dennis   508-362-2339
Yarmouth Port
Fax: 508-362-2689

MASSACHUSETTS (Eastern, west to and including Worcester county.)
W.P.Hanney Co.
South Easton   508-238-2030
Fax: 508-228-8353

MICHIGAN (Lower Peninsula)
RJM Sales and Marketing
Clarkston   313-625-2000
Fax: 313-625-8514
Ada   313-625-2000
Car   616-450-3038

MICHIGAN (Upper Peninsula)
See Wisconsin

MINNESOTA
J.L. Company
Edina   612-933-7768
Fax: 612-933-1069

MISSOURI (Eastern Missouri, west to and including the counties of: Putnam, Adair, Maco, Randolph, Howard, Cooper, Morgan, Camden, Lacledet, Texas and Howell.)
Sweeney-Fortwengler Associates, Inc.
Fenton   314-343-1243
               314-343-9509

MISSOURI (Western, east to and including the following counties: Ozark, Douglas, Wright, Dallas, Hickory, Benton, Pettis, Saline, Chariton, Linn, Sullivan and Mercer.)
See Kansas (Overland Park)

MONTANA
See Colorado
See Utah

NEW HAMPSHIRE
See Massachusetts (Eastern)

NEW JERSEY (Southern, including the following counties: Atlantic, Burlington, Camden, Gloucester, Salem, Cumberland, and Cap May.)
See Pennsylvania (Eastern)

NEW JERSEY (Excluding the following counties: Camden,

Gloucester, Atlantic, Salem, Cumberland and Cap May.)
Morco Sales Company
Linden   201-925-8888
               800-426-0239
Fax: 201-925-7321

NEW MEXICO
Rocky Mountain Marketing
Albuquerque   505-883-4405
Fax: 505-881-3767

NEW YORK (Including the counties of: Brooklyn, Queens, Manhattan, Bronx, Putnam, Dutchess, Ulster, and Sullivan, excluding Schmidt's Wholesale in Monticello, New York and Orange county Plumbing Supply in Middletown, New York and branches, and Fowler & Keith Supply in Kingston, New York.
Chasco Sales/Manhattan Sales
Woodmere   516-374-4884
Fax: 516-569-8480

NEW YORK (Upper state, down to and including the counties of: Delaware, Greene, and Columbia.)
Hydronics Sales, Inc.
Syracuse   315-638-8847
               315-638-0402
Fax: 351-638-1133

NEW YORK (Including counties of: Rockland and Richmond (Staten Island) and Orange county Plumbing Supply in Middletown, New York and branch, Fowler & Keith Supply in Kingston, New York.)
See New Jersey

NORTH DAKOTA
See Minnesota

OHIO (Including the city of Toledo.)
See Michigan (Lower Peninsula)

OHIO (Excluding the city of Toledo. Southwestern Ohio excluding the following counties: Prebble, Montgomery, Greene, Fayette, Highland and Adams.)
Fairview Sales Company
Fairview Park   216-226-3113

OHIO (Southwestern, having the following counties as its northern and eastern bounaries: Prebble, Montgomery, Greene, Fayette, Highland and Adams)
See Kentucky

OREGON
See Washington

PENNSYLVANIA (Eastern, having its westerly boundardy and including the following counties: Potter, Clinton, Centre, Huntington and Fulton.)
Leonard Woldoff, Inc.
Huntingdon Valley   215-673-1950
Fax: 215-947-6396
Philadelphia   215-843-6846
Fax: 215-843-9145

PENNSYLVANIA (Western, with eastern boundaries to include the counties of: McKean, Cameron, Clearfield, Blair and Bedford.
See Ohio

RHODE ISLAND
See Massachusetts (Eastern)

SOUTH DAKOTA
See Minnesota

TENNESSEE
See Georgia

TEXAS (City of El Paso)
See New Mexico

UTAH
Utah Branch
Salt Lake City   801-531-1717
Fax: 801-359-2936

VERMONT
See Massachusetts

VIRGINIA
See Maryland

WEST VIRGINIA
See Ohio

WISCONSIN
(West to, but not including the following counties: Superior, Burnett, Washburn, Polk, Barron, St. Croix, Dunn, Chippewa, Pierce, Pepin, Eau Claire, Buffalo, Trampealeau, LaCrosse, Vernon, Crawford, and Grand.)
Kissel & Associates
Green Bay   414-497-1555
Fax: 414-497-2292

WISCONSIN
(Western, having its easterly boundary and including the following counties: Superior, Burnett, Washburn, Polk, Barron, St. Croix, Dunn, Chippewa, Pierce, Pepin, Eau Claire, Buffalo, Trampealeau, LaCross, Vernon, Crawford and Grand.)
See Minnesota

WYOMING
See Colorado
See Utah

CANADA
Wesmech Technical Sales, Inc.
Edmonton, Alberta 403-486-0114
Fax: 403-486-0959

SASKATCHEWAN
See Canada

BRITISH COLUMBIA
See Canada

FORMICA CORPORATION

Please Contact Home Office:

Formica Corporation
10155 Reading Rd.
Cincinnati, OH 45241
               513-786-3533

FRANKE, INC.

Please Contact Home Office:

Franke, Inc.
Thomas M. Smith, V. Pres./Sls & Mkt.

Box 428
Hatfield, PA 19440 800-626-5771
Fax: 215-997-1220

GEBERIT

ALABAMA
Wooldridge & Associates
Birmingham   205-836-8706

ALASKA
See Washington

ARIZONA
Topline Sales
Tempe   602-254-7755

ARKANSAS
A. H. Deveney & Co.
Birmingham   205-870-5119

CALIFORNIA (Northern)
See Nevada

CALIFORNIA
Southern, Paragon Sales
Pacoima   818-890-0701

COLORADO
Carmco Sales
Arvada   303-424-2212

CONNECTICUT
DEBsco
Cheshire   203-272-4144

DELAWARE
R. A. Munder Co.
Conshohocken, PA 215-825-5666

FLORIDA
J. J. Ventures
Boca Raton   407-750-7413

GEORGIA
Patti Dawn Sales
Roswell   404-993-0909

HAWAII
Swords & Associates
Honolulu   808-845-6411

IDAHO
Frank W. Welsh & Associates
Bountiful   801-292-2416

ILLINOIS
H.O.K. Sales, Inc.
Villa Park   708-834-8483

INDIANA
See Illinois

IOWA
Jamesway Corporation
Blair, NE   402-426-4900

KANSAS
Gilbert Sales Associates
Stilwell   913-681-3225

KENTUCKY
Bob Day Sales Agency
Hixson, TN   615-842-4632

LOUISIANA
See Arkansas

MAINE
See Connecticut

MARYLAND
E. J. Dwyer Co., Inc.
Laurel   301-792-9307

MASSACHUSETTS
See Connecticut

MICHIGAN
Reliant Sales
Walled Lake 313-669-1010
MINNESOTA
Worley & Associates
Wayzata 612-473-5879
MISSISSIPPI
See Arkansas
MISSOURI
See Kansas
MONTANA
See Idaho
NEBRASKA
See Iowa
NEVADA
Capri Sales
Sacramento, CA 415-276-5097
NEW HAMPSHIRE
See Connecticut
NEW JERSEY (Northern)
Sales Associates
Union 201-686-0600
NEW JERSEY (Southern)
R. A. Munder Co.
Conshohocken, PA 215-825-5666
NEW MEXICO
MCA Associates
Phoenix, AZ 602-943-6927
NEW YORK (Long Island)
Laudin & Associates
Hollis 212-683-9221
NEW YORK (Western)
C & C Marketing
Rochester 716-328-1919
NORTH CAROLINA
Herrick & Co.
Greensboro 919-855-5600
NORTH DAKOTA
See Minnesota
OHIO (Northern)
J. Bastl & Associates
Westlake 216-871-2827
OHIO (Southern)
Hurley & Associates
Twinsburg 216-525-8443
OKLAHOMA
Rowell-Degrazier
Irving, TX 214-313-1688
OREGON
W. R. Mitchell & Co.
Everett, WA 206-365-9712
PENNSYLVANIA (Eastern)
See Delaware
PENNSYLVANIA (Western)
Weaver Agency
Pittsburgh 412-795-0600
RHODE ISLAND
See Connecticut
SOUTH CAROLINA
See North Carolina
SOUTH DAKOTA
See Minnesota
TENNESSEE
See Kentucky
TEXAS (Northern)
See Oklahoma
TEXAS (Southern)
See Oklahoma
UTAH
See Idaho

VERMONT
See Connecticut
VIRGINIA
See North Carolina
WASHINGTON
R. J. Hardin Co.
Seattle 206-623-7217
WEST VIRGINIA
See Western Pennsylvania
WISCONSIN
Charter Sales Agency
Whitefish Bay 414-962-7466
WYOMING
See Colorado
PUERTO RICO
Jose Gomez
Rio Piedras 809-761-4090
CANADA (Western)
Bartel Industries, LTD
N. Vancouver, British Columbia
604-980-3253
CANADA (Eastern)
LaPala, Inc.
Toronto, Ontario
416-798-0190

GENERAL ELECTRIC/ MONOGRAM

To obtain specific information on any Monogram product or service, call G.E. Answer Center® Information Service at 800-626-2000—anytime of day or night.

GERBER PLUMBING FIXTURES CORP.

Please Contact Home Office:

Gerber Rep
Ila Lewis
4656 West Touhy Avenue
Lincolnwood, IL 60646 708-675-6570
Fax: 1-800-5GERBER

GROHE AMERICA, INC.

NORTHERN UNITED STATES
NEW ENGLAND STATES (including: ME,VT,NH,CT,RI)
Urell, Inc.
Watertown, MA 617-923-9500
NEW YORK METRO AREA (including: New York City proper, Long Island)
J.R. Associates
Glen Cove, NY 516-671-6880
UPSTATE NEW YORK
C&C Marketing
Rochester, NY 716-328-1919
NORTHERN NEW JERSEY
A.L.P.
Fairfield, NJ 201-575-5844

SOUTHERN NEW JERSEY, EASTERN PENNSYLVANIA, DELAWARE
P.F. Valente and Associates
Vineland, NJ 609-692-3370
WESTERN PENNSYLVANIA, WEST VIRGINIA
Bertus Artman
Baden, PA 412-869-1300
HARRISBURG, YORK, PA
John Murphy
Harrisburg, PA 717-657-0462
VIRGINIA, MARYLAND, WASHINGTON, DC
Mid-South Marketing
Charlotte, VA 804-985-6084
SOUTHEASTERN UNITED STATES
NORTH AND SOUTH CAROLINA
Quality Plumbing Products, Inc.
Charlotte, NC 704-554-9000
GEORGIA
Carl McClendon
Norcross, GA 404-448-4954
ALABAMA
Tri-South, Inc.
Anniston, AL 205-237-7846
NORTHERN FLORIDA
M. Brian Marincov
Winter Park, FL 305-679-0346
FLORIDA PANHANDLE
Clarence "Chic" Rowland
Jacksonville, FL 904-733-6141
SOUTHERN FLORIDA
J.C. Robaina
Miami, FL 305-554-8706
LOUISIANA, ARKANSAS, MISSISSIPPI
Winders Sales, Inc.
Baton Rouge, LA 504-293-9705
MIDWESTERN UNITED STATES
MINNESOTA, NORTH AND SOUTH DAKOTA
Michel Sales Company, Inc.
St. Paul, MN 612-645-5584
MICHIGAN
Reliant Sales Agency
Walled Lake, MI 313-669-1010
NORTHERN ILLINOIS, WISCONSIN, INDIANA
Added Sales
Elk Grove Village, IL 708-640-0123
WESTERN MISSOURI, KANSAS
Berger Sales
Prairie Village, KS 913-649-2006
EASTERN MISSOURI, SOUTHERN ILLINOIS
Mid-America Marketing Associates
Manchester, MO 314-227-1387
OHIO
Kelly DeVaul
Fairfield, OH 513-829-1536
TENNESSEE
Ledford, Davis, Wamack and Assoc.
Chattanooga, TN 615-624-9068
KENTUCKY
Shannon Sales, Inc.
Louisville, KY 502-426-1041
IOWA, NEBRASKA
JM and Associates
Omaha, NE 402-592-3981

NORTHWESTERN UNITED STATES
WASHINGTON, OREGON, ALASKA
W.R. Mitchell
Everett, WA 206-365-9712
IDAHO, UTAH
BB&G Associates
Centerville, UT 801-298-1792
SOUTHWESTERN UNITED STATES
COLORADO, MONTANA, WYOMING
David Miles
Ft. Collins, CO 303-226-1870
ARIZONA, NEVADA
Joe Banks
Scottsdale, AZ 602-423-5664
NORTHERN CALIFORNIA
Western Sales
Union City, CA 415-794-9000
CENTRAL, SOUTHERN CALIFORNIA
Mike Baldwin
Costa Mesa, CA 714-751-8356
Patrick Gilmore
Lakewood, CA 213-496-2245
Mike Hutzler
Palm Desert, CA 619-346-3910
Roy Roberts
Santa Barbara, CA 805-683-4384
SOUTHERN TEXAS
S.M. Mellgren and Associates
Houston, TX 713-699-2411
NORTHERN TEXAS, OKLAHOMA
Ed DeSeamus
Carrollton, TX 214-394-1925
HAWAII, SOUTH PACIFIC
L.N. Sales
Honolulu, HI 808-531-6124
CANADA
Patrick O'Reilly
Hamilton, Ontario 416-545-7076

HALSTEAD INDUSTRIAL PRODUCTS

Please Contact Home Office:

John Holmgren
27565 Diaz Rd.
Temecula, AZ 92390
714-676-3000

HANSA AMERICA

Please Contact Home Office:

Hansa America
Michael Isaacs, President
931 West 19th Street
Chicago, IL 60608 312-733-0025
Fax: 312-733-4220

HASTINGS BATH COLLECTION

Please Contact Home Office

Hastings Bath Collection
Michael Homola
30 Commercial Street
Freeport, NY 11520   516-379-3500
Fax: 516-379-3187

ICI ACRYLICS/KSH INC.

Please Contact Home Office:

Richard Hanson
10091 Manchester road
St. Louis, MO 63122   314-966-3111
Fax: 314-966-3117

IN-SINK-ERATOR

ALABAMA
Southern Marketing
Anniston   205-236-9966
Birmingham   205-995-8181
ARIZONA
The Marketing Pro's, Inc.
Scottsdale   602-863-4302
CALIFORNIA (Southern)
Bluffiington & Associates
Hayward   415-786-1600
In-Sink-Erator Divisions
Chino   714-591-6431
COLORADO
Fanning & Associates
Denver   303-289-4191
CONNECTICUT
W.H. Falvey Associates
Southington   203-529-2325
DELAWARE
Ledgerwood-Herwig Assoc., Ltd.
Pat Ledgerwood
Wilmington   302-658-5418
Dick Herwig   215-874-0700
FLORIDA
Harry Warren, Inc.
Boca Raton   407-391-6129
Maitland   305-671-7172
Orlando   407-298-7803
Palm Bay   407-724-5322
St. Petersburg   813-398-5815
GEORGIA
Hunt Sales Co., Inc.
Avon Estates
Stone Mountain   404-296-0646
ILLINOIS
Added Sales Company
Elk Grove Village   312-640-0123
IOWA
Mid-America Sales Group
Des Moines   515-244-0812
KENTUCKY
Jebco Marketing, Inc.
Louisville   502-426-0676

LOUISIANA
Landers & Assoc.
Kenner   504-466-9376
MARYLAND
Quay Yendall
Sparks   301-771-4823
MASSACHUSETTS
E.T. Peck Corp.
Woburn   617-935-0030
MICHIGAN
Major Sales, Inc.
Troy   313-362-5010
MINNESOTA
Joseph J. Mechavich, DSM
Long Lake   612-333-4110
MISSOURI
Lang-Moran Co.
Ballwin   314-394-9798
    314-391-1826
NEW MEXICO
Desert Star Sales
Albuquerque   505-881-5204
NEW YORK
Wm. K. Near & Associates
Bronxville   212-295-1409
Twin "D" Associates
Latham   518-783-0634
Collins Associated LTD
Mandon   716-624-9430
NORTH CAROLINA
Hester & Messina, Inc.
Charlotte   704-525-2921
OHIO
Great Lakes Sales Co.
Cleveland   216-356-9200
The Libb Company
Columbus   614-451-1433
OKLAHOMA
Randy Harkins, DSM
Oklahoma City   405-728-0581
OREGON
DRS Inc.
Portland   503-285-2832
PENNSYLVANIA
Triangle Sales
Bridgeville   412-257-2300
TEXAS
BYK, Inc.
Carrollton   214-245-5533
Dallas Dist. Sales Center
In-Sink-Erator Division
Dallas   214-956-9277
Greg Blavat Sales Co., Inc.
Houston   713-224-4177
UTAH
John Armour Sales
Salt Lake City   801-487-1355
VIRGINIA
Jordan Sales
Marrifield
Fairfax   703-352-1440
Virginia Marketing Assoc.
Virginia Beach   804-428-2060
WASHINGTON
DRS Inc.
Kirkland   206-821-1123
WISCONSIN
Burton-Anderson Assoc., Inc.
New Berlin   414-782-2870

CANADA
Jones-Lindell & Assoc.
Winnipeg, Manitoba   204-786-1332

INTERBATH INC./ONDINE DIV.

ALABAMA
Seiferd Sales Company
Baton Rouge   504-928-4234
ALASKA
See Oregon
ARIZONA
R.D. Wager Company
Tempe   602-968-8586
ARKANSAS
See Louisiana
CALIFORNIA
Interbath, Inc.
City of Industry   818-369-1841
CALIFORNIA (Northern)
Harcro Sales, Ltd.
Hayward   415-786-2480
CALIFORNIA (Southern)
Summit Sales
Gardena   213-329-9029
COLORADO
Olin Sales
Denver   303-777-0585
CONNECTICUT
Pendleton & Associates
Manchester   203-646-4411
DELAWARE
See Pennsylvania
DISTRICT OF COLUMBIA
See Pennsylvania (Eastern)
FLORIDA
R.E. Grace & Company
Lake City   904-752-6492
GEORGIA
Cain Sales Company, Inc.
Atlanta   404-662-0755
HAWAII
Pacific Basin Marketing Company
Honolulu   808-847-1464
IDAHO
See Utah
ILLINOIS
Landsman & Associates, Ltd.
Bensenville   312-860-0989
INDIANA
H & K Sales
Evansville   812-867-6719
IOWA
Progressive Reps, Inc.
Des Moines   515-276-0749
KANSAS
See California
KENTUCKY (Northern)
See Ohio (Southern)
KENTUCKY (Southern)
See Indiana
LOUISIANA
Seiferd Sales Company
Baton Rouge   504-928-4234
MAINE
See Connecticut

MARYLAND
See Pennsylvania (Eastern)
MASSACHUSETTS (Eastern)
See Connecticut
MASSACHUSETTS (Western)
See Connecticut
MICHIGAN
Triad Sales, Inc.
Grand Rapids   616-453-2798
MICHIGAN (Upper Peninsula only)
See Illinois
MINNESOTA
Stabeck Company, The
Wayzata   612-475-0900
MISSISSIPPI
See Louisiana
MISSOURI (Eastern)
See California (City of Industry)
MISSOURI (Western)
See California (City of Industry)
MONTANA
See Utah
NEBRASKA
See Iowa
NEVADA (Northern)
See California (Northern)
NEVADA (Southern)
See California (Southern)
NEW HAMPSHIRE
See Connecticut
NEW JERSEY (Northern)
See New York (Metro)
NEW JERSEY (Southern)
See Pennsylvania (Eastern)
NEW YORK (Metro)
Wm. K. Near & Associates
Bronxville   212-295-1409
NEW YORK (Northern)
R.D. Wright
Delmar   518-475-1117
NEW MEXICO
See Colorado
NORTH CAROLINA
GPPI
Charlotte   704-554-9000
NORTH DAKOTA
See Minnesota
OHIO (Northern)
O'Carroll Sales Company
Columbus   614-888-8132
OHIO (Southern)
Cincinnati   513-922-0300
OKLAHOMA
See Texas
OREGON
Bailey Sales
Portland   503-222-1684
PENNSYLVANIA (Eastern)
Associated Marketing
Philadelphia   215-423-0202
PENNSYLVANIA (Western)
Musillo Sales Agency
West Homestead   412-461-4544
RHODE ISLAND
See Connecticut
SOUTH CAROLINA
See North Carolina
SOUTH DAKOTA
See Minnesota

TENNESSEE
See Louisiana

TEXAS
Manufacturer's General Sales
Fort Worth   817-535-2941

UTAH
Frank W. Welsh & Associates
Bountiful   801-292-2416

VERMONT
See Connecticut

VIRGINIA
Joesph H. Keller & Assoc., Inc.
Richmond   804-288-7004

WASHINGTON
Bailey Sales
Seattle   206-433-8885

WEST VIRGINIA
See Pennsylvania (Western)

WISCONSIN
See Illinois

WYOMING
See Colorado
Consumer Contact:
Ondine, Division of Interbath, Inc.
Steve Nozet, Dir. of Mkt
427 N. Baldwin Park Blvd
City of Industry, CA 91746   800-423-9485
(California)   800-828-7943

JACUZZI WHIRLPOOL BATH

Please Contact Home Office:

Jacuzzi Whirlpool Bath
Estraeilla Thorpe, Dir. of Mkt.
100 N. Wiget Lane
PO Drawer J
Walnut Creek, CA 94596   415-938-7070
Fax: 415-938-0130
Telex: 800-678-6889

JADO BATHROOM AND HARDWARE MFG. CORP.

Please Contact Home Office:

Jado Bathroom and Hardware Mfg. Corp.
4690 Calle Quetzal
Carmarillo, CA 93012   805-482-2666
Fax: 805-484-4799

JENN-AIR COMPANY

JENN-AIR DISTRIBUTORS:

ALABAMA
Bellow-Evans, Inc.
Birmingham   205-791-0890
Fax: 205-791-1022

ALASKA
See Oregon

ARIZONA
Paradies Distributing Co.
Southwest Division
Chandler   602-926-7901
Fax: 602-926-2049

CALIFORNIA
Jenn-Air West
Burlingame   415-259-1090
Fax: 415-692-7102
R & K Western, Inc.
Cerritos   213-921-0804
Fax: 714-521-6123

COLORADO
Roth Distributing Co., Inc.
Denver   303-373-9090
   800-821-6374
Fax: 303-373-2006

FLORIDA
Southeast Distributing Inc.
DBA: Jenn-Air Florida
Tampa   813-628-4022

GEORGIA
Cain & Bultman, Inc.
Atlanta   404-691-0730
   800-624-6686
Fax: 404-691-7579

HAWAII
Mutual Distributors, Ltd.
Honolulu   808-847-5941
Fax: 808-847-2487

ILLINOIS
Jenn-Air Central Distribution, Inc.
Bensenville   708-616-1000
Fax: 708-616-1003

INDIANA
Jack McDonough & Assoc.
Indianapolis   317-898-4200
Fax: 317-895-3165

KANSAS
Jenn-Air Midwest
Overland Park   913-339-6650
Fax: 913-339-6548

KENTUCKY
Roth Distributing Co., Inc.
Louisville   502-361-9211
Fax: 502-361-9211

MAINE
Dion Distributors
Lewiston   207-784-3531
Fax: 207-784-2820

MARYLAND
Paradies Distributing Co., The
Baltimore   301-576-7100
Fax: 301-576-8472

MASSACHUSETTS
Jenn-Air of New England
Westborough   508-898-9500
Fax: 508-898-9656

MICHIGAN
Jenn-Air Distributing
Wixom   313-347-6290
Fax: 313-347-6284

MINNESOTA
Roth Distributing Co., Inc.
Eden Prairie   612-937-9540
Fax: 612-937-2607

MISSOURI
Roth Distributing Co., Inc.
Earth City   314-291-1800
Fax: 314-291-7076

MONTANA
American Appliance Co.
Billings   406-252-0188
Fax: 406-252-0187

NEBRASKA
Affiliated Holdings, Inc.
Omaha   402-558-0988
Fax: 402-558-9850

NEW JERSEY
Carl Schaedel & Co., Inc.
West Caldwell   201-228-4300
Fax: 201-228-1152

NEW MEXICO
Fields & Company
Albuquerque   505-345-0171
Fax: 505-345-1556

NEW YORK
A.P. Distributors, Inc.
Mineola   516-742-9400
Fax: 516-746-5065
MKS Industries, Inc.
Syracuse   315-437-1511
Fax: 315-437-8273
Cheektowaga   716-895-2900
Latham   518-783-3864

NORTH CAROLINA
Jenn-Air of the Carolinas
Charlotte   704-588-6783
Fax: 704-333-3982
Raleigh   919-781-7743
Fax: 919-781-8127

OHIO
Jenn-Air Distributing, Inc. (JEDI)
Holland   419-865-5377
   419-865-4644
Fax: 419-865-8535
Jenn-Air Mid-States
(O'Connor and Klein)
Broadview Heights   216-526-0072
Fax: 216-526-7861
Columbus   614-848-4877
Fax: 614-848-3028
Cincinnati   513-771-1221
Fax: 513-771-4377

OKLAHOMA
Jenn-Air Midwest
Oklahoma City   405-949-9440
Fax: 405-949-9468

OREGON
Gene Whitelock Dist. Co.
Portland   503-624-1100
Fax: 503-684-0721

PENNSYLVANIA
S.S. Fretz, Jr., Inc.
Philadelphia   215-671-8300
Fax: 215-671-8340
Harrisburg Electric Supply
Harrisburg   717-564-5803
Fax: 717-558-9879
Jenn-Air Eastern Distributing
Mars   412-772-0580
Fax: 412-772-0498

SOUTH CAROLINA
Jenn-Air of the Carolinas, Inc.
Lexington   803-356-4710
   800-346-8481
Fax: 803-356-0796

TENNESSEE
Hermitage Electric Supply
Nashville   615-244-4167
Fax: 615-242-4443

Mid-South Jenn-Air Dist.
Memphis   901-377-6435
Fax: 901-386-9348

TEXAS
Jenn-Air Sales Co. of TX (Hankla)
Dallas   214-701-8181
Fax: 214-991-3788
South Texas Jenn-Air
(J.P. Edwards)
Houston   713-460-9500
Fax: 713-895-7211

UTAH
Roth Distributing Co., Inc.
Salt Lake City   801-972-9304
Fax: 801-972-9371

VERMONT
Blodgett Supply Co., Inc.
Burlington   802-864-9831
Fax: 802-864-3645

VIRGINIA
E.A. Holsten, Inc.
Richmond   804-359-3511
Fax: 804-358-9649

WASHINGTON
Gene Whitelock Distributing
Kent   206-656-2900

WEST VIRGINIA
Jenn-Air Eastern Dist.
St. Albans   304-722-4486

WISCONSIN
Roth Distributing Co., Inc.
Milwaukee   414-353-9000
Fax: 414-353-7818

CANADA

ALBERTA
K.J. Bradlee Distributors, Inc.
Calgary   403-297-1000
Fax: 403-252-8995

BRITISH COLUMBIA
G.P.M. Distributors, Ltd.
Burnaby   604-436-2626
Fax: 604-436-2636

MANITOBA
K.J. Bradlee Distributors, Inc.
Winnipeg   204-663-0631
Fax: 204-663-3183

ONTARIO
Euroclean Canada, Inc.
Cambridge   519-653-8880
Fax: 519-653-8691

QUEBEC
E.A.F. Distributors, Ltd.
LaSalle   514-364-1844
Fax: 514-364-2128

KABINART

Kabinart
Brad Liggett
3650 Trousdale Drive
Nashville, TN 37211   615-833-1961
Fax: 615-834-8268

KABINART REPRESENTATIVES:

ALABAMA
See Tennessee

ARKANSAS
See Tennessee

CALIFORNIA
Jack Hefler
Huntington Beach   714-840-1889
CONNECTICUT
See Tennessee
DELAWARE
See Pennsylvania
FLORIDA
Berry Lubel
Dania   305-920-3044
GEORGIA
See Tennessee
ILLINOIS
John Van Horn
Palatine   708-358-4979
INDIANA
See Ohio
IOWA
See Illinois
KANSAS
See Missouri
KENTUCKY
See Tennessee
MAINE
See Tennessee
MARYLAND
See Pennsylvania
MASSACHUSETTS
See Tennessee
MICHIGAN
Tom Doty
Grand Rapids   616-458-8119
MINNESOTA
Dick Rudeen
Minneapolis   612-546-0282
MISSISSIPPI
See Louisiana
MISSOURI
Lou Hittler
St. Louis   314-845-9579
NEBRASKA
See Minnesota
NEW HAMPSHIRE
See Tennessee
NEW JERSEY
See Tennessee
NEW YORK (New York City Area)
See Tennessee
NEW YORK (Upstate)
Douglas Brown
Cortland   607-756-2546
NORTH CAROLINA
See Tennessee
OHIO
Gary Lappin
Shaker Heights   216-295-1051
OKLAHOMA
See Tennessee
PENNSYLVANIA (Western)
See Ohio
PENNSYLVANIA (Eastern)
Jack Rankin
Hershey   717-533-7639
RHODE ISLAND
See Massachusetts
SOUTH CAROLINA
See North Carolina
TENNESSEE
David Maddux
Nashville   615-269-5105

TEXAS
See Tennessee
VERMONT
See Tennessee
VIRGINIA
See Pennsylvania
WEST VIRGINIA
See Ohio
WISCONSIN
See Minnesota

KING REFRIGERATOR CORPORATION

ALABAMA
Nel-Mac Sales Inc.
Birmingham   205-942-9757
ALASKA
See Washington
ARIZONA
Contact:King Home Office   718-897-2200
ARKANSAS
Fred Smith Co.
North Little Rock   501-753-7400
ARKANSAS (Eastern)
See Tennessee (Western)
ARKANSAS (Southwest)
See Louisiana (Northern)
CALIFORNIA (Northern)
Pacific Valley Sales, Inc.
San Rafael   415-453-9142
CALIFORNIA (Southern)
Barry Krauss Sales
Van Nuys   818-376-1500
COLORADO
Tom Brady Inc.
Denver   303-722-2893
CONNECTICUT (Fairfield County)
Contact King Home Office   718-897-2200
CONNECTICUT
Thormann Associates
Auburndale   617-332-0918
DELAWARE
See Pennsylvania (Eastern)
DISTRICT OF COLUMBIA
See Maryland
FLORIDA
Crabtree, Trippe & Assoc., Inc.
Jacksonville   904-778-8768
FLORIDA (Northwest)
Jim Nelson
Birmingham   205-942-9757
GEORGIA
Cain Sales Co., Inc.
Atlanta   404-662-0755
HAWAII
Keyline Sales of Hawaii
Honolulu   808-833-3558
IDAHO (Northern)
See Washington (Seattle)
IDAHO (Southern)
See Colorado
ILLINOIS (Central)
Frank Riddile & Assoc.
Peoria   309-688-2448
Chicago   312-705-8877

ILLINOIS (Northern)
Frank Riddile & Assoc.
Rockford   813-963-3335
ILLINOIS (Southern)
See Missouri (Eastern)
INDIANA
Aspinall Associates
Indianapolis   317-849-5757
INDIANA (Northwest)
See Illinois (Northeast)
IOWA (Mississippi River Area)
See Illinois (Central)
IOWA (Western)
McQueeney-Childs
Des Moines   515-255-6718
KANSAS
McQueeny-Jochens Co.
Kansas City   816-842-3503
KENTUCKY
Contact:King Home Office   718-897-2200
KENTUCKY (Covington Area)
See Ohio (Southwestern)
KENTUCKY (Paducah Area)
See Missouri (Eastern)
LOUISIANA (Northern)
Agent Service, Inc.
Shreveport   318-869-1626
LOUISIANA (Southern)
Bremermann Co., Inc.
New Orleans   504-899-3415
MAINE
See Massachusetts
MARYLAND
Burns Associates, Inc.
Severna Park   301-544-5585
MARYLAND (Western)
See Pennsylvania (Western)
MASSACHUSETTS
Thormann Associates
Auburndale   617-332-0918
MICHIGAN (Lower Peninsula)
Knight-Rummel Associates
Livonia   313-525-6530
MICHIGAN (Upper Peninsula)
See Wisconsin
MINNESOTA
Contact:King Home Office   718-897-2200
MISSISSIPPI
Butler Sales Co.
Jackson   601-939-2804
MISSISSIPPI (Northern)
See Tennessee (Western)
MISSOURI (Eastern)
McQueeny-Lock
St. Louis   314-569-3025
MISSOURI (Western)
McQueeny-Jochens Co.
Kansas City   816-842-3503
MONTANA (Eastern)
Vemco Sales Inc.
Billings   406-248-8373
MONTANA (Central)
Gene Mahn
Great Falls   406-727-5335
MONTANA (Western)
Missoula   406-549-6113
NEBRASKA
See Iowa (Western)
NEBRASKA (Western)
See Colorado

NEVADA (Eastern)
See Colorado
NEVADA (Western)
See California (San Rafael)
NEVADA (South)
See Arizona
NEW HAMPSHIRE
See Massachusetts
NEW JERSEY (South)
See Pennsylvania (Philadelphia)
NEW JERSEY
Maloney & Curcio
Summit   201-277-6400
NEW MEXICO
Tom Brady Inc.
Albuquerque   505-293-2375
NEW YORK (Southern)
Contact King Home Office: 718-897-2200
NEW YORK (Western)
Eastern Hydronics Specialties
Buffalo   716-668-8882
NEW YORK (Central)
Gesco Sales, Inc.
Syracuse   315-474-1089
NEW YORK (Northeastern)
Robco Specialties Inc.
Albany   518-463-6607
NORTH CAROLINA
Strickland Sales Co.
Charlotte   704-525-3043
NORTH DAKOTA
Hebert Sales
Fargo   701-235-8202
OHIO (Northern)
BWA Co., Inc.
Cleveland   216-781-4040
OHIO (Central)
John Armbruster
Hillard   614-876-2477
OHIO (Southwestern)
Dave Armbruster
Cincinnati   513-921-4343
OKLAHOMA
Donald Hodge
Moore   405-794-4560
OREGON
Contact:King Home Office   718-897-2200
PENNSYLVANIA (Eastern)
Rich-Tomkins Co., Inc.
Philadelphia   215-735-0132
PENNSYLVANIA (Western)
George Olszewski
Oakdale   412-221-2109
RHODE ISLAND
See Massachusetts
SOUTH CAROLINA
Strickland Sales Co.
Charlotte   704-525-3043
SOUTH DAKOTA
See North Dakota
TENNESSEE (Central)
Fox Sales Inc.
Nashville   615-254-7732
TENNESSEE (Eastern)
Ben O'Neal Co.
Chattanooga   615-624-3359
TENNESSEE (Western)
Dave Hill Associates
Memphis   601-349-8810

TEXAS
Paul Harmon & Assoc.
Houston   713-521-0350
TEXAS (Northern)
Braswell Sales
Dallas   214-239-7465
TEXAS (Northeastern)
See Louisiana (Shreveport)
TEXAS (Southern)
Melvin Mullens
Houston   713-491-4935
TEXAS (Southwestern)
See Colorado
TEXAS (Western)
Braswell Sales
Dallas   214-239-7465
UTAH
See Colorado
VERMONT
See Massachusetts
VIRGINIA
Joseph Keller & Assoc.
Richmond   804-288-7004
VIRGINIA (Fairfax City)
See Maryland
WASHINGTON
Stone-Drew/Ashe & Jones
Seattle   206-763-2850
WASHINGTON (Southwestern)
Contact:King Home Office   718-897-2200
WEST VIRGINIA
See Pennsylvania (Western)
WEST VIRGINIA (Martinsburg Area)
See Maryland
WISCONSIN
Professional Sls. Assoc.
Brookfield   414-782-9006
WISCONSIN (Northwestern)
Contact:King Home Office   718-897-2200
WYOMING (Northern)
See Montana (Billings)
WYOMING (Southern)
See Colorado
WYOMING (Western)
See Utah

KITCHENAID

CENTRAL DISTRICT SALES OFFICES
ILLINOIS
Naperville   708-505-7520
Fax: 708-505-1160
KANSAS
Lenexa   913-492-3883
Fax: 913-492-3978
MINNESOTA
Eagan   612-683-0080
Fax: 612-683-9388
TEXAS
Irving   214-506-8396
Fax: 214-869-9558
Houston   713-680-0497
Fax: 713-956-5767
EASTERN DISTRICT SALES OFFICES
MASSACHUSETTS
N. Billerica   508-663-0063
Fax: 508-663-6563

MICHIGAN
Farmington Hills   313-553-0440
Fax: 313-553-2141
NEW JERSEY
Englewood   201-871-5800
Fax: 201-871-6778
Mt. Laurel   609-778-7575
Fax: 609-235-5015
NEW YORK
See New Jersey
OHIO
Dayton   513-454-6766
Fax: 513-454-6634
PENNSYLVANIA
Mars   412-776-9200
Fax: 412-776-0046
SOUTHERN DISTRICT SALES OFFICES
FLORIDA
Deerfield Beach   305-426-6760
Fax: 305-426-6724
Altamonte Springs   407-767-5727
Fax: 407-830-0498
GEORGIA
Smyrna   404-434-1004
Fax: 404-434-1252
NORTH CAROLINA
Charlotte   704-522-8148
Fax: 704-525-7637
WESTERN DISTRICT SALES OFFICES
ARIZONA
Tempe   602-921-9310
Fax: 602-921-8693
CALIFORNIA
Irvine   714-261-1806
Fax: 714-261-6681
Pleasanton   415-426-5010
Fax: 415-426-5505
WASHINGTON
Seattle   206-433-0727
Fax: 206-439-7886

MAGIC CHEF

NORTH EAST REGION
Magic Chef
Matawan, NJ   201-566-8667
Fax: 201-566-4989
SOUTH CENTRAL REGION
Magic Chef
Irving, TX
GREAT LAKE REGION
Magic Chef
Hoffman Estates, IL   708-310-0770
Fax: 708-310-0014
NORTH CENTRAL REGION
Overland Park, KS   913-469-5737
Fax: 913-469-0323
SOUTHEAST REGION
Magic Chef
Marietta, GA   404-956-0683/4
Fax: 404-988-9341
WESTERN REGION
Magic Chef
City of Industry, CA   818-961-2290
Fax: 818-330-8160
Magic Chef
Cleveland, TN   615-478-4545
Fax: 615-478-4418

Magic Chef
Marietta, GA   404-956-0683
Fax: 404-988-9341

MAYTAG COMPANY

Please Contact Home Office:

Maytag Company
One Dependability Square
Newton, IA 50208   800-845-6564
Extention: 800

MEMRY PLUMBING PRODUCTS

Memry Plumbing Products
Brian D. Stearns, Gen. Mgr.
69 Armory Street
Worcester, MA 01603   508-799-9931
Fax: 508-753-0032
ALABAMA
All Seasons Marketing   404-565-2397
ALASKA
Memry Plumbing Products   800-582-5454
ARIZONA
M&M Sales   602-966-8812
ARKANSAS
Memry Plumbing Products   800-582-5454
CALIFORNIA (North)
R.D. Kincaide   415-861-9400
CALIFORNIA (South)
Paragon Marketing   818-890-0701
COLORADO
Jack Carruth   303-969-8263
CONNECTICUT
D.J. Lipkin Companies   603-673-9655
DISTRICT OF COLUMBIA
Memry Plumbing Products   800-582-5454
DELAWARE
Memry Plumbing Products   800-582-5454
FLORIDA
McKee Marketing Group, Inc.   305-941-0122
GEORGIA
All Seasons Marketing   404-565-2397
HAWAII
Memry Plumbing Products   800-582-5454
IDAHO
Memry Plumbing Products   800-582-5454
ILLINOIS
Professional Sales Assoc.   414-782-9006
INDIANA
Memry Plumbing Products   800-582-5454
IOWA
Memry Plumbing Products   800-582-5454
KANSAS
Memry Plumbing Products   800-582-5454
KENTUCKY
Memry Plumbing Products   800-582-5454
LOUISIANA
Memry Plumbing Products   800-582-5454
MAINE
D.J. Lipkin Companies   603-673-9655
MARYLAND
Memry Plumbing Products   800-582-5454

MASSACHUSETTS
D.J. Lipkin Companies   603-673-9655
MICHIGAN
Jim Brown & Associates   313-360-4000
MINNESOTA
Rakieten Sales, Inc.   612-933-2299
MISSISSIPPI
Memry Plumbing Products   800-582-5454
MISSOURI
Memry Plumbing Products   800-582-5454
MONTANA
Jack Carruth   303-969-8263
NEBRASKA
Memry Plumbing Products   800-582-5454
NEVADA
M & M Sales   602-699-8812
NEW HAMPSHIRE
D.J. Lipkin Companies   603-673-9655
NEW JERSEY (North)
Amante Sales Corp.   516-586-3800
NEW JERSEY (South)
R.L.C. Associates   215-670-0131
NEW MEXICO
M & M Sales   602-966-8812
NEW YORK (NY Metro)
Amante Sales Corp.   516-586-3800
Institutional
A.T. Pennco Sales   516-724-4628
NORTH CAROLINA
Stover Sales Co., Inc.   704-333-5800
NORTH DAKOTA
Rakieten Sales, Inc.   612-933-2299
OHIO
R.D. Scott & Associates   216-247-7368
OHIO (Toledo)
Jim Brown & Associates   313-360-4000
OKLAHOMA
J.D. Sales Corp.   214-341-4705
OREGON
R.D. Kincaide   415-861-9400
PENNSYLVANIA (East)
R.L.C. Associates   215-670-0131
PENNSYLVANIS (West)
R.D. Scott & Associates   216-347-7368
RHODE ISLAND
D.J. Lipkin Companies   603-673-9655
SOUTH CAROLINA
Stover Sales Co., M Inc.   704-333-5800
SOUTH DAKOTA
Rakieten Sales, Inc.   612-933-2299
TENNESSEE (East)
All Seasons Marketing   404-565-2397
TEXAS
J.D. Sales Corp.   214-341-4705
TEXAS (El Paso)
M & M Sales   602-966-8812
UTAH
Jack Carruth   303-969-8263
VERMONT
D.J. Lipkin Companies   603-673-9655
VIRGINIA
Memry Plumbing Products   800-582-5454
WASHINGTON
Memry Plumbing Products   800-582-5454
WEST VIRGINIA
Memry Plumbing Products   800-582-5454
WISCONSIN
Professional Sales Assoc.   414-782-9006

WYOMING
Jack Carruth   303-969-8263
CANADA
Thorndale International   416-940-2611

MERILLAT INDUSTRIES, INC.

Please Contact Home Office:

Merillat Industries, Inc.
Adrian, MI   517-263-0771

MIELE APPLIANCE INCORPORATED

To Locate Your Nearest MIELE Dealer
Please Call: 800-289-MIELE

MOEN INCORPORATED

Please Contact Home Office:

Moen Incorporated
Mike Rahrig
377 Woodland Ave.
Elyria, OH 44036
                800-321-8809 Ext. 2132
Fax: 216-329-2761

MONARCH TILE, INCORPORATED

Please Contact Home Office:

Monarch Tile, Incorporated
Barba B. Keene
834 Rickwood Road
Florence, AL 35630   205-764-6181
Fax: 205-760-8686

MYSON, INC.

ARKANSAS
P.C. Hardware
Little Rock
CALIFORNIA (Northern)
Plumbery, The
Dublin
WatConceptoncepts
Fremont
O'Hair Bath Showroom
Fresno
Los Altos Hardware-Plumbing
Los Altos

Fixture Perfect
Merced
CTW Designs
Novato
Plumbing Unique
Rancho Cordova
Bath & Spa Market
Redwood City
Plumbing N'Things
Redwood City
Fixture Gallery
Roseville
Plumbery, The
Sacramento
Bath & Beyond
San Francisco
Deluxe Kitchen & Bath
San Francisco
O'Hair Bath Showroom
San Francisco
Cornelia's Hardware & Plumbing
San Jose
Fixture Gallery
San Rafael
Jackson's Hardware
San Rafael
Western Nevada-Showroom
Sparks
General Plumbing Showroom
Walnut Creek
CALIFORNIA (Southern)
Familian Pipe & Supply
Anaheim
Eurobath & Tile
Costa Mesa
West End West
Laguna Beach
Altmans
Los Angeles
Ulti Bath
Los Angeles
Zone Inc.
Los Angeles
Georges Pipe & Supply
Pasadena
Familian Pipe & Supply
Riverside
Familian Pipe & Supply
Santa Monica
S & D Distributors
Santa Monica
Pacific Sales
Torrance
Familian Pipe & Supply
Van Nuys
Proline Sales
Woodland Hills
COLORADO
Water Systems
Denver
DELAWARE
Bell Supply Company, Inc.
Wilmington
DISTRICT OF COLUMBIA
Atlantic Plumbing
Ferguson-Lenz Supply
Union Hardware
FLORIDA
Elegant Hardware
Boca Raton
Peter Darras & Assoc.
Coral Springs

Designer's Plumbing & Hardware
Dania
Millers Fine Decorative Hardware
Fort Lauderdale
Ferguson Enterprises
Jacksonville
Quality Doors & Hardware
Miami
Farrey's Wholesale Hardware
North Miami
Ferguson Enterprises
West Palm Beach
GEORGIA
Ferguson Enterprises
Roswell
IDAHO
Consolidated SUpply
Boise
Familian N.W.
Boise
Fixture Gallery, The
Boise
Norman Supply
Boise
Paramount Supply
Boise
Plumbing Parts & Supply
Boise
Plumb-Co Supply
Coeur D'Alene
Falls Plumbing Supply
Idaho Falls
Norman Supply
Idaho Falls
Material Distributors
Lewiston
Norman Supply
Pocatello
Penquin Plumbing & Electric
Pocatello
Sandpoint Plumbing Supply
Sandpoint
Norman Supply
Twin Falls
ILLINOIS
Community Home Supply
Chicago
Vanity City
Evanston
Kitchen & Bath Mart
Niles
International Kitchen & Bath Design
Westmont
MARYLAND
Thomas Somerville
Annapolis
Schumacher & Seller
Balitmore
William Sigler Company
Baltimore
Ferguson Enterprises
Beltsville
Decorator Center
Bethesda
Ferguson Enterprises
Rockville
MICHIGAN
Warner Plumbing & Heating Supply Co.
Alpena
D & C Supply
Ann Arbor
Classic Baths
Birmingham

D & C Supply
Dearborn Heights
A & S Supply Company
Flint
Richards Plumbing & Heating Supply Co.
Grand Rapids
Wittock Supply
Iron Mountain
Richards Plumbing & Heating Supply Co.
Kalamazoo
Builders Plumbing Supply Co.
Midland
Herald Wholesale
Oak Park
Crest Supply Company
Owosso
Gage Company, The
Petoskey
Gage Company, The
Port Huron
Bath Magic
Royal Oak
E & J Supply
Travelers City
H.L. Claeys
Warren
MONTANA
Familian N.W.
Billings
Mountain Supply
Billings
Northwest Pipe
Billings
Plumbers Supply
Billings
Mountain Supply
Bozeman
M & L Supply
Butte
National General
Great Falls
Northwest Pipe
Great Falls
MDM Supply
Helena
Familian N.W.
Kalispel
MDM Supply
Kalispel
Familian N.W.
Missoula
Keller Supply
Missoula
Modern Plumbing
Missoula
Mountain Supply
Missoula
NEW YORK
Cancos Tile Corp.
Aqueboque
Imaginative Hardware
Bedminster
GUSA
Edgewood
Cancos Tile Corp.
Farmingville
Paul Associates Inc.
New York City
Plumbing Store, Inc., The
Spring Valley
Cancos Tile Corp.
Westbury

Cancos Tile Corp.
Westhampton
NORTH CAROLINA
Ferguson Enterprises
Durham
Ferguson Enterprises
Greenville
Ferguson Enterprises
Hendersonville
Ferguson Enterprises
Highpoint
OKLAHOMA
Designer Hardware by Faye
Oklahoma City
Its Company
Oklahoma City
OREGON
Superbath
Beaverton
Familian N.W.
Bend
Keller Supply
Clackamas
Familiam N.W.
Eugene
Familian N.W.
Medford
Familian N.W.
Portland
National Builder
Portland
Show Place, The
Portland
Familiam N.W.
Salem
Keller Supply
Salem
Familian N.W.
Tigard
Fixture Gallery, The
Tigard
PENNSYLVANIA
Ferguson Enterprises
King of Prussia
SOUTH CAROLINA
Ferguson Enterprises
Spartanburg
TEXAS
Ann Moore
Dallas
Dallas North Builders Hardware
Dallas
Ferguson Enterprises
Dallas
International Bath & Tile
Dallas
Nob Hill Decorative Hardware
Dallas
Pierce Hardware
Dallas
Unlimited Solutions
Dallas
A.D.R.
Houston
Custom Accessories
Houston
Ferguson Enterprises
Houston
Hollywood Builders Hardware
Houston
Allen & Allen
San Antonio

Wagner & Company
San Antonio
UTAH
Familian Pipe & Supply
Salt Lake City
VIRGINIA
Ferguson Enterprises
Charlottesville
Ferguson Enterprises
Herndon
Ferguson Enterprises
Lynchburg
Ferguson Enterprises
Richmond
Ferguson Enterprises
Winchester
WASHINGTON
Better Bath & Kitchen
Bellevue
Stove & Spa Shop, The
Port Orchard
Best Plumbing
Seattle
Coast Products
Seattle
Fixture Gallery, The
Seattle
Luxus
Seattle
Pacific Plumbing Supply
Woodinville
Familian N.W.
Woodinville
Keller Supply
Woodinville
WEST VIRGINIA
Ferguson Enterprises
Bluefield
WISCONSIN
W.S. Patterson Company
Appleton
Eau Claire Plumbing Supply
Eau Claire
LaCrosse Plumbing Supply
LaCrosse
W.A. Roosevelt Company
LaCrosse
Automatic Temperature Supply
Madison
Wisconsin Supply Company
Madison
W.S. Patterson Company
Milwaukee
W.S. Patterson Company
Rhine Lander
W.S. Patterson Company
Wisconsin Rapids
WYOMING
Plumbdustrial
Caspar

NEVAMAR CORPORATION

Customer Service Centers:
ALABAMA
Mills Distributing
Birmingham   205-251-0176
Mills Distributing
Mobile   205-639-0522

ALASKA
Hardware Specialties
Anchorage   907-563-1312
ARIZONA
West-Mar Distributors
Phoenix   602-252-8845
CALIFORNIA
West-Mar Distributors, Inc.
Cerritos   213-926-5111
West-mar Distributors, Inc.
Chula Vista   619-426-3100
J.E. Higgins Lumber Company
Fresno   209-264-1771
West-Mar Distributors, Inc.
Grand Terrace   714-783-4495
J.E. Higgins Lumber Co.
Sacramento   916-927 -2727
West-Mar Distributors, Inc.
San Francisco
West-Mar Distributors, Inc.
San Jose   408-434-0123
J.E. Higgins Lumber Co.
Santa Maria   815-674-9300
COLORADO
Aim Distributing, Inc.
Denver   303-572-3572
CONNECTICUT
Raybern Company
Rocky Hill   203-529-7704
FLORIDA
Dixie Plywood & Plastics, Inc.
Ft. Myers   813-334-3339
Deebo Products
Jacksonville   904-356-5826
Metro Associates
Jacksonville   904-731 -2188
Tech Products Company
Miami   305-685-5993
Tech Products Company
Orlando   407-422-4427
Tech Products Company
Riviera Beach   407-842-2408
Tech Products Company
Tampa   813-884-2503
GEORGIA
Morrison Supply Company
Chamblee   404-455-8244
HAWAII
Monarch Building Supply, Inc.
Honolulu   808-834-5678
Monarch Building Supply, Inc.
Kahului,Maui
IDAHO
Architectural Surfaces of Idaho
Boise   208-376-6691
ILLINOIS
All Tile, Inc.
Elk Grove Village   708-364-9191
INDIANA
International Paper Laminates
Elkhart   219-295-4105
Aetna Plywood
Indianapolis   317-353-6281
C & D Distributors, Inc.
New Salisbury   812-347-3278
IOWA
Central Distributors, Inc.
Des Moines   515-244-8103
KANSAS
Magic Woods, Inc.
Kansas City   913-281-5000

International Paper Laminates
Newton   316-283-0335
The Cramer Company
Wichita
KENTUCKY
Sommerville Distribution & Supply
Louisville   502-634-1247
LOUISIANA
Bacon Lumber Company
New Orleans   504-833-1924
Huttig Sash & Door
Shreveport   318-861-7604
MAINE
Neils Sorenson Hardware
Portland   207-797-0152
MARYLAND
Dixie Plywood & Plastics
Landover   301-322-9090
Dixie Plywood & Plastics
Linthicum   301-636-1001
MASSACHUSETTS
Atlantic Plywood Corporation
Woburn   617-933-3830
MICHIGAN
Millers Wholesale, Inc.
Battle Creek   616-965-0518
Genesee Ceramic Tile Distributor
Burton   313-742-4611
Custom Distributors, Inc.
Troy   313-362-2700
MINNESOTA
Youngblood Lumber Company
Minneapolis   612-789-3521
MISSISSIPPI
Sequoia Supply Company
Jackson   601-981-8612
MISSOURI
Plywood Supply Company
Springfield   417-866-6675
Plywood Supply
St. Louis   314-385-8696
MONTANA
American Distributors
Billings   406-245-6033
S & D Flooring Distributing Co.
Missoula   406-543-6671
NEBRASKA
Cubs Distributing Inc.
Lincoln   402-477-4411
Cubs Distributing Inc.
Omaha   402-592-0113
NEVADA
Peterman Lumber, Inc.
Las Vegas   702-733-4011
J.E. Higgins Lumber Company
Reno   702-329-1653
NEW JERSEY
Laminators Supply Corp.
Edison   201-906-8333
Plywood Wholesalers, Inc.
Lodi   201-845-5300
NEW YORK
Laminators Supply Corp.
Brooklyn   718-745-4540
Plunkett-Webster, Inc.
Cheektowaga   716-683-0284
HNH Distributors Inc.
Farmindale   516-293-1224
Sloan & Company
Rochester   716-475-1000
Plunkett-Webster, Inc.
Syracuse   315-463-5236

NORTH CAROLINA
Reynold Distributing Company
Charlotte 704-376-2483
Kitchen Pak, Inc.
Kernersville 919-993-8686
Eastern Millwork & Supply
Raleigh 919-781-0143
Cabinet Makers Supply Co., Inc.
Wilmington 919-251-8947
Eastern Millwork & Supply
Winterville 919-756-3150

NORTH DAKOTA
Fabricators Unlimited
Fargo 701-235-1185

OHIO
Tamarack Wholesale Distributors
Cincinnati 513-242-7722
Metal Mouldings
Cleveland 216-391-8400
Scioto Kitchen Sales
Columbus 614-237-0315

OKLAHOMA
Huttig Sash & Door
Oklahoma City 405-524-7636
Huttig Sash & Door
Tulsa 918-622-3131

OREGON
Trym-Tex
Portland 503-233-1181

PENNSYLVANIA
American Metal Moulding Corp.
Allentown 215-264-7447
D & H Distributing Co.
Camp Hill 717-255-7831
D.S.I.
Carnegie 412-279-7824
American Metal Moulding Corp.
Philadelphia 215-634-3100

RHODE ISLAND
Stiller Distributors, Inc.
Cranston 401-946-6600

SOUTH CAROLINA
Bird Sales, Inc.
Charleston 803-577-5440
Palmetto Tile Distributors
Columbia 803-771-4001
Greenville/Spartanburg Hrdwds Cntr
Greer 803-877-7328

TENNESSEE
Cabinet Manufacturers Supply Corp.
Chattanooga 615-698-8031
Modern Supply Company
Knoxville 615-966-4567
Winco
Knoxville 615-522-2181
CDI
Memphis 901-795-5161
CDI
Nashville 615-391-3015

TEXAS
Sun Supply Corp.
Abilene 915-673-2505
American Tile Supply of Austin
Austin 512-837-2843
Tex-Mar Inc.
Dallas 214-484-9984
Wholesale Building Materials Co.
El Paso 915-533-9721
Tex-Mar, Inc.
Ft. Worth 817-496-6996
Floor Tech
Houston 713-932-0092

Pan-Tex Plywood & Lumber Co., Inc.
Lubbock 806-747-2561
American Tile Supply
San Antonio 512-490-1927

UTAH
West-Mar Distributors, Inc.
Salt Lake City 801-487-0773

VIRGINIA
Plywood & Plastics
Chesapeake 804-547-4303
Plywood & Plastics
Richmond 804-359-1374

WASHINGTON
T & A Supply
Kent 206-872-3682
T & A Supply
Seattle 206-282-3770
Cochrane Northwest, Inc.
Spokane 509-534-5004

WEST VIRGINIA
Ohio Valley Industrial Supply
Ravenswood 304-372-2266

WISCONSIN
Lumber Dealers Service & Supply Co.
Sussex 414-246-6555
West-Twin Distributing, Inc.
Two Rivers 414-684-5535

CANADA
Panel Products
Alberta 403-250-5504
Panel Products
Alberta 403-451-6800
Ceratec, Inc.
Dartmouth 902-468-5192
Panel Products
Manitoba 204-694-1016
Cutler Forest Products
Mississauga 416-622-7321
Ceratec, Inc.
Quebec 514-956-0341
Ceratec, Inc.
Quebec QC 418-681-0101
Panel Products
Richmond 604-273-3108
Ceratec, Inc.
Weston 416-743-5514

NORMBAU INC.

Please Contact Home Office:

Normbau Inc.
John Diedam
186 Branham Way
Mt. Washington, KY 40047 502-538-7386
Fax: 502-538-6400

NUTONE, INC.

Please Contact Home Office:

NuTone Inc.
Tom O'Brien, Dir. of Mkt.
Madison and Red Bank Roads
Cincinnati, OH 45227 513-527-5100
Fax: 513-527-5376

OLSONITE CORPORATION

ALABAMA
John Doggett Mktg. Group
Birmingham 205-991-5927
ALASKA
See Washington (Redmond)
ARKANSAS
Jim Taylor Sales Co.
N. Little Rock 501-753-6543
ARIZONA
J.A. Smythe Company
Tempe 602-345-0001
CALIFORNIA
Benisek & Assoc.
Los Angeles 213-685-9900
Nussbaum & Associates
Millbrae 415-697-6330
COLORADO
Shyne & Associates
Denver 303-722-1300
CONNECTICUT
Burkholder & Assocs. Inc.
Simsbury 203-651-5667
DELAWARE
See Maryland (Annapolis)
See Pennsylvania (Huntingdon Valley)
DISTRICT OF COLUMBIA
See Maryland (Annapolis)
FLORIDA
See Alabama
Maco of Florida, Inc.
Tampa 813-989-2474
Jeff Nelson
Pompano Beach 305-960-0220
Lou Zangara
Jacksonville 904-396-7586
Tom McGuire
Orlando 407-295-5832
GEORGIA
Repco Sales of Georgia
Woodstock 404-591-1800
HAWAII
Toledo & Associates
Honolulu 808-524-7878
IDAHO
See Oregon
See Utah
See Washington (Redmond)
ILLINOIS
Frank Riddile & Assocs.
Peoria Heights 309-688-2448
Dale Toedt
Rockford 815-963-3335
Repco Associates
Des Plaines 708-298-1720
See Missouri (St. Louis)
INDIANA
Shadco, Inc.
Indianapolis 317-251-9045
See Illinois (Des Plaines)
IOWA
McQueeney-Childs Company
Des Moines 515-255-6718
KANSAS
Knechtel Sales
Merriam 913-362-6660
KENTUCKY
Shadco, Inc.
Louisville 502-426-9615
See Ohio (Cincinnati)

See Missouri (St. Louis)
LOUISIANA
Brennan Brothers Inc.
Kenner 504-466-9332
MAINE
See Massachusetts (Norwood)
MARYLAND
K/T Marketing, Inc.
Annapolis 301-261-2395
See Pennsylvania (Bridgeville)
MASSACHUSETTS
Serpa Corporation
Norwood 617-769-9988
See Connecticut
MICHIGAN
Burke Agency, Inc.
Walled Lake 313-669-2800
John Burke
Grandville 616-531-4966
See Wisconsin (Rhinelander)
MINNESOTA
Trio Sales
Bloomington 612-884-8190
MISSISSIPPI
See Louisiana
See Arkansas
MISSOURI
Heinkel Sales Inc.
St. Louis 314-845-0035
See Kansas
MONTANA
Doyle & Associates, Inc.
Billings 406-245-5381
NEBRASKA
See Iowa
See Colorado
NEVADA
Korner Company
Las Vegas 702-362-8503
See California (Millbrae)
NEW HAMPSHIRE
See Massachusetts (Norwood)
NEW JERSEY
Maloney & Curico Inc.
Summit 201-277-6400
See Pennsylvania (Huntingdon Valley)
NEW MEXICO
M & M Sales Inc.
Albuquerque 505-884-1733
NEW YORK
Empire State Associates
Clifton Park 518-371-4032
Snowden & Brower
Forest Hills 718-275-9367
NORTH CAROLINA
Rogers Sales Co.
Charlotte 704-543-7053
NORTH DAKOTA
See Minnesota
OHIO
Borosh Associates Inc.
Cleveland 216-888-4550
David O'Carroll
Columbus 614-888-8132
Select Specialty Sales
Cincinnati 513-471-7732
See Pennsylvania (Bridgeville)
OKLAHOMA
Brazeal, Dilbeck, Hoevelman
Oklahoma City 405-232-2940

Jack Dilbeck
Tulsa   918-664-4800

OREGON
Braley, Gray & Assocs.
Portland   503-249-6972

PENNSYLVANIA
Triangle Sales
Bridgeville   412-257-2300
B.F. Miller Co.
Huntingdon Valley   215-947-3363
See New York (Clifton Park)

RHODE ISLAND
See Massachusetts (Norwood)

SOUTH CAROLINA
See North Carolina

SOUTH DAKOTA
See Minnesota

TENNESSEE
Benefield Sales Company
Nashville   615-832-8114
See Georgia

TEXAS
Moore Sales Company
Plano   214-985-8400
Mena & Associates
Houston   713-699-4414
See New Mexico

UTAH
JWS Sales
Salt Lake City   801-359-2218

VERMONT
See Massachusetts (Norwood)

VIRGINIA
Virginia Marketing
Virginia Beach   804-428-2060
See Maryland (Annapolis)
Mundy-Murdock, Inc.
Mechanicsville   804-730-0003

WASHINGTON
Reid-Pacific Co.
Redmond   206-883-1663
See Oregon

WEST VIRGINIA
See Pennsylvania (Bridgeville)

WISCONSIN
MBA Corporation
Milwaukee   414-643-5383
Reed Later
Rhinelander   715-362-6762
See Minnesota

WYOMING
See Colorado

PANASONIC

Please Contact Home Office:

Panasonic
Carl Killian, Nat'l Mkt Mgr, Built-In
Appliances
One Panasonic Way
Secaucus, NJ 07094   201-348-7302
Fax: 201-348-7382

PARADISE WHIRLPOOL BATHS

HOME OFFICE
Lloyd F. Pugh & Assoc.
Mercer Island, WA   800-232-2552

REGIONAL OFFICES:

EAST
Lloyd F. Pugh & Assoc.
James Crawford
Winchester, VA   703-662-3023

WEST
Sterling Supply
Ron Cox
Sparks, NV   702-331-9493

DISTRIBUTORS

CALIFORNIA
Ginty Supply
John Ginty
Auburn   916-823-6010
Builder's Showplace
Ray Kremer
Concord   415-827-9422
Vista Building Products
Richard Khoury
Culver City   213-822-1333
Faucet Factory, The
Roxanne
Encinitas   619-436-0088
Creative Kitchen & Bath's LTD
Lawrence Klein
Fontana   714-822-2239
B & C Custom Hardware
Jerry
Laguna Hills   714-859-6073
Zone, Inc.
Corey
Los Angeles   213-652-7360
Windsor Plumbing Corp.
Steve
Manhattan Beach   213-374-9698
A Plumbing Experience
Al Kirtlink
Janet Kirtlink
Napa   707-252-0579
Bath & Spa Market
Bob Bredel
Redwood City   415-366-7528
Harrison's
Gail Harrison
Sacramento, CA   916-332-6770
International Bath & Tile
Raymond or Clive
San Diego   619-268-3723
Bath & Beyond
Jeff Burton
San Francisco   415-552-5001
Saratoga Plumbing #1
David
San Jose   408-996-1773
Saratoga Plumbing #2
Rich
San Jose   408-279-5202
Huntington Bath Concept
Gene or Anthony
San Marino   818-793-5297
Kitchen & Bath Showroom
Steven Batis
San Rafael   415-459-4777
Economy Supply Company
Tom Rademacher

Mary Rademacher
Santa Barbara   805-965-4319
Bath Fantasies
Kursh or Leslie
Santa Monica   213-393-4031
Waterwishes
Vance Littleton
Santa Rosa   707-545-0743
International Bath & Tile
Neala or Walter
Solana Beach   619-481-4984
Plumbing Bureau
Jerry Opray
Soquel   408-462-3536
Kelly's Plumbing Supply
Tim Kelly
Stockton   209-948-1524
Anchor Lighting
Charles Boghosian
Tulare   209-688-0696
Tiffany Bath & Spa Design Center
Ron Harris
Van Nuys   818-994-7211

HAWAII
Vikiing Recreational
Stan
Honolulu   808-949-3333

MARYLAND
Woodstove Johnny's
Gib Mason
Severna Park   301-647-0535

MICHIGAN
Kitchens By Starline
Mark Welch
Flushing   313-659-3107
N B C Supply
Bob Postema
Holland   616-396-1931
Scholten Kitchens & Bath
Duane Scholten
Kalamazoo   616-345-1166
Mathison Hardware
Frank Mathison
Livonia   313-522-5633
Central Plumbing
Carol Bissett
Ed Bissett
Mt. Pleasant   517-772-9190
Style Trend
Bob Szotko
Muskegon   616-755-3777
Stu Brown Builders, Inc.
Jim Faulker
Port Huron   313-982-0484
Kitchen Shop of South Haven Inc., The
Len Cramer
South Haven   616-637-8468
Oakland Hardware
The Plumbery
Keith or Kevin
Walled Lake   313-669-2022

MISSOURI
Falkner Plumbing
Bill Falkner
Saint Joseph   816-232-0138

NEW YORK
Gregory Bath & Kitchen Center
Jon Kirshner
Great Neck   516-487-1975

OHIO
Fireplace & Spa Center

Skip Manner
Toledo   419-475-7727

PENNSYLVANIA
Baumhauer's Kitchen & Bath Design Center
Joe Baumhauer
Ottsville   215-847-2626
C.B. Scott & Co.
Don Fish
Scranton   717-342-8221

TENNESSEE
Mini-Max Marble
Wayne or Jane
Bartlett   901-386-6868

WASHINGTON
Felton Plumbing
Dwight Felton
Port Angeles   206-457-7824

PORCHER, INC.

Please Contact Home Office:

Porcher, Inc.
13-160 Merchandise Mart
Chicago, IL 60654   312-923-0995
Toll Free: 800-338-1756
Fax: 312-923-1184
WESTERN REGIONAL OFFICE
Porcher, Inc.
650 Maple Avenue
Torrance, CA 90503   213-212-6112
Fax: 213-212-6775

QUAKER MAID, A DIVISION OF WCI, INC.

Please Contact Home Office:

Mary Ann Stewart
Marketing Manager
Route 61
Leesport, PA 19533   215-926-3011
Fax: 800-521-9505

RAPHAEL LTD.

Please Contact Home Office:

Raphael Ltd.
Casper de Jong, V.P. Sales
Box 386
Brookfield, WI 53008-0386
    414-786-5336
Fax: 414-786-5843

RALPH WILSON PLASTICS COMPANY INC.

Corporate Office:
Ralph Wilson Plastics Company, Inc.
David Hundley
Mktg. Communications Mgr.
600 South General Bruce Drive
Temple, Texas 76504

| | 817-778-2711 |
| Fax: | 817-770-2384 (24 hours) |

CALIFORNIA
Hayward 415-782-6055
Santa Fe Springs 213-771-8141

FLORIDA
Ralph Wilson Plastics Company, Inc.
Miami 305-477-8121

GEORGIA
Ralph Wilson Plastics Company, Inc.
Decatur 404-593-2424

ILLINOIS
Ralph Wilson Plastics Company, Inc.
Elk Grove Village 708-437-1500

MASSACHUSETTS
Ralph Wilson Plastics Company, Inc.
North Reading 617-662-9700

MICHIGAN
Ralph Wilson Plastics Company, Inc.
Westland 313-721-3600

NEW JERSEY
Ralph Wilson Plastics Company, Inc.
Pennsauken 609-662-4747

NEW YORK
Ralph Wilson Plastics Company, Inc.
Congers 914-268-4171

OHIO
Ralph Wilson Plastics Company, Inc.
Columbus 614-876-1515

TEXAS
Ralph Wilson Plastics Company, Inc.
Dallas 214-634-2310
Houston 713-699-4043
Temple 817-778-2322

WASHINGTON
Ralph Wilson Plastics Company, Inc.
Kent 206-872-8070

RUNTAL NORTH AMERICA

Please Contact Home Office For the Name of Your Local Representative:

Runtal North America
Owen Kantor, Nat'l Sales & Mktg Mgr
187 Neck Road
Ward Hill, MA 01835 508-373-1666
800-526-2621
Fax: 508-372-7140

RUSSELL RANGE

ALASKA
See Washington

ARIZONA (Northern)
Interwest
Phoenix 602-271-0100
ARIZONA (Southern)
Interwest
Tucson 602-747-0500
ARKANSAS
See Texas
CALIFORNIA (Northern)
Purcell-Murray
Brisbane 415-468-6620
CALIFORNIA (Southern)
Interwest
Bell 213-267-0700
COLORADO
See New Mexico
CONNECTICUT
A.D.C.
East Hartford 203-528-3781
DELAWARE
See Pennsylvania
FLORIDA
Major Appliances
Ft. Lauderdale 305-979-4700
GEORGIA
Wollaston Smith
Atlanta 404-451-7677
IDAHO (Northern)
See Washington
ILLINOIS
Leeland Dist.
Elmhurst 708-834-0888
INDIANA
See Michigan
LOUISIANA
See Mississippi
MAINE
See Connecticut
MARYLAND
Colonial Dist.
Beltsville 301-595-7300
MASSACHUSETTS
See Connecticut
MICHIGAN
A.D.I
Whitmore Lake 313-449-0080
MISSISSIPPI
Sunbelt Marketing
Bay St Louis 601-255-4985
NEVADA (Northern)
See California (Northern)
NEVADA (Southern)
Interwest
Las Vegas 702-897-1610
NEW HAMPSHIRE
See Connecticut
NEW JERSEY
Cooper Dist.
Newark 201-643-2680
NEW MEXICO
Interwest
Albuquerque 505-345-9001
NEW YORK (NYC Metro)
See New Jersey
NORTH CAROLINA
Warren Dist.
Raleigh 919-828-9100
OHIO
See Michigan

OREGON
BASCO
Portland 503-226-4377
PENNSYLVANIA
C & F Dist.
Columbia 717-684-3814
RHODE ISLAND
See Connecticut
SOUTH CAROLINA
See North Carolina
TENNESSEE
See Georgia
TEXAS (El Paso)
See New Mexico
TEXAS
Sunbelt Marketing
Arlington 817-261-9784
VERMONT
See Connecticut
VIRGINIA (DC area)
See Maryland
VIRGINIA
See North Carolina
WASHINGTON
Modern Supply
Seattle 206-285-0550
Wisconsin
See Illinois
CANADA (Western)
Can-West
Surrey 604-591-3321

SHARP ELECTRONICS CORPORATION

Sharp Corporation Headquarters & Executive Offices
Sharp Electronics Corp.
Sharp Plaza
Mahwah, NJ 07430-2135 201-529-8703
Regional Offices
MIDWEST OFFICE
Sharp Electronics Corp.
1300 Naperville Dr.
Romeoville, IL 60441 708-759-8555
WESTERN OFFICE
Sharp Electronics Corp.
20600 One Sharp Plaza
South Alameda Street
Carson, CA 90810 213-637-9488
SOUTHEASTERN OFFICE
Sharp Electronics Corp.
725 Old Norcross Rd.
Lawrenceville, GA 30245 404-995-0717
Distributors:
ALABAMA
R.P. McDavid Co., Inc.
Birmingham 205-251-3777
Fax: 205-251-5726
ALASKA
See Washington
ARIZONA
Noble Distributors, Inc.
Phoenix 602-273-7176
Fax: 602-273-7193
ARKANSAS
See Tennessee (Western)

CALIFORNIA (Southern)
Sues, Young & Brown Inc.
Baldwin Park 818-338-3800
Fax: 818-338-1967
CALIFORNIA (Northern)
Pacific Home Products
Burlingame 415-692-3062
Fax: 415-692-9469
COLORADO
Roth Distributing
Denver 303-373-9090
Fax: 303-373-2006
CONNECTICUT
See Massachusetts
DELAWARE
See Pennsylvania (Eastern)
FLORIDA
Raybro Electric Supplies
Tampa 813-223-7304
Fax: 813-221-7312
GEORGIA
Cain & Bultman, Inc.
Atlanta 404-691-0730
Fax: 404-691-7579
HAWAII
Delcrest, Inc.
Honolulu 808-848-0347
Fax: 808-841-4187
IDAHO (Northern)
See Montana
IDAHO (Southern)
See Utah
ILLINOIS (Northern)
Sharp Regional Office
Jeff Beyer
Romeoville 708-759-8555
Fax: 708-759-8340
ILLINOIS (Southern)
See Missouri (Fenton)
INDIANA
Wayne Distributing Co., Inc.
Indianapolis 317-871-6818
Fax: 317-875-6707
IOWA
Mid-State Distributing
Des Moines 515-244-7231
Fax: 515-244-0828
KANSAS
Liberty Distributors
Wichita 316-264-7393
Fax: 316-264-5210
KENTUCKY (Western)
Cooper Louisville Co., Inc.
Louisville 502-451-2117
Fax: 502-451-2290
KENTUCKY (Eastern)
See West Virginia
LOUISIANA
See Tennessee
MAINE
See Massachusetts
MARYLAND
The Selnick Corp.
Baltimore 301-796-1414
Fax: 301-796-1966
MASSACHUSETTS
Choquette & Co.
Seekonk 508-761-4300
Fax: 508-399-7450

MICHIGAN
Radio Distributing
Taylor 313-295-4500
Fax: 313-295-0298

MINNESOTA
Almo Minnesota
Brooklyn Center 612-566-2566
Fax: 612-566-9112

MISSISSIPPI
See Tennessee (Western)

MISSOURI
G.W. Ryan
Fenton 314-343-6002
Fax: 314-343-4023
Kansas City 816-241-3100
Fax: 816-241-3442

MONTANA
A.M.I.
Bozeman 406-586-2642
Fax: 406-586-7896

NEBRASKA
G.W. Ryan
Omaha 402-331-2526
Fax: 402-331-5635

NEVADA (Western)
See California (Northern)

NEW HAMPSHIRE
See Massachusetts

NEW JERSEY (Northern)
M. Rothman
Ramsey 201-818-1600
Fax: 201-825-7056

NEW JERSEY (Southern)
See Pennsylvania (Eastern)

NEW MEXICO
See Texas (Amarillo)

NEW YORK (Upstate)
Standard Electronics
Amherst 716-691-3061
Fax: 716-691-3170

NEW YORK (Metro & Long Island)
Wren Distributing
Mineola 516-746-5000
Fax: 516-746-5065

NEW YORK (Catskill Area)
Upstate Electronics
Newburgh 914-566-1660
Fax: 914-566-1619

NORTH CAROLINA
DistribuCon
Charlotte 704-527-8860
Fax: 704-522-8864

NORTH DAKOTA
Northern Plains Dist.
Fargo 701-282-7500
Fax: 701-281-1022

OHIO (Northern)
See Michigan

OHIO (Southern)
MAS, Inc.
Richfield 513-489-3090
Cleveland 216-659-3333
Fax: 216-659-4706

OKLAHOMA
See Texas (Amarillo)

OREGON
The Moore Company
Portland 503-234-5000
Fax: 503-238-1603

PENNSYLVANIA (Eastern)
Almo Distributing
Philadelphia 215-698-4000
Fax: 215-464-8567

PENNSYLVANIA (Pittsburgh Area)
See Ohio (Southern-Richfield)

PENNSYLVANIA (Northeastern)
Consolidated Dist.
Scranton 717-346-3831
Fax: 717-346-2890

PENNSYLVANIA (Southeastern)
Penn Appliance
Harrisburg 717-939-0451
Fax: 717-939-0459

RHODE ISLAND
See Massachusetts

SOUTH CAROLINA
See North Carolina

SOUTH DAKOTA
See North Dakota

TENNESSEE
W.L. Roberts
Memphis 901-362-2080
Fax: 901-366-7710

TEXAS
Amarillo Hardware
Amarillo 806-376-4722
Fax: 806-374-5520

TEXAS (North)
Michie Distributing Co.
Carrollton 214-245-0006
Fax: 214-245-0660

TEXAS (South)
StanCo
San Antonio 512-684-9688
Fax: 512-521-0004
Houston 713-224-8024
Fax: 713-224-3275

UTAH
Cowley Distributing Company
Salt Lake City 801-484-0317
Fax: 801-484-0491

VERMONT
Vermont Appliance
Burlington 802-864-9831
Fax: 802-864-3645

VIRGINIA (Eastern)
See Pennsylvania (Philadelphia)

VIRGINIA (Western)
See West Virginia

WASHINGTON
Sea-Pac Sales
Seattle 206-223-5353
Fax: 206-223-5307

WEST VIRGINIA
Bluefield Distributing
Bluefield 304-325-2437
Fax: 304-325-8344

WISCONSIN
Almo Wisconsin
Wauwatosa 414-462-8288
Fax: 414-438-4745

WYOMING
See Colorado

SIRO DESIGNS INCORPORATED

Please contact Home Office:

Siro Designs Incorporated
Jurgen Sikora
2010 NW 55th Ave.
Margate, FL 33063 305-968-0104
Fax: 305-968-0106

SKYMASTER SKYLIGHTS

CALIFORNIA
Skymaster Skylights
Ontario 714-947-0777

FLORIDA
Skymaster Skylights
Orlando 407-898-2881

SPEAKMAN COMPANY

NORTHEAST
Regional Mgr: Vincent Scriboni
3735 Hawkhurst Close
Chaddsford, PA 19317 215-558-2728

SOUTHEAST
Regional Mgr: Henry Spratlin
318 White Falls Drive
Columbia, SC 29212 803-781-6240

WEST COAST
Regional Mgr: Mark Tnuacale
29591 Squaw Valley Drive
Sun City, CA 92381
SALES REPRESENTATIVES:

ALABAMA
Commerical Sales Inc.
Birmingham 205-591-6296

ALASKA
See Washington

ARIZONA
The Keith Wharton Company
Phoenix 602-952-1030

ARKANSAS
Al Rathheim Sales
Memphis, TN 901-367-2912

CALIFORNIA (Northern)
R.D. Kincaide Inc.
San Francisco 415-861-9400

CALIFORNIA (Southern)
Proline Sales
Rancho Santa Fe 619-756-4993

COLORADO
Collison Berger, Inc.
Denver 303-286-1515

CONNECTICUT
Denber Associates
Wallingford 203-265-1563

DELAWARE
Speakman Company
Wilmington 302-764-7100

DISTRICT OF COLUMBIA
See Maryland

FLORIDA (Northern)
Merrell L. Poole Assoc.
Jacksonville 904-398-7334
Port Orange 904-756-0820

FLORIDA (Northwestern)
See Alabama

FLORIDA (Southeastern)
Merrell L. Poole Assoc.
Pompano Beach 305-946-6866
Miami 305-251-7240

FLORIDA (Orlando area & Mid-State)
Merrell L. Poole Assoc.
Orlando 407-297-3656

FLORIDA (Tampa area & Southwest)
Merrell L. Poole Assoc.
Temple Terrace 813-988-5040

GEORGIA
HEADCO
Dunwoody 404-393-0503

IDAHO (Northern)
See Washington

IDAHO (Southern)
See Utah

ILLINOIS (Central & Springfield)
John Sandberg Co., Inc.
East Moline 309-796-2371

ILLINOIS (Northwestern & Eastern)
Deery-Pardue & Assoc.
Franklin Park 708-671-9233

ILLINOIS (Southern)
See Missouri (Eastern)

INDIANA (Except Lake & Porter Counties)
R.C.I. Sales & Marketing
Indianapolis 317-841-7020

IOWA (Excluding Scotts County)
See Nebraska

IOWA (Scotts County)
See Illinois (Central & Springfield)

KANSAS
Knechtel Sales
Merriam 913-362-6660

KENTUCKY
See Ohio (Cincinnati)

LOUISIANA
Superior Products, Inc.
Baton Rouge 504-293-9773
Metairie 504-831-4451

MAINE
See Massachusetts

MARYLAND
Bay Distributing Company
Lutherville 301-825-6616

MASSACHUSETTS (Eastern)
E.R. Stephens
Billerica 508-667-6399

MASSACHUSETTS (Western)
See Connecticut

MICHIGAN (Excluding Lenawee & Monroe Counties)
R.E. Wallace, Inc.
Oak Park 313-398-2400

MICHIGAN (Lenawee & Monroe Counties)
See Ohio (Northern)

MISSISSIPPI
See Tennessee

MISSOURI (Eastern)
Donahue McGuire
St. Louis   314-664-2122

NEBRASKA (Except Panhandle)
William D. Anderson Co.
Omaha   402-330-3877

NEBRASKA (Panhandle)
See Colorado

NEVADA (Excluding Las Vegas)
See California (Northern)

NEVADA (Las Vegas only)
See California (Southern)

NEW HAMPSHIRE
See Massachusetts

NEW JERSEY (Southern)
See Pennsylvania (Central/Metro)

NEW JERSEY)North of Trenton & Trenton)
Dolan & Traynor Inc.
Clifton   201-696-8700

NEW YORK (Eastern)
GESCO Sales Company
Syracuse   315-474-1089

NEW YORK (Western)
Minic Sales, Inc.
Rochester   716-442-0606

NEW YORK (Export Agent)
John Prior, Inc.
Westbury   516-683-1020

NEW YORK (Metro area)
Salsbury Sales Co., Inc.
Long Island City   718-786-8260

NEW YORK (Rockland & Orange Counties)
See New Jersey (North of Trenton)

NORTH CAROLINA
Caveness Plyer & Associates
Greensboro   919-292-4873
Charlotte   704-372-4331

NORTH DAKOTA
See Minnesota

OHIO (Northern)
The Campbell Equip. Co.
Cleveland   216-696-1155

OHIO
Beauchamp & Associates
Cincinnati   513-232-7728

OKLAHOMA
See Texas (Dallas)

PENNSYLVANIA
CBA Associates
Vincentown   609-268-1478

RHODE ISLAND (Except Washington County)
See Maine

RHODE ISLAND (Washington County)
See Connecticut

SOUTH CAROLINA
See North Carolina

SOUTH DAKOTA
See Minnesota

TENNESSEE
Al Rathheim & Assoc.
Germantown   901-756-8667

TEXAS
Hugh M. Cunningham Inc.
Dallas   214-661-0222
Houston   713-923-2371
San Antonio   512-661-4161

TEXAS (El Paso)
See Arizona

UTAH
Western Sales Service
Salt Lake City   801-359-9600

VERMONT
See New York (Eastern)

VIRGINIA
Bay Distributing Co.
Virginia Beach   804-422-0752

WASHINGTON
Engineered Specification and Sales
Seattle   206-623-9508

WEST VIRGINIA
See Pennsylvania

WISCONSIN
Peck Sales
Berlin   414-782-1232

WYOMING
See Colorado

STERLING DOMESTIC APPLIANCES, INC.

Sterling Domestic Appliances
Graham Jones, Gen. Opr./Mkt. Mgr.
89 Access Road
Norwood, MA 02062   617-255-9909
    617-255-9910
Fax: 617-255-9911

MID-ATLANTIC

ILLINOIS
Leeland Int'l. Distributors
Elmhurst   708-834-0888
Fax: 708-834-0953

MICHIGAN
Radio Distributing Co., Inc.
Taylor
Outside MI   313-295-4500
Inside MI   800-462-1544
Fax: 313-295-0298

NORTHEAST

CONNECTICUT
See Massachusetts

DISTRICT OF COLUMBIA
See New Jersey

MAINE
See Massachusetts

MARYLAND
See New Jersey

MASSACHUSETTS
Wittenberg Distributors
Avon   617-479-3916
Outside MA   800-322-5002
Fax: 315-475-0130

NEW HAMPSHIRE
See Massachusetts

NEW JERSEY
Larsam, Inc.
Edison   201-249-8600
Fax: 201-248-9234

NEW YORK
See New Jersey

PENNSYLVANIA
See New Jersey

RHODE ISLAND
See Massachusetts

VERMONT
See Massachusetts

VIRGINIA
See New Jersey

WEST VIRGINIA
See New Jersey

PACIFIC WEST

CALIFORNIA (Northern)
Golden West Sales, Inc.
S. San Francisco   415-467-4880
Fax: 415-467-0280

OREGON
See Washington

WASHINGTON
Tri-State Distributors, Inc.
Kent   206-859-1800
Fax: 206-859-9488

SOUTH WESTERN

ARIZONA
Salmi Distributing
Scottsdale   602-949-7300
Fax: 602-949-8588

CALIFORNIA (Southern)
Sues, Young & Brown
Baldwin Park   818-338-3800
Fax: 818-338-1967

OKLAHOMA
See Texas

TEXAS (Except El Paso)
Ferguson Enterprises
Euless   817-540-1888
Fax: 817-354-4598

TEXAS—EL PASO
See Arizona

CANADA
Robert Morse Appliances, Ltd.
Richmond B.C.   604-278-3931
Fax: 604-278-1209
Calgary, Alberta   403-287-3191
Fax: 403-243-1713
Edmunton, Alberta   403-452-2950
Fax: 403-452-4389
Thomas Rathwell, Ltd.
Winnipeg, Manitoba   204-786-5571
Fax: 204-943-4384

SASKATCHEWAN
See Winnipeg, Manitoba
Euroline Appliances, Ltd.
Toronto, Ontario   416-867-1786
Fax: 416-360-5310
Radex, Ltd.
Montreal, Quebec   514-332-3250
Fax: 514-332-2660

SUB-ZERO FREEZER COMPANY

Please Contact Home Office:

Sub-Zero Freezer Company
P.O. Box 4130
4717 Hammersley Road
Madison, WI 53711   800-222-7820
    608-271-2233
Fax: 608-271-1538

SWIRL-WAY

ALABAMA
See Tennessee

ALASAKA
See Washington

ARIZONA
Double K Sales
Phoenix   602-893-8600

ARKANSAS
See Tennessee

CALIFORNIA (Northern)
Thomas D. Ramos
Santa Cruz   408-429-9506

CALIFORNIA (Southern)
Bob Rosenblume
Thousand Oaks   805-494-4427

COLORADO
Contact Sales Company
Lakewood   303-936-5515

CONNECTICUT
See Massachusetts

DELAWARE
See Pennsylvania (Eastern)

DISTRICT OF COLUMBIA
See Pennsylvania (Eastern)

FLORIDA (Minus Panhandle)
See Tennessee

GEORGIA
See Texas

ILLINOIS (Northern)
Ken Pacholski
Palo Park   708-385-3980

ILLINOIS (Southern)
See Missouri

INDIANA (Northern)
Battersby & Assoc.
Carmel   317-843-5700

INDIANA (Southern)
See Kentucky

IOWA
Mid-America Sales
Des Moines   515-244-0812

KANSAS (Western)
Summit Sales
Lenexa   913-492-7734
(Eastern 2/3)

KENTUCKY
Jebco Marketing
Louisville   502-426-0676

LOUISIANA
Denman Sales
Slidell   504-641-0751

MAINE
See Massachusetts

MARYLAND
See Pennsylvania

MASSACHUSETTS
Sales, Marketing Service, Inc.
Canton   617-821-1770

MICHIGAN
Preferred Sales Agency
Wyoming   616-243-2090

MINNESOTA
Preiss Co., The
Minnetonka   612-474-1570

MISSISSIPPI
See Tennessee

MISSOURI
Donahue-McGuire Sales Agency, Inc.
St. Louis   314-664-2122
MONTANA
Rocky Mountain Marketing
Missoula   406-542-3838
NEBRASKA
Mid-America Sales Group
Des Moines   515-244-0812
NEVADA (Clark County)
See Arizona
NEVADA (Northern)
See California
NEW HAMPSHIRE
See Massachusetts
NEW JERSEY (Northern)
See New York (Southern)
NEW JERSEY (Southern)
See Pennsylvania (East)
NEW MEXICO
Foster Sales Co.
Artesia   505-292-9098
NEW YORK (Northern)
Northern Marketing
Victor   716-924-2521
NEW YORK (Southern)
Alexanderson, Inc.
Hauppauge   516-361-9545
NORTH CAROLINA
Gillis, Teskey, Schaefer & Assoc.
Charlotte   704-522-0015
NORTH DAKOTA
See Minnesota
OHIO (Cincinnati)
See Kentucky
OHIO (Less Cincinnati)
Terry Baron
Cleveland   216-226-8418
OKLAHOMA
B & T Sales
Oklahoma City   405-843-0207
OREGON
Hollabaugh Bros. & Assoc.
Portland   503-238-0313
PENNSYLVANIA (Eastern)
Lenny Woldoff, Inc.
Huntingdon Valley   215-673-1950
PENNSYLVANIA (Western)
Triangle Sales
Bridgeville   412-257-2300
RHODE ISLAND
See Massachusetts
SOUTH CAROLINA
North Carolina
SOUTH DAKOTA
See Minnesota
TENNESSEE
Denman Sales Co.
Signal Mountain   615-886-1147
TEXAS (El Paso)
See New Mexico
TEXAS (North)
Moore Sales Co.
Plano   214-985-8400
TEXAS (South)
Paul Brewster
Henderson   800-999-1459
UTAH
Don Scott
Pleasant View   801-782-0100

VERMONT
See Massachusetts
VIRGINIA
W.G. Leseman & Son
Richmond   ·   804-752-6301
WEST VIRGINIA
See Pennsylvania (West)
WASHINGTON
Hollabaugh Bros. & Assocs.
Seattle   206-575-1277
WISCONSIN
See Minnesota
WYOMING
See Colorado
CANADA
Banique Dist. Inc.
Quebec   514-626-2001
PUERTO RICO
Delva Corp.
Rio Peidras   809-793-8081

TRAULSEN & CO., INC.

Please Contact Home Office:

Traulsen & Co., Inc.
Ultra Division
114-02 15th Avenue
College Point, NY 11356
                         718-463-9000
                         800-542-4022
Fax: 718-961-1390

TUB-MASTER CORPORATION

CALIFORNIA
Tub-Master Corporation
Ontario   714-947-0777
FLORIDA
Tub-Master Corporation
Orlando   407-898-2881

ULTRACRAFT, DIVISION OF ALSIDE

Please Contact Home Office:

UltraCraft, Division of Alside
Jeff Nesbitt
2109 N. Greensboro Street
Liberty, NC 27298   919-622-4281
Fax: 919-622-2132

WCI MAJOR APPLIANCE GROUP/EUROFLAIR BY FRIGIDAIRE

ALABAMA
See Louisiana
ARIZONA
All State Appliance, Inc.
Phoenix, 85017
ARKANSAS
See Louisiana
CALIFORNIA (Northern)
Excel Distributing
Petaluma   707-762-3392
CALIFORNIA (Southern)
Cal-Western Distributing 213-941-6056
CALIFORNIA (Central)
Built-In Distributing
Seaside   408-899-2666
CONNECTICUT
(See Massachusetts)
FLORIDA (East)
Coral Springs Appliance Co.
Coral Springs   305-752-3880
FLORIDA (Northwest)
Consolidated Electric Supply Inc.
Panama City   904-769-3381
GEORGIA
Kurtak Corporation
Atlanta   404-824-1200
IDAHO (Northern)
See Washington
IDAHO (Southern)
See Utah
ILLINOIS (Chicago)
Advance Refrigeration Co.
Bensenville   312-766-2000
INDIANA (Northern)
Cloud Brothers, Inc.
South Bend   219-289-0395
INDIANA (Northwest)
See Illinois (Chicago)
IOWA
Jones Distributing Company
Sioux City   712-277-8600
KENTUCKY
See Ohio (Southern)
LOUISIANA (Southern)
Glindmeyer Distributing Company
New Orleans   514-486-6646
MAINE
See Massachusetts
MARYLAND
See New Jersey
MASSACHUSETTS
Choquette & Company, Inc.
Seekonk   508-761-4300
MICHIGAN (Lower Peninsula)
Scandinavian Concepts
Rockford   616-866-3057
MICHIGAN (Upper Peninsula)
See Wisconsin
MINNESOTA
See Wisconsin
MISSISSIPPI
See Louisiana
NEBRASKA
See Iowa

NEVADA (Western)
See California (Northern)
NEVADA (Southern)
Econ, Inc.
Las Vegas   702-384-4684
NEW HAMPSHIRE
See Massachusetts
NEW JERSEY
M. Rothman & Co. Inc.
Ramsey   201-818-1600
NEW MEXICO
See Arizona
NEW YORK
See New Jersey
NORTH CAROLINA
Scan Am Design Inc.
Matthews   704-847-7987
NORTH DAKOTA
See Wisconsin
OHIO (Northeast)
C.C. Mitchell Supply Co.
Broadview Heights   216-526-2040
OHIO (North)
Don Walter Kitchen Distributors
Austintown   216-793-9338
OHIO (Southern)
Southern Ohio Kitchens
Dayton   513-222-2829
OKLAHOMA
See Texas (Northern)
OREGON
Builder Appliance Supply Company
Portland   503-226-4377
PENNSYLVANIA
See New Jersey
PENNSYLVANIA (Western)
See Ohio (North)
RHODE ISLAND
See Massachusetts
SOUTH DAKOTA
See Iowa
TEXAS (Northern)
Meletio Electric Company
Dallas   214-352-3900
UTAH
Familian Pipe & Supply
Salt Lake City   801-487-0761
VERMONT
See Massachusetts
VIRGINIA
See New Jersey
WASHINGTON D.C.
See New Jersey
WASHINGTON
Modern Supply Company
Seattle   206-285-0550
WEST VIRGINIA
See New Jersey
WISCONSIN
Morley-Murphy Company
Milwaukee   414-357-7900

WCI MAJOR APPLIANCE GROUP/FRIGIDAIRE

EASTERN REGION
WCI Builder Sales Division
Norm Hunt, Region Manager

116 E. Corporate Blvd.
Middlesex Business Park
South Plainfield, NJ 07080

MIDWEST REGION
WCI Builder Sales Division
Dan Trbovich, Region Manager
846 Algonquin Rd.
Shaumburg, IL 60173

SOUTHERN REGION
WCI Builder Sales Division
Wil Baning, Region Manager
3305 Breckenridge Blvd. Ste. 122
Duluth, GA 30136-5002

WESTERN REGION
WCI Builder Sales Division
Dennis Richards, Region Manager
4007 Paramount Blvd. Ste. 100
Lakewood, CA 90712

BUILDER DISTRIBUTORS

Joseph A. DeVita, Jr.	718-229-1552
	800-338-9333
Norman H. Hunt	717-575-3633
WCI	
Dennis Richards	213-425-8080

ALABAMA

Bell Supply Co. Inc.	
Dothan	205-793-4500
D & R Appliance	
Birmingham	205-942-3959

ARIZONA

All State Appliance	
Phoenix	602-233-0077

CALIFORNIA

Built-In Distributors	
Seaside	
L & D Appliance	
Santa Fe Springs	213-946-1105
McPhail's	
Petaluma	

CONNECTICUT

Contractor Home Appliance	
E. Granby	203-653-8266

DELAWARE

Craftway Kitchens	
Wilmington	302-998-3300

FLORIDA

Major Appliance Inc.	
Ft. Lauderdale	305-979-4700
Robbins Mfg. Co.	
Ft. Myers	813-334-1937
Broadway Appliance	
Riviera Beach	407-844-0081
Hess Appliances	
Satellite Beach	407-773-0222
Coral Springs Appliance Center	
Coral Springs	305-752-3880
Van's Appliances	
Lake Worth	407-582-6701
Westwood Appliance Center	
Jupiter	407-747-5662
Consolidated Electric Supply	
Ft. Walton Beach	904-243-7627
Consolidated Electric Supply	
Panama City	904-769-3381
Robbins Mfg. Co.	
Tampa	813-972-2448

GEORGIA

Shuman's Electric	
Baxley	912-367-7748
Shuman's Electric	
Jesup	912-427-8599

Shuman's Electric	
Vidalia	912-537-1834
Britt Home Furniture	
Snellville	404-972-2808
Collins Door Company	
Gainesville	404-534-4441
Forsyth Refrigeration Appliance Co.	
Cumming	404-889-9274
Hallman Wood Products	
Eatonton	404-485-6574
Howard Payne Co.	
Atlanta	404-451-0136
City Plumbing	
Gainesville	404-532-4123
Residential Construction Specialists	
Norcross	404-368-0646
All Star Insulation Co.	
Kingsland	912-729-6508

ILLINOIS

Contractors Service Supply	
Streamwood	708-289-4200
Kitchen Dist. of America	
Itasca	708-773-2010
Advance Refrigeration	
Bensenville	708-766-2000
Shipley Sales	
Wood Dale	708-766-9140
Northtowne Refrigeration	
Chicago	312-878-1122

INDIANA

Shilling Bros. Lumber	
St. Johns	219-365-6006
Cloud Brothers	
South Bend	219-289-0395
Hanners Appliances	
Indianapolis	317-634-1474
Mitchells Kitchen/Complete Lumber	
Evansville	812-473-6418

KENTUCKY

Kitchen Planning Center	
Lexington	606-252-0866

MARYLAND

Zamoiski Company, The	
Baltimore	301-539-3000
Easton Appliance Center	
Easton	301-822-1323
Bow Lighting and Supply Co.	
Hagerstown	301-739-7630

MASSACHUSETTS

Keystone Plumbing Supply Co.	
Springfield	413-781-1030
Boss Distributors	
Marlboro	
Valley Sales Co., Inc.	
W. Springfield	413-732-7754

MICHIGAN

Walters Appliance Dist.	
Union Lake	313-363-9083
Wicks Lumber	
Gaylord	517-732-5136

MISSISSIPPI

Sheppard Building Supply Co., Inc.	
Jackson	601-354-5510

MISSOURI

Roth Distributing Co.	
Earth City	314-291-1800
RSI Distributing Inc.	
St. Louis	314-644-5500

NEVADA

ECON	
Las Vegas	702-384-4682

Appliance Wholesale of NV	
Las Vegas	702-367-4330

NEW JERSEY

Sammans Electronics	
Wayne	201-696-8855
Johnson's Electric	
Ocean City	609-399-1598
IDI	
Pennsauken	609-662-9222

NEW YORK

Earl B. Fieden	
Latham	518-785-8555
Classic A/C & Refrig.	
New York City	212-947-4229
Glaser Bros.	
Brooklyn	718-774-5300
P.C. Richard	
c/o L.A.W. Bldr	
Hauppauge	516-582-6996
Dells House of Kitchens	
Rochester	716-338-2400
Fayette Distributing	
Syracuse	315-463-9955
Kitchen World	
Lockport	716-688-1334

NORTH CAROLINA

Builder Products	
Raleigh	919-755-0119
Lee Builder Mart	
Sanford	919-775-5955

OHIO

C C Mitchell Supply	
Broadview Heights	216-526-2040
Don Walter Kitchen Dist.	
Austintown	216-793-9338
Don Walter Kitchen Dist.	
Streetsboro	216-626-5557
Famous Supply	
Ashtabula	216-992-2116
Famous Supply	
Lorain	216-245-6874
Famous Supply	
Akron	216-434-5191
Famous Supply	
Canton	216-456-4500
Babin Building Center	
Mentor	216-951-4940
Babin Building Center	
Middleburg	216-842-1142
Babin Building Center	
Elyria	800-362-1163
Forest City/Babin Bldg. Co.	
Bedford Heights	216-292-2500
Famous Supply Co., The	
Steubenville	614-282-0951
Famous Supply Co., The	
Newark	614-345-9617
Famous Supply Co., The	
Sandusky	419-625-5354
Famous Supply Co., The	
Fremont	419-332-2636
Famous Supply Co., The	
Toledo	419-478-0343
Famous Supply Co., The	
Byesville	614-685-2535
Famous Supply Co., The	
Cleveland	216-529-1010
Famous Supply Co., The	
Warren	216-369-2563
Famous Supply Co., The	
Mansfield	419-524-0411
Famous Supply Co., The	
Cleveland	216-391-1600

Famous Supply Co., The	
Columbus	614-294-3500
London Kitchens	
Columbus	614-461-1820
Builder Appliance Supply Co.	
Columbus	614-235-5646
Powell Supply Inc.	
Mansfield	419-524-8211

PENNSYLVANIA

Peirce-Phelps Inc.	
Camp Hill	717-761-0240
American Kitchens Inc.	
Allentown	215-398-0666
Cliff Wood Kitchens	
Milroy	717-667-2141
Instant Kitchens	
Hazelton	215-455-1546
R & J Kitchens Distributors Inc.	
Mohnton	215-777-5717
Bentley Distributors	
Williamsport	717-322-6201
Mariotti Building Products	
Old Forge	717-457-6774
Kery Inc.	
Newtown Square	215-356-8897
Peirce-Phelps Inc.	
Philadelphia	215-879-7070
Walt Schandein	
Willow Grove	215-659-2110
S.S. Fretz, Jr. Inc.	
Philadelphia	215-671-8300
Don Walter Kitchen Dist.	
Wexford	412-935-3455
Don Walter Kitchen Dist.	
Erie	412-868-5407
Rea Jobber	
Clarion	814-226-9552
Famous Supply Co., The	
Uniontown	412-437-9806
Famous Supply Co., The	
Washington	412-225-8330

RHODE ISLAND

National Lumber Co.	
Providence	

TENNESSEE

Cleveland Building Materials	
Cleveland	615-476-6509
Siano Appliance Distributors	
Memphis	901-382-5831
Southern Kitchen & Supply	
Knoxville	615-525-0391

TEXAS

Capital Distributor Inc.	
Dallas	214-638-2681
Tarrant Appliance Builders Supply	
Ft. Worth	817-531-2703
Meletio Dist. Co.	
Dallas	214-352-3900
Johnson Burks Supply Co. Inc.	
Sherman	214-235-7432
Appliance Associates Service Center	
Austin	512-454-5896
Built-In Appliance Center	
Houston	713-782-5525
Ran-Mar Sales & Service	
Missouri City	713-464-3066
Sides Supply Inc./dba Builders Appl.	
Market	
San Antonio	512-926-7106
Webco Distributing Co. Inc.	
Austin	512-836-8476

WASHINGTON
Modern Supply Co.
Seattle

WEST VIRGINIA
Famous Supply Co., The
Wheeling   304-232-3310
Gray Lumber Co. Inc.
Beckley   304-252-6363

WISCONSIN
Morley-Murphy Co.
Milwaukee   414-357-7900

WCI MAJOR APPLIANCE GROUP/TAPPAN

EASTERN REGION
WCI Builder Sales Division
Norm Hunt, Region Manager
116 E. Corporate Blvd.
Middlesex Business Park
South Plainfield, NJ 07080

MIDWEST REGION
WCI Builder Sales Division
Dan Trbovich, Region Manager
846 Algonquin Rd.
Shaumburg, IL 60173

SOUTHERN REGION
WCI Builder Sales Division
Wil Baning, Region Manager
3305 Breckenridge Blvd. Ste. 122
Duluth, GA 30136-5002

WESTERN REGION
WCI Builder Sales Division
Dennis Richards, Region Manager
4007 Paramount Blvd. Ste. 100
Lakewood, CA 90712

BUILDER DISTRIBUTORS
Joseph A. DeVita, Jr.   718-229-1552
    800-338-9333
Norman H. Hunt   717-575-3633

ALABAMA
D & R Appliance
Birmingham   205-942-3959

ARIZONA
All State Appliance
Phoenix   602-233-0077

CALIFORNIA
Familian Pipe & Supply
N. Hollywood   818-982-6710
TFI-Hollywood Refrigeration
Los Angeles

DELAWARE
Craftway Kitchens
Wilmington   302-998-3300

GEORGIA
Shuman's Electric
Vidalia   912-537-1834
Collins Door Company
Gainesville   404-534-4441
Newton Showroom
Milledgeville   912-453-7561
Cain & Bultman
Atlanta   404-691-0730
Coley Electric
Alma   912-632-5942
Coley Electric
Douglas   912-384-2444
Coley Electric
Waycross   912-285-2883

Shumans Electric
Baxley   912-367-7748
Shumans Electric
Jesup   912-427-8599

ILLINOIS
American Kitchen & Bath
Posen   708-371-1400
Contractors Service Supply
Streamwood   708-289-4200
Kitchen Dist. of America
Itasca   708-773-2010
Custom Products
Lombard   708-629-3600
Advance Refrigeration
Bensenville   708-766-2000
Troller Cabinet Co.
Rockford   815-654-1488
Northtowne Refrigeration
Chicago   312-878-1122

INDIANA
Shilling Bros. Lumber
St. Johns   219-365-6006
Essig Bros. Distributors
Noblesville   317-776-0733
Mitchells Kitchens/Complete Lumber
Evansville   812-473-6418
Pittmans Home Service
Bloomfield   812-384-3187

LOUISIANA
Allen Appliance Distributors
Shreveport   318-868-6541
Campbell Cabinets
Harahan   504-733-4687

MASSACHUSETTS
Colonial Gas Co.
Lowell   508-458-3171
Colonial Gas Co.
Hyannis   617-771-8870

MICHIGAN
J D Lynn
Pontiac   313-335-0111

MINNESOTA
All Inc.
St. Paul   612-227-6331

NEVADA
ECON
Las Vegas   702-384-4682

NEW JERSEY
Union Stove Works
Hackettstown   201-850-5500
Johnson's Electric
Ocean City   609-399-1598
IDI
Pennsauken   609-662-9222

NEW YORK
Classic A/C & Refrig.
New York City   212-947-4229
Elgot Sales
New York City   212-879-1200

OHIO
Americo Supply
Cleveland   216-696-1910
Bloom Bros. Supply
Chesterland   216-729-7336
Custom Counter Top & Kitchens
Cortland   216-637-4856
Kitchen & Bath World
Canfield   216-533-1146
Myers Appliance Service
Stow   216-688-0261
Ohio Sanitary Supply
Warrensville Heights   216-587-1222

Ohio Sanitary Supply
Elyria   800-522-7524
Babin Building Center
Mentor   216-951-4940
Babin Building Center
Middleburg   216-842-1142
Babin Building Center
Elyria   800-362-1163
Forest City/Babin Bldg. Co.
Bedford Heights   216-292-2500
Nu Supply Inc.
Marion   614-387-2210
Southern Ohio Kitchens
Dayton   513-222-2829
Builder Appliance Supply Co.
Columbus   614-235-5646
Powell Supply Inc.
Mansfield   419-524-8211

OKLAHOMA
OK Distributing Co. Inc.
Oklahoma City   405-751-8833

PENNSYLVANIA
C & F Distributors Inc.
Columbia   717-684-3814
Quaker Maid Kitchens of Reading Inc.
Reading   215-921-2045
Kery Inc.
Newtown Square   215-356-8897
S S Fretz Jr. Inc.
Philadelphia   215-671-8300
C & C Builder's Supply
Tarrs   412-696-5757
Eckstein Co.
Pittsburgh   412-321-8300
Houston-Starr Co.
Wilkensburg   412-242-6000
Houston-Starr Co.
Altoona   814-942-5110
Rea Jobber
Clarion   814-226-9552

TENNESSEE
Summers Hardware & Supply
Johnson City   615-461-4700
Siano Appliance Distributors
Memphis   901-382-5831

TEXAS
Intrastate Sales Ent/dba Kitchen King
Dallas   214-357-6879
Texas Appliance Builder Supply Inc.
Arlington   817-469-6644
Tarrant Appliance Builders Supply
Ft. Worth   817-531-2703
Meletio Dist. Co.
Dallas   214-352-3900
Johnson Burks Supply Co. Inc.
Sherman   214-235-7432
Manna Distributing Inc.
Houston   713-977-3318
Metro Wholesale Distributors Inc.
Houston   713-433-7248
Ran-Mar Sales & Service
Missouri City   713-464-3066
Webco Distributing Co. Inc.
Austin   512-836-8476

WELLBORN CABINET INC.

Please Contact Home Office:

Wellborn Cabinet, Inc.
Angela Wellborn
R. 1 Box 37
Ashland, Alabama 36251

    205-354-7151

WHIRLPOOL CORPORATION

ARIZONA
Arizona Wholesale Supply Company
Phoenix   602-258-7901

HAWAII
Electrical Distributors, Inc.
Honolulu   808-836-0602

ILLINOIS
Klaus Radio, Inc.
Peoria   309-691-4840

MAINE
Eastco
Westbrook   207-854-0435

MARYLAND
D & H Distributing Company
Savage   301-498-0001

MASSACHUSETTS
Eastco
Westwood   617-329-3000

MINNESOTA
F.C. Hayer Company
Minneapolis   612-546-3777

NEW YORK
RTA Corporation
Albany   518-463-3251
Bruno Appliances Corporation
New York   212-564-2424

PENNSYLVANIA
Raymond Rosen & Co., Inc.
Conshohocken   215-941-5000
Hamburg Brothers, Inc.
Pittsburgh   412-227-6200

OKLAHOMA
Dulaney's Inc.
Oklahoma City   405-528-0511

OREGON
North Pacific Supply Co., Inc.
Clackamas   503-656-2940

SOUTH DAKOTA
Warren Supply Company
Souix Falls   605-336-1830

TENNESSEE
McDonald Bros. Co. Inc.
Memphis   901-948-2771

TEXAS
Nunn Electric Supply Corp.
Amarillo   806-376-4501

VIRGINIA
Goldberg Company, Inc.
Richmond   804-771-5700

WASHINGTON
Prudential Distributors, Inc.
Spokane   509-535-2401

WISCONSIN
Taylor Electric Company
Mequon   414-241-4321

EASTERN REGION

FLORIDA
Florida Sales Division
Deerfield   305-426-6715

GEORGIA
Atlanta Sales Division
Norcross   404-449-4360

NORTH CAROLINA
Charlotte Sales Division
Charlotte   704-393-5950

EAST CENTRAL REGION

ILLINOIS
Chicago Sales Division
Naperville   708-505-2600

KENTUCKY
Cincinnati Sales Division
Erlanger   606-283-8240
Louisville Sales Division
Erlanger   502-361-5011

MICHIGAN
Detroit Sales Division
Livonia   313-591-4810

WEST CENTRAL REGION

ARKANSAS
Little Rock Sales Division
North Little Rock   501-758-3094

COLORADO
Denver Sales Division
Denver   303-371-5550

KANSAS
Kansas City Sales Division
Lenexa   913-888-1020

MISSOURI
St. Louis Sales Division
Maryland Heights   314-739-3606

NEBRASKA
Omaha Sales Division
Omaha   402-592-1631

LOUISIANA
New Orleans Sales Division
Harahan   504-734-0215

TEXAS
Dallas Sales Division
Farmers Branch   214-233-2200
Houston Sales Division
Houston   713-464-9700

WESTERN REGION

CALIFORNIA
Southern California Sales Division
Anaheim   714-634-9696
Northern California Sales Division
Santa Clara   408-727-3700

UTAH
Salt Lake City Sales Division
Salt Lake City   801-537-1020

WASHINGTON
Seattle Sales Division
Remond   206-828-4666

WOLF RANGE COMPANY

Please contact home office:

Wolf Range Company
Bruce Hoegh
19600 S. Alameda Street
Compton, CA 90221   213-637-3737
Fax: 213-637-7931

WOOD-MODE CABINETRY

ALABAMA (Northern)
See Georgia

ALABAMA (Southern)
See Louisiana

ARIZONA
See New Mexico

ARKANSAS
See Texas

CALIFORNIA (Northern)
KB Associates
Pam Baird
1160 Chess Drive, Suite 11
Foster City,94404   415-570-6212

CALIFORNIA (Southern)
John W. Avram & Associates
John W. Avram
1328 South Santa Fe Avenue
Los Angeles,90021   213-939-2118

COLORADO
See New Mexico

CONNECTICUT
See New York

DELAWARE (Northern)
See Pennsylvania (Southwest)

DELAWARE (Southern)
See Pennsylvania (Central & Northeastern)

DISTRICT OF COLUMBIA
See Maryland (Rockville area)

FLORIDA (excluding Northwest)
Roger Jorn Associates, Inc.
Roger Jorn
1010 Tenth Avenue North
Box 1429
Lake Worth,33460   407-586-2310

FLORIDA (Northwest)
See Louisiana

GEORGIA
McKimmy & Associates
Mike McKimmy
2330 Shore View Way
Box 308
Suwanee,30174-0308   404-962-3530

HAWAII
See California (Southern)

ILLINOIS (Northern)
Krengel & Associates, Inc.
Ken Krengel
502 North Plum Grove Road
Palatine, 60067   708-202-0600

ILLINOIS (East St. Louis area)
See Iowa

INDIANA (Northeast)
See Ohio (Northwest)

INDIANA (Southeast)
See Ohio (Excluding Northwest)

INDIANA (Excluding Northeast & Southeast)
See Illinois (Northern)

IOWA
Swanco Enterprises, Inc.
Craig Swanson
815 North Third Ave.
Box 1030
Marshalltown,50158   515-752-1072

KANSAS (Northeast)
See Iowa)

KANSAS (Excluding Northeast)
See Texas (Northern)

KENTUCKY
See Ohio (Excluding Northwest)

LOUISIANA
David Broussard & Associates
Dadvid Broussard
4861 Magazine Street
New Orleans,70115   504-899-5829

MAINE
See Massachusetts

MARYLAND (Excluding Rockville/ Washington,D.C. areas)
See Pennsylvania (Central & Northeastern)

MARYLAND (Rockville area)
Collins & Company, Inc.
Scott Collins
5110 Ridgefield Road, Suite 409
Bethesda,20816   301-652-0822

MASSACHUSETTS
Cuccaro Associates, Inc.
Jim Cuccaro
2 Wesleyan Terrance
Box 1189
Shrewsbury,01545   508-842-4660

MICHIGAN (Lower)
See Ohio (Northwest)

MICHIGAN (Upper Penninsula)
See Wisconsin

MINNESOTA
See Iowa

MISSISSIPPI (Northern)
See Texas (Northern)

MISSISSIPPI (Southern)
See Louisiana

MISSOURI
See Iowa

NEBRASKA (Central & Eastern)
See Iowa

NEVADA
See California (Northern)

NEW HAMPSHIRE
See Massachusetts

NEW JERSEY (Northern)
See New York (Metropolitan area)

NEW JERSEY (Southern)
See Pennsylvania (Southwest)

NEW MEXICO
Robert Carr & Associates, Inc.
Bob Carr
1309 San Mateo, NE
Albuquerque,87110   505-256-7555

NEW YORK (Metropolitan area)
T.O. Gronlund Company, Inc.
Ted B. Gronlund
200 Lexington Avenue
New York,10016   212-679-3535

NEW YORK (Excluding Metro area)
R.F. Martino, Jr. & Associates, Inc.
Ray F. Martino, Jr.
5801 Court Street Road
Box 4948
Syracuse,13221   315-437-1511

NORTH CAROLINA (Central & Eastern)
See Maryland (Rockville area)

NORTH CAROLINA (Western)
See Georgia

NORTH DAKOTA
See Iowa

OHIO (Northwest)
Ram Marketing, Inc.
Dick McKimmy

6509-25 Angola Road
Box 506
Holland,43528   419-865-9282

OHIO (Excluding Northwest)
R.J. O'Connor & Associates, Inc.
Dick O'Connor
666 Redna Street
Cincinnati,45215   513-771-7405

OKLAHOMA
See Texas (Northern)

PENNSYLVANIA (Central & Northeastern)
Battram Company
Joseph E. Callender
Box 582
Kreamer,17833   717-374-5271

PENNSYLVANIA (Western)
Marcus Kitchens, Inc.
Joe Safyan
5954 Baum Blvd.
Pittsburgh,15206   412-661-9704

PENNSYLVANIA (Southwest)
Wall & Walsh, Inc.
Chuck Walsh
8320 West Chester Pike
Upper Darby,19082   215-789-8530

RHODE ISLAND
See Massachusetts

SOUTH CAROLINA (Charlotte, Gastonia, Rock Hill areas)
See Maryland (Rockville area)

SOUTH CAROLINA (Excluding Charlotte, Gastonia, Rock Hill)

SOUTH DAKOTA
See Iowa

TENNESSEE (Central & Eastern)
See Georgia

TENNESSEE (Western)
See Texas (Northern)

TEXAS (El Paso area)
See New Mexico

TEXAS (Northern)
Herman-Johns & Associates
Bob Johns
One Summit Avenue, Suite 1010
Fort Worth,76102   817-322-3593

TEXAS (Southern)
D.B. Steffan Associates
Dave Steffan
Box 219202
Houston,77218   713-497-8887

UTAH
See New Mexico

VERMONT
See Massachusetts

VIRGINIA (Central & Eastern)
See Maryland (Rockville area)

VIRGINA (Western)
See Georgia

WEST VIRGINIA
See Pennsylvania (Western)

WISCONSIN
Lakewood Distributors, Inc.
Dik Rossman
645 N. 36th Street
Milwaukee,53208   414-344-6100

WYOMING
See New Mexico

CANADA

WINDSOR & LONDON
See Ohio (Northwest)

MONTREAL & TORONTO
See New York (Excluding Metro area)

WORK RIGHT PRODUCTS, INC.

Please Contact Home Office:

Work Right Products, Inc.
4615 Work Right Circle
Lakeport, CA, 95453
USA: 800-358-9064
CA: 800-862-4995

Int'l: 707-263-0290
Fax: 707-263-4048

YORKTOWNE, INC.

Yorktowne, Inc.
John Stephenson
100 Redco Avenue
Red Lion, PA 17356   717-244-4011
Fax: 717-244-5497

YORKTOWNE BRANCHES
MARYLAND
Yorktowne Kitchens
Jeff Grove

5189 Raynor Avenue
Linthicum, 21090   301-789-5513
NEW JERSEY
Yorktowne Kitchens
George Gordon
124 A Tices Lane
E. Brunswick, 08816   201-390-0077
PENNSYLVANIA
Yorktowne Kitchens
Mike Cosmo
2225 Richmond Street
Philadelphia, 19125   215-739-7700
Yorktowne Kitchens
Jeff Grove
3405 Board Road
York, 17402   717-764-0799
                             717-764-0699

ZOELLER COMPANY

Please Contact Home Office:

Zoeller Company
Customer Service Department
3280 Old Millers Lane
Louisville, KY 40216   502-778-2731
Fax: 502-774-3624

Please check off the answers to the question below. This information is for demographic purposes only.

1. Amount you estimate spending on your remodeling job?
   _____ up to $5,000
   _____ $5,000–$10,000
   _____ $10,000–$20,000
   _____ $20,000–over

2. Which products do you plan to replace:
   _____ Bath Accessories
   _____ Cabinets
   _____ Countertops
   _____ Dishwasher
   _____ Disposal
   _____ Faucets
   _____ Flooring
   _____ A. Resilient
   _____ B. Tile/Marble
   _____ C. Wood
   _____ Freezer
   _____ Lighting
   _____ Microwave Oven
   _____ Oven
   _____ Range
   _____ Refrigerator
   _____ Shower doors
   _____ Shower Stalls
   _____ Toilets
   _____ Tubs
   _____ Vanities
   _____ Windows

3. Which product(s) do you plan to add:
   _____ Barbeque
   _____ Bidet
   _____ Cooktop
   _____ Disposal
   _____ Flooring
   _____ A. Resilient
   _____ B. Tile/Marble
   _____ C. Wood
   _____ His & Her Sinks
   _____ Hot Tub
   _____ Ice Machine
   _____ Microwave Oven
   _____ Sauna
   _____ Shower Door
   _____ Skylights
   _____ Sound System/ Intercom System
   _____ Steam Bath
   _____ Sun Room
   _____ Water purifier
   _____ Whirlpool tub

4. What is the approximate value of your home?
   _____ $50,000–$100,000
   _____ $100,000–$150,000
   _____ $150,000–$200,000
   _____ $200,000–$275,000
   _____ $275,000–$350,000
   _____ $350,000–$500,000
   _____ $500,000–$750,000
   _____ $750,000–Above

5. What is your approximate household income?
   _____ $25,000–$40,000
   _____ $40,000–$50,000
   _____ $50,000–$75,000
   _____ $75,000–$150,000
   _____ $150,000–Above

6. Are you a double income household?
   _____ Yes
   _____ No

7. How long have you lived in your home?
   _____ 0–2 years
   _____ 5–10 years
   _____ 20 years–Above
   _____ 2–5 years
   _____ 10–20 years

8. Would you like to be put on our mailing list in order to receive future information on home remodeling ideas?
   _____ Yes
   _____ No

9. Have you found this book to be:
   _____ Most helpful
   _____ Somewhat helpful
   _____ Not very helpful

   Comments: _____
   _____
   _____

10. Where did you buy this book?
    Name of store or book club: _____
    Location of store: City _____ State _____

Thank You

PLACE
STAMP
HERE

Name _____

Company _____

Address _____

City, State, Zip _____

MBC Data Distribution Publications (USA)
Attn: Judy Hamilton
3901 West 86th Street, Ste. 330
Indianapolis, IN 46268

(KBSB91)

- -
(FOLD THIS FLAP SECOND)

The Kitchen & Bathroom remodeling job is going to bring you and your family a host of decisions. Where should the refrigerator go? How much light will we need? Should we include a bidet, a whirlpool?

All these questions have sound answers which any of the NKBA (National Kitchen & Bath Association) members can provide for you. A complete listing of these individuals can be found in this book.

In the meantime you may need some "Helpful Hints" right now! For a complete packet of information designed to give you answers and ideas on your upcoming Kitchen or Bathroom remodeling job, please fill out and send in the attached card.

It's FREE . . . and we hope you find the "Helpful Hints" useful.

- -
(FOLD THIS FLAP FIRST)

Please send a free "Helpful Hints" packet on:

_____ Kitchen

_____ Bathroom

_____ Both

Send to: Name _____

Address _____

City _____   State _____   Zip _____

Phone _____